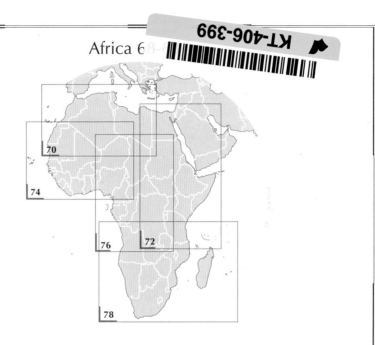

70

74

76 72

78

Europe 80-81

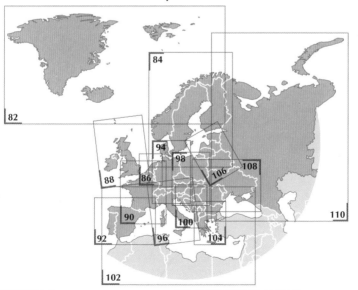

84

82

94

98

88 86 106 108

90

100

92 96 104

110

102

NC

WORLD
ATLAS

ESSENTIAL

LONDON, NEW YORK, MELBOURNE, MUNICH, DELHI

LONDON, NEW YORK, MELBOURNE, MUNICH, DELHI

FOR THE EIGHTH EDITION

SENIOR CARTOGRAPHIC EDITOR Simon Mumford
CARTOGRAPHY Encompass Graphics Ltd., Brighton, UK
PRODUCTION CONTROLLER Mandy Inness   PRODUCER, PRE-PRODUCTION Rebekah Parsons-King
INDEX DATABASE David Roberts   JACKET DESIGNER Mark Cavanagh
PUBLISHER Jonathan Metcalf   ART DIRECTOR Philip Ormerod
ASSOCIATE PUBLISHER Liz Wheeler

DORLING KINDERSLEY CARTOGRAPHY
PROJECT CARTOGRAPHY AND DESIGN
Julia Lunn, Julie Turner

CARTOGRAPHERS
James Anderson, Roger Bullen, Martin Darlison,
Simon Mumford, John Plumer, Peter Winfield

DESIGN
Katy Wall

INDEX-GAZETTEER
Natalie Clarkson, Ruth Duxbury, Margaret Hynes, Margaret Stevenson

PRODUCTION
Hilary Stephens, David Proffit

EDITORIAL DIRECTION
Andrew Heritage

ART DIRECTION
Chez Picthall

First published in Great Britain in 1997 by
Dorling Kindersley Limited,
80 Strand, London WC2R 0RL
Penguin Group (UK)

2 4 6 8 10 9 7 5 3 1

001 - 188128 - May/2013

Second edition 1998, Third edition 2001, Fourth edition 2003,
Fifth edition 2005, Sixth edition 2008, Seventh edition 2011, Eighth edition 2013.

Previously published as the Concise World Atlas

Printed and bound by Hung Hing, Hong Kong.

Discover more at **www.dk.com**

Key to map symbols

Physical features

Elevation

	6000m/19,686ft
	4000m/13,124ft
	3000m/9843ft
	2000m/6562ft
	1000m/3281ft
	500m/1640ft
	250m/820ft
	0
	Below sea level

△ Mountain

▽ Depression

⌂ Volcano

)(Pass/tunnel

▨ Sandy desert

Drainage features

— Major perennial river

— Minor perennial river

– – – Seasonal river

— Canal

│ Waterfall

◯ Perennial lake

◌ Seasonal lake

▨ Wetland

Ice features

	Permanent ice cap/ice shelf
	Winter limit of pack ice
	Summer limit of pack ice

Borders

▬▬▬ Full international border

▬ ▬ ▬ Disputed de facto border

• • • • • Territorial claim border

✕▬✕▬✕ Cease-fire line

▬ ▬ ▬ Undefined boundary

——— Internal administrative boundary

Communications

——— Major road

——— Minor road

——— Railway

✈ International airport

Settlements

▣ Above 500,000

◉ 100,000 to 500,000

◯ 50,000 to 100,000

○ Below 50,000

● National capital

◉ Internal administrative capital

Miscellaneous features

+ Site of interest

ᴖᴖᴖᴖ Ancient wall

Graticule features

——— Line of latitude/longitude/ Equator

– – – Tropic/Polar circle

25° Degrees of latitude/ longitude

Names

Physical features

Andes
Sahara   Landscape features
Ardennes

Land's End   Headland

Mont Blanc 4,807m   Elevation/volcano/pass

Blue Nile   River/canal/waterfall

Ross Ice Shelf   Ice feature

PACIFIC OCEAN
Sulu Sea   Sea features
Palk Strait

Chile Rise   Undersea feature

Regions

FRANCE   Country

JERSEY (to UK)   Dependent territory

KANSAS   Administrative region

Dordogne   Cultural region

Settlements

PARIS   Capital city

SAN JUAN   Dependent territory capital city

Chicago
Kettering   Other settlements
Burke

Inset map symbols

	Urban area
	City
	Park
▪	Place of interest
▫	Suburb/district

Contents

The World Today

Flags of the World..6-7
The Political World...8-9
The Physical World.......................................10-11
Time Zones...12-13
Geology & Structure.....................................14-15
World Climate...16-17
Ocean Currents...18-19
Life Zones...20-21
Population...22-23
Languages...24-25
Religion...26-27
The Global Economy....................................28-29
Politics and Conflict.....................................30-31

The World's Regions

North & Central America

North & Central America.............................34-35
Western Canada & Alaska...........................36-37
Eastern Canada...38-39
USA: The Northeast......................................40-41
USA: The Southeast.....................................42-43
  Bermuda
USA: Central States......................................44-45
USA: The West...46-47
  Los Angeles & Hawaii
USA: The Southwest......................................48-49
Mexico...50-51
Central America...52-53
The Caribbean...54-55
  Jamaica, St. Lucia, & Barbados

South America

South America..56-57
Northern South America..............................58-59
Western South America.................................60-61
  Galapagos Islands
Brazil..62-63
Southern South America...............................64-65
The Atlantic Ocean..66-67

Africa

Africa..68-69
Northwest Africa...70-71
Northeast Africa..72-73
West Africa...74-75
Central Africa...76-77
  Sao Tome & Principe
Southern Africa..78-79

Europe

Europe..80-81
The North Atlantic..82-83
Scandinavia & Finland..................................84-85
The Low Countries..86-87
The British Isles...88-89
  London

continued....

Europe *continued*

France, Andorra, & Monaco...............90-91
  Paris, Andorra, & Monaco
Spain & Portugal...........................92-93
  Azores & Gibraltar
Germany & the Alpine States.............94-95
  Liechtenstein
Italy.......................................96-97
  San Marino & Vatican City
Central Europe...........................98-99
Southeast Europe......................100-101
  Bosnia & Herzegovina
The Mediterranean....................102-103
  Malta & Cyprus
Bulgaria & Greece......................104-105
The Baltic States & Belarus...........106-107
Ukraine, Moldova,
  & Romania............................108-109
European Russia........................110-111

North & West Asia

North & West Asia......................112-113
Russia & Kazakhstan...................114-115
Turkey & the Caucasus.................116-117
The Near East...........................118-119
  West Bank
The Middle East.........................120-121
Central Asia.............................122-123

South & East Asia

South & East Asia.......................124-125
Western China & Mongolia............126-127

Eastern China & Korea..................128-129
  Hong Kong (Xianggang)
Japan....................................130-131
  Tokyo & Nansei-Shoto
South India & Sri Lanka.................132-133
North India, Pakistan,
  & Bangladesh.......................134-135
Mainland Southeast Asia...............136-137
Maritime Southeast Asia...............138-139
  Singapore
The Indian Ocean.......................140-141

Australasia & Oceania

Australasia & Oceania..................142-143
The Southwest Pacific..................144-145
Western Australia.......................146-147
Eastern Australia.......................148-149
  Sydney
New Zealand............................150-151
The Pacific Ocean.......................152-153
Antarctica.................................154
The Arctic Ocean...........................155

Index– Gazetteer

Overseas Territories
  & Dependencies.....................156-159
Glossary of Geographical
  Terms.................................160-161
Continental Factfiles...................162-163
Geographical Comparisons............164-166
Index-Gazetteer of Places
  & Countries...........................167-256

Flags of the World

NORTH & CENTRAL AMERICA

CANADA
PAGES 36-39

UNITED STATES OF AMERICA
PAGES 40-49

MEXICO
PAGES 50-51

BELIZE
PAGES 52-53

COSTA RICA
PAGES 52-53

EL SALVADOR
PAGES 52-53

GUATEMALA
PAGES 52-53

HONDURAS
PAGES 52-53

GRENADA
PAGES 54-55

HAITI
PAGES 54-55

JAMAICA
PAGES 54-55

ST KITTS & NEVIS
PAGES 54-55

ST LUCIA
PAGES 54-55

ST VINCENT & THE GRENADINES
PAGES 54-55

TRINIDAD & TOBAGO
PAGES 54-55

SOUTH AMERIC

COLOMBIA
PAGES 58-59

URUGUAY
PAGES 64-65

CHILE
PAGES 64-65

PARAGUAY
PAGES 64-65

AFRICA

ALGERIA
PAGES 70-71

LIBYA
PAGES 70-71

MOROCCO
PAGES 70-71

TUNISIA
PAGES 70-71

BURUNDI
PAGES 72-73

SUDAN
PAGES 72-73

TANZANIA
PAGES 72-73

UGANDA
PAGES 72-73

BENIN
PAGES 74-75

BURKINA FASO
PAGES 74-75

CAPE VERDE
PAGES 74-75

CÔTE D'IVOIRE (IVORY COAST)
PAGES 74-75

GAMBIA
PAGES 74-75

GHANA
PAGES 74-75

SIERRA LEONE
PAGES 74-75

TOGO
PAGES 74-75

CAMEROON
PAGES 76-77

CENTRAL AFRICAN REPUBLIC
PAGES 76-77

CHAD
PAGES 76-77

CONGO
PAGES 76-77

DEM. REP. CONGO
PAGES 76-77

EQUATORIAL GUINEA
PAGES 76-77

MAURITIUS
PAGES 78-79

MOZAMBIQUE
PAGES 78-79

NAMIBIA
PAGES 78-79

SEYCHELLES
PAGES 78-79

SOUTH AFRICA
PAGES 78-79

SWAZILAND
PAGES 78-79

ZAMBIA
PAGES 78-79

ZIMBABWE
PAGES 78-79

UNITED KINGDOM
PAGES 88-89

FRANCE
PAGES 90-91

MONACO
PAGES 90-91

ANDORRA
PAGES 90-91

PORTUGAL
PAGES 92-93

SPAIN
PAGES 92-93

AUSTRIA
PAGES 94-95

GERMANY
PAGES 94-95

POLAND
PAGES 98-99

SLOVAKIA
PAGES 98-99

ALBANIA
PAGES 100-101

BOSNIA & HERZEGOVINA
PAGES 100-101

CROATIA
PAGES 100-101

KOSOVO
PAGES 100-101

MACEDONIA
PAGES 100-101

MONTENEGRO
PAGES 100-101

MOLDOVA
PAGES 108-109

ROMANIA
PAGES 108-109

UKRAINE
PAGES 108-109

RUSSIAN FEDERATION
PAGES 110-115

ASIA

KAZAKHSTAN
PAGES 114-115

ARMENIA
PAGES 116-117

AZERBAIJAN
PAGES 116-117

GEORGIA
PAGES 116-117

KUWAIT
PAGES 120-121

OMAN
PAGES 120-121

QATAR
PAGES 120-121

SAUDI ARABIA
PAGES 120-121

UNITED ARAB EMIRATES
PAGES 120-121

YEMEN
PAGES 120-121

AFGHANISTAN
PAGES 122-123

KYRGYZSTAN
PAGES 122-123

JAPAN
PAGES 130-131

INDIA
PAGES 132-135

SRI LANKA
PAGES 132-133

MALDIVES
PAGES 132-133

PAKISTAN
PAGES 134-135

BANGLADESH
PAGES 134-135

BHUTAN
PAGES 134-135

NEPAL
PAGES 134-135

CAMBODIA
PAGES 136-137

PHILIPPINES
PAGES 138-139

SINGAPORE
PAGES 138-139

AUSTRALASIA & OCEANIA

FIJI
PAGES 144-145

KIRIBATI
PAGES 144-145

MARSHALL ISLANDS
PAGES 144-145

MICRONESIA
PAGES 144-145

NAURU
PAGES 144-145

PALAU
PAGES 144-145

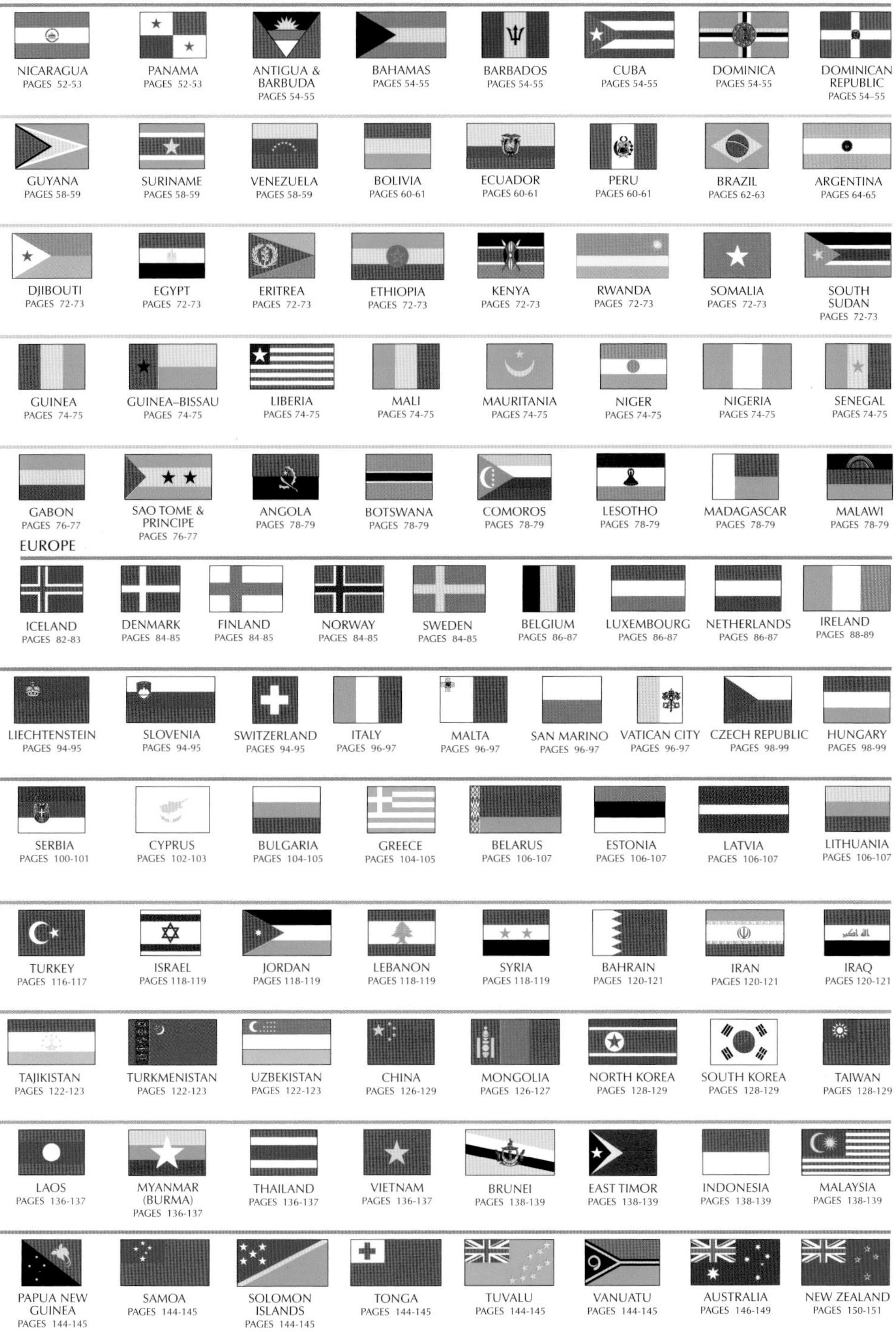
NICARAGUA PAGES 52-53
PANAMA PAGES 52-53
ANTIGUA & BARBUDA PAGES 54-55
BAHAMAS PAGES 54-55
BARBADOS PAGES 54-55
CUBA PAGES 54-55
DOMINICA PAGES 54-55
DOMINICAN REPUBLIC PAGES 54–55
GUYANA PAGES 58-59
SURINAME PAGES 58-59
VENEZUELA PAGES 58-59
BOLIVIA PAGES 60-61
ECUADOR PAGES 60-61
PERU PAGES 60-61
BRAZIL PAGES 62-63
ARGENTINA PAGES 64-65
DJIBOUTI PAGES 72-73
EGYPT PAGES 72-73
ERITREA PAGES 72-73
ETHIOPIA PAGES 72-73
KENYA PAGES 72-73
RWANDA PAGES 72-73
SOMALIA PAGES 72-73
SOUTH SUDAN PAGES 72-73
GUINEA PAGES 74-75
GUINEA–BISSAU PAGES 74-75
LIBERIA PAGES 74-75
MALI PAGES 74-75
MAURITANIA PAGES 74-75
NIGER PAGES 74-75
NIGERIA PAGES 74-75
SENEGAL PAGES 74-75
GABON PAGES 76-77
SAO TOME & PRINCIPE PAGES 76-77
ANGOLA PAGES 78-79
BOTSWANA PAGES 78-79
COMOROS PAGES 78-79
LESOTHO PAGES 78-79
MADAGASCAR PAGES 78-79
MALAWI PAGES 78-79
EUROPE
ICELAND PAGES 82-83
DENMARK PAGES 84-85
FINLAND PAGES 84-85
NORWAY PAGES 84-85
SWEDEN PAGES 84-85
BELGIUM PAGES 86-87
LUXEMBOURG PAGES 86-87
NETHERLANDS PAGES 86-87
IRELAND PAGES 88-89
LIECHTENSTEIN PAGES 94-95
SLOVENIA PAGES 94-95
SWITZERLAND PAGES 94-95
ITALY PAGES 96-97
MALTA PAGES 96-97
SAN MARINO PAGES 96-97
VATICAN CITY PAGES 96-97
CZECH REPUBLIC PAGES 98-99
HUNGARY PAGES 98-99
SERBIA PAGES 100-101
CYPRUS PAGES 102-103
BULGARIA PAGES 104-105
GREECE PAGES 104-105
BELARUS PAGES 106-107
ESTONIA PAGES 106-107
LATVIA PAGES 106-107
LITHUANIA PAGES 106-107
TURKEY PAGES 116-117
ISRAEL PAGES 118-119
JORDAN PAGES 118-119
LEBANON PAGES 118-119
SYRIA PAGES 118-119
BAHRAIN PAGES 120-121
IRAN PAGES 120-121
IRAQ PAGES 120-121
TAJIKISTAN PAGES 122-123
TURKMENISTAN PAGES 122-123
UZBEKISTAN PAGES 122-123
CHINA PAGES 126-129
MONGOLIA PAGES 126-127
NORTH KOREA PAGES 128-129
SOUTH KOREA PAGES 128-129
TAIWAN PAGES 128-129
LAOS PAGES 136-137
MYANMAR (BURMA) PAGES 136-137
THAILAND PAGES 136-137
VIETNAM PAGES 136-137
BRUNEI PAGES 138-139
EAST TIMOR PAGES 138-139
INDONESIA PAGES 138-139
MALAYSIA PAGES 138-139
PAPUA NEW GUINEA PAGES 144-145
SAMOA PAGES 144-145
SOLOMON ISLANDS PAGES 144-145
TONGA PAGES 144-145
TUVALU PAGES 144-145
VANUATU PAGES 144-145
AUSTRALIA PAGES 146-149
NEW ZEALAND PAGES 150-151

The Political World

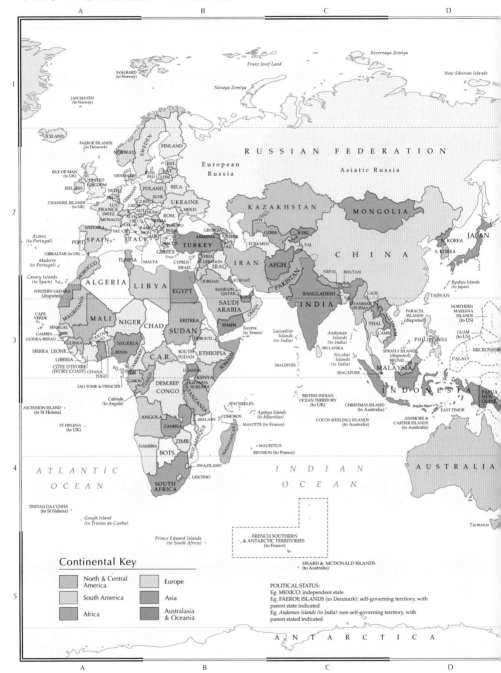

SVALBARD
(to Norway)

Franz Josef Land

Severnaya Zemlya

New Siberian Islands

JAN MAYEN
(to Norway)

Novaya Zemlya

ICELAND

FAEROE ISLANDS
(to Denmark)

NORWAY

SWEDEN

FINLAND

RUSSIAN FEDERATION

European
Russia

Asiatic Russia

ISLE OF MAN
(to UK)

UNITED
KINGDOM

DENMARK

EST.
LAT.
LITH.

RUSS.
FED.

IRELAND

NETH.

GERMANY

POLAND

BELA.

CHANNEL ISLANDS
(to UK)

LUX.
FRANCE
SWITZ.

CZ.REP.
AUT.HUNG.
SLVN.

SLVK.

UKRAINE

KAZAKHSTAN

MONGOLIA

MONACO

CRO.
B&H

ROM.

MOLD.

ANDORRA

VAT. CITY

SERBIA

MON.

BULG.

UZBEK.

KYRG.

Azores
(to Portugal)

PORT.

SPAIN

ITALY

ALB.

MAC.D

GEORGIA

ARMENIA

AZERB.

TURKMEN.

TAJ.

JAPAN

GREECE

TURKEY

AZ.

N. KOREA

GIBRALTAR (to UK)

SYRIA

LEBANON

S. KOREA

Madeira
(to Portugal)

TUNISIA

MALTA

CYPRUS

ISRAEL

IRAQ

IRAN

AFGH.

CHINA

Canary Islands
(to Spain)

MOROCCO

ALGERIA

LIBYA

EGYPT

JORDAN

KUWAIT

PAKISTAN

NEPAL

BHUTAN

Ryukyu Islands
(to Japan)

WESTERN SAHARA
(disputed)

BAHRAIN

QATAR

SAUDI
ARABIA

OMAN

BANGLADESH

INDIA

LAOS

TAIWAN

CAPE
VERDE

MAURITANIA

MALI

NIGER

CHAD

ERITREA

YEMEN

Socotra
(to Yemen)

Laccadive
Islands
(to India)

Andaman
Islands
(to India)

MYANMAR
(BURMA)

THAI.

NORTHERN
MARIANA
ISLANDS
(disputed)
(to US)

SENEGAL

BURKINA

SUDAN

DJIBOUTI

GUAM
(to US)

GAMBIA

GUINEA-BISSAU

GUINEA

NIGERIA

BENIN

SOUTH
SUDAN

ETHIOPIA

SRI LANKA

CAMB.

PHILIPPINES

MICRONESIA

SIERRA LEONE

CAMEROON

C.A.R.

Nicobar
Islands
(to India)

SPRATLY ISLANDS
(disputed)

PALAU

LIBERIA

CÔTE D'IVOIRE
(IVORY COAST)

GHANA

TOGO

EQ. GUINEA

MALDIVES

SINGAPORE

BRUNEI

MALAYSIA

SAO TOME & PRINCIPE

GABON

CONGO

DEM.REP.
CONGO

UGANDA

RWANDA

BURUNDI

KENYA

INDONESIA

PAPUA
NEW
GUINEA

Cabinda
(to Angola)

TANZANIA

SEYCHELLES

BRITISH INDIAN
OCEAN TERRITORY
(to UK)

CHRISTMAS ISLAND
(to Australia)

EAST TIMOR

ASCENSION ISLAND
(to St Helena)

ANGOLA

MALAWI

COMOROS

Agalega Islands
(to Mauritius)

MAYOTTE (to France)

COCOS (KEELING) ISLANDS
(to Australia)

ASHMORE &
CARTIER ISLANDS
(to Australia)

ST HELENA
(to UK)

ZAMBIA

MOZAMBIQUE

MADAGASCAR

AUSTRALIA

NAMIBIA

ZIMB.

BOTS.

MAURITIUS

REUNION (to France)

SWAZILAND

$ATLANTIC$

$OCEAN$

$INDIAN$

$OCEAN$

SOUTH
AFRICA

LESOTHO

TRISTAN DA CUNHA
(to St Helena)

Gough Island
(to Tristan da Cunha)

Tasmania

Prince Edward Islands
(to South Africa)

FRENCH SOUTHERN
& ANTARCTIC TERRITORIES
(to France)

HEARD & MCDONALD ISLANDS
(to Australia)

Continental Key

North & Central America	Europe
South America	Asia
Africa	Australasia & Oceania

POLITICAL STATUS:
Eg. MEXICO: independent state
Eg. FAEROE ISLANDS (to Denmark): self-governing territory, with
parent state indicated
Eg. *Andaman Islands (to India)*: non self-governing territory, with
parent stated indicated

$ANTARCTICA$

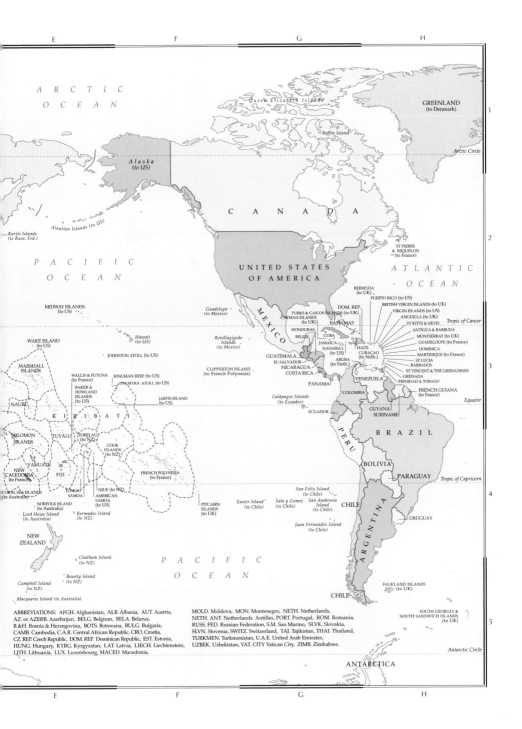

The Physical World

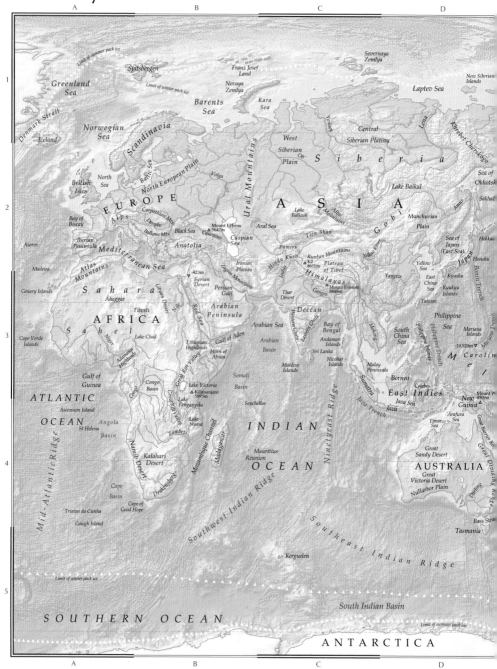

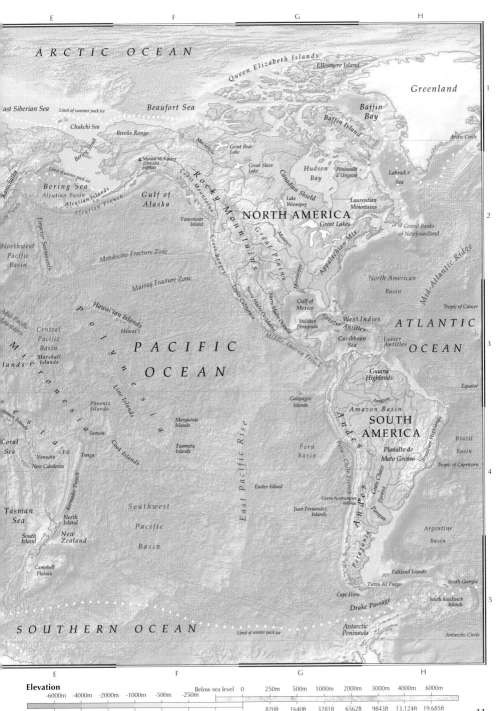

E   F   G   H

ARCTIC OCEAN

Queen Elizabeth Islands

Ellesmere Island

Greenland

East Siberian Sea

Limit of summer pack ice

Beaufort Sea

Baffin Island

Baffin Bay

Chukchi Sea

Brooks Range

Mackenzie

Great Bear Lake

Great Slave Lake

Hudson Bay

Péninsule d'Ungava

Labrador Sea

Arctic Circle

Limit of winter pack ice

△ Mount McKinley (Denali) 6194m

Rocky Mountains

Canadian Shield

Bering Sea

Aleutian Basin

Aleutian Islands

Aleutian Trench

Gulf of Alaska

Coast Mountains

Vancouver Island

Lake Winnipeg

NORTH AMERICA

Great Lakes

Laurentian Mountains

Grand Banks of Newfoundland

Emperor Seamounts

Northwest Pacific Basin

Mendocino Fracture Zone

Coast Ranges

Great Plains

Missouri

Appalachian Mts

North American Basin

Mid-Atlantic Ridge

Murray Fracture Zone

Mississippi

Sierra Madre Occidental

Sierra Madre Oriental

Tropic of Cancer

Mid-Pacific Mountains

Hawai'ian Islands

Hawai'i

Lower California

Gulf of Mexico

Middle America Trench

Yucatán Peninsula

West Indies

Greater Antilles

ATLANTIC

Central Pacific Basin

Marshall Islands

PACIFIC OCEAN

Polynesia

Caribbean Sea

Lesser Antilles

OCEAN

Micronesia

Islands

Guiana Highlands

Equator

Solomon Islands

Phoenix Islands

Line Islands

Samoa

Marquesas Islands

Galápagos Islands

Amazon

Amazon Basin

SOUTH AMERICA

Brazil Basin

Coral Sea

Vanuatu

Fiji

Tonga

Cook Islands

Tuamotu Islands

Peru Basin

Andes

Planalto de Mato Grosso

Brazilian Highlands

Tropic of Capricorn

New Caledonia

East Pacific Rise

Easter Island

Cerro Aconcagua 6959m

Juan Fernandez Islands

Peru-Chile Trench

Gran Chaco

Paraná

Argentine Basin

Tasman Sea

Kermadec Trench

North Island

Southwest Pacific Basin

Pampas

South Island

New Zealand

Patagonia

Falkland Islands

South Georgia

Campbell Plateau

Tierra del Fuego

Cape Horn

Drake Passage

South Sandwich Islands

SOUTHERN OCEAN

Limit of winter pack ice

Antarctic Peninsula

Antarctic Circle

E   F   G   H

Elevation

| -6000m | -4000m | -2000m | -1000m | -500m | -250m | Below sea level 0 | 250m | 500m | 1000m | 2000m | 3000m | 4000m | 6000m |

| -19,658ft | -13,124ft | -6562ft | -3281ft | -1640ft | -820ft | -328ft/-100m | 0 | 820ft | 1640ft | 3281ft | 6562ft | 9843ft | 13,124ft | 19,685ft |

Time Zones

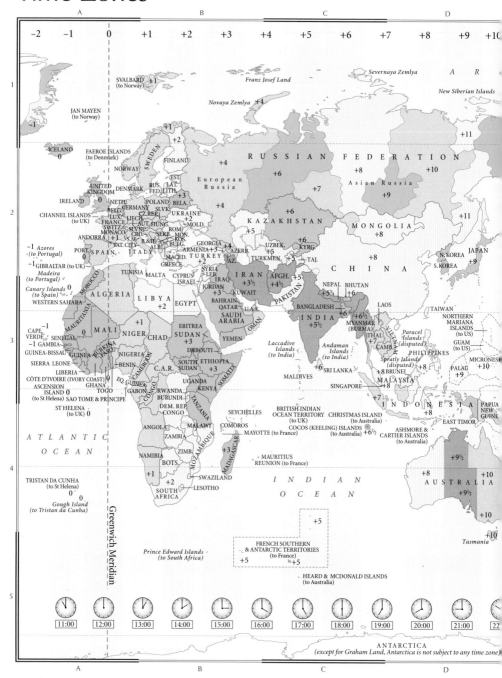

The numbers represented thus; +2/-2, indicate the number of hours each time zone is ahead or behind UCT (Coordinated Universal Time)

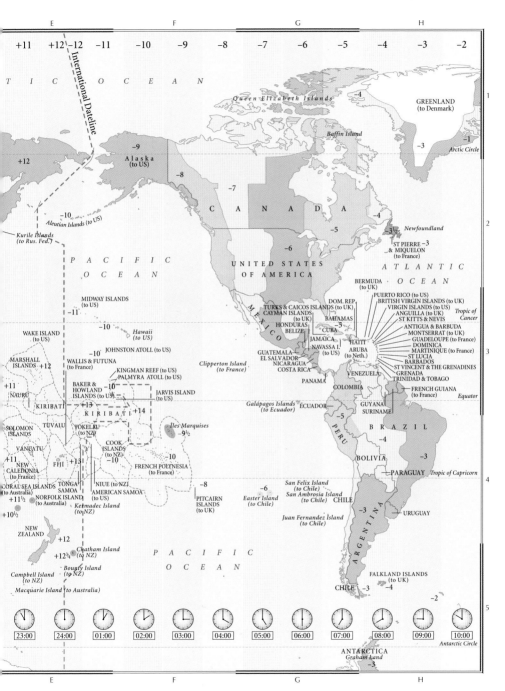

The clocks and 24-hour times given at the bottom of the map show time in each time zone when it is 12.00 hours noon UCT

Geology & Structure

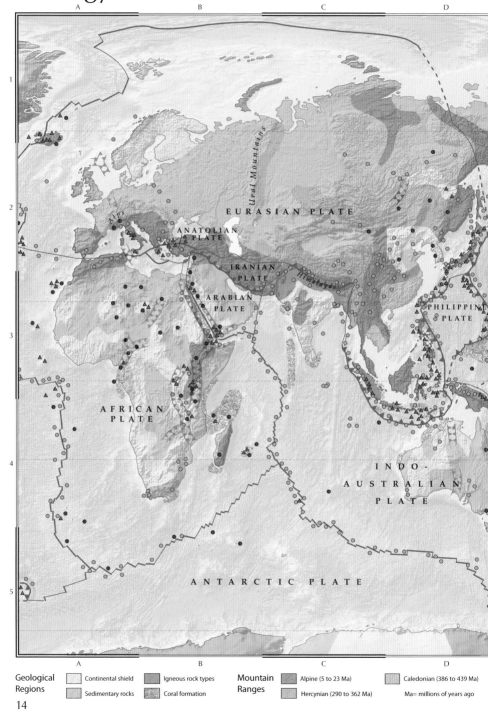

Ural Mountains

EURASIAN PLATE

Alps

ANATOLIAN PLATE

IRANIAN PLATE

Himalayas

ARABIAN PLATE

PHILIPPINE PLATE

AFRICAN PLATE

INDO- AUSTRALIAN PLATE

ANTARCTIC PLATE

Geological Regions			Mountain Ranges			
	Continental shield	Igneous rock types		Alpine (5 to 23 Ma)		Caledonian (386 to 439 Ma)
	Sedimentary rocks	Coral formation		Hercynian (290 to 362 Ma)		Ma= millions of years ago

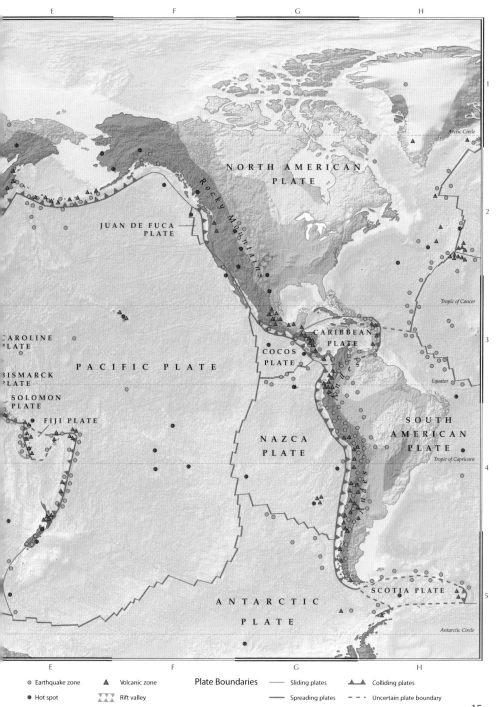

E   F   G   H

NORTH AMERICAN
PLATE

JUAN DE FUCA
PLATE

Rocky Mountains

CAROLINE
PLATE

PACIFIC PLATE

BISMARCK
PLATE

SOLOMON
PLATE

FIJI PLATE

CARIBBEAN
PLATE

COCOS
PLATE

SOUTH
AMERICAN
PLATE

NAZCA
PLATE

Andes

ANTARCTIC

PLATE

SCOTIA PLATE

Arctic Circle

Tropic of Cancer

Equator

Tropic of Capricorn

Antarctic Circle

1

2

3

4

5

E   F   G   H

●	Earthquake zone	▲	Volcanic zone
●	Hot spot	XXX	Rift valley

Plate Boundaries

—— Sliding plates
▲▲ Colliding plates
—— Spreading plates
- - - Uncertain plate boundary

15

World Climate

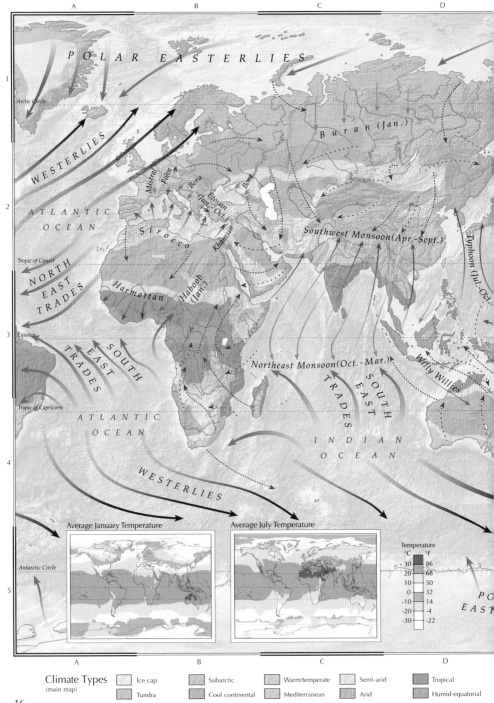

POLAR EASTERLIES

Arctic Circle

WESTERLIES

Buran (Jan.)

ATLANTIC OCEAN

Mistral
Föhn
Bora
Etesian (June-Oct.)
Bora
Sirocco
Khamsin
Southwest Monsoon (Apr.-Sept.)
Typhoon (Jul.-Oct.)

Tropic of Cancer

NORTH EAST TRADES

Harmattan
Haboob (Jan.)

Equator

SOUTH EAST TRADES

Northeast Monsoon (Oct.-Mar.)

Willy Willies

SOUTH EAST TRADES

Tropic of Capricorn

ATLANTIC OCEAN

INDIAN OCEAN

4

WESTERLIES

Average January Temperature

Average July Temperature

Temperature
°C	°F
30	86
20	68
10	50
0	32
-10	14
-20	-4
-30	-22

Antarctic Circle

PO
EAST

A   B   C   D

Climate Types
(main map)
- Ice cap
- Tundra
- Subarctic
- Cool continental
- Warm/temperate
- Mediterranean
- Semi-arid
- Arid
- Tropical
- Humid-equatorial

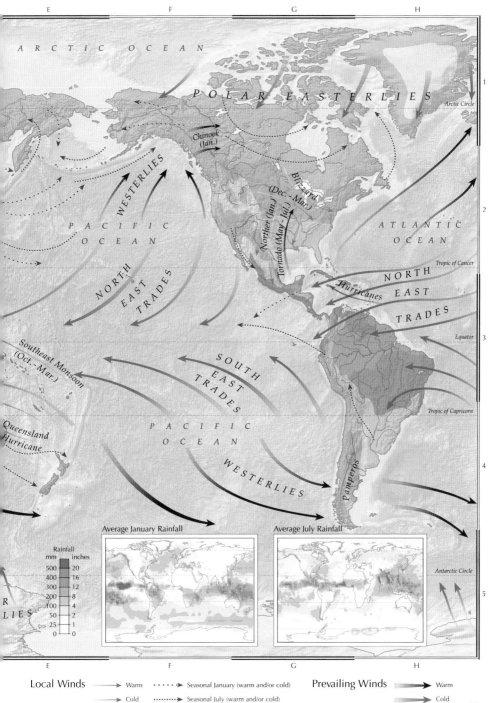

ARCTIC OCEAN

P O L A R   E A S T E R L I E S

Arctic Circle

Chinook
(Jan.)

Blizzard

WESTERLIES

Norther (Jan.) (Dec. - Mar.)

Tornado (May - Jul.)

PACIFIC
OCEAN

ATLANTIC
OCEAN

Tropic of Cancer

NORTH

NORTH

EAST

EAST

TRADES

Hurricanes

TRADES

Equator

Southeast Monsoon
(Oct. - Mar.)

SOUTH

EAST

TRADES

Tropic of Capricorn

PACIFIC
OCEAN

Queensland
Hurricane

WESTERLIES

Pamperos

Average January Rainfall

Average July Rainfall

Rainfall
mm   inches
500   20
400   16
300   12
200   8
100   4
50   2
25   1
0   0

Antarctic Circle

R

LIES

Local Winds
→ Warm
→ Cold
····▸ Seasonal January (warm and/or cold)
·····▸ Seasonal July (warm and/or cold)

Prevailing Winds
→ Warm
→ Cold

17

Ocean Currents

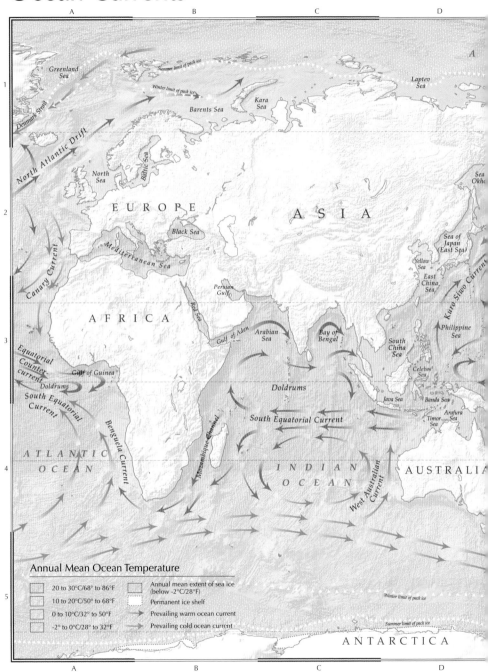

Annual Mean Ocean Temperature

20 to 30°C/68° to 86°F	Annual mean extent of sea ice (below -2°C/28°F)
10 to 20°C/50° to 68°F	Permanent ice shelf
0 to 10°C/32° to 50°F	Prevailing warm ocean current
-2° to 0°C/28° to 32°F	Prevailing cold ocean current

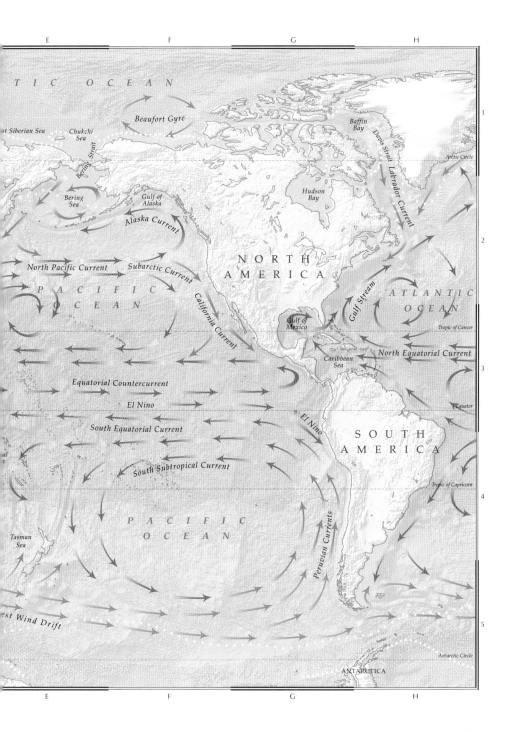

Life Zones

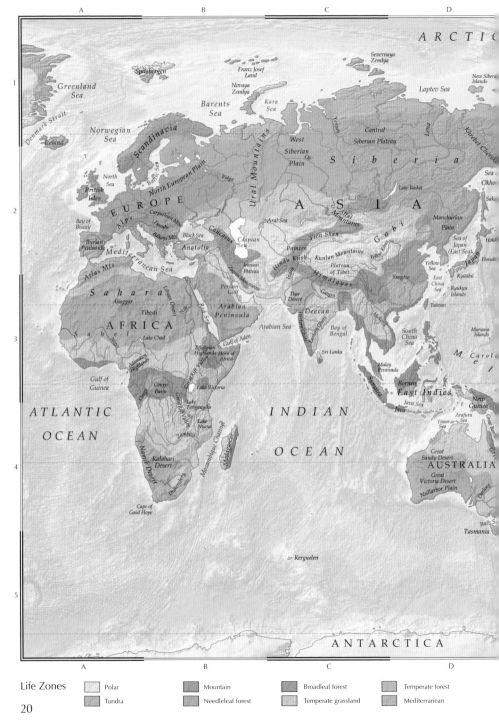

ARCTIC

Greenland Sea

Spitsbergen

Franz Josef Land

Severnaya Zemlya

New Siberia Islands

Laptev Sea

Denmark Strait

Iceland

Norwegian Sea

Scandinavia

Novaya Zemlya

Barents Sea

Kara Sea

Yenisey

West Siberian Plain

Ob

Central Siberian Plateau

Siberia

Khrebet Cherski

Sea Okho

North Sea

Baltic Sea

North European Plain

Ural Mountains

Lake Baikal

British Isles

EUROPE

ALPS

Carpathian Mts

Danube

Volga

ASIA

Altai Mountains

Gobi

Manchurian Plain

Sea of Japan (East Sea)

Hoki

Bay of Biscay

Balkans Mts

Black Sea

Caucasus

Aral Sea

Tien Shan

Yellow River

Japan

Honsh

Iberian Peninsula

Mediterranean Sea

Anatolia

Caspian Sea

Pamirs

Hindu Kush

Kunlun Mountains

Plateau of Tibet

Yangtze

Yellow Sea

Kyūshū

East China Sea

Ryukyu Islands

Atlas Mts

Iranian Plateau

Zagros Mountains

Indus

Himalayas

Taiwan

Mariana Islands

Sahara

Libyan Desert

Nile

Persian Gulf

Ganges

Thar Desert

Deccan

Western Ghats

Eastern Ghats

South China Sea

M Carol

Ahaggar

Tibesti

AFRICA

Lake Chad

Arabian Peninsula

Arabian Sea

Bay of Bengal

Mekong

Sahel

Niger

Sri Lanka

Malay Peninsula

Gulf of Guinea

Ethiopian Highlands

Horn of Africa

Gulf of Aden

Red Sea

Sumatra

Borneo

East Indies

New Guinea

Java Sea

Java

Timor Sea

Arafura Sea

Great

Adamawa Highlands

Congo

Congo Basin

Great Rift Valley

Lake Victoria

Lake Tanganyika

INDIAN

ATLANTIC

OCEAN

Lake Nyasa

Zambezi

Mozambique Channel

Madagascar

OCEAN

Great Sandy Desert

AUSTRALIA

Namib Desert

Kalahari Desert

Drakensberg

Great Victoria Desert

Nullarbor Plain

Darling

Cape of Good Hope

Bass S

Tasmania

Kerguelen

ANTARCTICA

Life Zones

	Polar		Mountain		Broadleaf forest		Temperate forest
	Tundra		Needleleaf forest		Temperate grassland		Mediterranean

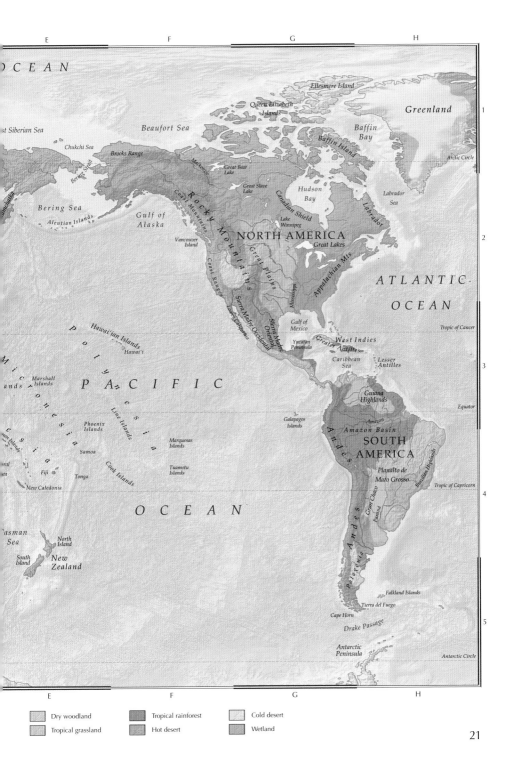

E   F   G   H

OCEAN

st Siberian Sea

Chukchi Sea

Beaufort Sea

Ellesmere Island

Queen Elizabeth Islands

Greenland

1

Baffin Bay

Brooks Range

Bering Strait

Baffin Island

Arctic Circle

Mackenzie

Great Bear Lake

Bering Sea

Aleutian Islands

Gulf of Alaska

Coast Mountains

Great Slave Lake

Canadian Shield

Hudson Bay

Labrador Sea

Labrador

Vancouver Island

Rocky Mountains

Lake Winnipeg

NORTH AMERICA

Great Lakes

2

Coast Range

Great Plains

Appalachian Mts

ATLANTIC OCEAN

Sierra Madre Occidental

Mississippi

Sierra Madre Oriental

Lower California

Gulf of Mexico

Tropic of Cancer

Hawai'ian Islands

Hawai'i

Yucatan Peninsula

Greater Antilles

West Indies

Caribbean Sea

Lesser Antilles

3

Micronesia

Marshall Islands

ands

P O L Y N E S I A

P A C I F I C

Phoenix Islands

Line Islands

Galapagos Islands

Guiana Highlands

Equator

nesia

Marquesas Islands

Amazon

Amazon Basin

SOUTH AMERICA

Andes

Samoa

oral ea

Fiji

Tonga

Cook Islands

Tuamotu Islands

Planalto de Mato Grosso

Brazilian Highlands

Tropic of Capricorn

4

New Caledonia

Gran Chaco

Pampa

O C E A N

asman Sea

North Island

New Zealand

Andes

Patagonia

South Island

Falkland Islands

Tierra del Fuego

Cape Horn

Drake Passage

5

Antarctic Peninsula

Antarctic Circle

E   F   G   H

Dry woodland	Tropical rainforest	Cold desert
Tropical grassland	Hot desert	Wetland

Population

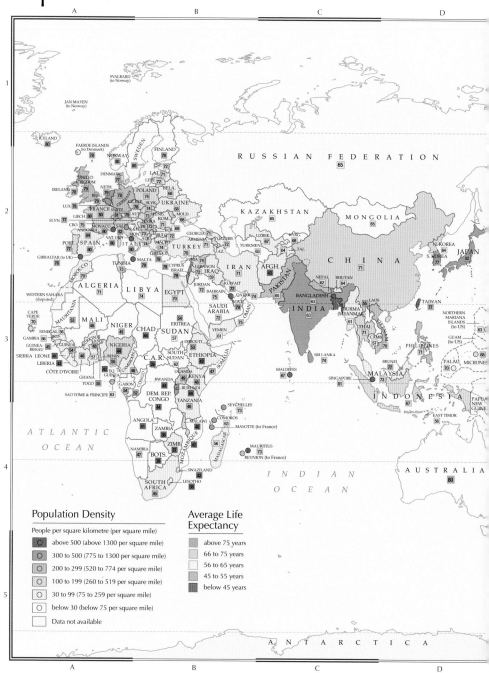

Population Density

People per square kilometre (per square mile)

- above 500 (above 1300 per square mile)
- 300 to 500 (775 to 1300 per square mile)
- 200 to 299 (520 to 774 per square mile)
- 100 to 199 (260 to 519 per square mile)
- 30 to 99 (75 to 259 per square mile)
- below 30 (below 75 per square mile)
- Data not available

Average Life Expectancy

- above 75 years
- 66 to 75 years
- 56 to 65 years
- 45 to 55 years
- below 45 years

ARCTIC
OCEAN

GREENLAND
(to Denmark)
67

Arctic Circle

Alaska
(to US)

PACIFIC
OCEAN

C A N A D A
80

UNITED STATES
OF AMERICA
77

ATLANTIC
OCEAN

MEXICO

Tropic of Cancer

Hawai'i
(to US)

BERMUDA
(to UK)
75

PUERTO RICO (to US)
74

CAYMAN ISLANDS
(to UK)
77

DOM. REP.
68

ST KITTS & NEVIS
72

ANTIGUA & BARBUDA
75

HONDURAS
BELIZE
72

BAHAMAS
75

CUBA
70

GUADELOUPE (to France)
75

DOMINICA
77

JAMAICA
71

HAITI

MARTINIQUE (to France)
76

CURAÇAO
(to Neth.)

ST LUCIA
73

GUATEMALA
68

EL SALVADOR 71

66

ARUBA
(to Neth.)
76

BARBADOS
75

ST VINCENT & THE
GRENADINES
71

MARSHALL
ISLANDS
70

NICARAGUA 70

COSTA RICA 79

PANAMA 75

COLOMBIA
73

VENEZUELA
74

73

GRENADA
73

TRINIDAD & TOBAGO
70

FRENCH GUIANA
(to France)
75

64

69

Equator

NAURU
63

WALLIS & FUTUNA
(to France)

ECUADOR
75

GUYANA
SURINAME

KIRIBATI
63

SOLOMON
ISLANDS
63

TUVALU
68

TOKELAU
(to NZ)
70

COOK
ISLANDS
(to NZ)

PERU
70

BRAZIL
71

VANUATU
69

FRENCH POLYNESIA
(to France)
70

BOLIVIA
65

PARAGUAY
71

Tropic of Capricorn

NEW
CALEDONIA
(to France)
74

FIJI
68

TONGA
SAMOA

72

NIUE (to NZ)

AMERICAN
SAMOA
(to US)

PITCAIRN
ISLANDS
(to UK)

CHILE
78

ARGENTINA

URUGUAY
75

75

NEW
ZEALAND
79

PACIFIC
OCEAN

CHILE

FALKLAND ISLANDS
(to UK)
76

SOUTH GEORGIA &
SOUTH SANDWICH ISLANDS
(to UK)

Antarctic Circle

ANTARCTICA

Languages

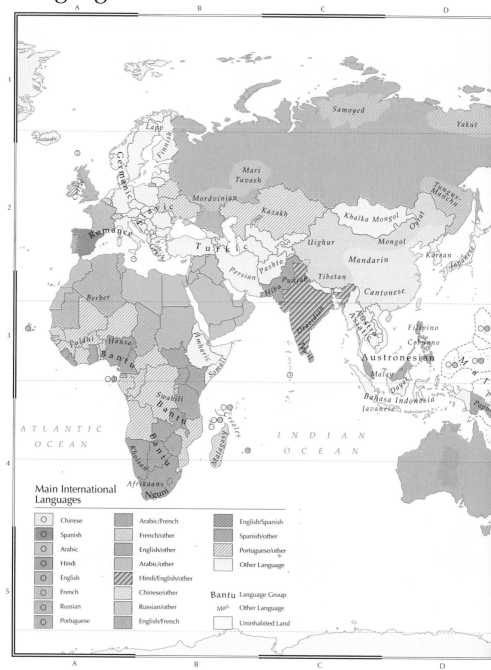

Main International Languages

○ Chinese	Arabic/French	English/Spanish
○ Spanish	French/other	Spanish/other
○ Arabic	English/other	Portuguese/other
○ Hindi	Arabic/other	Other Language
○ English	Hindi/English/other	
○ French	Chinese/other	
○ Russian	Russian/other	*Bantu* Language Group
○ Portuguese	English/French	*Mari* Other Language
		Uninhabited Land

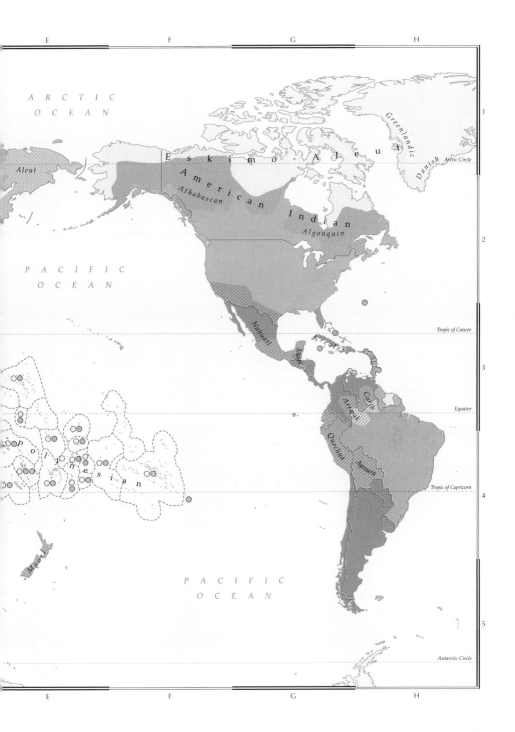

Religion

Majority Religions

- Protestant Christianity
- Catholic Christianity
- Orthodox Christianity
- Shi'a Islam
- Sunni Islam
- Hinduism
- Judaism
- Theravada Buddhism
- Mahayana Buddhism
- Tibetan Buddhism
- Other
- Marxism / Maoism

State Policy

- ▲ Secular ideologies governing
- ● Communist states during 20th century
- ■ Non-pluralist states

The Global Economy

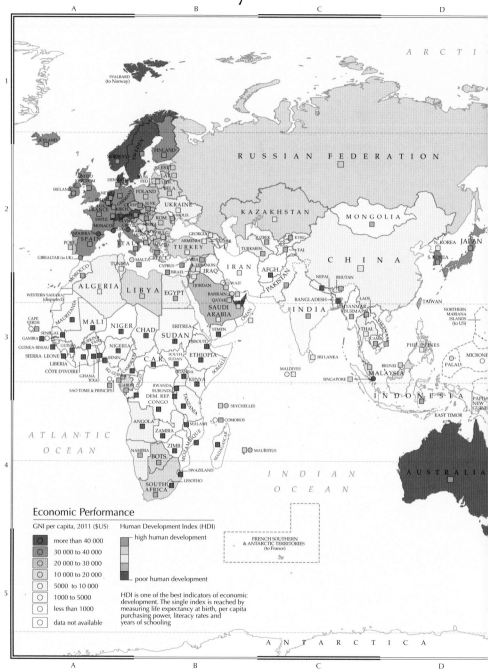

Economic Performance

GNI per capita, 2011 ($US)

- more than 40 000
- 30 000 to 40 000
- 20 000 to 30 000
- 10 000 to 20 000
- 5000 to 10 000
- 1000 to 5000
- less than 1000
- data not available

Human Development Index (HDI)

- high human development
- poor human development

HDI is one of the best indicators of economic development. The single index is reached by measuring life expectancy at birth, per capita purchasing power, literacy rates and years of schooling

Politics and Conflict

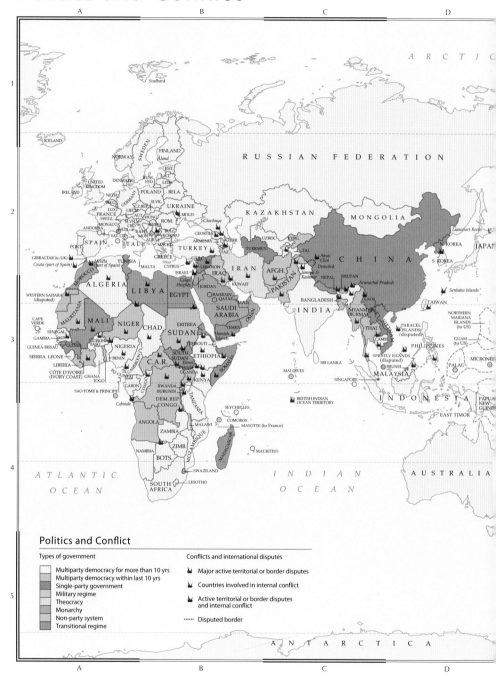

Politics and Conflict

Types of government

- Multiparty democracy for more than 10 yrs
- Multiparty democracy within last 10 yrs
- Single-party government
- Military regime
- Theocracy
- Monarchy
- Non-party system
- Transitional regime

Conflicts and international disputes

- Major active territorial or border disputes
- Countries involved in internal conflict
- Active territorial or border disputes and internal conflict
- ····· Disputed border

GREENLAND
(to Denmark)

Arctic Circle

Alaska
(to US)

C E A N

Kurile Islands
(part of Russ.Fed.)

P A C I F I C

O C E A N

C A N A D A

ST PIERRE
& MIQUELON
(to France)

UNITED STATES
OF AMERICA

A T L A N T I C

O C E A N

Tropic of Cancer

BAHAMAS

Hawai'i
(to US)

GUANTANAMO BAY
(to US)   CUBA

DOM. REP.

ST KITTS & NEVIS

ANTIGUA & BARBUDA

BELIZE JAMAICA
HAITI

DOMINICA

MARSHALL
ISLANDS

GUATEMALA
EL SALVADOR   HONDURAS

ST LUCIA

BARBADOS

NICARAGUA

ST VINCENT & THE GRENADINES

GRENADA

NAURU

COSTA RICA
PANAMA

VENEZUELA

TRINIDAD & TOBAGO

FRENCH GUIANA
(to France)

K I R I B A T I

COLOMBIA

Equator

ECUADOR

GUYANA

SURINAME

TUVALU

SOLOMON
ISLANDS

COOK
ISLANDS
(to NZ)

P E R U

B R A Z I L

VANUATU

SAMOA

BOLIVIA

NEW
CALEDONIA
(to France)

FIJI   TONGA

FRENCH POLYNESIA
(to France)

PARAGUAY

Tropic of Capricorn

CHILE

PITCAIRN
ISLANDS
(to UK)

URUGUAY

A R G E N T I N A

NEW
ZEALAND

P A C I F I C

O C E A N

FALKLAND ISLANDS
(to UK)

CHILE

Antarctic Circle

ANTARCTICA

31

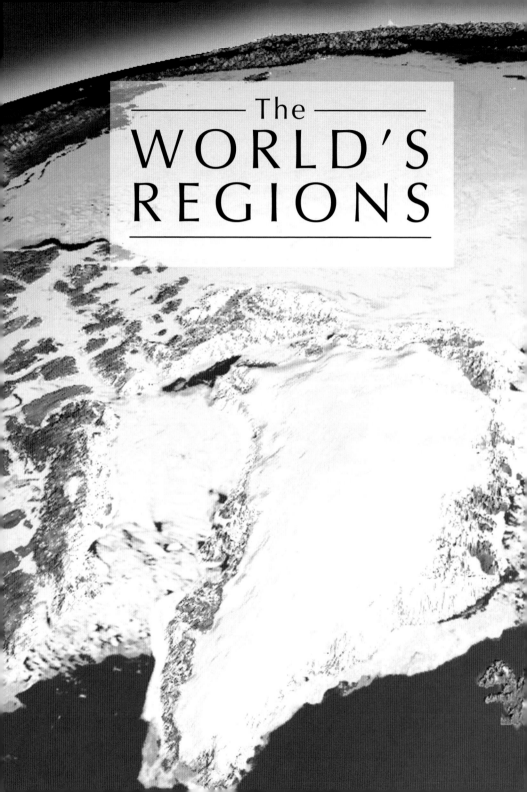

The
WORLD'S
REGIONS

North & Central America

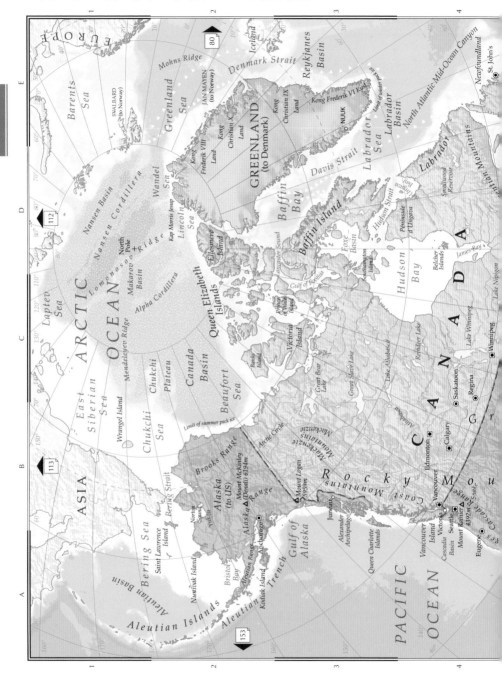

0 km 1000
0 miles 1000

Population ● National capital

o below 50,000 o 50,000 to 100,000 ◉ 100,000 to 500,000 ■ above 500,000

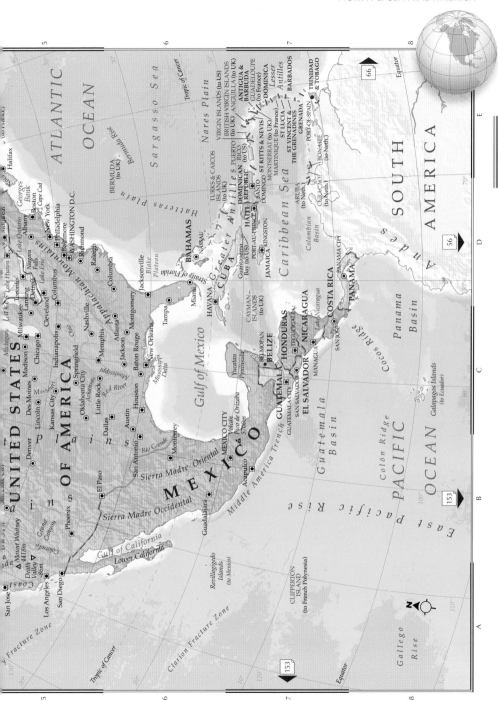

Western Canada & Alaska

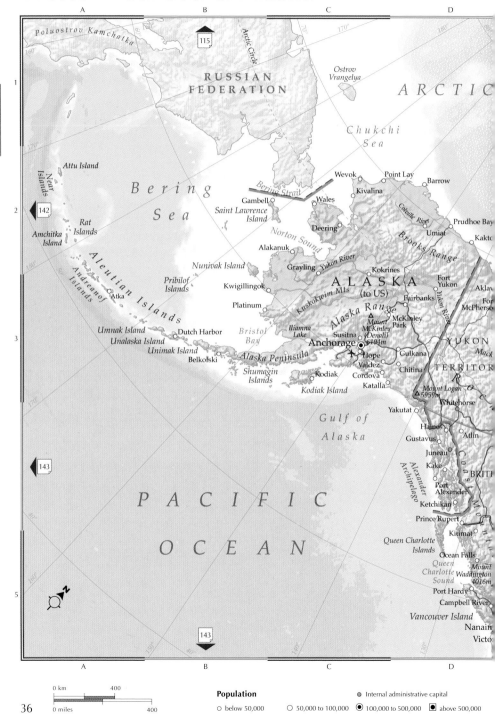

Poloustrov Kamchatka

115

Arctic Circle

RUSSIAN
FEDERATION

Ostrov
Vrangelya

ARCTIC

Chukchi
Sea

Attu Island

Near
Islands

142

Bering

Sea

Rat
Islands

Amchitka
Island

Andreanof
Islands

Aleutian Islands

Atka

Saint Lawrence
Island

Gambell

Norton Sound

Nunivak Island

Pribilof
Islands

Kwigillingok

Platinum

Wevok

Point Lay

Barrow

Kivalina

Bering Strait

Wales

Deering

Alakanuk

Grayling

Yukon River

Kokrines

Kuskokwim Mts

ALASKA
(to US)

Colville River

Brooks Range

Umiat

Prudhoe Bay

Kaktc

Fort
Yukon

Aklav

Fairbanks

Yukon River

For
McPherso

Alaska Range

Mount
McKinley
(Denali)
6194m

McKinley
Park

Umnak Island
Unalaska Island

Dutch Harbor

Unimak Island

Belkofski

Bristol
Bay

Iliamna
Lake

Susitna

Anchorage

Hope

Gulkana

YUKON

Alaska Peninsula

Shumagin
Islands

Kodiak

Valdez

Cordova

Katalla

Chitina

TERRITOR

Mack

Kodiak Island

Gulf of
Alaska

Mount Logan
△5959m

Whitehorse

Yakutat

Haines

143

PACIFIC

OCEAN

Gustavus

Atlin

Juneau

Kake

Alexander
Archipelago

Coast

Port
Alexander

Ketchikan

Prince Rupert

BRIT

Kitimat

Queen Charlotte
Islands

Queen
Charlotte
Sound

Ocean Falls

Mount
Waddington
4016m

Port Hardy

Campbell River

Vancouver Island

Nanain

Victo

143

0 km   400

0 miles   400

Population

○ below 50,000   ○ 50,000 to 100,000   ◉ 100,000 to 500,000   ■ above 500,000

◉ Internal administrative capital

Elevation

-6000m	-4000m	-2000m	-1000m	-500m		Below sea level	0		250m	500m	1000m	2000m	3000m	4000m	6000m
					-250m										
-19,658ft	-13,124ft	-6562ft	-3281ft	-1640ft	-820ft	-328ft/-100m	0		820ft	1640ft	3281ft	6562ft	9843ft	13,124ft	19,685ft

Eastern Canada

NORTHWEST TERRITORIES

NUNAVUT

Hudson Bay

Coats Island

Mansel Island

Ivujivik

Charles Island

Hu

Péninsule d' Ungave

SASKATCHEWAN

Churchill

Southern Indian Lake

Nelson

Hayes

Ottawa Islands

Inukjuak (Port Harrison)

Rivière Feu

Lac Minto

MANITOBA

Cedar Lake

Lake Winnipeg

Lake Winnipegosis

Lake Manitoba

Sandy Lake

Severn

Fort Severn

Peawanuk

Winisk

Belcher Islands

James Bay

Bien

QU

CANADA

ONTARIO

Attawapiskat

Attawapiskat

Albany

Akimiski Island

Fort Albany

Moosonee

Moose

Eastmain

Rivière de Rupert

Lac Mistassini

Chibougamau

Lac Seul

Kenora

Dryden

Armstrong

Hearst

Kapuskasing

Cochrane

Réservoir Gouin

Red River

Lake of the Woods

Lake Nipigon

Longlac

Nipigon

Amos

Rouyn-Noranda

Val-d'Or

NORTH DAKOTA

Fort Frances

Rainy Lake

Atikokan

Marathon

Tip Top Mountain △640m

Timmins

Foleyet

Kirkland Lake

Thunder Bay

Lake Superior

Wawa

MINNESOTA

Harricana

SOUTH DAKOTA

MICHIGAN

Sault Ste.Marie

Sudbury

North Bay

Pembroke

Gatineau

Hull

La

OTTAWA

UNITED STATES

WISCONSIN

Manitoulin Island

Georgian Bay

Lake Huron

Midland

Peterborough

Kingston

Oshawa

Lake Ontar

NEBRASKA

OF AMERICA

IOWA

Lake Michigan

Brampton

Kitchener

Hamilton

Sarnia

Windsor

London

Toronto

St.Catharines

Niagara Falls

NEW YORK

Mississippi River

ILLINOIS

Leamington

Lake Erie

INDIANA

OHIO

PENNSYLVANIA

0 km 300

0 miles 300

Population

● National capital ○ Internal administrative capital

○ below 50,000 ○ 50,000 to 100,000 ◉ 100,000 to 500,000 ◼ above 500,000

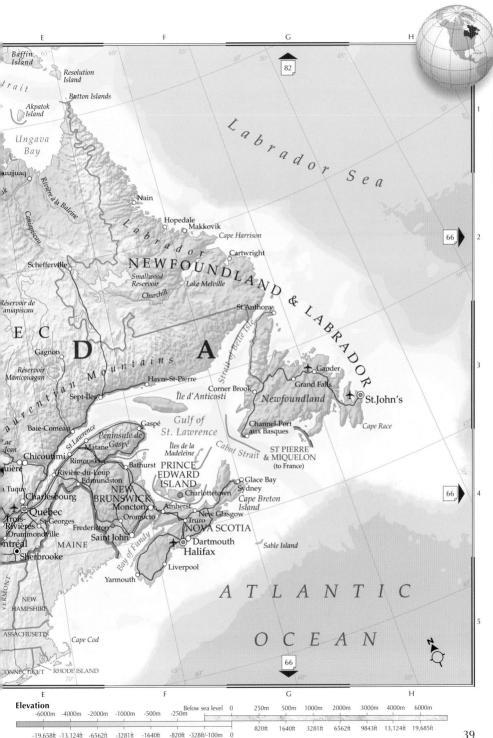

66

66

66

Labrador Sea

Baffin
Island
Resolution
Island
. Button Islands
trait
Akpatok
Island
*Ungava
Bay*
uujjuaq
Rivière à la Baleine
Nain
Hopedale
Makkovik
Cape Harrison
Scefferville
Cartwright
Caniapiscau
NEWFOUNDLAND
Réservoir de
aniapiscau
*Smallwood
Reservoir*
Lake Melville
Churchill
St.Anthony
E C D A
& LABRADOR
Gagnon
Réservoir
Manicouagan
Laurentian Mountains
Havre-St-Pierre
Strait of Belle Isle
Gander
Grand Falls
Sept-Îles
Île d'Anticosti
Corner Brook
Newfoundland
St.John's
Baie-Comeau
Gaspé
*Gulf of
St. Lawrence*
Cape Race
ac
lean
St.Lawrence
*Péninsule de
Gaspé*
Channel-Port
aux Basques
Chicoutimi
Matane
*Îles de la
Madeleine*
Cabot Strait
uière
Rimouski
Rivière-du-Loup
Bathurst
ST PIERRE
& MIQUELON
(to France)
a Tuque
Edmundston
PRINCE
EDWARD
ISLAND
Charlesbourg
NEW
BRUNSWICK
Charlottetown
Glace Bay
Sydney
Trois-
Rivières
Québec
Moncton
Amherst
*Cape Breton
Island*
St.Georges
Oromocto
New Glasgow
ntréal
Drummondville
Fredericton
Truro
NOVA SCOTIA
Sherbrooke
Saint John
Dartmouth
MAINE
Bay of Fundy
Halifax
Sable Island
VERMONT
Liverpool
NEW
HAMPSHIRE
Yarmouth
A T L A N T I C
ASSACHUSETTS
Cape Cod
O C E A N
CONNECTICUT
RHODE ISLAND

Elevation

-6000m	-4000m	-2000m	-1000m	-500m	-250m	Below sea level	0	250m	500m	1000m	2000m	3000m	4000m	6000m
-19,658ft	-13,124ft	-6562ft	-3281ft	-1640ft	-820ft	-328ft/-100m	0	820ft	1640ft	3281ft	6562ft	9843ft	13,124ft	19,685ft

USA: The Northeast

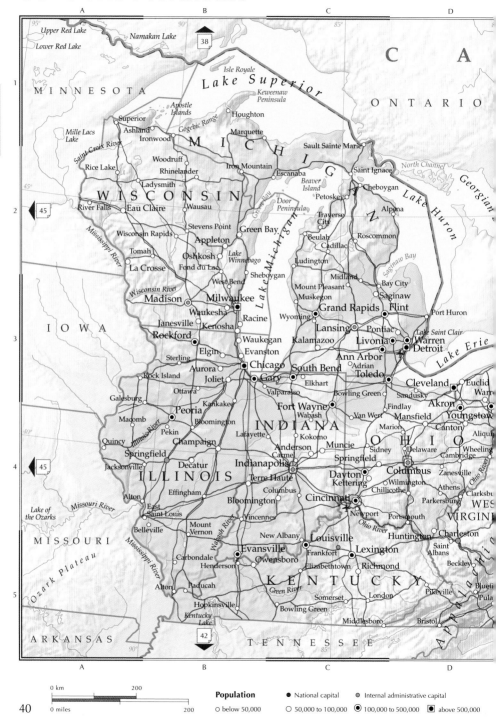

Upper Red Lake
Lower Red Lake
Namakan Lake
38
Isle Royale
Lake Superior
Keweenaw Peninsula
MINNESOTA
ONTARIO
CANADA
Apostle Islands
Houghton
Superior
Ashland
Ironwood
Marquette
Gogebic Range
Mille Lacs Lake
Sault Sainte Marie
Saint Ignace
North Channel
MICHIGAN
Georgian
Woodruff
Rhinelander
Iron Mountain
Escanaba
Beaver Island
Petoskey
Cheboygan
Lake Huron
Rice Lake
Ladysmith
Saint Croix River
WISCONSIN
Door Peninsula
Traverse City
Alpena
River Falls
Eau Claire
Wausau
Green Bay
Roscommon
Mississippi River
Wisconsin Rapids
Stevens Point
Appleton
Beulah
Cadillac
Saginaw Bay
IOWA
Tomah
Oshkosh
Lake Winnebago
Ludington
Midland
Bay City
La Crosse
Fond du Lac
Sheboygan
Mount Pleasant
Muskegon
Saginaw
Wisconsin River
West Bend
Madison
Milwaukee
Grand Rapids
Flint
Port Huron
Waukesha
Racine
Wyoming
Lansing
Pontiac
Lake Saint Clair
Janesville
Kenosha
Waukegan
Kalamazoo
Livonia
Warren
Rockford
Evanston
Ann Arbor
Detroit
Lake Erie
Elgin
Sterling
Aurora
Chicago
South Bend
Adrian
Toledo
Cleveland
Euclid
Warr
Rock Island
Joliet
Gary
Valparaiso
Elkhart
Bowling Green
Sandusky
Akron
Galesburg
Ottawa
Kankakee
Fort Wayne
Findlay
Mansfield
Youngstow
Peoria
Bloomington
Wabash
Van Wert
Canton
Aliqu
Macomb
Pekin
Lafayette
INDIANA
Kokomo
Marion
Sidney
Delaware
Wheeling
Quincy
Champaign
Anderson
Muncie
OHIO
Cambridge
Springfield
Carmel
Springfield
Columbus
Zanesville
WES
Jacksonville
Decatur
Indianapolis
Dayton
Athens
Clarksbu
Illinois River
ILLINOIS
Terre Haute
Kettering
Chillicothe
Ohio River
VIRGINIA
Alton
Effingham
Columbus
Dayton
Wilmington
Parkersburg
Lake of the Ozarks
Missouri River
East Saint Louis
Bloomington
Cincinnati
Portsmouth
Clarksbu
Belleville
Mount Vernon
Vincennes
Newport
New Albany
Huntington
Charleston
Saint Albans
MISSOURI
Carbondale
Evansville
Louisville
Frankfort
Lexington
Richmond
Beckley
Mississippi River
Henderson
Owensboro
Elizabethtown
Bluefi
Pula
Alton
Paducah
KENTUCKY
Pikeville
Ozark Plateau
Hopkinsville
Green River
Somerset
London
Bristol
Appalachi
Kentucky Lake
Bowling Green
Middlesboro
ARKANSAS
42
TENNESSEE

0 km   200
0 miles   200

Population
● National capital
○ Internal administrative capital
○ below 50,000
○ 50,000 to 100,000
◉ 100,000 to 500,000
■ above 500,000

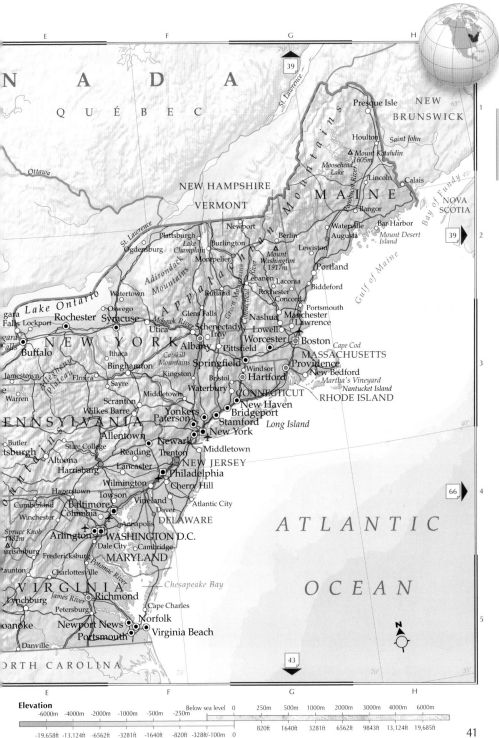

CANADA

QUÉBEC

NEW BRUNSWICK

Ottawa

St. Lawrence

Presque Isle

Houlton   Saint John

Mount Katahdin
1605m

Moosehead
Lake

Lincoln   Calais

NOVA
SCOTIA

NEW HAMPSHIRE

VERMONT

MAINE

Appalachian Mountains

Newport

Plattsburgh
Ogdensburg   Lake
          Champlain
          Burlington

Berlin

Montpelier

Mount
Washington
1917m

Waterville

Augusta

Bar Harbor

Mount Desert
Island

Lewiston

Portland

Biddeford

Gulf of Maine

Bay of Fundy

39

Adirondack
Mountains

St. Lawrence

Watertown

Lake Ontario

gara
Falls   Lockport

Rochester   Syracuse

Oswego

Mohawk River

Lebanon

Laconia

Rochester

Concord

Portsmouth

Green Mountains

Connecticut River

Rutland

Glens Falls

Utica

Schenectady

Nashua

Manchester

Lowell   Lawrence

Troy

NEW YORK

Ithaca

Binghamton

Albany

Pittsfield

Worcester   Boston

Cape Cod

MASSACHUSETTS

gara
Falls

Buffalo

Catskill
Mountains

Springfield

Windsor

Providence

RHODE ISLAND

Jamestown

Allegheny
Plateau

Elmira

Kingston

Bristol

Hartford

New Bedford

Martha's Vineyard

Nantucket Island

Warren

Sayre

Middletown

Waterbury

CONNECTICUT

New Haven

Scranton

Yonkers

Bridgeport

PENNSYLVANIA

Wilkes Barre

Paterson

Stamford

Long Island

Butler

State College

Allentown

Reading

Newark

New York

tsburgh

Altoona

Middletown

Harrisburg

Lancaster

Trenton

NEW JERSEY

Pittsburgh

Hagerstown

Wilmington

Philadelphia

Cherry Hill

Cumberland

Towson

Vineland

Atlantic City

Winchester

Baltimore

Columbia

Dover

DELAWARE

Spruce Knob
1482m

Annapolis

Arlington   WASHINGTON D.C.

arrisonburg

Fredericksburg   Dale City   Cambridge

ATLANTIC

66

taunton

Charlottesville

MARYLAND

Potomac River

Chesapeake Bay

OCEAN

VIRGINIA

James River

Richmond

Lynchburg

Petersburg

Cape Charles

oanoke

Newport News   Norfolk

Danville

Portsmouth   Virginia Beach

N

ORTH CAROLINA

43

Elevation

| -6000m | -4000m | -2000m | -1000m | -500m | -250m | Below sea level | 0 | 250m | 500m | 1000m | 2000m | 3000m | 4000m | 6000m |

-19,658ft   -13,124ft   -6562ft   -3281ft   -1640ft   -820ft   -328ft/-100m   0   820ft   1640ft   3281ft   6562ft   9843ft   13,124ft   19,685ft

USA: The Southeast

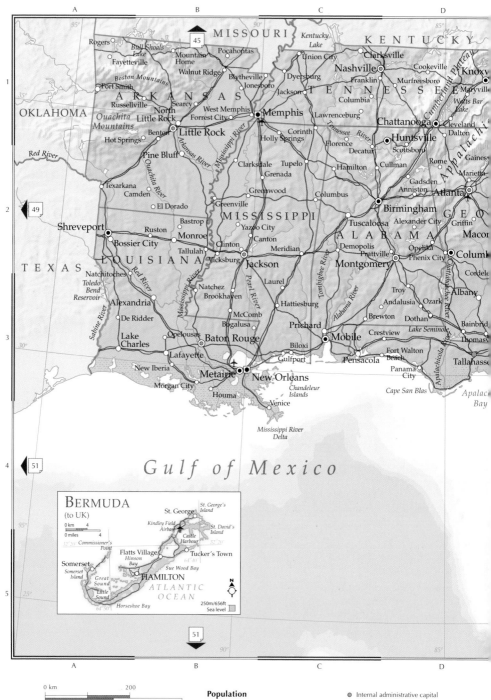

MISSOURI

KENTUCKY

Rogers
Bull Shoals Lake
Fayetteville
Mountain Home
Pocahontas
Walnut Ridge
Boston Mountains
Fort Smith
Russellville
ARKANSAS
North Little Rock
Searcy
West Memphis
Forrest City
Little Rock
Benton
Hot Springs
Pine Bluff
Ouachita Mountains
OKLAHOMA

Kentucky Lake
Union City
Clarksville
Nashville
Cookeville
Knoxv
Franklin
Murfreesboro
TENNESSEE
Columbia
Lawrenceburg
Chattanooga
Cleveland
Dalton
Huntsville
Florence
Decatur
Scottsboro
Cullman
Rome
Marietta

Blytheville
Jonesboro
Jackson
Dyersburg
Corinth
Holly Springs
Memphis
Clarksdale
Tupelo
Grenada
Greenwood
Columbus
Hamilton
Gadsden
Anniston
Atlanta

Red River
Texarkana
Camden
El Dorado
Greenville
MISSISSIPPI
Birmingham
Tuscaloosa
Alexander City
Griffin
GEO
Macon

Shreveport
Ruston
Bastrop
Yazoo City
ALABAMA
Bossier City
Monroe
Canton
Demopolis
Opelika
Columb
Tallulah
Clinton
Meridian
Prattville
Phenix City
Natchitoches
LOUISIANA
Vicksburg
Jackson
Montgomery
Cordele
TEXAS
Toledo Bend Reservoir
Alexandria
Natchez
Brookhaven
Laurel
Troy
Andalusia
Ozark
Albany
De Ridder
McComb
Hattiesburg
Brewton
Dothan
Lake Charles
Opelousas
Bogalusa
Prichard
Crestview
Fort Walton Beach
Bainbrid
Lafayette
Baton Rouge
Biloxi
Mobile
Pensacola
Thomas
New Iberia
Metairie
Gulfport
Panama City
Tallahasse
Morgan City
New Orleans
Cape San Blas
Apalac
Houma
Chandeleur Islands
Bay
Venice

Mississippi River Delta

Gulf of Mexico

BERMUDA
(to UK)

0 km   4
0 miles

St. George's Island
St. George
Kindley Field Airbase
St. David's Island
Commissioner's Point
Castle Harbour
Tucker's Town
Flatts Village
Hinson Bay
Sue Wood Bay
Somerset
Somerset Island
HAMILTON
ATLANTIC OCEAN
Great Sound
Little Sound
250m/656ft
Sea level
Horseshoe Bay

0 km   200
0 miles   200

Population
○ below 50,000
○ 50,000 to 100,000
◉ 100,000 to 500,000
■ above 500,000
● Internal administrative capital

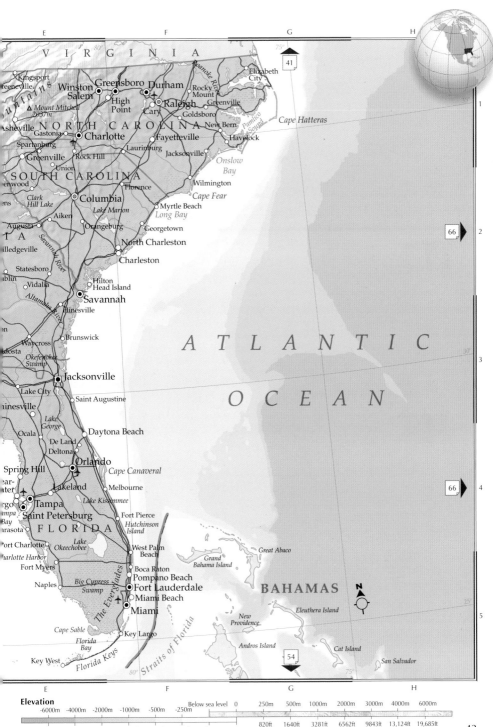

VIRGINIA

Kingsport
reeneville
Winston
Salem
Greensboro
Durham
High
Point
Raleigh
Cary
Goldsboro
Elizabeth
City
Rocky
Mount
Greenville
New Bern

△ Mount Mitchell
2037m

NORTH CAROLINA

Asheville
Gastonia
Charlotte
Fayetteville
Laurinburg
Jacksonville
Havelock
Cape Hatteras
Pamlico Sound
Roanoke River

Spartanburg
Greenville
Rock Hill
Union

SOUTH CAROLINA

enwood

Florence
Wilmington
Cape Fear
Onslow
Bay

Clark
Hill Lake
Columbia
Lake Marion
Myrtle Beach
Long Bay

ens
Aiken
Orangeburg
Georgetown

Augusta
ledgeville
TA
Savannah River
North Charleston
Charleston

Statesboro
ublin
Vidalia
Altamaha River
Hilton
Head Island
Savannah

on
Hinesville

Waycross
Brunswick

dosta
Okefenokee
Swamp

Jacksonville

Lake City
Saint Augustine

inesville

Ocala
Lake
George
De Land
Deltona
Daytona Beach

Spring Hill
Orlando
Cape Canaveral

ear-
ater
Lakeland
Melbourne
Lake Kissimmee

rgo
Tampa
ampa
Saint Petersburg
Fort Pierce

Bay
arasota
FLORIDA
Hutchinson
Island

ort Charlotte
Lake
Okeechobee
West Palm
Beach

arlotte Harbor
Fort Myers
Boca Raton

Naples
Big Cypress
Swamp
Pompano Beach
Fort Lauderdale
Miami Beach
Miami

Cape Sable
Key Largo
Florida
Bay

Key West
Florida Keys
Straits of Florida

ATLANTIC

OCEAN

BAHAMAS

Great Abaco

Grand
Bahama Island

New
Providence
Eleuthera Island

Andros Island
Cat Island
San Salvador

N

41

66

66

54

Elevation

-6000m -4000m -2000m -1000m -500m -250m Below sea level 0 250m 500m 1000m 2000m 3000m 4000m 6000m

820ft 1640ft 3281ft 6562ft 9843ft 13,124ft 19,685ft

-19,658ft -13,124ft -6562ft -3281ft -1640ft -820ft -328ft/-100m 0

43

USA: Central States

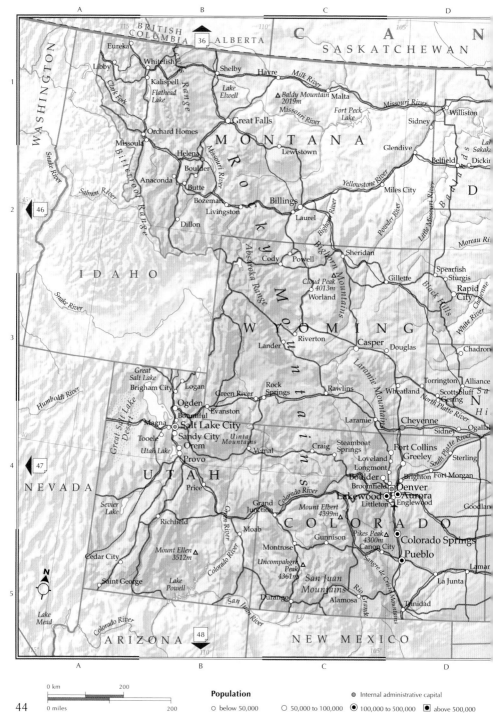

Population

○ below 50,000   ○ 50,000 to 100,000   ◉ 100,000 to 500,000   ▣ above 500,000

● Internal administrative capital

0 km   200

0 miles   200

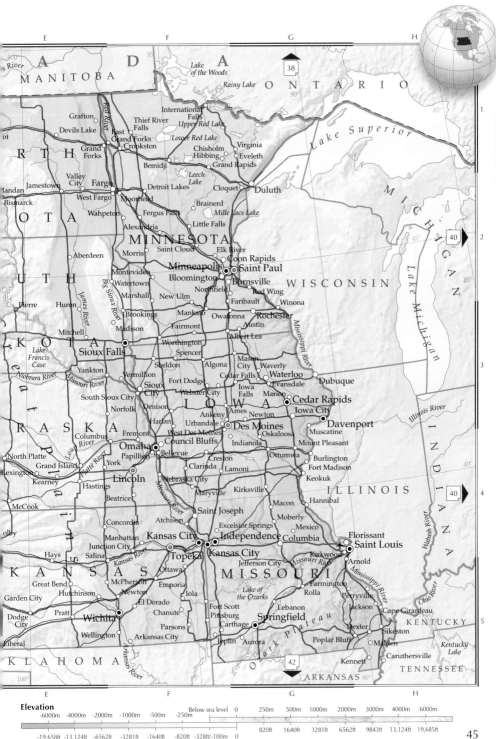

Elevation

					Below sea level	0	250m	500m	1000m	2000m	3000m	4000m	6000m
-6000m	-4000m	-2000m	-1000m	-500m	-250m								
-19,658ft	-13,124ft	-6562ft	-3281ft	-1640ft	-820ft	-328ft/-100m	0	820ft	1640ft	3281ft	6562ft	9843ft	13,124ft	19,685ft

USA: The West

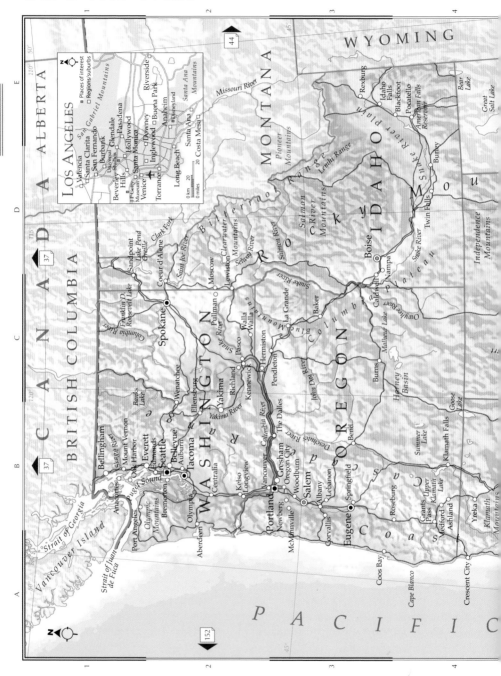

Inset map legend:

LOS ANGELES

- ■ Places of interest
- ▒ Regions/suburbs

Valencia
Santa Clarita
San Fernando
Burbank
Universal Studios
Beverley Hills
Getty Museum
Venice
Torrance

San Gabriel Mountains
Glendale
Pasadena
Hollywood
Santa Monica
Downey
Inglewood
Long Beach

Riverside
Santa Ana
Buena Park
Disneyland
Anaheim
Santa Ana Mountains
Costa Mesa

0 km 20
0 miles 20

Map labels:

WYOMING

MONTANA

IDAHO

OREGON

WASHINGTON

CANADA

ALBERTA

BRITISH COLUMBIA

Rexburg, Idaho Falls, Blackfoot, Pocatello, American Falls Reservoir, Burley, Twin Falls, Bear Lake, Great Salt Lake

Missouri River

Pioneer Mountains

Salmon River Mountains, Lemhi Range, Bitterroot Mountains, Clearwater Mountains, Selway River, Salmon River, Snake River

Boise, Nampa, Caldwell, Owyhee River, Malheur Lake, Independence Mountains, Snake River Plain

Sandpoint, Lake Pend Oreille, Coeur d'Alene, Saint Joe River, Clark Fork, Moscow, Lewiston, Pullman, Walla Walla

Franklin D. Roosevelt Lake, Columbia River, Spokane

Wenatchee, Banks Lake, Ellensburg, Yakima, Yakima River, Richland, Kennewick, Pasco, Hermiston, La Grande, Baker, John Day River, Burns, Harney Basin

Bellingham, Mount Vernon, Anacortes, Oak Harbor, Everett, Edmonds, Seattle, Bellevue, Bremerton, Tacoma, Olympia, Centralia, Aberdeen, Kelso, Longview

Snake River, Blue Mountains, Pendleton, Columbia River, Columbia Plateau

Port Angeles, Olympic Mountains, Puget Sound, Strait of Juan de Fuca, Strait of Georgia, Vancouver Island, Skagit River

Vancouver, Gresham, Portland, Oregon City, Woodburn, Newberg, McMinnville, Salem, Albany, Corvallis, Lebanon, Springfield, Eugene

The Dalles, Deschutes River, Bend, Summer Lake, Goose Lake, Klamath Falls, Upper Klamath Lake

Roseburg, Grants Pass, Medford, Ashland, Yreka, Klamath Mountains

Coos Bay, Cape Blanco, Crescent City

PACIFIC

Scale bar:

0 km 200
0 miles 200

Population

- ○ below 50,000
- ○ 50,000 to 100,000
- ◉ 100,000 to 500,000
- ■ above 500,000
- ● Internal administrative capital

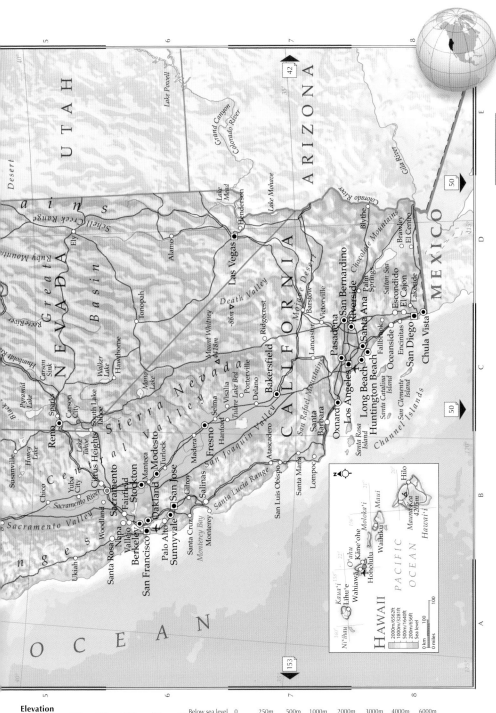

Elevation

-6000m	-4000m	-2000m	-1000m	-500m	-250m	Below sea level	0	250m	500m	1000m	2000m	3000m	4000m	6000m
-19,658ft	-13,124ft	-6562ft	-3281ft	-1640ft	-820ft	-328ft/-100m	0	820ft	1640ft	3281ft	6562ft	9843ft	13,124ft	19,685ft
						Sea level								

47

USA: The Southwest

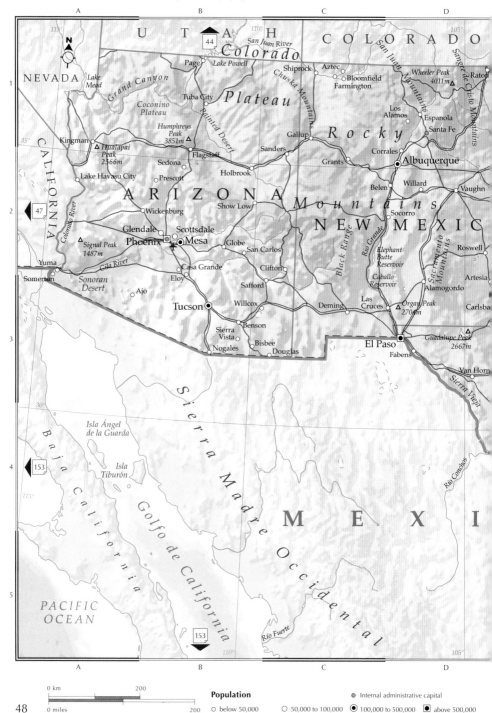

Population

- ○ below 50,000
- ○ 50,000 to 100,000
- ◉ 100,000 to 500,000
- ◼ above 500,000

● Internal administrative capital

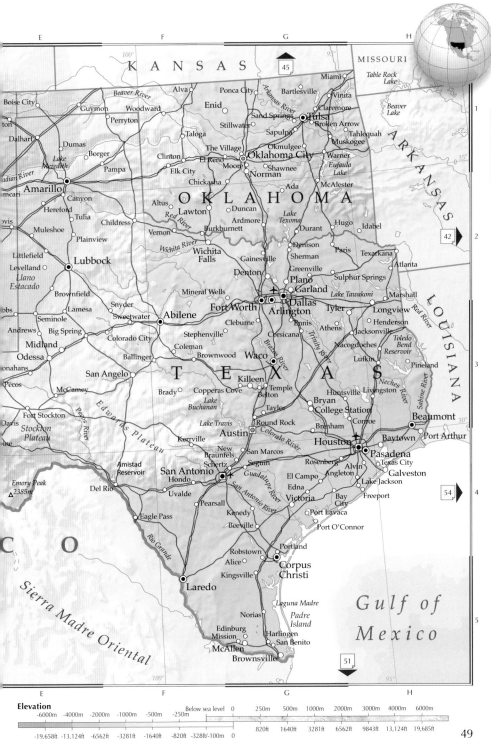

Elevation

-6000m	-4000m	-2000m	-1000m	-500m	-250m	Below sea level	0	250m	500m	1000m	2000m	3000m	4000m	6000m
-19,658ft	-13,124ft	-6562ft	-3281ft	-1640ft	-820ft	-328ft/-100m	0	820ft	1640ft	3281ft	6562ft	9843ft	13,124ft	19,685ft

Mexico

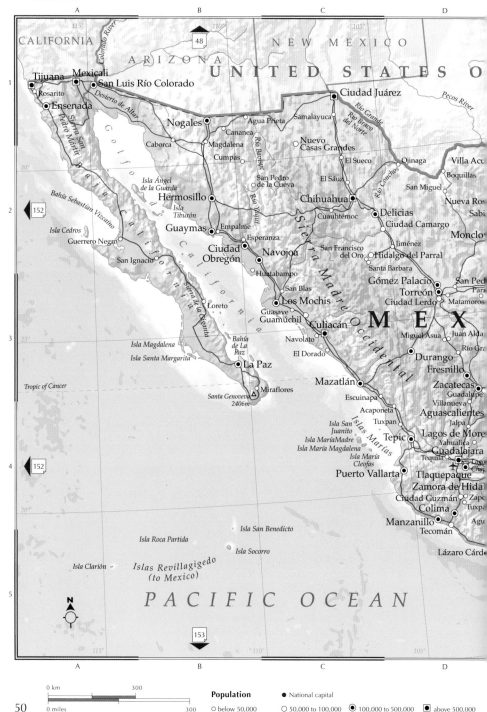

CALIFORNIA

ARIZONA

NEW MEXICO

UNITED STATES O

Tijuana
Mexicali
San Luis Río Colorado
Rosarito
Ensenada
Ciudad Juárez
Pecos River

Desierto de Altar
Nogales
Agua Prieta
Samalayuca
Río Grande del Norte
Ojinaga
Villa Acu
Boquillas
Cananea
Caborca
Magdalena
Nuevo Casas Grandes
El Sueco
San Miguel
Nueva Ros
Cumpas
San Pedro de la Cueva
El Sáuz
Sabi

Isla Ángel de la Guarda
Hermosillo
Chihuahua
Delicias
Monclo
Isla Tiburón
Cuauhtémoc
Ciudad Camargo
Bahía Sebastián Vizcaíno
Guaymas
Empalme
Esperanza
San Francisco del Oro
Jiménez
Isla Cedros
Ciudad Obregón
Navojoa
Hidalgo del Parral
Santa Bárbara
Guerrero Negro
Huatabampo
Gómez Palacio
San Ped
San Ignacio
San Blas
Torreón
Par
Los Mochis
Ciudad Lerdo
Matamoros
Loreto
Guasave
Guamúchil
M E X
Isla Magdalena
Bahía de La Paz
Culiacán
Miguel Asua
Juan Alda
Isla Santa Margarita
Navolato
Durango
Río Gra
El Dorado
Tropic of Cancer
La Paz
Fresnillo
Santa Genoveva
2406m
Miraflores
Mazatlán
Zacatecas
Guadalupe
Escuinapa
Villanueva
Acaponeta
Aguascalientes
Isla San Juanito
Tuxpan
Jalpa
Isla MaríaMadre
Tepic
Lagos de More
Isla María Magdalena
Yahualica
Isla María Cleofas
Guadalajara
Tequila
Puerto Vallarta
Tlaquepaque
Zamora de Hida
Ciudad Guzmán
Zapc
Colima
Tuxpa
Isla San Benedicto
Manzanillo
Agu
Isla Roca Partida
Tecomán
Isla Socorro
Lázaro Cárd
Isla Clarión
Islas Revillagigedo
(to Mexico)

PACIFIC OCEAN

N

Population
● National capital
○ below 50,000
○ 50,000 to 100,000
◉ 100,000 to 500,000
▣ above 500,000

0 km 300
0 miles 300

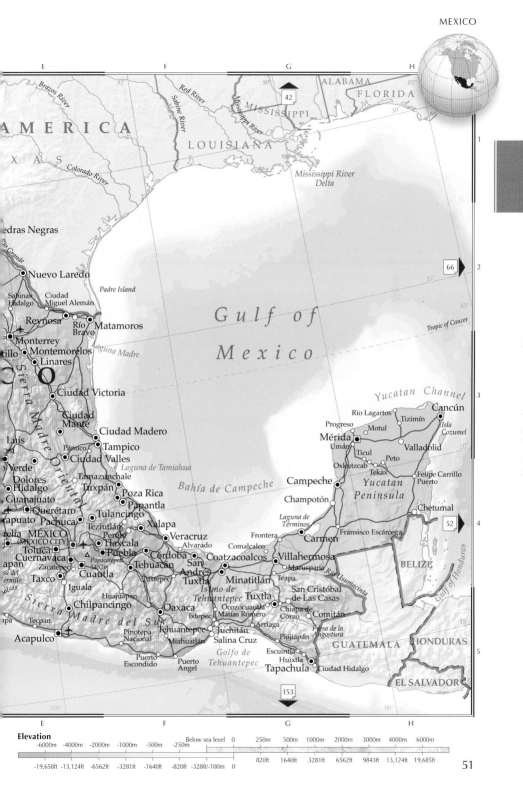

MEXICO

ALABAMA

FLORIDA

42

A M E R I C A

T E X A S

LOUISIANA

Brazos River

Red River

Sabine River

Mississippi River

M I S S I S S I P P I

Colorado River

Mississippi River Delta

edras Negras

io Grande

Nuevo Laredo

Padre Island

66

Gulf of

Sabinas Hidalgo

Ciudad Miguel Alemán

Reynosa

Río Bravo

Matamoros

Monterrey

Montemorelos

Linares

Laguna Madre

Mexico

Tropic of Cancer

illo

O

Sierra Madre Oriental

Ciudad Victoria

Ciudad Mante

Yucatan Channel

Cancún

Luis

251

Verde

Ciudad Madero

Pánuco

Tampico

Ciudad Valles

Dolores

Tamazunchale

Laguna de Tamiahua

Rio Lagartos

Tizimín

Progreso

Motul

Mérida

Umán

Ticul

Peto

Valladolid

Isla Cozumel

Hidalgo

Tuxpán

Guanajuato

Poza Rica

Papantla

Bahía de Campeche

Oxkutzcab

Tekax

Campeche

Champotón

Yucatan Peninsula

Felipe Carrillo Puerto

apuato

Querétaro

Tulancingo

Teziutlán

Chetumal

Pachuca

Xalapa

rélia

MÉXICO

(MEXICO CITY)

Perote

Tlaxcala

Veracruz

Laguna de Términos

52

Frontera

Comalcaleo

Carmen

Fransisco Escárcega

Popocatépetl

5452m

Puebla

Tehuacán

Córdoba

Alvarado

Coatzacoalcos

Villahermosa

BELIZE

Cuernavaca

Zacatepec

Córdoba

San Andrés Tuxtla

Macuspana

Gulf of Honduras

sa del rmillo

Taxco

Cuautla

Ixtepec

Minatitlán

Teapa

Río Usumacinta

olsas

Iguala

Huajuapan

Istmo de Tehuantepec

Tuxtla

San Cristóbal de Las Casas

Chilpancingo

Oaxaca

Ixtepec

Ocozocuautla

Matías Romero

Chiapa de Corzo

Comitán

Sierra Madre del Sur

Tecpan

Pinotepa Nacional

Tehuantepec

Juchitán

Arriaga

Presa de la Angostura

apa

Acapulco

Miahuatlán

Salina Cruz

Pijijiapán

GUATEMALA

HONDURAS

Puerto Escondido

Puerto Angel

Golfo de Tehuantepec

Escuintla

Huixtla

Tapachula

Ciudad Hidalgo

153

EL SALVADOR

Elevation

-6000m	-4000m	-2000m	-1000m	-500m	-250m	Below sea level	0	250m	500m	1000m	2000m	3000m	4000m	6000m
-19,658ft	-13,124ft	-6562ft	-3281ft	-1640ft	-820ft	-328ft/-100m	0	820ft	1640ft	3281ft	6562ft	9843ft	13,124ft	19,685ft

51

Central America

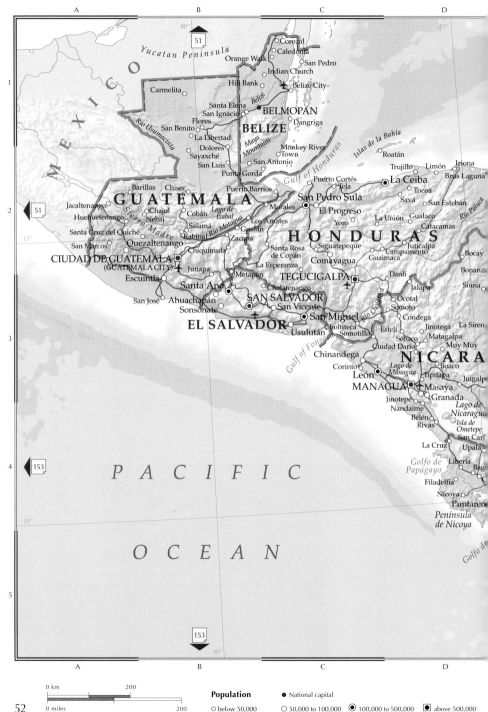

Yucatan Peninsula

MEXICO

Río Usumacinta

Carmelita

Santa Elena
San Ignacio
Flores
San Benito
La Libertad
Dolores
Sayaxché
San Luis

Corozal
Caledonia
Orange Walk
San Pedro
Indian Church
Hill Bank
Belize City

Santa Elena

BELMOPAN

BELIZE

Dangriga

Maya
Mountains

Monkey River
Town
San Antonio

Punta Gorda

Gulf of Honduras

Islas de la Bahía

Roatán

Barillas Chisec
Jacaltenango
Huehuetenango
Santa Cruz del Quiché
San Marcos

Chajul
Nebaj
Cobán

Salamá
Rabinal
Chiquimula

GUATEMALA

Sierra Madre

Lago de
Izabal

Río Motagua

Puerto Barrios

Morales

Los Amates
Gualán
Zacapa

Puerto Cortés
Tela

San Pedro Sula

El Progreso

Yoro

La Unión

Trujillo Limón Iriona
Brus Laguna
La Ceiba
Tocoa
Savá San Esteban
Gualaco
Catacamas

HONDURAS

Río Patuca

Bocay

Bonanza

Siuna

Quezaltenango

CIUDAD DE GUATEMALA
(GUATEMALA CITY)
Escuintla
San José
Ahuachapán
Sonsonate

Jutiapa

Metapán

Santa Ana

EL SALVADOR

Santa Rosa
de Copán
La Esperanza

Chalatenango

SAN SALVADOR
San Vicente

San Miguel
Usulután Choluteca
Somotillo

Comayagua

TEGUCIGALPA

Siguatepeque

Guaimaca

Campamento

Juticalpa

Danlí

Jalapa

Ocotal
Somoto
Condega
Estelí
Sébaco
Ciudad Darío

Jinotega La Siren
Matagalpa
Muy Muy

Gulf of Fonseca

Río Choluteca

Chinandega
Corinto

León

MANAGUA

Jinotepe
Nandaime

Lago de
Managua
Tipitapa
Masaya

Granada

Belén
Rivas

La Cruz

NICARAGUA

Boaco
Juigalpa

Lago de
Nicaragua
Isla de
Ometepe
San Carlos
Upala

PACIFIC

Golfo de
Papagayo

Liberia
Bag

Filadelfia

Nicoya
Puntaren

Península
de Nicoya

OCEAN

Golfo de

Population

● National capital

○ below 50,000 ○ 50,000 to 100,000 ◉ 100,000 to 500,000 ▣ above 500,000

0 km 200
0 miles 200

54

s Santanilla
(Honduras)

Bajo Nuevo
(to Colombia)

Cayo de Serranilla
(to Colombia)

15°

na de Caratasca
Puerto Lempira

Coco

55

Cayo de Serrana
(to Colombia)

75°

spam

Cayos Miskitos

Tuapi

ablis

Puerto Cabezas

C a r i b b e a n

Isla de Providencia
(to Colombia)

Mosquito Coast

Prinzapolka

Barra de Río Grande

S e a

Isla de San Andrés
(to Colombia)

A

Laguna de Perlas

Rama

Islas del Maíz

Bluefields

Punta Gorda

San Juan del Norte

an Juan
to
ejo
esada

58

COSTA RICA

Istmo de Panamá

Gulf of

ela

Siquirres

Portobelo

El Porvenir

Heredia

Limón

Colón

Aligandí

Darien

SAN JOSÉ

Cristóbal

Cordillera de San Blas

Cartago

Guabito

Panama Canal

Lago Bayano

Puerto Obaldía

erro Chirripó

Grande

Almirante

Lago Gatún

Balboa

San Miguelito

Chimán

Serranía del Darién

3819m

Laguna

Golfo de los

Capira

PANAMÁ

COLOMBIA

epos

Buenos Aires

de Chiriquí

Mosquitos

(PANAMA CITY)

Cortés

Volcán Barú 3475m

Penonomé

La Palma

Yaviza

Palmar Sur

Boquete

Cordillera Central

Archipiélago

Isla

El Real

Bahía

David

Aguadulce

de las Perlas

del Rey

Coronado

La Concepción

P A N A M A

Garachiné

nínsula de Osa

Santiago

Chitré

Golfo

Golfo Dulce

Golfo

Guarumal

Ocú

Golfo

de Panamá

Jaqué

de Chiriquí

Las Tablas

Isla de Coiba

Península de
Azuero

58

Isla
Cébaco

80°

Elevation

-6000m	-4000m	-2000m	-1000m	-500m	-250m	Below sea level	0	250m	500m	1000m	2000m	3000m	4000m	6000m
-19,658ft	-13,124ft	-6562ft	-3281ft	-1640ft	-820ft	-328ft/-100m	0	820ft	1640ft	3281ft	6562ft	9843ft	13,124ft	19,685ft

The Caribbean

UNITED STATES OF AMERICA

Gulf of Mexico

Tropic of Cancer

Yucatan Channel

LA HABANA
(HAVANA)

Pinar del Río

La Fé

Consolación del Sur

Artemisa

Guanabacoa

Cárdenas

Matanzas

Cienfuegos

Santa Clara

Placetas

Sagua la Grande

Nueva Gerona

Isla de la Juventud

Cayo Largo

Archipiélago de los Canarreos

Bahía de Cochinos

Sancti Spíritus

Morón

Ciego de Ávila

C U B A

Camagüey

Nuevitas

Archipiélago de Camagüey

Ragged Island Range

Archipiélago de los Jardines de la Reina

Las Tunas

Holguín

Manzanillo

Bayamo

Palma Soriano

Santiago de Cuba

Guantánamo

Guantánamo Bay
(to US)

Windward Passage

Little Cayman

Cayman Brac

GEORGE TOWN

Grand Cayman

CAYMAN ISLANDS
(to UK)

Montego Bay

Spanish Town

Portmore

KINGSTON

JAMAICA

Pedro Cays

NAVASSA ISLAND
(to US)

Île de la Gonâve

Jérémie

PORT-AU-PRINCE

Cayes

Gonaïves

HAI

Haïtie

Jacm

Ca

Great Inag

Jamaica Channel

G   r   e   a   t   e   r

C   a   r   i   b   b   e   a   n

The Everglades

Florida Keys

Straits of Florida

Cay Sal

Grand Bahama Island

Freeport

Marsh Harbour

Great Abaco

Bimini Islands

Berry Islands

Northeast Providence Channel

Nicholls Town

NASSAU

New Providence

Eleuthera Island

Rock Sound

Cat Island

Andros Town

Andros Island

Anguilla Cays

Exuma Cays

Exuma Sound

B A H A M A S

George Town

Great Exuma Island

Clarence Town

Crooked Island Passage

San Salvador

Rum Cay

Long Island

Crooked Island

Acklins Island

Mayaguana Passage

Caicos Passa

Mayagu

Little Inagua

Lake Rosa

Matthew Town

HONDURAS

NICARAGUA

COSTA RICA

COLOMBI

JAMAICA

Montego Bay

Lucea

Falmouth

Discovery Bay

St Ann's Bay

Ocho Rios

Annotto Bay

Buff Bay

Port Antonio

The Cockpit Country

Cambridge

Christiana

Ewarton

Spanish Town

Savanna-La-Mar

Mandeville

Black River

May Pen

Old Harbour

Portmore

Morant Bay

KINGSTON

Blue Mountain Peak
△2258m

Portland Bight

Caribbean Sea

Caribbean Sea

2000m/6562ft	
1000m/3281ft	
500m/1640ft	
200m/656ft	
Sea level	

0 km   20
0 miles   20

0 km   200
0 miles   200

Population
○ below 50,000
○ 50,000 to 100,000
◉ 100,000 to 500,000
▣ above 500,000

● National capital

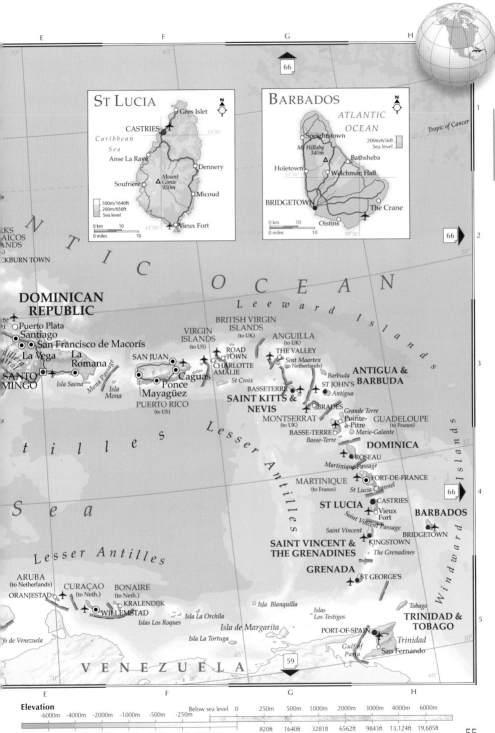

St Lucia

Gros Islet
CASTRIES
Caribbean Sea
Anse La Raye
Dennery
Soufrière
Mount Gimie 950m
Micoud
Vieux Fort

500m/1640ft
200m/656ft
Sea level

Barbados

ATLANTIC OCEAN
Speightstown
Mt Hillaby 340m
Holetown
Bathsheba
Welchman Hall
BRIDGETOWN
Oistins
The Crane

200m/656ft
Sea level

66

TURKS & CAICOS ISLANDS
COCKBURN TOWN

DOMINICAN REPUBLIC

Puerto Plata
Santiago
San Francisco de Macorís
La Vega
La Romana
SANTO DOMINGO
Isla Saona
Mona Passage
Isla Mona

SAN JUAN
Caguas
Ponce
Mayagüez
PUERTO RICO (to US)

VIRGIN ISLANDS (to US)
BRITISH VIRGIN ISLANDS (to UK)
ROAD TOWN
CHARLOTTE AMALIE
St Croix
ANGUILLA (to UK)
THE VALLEY
Sint Maarten (to Netherlands)
BASSETERRE
SAINT KITTS & NEVIS
Barbuda
ST JOHN'S
Antigua
ANTIGUA & BARBUDA
BRADES
MONTSERRAT (to UK)
Pointe-à-Pitre
Grande Terre
BASSE-TERRE
Basse-Terre
Marie-Galante
GUADELOUPE (to France)
DOMINICA
ROSEAU
Martinique Passage
MARTINIQUE (to France)
FORT-DE-FRANCE
St Lucia Channel
ST LUCIA
CASTRIES
Vieux Fort
Saint Vincent Passage
Saint Vincent
BARBADOS
BRIDGETOWN
SAINT VINCENT & THE GRENADINES
KINGSTOWN
The Grenadines
GRENADA
ST GEORGE'S

ARUBA (to Netherlands)
ORANJESTAD
CURAÇAO (to Neth.)
BONAIRE (to Neth.)
KRALENDIJK
WILLEMSTAD
Islas Los Roques
Isla La Orchila
Isla Blanquilla
Islas Los Testigos
Isla de Margarita
Isla La Tortuga
Tobago
TRINIDAD & TOBAGO
PORT-OF-SPAIN
Trinidad
Gulf of Paria
San Fernando

VENEZUELA

Lesser Antilles
Leeward Islands
Windward Islands
ATLANTIC OCEAN
Caribbean Sea

Elevation

55

South America

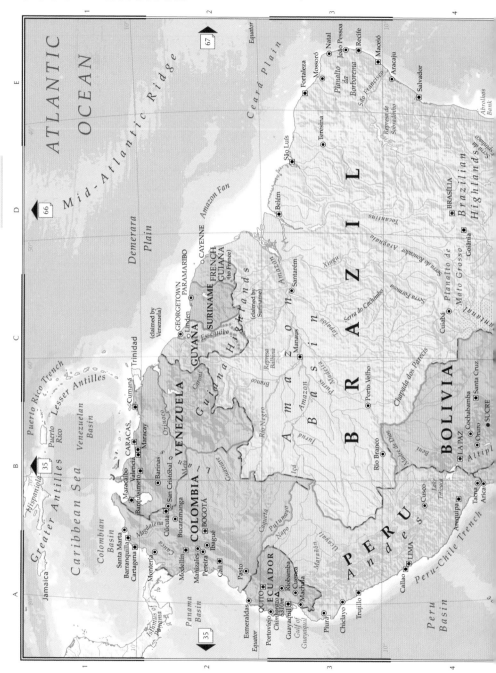

Population   • National capital

o below 50,000   o 50,000 to 100,000   ◉ 100,000 to 500,000   ◾ above 500,000

0 km   500

0 miles   500

Tropic of Capricorn

PACIFIC OCEAN

Chile Basin

Chile Rise

Isla San Félix (to Chile)
Isla San Ambrosio (to Chile)
Islas Juan Fernández (to Chile)

Antofagasta
La Serena
Coquimbo
Viña del Mar
Valparaíso
SANTIAGO
Concepción
Temuco
Valdivia
Puerto Montt
Isla de Chiloé

C H I L E

Atacama

San Salvador de Jujuy
Salta
San Miguel de Tucumán
Cerro Ojos del Salado 6880m
Santiago del Estero
La Rioja
San Juan
Cerro Aconcagua 6959m
Mendoza
Neuquén

A R G E N T I N A

Patagonia

Pampas

Gran Chaco

Formosa
Resistencia
Corrientes
Santa Fe
Córdoba
Rosario
Santa María
La Plata
Bahía Blanca

Rawson
Chubut
Río Negro
Colorado
Chico
Deseado
Laguna del Carbón -105m
Río Chico

Bahía Grande
West Falkland
Bahía Blanca
Gulf of San Jorge
Golfo San Matías

PARAGUAY
ASUNCIÓN
Pilcomayo
Pilacomayo
Bermejo
Paraná
Ciudad del Este
Posadas
Mesopotamia
URUGUAY
MONTEVIDEO
BUENOS AIRES
Río de la Plata
Mar del Plata
Negro
Mirim Lagoon
Lagoa dos Patos

Serra Geral
Londrina
Campinas
São Paulo
Curitiba
Florianópolis
Porto Alegre
Rio de Janeiro
Santos
Salta

Santos Plateau

Rio Grande Rise

ATLANTIC OCEAN

Argentine Basin

Falkland Plateau

FALKLAND ISLANDS (to UK)
STANLEY
East Falkland
Strait of Magellan
Tierra del Fuego
Cape Horn
Punta Arenas

Scotia Sea
Drake Passage
South Shetland Islands
South Orkney Islands

SOUTH GEORGIA (to UK)
South Sandwich Trench
SOUTH SANDWICH ISLANDS (to UK)

Winter limit of pack ice
Summer limit of pack ice

ANTARCTICA

Tropic of Capricorn

Z

67
153
154
154

57

Northern South America

0 km   200

0 miles   200

Population   ● National capital

○ below 50,000   ◎ 50,000 to 100,000   ◉ 100,000 to 500,000   ■ above 500,000

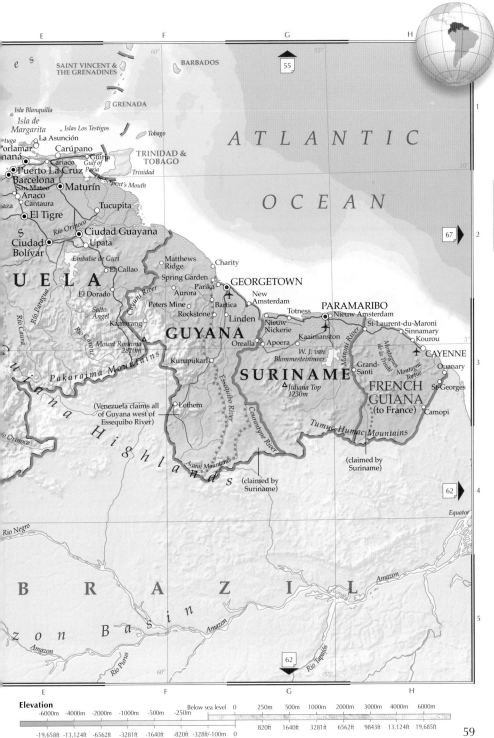

ATLANTIC

OCEAN

SAINT VINCENT & THE GRENADINES

BARBADOS

GRENADA

Isla Blanquilla

Islas Los Testigos

Isla de Margarita

La Asunción

Tobago

TRINIDAD & TOBAGO

orlamar

Carúpano

naná

Cariaco

Güiria

Gulf of Paria

Puerto La Cruz

Barcelona

San Mateo

Anaco

Cantaura

Trinidad

Serpent's Mouth

Maturín

aza

El Tigre

Tucupita

Río Orinoco

Ciudad Guayana

S

Ciudad Bolívar

Upata

Embalse de Guri

Matthews Ridge

Charity

U E L A

El Callao

Spring Garden

Parika

GEORGETOWN

El Dorado

Caroní River

Aurora

New Amsterdam

PARAMARIBO

Río Paragua

Peters Mine

Bartica

Totness

Nieuw Amsterdam

Salto Angel

Rockstone

Linden

Nieuw Nickerie

St-Laurent-du-Maroni

Sinnamary

Kamarang

Río Caroní

Río Caura

Mount Roraima 2810m

GUYANA

Orealla

Apoera

Kaaimanston

Kourou

Maroni River

Montagnes de la Trinité

CAYENNE

Kurupukari

SURINAME

W. J. van Blommesteinmeer

Grand-Santi

Ouanary

Pakaraima Mountains

Juliana Top 1230m

Montagne Tortue

St-Georges

(Venezuela claims all of Guyana west of Essequibo River)

Lethem

Essequibo River

FRENCH GUIANA (to France)

Camopi

G u i a n a   H i g h l a n d s

Tumuc-Humac Mountains

(claimed by Suriname)

Acarai Mountains

Courantyne River

(claimed by Suriname)

Río Negro

Equator

o Orinoco

B   R   A   Z   I   L

Amazon

z o n   B a s i n

Amazon

Amazon

Rio Purus

Rio Tapajós

Elevation

-6000m	-4000m	-2000m	-1000m	-500m	-250m	Below sea level	0	250m	500m	1000m	2000m	3000m	4000m	6000m
-19,658ft	-13,124ft	-6562ft	-3281ft	-1640ft	-820ft	-328ft/-100m	0	820ft	1640ft	3281ft	6562ft	9843ft	13,124ft	19,685ft

Western South America

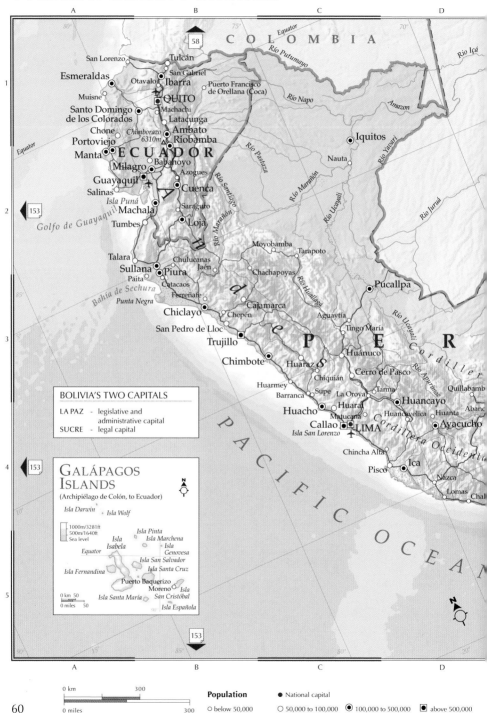

BOLIVIA'S TWO CAPITALS

LA PAZ - legislative and
          administrative capital
SUCRE - legal capital

GALÁPAGOS
ISLANDS
(Archipiélago de Colón, to Ecuador)

Isla Darwin
    Isla Wolf

1000m/3281ft
500m/1640ft
Sea level

Isla Pinta
Isla   Isla Marchena
Isabela   Isla
Equator   Genovesa
    Isla San Salvador
Isla Fernandina   Isla Santa Cruz
Puerto Baquerizo
    Moreno   Isla
Isla Santa María   San Cristóbal
    Isla Española

0 km 50
0 miles 50

Population   ● National capital

○ below 50,000   ○ 50,000 to 100,000   ◉ 100,000 to 500,000   ◼ above 500,000

0 km   300
0 miles   300

BRAZIL

Amazon Basin

Amazon

Rio Madeira

Serra do Cachimbo

Rio São Manuel

Rio Purus

Rio Juruena

Chapada dos Parecis

Rio Abunã

Fortaleza
Villa Bella

Rio Guaporé

Rio Madre de Dios

Riberalta

Cobija
Porvenir
Rio Beni

Magdalena

Puerto
Maldonado

Santa Ana

Rio Mamoré

San Matías

Reyes
San Ignacio
Trinidad

Rio San Miguel

Concepción

Pantanal

BOLIVIA

riental

sco

Sicuani
Nevado Pupuya
△ 5818m

Ayaviri
Moho
Puerto Acosta
Achacachi

Juliaca
Lago
Titicaca
Copacabana

Portachuelo
Buena Vista

Montero
Warnes
Santa Cruz

San José

Puerto
Suárez

Puno
Ilave
Viacha

Cochabamba

Comarapa
Aiquile

Nevado Ampato
6310m

Corocoro

Oruro
Huanuni

SUCRE

Lagunillas

Arequipa
Volcán Misti
5822m

Moquegua

Nevado
Sajama
6520m

Lincia
Challapata

Monteagudo

aná

Tacna

Lago
Poopó

Potosí

PARAGUAY

Mollendo
Ilo
La Yarada

Sabaya

Cotagaita

Villa Martín

Uyuni

San Lorenzo

Tarija

Pilcomayo

Tropic of Capricorn

San Pablo

Tupiza

Villazón

Gran Chaco

Paraguay

CHILE

Desierto de Atacama

Tropic of Capricorn

ARGENTINA

Elevation

-6000m	-4000m	-2000m	-1000m	-500m	-250m	Below sea level	0	250m	500m	1000m	2000m	3000m	4000m	6000m
-19,658ft	-13,124ft	-6562ft	-3281ft	-1640ft	-820ft	-328ft/-100m	0	820ft	1640ft	3281ft	6562ft	9843ft	13,124ft	19,685ft

Brazil

VENEZUELA

COLOMBIA

Cordillera Occidental

Cordillera Oriental

Guiana Highlan

Uraricoera
Boa Vista

Caracora

Pico da Neblina
3014m

Roraima

Río Putumayo

ECUADOR

Río Napo

Río Japurá

Río Içá

Río Negro

Represa Ba

Tefé

Amazon

Manaus

Equator

Galapagos Islands
(Archipiélago de Colón)
(to Ecuador)

Coari

Río Juruá

Río Purus

Río Madeira

58

153

Río Marañón

Río Yavari

A m a z o n

Humaitá

Japiim

Feijó

B **Porto Velho** **R**

Río Ucayali

A c r e

Río Abunã

R o n d ô n i a

PERU

Chapada dos Parec

Vilhen

Río Guaporé

Cordillera

A n d e s

Lake
Titicaca

Cordillera

Río Mamoré

B O **L I V I A** **O**

Lago
Poopó

C e n t r a l

P A R A

153

Desierto de Atacama

Oriental

Pilcomayo

Río Bermejo

Río

Tropic of Capricorn

CHILE

A n d e s

G

Río Salado

Pan

A R G E N T I N A

P A C I F I C   O C E A N

153

N

0 km	600
0 miles	600

Population

● National capital

○ below 50,000

○ 50,000 to 100,000

◉ 100,000 to 500,000

◼ above 500,000

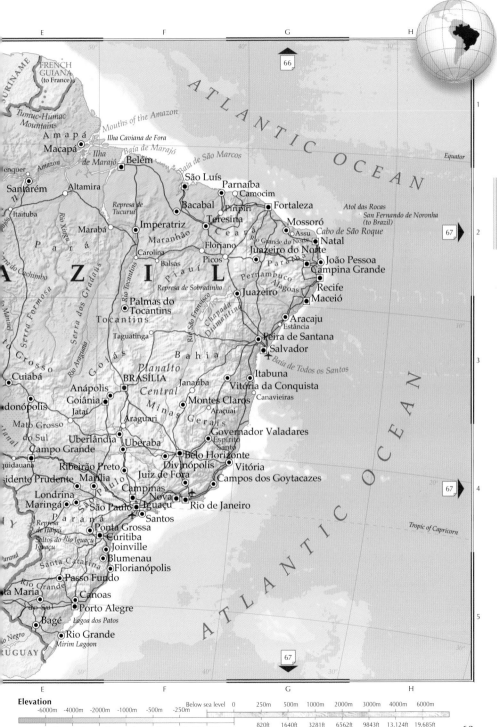

Southern South America

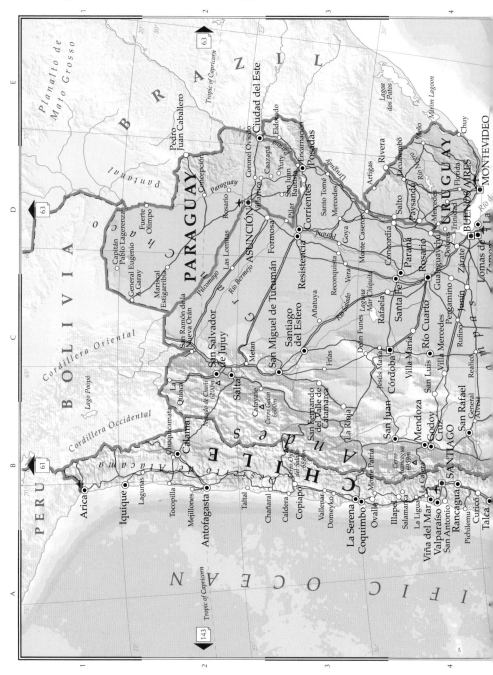

Population

○ below 50,000   ○ 50,000 to 100,000   ◉ 100,000 to 500,000   ■ above 500,000

● National capital

0 km   200

0 miles   200

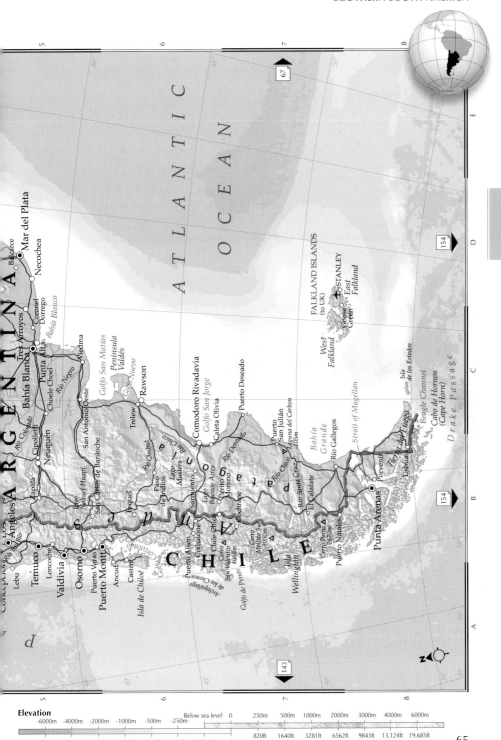

ARGENTINA

Mar del Plata
Balcarce
Necochea
Coronel
Dorrego
Tres Arroyos
Punta Alta
Bahía Blanca
Bahía Blanca
Choele Choel
Río Negro
Cipolletti
Neuquén
Zapala
Río Colorado
San Antonio Oeste
Viedma
Golfo San Matías
Península
Valdés
Golfo Nuevo
Rawson
Trelew
Río Chubut
Lago
Musters
Comodoro Rivadavia
Golfo San Jorge
Caleta Olivia
Puerto Deseado
Río Deseado
Puerto
San Julián
Laguna del Carbón
105m
Bahía
Grande
Río Gallegos
Río Chico
Río Santa Cruz
El Calafate
Puerto Natales

ATLANTIC
OCEAN

FALKLAND ISLANDS
(to UK)
STANLEY
Goose
Green
East
Falkland
West
Falkland

Isla
de los Estados
Beagle Channel
Cabo de Hornos
(Cape Horn)
Drake Passage

Strait of Magellan

Porvenir
Punta Arenas
Tierra del Fuego
Ushuaia

67
154
154
154
143

Concepción
Los
Ángeles
Lebu
Temuco
Loncoche
Valdivia
Osorno
Puerto Varas
Puerto Montt
Ancud
Castro
Isla de Chiloé
Puerto Aisén
Coihaique
Chile Chico
Archipiélago
de los Chonos
Golfo de Penas
Isla
Wellington
Cerro
Melizo Sur
2670m
Cerro
San Valentín
4058m
Cerro Fitzroy
3050m

CHILE

Lago
Nahuel Huapí
San Carlos de Bariloche
Esquel
Paso
de Indios
Lago
Buenos Aires
Cerrito
Moreno
Cochrane
Sarmiento

Elevation

						Below sea level								
-6000m	-4000m	-2000m	-1000m	-500m	-250m	0	250m	500m	1000m	2000m	3000m	4000m	6000m
-19,658ft	-13,124ft	-6562ft	-3281ft	-1640ft	-820ft	-328ft/-100m	0	820ft	1640ft	3281ft	6562ft	9843ft	13,124ft	19,685ft

The Atlantic Ocean

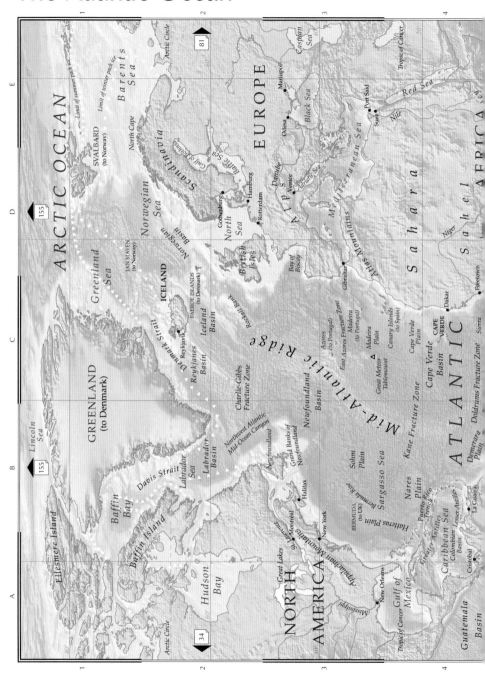

0 km 1000

0 miles 1000

• Major port

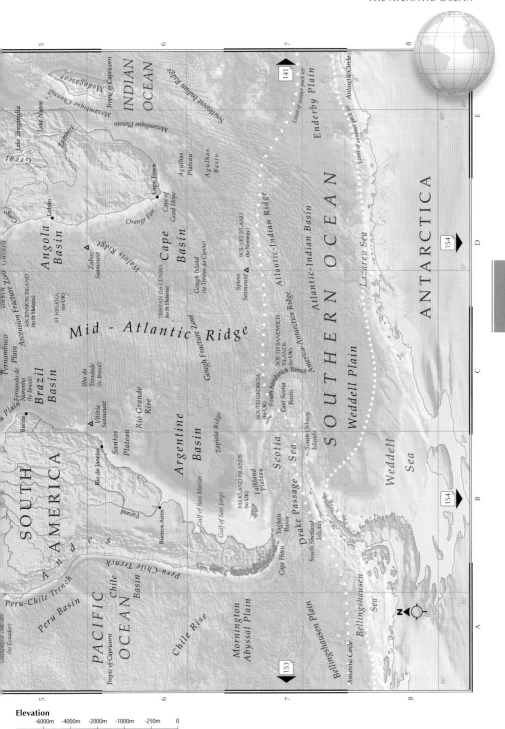

SOUTHERN OCEAN

ANTARCTICA

INDIAN OCEAN

Tropic of Capricorn

Madagascar

Mozambique Channel

Lake Nyasa

Lake Tanganyika

Zambezi

Great

Mozambique Plateau

Southwest Indian Ridge

141

Limit of winter pack ice

Antarctic Circle

Enderby Plain

Limit of summer pack ice

Cape Town

Agulhas Plateau

Agulhas Basin

Cape of Good Hope

Orange Fan

Angola Basin

Luanda

Congo

Walvis Ridge

Cape Basin

Zubov Seamount

BOUVET ISLAND (to Norway)

154

Atlantic-Indian Ridge

Atlantic-Indian Basin

Lazarev Sea

Gough Island (to Tristan da Cunha)

TRISTAN DA CUNHA (to St Helena)

Spiess Seamount

ST HELENA (to UK)

ASCENSION ISLAND (to St Helena)

Ascension Fracture Zone

Guinea

Fernando de Noronha (to Brazil)

Brazil Basin

Pernambuco Plain

Recife

Ilha da Trindade (to Brazil)

Vitória Seamount

Mid - Atlantic Ridge

Gough Fracture Zone

SOUTH GEORGIA (to UK)

SOUTH SANDWICH ISLANDS (to UK)

America-Antarctica Ridge

South Sandwich Trench

Weddell Plain

Rio de Janeiro

Santos Plateau

Rio Grande Rise

Argentine Basin

Zapiola Ridge

East Scotia Basin

Scotia Sea

South Orkney Islands

Weddell Sea

SOUTH AMERICA

Andes

Paraná

Buenos Aires

Gulf of San Matías

Gulf of San Jorge

FALKLAND ISLANDS (to UK)

Falkland Plateau

Drake Passage

South Shetland Islands

Yaghan Basin

Cape Horn

Peru-Chile Trench

Peru-Chile Trench

Chile Basin

Peru Basin

PACIFIC OCEAN

Tropic of Capricorn

Galápagos Islands (to Ecuador)

Chile Rise

Mornington Abyssal Plain

Bellingshausen Plain

Bellingshausen Sea

Antarctic Circle

153

154

154

Elevation

-6000m	-4000m	-2000m	-1000m	-250m	0
-19,658ft	-13,124ft	-6562ft	-3281ft	-820ft	0

Africa

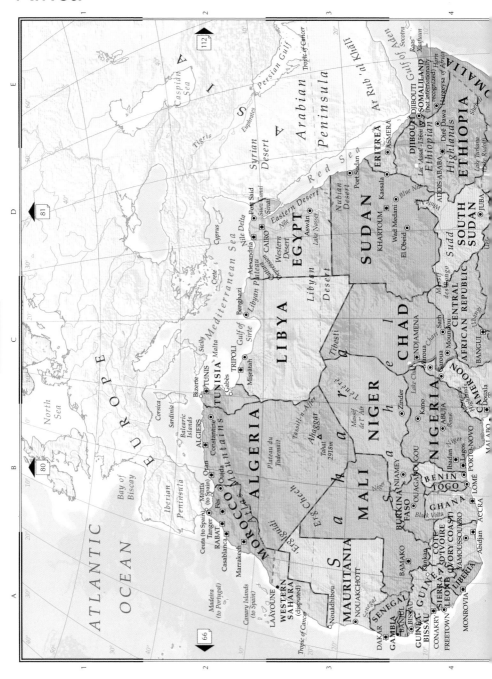

0 km   1000

0 miles   1000

Population   ● National capital

○ below 50,000   ○ 50,000 to 100,000   ◉ 100,000 to 500,000   ◼ above 500,000

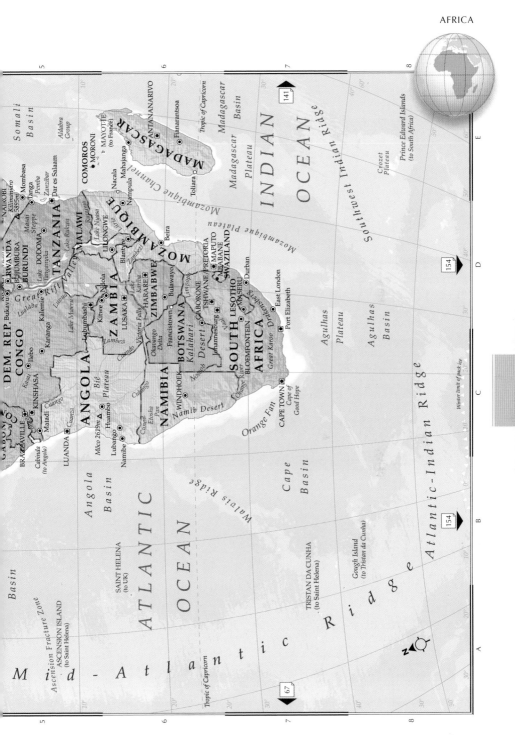

Northwest Africa

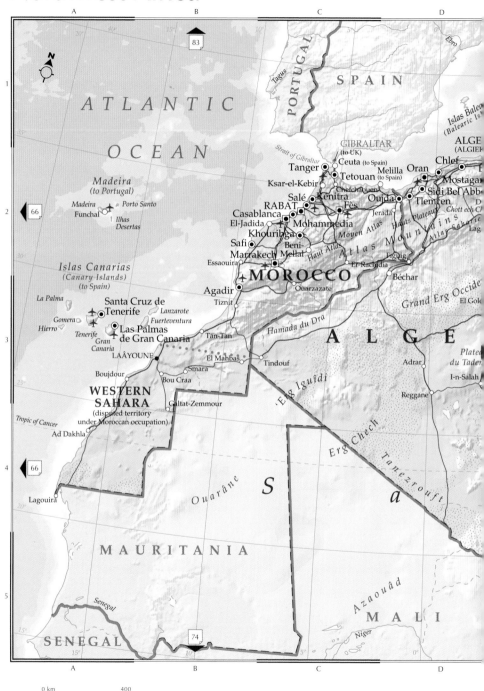

ATLANTIC OCEAN

PORTUGAL

SPAIN

Tagus

Strait of Gibraltar

GIBRALTAR (to UK)

Ceuta (to Spain)

Tanger
Tetouan
Melilla (to Spain)
Ksar-el-Kebir
Chefchaouen

ALGE (ALGIE

Chlef

Oran
Mostaga

Sidi Bel Abb
Tlemcen
Oujda
Jerada
Chott ech Cl

Salé
Kenitra
RABAT
Fès

Casablanca
El-Jadida
Mohammedia

Moyen Atlas
Hauts Plateaux

Atlas Mountains
Atlas Saharien

Khouribga
Safi
Beni-
Mellal

Haut Atlas

Figuig

Er-Rachidia

Marrakech
Essaouira

MOROCCO

Agadir
Tiznit

Ouarzazate

Béchar

Grand Erg Occide

El Gole

Islas Baleares
(Balearic Is

Madeira
(to Portugal)

Madeira
Funchal
Porto Santo
Ilhas
Desertas

Islas Canarias
(Canary Islands)
(to Spain)

La Palma
Gomera
Hierro
Tenerife
Gran
Canaria
Santa Cruz de
Tenerife
Lanzarote
Fuerteventura
Las Palmas
de Gran Canaria

Tan-Tan
El Mahbaş
Tindouf

Hamada du Dra

A L G E

Plate
du Tader

Adrar
I-n-Salah

Reggane

LAÂYOUNE

Boujdour
Bou Craa
Smara

WESTERN
SAHARA
(disputed territory
under Moroccan occupation)
Galtat-Zemmour

'Erg Iguîdi

Erg Chech

Tanezrouft

Tropic of Cancer
Ad Dakhla

66

Lagouira

Ouarâne

S

a

Azouâd

M A U R I T A N I A

M A L I

Senegal

Niger

SENEGAL

83

66

74

Population

● National capital

○ below 50,000   ○ 50,000 to 100,000   ◎ 100,000 to 500,000   ▣ above 500,000

0 km   400
0 miles   400

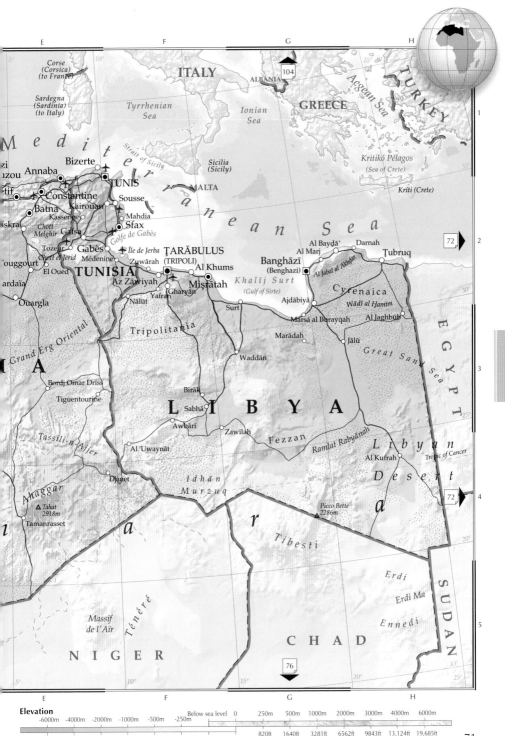

Elevation

-6000m	-4000m	-2000m	-1000m	-500m	-250m	Below sea level 0	250m	500m	1000m	2000m	3000m	4000m	6000m
-19,658ft	-13,124ft	-6562ft	-3281ft	-1640ft	-820ft	-328ft/-100m 0	820ft	1640ft	3281ft	6562ft	9843ft	13,124ft	19,685ft

Northeast Africa

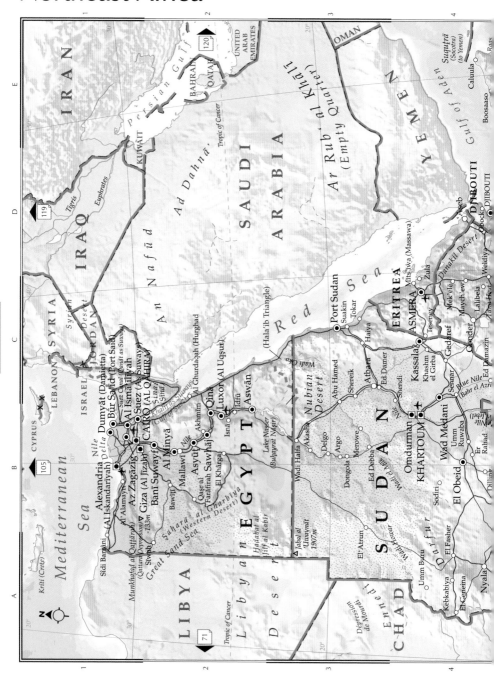

IRAN

IRAQ

SYRIA

LEBANON

CYPRUS

ISRAEL

JORDAN

KUWAIT

BAHRAIN

QATAR

UNITED ARAB EMIRATES

OMAN

SAUDI ARABIA

YEMEN

Suqutrā (Socotra) (to Yemen)

Raas

Calula

Boosaaso

DJIBOUTI

DJIBOUTI

Asseb

Gulf of Aden

Obock

Persian Gulf

Tigris

Euphrates

Syrian Desert

An Nafūd

Ad Dahnā'

Ar Rub' al Khālī (Empty Quarter)

Tropic of Cancer

Red Sea

ERITREA

ASMARA

Mits'iwa (Massawa)

Zula

Danakil Desert

Weldiya

Mek'ele

Maych'ew

Lalibela

Teseney

Gonder

Bahir Dar

Tāna, Lake

Blue Nile

Gedaref

Ed Damazin

Port Sudan

Suakin

Tokar

(Hala'ib Triangle)

Haiya

Kassala

Khashm el Girba

Wadi Oro

Abu Hamed

Shereik

Atbara

Ed Damer

Shendi

Nile

Nubian Desert

Wadi Halfa

Akasha

Delgo

Argo

Dongola

Merowe

Ed Debba

Sodiri

SUDAN

Omdurman

KHARTOUM

Wad Medani

Umm Ruwaba

Sennar

Bahr el Azraq

Nile el Abyad (White Nile)

Er Rahad

El Obeid

Dilling

Mediterranean Sea

Kriti (Crete)

Sidi Barāni

Al'Alamayn

Marsá Matrūh

(Qattarah Depression) Munkhafad al Qattārah –133m

Siwah

Nile

Alexandria (Al Iskandariyah)

Būr Sa'īd (Port Said)

Dumyāt (Damietta)

Al Ismā'īlīyah

Suez Canal (Qanāt as Suways)

Suez (As Suways)

CAIRO (AL QĀHIRA)

Az Zaqāzīq

Giza (Al Jizah)

Banī Suwayf

Al Minyā

Mallawī

Asyūt

Qasr al Farāfirah

El Khārga

Akhmīm

Sohâg

Qinā

Luxor (Al Uqsur)

Idfū

Isnā

Aswān

Lake Nasser (Buhayrat Nāsir)

Gulf of Suez

Sinai (Sīnā')

Chaîne arabique

Al Ghurdaqah (Hurghad)

Bawiti

Sahara al Gharbiya (Western Desert)

Hādabat al Jilf al Kabīr

△ Jabal al 'Uwaynāt 1907m

El'Atrun

LIBYA

Tropic of Cancer

EGYPT

Libyan Desert

Great Sand Sea

Dépression de Mourdi

Ennedi

CHAD

Umbūra

Kebkabiya

El Geneina

El Fasher

Nyala

Darfur

Wadi Howar

Wadi al Milk

Population

| 0 km | 400 |
| 0 miles | 400 |

● National capital

○ below 50,000

○ 50,000 to 100,000

◉ 100,000 to 500,000

■ above 500,000

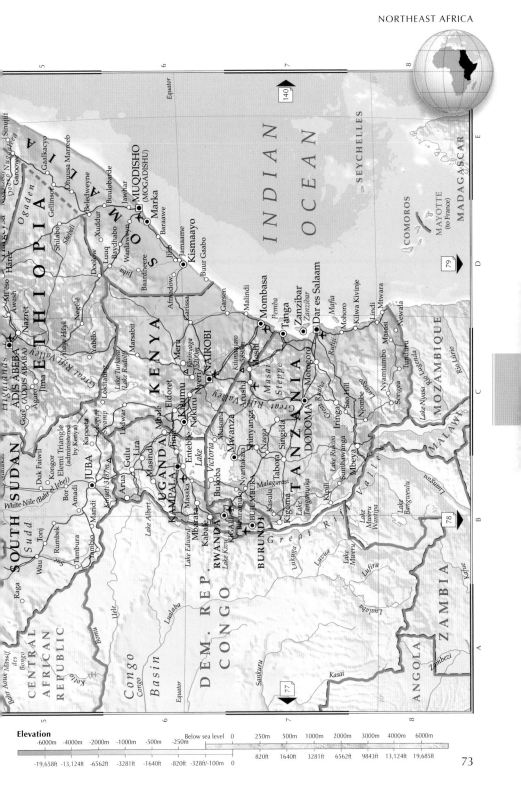

Elevation

-6000m	-4000m	-2000m	-1000m	-500m	-250m	Below sea level	0	250m	500m	1000m	2000m	3000m	4000m	6000m
-19,658ft	-13,124ft	-6562ft	-3281ft	-1640ft	-820ft	-328ft/-100m	0	820ft	1640ft	3281ft	6562ft	9843ft	13,124ft	19,685ft

73

West Africa

Tropic of Cancer

WESTERN
SAHARA
(disputed territory
under Moroccan occupation)

Aïn Ben Tili

Bîr Mogreïn

'Erg

Kâghet

El Hank

Fdérik Zouérat
Touâjil

Ouarâne

S

Nouâdhibou

Choûm

Akchâr Atâr
Chinguetti

El Mreyyé

Akjoujt Oujeft

MAURITANIA

CAPE
VERDE

Ilhas de Barlavento
Santo Antão
Mindelo
São Pedra Lume
Vicente Sal
São Boa Vista
Nicolau

Santiago
Fogo
PRAIA
Ilhas de Sotavento

ATLANTIC

NOUAKCHOTT Idîni
Boutilimit Magta'
Lahjar

Tidjikja Tîchît

Boûmdeïd
Aoukâr Oualâta
Rkîz Tâmchekket
Rosso Aleg Kiffa Ayoûn el 'Atroûs Nêma
Richard Toll Sénégal Kaédi Amourj
Dagana Timbedgha
Saint Louis Matam Kobenni Bassikou
Louga Schibabi
Mékhé Nioro
DAKAR Thiès Mbaké
Mbour Diourbel S Ténenkou
Kaolack Kayes Niger
Sokone Kolokani Ségou
BANJUL GAMBIA Tambacounda Toukoto Koulikoro
Bignona Kolda Gambia Kita
Ziguinchor Sédhiou Bô
Balata BAMAKO
BISSAU Gaoual Kouti
Boké Dinguiraye Bougouni Si
GUINEA- Labé Pita Tikinsso Siguiri
BISSAU Boffa
GUINEA
Kindia Mamou Kankan
CONAKRY Tokounou Odienné Tengréla Ferkessédou
Faranah Korh
SIERRA Makeni Kissidougou Boundiali CÔTE
FREETOWN LEONE Beyla D'IVOIRE
Bo Kenema Katiola
Nzérékoré IVORY COAST
Gbanga Danané
Tubmanburg YAMOUSSOUKRO
MONROVIA Harbel Gagnoa
Buchanan Zwedru
LIBERIA Divo

Sassan
Harper San-Pédro

ATLANTIC OCEAN

Population

● National capital

○ below 50,000   ○ 50,000 to 100,000   ◉ 100,000 to 500,000   ◾ above 500,000

0 km   400

0 miles   400

ALGERIA

LIBYA

Tanezrouft

Tassili-n-Ajjer

Tropic of Cancer

A h a g g a r

Tibesti

71

Tenezrouft

S a h a r a

Ténéré du Tafassâsset

Séguédine

76

'Erg I-n-Sâkâne

Tessalit

Assamakka

Iferouâne

Adrar des Ifôghas

Massif de l'Aïr

Araouane

Ténéré

MALI

Azaouâd

Monts Bagzane 2022m △

Grand Erg de Bilma

Tombouctou

Gao

Ménaka

Agadez

Ngourti

CHAD

Goundam

Lac Niangay

Ansongo

N I G E R

Dilia

Nguigmi

Hombori

Tahoua

Keita

Dakoro

Lake Chad

audiagara

Ayorou

Tillabéri

Birnin Konni

l

Ouahigouya

Dogondoutchi

Maradi

Tessaoua

Zinder

Gouré

URKINA

NIAMEY

Sokoto

Guidimouni

Hadejia

Kaya

Sokoto

Katsina

Nguru

Maiduguri

dougou

OUAGADOUGOU

Gusau

Kano

Hadejia

Potiskum

FASO

Fada-Ngourma

Koko

Zaria

Gongola

Biu

o-Dioulasso

Tenkodogo

Kaduna

Bauchi

Kumo

Banfora

Yelwa

Gombi

Bolgatanga

Sansanné-Mango

Kandi

Kainji Reservoir

Jos

Wa

Natitingou

N I G E R I A

Yendi

BENIN

Parakou

Minna

Jos Plateau

Yola

Tamale

Sokodé

Ilorin

Jebba

ABUJA

Lafia

Mandara Mountains

Adamawa Highlands

GHANA

Lake Volta

Oyo

Ogbomosho

Lokoja

Makurdi

Wukari

Kumasi

Abomey

PORTO-NOVO

Ede

Niger

Benue

CAMEROON

Nsawam

Kpalimé

Ibadan

Owo

Benin City

Enugu

C.A.R.

Asamankese

ACCRA

LOMÉ

Cotonou

Lagos

Sapele

Onitsha

Cape Coast

Warri

Owerri

Aba

Calabar

Sekondi-Takoradi

Bight of Benin

Port Harcourt

Uyo

EQUATORIAL GUINEA

Gulf of Guinea

Mouths of the Niger

Isla de Bioco

77

Elevation

| -6000m | -4000m | -2000m | -1000m | -500m | -250m | Below sea level | 0 | 250m | 500m | 1000m | 2000m | 3000m | 4000m | 6000m |

| -19,658ft | -13,124ft | -6562ft | -3281ft | -1640ft | -820ft | -328ft/-100m | 0 | 820ft | 1640ft | 3281ft | 6562ft | 9843ft | 13,124ft | 19,685ft |

Central Africa

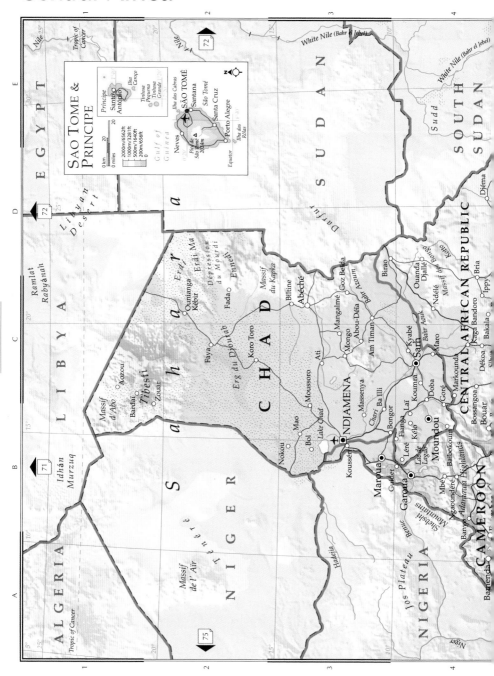

SÃO TOMÉ & PRÍNCIPE

Príncipe
Santo
António
Ilha
Caroço
Tinhosa
Pequena
Tinhosa
Grande
Ilha das Cabras
SÃO TOMÉ
Santana
Santa Cruz
Neves
Pico de
São Tomé
2024m
Porto Alegre
Ilha das
Rôlas
Equator

Gulf of Guinea

2000m/6562ft
1000m/3281ft
500m/1640ft
200m/656ft
0

EGYPT

LIBYA

Libyan Desert

Ramlat Rabyânah

Idhân Murzuq

Massif de l'Aïr

ALGERIA

NIGER

Ténéré

Tropic of Cancer

Nile

White Nile (Bahr el Jebel)

SUDAN

SOUTH SUDAN

Sudd

Darfur

CHAD

Sahara

Tibesti

Massif d'Abo
Aozou
Bardaï
Zouar

Erg du Djourab

Faya
Koro Toro
Ouanianga
Kébir
Erdi Ma
Erdi
Fadao
Enneddi
Depression du Mourdi
Massif du Kapka

Biltine
Abéché
Goz Beïda
Bitao
Ouanda
Djallé
Ndélé
Koho
Bongo
Bria
Ippy
Massif Bandoro
Bakala
Dékoa
Bossangoa
Bouar
Bossembélé
CENTRAL AFRICAN REPUBLIC
Djéma

Mangalmé
Abou-Déïa
Am Timan
Mongo
Bahr Azoum
Bahr Aouk
Kyabé
Sarh
Maro
Koumra
Doba
Goré
Moundou
Markounda

Ati
Moussoro
Mao
Bol
Nokou
Lake Chad
NDJAMENA
Kousséri
Massenya
Ba Illi
Bongor
Chari
Fianga
Léré
Lai
Kélo
Laï
Bénoué
Garoua
Maroua
Guider
Mbé
Ngaoundéré
Adamawa Highlands
Banyo
Shebshi Mountains
Bamenda
CAMEROON
NIGERIA
Jos Plateau
Hadejia
Niger
Benue
Batokoum

Population

● National capital

○ below 50,000
◎ 50,000 to 100,000
◉ 100,000 to 500,000
◼ above 500,000

0 km   400
0 miles   400

Great Rift Valley

TANZANIA

RWANDA
BURUNDI

73

Watsi
Isiro
Mungbere
Beni
Butembo
Bunia
Equator
Lake Albert
Lake Edward
Lake Kivu
Goma
Bukavu
Kalima
Kindu
Kasongo
Kongolo
Kibombo
Kalemie
Lake Tanganyika
Moba
Lake Mweru Wantipa
Lake Bangweulu

Luapula

ZAMBIA

Zambezi

M u c h i n g a   M o u n t s

Lake Mweru
Lufira
Likasi
Lubumbashi
Kipushi
Kolwezi

Titule
Nia-Nia
Kisangani
Yangambi
Lubutu
Lualaba
Lomami
Kela
Tshuapa
Lodja
Lubao
Kabinda
Gandajika
Kamina
Kasaji
Dilolo
Zambezi
Kafue

78

DEM. REP.
CONGO

Congo Basin

Buta
Bumba
Lisala
Akula
Gemena
Mbandaka
Boende
Congo
Lulonga
Impfondo
Dongou
Epéna
Owando
Makoua
Gamboma
Ngo
Bandundu
Lac Mai-Ndombe
Lac Tumba
Lomela
Lukenie
Ilebo
Mangai
Kikwit
Luebo
Kananga
Mbuji-Mayi
Mwene-Ditu
Ishikapa
Tshikapa
Lulua
Kasai
Lulua
Demba
Lusambo
Mweka
Sankuru
Kasongo-Lunda
Kenge
Kwilu
Kwango
Mbanza-Ngungu
KINSHASA
BRAZZAVILLE
Matadi

CONGO

Ouesso
Bétou
Mbaïki
Nola
Nola
Ngoko
Souanké
Sembé
Bélinga
Koumou
Mpouya
Djambala
Plateaux
Batéké
Sibiti
Kibangou
Franceville
Koulamoutou
Moanda
Mayoko
Massif du
Chaillu
Mouila
Lambaréné
Fougamou
Ndendé
Omboué
Setté Cama
Port-Gentil

Kibangou
Dolisie
Loubomo
Mossendjo
Nkayi
Tshela
Boma
Pointe-Noire
Cabinda
(to Angola)

GABON

Edéa
Ebolowa
Ambam
Bitam
Oyem
Mitzic
LIBREVILLE
Ndjolé
Kango
Cocobeach
Oyan
Alalayong

EQUATORIAL GUINEA

Isla
de Bioco
MALABO
Gulf of
Guinea
SAO TOME &
PRINCIPE
Príncipe
São Tomé
SÃO TOMÉ
Equator

ANGOLA

Planalto
do Biê
Cuanza
Kwango
Lungué-Bungo

ATLANTIC

OCEAN

N

67

78

Elevation

| -6000m | -4000m | -2000m | -1000m | -500m | -250m | Below sea level | 0 | 250m | 500m | 1000m | 2000m | 3000m | 4000m | 6000m |

| -19,658ft | -13,124ft | -6562ft | -3281ft | -1640ft | -820ft | -328ft/-100m | 0 | 820ft | 1640ft | 3281ft | 6562ft | 9843ft | 13,124ft | 19,685ft |

Southern Africa

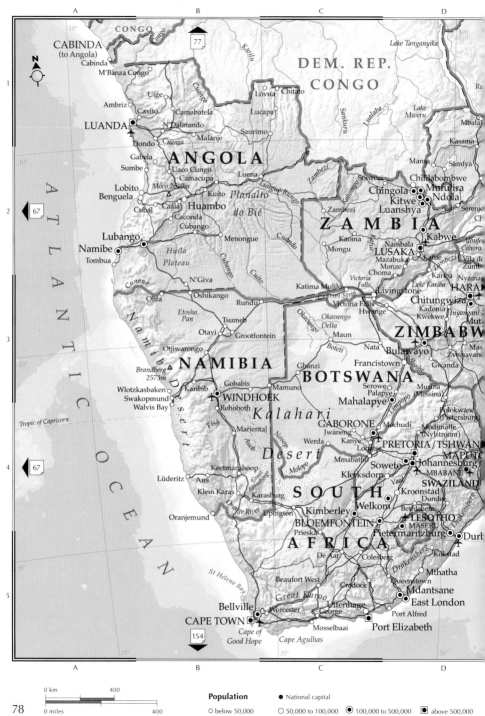

CABINDA
(to Angola)
Cabinda

M'Banza Congo

Uíge

Ambriz

Caxito

Camabatela

Lúvua

Chitato

LUANDA

N'Dalatando

Lucapa

Dondo

Malanje

Saurimo

Gabela

Sumbe

Uaco Cungo

Camacupa

Luena

Lobito

Benguela

Móco 2610m

Kuito

Cubal

Caála

Huambo

Planalto
do Bié

Caconda

Cubango

Lubango

Menongue

Ciubindo

Namibe

Huíla
Plateau

Mongu

Tombua

N'Giva

Olita

Oshikango

Rundu

Katima Mulilo

DEM. REP.
CONGO

Lake Tanganyika

Mbala

Kasama

Mansa

Samfya

Solwezi

Chililabombwe

Chingola

Mufulira

Kitwe

Ndola

Luanshya

Serenje

ZAMBIA

Kabwe

Kaoma

Nambala

LUSAKA

Mazabuka

Monze

Choma

Kafue

Vila do
Zumb

Kariba

Nyama

HARA

Lake Kariba

Livingstone

Chitungwiza

Victoria Falls

Hwange

ZIMBABW

Kadoma

Kwekwe

Inyangani

Mut

Etosha
Pan

Tsumeb

Otavi

Grootfontein

Okavango
Delta

Maun

Nata

Bulawayo

Mas

Otjiwarongo

Boteti

Francistown

Gwanda

Zvishavane

NAMIBIA

Ghanzi

BOTSWANA

Brandberg
2573m

Wlotzkasbaken

Karibib

Gobabis

Mamuno

Serowe

Palapye

Musina
(Messina)

Swakopmund

Walvis Bay

WINDHOEK

Rehoboth

Mahalapye

Limpopo

Polokwane
(Pietersburg)

Kalahari

GABORONE

Mochudi

Modimolle
(Nylstroom)

Mariental

Jwaneng

Kanye

Lobatse

PRETORIA / TSHWAN

Werda

Mmabatho

Soweto

Johannesburg

MAPUT

Desert

Nosop

Molopo

Klerksdorp

MBABANE

Lüderitz

Aus

Keetmanshoop

Kroonstad

SWAZILAND

Klein Karas

Karasburg

Vaal

Dundee

Welkom

Kimberley

Bethlehem

LESOTHO

Oranjemund

Upington

BLOEMFONTEIN

MASERU

Prieska

Pietermaritzburg

Durb

SOUTH

De Aar

Colesberg

Kokstad

AFRICA

Cradock

Mthatha

Beaufort West

Queenstown

Mdantsane

Bellville

Great Karoo

Uitenhage

East London

Worcester

George

CAPE TOWN

Cape of
Good Hope

Mosselbaai

Cape Agulhas

Port Alfred

Port Elizabeth

Population ● National capital
○ below 50,000 ○ 50,000 to 100,000 ◉ 100,000 to 500,000 ▣ above 500,000

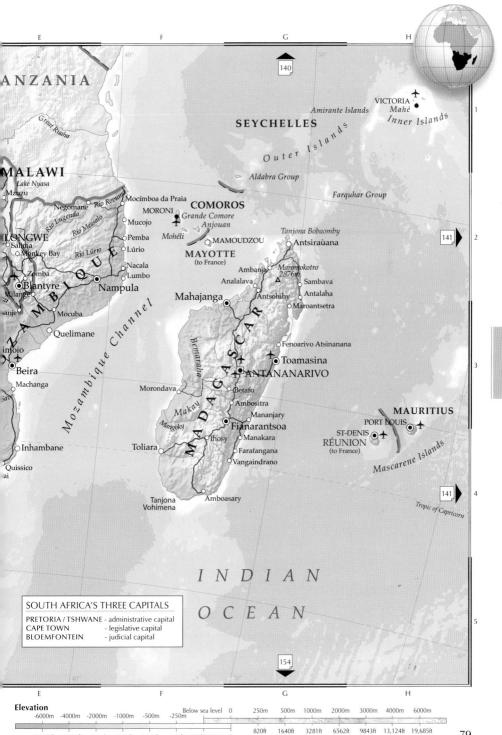

ANZANIA

Great Ruaha

MALAWI
Lake Nyasa
Mzuzu

Negomane *Rio Rovuma*
Rio Lugenda
LONGWE *Rio Messalo*
Salima
Monkey Bay *Rio Lúrio*
Zomba
Milange
Blantyre Nampula
sanje
Mocuba
Quelimane
Beira
Machanga
Inhambane
Quissico
ai

SEYCHELLES

Amirante Islands
VICTORIA
Mahé
Inner Islands

O u t e r   I s l a n d s

Aldabra Group

Farquhar Group

Mocímboa da Praia
COMOROS
MORONI
Grande Comore
Mucojo *Anjouan*
Pemba *Mohéli*
Lúrio MAMOUDZOU
Nacala **MAYOTTE**
Lumbo (to France)
Ambanja
Analalava
Mahajanga Antsohihy

Tanjona Bobaomby
Antsiraùana

Maromokotro
2876m
Sambava
Antalaha
Maroantsetra

M O Z A M B I Q U E

Mozambique Channel

Bemaraha

M A D A G A S C A R

Makay
Mangoky

Morondava
Betafo
Ambositra
Mananjary
Fianarantsoa
Ihosy
Manakara
Toliara Farafangana
Vangaindrano

Tanjona
Vohimena
Amboasary

Fenoarivo Atsinanana

Toamasina
ANTANANARIVO

MAURITIUS
PORT LOUIS
ST-DENIS
RÉUNION
(to France)

Mascarene Islands

Tropic of Capricorn

I N D I A N

O C E A N

SOUTH AFRICA'S THREE CAPITALS
PRETORIA / TSHWANE   - administrative capital
CAPE TOWN   - legislative capital
BLOEMFONTEIN   - judicial capital

Elevation

							Below sea level	0		250m	500m	1000m	2000m	3000m	4000m	6000m
-6000m	-4000m	-2000m	-1000m	-500m	-250m											
-19,658ft	-13,124ft	-6562ft	-3281ft	-1640ft	-820ft	-328ft/-100m	0		820ft	1640ft	3281ft	6562ft	9843ft	13,124ft	19,685ft

Europe

155

66

REYKJAVÍK ●
ICELAND
Vatnajökull

Limit of winter pack ice

Arctic Circle

Reykjanes Ridge

Charlie - Gibbs Fracture Zone

Iceland Basin

Faeroe-Iceland Ridge

FAEROE ISLANDS
(to Denmark)

Norwegian Basin

Norwegian Sea

Trondheim ●

Hatton Ridge

Faeroe-Shetland Trough

Shetland Islands

Bergen ●

Stavanger ●

OSLO ●

Mid - Atlantic Ridge

Rockall Bank

Rockall Trough

Outer Hebrides

Orkney Islands

British Isles

Glasgow ●
● Edinburgh

Gothenburg ●
Aalborg ●

Jönkö

North Sea

ATLANTIC

Ireland

Porcupine Plain

Belfast ●

IRELAND
DUBLIN ■

ISLE OF MAN
(to UK)

UNITED KINGDOM

Jutland

DENMARK COPENH

Odense ●

Malr

OCEAN

Liverpool ● ● Manchester

Britain

Celtic Sea

Cardiff ●

● Birmingham

LONDON ■

Hamburg ●

NETHERLANDS

THE
HAGUE ●

● AMSTERDAM
● Rotterdam

Hanover ●

N

Azores-Biscay Rise

Charcot Seamounts

Biscay Plain

Celtic Shelf

English Channel

CHANNEL IS.
(to UK)

le Havre ●

BELGIUM
Liège ●

BRUSSELS ■
● Düsseldorf

BERLIN ■

Wroc

Iberian Plain

Rennes ●

LUXEMBOURG

LUXEMBOURG ■
● Bonn

GERMANY

PRA

Nantes ●

PARIS ■

Frankfurt
am Main ●

CZE

Loire

● Orléans

Strasbourg ●

Stuttgart ●

REPU

A Coruña ■

Galicia Bank

Bordeaux ●

FRANCE

Zurich ●

Munich ●

BRAT

VIENNA ●

Bay of Biscay

Bilbao ●

Garonne

Lyon ●

SWITZERLAND

BERN ■

Innsbruck ●

Salzburg ●

Porto ■

Cordillera Cantábrica

Duero

Rhône

Mont Blanc
4807m ▲

Milan ●

AUSTRIA

Massif Central

Turin ●

Venice ●

LJUBLJA ●

Trieste ●

PORTUGAL

Iberian
Zaragoza ●

ANDORRA

Nice ●

Bologna ●

Tagus Plain

Tagus

MADRID ■

Ebro

Toulouse ●

Pyrenees

Marseille ●

MONACO ■

Pisa ●

SAN MARINO ●

LISBON ■

SPAIN

Barcelona ■

Corsica

VATICAN CITY ●
ROME ■

Madeira
(to Portugal)

Peninsula

Valencia ■

Sardinia

Naples ●

Bari ●

Seville ■

Guadalquivir

Palma ●

Balearic Islands

Algerian Basin

Cagliari ●

Tyrrhenian Sea

Cosenza ●

Horseshoe Seamounts

Málaga ●

GIBRALTAR
(to UK)

Ceuta
(to Spain)

Strait of Gibraltar

Melilla
(to Spain)

Palermo ●

Sicily

Mount Etna
3340m ▲

Catania ●

Canary Islands
(to Spain)

N

MALTA ●
VALLETTA

Mediterra

Atlas Mountains

68

AFRICA

M e d i t e r r a

0 km — 500
0 miles — 500

Population   ● National capital

○ below 50,000   ◉ 50,000 to 100,000   ◉ 100,000 to 500,000   ■ above 500,000

E   F   G   H

20°   30°   40°   50°   60°   70°   80°

Barents Sea

20°

155

70°

North Cape

Ostrov Kolguyev

Arctic Circle

Ob'

80°

1

Murmansk

Irtysh

Kola Peninsula

Ural Mountains

White Sea

Archangel

Northern Dvina

R   U   S   S   I   A   N

112

Tampere

Lake Onega

Perm'

2

70°

Turku HELSINKI

Lake Ladoga

F   E   D   E   R   A   T   I   O   N

60°

TALLINN

Saint Petersburg

Vologda

Ufa

CKHOLM

ESTONIA

Yaroslavl'

Kazan'

LATVIA

Nizhniy Novgorod

Ul'yanovsk

Orenburg

RIGA

MOSCOW

Samara

Ural

LITHUANIA

Vitsyebsk

Central Russian Upland

Volga Uplands

Syr Darya

3

Aral Sea

Kaunas

Volga

VILNIUS

KALININGRAD
(to Russ.Fed.)

MINSK

Babruysk

Homyel'

Voronezh

Amu Darya

szcz

BELARUS

Don

60°

WARSAW

Brest

Pripet Marshes

Bug

Dnieper Lowlands

Ural

LAND

Dniester

KIEV

Kharkiv

Volgograd

Dnieper

40°

Kraków

L'viv

UKRAINE

Dnipropetrovs'k

Astrakhan'

A

4

112

AKIA

Chernivtsi

Donets'k

*Volga Delta
-28m*

APEST

MOLDOVA

Rostov-na-Donu

Caspian Sea

GARY

Cluj-Napoca

CHIŞINĂU

Stavropol'

S

ROMANIA

Odesa

Sea of Azov

Crimea

BELGRADE

Braşov

Simferopol

C a u c a s u s

El'brus 5642m △

30°

BUCHAREST

Constanţa

Black Sea

I

BIA

Danube

OSOVO
(disputed)

BULGARIA

Varna

Balkan Mountains

PRISTINE

Burgas

5

OFI A SOFIA

SKOPJE

MACED

TURKEY

Zagros Mountains

ANIA

Aegean Sea

A n a t o l i a

Tigris

30°

Pindus Mountains

GREECE

ATHENS

Piraeus

Peloponnese

Cyprus

118

Euphrates

50°

e a

Irákleio

Crete

30°   40°   50°

E   F   G   H

The North Atlantic

A | B | C | D

37

Gulf of Boothia

Devon Island

Ellesmere Island

Arctic Circle

Nares Strait

N U N A V U T

Qaanaaq

Knud Rasmussen

Hudson Bay

Innaanganeq

Savissivik

Southampton Island

Qimusseriarsuaq

Foxe Basin

Baffin Bay

Kullorsuaq

38 C A N A D A

Baffin Island

Upernavik

Péninsule d'Ungava

Hudson Strait

QUÉBEC

Uummannaq

Qeqertarsuaq

Qeqertarsuaq

Arnaud

Cumberland Sound

Qeqertarsuup Tunua

Qasigiannguit

Frobisher Bay

Davis Strait

Sisimiut

Kong Frederik IX Land

Qasigiannguit

G R E E N L A N D

(to Denmark)

Ungava Bay

Limit of summer pack ice

Maniitsoq

Kong Christian IX Land

Gunnbjørn

Mont Forel 3360m

George

NUUK

39

NEWFOUNDLAND & LABRADOR

Paamiut

Kong Frederik VI Kyst

Ammassalik

Ivittuut

Denma

Labrador Sea

Qaqortoq

Nanortalik

Reykjanes Basin

Nunap Isua (Kap Farvel)

Limit of winter pack ice

A T L A N T I C

66

O C E A N

A | B | C | D

0 km 400

0 miles 400

Population

● National capital

○ below 50,000

○ 50,000 to 100,000

◉ 100,000 to 500,000

■ above 500,000

ARCTIC OCEAN

Kap Morris Jesup

Lincoln Sea

Wandel Sea

Independence Fjord

Nord

Zemlya Frantsa-Iosifa

Kvitøya

Novaya Zemlya

SVALBARD
(to Norway)

Nordaustlandet

Kong Karls Land

Spitsbergen

Barentsøya

Edgeøya

Barents Sea

LONGYEARBYEN
Barentsburg

Storfjorden

Limit of winter pack ice

Greenland Sea

Bjørnøya
(to Norway)

Nordkapp
(North Cape)

Kong Frederik VIII Land

Daneborg

Petermann Bjerg
2940m

Limit of summer pack ice

Mohns Ridge

FINLAND

Kong Oscar Fjord

Kangertittivaq

Ittoqqortoormiit

Kangikajik

JAN MAYEN
(to Norway)

Norwegian Sea

Vestfjorden

Arctic Circle

Strait

ICENLAND

Bolungarvík
Siglufjördhur   Raufarhöfn
Bordhur
Húsavík
Akureyri
Stykkishólmur   Seydhisfjördhur
Neskaupstadhur
REYKJAVÍK
Selfoss   Vatnajökull   Djúpivogur
Dorlákshöfn
Hvannadalshnúkur
2119m
Surtsey   Vestmannaeyjar

Norwegian Basin

SWEDEN

Gulf of Bothnia

NORWAY

FAEROE ISLANDS
(to Denmark)

TÓRSHAVN

N

Shetland Islands

Elevation

-6000m	-4000m	-2000m	-1000m	-500m	-250m	Below sea level 0	250m	500m	1000m	2000m	3000m	4000m	6000m
-19,658ft	-13,124ft	-6562ft	-3281ft	-1640ft	-820ft	-328ft/-100m 0	820ft	1640ft	3281ft	6562ft	9843ft	13,124ft	19,685ft

Scandinavia & Finland

Population

- National capital

○ below 50,000   ○ 50,000 to 100,000   ◉ 100,000 to 500,000   ■ above 500,000

0 km   200

0 miles   200

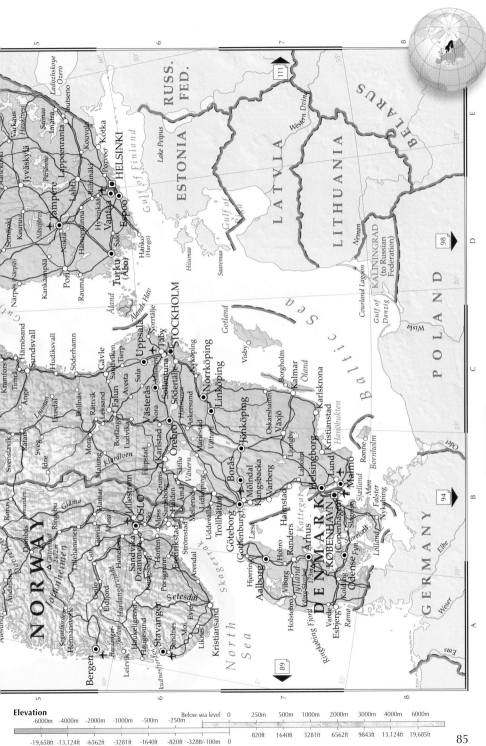

Elevation

Below sea level						0	250m	500m	1000m	2000m	3000m	4000m	6000m
-6000m	-4000m	-2000m	-1000m	-500m	-250m								
-19,658ft	-13,124ft	-6562ft	-3281ft	-1640ft	-820ft	-328ft/-100m	0	820ft	1640ft	3281ft	6562ft	9843ft	13,124ft	19,685ft

The Low Countries

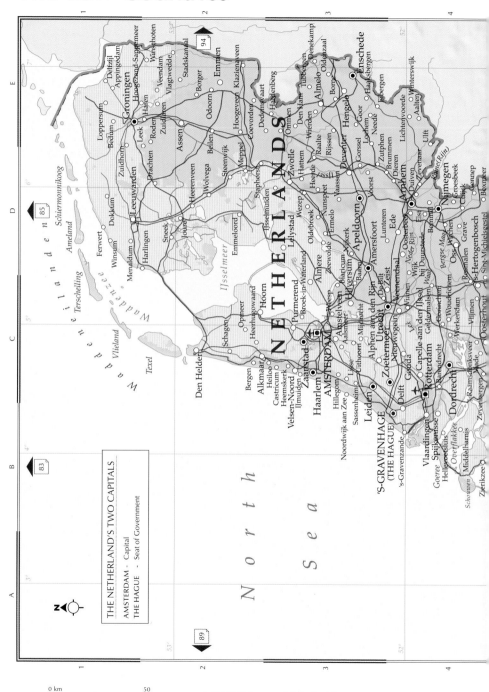

THE NETHERLAND'S TWO CAPITALS

AMSTERDAM - Capital
THE HAGUE - Seat of Government

Population

○ below 50,000 ○ 50,000 to 100,000 ◉ 100,000 to 500,000 ■ above 500,000

● National capital

0 km ____ 50
0 miles ____ 50

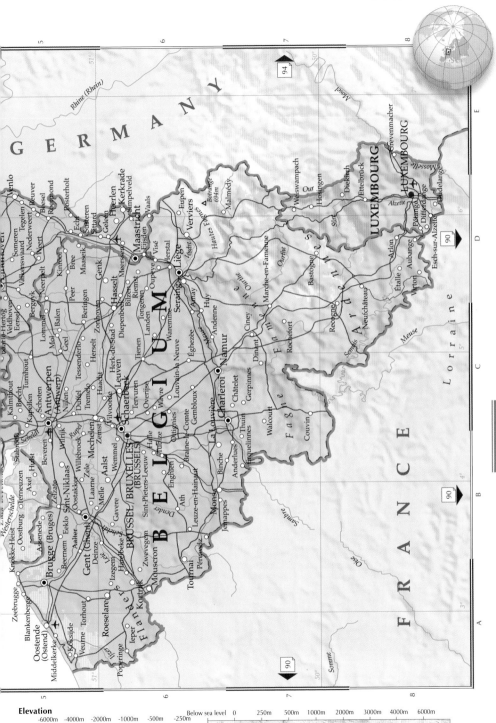

Elevation

						Below sea level	0	250m	500m	1000m	2000m	3000m	4000m	6000m
-6000m	-4000m	-2000m	-1000m	-500m	-250m									
-19,658ft	-13,124ft	-6562ft	-3281ft	-1640ft	-820ft	-328ft/-100m	0	820ft	1640ft	3281ft	6562ft	9843ft	13,124ft	19,685ft

North Sea

Atlantic Ocean

Shetland Islands
Unst
Fetlar
Yell
Mainland
Lerwick
Fair Isle

Orkney Islands
Sanday
Kirkwall
Mainland
Hoy
John o'Groats

Thurso
Ben Hope 927 m △
North West Highlands
Ullapool
Inverness
Aviemore
Loch Ness
Grampian Mountains
Ben Nevis 1343 m △
Fort William
Oban
Loch Lomond
Mallaig
Stromeferry
Isle of Skye
Rhum
Eigg
Coll
Tiree
Isle of Mull
Firth of Lorn
Jura
Islay
Kintyre

The Minch
The Little Minch
Isle of Lewis
Stornoway
Harris
North Uist
South Uist
Barra
St Kilda
Outer Hebrides
Inner Hebrides

SCOTLAND
Fraserburgh
Peterhead
Aberdeen
Elgin
Montrose
Arbroath
St Andrews
Dee
Forfar
Dundee
Tay
Perth
Dunfermline
Firth of Forth
Edinburgh
Stirling
Forth
Glasgow
Hamilton
Clyde
Paisley
East Kilbride
Greenock
Prestwick
Ayr
Kilmarnock
Isle of Arran
Berwick-upon-Tweed
Galashiels
Hawick
Cheviot Hills
Southern Uplands
Coleraine
NORTHERN
Newcastle upon Tyne

Moray Firth

82
82
82
84

N

0 km   100
0 miles   100

Population

National capital
Internal administrative capital

○ below 50,000
○ 50,000 to 100,000
◉ 100,000 to 500,000
◼ above 500,000

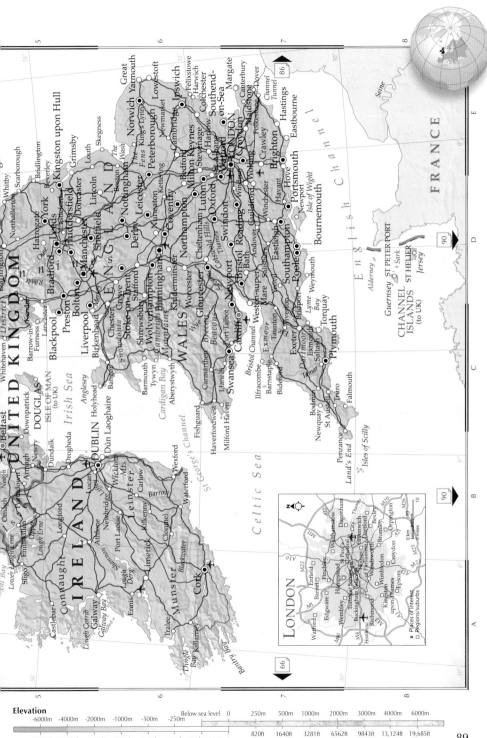

Elevation

Below sea level						0	250m	500m	1000m	2000m	3000m	4000m	6000m
-6000m	-4000m	-2000m	-1000m	-500m	-250m								
-19,658ft	-13,124ft	-6562ft	-3281ft	-1640ft	-820ft	-328ft/-100m	0	820ft	1640ft	3281ft	6562ft	9843ft	13,124ft	19,685ft

89

France, Andorra & Monaco

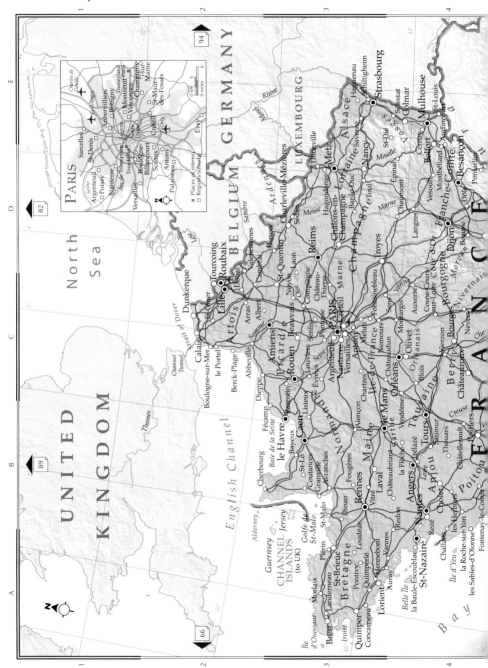

Population   ● National capital

○ below 50,000   ○ 50,000 to 100,000   ◉ 100,000 to 500,000   ▣ above 500,000

0 km   100

0 miles   100

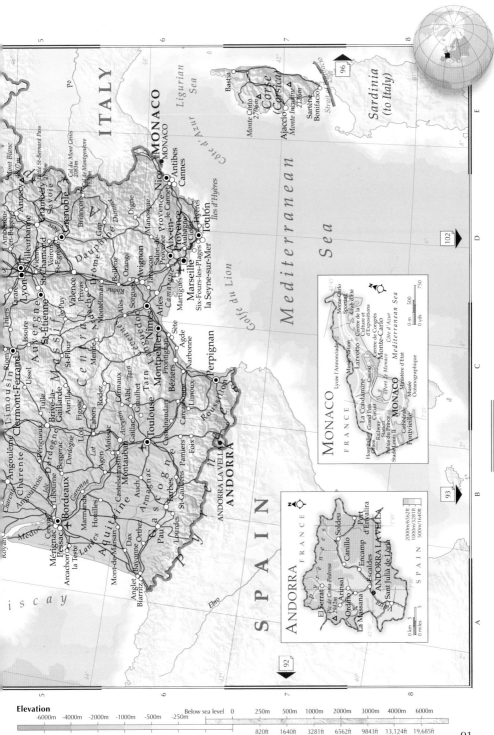

Elevation

-6000m	-4000m	-2000m	-1000m	-500m	Below sea level	0	250m	500m	1000m	2000m	3000m	4000m	6000m
-19,658ft	-13,124ft	-6562ft	-3281ft	-1640ft	-820ft -328ft/-100m	0	820ft	1640ft	3281ft	6562ft	9843ft	13,124ft	19,685ft

Spain & Portugal

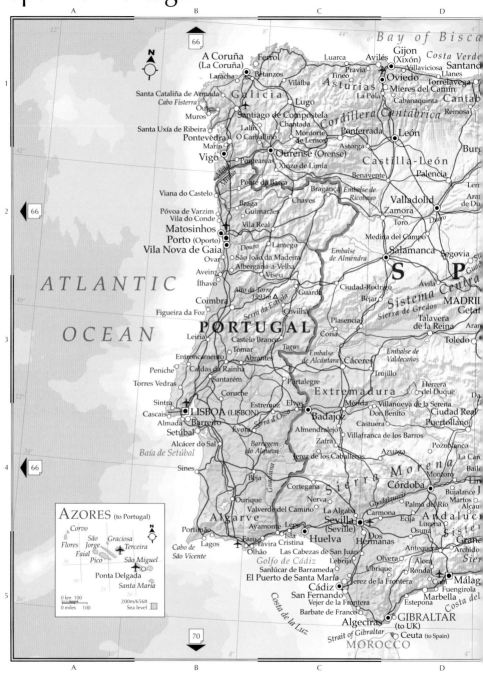

Bay of Biscay

A Coruña (La Coruña)
Laracha
Betanzos
Ferrol
Vilalba
Luarca
Tineo
Pravia
Avilés
La Pola
Gijon (Xixón)
Villaviciosa
Santand
Costa Verde
Llanes
Oviedo
Torrelavega
Mieres del Camín
Cabanaquinta
Reinosa
Asturias
Cantab

Santa Cataliña de Armada
Cabo Fisterra
Oules
Muros
Galicia
Lugo
Chantada
Santiago de Compostela
Cordillera Cantábrica

Santa Uxía de Ribeira
Pontevedra
Marín
Lalín
Monforte de Lemos
O Carballiño
Ponferrada
Astorga
León
Castilla-León
Burg

Vigo
Ponteareas
Ourense (Orense)
Xinzo de Limia
Benavente
Palencia
Lerr
Aran
de Du

Viana do Castelo
Ponte da Barca
Bragança
Embalse de Ricobayo
Valladolid
Zamora
Toro
Medina del Campo
Duero
Salamanca
Segovia
Sta

Póvoa de Varzim
Vila do Conde
Braga
Guimarães
Vila Real
Chaves

Matosinhos
Porto (Oporto)
Vila Nova de Gaia
Ovar
Douro
São João da Madeira
Albergaria-a-Velha
Lamego
Viseu
Embalse de Almendra
S   **P**

ATLANTIC
Aveiro
Ílhavo
Alto da Torre 1993m
Guarda
Ciudad-Rodrigo
Béjar
Ávila
MADRII
Getal
Ceuta

OCEAN
Coimbra
Figueira da Foz
Serra da Estrela
Covilhã
Plasencia
Sistema Central
Sierra de Gredos
Talavera de la Reina
Aran

Leiria
Castelo Branco
Coria
Toledo

Entroncamento
Tomar
Tagus
Cáceres
Embalse de Valdecañas

PORTUGAL
Abrantes
Embalse de Alcántara
Trujillo

Peniche
Caldas da Rainha
Santarém
Portalegre
Extremadura
Herrera del Duque
Da

Torres Vedras
Coruche
Mérida
Villanueva de la Serena

Sintra
Cascais
Almada
LISBOA (LISBON)
Barreiro
Estremoz
Serra d'Ossa
Elvas
Badajoz
Don Benito
Castuera
Ciudad Real
Puertollano

Setúbal
Évora
Almendralejo
Zafra
Villafranca de los Barros
Pozoblanco
La Card

Alcácer do Sal
Barragem do Alqueva
Jerez de los Caballeros
Azuaga
Baile

Baía de Setúbal
Sines
Beja
Cortegana
Nerva
Sierra Morena
Córdoba
Montoro
Lin
Bujalance
Martos
Alcau

Ourique
Valverde del Camino
La Algaba
Ghadalquivir
Palma del Río
Andaluc
Sister
Grana

Algarve
Portimão
Lagos
Cabo de São Vicente
Ayamonte
Lepe
Faro
Isla Cristina
Tavira
Olhão
Huelva
Dos Hermanas
Sevilla (Seville)
Carmona
Ecija
Osuna
Antequera
Archido

Golfo de Cádiz
Las Cabezas de San Juan
Lebrija
Olvera
Álora
Ronda
Sierra

Sanlúcar de Barrameda
El Puerto de Santa María
Jerez de la Frontera
Ubrique
C
Málag
Fuengirola

Cádiz
San Fernando
Vejer de la Frontera
Estepona
Marbella
Costa del

Costa de la Luz
Barbate de Franco
Algeciras
GIBRALTAR (to UK)
Strait of Gibraltar
Ceuta (to Spain)
MOROCCO

AZORES (to Portugal)

Corvo
Flores
São Jorge
Graciosa
Terceira
Faial
Pico
São Miguel
Ponta Delgada
Santa Maria

0 km 100
0 miles 100
200m/656ft
Sea level

0 km 100
0 miles 100

Population   • National capital

○ below 50,000   ○ 50,000 to 100,000   ◉ 100,000 to 500,000   ◼ above 500,000

E   F   G   H

F R A N C E

Bermeo
Zarautz
Donostia/San Sebastián
Eibar
Irun
Tolosa
Bergara
País Vasco
Pamplona
(Iruña)
toria-Gasteiz
Miranda
de Ebro
Estella
Jaca
P y r e n e e s
Monte Perdido
3348m
La Seu d'Urgell
ANDORRA
ogroño
N a v a r r a
Huesca
Barbastro
Berga
Manlleu
Ripoll
Figueres
Banyoles
Girona
(Gerona)
Arnedo
Calahorra
La Rioja
Tudela
Tarazona
Soria
Ejea de
los Caballeros
Ebro
Monzón
Balaguer
Cervera
Vic
Cataluña
Palafrugell
Palamós
Burgo
Osma
Zaragoza
Lleida
(Lérida)
Tàrrega
Terrassa
Sabadell
Blanes
Arenys de Mar
Costa Brava
Medinaceli
Sistema Ibérico
Calatayud
Daroca
Aragón
Fraga
Vilafranca del Penedès
Mataró
Barcelona
L'Hospitalet de Llobregat
Alcañiz
Reus
Valls
Sitges
El Vendrell
Tarragona
Guadalajara
calá de Henares
ejón de Ardoz
N
Teruel
Tortosa
Amposta
Sant Carles de la Ràpita
Vinaròs
Tarancón
Cuenca
Javalambre
2020m △
Onda
País Valenciano
Castellón de la Plana
Ciutadella
(Minorca)
Menorca
(Minorca)
Maó
Pollença
Sa Pobla
stilla-La Mancha
Mota del Cuervo
Campo de Criptana
Socuéllamos
La Roda
Júcar
Vall d'Uxó
Burjassot
Sagunto
(Sagunt)
Valencia
Catarroja
Sueca
Cullera
Costa del Azahar
Palma
Lluçmajor
Manacor
Felanitx
*Illa de
Cabrera*
Mallorca
(Majorca)
*Golfo de
Valencia*
Islas Baleares
(Balearic Islands)
nzanares
a Solana
peñas
Albacete
Almansa
Xàtiva
Algemesí
Gandia
Oliva
Dénia
Ibiza
Eivissa (Ibiza)
Formentera
Villanueva de los Infantes
Hellín
Segura
Ontinyent
Villena
Alcoy
Jumilla
Elda
Benidorm
Villajoyosa (La Vila Joíosa)
Sant Joan d'Alacant
Beas de Segura
Moratalla
Cieza
Monóvar
Elche
(Elx)
Alicante (Alacant)
Mula
Callosa de Segura
Orihuela
Costa Blanca
Villacarrillo
Cazorla
éticos
Murcia
Murcia
Huéscar
Totana
La Unión
Baza
Lorca
Aguilas
Cartagena
Guadix
*nbacén
81m*
vada
Mojácar
Berja
Almería
Adra

M e d i t e r r a n e a n   S e a

A L G E R I A

Golfe du Lion

96 ▶ 2

97 ▶ 4

GIBRALTAR (to UK)

SPAIN
Gibraltar
Airport
North Mole
The Rock
Gibraltar
Harbour
Catalan Bay
Catalan
Bay
Sandy
Bay
Rosia
Summit Area △
Rosia
Bay
Little
Bay
Buena Vista
Europa Point

□ 200m/656ft
Sea level
0 km   1
0 mile   1

Bay of Gibraltar

Strait of Gibraltar

Elevation

-6000m	-4000m	-2000m	-1000m	-500m	-250m	Below sea level	0	250m	500m	1000m	2000m	3000m	4000m	6000m
-19,658ft	-13,124ft	-6562ft	-3281ft	-1640ft	-820ft	-328ft/-100m	0	820ft	1640ft	3281ft	6562ft	9843ft	13,124ft	19,685ft

Germany & the Alpine States

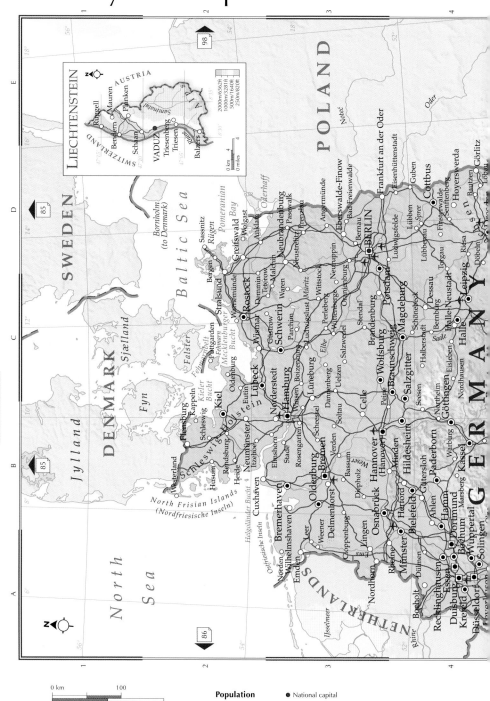

LIECHTENSTEIN

2000m/6562ft
1000m/3281ft
500m/1640ft
250m/820ft

Roggell · Mauren · Planken
Bendern · Schaan · VADUZ · Triesenberg · Triesen · Balzers

AUSTRIA
SWITZERLAND

Saminatal

ALPS
Rhine

0 km 4
0 miles 4

**Bornholm
(to Denmark)**

Baltic Sea

SWEDEN

POLAND

Oder
Noteć

Sassnitz
Rügen · Bergen
Stralsund · Greifswald Bay · Greifswald
Wolgast
Pomeranian Bay
Oderhaff

Wittow
Wolgast
Anklam
Pasewalk
Angermünde
Eberswalde-Finow
Bad Freienwalde
Frankfurt an der Oder
Eisenhüttenstadt
Guben
Cottbus
Eisenwalde
Senftenberg
Hoyerswerda
Bautzen · Görlitz
Löbau

Zingst
Wismar
Rostock
Warnemünde
Güstrow
Teterow
Waren
Müritz
Witstock
Neustrelitz
Neuruppin
Oranienburg
Bernau
BERLIN
Ludwigsfelde
Lübben
Lübbenau
Spree
Finsterwalde
Riesa
Döbeln
Leipzig

Schwerin
Parchim
Ludwigslust
Perleberg
Wittenberge
Stendal
Brandenburg
Potsdam
Magdeburg
Wolfsburg
Braunschweig
Salzgitter
Schönebeck
Halberstadt
Bernburg
Dessau
Halle-Neustadt
Eisleben
Halle
Nordhausen
Göttingen

Falster

DENMARK

Sjælland

Fyn

Jylland

North Frisian Islands
(Nordfriesische Inseln)

Ostfriesische Inseln
Helgoländer Bucht

Westerland
Husum
Heide
Rendsburg
Schleswig
Kappeln
Flensburg
Eckernförde
Kiel
Kieler Bucht
Eutin
Neumünster
Itzehoe
Elmshorn
Stade
Rosengarten
Scheessel
Zeven

Fehmarn
Puttgarden
Oldenburg
Mecklenburg Bucht
Lübeck
Norderstedt
Hamburg
Buchen
Lüneburg
Dannenberg
Boizenburg
Uelzen
Salzwedel
Soltau
Celle

Cuxhaven
Bremerhaven
Wilhelmshaven
Norden
Emden
Leer
Weener
Cloppenburg
Delmenhorst
Oldenburg
Bassum
Diepholz
Nienburg
Verden
Bremen
Osnabrück
Hannover
Minden
Hameln
Hildesheim
Peine
Seesen
Northeim
Warburg
Kassel

NETHERLANDS

Rhine
Nordhorn
Rheine
Lingen
Ems
Weser
Bocholt
Borken
Dülmen
Münster
Gütersloh
Bielefeld
Herford
Paderborn
Ahlen
Hamm
Marsberg
Recklinghausen
Duisburg
Essen
Bochum
Dortmund
Krefeld
Düsseldorf
Wuppertal
Solingen

G E R M A N Y

IJsselmeer

*N o r t h
S e a*

0 km 100
0 miles 100

Population ● National capital

○ below 50,000 ○ 50,000 to 100,000 ◉ 100,000 to 500,000 ▣ above 500,000

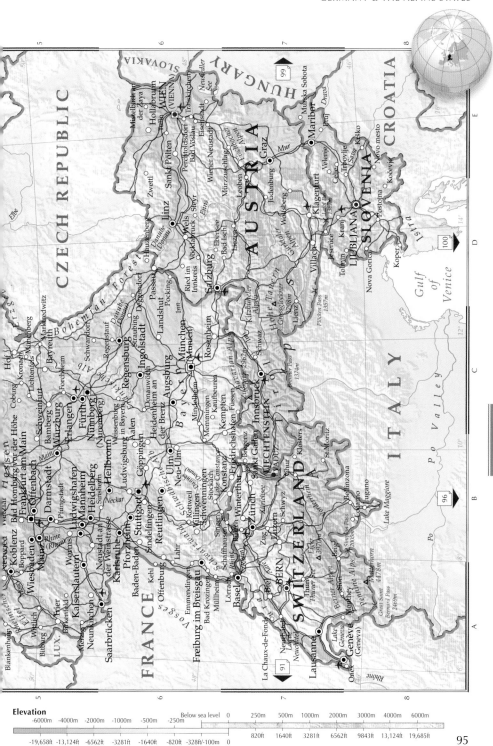

Elevation

					Below sea level	0	250m	500m	1000m	2000m	3000m	4000m	6000m
-6000m	-4000m	-2000m	-1000m	-500m	-250m								

						820ft	1640ft	3281ft	6562ft	9843ft	13,124ft	19,685ft
-19,658ft	-13,124ft	-6562ft	-3281ft	-1640ft	-820ft	-328ft/-100m	0					

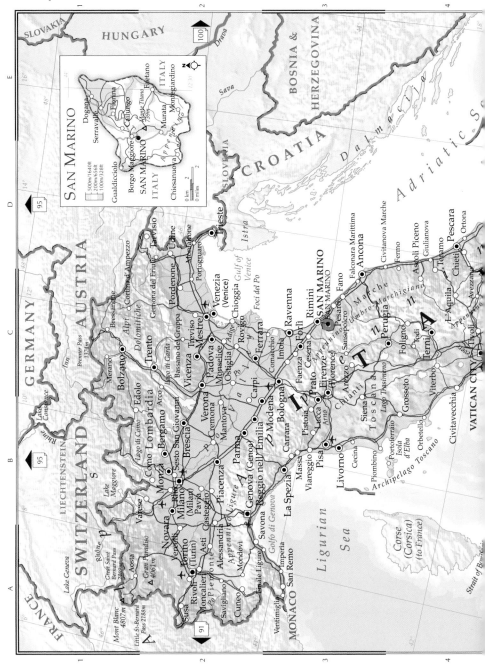

Population

● National capital

○ below 50,000 ○ 50,000 to 100,000 ◉ 100,000 to 500,000 ■ above 500,000

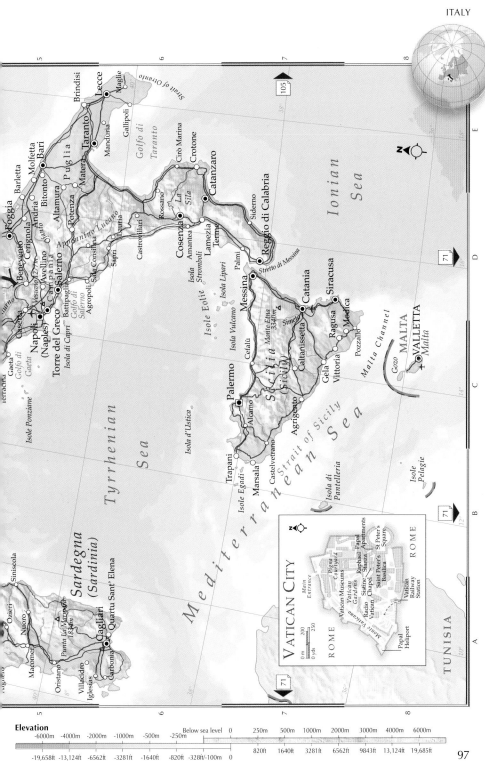

Strait of Otranto

Maglie
Lecce
Brindisi
Gallipoli
Manduria
Taranto
Golfo di Taranto
Molfetta
Bari
Barletta
Bitonto
Andria
Altamura
Matera
Puglia
Ciro Marina
Crotone
Rossano
La Sila
Catanzaro
Sidermo
Reggio di Calabria

Ionian Sea

Foggia
Cerignola
Benevento
Avellino
Vesuvio 1277m
Potenza
Sala Consilina
Campania
Salerno
Caserta
Napoli (Naples)
Torre del Greco
Appennino Lucano
Sapri
Castrovillari
Amantea
Cosenza
Lamezia Terme
Palmi
Stretto di Messina
Messina
Catania
Siracusa

Terracina
Gaeta
Golfo di Gaeta
Isole Ponziane
Isola di Capri
Golfo di Salerno
Agropoli
Battipaglia
Isola Stromboli
Isole Eolie
Isola Lipari
Isola Vulcano
Cefalù
Monte Etna 3340m
Simeto
Ragusa
Medica
Pozzallo

MALTA
VALLETTA
Malta

Malta Channel
Gozo

Tyrrhenian Sea

Palermo
Alcamo
Sicilia (Sicily)
Caltanissetta
Gela
Vittoria

Isola d'Ustica

Trapani
Isole Egadi
Marsala
Castelvetrano
Agrigento
Strait of Sicily

Mediterranean Sea

Isola di Pantelleria
Isole Pelagie

Sardegna (Sardinia)
Siniscola
Ozieri
Nuoro
Macomer
Oristano
Villacidro
Iglesias
Carbonia
Punta La Marmora 1834m
Cagliari
Quartu Sant'Elena

TUNISIA

VATICAN CITY

ROME

Main Entrance
Pigna Courtyard
Vatican Museums
Vatican Gardens
Radio Vatican
Raphael Stanza
Sistine Chapel
Papal Apartments
Saint Peter's Basilica
St Peter's Square
Vatican Railway Station
Monte Vaticano
Papal Heliport

ROME

0 m   200
0 yds   250

Elevation

-6000m	-4000m	-2000m	-1000m	-500m	-250m	Below sea level	0	250m	500m	1000m	2000m	3000m	4000m	6000m
-19,658ft	-13,124ft	-6562ft	-3281ft	-1640ft	-820ft	-328ft/-100m	0	820ft	1640ft	3281ft	6562ft	9843ft	13,124ft	19,685ft

Central Europe

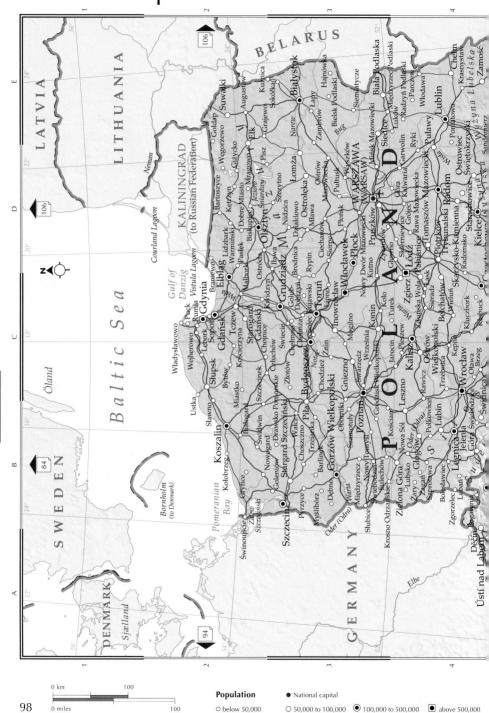

Population

● National capital

○ below 50,000   ○ 50,000 to 100,000   ◉ 100,000 to 500,000   ■ above 500,000

0 km   100

0 miles   100

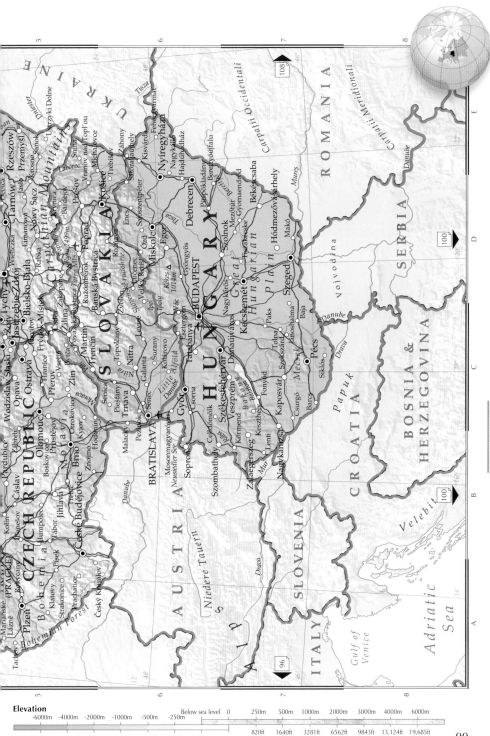

Elevation

							Below sea level	0	250m	500m	1000m	2000m	3000m	4000m	6000m
-6000m	-4000m	-2000m	-1000m	-500m	-250m										
-19,658ft	-13,124ft	-6562ft	-3281ft	-1640ft	-820ft	-328ft/-100m	0		820ft	1640ft	3281ft	6562ft	9843ft	13,124ft	19,685ft

Southeast Europe

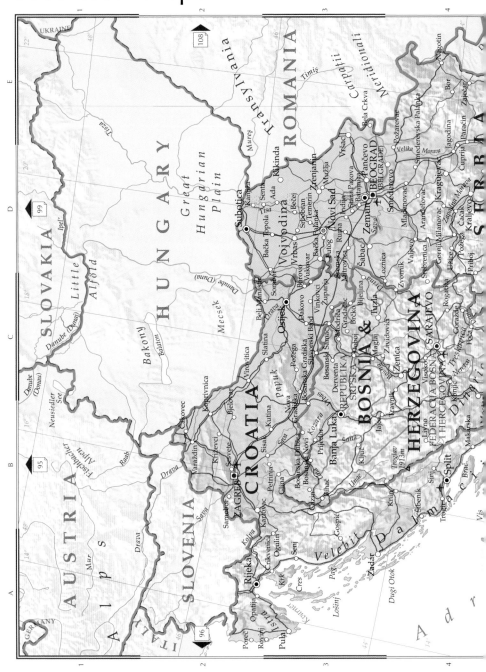

Population

- National capital
- Internal administrative capital

○ below 50,000 ○ 50,000 to 100,000 ◉ 100,000 to 500,000 ■ above 500,000

0 km   100

0 miles   100

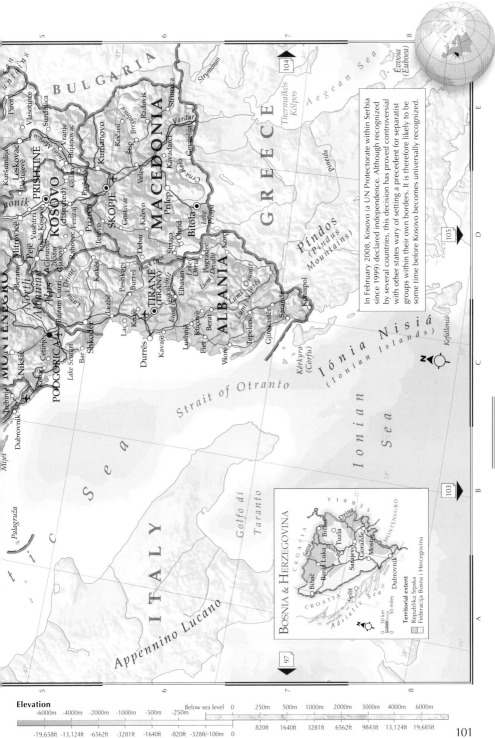

The Mediterranean

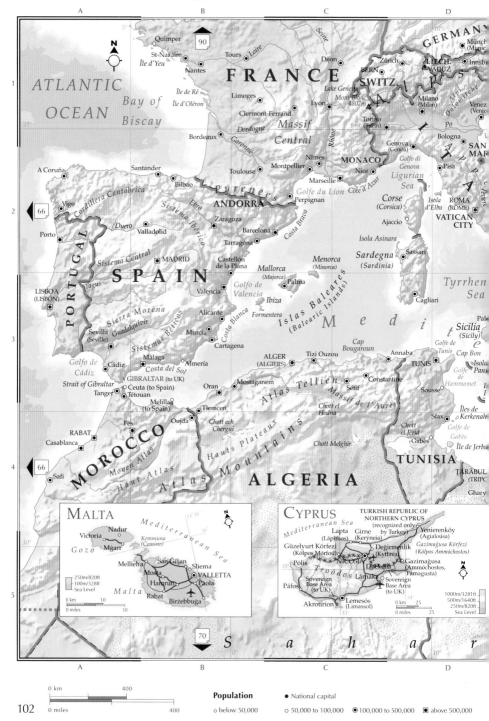

ATLANTIC
OCEAN

Bay of
Biscay

Île d'Yeu
Quimper
St-Nazaire
Nantes
Tours
Loire
Dijon
Zürich
BERN
SWITZ.
LIECH.
VADUZ
Innsb
Münc
(Munic)
GERMANY

FRANCE

Île de Ré
Île d'Oléron
Limoges
Clermont-Ferrand
Dordogne
Lyon
Mont Blanc
4807m
Torino
(Turin)
Milano
(Milan)
Po
Venez
(Venic)

Bordeaux
Garonne
Massif
Central
Rhône
Genova
(Genoa)
Bologna
SAN
MAF

A Coruña
Santander
Bilbao
Toulouse
Montpellier
Nîmes
MONACO
Nice
Marseille
Perpignan
Golfo di
Genova
Côte d'Azur
Pisa
ROMA
(ROME)
VATICAN
CITY

Vigo
Porto
Duero
Valladolid
Cordillera Cantábrica
Sistema Ibérico
Ebro
Zaragoza
Barcelona
Tarragona
ANDORRA
Costa Brava
Ligurian
Sea
Corse
(Corsica)
Ajaccio
Isola
d'Elba
Isola Asinara
Sardegna
(Sardinia)
Sassari

66

LISBOA
(LISBON)
PORTUGAL
Tagus
Sistema Central
MADRID
SPAIN
Castellón
de la Plana
Valencia
Golfo de
Valencia
Mallorca
(Majorca)
Palma
Ibiza
Menorca
(Minorca)
Tyrrhen
Sea
Cagliari

Sevilla
(Seville)
Sierra Morena
Guadalquivir
Sistemas Béticos
Málaga
Almería
Murcia
Cartagena
Alicante
Costa Blanca
Formentera
Islas Baleares
(Balearic Islands)
Ibiza
M   e   d   i   t   e
Sicilia
(Sicily)
Pale
Isola
Pan

Golfo de
Cádiz
Cádiz
Costa del Sol
GIBRALTAR (to UK)
Ceuta (to Spain)
Tanger
Tétouan
Strait of Gibraltar
Melilla
(to Spain)
Oran
Mostaganem
ALGER
(ALGIERS)
Tizi Ouzou
Cap
Bougaroun
Annaba
Constantine
Sétif
TUNIS
Golfe de
Tunis
Cap Bon
Golfe
de
Hammamet
Sousse
Sfax
Îles de
Kerkenah

RABAT
Casablanca
Fes
Oujda
Tlemcen
Chott ech
Chergui
Atlas Tellien
Massif de l'Aurès
Chott el
Hodna
Chott
el Jerid
Golfe de
Gabès
Gabès
Île de Jerba

Safi
MOROCCO
Moyen Atlas
Haut Atlas
Atlas Mountains
Hauts Plateaux
ALGERIA
Chott Melghir
TUNISIA
TARABUL
(TRIPC
Ghary

66

MALTA

Mediterranean Sea
Kemmuna
(Comino)
Victoria
Nadur
Mġarr
Gozo
Mellieħa
Mosta
Ħamrun
Rabat
San Ġiljan
Sliema
VALLETTA
Paola
Birżebbuġa
Malta

250m/820ft
100m/328ft
Sea Level

0 km   10
0 miles   10

CYPRUS

Mediterranean Sea
TURKISH REPUBLIC OF
NORTHERN CYPRUS
(recognized only
by Turkey)
Lapta
(Lápithos)
Girne
(Kerýneia)
Yenierenköy
(Agialoúsa)
Güzelyurt Körfezi
(Kólpos Mórfou)
Dğirmenlik
(Kythréa)
Gazimağusa Körfezi
(Kólpos Ammóchostos)
Pólis
NICOSIA
Dikelia
Gazimağusa
(Ammóchostos,
Famagusta)
Tróodos
Páfos
Sovereign
Base Area
(to UK)
Larnaka
Sovereign
Base Area
(to UK)
Akrotírion
Lemesós
(Limassol)

1000m/3281ft
500m/1640ft
250m/820ft
Sea Level

0 km   25
0 miles   25

70

S   a   h   a   r

0 km   400
0 miles   400

Population   • National capital

o below 50,000   ○ 50,000 to 100,000   ◉ 100,000 to 500,000   ▣ above 500,000

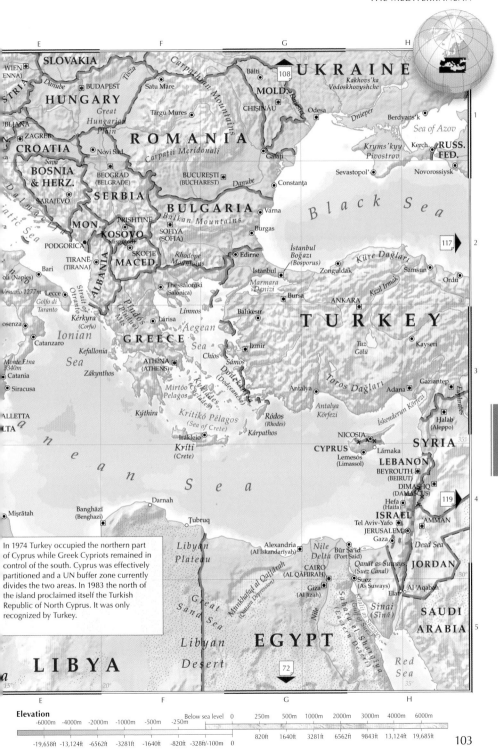

In 1974 Turkey occupied the northern part of Cyprus while Greek Cypriots remained in control of the south. Cyprus was effectively partitioned and a UN buffer zone currently divides the two areas. In 1983 the north of the island proclaimed itself the Turkish Republic of North Cyprus. It was only recognized by Turkey.

Elevation

-6000m	-4000m	-2000m	-1000m	-500m		Below sea level	0		250m	500m	1000m	2000m	3000m	4000m	6000m
					-250m										
-19,658ft	-13,124ft	-6562ft	-3281ft	-1640ft	-820ft	-328ft/-100m	0		820ft	1640ft	3281ft	6562ft	9843ft	13,124ft	19,685ft

103

Bulgaria & Greece

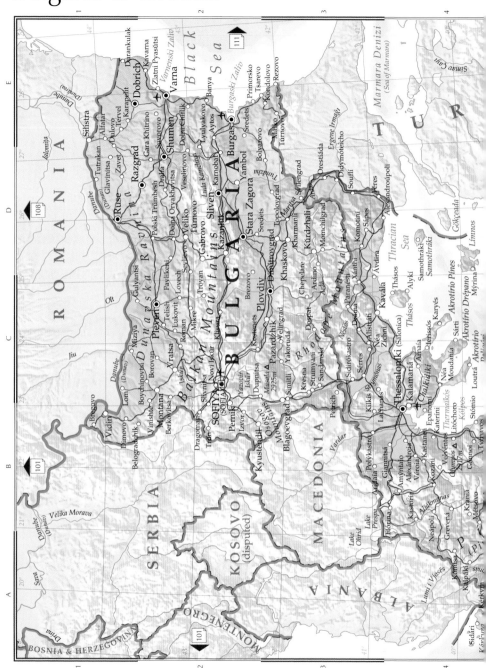

0 km 100

0 miles 100

Population

● National capital

○ below 50,000   ○ 50,000 to 100,000   ◉ 100,000 to 500,000   ▣ above 500,000

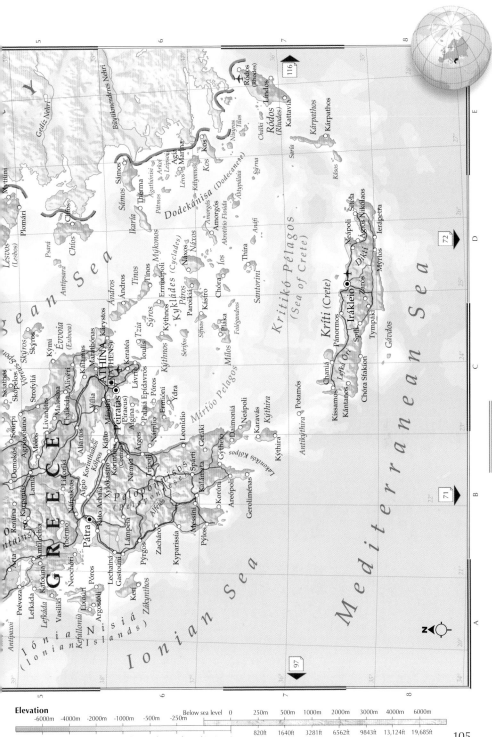

Ródos (Rhodes)
Lindos
Kattaviá
Kárpathos
Kárpathos

Ródos (Rhodes)
Chálki
Sími

Kos
Kos
Léros
Agía Marína
Lípsoi
Arkói
Agathónisi
Pátmos

Mýrtilum
Gediz Nehri
Büyükmenderes Nehri

Léstos (Lesbos)
Plomári
Psará
Chíos
Chíos

Sámos
Sámos
Ikaría

Dodekánisa (Dodecanese)
Amorgós
Astypálaia
Akrotírio Floúda
Anáfi

Sária
Kásos

Kritikó Pélagos (Sea of Crete)
Thíra

Antípsara

Antípaxoi
Préveza
Lefkáda
Vasilikí
Katoúna

Árta
Renína
Karpenisi
Lamía
Domokós
Agrínio
Mesolóngi
Thérmo
Vónitsa

Neochóri
Lidoríki
Amfíklia
Lechainá
Gastoúni
Ikoúrt
Lampeia
Pátra
Káto Acháïa
Aígio

Korinthiakós Kólpos (Corinth)
Kíato
Korínthos (Corinth)
Xylókastro
Nemea
Argos
Náfplio
Tírypoli

Préveza
Pýrgos
Zácharo
Kyparissía
Pýlos
Messíni
Kalamáta
Koróni

Spárti
Geráki
Gýtheio
Areópoli
Gerolímenas

Neochóri
Kefalloniá
Zákynthos
Argostóli
Kéri

Iónia Nisiá (Ionian Islands)

Ionian Sea

GREECE

Peloponnísos

Lakonikós Kólpos

Antikýthira
Kýthira
Kýthira
Potamós
Neápoli
Karavás
Daimoniá

Myrtóo Pélagos

Skíathos
Skópelos
Skýros
Skýros
Kými
Chalkída
Alíveri
Évvoia (Euboea)
Marathónas
Karystos
Keratéa
Lávrio
Pórto
Ýdra
Ermióni
Palaiá Epídavros
Póros
Aígina
Salamína
Peiraiás (Piraeus)
ATHÍNA (ATHENS)
Mégara
Élefsína
Ília

Andros
Andros
Tínos
Tínos
Mýkonos
Sýros
Tzía
Kýthnos
Kéa
Séarifos
Sifnos
Mílos

Kykládes (Cyclades)
Páros
Paroikía
Náxos
Náxos
Ermoúpoli
Kástro
Folégandros
Chóra
Íos
Píaka

Santorini

Kríti (Crete)
Néápoli
Siteía
Ágios Nikólaos
Ierápetra
Myrtos
Dikti
Zarós
Irákleio
Spíli
Tympáki
Gávdos
Chaniá
Réthymno
Lefká Óri
Kíssamos
Kántanos
Chóra Sfakíon

Kritikó Pélagos (Sea of Crete)
Pánormos

Mediterranean Sea

Elevation

-6000m	-4000m	-2000m	-1000m	-500m	-250m	Below sea level	0	250m	500m	1000m	2000m	3000m	4000m	6000m
-19,658ft	-13,124ft	-6562ft	-3281ft	-1640ft	-820ft	-328ft/-100m	0	820ft	1640ft	3281ft	6562ft	9843ft	13,124ft	19,685ft

105

The Baltic States & Belarus

Population

● National capital

○ below 50,000 ○ 50,000 to 100,000 ◉ 100,000 to 500,000 ◼ above 500,000

0 km — 100
0 miles — 100

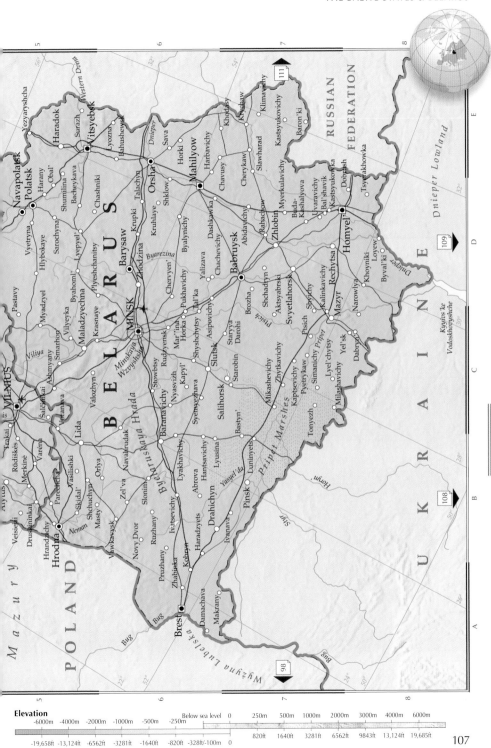

109

108

98

Elevation

| Below sea level | 0 | 250m | 500m | 1000m | 2000m | 3000m | 4000m | 6000m |

-6000m -4000m -2000m -1000m -500m -250m

-19,658ft -13,124ft -6562ft -3281ft -1640ft -820ft -328ft/-100m 0

820ft 1640ft 3281ft 6562ft 9843ft 13,124ft 19,685ft

Ukraine, Moldova & Romania

Population ● National capital

○ below 50,000 ○ 50,000 to 100,000 ◉ 100,000 to 500,000 ■ above 500,000

Elevation

-6000m	-4000m	-2000m	-1000m	-500m	-250m	Below sea level 0	250m	500m	1000m	2000m	3000m	4000m	6000m
-19,658ft	-13,124ft	-6562ft	-3281ft	-1640ft	-820ft	-328ft/-100m 0	820ft	1640ft	3281ft	6562ft	9843ft	13,124ft	19,685ft

European Russia

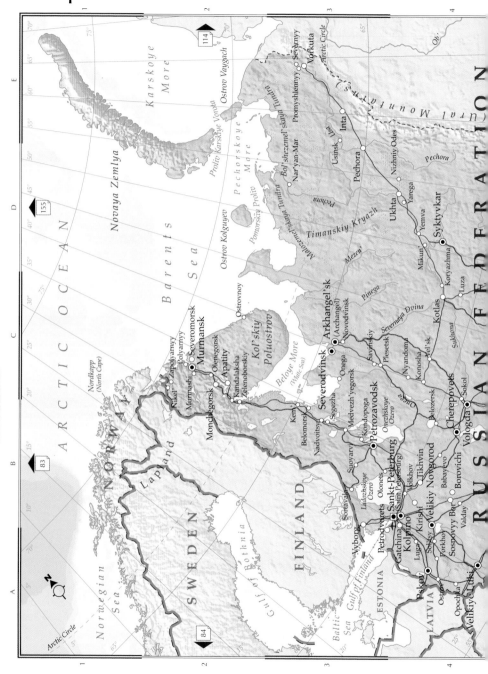

Population

● National capital

○ below 50,000   ○ 50,000 to 100,000   ◉ 100,000 to 500,000   ◼ above 500,000

0 km ———— 300

0 miles ———— 300

Elevation

-6000m	-4000m	-2000m	-1000m	-500m	-250m	Below sea level	0	250m	500m	1000m	2000m	3000m	4000m	6000m
-19,658ft	-13,124ft	-6562ft	-3281ft	-1640ft	-820ft	-328ft/-100m	0	820ft	1640ft	3281ft	6562ft	9843ft	13,124ft	19,685ft

111

North & West Asia

A   B   C   D

ARCTI

Franz Josef Land

155

Ostrov Komsomolets

Severnaya Z

Ostrov Oktyabr'skoy Revolyyutsii

Ostrov Bol'shevik

Summer limit of pack ice

Winter limit of pack ice

Norwegian Sea

North Cape

Barents Sea

Ostrov Kolguyev

Kara Sea

East Novaya Zemlya Trench

Novaya Zemlya

Poluostrov Yamal

Poluostrov Taym

North Sibe

Kheta

Murmansk

Kola Peninsula

White Sea

Archangel

81

Arctic Circle

Gulf of Bothnia

Northern Dvina

Lake Onega

Lake Ladoga

Saint Petersburg

Yaroslavl

Vologda

Nizhniy Novgorod

Perm

R U S S I A N

Ural Mountains

West Siberian Plain

Ob'

Irtysh

Ob'

Noril'sk

Kureyka

Centra Siberia Platea

Lower Tunguska

Stony Tunguska

Yenisey

Angara

Chulym

MOSCOW

Kaliningrad

KALININGRAD (to Russ. Fed.)

Baltic Sea

Central Russian Upland

Voronezh

Kazan

Ul'yanovsk

Samara

Ufa

Volga

Yekaterinburg

Chelyabinsk

Omsk

Novosibirsk

Tomsk

Krasnoyarsk

Novokuznetsk

Irk

Sayanskiy Khrebet

ASTANA

Saratov

Volgograd

Ural'sk

Orenburg

Ural

E U R O P E

Rostov-na-Donu

Don

Astrakhan

Kirghiz Steppe

Karagandy

Kazakh Uplands

Semipalatinsk

A

Altai Mountains

Ozero Zaysan

S

Stavropol

El'brus 5642m

Danube

Black Sea

Istanbul

Caucasus

Aral'sk

KAZAKHSTAN

Aral Sea

Syr Darya

Kyzylorda

Lake Balkhash

Ili

Taraz

Almaty

Tien Shan

Pik Pobedy 7443m

Ustyurt Plateau

Aktau

Kyzyl Kum

UZBEKISTAN

Daşoguz

BISHKEK

KYRGYZSTAN

TBILISI

BAKU

AZERB.

TASHKENT

TURKMENISTAN

Garagum

Amu Darya

DUSHANBE

TAJIKISTAN

Mediterranean Sea

GEORGIA

ARMENIA

ANKARA

YEREVAN

TURKEY

Adana

Gaziantep

Tabriz

AŞGABAT

Küre Dağları

Caspian Sea

Kopet Dag

KABUL

Jalalabad

Hindu Kush

Kunlun Mountains

Aleppo

SYRIA

IRAQ

Mosul

Qom

TEHRAN

IRAN

Herat

AFGHANISTAN

Khyber Pass

CYPRUS

DAMASCUS

BEIRUT

LEBANON

ISRAEL

BAGHDAD

Syrian Desert

Isfahan

Iranian Plateau

Zagros Mountains

Thar Desert

Himalayas

JERUSALEM

AMMAN

JORDAN

Basra

Dead Sea −423m

An Nafud

KUWAIT

KUWAIT

Shiraz

Zahedan

Bandar-e 'Abbas

Persian Gulf

Dubai

Indus Fan

Ganges

MANAMA

BAHRAIN

SAUDI ARABIA

RIYADH

QATAR

DOHA

U.A.E.

ABU DHABI

MUSCAT

Gulf of Oman

Sur

Jedda

Tropic of Cancer

Nile

Arabian Peninsula

At Ta'if

Red Sea

Ar Rub' al Khali

O M A N

Murray Ridge

Arabian Sea

Ganges Fan

Bay of Bengal

A F R I C A

SANA

YEMEN

Ta'izz

Aden

Gulf of Aden

Socotra (to Yemen)

69

N

A   B   C   D

103

0 km   800
0 miles   800

Population   ● National capital

○ below 50,000   ◌ 50,000 to 100,000   ◉ 100,000 to 500,000   ▣ above 500,000

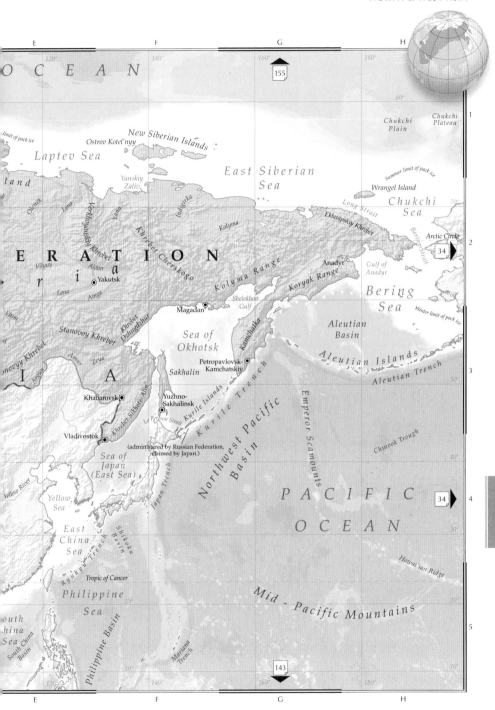

E   120°   F   140°   G   160°   H   180°

155

O C E A N

80°

Chukchi
Plain

Chukchi
Plateau

1

limit of pack ice

New Siberian Islands

Laptev Sea

Ostrov Kotel'nyy

*East Siberian
Sea*

Summer limit of pack ice

Wrangel Island

70°

*Chukchi
Sea*

Yanskiy
Zaliv

Indigirka

Long Strait

Ekiatapskiy Khrebet

Bering Strait

Arctic Circle

34

2

Olenek

Lena

Verkhoyanskiy Khrebet

Yana

Kolyma

Khrebet Cherskogo

Kolyma Range

Koryak Range

Anadyr

Gulf of
Anadyr

60°

*Bering
Sea*

Vilyuy

Aldan

Yakutsk

Lena

Amga

Shelekhov
Gulf

*Aleutian
Basin*

Winter limit of pack ice

E R A T I O N

r i a

I A

Stanovoy Khrebet

Khrebet Dzhugdzhur

Magadan

*Sea of
Okhotsk*

Kamchatka

Aleutian Islands

Aleutian Trench

50°

3

Amur

Zeya

Petropavlovsk-
Kamchatskiy

Sakhalin

Emperor Seamounts

Chinook Trough

Khabarovsk

Yuzhno-
Sakhalinsk

Kurile Islands

Kurile Trench

*Northwest Pacific
Basin*

40°

Vladivostok

Khrebet Sikhote-Alin'

La Pérouse Strait

(administered by Russian Federation,
claimed by Japan.)

Yellow River

*Sea of
Japan
(East Sea)*

Japan Trench

P A C I F I C

30°

34

4

*Yellow
Sea*

*East
China
Sea*

Shikoku
Basin

O C E A N

Hawai'ian Ridge

Tropic of Cancer

20°

Ryukyu Trench

Philippine Basin

*Philippine
Sea*

Mid - Pacific Mountains

outh
hina
Sea

South
China
Sea
Basin

140°

Mariana
Trench

160°

143

180°

10°

E   F   G   H

Russia & Kazakhstan

ARCTIC

SVALBARD
(to Norway)

Zemlya Fra
Iosifa

NETH.

DENMARK

GERMANY

NORWAY

SWEDEN

Arctic Circle

Winter limit of pack ice

Summer limit of pack ice

Nordkapp
(North Cape)

Barents
Sea

Murmansk

Novaya Zemlya

KALININGRAD
(to Russ. Fed.)

Kaliningrad

POLAND

LITH.

LAT.

EST.

Sankt-Peterburg

Pskov

Velikiy Novgorod

BELARUS

Smolensk

MOLDOVA

UKRAINE

Bryansk

Belgorod

Voronezh

Sea of Azov

Rostov-na-
Donu

Krasnodar

Sochi

Stavropol'

Nal'chik

Elbrus
5642m

Vladikavkaz

GEORGIA

Groznyy

ARM.

Makhachkala

AZERBAIJAN

Fort-Shevchenko

Aktau

Zhanaozen

Gulf of Bothnia

Gulf of Finland

FINLAND

Ladozhskoye
Ozero

Petrozavodsk

Onezhskoye
Ozero

Cherepovets

MOSKVA
(MOSCOW)

Tula

Ryazan'

Tambov

Penza

Mikhaylovka

Saratov

Balakovo

Volgograd

Kaliningrad

Kandalaksha

Severodvinsk

Arkhangel'sk

Vel'sk

Severnaya
Dvina

Tver

Vologda

Yaroslavl'

Kineshma

Vladimir

Nizhniy Novgorod

Kirov

Glazov

Kazan'

Ul'yanovsk

Izhevsk

Tol'yatti

Naberezhnyye
Chelny

Samara

Ufa

Sterlitamak

Ural'sk

Orenburg

Astrakhan'

Ural

Zhayyq

Baltic Sea

Beloye More

Kotlas

Ukhta

Syktyvkar

Solikamsk

Perm'

Serov

Lesnoy

Yekaterinburg

Khanty-Mansiysk

Surgut

Nyagan'

Nar'yan-Mar

Pechora

Vorkuta

Salekhard

Ostrov
Kolguyev

Kol'skiy
Poluostrov

Ostrov Belyy

Diks

Ostrov Vaygach

Poluostrov Yamal

Nadym

Zapadno-
Sibirskaya
Ravnina

Ob'

Noril

Igarka

Ta

Karskoye More

Yenisey

Tol'ka

Kolyma

Nizhnevartovsk

RUSSIA

Magnitogorsk

Orsk

Alga

Emba

Atyrau

Aktobe
(Aktyubinsk)

Rudnyy

Kostanay

Kokshetau

Atbasar

Shalkar

Ustyurt
Plateau

Aral
Sea

Caspian Sea

IRAN

TURKMENISTAN

Amu Darya

UZBEKISTAN

Syr Darya

Aral'sk

Ayteke Bi

Zhosaly

Kyzylorda

Kyzyl Kum

Turkistan

Karatau

Arys

Shymkent

Kentau

TAJIKISTAN

AFGHANISTAN

Tyumen'

Tobol'sk

Chelyabinsk

Ishim

Tobol

Irtysh

Ishim

Petropavlovsk

Omsk

Severska

Tomsk

Krasno

Kemero

Novosibirsk

Barnaul

Novokuznetsk

Ab

Chulym

Ob'

KAZAKHSTAN

ASTANA

Pavlodar

Temirtau

Saran'

Karagandy

Zhezkazgan

Kazakhskiy
Melkosopochnik

Balkhash

Shar

Ozero
Zaysan

Ayagoz

Semey

Ridder

Zyryanovsk

Ust'-Kamenogorsk

Gora Belukha
4506m

Altai
Mountain

K

Shar

Shuchinsk

Saryarka

Ozero
Balkash

Shu

Taraz

Tekeli

Taldykorgan

Almaty
(Alma-Ata)

Kirghiz Range

Tien Shan

KYRGYZSTAN

CHINA

0 km   600

0 miles   600

Population   ● National capital

○ below 50,000   ○ 50,000 to 100,000   ◉ 100,000 to 500,000   ▣ above 500,000

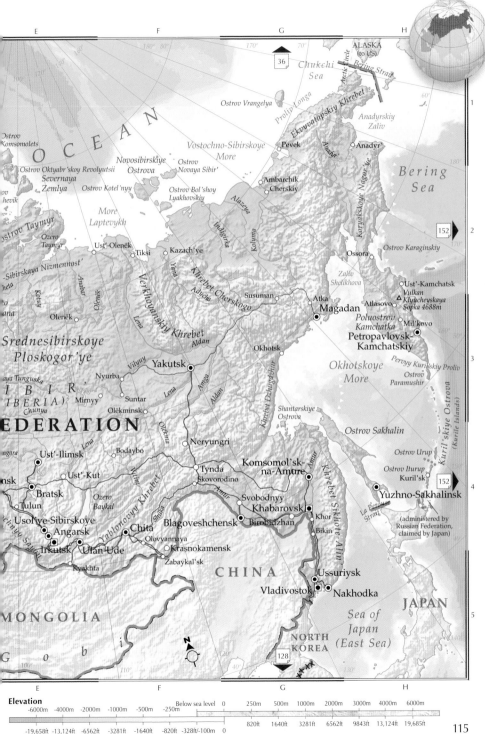

ALASKA
(to US)

*Chukchi
Sea*

Ostrov Vrangelya

A R C T I C

O C E A N

*Ostrov
Komsomolets*

*Vostochno-Sibirskoye
More*

Pevek

Ekvyvatapskiy Khrebet

*Anadyrskiy
Zaliv*

*Bering
Sea*

*Novosibirskiye
Ostrova*

*Ostrov
Novaya Sibir'*

Ostrov Oktyabr'skoy Revolyutsii

Severnaya
Zemlya

Ostrov Kotel'nyy

*Ostrov Bol'shoy
Lyakhovskiy*

Ambarchik
Cherskiy

Anadyr'

152

*Ostrov
Komsomolets*

Ostrov Taymyr

*More
Laptevykh*

Alazeya

Indigirka

Kolyma

Ossora

Ostrov Karaginskiy

*Ozero
Taymyr*

Ust'-Olenëk

Tiksi

Kazach'ye

Anabar

Olenëk

Lena

Yana

Khrebet Cherskogo

Adycha

Susuman

Atka

Magadan

*Zaliv
Shelikhova*

Ust'-Kamchatsk
*Vulkan
Klyuchevskaya
Sopka 4688m*

*Srednesibirskoye
Ploskogor'ye*

Verkhoyanskiy Khrebet

Aldan

Yakutsk

Okhotsk

Atlasovo

*Poluostrov
Kamchatka*

Mil'kovo

Petropavlovsk-
Kamchatskiy

Nyurba

Vilyuy

Lena

Amga

Aldan

Khrebet Dzhugdzhur

*Okhotskoye
More*

Pervyy Kuril'skiy Proliv

*Ostrov
Paramushir*

SIBIR'
IBERIA)

Mirnyy

Suntar

Olëkminsk

Olëkma

Neryungri

*Shantarskiye
Ostrova*

Ostrov Sakhalin

*Kuril'skiye Ostrova
(Kurile Islands)*

FEDERATION

Lena

Bodaybo

Tynda
Skovorodino

Komsomol'sk-
na-Amure

Amur

Ostrov Urup

Ostrov Iturup
Kuril'sk

152

Ust'-Ilimsk

Ust'-Kut

Vitim

Yablonovyy Khrebet

Amur

Svobodnyy

Khabarovsk

Khrebet Sikhote-Alin'

Yuzhno-Sakhalinsk

Bratsk

Tulun

*Ozero
Baykal*

Shilka

Blagoveshchensk

Birobidzhan

Khor

(administered by
Russian Federation,
claimed by Japan)

Usol'ye-Sibirskoye

Angarsk

Chita

Olovyannaya

Bikin

*La Pérouse
Strait*

Irkutsk

Ulan-Ude

Krasnokamensk

CHINA

Ussuriysk

MONGOLIA

Kyakhta

Zabaykal'sk

Vladivostok

Nakhodka

JAPAN

G   o   b   i

*Sea of
Japan
(East Sea)*

NORTH
KOREA

128

Elevation

-6000m	-4000m	-2000m	-1000m	-500m	-250m	Below sea level 0	250m	500m	1000m	2000m	3000m	4000m	6000m
-19,658ft	-13,124ft	-6562ft	-3281ft	-1640ft	-820ft	-328ft/-100m 0	820ft	1640ft	3281ft	6562ft	9843ft	13,124ft	19,685ft

Turkey & the Caucasus

ROMANIA

Tacul Sinoie

UKRAINE

Kryms'kyy
Pivostriv

Danube

BULGARIA

Varnenski
Zaliv

Black   Sea

Burgaski
Zaliv

Maritsa

104

Kırklareli

Edirne

Cide   İnebolu   Sinop

Bartın   Gerze

Zonguldak   Küre Dağları   Bafra

Ergene Çayi

Çorlu

Devrek   Karabük   Kastamonu   Samsun

Tekirdağ

Marmara Denizi
(Sea of Marmara)

İstanbul

İzmit   Adapazarı

Çerkeş   Kargı

İstanbul Boğazı
(Bosporus)

Bandırma   Yalova   İznik Gölü   Bolu   Gerede   Çankırı   Merzifon

Canik Dağları

Çanakkale

Bursa   Bilecik   Çankırı   Kızıl Irmak   Çorum   Tokat

Çanakkale
Boğazı
(Dardanelles)

Balıkesir

Bozüyük   Eskişehir   ANKARA   Kalecik   Alaca   Yıldızeli

Edremit

Kütahya   Polatlı   Kırıkkale   Sorgun   Si

Ayvalık

TURK

Lésvos

Akhisar   Simav   Gediz   Hirfanlı
Barajı   Şarkışla

Bogazlıyan   K

Menemen

Manisa   Uşak   Afyon   Kulu   Tuz Gölü   İncesu   Bünyan   Gürün

Chíos

İzmir   Ödemiş   Cihanbeyli   Nevşehir   Kayseri

Sámos

Alaşehir   Akşehir   Aksaray   Göksun   G   il

Aydın   Nazilli   Dinar   Anatolia   Niğde   Kahramann

Söke

Büyük Menderes Nehri   Denizli   Beyşehir
Gölü   Konya   Ereğli

Milas   Tavas   Burdur   Isparta   Karaman   Gaz

105   Bodrum   Muğla   Burdur
Gölü   Suğla Gölü   Toros   Dağları   Ceyhan

Marmaris   Dalaman   Antalya   Karaman   Tarsus   Adana   Osmaniy

Fethiye   Manavgat   Mut   Mersin (İçel)   İskenderun   Kilis

Kaş   Finike   Alanya   Antakya   Kırıkhan

Dodekánisa
(Dodecánese)

Ródos
(Rhodes)   Antalya
Körfezi   Silifke

Anamur   Orantes

Kárpathos

TURKISH REPUBLIC OF
NORTHERN CYPRUS
(recognized only by Turkey)

CYPRUS

Mediterranean

Sea

LEBANON

72

Population   ● National capital

0 km   200

0 miles   200

○ below 50,000   ○ 50,000 to 100,000   ◉ 100,000 to 500,000   ◼ above 500,000

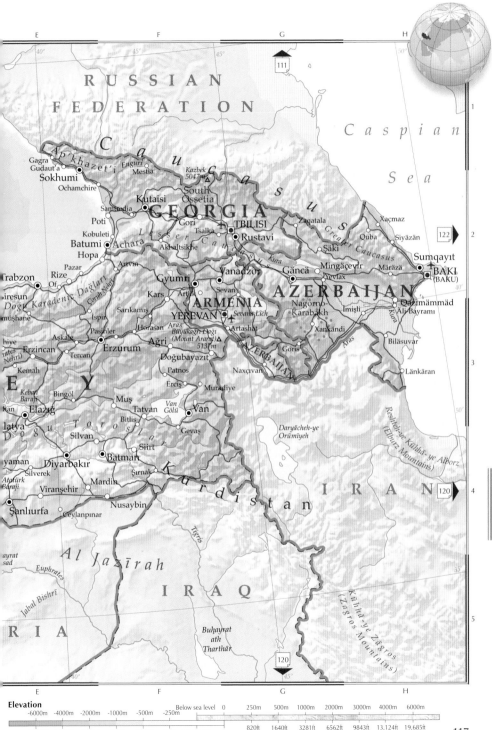

RUSSIAN

FEDERATION

C a u c a s u s

Gagra
Gudaut'a
Sokhumi
Ochamchire

Ap'khazet'i   *Enguri*

Mestia

Kazbek
5047m △

GEORGIA

Kutaisi

Samtredia

South
Ossetia

Poti

Lesser   Cau

Gori

Tsalka

TBILISI

Rustavi

Zaqatala

Xaçmaz

122

Kobuleti

Batumi **Achara**

Hopa

Akhaltsikhe

Säki

Quba

Siyäzän

Sumqayıt

Artvin

Pazar

Rize

Trabzon

Of

Doğu Karadeniz Dağları

Çoruh Nehri

Gyumri

Kars

Artik

Vanadzor

Sevan

Kura

Gäncä

Yevlax

Mingäçevir

Märäzä

BAKI
(BAKU)

Giresun

müşhane

*Euphrates
(Nehri)*

İspir

Sarıkamış

ARMENIA

Sevan

AZERBAIJAN

Nagorno-
Karabakh

İmişli

Qazimämmäd
Ali-Bayramı

Aşkale

Erzincan

Pasinler

Horasan

YEREVAN

Sevani Lich

Artashat

Xankändi

Biläsuvar

Erzurum

Tercan

Aras

Ağrı

*Büyükağrı Dağı
(Mount Ararat)* △
5137m

Goris

Aras

Länkäran

Kemah

Doğubayazıt

AZERBAIJAN

Patnos

Naxçıvan

Bingöl

Erciş

Muradiye

Elazığ

Muş

*Van
Gölü*

Van

*Daryácheh-ye
Orümiyeh*

*Reshteh-ye Kühhä-ye Alborz
(Elburz Mountains)*

İatya

Doğu

Toroslar

Tatvan

Bitlis

Gevaş

Silvan

Siirt

I R A N

120

Silverek

Diyarbakır

Batman

Şırnak

Kürdistan

yaman

Atatürk
Baraji

Mardin

Viranşehir

Nusaybin

Şanlıurfa

Ceylanpınar

Tigris

Al Jazīrah

Euphrates

Jabal Bishrī

I R A Q

ayrat
sad

*Buhayrat
ath
Tharthār*

120

R I A

Caspian

Sea

Greater Caucasus

*Kühhä-ye Zagros
(Zagros Mountains)*

Elevation

-6000m	-4000m	-2000m	-1000m	-500m	Below sea level	0	250m	500m	1000m	2000m	3000m	4000m	6000m
					-250m								
-19,658ft	-13,124ft	-6562ft	-3281ft	-1640ft	-820ft	-328ft/-100m	0	820ft	1640ft	3281ft	6562ft	9843ft	13,124ft	19,685ft

The Near East

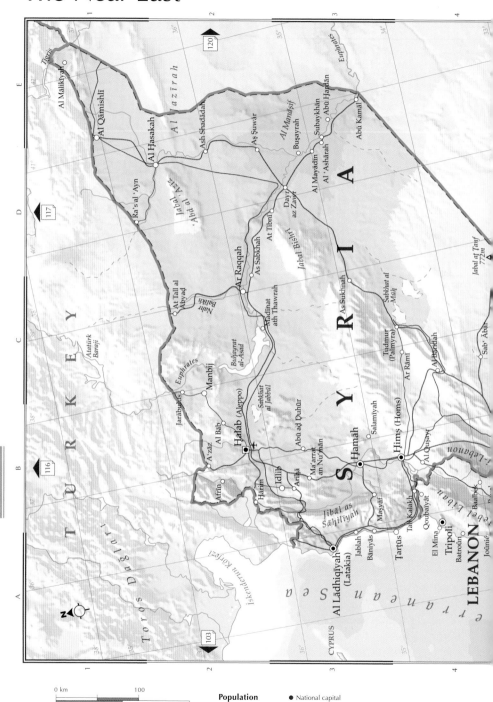

Population

- National capital

○ below 50,000   ○ 50,000 to 100,000   ◉ 100,000 to 500,000   ◼ above 500,000

0 km   100
0 miles   100

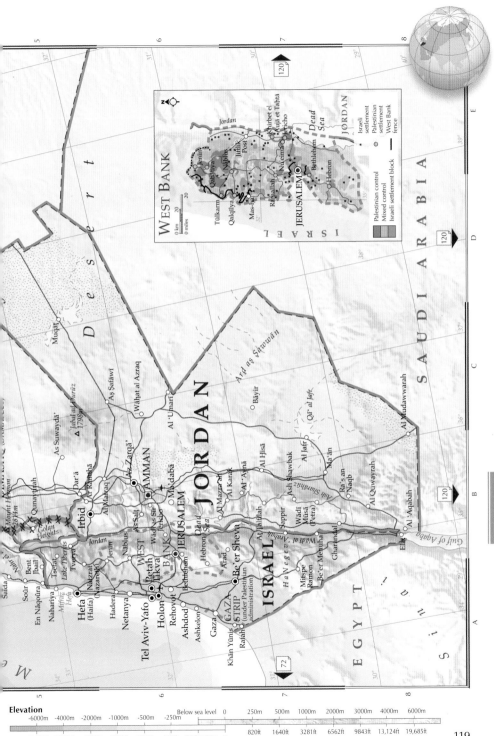

WEST BANK

Jordan

Khirbet el
'Auja et Tahtā
Post

Dead
Sea

Jenin

Nāblus
Qabāțiya
Zufūt
Nu'eimā
Jericho

JORDAN

Ţulkarm
Qalqilya
Mas-ḥa
Ramallah
Bethlehem
Hebron

JERUSALEM

ISRAEL

0 km   20
0 miles   20

Israeli settlement
Palestinian settlement
West Bank fence

Palestinian control
Mixed control
Israeli settlement block

Elevation

-6000m	-4000m	-2000m	-1000m	-500m	-250m	Below sea level 0	250m	500m	1000m	2000m	3000m	4000m	6000m

-19,658ft	-13,124ft	-6562ft	-3281ft	-1640ft	-820ft	-328ft/-100m 0	820ft	1640ft	3281ft	6562ft	9843ft	13,124ft	19,685ft

The Middle East

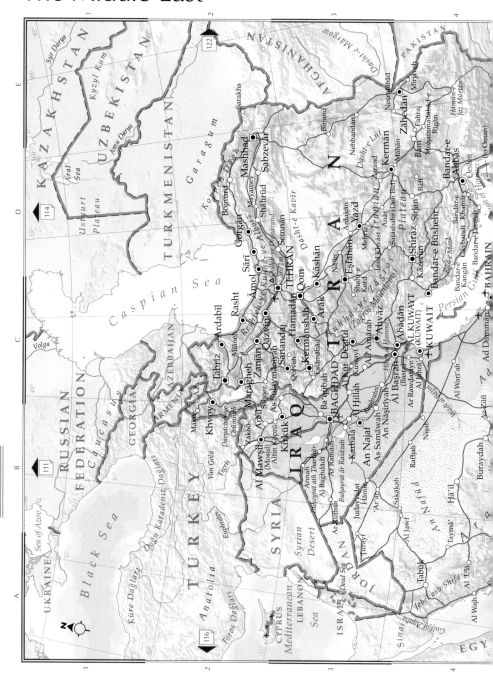

0 km 400

0 miles 400

Population ● National capital

○ below 50,000 ○ 50,000 to 100,000 ◉ 100,000 to 500,000 ■ above 500,000

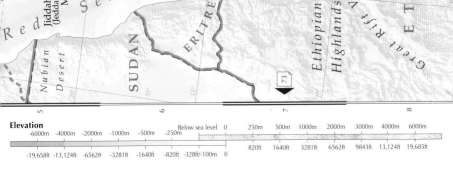

Ṣūr
Al Rustāq
Jabal al Ghubḥ
Rams
Al Wāhibah
Jazīrat
Maşīrah
Al Ghābah
Khalūf
Jazīrat Maşīrah
Duqm
Ṣawqirah

Arabian Sea

UNITED ARAB EMIRATES

O M A N

Thamarīt
Salālah
Jūzur al Ḥalāniyāt

140

INDIAN

OCEAN

140

Damqawt
Sayḥūt
Raas Xaafuun

Suquṭrā
(Socotra)
(to Yemen)

SAUDI ARABIA

(RIYADH)

Layla
Jabal Ṭuwayq

As Sulayyil

Ar Rub' al Khālī
(Empty Quarter)

e n i n s u l a

P

Sanāw

Wuday'ah
Al Mahrah

Al Mahrah

Ash Shiḥr
Al Mukallā
Tarīm
Say'ūn

Y E M E N
Ḥadhramawt

Ḥadhramawt

Gulf of Aden

Ramlat Dahm

Ramlat
as Sab'atayn

Najrān

Tathlīth
Khamīs Mushayṭ

Qal 'at Bīshah

Abhā
Ṣabyā
Jīzān
Abū 'Arīsh

Zabīd
Al Hudaydah
(Hodeida)

SAN'Ā'
(SANA)
Ta'izz
Shuqrah
Adan
(Aden)

SOMALILAND
(not internationally
recognized)

S O M A L I A

73

Ogaden

Turabah
Zalim

Ṭabāb al Bishāh

Harrat Rahaṭ

Makkah
(Mecca)
Aṭ Ṭā'if

Jiddah
(Jedda)

Al Lith
Al Bāḥah

Jazā'ir
Farasān

Bāb el Mandeb

DJIBOUTI

Danakil Desert

ERITREA

Ethiopian Highlands

Great Rift Valley

E T H I O P I A

73

R e d   S e a

Nubian
Desert

S U D A N

Elevation

-6000m	-4000m	-2000m	-1000m	-500m	-250m	Below sea level	0	250m	500m	1000m	2000m	3000m	4000m	6000m
-19,658ft	-13,124ft	-6562ft	-3281ft	-1640ft	-820ft	-328ft/-100m	0	820ft	1640ft	3281ft	6562ft	9843ft	13,124ft	19,685ft

121

Central Asia

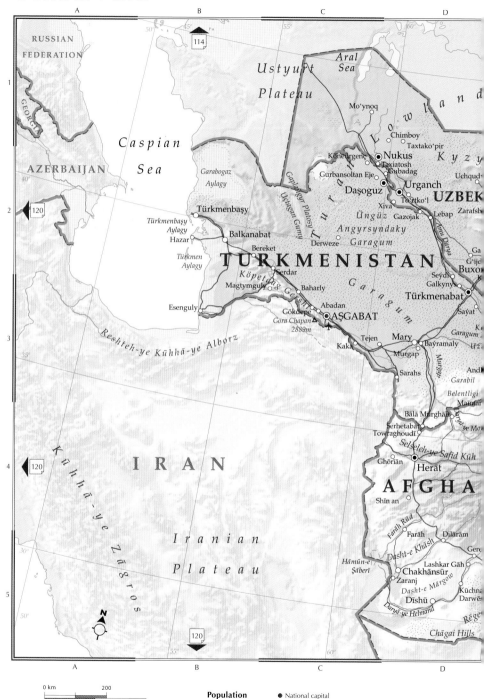

RUSSIAN
FEDERATION

GEORGIA

AZERBAIJAN

Caspian

Sea

Ustyurt
Plateau

*Aral
Sea*

Turan Lowland

Mo'ynoq

Chimboy
Taxtako'pir

Köneürgenç **Nukus**
Taxiatosh
Gurbansoltan Eje Qubadag
Daşoguz
Xiva **Urganch**
To'rtko'l
UZBEK
Zarafsh
Üngüz Gazojak Lebap
Angyrsyndaky
Garagum
Uchqud

*Garabogaz
Aylagy*

Gaplaňgyr Platosy

Uňüzan Gumy

Türkmenbaşy

*Türkmenbaşy
Aylagy*
Hazar

*Türkmen
Aylagy*

Balkanabat

Bereket
Derweze

Köpetdag Gerşi

Magtymguly
Serdar

Baharly

TURKMENISTAN

Garagum

Seýdi
Galkynyş
Türkmenabat

Ga
G'ijd
Buxo
k

Sayat

Esenguly

Gökdepe
*Gora Chapan
2889m*

Abadan
⊙**AŞGABAT**

Tejen **Mary**

Kaka

Murgap
Bayramaly

Garagum
Uz

Murgap

And
Garabil

Sarahs

Belentligi
Maimar

Reshteh-ye Kūhhā-ye Alborz

Bālā Murghāb

Darya-ye Mo

Serhetabat
Towraghoudī

Selseleh-ye Safid Kūh

I R A N

Ghōriān
Herāt

AFGHA

Shīn an

Kūhhā-ye Zāgros

Iranian

Plateau

Farāh Rūd

Farāh Dilārām

Gerc

Dasht-e Khāsh

*Hāmūn-e
Şāberī*

Lashkar Gāh
Chakhānsūr
Zaranj

Dasht-e Mārgow

Kuchn
Darwē

Dīshū

Darya-ye Helmand

Rēge

Chāgai Hills

N

0 km   200

0 miles   200

Population   ● National capital

○ below 50,000   ○ 50,000 to 100,000   ◉ 100,000 to 500,000   ◼ above 500,000

KAZAKHSTAN

Ozero Balkash

Peski Saryyesik-Atyrau

Peski Taukum

115

Borohoro Shan

Peski Moyynkum

Ili

Syr Darya

BISHKEK △ Tokmak
Kara-Balta Tyup
Kemin Ozero Issyk- Dzhergalan
Talas Kul' Karakol
Teninpol Balykchy Kyzyl-Suu
Gora Manas Kadzhi-Say Pik Pobedy
4482m KYRGYZSTAN Kara-Say 7443m
Chatkal Range Tash-Kumyr Khrebet Moldo-Too Karakol 126
TOSHKENT Chirchiq Naryn Kokshaal-Tau
(TASHKENT) Angren Dzhalal-Abad Chatyr-Tash
Yangiyo'l Namangan
ko'l Ko'li Olmaliq Qo'qon Andijon Kök-Art
Nurota Bekobod Osh
Langar Guliston
Javoiy Jizzax Sulyukta XINJIANG *Taklimakan*
Kattaqo'rg'on Urotteppa Khaydarkan Sary-Tash UYGUR *Shamo*
son Samarqand Zeravshan Daroot-Korgon ZIZHIQU
Urgut Surkhob Qarokül C
Qarshi Kitob DUSHANBE Qal'aikhum Ghüdara Murghob H
Denov TAJIKISTAN Qizilrabot I
derya Boysun Norak Dzhelandy N
rat Danghara Bartang (claimed by India) A
Qürghonteppa Kŭlob Moskva AKSAI CHIN
Termiz Jarqo'rg'on Dŭsti Farkhor Khorugh (administered by China,
sah Balkh Konduz Feyzābād Ishkoshim claimed by India)
rghān Mazār-e Khulm Tāloqān Baroghil Pass Aksai
Sharif Khānābād 3777m Chin 126
Pol-e Khumrī Baghlān Karakoram Range
Hindu Kush Indus DEMCHOK/
Barikowt DÊMQOG
Charikār Mahmūd-e Rāqī (administered by China,
KABUL Asadābād claimed by India)
(KABUL) Mehtar Lām
Maidān Shahr Jalālābād XIZANG
Ghaznī Gardēz Khyber Pass ZIZHIQU
STAN 1080m (Tibet)
Khōst
(A 'line of control' (administered by China,
ye Arghandāb was agreed between claimed by India)
Zarghūn India and Pakistan
Shahr in 1972)
Qalāt
Spin Būldak Indus
ndahār Toba Kākar Range Ravi
PAKISTAN INDIA H
Sulaimān i
Range m
a
134 l
a
y
a
NEPAL s

Elevation

| -6000m | -4000m | -2000m | -1000m | -500m | -250m | Below sea level | 0 | 250m | 500m | 1000m | 2000m | 3000m | 4000m | 6000m |

| -19,658ft | -13,124ft | -6562ft | -3281ft | -1640ft | -820ft | -328ft/-100m | 0 | 820ft | 1640ft | 3281ft | 6562ft | 9843ft | 13,124ft | 19,685ft |

123

South & East Asia

| 0 km | 1000 |
| 0 miles | 1000 |

Population • National capital

o below 50,000 o 50,000 to 100,000 ◉ 100,000 to 500,000 ■ above 500,000

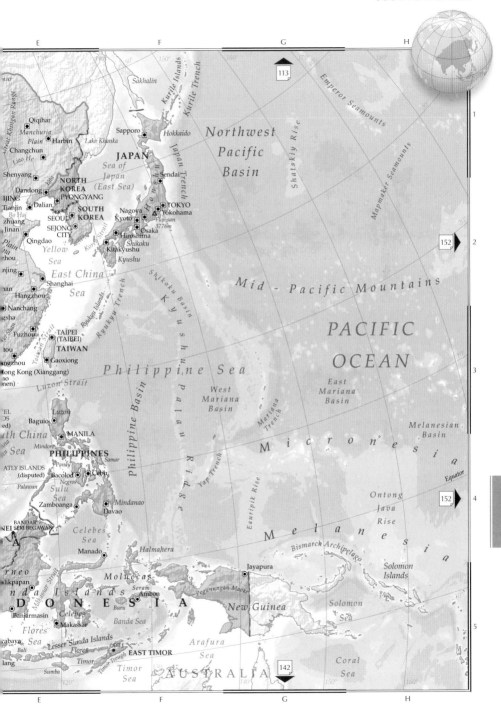

E F G H

113

1

Sakhalin

Kurile Islands

Kurile Trench

Qiqihar
Manchuria
Plain Harbin *Lake Khanka* Sapporo Hokkaido

Northwest Pacific Basin

Great Khingan Range
Changchun

Shenyang

Liao He

JAPAN

Sea of Japan (East Sea) Sendai

Emperor Seamounts

Shatskiy Rise

Japan Trench

Mapmaker Seamounts

NORTH KOREA
Dandong **PYONGYANG**

IJING
Tianjin Dalian
Bo Hai

152 2

zhuang **SOUTH**
Jinan **KOREA** **SEOUL** Nagoya **TOKYO** Yokohama
SEJONG Kyoto *Osaka* Yokohama
CITY Hiroshima Fuji-san
Qingdao *Shikoku* 3776m
Yellow Kitakyushu
nja *Sea* *Kyushu*

Mid - Pacific Mountains

njing

East China Sea Shanghai

Hangzhou

Nanchang
gsha *Shikoku Basin*

Fuzhou
tou **TAIPEI (TAIBEI)**
angzhou **TAIWAN**
ao Gaoxiong
nen) Hong Kong (Xianggang)

Luzon Strait

PACIFIC OCEAN

Kyushu-Palau Ridge

Ryukyu Trench
Ryukyu Islands

Taiwan Strait

3

Philippine Sea

Philippine Basin

West Mariana Basin

East Mariana Basin

Mariana Trench

EL Luzon
OS Baguio
ed)

th China **MANILA**
n Sea *Mindoro*

PHILIPPINES

ATLY ISLANDS *Panay* Samar
(disputed) Bacolod Cebu
Palawan *Negros*

M i c r o n e s i a

Yap Trench

Melanesian Basin

Equator

152 4

Sulu Sea
Zamboanga *Mindanao*
Davao

BANDAR
NEI SERI BEGAWAN

A

Eauripik Rise

Ontong Java Rise

Celebes Sea
Manado

Halmahera

M e l a n e s i a

Bismarck Archipelago

Jayapura

Solomon Islands

rneo
likpapan

Banjarmasin *Celebes*

Moluccas

Seram
Buru Ambon

Pegunungan Maoke

New Guinea

Solomon Sea

5

aya *Flores*
abaya Makassar *Banda Sea*
lang *Bali* *Lesser Sunda Islands*
Flores

Makassar Strait

ndaI s l a n d s

I N D O N E S I A

Arafura Sea

Sumba *Timor* DILI **EAST TIMOR**
Timor Trough

Timor Sea

AUSTRALIA

142

Coral Sea

E F G H

Western China & Mongolia

RUSSIAN FE

Kulunda Steppe

Yenisey

Zapadnyy Sayan

KAZAKHSTAN

Kazakhskiy

Melkosopochnik

Ozero Balkash

Ozero Zaysan

Altai Mountains

Hövsgöl Nuur

Uvs Nuur

Ulaangom

Ölgiy

Har Us Nuur

Hyargas Nuur

Har Nuur

Möi

Altay

Hovd

MON

Hangayn Nuruu

Tsetserle

Altay

Bayanhongor

Ulungur Hü

Karamay

Gurbantünggüt Shamo

△ *Aj Bogd Uul 3802m*

△ *Atas Bogd 2695m*

G

Borohoro Shan

Kuytun

Shihezi

Fukang

Jimsar

Yining

Ozero Issyk-Kul'

KYRGYZSTAN

Tien Shan

△ *Tomür Feng 7443m*

Korla

Ürümqi

Qitai

Turpan

Hami

Turpan Pendi

Bosten Hu

Kuruktag

Xingxingxia

Dalian H

TAJIKISTAN

Kashi

Yengisar

Shache

Tarim He

Tarim Basin

XINJIANG UYGUR

ZIZHIQU

Ruoqiang

Lop Nur

GANSU

Qilian Shan

AIGH

Yecheng

(claimed by India)

Pishan

Moyu

Hotan

Taklimakan Shamo

Qira

Altun Shan

Danghe Nanshan

Qaidam Pendi

Qinghai I

PAKISTAN

Karakoram Range

K2

△ *8611m*

K a

Kunlun Shan

Golmud

Burhan Budai Shan

Anyêmaqên

Dulan

C

QINGHAI

H

JAMMU AND KASHMIR

AKSAI CHIN

AKSAI CHIN

(administered by China, claimed by India)

Qingzang Gaoyuan

(Plateau of Tibet)

Tongtian He

Bayan Har Sh

Yushu

Mekong

Rutog

DEMCHOK/DÊMQOG

(administered by China, claimed by India)

Gar Xincun

Zanda

XIZANG

ZIZHIQU

(Tibet)

Tanggula Shan

Gozhê

Siling Co

Amdo

Qamdo

Salween

Jinsha Jiang

Himalaya

Yamuna

Ganges

Brahmaputra

NEPAL

Lhazê

Xigazê

Tangra Yumco

Ngangzê Co

Gyaring Co

Nam Co

Nagqu

Damxung

Nyainqêntanglha Shan

Maizhokunggar

Lhasa

Gonggar

ARUNACHAL PRADESH

(claimed by China)

Gyangzê

a

s

△ *Mount Everest 8848m*

INDIA

BHUTAN

INDIA

MYANMAR

(BURMA)

0 km   400

0 miles   400

Population

● National capital   ◉ Internal administrative capital

○ below 50,000   ○ 50,000 to 100,000   ◉ 100,000 to 500,000   ■ above 500,000

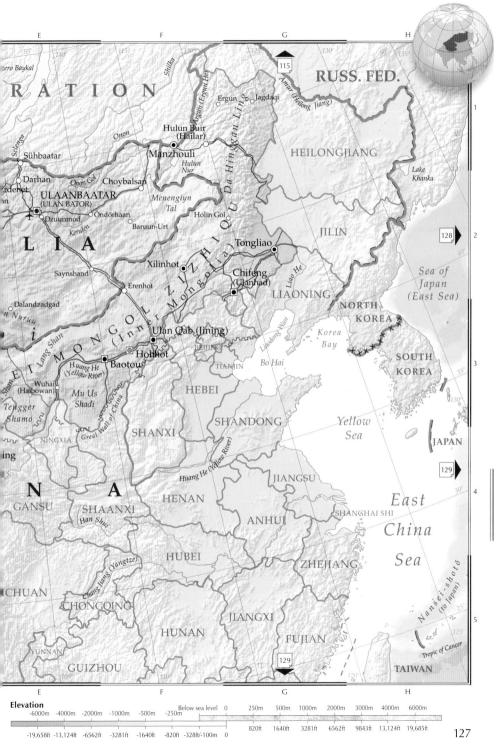

ozero Baykal

RATION

RUSS. FED.

115

Shilka

Amur (Heilong Jiang)

Ergun (Erguni He)

Ergun

Jagdaqi

HEILONGJIANG

Lake
Khanka

Hulun Buir
(Hailar)

Manzhouli

Hulun
Nur

Selenga

Onon

Sühbaatar

Darhan

Onon Gol

Choybalsan

Menengiyn
Tal

Holin Gol

JILIN

128

rdenet

ULAANBAATAR
(ULAN BATOR)

Dzuunmod

Öndörhaan

Baruun-Urt

Tongliao

n

LIA

Kerulen

Saynshand

Xilinhot

Chifeng
(Ulanhad)

Sea of
Japan
(East Sea)

Erenhot

LIAONING

Dalandzadgad

Liao He

NORTH
KOREA

n Nuruu

MONGOL

ZIZHIQU

Da Hingqan Ling

Ulan Qab (Jining)

(Inner Mongolia)

Korea
Bay

SOUTH
KOREA

Shan

EI Lang Shan

Hohhot

BEIJING

Liaodong Wan

3

Huang He
(Yellow River)

Baotou

TIANJIN

Bo Hai

129

Wuhai
(Haibowan)

Mu Us
Shadi

HEBEI

Tengger
Shamo

NINGXIA

Great Wall of China

SHANXI

SHANDONG

Yellow
Sea

JAPAN

ing

Huang He (Yellow River)

JIANGSU

129

N

GANSU

SHAANXI

Han Shui

HENAN

ANHUI

SHANGHAI SHI

East

4

A

China

CHUAN

Chang Jiang (Yangtze)

HUBEI

ZHEJIANG

Sea

CHONGQING

JIANGXI

Nansei-shotō
(to Japan)

5

YUNNAN

HUNAN

FUJIAN

129

Tropic of Cancer

GUIZHOU

TAIWAN

Elevation

| -6000m | -4000m | -2000m | -1000m | -500m | -250m | Below sea level | 0 | 250m | 500m | 1000m | 2000m | 3000m | 4000m | 6000m |

| -19,658ft | -13,124ft | -6562ft | -3281ft | -1640ft | -820ft | -328ft/-100m | 0 | 820ft | 1640ft | 3281ft | 6562ft | 9843ft | 13,124ft | 19,685ft |

127

Eastern China & Korea

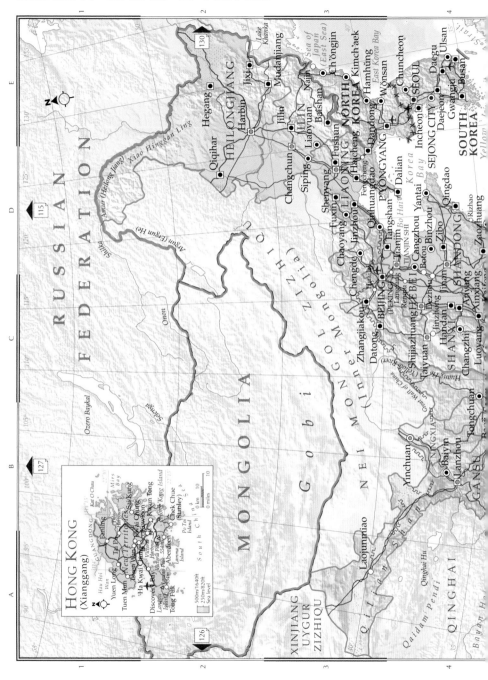

RUSSIAN FEDERATION

HEILONGJIANG

Hegang

Qiqihar

Harbin

Jixi

Mudanjiang

Lake Khanka

Sea of Japan (East Sea)

JILIN

Changchun

Jilin

Liaoyuan

Baishan

Siping

Shenyang

Fushun

LIAONING

Chaoyang

Fuxin

Jinzhou

Fengcheng

Haicheng

Yingkou

Qinhuangdao

Tangshan

Chengde

Zhangjiakou

Datong

Taiyuan

SHANXI

Changzhi

Luoyang

BEIJING

(PEKING)

HEBEI

TIANJIN

TIANJIN SHI

Langfang

Shijiazhuang

Handan

Jinzhong

Anyang

Xinxiang

Zhengzhou

HENAN

Huang He (Yellow River)

NEI MONGOL (Inner Mongolia)

Gobi

MONGOLIA

Hamhŭng

Wŏnsan

Dandong

Dalian

Yantai

Cangzhou

Binzhou

Zibo

Qingdao

SHANDONG

Rizhao

Zaozhuang

Jining

PYONGYANG

NORTH KOREA

Najin

Ch'ŏngjin

Kimch'aek

SOUTH KOREA

SEOUL

Incheon

SEJONG CITY

Daejeon

Chuncheon

Gwangju

Daegu

Ulsan

Busan

East Korea Bay

Korea Bay

Bo Hai

Yellow Sea

YINCHUAN

NINGXIA

Baiyin

Lanzhou

GANSU

Qilian Shan

QINGHAI

Qinghai Hu

Qaidam Pendi

Bayan Har

XINJIANG UYGUR ZIZHIQU

Laojunmiao

Great Wall of China

Amur (Heilong Jiang)

Argun (Ergun He)

Shilka

Onon

Selenga

Ozero Baykal

Xiao Hinggan Ling

Tongchuan

Yongchuan

Bayin

HONG KONG (Xianggang)

Kat O Chau
Mirs Bay
Hau Hoi Wan
Yuen Long
GUANGDONG
Panling
Tai Po
Fanling
Tsuen Wan
Sha Tin
Sai Kung
Kwai Chung
Kwun Tong
Kowloon
Victoria Harbour
Lamma Island
Aberdeen
Cheung Chau
Discovery Bay
Ha Kwai Chung
Tung Chung
Tuen Mun
Chek Chue (Stanley)
Po Toi Island
Hong Kong Island
Lantau Island
Tong Fuk

500m/1640ft
250m/820ft
Sea level

0 km 10
0 miles 10

South China Sea

Population

● National capital   ● Internal administrative capital

○ below 50,000   ○ 50,000 to 100,000   ◉ 100,000 to 500,000   ■ above 500,000

0 km 400

0 miles 400

East China
Sea

Nansei-shoto (Japan)

Okinawa

Tropic of Cancer

PACIFIC OCEAN

TAIWAN

TAIPEI (T'AIBEI)

Jilong
Taizhong
Jiayi
Tainan
Gaoxiong

(China and Taiwan claim
all of each other's territory)

Luzon Strait

PHILIPPINES

SOUTH KOREA'S TWO CAPITALS

SEOUL - Capital
SEJONG CITY - Administrative capital

South China
Sea

SPRATLY ISLANDS
(disputed by China,
Malaysia, Philippines,
Taiwan and Vietnam)

Flat Island
Nanshan Island
Thitu
Island
Loaita Island
Namyit Island   Len Dao
Spratly Island

PARACEL
ISLANDS
(disputed by China,
Taiwan and Vietnam)
Amphitrite Group
Crescent Group
Triton Island

Hainan Dao

HAINAN

Xuwen
Danzhou
Dongfang

Gulf of Tongking

VIETNAM

Shanghai
Suzhou
Wuxi
Jiaxing
Ningbo
Wubu
Hangzhou
Jinhua
Wenzhou
Shangrao
ZHEJIANG

ANHUI
Hefei
Anqing
Tongling
Shangshi
Jingdezhen
Nanchang
Fuzhou
Longyan
Yong'an
Quanzhou
Xiamen
Shantou
Zhangzhou

FUJIAN
JIANGXI

HUBEI
Xinyang
Yichang
Wuhan
Wanzhou
Lichuan
Chongqing
CHONGQINGSHI

Dongting Hu
Changsha
Loudi
Yueyang
Huaihua
Hengyang
Yongzhou
Chenzhou
Shaoguan

HUNAN

GUIZHOU
Zunyi
Anshun
Guiyang

GUANGXI
ZHUANGZU

Liuzhou
Guilin
Zhaoqing
Yulin

GUANGDONG
Guangzhou
Dongguan
Hong Kong
(Xianggang)
Macao
(Aomen)
Jiangmen
Maoming
Zhanjiang
Haikou
Beihai
Qinzhou
Nanning
Gejiu

Hong Kong
(Xianggang)

Red River

SICHUAN
(Tibet)
Mianyang
Chengdu
Ya'an
Leshan
Zigong
Neijiang

Sichuan
Pendi

Chang Jiang
Xichang
Dali
Baoshan

YUNNAN
Kunming
Jinghong
Wuliang Shan
Mekong

Salween
Hengduan Shan

INDIA

MYANMAR
(BURMA)

Tropic of Cancer

LAOS

THAILAND

Mekong

CAMBODIA

Gulf of Thailand

152
139
136
136

Elevation

-6000m	-4000m	-2000m	-1000m	-500m	-250m	Below sea level	0	250m	500m	1000m	2000m	3000m	4000m	6000m
-19,658ft	-13,124ft	-6562ft	-3281ft	-1640ft	-820ft	-328ft/-100m	0	820ft	1640ft	3281ft	6562ft	9843ft	13,124ft	19,685ft

Japan

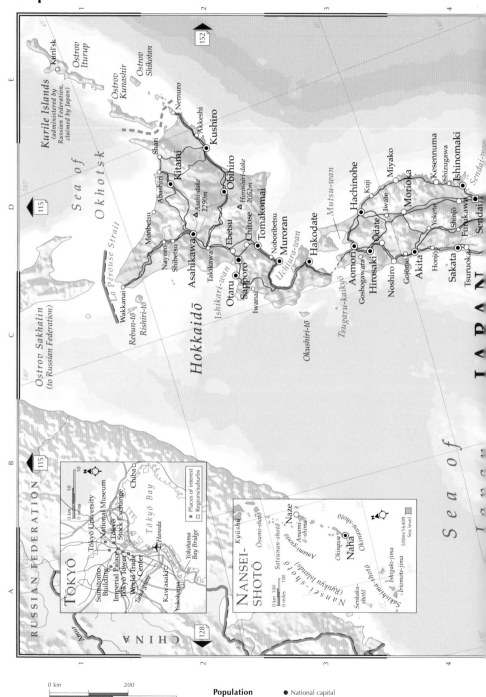

Kuril Islands
(administered by
Russian Federation,
claimed by Japan)

Ostrov Iturup

Kuril'sk

Ostrov Shikotan

Ostrov Kunashir

Nemuro

Akkeshi

Kushiro

Shari

Kitami

Obihiro

Abashiri

△ Asahi-dake 2290m

△ Horoshiri-dake 2052m

Sea of Okhotsk

Monbetsu

Nayoro

Shibetsu

Asahikawa

Takikawa

Ebetsu

Chitose

Tomakomai

Noboribetsu

Muroran

Hakodate

Uchiura-wan

Mutsu-wan

Kesennuma

Shizugawa

Ishinomaki

Sendai-wan

Miyako

Morioka

Kuji

Iwate

Yokote

Shinjō

Furukawa

Sendai

Hachinohe

Odate

Aomori

Goshogawara

Hirosaki

Noshiro

Gojōme

Akita

Honjō

Sakata

Tsuruoka

La Pérouse Strait

Wakkanai

Rebun-tō

Rishiri-tō

Ishikari-wan

Otaru

Sapporo

Iwanai

Okushiri-tō

Hokkaidō

Tsugaru-kaikyō

Okushiri-tō

Ostrov Sakhalin
(to Russian Federation)

Amur

RUSSIAN FEDERATION

Sea of Japan

JAPAN

TŌKYŌ (inset)

Tōkyō Bay

Chiba

Tōkyō University

National Museum

Tōkyō Stock Exchange

Sumitomo Building

Imperial Palace

Tōkyō Tower

World Trade Center

Kawasaki

Yokohama

Yokohama Bay Bridge

Haneda

Places of interest

Regions/suburbs

CHINA

NANSEI-SHOTŌ (inset)

Kyūshū

Ōsumi-shotō

Naze

Amami-ō-shima

Satsunan-shotō

Naha

Okinawa

Okinawa-shotō

Tokara-rettō

Sakishima-shotō

Ishigaki-jima

Iriomote-shima

Senkaku-shotō

Nansei-shotō (Ryūkyū Islands)

500m/1640ft
Sea level

0 km 200

0 miles 200

Population

● National capital

○ below 50,000

○ 50,000 to 100,000

◉ 100,000 to 500,000

◼ above 500,000

PACIFIC

OCEAN

Honshu

Hitachi
Utsunomiya
Mito
Chōshi
Ōyama
Chiba
Kawagoe
Yokohama
Mikuni-sanmyaku
Kasumiga-ura
Maebashi
Bōsō-hantō
TOKYO
Kawasaki
Izu-hantō
Sagami-nada
Miyake-jima
Mikura-jima
Hachijō-jima
Nii-jima
Ō-shima
Kōzu-shima
Izu-shotō
Jōetsu
Iïoïgawa
Nagano
Toyama
Matsumoto
Kōfu
Fuji-san
3776m
Fuji
Shizuoka
Hamamatsu
Enshū-nada
Hida
Toyota
sanmyaku
Nakatsugawa
Okazaki
Gifu
Nagoya
Ō-gaki
Tsu
Ise
Owase
Shingū
Takaoka
Kanazawa
Komatsu
Fukui
Tsuruga
Biwa-ko
Kyōto
Kōbe
Ōsaka
Wakayama
Gobō
Tanabe
Ise-wan
Toyama-wan
Wakasa-wan
Kii-suidō
Shikoku
Tottori
Chūgoku-sanchi
Okayama
Kurashiki
Himeji
Kii-hanto
Awaji-shima
Harima-nada
Tokushima
Niihama
Matsuyama
Kōchi
Nakamura
Sukumo
Tosa-wan
Bungo-suidō
Kyūshū
Miyazaki
Miyakonojō
Shibushi-wan
Tanega-shima
Yaku-shima
Yonago
Dōgo
Dōzen
Oki-shotō
Matsue
Gōtsu
Hamada
Masuda
Hiroshima
Iwakuni
Hōfu
Ōita
Nobeoka
Satsushin
Kagoshima
Kurume
Ōmuta
Kumamoto
Satsuma-Sendai
Osumi-shotō
Kagoshima-wan
Ōsumi-hantō
Liancourt Rocks
(under South
Korean control)
Tsushima
Nagato
Yamaguchi
Ube
Shimonoseki
Kitakyūshū
Iki
Fukuoka
Sasebo
Nagasaki
Amakusa-nada
Koshikijima-rettō
Tanega-shima
East
China Sea
Kō-saki
Tsushima
Tsushima Strait
Iki-suidō
Gotō-rettō
Korea Strait
SOUTH
KOREA

152
128

N

Elevation

-6000m	-4000m	-2000m	-1000m	-500m	Below sea level	0	250m	500m	1000m	2000m	3000m	4000m	6000m
-19,658ft	-13,124ft	-6562ft	-3281ft	-1640ft	-820ft -328ft/-100m	0	820ft	1640ft	3281ft	6562ft	9843ft	13,124ft	19,685ft

Southern India & Sri Lanka

SRI LANKA'S TWO CAPITALS

COLOMBO - Capital
SRI JAYEWARDENAPURA KOTTE - Administrative capital

Population

- National capital

○ below 50,000
○ 50,000 to 100,000
◉ 100,000 to 500,000
◼ above 500,000

0 km   300
0 miles   300

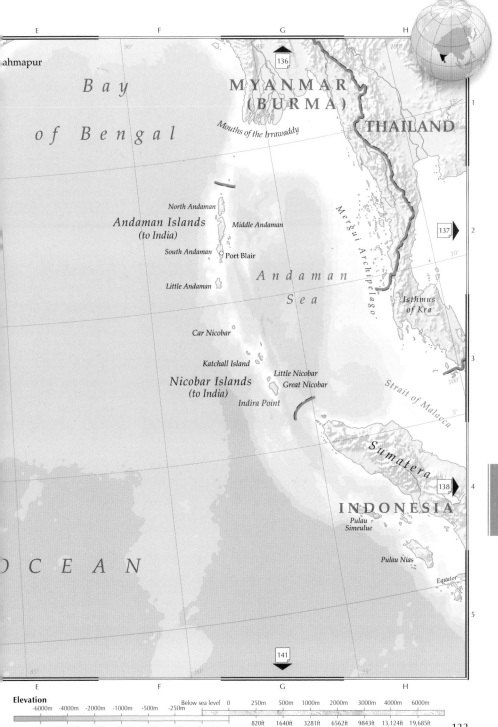

ahmapur

Bay

of Bengal

MYANMAR
(BURMA)

THAILAND

Mouths of the Irrawaddy

136

137

North Andaman

Andaman Islands
(to India)

Middle Andaman

South Andaman

Port Blair

Mergui Archipelago

Little Andaman

A n d a m a n

S e a

*Isthmus
of Kra*

Car Nicobar

Katchall Island

Nicobar Islands
(to India)

Little Nicobar

Great Nicobar

Indira Point

Strait of Malacca

Sumatera

138

INDONESIA

*Pulau
Simeulue*

O C E A N

Pulau Nias

Equator

141

Elevation

| -6000m | -4000m | -2000m | -1000m | -500m | -250m | Below sea level | 0 | 250m | 500m | 1000m | 2000m | 3000m | 4000m | 6000m |

| -19,658ft | -13,124ft | -6562ft | -3281ft | -1640ft | -820ft | -328ft/-100m | 0 | 820ft | 1640ft | 3281ft | 6562ft | 9843ft | 13,124ft | 19,685ft |

Northern India, Pakistan & Bangladesh

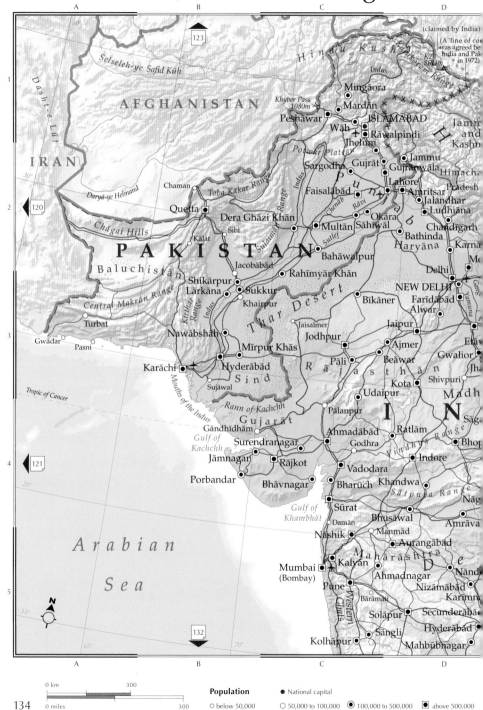

A   B   C   D

(claimed by India)

(A line of co
was agreed be
India and Pak
in 1972)

AFGHANISTAN

Hindu Kush

Selseleh-ye Safid Kūh

Indus

Mingāora

Khyber Pass
1080m ▲

Mardān

Peshāwar

ISLĀMĀBĀD

Wāh

Rāwalpindi

Jhelum

Jhelum

IRAN

Daryā-ye Helmand

Chaman

Toba Kākar Range

Quetta

Dera Ghāzi Khān

Chāgai Hills

Kālat

Sibi

PAKISTAN

Baluchistān

Jacobābād

Central Makrān Range

Shikārpur

Lārkāna

Sukkur

Khairpur

Turbat

Gwādar

Pasni

Nawābshāh

Mīrpur Khās

Karāchi

Hyderābād

Sind

Sujāwal

Mouths of the Indus

Rann of Kachchh

Sargodha

Gujrāt

Jammu

Gujrānwāla

Lahore

Amritsar

Faisalābād

Jalandhar

Ludhiāna

Chenāb

Rāvi

Okāra

Sāhiwāl

Chandīgarh

Multān

P   u   n   j   a   b

Bathinda

Haryāna

Karna

Bahāwalpur

Delhi

Rahīmyār Khān

Bīkāner

NEW DELHI

Farīdābād

Alwar

Thar Desert

Jaisalmer

Jaipur

Jodhpur

Ajmer

Eta

Pāli

Beāwar

Gwalior

Jh

R   ā   j   a   s   t   h   ā   n

Kota

Shivpuri

Udaipur

I   N

Madh

Pālanpur

Sāg

Tropic of Cancer

Gāndhīdhām

Gujarāt

Ahmadābād

Ratlām

*Gulf of
Kachchh*

Surendranagar

Godhra

Bhoj

Jāmnagar

Rājkot

Vindhya   Range

Indore

Porbandar

Vadodara

Bhāvnagar

Bharūch

Khandwa

Nāg

Satpura Range

*Gulf of
Khambhāt*

Sūrat

Bhusāwal

Amrāva

Damān

Manmād

Arabian

Nāshik

Aurangābād

Sea

Mahārāshtra

D e

Mumbai
(Bombay)

Kalyān

Nānd

Ahmadnagar

Nizāmābād

Pune

Karīmn

Bārāmati

Secunderābā

Solāpur

Hyderābād

Kolhāpur

Sāngli

Mahbūbnagar

Jammu
and
Kashn

Indus

Karakoram Range

K2
8611m ▲

**Jam
and
Kashn**

Himacha
Pradesh

Ganges

Yamuna

Me

Western Ghāts

A   B   C   D

0 km   300

0 miles   300

Population

● National capital

○ below 50,000

○ 50,000 to 100,000

◉ 100,000 to 500,000

■ above 500,000

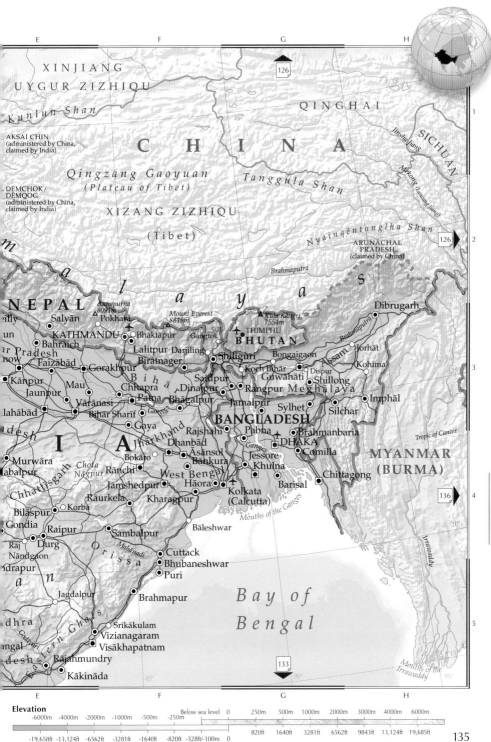

XINJIANG
UYGUR ZIZHIQU

Kunlun Shan

AKSAI CHIN
(administered by China,
claimed by India)

QINGHAI

Jinsha Jiang

SICHUAN

C H I N A

Qingzang Gaoyuan
(Plateau of Tibet)

Tanggula Shan

Mekong (Lancang Jiang)

DEMCHOK/
DÊMQOG
(administered by China,
claimed by India)

XIZANG ZIZHIQU

(Tibet)

Nyaingêntanglha Shan

ARUNÁCHAL
PRADESH
(claimed by China)

Brahmaputra

H   i   m   a   l   a   y   a   s

NEPAL
△ Annapurna
  8091m
Salyān ● Pokhara
Mount Everest
8848m △
△ Kula Kangri
  7554m
Dibrugarh

reilly
●Bahraich
KATHMANDU
Bhaktapur
Gangtok
THIMPHU
BHUTAN
Assam
Jorhāt

un
r Pradesh
now
Faizābād ●
Lalitpur Darjiling ●
●Shiliguri
Bongaigaon
Guwāhāti ● Dispur
Shillong
Kohīma

Kānpur ●
●Gorakhpur
Biratnager
Koch Bihār
Rangpur *Meghalaya*

Jaunpur ●
B   i   h   a   r
Saidpur
Dinajpur
Imphāl

Mau ●
Chhapra
Pātna
●Bhāgalpur
Jamālpur
Sylhet ●
Silchar

●Vārānasi
●Bihar Sharīf
Ganges
BANGLADESH

lahābād
Gaya ●
Rājshāhi
Pabna
●Brahmanbaria
Tropic of Cancer

desh
Jharkhand
Dhanbād
Ganges
DHAKA
Comilla
MYANMAR
(BURMA)

●Murwāra
Chota
Nāgpur
Bokāro
●Āsānsol
Bānkura
Jessore ●
Khulna
Chittagong

abalpur
Ranchī
West Bengal
Kolkata
Barisal

Bilāspur ●
●Korba
Jamshedpur
Hāora ●
(Calcutta)

Chhattisgarh
Rāurkela
Kharagpur
Mouths of the Ganges

Gondia ●
Raipur ●
Sambalpur
Bāleshwar

Rāj
Durg ●
Mahanadi
Irrawaddy

Nāndgaon
O r i s s a
Cuttack
Bay of
Bengal

drapur
Jagdalpur
Bhubaneshwar
Puri

Brahmapur

dhra
Srikākulam

ngal
Vizianagaram
Visākhapatnam
Mouths of the
Irrawaddy

desh
Rājahmundry ●
Kākināda ●

Elevation
-6000m -4000m -2000m -1000m -500m -250m   Below sea level 0   250m 500m 1000m 2000m 3000m 4000m 6000m
-19,658ft -13,124ft -6562ft -3281ft -1640ft -820ft -328ft/-100m 0   820ft 1640ft 3281ft 6562ft 9843ft 13,124ft 19,685ft

Mainland Southeast Asia

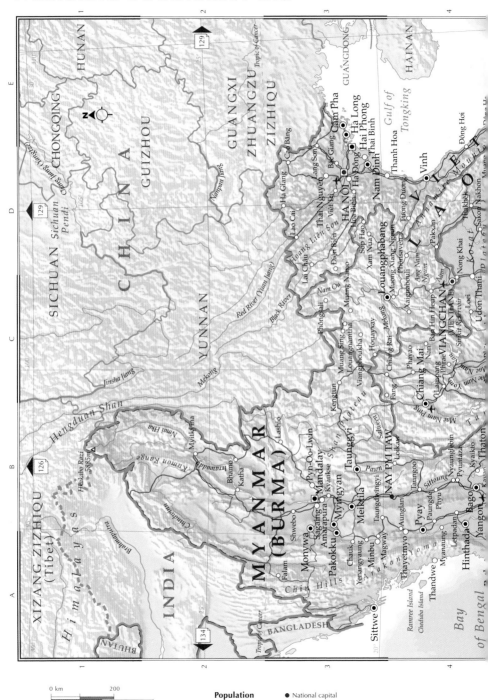

0 km   200

0 miles   200

Population

● National capital

○ below 50,000   ◉ 100,000 to 500,000

○ 50,000 to 100,000   ▣ above 500,000

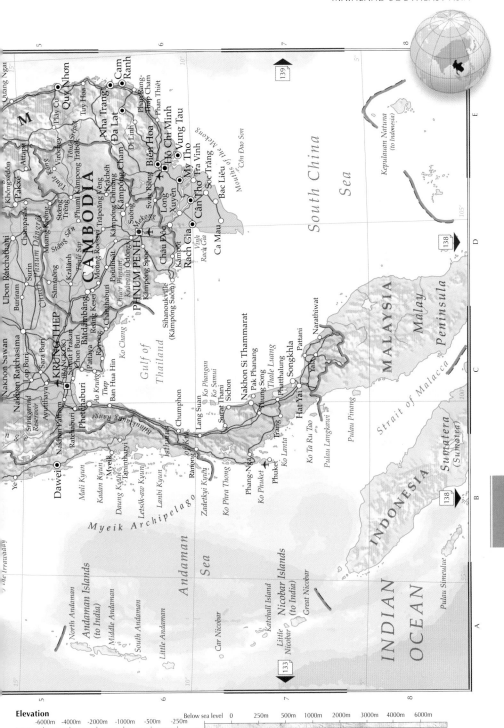

Elevation

-6000m	-4000m	-2000m	-1000m	-500m	Below sea level	0	250m	500m	1000m	2000m	3000m	4000m	6000m
					-250m								
-19,658ft	-13,124ft	-6562ft	-3281ft	-1640ft	-820ft	-328ft/-100m	0	820ft	1640ft	3281ft	6562ft	9843ft	13,124ft	19,685ft

Maritime Southeast Asia

Luzon Strait
Babuyan Island
Babuyan Channel
Cordillera Central
Tuguegarao
Ilagan
uio
Luzon
Dagupan
les
Cabanatuan
NILA
Lucena
PHILIPPINES
ngas
Naga
Legazpi City
Mindoro
Sibuyan Sea
Calbayog
Samar
Roxas City
Panay Island
Cadiz
Tacloban
Leyte
Iloilo
Palawan
erto
ncesa
Bacolod City
Cebu
Negros
Bohol Sea
Butuan
Sulu Sea
Iligan
Cagayan de Oro
Bislig
Mindanao
amboanga
Moro Gulf
Davao
Basilan
Lebak
Davao Gulf
kan
Sulu Archipelago
General Santos

Philippine
Sea

131

NORTHERN MARIANA ISLANDS
(to US)

GUAM
(to US)

Yap

144

MICRONESIA

P   A   C   I   F   I   C

Babeldaob

PALAU

O   C   E   A   N

Equator

Kepulauan Talaud

elebes Sea
Manado
Bitung
Gorontalo
Molucca Sea
Pulau Morotai
Pulau Halmahera
Pulau Waigeo
Sorong
Jazirah Doberai
Manokwari
Pulau Biak
Pulau Yapen
Jayapura

Tomini Teluk
Kepulauan Banggai
Sulawesi
(Celebes)
Kepulauan Sula
Laut Halmahera
Selat Dampier
Laut Seram
Pulau Misool
Teluk Berau
Teluk Cenderawasih
Sungai Mamberamo
Pegunungan Maoke
Papua
(Irian Jaya)
PAPUA

Danau Towuti
Waflia
Tifu
Wahai
Puncak Jaya 5030m

N   E   S   I   A

are
Kolaka
Kendari
Pulau Buru
Ambon
Pulau Seram

Watampone
Pulau Buton
Kepulauan Kai
Kepulauan Aru
New Guinea
GUINEA

Makassar
Bulukumba
Banda Sea

NEW

es
Kepulauan Tanimbar
Pulau Yamdena
Sungai Digul

T e n g g a r a
Flores
Kepulauan Alor
Pulau Wetar
Kepulauan Leti

A r a f u r a   S e a
Torres Strait

Sumba
Savu Sea
DILI
Timor
EAST TIMOR

au
Nikiniki
Kupang

Timor Sea

Timor Sea

148

AUSTRALIA

Elevation
-6000m -4000m -2000m -1000m -500m -250m   Below sea level 0   250m   500m 1000m 2000m 3000m 4000m 6000m

-19,658ft -13,124ft -6562ft -3281ft -1640ft -820ft -328ft/-100m 0   820ft 1640ft 3281ft 6562ft 9843ft 13,124ft 19,685ft

139

The Indian Ocean

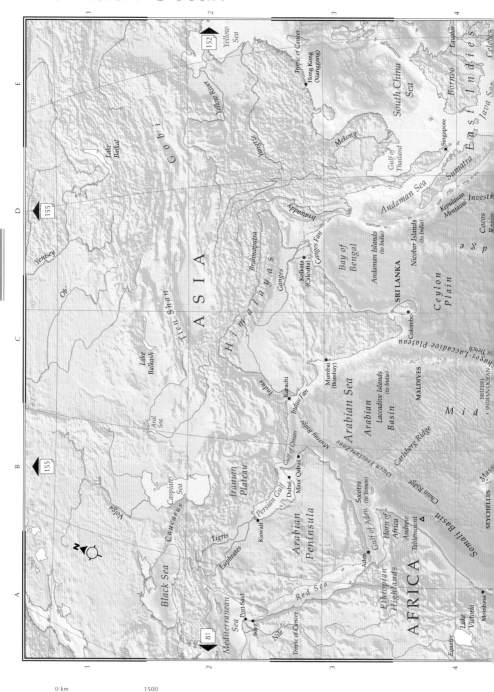

152

155

155

81

Yellow
Sea

Yellow River

Tropic of Cancer

Hong Kong
(Xianggang)

South China
Sea

Borneo

Equator

East Indies

Celebes

Java Sea

Sumatra

Singapore

Gulf of
Thailand

Mekong

Yangtze

Gobi

Lake
Baikal

Irrawaddy

Andaman Sea

Kepulauan
Mentawai

Investi

Cocos

Brahmaputra

Ganges Fan

Andaman Islands
(to India)

Nicobar Islands
(to India)

ASIA

Yenisey

Himalayas

Ganges

Kolkata
(Calcutta)

Bay of
Bengal

SRI LANKA

Ceylon
Plain

Tien Shan

Ob'

Lake
Balkhash

Indus

Karachi

Indus Fan

Mumbai
(Bombay)

Colombo

Chagos-Laccadive Plateau

os Trench

BRITISH
INDIAN OCEAN

Aral
Sea

Arabian Sea

Laccadive Islands
(to India)

MALDIVES

Mid

Caspian
Sea

Iranian
Plateau

Murray Ridge

Arabian
Basin

Carlsberg Ridge

Volga

Caucasus

Persian Gulf

Dubai

Mina Qabus

Gulf of Oman

Queen Fracture Zone

Socotra
(to Yemen)

Chain Ridge

Mas

Somali Basin

SEYCHELLES

Black Sea

Tigris

Kuwait

Euphrates

Arabian
Peninsula

Gulf of Aden

Horn of
Africa

Andreta
Tablemount

Aden

Mediterranean
Sea

Port Said

Suez

Nile

Tropic of Cancer

Red Sea

Ethiopian
Highlands

AFRICA

Equator

Lake
Victoria

Mombasa

0 km	1500
0 miles	1500

• Major port

152

AUSTRALIA

Tropic of Capricorn
Fremantle
Australian Basin
Exmouth Plateau
Cuvier Plateau
Perth Basin
Naturaliste Plateau
Wharton Basin
East Indiaman Ridge
Diamantina Fracture Zone
Broken Ridge
Southeast Indian Ridge
South Indian Basin
Limit of winter pack ice
Limit of summer pack ice
Antarctic Circle

154

Ninetyeast Ridge
Osborn Plateau
INDIAN
OCEAN
SOUTHERN OCEAN
ANTARCTICA
Amsterdam Island
St-Paul Island
Crozet Basin
FRENCH SOUTHERN & ANTARCTIC TERRITORIES (to France)
Kerguelen Plateau
Kerguelen
HEARD & McDONALD ISLANDS (to Australia)
Banzare Seamounts
Argo Plateau
Vityaz Fracture Zone
Egeria Fracture Zone
MAURITIUS
RÉUNION (to France)
Mascarene Plateau
Madagascar Basin
Southwest Indian Ridge
Crozet Islands
Crozet Plateau
Lena Tablemount
Enderby Plain
154
Basin
Madagascar Plateau
Indomed Fracture Zone
Ob' Tablemount
Natal Basin
MADAGASCAR
MAYOTTE (to France)
Davie Ridge
Mozambique Channel
Mozambique Plateau
Prince Edward Islands (to South Africa)
Atlantic-Indian Basin
Antarctic Circle
Zambezi
Tropic of Capricorn
Durban
Africana Seamount
Agulhas
Aguhlas Plateau
Aguhlas Basin
Farafangana
67

Elevation

-6000m	-4000m	-2000m	-1000m	-250m	0
-19,658ft	-13,124ft	-6562ft	-3281ft	-820ft	0

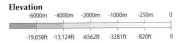

141

Australasia & Oceania

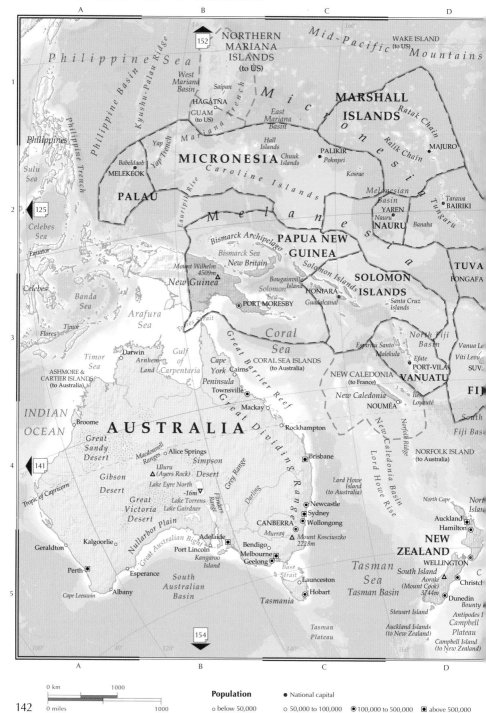

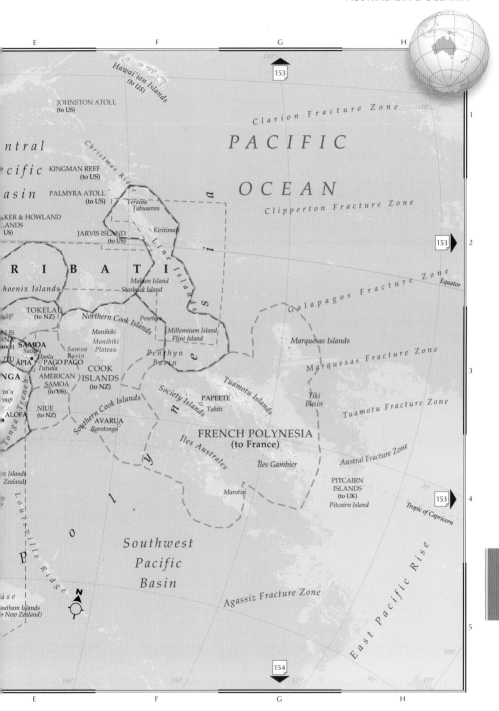

E   F   G   H

JOHNSTON ATOLL
(to US)

Hawaiian Islands
(to US)

Clarion Fracture Zone

ntral

cific

asin

KINGMAN REEF
(to US)

PALMYRA ATOLL
(to US)

PACIFIC

OCEAN

Clipperton Fracture Zone

Christmas Ridge

Teraina
Tabuaeran

KER & HOWLAND
LANDS
US)

JARVIS ISLAND
(to US)

Kiritimati

Line Islands

153

R I B A T I

hoenix Islands

Malden Island
Starbuck Island

Galapagos Fracture Zone

Equator

TOKELAU
(to NZ)

Northern Cook Islands

Penrhyn

Marquesas Islands

LIS
INA
ance)

ITU

SAMOA
Savai'i
Upolu
Tutuila

Manihiki
Manihiki
Plateau

Millennium Island
Flint Island

Samoa
Basin

Marquesas Fracture Zone

NGA

ALOFA

PAGO PAGO

AMERICAN
SAMOA
(to US)

NIUE
(to NZ)

COOK
ISLANDS
(to NZ)

Penrhyn
Basin

Tuamotu Islands

Society Islands

PAPEETE
Tahiti

Tiki
Basin

Tuamotu Fracture Zone

ÁPIA

'va'u
roup

Tonga Trench

Southern Cook Islands

AVARUA
Rarotonga

FRENCH POLYNESIA
(to France)

Îles Australes

Îles Gambier

Austral Fracture Zone

PITCAIRN
ISLANDS
(to UK)
Pitcairn Island

Tropic of Capricorn

153

ec Islands
Zealand)

Southwest

Pacific

Basin

Marotiri

Louisville Ridge

ise
atham Islands
New Zealand)

N

Agassiz Fracture Zone

East Pacific Rise

E   F   G   H

The Southwest Pacific

Population
○ below 50,000 ○ 50,000 to 100,000 ◉ 100,000 to 500,000 ▣ above 500,000
● National capital

0 km — 750
0 miles — 750

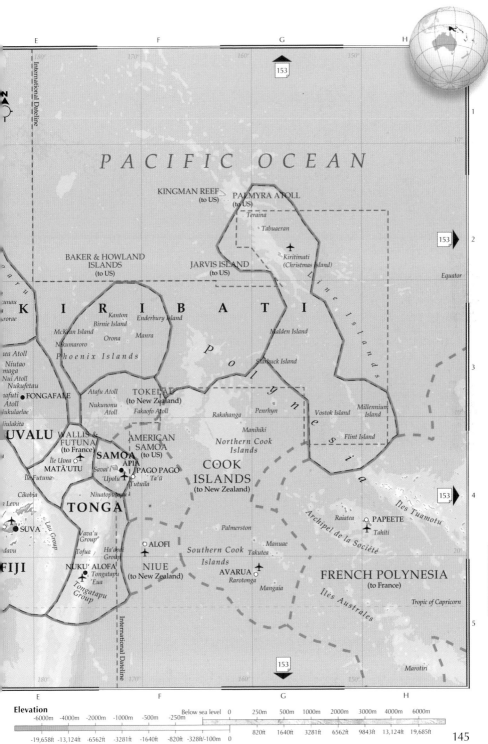

PACIFIC OCEAN

KINGMAN REEF
(to US)

PALMYRA ATOLL
(to US)

Teraina

Tabuaeran

BAKER & HOWLAND
ISLANDS
(to US)

JARVIS ISLAND
(to US)

Kiritimati
(Christmas Island)

Equator

K I R I B A T I

Kanton

Birnie Island   *Enderbury Island*

McKean Island   *Orona*   *Manra*

Nikumaroro

Phoenix Islands

Malden Island

Line Islands

P
o
l
y
n
e
s
i
a

ea Atoll
Niutao
maga
Nui Atoll
Nukufetau
FONGAFALE   *Atafu Atoll*

TOKELAU
(to New Zealand)

Starbuck Island

uafuti
Atoll
ukulaelae

Nukunonu
Atoll

Fakaofo Atoll

Rakahanga   *Penrhyn*   *Vostok Island*   *Millennium*
Island

jiulakita

UVALU

WALLIS &
FUTUNA
(to France)

AMERICAN
SAMOA
(to US)

Manihiki

Northern Cook
Islands

Flint Island

Île Uvea   SAMOA   *Savai'i*   APIA

MATĀ'UTU

Upolu   PAGO PAGO   *Ta'ū*

Île Futuna   *Tutuila*

COOK
ISLANDS
(to New Zealand)

Cikobia
a Levu

Niuatoputapu

TONGA

PAPEETE

Raiatea

Tahiti

Archipel de la Société

Îles Tuamotu

SUVA

Vava'u
Group

Palmerston

Manuae

Tofua   *Ha'apai*
Group

ALOFI

Southern Cook
Islands

Takutea

davu

FIJI

Lau Group

NUKU'ALOFA

NIUE
(to New Zealand)

AVARUA
Rarotonga

FRENCH POLYNESIA
(to France)

Tongatapu
'Eua

Mangaia

Îles Australes

Tongatapu
Group

Marotiri

Tropic of Capricorn

International Dateline

153

Elevation

					Below sea level	0	250m	500m	1000m	2000m	3000m	4000m	6000m
-6000m	-4000m	-2000m	-1000m	-500m	-250m								
-19,658ft	-13,124ft	-6562ft	-3281ft	-1640ft	-820ft	-328ft/-100m	0	820ft	1640ft	3281ft	6562ft	9843ft	13,124ft	19,685ft

Western Australia

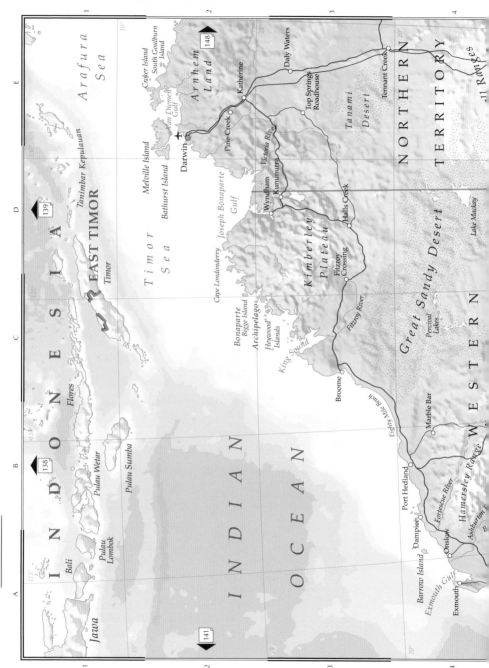

Arafura Sea

Croker Island
South Goulburn Island
Arnhem Land

148

Tanimbar Kepulauan

Van Diemen Gulf

EAST TIMOR

139

Timor

Katherine
Daly Waters
Tennant Creek

NORTHERN TERRITORY

Tanami Desert

Top Springs Roadhouse

ll Ranges

Timor Sea

Melville Island
Bathurst Island

Darwin

Pine Creek

Victoria River

Wyndham
Kununurra

Halls Creek

Lake Mackay

INDONESIA

Bonaparte Gulf
Cape Londonderry

Joseph Bonaparte Gulf

Kimberley Plateau

Fitzroy Crossing

Great Sandy Desert

Percival Lakes

Bonaparte Archipelago
Bigge Island
Heywood Islands

King Sound

Fitzroy River

Pulau Wetar

Flores

Pulau Sumba

138

Broome

Eighty Mile Beach

WESTERN

Bali
Pulau Lombok

INDIAN OCEAN

Marble Bar

Hamersley Range

Port Hedland

Fortescue River

Ashburton R

Jawa

Dampier

Barrow Island

Onslow

Exmouth Gulf

Exmouth

141

0 km 300
0 miles 300

Population

○ below 50,000   ○ 50,000 to 100,000   ◉ 100,000 to 500,000   ■ above 500,000

● Internal administrative capital

A U S T R A L I A

SOUTH

AUSTRALIA

Musgrave Ranges

△ Uluru (Ayers Rock) 863m

Great Victoria Desert

Nullarbor Plain

INDIAN OCEAN

Great Australian Bight

Coober Pedy

Tarcoola

Penong

Lake Everard

Lake Gairdner

Ceduna

Elliston

Port Lincoln

Eucla

Reid

Balladonia

Zanthus

Lake Carnegie

Lake Wells

Lake Carey

Lake Rebecca

Kalgoorlie

Coolgardie

Lake Cowan

Norseman

Esperance

Southern Cross

Lake Barlee

Lake Moore

Robinson Range

Meekatharra

Mount Magnet

Meredin

Brookton

Narrogin

Wagin

Katanning

Manjimup

Albany

Northam

Collie

Bunbury

Busselton

Augusta

Perth

Fremantle

Rockingham

Mandurah

Gingin

Moora

Murchison River

Geraldton

Kalbarri

Carnarvon

Denham

Shark Bay

Dorre Island

Dirk Hartog Island

149

154

154

141

N

Elevation

						Below sea level	0	250m	500m	1000m	2000m	3000m	4000m	6000m
-6000m	-4000m	-2000m	-1000m	-500m	-250m									
-19,658ft	-13,124ft	-6562ft	-3281ft	-1640ft	-820ft	-328ft/-100m	0	820ft	1640ft	3281ft	6562ft	9843ft	13,124ft	19,685ft

Eastern Australia

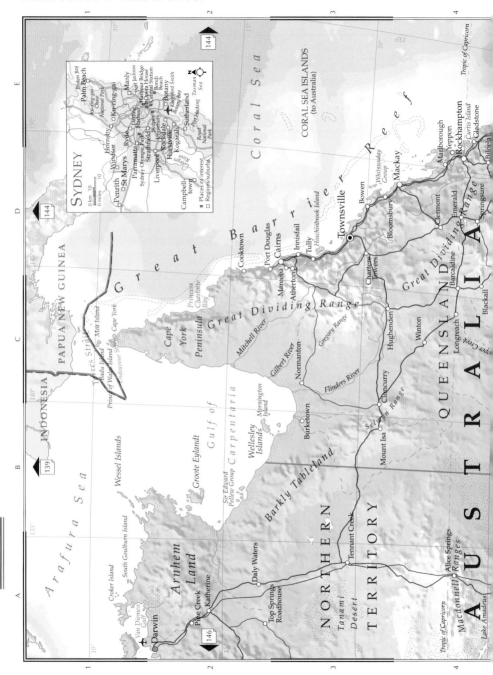

SYDNEY

Broken Bay
Palm Beach
Kuring-gai
National Park
Ku-ring-gai
Manly
Port Jackson
Harbour Bridge
Opera House
Bondi Beach
Botany
Kingsford Smith
Botany Bay
Port Hacking
Royal National Park

Hornsby
Windsor
Ryde
Penrith
St Marys
Parramatta
Sydney Olympic Park
University
Liverpool
Rockdale
Hurstville
Kogarah
Sutherland

Campbelltown

Tasman Sea

Places of interest
Regions/suburbs

0 km   10
0 miles   10

PAPUA NEW GUINEA

INDONESIA

Arafura Sea

Coral Sea

CORAL SEA ISLANDS
(to Australia)

Great Barrier Reef

Torres Strait

Moa Island
Prince of Wales Island
Badu Island
Endeavour Strait
Cape York

Cape York Peninsula

Princess Charlotte Bay

Great Dividing Range

Cooktown
Port Douglas
Cairns
Innisfail
Tully
Hinchinbrook Island
Townsville
Bowen
Whitsunday Group
Mackay
Bloomsbury
Bowen
Charters Towers
Hughenden
Winton
Clermont
Emerald
Barcaldine
Longreach
Blackall
Marlborough
Yeppoon
Rockhampton
Curtis Island
Gladstone
Biloela
Springsure

Mareeba
Atherton

Mitchell River
Gilbert River
Gregory Range
Flinders River
Normanton
Burketown
Cloncurry
Selwyn Range
Mount Isa
Copper Creek

Gulf of Carpentaria

Wellesley Islands
Mornington Island
Sir Edward Pellew Group
Groote Eylandt
Wessel Islands

Barkly Tableland

Tennant Creek

NORTHERN TERRITORY

Tanami Desert

QUEENSLAND

AUSTRALIA

Arnhem Land

Van Diemen Gulf
Croker Island
South Goulburn Island

Darwin
Pine Creek
Katherine
Daly Waters
Top Springs Roadhouse

Alice Springs
Macdonnell Ranges
Lake Amadeus

Tropic of Capricorn

Population

● National capital	◉ Internal administrative capital	
○ below 50,000	○ 50,000 to 100,000	◉ 100,000 to 500,000	■ above 500,000

0 km   300
0 miles   300

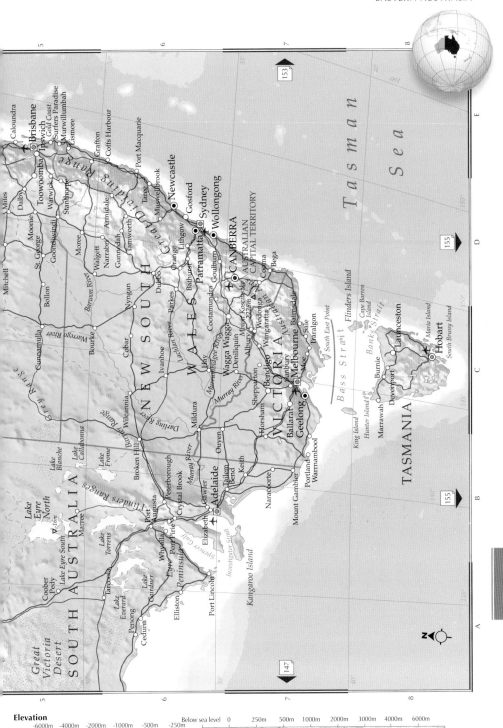

153

155

155

155

147

Tasman Sea

Caloundra
Brisbane
Ipswich
Gold Coast
Surfers Paradise
Murwillumbah
Lismore
Toowoomba
Warwick
Stanthorpe
Grafton
Coffs Harbour
Port Macquarie

Miles
Dalby
Moonie
St. George
Goondiwindi
Moree
Narrabri
Gunnedah
Tamworth
Armidale
Muswellbrook
Taree
Newcastle
Gosford
Sydney
Parramatta
Wollongong

Mitchell
Bollon
Walgett
Dubbo
Orange
Bathurst
Lithgow
Goulburn
CANBERRA
AUSTRALIAN CAPITAL TERRITORY
Cooma
Bega

Cunnamulla
Bourke
Cobar
Ivanhoe
Parkes
Lachlan River
Cootamundra
Wagga Wagga
Mount Kosciuszko
2228m
Albury
Wodonga
Wangaratta
Bairnsdale
Sale
Traralgon
South East Point

Warrego River
Barwon River
Nyngan
Hay
Deniliquin
Murrumbidgee River
Shepparton
Benalla

Darling River
Wilcannia
Menindee
Broken Hill
Mildura
Murray River
Ouyen
Horsham
Bendigo
Sunbury
Melbourne
Moe
Geelong
Ballarat

NEW SOUTH WALES

Great Dividing Range

VICTORIA

Great Artesian Basin

Lake Eyre North
Lake Eyre South
Marree
Lake Blanche
Lake Callabonna
Lake Frome
Lake Torrens
Peterborough
Crystal Brook
Port Augusta
Whyalla
Port Pirie
Gawler
Adelaide
Elizabeth
Tailem Bend
Keith
Naracoorte
Mount Gambier
Portland
Warrnambool

Coober Pedy
Tarcoola
Lake Everard
Lake Gairdner
Penong
Ceduna
Elliston
Port Lincoln
Eyre Peninsula
Kangaroo Island
Investigator Strait
Spencer Gulf

Flinders Ranges

SOUTH AUSTRALIA

Great Victoria Desert

Bass Strait
Banks' Strait
King Island
Hunter Island
Marrawah
Burnie
Devonport
Launceston
Hobart
South Bruny Island
Maria Island
Flinders Island
Cape Barren Island

TASMANIA

Elevation

Below sea level													
-6000m	-4000m	-2000m	-1000m	-500m	-250m	0	250m	500m	1000m	2000m	3000m	4000m	6000m
-19,658ft	-13,124ft	-6562ft	-3281ft	-1640ft	-820ft	-328ft/-100m	0	820ft	1640ft	3281ft	6562ft	9843ft	13,124ft	19,685ft

149

New Zealand

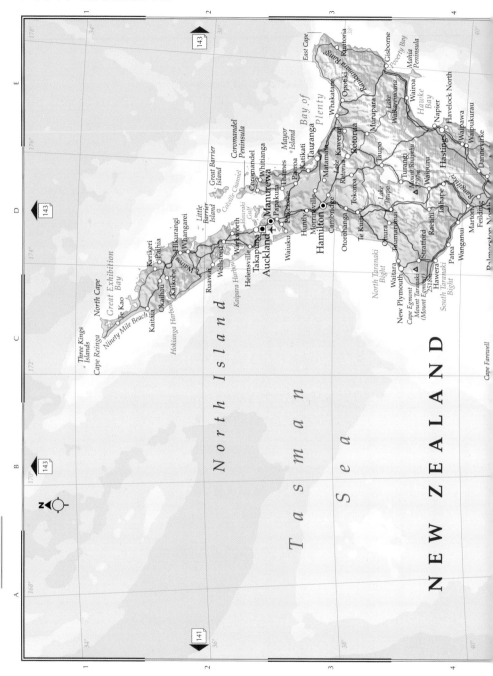

0 km   100

0 miles   100

Population

● National capital

○ below 50,000   ○ 50,000 to 100,000   ◉ 100,000 to 500,000   ◼ above 500,000

143

154

154

154

142

South Island

WELLINGTON
Lower Hutt
Cape Palliser
Cape Campbell
Seddon
Clarence
Blenheim
Richmond
Mount Owen
1875m
Kaikoura
Kaikoura Peninsula

Richmond Range
Kaikoura
Seddonville
Westport
Cape Foulwind
Reefton
Springs Junction
Hanmer Springs
Lewis Pass
907m
Rangiora
Waipara
Christchurch
Lyttelton
Banks Peninsula
Kaiapoi
Lake Ellesmere

Runanga
Greymouth
Hokitika
Ross
Lake Brunner
Otira
Arthur's Pass
920m
Darfield
Oxford
Methven
Mayfield
Canterbury Plains
Ashburton
Hinds
Geraldine
Temuka
Timaru

Rakaia
Southern Alps
Mount Cook
(Aoraki)
3754m
Mount Cook
Fairlie
Pleasant Point
Waihi
Waimate
Studholme
Oamaru
Hampden

Abut Head
Fox Glacier
Whataroa
Haast
Jackson Head
Lake Pukaki
Lake Hawea
Wanaka
Lake Wanaka
Lake Wakatipu
Queenstown
Cromwell
Alexandra
Clutha
Taieri
Dunedin
Mosgiel
Milton
Balclutha
Otago Peninsula

Milford Sound
Milford Sound
George Sound
Caswell Sound
Lake Te Anau
Te Anau
Lake Manapouri
Livingstone Mts
Eyre Mts
Lumsden
Mataura
Gore
Clinton
Balclutha
Te Waewae Bay
West Cape
Resolution Island
Waiau
Riverton
Wallace
Invercargill
Mataura
Tokanui
Lake Hauroka
Foveaux Strait
Halfmoon Bay
Codfish Island
Ruapuke Island
Stewart Island
South West Cape
Muttonbird Islands

Fiordland

Pegasus Bay
Canterbury Bight

PACIFIC OCEAN

Cook Strait
Golden Bight
Tasman Bight

Elevation

-6000m	-4000m	-2000m	-1000m	-500m	-250m	Below sea level	0	250m	500m	1000m	2000m	3000m	4000m	6000m
-19,658ft	-13,124ft	-6562ft	-3281ft	-1640ft	-820ft	-328ft/-100m	0	820ft	1640ft	3281ft	6562ft	9843ft	13,124ft	19,685ft

151

The Pacific Ocean

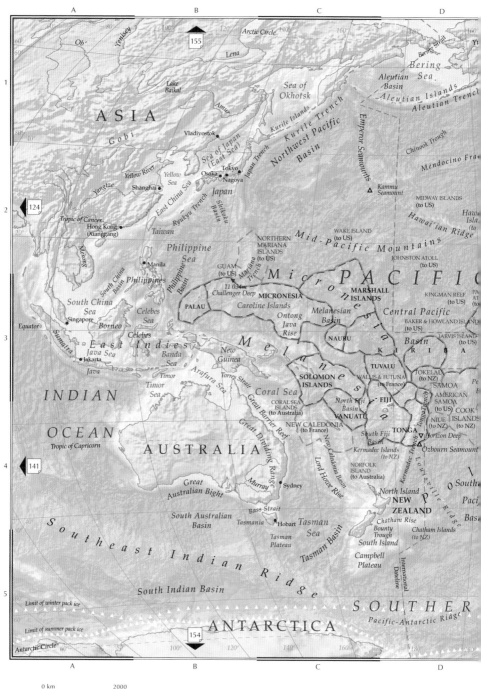

Major port

0 km   2000
0 miles   2000

152

E　　　　　F　　　　　G　　　　　H

155

Arctic Circle

Hudson
Bay

Labrador
Sea

Rocky Mountains

NORTH
AMERICA

Vancouver

Cascadia
Basin

Great Lakes

ATLANTIC

San Francisco

Colorado

Appalachian Mountains

OCEAN

y Fracture Zone

Long Beach

Mississippi

Tropic of Cancer

66

kai Fracture Zone

Gulf of California

Gulf of
Mexico

Greater Antilles

Lesser Antilles

Clarion Fracture Zone

Middle America Trench

Caribbean Sea

O C E A N

Clipperton Fracture Zone

CLIPPERTON ISLAND
(to France)

Guatemala
Basin

Panama City

Cocos Ridge

N

Galapagos Fracture Zone

Galápagos Islands
(to Ecuador)

Peru Basin

Amazon

Equator

Gallego Rise

SOUTH

Marquesas
Islands

Marquesas
Fracture Zone

Bauer
Basin

Galapagos
Rise

Peru-Chile Trench

Callao

AMERICA

Tiki
Basin

Mendaña Fracture Zone

Nazca Ridge

FRENCH
POLYNESIA
(to France)

Austral
Fracture Zone

Sala y Gomez
(to Chile)

Sala y Gomez Ridge

Andes

Iles Gambier

Easter Fracture Zone

Chile Basin

Australes

PITCAIRN ISLANDS
(to UK)

Easter Island
(to Chile)

Isla San Félix
(to Chile)

Isla San Ambrosio
(to Chile)

Tropic of Capricorn

67

Islas Juan Fernández
(to Chile)

Paraná

Valparaiso

East Pacific Rise

Challenger Fracture Zone

Agassiz Fracture Zone

Chile Rise

ATLANTIC

Mornington
Abyssal
Plain

OCEAN

Eltanin Fracture Zone

Cape Horn

O C E A N

Drake Passage

Southeast Pacific Basin

Bellingshausen Plain

PETER I ØY
(to Norway)

154

Amundsen Plain

Antarctic Circle

Elevation

-6000m	-4000m	-2000m	-1000m	-250m	0
-19,658ft	-13,124ft	-6562ft	-3281ft	-820ft	0

Antarctica

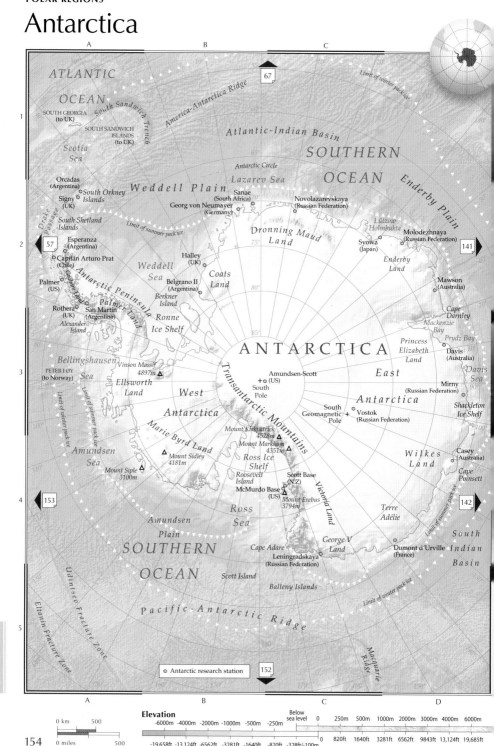

ATLANTIC OCEAN

SOUTH GEORGIA (to UK)

SOUTH SANDWICH ISLANDS (to UK)

Scotia Sea

South Sandwich Trench

America-Antarctica Ridge

67

Limit of winter pack ice

Atlantic-Indian Basin

Antarctic Circle

Lazarev Sea

SOUTHERN OCEAN

Enderby Plain

Orcadas (Argentina)

South Orkney Islands

Signy (UK)

Weddell Plain

Sanae (South Africa)

Georg von Neumayer (Germany)

Novolazarevskaya (Russian Federation)

Lützow Holmbukta

Molodezhnaya (Russian Federation)

South Shetland Islands

Limit of summer pack ice

57

Esperanza (Argentina)

Capitán Arturo Prat (Chile)

Halley (UK)

Weddell Sea

Coats Land

Dronning Maud Land

Syowa (Japan)

Enderby Land

141

Palmer (US)

Rothera (UK)

San Martín (Argentina)

Belgrano II (Argentina)

Berkner Island

Ronne Ice Shelf

Mawson (Australia)

Cape Darnley

Mackenzie Bay

Prydz Bay

Antarctic Peninsula

Graham Land

Palmer Land

Alexander Island

Bellingshausen Sea

PETER I ØY (to Norway)

Vinson Massif 4897m △

Ellsworth Land

West Antarctica

Transantarctic Mountains

Amundsen-Scott (US)

South Pole

ANTARCTICA

East

Antarctica

Princess Elizabeth Land

Davis (Australia)

Davis Sea

Mirny (Russian Federation)

Shackleton Ice Shelf

153

Marie Byrd Land

Mount Sidley 4181m △

Amundsen Sea

Mount Siple 3100m △

Mount Kirkpatrick 4528m △

Mount Markham 4351m △

Ross Ice Shelf

South Geomagnetic Pole

Vostok (Russian Federation)

Wilkes Land

Casey (Australia)

Cape Poinsett

Roosevelt Island

McMurdo Base (US)

Scott Base (N.Z.)

Mount Erebus 3794m △

Ross Sea

Victoria Land

Terre Adélie

142

Amundsen Plain

SOUTHERN OCEAN

Cape Adare

Leningradskaya (Russian Federation)

Scott Island

George V Land

Dumont d'Urville (France)

South Indian Basin

Balleny Islands

Limit of winter pack ice

Pacific-Antarctic Ridge

Eltanin Fracture Zone

Udintsev Fracture Zone

Macquarie Ridge

○ Antarctic research station

152

Drake Passage

Scotia Sea

A B C D

0 km   500
0 miles   500

Elevation

| -6000m | -4000m | -2000m | -1000m | -500m | -250m | Below sea level 0 | 250m | 500m | 1000m | 2000m | 3000m | 4000m | 6000m |

-19,658ft -13,124ft -6562ft -3281ft -1640ft -820ft -328ft/-100m   0   820ft 1640ft 3281ft 6562ft 9843ft 13,124ft 19,685ft

Arctic Ocean

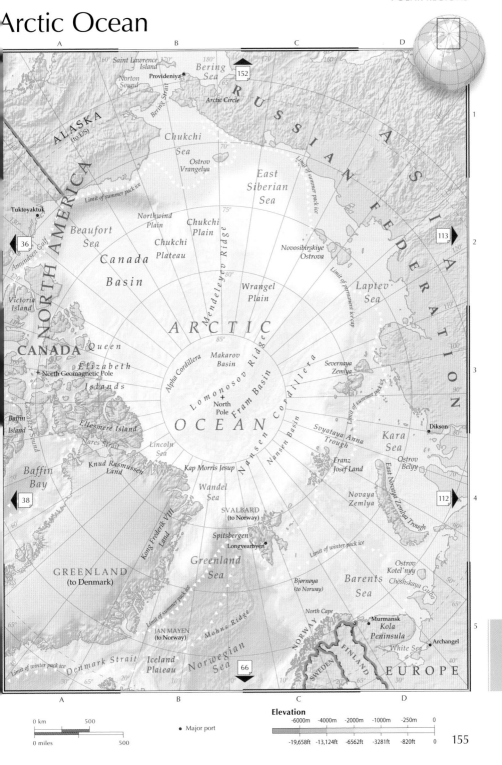

Elevation
-6000m   -4000m   -2000m   -1000m   -250m   0
-19,658ft   -13,124ft   -6562ft   -3281ft   -820ft   0

0 km   500
0 miles   500

● Major port

Overseas territories & dependencies

Despite the rapid process of global decolonization since the Second World War, around 8 million people in more than 50 territories around the world continue to live under the protection of France, Australia, the Netherlands, Denmark, Norway, New Zealand, the UK, or the USA. These remnants of former colonial empires may have persisted for economic, strategic or political reasons and are administered in a variety of ways.

AUSTRALIA

Australia's overseas territories have not been an issue since Papua New Guinea became independent in 1975. Consequently there is no overriding policy toward them. Norfolk Island is inhabited by descendants of the H.M.S Bounty mutineers and more recent Australian migrants.

Ashmore & Cartier Islands
Indian Ocean
Status: External territory
Claimed: 1931
Capital: Not applicable
Population: None
Area: 2 sq miles
(5.2 sq km)

Christmas Island
Indian Ocean
Status: External territory
Claimed: 1958
Capital: The Settlement
Population: 1403
Area: 52 sq miles
(135 sq km)

Cocos Islands
Indian Ocean
Status: External territory
Claimed: 1955
Capital: No official capital
Population: 596
Area: 5.5 sq miles
(14 sq km)

Coral Sea Islands
South Pacific
Status: External territory
Claimed: 1969
Capital: None
Population: 8 (meteorologists)
Area: Less than 1.2 sq miles
(3 sq km)

Heard & McDonald Is.
Indian Ocean
Status: External territory
Claimed: 1947
Capital: Not applicable
Population: None
Area: 161 sq miles
(417 sq km)

Norfolk Island
South Pacific
Status: External territory
Claimed: 1774
Capital: Kingston
Population: 2141
Area: 13 sq miles
(34 sq km)

DENMARK

The Faeroe Islands have been under Danish administration since Queen Margreth I of Denmark inherited Norway in 1380. The Home Rule Act of 1948 gave the Faeroese control over all their internal affairs. Greenland first came under Danish rule in 1380. Today, Denmark is responsible for the island's foreign affairs and defense.

Faeroe Islands
North Atlantic
Status: External territory
Claimed: 1380
Capital: Tórshavn
Population: 48,917
Area: 540 sq miles
(1399 sq km)

Greenland
North Atlantic
Status: External territory
Claimed: 1380
Capital: Nuuk
Population: 56,452
Area: 840,000 sq miles
(2,175,516 sq km)

FRANCE

France has developed economic ties with its *Territoires d'Outre-Mer,* thereby stressing interdependence over independence. Overseas *départements,* officially part of France, have their own governments. Territorial *collectivités* and overseas *territoires* have varying degrees of autonomy.

Clipperton Island
East Pacific
Status: Dependency of French Polynesia
Claimed: 1935
Capital: Not applicable
Population: None
Area: 2.7 sq miles
(7 sq km)

French Guiana
South America
Status: Overseas department
Claimed: 1817
Capital: Cayenne
Population: 229,000
Area: 32,253 sq miles
(83,534 sq km)

French Polynesia
South Pacific
Status: Overseas territory
Claimed: 1843
Capital: Papeete
Population: 264,000
Area: 1608 sq miles
(4165 sq km)

Guadeloupe
West Indies
Status: Overseas department
Claimed: 1635
Capital: Basse-Terre
Population: 405,500
Area: 687 sq miles
(1780 sq km)

Martinique
West Indies
Status: Overseas department
Claimed: 1635
Capital: Fort-de-France
Population: 397,000
Area: 425 sq miles (1100 sq km)

Mayotte
Indian Ocean
Status: Territorial collectivity
Claimed: 1843
Capital: Mamoudzou
Population: 194,000
Area: 144 sq miles (374 sq km)

New Caledonia
South Pacific
Status: Overseas territory
Claimed: 1853
Capital: Nouméa
Population: 249,000
Area: 7374 sq miles (19,100 sq km)

Réunion
Indian Ocean
Status: Overseas department
Claimed: 1638
Capital: Saint-Denis
Population: 827,000
Area: 970 sq miles (2500 sq km)

St. Pierre & Miquelon
North America
Status: Territorial collectivity
Claimed: 1604
Capital: Saint-Pierre
Population: 7063
Area: 93 sq miles (242 sq km)

Wallis & Futuna
South Pacific
Status: Overseas territory
Claimed: 1842
Capital: Matá'Utu
Population: 15,289
Area: 106 sq miles (274 sq km)

NETHERLANDS

The country's remaining overseas territories were formerly part of the Dutch West Indies. The Netherlands Antilles dissolved in 2010 leaving the constituent islands with varying degrees of autonomy, but the Netherlands remains responsible for their security.

Aruba
West Indies
Status: Autonomous part of the Netherlands
Claimed: 1643
Capital: Oranjestad
Population: 103,065
Area: 75 sq miles (194 sq km)

Bonaire
West Indies
Status: Special municipality of the Netherlands
Claimed: 1816
Capital: Kralendijk
Population: 14,006
Area: 113 sq miles (294 sq km)

Curaçao
West Indies
Status: Autonomous part of the Netherlands
Claimed: 1816
Capital: Willemstad
Population: 141,766
Area: 171 sq miles (444 sq km)

Sint Maarten
West Indies
Status: Autonomous part of the Netherlands
Claimed: 1816
Capital: Philipsburg
Population: 40,917
Area: 13 sq miles (34 sq km)

NEW ZEALAND

New Zealand's government has no desire to retain any overseas territories. However, the economic weakness of its dependent territory Tokelau and its freely associated states, Niue and the Cook Islands, has forced New Zealand to remain responsible for their foreign policy and defense.

Cook Islands
South Pacific
Status: Associated territory
Claimed: 1901
Capital: Avarua
Population: 19,596
Area: 91 sq miles (235 sq km)

Niue
South Pacific
Status: Associated territory
Claimed: 1901
Capital: Alofi
Population: 1398
Area: 102 sq miles (264 sq km)

Tokelau
South Pacific
Status: Dependent territory
Claimed: 1926
Capital: Not applicable
Population: 1416
Area: 4 sq miles (10 sq km)

NORWAY

In 1920, 41 nations signed the Spits-bergen Treaty recognizing Norwegian sovereignty over Svalbard. There is a NATO base on Jan Mayen. Bouvet Island is a nature reserve.

Bouvet Island
South Atlantic
Status: Dependency
Claimed: 1928
Capital: Not applicable
Population: None
Area: 22 sq miles (58 sq km)

Jan Mayen
North Atlantic
Status: Dependency
Claimed: 1929
Capital: Not applicable
Population: None
Area: 147 sq miles (381 sq km)

Continued on page158

Overseas territories & dependencies

Peter I. Island
Southern Ocean
Status: Dependency
Claimed: 1931
Capital: Not applicable
Population: None
Area: 69 sq miles (180 sq km)

Svalbard
Arctic Ocean
Status: Dependency
Claimed: 1920
Capital: Longyearbyen
Population: 2572
Area: 24,289 sq miles
(62,906 sq km)

UNITED KINGDOM

The UK still has the largest number of overseas territories. These are locally-governed by a mixture of elected representatives and appointed officials, and they all enjoy a large measure of internal self-government, but certain powers, such as foreign affairs and defense, are reserved for Governors of the British Crown.

Anguilla
West Indies
Status: Dependent territory
Claimed: 1650
Capital: The Valley
Population: 13,600
Area: 37 sq miles
(96 sq km)

Ascension Island
South Atlantic
Status: Dependency of St. Helena
Claimed: 1673
Capital: Georgetown
Population: 940
Area: 34 sq miles
(88 sq km)

Bermuda
North Atlantic
Status: Crown colony
Claimed: 1612
Capital: Hamilton
Population: 67,837
Area: 20 sq miles (53 sq km)

British Indian Ocean Territory
Status: Dependent territory
Claimed: 1814
Capital: Diego Garcia
Population: 4000
Area: 23 sq miles
(60 sq km)

British Virgin Islands
West Indies
Status: Dependent territory
Claimed: 1672
Capital: Road Town
Population: 27,000
Area: 59 sq miles
(153 sq km)

Cayman Islands
West Indies
Status: Dependent territory
Claimed: 1670
Capital: George Town
Population: 60,456
Area: 100 sq miles (259 sq km)

Falkland Islands
South Atlantic
Status: Dependent territory
Claimed: 1832
Capital: Stanley
Population: 3140
Area: 4699 sq miles
(12,173 sq km)

Gibraltar
Southwest Europe
Status: Crown colony
Claimed: 1713
Capital: Gibraltar
Population: 29,286
Area: 2.5 sq miles (6.5 sq km)

Guernsey
Channel Islands
Status: Crown dependency
Claimed: 1066
Capital: St. Peter Port
Population: 65,573
Area: 25 sq miles (65 sq km)

Isle of Man
British Isles
Status: Crown dependency
Claimed: 1765
Capital: Douglas
Population: 80,085
Area: 221 sq miles (572 sq km)

Jersey
Channel Islands
Status: Crown dependency
Claimed: 1066
Capital: St. Helier
Population: 91,626
Area: 45 sq miles (116 sq km)

Montserrat
West Indies
Status: Dependent territory
Claimed: 1632
Capital: Plymouth *(de jure)*, Brades *(de facto)*
Population: 4655
Area: 40 sq miles (102 sq km)

Pitcairn Islands
South Pacific
Status: Dependent territory
Claimed: 1887
Capital: Adamstown
Population: 50
Area: 18 sq miles (47 sq km)

St. Helena
South Atlantic
Status: Dependent territory
Claimed: 1673
Capital: Jamestown
Population: 4255
Area: 47 sq miles (122 sq km)

South Georgia & The South Sandwich Islands
South Atlantic
Status: Dependent territory
Claimed: 1775
Capital: Not applicable
Population: No permanent residents
Area: 1387 sq miles
(3592 sq km)

Tristan da Cunha
South Atlantic
Status: Dependency
of St. Helena
Claimed: 1612
Capital: Edinburgh
Population: 276
Area: 38 sq miles (98 sq km)

Turks & Caicos Islands
West Indies
Status: Dependent territory
Claimed: 1766
Capital: Cockburn Town
Population: 36,605
Area: 166 sq miles
(430 sq km)

UNITED STATES OF AMERICA

America's overseas territories
have been seen as strategically
useful, if expensive, links with its
"backyards." The US has, in most
cases, given the local population a
say in deciding their own status.
A US Commonwealth territory, such
as Puerto Rico, has a greater level
of independence than that of a US
unincorporated or external territory.

American Samoa
South Pacific
Status: Unincorporated
territory
Claimed: 1900
Capital: Pago Pago
Population: 65,628
Area: 75 sq miles (195 sq km)

Baker & Howland Islands
South Pacific
Status: Unincorporated
territory
Claimed: 1856
Capital: Not applicable
Population: None
Area: 0.5 sq miles (1.4 sq km)

Guam
West Pacific
Status: Unincorporated
territory
Claimed: 1898
Capital: Hagåtña
Population: 178,000
Area: 212 sq miles
(549 sq km)

Jarvis Island
South Pacific
Status: Unincorporated territory
Claimed: 1856
Capital: Not applicable
Population: None
Area: 1.7 sq miles (4.5 sq km)

Johnston Atoll
Central Pacific
Status: Unincorporated
territory
Claimed: 1858
Capital: Not applicable
Population: Not applicable
Area: 1 sq mile (2.8 sq km)

Kingman Reef
Central Pacific
Status: Administered territory
Claimed: 1856
Capital: Not applicable
Population: None
Area: 0.4 sq mile
(1 sq km)

Midway Islands
Central Pacific
Status: Administered
territory
Claimed: 1867
Capital: Not applicable
Population: None
Area: 2 sq miles
(5.2 sq km)

Navassa Island
West Indies
Status: Unincorporated
territory
Claimed: 1856
Capital: Not applicable
Population: None
Area: 2 sq miles (5.2 sq km)

Northern Mariana Islands
West Pacific
Status: Commonwealth
territory
Claimed: 1947
Capital: Saipan
Population: 86,616
Area: 177 sq miles (457 sq km)

Palmyra Atoll
Central Pacific
Status: Unincorporated
territory
Claimed: 1898
Capital: Not applicable
Population: None
Area: 5 sq miles (12 sq km)

Puerto Rico
West Indies
Status: Commonwealth
territory
Claimed: 1898
Capital: San Juan
Population: 4.0 million
Area: 3515 sq miles
(9104 sq km)

Virgin Islands
West Indies
Status: Unincorporated
territory
Claimed: 1917
Capital: Charlotte Amalie
Population: 108,448
Area: 137 sq miles
(355 sq km)

Wake Island
Central Pacific
Status: Unincorporated
territory
Claimed: 1898
Capital: Not applicable
Population: 200
Area: 2.5 sq miles
(6.5 sq km)

Glossary of geographical terms

The following glossary lists all geographical terms occuring on the maps and in the main-entry names in the Index–Gazetteer. These terms may precede, follow or be run together with the proper elements of the name; where they precede it the term is reversed for indexing purposes – thus Poluostov Yamal is indexed as Yamal, Poluostrov.

A

Å *Danish, Norwegian,* River
Alpen *German,* Alps
Altiplanicie *Spanish,* Plateau
Älv(en) *Swedish,* River
Anse *French,* Bay
Archipiélago *Spanish,* Archipelago
Arcipelago *Italian,* Archipelago
Arquipélago *Portuguese,* Archipelago
Aukštuma *Lithuanian,* Upland

B

Bahía *Spanish,* Bay
Baía *Portuguese,* Bay
Baḥr *Arabic,* River
Baie *French,* Bay
Bandao *Chinese,* Peninsula
Banjaran *Malay,* Mountain range
Batang *Malay,* Stream
-berg *Afrikaans, Norwegian,* Mountain
Birket *Arabic,* Lake
Boğazı *Turkish,* Strait
Bucht *German,* Bay
Bugten *Danish,* Bay
Buḩayrat *Arabic,* Lake, reservoir
Buḩeiret *Arabic,* Lake
Bukit *Malay,* Mountain
-bukta *Norwegian,* Bay
bukten *Swedish,* Bay
Burnu *Turkish,* Cape, point
Buuraha *Somali,* Mountains

C

Cabo *Portuguese,* Cape
Cap *French,* Cape
Cascada *Portuguese,* Waterfall
Cerro *Spanish,* Hill
Chaîne *French,* Mountain range
Chau *Cantonese,* Island
Cháy *Turkish,* Stream
Chhâk *Cambodian,* Bay
Chhu *Tibetan,* River
-chôsuji *Korean,* Reservoir

Chott *Arabic,* Salt lake, depression
Ch'ün-tao *Chinese,* Island group
**Cambodian,* Mountains
Cordillera *Spanish,* Mountain range
Costa *Spanish,* Coast
Côte *French,* Coast
Cuchilla *Spanish,* Mountains

D

Dağı *Azerbaijani, Turkish,* Mountain
Dağları *Azerbaijani, Turkish,* Mountains
-dake *Japanese,* Peak
Danau *Indonesian,* Lake
Đao *Vietnamese,* Island
Daryá *Persian,* River
Daryácheh *Persian,* Lake
Dasht *Persian,* Plain, desert
Dawḩat *Arabic,* Bay
Dere *Turkish,* Stream
Dili *Azerbaijani,* Spit
-do *Korean,* Island
Dooxo *Somali,* Valley
Düzü *Azerbaijani,* Steppe
-dwíp *Bengali,* Island

E

Embalse *Spanish,* Reservoir
Erg *Arabic,* Dunes
Estany *Catalan,* Lake
Estrecho *Spanish,* Strait
-ey *Icelandic,* Island
Ezero *Bulgarian, Macedonian,* Lake

F

Fjord *Danish,* Fjord
-fjorden *Norwegian,* Fjord
-fjordhur *Faeroese,* Fjord
Fleuve *French,* River
Fliegu *Maltese,* Channel
-fljór *Icelandic,* River

G

-gang *Korean,* River
Ganga *Nepali, Sinhala,* River
Gaoyuan *Chinese,* Plateau
-gawa *Japanese,* River

Gebel *Arabic,* Mountain
-gebirge *German,* Mountains
Ghubbat *Arabic,* Bay
Gjiri *Albanian,* Bay
Gol *Mongolian,* River
Golfe *French,* Gulf
Golfo *Italian, Spanish,* Gulf
Gora *Russian, Serbian,* Mountain
Gory *Russian,* Mountains
Guba *Russian,* Bay
Gunung *Malay,* Mountain

H

Ḩadd *Arabic,* Spit
-haehyôp *Korean,* Strait
Haff *German,* Lagoon
Hai *Chinese,* Sea, bay
Ḩammádat *Arabic,* Plateau
Hámún *Persian,* Lake
Hawr *Arabic,* Lake
Háyk' *Amharic,* Lake
He *Chinese,* River
Helodrano *Malagasy,* Bay
-hegység *Hungarian,* Mountain range
Hka *Burmese,* River
-ho *Korean,* Lake
Hô *Korean,* Reservoir
/olot *Hebrew,* Dunes
Hora *Belorussian,* Mountain
Hrada *Belorussian,* Mountains, ridge
Hsi *Chinese,* River
Hu *Chinese,* Lake

I

Île(s) *French,* Island(s)
Ilha(s) *Portuguese,* Island(s)
Ilhéu(s) *Portuguese,* Islet(s)
Irmak *Turkish,* River
Isla(s) *Spanish,* Island(s)
Isola (Isole) *Italian,* Island(s)

J

Jabal *Arabic,* Mountain
Jál *Arabic,* Ridge
-järvi *Finnish,* Lake
Jazírat *Arabic,* Island
Jazíreh *Persian,* Island

Jebel *Arabic,* Mountain
Jezero *Serbian/Croatian,* Lake
Jiang *Chinese,* River
-joki *Finnish,* River
-jökull *Icelandic,* Glacier
Juzur *Arabic,* Islands

K

Kaikyó *Japanese,* Strait
-kaise *Lappish,* Mountain
Kali *Nepali,* River
Kalnas *Lithuanian,* Mountain
Kalns *Latvian,* Mountain
Kang *Chinese,* Harbor
Kangri *Tibetan,* Mountain(s)
Kaôh *Cambodian,* Island
Kapp *Norwegian,* Cape
Kavír *Persian,* Desert
K'edi *Georgian,* Mountain range
Kediet *Arabic,* Mountain
Kepulauan *Indonesian, Malay,* Island group
Khalíg, Khalíj *Arabic,* Gulf
Khawr *Arabic,* Inlet
Khola *Nepali,* River
Khrebet *Russian,* Mountain range
Ko *Thai,* Island
Kolpos *Greek,* Bay
-kopf *German,* Peak
Körfäzi *Azerbaijani,* Bay
Körfezi *Turkish,* Bay
Kõrgustik *Estonian,* Upland
Koshi *Nepali,* River
Kowtal *Persian,* Pass
Kúh(há) *Persian,* Mountain(s)
-kundo *Korean,* Island group
-kysten *Norwegian,* Coast
Kyun *Burmese,* Island

L

Laaq *Somali,* Watercourse
Lac *French,* Lake
Lacul *Romanian,* Lake
Lago *Italian, Portuguese, Spanish,* Lake

Laguna *Spanish,* Lagoon, Lake
Laht *Estonian,* Bay
Laut *Indonesian,* Sea
Lembalemba *Malagasy,* Plateau
Lerr *Armenian,* Mountain
Lerrnashght'a *Armenian,* Mountain range
Les *Czech,* Forest
Lich *Armenian,* Lake
Liqeni *Albanian,* Lake
Lumi *Albanian,* River
Lyman *Ukrainian,* Estuary

M
Mae Nam *Thai,* River
-mägi *Estonian,* Hill
Maja *Albanian,* Mountain
-man *Korean,* Bay
Marios *Lithuanian,* Lake
-meer *Dutch,* Lake
Melkosopochnik *Russian,* Plain
-meri *Estonian,* Sea
Mifraz *Hebrew,* Bay
Monkhafad *Arabic,* Depression
Mont(s) *French,* Mountain(s)
Monte *Italian, Portuguese,* Mountain
More *Russian,* Sea
Mörön *Mongolian,* River

N
Nagor'ye *Russian,* Upland
Najal *Hebrew,* River
Nahr *Arabic,* River
Nam *Laotian,* River
Nehri *Turkish,* River
Nevado *Spanish,* Mountain (snow-capped)
Nisoi *Greek,* Islands
Nizmennost' *Russian,* Lowland, plain
Nosy *Malagasy,* Island
Nur *Mongolian,* Lake
Nuruu *Mongolian,* Mountains
Nuur *Mongolian,* Lake
Nyzovyna *Ukrainian,* Lowland, plain

O
Ostrov(a) *Russian,* Island(s)
Oued *Arabic,* Watercourse
-oy *Faeroese,* Island
-øy(a) *Norwegian,* Island
Oya *Sinhala,* River
Ozero *Russian, Ukrainian,* Lake

P
Passo *Italian,* Pass
Pegunungan *Indonesian, Malay,* Mountain range
Pelagos *Greek,* Sea
Penisola *Italian,* Peninsula
Peski *Russian,* Sands
Phanom *Thai,* Mountain
Phou *Laotian,* Mountain
Pic *Catalan,* Peak
Pico *Portuguese, Spanish,* Peak
Pik *Russian,* Peak
Planalto *Portuguese,* Plateau
Planina, Planini *Bulgarian, Macedonian, Serbian, Croatian,* Mountain range
Ploskogor'ye *Russian,* Upland
Poluostrov *Russian,* Peninsula
Potamos *Greek,* River
Proliv *Russian,* Strait
Pulau *Indonesian, Malay,* Island
Pulu *Malay,* Island
Punta *Portuguese, Spanish,* Point

Q
Qá' *Arabic,* Depression
Qolleh *Persian,* Mountain

R
Raas *Somali,* Cape
-rags *Latvian,* Cape
Ramlat *Arabic,* Sands
Ra's *Arabic,* Cape, point, headland
Ravnina *Bulgarian, Russian,* Plain
Récif *French,* Reef
Represa (Rep.) *Spanish, Portuguese,* Reservoir
-rettō *Japanese,* Island chain
Riacho *Spanish,* Stream
Riban' *Malagasy,* Mountains
Rio *Portuguese,* River
Río *Spanish,* River
Riu *Catalan,* River
Rivier *Dutch,* River
Rivière *French,* River
Rowd *Pashtu,* River
Rúd *Persian,* River
Rudohorie *Slovak,* Mountains
Ruisseau *French,* Stream

S
Sabkhat *Arabic,* Salt marsh
Şaḥrá' *Arabic,* Desert
Samudra *Sinhala,* Reservoir
-san *Japanese, Korean,* Mountain
-sanchi *Japanese,* Mountains
-sanmaek *Korean,* Mountains
Sarír *Arabic,* Desert
Sebkha, Sebkhet *Arabic,* Salt marsh, depression
See *German,* Lake
Selat *Indonesian,* Strait
-selkä *Finnish,* Ridge
Selseleh *Persian,* Mountain range
Serra *Portuguese,* Mountain
Serranía *Spanish,* Mountain
Sha'íb *Arabic,* Watercourse
Shamo *Chinese,* Desert
Shan *Chinese,* Mountain(s)
Shan-mo *Chinese,* Mountain range
Shaṭṭ *Arabic,* Distributary
-shima *Japanese,* Island
Shui-tao *Chinese,* Channel
Sierra *Spanish,* Mountains
Sòn *Vietnamese,* Mountain
Sông *Vietnamese,* River
-spitze *German,* Peak
Štít *Slovak,* Peak
Stoeng *Cambodian,* River
Stretto *Italian,* Strait
Su Anbarı *Azerbaijani,* Reservoir
Sungai *Indonesian, Malay,* River
Suu *Turkish,* River

T
Tal *Mongolian,* Plain
Tandavan' *Malagasy,* Mountain range
Tangorombohitr' *Malagasy,* Mountain massif
Tao *Chinese,* Island
Tassili *Berber,* Plateau, mountain
Tau *Russian,* Mountain(s)
Taungdan *Burmese,* Mountain range

Teluk *Indonesian, Malay,* Bay
Terara *Amharic,* Mountain
Tog *Somali,* Valley
Tônlé *Cambodian,* Lake
Top *Dutch,* Peak
-tunturi *Finnish,* Mountain
Tur'at *Arabic,* Channel

V
Väin *Estonian,* Strait
-vatn *Icelandic,* Lake
-vesi *Finnish,* Lake
Vinh *Vietnamese,* Bay
Vodokhranilishche (Vdkhr.) *Russian,* Reservoir
Vodoskhovyshche (Vdskh.) *Ukrainian,* Reservoir
Volcán *Spanish,* Volcano
Vozvyshennost' *Russian,* Upland, plateau
Vrh *Macedonian,* Peak
Vysochyna *Ukrainian,* Upland
Vysočina *Czech,* Upland

W
Waadi *Somali,* Watercourse
Wádí *Arabic,* Watercourse
Wáḥat, Wâhat *Arabic,* Oasis
Wald *German,* Forest
Wan *Chinese,* Bay
Wyżyna *Polish,* Upland

X
Xé *Laotian,* River

Y
Yarımadası *Azerbaijani,* Peninsula
Yazovir *Bulgarian,* Reservoir
Yoma *Burmese,* Mountains
Yu *Chinese,* Islet

Z
Zaliv *Bulgarian, Russian,* Bay
Zatoka *Ukrainian,* Bay
Zemlya *Russian,* Land

Continental factfile

North & Central America

Total area:
9,400,000 sq miles
(24,346,000 sq km)

Total number of countries: 23

Total population:
512 million

Largest city with population: Mexico City, Mexico 20.1 million

Country with highest population density: Barbados 1807 people per sq mile (698 people per sq km)

Largest country:
Canada 3,855,171 sq miles
(9,984,670 sq km)

Smallest country:
St. Kitts & Nevis 101 sq miles
(261 sq km)

Largest lake: Lake Superior, Canada/ USA 32,151 sq miles (83,270 sq km)

Longest river: Mississippi-Missouri, USA 3710 miles (5969 km)

Highest point: Mt. McKinley (Denali), Alaska, USA 20,322 ft (6194 m)

lowest point: Death Valley, California, USA 282 ft (86 m) below sea level

South America

Total area:
6,880,000 sq miles
(17,819,000 sq km)

Total number of countries: 12

Total population:
375 million

Largest city with population: São Paulo, Brazil 19.6 million

Country with highest population density: Ecuador 138 people per sq mile (53 people per sq km)

Largest country:
Brazil 3,286,470 sq miles
(8,511,965 sq km)

Smallest country:
Suriname 63,039 sq miles
(163,270 sq km)

Largest lake: Lake Titicaca, Bolivia/Peru 3220 sq miles (8340 sq km)

Longest river: Amazon, Brazil 4049 miles (6516 km)

Highest point: Cerro Aconcagua, Argentina 22,831 ft (6959 m)

Lowest point: Laguna del Carbón, Argentina 344 ft (105 m) below sea level

Africa

Total area:
11,677,250 sq miles
(30,244,050 sq km)

Total number of countries: 57

Total population:
910 million

Largest city with population: Cairo, Egypt 11.4 million

Country with highest population density: Mauritius 1811 people per sq mile (699 people per sq km)

Largest country:
Algeria 919,590 sq miles
(2,381,740 sq km)

Smallest country:
Seychelles 176 sq miles
(455 sq km)

Largest lake: Lake Victoria, Uganda, Kenya, Tanzania 26,828 sq miles (69,484 sq km)

Longest river: Nile, Uganda/Sudan/Egypt 4160 miles (6695 km)

Highest point: Kilimanjaro, Tanzania 19,340 ft (5895 m)

Lowest point: Lac', Assal, Djibouti 512 ft (156 m) below sea level

Europe

Total area:
4,809,200 sq miles
(12,456,000 sq km)

Total number of countries: 46

Total population:
697 million

Largest city with population: Moscow, Euro Russia 11.5 million

Country with highest population density: Monaco 40,680 people per sq mile (15,641 people per sq km)

Largest country: European Russia 1,527,341 sq miles (3,955,818 sq km)

Smallest country:
Vatican City, Italy 0.17 sq miles
(0.44 sq km)

Largest lake: Ladoga, European Russia 7100 sq miles (18,390 sq km)

Longest river: Volga, European Russia 2290 miles (3688 km)

Highest point: El'brus, Caucasus Mts, European Russia 18,510 ft (5642 m)

Lowest point: Volga Delta, Caspian Sea, European Russia 92 ft (28 m) below sea level

North & West Asia

 Total area:
9,585,500 sq miles
(24,826,600 sq km)

 Total number of
countries: 24

 Total population:
398 million

 Largest city with
population: Tehran, Iran
8.4 million

 Country with highest
population density: Bahrain
4762 people per sq mile
(1841 people per sq km)

 Largest country: Asiatic
Russia 5,065,471 sq miles
(13,119,582 sq km)

 Smallest country:
Bahrain 239 sq miles
(620 sq km)

 Largest lake:
Caspian Sea 142,243 sq miles
(371,000 sq km)

 Longest river: Ob'-Irtysh,
Asiatic Russia 3461 miles
(5570 km)

 Highest point: Pik Pobedy,
Kyrgyzstan/China 24,408 ft
(7439 m)

 Lowest point: Dead Sea,
Israel/Jordan 1388 ft
(423 m) below sea level

South & East Asia

 Total area:
7,936,200 sq miles
(20,554,700 sq km)

 Total number of
countries: 24

 Total population:
3979 million

 Largest city with
population: Tokyo,
Japan 36.9 million

 Country with highest
population density: Singapore
22,034 people per sq mile
(8525 people per sq km)

 Largest country:
China 3,705,386 sq miles
(9,596,960 sq km)

 Smallest country:
Maldives 116 sq miles
(300 sq km)

 Largest lake: Tonle Sap,
Cambodia 1000 sq miles
(2850 sq km)

 Longest river: Chang Jiang
(Yangtze) 3965 miles
(6380 km)

 Highest point:
Mount Everest, Nepal
29,035 ft (8850 m)

 Lowest point: Turpan Hami,
(Turfan basin), China 505 ft
(154 m) below sea level

Australasia & Oceania

 Total area:
3,376,700 sq miles
(8,745,750 sq km)

 Total number of
countries: 14

 Total population:
32 million

Largest city with
population: Sydney,
Australia 4.4 million

 Country with highest
population density: Nauru
1670 people per sq mile
(644 people per sq km)

 Largest country:
Australia 2,967,893 sq miles
(7,686,850 sq km)

 Smallest country:
Nauru 8 sq miles
(21 sq km)

 Largest lake: Lake Eyre,
Australia 3700 sq miles
(9583 sq km)

 Longest river: Murray-
Darling, Australia
2330 miles (3750 km)

 Highest point: Mt. Wilhelm,
Papua New Guinea 14,795 ft
(4509 m)

 Lowest point: Lake Eyre,
Australia 52 ft
(16 m) below sea level

Antarctica

 Total area: 5,450,500 sq miles (14,000,000 sq km)
of which approx. 324,300 sq miles
(840,000 sq km) is ice-free.

 Total number of countries: The Antarctic Treaty has
30 participating nations and 14 with observer status.
Claims by Australia, France, New Zealand, Norway,
Argentina, Chile, and the UK are not recognized by
other member states.

 Total Population: No indigenous population.
74 research stations, (42 are staffed all year-round).
Population varies between about 1000 (winter)
and 4000 (summer).

Total volume of ice:
7,200,000 cu miles (30,000,000 cu km):
contains 90% of Earth's fresh water

Sea ice: 1,158,300 sq miles (3,000,000
sq km) in February. 7,722,000 sq miles
(20,000,000 sq km) in October

Lowest temperature: Vostok station
-89.5°C (-129°F)

Highest point: Vinson Massif
16,072 ft (4897 m)

Lowest Point: Coastline 0ft/m

Geographical comparisons

Largest countries

Russ. Fed.	6,592,735 sq miles	(17,075,200 sq km)
Canada	3,855,171 sq miles	(9,984,670 sq km)
USA	3,717,792 sq miles	(9,629,091 sq km)
China	3,705,386 sq miles	(9,596,960 sq km)
Brazil	3,286,470 sq miles	(8,511,965 sq km)
Australia	2,967,893 sq miles	(7,686,850 sq km)
India	1,269,339 sq miles	(3,287,590 sq km)
Argentina	1,068,296 sq miles	(2,766,890 sq km)
Kazakhstan	1,049,150 sq miles	(2,717,300 sq km)
Algeria	919,590 sq miles	(2,381,740 sq km)

Smallest countries

Vatican City	0.17 sq miles	(0.44 sq km)
Monaco	0.75 sq miles	(1.95 sq km)
Nauru	8 sq miles	(21 sq km)
Tuvalu	10 sq miles	(26 sq km)
San Marino	24 sq miles	(61 sq km)
Liechtenstein	62 sq miles	(160 sq km)
Marshall Islands	70 sq miles	(181 sq km)
St. Kitts & Nevis	101 sq miles	(261 sq km)
Maldives	116 sq miles	(300 sq km)
Malta	124 sq miles	(320 sq km)

Largest islands

Greenland	849,400 sq miles	(2,200,000 sq km)
New Guinea	312,000 sq miles	(808,000 sq km)
Borneo	292,222 sq miles	(757,050 sq km)
Madagascar	229,300 sq miles	(594,000 sq km)
Sumatra	202,300 sq miles	(524,000 sq km)
Baffin Island	183,800 sq miles	(476,000 sq km)
Honshu	88,800 sq miles	(230,000 sq km)
Britain	88,700 sq miles	(229,800 sq km)
Victoria Island	81,900 sq miles	(212,000 sq km)
Ellesmere Island	75,700 sq miles	(196,000 sq km)

Richest countries (GNI per capita, in US$)

Monaco	188,150
Liechtenstein	137,070
Norway	88,890
Qatar	80,440
Luxembourg	78,130
Switzerland	76,380
Denmark	60,390
Sweden	52,230
Netherlands	49,730
Kuwait	48,900

Poorest countries (GNI per capita, in US$)

Congo, Dem. Rep	190
Liberia	240
Burundi	250
Sierra Leone	340
Malawi	340
Niger	360
Ethiopia	400
Afghanistan	400
Madagascar	430
Eritrea	430

Most populous countries

China	1,347,300,000
India	1,240,000,000
USA	314,500,000
Indonesia	237,600,000
Brazil	193,300,000
Pakistan	180,800,000
Nigeria	166,500,000
Bangladesh	152,500,000
Russian Federation	143,200,000
Japan	127,500,000

Least populous countries

Vatican City	821
Nauru	9,378
Tuvalu	10,619
Palau	21,032
Monaco	30,510
San Marino	32,140
Liechtenstein	36,713
St. Kitts & Nevis	50,726
Marshall Islands	64,480
Dominica	73,126

Most densely populated countries

Monaco	40,680 people per sq mile	(15,641 per sq km)
Singapore	22,034 people per sq mile	(8525 per sq km)
Vatican City	4918 people per sq mile	(1900 per sq km)
Bahrain	4762 people per sq mile	(1841 per sq km)
Maldives	3400 people per sq mile	(1315 per sq km)
Malta	3226 people per sq mile	(1250 per sq km)
Bangladesh	2911 people per sq mile	(1124 per sq km)
Taiwan	1860 people per sq mile	(718 per sq km)
Mauritius	1811 people per sq mile	(699 per sq km)
Barbados	1807 people per sq mile	(698 per sq km)

Most sparsely populated countries

Mongolia.........5 people per sq mile......... (2 per sq km)
Namibia...........7 people per sq mile......... (3 per sq km)
Australia ....8 people per sq mile......... (3 per sq km)
Suriname.........8 people per sq mile......... (3 per sq km)
Iceland ....8 people per sq mile......... (3 per sq km)
Mauritania ......9 people per sq mile......... (4 per sq km)
Botswana.........9 people per sq mile......... (4 per sq km)
Libya ....9 people per sq mile......... (4 per sq km)
Canada ....10 people per sq mile......... (4 per sq km)
Guyana ....11 people per sq mile......... (4 per sq km)

Most widely spoken languages

1. Chinese (Mandarin)	6. Arabic
2. English	7. Bengali
3. Hindi	8. Portuguese
4. Spanish	9. Malay-Indonesian
5. Russian	10. French

Largest conurbations

Tokyo 36,900,000
Delhi 21,900,000
Mexico City 20,100,000
New York - Newark 20,100,000
São Paulo 19,600,000
Shanghai..19,500,000
Mumbai 19,400,000
Beijing 15,000,000
Dhaka 14,900,000
Kolkata...14,300,000
Karachi...13,500,000
Buenos Aires 13,400,000
Los Angeles 13,200,000
Rio de Janeiro..11,800,000
Manilla...11,600,000
Moscow..11,500,000
Osaka 11,400,000
Cairo 11,400,000
Istanbul 10,900,000
Lagos 10,800,000
Paris 10,500,000
Guangzhou...10,500,000
Shenzhen 10,200,000
Seoul 9,700,000
Chongqing 9,700,000

Longest rivers

Nile (NE Africa) .... 4160 miles ...... (6695 km)
Amazon (South America) .... 4049 miles ...... (6516 km)
Yangtze (China)........................... 3915 miles ...... (6299 km)
Mississippi/Missouri (USA).......... 3710 miles........ (5969 km)
Ob'-Irtysh (Russ. Fed.) .... 3461 miles ...... (5570 km)
Yellow River (China) .... 3395 miles ...... (5464 km)
Congo (Central Africa) .... 2900 miles ...... (4667 km)
Mekong (Southeast Asia) .... 2749 miles ...... (4425 km)
Lena (Russian Federation)........ 2734 miles ...... (4400 km)
Mackenzie (Canada) .... 2640 miles ...... (4250 km)
Yenisey (Russ. Federation) ...... 2541 miles....... (4090 km)

Highest mountains   (Height above sea level)

Everest.................................... 29,029 ft....... (8848 m)
K2 .... 28,253 ft....... (8611 m)
Kanchenjunga I........................ 28,210 ft....... (8598 m)
Makalu I .... 27,767 ft....... (8463 m)
Cho Oyu .... 26,907 ft....... (8201 m)
Dhaulagiri I.............................. 26,796 ft....... (8167 m)
Manaslu I................................. 26,783 ft....... (8163 m)
Nanga Parbat I......................... 26,661 ft....... (8126 m)
Annapurna I .... 26,547 ft....... (8091 m)
Gasherbrum I........................... 26,471 ft....... (8068 m)

Largest bodies of inland water (Area & depth)

Caspian Sea
143,243 sq miles (371,000 sq km).......3215 ft (980 m)
Lake Superior
32,151 sq miles (83,270 sq km).......1289 ft (393 m)
Lake Victoria
26,560 sq miles (68,880 sq km).........328 ft (100 m)
Lake Huron
23,436 sq miles (60,700 sq km).........751 ft (229 m)
Lake Michigan
22,402 sq miles (58,020 sq km).........922 ft (281 m)
Lake Tanganyika
12,703 sq miles (32,900 sq km).... 4700 ft (1435 m)
Great Bear Lake
12,274 sq miles (31,790 sq km)..... 1047 ft (319 m)
Lake Baikal
11,776 sq miles (30,500 sq km).... 5712 ft (1741 m)
Great Slave Lake
10,981 sq miles (28,440 sq km).........459 ft (140 m)
Lake Erie
9915 sq miles (25,680 sq km)..........197 ft (60 m)

......continued on page 166

Geographical comparisons continued

Deepest ocean features

Challenger Deep, Mariana Trench (Pacific)
36,201 ft .... (11,034 m)
Vityaz III Depth, Tonga Trench (Pacific)
35,704 ft .... (10,882 m)
Vityaz Depth, Kurile-Kamchatka Trench (Pacific)
34,588 ft .... (10,542 m)
Cape Johnson Deep, Philippine Trench (Pacific)
34,441 ft .... (10,497 m)
Kermadec Trench (Pacific)
32,964 ft .... (10,047 m)
Ramapo Deep, Japan Trench (Pacific)
32,758 ft .... (9984 m)
Milwaukee Deep, Puerto Rico Trench (Atlantic)
30,185 ft .... (9200 m)
Argo Deep, Torres Trench (Pacific)
30,070 ft .... (9165 m)
Meteor Depth, South Sandwich Trench (Atlantic)
30,000 ft .... (9144 m)
Planet Deep, New Britain Trench (Pacific)
29,988 ft .... (9140 m)

Greatest waterfalls (Mean flow of water)

Boyoma (D.R. Congo).....600,400 cu. ft/sec (17,000 cu.m/sec)
Khône (Laos/Cambodia) ... 410,000 cu. ft/sec (11,600 cu.m/sec)
Niagara (USA/Canada).........195,000 cu. ft/sec (5500 cu.m/sec)
Grande, Salto (Uruguay) ..... 160,000 cu. ft/sec (4500 cu.m/sec)
Paulo Afonso (Brazil)........... 100,000 cu. ft/sec(2800 cu.m/sec)
Urubupungá (Brazil)............97,000 cu. ft/sec (2750 cu.m/sec)
Iguaçu (Argentina/Brazil).........62,000 cu. ft/sec (1700 cu.m/sec)
Maribondo (Brazil)................53,000 cu. ft/sec (1500 cu.m/sec)
Victoria (Zimbabwe)................39,000 cu. ft/sec (1100 cu.m/sec)
Murchison Falls (Uganda).....42,000 cu. ft/sec (1200 cu.m/sec)
Churchill (Canada)................35,000 cu. ft/sec (1000 cu.m/sec)
Kaveri Falls (India)....................33,000 cu. ft/sec (900 cu.m/sec)

Highest waterfalls

Angel (Venezuela) ....3212 ft............. (979 m)
Tugela (South Africa)...................3110 ft............. (948 m)
Utigard (Norway)...........................2625 ft............. (800 m)
Mongefossen (Norway) ....2539 ft............. (774 m)
Mtarazi (Zimbabwe) ....2500 ft............. (762 m)
Yosemite (USA) ....2425 ft............. (739 m)
Ostre Mardola Foss (Norway) .....2156 ft............. (657 m)
Tyssestrengane (Norway)...........2119 ft............. (646 m)
*Cuquenan (Venezuela)...............2001 ft............. (610 m)
Sutherland (New Zealand)..........1903 ft............. (580 m)
*Kjellfossen (Norway) ....1841 ft............(561 m)

indicates that the total height is a single leap

Largest deserts

Sahara................3,450,000 sq miles (9,065,000 sq km)
Gobi.................... 500,000 sq miles (1,295,000 sq km)
Ar Rub al Khali ...... 289,600 sq miles (750,000 sq km)
Great Victorian ..... 249,800 sq miles (647,000 sq km)
Sonoran .... 120,000 sq miles (311,000 sq km)
Kalahari .... 120,000 sq miles (310,800 sq km)
Kara Kum............... 115,800 sq miles (300,000 sq km)
Takla Makan .... 100,400 sq miles (260,000 sq km)
Namib......................52,100 sq miles (135,000 sq km)
Thar......................33,670 sq miles (130,000 sq km)

NB – Most of Antarctica is a polar desert, with only 2 inches (50 mm) of precipitation annually

Hottest inhabited places

Djibouti (Djibouti) .... 86.0°F .... (30.0°C)
Tombouctou (Mali) .... 84.7°F .... (29.3°C)
Tirunelveli (India) .... 84.7°F .... (29.3°C)
Tuticorin (India)........................ 84.7°F .... (29.3°C)
Nellore (India)........................... 84.5°F .... (29.2°C)
Santa Marta (Colombia) .... 84.5°F .... (29.2°C)
Aden (Yemen)............................ 84.0°F .... (29.0°C)
Madurai (India).......................... 84.0°F .... (29.0°C)
Niamey (Niger).......................... 84.0°F .... (29.0°C)

Driest inhabited places

Aswân (Egypt)............................0.02 in ....(0.5 mm)
Luxor (Egypt)............................0.03 in ....(0.7 mm)
Arica (Chile)...............................0.04 in ....(1.1 mm)
Ica (Peru)..................................0.10 in ....(2.3 mm)
Antofagasta (Chile)....................0.20 in ....(4.9 mm)
El Minya (Egypt) ....0.20 in ....(5.1 mm)
Asyut (Egypt)............................0.20 in ....(5.2 mm)
Callao (Peru)..............................0.50 in ....(12.0 mm)
Trujillo (Peru)............................0.55 in .....(14.0 mm)
Al Fayyum (Egypt)......................0.80 in .....(19.0 mm)

Wettest inhabited places

Mawsynram (India) .... 467 in ..(11,862 mm)
Mt Waialeale (Hawaii, USA)....... 460 in ..(11,684 mm)
Cherrapunji (India) .... 450 in ..(11,430 mm)
Cape Debundsha (Cameroon) .... 405 in ..(10,290 mm)
Quibdo (Colombia) .... 354 in ..(8892 mm)
Buenaventura (Colombia) .... 265 in ..(6743 mm)
Monrovia (Liberia) .... 202 in ..(5131 mm)
Pago Pago (American Samoa) .... 196 in ..(4990 mm)
Moulmein (Myanmar) .... 191 in ..(4852 mm)
Lae (Papua New Guinea)............. 183 in ....(4645 mm)

GLOSSARY OF ABBREVIATIONS

This Glossary provides a comprehensive guide to the abbreviations used in this Atlas, and in the Index.

A
abbrev. abbreviated
Afr. Afrikaans
Alb. Albanian
Amh. Amharic
anc. ancient
Ar. Arabic
Arm. Armenian
Az. Azerbaijani

B
Basq. Basque
Bel. Belorussian
Ben. Bengali
Bibl. Biblical
Bret. Breton
Bul. Bulgarian
Bur. Burmese

C
Cam. Cambodian
Cant. Cantonese
Cast. Castilian
Cat. Catalan
Chin. Chinese
Cro. Croat
Cz. Czech

D
Dan. Danish
Dut. Dutch

E
Eng. English
Est. Estonian
est. estimated

F
Faer. Faeroese
Fij. Fijian
Fin. Finnish
Flem. Flemish
Fr. French
Fris. Frisian

G
Geor. Georgian
Ger. German
Gk. Greek
Guj. Gujarati

H
Haw. Hawaiian
Heb. Hebrew
Hind. Hindi
hist. historical
Hung. Hungarian

I
Icel. Icelandic
Ind. Indonesian
In. Inuit
Ir. Irish
It. Italian

J
Jap. Japanese

K
Kaz. Kazakh
Kir. Kirghiz
Kor. Korean
Kurd. Kurdish

L
Lao. Laotian
Lapp. Lappish
Lat. Latin
Latv. Latvian

Lith. Lithanian
Lus. Lusatian

M
Mac. Macedonian
Mal. Malay
Malg. Malagasy
Malt. Maltese
Mon. Montenegro
Mong. Mongolian

N
Nepali. Nepali
Nor. Norwegian

O
off. officially

P
Pash. Pashtu
Per. Persian
Pol. Polish
Port. Portuguese
prev. previously

R
Rmsch. Romansch
Roman. Romanian
Rus. Russian

S
SCr. Serbo - Croatian
Serb. Serbian
Slvk. Slovak
Slvn. Slovene
Som. Somali
Sp. Spanish
Swa. Swahili
Swe. Swedish

T
Taj. Tajik
Th. Thai
Tib. Tibetan
Turk. Turkish
Turkm. Turkmenistan

U
Uigh. Uighur
Ukr. Ukrainian
Uzb. Uzbek

V
var. variant
Vtn. Vietnamese

W
Wel. Welsh

X
Xh. Xhosa

Key to country factboxes within the Index:

Formation
Date of independence

Population
Total population / population density - based on total land area .

Calorie consumption
Average number of calories consumed daily per person.

A

Aa *see* Gauja
Aachen 94 A4 *Dut.* Aken, *Fr.* Aix-la-Chapelle; *anc.* Aquae Grani, Aquisgranum. Nordrhein-Westfalen, W Germany
Aaiún *see* Laâyoune
Aalborg 85 B7 *var.* Ålborg, Ålborg-Nørresundby; *anc.* Alburgum. Nordjylland, N Denmark
Aalen 95 B6 Baden-Württemberg, S Germany
Aalsmeer 86 C3 Noord-Holland, C Netherlands
Aalst 87 B6 Oost-Vlaanderen, C Belgium
Aalten 86 E4 Gelderland, E Netherlands
Aalter 87 B5 Oost-Vlaanderen, NW Belgium
Aanaarjävri *see* Inarijärvi
Äänekoski 85 D5 Länsi-Suomi, W Finland
Aar *see* Aare
Aare 95 A7 *var.* Aar. *river* W Switzerland
Aarhus *see* Århus
Aarlen *see* Arlon
Aat *see* Ath
Aba 77 E5 Orientale, NE Dem. Rep. Congo
Aba 75 G5 Abia, S Nigeria
Abā as Su'ūd *see* Najrān
Abaco Island *see* Great Abaco, N Bahamas
Ābādān 120 C4 Khūzestān, SW Iran
Abadan 122 C3 *prev.* Bezmein, Büzmeyin, *Rus.* Byuzmeyin. Ahal Welaýaty, C Turkmenistan
Abai *see* Blue Nile
Abakan 114 D4 Respublika Khakasiya, S Russian Federation
Abancay 60 D4 Apurímac, SE Peru
Abariringa *see* Kanton
Abashiri 130 D2 *var.* Abasiri. Hokkaidō, NE Japan
Abasiri *see* Abashiri
Ābay Wenz *see* Blue Nile
Abbaia *see* Ābaya Hāyk'
Abbatis Villa *see* Abbeville
Abbazia *see* Opatija
Abbeville 90 C2 *anc.* Abbatis Villa. Somme, N France
'Abd al 'Azīz, Jabal 118 D2 *mountain range* NE Syria
Abéché 76 C3 *var.* Abécher, Abeshr. Ouaddaï, SE Chad
Abécher *see* Abéché
Abela *see* Ávila
Abellinum *see* Avellino
Abemama 144 D2 *var.* Apamama; *prev.* Roger Simpson Island. *atoll* Tungaru, W Kiribati
Abengourou 75 E5 E Côte d'Ivoire
Aberbrothock *see* Arbroath
Abercorn *see* Mbala
Aberdeen 88 D3 *anc.* Devana. NE Scotland, United Kingdom
Aberdeen 45 E2 South Dakota, N USA
Aberdeen 46 B2 Washington, NW USA
Abergwaun *see* Fishguard
Abertawe *see* Swansea
Aberystwyth 89 C6 W Wales, United Kingdom
Abeshr *see* Abéché
Abhā 121 B6 'Asīr, SW Saudi Arabia
Abidavichy 107 D7 *Rus.* Obidovichi. Mahilyowskaya Voblasts', E Belarus
Abidjan 75 E5 S Côte d'Ivoire
Abilene 49 F3 Texas, SW USA
Abingdon *see* Pinta, Isla
Abkhazia *see* Apkhazeti
Åbo *see* Turku
Aboisso 75 E5 SE Côte d'Ivoire
Abo, Massif d' 76 B1 *mountain range* NW Chad
Abomey 75 F5 S Benin
Abou-Déïa 76 C3 Salamat, SE Chad
Aboudouhour *see* Abū aḑ Ḑuhūr
Abou Kémal *see* Abū Kamāl
Abrantes 92 B3 *var.* Abrántes. Santarém, C Portugal
Abrashlare *see* Brezovo
Abrolhos Bank 56 E4 *undersea bank* W Atlantic Ocean
Abrova 107 B6 *Rus.* Obrovo. Brestskaya Voblasts', SW Belarus
Abrud 108 B4 *Ger.* Gross-Schlatten, *Hung.* Abrudbánya. Alba, SW Romania
Abrudbánya *see* Abrud

Abruzzese, Appennino 96 C4 *mountain range* C Italy
Absaroka Range 44 B2 *mountain range* Montana/Wyoming, NW USA
Abū aḑ Ḑuhūr 118 B3 *Fr.* Aboudouhour. Idlib, NW Syria
Abu Dhabi *see* Abū Z̧abī
Abu Hamed 72 C3 River Nile, N Sudan
Abū Ḩardān 118 E3 *var.* Hajîne. Dayr az Zawr, E Syria
Abuja 75 G4 *country capital* (Nigeria) Federal Capital District, C Nigeria
Abū Kamāl 118 E3 *Fr.* Abou Kémal. Dayr az Zawr, E Syria
Abula *see* Ávila
Abunã, Rio 62 C2 *var.* Río Abuná. *river* Bolivia/Brazil
Abut Head 151 B6 *headland* South Island, New Zealand
Abuye Meda 72 D4 *mountain* C Ethiopia
Abū Z̧abī 121 C5 *var.* Abū Z̧abī, *Eng.* Abu Dhabi. *country capital* (United Arab Emirates) Abū Z̧aby, C United Arab Emirates
Abū Z̧aby *see* Abū Z̧abī
Abyad, Al Baḩr al *see* White Nile
Abyei Area 73 B5 *disputed region* Southern Kordofan, S Sudan
Abyla *see* Ávila
Abyssinia *see* Ethiopia
Acalayong 77 A5 SW Equatorial Guinea
Acaponeta 50 D4 Nayarit, C Mexico
Acapulco 51 E5 *var.* Acapulco de Juárez. Guerrero, S Mexico
Acapulco de Juárez *see* Acapulco
Acarai Mountains 59 F4 *Sp.* Serra Acaraí. *mountain range* Brazil/Guyana
Acaraí, Serra *see* Acarai Mountains
Acarigua 58 D2 Portuguesa, N Venezuela
Accra 75 E5 *country capital* (Ghana) SE Ghana
Achacachi 61 E4 La Paz, W Bolivia
Ach'ara 117 F2 *prev.* Achara, *var.* Ajaria. *autonomous republic* SW Georgia
Achara *see* Ach'ara
Acklins Island 54 C2 *island* SE Bahamas
Aconcagua, Cerro 64 B4 *mountain* W Argentina
Açores/Açores, Arquipélago dos/Açores, Ilhas dos *see* Azores
A Coruña 92 B1 *Cast.* La Coruña, *Eng.* Corunna; *anc.* Caronium. Galicia, NW Spain
Acre 62 C2 *off.* Estado do Acre. *state* W Brazil
Acre 62 C2 *off.* Estado do Acre. *region* W Brazil
Açu *see* Assu
Acunum Acusio *see* Montélimar
Ada 100 D3 Vojvodina, N Serbia
Ada 49 G2 Oklahoma, C USA
Ada Bazar *see* Adapazarı
Adalia *see* Antalya
Adalia, Gulf of *see* Antalya Körfezi
Adama *see* Nazrēt
'Adan 121 B7 *Eng.* Aden. SW Yemen
Adana 116 D4 *var.* Seyhan. Adana, S Turkey
Adâncata *see* Horlivka
Adapazarı 116 B2 *prev.* Ada Bazar. Sakarya, NW Turkey
Adare, Cape 154 B4 *cape* Antarctica
Ad Dahna 120 C4 *desert* E Saudi Arabia
Ad Dakhla 70 A4 *var.* Dakhla. SW Western Sahara
Ad Dalanj *see* Dilling
Ad Damar *see* Ed Damer
Ad Damazīn *see* Ed Damazin
Ad Dāmir *see* Ed Damer
Ad Dammām 120 C4 *var.* Dammām. Ash Sharqīyah, NE Saudi Arabia
Ad Dāmūr *see* Damoûr
Ad Dawḩah 120 C4 *Eng.* Doha. *country capital* (Qatar) C Qatar
Ad Diffah *see* Libyan Plateau
Addis Ababa *see* Ādīs Ābeba
Addoo Atoll *see* Addu Atoll
Addu Atoll 132 A5 *var.* Addoo Atoll, Seenu Atoll. *atoll* S Maldives
Adelaide 149 B6 *state capital* South Australia
Adelsberg *see* Postojna
Aden *see* 'Adan
Aden, Gulf of 121 C7 *gulf* SW Arabian Sea
Adige 96 C2 *Ger.* Etsch. *river* N Italy
Adirondack Mountains 41 F2 *mountain range* New York, NE USA

Ādīs Ābeba *73 C5 Eng.* Addis Ababa. *country capital* (Ethiopia) Ādīs Ābeba, C Ethiopia
Adıyaman *117 E4* Adıyaman, SE Turkey
Adjud *108 C4* Vrancea, E Romania
Admiralty Islands *144 B3 island group* N Papua New Guinea
Adra *93 E5* Andalucía, S Spain
Adrar *70 D3* C Algeria
Adrian *40 C3* Michigan, N USA
Adrianople/Adrianopolis *see* Edirne
Adriatico, Mare *see* Adriatic Sea
Adriatic Sea *103 E2 Alb.* Deti Adriatik, *It.* Mare Adriatico, *SCr.* Jadransko More, *Slvn.* Jadransko Morje. *sea* N Mediterranean Sea
Adriatik, Deti *see* Adriatic Sea
Adycha *115 F2 river* NE Russian Federation
Aegean Sea *105 C5 Gk.* Aigaíon Pelagos, Aigaío Pelagos, *Turk.* Ege Denizi. *sea* NE Mediterranean Sea
Aegviidu *106 D2 Ger.* Charlottenhof. Harjumaa, NW Estonia
Aegyptus *see* Egypt
Aelana *see* Al 'Aqabah
Aelok *see* Ailuk Atoll
Aelönlaplap *see* Ailinglaplap Atoll
Aemona *see* Ljubljana
Aeolian Islands *97 C6 var.* Isole Lipari, *Eng.* Aeolian Islands, Lipari Islands. *island group* S Italy
Aeolian Islands *see* Eolie, Isole
Æsernia *see* Isernia
Afar Depression *see* Danakil Desert
Afars et des Issas, Territoire Français des *see* Djibouti
Afghänestän, Dowlat-e Eslāmī-ye *see* Afghanistan
Afghanistan *122 C4 off.* Islamic Republic of Afghanistan, *Per.* Dowlat-e Eslāmī-ye Afghänestän; *prev.* Republic of Afghanistan. *country* C Asia

AFGHANISTAN
Central Asia

Official name The Islamic Republic of Afghanistan
Formation 1919 / 1919
Capital Kabul
Population 32.4 million / 129 people per sq mile (50 people per sq km)
Total area 250,000 sq. miles (647,500 sq. km)
Languages Pashtu*, Tajik, Dari*, Farsi, Uzbek, Turkmen
Religions Sunni Muslim 80%, Shi'a Muslim 19%, Other 1%
Ethnic mix Pashtun 38%, Tajik 25%, Hazara 19%, Uzbek and Turkmen 15%, Other 3%
Government Nonparty system
Currency Afghani = 100 puls
Literacy rate 28%
Calorie consumption 1539 kilocalories

Afmadow *73 D6* Jubbada Hoose, S Somalia
Africa *68 continent*
Africa, Horn of *68 E4 physical region* Ethiopia/Somalia
Africana Seamount *141 A6 seamount* SW Indian Ocean
'Afrīn *118 B2* Ḥalab, N Syria
Afyon *116 B3 prev.* Afyonkarahisar. Afyon, W Turkey
Agadès *see* Agadez
Agadez *75 G3 prev.* Agadès. Agadez, C Niger
Agadir *70 B3* SW Morocco
Agana/Agaña *see* Hagåtña
Agaro *73 C5* Oromīya, C Ethiopia
Agassiz Fracture Zone *143 G5 fracture zone* S Pacific Ocean
Agatha *see* Agde
Agathónisi *105 D6 island* Dodekánisa, Greece, Aegean Sea
Agde *91 C6 anc.* Agatha. Hérault, S France
Agedabia *see* Ajdābiyā
Agen *91 B5 anc.* Aginnum. Lot-et-Garonne, SW France
Agendicum *see* Sens
Aghri Dagh *see* Büyükağrı Dağı
Agiá *104 B4 var.* Ayiá. Thessalía, C Greece
Agialoúsa *see* Yenierenköy

Agía Marína *105 E6* Léros, Dodekánisa, Greece, Aegean Sea
Aginnum *see* Agen
Ágios Efstrátios *104 D4 var.* Áyios Evstrátios, Hagios Evstrátios. *island* E Greece
Ágios Nikólaos *105 D8 var.* Áyios Nikólaos. Kríti, Greece, E Mediterranean Sea
Āgra *134 D3* Uttar Pradesh, N India
Agra and Oudh, United Provinces of *see* Uttar Pradesh
Agram *see* Zagreb
Ağrı *117 F3 var.* Karaköse; *prev.* Karakılıssse. Ağrı, NE Turkey
Agri Dagi *see* Büyükağrı Dağı
Agrigento *97 C7 Gk.* Akragas; *prev.* Girgenti. Sicilia, Italy, C Mediterranean Sea
Agriovótano *105 C5* Évvoia, C Greece
Agropoli *97 D5* Campania, S Italy
Aguachica *58 B2* Cesar, N Colombia
Aguadulce *53 F5* Coclé, S Panama
Agua Prieta *50 B1* Sonora, NW Mexico
Aguascalientes *50 D4* Aguascalientes, C Mexico
Aguaytía *60 C3* Ucayali, C Peru
Aguilas *93 E4* Murcia, SE Spain
Aguililla *50 D4* Michoacán, SW Mexico
Agulhas Basin *69 D8 undersea basin* SW Indian Ocean
Agulhas Plateau *67 D6 undersea plateau* SW Indian Ocean
Ahaggar *75 F2 high plateau region* SE Algeria
Ahlen *94 B4* Nordrhein-Westfalen, W Germany
Ahmadābād *134 C4 var.* Ahmedabad. Gujarāt, W India
Ahmadnagar *134 C5 var.* Ahmednagar. Mahārāshtra, W India
Ahmedabad *see* Ahmadābād
Ahmednagar *see* Ahmadnagar
Ahuachapán *52 B3* Ahuachapán, W El Salvador
Ahvāz *120 C3 var.* Ahwāz; *prev.* Nāsiri. Khūzestān, SW Iran
Ahvenanmaa *see* Åland
Ahwāz *see* Ahvāz
Aigaíon Pelagos/Aigaío Pélagos *see* Aegean Sea
Aígina *105 C6 var.* Aíyina, Egina. Aígina, C Greece
Aígio *105 B5 var.* Egio; *prev.* Aíyion. Dytikí Elláda, S Greece
Aiken *43 E2* South Carolina, SE USA
Ailinglaplap Atoll *144 D2 var.* Aelönlaplap. *atoll* Ralik Chain, S Marshall Islands
Ailuk Atoll *144 D1 var.* Aelok. *atoll* Ratak Chain, NE Marshall Islands
Ainaži *106 D3 Est.* Heinaste, *Ger.* Hainasch. N Latvia
'Aïn Ben Tili *74 D1* Tiris Zemmour, N Mauritania
Aintab *see* Gaziantep
Aïoun el Atrous/Aïoun el Atroûss *see* 'Ayoûn el 'Atroûs
Aiquile *61 F4* Cochabamba, C Bolivia
Aïr *see* Aïr, Massif de l'
Air du Azbine *see* Aïr, Massif de l'
Aïr, Massif de l' *75 G2 var.* Aïr, Air du Azbine, Asben. *mountain range* NC Niger
Aiud *108 B4 Ger.* Strassburg, *Hung.* Nagyenyed; *prev.* Engeten. Alba, SW Romania
Aix *see* Aix-en-Provence
Aix-en-Provence *91 D6 var.* Aix; *anc.* Aquae Sextiae. Bouches-du-Rhône, SE France
Aix-la-Chapelle *see* Aachen
Aíyina *see* Aígina
Aíyion *see* Aígio
Aizkraukle *106 C4* S Latvia
Ajaccio *91 E7* Corse, France, C Mediterranean Sea
Ajaria *see* Ach'ara
Ajastan *see* Armenia
Aj Bogd Uul *126 D2 mountain* SW Mongolia
Ajdābiyā *71 G2 var.* Agedabia, Ajdābiyah. NE Libya
Ajdābiyah *see* Ajdābiyā
Ajjinena *see* El Geneina
Ajmer *134 D3 var.* Ajmere. Rājasthān, N India
Ajo *48 A3* Arizona, SW USA

Akaba *see* Al 'Aqabah
Akamagaseki *see* Shimonoseki
Akasha *72 B3* Northern, N Sudan
Akchâr *74 C2 desert* W Mauritania
Aken *see* Aachen
Akermanceaster *see* Bath
Akhaltsikhe *117 F2 prev.* Akhalts'ikhe. SW Georgia
Akhalts'ikhe *see* Akhaltsikhe
Akhisar *116 A3* Manisa, W Turkey
Akhmîm *72 B2 var.* Akhmim; *anc.* Panopolis. C Egypt
Akhtubinsk *111 C7* Astrakhanskaya Oblast', SW Russian Federation
Akhtyrka *see* Okhtyrka
Akimiski Island *38 C3 island* Nunavut, C Canada
Akinovka *109 F4* Zaporiz'ka Oblast', S Ukraine
Akita *130 D4* Akita, Honshū, C Japan
Akjoujt *74 C2 prev.* Fort-Repoux. Inchiri, W Mauritania
Akkeshi *130 E2* Hokkaidō, NE Japan
Aklavik *36 D3* Northwest Territories, NW Canada
Akmola *see* Astana
Akmolinsk *see* Astana
Aknavásár *see* Târgu Ocna
Akpatok Island *39 E1 island* Nunavut, E Canada
Akragas *see* Agrigento
Akron *40 D4* Ohio, N USA
Akrotiri *see* Akrotírion
Akrotírion *102 C5 var.* Akrotiri. UK air base S Cyprus
Aksai Chin *124 B2 Chin.* Aksayqin. disputed region China/India
Aksaray *116 C4* Aksaray, C Turkey
Aksayqin *see* Aksai Chin
Akşehir *116 B4* Konya, W Turkey
Aktash *see* Oqtosh
Aktau *114 A4 Kaz.* Aqtaū; *prev.* Shevchenko. Mangistau, W Kazakhstan
Aktjubinsk/Aktyubinsk *see* Aktobe
Aktobe *114 B4 Kaz.* Aqtöbe; *prev.* Aktjubinsk, Aktyubinsk. NW Kazakhstan
Aktsyabrski *107 C7 Rus.* Oktyabr'skiy; *prev.* Karpilovka. Homyel'skaya Voblasts', SE Belarus
Aktyubinsk *see* Aktobe
Akula *77 C5* Equateur, NW Dem. Rep. Congo
Akureyri *83 E4* Nordhurland Eystra, N Iceland
Akyab *see* Sittwe
Alabama *42 C2 off.* State of Alabama, also known as Camellia State, Heart of Dixie, The Cotton State, Yellowhammer State. *state* S USA
Alabama River *42 C3 river* Alabama, S USA
Alaca *116 C3* Çorum, N Turkey
Alacant *see* Alicante
Alagoas *63 G2 off.* Estado de Alagoas. *region* E Brazil
Alagoas *63 G2 off.* Estado de Alagoas. *state* E Brazil
Alais *see* Alès
Alajuela *53 E4* Alajuela, C Costa Rica
Alakanuk *36 C2* Alaska, USA
Al 'Alamayn *72 B1 var.* El 'Alamein. N Egypt
Al 'Amārah *120 C3 var.* Amara. Maysān, E Iraq
Alamo *47 D6* Nevada, W USA
Alamogordo *48 D3* New Mexico, SW USA
Alamosa *44 C5* Colorado, C USA
Åland Islands *85 C6 var.* Aland Islands, *Fin.* Ahvenanmaa. *island group* SW Finland
Aland Islands *see* Åland Islands
Aland Sea *85 C6 var.* Aland Sea. *strait* Baltic Sea/Gulf of Bothnia
Aland Sea *see* Ålands Hav
Alanya *116 C4* Antalya, S Turkey
Alappuzha *132 C3 prev.* Alleppey. Kerala, SW India
Al 'Aqabah *119 B8 var.* Akaba, Aqaba; *anc.* Aelana, Elath. Al 'Aqabah, SW Jordan
Al 'Arabīyah as Su'ūdīyah *see* Saudi Arabia
Alasca, Golfo de *see* Alaska, Gulf of
Alaşehir *116 A4* Manisa, W Turkey
Al 'Ashārah *118 E3 var.* Ashara. Dayr az Zawr, E Syria

Alaska *36 C3 off.* State of Alaska, also known as Land of the Midnight Sun, The Last Frontier, Seward's Folly; *prev.* Russian America. *state* NW USA
Alaska, Gulf of *36 C4 var.* Golfo de Alasca. *gulf* Canada/USA
Alaska Peninsula *36 C3 peninsula* Alaska, USA
Alaska Range *34 B2 mountain range* Alaska, USA
Al-Asnam *see* Chlef
Alattio *see* Alta
Al Awaynāt *see* Al 'Uwaynāt
Alaykel'/Alay-Kuu *see* Kök-Art
Al 'Aynā *119 B7* Al Karak, W Jordan
Alazeya *115 G2 river* NE Russian Federation
Al Bāb *118 B2* Ḥalab, N Syria
Albacete *93 E3* Castilla-La Mancha, C Spain
Al Baghdādī *120 B3 var.* Khān al Baghdādī. Al Anbār, SW Iraq
Al Bāha *see* Al Bāḥah
Al Bāḥah *121 B5 var.* Al Bāha. Al BāḤah, SW Saudi Arabia
Al Baḥrayn *see* Bahrain
Alba Iulia *108 B4 Ger.* Weissenburg, *Hung.* Gyulafehérvár; *prev.* Bálgrad, Karlsburg, Károly-Fehérvár. Alba, W Romania
Albania *101 C7 off.* Republic of Albania, *Alb.* Republika e Shqipqërisë, Shqipëria; *prev.* People's Socialist Republic of Albania. *country* SE Europe

ALBANIA
Southeast Europe

Official name Republic of Albania
Formation 1912 / 1921
Capital Tirana
Population 3.2 million / 302 people per sq mile (117 people per sq km)
Total area 11,100 sq. miles (28,748 sq. km)
Languages Albanian*, Greek
Religions Sunni Muslim 70%, Albanian Orthodox 20%, Roman Catholic 10%
Ethnic mix Albanian 98%, Greek 1%, Other 1%
Government Parliamentary system
Currency Lek = 100 qindarka (qintars)
Literacy rate 96%
Calorie consumption 2903 kilocalories

Albania *see* Aubagne
Albany *147 B7* Western Australia
Albany *42 D3* Georgia, SE USA
Albany *41 F3 state capital* New York, NE USA
Albany *46 B3* Oregon, NW USA
Albany *38 C3 river* Ontario, S Canada
Alba Regia *see* Székesfehérvár
Al Bārīdah *118 C4 var.* Bāridah. Ḥimṣ, C Syria
Al Baṣrah *120 C3 Eng.* Basra, *hist.* Busra, Bussora. Al Baṣrah, SE Iraq
Al Batrūn *see* Batroûn
Al Baydā' *71 G2 var.* Beida. NE Libya
Albemarle Island *see* Isabela, Isla
Albemarle Sound *43 G1 inlet* W Atlantic Ocean
Albergaria-a-Velha *92 B2* Aveiro, N Portugal
Albert *90 C3* Somme, N France
Alberta *37 E4 province* SW Canada
Albert Edward Nyanza *see* Edward, Lake
Albert, Lake *73 B6 var.* Albert Nyanza, Lac Mobutu Sese Seko. *lake* Uganda/Dem. Rep. Congo
Albert Lea *45 F3* Minnesota, N USA
Albert Nyanza *see* Albert, Lake
Albertville *see* Kalemie
Albi *91 C6 anc.* Albiga. Tarn, S France
Albiga *see* Albi
Ålborg *see* Aalborg
Ålborg-Nørresundby *see* Aalborg
Albuquerque *48 D2* New Mexico, SW USA
Al Burayqah *see* Marsá al Burayqah
Alburgum *see* Aalborg
Albury *149 C7* New South Wales, SE Australia
Alcácer do Sal *92 B4* Setúbal, W Portugal
Alcalá de Henares *93 E3 Ar.* Alkal'a; *anc.* Complutum. Madrid, C Spain
Alcamo *97 C7* Sicilia, Italy, C Mediterranean Sea
Alcañiz *93 F2* Aragón, NE Spain

Alcántara, Embalse de 92 C3 *reservoir* W Spain
Alcaudete 92 D4 Andalucía, S Spain
Alcázar *see* Ksar-el-Kebir
Alcazarquivir *see* Ksar-el-Kebir
Alcoi *see* Alcoy
Alcoy 93 F4 *Cat.* Alcoi. Valenciana, E Spain
Aldabra Group 79 G2 *island group* SW Seychelles
Aldan 115 F3 *river* NE Russian Federation
al Dar al Baida *see* Rabat
Alderney 90 A2 *island* Channel Islands
Aleg 74 C3 Brakna, SW Mauritania
Aleksandriya *see* Oleksandriya
Aleksandropol' *see* Gyumri
Aleksandrovka *see* Oleksandrivka
Aleksandrovsk *see* Zaporizhzhya
Aleksin 111 B5 Tul'skaya Oblast', W Russian Federation
Aleksinac 100 E4 Serbia, SE Serbia
Alençon 90 B3 Orne, N France
Alenquer 62 E2 Pará, NE Brazil
Alep/Aleppo *see* Ḥalab
Alert 37 F1 Ellesmere Island, Nunavut, N Canada
Alès 91 C6 *prev.* Alais. Gard, S France
Aleşd 108 B3 *Hung.* Élesd. Bihor, SW Romania
Alessandria 96 B2 *Fr.* Alexandrie. Piemonte, N Italy
Ålesund 85 A5 Møre og Romsdal, S Norway
Aleutian Basin 113 G3 *undersea basin* Bering Sea
Aleutian Islands 36 A3 *island group* Alaska, USA
Aleutian Range 34 A2 *mountain range* Alaska, USA
Aleutian Trench 113 H3 *trench* S Bering Sea
Alexander Archipelago 36 D4 *island group* Alaska, USA
Alexander City 42 D2 Alabama, S USA
Alexander Island 154 A3 *island* Antarctica
Alexander Range *see* Kirghiz Range
Alexandra 151 B7 Otago, South Island, New Zealand
Alexándreia 104 B4 *var.* Alexándria. Kentrikí Makedonía, N Greece
Alexandretta *see* Iskenderun
Alexandretta, Gulf of *see* Iskenderun Körfezi
Alexandria 72 B1 *Ar.* Al Iskandarīyah. N Egypt
Alexandria 108 C5 Teleorman, S Romania
Alexandria 42 B3 Louisiana, S USA
Alexandria 45 F2 Minnesota, N USA
Alexándria *see* Alexándreia
Alexandrie *see* Alessandria
Alexandroúpoli 104 D3 *var.* Alexandroúpolis, *Turk.* Dedeagaç, Dedeagach. Anatolikí Makedonía kai Thráki, NE Greece
Alexandroúpolis *see* Alexandroúpoli
Al Fāshir *see* El Fasher
Alfatar 104 E1 Silistra, NE Bulgaria
Alfeiós 105 B6 *prev.* Alfiós; *anc.* Alpheius, Alpheus. *river* S Greece
Alfiós *see* Alfeiós
Alföld *see* Great Hungarian Plain
Al-Furāt *see* Euphrates
Alga 114 B2 *Kaz.* Algha. Aktyubinsk, NW Kazakhstan
Algarve 92 C5 *cultural region* S Portugal
Algeciras 92 C5 Andalucía, SW Spain
Algemesí 93 F3 Valenciana, E Spain
Al-Genain *see* El Geneina
Alger 71 E1 *var.* Algiers, El Djazaïr, Al Jazair. *country capital* (Algeria) N Algeria
Algeria 70 C3 *off.* Democratic and Popular Republic of Algeria. *country* N Africa

ALGERIA
North Africa

Official name People's Democratic Republic of Algeria
Formation 1962 / 1962
Capital Algiers
Population 36 million / 39 people per sq mile (15 people per sq km)
Total area 919,590 sq. miles (2,381,740 sq. km)

ALGERIA
(continued)

Languages Arabic*, Tamazight (Kabyle, Shawia, Tamashek), French
Religions Sunni Muslim 99%, Christian and Jewish 1%
Ethnic mix Arab 75%, Berber 24%, European and Jewish 1%
Government Presidential system
Currency Algerian dinar = 100 centimes
Literacy rate 75%
Calorie consumption 3239 kilocalories

Algeria, Democratic and Popular Republic of *see* Algeria
Algerian Basin 80 C5 *var.* Balearic Plain. *undersea basin* W Mediterranean Sea
Algha *see* Alga
Al Ghābah 121 E5 *var.* Ghaba. C Oman
Alghero 97 A5 Sardegna, Italy, C Mediterranean Sea
Al Ghurdaqah 72 C2 *var.* Ghurdaqah, Hurghada. E Egypt
Algiers *see* Alger
Al Golea *see* El Goléa
Algona 45 F3 Iowa, C USA
Al Hajar al Gharbi 121 D5 *mountain range* N Oman
Al Hamad *see* Syrian Desert
Al Ḥasakah 118 D2 *var.* Al Hasijah, El Haseke, *Fr.* Hassetché. Al Ḥasakah, NE Syria
Al Hasijah *see* Al Ḥasakah
Al Ḥillah 120 B3 *var.* Hilla. Bābil, C Iraq
Al Ḥisā 119 B7 At Ṭafilah, W Jordan
Al Ḥudaydah 121 B6 *Eng.* Hodeida. W Yemen
Al Hufūf 120 C4 *var.* Hofuf. Ash Sharqīyah, NE Saudi Arabia
Aliákmon *see* Aliákmonas
Aliákmonas 104 B4 *prev.* Aliákmon; *anc.* Haliacmon. *river* N Greece
Alíartos 105 C5 Stereá Elláda, C Greece
Alicante 93 F4 *Cat.* Alacant, *Lat.* Lucentum. Valenciana, SE Spain
Alice 49 G5 Texas, SW USA
Alice Springs 148 A4 Northern Territory, C Australia
Alifu Atoll *see* Ari Atoll
Aligandí 53 G4 Kuna Yala, NE Panama
Aliki *see* Alykí
Alima 77 B6 *river* C Congo
Al Imārāt al 'Arabīyah al Muttaḥidah *see* United Arab Emirates
Alindao 76 C4 Basse-Kotto, S Central African Republic
Aliquippa 40 D4 Pennsylvania, NE USA
Al Iskandarīyah *see* Alexandria
Al Ismā'īliya 72 B1 *var.* Ismailia, Ismā'īliya. N Egypt
Alistráti 104 C3 Kentrikí Makedonía, NE Greece
Alivéri 105 C5 *var.* Alivérion. Évvoia, C Greece
Alivérion *see* Alivéri
Al Jabal al Akhḍar 71 G2 *mountain range* NE Libya
Al Jafr 119 B7 Ma'ān, S Jordan
Al Jaghbūb 71 H3 NE Libya
Al Jahrā' 120 C4 *var.* Al Jahrah, Jahra. C Kuwait
Al Jahrah *see* Al Jahrā'
Al Jamāhīrīyah al 'Arabīyah al Lībīyah ash Sha'bīyah al Ishtirākīy *see* Libya
Al Jawf 120 B4 *off.* Jauf. Al Jawf, NW Saudi Arabia
Al Jawlān *see* Golan Heights
Al Jazair *see* Alger
Al Jazirah 118 E2 *physical region* Iraq/Syria
Al Jīzah *see* Giza
Alkal'a *see* Alcalá de Henares
Al Karak 119 B7 *var.* El Kerak, Karak, Kerak; *anc.* Kir Moab, Kir of Moab. Al Karak, W Jordan
Al-Kasr al-Kebir *see* Ksar-el-Kebir
Al Khalil *see* Hebron
Al Khārijah 72 B2 *var.* El Khârga. C Egypt
Al Khums 71 F2 *var.* Homs, Khoms, Khums. NW Libya
Alkmaar 86 C3 Noord-Holland, NW Netherlands
Al Kufrah 71 H4 SE Libya
Al Kūt 120 C3 *var.* Kūt al 'Amārah, Kut al Imara. Wāsiṭ, E Iraq

Al-Kuwait *see* Al Kuwayt
Al Kuwayt 120 C4 *var.* Al-Kuwait, *Eng.* Kuwait, Kuwait City; *prev.* Qurein. *country capital* (Kuwait) E Kuwait
Al Lādhiqīyah 118 A3 *Eng.* Latakia, *Fr.* Lattaquié; *anc.* Laodicea, Laodicea ad Mare. Al Lādhiqīyah, W Syria
Allahābād 135 E3 Uttar Pradesh, N India
Alanmyo *see* Aunglan
Allegheny Plateau 41 E3 *mountain range* New York/Pennsylvania, NE USA
Allenstein *see* Olsztyn
Allentown 41 F4 Pennsylvania, NE USA
Alleppey *see* Alappuzha
Alliance 44 D3 Nebraska, C USA
Al Lith 121 B5 Makkah, SW Saudi Arabia
Al Lubnān *see* Lebanon
Alma-Ata *see* Almaty
Almada 92 B4 Setúbal, W Portugal
Al Madīnah 121 A5 *Eng.* Medina. Al Madīnah, W Saudi Arabia
Al Mafraq 119 B6 *var.* Mafraq. Al Mafraq, N Jordan
Al Mahdīyah *see* Mahdia
Al Mahrah 121 C6 *mountain range* E Yemen
Al Majma'ah 120 B4 Ar Riyāḍ, C Saudi Arabia
Al Mālikīyah 118 E1 *var.* Malkiye. Al Ḥasakah, N Syria
Almalyk *see* Olmaliq
Al Mamlakah *see* Morocco
Al Mamlaka al Urdunīya al Hashemīyah *see* Jordan
Al Manāmah 120 C4 *Eng.* Manama. *country capital* (Bahrain) N Bahrain
Al Manāṣif 118 E3 *mountain range* E Syria
Almansa 93 F4 Castilla-La Mancha, C Spain
Al-Mariyya *see* Almería
Al Marj 71 G2 *var.* Barka, *It.* Barce. NE Libya
Almaty 114 C5 *var.* Alma-Ata. Almaty, SE Kazakhstan
Al Mawṣil 120 B2 *Eng.* Mosul. Nīnawá, N Iraq
Al Mayādīn 118 D3 *var.* Mayadin, *Fr.* Meyadine. Dayr az Zawr, E Syria
Al Mazra' *see* Al Mazra'ah
Al Mazra'ah 119 B6 *var.* Al Mazra', Mazra'a. Al Karak, W Jordan
Almelo 86 E3 Overijssel, E Netherlands
Almendra, Embalse de 92 C2 *reservoir* Castilla y León, NW Spain
Almendralejo 92 C4 Extremadura, W Spain
Almere 86 C3 *var.* Almere-stad. Flevoland, C Netherlands
Almere-stad *see* Almere
Almería 93 E5 *Ar.* Al-Mariyya; *anc.* Unci, *Lat.* Portus Magnus. Andalucía, S Spain
Al'met'yevsk 111 D5 Respublika Tatarstan, W Russian Federation
Al Mīnā' *see* El Mina
Al Minyā 72 B2 *var.* El Minya, Minya. C Egypt
Almirante 53 E4 Bocas del Toro, NW Panama
Al Mudawwarah 119 B8 Ma'ān, SW Jordan
Al Mukallā 121 C6 *var.* Mukalla. SE Yemen
Al Obayyid *see* El Obeid
Alofi 145 F4 *dependent territory capital* (Niue) W Niue
Aloha State *see* Hawai'i
Aloja 106 D3 N Latvia
Alónnisos 105 C5 *island* Vóreies Sporádes, Greece, Aegean Sea
Álora 92 D5 Andalucía, S Spain
Alor, Kepulauan 139 E5 *island group* E Indonesia
Al Oued *see* El Oued
Alpen *see* Alps
Alpena 40 D2 Michigan, N USA
Alpes *see* Alps
Alpha Cordillera 155 B3 *var.* Alpha Ridge. *seamount range* Arctic Ocean
Alpha Ridge *see* Alpha Cordillera
Alpheius *see* Alfeiós
Alphen *see* Alphen aan den Rijn
Alphen aan den Rijn 86 C3 *var.* Alphen. Zuid-Holland, C Netherlands
Alpheus *see* Alfeiós
Alpi *see* Alps
Alpine 49 E4 Texas, SW USA

Alps 102 C1 *Fr.* Alpes, *Ger.* Alpen, *It.* Alpi. *mountain range* C Europe
Al Qaḍārif *see* Gedaref
Al Qāhirah *see* Cairo
Al Qāmishlī 118 E1 *var.* Kamishli, Qamishly. Al Ḥasakah, NE Syria
Al Qaṣrayn *see* Kasserine
Al Qayrawān *see* Kairouan
Al-Qsar al-Kbir *see* Ksar-el-Kebir
Al Qubayyāt *see* Qoubaïyât
Al Quds/Al Quds ash Sharif *see* Jerusalem
Alqueva, Barragem do 92 C4 *reservoir* Portugal/Spain
Al Qunayṭirah 119 B5 *var.* El Kuneitra, El Quneitra, Kuneitra, Qunaytra. Al Qunayṭirah, SW Syria
Al Quṣayr 118 B4 *var.* El Quseir, Quṣayr, *Fr.* Kousseir. Ḥimṣ, W Syria
Al Quwayrah 119 B8 *var.* El Quweira. Al 'Aqabah, SW Jordan
Alsace 90 E3 *Ger.* Elsass; *anc.* Alsatia. *cultural region* NE France
Alsatia *see* Alsace
Alsdorf 94 A4 Nordrhein-Westfalen, W Germany
Alt *see* Olt
Alta 84 D2 *Fin.* Alattio. Finnmark, N Norway
Altai *see* Altai Mountains
Altai Mountains 126 C2 *var.* Altai, *Chin.* Altay Shan, *Rus.* Altay. *mountain range* Asia/Europe
Altamaha River 43 E3 *river* Georgia, SE USA
Altamira 63 E2 Pará, NE Brazil
Altamura 97 E5 *anc.* Lupatia. Puglia, SE Italy
Altay 126 C2 Xinjiang Uygur Zizhiqu, NW China
Altay 126 C2 *var.* Yösönbulag. Govĭ-Altay, W Mongolia
Altay Altai Mountains, Asia/Europe
Altay Shan *see* Altai Mountains
Altbetsche *see* Bečej
Altenburg 94 D4 Sachsen, E Germany
Altın Köprü 120 B3 *var.* Altun Kupri. At Ta'mím, N Iraq
Altiplano 61 F4 *physical region* W South America
Altkanischa *see* Kanjiža
Alton 40 B5 Illinois, N USA
Alton 44 B4 Missouri, C USA
Altoona 41 E4 Pennsylvania, NE USA
Alto Paraná *see* Paraná
Altpasua *see* Stara Pazova
Alt-Schwanenburg *see* Gulbene
Altsohl *see* Zvolen
Altun Kupri *see* Altın Köprü
Altun Shan 126 C3 *var.* Altyn Tagh. *mountain range* NW China
Altus 49 F2 Oklahoma, C USA
Altyn Tagh *see* Altun Shan
Al Ubayyiḍ *see* El Obeid
Alūksne 106 D3 *Ger.* Marienburg. NE Latvia
Al 'Ulā 120 A4 Al Madīnah, NW Saudi Arabia
Al 'Umarī 119 C6 'Ammān, E Jordan
Alupka 109 F5 Avtonomna Respublika Krym, S Ukraine
Al Uqṣur *see* Luxor
Al Urdunn *see* Jordan
Alushta 109 F5 Avtonomna Respublika Krym, S Ukraine
Al 'Uwaynāt 71 F4 *var.* Al Awaynāt. SW Libya
Alva 49 F1 Oklahoma, C USA
Alvarado 51 F4 Veracruz-Llave, E Mexico
Alvin 49 H4 Texas, SW USA
Al Wajh 120 A4 Tabūk, NW Saudi Arabia
Alwar 134 D3 Rājasthān, N India
Al Wari'ah 120 C4 Ash Sharqīyah, N Saudi Arabia
Al Yaman *see* Yemen
Alykí 104 C4 *var.* Aliki. Thásos, N Greece
Alytus 107 B5 *Pol.* Olita. Alytus, S Lithuania
Alzette 87 D8 *river* S Luxembourg
Amadeus, Lake 147 D5 *seasonal lake* Northern Territory, C Australia
Amadi 73 B5 Western Equatoria, SW South Sudan

Amadjuak Lake 37 G3 *lake* Baffin Island, Nunavut, N Canada
Amakusa-nada 131 A7 *gulf* SW Japan
Åmål 85 B6 Västra Götaland, S Sweden
Amami-gunto 130 A3 *island group* SW Japan
Amami-o-shim 130 A3 *island* S Japan
Amantea 97 D6 Calabria, SW Italy
Amapá 63 E1 *off.* Estado de Amapá; *prev.* Território de Amapá. *region* NE Brazil
Amapá 63 E1 *off.* Estado de Amapá; *prev.* Território de Amapá. *state* NE Brazil
Amapá, Estado de *see* Amapá
Amapá, Território de *see* Amapá
Amara *see* Al 'Amārah
Amarapura 136 B3 Mandalay, C Myanmar (Burma)
Amarillo 49 E2 Texas, SW USA
Amay 87 C6 Liège, E Belgium
Amazon 63 E1 *Sp.* Amazonas. *river* Brazil/Peru
Amazonas *see* Amazon
Amazon Basin 62 D2 *basin* N South America
Amazon, Mouths of the 63 F1 *delta* NE Brazil
Ambam 77 B5 Sud, S Cameroon
Ambanja 79 G2 Antsiñaña, N Madagascar
Ambarchik 115 G2 Respublika Sakha (Yakutiya), NE Russian Federation
Ambato 60 B1 Tungurahua, C Ecuador
Ambérieu-en-Bugey 91 D5 Ain, E France
Ambianum *see* Amiens
Amboasary 79 F4 Toliara, S Madagascar
Amboina *see* Ambon
Ambon 139 F4 *prev.* Amboina, Amboyna. Pulau Ambon, E Indonesia
Ambositra 79 G3 Fianarantsoa, SE Madagascar
Amboyna *see* Ambon
Ambracia *see* Árta
Ambre, Cap d' *see* Bobaomby, Tanjona
Ambrim *see* Ambrym
Ambriz 78 A1 Bengo, NW Angola
Ambrym 144 D4 *var.* Ambrim. *island* C Vanuatu
Amchitka Island 36 A2 *island* Aleutian Islands, Alaska, USA
Amdo 126 C5 Xizang Zizhiqu, W China
Ameland 86 D1 *Fris.* It Amelân. *island* Waddeneilanden, N Netherlands
Amelân, It *see* Ameland
America *see* United States of America
America-Antarctica Ridge 67 C7 *undersea ridge* S Atlantic Ocean
America in Miniature *see* Maryland
American Falls Reservoir 46 E4 *reservoir* Idaho, NW USA
American Samoa 145 E4 *US unincorporated territory* W Polynesia
Amersfoort 86 D3 Utrecht, C Netherlands
Ames 45 F3 Iowa, C USA
Amfilochía 105 A5 *var.* Amfilokhía. Dytiki Elláda, C Greece
Amfilokhía *see* Amfilochía
Amga 115 F3 *river* NE Russian Federation
Amherst 39 F4 Nova Scotia, SE Canada
Amherst *see* Kyaikkami
Amida *see* Diyarbakır
Amiens 90 C3 *anc.* Ambianum, Samarobriva. Somme, N France
Amíndaion/Amindeo *see* Amýntaio
Amindivi Islands 132 A2 *island group* Lakshadweep, India, N Indian Ocean
Amirante Islands 79 G1 *var.* Amirantes Group. *island group* C Seychelles
Amirantes Group *see* Amirante Islands
Amistad, Presa de la *see* Amistad Reservoir
Amistad Reservoir 49 F4 *var.* Presa de la Amistad. *reservoir* Mexico/USA
Amisus *see* Samsun
Ammaia *see* Portalegre
'Amman 119 B6 *var.* Amman; *anc.* Philadelphia, *Bibl.* Rabbah Ammon, Rabbath Ammon. *country capital* (Jordan) 'Ammān, NW Jordan
Ammassalik 82 D4 *var.* Angmagssalik. Tunu, S Greenland
Ammóchostos *see* Gazimağusa
Ammóchostos, Kólpos *see* Gazimağusa Körfezi
Amnok-kang *see* Yalu

Amoea *see* Portalegre
Amoentai *see* Amuntai
Āmol 120 D2 *var.* Amul. Māzandarān, N Iran
Amorgós 105 D6 Amorgós, Kykládes, Greece, Aegean Sea
Amorgós 105 D6 *island* Kykládes, Greece, Aegean Sea
Amos 38 D4 Québec, SE Canada
Amourj 74 D3 Hodh ech Chargui, SE Mauritania
Amoy *see* Xiamen
Ampato, Nevado 61 E4 *mountain* S Peru
Amposta 93 F2 Cataluña, NE Spain
Amraoti *see* Amrāvati
Amrāvati 134 D4 *prev.* Amraoti. Mahārāshtra, C India
Amritsar 134 D2 Punjab, N India
Amstelveen 86 C3 Noord-Holland, C Netherlands
Amsterdam 86 C3 *country capital* (Netherlands) Noord-Holland, C Netherlands
Amsterdam Island 141 C6 *island* NE French Southern and Antarctic Territories
Am Timan 76 C3 Salamat, SE Chad
Amu Darya 122 D2 *Rus.* Amudar'ya, *Taj.* Dar"yoi Amu, *Turkm.* Amyderya, *Uzb.* Amudaryo; *anc.* Oxus. *river* C Asia
Amu-Dar'ya *see* Amyderýa
Amudar'ya/Amudaryo/Amu, Dar"yoi *see* Amu Darya
Amul *see* Āmol
Amund Ringnes Island 37 F2 *Island* Nunavut, N Canada
Amundsen Basin *see* Fram Basin
Amundsen Plain 154 A4 *abyssal plain* S Pacific Ocean
Amundsen-Scott 154 B3 *US research station* Antarctica
Amundsen Sea 154 A4 *sea* S Pacific Ocean
Amuntai 138 D4 *prev.* Amoentai. Borneo, C Indonesia
Amur 115 G4 *Chin.* Heilong Jiang. *river* China/Russian Federation
Amvrosiyevka *see* Amvrosiyivka
Amvrosiyivka 109 H3 *Rus.* Amvrosiyevka. Donets'ka Oblast', SE Ukraine
Amyderýa 123 E3 *Rus.* Amu-Dar'ya. Lebap Welaýaty, NE Turkmenistan
Amyderya *see* Amu Darya
Amýntaio 104 B4 *var.* Amindeo; *prev.* Amíndaion. Dytiki Makedonía, N Greece
Anabar 115 E2 *river* NE Russian Federation
An Abhainn Mhór *see* Blackwater
Anaco 59 E2 Anzoátegui, NE Venezuela
Anaconda 44 B2 Montana, NW USA
Anacortes 46 B1 Washington, NW USA
Anadolu Dağları *see* Doğu Karadeniz Dağları
Anadyr' 115 H1 Chukotskiy Avtonomnyy Okrug, NE Russian Federation
Anadyr' 115 G1 *river* NE Russian Federation
Anadyr, Gulf of 115 H1 *Eng.* Gulf of Anadyr. *gulf* NE Russian Federation
Anadyr, Gulf of *see* Anadyrskiy Zaliv
Anáfi 105 D7 *anc.* Anaphe. *island* Kykládes, Greece, Aegean Sea
'Ānah *see* 'Annah
Anaheim 46 E2 California, W USA
Anaiza *see* 'Unayzah
Analalava 79 G2 Mahajanga, NW Madagascar
Anamur 116 C5 İçel, S Turkey
Anantapur 132 C2 Andhra Pradesh, S India
Anaphe *see* Anáfi
Anápolis 63 F3 Goiás, C Brazil
Anār 120 D3 Kermān, C Iran
Anatolia 116 C4 *plateau* C Turkey
Anatom *see* Aneityum
Añatuya 64 C3 Santiago del Estero, N Argentina
An Bhearú *see* Barrow
Anchorage 36 C3 Alaska, USA
Ancona 96 C3 Marche, C Italy
Ancud 65 B6 *prev.* San Carlos de Ancud. Los Lagos, S Chile
Ancyra *see* Ankara
Åndalsnes 85 A5 Møre og Romsdal, S Norway

Andalucía 92 D4 *cultural region* S Spain
Andalusia 42 C3 Alabama, S USA
Andaman Islands 124 B4 *island group* India, NE Indian Ocean
Andaman Sea 124 C4 *sea* NE Indian Ocean
Andenne 87 C6 Namur, SE Belgium
Anderlues 87 B7 Hainaut, S Belgium
Anderson 40 C4 Indiana, N USA
Andes 64 B3 *mountain range* W South America
Andhra Pradesh 135 E5 *cultural region* E India
Andijon 123 F2 *Rus.* Andizhan. Andijon Viloyati, E Uzbekistan
Andikíthira *see* Antikýthira
Andipaxi *see* Antípaxoi
Andípsara *see* Antípsara
Ándissa *see* Ántissa
Andizhan *see* Andijon
Andkhvóy 122 D3 *prev.* Andkhvoy. Fāryāb, N Afghanistan
Andorra 91 A7 *off.* Principality of Andorra, *Cat.* Valls d'Andorra, Vallée d'Andorre. *country* SW Europe

ANDORRA
Southwest Europe

Official name Principality of Andorra
Formation 1278 / 1278
Capital Andorra la Vella
Population 85,082 / 473 people per sq mile (183 people per sq km)
Total area 181 sq. miles (468 sq. km)
Languages Spanish, Catalan*, French, Portuguese
Religions Roman Catholic 94%, Other 6%
Ethnic mix Spanish 46%, Andorran 28%, Other 18%, French 8%
Government Parliamentary system
Currency Euro = 100 cents
Literacy rate 99%
Calorie consumption Not available

Andorra *see* Andorra la Vella
Andorra la Vella 91 A8 *var.* Andorra, *Fr.* Andorre la Vielle, *Sp.* Andorra la Vieja. *country capital* (Andorra) C Andorra
Andorra la Vieja *see* Andorra la Vella
Andorra, Principality of *see* Andorra
Andorra, Valls d'/Andorra, Vallée d' *see* Andorra
Andorre la Vielle *see* Andorra la Vella
Andover 89 D7 S England, United Kingdom
Andøya 84 C2 *island* C Norway
Andreanof Islands 36 A3 *island group* Aleutian Islands, Alaska, USA
Andrews 49 E3 Texas, SW USA
Andrew Tablemount 140 A4 *var.* Gora Andryu. *seamount* W Indian Ocean
Andria 97 D5 Puglia, SE Italy
An Droichead Nua *see* Newbridge
Andropov *see* Rybinsk
Ándros 105 D6 Ándros, Kykládes, Greece, Aegean Sea
Ándros 105 C6 *island* Kykládes, Greece, Aegean Sea
Andros Island 54 B2 *island* NW Bahamas
Andros Town 54 C1 Andros Island, NW Bahamas
Andryu, Gora *see* Andrew Tablemount
Aneityum 144 D5 *var.* Anatom; *prev.* Kéamu. *island* S Vanuatu
Ánewetak *see* Enewetak Atoll
Angara 115 E4 *river* C Russian Federation
Angarsk 115 E4 Irkutskaya Oblast', S Russian Federation
Ånge 85 C5 Västernorrland, C Sweden
Ángel de la Guarda, Isla 50 B2 *island* NW Mexico
Angeles 139 E1 *off.* Angeles City. Luzon, N Philippines
Angeles City *see* Angeles
Angel Falls 59 E3 *Eng.* Angel Falls. *waterfall* E Venezuela
Angel Falls *see* Ángel, Salto
Angerburg *see* Węgorzewo
Ångermanälven 84 C4 *river* N Sweden
Angermünde 94 D3 Brandenburg, NE Germany
Angers 90 B4 *anc.* Juliomagus. Maine-et-Loire, NW France
Anglesey 89 C5 *island* NW Wales, United Kingdom

Anglet 91 A6 Pyrénées-Atlantiques, SW France
Angleton 49 H4 Texas, SW USA
Anglia *see* England
Anglo-Egyptian Sudan *see* Sudan
Angmagssalik *see* Ammassalik
Ang Nam Ngum 136 C4 *lake* C Laos
Angola 78 B2 *off.* Republic of Angola; *prev.* People's Republic of Angola, Portuguese West Africa. *country* SW Africa

ANGOLA
Southern Africa

Official name Republic of Angola
Formation 1975 / 1975
Capital Luanda
Population 16.9 million / 41 people per sq mile (16 people per sq km)
Total area 481,351 sq. miles (1,246,700 sq. km)
Languages Portuguese*, Umbundu, Kimbundu, Kikongo
Religions Roman Catholic 68%, Protestant 20%, Indigenous beliefs 12%
Ethnic mix Ovimbundu 37%, Other 25%, Kimbundu 25%, Bakongo 13%
Government Presidential system
Currency Readjusted kwanza = 100 lwei
Literacy rate 70%
Calorie consumption 2079 kilocalories

Angola Basin 69 B5 *undersea basin* E Atlantic Ocean
Angola, People's Republic of *see* Angola
Angola, Republic of *see* Angola
Angora *see* Ankara
Angostura *see* Ciudad Bolívar
Angostura, Presa de la 51 G5 *reservoir* SE Mexico
Angoulême 91 B5 *anc.* Iculisma. Charente, W France
Angoumois 91 B5 *cultural region* W France
Angra Pequena *see* Lüderitz
Angren 123 F2 Toshkent Viloyati, E Uzbekistan
Anguilla 55 G3 *UK dependent territory* E West Indies
Anguilla Cays 54 B2 *islets* SW Bahamas
Anhui 128 C5 *var.* Anhui Sheng, Anhwei, Wan. *province* E China
Anhui Sheng/Anhwei Wan *see* Anhui
Anicium *see* le Puy
Anina 108 A4 *Ger.* Steierdorf, *Hung.* Stájerlakanina; *prev.* Stájerdorf-Anina, Steierdorf-Anina, Steyerlak-Anina. Caraş-Severin, SW Romania
Anjou 90 B4 *cultural region* NW France
Anjouan *see* Nzwani
Ankara 116 C3 *prev.* Angora; *anc.* Ancyra. *country capital* (Turkey) Ankara, C Turkey
Ankeny 45 F3 Iowa, C USA
Anklam 94 D2 Mecklenburg-Vorpommern, NE Germany
An Muir Cheilteach *see* Celtic Sea
Annaba 71 E1 *prev.* Bône. NE Algeria
An Nafud 120 B4 *desert* NW Saudi Arabia
'Annah 120 B3 *var.* 'Ānah. Al Anbār, NW Iraq
An Najaf 120 B3 *var.* Najaf. An Najaf, S Iraq
Annamite Mountains 136 D4 *var.* annamsescordillera, *Fr.* Chaîne Annamitique, *Lao.* Phou Louang. *mountain range* C Laos
Annamitique, Chaîne *see* Annamite Mountains
Annamses Cordillera *see* Annamite Mountains
Annapolis 41 F4 *state capital* Maryland, NE USA
Annapurna 135 E3 *mountain* C Nepal
An Náqúrah *see* En Nâqoûra
Ann Arbor 40 C3 Michigan, N USA
An Nāşiriyah 120 C3 *var.* Nasiriya. Dhī Qār, SE Iraq
Anneciacum *see* Annecy
Annecy 91 D5 *anc.* Anneciacum. Haute-Savoie, E France
An Níl al Abyaḍ *see* White Nile
An Níl al Azraq *see* Blue Nile
Anniston 42 D2 Alabama, S USA
Annotto Bay 54 B4 C Jamaica
An Ómaigh *see* Omagh

Anqing *128 D5* Anhui, E China
Anse La Raye *55 F1* NW Saint Lucia
Anshun *128 B6* Guizhou, S China
Ansongo *75 E3* Gao, E Mali
An Srath Bán *see* Strabane
Antakya *116 D4 anc.* Antioch, Antiochia. Hatay, S Turkey
Antalaha *79 G2* Antsirañana, NE Madagascar
Antalya *116 B4 prev.* Adalia; *anc.* Attaleia, *Bibl.* Attalia. Antalya, SW Turkey
Antalya, Gulf of *116 B4 var.* Gulf of Adalia, *Eng.* Gulf of Antalya. *gulf* SW Turkey
Antalya, Gulf of *see* Antalya Körfezi
Antananarivo *79 G3 prev.* Tananarive. *country capital* (Madagascar) Antananarivo, C Madagascar
Antarctica *154 B3 continent*
Antarctic Peninsula *154 A2 peninsula* Antarctica
Antep *see* Gaziantep
Antequera *92 D5 anc.* Anticaria, Antiquaria. Andalucía, S Spain
Antequera *see* Oaxaca
Antibes *91 D6 anc.* Antipolis. Alpes-Maritimes, SE France
Anticaria *see* Antequera
Anticosti, Île d' *39 F3 Eng.* Anticosti Island. *island* Québec, E Canada
Anticosti Island *see* Anticosti, Île d'
Antigua *55 G3 island* S Antigua and Barbuda, Leeward Islands
Antigua and Barbuda *55 G3 country* E West Indies

ANTIGUA & BARBUDA
West Indies

Official name Antigua and Barbuda
Formation 1981 / 1981
Capital St. John's
Population 89,018 / 524 people per sq mile (202 people per sq km)
Total area 170 sq. miles (442 sq. km)
Languages English*, English patois
Religions Anglican 45%, Other Protestant 42%, Roman Catholic 10%, Other 2%, Rastafarian 1%
Ethnic mix Black African 95%, Other 5%
Government Parliamentary system
Currency Eastern Caribbean dollar = 100 cents
Literacy rate 99%
Calorie consumption 2373 kilocalories

Antikythira *105 B7 var.* Andikíthira. *island* S Greece
Anti-Lebanon *118 B4 var.* Jebel esh Sharqi, *Ar.* Al Jabal ash Sharqī, *Fr.* Anti-Liban. *mountain range* Lebanon/Syria
Anti-Liban *see* Anti-Lebanon
Antioch *see* Antakya
Antiochia *see* Antakya
Antípaxoi *105 A5 var.* Andipaxi. *island* Iónia Nisiá, Greece, C Mediterranean Sea
Antipodes Islands *142 D5 island group* S New Zealand
Antipolis *see* Antibes
Antípsara *105 D5 var.* Andípsara. *island* E Greece
Antiquaria *see* Antequera
Ántissa *105 D5 var.* Ándissa. Lésvos, E Greece
An tIúr *see* Newry
Antivari *see* Bar
Antofagasta *64 B2* Antofagasta, N Chile
Antony *90 E2* Hauts-de-Seine, N France
An tSionainn *see* Shannon
Antsirañana *79 G2 province* N Madagascar
Antsohihy *79 G2* Mahajanga, NW Madagascar
An-tung *see* Dandong
Antwerpen *87 C5 Eng.* Antwerp, *Fr.* Anvers. Antwerpen, N Belgium
Anuradhapura *132 D3* North Central Province, C Sri Lanka
Anvers *see* Antwerpen
Anyang *128 C4* Henan, C China
A'nyêmaqên Shan *126 D4 mountain range* C China
Anykščiai *106 C4* Utena, E Lithuania
Anzio *97 C5* Lazio, C Italy
Ao Krung Thep *137 C5 var.* Krung Thep Mahanakhon, *Eng.* Bangkok. *country capital* (Thailand) Bangkok, C Thailand
Aomen *see* Macao
Aomori *130 D3* Aomori, Honshū, C Japan
Aóos *see* Vjosës, Lumi i
Aoraki *151 B6 prev.* Aorangi, Mount Cook. *mountain* South Island, New Zealand
Aorangi *see* Aoraki
Aosta *96 A1 anc.* Augusta Praetoria. Valle d'Aosta, NW Italy
Aoukâr *74 D3 var.* Aouker. *plateau* C Mauritania
Aouk, Bahr *76 C4 river* Central African Republic/Chad
Aouker *see* Aoukâr
Aozou *76 C1* Borkou-Ennedi-Tibesti, N Chad
Apalachee Bay *42 D3 bay* Florida, SE USA
Apalachicola River *42 D3 river* Florida, SE USA
Apamama *see* Abemama
Apaporis, Río *58 C4 river* Brazil/Colombia
Apatity *110 C2* Murmanskaya Oblast', NW Russian Federation
Ape *106 D3* NE Latvia
Apeldoorn *86 D3* Gelderland, E Netherlands
Apennines *96 E2 Eng.* Apennines. *mountain range* Italy/San Marino
Apennines *see* Appennino
Āpia *145 F4 country capital* (Samoa) Upolu, SE Samoa
Apkhazeti *117 E1 var.* Abkhazia; *prev.* Ap'khazet'i. *autonomous republic* NW Georgia
Ap'khazet'i *see* Apkhazeti
Apoera *59 G3* Sipaliwini, NW Suriname
Apostle Islands *40 B1 island group* Wisconsin, N USA
Appalachian Mountains *35 D5 mountain range* E USA
Appingedam *86 E1* Groningen, NE Netherlands
Appleton *40 B2* Wisconsin, N USA
Apulia *see* Puglia
Apure, Río *58 C2 river* W Venezuela
Apurímac, Río *60 D3 river* S Peru
Apuseni, Munții *108 A4 mountain range* W Romania
Aqaba/'Aqaba *see* Al 'Aqabah
Aqaba, Gulf of *120 A4 var.* Gulf of Elat, *Ar.* Khalīj al 'Aqabah; *anc.* Sinus Aelaniticus. *gulf* NE Red Sea
'Aqabah, Khalīj al *see* Aqaba, Gulf of
Āqchah *123 E3 var.* Āqcheh. Jowzjān, N Afghanistan
Āqcheh *see* Āqchah
Aqmola *see* Astana
Aqtöbe *see* Aktobe
Aquae Augustae *see* Dax
Aquae Calidae *see* Bath
Aquae Flaviae *see* Chaves
Aquae Grani *see* Aachen
Aquae Sextiae *see* Aix-en-Provence
Aquae Solis *see* Bath
Aquae Tarbelicae *see* Dax
Aquidauana *63 E4* Mato Grosso do Sul, S Brazil
Aquila/Aquila degli Abruzzi *see* L'Aquila
Aquisgranum *see* Aachen
Aquitaine *91 B6 cultural region* SW France
'Arabah, Wadi al *119 B7 Heb.* Ha'Arava. *dry watercourse* Israel/Jordan
Arabian Basin *124 A4 undersea basin* N Arabian Sea
Arabian Desert *see* Sahara el Sharqîya
Arabian Peninsula *121 B5 peninsula* SW Asia
Arabian Sea *124 A3 sea* NW Indian Ocean
Arabicus, Sinus *see* Red Sea
'Arabī, Khalīj al *see* Persian Gulf
'Arabīyah as Su'ūdīyah, Al Mamlakah al *see* Saudi Arabia
'Arabīyah Jumhūrīyah, Miṣr al *see* Egypt
Arab Republic of Egypt *see* Egypt
Aracaju *63 G3 state capital* Sergipe, E Brazil
Araçuai *63 F3* Minas Gerais, SE Brazil
Arad *119 B7* Southern, S Israel
Arad *108 A4* Arad, W Romania
Arafura Sea *142 A3 Ind.* Laut Arafuru. *sea* W Pacific Ocean
Arafuru, Laut *see* Arafura Sea
Aragón *93 E2 autonomous community* E Spain
Araguaia, Río *63 E3 var.* Araguaya. *river* C Brazil
Araguari *63 F3* Minas Gerais, SE Brazil
Araguaya *see* Araguaia, Río
Ara Jovis *see* Aranjuez
Arāk *120 C3 prev.* Sultānābād. Markazī, W Iran
Arakan Yoma *136 A3 mountain range* W Myanmar (Burma)
Araks/Arak's *see* Aras
Aral *see* Aralsk, Kazakhstan
Aral Sea *122 C1 Kaz.* Aral Tengizi, *Rus.* Aral'skoye More, *Uzb.* Orol Dengizi. *inland sea* Kazakhstan/Uzbekistan
Aral'sk *114 B4 Kaz.* Aral. Kzylorda, SW Kazakhstan
Aral'skoye More/Aral Tengizi *see* Aral Sea
Aranda de Duero *92 D2* Castilla y León, N Spain
Aranđelovac *100 D4 prev.* Arandjelovac. Serbia, C Serbia
Arandjelovac *see* Aranđelovac
Aranjuez *92 D3 anc.* Ara Jovis. Madrid, C Spain
Araouane *75 E2* Tombouctou, N Mali
'Ar'ar *120 B3* Al Ḥudūd ash Shamālīyah, NW Saudi Arabia
Mount Ararat *117 F3 var.* Aghri Dagh, Agri Dagi, Koh I Noh, Masis, *Eng.* Great Ararat, Mount Ararat. *mountain* E Turkey
Ararat, Mount *see* Büyükağrı Dağı
Aras *117 G3 Arm.* Arak's, *Az.* Araz Nehri, *Per.* Rūd-e Aras, *Rus.* Araks; *prev.* Araxes. *river* SW Asia
Aras, Rūd-e *see* Aras
Arauca *58 C2* Arauca, NE Colombia
Arauca, Río *58 C2 river* Colombia/Venezuela
Arausio *see* Orange
Araxes *see* Aras
Araz Nehri *see* Aras
Arbela *see* Arbīl
Arbīl *120 B2 var.* Erbil, Irbīl, *Kurd.* Hawlēr; *anc.* Arbela. Arbīl, N Iraq
Arbroath *88 D3 anc.* Aberbrothock. E Scotland, United Kingdom
Arbuzinka *see* Arbuzynka
Arbuzynka *109 E3 Rus.* Arbuzinka. Mykolayivs'ka Oblast', S Ukraine
Arcachon *91 B5* Gironde, SW France
Arcae Remorum *see* Châlons-en-Champagne
Arcata *46 A4* California, W USA
Archangel *see* Arkhangel'sk
Archangel Bay *see* Chëshskaya Guba
Archidona *92 D5* Andalucía, S Spain
Arco *96 C2* Trentino-Alto Adige, N Italy
Arctic Mid Oceanic Ridge *see* Nansen Cordillera
Arctic Ocean *155 B3 ocean*
Arda *104 C3 var.* Ardhas, *Gk.* Ardas. *river* Bulgaria/Greece
Ardabīl *120 C2 var.* Ardebil. Ardabīl, NW Iran
Ardakān *120 D3* Yazd, C Iran
Ardas *104 D3 var.* Ardhas, *Bul.* Arda. *river* Bulgaria/Greece
Arḍ aṣ Ṣawwān *119 C7 var.* Ardh es Suwwān. *plain* S Jordan
Ardeal *see* Transylvania
Ardebil *see* Ardabīl
Ardèche *91 C5 cultural region* E France
Ardennes *87 C8 physical region* Belgium/France
Ardhas *see* Arda/Ardas
Ardh es Suwwān *see* Arḍ aṣ Ṣawwān
Ardino *104 D3* Kŭrdzhali, S Bulgaria
Ard Mhacha *see* Armagh
Ardmore *49 G2* Oklahoma, C USA
Arel *see* Arlon
Arelas/Arelate *see* Arles
Arendal *85 A6* Aust-Agder, S Norway
Arensburg *see* Kuressaare
Arenys de Mar *93 G2* Cataluña, NE Spain
Areópoli *105 B7 prev.* Areópolis. Pelopónnisos, S Greece
Areópolis *see* Areópoli
Arequipa *61 E4* Arequipa, SE Peru
Arezzo *96 C3 anc.* Arretium. Toscana, C Italy
Argalastí *105 C5* Thessalía, C Greece
Argenteuil *90 D1* Val-d'Oise, N France
Argentina *65 B5 off.* Argentine Republic. *country* S South America

ARGENTINA
South America

Official name The Argentine Republic
Formation 1816 / 1816
Capital Buenos Aires
Population 40.8 million / 39 people per sq mile (15 people per sq km)
Total area 1,068,296 sq. miles (2,766,890 sq. km)
Languages Spanish*, Italian, Amerindian languages
Religions Roman Catholic 70%, Other 18%, Protestant 9%, Muslim 2%, Jewish 2%
Ethnic mix Indo-European 97%, Mestizo 2%, Amerindian 1%
Government Presidential system
Currency Argentine peso = 100 centavos
Literacy rate 98%
Calorie consumption 2918 kilocalories

Argentina Basin *see* Argentine Basin
Argentine Basin *57 C7 var.* Argentina Basin. *undersea basin* SW Atlantic Ocean
Argentine Republic *see* Argentina
Argentine Rise *see* Falkland Plateau
Argentoratum *see* Strasbourg
Darya-ye Arghandab *123 E5 river* SE Afghanistan
Argirocastro *see* Gjirokastër
Argo *72 B3* Northern, N Sudan
Argo Fracture Zone *141 C5 tectonic Feature* C Indian Ocean
Árgos *105 B6* Pelopónnisos, S Greece
Argostóli *105 A5 var.* Argostólion. Kefallonía, Iónia Nisiá, Greece, C Mediterranean Sea
Argostólion *see* Argostóli
Argun *125 E1 Chin.* Ergun He, *Rus.* Argun'. *river* China/Russian Federation
Argyrokastron *see* Gjirokastër
Århus *85 B7 var.* Aarhus. Midtjylland, C Denmark
Aria *see* Herāt
Ari Atoll *132 A4 var.* Alifu Atoll. *atoll* C Maldives
Arica *64 B1 hist.* San Marcos de Arica. Arica y Parinacota, N Chile
Aridaía *104 B3 var.* Aridea, Aridhaía. Dytikí Makedonía, N Greece
Aridea *see* Aridaía
Aridhaía *see* Aridaía
Arīhā *118 B3* Al Karak, W Jordan
Arīḥā *see* Jericho
Ariminum *see* Rimini
Arinsal *91 A7* NW Andorra Europe
Arizona *48 A2 off.* State of Arizona, *also known as* Copper State, Grand Canyon State. *state* SW USA
Arkansas *42 A1 off.* State of Arkansas, *also known as* The Land of Opportunity. *state* S USA
Arkansas City *45 F5* Kansas, C USA
Arkansas River *49 G1 river* C USA
Arkhangel'sk *114 B2 Eng.* Archangel. Arkhangel'skaya Oblast', NW Russian Federation
Arkoí *105 E6 island* Dodekánisa, Greece, Aegean Sea
Arles *91 D6 var.* Arles-sur-Rhône; *anc.* Arelas, Arelate. Bouches-du-Rhône, SE France
Arles-sur-Rhône *see* Arles
Arlington *49 G2* Texas, SW USA
Arlington *41 E4* Virginia, NE USA
Arlon *87 D8 Dut.* Aarlen, *Ger.* Arel, *Lat.* Orolaunum. Luxembourg, SE Belgium
Armagh *89 B5 Ir.* Ard Mhacha. S Northern Ireland, United Kingdom
Armagnac *91 B6 cultural region* S France
Armenia *58 B3* Quindío, W Colombia
Armenia *117 F3 off.* Republic of Armenia, *var.* Ajastan, *Arm.* Hayastani Hanrapetut'yun; *prev.* Armenian Soviet Socialist Republic. *country* SW Asia

ARMENIA
Southwest Asia

Official name Republic of Armenia
Formation 1991 / 1991

ARMENIA
(continued)

Capital Yerevan
Population 3.1 million / 269 people
per sq mile (104 people per sq km)
Total area 11,506 sq. miles (29,800 sq. km)
Languages Armenian*, Azeri, Russian
Religions Armenian Apostolic Church
(Orthodox) 88%, Other 6%, Armenian
Catholic Church 6%, Other 6%
Ethnic mix Armenian 98%, Other 1%,
Yezidi 1%
Government Parliamentary system
Currency Dram = 100 luma
Literacy rate 99%
Calorie consumption 2806 kilocalories

Armenian Soviet Socialist Republic
see Armenia
Armenia, Republic of *see* Armenia
Armidale 149 *D6* New South Wales,
SE Australia
Armstrong 38 *B3* Ontario, S Canada
Armyans'k 109 *F4 Rus.* Armyansk.
Avtonomna Respublika Krym,
S Ukraine
Arnaía 104 *C4 Cont.* Arnea. Kentrikí
Makedonía, N Greece
Arnaud 82 *A3 river* Québec, E Canada
Arnea *see* Arnaía
Arnedo 93 *E2* La Rioja, N Spain
Arnhem 86 *D4* Gelderland,
SE Netherlands
Arnhem Land 148 *A2 physical region*
Northern Territory, N Australia
Arno 96 *B3 river* C Italy
Arnold 45 *G4* Missouri, C USA
Arnswalde *see* Choszczno
Aroe Islands *see* Aru, Kepulauan
Arorae 145 *E3 atoll* Tungaru,
W Kiribati
Arrabona *see* Győr
Ar Rahad *see* Er Rahad
Ar Ramādī 120 *C4 var.* Ramadi,
Rumadiya. Al Anbār, SW Iraq
Ar Rāmi 118 *C4* Ḩimṣ, C Syria
Ar Ramtha 119 *B5 var.* Ramtha. Irbid,
N Jordan
Arran, Isle of 88 *C4 island* SW Scotland,
United Kingdom
Ar Raqqah 118 *C2 var.* Rakka; *anc.*
Nicephorium. Ar Raqqah, N Syria
Arras 90 *C2 anc.* Nemetocenna. Pas-de-
Calais, N France
Ar Rawdatayn 120 *C4 var.* Raudhatain.
N Kuwait
Arretium *see* Arezzo
Arriaca *see* Guadalajara
Arriaga 51 *G5* Chiapas, SE Mexico
Ar Riyāḍ 121 *C5 Eng.* Riyadh. *country
capital* (Saudi Arabia) Ar Riyāḍ,
C Saudi Arabia
Ar Rub 'al Khali 121 *C6 Eng.* Empty
Quarter, Great Sandy Desert. *desert*
SW Asia
Ar Rustāq 121 *E5 var.* Rostak, Rustaq.
N Oman
Ar Ruṭbah 120 *B3 var.* Rutba. Al Anbār,
SW Iraq
Árta 105 *A5 anc.* Ambracia. Ípeiros,
W Greece
Artashat 117 *F3* S Armenia
Artemisa 54 *B2* La Habana, W Cuba
Artesia 48 *D3* New Mexico, SW USA
Arthur's Pass 151 *C6 pass* South Island,
New Zealand
Artigas 64 *D3 prev.* San Eugenio,
San Eugenio del Cuareim. Artigas,
N Uruguay
Art'ik 117 *F2* W Armenia
Artois 90 *C2 cultural region* N France
Artsiz *see* Artsyz
Artsyz 108 *D4 Rus.* Artsiz. Odes'ka
Oblast', SW Ukraine
Artvin 117 *F2* Artvin, NE Turkey
Arua 73 *B6* NW Uganda
Aruba 58 *C1 var.* Oruba. *Dutch
autonomous region* S West Indies
Aru Islands *see* Aru, Kepulauan
Aru, Kepulauan 139 *G4 Eng.* Aru
Islands; *prev.* Aroe Islands. *island
group* E Indonesia
Arunāchal Pradesh 135 *G3 prev.* North
East Frontier Agency, North East
Frontier Agency of Assam. *cultural
region* NE India
Arusha 73 *C7* Arusha, N Tanzania

Arviat 37 *G4 prev.* Eskimo Point.
Nunavut, C Canada
Arvidsjaur 84 *C4* Norrbotten, N Sweden
'Arys' 114 *B5 prev.* Arys'. Yuzhnyy
Kazakhstan, S Kazakhstan
Arys' *see* 'Arys'
Asadābād 123 *F4 var.* Asaḍābād; *prev.*
Chaghasarāy. Kunar, E Afghanistan
Asaḍābād *see* Asadābād
Asahi-dake 130 *D2 mountain* Hokkaidō,
N Japan
Asahikawa 130 *D2* Hokkaidō, N Japan
Asamankese 75 *E5* SE Ghana
Āsānsol 135 *F4* West Bengal, NE India
Asben *see* Aïr, Massif de l'
Ascension Fracture Zone 69 *A5 tectonic
Feature* C Atlantic Ocean
Ascension Island 67 *C5 dependency of
St.Helena* C Atlantic Ocean
Ascoli Piceno 96 *C4 anc.* Asculum
Picenum. Marche, C Italy
Asculum Picenum *see* Ascoli Piceno
'Aseb 72 *D4 var.* Assab, *Amh.* Āseb.
SE Eritrea
Assen 86 *E2* Drenthe, NE Netherlands
A Serra de Outes 92 *B1* Galicia,
NW Spain
Aşgabat 122 *C3 prev.* Ashgabat,
Ashkhabad, Poltoratsk. *country
capital* (Turkmenistan) Ahal Welaýaty,
C Turkmenistan
Ashara *see* Al 'Ashārah
Ashburton 151 *C6* Canterbury, South
Island, New Zealand
Ashburton River 146 *A4 river* Western
Australia
Ashdod 119 *A6 anc.* Azotos, *Lat.* Azotus.
Central, W Israel
Asheville 43 *E1* North Carolina, SE USA
Ashgabat *see* Aşgabat
Ashkelon 119 *A6 prev.* Ashqelon.
Southern, C Israel
Ashkhabad *see* Aşgabat
Ashland 46 *B4* Oregon, NW USA
Ashland 40 *B1* Wisconsin, N USA
Ashmore and Cartier Islands 142 *A3
Australian external territory* E Indian
Ocean
Ashmyany 107 *C5 Rus.* Oshmyany.
Hrodzyenskaya Voblasts', W Belarus
Ashqelon *see* Ashkelon
Ash Shaddādah 118 *D2 var.* Ash
Shaddādah, Jisr ash Shadadi, Shaddādi,
Shedadi, Tell Shedadi. Al Ḩasakah,
NE Syria
Ash Shaddādah *see* Ash Shaddādah
Ash Sharah 119 *B7 var.* Esh Sharā.
mountain range W Jordan
Ash Shāriqah 120 *D4 Eng.* Sharjah. Ash
Shāriqah, NE United Arab Emirates
Ash Shawbak 119 *B7* Ma'ān, W Jordan
Ash Shiḩr 121 *C6* SW Yemen
Asia 112 *continent*
Asinara 96 *A4 island* W Italy
Asipovichy 107 *D6 Rus.* Osipovichi.
Mahilyowskaya Voblasts', C Belarus
Aşkale 117 *E3* Erzurum, NE Turkey
Askersund 85 *C6* Örebro, C Sweden
Asmara *see* Asmera
Asmera 72 *C4 var.* Asmara. *country
capital* (Eritrea) C Eritrea
Aspadana *see* Eşfahān
Asphaltites, Lacus *see* Dead Sea
Aspinwall *see* Colón
Assab *see* 'Aseb
As Sabkhah 118 *D2 var.* Sabkha. Ar
Raqqah, NE Syria
As Salamīyah *see* Salamīyah
'Assal, Lac 68 *E4 lake* C Djibouti
As Salṭ 119 *B6 var.* Salt. Al Balqā',
NW Jordan
Assamaka *see* Assamakka
Assamakka 75 *F2 var.* Assamaka.
Agadez, NW Niger
As Samāwah 120 *B3 var.* Samawa. Al
Muthanná, S Iraq
Assenede 87 *B5* Oost-Vlaanderen,
NW Belgium
Assiout *see* Asyūṭ
Assiut *see* Asyūṭ
Assling *see* Jesenice
Assouan *see* Aswān
Assu 63 *G2 var.* Açu. Rio Grande do
Norte, E Brazil

Assuan *see* Aswān
As Sukhnah 118 *C3 var.* Sukhne, *Fr.*
Soukhné. Ḩimṣ, C Syria
As Sulaymāniyah 120 *C3 var.*
Sulaimaniya, *Kurd.* Slēmānī. As
Sulaymāniyah, NE Iraq
As Sulayyil 121 *B5* Ar Riyāḍ, S Saudi
Arabia
Aş Şuwār 118 *D2 var.* Şuwār. Dayr az
Zawr, E Syria
As Suwaydā' 119 *B5 var.* El Suweida,
Es Suweida, Suweida, *Fr.* Soueida. As
Suwaydā', SW Syria
As Suways *see* Suez
Asta Colonia *see* Asti
Astacus *see* İzmit
Astana 114 *C4 prev.* Akmola,
Akmolinsk, Tselinograd, Aqmola.
country capital (Kazakhstan) Akmola,
N Kazakhstan
Asta Pompeia *see* Asti
Astarabad *see* Gorgān
Asterābād *see* Gorgān
Asti 96 *A2 anc.* Asta Colonia, Asta
Pompeia, Hasta Colonia, Hasta
Pompeia. Piemonte, NW Italy
Astigi *see* Ecija
Astipálaia *see* Astypálaia
Astorga 92 *C1 anc.* Asturica Augusta.
Castilla y León, N Spain
Astrabad *see* Gorgān
Astrakhan' 111 *C7* Astrakhanskaya
Oblast', SW Russian Federation
Asturias 92 *C1 autonomous community*
NW Spain
Asturias *see* Oviedo
Asturica Augusta *see* Astorga
Astypálaia 105 *D7 var.* Astipálaia, *It.*
Stampalia. *island* Kykládes, Greece,
Aegean Sea
Asunción 64 *D2 country capital*
(Paraguay) Central, S Paraguay
Aswān 72 *B2 var.* Assouan, Assuan,
Aswân; *anc.* Syene. SE Egypt
Aswân *see* Aswān
Asyūṭ 72 *B2 var.* Assiout, Assiut, Asyût,
Siut; *anc.* Lycopolis. C Egypt
Asyût *see* Asyūṭ
Atacama Desert 64 *B2 Eng.* Atacama
Desert. *desert* N Chile
Atacama Desert *see* Atacama, Desierto de
Atafu Atoll 145 *E3 island* NW Tokelau
Atamyrat 122 *D3 prev.* Kerki. Lebap
Welaýaty, E Turkmenistan
Aṭār 74 *C2* Adrar, W Mauritania
Atas Bogd 126 *D3 mountain*
SW Mongolia
Atascadero 47 *B7* California, W USA
Atbara 72 *C3 var.* 'Aṭbārah. River Nile,
NE Sudan
'Aṭbārah/'Aṭbarah, Nahr *see* Atbara
Atbasar 114 *C4* Akmola,
N Kazakhstan
Atchison 45 *F4* Kansas, C USA
Aternum *see* Pescara
Ath 87 *B6 var.* Aat. Hainaut, SW Belgium
Athabasca 37 *E5* Alberta, SW Canada
Athabasca 37 *E5 var.* Athabaska. *river*
Alberta, SW Canada
Athabasca, Lake 37 *F4 lake* Alberta/
Saskatchewan, SW Canada
Athabaska *see* Athabasca
Athenae *see* Athína
Athens 43 *E2* Georgia, SE USA
Athens 40 *D4* Ohio, N USA
Athens 49 *G3* Texas, SW USA
Athens *see* Athína
Atherton 148 *D3* Queensland,
NE Australia
Athína 105 *C6 Eng.* Athens, *prev.*
Athínai; *anc.* Athenae. *country capital*
(Greece) Attikí, C Greece
Athínai *see* Athína
Athlone 89 *B5 Ir.* Baile Átha Luain.
C Ireland
Ath Thawrah *see* Madinat ath Thawrah
Ati 76 *C3* Batha, C Chad
Atikokan 38 *B4* Ontario, S Canada
Atka 115 *G3* Magadanskaya Oblast',
E Russian Federation
Atka 36 *A3* Atka Island, Alaska, USA
Atlanta 42 *D2 state capital* Georgia,
SE USA
Atlanta 49 *H2* Texas, SW USA
Atlantic City 41 *F4* New Jersey, NE USA
Atlantic-Indian Basin 67 *D7 undersea
basin* SW Indian Ocean

Atlantic-Indian Ridge 69 *B8 undersea
ridge* SW Indian Ocean
Atlantic Ocean 66 *B4 ocean*
Atlas Mountains 70 *C2 mountain range*
NW Africa
Atlasovo 115 *H3* Kamchatskiy Kray,
E Russian Federation
Atlas, Tell 102 *C3 Eng.* Tell Atlas.
mountain range N Algeria
Atlas, Tell *see* Atlas Tellien
Atlin 36 *D4* British Columbia, W Canada
Aṭ Ṭafīlah 119 *B7 var.* Et Tafila, Tafila.
Aṭ Ṭafīlah, W Jordan
Aṭ Ṭā'if 121 *B5* Makkah, W Saudi Arabia
Attaleia/Attalia *see* Antalya
At Tall al Abyaḍ 118 *C2 var.* Tall al
Abyaḍ, Tell Abyaḍ, Tell Abiad. Ar
Raqqah, N Syria
Aṭ Ṭanf 118 *D4* Ḩimṣ, S Syria
Attapu 137 *E5 var.* Attopeu, Samakhixai.
Attapu, S Laos
Attawapiskat 38 *C3* Ontario, C Canada
Attawapiskat 38 *C3 river* Ontario,
S Canada
At Tibnī 118 *D2 var.* Tibni. Dayr az
Zawr, NE Syria
Attopeu *see* Attapu
Attu Island 36 *A2 island* Aleutian
Islands, Alaska, USA
Atyrau 114 *B4 prev.* Gur'yev. Atyrau,
W Kazakhstan
Aubagne 91 *D6 anc.* Albania. Bouches-
du-Rhône, SE France
Aubange 87 *D8* Luxembourg,
SE Belgium
Aubervilliers 90 *E1* Seine-St-Denis,
Île-de-France, N France Europe
Auburn 46 *B2* Washington, NW USA
Auch 91 *B6 Lat.* Augusta Auscorum,
Elimberrum. Gers, S France
Auckland 150 *D2* Auckland, North
Island, New Zealand
Auckland Islands 142 *C5 island group*
S New Zealand
Audern *see* Audru
Audincourt 90 *E4* Doubs, E France
Audru 106 *D2 Ger.* Audern. Pärnumaa,
SW Estonia
Augathella 149 *D5* Queensland,
E Australia
Augsbourg *see* Augsburg
Augsburg 95 *C6 Fr.* Augsbourg; *anc.*
Augusta Vindelicorum. Bayern,
S Germany
Augusta 147 *A7* Western Australia
Augusta 43 *E2* Georgia, SE USA
Augusta 41 *G2 state capital* Maine,
NE USA
Augusta *see* London
Augusta Auscorum *see* Auch
Augusta Emerita *see* Mérida
Augusta Praetoria *see* Aosta
Augusta Trajana *see* Stara Zagora
Augusta Treverorum *see* Trier
Augusta Vangionum *see* Worms
Augusta Vindelicorum *see* Augsburg
Augustobona Tricassium *see* Troyes
Augustodurum *see* Bayeux
Augustoritum Lemovicensium *see*
Limoges
Augustów 98 *E2 Rus.* Avgustov.
Podlaskie, NE Poland
Aulie Ata/Auliye-Ata *see* Taraz
Aunglan 136 *B4 var.* Allanmyo, Myaydo.
Magway, C Myanmar (Burma)
Auob 78 *B4 var.* Oup. *river* Namibia/
South Africa
Aurangābād 134 *D5* Mahārāshtra,
C India
Auray 90 *A3* Morbihan, NW France
Aurelia Aquensis *see* Baden-Baden
Aurelianum *see* Orléans
Aurès, Massif de l' 102 *C4 mountain
range* NE Algeria
Aurillac 91 *C5* Cantal, C France
Aurium *see* Ourense
Aurora 59 *F2* NW Guyana
Aurora 44 *D4* Colorado, C USA
Aurora 40 *B3* Illinois, N USA
Aurora 45 *G5* Missouri, C USA
Aurora *see* Maéwo, Vanuatu
Ausa *see* Vic
Aussig *see* Ústí nad Labem
Austin 45 *G3* Minnesota, N USA
Austin 49 *G3 state capital* Texas, SW USA
Australes, Archipel des *see* Australes, Îles
**Australes et Antarctiques Françaises,
Terres** *see* French Southern and
Antarctic Territories

Australes, Îles 143 F4 var. Archipel des Australes, Îles Tubuai, Tubuai Islands, Eng. Austral Islands. island group SW French Polynesia

Austral Fracture Zone 143 H4 tectonic feature S Pacific Ocean

Australia 142 A4 off. Commonwealth of Australia. country

AUSTRALIA
Australasia & Oceania

Official name Commonwealth of Australia
Formation 1901 / 1901
Capital Canberra
Population 22.6 million / 8 people per sq mile (3 people per sq km)
Total area 2,967,893 sq. miles (7,686,850 sq. km)
Languages English*, Italian, Cantonese, Greek, Arabic, Vietnamese, Aboriginal languages
Religions Roman Catholic 26%, Nonreligious 19%, Anglican 19%, Other 17%, Other Christian 13%, United Church 6%
Ethnic mix European 92%, Asian 7%, Aboriginal and other 1%
Government Parliamentary system
Currency Australian dollar = 100 cents
Literacy rate 99%
Calorie consumption 3261 kilocalories

Australia, Commonwealth of see Australia

Australian Alps 149 C7 mountain range SE Australia

Australian Capital Territory 149 D7 prev. Federal Capital Territory. territory SE Australia

Australie, Bassin Nord de l' see North Australian Basin

Austral Islands see Australes, Îles

Austrava see Ostrov

Austria 95 D7 off. Republic of Austria, Ger. Österreich. country C Europe

AUSTRIA
Central Europe

Official name Republic of Austria
Formation 1918 / 1919
Capital Vienna
Population 8.4 million / 263 people per sq mile (102 people per sq km)
Total area 32,378 sq. miles (83,858 sq. km)
Languages German*, Croatian, Slovenian, Hungarian (Magyar)
Religions Roman Catholic 78%, Nonreligious 9%, Other (including Jewish and Muslim) 8%, Protestant 5%
Ethnic mix Austrian 93%, Croat, Slovene, and Hungarian 6%, Other 1%
Government Parliamentary system
Currency Euro = 100 cents
Literacy rate 99%
Calorie consumption 3800 kilocalories

Austria, Republic of see Austria

Autesiodorum see Auxerre

Autissiodorum see Auxerre

Autricum see Chartres

Auvergne 91 C5 cultural region C France

Auxerre 90 C4 anc. Autesiodorum, Autissiodorum. Yonne, C France

Avaricum see Bourges

Avarua 145 G5 dependent territory capital (Cook Islands) Rarotonga, S Cook Islands

Avasfelsöfalu see Negreşti-Oaş

Ávdira 104 C3 Anatolikí Makedonía kai Thráki, NE Greece

Aveiro 92 B2 anc. Talabriga. Aveiro, W Portugal

Avela see Ávila

Avellino 97 D5 anc. Abellinum. Campania, S Italy

Avenio see Avignon

Avesta 85 C6 Dalarna, C Sweden

Aveyron 91 C6 river S France

Avezzano 96 C4 Abruzzo, C Italy

Avgustov see Augustów

Aviemore 88 C3 N Scotland, United Kingdom

Avignon 91 D6 anc. Avenio. Vaucluse, SE France

Ávila 92 D3 var. Avila; anc. Abela, Abula, Abyla, Avela. Castilla y León, C Spain

Avilés 92 C1 Asturias, NW Spain

Avranches 90 B3 Manche, N France

Avveel see Ivalo, Finland

Avvil see Ivalo

Awaji-shima 131 C6 island SW Japan

Awash 73 D5 Afar, NE Ethiopia

Awbári 71 F3 SW Libya

Ax see Dax

Axel 87 B5 Zeeland, SW Netherlands

Axel Heiberg Island 37 E1 var. Axel Heiburg. island Nunavut, N Canada

Axel Heiburg see Axel Heiberg Island

Axiós see Vardar

Ayacucho 60 D4 Ayacucho, S Peru

Ayagoz 114 C5 var. Ayaguz, Kaz. Ayakoz. river E Kazakhstan

Ayamonte 92 C4 Andalucía, S Spain

Ayaviri 61 E4 Puno, S Peru

Aydarko'l Ko'li 123 E2 Rus. Ozero Aydarkul'. lake C Uzbekistan

Aydarkul', Ozero see Aydarko'l Ko'li

Aydın 116 A4 var. Aïdin; anc. Tralles Aydin. Aydın, SW Turkey

Ayers Rock see Uluṟu

Ayeyarwady see Irrawaddy

Ayiá see Agiá

Áyios Evstrátios see Ágios Efstrátios

Áyios Nikólaos see Ágios Nikólaos

Ayorou 75 E3 Tillabéri, W Niger

'Ayoûn el 'Atroûs 74 D3 var. Aïoun el Atrous, Aïoun el Atroûss. Hodh el Gharbi, SE Mauritania

Ayr 88 C4 W Scotland, United Kingdom

Ayteke Bi 114 B4 Kaz. Zhangaqazaly; prev. Novokazalinsk. Kzylorda, SW Kazakhstan

Aytos 104 E2 Burgas, E Bulgaria

Ayutthaya 137 C5 var. Phra Nakhon Si Ayutthaya. Phra Nakhon Si Ayutthaya, C Thailand

Ayvalık 116 A3 Balıkesir, W Turkey

Azahar, Costa del 93 F3 coastal region E Spain

Azaouâd 75 E3 desert C Mali

Azärbaycan/Azärbaycan Respublikasi see Azerbaijan

A'zäz 118 B2 Ḥalab, NW Syria

Azerbaijan 117 G2 off. Azerbaijani Republic, Az. Azärbaycan, Azärbaycan Respublikasi; prev. Azerbaijan SSR. country SE Asia

AZERBAIJAN
Southwest Asia

Official name Republic of Azerbaijan
Formation 1991 / 1991
Capital Baku
Population 9.3 million / 278 people per sq mile (107 people per sq km)
Total area 33,436 sq. miles (86,600 sq. km)
Languages Azeri*, Russian
Religions Shi'a Muslim 68%, Sunni Muslim 26%, Russian Orthodox 3%, Armenian Apostolic Church (Orthodox) 2%, Other 1%
Ethnic mix Azeri 91%, Other 3%, Lazs 2%, Armenian 2%, Russian 2%
Government Presidential system
Currency New manat = 100 gopik
Literacy rate 99%
Calorie consumption 3072 kilocalories

Azerbaijani Republic see Azerbaijan

Azerbaijan SSR see Azerbaijan

Azimabad see Patna

Azizie see Telish

Azogues 60 B2 Cañar, S Ecuador

Azores 92 A5 var. Açores, Ilhas dos Açores, Port. Arquipélago dos Açores. island group Portugal, NE Atlantic Ocean

Azores-Biscay Rise 80 A3 undersea rise E Atlantic Ocean

Azotos/Azotus see Ashdod

Azoum, Bahr 76 C3 seasonal river SE Chad

Azov, Sea of 103 H1 Rus. Azovskoye More, Ukr. Azovs'ke More. sea NE Black Sea

Azovs'ke More/Azovskoye More see Azov, Sea of

Azraq, Wāḥat as 119 C6 oasis N Jordan

Aztec 48 C1 New Mexico, SW USA

Azuaga 92 C4 Extremadura, W Spain

Azuero, Península de 53 F5 peninsula S Panama

Azul 65 D5 Buenos Aires, E Argentina

Azur, Côte d' 91 E6 coastal region SE France

'Azza see Gaza

Az Zaqāziq 72 B1 var. Zagazig. N Egypt

Az Zarqā' 119 B6 var. Zarqa. Az Zarqā', NW Jordan

Az Zāwiyah 71 F2 var. Zawia. NW Libya

Az Zilfi 120 B4 Ar Riyāḍ, N Saudi Arabia

B

Baalbek 118 B4 var. Ba'labakk; anc. Heliopolis. E Lebanon

Baardheere 73 D6 var. Bardere, It. Bardera. Gedo, SW Somalia

Baarle-Hertog 87 C5 Antwerpen, N Belgium

Baarn 86 C3 Utrecht, C Netherlands

Babadag 108 D5 Tulcea, SE Romania

Babahoyo 60 B2 prev. Bodegas. Los Ríos, C Ecuador

Bābā, Kūh-e 123 E4 mountain range C Afghanistan

Babayevo 110 B4 Vologodskaya Oblast', NW Russian Federation

Babeldaob 144 A1 var. Babeldaop, Babelthuap. island N Palau

Babeldaop see Babeldaob

Bab el Mandeb 121 B7 strait Gulf of Aden/Red Sea

Babelthuap see Babeldaob

Babian Jiang see Black River

Babruysk 107 D7 Rus. Bobruysk. Mahilyowskaya Voblasts', E Belarus

Babuyan Channel 139 E1 channel N Philippines

Babuyan Islands 139 E1 island group N Philippines

Bacabal 63 F2 Maranhão, E Brazil

Bacău 108 C4 Hung. Bákó. Bacău, NE Romania

Bắc Bộ, Vịnh see Tongking, Gulf of

Bắc Giang 136 D3 Ha Bắc, N Vietnam

Bacheykava 107 D5 Rus. Bocheykovo. Vitsyebskaya Voblasts', N Belarus

Back 37 F3 river Nunavut, N Canada

Bačka Palanka 100 D3 prev. Palanka. Serbia, NW Serbia

Bačka Topola 100 D3 Hung. Topolya; prev. Hung. Bácstopolya. Vojvodina, N Serbia

Bạc Liêu 137 D6 var. Vinh Loi. Minh Hai, S Vietnam

Bacolod 125 E4 off. Bacolod City. Negros, C Philippines

Bacolod City see Bacolod

Bácsszenttamás see Srbobran

Bácstopolya see Bačka Topola

Bactra see Balkh

Badajoz 92 C4 anc. Pax Augusta. Extremadura, W Spain

Baden-Baden 95 B6 anc. Aurelia Aquensis. Baden-Württemberg, SW Germany

Badger State see Wisconsin

Bad Hersfeld 94 B4 Hessen, C Germany

Bad Homburg see Bad Homburg vor der Höhe

Bad Homburg vor der Höhe 95 B5 var. Bad Homburg. Hessen, W Germany

Bad Ischl 95 D7 Oberösterreich, N Austria

Bad Krozingen 95 A6 Baden-Württemberg, SW Germany

Badlands 44 D2 physical region North Dakota/South Dakota, N USA

Badu Island 148 C1 island Queensland, NE Australia

Bad Vöslau 95 E6 Niederösterreich, NE Austria

Baeterrae/Baeterrae Septimanorum see Béziers

Baetic Cordillera/Baetic Mountains see Béticos, Sistemas

Bafatá 74 C3 C Guinea-Bissau

Baffin Bay 37 G2 bay Canada/Greenland

Baffin Island 37 G2 island Nunavut, NE Canada

Bafing 74 C3 river W Africa

Bafoussam 76 B4 Ouest, W Cameroon

Bafra 116 D2 Samsun, N Turkey

Bāft 120 D4 Kermān, S Iran

Bagaces 52 D4 Guanacaste, NW Costa Rica

Bagdad see Baghdad

Bagé 63 E5 Rio Grande do Sul, S Brazil

Baghdad 120 B3 var. Bagdad, Eng. Baghdad. country capital (Iraq) Baghdād, C Iraq

Baghdad see Baghdad

Baghlān 123 E3 Baghlān, NE Afghanistan

Bago 136 B4 var. Pegu. Bago, SW Myanmar (Burma)

Bagoé 74 D4 river Côte d'Ivoire/Mali

Bagrationovsk 106 A4 Ger. Preussisch Eylau. Kaliningradskaya Oblast', W Russian Federation

Bagrax Hu see Bosten Hu

Baguio 139 E1 off. Baguio City. Luzon, N Philippines

Baguio City see Baguio

Bagzane, Monts 75 F3 mountain N Niger

Bahama Islands see Bahamas

Bahamas 54 C2 off. Commonwealth of the Bahamas. country N West Indies

Bahamas 53 D6 var. Bahama Islands. island group N West Indies

BAHAMAS
West Indies

Official name Commonwealth of the Bahamas
Formation 1973 / 1973
Capital Nassau
Population 300,000 / 78 people per sq mile (30 people per sq km)
Total area 5382 sq. miles (13,940 sq. km)
Languages English*, English Creole, French Creole
Religions Baptist 32%, Anglican 20%, Roman Catholic 19%, Other 17%, Methodist 6%, Church of God 6%
Ethnic mix Black African 85%, Other 15%
Government Parliamentary system
Currency Bahamian dollar = 100 cents
Literacy rate 96%
Calorie consumption 2750 kilocalories

Bahamas, Commonwealth of the see Bahamas

Baharly 122 C3 var. Bäherden, Rus. Bakharden; prev. Bakherden. Ahal Welaýaty, C Turkmenistan

Bahāwalpur 134 C2 Punjab, E Pakistan

Bäherden see Baharly

Bahia 63 F3 off. Estado da Bahia. state E Brazil

Bahia 63 F3 off. Estado da Bahia. region E Brazil

Bahía Blanca 65 C5 Buenos Aires, E Argentina

Bahia, Estado da see Bahia

Bahir Dar 72 C4 var. Bahr Dar, Bahrdar Giyorgis. Āmara, N Ethiopia

Bahraich 135 E3 Uttar Pradesh, N India

Bahrain 120 C4 off. State of Bahrain, Dawlat al Bahrayn, Ar. Al Baḥrayn, prev. Bahrein; anc. Tylos, Tyros. country SW Asia

BAHRAIN
Southwest Asia

Official name Kingdom of Bahrain
Formation 1971 / 1971
Capital Manama
Population 1.3 million / 4762 people per sq mile (1841 people per sq km)
Total area 239 sq. miles (620 sq. km)
Languages Arabic
Religions Muslim (mainly Shi'a) 99%, Other 1%
Ethnic mix Bahraini 63%, Asian 19%, Other Arab 10%, Iranian 8%
Government Mixed monarchical–parliamentary system
Currency Bahraini dinar = 1000 fils
Literacy rate 91%
Calorie consumption Not available

Bahrain, State of see Bahrain

Bahrayn, Dawlat al see Bahrain

Bahr Dar/Bahrdar Giyorgis see Bahir Dar

Bahrein see Bahrain

Bahr el, Azraq see Blue Nile

Bahr Tabariya, Sea of see Tiberias, Lake

Bahushewsk 107 E6 Rus. Bogushëvsk. Vitsyebskaya Voblasts', NE Belarus

Baia Mare 108 B3 Ger. Frauenbach,
Hung. Nagybánya; prev. Neustadt.
Maramureş, NW Romania
Baia Sprie 108 B3 Ger. Mittelstadt,
Hung. Felsőbánya. Maramureş,
NW Romania
Baïbokoum 76 B4 Logone-Oriental,
SW Chad
Baidoa see Baydhabo
Baie-Comeau 39 E3 Québec, SE Canada
Baikal, Lake 115 E4 Eng. Lake Baikal.
lake S Russian Federation
Baikal, Lake see Baykal, Ozero
Baile Átha Cliath see Dublin
Baile Átha Fhada see Athlone
Bailén 92 D4 Andalucía, S Spain
Baile na Mainistreach see Newtownabbey
Băileşti 108 B5 Dolj, SW Romania
Ba Illi 76 B3 Chari-Baguirmi, SW Chad
Bainbridge 42 D3 Georgia, SE USA
Bā'ir see Bāyir
Baireuth see Bayreuth
Bairiki 144 D2 country capital (Kiribati)
Tarawa, NW Kiribati
Bairnsdale 149 C7 Victoria, SE Australia
Baishan 129 E3 prev. Hunjiang. Jilin,
NE China
Baiyin 128 B4 Gansu, C China
Baja 99 C7 Bács-Kiskun, S Hungary
Baja California Norte 50 B2 state
NW Mexico
Bajo Boquete see Boquete
Bajram Curri 101 D5 Kukës, N Albania
Bakala 76 C4 Ouaka, C Central African
Republic
Bakan see Shimonoseki
Baker 46 C3 Oregon, NW USA
Baker and Howland Islands 145 E2 US
unincorporated territory W Polynesia
Baker Lake 37 F3 var. Qamanittuaq.
Nunavut, N Canada
Bakersfield 47 C7 California, W USA
Bakharden see Baharly
Bakhchisaray see Bakhchysaray
Bakhchysaray 109 F5 Rus. Bakhchisaray.
Avtonomna Respublika Krym,
S Ukraine
Bakherden see Baharly
Bakhmach 109 F1 Chernihivs'ka Oblast',
N Ukraine
Bäkhtärän see Kermänshäh
Bakı 117 H2 Eng. Baku. country capital
(Azerbaijan) E Azerbaijan
Bákó see Bacău
Bakony 99 C7 Eng. Bakony Mountains,
Ger. Bakonywald. mountain range
W Hungary
Bakony Mountains/Bakonywald see
Bakony
Baku see Bakı
Bakwanga see Mbuji-Mayi
Balabac Island 129 C8 island
W Philippines
Balabac, Selat see Balabac Strait
Balabac Strait 138 D2 var. Selat Balabac.
strait Malaysia/Philippines
Ba'labakk see Baalbek
Balaguer 93 F2 Cataluña, NE Spain
Balakovo 111 C6 Saratovskaya Oblast',
W Russian Federation
Bālā Morghāb see Bālā Murghāb
Bālā Murghāb 122 D4 prev. Bālā
Morghāb. Laghmān, NW Afghanistan
Balashov 111 B6 Saratovskaya Oblast',
W Russian Federation
Balasore see Bāleshwar
Balaton, Lake 99 C7 var. Lake Balaton,
Ger. Plattensee. lake W Hungary
Balaton, Lake see Balaton
Balbina, Represa 62 D1 reservoir
NW Brazil
Balboa 53 G4 Panamá, C Panama
Balcarce 65 D5 Buenos Aires,
E Argentina
Balclutha 151 B7 Otago, South Island,
New Zealand
Baldy Mountain 44 C1 mountain
Montana, NW USA
Bâle see Basel
Balearic Plain see Algerian Basin
Baleares Major see Mallorca
Balearic Islands 93 G3 Eng. Balearic
Islands. island group Spain,
W Mediterranean Sea
Balearic Islands see Baleares, Islas
Baleares Minor see Menorca
Baleine, Rivière à la 39 E2 river Québec,
E Canada
Balen 87 C5 Antwerpen, N Belgium

Bāleshwar 135 F4 prev. Balasore. Orissa,
E India
Bălgrad see Alba Iulia
Bali 138 D5 island C Indonesia
Balıkesir 116 A3 Balıkesir, W Turkey
Balikh, Nahr 118 C2 river N Syria
Balikpapan 138 D4 Borneo, C Indonesia
Balkanabat 122 B2 Rus. Nebitdag.
Balkan Welaýaty, W Turkmenistan
Balkan Mountains 104 C2 Bul./
SCr. Stara Planina. mountain range
Bulgaria/Serbia
Balkash 114 C5 Kaz. Balqash; prev.
Balkhash. Karagandy, SE Kazakhstan
Balkash, Ozero 114 C5 Eng. Lake
Balkhash, Kaz. Balqash; prev. Ozero
Balkhash. lake SE Kazakhstan
Balkh 123 E3 anc. Bactra. Balkh,
N Afghanistan
Balkhash see Balkash
Balkhash, Lake see Balkash, Ozero
Balkhash, Ozero see Balkash, Ozero
Balladonia 147 C6 Western Australia
Ballarat 149 C7 Victoria, SE Australia
Balleny Islands 154 B5 island group
Antarctica
Ballinger 49 F3 Texas, SW USA
Balochistan 134 B3 prev. Baluchistan,
Beluchistan. province SW Pakistan
Balqash see Balkhash/Balkhash, Ozero
Balş 108 B5 Olt, S Romania
Balsas 63 F2 Maranhão, E Brazil
Balsas, Río 51 E5 var. Río Mexcala. river
S Mexico
Bal'shavik 107 D7 Rus. Bol'shevik.
Homyel'skaya Voblasts', SE Belarus
Balta 108 D3 Odes'ka Oblast',
SW Ukraine
Bălţi 108 D3 Rus. Bel'tsy. N Moldova
Baltic Port see Paldiski
Baltic Sea 85 D7 Ger. Ostee, Rus.
Baltiskoye More. sea N Europe
Baltimore 41 F4 Maryland, NE USA
Baltischport/Baltiski see Paldiski
Baltiskoye More see Baltic Sea
Baltkrievija see Belarus
Baluchistan see Balochistan
Balvi 106 D4 NE Latvia
Balykchy 123 G2 Kir. Ysyk-Köl; prev.
Issyk-Kul', Rybach'ye. Issyk-Kul'skaya
Oblast', NE Kyrgyzstan
Balzers 94 E2 S Liechtenstein
Bam 120 E4 Kermān, SE Iran
Bamako 74 D4 country capital (Mali)
Capital District, SW Mali
Bambari 76 C4 Ouaka, C Central African
Republic
Bamberg 95 C5 Bayern, SE Germany
Bamenda 76 A4 Nord-Ouest,
W Cameroon
Banaba 144 D2 var. Ocean Island. island
Tungaru, W Kiribati
Banaras see Vārānasi
Banda Aceh 138 A3 var. Banda Atjeh;
prev. Koetaradja, Kutaradja, Kutaraja.
Sumatera, W Indonesia
Banda Atjeh see Banda Aceh
Banda, Laut see Banda Sea
Bandama 74 D5 var. Bandama Fleuve.
river S Côte d'Ivoire
Bandama Fleuve see Bandama
Bandar 'Abbās see Bandar-e 'Abbās
Bandarbeyla 73 E5 var. Bender Beila,
Bender Beyla. Bari, NE Somalia
Bandar-e 'Abbās 120 D4 var. Bandar
'Abbās; prev. Gombroon. Hormozgān,
S Iran
Bandar-e Büshehr 120 C4 var. Büshehr,
Eng. Bushire. Büshehr, S Iran
Bandar-e Kangān 120 D4 var. Kangān.
Büshehr, S Iran
Bandar-e Khamīr 120 D4 Hormozgān,
S Iran
Bandar-e Langeh see Bandar-e Lengeh
Bandar-e Lengeh 120 D4 var. Bandar-e
Langeh, Lingeh. Hormozgān, S Iran
Bandar Kassim see Boosaaso
Bandar Lampung 138 C4 var.
Bandarlampung, Tanjungkarang-
Telukbetung; prev. Tandjoengkarang,
Tanjungkarang, Teloekbetoeng,
Telukbetung. Sumatera, W Indonesia
Bandarlampung see Bandar Lampung
Bandar Maharani see Muar
Bandar Masulipatnam see
Machilipatnam
Bandar Penggaram see Batu Pahat
Bandar Seri Begawan 138 D3 prev.
Brunei Town. country capital (Brunei)
N Brunei

Banda Sea 139 F5 var. Laut Banda. sea
E Indonesia
Bandiagara 75 E3 Mopti, C Mali
Bandırma 116 A3 var. Penderma.
Balıkesir, NW Turkey
Bandjarmasin see Banjarmasin
Bandoeng see Bandung
Bandundu 77 C6 prev. Banningville.
Bandundu, W Dem. Rep. Congo
Bandung 138 C5 prev. Bandoeng. Jawa,
C Indonesia
Bangalore 132 C2 var. Bengalooru. state
capital Karnātaka, S India
Bangassou 76 D4 Mbomou, SE Central
African Republic
Banggai, Kepulauan 139 E4 island
group C Indonesia
Banghāzī 71 G2 Eng. Bengazi, Benghazi,
It. Bengasi. NE Libya
Bangka, Pulau 138 C4 island
W Indonesia
Bangkok see Ao Krung Thep
Bangkok, Bight of see Krung Thep, Ao
Bangladesh 135 G3 off. People's
Republic of Bangladesh; prev. East
Pakistan. country S Asia

BANGLADESH
South Asia

Official name People's Republic
of Bangladesh
Formation 1971 / 1971
Capital Dhaka
Population 150 million / 2911 people
per sq mile (1124 people per sq km)
Total area 55,598 sq. miles
(144,000 sq. km)
Languages Bengali*, Urdu, Chakma,
Marma (Magh), Garo, Khasi, Santhali,
Tripuri, Mro
Religions Muslim (mainly Sunni) 88%,
Hindu 11%, Other 1%
Ethnic mix Bengali 98%, Other 2%
Government Parliamentary system
Currency Taka = 100 poisha
Literacy rate 56%
Calorie consumption 2481 kilocalories

Bangladesh, People's Republic of see
Bangladesh
Ba Ngoi see Cam Ranh
Bangor 89 C6 NW Wales, United
Kingdom
Bangor 89 B5 Ir. Beannchar. E Northern
Ireland, United Kingdom
Bangor 41 G2 Maine, NE USA
Bang Pla Soi see Chon Buri
Bangui 77 B5 country capital
(Central African Republic)
Ombella-Mpoko, SW Central
African Republic
Bangweulu, Lake 73 B8 var. Lake
Bengwelu. lake N Zambia
Ban Hat Yai see Hat Yai
Ban Hin Heup 136 C4 Viangchan,
C Laos
Ban Houayxay/Ban Houei Sai see
Houayxay
Ban Hua Hin 137 C6 var. Hua Hin.
Prachuap Khiri Khan, SW Thailand
Bani 74 D3 river S Mali
Banias see Bāniyās
Banijska Palanka see Glina
Bani Suwayf 72 B2 var. Beni Suef.
N Egypt
Bāniyās 118 B3 var. Banias, Baniyas,
Paneas. Tarţūs, W Syria
Banjak, Kepulauan see Banyak,
Kepulauan
Banja Luka 100 B3 Republika Srpska,
NW Bosnia and Herzegovina
Banjarmasin 138 D4 prev.
Bandjarmasin. Borneo, C Indonesia
Banjul 74 B3 prev. Bathurst. country
capital (Gambia) W Gambia
Banks, Îles see Banks Islands
Banks Island 37 E2 island Northwest
Territories, NW Canada
Banks Islands 144 D4 Fr. Îles Banks.
island group N Vanuatu
Banks Lake 46 B1 reservoir Washington,
NW USA
Banks Peninsula 151 C6 peninsula
South Island, New Zealand
Banks Strait 149 C8 strait SW Tasman
Sea
Bānkura 135 F4 West Bengal, NE India
Ban Mak Khaeng see Udon Thani

Banmo see Bhamo
Banningville see Bandundu
Bañolas see Banyoles
Ban Pak Phanang see Pak Phanang
Ban Sichon see Sichon
Banská Bystrica 99 C6 Ger.
Neusohl, Hung. Besztercebánya.
Banskobystricky Kraj, C Slovakia
Bantry Bay 89 A7 Ir. Bá Bheanntraí. bay
SW Ireland
Banya 104 E2 Burgas, E Bulgaria
Banyak, Kepulauan 138 A3 prev.
Kepulauan Banjak. island group
NW Indonesia
Banyo 76 B4 Adamaoua, NW Cameroon
Banyoles 93 G2 var. Bañolas. Cataluña,
NE Spain
Banzare Seamounts 141 C7 seamount
range S Indian Ocean
Banzart see Bizerte
Baoji 128 B4 var. Pao-chi, Paoki.
Shaanxi, C China
Baoro 76 B4 Nana-Mambéré, W Central
African Republic
Baoshan 128 A6 var. Pao-shan. Yunnan,
SW China
Baotou 127 F3 var. Pao-t'ou, Paotow.
Nei Mongol Zizhiqu, N China
Ba'qubah 120 B3 var. Qubba. Diyālá,
C Iraq
Baquerizo Moreno see Puerto Baquerizo
Moreno
Bar 101 C5 It. Antivari. S Montenegro
Baraawe 73 D6 It. Brava. Shabeellaha
Hoose, S Somalia
Bārāmati 134 C5 Mahārāshtra, W India
Baranavichy 107 B6 Pol. Baranowicze,
Rus. Baranovichi. Brestskaya Voblasts',
SW Belarus
Baranovichi/Baranowicze see
Baranavichy
Barbados 55 G1 country SE West Indies

BARBADOS
West Indies

Official name Barbados
Formation 1966 / 1966
Capital Bridgetown
Population 300,000 / 1807 people
per sq mile (698 people per sq km)
Total area 166 sq. miles (430 sq. km)
Languages Bajan (Barbadian English),
English*
Religions Anglican 40%, Other 24%,
Nonreligious 17%, Pentecostal 8%,
Methodist 7%, Roman Catholic 4%
Ethnic mix Black African 92%, White 3%,
Other 3%, Mixed race 2%
Government Parliamentary system
Currency Barbados dollar = 100 cents
Literacy rate 99%
Calorie consumption 3021 kilocalories

Barbastro 93 F2 Aragón, NE Spain
Barbate de Franco 92 C5 Andalucía,
S Spain
Barbuda 55 G3 island N Antigua and
Barbuda
Barcaldine 148 C4 Queensland,
E Australia
Barcarozsnyó see Râşnov
Barcău see Berettyó
Barce see Al Marj
Barcelona 93 G2 anc. Barcino,
Barcinona. Cataluña, E Spain
Barcelona 59 E2 Anzoátegui,
NE Venezuela
Barcino/Barcinona see Barcelona
Barcoo see Cooper Creek
Barcs 99 C7 Somogy, SW Hungary
Bardai 76 C1 Borkou-Ennedi-Tibesti,
N Chad
Bardejov 99 D5 Ger. Bartfeld, Hung.
Bártfa. Presovský Kraj, E Slovakia
Bardera/Bardere see Baardheere
Barduli see Barletta
Bareilly 135 E3 var. Bareli. Uttar
Pradesh, N India
Bareli see Bareilly
Barendrecht 86 C4 Zuid-Holland,
SW Netherlands
Barentin 90 C3 Seine-Maritime,
N France
Barentsburg 83 G2 Spitsbergen,
W Svalbard
Barentsevo More/Barents Havet see
Barents Sea
Barentsøya 83 G2 island E Svalbard

Barents Sea 110 C2 Nor. Barents Havet, Rus. Barentsevo More. sea Arctic Ocean
Bar Harbor 41 H2 Mount Desert Island, Maine, NE USA
Bari 97 E5 var. Bari delle Puglie; anc. Barium. Puglia, SE Italy
Bäridah see Al Bāridah
Bari delle Puglie see Bari
Barikot see Barikowţ
Barikowţ 123 F4 var. Barikot. Kunar, NE Afghanistan
Barillas 52 A2 var. Santa Cruz Barillas. Huehuetenango, NW Guatemala
Barinas 58 C2 Barinas, W Venezuela
Barisal 135 G4 Barisal, S Bangladesh
Barisan, Pegunungan 138 B4 mountain range Sumatera, W Indonesia
Barito, Sungai 138 D4 river Borneo, C Indonesia
Barium see Bari
Barka see Al Marj
Barkly Tableland 148 B3 plateau Northern Territory/Queensland, N Australia
Bârlad 108 D4 prev. Bîrlad. Vaslui, E Romania
Barlavento, Ilhas de 74 A2 var. Windward Islands. island group N Cape Verde
Bar-le-Duc 90 D3 var. Bar-sur-Ornain. Meuse, NE France
Barlee, Lake 147 B6 lake Western Australia
Barlee Range 146 A4 mountain range Western Australia
Barletta 97 D5 anc. Barduli. Puglia, SE Italy
Barlinek 98 B3 Ger. Berlinchen. Zachodnio-pomorskie, NW Poland
Barmen-Elberfeld see Wuppertal
Barmouth 89 C6 NW Wales, United Kingdom
Barnaul 114 D4 Altayskiy Kray, C Russian Federation
Barnet 89 A7 United Kingdom
Barnstaple 89 C7 SW England, United Kingdom
Baroda see Vadodara
Baroghil Pass 123 F3 var. Kowtal-e Barowghil. pass Afghanistan/Pakistan
Baron'ki 107 F2 Rus. Boron'ki. Mahilyowskaya Voblasts', E Belarus
Barowghil, Kowtal-e see Baroghil Pass
Barquisimeto 58 C2 Lara, NW Venezuela
Barra 88 B3 island NW Scotland, United Kingdom
Barra de Río Grande 53 E3 Región Autónoma Atlántico Sur, E Nicaragua
Barranca 60 C3 Lima, W Peru
Barrancabermeja 58 B2 Santander, N Colombia
Barranquilla 58 B1 Atlántico, N Colombia
Barreiro 92 B4 Setúbal, W Portugal
Barrier Range 149 C6 hill range New South Wales, SE Australia
Barrow 36 D2 Alaska, USA
Barrow 89 B6 Ir. An Bhearú. river SE Ireland
Barrow-in-Furness 89 C5 NW England, United Kingdom
Barrow Island 146 A4 island Western Australia
Barstow 47 C7 California, W USA
Bartang 123 F3 river SE Tajikistan
Bartenstein see Bartoszyce
Bártfa/Bartfeld see Bardejov
Bartica 59 F3 N Guyana
Bartın 116 C2 Bartın, NW Turkey
Bartlesville 49 G1 Oklahoma, C USA
Bartoszyce 98 D2 Ger. Bartenstein. Warmińsko-mazurskie, NE Poland
Baruun-Urt 127 F2 Sühbaatar, E Mongolia
Barú, Volcán 53 E5 var. Volcán de Chiriquí. volcano W Panama
Barwon River 149 D5 river New South Wales, SE Australia
Barysaw 107 D6 Rus. Borisov. Minskaya Voblasts', NE Belarus
Basarabeasca 108 D4 Rus. Bessarabka. SE Moldova
Basel 95 A7 Eng. Basle, Fr. Bâle. Basel Stadt, NW Switzerland
Basilan 139 E3 island Sulu Archipelago, SW Philippines

Basle see Basel
Basra see Al Başrah
Bassano del Grappa 96 C2 Veneto, NE Italy
Bassein see Pathein
Basseterre 55 G4 country capital (Saint Kitts and Nevis) Saint Kitts, Saint Kitts and Nevis
Basse-Terre 55 G3 dependent territory capital (Guadeloupe) Basse Terre, SW Guadeloupe
Basse Terre 55 G4 island W Guadeloupe
Bassikounou 74 D3 Hodh ech Chargui, SE Mauritania
Bass, Îlots de see Marotiri
Bass Strait 149 C7 strait SE Australia
Bassum 94 B3 Niedersachsen, NW Germany
Bastia 91 E7 Corse, France, C Mediterranean Sea
Bastogne 87 D7 Luxembourg, SE Belgium
Bastrop 42 B2 Louisiana, S USA
Bastyn' 107 B7 Rus. Bostyn'. Brestskaya Voblasts', SW Belarus
Basuo see Dongfang
Basutoland see Lesotho
Bata 77 A5 NW Equatorial Guinea
Batae Coritanorum see Leicester
Batajnica 100 D3 Vojvodina, N Serbia
Batangas 139 E2 off. Batangas City. Luzon, N Philippines
Batangas City see Batangas
Batavia see Jakarta
Bătdâmbâng 137 C5 prev. Battambang. Bătdâmbâng, NW Cambodia
Batéké, Plateaux 77 B6 plateau S Congo
Bath 89 D7 hist. Akermanceaster; anc. Aquae Calidae, Aquae Solis. SW England, United Kingdom
Bathinda 134 D2 Punjab, NW India
Bathsheba 55 G1 E Barbados
Bathurst 149 D6 New South Wales, SE Australia
Bathurst 39 F4 New Brunswick, SE Canada
Bathurst see Banjul
Bathurst Island 146 D2 island Northern Territory, N Australia
Bathurst Island 37 F2 island Parry Islands, Nunavut, N Canada
Wadi al Bātin 120 C4 dry watercourse SW Asia
Batman 117 E4 var. Iluh. Batman, SE Turkey
Batna 71 E2 NE Algeria
Baton Rouge 42 B3 state capital Louisiana, S USA
Batroûn 118 A4 var. Al Batrūn. N Lebanon
Battambang see Bătdâmbâng
Batticaloa 132 D3 Eastern Province, E Sri Lanka
Battipaglia 97 D5 Campania, S Italy
Battle Born State see Nevada
Batumi 117 F2 W Georgia
Batu Pahat 138 B3 prev. Bandar Penggaram. Johor, Peninsular Malaysia
Bauchi 75 G4 Bauchi, NE Nigeria
Bauer Basin 153 F3 undersea basin E Pacific Ocean
Bauska 106 C3 Ger. Bauske. S Latvia
Bauske see Bauska
Bautzen 94 D4 Lus. Budyšin. Sachsen, E Germany
Bauzanum see Bolzano
Bavaria see Bayern
Bavarian Alps 95 C7 Ger. Bayrische Alpen. mountain range Austria/Germany
Bavière see Bayern
Bavispe, Río 50 C2 river NW Mexico
Bawiţi 72 B2 var. Bawîti. N Egypt
Bawîti see Bawiţi
Bawku 75 E4 N Ghana
Bayamo 54 C3 Granma, E Cuba
Bayan Har Shan 126 D4 var. Bayan Khar. mountain range C China
Bayanhongor 126 D2 Bayanhongor, C Mongolia
Bayan Khar see Bayan Har Shan
Bayano, Lago 53 G4 lake E Panama
Bay City 40 C3 Michigan, N USA
Bay City 49 G4 Texas, SW USA
Baydhabo 73 D6 var. Baydhowa, Isha Baydhabo, It. Baidoa. Bay, SW Somalia
Baydhowa see Baydhabo

Bayeux 90 B3 anc. Augustodurum. Calvados, N France
Bâyir 119 C7 var. Bā'ir. Ma'ān, S Jordan
Bay Islands 52 C1 Eng. Bay Islands. island group N Honduras
Bay Islands see Bahía, Islas de la
Baymak 111 D6 Respublika Bashkortostan, W Russian Federation
Bayonne 91 A6 anc. Lapurdum. Pyrénées-Atlantiques, SW France
Bayou State see Louisiana
Bayram-Ali see Baýramaly
Baýramaly 122 D3 var. Bayramaly; prev. Bayram-Ali. Mary Welaýaty, S Turkmenistan
Bayreuth 95 C5 var. Baireuth. Bayern, SE Germany
Bayrische Alpen see Bavarian Alps
Bayrūt see Beyrouth
Bay State see Massachusetts
Baysun see Boysun
Bayt Laḥm see Bethlehem
Baytown 49 H4 Texas, SW USA
Baza 93 E4 Andalucía, S Spain
Bazargic see Dobrich
Bazin see Pezinok
Beagle Channel 65 C8 channel Argentina/Chile
Béal Feirste see Belfast
Beannchar see Bangor, Northern Ireland, UK
Bear Island see Bjørnøya
Bear Lake 46 E4 lake Idaho/Utah, NW USA
Beas de Segura 93 E4 Andalucía, S Spain
Beata, Isla 55 E3 island SW Dominican Republic
Beatrice 45 F4 Nebraska, C USA
Beaufort Sea 36 D2 sea Arctic Ocean
Beaufort-Wes see Beaufort West
Beaufort West 78 C5 Afr. Beaufort-Wes. Western Cape, SW South Africa
Beaumont 49 H3 Texas, SW USA
Beaune 90 D4 Côte d'Or, C France
Beauvais 90 C3 anc. Bellovacum, Caesaromagus. Oise, N France
Beaver Island 40 C2 island Michigan, N USA
Beaver Lake 49 H1 reservoir Arkansas, C USA
Beaver River 49 F1 river Oklahoma, C USA
Beaver State see Oregon
Beäwar 134 C3 Rājasthān, N India
Bečej 100 D3 Ger. Altbetsche, Hung. Óbecse, Rácz-Becse; prev. Magyar-Becse, Stari Bečej. Vojvodina, N Serbia
Béchar 70 D2 prev. Colomb-Béchar. W Algeria
Beckley 40 D5 West Virginia, NE USA
Bécs see Wien
Bedford 89 D6 E England, United Kingdom
Bedum 86 E1 Groningen, NE Netherlands
Beehive State see Utah
Be'er Menuha 119 B7 prev. Be'ér Menuẖa. Southern, S Israel
Be'ér Menuẖa see Be'er Menuha
Beernem 87 A5 West-Vlaanderen, NW Belgium
Beersheba see Be'er Sheva
Be'er Sheva 119 A7 var. Beersheba, Ar. Bir es Saba; prev. Be'ér Sheva'. Southern, S Israel
Be'ér Sheva' see Be'er Sheva
Beesel 87 D5 Limburg, SE Netherlands
Beeville 49 G4 Texas, SW USA
Bega 149 D7 New South Wales, SE Australia
Begoml' see Byahoml'
Begovat see Bekobod
Behagle see Laï
Behar see Bihār
Beibu Wan see Tongking, Gulf of
Beida see Al Baydā'
Beihai 128 B6 Guangxi Zhuangzu Zizhiqu, S China
Beijing 128 C3 var. Pei-ching, Eng. Peking; prev. Pei-p'ing. country capital (China) Beijing Shi, E China
Beilen 86 E2 Drenthe, NE Netherlands
Beira 79 E3 Sofala, C Mozambique
Beirut see Beyrouth
Beit Lekhem see Bethlehem
Beiuş 108 B3 Hung. Belényes. Bihor, NW Romania
Beja 92 B4 anc. Pax Julia. Beja, SE Portugal

Béjar 92 C3 Castilla y León, N Spain
Bejraburi see Phetchaburi
Bekabad see Bekobod
Békás see Bicaz
Bek-Budi see Qarshi
Békéscsaba 99 D7 Rom. Bichiş-Ciaba. Békés, SE Hungary
Bekobod 123 E2 Rus. Bekabad; prev. Begovat. Toshkent Viloyati, E Uzbekistan
Bela Crkva 100 E3 Ger. Weisskirchen, Hung. Fehértemplom. Vojvodina, W Serbia
Belarus 107 B5 off. Republic of Belarus, var. Belorussia, Latv. Baltkrievija; prev. Belorussian SSR, Rus. Belorusskaya SSR. country E Europe

BELARUS	
Eastern Europe	
Official name Republic of Belarus	
Formation 1991 / 1991	
Capital Minsk	
Population 9.6 million / 120 people per sq mile (46 people per sq km)	
Total area 80,154 sq. miles (207,600 sq. km)	
Languages Belarussian*, Russian*	
Religions Orthodox Christian 80%, Roman Catholic 14%, Other 6%	
Ethnic mix Belorussian 81%, Russian 11%, Polish 4%, Ukrainian 2%, Other 2%	
Government Presidential system	
Currency Belarussian rouble = 100 kopeks	
Literacy rate 99%	
Calorie consumption 3186 kilocalories	

Belarus, Republic of see Belarus
Belau see Palau
Belaya Tserkov' see Bila Tserkva
Bełchatów 98 C4 var. Belchatow. Łódzskie, C Poland
Belchatow see Bełchatów
Belcher, Îles see Belcher Islands
Belcher Islands 38 C2 Fr. Îles Belcher. island group Nunavut, SE Canada
Beledweyne 73 D5 var. Belet Huen, It. Belet Uen. Hiiraan, C Somalia
Belém 63 F1 var. Pará. state capital Pará, N Brazil
Belén 52 D4 Rivas, SW Nicaragua
Belen 48 D2 New Mexico, SW USA
Belényes see Beiuş
Belet Huen/Belet Uen see Beledweyne
Belfast 89 B5 Ir. Béal Feirste. national capital E Northern Ireland, United Kingdom
Belfield 44 D2 North Dakota, N USA
Belfort 90 E4 Territoire-de-Belfort, E France
Belgard see Białogard
Belgaum 132 B1 Karnātaka, W India
Belgian Congo see Congo (Democratic Republic of)
België/Belgique see Belgium
Belgium 87 B6 off. Kingdom of Belgium, Dut. België, Fr. Belgique. country NW Europe

BELGIUM	
Northwest Europe	
Official name Kingdom of Belgium	
Formation 1830 / 1919	
Capital Brussels	
Population 10.8 million / 852 people per sq mile (329 people per sq km)	
Total area 11,780 sq. miles (30,510 sq. km)	
Languages Dutch*, French*, German*	
Religions Roman Catholic 88%, Other 10%, Muslim 2%	
Ethnic mix Fleming 58%, Walloon 33%, Other 6%, Italian 2%, Moroccan 1%	
Government Parliamentary system	
Currency Euro = 100 cents	
Literacy rate 99%	
Calorie consumption 3721 kilocalories	

Belgium, Kingdom of see Belgium
Belgorod 111 A6 Belgorodskaya Oblast', W Russian Federation
Belgrano II 154 A2 Argentinian research station Antarctica
Belice see Belize/Belize City
Beligrad see Berat
Beli Manastir 100 C3 Hung. Pélmonostor; prev. Monostor. Osijek-Baranja, NE Croatia

Bélinga 77 B5 Ogooué-Ivindo, NE Gabon
Belitung, Pulau 138 C4 *island* W Indonesia
Belize 52 B1 *Sp.* Belice; *prev.* British Honduras, Colony of Belize. *country* Central America

BELIZE
Central America

Official name Belize
Formation 1981 / 1981
Capital Belmopan
Population 294,385 / 33 people per sq mile (13 people per sq km) / 48%
Total area 8867 sq. miles (22,966 sq. km)
Languages English*, English Creole, Spanish, Mayan, Garifuna (Carib)
Religions Roman Catholic 62%, Other 13%, Anglican 12%, Methodist 6%, Mennonite 4%, Seventh-day Adventist 3%
Ethnic mix Mestizo 49%, Creole 25%, Maya 11%, Other 6%, Garifuna 6%, Asian Indian 3%
Government Parliamentary system
Currency Belizean dollar = 100 cents
Literacy rate 75%
Calorie consumption 2869 kilocalories

Belize 52 B1 *river* Belize/Guatemala
Belize *see* Belize City
Belize City 52 C1 *var.* Belize, *Sp.* Belice. Belize, NE Belize
Belize, Colony of *see* Belize
Beljak *see* Villach
Belkofski 36 B3 Alaska, USA
Belle Île 90 A4 *island* NW France
Belle Isle, Strait of 39 G3 *strait* Newfoundland and Labrador, E Canada
Bellenz *see* Bellinzona
Belleville 40 B4 Illinois, N USA
Bellevue 45 F4 Iowa, C USA
Bellevue 46 B2 Washington, NW USA
Bellingham 46 B1 Washington, NW USA
Belling Hausen Mulde *see* Southeast Pacific Basin
Bellingshausen Abyssal Plain *see* Bellingshausen Plain
Bellingshausen Plain 153 F5 *var.* Bellingshausen Abyssal Plain. *abyssal plain* SE Pacific Ocean
Bellingshausen Sea 154 A3 *sea* Antarctica
Bellinzona 95 B8 *Ger.* Bellenz. Ticino, S Switzerland
Bello 58 B2 Antioquia, W Colombia
Belo Horizonte *see* Belo Horizonte
Bellovacum *see* Beauvais
Bellville 78 B5 Western Cape, SW South Africa
Belmopan 52 C1 *country capital* (Belize) Cayo, C Belize
Belogradchik 104 B1 Vidin, NW Bulgaria
Belo Horizonte 63 F4 *prev.* Bello Horizonte. *state capital* Minas Gerais, SE Brazil
Belomorsk 110 B3 Respublika Kareliya, NW Russian Federation
Beloretsk 111 D6 Respublika Bashkortostan, W Russian Federation
Belorussia/Belorussian SSR *see* Belarus
Belorusskaya Gryada *see* Byelaruskaya Hrada
Belorusskaya SSR *see* Belarus
Beloshchel'ye *see* Nar'yan-Mar
Belostok *see* Białystok
Belovár *see* Bjelovar
Belozërsk 110 B4 Vologodskaya Oblast', NW Russian Federation
Belton 49 G3 Texas, SW USA
Bel'tsy *see* Bălţi
Beluchistan *see* Balochistan
Belukha, Gora 114 D5 *mountain* Kazakhstan/Russian Federation
Belynichi *see* Byalynichy
Belyy, Ostrov 114 D2 *island* N Russian Federation
Bemaraha 79 F3 *var.* Plateau du Bemaraha. *mountain range* W Madagascar
Bemaraha, Plateau du *see* Bemaraha
Bemidji 45 F1 Minnesota, N USA
Bemmel 86 D4 Gelderland, SE Netherlands
Benaco *see* Garda, Lago di
Benares *see* Vārānasi
Benavente 92 D2 Castilla y León, N Spain

Bend 46 B3 Oregon, NW USA
Bender *see* Tighina
Bender Beila/Bender Beyla *see* Bandarbeyla
Bender Cassim/Bender Qaasim *see* Boosaaso
Bendern 94 E1 NW Liechtenstein Europe
Bendery *see* Tighina
Bendigo 149 C7 Victoria, SE Australia
Beneschau *see* Benešov
Beneški Zaliv *see* Venice, Gulf of
Benešov 99 B5 *Ger.* Beneschau. Středočeský Kraj, W Czech Republic
Benevento 97 D5 *anc.* Beneventum, Malventum. Campania, S Italy
Beneventum *see* Benevento
Bengal, Bay of 124 C4 *bay* N Indian Ocean
Bengalooru *see* Bangalore
Bengasi *see* Banghāzī
Bengazi *see* Banghāzī
Bengbu 128 D5 *var.* Peng-pu. Anhui, E China
Benghazi *see* Banghāzī
Bengkulu 138 B4 *prev.* Bengkoeloe, Benkoelen, Benkulen. Sumatera, W Indonesia
Benguela 78 A2 *var.* Benguella. Benguela, W Angola
Benguella *see* Benguela
Bengweulu, Lake *see* Bangweulu, Lake
Ben Hope 88 B2 *mountain* N Scotland, United Kingdom
Beni 77 E5 Nord-Kivu, NE Dem. Rep. Congo
Benidorm 93 F4 Valenciana, SE Spain
Beni-Mellal 70 C2 C Morocco
Benin 75 F4 *off.* Republic of Benin; *prev.* Dahomey. *country* W Africa

BENIN
West Africa

Official name Republic of Benin
Formation 1960 / 1960
Capital Porto-Novo
Population 9.1 million / 213 people per sq mile (82 people per sq km)
Total area 43,483 sq. miles (112,620 sq. km)
Languages Fon, Bariba, Yoruba, Adja, Houeda, Somba, French*
Religions Indigenous beliefs and Voodoo 50%, Christian 30%, Muslim 20%
Ethnic mix Fon 41%, Other 21%, Adja 16%, Yoruba 12%, Bariba 10%
Government Presidential system
Currency CFA franc = 100 centimes
Literacy rate 42%
Calorie consumption 2592 kilocalories

Benin, Bight of 75 F5 *gulf* W Africa
Benin City 75 F5 Edo, SW Nigeria
Benin, Republic of *see* Benin
Beni, Río 61 E3 *river* N Bolivia
Beni Suef *see* Banī Suwayf
Ben Nevis 88 C3 *mountain* N Scotland, United Kingdom
Bénoué *see* Benue
Benson 48 B3 Arizona, SW USA
Bent Jbaïl 119 A5 *var.* Bint Jubayl. S Lebanon
Benton 42 B1 Arkansas, C USA
Benue 76 B4 *Fr.* Bénoué. *river* Cameroon/Nigeria
Beograd 100 D3 *Eng.* Belgrade. Serbia, N Serbia
Berane 101 D5 *prev.* Ivangrad. E Montenegro
Berat 101 C6 *var.* Berati, *SCr.* Beligrad. Berat, C Albania
Berätäu *see* Berettyó
Berati *see* Berat
Berau, Teluk 139 G4 *var.* MacCluer Gulf. *bay* Papua, E Indonesia
Berbera 72 D4 Woqooyi Galbeed, NW Somalia
Berbérati 77 B5 Mambéré-Kadéï, SW Central African Republic
Berck-Plage 90 C2 Pas-de-Calais, N France
Berdichev *see* Berdychiv
Berdyans'k 109 G4 *Rus.* Berdyansk; *prev.* Osipenko. Zaporiz'ka Oblast', SE Ukraine
Berdychiv 108 D2 *Rus.* Berdichev. Zhytomyrs'ka Oblast', N Ukraine
Beregovo/Beregszász *see* Berehove
Berehove 108 B3 *Cz.* Berehovo, *Hung.* Beregszász, *Rus.* Beregovo. Zakarpats'ka Oblast', W Ukraine

Berehovo *see* Berehove
Bereket 122 B2 *prev. Rus.* Gazandzhyk, Kazandzhik, *Turkm.* Gazanjyk. Balkan Welaýaty, W Turkmenistan
Beretäu *see* Berettyó
Berettyó 99 D7 *Rom.* Barcău; *prev.* Berătău, Beretău. *river* Hungary/Romania
Berettyóújfalu 99 D6 Hajdú-Bihar, E Hungary
Berezhany 108 C2 Pol. Brzeżany. Ternopil's'ka Oblast', W Ukraine
Berezina *see* Byarezina
Berezniki 111 D5 Permskiy Kray, NW Russian Federation
Berga 93 G2 Cataluña, NE Spain
Bergamo 96 B2 *anc.* Bergomum. Lombardia, N Italy
Bergara 93 E1 País Vasco, N Spain
Bergen 94 D2 Mecklenburg-Vorpommern, NE Germany
Bergen 86 C2 Noord-Holland, NW Netherlands
Bergen 85 A5 Hordaland, S Norway
Bergen *see* Mons
Bergerac 91 B5 Dordogne, SW France
Bergeyk 87 C5 Noord-Brabant, S Netherlands
Bergomum *see* Bergamo
Bergse Maas 86 D4 *river* S Netherlands
Beringen 87 C5 Limburg, NE Belgium
Beringov Proliv *see* Bering Strait
Bering Sea 36 A2 *sea* N Pacific Ocean
Bering Strait 36 C2 *Rus.* Beringov Proliv. *strait* Bering Sea/Chukchi Sea
Berja 93 E5 Andalucía, S Spain
Berkeley 47 B6 California, W USA
Berkner Island 154 A2 *island* Antarctica
Berkovitsa 104 C2 Montana, NW Bulgaria
Berlin 94 D3 *country capital* (Germany) Berlin, NE Germany
Berlin 41 G2 New Hampshire, NE USA
Berlinchen *see* Barlinek
Bermejo, Río 64 C2 *river* N Argentina
Bermeo 93 E1 País Vasco, N Spain
Bermuda 35 D6 *var.* Bermuda Islands, Bermudas; *prev.* Somers Islands. *UK crown colony* NW Atlantic Ocean
Bermuda Islands *see* Bermuda
Bermuda Rise 35 E6 *undersea rise* C Sargasso Sea
Bermudas *see* Bermuda
Bern 95 A7 *Fr.* Berne. *country capital* (Switzerland) Bern, W Switzerland
Bernau 94 D3 Brandenburg, NE Germany
Bernburg 94 C4 Sachsen-Anhalt, C Germany
Berne *see* Bern
Berner Alpen 95 A7 *var.* Berner Oberland, *Eng.* Bernese Oberland. *mountain range* SW Switzerland
Berner Oberland/Bernese Oberland *see* Berner Alpen
Bernier Island 147 A5 *island* Western Australia
Beroea *see* Ḥalab
Berry 90 C4 *cultural region* C France
Berry Islands 54 C1 *island group* N Bahamas
Bertoua 77 B5 Est, E Cameroon
Beru 145 E2 *var.* Peru. *atoll* Tungaru, W Kiribati
Berwick-upon-Tweed 88 D4 N England, United Kingdom
Berytus *see* Beyrouth
Besançon 90 D4 *anc.* Besontium, Vesontio. Doubs, E France
Beskra *see* Biskra
Besontium *see* Besançon
Bessarabka *see* Basarabeasca
Besztercze *see* Bistriţa
Besztercebánya *see* Banská Bystrica
Betafo 79 G3 Antananarivo, C Madagascar
Betanzos 92 B1 Galicia, NW Spain
Bethlehem 78 D4 Free State, C South Africa
Bethlehem 119 B6 *var.* Beit Lekhem, *Ar.* Bayt Laḥm, *Heb.* Bet Leḥem. C West Bank
Béticos, Sistemas 92 D4 *var.* Sistema Penibético, *Eng.* Baetic Cordillera, Baetic Mountains. *mountain range* S Spain
Bet Leḥem *see* Bethlehem
Bétou 77 C5 Likouala, N Congo

Bette, Pic *see* Bette, Picco
Bette, Picco 71 G4 *var.* Bīkkū Bīttī, Pic Bette. *mountain* S Libya
Beulah 40 C2 Michigan, N USA
Beuthen *see* Bytom
Beveren 87 B5 Oost-Vlaanderen, N Belgium
Beverley 89 D5 E England, United Kingdom
Bexley 89 B8 Bexley, SE England, United Kingdom
Beyla 74 D4 SE Guinea
Beyrouth 118 A4 *var.* Bayrūt, *Eng.* Beirut; *anc.* Berytus. *country capital* (Lebanon) W Lebanon
Beyşehir 116 B4 Konya, SW Turkey
Beyşehir Gölü 116 B4 *lake* C Turkey
Béziers 91 C6 *anc.* Baeterrae, Baeterrae Septimanorum, Julia Beterrae. Hérault, S France
Bezmein *see* Abadan
Bezwada *see* Vijayawāda
Bhadrāvati 132 C2 Karnātaka, SW India
Bhāgalpur 135 F3 Bihār, NE India
Bhaktapur 135 F3 Central, C Nepal
Bhamo 136 B2 *var.* Banmo. Kachin State, N Myanmar (Burma)
Bhārat *see* India
Bharūch 134 C4 Gujarāt, W India
Bhaunagar *see* Bhāvnagar
Bhāvnagar 134 C4 *prev.* Bhaunagar, Gujarāt, W India
Bheanntraí, Bá *see* Bantry Bay
Bhopāl 134 D4 *state capital* Madhya Pradesh, C India
Bhubaneshwar 135 F5 *prev.* Bhubaneswar, Bhuvaneshwar. *state capital* Orissa, E India
Bhubaneswar *see* Bhubaneshwar
Bhuket *see* Phuket
Bhusaval *see* Bhusāwal
Bhusāwal 134 D4 *prev.* Bhusaval. Mahārāshtra, C India
Bhutan 135 G3 *off.* Kingdom of Bhutan, *var.* Druk-yul. *country* S Asia

BHUTAN
South Asia

Official name Kingdom of Bhutan
Formation 1656 / 1865
Capital Thimphu
Population 700,000 / 39 people per sq mile (15 people per sq km)
Total area 18,147 sq. miles (47,000 sq. km)
Languages Dzongkha*, Nepali, Assamese
Religions Mahayana Buddhist 75%, Hindu 25%
Ethnic mix Bhutanese 50%, Nepalese 35%, Other 15%
Government Mixed monarchical-parliamentary system
Currency Ngultrum = 100 chetrum
Literacy rate 56%
Calorie consumption Not available

Bhutan, Kingdom of *see* Bhutan
Bhuvaneshwar *see* Bhubaneshwar
Biak, Pulau 139 G4 *island* E Indonesia
Biała Podlaska 98 E3 Lubelskie, E Poland
Białogard 98 B2 *Ger.* Belgard. Zachodnio-pomorskie, NW Poland
Białystok 98 E3 *Rus.* Belostok, Bielostok. Podlaskie, NE Poland
Bianco, Monte *see* Blanc, Mont
Biarritz 91 A6 Pyrénées-Atlantiques, SW France
Bicaz 108 C3 *Hung.* Békás. Neamţ, NE Romania
Bichiş-Ciaba *see* Békéscsaba
Biddeford 41 G2 Maine, NE USA
Bideford 89 C7 SW England, United Kingdom
Biel 95 A7 *Fr.* Bienne. Bern, W Switzerland
Bielefeld 94 B3 Nordrhein-Westfalen, NW Germany
Bielitz/Bielitz-Biala *see* Bielsko-Biała
Bielostok *see* Białystok
Bielsko-Biała 99 C5 *Ger.* Bielitz, Bielitz-Biala. Śląskie, S Poland
Bielsk Podlaski 98 E3 Białystok, E Poland
Bien Bien *see* Điện Biên Phu
Biên Đông *see* South China Sea
Biên Hoa 137 E6 Đông Nai, S Vietnam
Bienne *see* Biel

Bienville, Lac *38 D2 lake* Québec,
C Canada
Bié Plateau *78 B2 var.* Bié Plateau.
plateau C Angola
Bié Plateau *see* Bié, Planalto do
Big Cypress Swamp *43 E5 wetland*
Florida, SE USA
Bigge Island *146 C2 island* Western
Australia
Bighorn Mountains *44 C2 mountain
range* Wyoming, C USA
Bighorn River *44 C2 river* Montana/
Wyoming, NW USA
Bignona *74 B3* SW Senegal
Bigorra *see* Tarbes
Bigosovo *see* Bihosava
Big Sioux River *45 E2 river* Iowa/South
Dakota, N USA
Big Spring *49 E3* Texas, SW USA
Bihać *100 B3* Federacija Bosna I
Hercegovina, NW Bosnia and
Herzegovina
Bihār *135 F3 prev.* Behar. *cultural
region* N India
Bihār Sharīf *see* Bihār Sharīf
Biharamulo *73 B7* Kagera, NW Tanzania
Bihār Sharīf *135 F3 var.* Bihār. Bihār,
N India
Bihosava *107 D5 Rus.* Bigosovo.
Vitsyebskaya Voblasts', NW Belarus
Bijeljina *100 C3* Republika Srpska,
NE Bosnia and Herzegovina
Bijelo Polje *101 D5* E Montenegro
Bikāner *134 C3* Rājasthān, NW India
Bikin *115 G4* Khabarovskiy Kray,
SE Russian Federation
Bikini Atoll *144 C1 var.* Pikinni. *atoll*
Ralik Chain, NW Marshall Islands
Bikkū Bitti *see* Bette, Picco
Bilāspur *135 E4* Chhattīsgarh, C India
Bilāsuvar *117 H3 Rus.* Bilyasuvar; *prev.*
Pushkino. SE Azerbaijan
Bila Tserkva *109 E2 Rus.* Belaya
Tserkov'. Kyyivs'ka Oblast', N Ukraine
Bilauktaung Range *137 C6 var.*
Thanintari Taungdan. *mountain range*
Myanmar (Burma)/Thailand
Bilbao *93 E1 Basq.* Bilbo. País Vasco,
N Spain
Bilbo *see* Bilbao
Bilecik *116 B3* Bilecik, NW Turkey
Billings *44 C2* Montana, NW USA
Bilma, Grand Erg de *75 H3 desert*
NE Niger
Biloela *148 D4* Queensland, E Australia
Biloxi *42 C3* Mississippi, S USA
Biltine *76 C3* Biltine, E Chad
Bilwi *see* Puerto Cabezas
Bilyasuvar *see* Bilāsuvar
Bilzen *87 D6* Limburg, NE Belgium
Bimini Islands *54 C1 island group*
W Bahamas
Binche *87 B7* Hainaut, S Belgium
Bindloe Island *see* Marchena, Isla
Bin Ghalfān, Jazā'ir *see* Ḥalānīyāt,
Juzur al
Binghamton *41 F3* New York, NE USA
Bingöl *117 E3* Bingöl, E Turkey
Bint Jubayl *see* Bent Jbaïl
Bintulu *138 D3* Sarawak, East Malaysia
Binzhou *128 D4* Shandong, E China
Bío Bío, Río *65 B5 river* C Chile
Bioco, Isla de *77 A5 var.* Bioko, *Eng.*
Fernando Po, *Sp.* Fernando Póo;
prev. Macías Nguema Biyogo. *island*
NW Equatorial Guinea
Bioko *see* Bioco, Isla de
Birāk *71 F3 var.* Brak. C Libya
Birao *76 D3* Vakaga, NE Central African
Republic
Birātnagar *135 F3* Eastern, SE Nepal
Bir es Saba *see* Be'er Sheva
Birjand *120 E3* Khorāsān-e Janūbī,
E Iran
Birkenfeld *95 A5* Rheinland-Pfalz,
SW Germany
Birkenhead *89 C5* NW England, United
Kingdom
Bîrlad *see* Bârlad
Birmingham *89 C6* C England, United
Kingdom
Birmingham *42 C2* Alabama, S USA
Bir Moghrein *see* Bîr Moghreïn
Bir Mogrein *74 C1 var.* Bir Moghrein;
prev. Fort-Trinquet. Tiris Zemmour,
N Mauritania
Birnie Island *145 E3 atoll* Phoenix
Islands, C Kiribati
Birnin Konni *75 F3 var.* Birni-Nkonni.
Tahoua, SW Niger

Birni-Nkonni *see* Birnin Konni
Birobidzhan *115 G4* Yevreyskaya
Avtonomnaya Oblast', SE Russian
Federation
Birsen *see* Biržai
Birsk *111 D5* Respublika Bashkortostan,
W Russian Federation
Biržai *106 C4 Ger.* Birsen. Panevėžys,
NE Lithuania
Birżebbuġa *102 B5* SE Malta
Bisanthe *see* Tekirdağ
Bisbee *48 B3* Arizona, SW USA
Biscaia, Baía de *see* Biscay, Bay of
Biscay, Bay of *80 B4 Sp.* Golfo de
Vizcaya, *Port.* Baía de Biscaia. *bay*
France/Spain
Biscay Plain *80 B3 abyssal plain* SE Bay
of Biscay
Bischofsburg *see* Biskupiec
Bishah, Wadi *121 B5 dry watercourse*
C Saudi Arabia
Bishkek *123 G2 var.* Pishpek; *prev.*
Frunze. *country capital* (Kyrgyzstan)
Chuyskaya Oblast', N Kyrgyzstan
Bishop's Lynn *see* King's Lynn
Bishrī, Jabal *118 D3 mountain range*
E Syria
Biskara *see* Biskra
Biskra *71 E2 var.* Beskra, Biskara.
NE Algeria
Biskupiec *98 D2 Ger.* Bischofsburg.
Warmińsko-Mazurskie,
NE Poland
Bislig *139 F2* Mindanao, S Philippines
Bismarck *45 E2 state capital* North
Dakota, N USA
Bismarck Archipelago *144 B3 island
group* NE Papua New Guinea
Bismarck Sea *144 B3 sea* W Pacific
Ocean
Bisnulok *see* Phitsanulok
Bissau *74 B4 country capital* (Guinea-
Bissau) W Guinea-Bissau
Bistriţa *108 B3 Ger.* Bistritz, *Hung.*
Besztercze; *prev.* Nösen. Bistriţa-
Năsăud, N Romania
Bistritz *see* Bistriţa
Bitam *77 B5* Woleu-Ntem, N Gabon
Bitburg *95 A5* Rheinland-Pfalz,
SW Germany
Bitlis *117 F3* Bitlis, SE Turkey
Bitoeng *see* Bitung
Bitola *101 D6 Turk.* Monastir; *prev.*
Bitolj. S FYR Macedonia
Bitolj *see* Bitola
Bitonto *97 D5 anc.* Butuntum. Puglia,
SE Italy
Bitterroot Range *46 D2 mountain range*
Idaho/Montana, NW USA
Bitung *139 F3 prev.* Bitoeng. Sulawesi,
C Indonesia
Biu *75 H4* Borno, E Nigeria
Biwa-ko *131 C6 lake* Honshū,
SW Japan
Bizerta *see* Bizerte
Bizerte *71 E1 Ar.* Banzart, *Eng.* Bizerta.
N Tunisia
Bjelovar *100 B2 Hung.* Belovár.
Bjelovar-Bilogora, N Croatia
Bjeshkët e Namuna *see* North Albanian
Alps
Björneborg *see* Pori
Bjørnøya *83 F3 Eng.* Bear Island. *island*
N Norway
Blackall *148 C4* Queensland, E Australia
Black Drin *101 D6 Alb.* Lumi i Drinit të
Zi, SCr. Crni Drim. *river* Albania/FYR
Macedonia
Blackfoot *46 E4* Idaho, NW USA
Black Forest *95 B6 Eng.* Black Forest.
mountain range SW Germany
Black Forest *see* Schwarzwald
Black Hills *44 D3 mountain range* South
Dakota/Wyoming, N USA
Blackpool *89 C5* NW England, United
Kingdom
Black Range *48 C2 mountain range* New
Mexico, SW USA
Black River *54 A5* W Jamaica
Black River *136 C3* Chin. Babian Jiang,
Lixian Jiang, *Fr.* Rivière Noire, *Vtn.*
Sông Ɖa. *river* China/Vietnam
Black Rock Desert *47 C5 desert* Nevada,
W USA
Black Sand Desert *see* Garagum
Black Sea *116 B1 var.* Euxine Sea, *Bul.*
Cherno More, *Rom.* Marea Neagrǎ, *Rus.*
Chernoye More, *Turk.* Karadeniz, *Ukr.*
Chorne More. *sea* Asia/Europe

Black Sea Lowland *109 E4 Ukr.*
Prychornomor'ska Nyzovyna.
depression SE Europe
Black Volta *75 E4 var.* Borongo,
Mouhoun, Moun Hou, *Fr.* Volta Noire.
river W Africa
Blackwater *89 A6 Ir.* An Abhainn Mhór.
river S Ireland
Blackwater State *see* Nebraska
Blagoevgrad *104 C3 prev.* Gorna
Dzhumaya. Blagoevgrad, W Bulgaria
Blagoveshchensk *115 G4* Amurskaya
Oblast', SE Russian Federation
Blake Plateau *35 D6 var.* Blake Terrace.
undersea plateau W Atlantic Ocean
Blake Terrace *see* Blake Plateau
Blanca, Bahía *65 C5 bay* E Argentina
Blanca, Costa *93 F4 physical region*
SE Spain
Blanche, Lake *149 B5 lake* South
Australia
Blanc, Mont *91 D5 It.* Monte Bianco.
mountain France/Italy
Blanco, Cape *46 A4 headland* Oregon,
NW USA
Blanes *93 G2* Cataluña, NE Spain
Blankenberge *87 A5* West-Vlaanderen,
NW Belgium
Blankenheim *95 A5* Nordrhein-
Westfalen, W Germany
Blanquilla, Isla *59 E1 var.* La Blanquilla.
island N Venezuela
Blanquilla, La *see* Blanquilla, Isla
Blantyre *79 E2 var.* Blantyre-Limbe.
Southern, S Malawi
Blantyre-Limbe *see* Blantyre
Blaricum *86 C3* Noord-Holland,
C Netherlands
Blatnitsa *see* Durankulak
Blenheim *151 C5* Marlborough, South
Island, New Zealand
Blesae *see* Blois
Blida *70 D2 var.* El Boulaida, El
Boulaïda. N Algeria
Bloemfontein *78 C4 var.* Mangaung.
country capital (South Africa-judicial
capital) Free State, C South Africa
Blois *90 C4 anc.* Blesae. Loir-et-Cher,
C France
Bloomfield *48 C1* New Mexico, SW USA
Bloomington *40 B4* Illinois, N USA
Bloomington *40 C4* Indiana, N USA
Bloomington *45 F2* Minnesota, N USA
Bloomsbury *148 D3* Queensland,
NE Australia
Bluefield *40 D5* West Virginia, NE USA
Bluefields *53 E3* Región Autónoma
Atlántico Sur, SE Nicaragua
Bluegrass State *see* Kentucky
Blue Hen State *see* Delaware
Blue Law State *see* Connecticut
Blue Mountain Peak *54 B5 mountain*
E Jamaica
Blue Mountains *46 C3 mountain range*
Oregon/Washington, NW USA
Blue Nile *72 C4 var.* Abai, Bahr el,
Azraq, *Amh.* Ābay Wenz, *Ar.* An Nīl al
Azraq, Bahr el Azraq/Sudan
Blumenau *63 E5* Santa Catarina,
S Brazil
Blythe *47 D8* California, W USA
Blytheville *42 C1* Arkansas, C USA
Bo *74 C4* S Sierra Leone
Boaco *52 D3* Boaco, S Nicaragua
Boa Vista *62 D1 state capital* Roraima,
NW Brazil
Boa Vista *74 A3 island* Ilhas de
Barlavento, E Cape Verde
Bobaomby, Tanjona *79 G2 Fr.* Cap
d'Ambre. *headland* N Madagascar
Bobigny *90 E1* Seine-St-Denis, N France
Bobo-Dioulasso *74 D4* SW Burkina Faso
Bobrinets *see* Bobrynets'
Bobruysk *see* Babruysk
Bobrynets' *109 E3 Rus.* Bobrinets.
Kirovohrads'ka Oblast', C Ukraine
Boca Raton *43 F5* Florida, SE USA
Bocay *52 D2* Jinotega, N Nicaragua
Bocheykovo *see* Bacheyka
Bocholt *94 A4* Nordrhein-Westfalen,
W Germany
Bochum *94 A4* Nordrhein-Westfalen,
W Germany
Bocşa *108 A4 Ger.* Bokschen, *Hung.*
Boksánbánya. Caraş-Severin,
SW Romania
Bodajbo *115 F4* Irkutskaya Oblast',
E Russian Federation
Bodegas *see* Babahoyo

Boden *84 D4* Norrbotten, N Sweden
Bodensee *see* Constance, Lake,
C Europe
Bodmin *89 C7* SW England, United
Kingdom
Bodø *84 C3* Nordland, C Norway
Bodrum *116 A4* Muğla, SW Turkey
Boeloekoemba *see* Bulukumba
Boende *77 C5* Equateur, C Dem. Rep.
Congo
Boeroe *see* Buru, Pulau
Boetoeng *see* Buton, Pulau
Bogale *136 B4* Ayeyarwady,
SW Myanmar (Burma)
Bogalusa *42 B3* Louisiana, S USA
Bogatynia *98 B4 Ger.* Reichenau.
Dolnośląskie, SW Poland
Boğazlıyan *116 D3* Yozgat, C Turkey
Bogendorf *see* Łuków
Bogor *138 C5 Dut.* Buitenzorg. Jawa,
C Indonesia
Bogotá *58 B3 prev.* Santa Fe, Santa Fe
de Bogotá. *country capital* (Colombia)
Cundinamarca, C Colombia
Bogushëvsk *see* Bahushewsk
Bo Hai *128 D4 var.* Gulf of Chihli. *gulf*
NE China
Bohemia *99 A5 Cz.* Čechy, Ger. Böhmen.
W Czech Republic
Bohemian Forest *95 C5 Cz.* Český Les,
Šumava, Ger. Böhmerwald. *mountain
range* C Europe
Böhmen *see* Bohemia
Böhmerwald *see* Bohemian Forest
Böhmisch-Krumau *see* Český Krumlov
Bohol Sea *139 E2 var.* Mindanao Sea. *sea*
S Philippines
Bohuslav *109 E2 Rus.* Boguslav.
Kyyivs'ka Oblast', N Ukraine
Boise *46 D3 var.* Boise City. *state capital*
Idaho, NW USA
Boise City *49 E1* Oklahoma, C USA
Boise City *see* Boise
Bois, Lac des *36 D3* Woods, Lake of the
Bois-le-Duc *see* 's-Hertogenbosch
Boizenburg *94 C3* Mecklenburg-
Vorpommern, N Germany
Bojador *see* Boujdour
Bojnūrd *120 D2 var.* Bujnurd.
Khorāsān-e Shemālī, N Iran
Bokāro *135 F4* Jhārkhand, N India
Boké *74 C4* W Guinea
Bokhara *see* Buxoro
Bokonbayevo *123 G2 Kir.* Kajisay; *prev.*
Kadzhi-Say. Issyk-Kul'skaya Oblast',
NE Kyrgyzstan
Boksánbánya/Bokschen *see* Bocşa
Bol *76 B3* Lac, W Chad
Bolgatanga *75 E4* N Ghana
Bolgrad *see* Bolhrad
Bolhrad *108 D4 Rus.* Bolgrad. Odes'ka
Oblast', SW Ukraine
Bolívar, Pico *58 C2 mountain*
W Venezuela
Bolivia *61 F3 off.* Republic of Bolivia.
country W South America

BOLIVIA
South America

Official name Plurinational State
of Bolivia
Formation 1825 / 1938
Capital La Paz (administrative);
Sucre (judicial)
Population 10.1 million / 24 people
per sq mile (9 people per sq km)
Total area 424,162 sq. miles
(1,098,580 sq. km)
Languages Aymara*, Quechua*, Spanish*
Religions Roman Catholic 93%, Other 7%
Ethnic mix Quechua 37%, Aymara 32%,
Mixed race 13%, European 10%, Other 8%
Government Presidential system
Currency Boliviano = 100 centavos
Literacy rate 91%
Calorie consumption 2172 kilocalories

Bolivia, Republic of *see* Bolivia
Bollène *91 D6* Vaucluse, SE France
Bollnäs *85 C5* Gävleborg, C Sweden
Bollon *149 D5* Queensland, C Australia
Bologna *96 C3* Emilia-Romagna,
N Italy
Bol'shevik *see* Bal'shavik
Bol'shevik, Ostrov *115 E2 island*
Severnaya Zemlya, N Russian
Federation

Bol'shezemel'skaya Tundra 110 E3 *physical region* NW Russian Federation
Bol'shoy Lyakhovskiy, Ostrov 115 F2 *island* NE Russian Federation
Bolton 89 D5 *prev.* Bolton-le-Moors. NW England, United Kingdom
Bolton-le-Moors *see* Bolton
Bolu 116 B3 Bolu, NW Turkey
Bolungarvík 83 E4 Vestfirðhir, NW Iceland
Bolyarovo 104 D3 *prev.* Pashkeni. Yambol, E Bulgaria
Bolzano 96 C1 *Ger.* Bozen; *anc.* Bauzanum. Trentino-Alto Adige, N Italy
Boma 77 B6 Bas-Congo, W Dem. Rep. Congo
Bombay *see* Mumbai
Bomu 76 D4 *var.* Mbomou, Mbomu, M'Bomu. *river* Central African Republic/Dem. Rep. Congo
Bonaire 55 F5 *island* Lesser Antilles
Bonanza 52 D2 Región Autónoma Atlántico Norte, NE Nicaragua
Bonaparte Archipelago 146 C2 *island group* Western Australia
Bon, Cap 102 D3 *headland* N Tunisia
Bonda 77 B6 Ogooué-Lolo, C Gabon
Bondoukou 75 E4 E Côte d'Ivoire
Bône *see* Annaba, Algeria
Bone *see* Watampone, Indonesia
Bone, Teluk 139 E4 *bay* Sulawesi, C Indonesia
Bongaigaon 135 G3 Assam, NE India
Bongo, Massif des 76 D4 *var.* Chaîne des Mongos. *mountain range* NE Central African Republic
Bongor 76 B3 Mayo-Kébbi, SW Chad
Bonifacio 91 E7 Corse, France, C Mediterranean Sea
Bonifacio, Bocche de/Bonifacio, Bouches de *see* Bonifacio, Strait of
Bonifacio, Strait of 96 A4 *Fr.* Bouches de Bonifacio, *It.* Bocche di Bonifacio. *strait* C Mediterranean Sea
Bonn 95 A5 Nordrhein-Westfalen, W Germany
Bononia *see* Vidin, Bulgaria
Bononia *see* Boulogne-sur-Mer, France
Boosaaso 72 E4 *var.* Bandar Kassim, Bender Qaasim, Bosaso, *It.* Bender Cassim. Bari, N Somalia
Boothia Felix *see* Boothia Peninsula
Boothia, Gulf of 37 F2 *gulf* Nunavut, NE Canada
Boothia Peninsula 37 F2 *prev.* Boothia Felix. *peninsula* Nunavut, NE Canada
Boppard 95 A5 Rheinland-Pfalz, W Germany
Boquete 53 E5 *var.* Bajo Boquete. Chiriquí, W Panama
Boquillas 50 D2 *var.* Boquillas del Carmen. Coahuila, NE Mexico
Boquillas del Carmen *see* Boquillas
Bor 100 E4 Serbia, E Serbia
Bor 73 B5 Jonglei, E South Sudan
Borås 85 B7 Västra Götaland, S Sweden
Borbetomagus *see* Worms
Borborema, Planalto da 56 E3 *plateau* NE Brazil
Bordeaux 91 B5 *anc.* Burdigala. Gironde, SW France
Bordj Omar Driss 71 E3 E Algeria
Borgå *see* Porvoo
Borgefjell 84 C4 *mountain range* C Norway
Borger 86 E2 Drenthe, NE Netherlands
Borger 49 F1 Texas, SW USA
Borgholm 85 C7 Kalmar, S Sweden
Borgo Maggiore 96 E1 NW San Marino
Borislav *see* Boryslav
Borisoglebsk 111 B6 Voronezhskaya Oblast', W Russian Federation
Borisov *see* Barysaw
Borlänge 85 C6 Dalarna, C Sweden
Borne 86 E3 Overijssel, E Netherlands
Borneo 138 C4 *island* Brunei/Indonesia/Malaysia
Bornholm 85 B8 *island* E Denmark
Borohoro Shan 126 B2 *mountain range* NW China
Borongo *see* Black Volta
Boron'ki *see* Baron'ki
Borosjenő *see* Ineu
Borovan 104 C2 Vratsa, NW Bulgaria
Borovichi 110 B4 Novgorodskaya Oblast', W Russian Federation
Borovo 100 C3 Vukovar-Srijem, NE Croatia

Borriana 93 F3 *var.* Burriana. Valenciana, E Spain
Borşa 108 C3 *Hung.* Borsa. Maramureş, N Romania
Boryslav 108 B2 *Pol.* Borysław, *Rus.* Borislav. L'vivs'ka Oblast', NW Ukraine
Borysław *see* Boryslav
Bosanska Dubica 100 B3 *var.* Kozarska Dubica. Republika Srpska, NW Bosnia and Herzegovina
Bosanska Gradiška 100 B3 *var.* Gradiška. Republika Srpska, N Bosnia and Herzegovina
Bosanski Novi 100 B3 *var.* Novi Grad. Republika Srpska, NW Bosnia and Herzegovina
Bosanski Šamac 100 C3 *var.* Šamac. Republika Srpska, N Bosnia and Herzegovina
Bosaso *see* Boosaaso
Bösing *see* Pezinok
Boskovice 99 B5 *Ger.* Boskowitz. Jihomoravský Kraj, SE Czech Republic
Boskowitz *see* Boskovice
Bosna 100 C4 *river* N Bosnia and Herzegovina
Bosnia and Herzegovina 100 B3 *off.* Republic of Bosnia and Herzegovina. *country* SE Europe

BOSNIA & HERZEGOVINA
Southeast Europe

Official name Bosnia and Herzegovina
Formation 1992 / 1992
Capital Sarajevo
Population 3.8 million / 192 people per sq mile (74 people per sq km)
Total area 19,741 sq. miles (51,129 sq. km)
Languages Bosnian*, Serbian*, Croatian*
Religions Muslim (mainly Sunni) 40%, Orthodox Christian 31%, Roman Catholic 15%, Other 10%, Protestant 4%
Ethnic mix Bosniak 48%, Serb 34%, Croat 16%, Other 2%
Government Parliamentary system
Currency Marka = 100 pfeninga
Literacy rate 98%
Calorie consumption 3070 kilocalories

Bosnia and Herzegovina, Republic of *see* Bosnia and Herzegovina
Boso-hantō 131 D6 *peninsula* Honshū, S Japan
Bosphorus/Bosporus *see* İstanbul Boğazı
Bosporus 116 B2 *var.* Bosporus Thracius, *Eng.* Bosphorus, Bosporus, *Turk.* Karadeniz Boğazı. *strait* NW Turkey
Bosporus Cimmerius *see* Kerch Strait
Bosporus Thracius *see* İstanbul Boğazı
Bossangoa 76 C4 Ouham, C Central African Republic
Bossembélé 76 C4 Ombella-Mpoko, C Central African Republic
Bossier City 42 A2 Louisiana, S USA
Bosten Hu 126 C3 *var.* Bagrax Hu. *lake* NW China
Boston 89 E6 *prev.* St.Botolph's Town. E England, United Kingdom
Boston 41 G3 *state capital* Massachusetts, NE USA
Boston Mountains 42 B1 *mountain range* Arkansas, C USA
Bostyn' *see* Bastyn'
Botany 148 E2 New South Wales, E Australia
Botany Bay 148 E2 *inlet* New South Wales, SE Australia
Boteti 78 C3 *var.* Botletle. *river* N Botswana
Bothnia, Gulf of 85 D5 *Fin.* Pohjanlahti, *Swe.* Bottniska Viken. *gulf* N Baltic Sea
Botletle *see* Boteti
Botoşani 108 C3 *Hung.* Botosány. Botoşani, NE Romania
Botosány *see* Botoşani
Botou 128 C4 *prev.* Bozhen. Hebei, E China
Botrange 87 D6 *mountain* E Belgium
Botswana 78 C3 *off.* Republic of Botswana. *country* S Africa

BOTSWANA
Southern Africa

Official name Republic of Botswana
Formation 1966 / 1966
Capital Gaborone

BOTSWANA
(continued)

Population 2 million / 9 people per sq mile (4 people per sq km)
Total area 231,803 sq. miles (600,370 sq. km)
Languages Setswana, English*, Shona, San, Khoikhoi, isiNdebele
Religions Christian 70%, Nonreligious 20%, Traditional beliefs 6%, Other 4%
Ethnic mix Tswana 79%, Kalanga 11%, Other 10%
Government Presidential system
Currency Pula = 100 thebe
Literacy rate 84%
Calorie consumption 2164 kilocalories

Botswana, Republic of *see* Botswana
Bottniska Viken *see* Bothnia, Gulf of
Bouar 76 B4 Nana-Mambéré, W Central African Republic
Bou Craa 70 B3 *var.* Bu Craa. NW Western Sahara
Bougainville Island 142 B3 *island* NE Papua New Guinea
Bougaroun, Cap 102 C3 *headland* NE Algeria
Bougouni 74 D4 Sikasso, SW Mali
Boujdour 70 A3 *var.* Bojador. W Western Sahara
Boulder 44 C4 Colorado, C USA
Boulder 44 B2 Montana, NW USA
Boulogne *see* Boulogne-sur-Mer
Boulogne-Billancourt 90 D1 Île-de-France, N France Europe
Boulogne-sur-Mer 90 C2 *var.* Boulogne; *anc.* Bononia, Gesoriacum, Gessoriacum. Pas-de-Calais, N France
Boûmdeïd 74 C3 *var.* Boumdeit. Assaba, S Mauritania
Boumdeit *see* Boûmdeïd
Boundiali 74 D4 N Côte d'Ivoire
Bountiful 44 B4 Utah, W USA
Bounty Basin *see* Bounty Trough
Bounty Islands 142 D5 *island group* S New Zealand
Bounty Trough 152 C5 *var.* Bounty Basin. *trough* S Pacific Ocean
Bourbonnais 90 C4 *cultural region* C France
Bourbon Vendée *see* la Roche-sur-Yon
Bourg *see* Bourg-en-Bresse
Bourgas *see* Burgas
Bourge-en-Bresse 91 D5 *var.* Bourg, Bourge-en-Bresse. Ain, E France
Bourges 90 C4 *anc.* Avaricum. Cher, C France
Bourgogne 90 C4 *Eng.* Burgundy. *cultural region* E France
Bourke 149 C5 New South Wales, SE Australia
Bournemouth 89 D7 S England, United Kingdom
Boutilimit 74 C3 Trarza, SW Mauritania
Bouvet Island 67 D7 *Norwegian dependency* S Atlantic Ocean
Bowen 148 D3 Queensland, NE Australia
Bowling Green 40 B5 Kentucky, S USA
Bowling Green 40 C3 Ohio, N USA
Boxmeer 86 D4 Noord-Brabant, SE Netherlands
Boyarka 109 E2 Kyyivs'ka Oblast', N Ukraine
Boysun 123 E3 *Rus.* Baysun. Surkhondaryo Viloyati, S Uzbekistan
Bozeman 44 B2 Montana, NW USA
Bozen *see* Bolzano
Bozhen *see* Botou
Bozüyük 116 B3 Bilecik, NW Turkey
Brač 100 B4 *var.* Brach, *It.* Brazza; *anc.* Brattia. *island* S Croatia
Bracara Augusta *see* Braga
Brach *see* Brač
Brades 55 G3 *de facto country capital*, (Montserrat) *(de jure capital, Plymouth, destroyed by volcano in 1995)* SW Montserrat
Bradford 89 D5 N England, United Kingdom
Brady 49 F3 Texas, SW USA
Braga 92 B2 *anc.* Bracara Augusta. Braga, NW Portugal
Bragança 92 C2 *Eng.* Braganza; *anc.* Julio Briga. Bragança, NE Portugal
Braganza *see* Bragança
Brahestad *see* Raahe

Brahmanbaria 135 G4 Chittagong, E Bangladesh
Brahmapur 135 F5 Orissa, E India
Brahmaputra 135 H3 *var.* Padma, Tsangpo, *Ben.* Jamuna, *Chin.* Yarlung Zangbo Jiang, *Ind.* Bramaputra, Dihang, Siang. *river* S Asia
Bräila 108 D4 Brăila, E Romania
Braine-le-Comte 87 B6 Hainaut, SW Belgium
Brainerd 45 F2 Minnesota, N USA
Brak *see* Birāk
Bramaputra *see* Brahmaputra
Brampton 38 D5 Ontario, S Canada
Branco, Rio 56 C3 *river* N Brazil
Brandberg 78 A3 *mountain* NW Namibia
Brandenburg 94 C3 *var.* Brandenburg an der Havel. Brandenburg, NE Germany
Brandenburg an der Havel *see* Brandenburg
Brandon 37 F5 Manitoba, S Canada
Braniewo 98 D2 *Ger.* Braunsberg. Warmińsko-mazurskie, N Poland
Brasil *see* Brazil
Brasília 63 F3 *country capital* (Brazil) Distrito Federal, C Brazil
Brasil, República Federativa do *see* Brazil
Braşov 108 C4 *Ger.* Kronstadt, *Hung.* Brassó; *prev.* Oraşul Stalin. Braşov, C Romania
Brassó *see* Braşov
Bratislava 99 C6 *Ger.* Pressburg, *Hung.* Pozsony. *country capital* (Slovakia) Bratislavský Kraj, W Slovakia
Bratsk 115 E4 Irkutskaya Oblast', C Russian Federation
Brattia *see* Brač
Braunsberg *see* Braniewo
Braunschweig 94 C4 *Eng./Fr.* Brunswick. Niedersachsen, N Germany
Brava *see* Baraawe
Brava, Costa 93 H2 *coastal region* NE Spain
Bravo del Norte, Río/Bravo, Río *see* Grande, Rio
Bravo, Río 50 C1 *river* Mexico/USA North America
Brawley 47 D8 California, W USA
Brazil 62 C2 *off.* Federative Republic of Brazil, *Port.* República Federativa do Brasil, *Sp.* Brasil; *prev.* United States of Brazil. *country* South America

BRAZIL
South America

Official name Federative Republic of Brazil
Formation 1822 / 1828
Capital Brasília
Population 197 million / 60 people per sq mile (23 people per sq km)
Total area 3,286,470 sq. miles (8,511,965 sq. km)
Languages Portuguese*, German, Italian, Spanish, Polish, Japanese, Amerindian languages
Religions Roman Catholic 74%, Protestant 15%, Atheist 7%, Other 4%
Ethnic mix White 54%, Mixed race 38%, Black 6%, Other 2%
Government Presidential system
Currency Real = 100 centavos
Literacy rate 90%
Calorie consumption 3173 kilocalories

Brazil Basin 67 C5 *var.* Brazilian Basin, Brazil'skaya Kotlovina. *undersea basin* W Atlantic Ocean
Brazil, Federative Republic of *see* Brazil
Brazilian Basin *see* Brazil Basin
Brazilian Highlands 63 F3 *var.* Brazilian Highlands. *mountain range* E Brazil
Brazilian Highlands *see* Central, Planalto
Brazil'skaya Kotlovina *see* Brazil Basin
Brazil, United States of *see* Brazil
Brazos River 49 G3 *river* Texas, SW USA
Brazza *see* Brač
Brazzaville 77 B6 *country capital* (Congo) Capital District, S Congo
Brčko 100 C3 Republika Srpska, NE Bosnia and Herzegovina
Brecht 87 C5 Antwerpen, N Belgium
Brecon Beacons 89 C6 *mountain range* S Wales, United Kingdom

Breda 86 C4 Noord-Brabant,
S Netherlands
Bree 87 D5 Limburg, NE Belgium
Bregalnica 101 E6 *river* E FYR
Macedonia
Bregenz 57 B7 *anc.* Brigantium.
Vorarlberg, W Austria
Bregovo 104 B1 Vidin, NW Bulgaria
Bremen 94 B3 *Fr.* Brême. Bremen,
NW Germany
Bremerhaven 94 B3 Bremen,
NW Germany
Bremerton 46 B2 Washington, NW USA
Brenham 49 G3 Texas, SW USA
Brenner, Col du/Brennero, Passo del
see Brenner Pass
Brenner Pass 96 C1 *var.* Brenner Sattel,
Fr. Col du Brenner, *Ger.* Brennerpass,
It. Passo del Brennero. *pass* Austria/
Italy
Brennerpass *see* Brenner Pass
Brenner Sattel *see* Brenner Pass
Brescia 96 B2 *anc.* Brixia. Lombardia,
N Italy
Breslau *see* Wrocław
Bressanone 96 C1 *Ger.* Brixen.
Trentino-Alto Adige, N Italy
Brest 107 A6 Pol. Brześć nad Bugiem,
Rus. Brest-Litovsk; *prev.* Brześć
Litewski. Brestskaya Voblasts',
SW Belarus
Brest 90 A3 Finistère, NW France
Brest-Litovsk *see* Brest
Bretagne 90 A3 *Eng.* Brittany, *Lat.*
Britannia Minor. *cultural region*
NW France
Brewster, Kap *see* Kangikajik
Brewton 42 C3 Alabama, S USA
Brezhnev *see* Naberezhnyye Chelny
Brezovo 104 D2 *prev.* Abrashlare.
Plovdiv, C Bulgaria
Bria 76 D4 Haute-Kotto, C Central
African Republic
Briançon 91 D5 *anc.* Brigantio. Hautes-
Alpes, SE France
Bricgstow *see* Bristol
Bridgeport 41 F3 Connecticut, NE USA
Bridgetown 55 G2 *country capital*
(Barbados) SW Barbados
Bridlington 89 D5 E England, United
Kingdom
Bridport 89 D7 S England, United
Kingdom
Brieg *see* Brzeg
Brig 95 A7 *Fr.* Brigue, *It.* Briga. Valais,
SW Switzerland
Briga *see* Brig
Brigantio *see* Briançon
Brigantium *see* Bregenz
Brigham City 44 B3 Utah, W USA
Brighton 89 E7 SE England, United
Kingdom
Brighton 44 D4 Colorado, C USA
Brigue *see* Brig
Brindisi 97 E5 *anc.* Brundisium,
Brundusium. Puglia, SE Italy
Brisbane 149 E5 *state capital*
Queensland, E Australia
Bristol 89 D7 *anc.* Bricgstow.
SW England, United Kingdom
Bristol 41 F3 Connecticut, NE USA
Bristol 40 D5 Tennessee, S USA
Bristol Bay 36 B3 *bay* Alaska, USA
Bristol Channel 89 C7 *inlet* England/
Wales, United Kingdom
Britain 80 C3 *var.* Great Britain. *island*
United Kingdom
Britannia Minor *see* Bretagne
British Columbia 36 D4 *Fr.* Colombie-
Britannique. *province* SW Canada
British Guiana *see* Guyana
British Honduras *see* Belize
British Indian Ocean Territory 141 B5
UK dependent territory C Indian Ocean
British Isles 89 *island group* NW Europe
British North Borneo *see* Sabah
British Solomon Islands Protectorate
see Solomon Islands
British Virgin Islands 55 F3 *var.*
Virgin Islands. *UK dependent territory*
E West Indies
Brittany *see* Bretagne
Briva Curretia *see* Brive-la-Gaillarde
Briva Isarae *see* Pontoise
Brive *see* Brive-la-Gaillarde
Brive-la-Gaillarde 91 C5 *prev.* Brive;
anc. Briva Curretia. Corrèze, C France
Brixen *see* Bressanone

Brixia *see* Brescia
Brno 99 B5 *Ger.* Brünn. Jihomoravský
Kraj, SE Czech Republic
Brocēni 106 B3 SW Latvia
Brod/Bród *see* Slavonski Brod
Brodeur Peninsula 37 F2 *peninsula*
Baffin Island, Nunavut, NE Canada
Brod na Savi *see* Slavonski Brod
Brodnica 98 C3 *Ger.* Buddenbrock.
Kujawski-pomorskie, C Poland
Broek-in-Waterland 86 C3 Noord-
Holland, C Netherlands
Broken Arrow 49 G1 Oklahoma, C USA
Broken Bay 148 E1 *bay* New South
Wales, SE Australia
Broken Hill 149 B6 New South Wales,
SE Australia
Broken Ridge 141 D6 *undersea plateau*
S Indian Ocean
Bromberg *see* Bydgoszcz
Bromley 89 B8 United Kingdom
Brookhaven 42 B3 Mississippi, S USA
Brookings 45 F3 South Dakota, N USA
Brooks Range 36 D2 *mountain range*
Alaska, USA
Brookton 147 B6 Western Australia
Broome 146 B3 Western Australia
Broomfield 44 D4 Colorado, C USA
Broucsella *see* Brussel/Bruxelles
Brovary 109 E2 Kyyivs'ka Oblast',
N Ukraine
Brownfield 49 E2 Texas, SW USA
Brownsville 49 G5 Texas, SW USA
Brownwood 49 F3 Texas, SW USA
Brozha 107 D7 Mahilyowskaya Voblasts',
E Belarus
Bruges *see* Brugge
Brugge 87 A5 *Fr.* Bruges. West-
Vlaanderen, NW Belgium
Brummen 86 D3 Gelderland,
E Netherlands
Brundisium/Brundusium *see* Brindisi
Brunei 138 D3 *off.* Brunei Darussalam,
Mal. Negara Brunei Darussalam.
country SE Asia

BRUNEI
Southeast Asia

Official name Brunei Darussalam
Formation 1984 / 1984
Capital Bandar Seri Begawan
Population 400,000 / 197 people
per sq mile (76 people per sq km)
Total area 2228 sq. miles (5770 sq. km)
Languages Malay*, English, Chinese
Religions Muslim (mainly Sunni) 66%,
Buddhist 14%, Christian 10%, Other 10%
Ethnic mix Malay 67%, Chinese 16%,
Other 11%, Indigenous 6%
Government Monarchy
Currency Brunei dollar = 100 cents
Literacy rate 95%
Calorie consumption 3088 kilocalories

Brunei Darussalam *see* Brunei
Brunei Town *see* Bandar Seri Begawan
Brünn *see* Brno
Brunner, Lake 151 C5 *lake* South Island,
New Zealand
Brunswick 43 E3 Georgia, SE USA
Brunswick *see* Braunschweig
Brusa *see* Bursa
Brus Laguna 52 D2 Gracias a Dios,
E Honduras
Brussa *see* Bursa
Brussel 87 C6 *var.* Brussels,
Fr. Bruxelles, *Ger.* Brüssel; *anc.*
Broucsella. *country capital*
(Belgium) Brussels, C Belgium
Brüssel/Brussels *see* Brussel/Bruxelles
Brüx *see* Most
Bruxelles *see* Brussel
Bryan 49 G3 Texas, SW USA
Bryansk 111 A5 Bryanskaya Oblast',
W Russian Federation
Brzeg 98 C4 *Ger.* Brieg; *anc.* Civitas Altae
Ripae. Opolskie, S Poland
Brześć Litewski/Brześć nad Bugiem
see Brest
Brzeżany *see* Berezhany
Bucaramanga 58 B2 Santander,
N Colombia
Buchanan 74 C5 *prev.* Grand Bassa.
SW Liberia
Buchanan, Lake 49 F3 *reservoir* Texas,
SW USA
Bucharest *see* București
Buckeye State *see* Ohio

Bu Craa *see* Bou Craa
București 108 C5 *Eng.* Bucharest, *Ger.*
Bukarest, *prev.* Altenburg; *anc.* Cetatea
Dâmboviţei. *country capital* (Romania)
București, S Romania
Buda-Kashalyova 107 D7 *Rus.* Buda-
Koshelëvo. Homyel'skaya Voblasts',
SE Belarus
Buda-Koshelëvo *see* Buda-Kashalyova
Budapest 99 C6 *off.* Budapest Főváros,
SCr. Budimpešta. *country capital*
(Hungary) Pest, N Hungary
Budapest Főváros *see* Budapest
Budaun 134 D3 Uttar Pradesh, N India
Buddenbrock *see* Brodnica
Budějovice *see* Budweis
Budweis *see* České Budějovice
Budyšin *see* Bautzen
Buena Park 46 E2 California, W USA
North America
Buenaventura 58 A3 Valle del Cauca,
W Colombia
Buena Vista 61 G4 Santa Cruz, S Bolivia
Buena Vista 93 H5 S Gibraltar Europe
Buena Vista 93 H5 S Gibraltar Europe
Buenavista 93 H5 Western Europe
NW Mexico
Buenavista 93 H5 Sonora, NW Mexico
Buena Vista 93 H5 Cerro Largo,
Uruguay
Buena Vista 93 H5 Colorado, C USA
Buena Vista 93 H5 Georgia, SE USA
Buena Vista 93 H5 Virginia, NE USA
Buenos Aires 64 D4 *var.* Santa Maria del
Buen Aire. *country capital* (Argentina)
Buenos Aires, E Argentina
Buenos Aires 53 E5 Puntarenas,
SE Costa Rica
Buenos Aires, Lago 65 B6 *var.* Lago
General Carrera. *lake* Argentina/Chile
Buffalo 41 E3 New York, NE USA
Buffalo Narrows 37 F4 Saskatchewan,
C Canada
Buff Bay 54 B5 E Jamaica
Buftea 108 C5 Ilfov, S Romania
Bug 81 E3 *Bel.* Zakhodni Buh, *Eng.*
Western Bug, *Rus.* Zapadnyy Bug, *Ukr.*
Zakhidnyy Buh. *river* E Europe
Buga 58 B3 Valle del Cauca,
W Colombia
Bughotu *see* Santa Isabel
Buguruslan 111 D6 Orenburgskaya
Oblast', W Russian Federation
Buitenzorg *see* Bogor
Bujalance 92 D4 Andalucía, S Spain
Bujanovac 101 E5 SE Serbia
Bujnurd *see* Bojnūrd
Bujumbura 73 B7 *prev.* Usumbura.
country capital (Burundi) W Burundi
Bukarest *see* București
Bukavu 77 E6 *prev.* Costermansville.
Sud-Kivu, E Dem. Rep. Congo
Bukhara *see* Buxoro
Bukoba 73 B6 Kagera, NW Tanzania
Bülach 95 B7 Zürich, NW Switzerland
Bulawayo 78 D3 Matabeleland North,
SW Zimbabwe
Bulgan 127 E2 Bulgan, N Mongolia
Bulgaria 104 C2 *off.* Republic of Bulgaria,
Bul. Bŭlgariya; *prev.* People's Republic
of Bulgaria. *country* SE Europe

BULGARIA
Southeast Europe

Official name Republic of Bulgaria
Formation 1908 / 1947
Capital Sofia
Population 7.4 million / 173 people
per sq mile (67 people per sq km)
Total area 42,822 sq. miles (110,910 sq. km)
Languages Bulgarian*, Turkish, Romani
Religions Bulgarian Orthodox 83%,
Muslim 12%, Other 4%,
Roman Catholic 1%
Ethnic mix Bulgarian 84%, Turkish 9%,
Roma 5%, Other 2%
Government Parliamentary system
Currency Lev = 100 stotinki
Calorie consumption 2791 kilocalories

Bulgaria, People's Republic of *see*
Bulgaria
Bulgaria, Republic of *see* Bulgaria
Bŭlgariya *see* Bulgaria
Bullion State *see* Missouri
Bull Shoals Lake 42 B1 *reservoir*
Arkansas/Missouri, C USA

Bulukumba 139 E4 *Prev.* Boeloekoemba.
Sulawesi, C Indonesia
Bumba 77 D5 Equateur, N Dem. Rep.
Congo
Bunbury 147 A7 Western Australia
Bundaberg 148 E4 Queensland,
E Australia
Bungo-suido 131 B7 *strait* SW Japan
Bunia 77 E5 Orientale, NE Dem. Rep.
Congo
Bünyan 116 D3 Kayseri, C Turkey
Buraida *see* Buraydah
Buraydah 120 B4 *var.* Buraida. Al
Qasim, N Saudi Arabia
Burdigala *see* Bordeaux
Burdur 116 B4 *var.* Buldur. Burdur,
SW Turkey
Burdur Turkey
Burdur Gölü 116 B4 *salt lake* SW Turkey
Burē 72 C4 Āmara, N Ethiopia
Burgas 104 E2 *var.* Bourgas. Burgas,
E Bulgaria
Burgaski Zaliv 104 E2 *gulf* E Bulgaria
Burgos 92 D2 Castilla y León, N Spain
Burgundy *see* Bourgogne
Burhan Budai Shan 126 D4 *mountain*
range C China
Buriram 137 D5 *var.* Buri Ram,
Puriramya. Buri Ram, E Thailand
Buri Ram *see* Buriram
Burjassot 93 F3 Valenciana, E Spain
Burkburnett 49 F2 Texas, SW USA
Burketown 148 B3 Queensland,
NE Australia
Burkina *see* Burkina Faso
Burkina Faso 75 E4 *off.* Burkina Faso;
var. Burkina, *prev.* Upper Volta.
country W Africa

BURKINA FASO
West Africa

Official name Burkina Faso
Formation 1960 / 1960
Capital Ouagadougou
Population 17 million / 161 people
per sq mile (62 people per sq km)
Total area 105,869 sq. miles
(274,200 sq. km)
Languages Mossi, Fulani, French*,
Tuareg, Dyula, Songhai
Religions Muslim 55%, Christian 25%,
Traditional beliefs 20%
Ethnic mix Mossi 48%, Other 21%,
Peul 10%, Lobi 7%, Bobo 7%,
Mande 7%
Government Presidential system
Currency CFA franc = 100 centimes
Literacy rate 29%
Calorie consumption 2647 kilocalories

Burley 46 D4 Idaho, NW USA
Burlington 45 G4 Iowa, C USA
Burlington 41 F2 Vermont, NE USA
Burma 136 A3 *off.* Union of Myanmar.
country SE Asia. *See also* Myanmar
Burnie 149 C8 Tasmania, SE Australia
Burns 46 C3 Oregon, NW USA
Burnside 37 F3 *river* Nunavut,
NW Canada
Burnsville 45 F2 Minnesota, N USA
Burrel 101 D6 *var.* Burreli. Dibër,
C Albania
Burreli *see* Burrel
Burriana *see* Borriana
Bursa 116 B3 *var.* Brussa, *prev.* Brusa;
anc. Prusa. Prusa. Bursa, NW Turkey
Būr Sa'īd 72 B1 *var.* Port Said. N Egypt
Burtnieks 106 C3 *var.* Burtnieks Ezers.
lake N Latvia
Burtnieks Ezers *see* Burtnieks
Burundi 73 B7 *off.* Republic of Burundi;
prev. Kingdom of Burundi, Urundi.
country C Africa

BURUNDI
Central Africa

Official name Republic of Burundi
Formation 1962 / 1962
Capital Bujumbura
Population 8.6 million / 868 people
per sq mile (335 people per sq km)
Total area 10,745 sq. miles (27,830 sq. km)
Languages Kirundi*, French*, Kiswahili
Religions Roman Catholic 62%,
Traditional beliefs 23%, Muslim 10%,
Protestant 5%
Ethnic mix Hutu 85%, Tutsi 14%, Twa 1%
Government Presidential system

BURUNDI
(continued)

Currency Burundian franc = 100 centimes
Literacy rate 67%
Calorie consumption 1604 kilocalories

Burundi, Kingdom of *see* Burundi
Burundi, Republic of *see* Burundi
Buru, Pulau *139 F4 prev.* Boeroe. *island* E Indonesia
Busan *129 E4 off.* Pusan-gwangyŏksi, *var.* Vusan; *prev.* Pusan, *Jap.* Fusan. SE South Korea
Buşayrah *118 D3* Dayr az Zawr, E Syria
Büshehr/Bushire *see* Bandar-e Būshehr
Busra *see* Al Başrah, Iraq
Busselton *147 A7* Western Australia
Bussora *see* Al Başrah
Buta *77 D5* Orientale, N Dem. Rep. Congo
Butembo *77 E5* Nord-Kivu, NE Dem. Rep. Congo
Butler *41 E4* Pennsylvania, NE USA
Buton, Pulau *139 E4 var.* Pulau Butung; *prev.* Boetoeng. *island* C Indonesia
Bütow *see* Bytów
Butte *44 B2* Montana, NW USA
Butterworth *138 B3* Pinang, Peninsular Malaysia
Button Islands *39 E1 island group* Nunavut, NE Canada
Butuan *139 F2 off.* Butuan City. Mindanao, S Philippines
Butuan City *see* Butuan
Butung, Pulau *see* Buton, Pulau
Butuntum *see* Bitonto
Buulobarde *73 D5 var.* Buulo Berde. Hiiraan, C Somalia
Buulo Berde *see* Buulobarde
Buur Gaabo *73 D6* Jubbada Hoose, S Somalia
Buxoro *122 D2 var.* Bokhara, *Rus.* Bukhara. Buxoro Viloyati, C Uzbekistan
Buynaksk *111 B8* Respublika Dagestan, SW Russian Federation
Büyükmenderes Nehri *116 A4 river* SW Turkey
Buzău *108 C4* Buzău, SE Romania
Büzmeyin *see* Abadan
Buzuluk *111 D6* Orenburgskaya Oblast', W Russian Federation
Byahoml' *107 D5 Rus.* Begoml'. Vitsyebskaya Voblasts', N Belarus
Byalynichy *107 D6 Rus.* Belynichi. Mahilyowskaya Voblasts', E Belarus
Byan Tumen *see* Choybalsan
Byarezina *107 D6 prev.* Byerezino, *Rus.* Berezina. *river* C Belarus
Bydgoszcz *98 C3 Ger.* Bromberg. Kujawski-pomorskie, C Poland
Byelaruskaya Hrada *107 B6 Rus.* Belorusskaya Gryada. *ridge* N Belarus
Byerezino *see* Byarezina
Byron Island *see* Nikunau
Bystrovka *see* Kemin
Bytča *99 C5* Žilinský Kraj, N Slovakia
Bytom *99 C5 Ger.* Beuthen. Śląskie, S Poland
Bytów *98 C2 Ger.* Bütow. Pomorskie, N Poland
Byuzmeyin *see* Abadan
Byval'ki *107 D8* Homyel'skaya Voblasts', SE Belarus
Byzantium *see* Istanbul

C

Caála *78 B2 var.* Kaala, Robert Williams, *Port.* Vila Robert Williams. Huambo, C Angola
Caazapá *64 D3* Caazapá, S Paraguay
Caballo Reservoir *48 C3 reservoir* New Mexico, SW USA
Cabanaquinta *92 D1* Asturias, N Spain
Cabanatuan *139 E1 off.* Cabanatuan City. Luzon, N Philippines
Cabanatuan City *see* Cabanatuan
Cabillonum *see* Chalon-sur-Saône
Cabimas *58 C1* Zulia, NW Venezuela
Cabinda *78 A1 var.* Kabinda. Cabinda, NW Angola
Cabinda *78 A1 var.* Kabinda. *province* NW Angola
Lake Cabora Bassa *78 D2 var.* Lake Cabora Bassa. *reservoir* NW Mozambique

Cabora Bassa, Lake *see* Cahora Bassa, Albufeira de
Caborca *50 B1* Sonora, NW Mexico
Cabot Strait *39 G4 strait* E Canada
Cabo Verde, Ilhas do *see* Cape Verde
Cabras, Ilha das *76 E2 island* S Sao Tome and Principe, Africa, E Atlantic Ocean
Cabrera *93 G3 river* NW Spain
Cáceres *92 C3 Ar.* Qazris. Extremadura, W Spain
Cachimbo, Serra do *63 E2 mountain range* C Brazil
Caconda *78 B2* Huíla, C Angola
Čadca *99 C5 Hung.* Csaca. Žilinský Kraj, N Slovakia
Cadillac *40 C2* Michigan, N USA
Cadiz *139 E2 off.* Cadiz City. Negros, C Philippines
Cádiz *92 C5 anc.* Gades, Gadier, Gadir, Gadire. Andalucía, SW Spain
Cadiz City *see* Cadiz
Gulf of Cadiz *92 B5 Eng.* Gulf of Cadiz. *gulf* Portugal/Spain
Cádiz, Gulf of *see* Cádiz, Golfo de
Cadurcum *see* Cahors
Caen *90 B3* Calvados, N France
Caene/Caenepolis *see* Qinā
Caerdydd *see* Cardiff
Caer Glou *see* Gloucester
Caer Gybi *see* Holyhead
Caerleon *see* Chester
Caer Luel *see* Carlisle
Caesaraugusta *see* Zaragoza
Caesarea Mazaca *see* Kayseri
Caesarobriga *see* Talavera de la Reina
Caesarodunum *see* Tours
Caesaromagus *see* Beauvais
Caesena *see* Cesena
Cafayate *64 C2* Salta, N Argentina
Cagayan de Oro *139 E2 off.* Cagayan de Oro City. Mindanao, S Philippines
Cagayan de Oro City *see* Cagayan de Oro
Cagliari *97 A6 anc.* Caralis. Sardegna, Italy, C Mediterranean Sea
Caguas *55 F3* E Puerto Rico
Cahors *91 C5 anc.* Cadurcum. Lot, S France
Cahul *108 D4 Rus.* Kagul. S Moldova
Caicos Passage *54 D2 strait* Bahamas/ Turks and Caicos Islands
Caiffa *see* Hefa
Cailungo *96 E1* N San Marino
Caiphas *see* Hefa
Cairns *148 D3* Queensland, NE Australia
Cairo *72 B2 var.* El Qâhira, *Ar.* Al Qâhirah. *country capital* (Egypt) N Egypt
Caislean an Bharraigh *see* Castlebar
Cajamarca *60 B3 prev.* Caxamarca. Cajamarca, NW Peru
Čakovec *100 B2 Ger.* Csakathurn, *Hung.* Csáktornya; *prev. Ger.* Tschakathurn. Medimurje, N Croatia
Calabar *75 G5* Cross River, S Nigeria
Calabozo *58 D2* Guárico, C Venezuela
Calafat *108 B5* Dolj, SW Romania
Calafate *see* El Calafate
Calahorra *93 E2* La Rioja, N Spain
Calais *90 C2* Pas-de-Calais, N France
Calais *41 H2* Maine, NE USA
Calais, Pas de *see* Dover, Strait of
Calama *64 B2* Antofagasta, N Chile
Cālāraşi *108 D4 var.* Cālāraş, SE Romania
Cālāraşi *108 D4 var.* Cālāraş, *Rus.* Kalarash. C Moldova
Calatayud *93 E2* Aragón, NE Spain
Calbayog *139 E2 off.* Calbayog City. Samar, C Philippines
Calbayog City *see* Calbayog
Calcutta *135 G4* West Bengal, N India
Caldas da Rainha *92 B3* Leiria, W Portugal
Caldera *64 B3* Atacama, N Chile
Caldwell *46 C3* Idaho, NW USA
Caledonia *52 C1* Corozal, N Belize
Caleta Olivia *65 B6* Santa Cruz, SE Argentina
Calgary *37 E5* Alberta, SW Canada
Cali *58 B3* Valle del Cauca, W Colombia
Calicut *see* Kozhikode
California *47 B7 off.* State of California, *also known as* El Dorado, The Golden State. *state* W USA
Gulf of California *50 B2 Eng.* Gulf of California; *prev.* Sea of Cortez. *gulf* W Mexico

California, Gulf of *see* California, Golfo de
Călimăneşti *108 B4* Vâlcea, SW Romania
Calisia *see* Kalisz
Callabonna, Lake *149 B5 lake* South Australia
Callao *60 C4* Callao, W Peru
Callatis *see* Mangalia
Callosa de Segura *93 F4* Valencia, E Spain
Calmar *see* Kalmar
Caloundra *149 E5* Queensland, E Australia
Caltanissetta *97 C7* Sicilia, Italy, C Mediterranean Sea
Caluula *72 E4* Bari, NE Somalia
Camabatela *78 B1* Cuanza Norte, NW Angola
Camacupa *78 B2 var.* General Machado, *Port.* Vila General Machado. Bié, C Angola
Camagüey *54 C2 prev.* Puerto Príncipe. Camagüey, C Cuba
Camagüey, Archipiélago de *54 C2 island group* C Cuba
Camana *61 E4 var.* Camaná. Arequipa, SW Peru
Camargue *91 D6 physical region* SE France
Ca Mau *137 D6 var.* Quan Long. Minh Hai, S Vietnam
Cambay, Gulf of *see* Khambhāt, Gulf of
Camberia *see* Chambéry
Cambodia *137 D5 off.* Kingdom of Cambodia, *var.* Democratic Kampuchea, Roat Kampuchea, *Cam.* Kampuchea; *prev.* People's Democratic Republic of Kampuchea. *country* SE Asia

CAMBODIA
Southeast Asia

Official name Kingdom of Cambodia
Formation 1953 / 1953
Capital Phnom Penh
Population 14.3 million / 210 people per sq mile (81 people per sq km)
Total area 69,900 sq. miles (181,040 sq. km)
Languages Khmer*, French, Chinese, Vietnamese, Cham
Religions Buddhist 93%, Muslim 6%, Christian 1%
Ethnic mix Khmer 90%, Other 5%, Vietnamese 4%, Chinese 1%
Government Parliamentary system
Currency Riel = 100 sen
Literacy rate 78%
Calorie consumption 2382 kilocalories

Cambodia, Kingdom of *see* Cambodia
Cambrai *90 C2 Flem.* Kambryk, *prev.* Cambray; *anc.* Cameracum. Nord, N France
Cambray *see* Cambrai
Cambrian Mountains *89 C6 mountain range* C Wales, United Kingdom
Cambridge *54 A4* W Jamaica
Cambridge *150 D3* Waikato, North Island, New Zealand
Cambridge *89 E6 Lat.* Cantabrigia. E England, United Kingdom
Cambridge *41 F4* Maryland, NE USA
Cambridge *40 D4* Ohio, NE USA
Cambridge Bay *37 F3 var.* Ikaluktutiak. Victoria Island, Nunavut, NW Canada
Camden *42 B2* Arkansas, C USA
Camellia State *see* Alabama
Cameracum *see* Cambrai
Cameroon *76 A4 off.* Republic of Cameroon, *Fr.* Cameroun. *country* W Africa

CAMEROON
Central Africa

Official name Republic of Cameroon
Formation 1960 / 1961
Capital Yaoundé
Population 20 million / 111 people per sq mile (43 people per sq km)
Total area 183,567 sq. miles (475,400 sq. km)
Languages Bamileke, Fang, Fulani, French*, English*
Religions Roman Catholic 35%, Traditional beliefs 25%, Muslim 22%, Protestant 18%
Ethnic mix Cameroon highlanders 31%,

CAMEROON
(continued)

Other 21%, Equatorial Bantu 19%, Kirdi 11%, Fulani 10%, Northwestern Bantu 8%
Government Presidential system
Currency CFA franc = 100 centimes
Literacy rate 71%
Calorie consumption 2457 kilocalories

Cameroon, Republic of *see* Cameroon
Cameroun *see* Cameroon
Camocim *63 F2* Ceará, E Brazil
Camopi *59 H3* E French Guiana
Campamento *52 C2* Olancho, C Honduras
Campania *97 D5 Eng.* Champagne. *region* S Italy
Campbell, Cape *151 D5 headland* South Island, New Zealand
Campbell Island *142 D5 island* S New Zealand
Campbell Plateau *142 D5 undersea plateau* SW Pacific Ocean
Campbell River *36 D5* Vancouver Island, British Columbia, SW Canada
Campeche *51 G4* Campeche, SE Mexico
Bay of Campeche *51 F4 Eng.* Bay of Campeche. *bay* E Mexico
Campeche, Bay of *see* Campeche, Bahía de
Câm Pha *136 E3* Quang Ninh, N Vietnam
Câmpina *108 C4 prev.* Cîmpina. Prahova, SE Romania
Campina Grande *63 G2* Paraíba, E Brazil
Campinas *63 F4* São Paulo, S Brazil
Campobasso *97 D5* Molise, C Italy
Campo Criptana *see* Campo de Criptana
Campo de Criptana *93 E3 var.* Campo Criptana. Castilla-La Mancha, C Spain
Campo Grande *63 E4 state capital* Mato Grosso do Sul, SW Brazil
Campos dos Goytacazes *63 F4* Rio de Janeiro, SE Brazil
Câmpulung *108 B4 prev.* Cîmpulung-Muscel, Cîmpulung. Argeş, S Romania
Câmpulung-Muscel *see* Câmpulung
Campus Stellae *see* Santiago de Compostela
Cam Ranh *137 E6 prev.* Ba Ngoi. Khanh Hoa, S Vietnam
Canada *34 B4 country* N North America

CANADA
North America

Official name Canada
Formation 1867 / 1949
Capital Ottawa
Population 34.3 million / 10 people per sq mile (4 people per sq km)
Total area 3,854,085 sq. miles (9,984,670 sq. km)
Languages English*, French*, Chinese, Italian, German, Ukrainian, Portuguese, Inuktitut, Cree
Religions Roman Catholic 44%, Protestant 29%, Other and nonreligious 27%
Ethnic mix European 66%, Other 32%, Amerindian 2%
Government Parliamentary system
Currency Canadian dollar = 100 cents
Literacy rate 99%
Calorie consumption 3399 kilocalories

Canada Basin *34 C2 undersea basin* Arctic Ocean
Canadian River *49 E2 river* SW USA
Çanakkale *116 A3 var.* Dardanelli; *prev.* Chanak, Kale Sultanie. Çanakkale, W Turkey
Cananea *50 B1* Sonora, NW Mexico
Canarreos, Archipiélago de los *54 B2 island group* W Cuba
Canary Islands *70 A2 Eng.* Canary Islands. *island group* Spain, NE Atlantic Ocean
Canary Islands *see* Canarias, Islas
Cañas *52 D4* Guanacaste, NW Costa Rica
Canaveral, Cape *43 E4 headland* Florida, SE USA
Canavieiras *63 G3* Bahia, E Brazil
Canberra *142 C4 country capital* (Australia) Australian Capital Territory, SE Australia
Cancún *51 H3* Quintana Roo, SE Mexico
Candia *see* Irákleio

Canea see Chaniá
Cangzhou 128 D4 Hebei, E China
Caniapiscau 39 E2 river Québec, E Canada
Caniapiscau, Réservoir de 38 D3 reservoir Québec, C Canada
Canik Dağları 116 D2 mountain range N Turkey
Canillo 91 A7 Canillo, C Andorra Europe
Çankırı 116 C3 var. Chankiri; anc. Gangra, Germanicopolis. Çankın, N Turkey
Cannanore see Kannur
Cannes 91 D6 Alpes-Maritimes, SE France
Canoas 63 E5 Rio Grande do Sul, S Brazil
Canon City 44 C5 Colorado, C USA
Cantabria 92 D1 autonomous community N Spain
Cantábrica, Cordillera 92 C1 mountain range N Spain
Cantabrigia see Cambridge
Cantaura 59 E2 Anzoátegui, NE Venezuela
Canterbury 89 E7 hist. Cantwaraburh; anc. Durovernum, Lat. Cantuaria. SE England, United Kingdom
Canterbury Bight 151 C6 bight South Island, New Zealand
Canterbury Plains 151 C6 plain South Island, New Zealand
Cân Thơ 137 E6 Cân Thơ, S Vietnam
Canton 42 B2 Mississippi, S USA
Canton 40 D4 Ohio, N USA
Canton see Guangzhou
Canton Island see Kanton
Cantuaria/Cantwaraburh see Canterbury
Canyon 49 E2 Texas, SW USA
Cao Băng 136 D3 var. Caobang. Cao Băng, N Vietnam
Caobang see Cao Băng
Cap-Breton, Île du see Cape Breton Island
Cape Barren Island 149 C8 island Furneaux Group, Tasmania, SE Australia
Cape Basin 69 B7 undersea basin S Atlantic Ocean
Cape Breton Island 39 G4 Fr. Île du Cap-Breton. island Nova Scotia, SE Canada
Cape Charles 41 F5 Virginia, NE USA
Cape Coast 75 E5 prev. Cape Coast Castle. S Ghana
Cape Coast Castle see Cape Coast
Cape Girardeau 45 H5 Missouri, C USA
Capelle aan den IJssel 86 C4 Zuid-Holland, SW Netherlands
Cape Palmas see Harper
Cape Saint Jacques see Vung Tau
Cape Town 78 B5 var. Ekapa, Afr. Kaapstad, Kapstad. country capital (South Africa-legislative capital) Western Cape, SW South Africa
Cape Verde 74 A2 off. Republic of Cape Verde, Port. Cabo Verde, Ilhas do Cabo Verde. country E Atlantic Ocean

CAPE VERDE
Atlantic Ocean

Official name Republic of Cape Verde
Formation 1975 / 1975
Capital Praia
Population 500,000 / 321 people per sq mile (124 people per sq km)
Total area 1557 sq. miles (4033 sq. km)
Languages Portuguese Creole, Portuguese*
Religions Roman Catholic 97%, Other 2%, Protestant (Church of the Nazarene) 1%
Ethnic mix Mestiço 71%, African 28%, European 1%
Government Mixed presidential–parliamentary system
Currency Cape Verde escudo = 100 centavos
Literacy rate 85%
Calorie consumption 2644 kilocalories

Cape Verde Basin 66 C4 undersea basin E Atlantic Ocean
Cape Verde Plain 66 C4 abyssal plain E Atlantic Ocean
Cape Verde, Republic of see Cape Verde
Cape York Peninsula 148 C2 peninsula Queensland, N Australia
Cap-Haïtien 54 D3 var. Le Cap. N Haiti
Capira 53 G5 Panamá, C Panama
Capitán Arturo Prat 154 A2 Chilean research station South Shetland Islands, Antarctica
Capitán Pablo Lagerenza 64 D1 var. Mayor Pablo Lagerenza. Chaco, N Paraguay
Capodistria see Koper
Capri 97 C5 island S Italy
Caprivi Concession see Caprivi Strip
Caprivi Strip 78 C3 Ger. Caprivizipfel; prev. Caprivi Concession. cultural region NE Namibia
Caprivizipfel see Caprivi Strip
Cap Saint-Jacques see Vung Tau
Caquetá, Río 58 C5 var. Rio Japurá, Yapurá. river Brazil/Colombia
Caquetá, Río see Japurá, Rio
CAR see Central African Republic
Caracal 108 B5 Olt, S Romania
Caracaraí 62 D1 Rondônia, W Brazil
Caracas 58 D1 country capital (Venezuela) Distrito Federal, N Venezuela
Caralis see Cagliari
Caratasca, Laguna de 53 E2 lagoon NE Honduras
Carballiño see O Carballiño
Carbondale 40 B5 Illinois, N USA
Carbon, Laguna del 64 B7 depression S Argentina
Carbonia 97 A6 var. Carbonia Centro. Sardegna, Italy, C Mediterranean Sea
Carbonia Centro see Carbonia
Carcaso see Carcassonne
Carcassonne 91 C6 anc. Carcaso. Aude, S France
Cardamomes, Chaîne des see Krâvanh, Chuŏr Phnum
Cardamom Mountains see Krâvanh, Chuŏr Phnum
Cárdenas 54 B2 Matanzas, W Cuba
Cardiff 89 C7 Wel. Caerdydd. national capital S Wales, United Kingdom
Cardigan Bay 89 C6 bay W Wales, United Kingdom
Carei 108 B3 Ger. Gross-Karol, Karol, Hung. Nagykároly; prev. Careii-Mari. Satu Mare, NW Romania
Careii-Mari see Carei
Carey, Lake 147 B6 lake Western Australia
Cariaco 59 E1 Sucre, NE Venezuela
Caribbean Sea 54 C4 sea W Atlantic Ocean
Caribrod see Dimitrovgrad
Carlisle 88 C4 anc. Caer Luel, Luguvallium, Luguvallum. NW England, United Kingdom
Carlow 89 B6 Ir. Ceatharlach. SE Ireland
Carlsbad 48 D3 New Mexico, SW USA
Carlsbad see Karlovy Vary
Carlsberg Ridge 140 B4 undersea ridge S Arabian Sea
Carlsruhe see Karlsruhe
Carmana/Carmania see Kermān
Carmarthen 89 C6 SW Wales, United Kingdom
Carmaux 91 C6 Tarn, S France
Carmel 40 C4 Indiana, N USA
Carmelita 52 B1 Petén, N Guatemala
Carmen 51 G4 var. Ciudad del Carmen. Campeche, SE Mexico
Carmona 92 C4 Andalucía, S Spain
Carmona see Uíge
Carnaro see Kvarner
Carnarvon 147 A5 Western Australia
Carnegie, Lake 147 B5 salt lake Western Australia
Car Nicobar 133 F3 island Nicobar Islands, India, NE Indian Ocean
Caroąo, Ilha 76 E1 island N Sao Tome and Principe, Africa, E Atlantic Ocean
Carolina 63 F2 Maranhão, E Brazil
Caroline Island see Millennium Island
Caroline Islands 144 B2 island group C Micronesia
Carolopois see Châlons-en-Champagne
Caroní, Río 59 E3 river E Venezuela
Caronium see A Coruña
Carora 58 C1 Lara, N Venezuela
Carpathian Mountains 81 E4 var. Carpathians, Cz./Pol. Karpaty, Ger. Karpaten. mountain range E Europe
Carpathians see Carpathian Mountains
Carpathos/Carpathus see Kárpathos
Carpații Sudici see Carpații Meridionalii
Carpentaria, Gulf of 148 B2 gulf N Australia
Carpi 96 C2 Emilia-Romagna, N Italy
Carrara 96 B3 Toscana, C Italy
Carson City 47 C5 state capital Nevada, W USA
Carson Sink 47 C5 salt flat Nevada, W USA
Carstensz, Puntjak see Jaya, Puncak
Cartagena 58 B1 var. Cartagena de los Indes. Bolívar, NW Colombia
Cartagena 93 F4 anc. Carthago Nova. Murcia, SE Spain
Cartagena de los Indes see Cartagena
Cartago 53 E4 Cartago, C Costa Rica
Carthage 45 F5 Missouri, C USA
Carthago Nova see Cartagena
Cartwright 39 F2 Newfoundland and Labrador, E Canada
Carúpano 59 E1 Sucre, NE Venezuela
Carusbur see Cherbourg
Caruthersville 45 H5 Missouri, C USA
Cary 43 F1 North Carolina, SE USA
Casablanca 70 C2 Ar. Dar-el-Beida. NW Morocco
Casa Grande 48 B2 Arizona, SW USA
Cascade Range 46 B3 mountain range Oregon/Washington, NW USA
Cascadia Basin 34 A4 undersea basin NE Pacific Ocean
Cascais 92 B4 Lisboa, C Portugal
Caserta 97 D5 Campania, S Italy
Casey 154 D4 Australian research station Antarctica
Čáslav 99 B5 Ger. Tschaslau. Střední Čechy, C Czech Republic
Casper 44 C3 Wyoming, C USA
Caspian Depression 111 B7 Kaz. Kaspīy Mangy Oypaty, Rus. Prikaspiyskaya Nizmennost'. depression Kazakhstan/Russian Federation
Caspian Sea 114 A4 Az. Xäzär Dänizi, Kaz. Kaspiy Tengizi, Per. Baḩr-e Khazar, Daryā-ye Khazar, Rus. Kaspiyskoye More. inland sea Asia/Europe
Cassai see Kasai
Cassel see Kassel
Castamoni see Kastamonu
Casteggio 96 B2 Lombardia, N Italy
Castelló de la Plana see Castellón de la Plana
Castellón see Castellón de la Plana
Castellón de la Plana 93 F3 var. Castellón, Cat. Castelló de la Plana. Valenciana, E Spain
Castelnaudary 91 C6 Aude, S France
Castelo Branco 92 C3 Castelo Branco, C Portugal
Castelsarrasin 91 B6 Tarn-et-Garonne, S France
Castelvetrano 97 C7 Sicilia, Italy, C Mediterranean Sea
Castilla-La Mancha 93 E3 autonomous community NE Spain
Castilla y León 92 C2 var. Castillia Leon. autonomous community NW Spain
Castillia Leon see Castilla y León
Castlebar 89 A5 Ir. Caisleán an Bharraigh. W Ireland
Castleford 89 D5 N England, United Kingdom
Castle Harbour 42 B5 inlet Bermuda, NW Atlantic Ocean
Castra Regina see Regensburg
Castricum 86 C3 Noord-Holland, W Netherlands
Castries 55 F1 country capital (Saint Lucia) N Saint Lucia
Castro 65 B6 Los Lagos, W Chile
Castrovillari 97 D6 Calabria, SW Italy
Castuera 92 D4 Extremadura, W Spain
Caswell Sound 151 A7 sound South Island, New Zealand
Catacamas 52 D2 Olancho, C Honduras
Catacaos 60 B3 Piura, NW Peru
Catalan Bay 93 H4 bay E Gibraltar, Mediterranean Sea
Cataluña 93 G2 N Spain
Catamarca see San Fernando del Valle de Catamarca
Catania 97 D7 Sicilia, Italy, C Mediterranean Sea
Catanzaro 97 D6 Calabria, SW Italy
Catarroja 93 F3 Valenciana, E Spain
Cat Island 54 C1 island C Bahamas
Catskill Mountains 41 F3 mountain range New York, NE USA
Cattaro see Kotor
Cauca, Río 58 B2 river N Colombia
Caucasia 58 B2 Antioquia, NW Colombia
Caucasus 81 G4 Rus. Kavkaz. mountain range Georgia/Russian Federation
Caura, Río 59 E3 river C Venezuela
Cavaia see Kavajë
Cavalla 74 D5 var. Cavally, Cavally Fleuve. river Côte d'Ivoire/Liberia
Cavally/Cavally Fleuve see Cavalla
Caviana de Fora, Ilha 63 E1 var. Ilha Caviana. island N Brazil
Caviana, Ilha see Caviana de Fora, Ilha
Cawnpore see Kānpur
Caxamarca see Cajamarca
Caxito 78 B1 Bengo, NW Angola
Cayenne 59 H3 dependent territory/arrondissement capital (French Guiana) NE French Guiana
Cayes 54 D3 var. Les Cayes. SW Haiti
Cayman Brac 54 B3 island E Cayman Islands
Cayman Islands 54 B3 UK dependent territory W West Indies
Cayo see San Ignacio
Cay Sal 54 B2 islet SW Bahamas
Cazin 100 B3 Federacija Bosna I Hercegovina, NW Bosnia and Herzegovina
Cazorla 93 E4 Andalucía, S Spain
Ceadâr-Lunga see Ciadîr-Lunga
Ceará 63 F2 off. Estado do Ceará. region C Brazil
Ceará 63 F2 off. Estado do Ceará. state C Brazil
Ceará see Fortaleza
Ceara Abyssal Plain see Ceará Plain
Ceará, Estado do see Ceará
Ceará Plain 56 E3 var. Ceara Abyssal Plain. abyssal plain W Atlantic Ocean
Ceatharlach see Carlow
Cébaco, Isla 53 F5 island SW Panama
Cebu 139 E2 off. Cebu City. Cebu, C Philippines
Cebu City see Cebu
Čechy see Bohemia
Cecina 96 B3 Toscana, C Italy
Cedar City 44 A5 Utah, W USA
Cedar Falls 45 G3 Iowa, C USA
Cedar Lake 38 A2 lake Manitoba, C Canada
Cedar Rapids 45 G3 Iowa, C USA
Cedros, Isla 50 A2 island W Mexico
Ceduna 149 A6 South Australia
Cefalù 97 C7 anc. Cephaloedium. Sicilia, Italy, C Mediterranean Sea
Celebes 139 E4 Eng. Celebes. island C Indonesia
Celebes see Sulawesi
Celebes Sea 139 E3 Ind. Laut Sulawesi. sea Indonesia/Philippines
Celje 95 E7 Ger. Cilli. C Slovenia
Celldömölk 99 C6 Vas, W Hungary
Celle 94 B3 var. Zelle. Niedersachsen, N Germany
Celovec see Klagenfurt
Celtic Sea 89 B7 Ir. An Mhuir Cheilteach. sea SW British Isles
Celtic Shelf 80 B3 continental shelf E Atlantic Ocean
Cenderawasih, Teluk 139 G4 var. Teluk Irian, Teluk Sarera. bay W Pacific Ocean
Cenon 91 B5 Gironde, SW France
Centennial State see Colorado
Centrafricaine, République see Central African Republic
Central African Republic 76 C4 var. République Centrafricaine, abbrev. CAR; prev. Ubangi-Shari, Oubangui-Chari, Territoire de l'Oubangui-Chari. country C Africa

CENTRAL AFRICAN REPUBLIC
Central Africa

Official name Central African Republic
Formation 1960 / 1960
Capital Bangui
Population 4.5 million / 19 people per sq mile (7 people per sq km)
Total area 240,534 sq. miles (622,984 sq. km)
Languages Sango, Banda, Gbaya, French*
Religions Traditional beliefs 35%, Roman Catholic 25%, Protestant 25%, Muslim 15%
Ethnic mix Baya 33%, Banda 27%, Other 17%, Mandjia 13%, Sara 10%,
Government Presidential system

CENTRAL AFRICAN REPUBLIC
(continued)

Currency CFA franc = 100 centimes
Literacy rate 55%
Calorie consumption 2181 kilocalories

Central, Cordillera 58 B3 *mountain range* W Colombia
Cordillera Central 55 E3 *mountain range* C Dominican Republic
Cordillera Central 53 F5 *mountain range* C Panama
Central, Cordillera 139 E1 *mountain range* Luzon, N Philippines
Central Group see Inner Islands
Centralia 46 B2 Washington, NW USA
Central Indian Ridge see Mid-Indian Ridge
Central Makran Range 134 A3 *mountain range* W Pakistan
Central Pacific Basin 142 D1 *undersea basin* C Pacific Ocean
Central Provinces and Berar see Madhya Pradesh
Central Range 144 B3 *mountain range* NW Papua New Guinea
Central Russian Upland 109 G1 *Eng.* Central Russian Upland. *mountain range* W Russian Federation
Central Russian Upland see Srednerusskaya Vozvyshennost'
Central Siberian Plateau 114 D3 *var.* Central Siberian Uplands, *Eng.* Central Siberian Plateau. *mountain range* N Russian Federation
Central Siberian Plateau/Central Siberian Uplands see Srednesibirskoye Ploskogor'ye
Central, Sistema 92 D3 *mountain range* C Spain
Central Valley 47 B6 *valley* California, W USA
Centum Cellae see Civitavecchia
Ceos see Tziá
Cephaloedium see Cefalù
Ceram see Seram, Pulau
Ceram Sea see Seram, Laut
Cerasus see Giresun
Cereté 58 B2 Córdoba, NW Colombia
Cergy-Pontoise see Pontoise
Cerignola 97 D5 Puglia, SE Italy
Çerkeş 116 C2 Çankin, N Turkey
Cernăuţi see Chernivtsi
Cernay 90 E4 Haut-Rhin, NE France
Cerro de Pasco 60 C3 Pasco, C Peru
Cervera 93 F2 Cataluña, NE Spain
Cervino, Monte see Matterhorn
Cesena 96 C3 *anc.* Caesena. Emilia-Romagna, N Italy
Cēsis 106 D3 *Ger.* Wenden. C Latvia
Česká Republika see Czech Republic
České Budějovice 99 B5 *Ger.* Budweis. Jihočeský Kraj, S Czech Republic
Český Krumlov 99 A5 *var.* Böhmisch-Krumau, *Ger.* Krummau. Jihočeský Kraj, S Czech Republic
Český Les see Bohemian Forest
Cetatea Damboviţei see Bucureşti
Cetinje 101 C5 *It.* Cettigne. S Montenegro
Cette see Sète
Cettigne see Cetinje
Ceuta 70 C2 *enclave* Spain, N Africa
Cévennes 91 C6 *mountain range* S France
Ceyhan 116 D4 Adana, S Turkey
Ceylanpınar 117 E4 Şanlıurfa, SE Turkey
Ceylon see Sri Lanka
Ceylon Plain 124 B4 *abyssal plain* N Indian Ocean
Ceyre to the Caribs see Marie-Galante
Chachapoyas 60 B2 Amazonas, NW Peru
Chachevichy 107 D6 *Rus.* Chechevichi. Mahilyowskaya Voblasts', E Belarus
Chaco see Gran Chaco
Chad 76 C3 *off.* Republic of Chad, *Fr.* Tchad. *country* C Africa

CHAD
Central Africa

Official name Republic of Chad
Formation 1960 / 1960
Capital N'Djamena
Population 11.5 million / 24 people per sq mile (9 people per sq km)
Total area 495,752 sq. miles

CHAD
(continued)

(1,284,000 sq. km)
Languages French*, Sara, Arabic*, Maba
Religions Muslim 51%, Christian 35%, Animist 7%, Traditional beliefs 7%
Ethnic mix Other 30%, Sara 28%, Mayo-Kebbi 12%, Arab 12%, Ouaddai 9%, Kanem-Bornou 9%
Government Presidential system
Currency CFA franc = 100 centimes
Literacy rate 34%
Calorie consumption 2074 kilocalories

Chad, Lake 76 B3 *Fr.* Lac Tchad. *lake* C Africa
Chad, Republic of see Chad
Chadron 44 D3 Nebraska, C USA
Chadyr-Lunga see Ciadir-Lunga
Chagai Hills 134 A2 *var.* Chāh Gay. *mountain range* Afghanistan/Pakistan
Chaghasarāy see Asadābād
Chagos-Laccadive Plateau 124 B4 *undersea plateau* N Indian Ocean
Chagos Trench 141 C5 *trench* N Indian Ocean
Chāh Gay see Chāgai Hills
Chaillu, Massif du 77 B6 *mountain range* C Gabon
Chain Ridge 140 B4 *undersea ridge* W Indian Ocean
Chajul 52 B2 Quiché, W Guatemala
Chakhānsūr 122 D5 Nīmrōz, SW Afghanistan
Chala 60 D4 Arequipa, SW Peru
Chalatenango 52 C3 Chalatenango, N El Salvador
Chalcidice see Chalkidikí
Chalcis see Chalkída
Chalki 105 E7 *island* Dodekánisa, Greece, Aegean Sea
Chalkída 105 C5 *var.* Halkida, *prev.* Khalkís; *anc.* Chalcis. Evvoia, E Greece
Chalkidikí 104 C4 *var.* Khalkidhikí; *anc.* Chalcidice. *peninsula* NE Greece
Challans 90 B4 Vendée, NW France
Challapata 61 F4 Oruro, SW Bolivia
Challenger Deep 152 B3 *trench* W Pacific Ocean
Challenger Deep see Mariana Trench
Challenger Fracture Zone 153 F4 *tectonic feature* SE Pacific Ocean
Châlons-en-Champagne 90 D3 *prev.* Châlons-sur-Marne, *hist.* Arcae Remorum; *anc.* Carolopois. Marne, NE France
Châlons-sur-Marne see Châlons-en-Champagne
Chalon-sur-Saône 90 D4 *anc.* Cabillonum. Saône-et-Loire, C France
Cha Mai see Thung Song
Chaman 134 B2 Baluchistān, SW Pakistan
Chambéry 91 D5 *anc.* Camberia. Savoie, E France
Champagne 90 D3 *cultural region* N France
Champagne see Campania
Champaign 40 B4 Illinois, N USA
Champasak 137 D5 Champasak, S Laos
Champlain, Lake 41 F2 *lake* Canada/USA
Champotón 51 G4 Campeche, SE Mexico
Chanak see Çanakkale
Chañaral 64 B3 Atacama, N Chile
Chan-chiang/Chanchiang see Zhanjiang
Chandeleur Islands 42 C3 *island group* Louisiana, S USA
Chandigarh 134 D2 *state capital* Punjab, N India
Chandrapur 135 E5 Mahārāshtra, C India
Changan see Xi'an, Shaanxi, China
Changane 79 E3 *river* S Mozambique
Changchun 128 D3 *var.* Ch'angch'un, Ch'ang-ch'un; *prev.* Hsinking. *province capital* Jilin, NE China
Ch'angch'un/Ch'ang-ch'un see Changchun
Chang Jiang 128 A5 *Eng.* Yangtze. *river* SW China
Changkiakow see Zhangjiakou
Chang, Ko 137 C6 *island* S Thailand
Changsha 128 C6 *var.* Ch'angsha, Ch'ang-sha. *province capital* Hunan, S China

Ch'angsha/Ch'ang-sha see Changsha
Changzhi 128 C4 Shanxi, C China
Chaniá 105 C7 *var.* Hania, Khaniá, *Eng.* Canea; *anc.* Cydonia. Kríti, Greece, E Mediterranean Sea
Chañi, Nevado de 64 B2 *mountain* NW Argentina
Chankiri see Çankırı
Channel Islands 89 C8 *Fr.* Iles Normandes. *island group* S English Channel
Channel Islands 47 B8 *island group* California, W USA
Channel-Port aux Basques 39 G4 Newfoundland and Labrador, SE Canada
Channel, The see English Channel
Channel Tunnel 90 C2 *tunnel* France/United Kingdom
Chantabun/Chantaburi see Chanthaburi
Chantada 92 C1 Galicia, NW Spain
Chanthaburi 137 C6 *var.* Chantabun, Chantaburi. Chantaburi, S Thailand
Chanute 45 F5 Kansas, C USA
Chaouën see Chefchaouen
Chaoyang 128 D3 Liaoning, NE China
Chapala, Lago de 50 D4 *lake* C Mexico
Chapan, Gora 122 B3 *mountain* C Turkmenistan
Chapayevsk 111 C6 Samarskaya Oblast', W Russian Federation
Chaplynka 109 F4 Khersons'ka Oblast', S Ukraine
Chapra see Chhapra
Charcot Seamounts 80 B3 *seamount range* E Atlantic Ocean
Chardzhev see Türkmenabat
Chardzhou/Chardzhui see Türkmenabat
Charente 91 B5 *cultural region* W France
Charente 91 B5 *river* W France
Chari 76 B3 *var.* Shari. *river* Central African Republic/Chad
Chārīkār 123 E4 Parwān, NE Afghanistan
Charity 59 F2 NW Guyana
Charkhlik/Charklik see Ruoqiang
Charleroi 87 C7 Hainaut, S Belgium
Charlesbourg 39 E4 Québec, SE Canada
Charles de Gaulle 90 E1 (Paris) Seine-et-Marne, N France
Charles Island 38 D1 *island* Nunavut, NE Canada
Charles Island see Santa María, Isla
Charleston 43 F2 South Carolina, SE USA
Charleston 40 D5 *state capital* West Virginia, NE USA
Charleville 149 D5 Queensland, E Australia
Charleville-Mézières 90 D3 Ardennes, N France
Charlie-Gibbs Fracture Zone 66 C2 *tectonic feature* N Atlantic Ocean
Charlotte 43 E1 North Carolina, SE USA
Charlotte Amalie 55 F3 *prev.* Saint Thomas. *dependent territory capital* (Virgin Islands (US)) Saint Thomas, N Virgin Islands (US)
Charlotte Harbor 43 E5 *inlet* Florida, SE USA
Charlottenhof see Aegviidu
Charlottesville 41 E5 Virginia, NE USA
Charlottetown 39 F4 *province capital* Prince Edward Island, Prince Edward Island, SE Canada
Charlotte Town see Roseau, Dominica
Charsk see Shar
Charters Towers 148 D3 Queensland, NE Australia
Chartres 90 C3 *anc.* Autricum, Civitas Carnutum. Eure-et-Loir, C France
Chashniki 107 D5 Vitsyebskaya Voblasts', N Belarus
Châteaubriant 90 B4 Loire-Atlantique, NW France
Châteaudun 90 C3 Eure-et-Loir, C France
Châteauroux 90 C4 *prev.* Indreville. Indre, C France
Château-Thierry 90 C3 Aisne, N France
Châtelet 87 C7 Hainaut, S Belgium
Châtelherault see Châtellerault
Châtellerault 90 B4 *var.* Châtelherault. Vienne, W France

Chatham Islands 143 E5 *island group* New Zealand, SW Pacific Ocean
Chatham Rise 142 D5 *var.* Chatham Island Rise. *undersea rise* S Pacific Ocean
Chatkal Range 123 F2 *Rus.* Chatkal'skiy Khrebet. *mountain range* Kyrgyzstan/Uzbekistan
Chatkal'skiy Khrebet see Chatkal Range
Chāttagām see Chittagong
Chattahoochee River 42 D3 *river* SE USA
Chattanooga 42 D1 Tennessee, S USA
Chatyr-Tash 123 G2 Narynskaya Oblast', C Kyrgyzstan
Châu Đôc 137 D6 *var.* Chauphu, Chau Phu. An Giang, S Vietnam
Chauk 136 A3 Magway, W Myanmar (Burma)
Chaumont 90 D4 *prev.* Chaumont-en-Bassigny. Haute-Marne, N France
Chaumont-en-Bassigny see Chaumont
Chau Phu see Châu Đôc
Chausy see Chavusy
Chaves 92 C2 *anc.* Aquae Flaviae. Vila Real, N Portugal
Chávez, Isla see Santa Cruz, Isla
Chavusy 107 E6 *Rus.* Chausy. Mahilyowskaya Voblasts', E Belarus
Chaykovskiy 111 D5 Permskiy Kray, NW Russian Federation
Cheb 99 A5 *Ger.* Eger. Karlovarský Kraj, W Czech Republic
Cheboksary 111 C5 Chuvashskaya Respublika, W Russian Federation
Cheboygan 40 C2 Michigan, N USA
Chechaouèn see Chefchaouen
Chech, Erg 74 D1 *desert* Algeria/Mali
Chechevichi see Chachevichy
Che-chiang see Zhejiang
Cheduba Island 136 A4 *island* W Myanmar (Burma)
Chefchaouen 70 C2 *var.* Chaouèn, Chechaouèn, *Sp.* Xauen. N Morocco
Chefoo see Yantai
Cheju-do see Jeju-do
Cheju Strait see Jeju Strait
Chekiang see Zhejiang
Cheleken see Hazar
Chelkar see Shalkar
Chełm 98 E4 *Rus.* Kholm. Lubelskie, SE Poland
Chełmno 98 C3 *Ger.* Culm, Kulm. Kujawski-pomorskie, C Poland
Chełmża 98 C3 *Ger.* Culmsee, Kulmsee. Kujawski-pomorskie, C Poland
Cheltenham 89 D6 C England, United Kingdom
Chelyabinsk 114 C3 Chelyabinskaya Oblast', C Russian Federation
Chemnitz 94 D4 *prev.* Karl-Marx-Stadt. Sachsen, E Germany
Chemulpo see Incheon
Chenāb 134 C2 *river* India/Pakistan
Chengchiatun see Liaoyuan
Ch'eng-chou/Chengchow see Zhengzhou
Chengde 128 D3 *var.* Jehol. Hebei, E China
Chengdu 128 B5 *var.* Chengtu, Ch'eng-tu. *province capital* Sichuan, C China
Chenghsien see Zhengzhou
Chengtu/Ch'eng-tu see Chengdu
Chennai 132 D2 *prev.* Madras. *state capital* Tamil Nādu, S India
Chenstokhov see Częstochowa
Chen Xian/Chenxian/Chen Xiang see Chenzhou
Chenzhou 128 C6 *var.* Chenxian, Chen Xian, Chen Xiang. Hunan, S China
Chepelare 104 C3 Smolyan, S Bulgaria
Chepén 60 B3 La Libertad, C Peru
Cher 90 C4 *river* C France
Cherbourg 90 B3 *anc.* Carusbur. Manche, N France
Cherepovets 110 B4 Vologodskaya Oblast', NW Russian Federation
Chergui, Chott ech 70 D2 *salt lake* NW Algeria
Cherikaw see Cherykaw
Cherkassy see Cherkasy
Cherkasy 109 E2 *Rus.* Cherkassy. Cherkas'ka Oblast', C Ukraine
Cherkessk 111 B7 Karachayevo-Cherkesskaya Respublika, SW Russian Federation
Chernigov see Chernihiv
Chernihiv 109 E1 *Rus.* Chernigov. Chernihivs'ka Oblast', NE Ukraine
Chernivtsi 108 C3 *Ger.* Czernowitz, *Rom.* Cernăuţi, *Rus.* Chernovtsy. Chernivets'ka Oblast', W Ukraine

Cherno More see Black Sea
Chernomorskoye see Chornomors'ke
Chernovtsy see Chernivtsi
Chernoye More see Black Sea
Chernyakhovsk 106 A4 Ger. Insterburg. Kaliningradskaya Oblast', W Russian Federation
Cherry Hill 41 F4 New Jersey, NE USA
Cherski Range see Cherskogo, Khrebet
Cherskiy 115 G2 Respublika Sakha (Yakutiya), NE Russian Federation
Cherskogo, Khrebet 111 F2 var. Cherski Range. mountain range NE Russian Federation
Cherso see Cres
Cherven' see Chervyen'
Chervonograd see Chervonohrad
Chervonohrad 108 C2 Rus. Chervonograd. L'vivs'ka Oblast', NW Ukraine
Chervyen' 107 D6 Rus. Cherven'. Minskaya Voblasts', C Belarus
Cherykaw 107 E7 Rus. Cherikov. Mahilyowskaya Voblasts', E Belarus
Chesapeake Bay 41 F5 inlet NE USA
Chesha Bay see Chёshskaya Guba
Chёshskaya Guba 155 D5 var. Archangel Bay, Chesha Bay, Dvina Bay. bay NW Russian Federation
Chester 89 C6 Wel. Caerleon, hist. Legaceaster, Lat. Deva, Devana Castra. C England, United Kingdom
Chetumal 51 H4 var. Payo Obispo. Quintana Roo, SE Mexico
Cheviot Hills 88 D4 hill range England/ Scotland, United Kingdom
Cheyenne 44 D4 state capital Wyoming, C USA
Cheyenne River 44 D3 river South Dakota/Wyoming, N USA
Chezdi-Oşorheiu see Târgu Secuiesc
Chhapra 135 F3 prev. Chapra. Bihār, N India
Chhattisgarh 135 E4 cultural region E India
Chia-i see Jiayi
Chiai see Jiayi
Chiang-hsi see Jiangxi
Chiang Mai 136 B4 var. Chiangmai, Chiengmai, Kiangmai. Chiang Mai, NW Thailand
Chiangmai see Chiang Mai
Chiang Rai 136 C3 var. Chianpai, Chienrai, Muang Chiang Rai. Chiang Rai, NW Thailand
Chiang-su see Jiangsu
Chianning/Chian-ning see Nanjing
Chianpai see Chiang Rai
Chianti 96 C3 cultural region C Italy
Chiapa see Chiapa de Corzo
Chiapa de Corzo 51 G5 var. Chiapa. Chiapas, SE Mexico
Chiayi see Jiayi
Chiba 130 B1 var. Tiba. Chiba, Honshū, S Japan
Chibougamau 38 D3 Québec, SE Canada
Chicago 40 B3 Illinois, N USA
Ch'i-ch'i-ha-erh see Qiqihar
Chickasha 49 G2 Oklahoma, C USA
Chiclayo 60 B3 Lambayeque, NW Peru
Chico 47 B5 California, W USA
Chico, Río 65 B7 river SE Argentina
Chico, Río 65 B6 river S Argentina
Chicoutimi 39 E4 Québec, SE Canada
Chiengmai see Chiang Mai
Chienrai see Chiang Rai
Chiesanuova 96 D2 SW San Marino
Chieti 96 D4 var. Teate. Abruzzo, C Italy
Chifeng 127 G2 var. Ulanhad. Nei Mongol Zizhiqu, N China
Chigirin see Chyhyryn
Chih-fu see Yantai
Chihli see Hebei
Chihli, Gulf of see Bo Hai
Chihuahua 50 C2 Chihuahua, NW Mexico
Childress 49 F2 Texas, SW USA
Chile 64 B3 off. Republic of Chile. country SW South America

CHILE
South America

Official name Republic of Chile
Formation 1818 / 1883
Capital Santiago
Population 17.3 million / 60 people per sq mile (23 people per sq km)
Total area 292,258 sq. miles

CHILE
(continued)

(756,950 sq. km)
Languages Spanish*, Amerindian languages
Religions Roman Catholic 89%, Other and nonreligious 11%
Ethnic mix Mestizo and European 90%, Other Amerindian 9%, Mapuche 1%
Government Presidential system
Currency Chilean peso = 100 centavos
Literacy rate 99%
Calorie consumption 2908 kilocalories

Chile Basin 57 A5 undersea basin E Pacific Ocean
Chile Chico 65 B6 Aisén, W Chile
Chile, Republic of see Chile
Chile Rise 57 A7 undersea rise SE Pacific Ocean
Chilia-Nouă see Kiliya
Chililabombwe 78 D2 Copperbelt, C Zambia
Chi-lin see Jilin
Chillán 65 B5 Bío Bío, C Chile
Chillicothe 40 D4 Ohio, N USA
Chill Mhantáin, Sléibhte see Wicklow Mountains
Chiloé, Isla de 65 A6 var. Isla Grande de Chiloé. island W Chile
Chilpancingo 51 E5 var. Chilpancingo de los Bravos. Guerrero, S Mexico
Chilpancingo de los Bravos see Chilpancingo
Chilung see Jilong
Chimán 53 G5 Panamá, E Panama
Chimbay see Chimboy
Chimborazo 60 A1 volcano C Ecuador
Chimbote 60 C3 Ancash, W Peru
Chimboy 122 D1 Rus. Chimbay. Qoraqalpog'iston Respublikasi, NW Uzbekistan
Chimkent see Shymkent
Chimoio 79 E3 Manica, C Mozambique
China 124 C2 off. People's Republic of China, Chin. Chung-hua Jen-min Kung-ho-kuo, Zhonghua Renmin Gongheguo; prev. Chinese Empire. country E Asia

CHINA
East Asia

Official name People's Republic of China
Formation 960 / 1999
Capital Beijing
Population 1.35 billion / 374 people per sq mile (144 people per sq km)
Total area 3,705,386 sq. miles (9,596,960 sq. km)
Languages Mandarin*, Wu, Cantonese, Hsiang, Min, Hakka, Kan
Religions Nonreligious 59%, Traditional beliefs 20%, Other 13%, Buddhist 6%, Muslim 2%
Ethnic mix Han 92%, Other 4%, Hui 1%, Miao 1%, Manchu 1%, Zhuang 1%
Government One-party state
Currency Renminbi (known as yuan) = 10 jiao = 100 fen
Literacy rate 94%
Calorie consumption 3036 kilocalories

Chi-nan/Chinan see Jinan
Chinandega 52 C3 Chinandega, NW Nicaragua
China, People's Republic of see China
China, Republic of see China
Chincha Alta 60 D4 Ica, SW Peru
Chin-chiang see Quanzhou
Chin-chou/Chinchow see Jinzhou
Chindwin see Chindwinn
Chindwinn 136 B2 var. Chindwin. river N Myanmar (Burma)
Chinese Empire see China
Chinghai see Qinghai
Ch'ing Hai see Qinghai Hu, China
Chingola 78 D2 Copperbelt, C Zambia
Ching-Tao/Ch'ing-tao see Qingdao
Chinguetti 74 C2 var. Chinguetti. Adrar, C Mauritania
Chin Hills 131 D5 mountain range W Myanmar (Burma)
Chinhsien see Jinzhou
Chinnereth see Tiberias, Lake
Chinook Trough 113 H4 trough N Pacific Ocean

Chioggia 96 C2 anc. Fossa Claudia. Veneto, NE Italy
Chíos 105 D5 var. Hios, Khíos, It. Scio, Turk. Sakiz-Adasi. Chíos, E Greece
Chíos 105 D5 var. Khíos. island E Greece
Chipata 78 D2 prev. Fort Jameson. Eastern, E Zambia
Chiquián 60 C3 Ancash, W Peru
Chiquimula 52 B2 Chiquimula, SE Guatemala
Chīrāla 132 D1 Andhra Pradesh, E India
Chirchik see Chirchiq
Chirchiq 123 E2 Rus. Chirchik. Toshkent Viloyati, E Uzbekistan
Chiriqui Gulf 53 E5 Eng. Chiriqui Gulf. gulf SW Panama
Chiriquí Gulf see Chiriquí, Golfo de
Chiriquí, Laguna de 53 E5 lagoon NW Panama
Chiriquí, Volcán de see Barú, Volcán
Chirripó, Cerro see Chirripó Grande, Cerro
Chirripó Grande, Cerro 52 D4 var. Cerro Chirripó. mountain SE Costa Rica
Chisec 52 B2 Alta Verapaz, C Guatemala
Chisholm 45 F1 Minnesota, N USA
Chisimaio/Chisimayu see Kismaayo
Chişinău 108 D4 Rus. Kishinev. country capital (Moldova) C Moldova
Chita 117 F4 Zabaykal'skiy Kray, S Russian Federation
Chitangwiza see Chitungwiza
Chitato 78 C1 Lunda Norte, NE Angola
Chitina 36 D3 Alaska, USA
Chitose 130 D2 var. Titose. Hokkaidō, NE Japan
Chitré 53 F5 Herrera, S Panama
Chittagong 135 G4 Ben. Chāttagām. Chittagong, SE Bangladesh
Chitungwiza 78 D3 prev. Chitangwiza. Mashonaland East, NE Zimbabwe
Chkalov see Orenburg
Chlef 70 D2 var. Ech Cheliff, Ech Cliff; prev. Al-Asnam, El Asnam, Orléansville. NW Algeria
Chocolate Mountains 47 D8 mountain range California, W USA
Chodorów see Khodoriv
Chodzież 98 C3 Wielkopolskie, C Poland
Choele Choel 65 C5 Río Negro, C Argentina
Choiseul 144 C3 var. Lauru. island NW Solomon Islands
Chojnice 98 C2 Ger. Konitz. Pomorskie, N Poland
Ch'ok'ē 72 C4 var. Choke Mountains. mountain range NW Ethiopia
Choke Mountains see Ch'ok'ē
Cholet 90 B4 Maine-et-Loire, NW France
Choluteca 52 C3 Choluteca, S Honduras
Choluteca, Río 52 C3 river SW Honduras
Choma 78 D2 Southern, S Zambia
Chomutov 98 A4 Ger. Komotau. Ústecký Kraj, NW Czech Republic
Chona 113 E2 river E Russian Federation
Chon Buri 137 C5 prev. Bang Pla Soi. Chon Buri, S Thailand
Chone 60 A1 Manabí, W Ecuador
Ch'ŏngjin 129 E3 NE North Korea
Chongqing 128 B5 var. Ch'ung-ching, Ch'ung-ch'ing, Chungking, Pahsien, Tchongking, Yuzhou. Chongqing Shi, C China
Chonnacht see Connaught
Chonos, Archipiélago de los 65 A6 island group S Chile
Chóra Sfakíon 105 C8 var. Sfakiá. Kríti, Greece, E Mediterranean Sea
Chorne More see Black Sea
Chornomors'ke 109 E4 Rus. Chernomorskoye. Avtonomna Respublika Krym, S Ukraine
Chorokh/Chorokhi see Çoruh Nehri
Chortkiv 108 C2 Rus. Chortkov. Ternopil's'ka Oblast', W Ukraine
Chortkov see Chortkiv
Chorzów 99 C5 Ger. Königshütte; prev. Królewska Huta. Śląskie, S Poland
Chósebuz see Cottbus
Chōsen-kaikyō see Korea Strait
Chōshi 131 D5 var. Tyōsi. Chiba, Honshū, S Japan
Chosŏn-minjujuŭi-inmin-kanghwaguk see North Korea
Choszczno 98 B3 Ger. Arnswalde. Zachodnio-pomorskie, NW Poland

Chota Nagpur 135 E4 plateau N India
Choûm 74 C2 Adrar, C Mauritania
Choybalsan 127 F2 prev. Byan Tumen. Dornod, E Mongolia
Christchurch 151 C6 Canterbury, South Island, New Zealand
Christiana 54 B5 C Jamaica
Christiania see Oslo
Christiansand see Kristiansand
Christianshåb see Qasigiannguit
Christiansund see Kristiansund
Christmas Island 141 D5 Australian external territory E Indian Ocean
Christmas Island see Kiritimati
Christmas Ridge 143 E1 undersea ridge C Pacific Ocean
Chuan see Sichuan
Ch'uan-chou see Quanzhou
Chubek see Moskva
Chubut, Río 65 B6 river SE Argentina
Chudskoye Ozero see Peipus, Lake
Chugoku-sanchi 131 B6 mountain range Honshū, SW Japan
Chuí see Chuy
Chukai see Cukai
Chukchi Plain 155 B2 abyssal plain Arctic Ocean
Chukchi Plateau 34 C2 undersea plateau Arctic Ocean
Chukchi Sea 34 B2 Rus. Chukotskoye More. sea Arctic Ocean
Chukotskoye More see Chukchi Sea
Chula Vista 47 C8 California, W USA
Chulucanas 60 B2 Piura, NW Peru
Chulym 114 D4 river C Russian Federation
Chumphon 137 C6 var. Jumporn. Chumphon, SW Thailand
Chuncheon 129 E4 Jap. Shunsen; prev. Ch'unch'ŏn. N South Korea
Ch'unch'ŏn see Chuncheon
Ch'ung-ch'ing/Ch'ung-ching see Chongqing
Chung-hua Jen-min Kung-ho-kuo see China
Chungking see Chongqing
Chunya 115 E3 river C Russian Federation
Chuquicamata 64 B2 Antofagasta, N Chile
Chuquisaca see Sucre
Chur 95 B7 Fr. Coire, It. Coira, Rmsch. Cuera, Quera; anc. Curia Rhaetorum. Graubünden, E Switzerland
Churchill 37 G4 Manitoba, C Canada
Churchill 38 B2 river Manitoba/ Saskatchewan, C Canada
Churchill 39 F2 river Newfoundland and Labrador, E Canada
Chuska Mountains 48 C1 mountain range Arizona/New Mexico, SW USA
Chusovoy 111 D5 Permskiy Kray, NW Russian Federation
Chust see Khust
Chuuk Islands 144 B2 var. Hogoley Islands; prev. Truk Islands. island group Caroline Islands, C Micronesia
Chuy 64 E4 var. Chuí. Rocha, E Uruguay
Chyhyryn 109 E2 Rus. Chigirin. Cherkas'ka Oblast', N Ukraine
Ciadâr-Lunga 108 D4 var. Ceadâr-Lunga, Rus. Chadyr-Lunga. S Moldova
Cide 116 C2 Kastamonu, N Turkey
Ciechanów 98 D3 prev. Zichenau. Mazowieckie, C Poland
Ciego de Ávila 54 C2 Ciego de Ávila, C Cuba
Ciénaga 58 B1 Magdalena, N Colombia
Cienfuegos 54 B2 Cienfuegos, C Cuba
Cieza 93 E4 Murcia, SE Spain
Cihanbeyli 116 C3 Konya, C Turkey
Cikobia 145 E4 prev. Thikombia. island N Fiji
Cilacap 138 C5 prev. Tjilatjap. Jawa, C Indonesia
Cill Airne see Killarney
Cill Chainnigh see Kilkenny
Cilli see Celje
Cill Mhantáin see Wicklow
Cîmpina see Câmpina
Cîmpulung see Câmpulung
Cina Selatan, Laut see South China Sea
Cincinnati 40 C4 Ohio, N USA
Ciney 87 C7 Namur, SE Belgium
Cinto, Monte 91 E7 mountain Corse, France, C Mediterranean Sea
Cintra see Sintra
Cipolletti 65 B5 Río Negro, C Argentina

Cirebon *138 C4 prev.* Tjirebon. Jawa, S Indonesia
Cirkvenica *see* Crikvenica
Cirò Marina *97 E6* Calabria, S Italy
Cirquenizza *see* Crikvenica
Cisnădie *108 B4 Ger.* Heltau, *Hung.* Nagydisznód. Sibiu, SW Romania
Citharista *see* la Ciotat
Citlaltépetl *see* Orizaba, Volcán Pico de
Citrus Heights *47 B5* California, W USA
Ciudad Acuña *see* Villa Acuña
Ciudad Bolívar *59 E2 prev.* Angostura. Bolívar, E Venezuela
Ciudad Camargo *50 D2* Chihuahua, N Mexico
Ciudad Cortés *see* Cortés
Ciudad Darío *52 D3 var.* Dario. Matagalpa, W Nicaragua
Ciudad de Dolores Hidalgo *see* Dolores Hidalgo
Ciudad de Guatemala *52 B2 Eng.* Guatemala City; *prev.* Santiago de los Caballeros. *country capital* (Guatemala) Guatemala, C Guatemala
Ciudad del Carmen *see* Carmen
Ciudad del Este *64 E2 prev.* Ciudad Presidente Stroessner, Presidente Stroessner, Puerto Presidente Stroessner. Alto Paraná, SE Paraguay
Ciudad Delicias *see* Delicias
Ciudad de México *see* México
Ciudad de Panama *see* Panamá
Ciudad Guayana *59 E2 prev.* San Tomé de Guayana, Santo Tomé de Guayana. Bolívar, NE Venezuela
Ciudad Guzmán *50 D4* Jalisco, SW Mexico
Ciudad Hidalgo *51 G5* Chiapas, SE Mexico
Ciudad Juárez *50 C1* Chihuahua, N Mexico
Ciudad Lerdo *50 D3* Durango, C Mexico
Ciudad Madero *51 F3 var.* Villa Cecilia. Tamaulipas, C Mexico
Ciudad Mante *51 E3* Tamaulipas, C Mexico
Ciudad Miguel Alemán *51 E2* Tamaulipas, C Mexico
Ciudad Obregón *50 B2* Sonora, NW Mexico
Ciudad Ojeda *58 C1* Zulia, NW Venezuela
Ciudad Porfirio Díaz *see* Piedras Negras
Ciudad Presidente Stroessner *see* Ciudad del Este
Ciudad Quesada *see* Quesada
Ciudad Real *92 D3* Castilla-La Mancha, C Spain
Ciudad-Rodrigo *92 C3* Castilla y León, N Spain
Ciudad Trujillo *see* Santo Domingo
Ciudad Valles *51 E3* San Luis Potosí, C Mexico
Ciudad Victoria *51 E3* Tamaulipas, C Mexico
Ciutadella *93 H3 var.* Ciutadella de Menorca. Menorca, Spain, W Mediterranean Sea
Ciutadella Ciutadella de Menorca *see* Ciutadella
Civitanova Marche *96 D3* Marche, C Italy
Civitas Altae Ripae *see* Brzeg
Civitas Carnutum *see* Chartres
Civitas Eburovicum *see* Évreux
Civitavecchia *96 C4 anc.* Centum Cellae, Trajani Portus. Lazio, C Italy
Claremore *49 G1* Oklahoma, C USA
Clarence *151 C5 river* South Island, New Zealand
Clarence *151 C5 river* South Island, New Zealand
Clarence Town *54 D2* Long Island, C Bahamas
Clarinda *45 F4* Iowa, C USA
Clarion Fracture Zone *153 E2 tectonic feature* NE Pacific Ocean
Clarión, Isla *50 A5 island* W Mexico
Clark Fork *44 A1 river* Idaho/Montana, NW USA
Clark Hill Lake *43 E2 var.* J.Storm Thurmond Reservoir. *reservoir* Georgia/South Carolina, SE USA
Clarksburg *40 D4* West Virginia, NE USA
Clarksdale *42 B2* Mississippi, S USA
Clarksville *42 C1* Tennessee, S USA
Clausentum *see* Southampton

Clayton *49 E1* New Mexico, SW USA
Clearwater *43 E4* Florida, SE USA
Clearwater Mountains *46 D2 mountain range* Idaho, NW USA
Cleburne *49 G3* Texas, SW USA
Clermont *148 D4* Queensland, E Australia
Clermont-Ferrand *91 C5* Puy-de-Dôme, C France
Cleveland *40 D3* Ohio, N USA
Cleveland *42 D1* Tennessee, S USA
Clifton *48 C2* Arizona, SW USA
Clinton *42 B2* Mississippi, S USA
Clinton *49 F1* Oklahoma, C USA
Clipperton Fracture Zone *153 E3 tectonic feature* E Pacific Ocean
Clipperton Island *35 A7 French dependency* of French Polynesia E Pacific Ocean
Cloncurry *148 B3* Queensland, C Australia
Clonmel *89 B6 Ir.* Cluain Meala. S Ireland
Cloppenburg *94 B3* Niedersachsen, NW Germany
Cloquet *45 G2* Minnesota, N USA
Cloud Peak *44 C3 mountain* Wyoming, C USA
Clovis *49 E2* New Mexico, SW USA
Cluain Meala *see* Clonmel
Cluj *see* Cluj-Napoca
Cluj-Napoca *108 B3 Ger.* Klausenburg, *Hung.* Kolozsvár; *prev.* Cluj. Cluj, NW Romania
Clutha *151 B7 river* South Island, New Zealand
Clyde *88 C4 river* W Scotland, United Kingdom
Coari *62 D2* Amazonas, N Brazil
Coast Mountains *36 D4 Fr.* Chaîne Côtière. *mountain range* Canada/USA
Coast Ranges *46 A4 mountain range* W USA
Coats Island *37 G3 island* Nunavut, NE Canada
Coats Land *154 B2 physical region* Antarctica
Coatzacoalcos *51 G4 var.* Quetzalcoalco; *prev.* Puerto México. Veracruz-Llave, E Mexico
Cobán *52 B2* Alta Verapaz, C Guatemala
Cobar *149 C6* New South Wales, SE Australia
Cobija *61 E3* Pando, NW Bolivia
Coblence/Coblenz *see* Koblenz
Coburg *95 C5* Bayern, SE Germany
Cocanada *see* Kākināda
Cochabamba *61 F4 hist.* Oropeza. Cochabamba, C Bolivia
Cochin *see* Kochi
Cochrane *38 C4* Ontario, S Canada
Cochrane *65 B7* Aisén, S Chile
Cocibolca *see* Nicaragua, Lago de
Cockade State *see* Maryland
Cockburn Town *55 E2* San Salvador, E Bahamas
Cockpit Country, The *54 A4 physical region* W Jamaica
Cocobeach *77 A5* Estuaire, NW Gabon
Coconino Plateau *48 B1 plain* Arizona, SW USA
Coco, Río *52 E2 var.* Rio Wanki, Segoviao Wangkí. *river* Honduras/ Nicaragua
Cocos Basin *124 C5 undersea basin* E Indian Ocean
Cocos Island Ridge *see* Cocos Ridge
Cocos Islands *141 D5 island group* E Indian Ocean
Cocos Ridge *35 C8 var.* Cocos Island Ridge. *undersea ridge* E Pacific Ocean
Cod, Cape *41 G3 headland* Massachusetts, NE USA
Codfish Island *151 A8 island* SW New Zealand
Codlea *108 C4 Ger.* Zeiden, *Hung.* Feketehalom. Brașov, C Romania
Cody *44 C2* Wyoming, C USA
Coeur d'Alene *46 C2* Idaho, NW USA
Coevorden *86 E2* Drenthe, NE Netherlands
Coffs Harbour *149 E6* New South Wales, SE Australia
Cognac *91 B5 anc.* Compniacum. Charente, W France
Cohalm *see* Rupea
Coiba, Isla de *53 E5 island* SW Panama
Coihaique *65 B6 var.* Coyhaique. Aisén, S Chile

Coimbatore *132 C3* Tamil Nādu, S India
Coimbra *92 B3 anc.* Conimbria, Conimbriga. Coimbra, W Portugal
Coín *92 D5* Andalucía, S Spain
Coirib, Loch *see* Corrib, Lough
Colby *45 E4* Kansas, C USA
Colchester *89 E6* Connecticut, NE USA
Coleman *49 F3* Texas, SW USA
Coleraine *88 B4 Ir.* Cúil Raithin. N Northern Ireland, United Kingdom
Colesberg *78 C5* Northern Cape, C South Africa
Colima *50 D4* Colima, S Mexico
Coll *88 B3 island* W Scotland, United Kingdom
College Station *49 G3* Texas, SW USA
Collie *147 A7* Western Australia
Collipo *see* Leiria
Colmar *90 E4 Ger.* Kolmar. Haut-Rhin, NE France
Cöln *see* Köln
Cologne *see* Köln
Colomb-Béchar *see* Béchar
Colombia *58 B3 off.* Republic of Colombia. *country* N South America

---

COLOMBIA
South America

Official name Republic of Colombia
Formation 1819 / 1903
Capital Bogotá
Population 46.9 million / 117 people per sq mile (45 people per sq km) / 77%
Total area 439,733 sq. miles (1,138,910 sq. km)
Languages Spanish*, Wayuu, Páez, and other Amerindian languages
Religions Roman Catholic 95%, Other 5%
Ethnic mix Mestizo 58%, White 20%, European–African 14%, African 4%, African–Amerindian 3%, Amerindian 1%
Government Presidential system
Currency Colombian peso = 100 centavos
Literacy rate 93%
Calorie consumption 2717 kilocalories

Colombian Basin *56 A1 undersea basin* SW Caribbean Sea
Colombia, Republic of *see* Colombia
Colombie-Britannique *see* British Columbia
Colombo *132 C4 country capital* (Sri Lanka) Western Province, W Sri Lanka
Colón *53 G4 prev.* Aspinwall. Colón, C Panama
Colonia Agrippina *see* Köln
Colón Ridge *35 B8 undersea ridge* E Pacific Ocean
Colorado *44 C4 off.* State of Colorado, *also known as* Centennial State, Silver State. *state* C USA
Colorado City *49 F3* Texas, SW USA
Colorado Plateau *48 B1 plateau* W USA
Colorado, Río *65 C5 river* E Argentina
Colorado, Río *see* Colorado River
Colorado River *35 B5 var.* Río Colorado. *river* Mexico/USA
Colorado River *49 G4 river* Texas, SW USA
Colorado Springs *44 D5* Colorado, C USA
Columbia *41 E4* Maryland, NE USA
Columbia *45 G4* Missouri, C USA
Columbia *43 E2 state capital* South Carolina, SE USA
Columbia *42 C1* Tennessee, S USA
Columbia River *46 B3 river* Canada/ USA
Columbia Plateau *46 C3 plateau* Idaho/ Oregon, NW USA
Columbus *42 D2* Georgia, SE USA
Columbus *40 C4* Indiana, N USA
Columbus *42 C2* Mississippi, S USA
Columbus *45 F4* Nebraska, C USA
Columbus *40 D4 state capital* Ohio, N USA
Colville Channel *150 D2 channel* North Island, New Zealand
Colville River *36 D2 river* Alaska, USA
Comacchio *96 C3 var.* Commachio; *anc.* Comactium. Emilia-Romagna, N Italy
Comactium *see* Comacchio
Comalcalco *51 G4* Tabasco, SE Mexico
Coma Pedrosa, Pic de *91 A7 mountain* NW Andorra
Comarapa *61 F4* Santa Cruz, C Bolivia

Comayagua *52 C2* Comayagua, W Honduras
Comer See *see* Como, Lago di
Comilla *135 G4 Ben.* Kumillā. Chittagong, E Bangladesh
Comino *see* Kemmuna
Comitán *51 G5 var.* Comitán de Domínguez. Chiapas, SE Mexico
Comitán de Domínguez *see* Comitán
Commachio *see* Comacchio
Commissioner's Point *42 A5 headland* W Bermuda
Communism Peak *123 F3 prev.* Qullai Kommunizm. *mountain* E Tajikistan
Como *96 B2 anc.* Comum. Lombardia, N Italy
Comodoro Rivadavia *65 B6* Chubut, SE Argentina
Como, Lake *96 B2 var.* Lario, *Eng.* Lake Como, *Ger.* Comer See. *lake* N Italy
Como, Lake *see* Como, Lago di
Comores, République Fédérale Islamique des *see* Comoros
Comoros *79 F2 off.* Federal Islamic Republic of the Comoros, *Fr.* République Fédérale Islamique des Comores. *country* W Indian Ocean

---

COMOROS
Indian Ocean

Official name Union of the Comoros
Formation 1975 / 1975
Capital Moroni
Population 800,000 / 929 people per sq mile (359 people per sq km)
Total area 838 sq. miles (2170 sq. km)
Languages Arabic*, Comoran*, French*
Religions Muslim (mainly Sunni) 98%, Other 1%, Roman Catholic 1%
Ethnic mix Comoran 97%, Other 3%
Government Presidential system
Currency Comoros franc = 100 centimes
Literacy rate 74%
Calorie consumption 2139 kilocalories

Comoros, Federal Islamic Republic of the *see* Comoros
Compiègne *90 C3* Oise, N France
Complutum *see* Alcalá de Henares
Compniacum *see* Cognac
Compostela *see* Santiago de Compostela
Comrat *108 D4 Rus.* Komrat. S Moldova
Comum *see* Como
Conakry *74 C4 country capital* (Guinea) SW Guinea
Conca *see* Cuenca
Concarneau *90 A3* Finistère, NW France
Concepción *61 G3* Santa Cruz, E Bolivia
Concepción *65 B5* Bío Bío, C Chile
Concepción *64 D2 var.* Villa Concepción. Concepción, C Paraguay
Concepción *see* La Concepción
Concepción de la Vega *see* La Vega
Conchos, Río *48 D4 river* NW Mexico
Conchos, Río *50 D2 river* C Mexico
Concord *41 G3 state capital* New Hampshire, NE USA
Concordia *64 D4* Entre Ríos, E Argentina
Concordia *45 E4* Kansas, C USA
Côn Dao Sơn *137 E2 var.* Con Son. *island* S Vietnam
Condate *see* Rennes, Ille-et-Vilaine, France
Condate *see* St-Claude, Jura, France
Condega *52 D3* Estelí, NW Nicaragua
Condivincum *see* Nantes
Confluentes *see* Koblenz
Công Hoa Xa Hôi Chu Nghia Viêt Nam *see* Vietnam
Congo *77 D5 off.* Republic of the Congo, *Fr.* Moyen-Congo; *prev.* Middle Congo. *country* C Africa

---

CONGO
Central Africa

Official name Republic of the Congo
Formation 1960 / 1960
Capital Brazzaville
Population 4.1 million / 31 people per sq mile (12 people per sq km)
Total area 132,046 sq. miles (342,000 sq. km)
Languages Kongo, Teke, Lingala, French*
Religions Traditional beliefs 50%, Roman Catholic 35%, Protestant 13%, Muslim 2%
Ethnic mix Bakongo 51%, Teke 17%, Other 16%, Mbochi 11%, Mbédé 5%

CONGO
(continued)

Government Presidential system
Currency CFA franc = 100 centimes
Literacy rate 87%
Calorie consumption 2056 kilocalories

Congo, Dem. Rep. 77 C6 *off.* Democratic
Republic of Congo; *prev.* Zaire, Belgian
Congo, Congo (Kinshasa). *country*
C Africa

CONGO, DEM. REP.
Central Africa

Official name Democratic Republic of
the Congo
Formation 1960 / 1960
Capital Kinshasa
Population 67.8 million / 77 people
per sq mile (30 people per sq km)
Total area 905,563 sq. miles
(2,345,410 sq. km)
Languages Kiswahili, Tshiluba, Kikongo,
Lingala, French*
Religions Roman Catholic 50%,
Protestant 20%, Traditional beliefs and
other 10%, Muslim 10%, Kimbanguist 10%
Ethnic mix Other 55%, Mongo, Luba,
Kongo, and Mangbetu-Azande 45%
Government Presidential system
Currency Congolese franc = 100 centimes
Literacy rate 67%
Calorie consumption 1585 kilocalories

Congo 77 C6 *var.* Kongo, *Fr.* Zaire.
river C Africa
Congo Basin 77 C6 *drainage basin*
W Dem. Rep. Congo
Congo/Congo (Kinshasa) *see* Congo
(Democratic Republic of)
Coni *see* Cuneo
Conimbria/Conimbriga *see* Coimbra
Conjeeveram *see* Kānchipuram
Connacht *see* Connaught
Connaught 89 A5 *var.* Connacht, *Ir.*
Chonnacht, Cúige. *province*
W Ireland
Connecticut 41 F3 *off.* State of
Connecticut, *also known as* Blue Law
State, Constitution State, Land of
Steady Habits, Nutmeg State. *state*
NE USA
Connecticut 41 G3 *river* Canada/USA
Conroe 49 G3 Texas, SW USA
Consentia *see* Cosenza
Consolación del Sur 54 A2 Pinar del
Río, W Cuba
Con Son *see* Côn Dao Sơn
Constance *see* Konstanz
Constance, Lake 95 B7 *Ger.* Bodensee.
lake C Europe
Constanţa 108 D5 *var.* Küstendje, *Eng.*
Constanza, *Ger.* Konstanza, *Turk.*
Küstence. Constanţa, SE Romania
Constantia *see* Coutances
Constantia *see* Konstanz
Constantine 71 E2 *var.* Qacentina, *Ar.*
Qoussantina. NE Algeria
Constantinople *see* İstanbul
Constantiola *see* Olteniţa
Constanz *see* Konstanz
Constanza *see* Constanţa
Constitution State *see* Connecticut
Coo *see* Kos
Coober Pedy 149 A5 South Australia
Cookeville 42 D1 Tennessee, S USA
Cook Islands 145 F4 *territory in free
association with* New Zealand S Pacific
Ocean
Cook, Mount *see* Aoraki
Cook Strait 151 D5 *var.* Raukawa. *strait*
New Zealand
Cooktown 148 D2 Queensland,
NE Australia
Coolgardie 147 B6 Western Australia
Cooma 149 D7 New South Wales,
SE Australia
Coomassie *see* Kumasi
Coon Rapids 45 F2 Minnesota, N USA
Cooper Creek 148 C4 *var.* Barcoo,
Cooper's Creek. *seasonal river*
Queensland/South Australia
Cooper's Creek *see* Cooper Creek
Coos Bay 46 A3 Oregon, NW USA
Cootamundra 149 D6 New South Wales,
SE Australia

Copacabana 61 E4 La Paz, W Bolivia
Copenhagen *see* København
Copiapó 64 B3 Atacama, N Chile
Copperas Cove 49 G3 Texas, SW USA
Coppermine *see* Kugluktuk
Copper State *see* Arizona
Coquilhatville *see* Mbandaka
Coquimbo 64 B3 Coquimbo, N Chile
Corabia 108 B5 Olt, S Romania
Coral Harbour 37 G3 *var.* Salliq.
Southampton Island, Nunavut,
NE Canada
Coral Sea 142 B3 *sea* SW Pacific Ocean
Coral Sea Islands 144 B4 *Australian
external territory* SW Pacific Ocean
Corantijn Rivier *see* Courantyne River
Corcovado, Golfo 65 B6 *gulf* S Chile
Corcyra Nigra *see* Korčula
Cordele 42 D3 Georgia, SE USA
Córdoba 64 C3 Córdoba, C Argentina
Córdoba 51 F4 Veracruz-Llave, E Mexico
Córdoba 92 D4 *var.* Cordoba, *Eng.*
Cordova; *anc.* Corduba. Andalucía,
SW Spain
Cordova 36 C3 Alaska, USA
Cordova/Cordoba *see* Córdoba
Corduba *see* Córdoba
Corentyne River *see* Courantyne River
Corfu 104 A4 *var.* Kérkira, *Eng.*
Corfu. *island* Iónia Nisiá, Greece,
C Mediterranean Sea
Corfu *see* Kérkyra
Coria 92 C3 Extremadura, W Spain
Corinth 42 C1 Mississippi, S USA
Corinth *see* Kórinthos
Corinth, Gulf of 105 B5 *Eng.* Gulf of
Corinth; *anc.* Corinthiacus Sinus. *gulf*
C Greece
Corinth, Gulf of/Corinthiacus Sinus *see*
Korinthiakós Kólpos
Corinthus *see* Kórinthos
Corinto 52 C3 Chinandega,
NW Nicaragua
Cork 89 A6 *Ir.* Corcaigh. S Ireland
Çorlu 116 A2 Tekirdağ, NW Turkey
Corner Brook 39 F3 Newfoundland,
Newfoundland and Labrador, E Canada
Cornhusker State *see* Nebraska
Corn Islands 53 E3 *var.* Corn Islands.
island group SE Nicaragua
Corn Islands *see* Maíz, Islas del
Cornwallis Island 37 F2 *Island* Nunavut,
N Canada
Coro 58 C1 *prev.* Santa Ana de Coro.
Falcón, NW Venezuela
Corocoro 61 F4 La Paz, W Bolivia
Coromandel 150 D2 Waikato, North
Island, New Zealand
Coromandel Coast 132 D2 *coast* E India
Coromandel Peninsula 150 D2
peninsula North Island, New Zealand
Coronado, Bahía de 52 D5 *bay*
S Costa Rica
Coronel Dorrego 65 C5 Buenos Aires,
E Argentina
Coronel Oviedo 64 D2 Caaguazú,
SE Paraguay
Corozal 52 C1 Corozal, N Belize
Corpus Christi 49 G4 Texas, SW USA
Corrales 48 D2 New Mexico, SW USA
Corrib, Lough 89 A5 *Ir.* Loch Coirib.
lake W Ireland
Corrientes 64 D3 Corrientes,
NE Argentina
Corriza *see* Korçë
Corsica 91 E7 *Eng.* Corsica. *island*
France, C Mediterranean Sea
Corsica *see* Corse
Corsicana 49 G3 Texas, SW USA
Cortegana 92 C4 Andalucía, S Spain
Cortés 53 E5 *var.* Ciudad Cortés.
Puntarenas, SE Costa Rica
Cortez, Sea of *see* California, Golfo de
Cortina d'Ampezzo 96 C1 Veneto,
NE Italy
Coruche 92 B3 Santarém, C Portugal
Çoruh Nehri 117 E3 *Geor.* Chorokh,
Rus. Chorokhi. *river* Georgia/Turkey
Çorum 116 D3 *var.* Chorum. Çorum,
N Turkey
Corunna *see* A Coruña
Corvallis 46 A3 Oregon, NW USA
Corvo 92 A5 *var.* Ilha do Corvo. *island*
Azores, Portugal, NE Atlantic Ocean
Corvo, Ilha do *see* Corvo
Cos *see* Kos
Cosenza 97 D6 *anc.* Consentia. Calabria,
SW Italy
Cosne-Cours-sur-Loire 90 C4 Nièvre,
Bourgogne, C France Europe

Costa Mesa 46 D2 California, W USA
North America
Costa Rica 53 E4 *off.* Republic of Costa
Rica. *country* Central America

COSTA RICA
Central America

Official name Republic of Costa Rica
Formation 1838 / 1838
Capital San José
Population 4.7 million / 238 people
per sq mile (92 people per sq km)
Total area 19,730 sq. miles (51,100 sq. km)
Languages Spanish*, English Creole,
Bribri, Cabecar
Religions Roman Catholic 71%,
Evangelical 14%, Nonreligious 11%,
Other 4%
Ethnic mix Mestizo and European
94%, Black 3%, Other 1%, Chinese 1%,
Amerindian 1%
Government Presidential system
Currency Costa Rican colón
= 100 céntimos
Literacy rate 95%
Calorie consumption 2876 kilocalories

Costa Rica, Republic of *see* Costa Rica
Costermansville *see* Bukavu
Cotagaita 61 F5 Potosí, S Bolivia
Côte d'Ivoire 74 D4 *off.* Republic of
Côte d'Ivoire; *Fr.* Républic de la Côte
d'Ivoire, *Eng* Ivory Coast. *country*
W Africa

CÔTE D'IVOIRE (IVORY COAST)
West Africa

Official name Republic of Côte d'Ivoire
Formation 1960 / 1960
Capital Yamoussoukro
Population 20.2 million / 165 people
per sq mile (64 people per sq km)
Total area 124,502 sq. miles
(322,460 sq. km)
Languages Akan, French*, Krou, Voltaïque
Religions Muslim 38%, Traditional beliefs
25%, Roman Catholic 25%, Other 6%,
Protestant 6%
Ethnic mix Akan 42%, Voltaïque 18%,
Mandé du Nord 17%, Krou 11%, Mandé
du Sud 10%, Other 2%
Government Presidential system
Currency CFA franc = 100 centimes
Literacy rate 55%
Calorie consumption 2670 calories

Côte d'Ivoire, République de la *see*
Côte d'Ivoire
Côte d'Or 90 D4 *cultural region* C France
Côte Française des Somalis *see* Djibouti
Côtière, Chaine *see* Coast Mountains
Cotonou 75 F5 *var.* Kotonu. S Benin
Cotrone *see* Crotone
Cotswold Hills 89 D6 *var.* Cotswolds.
hill range S England, United Kingdom
Cotswolds *see* Cotswold Hills
Cottbus 94 D4 *Lus.* Chośebuz; *prev.*
Kottbus. Brandenburg, E Germany
Cotton State, The *see* Alabama
Cotyora *see* Ordu
Couentrey *see* Coventry
Council Bluffs 45 F4 Iowa, C USA
Courantyne River 59 G4 *var.* Corantijn
Rivier, Corentyne River. *river* Guyana/
Suriname
Courland Lagoon 106 A4 *Ger.* Kurisches
Haff, *Rus.* Kurskiy Zaliv. *lagoon*
Lithuania/Russian Federation
Courtrai *see* Kortrijk
Coutances 90 B3 *anc.* Constantia.
Manche, N France
Couvin 87 C7 Namur, S Belgium
Coventry 89 D6 *anc.* Couentrey.
C England, United Kingdom
Covilhã 92 C3 Castelo Branco, E Portugal
Cowan, Lake 147 B6 *lake* Western
Australia
Coxen Hole *see* Roatán
Coxin Hole *see* Roatán
Coyhaique *see* Coihaique
Coyote State, The *see* South Dakota
Cozhê 126 C2 Xizang, W China
Cozumel, Isla 51 H3 *island* SE Mexico
Cracovia/Cracow *see* Kraków
Cradock 78 C5 Eastern Cape, S South
Africa
Craig 44 C4 Colorado, C USA

Craiova 108 B5 Dolj, SW Romania
Cranbrook 37 E5 British Columbia,
SW Canada
Crane *see* The Crane
Cranz *see* Zelenogradsk
Crawley 89 E7 SE England, United
Kingdom
Cremona 96 B2 Lombardia, N Italy
Creole State *see* Louisiana
Cres 100 A3 *It.* Cherso; *anc.* Crexa.
island W Croatia
Crescent City 46 A4 California, W USA
Crescent Group 128 C7 *island group*
C Paracel Islands
Creston 45 F4 Iowa, C USA
Crestview 42 D3 Florida, SE USA
Crete 105 C7 *Eng.* Crete. *island* Greece,
Aegean Sea
Créteil 90 E2 Val-de-Marne, N France
Sea of Crete 105 D7 *var.* Kretikon
Delagos, *Eng.* Sea of Crete; *Mare*
Creticum. *sea* Greece, Aegean Sea
Crete, Sea of/Creticum, Mare *see* Kritikó
Pélagos
Creuse 90 B4 *river* C France
Crewe 89 D6 C England, United
Kingdom
Crexa *see* Cres
Crikvenica 100 A3 *It.* Cirquenizza; *prev.*
Cirkvenica, Crikvenica. Primorje-
Gorski Kotar, NW Croatia
Crimea 81 F4 *peninsula* SE Ukraine
Europe
Cristóbal 53 G4 Colón, C Panama
Cristóbal Colón, Pico 58 B1 *mountain*
N Colombia
Cristur/Cristuru Săcuiesc *see* Cristuru
Secuiesc
Cristuru Secuiesc 108 C4 *prev.* Cristur,
Cristuru Săcuiesc, Sitaş Cristuru, *Ger.*
Kreutz, *Hung.* Székelykeresztúr, Szitás-
Keresztúr. Harghita, C Romania
Crjkvenica *see* Crikvenica
Crna Gora *see* Montenegro
Crna Reka 101 D6 *river* S FYR
Macedonia
Crni Drim *see* Black Drin
Croatia 100 B3 *off.* Republic of Croatia,
Ger. Kroatien, *SCr.* Hrvatska. *country*
SE Europe

CROATIA
Southeast Europe

Official name Republic of Croatia
Formation 1991 / 1991
Capital Zagreb
Population 4.4 million / 202 people
per sq mile (78 people per sq km)
Total area 21,831 sq. miles (56,542 sq. km)
Languages Croatian*
Religions Roman Catholic 88%,
Other 7%, Orthodox Christian 4%,
Muslim 1%
Ethnic mix Croat 90%, Other 5%,
Serb 5%
Government Parliamentary system
Currency Kuna = 100 lipa
Literacy rate 99%
Calorie consumption 3130 kilocalories

Croatia, Republic of *see* Croatia
Crocodile *see* Limpopo
Croia *see* Krujë
Croker Island 146 E2 *island* Northern
Territory, N Australia
Cromwell 151 B7 Otago, South Island,
New Zealand
Crooked Island 54 D2 *island*
SE Bahamas
Crooked Island Passage 54 D2 *channel*
SE Bahamas
Crookston 45 F1 Minnesota, N USA
Crossen *see* Krosno Odrzańskie
Croton/Crotona *see* Crotone
Crotone 97 E6 *var.* Cotrone; *anc.* Croton,
Crotona. Calabria, SW Italy
Croydon 89 A8 SE England, United
Kingdom
Crozet Basin 141 B6 *undersea basin*
S Indian Ocean
Crozet Islands 141 B7 *island group*
French Southern and Antarctic
Territories
Crozet Plateau 141 B7 *var.* Crozet
Plateaus. *undersea plateau* SW Indian
Ocean
Crozet Plateaus *see* Crozet Plateau
Crystal Brook 149 B6 South Australia
Csaca *see* Čadca

185

Csakathurn/Csáktornya *see* Čakovec
Csíkszereda *see* Miercurea-Ciuc
Csorna 99 C6 Győr-Moson-Sopron, NW Hungary
Csurgó 99 C7 Somogy, SW Hungary
Cuando 78 C2 *var.* Kwando. *river* S Africa
Cuango 78 B1 *var.* Kwango. *river* Angola/Dem. Rep. Congo
Cuango *see* Kwango
Cuanza 78 B1 *var.* Kwanza. *river* C Angola
Cuauhtémoc 50 C2 Chihuahua, N Mexico
Cuautla 51 E4 Morelos, S Mexico
Cuba 54 B2 *off.* Republic of Cuba. *country* W West Indies

CUBA
West Indies

Official name Republic of Cuba
Formation 1902 / 1902
Capital Havana
Population 11.3 million / 264 people per sq mile (102 people per sq km) / 76%
Total area 42,803 sq. miles (110,860 sq. km)
Languages Spanish
Religions Nonreligious 49%, Roman Catholic 40%, Atheist 6%, Other 4%, Protestant 1%
Ethnic mix Mulatto (mixed race) 51%, White 37%, Black 11%, Chinese 1%
Government One-party state
Currency Cuban peso = 100 centavos
Literacy rate 99%
Calorie consumption 3258 kilocalories

Cubal 78 B2 Benguela, W Angola
Cubango 78 B2 *var.* Kuvango, *Port.* Vila Artur de Paiva, Vila da Ponte. Huíla, SW Angola
Cubango 78 B2 *var.* Kavango, Kavengo, Kubango, Okavango, Okavanggo. *river* S Africa
Cuba, Republic of *see* Cuba
Cúcuta 58 C2 *var.* San José de Cúcuta. Norte de Santander, N Colombia
Cuddapah 132 C2 Andhra Pradesh, S India
Cuenca 60 B2 Azuay, S Ecuador
Cuenca 93 E3 *anc.* Conca. Castilla-La Mancha, C Spain
Cuera *see* Chur
Cuernavaca 51 E4 Morelos, S Mexico
Cuiabá 63 E3 *prev.* Cuyabá. *state capital* Mato Grosso, SW Brazil
Cúige *see* Connaught
Cúige Laighean *see* Leinster
Cúige Mumhan *see* Munster
Cuijck 86 D4 Noord-Brabant, SE Netherlands
Cúil Raithin *see* Coleraine
Cuito 78 B2 *var.* Kwito. *river* SE Angola
Cukai 138 B3 *var.* Chukai, Kemaman. Terengganu, Peninsular Malaysia
Cularo *see* Grenoble
Culiacán 50 C3 *var.* Culiacán Rosales, Culiacán-Rosales. Sinaloa, C Mexico
Culiacán-Rosales/Culiacán Rosales *see* Culiacán
Cullera 93 F3 Valenciana, E Spain
Cullman 42 C2 Alabama, S USA
Culm *see* Chełmno
Culmsee *see* Chełmża
Cumaná 59 E1 Sucre, NE Venezuela
Cumbal, Nevado de 58 A4 *elevation* S Colombia
Cumberland 41 E4 Maryland, NE USA
Cumberland Plateau 42 D1 *plateau* E USA
Cumberland Sound 37 H3 *inlet* Baffin Island, Nunavut, NE Canada
Cumpas 50 B2 Sonora, NW Mexico
Cuneo 96 A2 *Fr.* Coni. Piemonte, NW Italy
Cunnamulla 149 C5 Queensland, E Australia
Čuprija 100 E4 Serbia, E Serbia
Curaçao 55 E5 *prev.* Dutch West Indies. *Dutch autonomous region* S Caribbean Sea
Curaçao 55 E5 *island* Lesser Antilles
Curia Rhaetorum *see* Chur
Curicó 64 B4 Maule, C Chile
Curieta *see* Krk
Curitiba 63 E4 *prev.* Curytiba. *state capital* Paraná, S Brazil
Curtbunar *see* Tervel

Curtea de Argeş 108 C4 *var.* Curtea-de-Arges. Argeş, S Romania
Curtea-de-Arges *see* Curtea de Argeş
Curtici 108 A4 *Ger.* Kurtitsch, *Hung.* Kürtös. Arad, W Romania
Curtis Island 148 E4 *island* Queensland, SE Australia
Curytiba *see* Curitiba
Curzola *see* Korčula
Cusco 60 D3 *var.* Cuzco. Cusco, C Peru
Cusset 91 C5 Allier, C France
Cutch, Gulf of *see* Kachchh, Gulf of
Cuttack 135 F4 Orissa, E India
Cuvier Plateau 141 E6 *undersea plateau* E Indian Ocean
Cuxhaven 94 B2 Niedersachsen, NW Germany
Cuyabá *see* Cuiabá
Cuyuni, Río *see* Cuyuni River
Cuyuni River 59 F3 *var.* Río Cuyuni. *river* Guyana/Venezuela
Cuzco *see* Cusco
Cyclades 105 D6 *var.* Kikládhes, *Eng.* Cyclades. *island group* SE Greece
Cyclades *see* Kykládes
Cydonia *see* Chaniá
Cymru *see* Wales
Cyprus 102 C4 *off.* Republic of Cyprus, *Gk.* Kypros, *Turk.* Kıbrıs, Kıbrıs Cumhuriyeti. *country* E Mediterranean Sea

CYPRUS
Southeast Europe

Official name Republic of Cyprus
Formation 1960 / 1960
Capital Nicosia
Population 1.1 million / 308 people per sq mile (119 people per sq km)
Total area 3571 sq. miles (9250 sq. km)
Languages Greek*, Turkish*
Religions Orthodox Christian 78%, Muslim 18%, Other 4%
Ethnic mix Greek 81%, Turkish 11%, Other 8%
Government Presidential system
Currency Euro (Turkish lira in TRNC) = 100 cents (euro); 100 kurus (Turkish lira)
Literacy rate 98%
Calorie consumption 2678 kilocalories

Cyprus, Republic of *see* Cyprus
Cythnos *see* Kýthnos
Czech Republic 99 A5 *Cz.* Česká Republika. *country* C Europe

CZECH REPUBLIC
Central Europe

Official name Czech Republic
Formation 1993 / 1993
Capital Prague
Population 10.5 million / 345 people per sq mile (133 people per sq km)
Total area 30,450 sq. miles (78,866 sq. km)
Languages Czech*, Slovak, Hungarian (Magyar)
Religions Roman Catholic 39%, Atheist 38%, Other 18%, Protestant 3%, Hussite 2%
Ethnic mix Czech 90%, Other 4%, Moravian 4%, Slovak 2%
Government Parliamentary system
Currency Czech koruna = 100 haleru
Literacy rate 99%
Calorie consumption 3305 kilocalories

Czenstochau *see* Częstochowa
Czernowitz *see* Chernivtsi
Częstochowa 98 C4 *Ger.* Czenstochau, Tschenstochau, *Rus.* Chenstokhov. Śląskie, S Poland
Człuchów 98 C3 *Ger.* Schlochau. Pomorskie, NW Poland

D

Dabajuro 58 C1 Falcón, NW Venezuela
Dabeiba 58 B2 Antioquia, NW Colombia
Dąbrowa Tarnowska 99 D5 Małopolskie, S Poland
Dabryn' 107 C8 *Rus.* Dobryn'. Homyel'skaya Voblasts', SE Belarus
Dacca *see* Dhaka
Daegu 129 E4 , *Jap.* Taikyū; *prev.* Taegu. SE South Korea

Daejeon 129 E4 , *Jap.* Taiden; *prev.* Taejŏn. C South Korea
Dagana 74 B3 N Senegal
Dagda 106 D4 SE Latvia
Dagden *see* Hiiumaa
Dagenham 89 B8 United Kingdom
Dağlıq Quarabağ *see* Nagorno-Karabakh
Dagö *see* Hiiumaa
Dagupan 139 E1 *off.* Dagupan City. Luzon, N Philippines
Dagupan City *see* Dagupan
Dahm, Ramlat 121 B6 *desert* NW Yemen
Dahomey *see* Benin
Daihoku *see* T'aipei
Daimiel 92 D3 Castilla-La Mancha, C Spain
Daimonia 105 B7 Pelopónnisos, S Greece
Dainan *see* Tainan
Daingin, Bá an *see* Dingle Bay
Dairen *see* Dalian
Dakar 74 B3 *country capital* (Senegal) W Senegal
Dakhla *see* Ad Dakhla
Dakoro 75 G3 Maradi, S Niger
Đakovica *see* Gjakovë
Đakovo 100 C3 *var.* Djakovo, *Hung.* Diakovár. Osijek-Baranja, E Croatia
Dakshin *see* Deccan
Dalain Hob 126 D3 *var.* Ejin Qi. Nei Mongol Zizhiqu, N China
Dalai Nor *see* Hulun Nur
Dalaman 116 A4 Muğla, SW Turkey
Dalandzadgad 127 E3 Ömnögovĭ, S Mongolia
Đa Lat 137 E6 Lâm Đông, S Vietnam
Dalby 149 D5 Queensland, E Australia
Dale City 41 E4 Virginia, NE USA
Dalhart 49 E1 Texas, SW USA
Dali 128 A6 *var.* Xiaguan. Yunnan, SW China
Dalian 128 D4 *var.* Dairen, Dalien, Jay Dairen, Lüda, Ta-lien, *Rus.* Dalny. Liaoning, NE China
Dalien *see* Dalian
Dallas 49 G2 Texas, SW USA
Dalmacija 100 B4 *Eng.* Dalmatia, *Ger.* Dalmatien, *It.* Dalmazia. *cultural region* S Croatia
Dalmatia/Dalmatien/Dalmazia *see* Dalmacija
Dalny *see* Dalian
Dalton 42 D1 Georgia, SE USA
Dälvvadis *see* Jokkmokk
Daly Waters 148 A2 Northern Territory, N Australia
Damachava 107 A6 *var.* Damachova, *Pol.* Domaczewo, *Rus.* Domachëvo. Brestskaya Voblasts', SW Belarus
Damachova *see* Damachava
Damān 134 C4 Damān and Diu, W India
Damara 76 C4 Ombella-Mpoko, S Central African Republic
Damas *see* Dimashq
Damasco *see* Dimashq
Damascus *see* Dimashq
Qolleh-ye Damavand 120 D3 *mountain* N Iran
Damietta *see* Dumyât
Dammām *see* Ad Dammām
Damoûr 119 A5 *var.* Ad Dāmūr. W Lebanon
Dampier 146 A4 Western Australia
Dampier, Selat 139 F4 *strait* Papua, E Indonesia
Damqawt 121 D6 *var.* Damqut. E Yemen
Damqut *see* Damqawt
Damxung 126 C5 *var.* Gongtang. Xizang Zizhiqu, W China
Danakil Desert 72 D4 *var.* Afar Depression, Danakil Plain. *desert* E Africa
Danakil Plain *see* Danakil Desert
Danané 74 D5 W Côte d'Ivoire
Đà Nẵng 137 E5 *prev.* Tourane. Quang Nam-Đa Nẵng, C Vietnam
Danborg *see* Daneborg
Dandong 128 D3 *var.* Tan-tung; *prev.* An-tung. Liaoning, NE China
Daneborg 83 E3 *var.* Danborg. Tunu, N Greenland
Dänew *see* Galkynyş
Dangara *see* Danghara
Dangerous Archipelago *see* Tuamotu, Îles
Danghara 123 E3 *Rus.* Dangara. SW Tajikistan
Danghe Nanshan 126 D3 *mountain range* W China

Dang Raek, Phanom/Dangrek, Chaîne des *see* Đăngrêk, Chuôr Phnum
Chuor Phnum Dangrek 137 D5 *var.* Phanom Dang Raek, Phanom Dong Rak, *Fr.* Chaîne des Dangrek. *mountain range* Cambodia/Thailand
Dangriga 52 C1 *prev.* Stann Creek. Stann Creek, E Belize
Danish West Indies *see* Virgin Islands (US)
Danlí 52 D2 El Paraíso, S Honduras
Danmark *see* Denmark
Danmarksstraedet *see* Denmark Strait
Dannenberg 94 C3 Niedersachsen, N Germany
Dannevirke 150 D4 Manawatu-Wanganui, North Island, New Zealand
Dantzig *see* Gdańsk
Danube 81 E4 *Bul.* Dunav, *Cz.* Dunaj, *Ger.* Donau, *Hung.* Duna, *Rom.* Dunărea. *river* C Europe
Danubian Plain 104 C2 *Eng.* Danubian Plain. *lowlands* N Bulgaria
Danubian Plain *see* Dunavska Ravnina
Danum *see* Doncaster
Danville 41 E5 Virginia, NE USA
Danxian/Dan Xian *see* Danzhou
Danzhou 128 C7 *prev.* Danxian, Dan Xian, Nada. Hainan, S China
Danzig *see* Gdańsk
Danziger Bucht *see* Danzig, Gulf of
Danzig, Gulf of 98 C2 *var.* Gulf of Gdańsk, *Ger.* Danziger Bucht, *Pol.* Zakota Gdańska, *Rus.* Gdan'skaya Bukhta. *gulf* N Poland
Daqm *see* Duqm
Daraʻ 119 B5 *var.* Derʻa, *Fr.* Déraa. Darʻā, SW Syria
Darabani 108 C3 Botoşani, NW Romania
Daraut-Kurgan *see* Daroot-Korgon
Dardanelles 116 A2 *Eng.* Dardanelles. *strait* NW Turkey
Dardanelles *see* Çanakkale Boğazı
Dardanelli *see* Çanakkale
Dar-el-Beida *see* Casablanca
Dar es Salaam 73 C7 Dar es Salaam, E Tanzania
Darfield 151 C6 Canterbury, South Island, New Zealand
Darfur 72 A4 *var.* Darfur Massif. *cultural region* W Sudan
Darfur Massif *see* Darfur
Darhan 127 E2 Darhan Uul, N Mongolia
Darién, Golfo del *see* Darien, Gulf of
Darien, Gulf of 58 A2 Sp. Golfo del Darién. *gulf* S Caribbean Sea
Darien, Isthmus of *see* Panama, Istmo de
Darién, Serranía del 53 H5 *mountain range* Colombia/Panama
Dario *see* Ciudad Darío
Dariorigum *see* Vannes
Darjeeling *see* Dārjiling
Dārjiling 135 F3 *prev.* Darjeeling. West Bengal, NE India
Darling River 149 C6 *river* New South Wales, SE Australia
Darlington 89 D5 N England, United Kingdom
Darmstadt 95 B5 Hessen, SW Germany
Darnah 71 G2 *var.* Dérna. NE Libya
Darnley, Cape 154 D2 *cape* Antarctica
Daroca 93 E2 Aragón, NE Spain
Daroot-Korgon 123 F3 *var.* Daraut-Kurgan. Oshskaya Oblast', SW Kyrgyzstan
Dartford 89 B8 SE England, United Kingdom
Dartmoor 89 C7 *moorland* SW England, United Kingdom
Dartmouth 39 F4 Nova Scotia, SE Canada
Darvaza *see* Derweze, Turkmenistan
Darwin 146 D2 *prev.* Palmerston, Port Darwin. *territory capital* Northern Territory, N Australia
Darwin, Isla 60 A4 *island* Galápagos, Galápagos Islands, W Ecuador
Dashhowuz *see* Daşoguz
Dashkawka 107 D6 *Rus.* Dashkovka. Mahilyowskaya Voblasts', E Belarus
Dashkovka *see* Dashkawka
Daşoguz 122 C2 *Rus.* Dashkhovuz, *Turkm.* Dashhowuz; *prev.* Tashauz. Daşoguz Welaýaty, N Turkmenistan
Đa, Sông *see* Black River
Datong 128 C3 *var.* Tatung, Ta-t'ung. Shanxi, C China
Daugava *see* Western Dvina

Daugavpils *106 D4 Ger.* Dünaburg; *prev. Rus.* Dvinsk. SE Latvia
Daung Kyun *137 B6 island* S Myanmar (Burma)
Dauphiné *91 D5 cultural region* E France
Dāvangere *132 C2* Karnātaka, W India
Davao *139 F3 off.* Davao City. Mindanao, S Philippines
Davao City *see* Davao
Davao Gulf *139 F3 gulf* Mindanao, S Philippines
Davenport *45 G3* Iowa, C USA
David *53 E5* Chiriquí, W Panama
Davie Ridge *141 A5 undersea ridge* W Indian Ocean
Davis *154 D3 Australian research station* Antarctica
Davis Sea *154 D3 sea* Antarctica
Davis Strait *82 B3 strait* Baffin Bay/Labrador Sea
Dawei *137 B5 var.* Tavoy, Htawei. Tanintharyi, S Myanmar (Burma)
Dawlat Qaṭar *see* Qatar
Dax *91 B6 var. anc.* Aquae Augustae, Aquae Tarbelicae. Landes, SW France
Dayr az Zawr *118 D3 var.* Deir ez Zor. Dayr az Zawr, E Syria
Dayton *40 C4* Ohio, N USA
Daytona Beach *43 E4* Florida, SE USA
De Aar *78 C5* Northern Cape, C South Africa
Dead Sea *119 B6 var.* Bahret Lut, Lacus Asphaltites, *Ar.* Al Baḥr al Mayyit, Baḥrat Lūṭ, *Heb.* Yam HaMelaḥ. *salt lake* Israel/Jordan
Deán Funes *64 C3* Córdoba, C Argentina
Death Valley *47 C7 valley* California, W USA
Deatnu *84 D2 Fin.* Tenojoki, *Nor.* Tana. *river* Finland/Norway
Debar *101 D6 Ger.* Dibra, *Turk.* Debre. W FYR Macedonia
De Behagle *see* Laï
Dębica *99 D5* Podkarpackie, SE Poland
De Bildt *see* De Bilt
De Bilt *86 C3 var.* De Bildt. Utrecht, C Netherlands
Dębno *98 B3* Zachodnio-pomorskie, NW Poland
Debre *see* Debar
Debrecen *99 D6 Ger.* Debreczin, *Rom.* Debreţin; *prev.* Debreczen. Hajdú-Bihar, E Hungary
Debreczen/Debreczin *see* Debrecen
Debreţin *see* Debrecen
Decatur *42 C1* Alabama, S USA
Decatur *40 B4* Illinois, N USA
Deccan *134 D5 Hind.* Dakshin. *plateau* C India
Děčín *98 B4 Ger.* Tetschen. Ústecký Kraj, NW Czech Republic
Dedeagaç/Dedeagach *see* Alexandroúpoli
Dedemsvaart *86 E3* Overijssel, E Netherlands
Dee *88 C3 river* NE Scotland, United Kingdom
Deering *36 C2* Alaska, USA
Deés *see* Dej
Deggendorf *95 D6* Bayern, SE Germany
Değirmenlik *102 C5 Gk.* Kythréa. N Cyprus
Deh Bīd *see* Ṣafāshahr
Dehli *see* Delhi
Deh Shū *see* Dishū
Deinze *87 B5* Oost-Vlaanderen, NW Belgium
Deir ez Zor *see* Dayr az Zawr
Deirgeirt, Loch *see* Derg, Lough
Dej *108 B3 Hung.* Dés; *prev.* Deés. Cluj, NW Romania
De Jouwer *see* Joure
Dekéleia *see* Dhekélia
Dékoa *76 C4* Kémo, C Central African Republic
De Land *43 E4* Florida, SE USA
Delano *47 C7* California, W USA
Delārām *see* Dilārām
Delaware *40 D4* Ohio, N USA
Delaware *41 F4 off.* State of Delaware, *also known as* Blue Hen State, Diamond State, First State. *state* NE USA
Delft *86 B4* Zuid-Holland, W Netherlands
Delfzijl *86 E1* Groningen, NE Netherlands
Delgo *72 B3* Northern, N Sudan
Delhi *134 D3 var.* Dehli, *Hind.* Dilli, *hist.* Shahjahanabad. *union territory capital* Delhi, N India

Delicias *50 D2 var.* Ciudad Delicias. Chihuahua, N Mexico
Déli-Kárpátok *see* Carpaţii Meridionalii
Delmenhorst *94 B3* Niedersachsen, NW Germany
Del Rio *49 F4* Texas, SW USA
Deltona *43 E4* Florida, SE USA
Demba *77 D6* Kasai-Occidental, C Dem. Rep. Congo
Dembia *76 D4* Mbomou, SE Central African Republic
Demchok *126 A5 var.* Dêmqog. *disputed region* China/India
Demerara Plain *56 C2 abyssal plain* W Atlantic Ocean
Deming *48 C3* New Mexico, SW USA
Demmin *94 C2* Mecklenburg-Vorpommern, NE Germany
Demopolis *42 C2* Alabama, S USA
Dêmqog *126 A5 var.* Demchok. China/India
Denali *see* McKinley, Mount
Denau *see* Denov
Dender *87 B6 Fr.* Dendre. *river* W Belgium
Dendre *see* Dender
Denekamp *86 E3* Overijssel, E Netherlands
Den Haag *see* 's-Gravenhage
Denham *147 A5* Western Australia
Den Ham *86 E3* Overijssel, E Netherlands
Den Helder *86 C2* Noord-Holland, NW Netherlands
Dénia *93 F4* Valenciana, E Spain
Deniliquin *149 C7* New South Wales, SE Australia
Denison *45 F3* Iowa, C USA
Denison *49 G2* Texas, SW USA
Denizli *116 B4* Denizli, SW Turkey
Denmark *85 A7 off.* Kingdom of Denmark, *Dan.* Danmark; *anc.* Hafnia. *country* N Europe

DENMARK
Northern Europe

Official name Kingdom of Denmark
Formation 950 / 1944
Capital Copenhagen
Population 5.6 million / 342 people per sq mile (132 people per sq km)
Total area 16,639 sq. miles (43,094 sq. km)
Languages Danish
Religions Evangelical Lutheran 95%, Roman Catholic 3%, Muslim 2%
Ethnic mix Danish 96%, Other (including Scandinavian and Turkish) 3%, Faeroese and Inuit 1%
Government Parliamentary system
Currency Danish krone = 100 øre
Literacy rate 99%
Calorie consumption 3378 kilocalories

Denmark, Kingdom of *see* Denmark
Denmark Strait *82 D4 var.* Danmarksstraedet. *strait* Greenland/Iceland
Dennery *55 F1* E Saint Lucia
Denov *123 E3 Rus.* Denau. Surkhondaryo Viloyati, S Uzbekistan
Denpasar *138 D5 prev.* Paloe. Bali, C Indonesia
Denton *49 G2* Texas, SW USA
D'Entrecasteaux Islands *144 B3 island group* SE Papua New Guinea
Denver *44 D4 state capital* Colorado, C USA
Der'a/Derā/Déraa *see* Dar'ā
Dera Ghāzi Khān *134 C2 var.* Dera Ghāzikhān. Punjab, C Pakistan
Dera Ghāzikhān *see* Dera Ghāzi Khān
Đeravica *see* Gjeravicë
Derbent *111 B8* Respublika Dagestan, SW Russian Federation
Derby *89 D6 C* England, United Kingdom
Dereli *see* Gónnoi
Dergachi *see* Derhachi
Derg, Lough *89 A6 Ir.* Loch Deirgeirt. *lake* W Ireland
Derhachi *109 G2 Rus.* Dergachi. Kharkivs'ka Oblast', E Ukraine
De Ridder *42 A3* Louisiana, S USA
Dérna *see* Darnah
Dertosa *see* Tortosa
Derventa *100 B3* Republika Srpska, N Bosnia and Herzegovina

Derweze *122 C2 Rus.* Darvaza. Ahal Welaýaty, C Turkmenistan
Dés *see* Dej
Deschutes River *46 B3 river* Oregon, NW USA
Desê *72 C4 var.* Desse, *It.* Dessie. Āmara, N Ethiopia
Deseado, Río *65 B7 river* S Argentina
Desertas, Ilhas *70 A2 island group* Madeira, Portugal, NE Atlantic Ocean
Deshu *see* Dishū
Des Moines *45 F3 state capital* Iowa, C USA
Desna *109 E2 river* Russian Federation/Ukraine
Dessau *94 C4* Sachsen-Anhalt, E Germany
Desse *see* Desê
Dessie *see* Desê
Destêrro *see* Florianópolis
Detroit *40 D3* Michigan, N USA
Detroit Lakes *45 F2* Minnesota, N USA
Deurne *87 B5* Noord-Brabant, SE Netherlands
Deutschendorf *see* Poprad
Deutsch-Eylau *see* Iława
Deutsch Krone *see* Wałcz
Deutschland/Deutschland, Bundesrepublik *see* Germany
Deutsch-Südwestafrika *see* Namibia
Deva *108 B4 Ger.* Diemrich, *Hung.* Déva. Hunedoara, W Romania
Déva *see* Deva
Deva *see* Chester
Devana *see* Aberdeen
Devana Castra *see* Chester
Đevđelija *see* Gevgelija
Deventer *86 D3* Overijssel, E Netherlands
Devils Lake *45 E1* North Dakota, N USA
Devoll *see* Devollit, Lumi i
Devollit, Lumi i *101 D6 var.* Devoll. *river* SE Albania
Devon Island *37 F2 prev.* North Devon Island. *island* Parry Islands, Nunavut, NE Canada
Devonport *149 C8* Tasmania, SE Australia
Devrek *116 C2* Zonguldak, N Turkey
Dexter *45 H5* Missouri, C USA
Deynau *see* Dänew
Dezfūl *120 C3 var.* Dizful. Khūzestān, SW Iran
Dezhou *128 D4* Shandong, E China
Dhaka *135 G4 prev.* Dacca. *country capital* (Bangladesh) Dhaka, C Bangladesh
Dhanbād *135 F4* Jhārkhand, NE India
Dhekélia *102 C5 Eng.* Dhekelia, *Gk.* Dekéleia. *UK air base* SE Cyprus *see* Dhekélia
Dhidhimótikhon *see* Didymóteicho
Dhíkti Ori *see* Díkti
Dhodhekánisos *see* Dodekánisa
Dhomokós *see* Domokós
Dhráma *see* Dráma
Dhrepanon, Akrotírio *see* Drépano, Akrotírio
Dhún na nGall, Bá *see* Donegal Bay
Dhuusa Marreeb *73 E5 var.* Dusa Marreb, *It.* Dusa Mareb. Galguduud, C Somalia
Diakovár *see* Đakovo
Diamantina, Chapada *63 F3 mountain range* E Brazil
Diamantina Fracture Zone *141 E6 tectonic feature* E Indian Ocean
Diamond State *see* Delaware
Diarbekr *see* Diyarbakır
Dibio *see* Dijon
Dibra *see* Debar
Dibrugarh *135 H3* Assam, NE India
Dickinson *44 D2* North Dakota, N USA
Dicle *see* Tigris
Didimotico *see* Didymóteicho
Didymóteicho *104 D3 var.* Dhidhimótikhon, Didimotího. Anatolikí Makedonía kai Thráki, NE Greece
Diedenhofen *see* Thionville
Diekirch *87 D7* Diekirch, C Luxembourg
Diemrich *see* Deva
Điện Biên *see* Điện Biên Phu
Điện Biên Phu *136 D3 var.* Bien Bien, Điện Biên. Lai Châu, N Vietnam
Diepenbeek *87 D6* Limburg, NE Belgium
Diepholz *94 B3* Niedersachsen, NW Germany
Dieppe *90 C2* Seine-Maritime, N France
Dieren *86 D4* Gelderland, E Netherlands

Differdange *87 D8* Luxembourg, SW Luxembourg
Digne *91 D6 var.* Digne-les-Bains. Alpes-de-Haute-Provence, SE France
Digne-les-Bains *see* Digne
Digoel *see* Digul, Sungai
Digoin *90 C4* Saône-et-Loire, C France
Digul, Sungai *139 H5 prev.* Digoel. *river* Papua, E Indonesia
Dihang *see* Brahmaputra
Dijlah *see* Tigris
Dijon *90 D4 anc.* Dibio. Côte d'Or, C France
Dikhil *72 D4* SW Djibouti
Dikson *114 D2* Krasnoyarskiy Kray, N Russian Federation
Dikti *105 D8 var.* Dhíkti Ori. *mountain range* Kríti, Greece, E Mediterranean Sea
Dilārām *122 D5 prev.* Delārām. Nīmrōz, SW Afghanistan
Dili *139 F5 var.* Dilli, Dilly. *country capital* (East Timor) N East Timor
Dilia *75 G3 var.* Dilli. *river* SE Niger
Dilli *see* Dili, East Timor
Dilli *see* Delhi, India
Dillia *see* Dilia
Dilling *72 B4 var.* Ad Dalanj. Southern Kordofan, C Sudan
Dillon *44 B2* Montana, NW USA
Dilly *see* Dili
Dilolo *77 D7* Katanga, S Dem. Rep. Congo
Dimashq *119 B5 var.* Ash Shām, Esh Sham, *Eng.* Damascus, *Fr.* Damas, *It.* Damasco. *country capital* (Syria) Rīf Dimashq, SW Syria
Dimitrovgrad *104 D3* Khaskovo, S Bulgaria
Dimitrovgrad *111 C6 prev.* Caribrod. Serbia, SE Serbia
Dimitrovo *see* Pernik
Dimovo *104 B1* Vidin, NW Bulgaria
Dinajpur *135 F3* Rajshahi, NW Bangladesh
Dinan *90 B3* Côtes d'Armor, NW France
Dinant *87 C7* Namur, S Belgium
Dinar *116 B4* Afyon, SW Turkey
Dinara *see* Dinaric Alps
Dinaric Alps *100 C4 var.* Dinara. *mountain range* Bosnia and Herzegovina/Croatia
Dindigul *132 C3* Tamil Nādu, SE India
Dingle Bay *89 A6 Ir.* Bá an Daingin. *bay* SW Ireland
Dinguiraye *74 C4* N Guinea
Diourbel *74 B3* W Senegal
Dirê Dawa *73 D5* Dirê Dawa, E Ethiopia
Dirk Hartog Island *147 A5 island* Western Australia
Dirschau *see* Tczew
Disappointment, Lake *146 C4 salt lake* Western Australia
Discovery Bay *54 B4* Middlesex, Jamaica, Greater Antilles, C Jamaica Caribbean Sea
Dishū *122 D5 var.* Deshu; *prev.* Deh Shū. Helmand, S Afghanistan
Dispur *135 G3 state capital* Assam, NE India
Divinópolis *63 F4* Minas Gerais, SE Brazil
Divo *74 D5* S Côte d'Ivoire
Divodurum Mediomatricum *see* Metz
Diyarbakır *117 F4 var. anc.* Amida. Diyarbakır, SE Turkey
Dizful *see* Dezfūl
Djailolo *see* Halmahera, Pulau
Djajapura *see* Jayapura
Djakarta *see* Jakarta
Djakovo *see* Đakovo
Djambala *77 B6* Plateaux, C Congo
Djambi *see* Hari, Batang
Djambi *see* Jambi
Djanet *71 E4 prev.* Fort Charlet. SE Algeria
Djébel *see* Jablah
Djelfa *70 D2 var.* El Djelfa. N Algeria
Djéma *76 D4* Haut-Mbomou, E Central African Republic
Djember *see* Jember
Djérablous *see* Jarāblus
Djerba *see* Jerba, Île de
Djerba *71 F2 var.* Djerba, Jazīrat Jarbah. *island* E Tunisia
Djerba *see* Jerba, Île de
Djérem *76 B4 river* C Cameroon

Djevdjelija see Gevgelija
Djibouti 72 D4 var. Jibuti. country capital (Djibouti) E Djibouti
Djibouti 72 D4 off. Republic of Djibouti, var. Jibuti; prev. French Somaliland, French Territory of the Afars and Issas, Fr. Côte Française des Somalis, Territoire Français des Afars et des Issas. country E Africa

DJIBOUTI
East Africa

Official name Republic of Djibouti
Formation 1977 / 1977
Capital Djibouti
Population 900,000 / 101 people per sq mile (39 people per sq km)
Total area 8494 sq. miles (22,000 sq. km)
Languages Somali, Afar, French*, Arabic*
Religions Muslim (mainly Sunni) 94%, Christian 6%
Ethnic mix Issa 60%, Afar 35%, Other 5%
Government Presidential system
Currency Djibouti franc = 100 centimes
Literacy rate 70%
Calorie consumption 2419 kilocalories

Djibouti, Republic of see Djibouti
Djokjakarta see Yogyakarta
Djourab, Erg du 76 C2 desert N Chad
Djupivogur 83 E5 Austurland, SE Iceland
Dmitriyevsk see Makiyivka
Dnepr see Dnieper
Dneprodzerzhinsk see Romaniv
Dneprodzerzhinskoye Vodokhranilishche see Dniprodzerzhyns'ke Vodoskhovyshche
Dnepropetrovsk see Dnipropetrovs'k
Dneprorudnoye see Dniprorudne
Dnestr see Dniester
Dnieper 81 F4 Bel. Dnyapro, Rus. Dnepr, Ukr. Dnipro. river E Europe
Dnieper Lowland 109 E2 Bel. Prydnyapowskaya Nizina, Ukr. Prydniprovs'ka Nyzovyna. lowlands Belarus/Ukraine
Dniester 81 E4 Rom. Nistru, Rus. Dnestr, Ukr. Dnister; anc. Tyras. river Moldova/Ukraine
Dnipro see Dnieper
Dniprodzerzhyns'k see Romaniv
Dniprodzerzhyns'ke Vodoskhovyshche 109 F3 Rus. Dneprodzerzhinskoye Vodokhranilishche. reservoir C Ukraine
Dnipropetrovs'k 109 F3 Rus. Dnepropetrovsk; prev. Yekaterinoslav. Dnipropetrovs'ka Oblast', E Ukraine
Dniprorudne 109 F3 Rus. Dneprorudnoye. Zaporiz'ka Oblast', SE Ukraine
Dnister see Dnieper
Dnyapro see Dnieper
Doba 76 C4 Logone-Oriental, S Chad
Döbeln 94 D4 Sachsen, E Germany
Doberai Peninsula 139 G4 Dut. Vogelkop. peninsula Papua, E Indonesia
Doboj 100 C3 Republiks Srpska, N Bosnia and Herzegovina
Dobre Miasto 98 D2 Ger. Guttstadt. Warmińsko-mazurskie, NE Poland
Dobrich 104 E1 Rom. Bazargic; prev. Tolbukhin. Dobrich, NE Bulgaria
Dobrush 107 D7 Homyel'skaya Voblasts', SE Belarus
Dobryn' see Dabryn'
Dodecanese 105 D6 var. Nóties Sporádes, Eng. Dodecanese; prev. Dhodhekánisos, Dodekánisos. island group SE Greece
Dodecanese see Dodekánisa
Dodekanisos see Dodekánisa
Dodge City 45 E5 Kansas, C USA
Dodoma 69 D5 country capital (Tanzania) Dodoma, C Tanzania
Dogana 96 E1 NE San Marino Europe
Dogo 131 B6 island Oki-shotō, SW Japan
Dogondoutchi 75 F3 Dosso, SW Niger
Dogrular see Pravda
Doğubayazıt 117 F3 Ağrı, E Turkey
Doğu Karadeniz Dağları 117 E3 var. Anadolu Dağları. mountain range NE Turkey
Doha see Ad Dawḥah
Doire see Londonderry

Dokkum 86 D1 Fryslân, N Netherlands
Dokuchayevs'k 109 G3 var. Dokuchayevsk. Donets'ka Oblast', SE Ukraine
Dokuchayevsk see Dokuchayevs'k
Doldrums Fracture Zone 66 C4 fracture zone W Atlantic Ocean
Dôle 90 D4 Jura, E France
Dolina see Dolyna
Dolinskaya see Dolyns'ka
Dolisie 77 B6 prev. Loubomo. Niari, S Congo
Dolomites 96 C1 var. Dolomiti, Eng. Dolomites. mountain range NE Italy
Dolomites/Dolomiti see Dolomitiche, Alpi
Dolores 64 D4 Buenos Aires, E Argentina
Dolores 52 B1 Petén, N Guatemala
Dolores 64 D4 Soriano, SW Uruguay
Dolores Hidalgo 51 E4 var. Ciudad de Dolores Hidalgo. Guanajuato, C Mexico
Dolyna 108 B2 Rus. Dolina. Ivano-Frankivs'ka Oblast', W Ukraine
Dolyns'ka 109 F3 Rus. Dolinskaya. Kirovohrads'ka Oblast', C Ukraine
Domachëvo/Domaczewo see Damachava
Dombås 85 B5 Oppland, S Norway
Domel Island see Letsôk-aw Kyun
Domesnes, Cape see Kolkasrags
Domeyko 64 B3 Atacama, N Chile
Dominica 55 H4 off. Commonwealth of Dominica. country E West Indies

DOMINICA
West Indies

Official name Commonwealth of Dominica
Formation 1978 / 1978
Capital Roseau
Population 73,126 / 252 people per sq mile (98 people per sq km)
Total area 291 sq. miles (754 sq. km)
Languages French Creole, English*
Religions Roman Catholic 77%, Protestant 15%, Other 8%
Ethnic mix Black 87%, Mixed race 9%, Carib 3%, Other 1%
Government Parliamentary system
Currency East Caribbean dollar = 100 cents
Literacy rate 88%
Calorie consumption 3147 kilocalories

Dominica Channel see Martinique Passage
Dominica, Commonwealth of see Dominica
Dominican Republic 55 E2 country C West Indies

DOMINICAN REPUBLIC
West Indies

Official name Dominican Republic
Formation 1865 / 1865
Capital Santo Domingo
Population 10.1 million / 541 people per sq mile (209 people per sq km)
Total area 18,679 sq. miles (48,380 sq. km)
Languages Spanish*, French Creole
Religions Roman Catholic 95%, Other and nonreligious 5%
Ethnic mix Mixed race 73%, European 16%, African 11%
Government Presidential system
Currency Dominican Republic peso = 100 centavos
Literacy rate 88%
Calorie consumption 2491 kilocalories

Domokós 105 B5 var. Dhomokós. Stereá Elláda, C Greece
Don 111 B6 var. Duna, Tanais. river SW Russian Federation
Donau see Danube
Donauwörth 95 C6 Bayern, S Germany
Don Benito 92 C3 Extremadura, W Spain
Doncaster 89 D5 anc. Danum. N England, United Kingdom
Dondo 78 B1 Cuanza Norte, NW Angola
Donegal 89 B5 Ir. Dún na nGall. Donegal, NW Ireland
Donegal Bay 89 A5 Ir. Bá Dhún na nGall. bay NW Ireland
Donets 109 G2 river Russian Federation/Ukraine

Donets'k 109 G3 Rus. Donetsk; prev. Stalino. Donets'ka Oblast', E Ukraine
Dongfang 128 B7 var. Basuo. Hainan, S China
Dongguan 128 C6 Guangdong, S China
Đông Ha 136 E4 Quang Tri, C Vietnam
Dong Hai see East China Sea
Đông Hơi 136 D4 Quang Binh, C Vietnam
Dongliao see Liaoyuan
Dongola 72 B3 var. Donqola, Dunqulah. Northern, N Sudan
Dongou 77 C5 Likouala, NE Congo
Dong Rak, Phanom see Dângrêk, Chuôr Phnum
Dongting Hu 128 C5 var. Tung-t'ing Hu. lake S China
Donostia/San Sebastián 93 E1 País Vasco, N Spain
Donqola see Dongola
Doolow 73 D5 Sumalē, E Ethiopia
Doornik see Tournai
Door Peninsula 40 C2 peninsula Wisconsin, N USA
Dooxo Nugaaleed 73 E5 var. Nogal Valley. valley E Somalia
Dordogne 91 B5 cultural region SW France
Dordogne 91 B5 river W France
Dordrecht 86 C4 var. Dordt, Dort. Zuid-Holland, SW Netherlands
Dordt see Dordrecht
Dorohoi 108 C3 Botoşani, NE Romania
Dorotea 84 C4 Västerbotten, N Sweden
Dorpat see Tartu
Dorre Island 147 A5 island Western Australia
Dort see Dordrecht
Dortmund 94 A4 Nordrhein-Westfalen, W Germany
Dos Hermanas 92 C4 Andalucía, S Spain
Dospad Dagh see Rhodope Mountains
Dospat 104 C3 Smolyan, S Bulgaria
Dothan 42 D3 Alabama, S USA
Dotnuva 106 B4 Kaunas, C Lithuania
Douai 90 C2 prev. Douay; anc. Duacum. Nord, N France
Douala 77 A5 var. Duala. Littoral, W Cameroon
Douay see Douai
Douglas 89 C5 dependent territory capital (Isle of Man) E Isle of Man
Douglas 43 C3 Arizona, SW USA
Douglas 44 D3 Wyoming, C USA
Douma see Dūmā
Douro see Duero
Douvres see Dover
Dover 89 E7 Fr. Douvres, Lat. Dubris Portus. SE England, United Kingdom
Dover 41 F4 state capital Delaware, NE USA
Dover, Strait of 90 C2 var. Straits of Dover, Fr. Pas de Calais. strait England, United Kingdom/France
Dover, Straits of see Dover, Strait of
Dovrefjell 85 B5 plateau S Norway
Downpatrick 89 B5 Ir. Dún Pádraig. SE Northern Ireland, United Kingdom
Dozen 131 B6 island Oki-shotō, SW Japan
Drâa, Hammada du see Dra, Hamada du
Drač/Draç see Durrës
Drachten 86 D2 Fryslân, N Netherlands
Drăgăşani 108 B5 Vâlcea, SW Romania
Dragoman 104 B2 Sofiya, W Bulgaria
Dra, Hamada du 70 C3 var. Hammada du Drâa, Haut Plateau du Dra. plateau W Algeria
Dra, Haut Plateau du see Dra, Hamada du
Drahichyn 107 B6 Pol. Drohiczyn Poleski, Rus. Drogichin. Brestskaya Voblasts', SW Belarus
Drakensberg 78 D5 mountain range Lesotho/South Africa
Drake Passage 57 B8 passage Atlantic Ocean/Pacific Ocean
Dralfa 104 D2 Türgovishte, N Bulgaria
Dráma 104 C3 var. Dhráma. Anatolikí Makedonía kai Thráki, NE Greece
Dramburg see Drawsko Pomorskie
Drammen 85 B6 Buskerud, S Norway
Drau see Drava
Drava 100 C3 var. Drau, Eng. Drave, Hung. Dráva. river C Europe
Dráva/Drave see Drava/Drava
Drawsko Pomorskie 98 B3 Ger. Dramburg. Zachodnio-pomorskie, NW Poland

Drépano, Akrotírio 104 C4 var. Akrotírio Dhrepanon. headland N Greece
Drepanum see Trapani
Dresden 94 D4 Sachsen, E Germany
Drin see Drinit, Lumi i
Drina 100 C3 river Bosnia and Herzegovina/Serbia
Drinit, Lumi i 101 D5 var. Drin. river NW Albania
Drinit të Zi, Lumi i see Black Drin
Drissa see Drysa
Drobeta-Turnu Severin 108 B5 prev. Turnu Severin. Mehedinţi, SW Romania
Drogheda 89 B5 Ir. Droichead Átha. NE Ireland
Drogichin see Drahichyn
Drogobych see Drohobych
Drohiczyn Poleski see Drahichyn
Drohobych 108 B2 Pol. Drohobycz, Rus. Drogobych. L'vivs'ka Oblast', NW Ukraine
Drohobycz see Drohobych
Droichead Átha see Drogheda
Drôme 91 D5 cultural region E France
Dronning Maud Land 154 B2 physical region Antarctica
Drontheim see Trondheim
Drug see Durg
Druk-yul see Bhutan
Drummondville 39 E4 Québec, SE Canada
Druskieniki see Druskininkai
Druskininkai 107 B5 Pol. Druskienniki. Alytus, S Lithuania
Dryden 38 B3 Ontario, C Canada
Drysa 107 D5 Rus. Drissa. river N Belarus
Duacum see Douai
Duala see Douala
Dubai see Dubayy
Dubăsari 108 D3 Rus. Dubossary. NE Moldova
Dubawnt 37 F4 river Nunavut, NW Canada
Dubayy 120 D4 Eng. Dubai. Dubayy, NE United Arab Emirates
Dubbo 149 D6 New South Wales, SE Australia
Dublin 89 B5 Ir. Baile Átha Cliath; anc. Eblana. country capital (Ireland) Dublin, E Ireland
Dublin 43 E2 Georgia, SE USA
Dubno 108 C2 Rivnens'ka Oblast', NW Ukraine
Dubossary see Dubăsari
Dubris Portus see Dover
Dubrovnik 101 B5 It. Ragusa. Dubrovnik-Neretva, SE Croatia
Dubuque 45 G3 Iowa, C USA
Dudelange 87 D8 var. Forge du Sud, Ger. Dudelingen. Luxembourg, S Luxembourg
Duero 92 D2 Port. Douro. river Portugal/Spain
Duesseldorf see Düsseldorf
Duffel 87 C5 Antwerpen, C Belgium
Dugi Otok 100 A4 var. Isola Grossa, It. Isola Lunga. island W Croatia
Duinekerke see Dunkerque
Duisburg 94 A4 prev. Duisburg-Hamborn. Nordrhein-Westfalen, W Germany
Duisburg-Hamborn see Duisburg
Duiven 86 D4 Gelderland, E Netherlands
Duk Faiwil 73 B5 Jonglei, E South Sudan
Dulan 126 D4 var. Qagan Us. Qinghai, C China
Dulce, Golfo 53 E5 gulf S Costa Rica
Dulce, Golfo de see Izabal, Lago de
Dülmen 94 A4 Nordrhein-Westfalen, W Germany
Dulovo 104 D1 Silistra, NE Bulgaria
Duluth 45 G2 Minnesota, N USA
Dūmā 119 B5 Fr. Douma. Rif Dimashq, SW Syria
Dumas 49 E1 Texas, SW USA
Dumfries 88 C4 S Scotland, United Kingdom
Dumont d'Urville 154 C4 French research station Antarctica
Dumyât 72 B1 var. Dumyât, Eng. Damietta. N Egypt
Duna see Danube, C Europe
Düna see Western Dvina
Duna see Don, Russian Federation
Dünaburg see Daugavpils

Dunaj see Wien, Austria
Dunaj see Danube, C Europe
Dunapentele see Dunaújváros
Dunărea see Danube
Dunaújváros 99 C7 prev. Dunapentele, Sztálinváros. Fejér, C Hungary
Dunav see Danube
Duncan 49 G2 Oklahoma, C USA
Dundalk 89 B5 Ir. Dún Dealgan. Louth, NE Ireland
Dún Dealgan see Dundalk
Dundee 78 D4 KwaZulu/Natal, E South Africa
Dundee 88 C4 E Scotland, United Kingdom
Dunedin 151 B7 Otago, South Island, New Zealand
Dunfermline 88 C4 C Scotland, United Kingdom
Dungu 77 E5 Orientale, NE Dem. Rep. Congo
Dungun 138 B3 var. Kuala Dungun. Terengganu, Peninsular Malaysia
Dunholme see Durham
Dunkerque 90 C2 Eng. Dunkirk, Flem. Duinekerke; prev. Dunquerque. Nord, N France
Dunkirk see Dunkerque
Dún Laoghaire 89 B6 Eng. Dunleary; prev. Kingstown. E Ireland
Dunleary see Dún Laoghaire
Dún Pádraig see Downpatrick
Dunquerque see Dunkerque
Dunqulah see Dongola
Dupnitsa 104 C2 prev. Marek, Stanke Dimitrov. Kyustendil, W Bulgaria
Duqm 121 E5 var. Daqm. E Oman
Durance 91 D6 river SE France
Durango 50 D3 var. Victoria de Durango. Durango, W Mexico
Durango 44 C5 Colorado, C USA
Durankulak 104 E1 Rom. Răcari; prev. Blatnitsa, Duranulac. Dobrich, NE Bulgaria
Durant 49 G2 Oklahoma, C USA
Duranulac see Durankulak
Durazzo see Durrës
Durban 78 D4 var. Port Natal. KwaZulu/Natal, E South Africa
Durbe 106 B3 Ger. Durben. W Latvia
Durben see Durbe
Durg 135 E4 prev. Drug. Chhattīsgarh, C India
Durham 89 D5 hist. Dunholme. N England, United Kingdom
Durham 43 F1 North Carolina, SE USA
Durocortorum see Reims
Durostorum see Silistra
Durovernum see Canterbury
Durrës 101 C6 var. Durrësi, Dursi, It. Durazzo, SCr. Drač, Turk. Draç. Durrës, W Albania
Durrësi see Durrës
Dursi see Durrës
Durúz, Jabal ad 119 C5 mountain SW Syria
D'Urville Island 150 C4 island C New Zealand
Dusa Mareb/Dusa Marreb see Dhuusa Marreeb
Dushanbe 123 E3 var. Dyushambe; prev. Stalinabad, Taj. Stalinobod. country capital (Tajikistan) W Tajikistan
Düsseldorf 94 A4 var. Duesseldorf. Nordrhein-Westfalen, W Germany
Düsti 123 E3 Rus. Dusti. SW Tajikistan
Dutch East Indies see Indonesia
Dutch Guiana see Suriname
Dutch Harbor 36 B3 Unalaska Island, Alaska, USA
Dutch New Guinea see Papua
Dutch West Indies see Curaçao
Duzdab see Zāhedān
Dvina Bay see Chëshskaya Guba
Dvinsk see Daugavpils
Dyanev see Galkynyş
Dyersburg 42 C1 Tennessee, S USA
Dyushambe see Dushanbe
Dza Chu see Mekong
Dzaudzhikau see Vladikavkaz
Dzerzhinsk 111 C5 Nizhegorodskaya Oblast', W Russian Federation
Dzerzhinskiy see Nar'yan-Mar
Dzhalal-Abad 123 F2 Kir. Jalal-Abad. Dzhalal-Abadskaya Oblast', W Kyrgyzstan
Dzhambul see Taraz

Dzhankoy 109 F4 Avtonomna Respublika Krym, S Ukraine
Dzharkurgan see Jarqo'rg'on
Dzhelandy 123 F3 SE Tajikistan
Dzhergalan 123 G2 Kir. Jyrgalan. Issyk-Kul'skaya Oblast', NE Kyrgyzstan
Dzhezkazgan see Zhezkazgan
Dzhizak see Jizzax
Dzhugdzhur, Khrebet 115 G3 mountain range E Russian Federation
Dzhusaly see Zhosaly
Działdowo 98 D3 Warmińsko-Mazurskie, C Poland
Dzuunmod 127 E2 Töv, C Mongolia
Dzüün Soyonï Nuruu see Vostochnyy Sayan
Dzvina see Western Dvina

E

Eagle Pass 49 F4 Texas, SW USA
East Açores Fracture Zone see East Azores Fracture Zone
East Antarctica 154 C3 prev. Greater Antarctica. physical region Antarctica
East Australian Basin see Tasman Basin
East Azores Fracture Zone 66 C3 var. East Açores Fracture Zone. tectonic feature E Atlantic Ocean
Eastbourne 89 E7 SE England, United Kingdom
East Cape 150 E3 headland North Island, New Zealand
East China Sea 125 E2 Chin. Dong Hai. sea W Pacific Ocean
Easter Fracture Zone 153 G4 tectonic feature E Pacific Ocean
Easter Island 153 F4 var. Rapa Nui, Easter Island. island E Pacific Ocean
Easter Island see Pascua, Isla de
Eastern Desert 68 D3 var. Aş Şaḩrā' ash Sharqīyah, Eng. Arabian Desert, Eastern Desert. desert E Egypt
Eastern Desert see Sahara el Sharqīya
Eastern Ghats 124 B3 mountain range SE India
Eastern Sayans see Vostochnyy Sayan
Eastern Sierra Madre see Madre Oriental, Sierra
East Falkland 65 D8 var. Isla Soledad. island E Falkland Islands
East Frisian Islands 94 A3 Eng. East Frisian Islands. island group NW Germany
East Frisian Islands see Ostfriesische Inseln
East Grand Forks 45 E1 Minnesota, N USA
East Indiaman Ridge 141 D6 undersea ridge E Indian Ocean
East Indies 152 A3 island group SE Asia
East Kilbride 88 C4 S Scotland, United Kingdom
East Korea Bay 129 E3 bay E North Korea
Eastleigh 89 D7 S England, United Kingdom
East London 78 D5 Afr. Oos-Londen; prev. Emonti, Port Rex. Eastern Cape, S South Africa
Eastmain 38 D3 river Québec, C Canada
East Mariana Basin 142 B1 undersea basin W Pacific Ocean
East Novaya Zemlya Trough 112 C1 var. Novaya Zemlya Trough. trough W Kara Sea
East Pacific Rise 153 F4 undersea rise E Pacific Ocean
East Pakistan see Bangladesh
East Saint Louis 40 B4 Illinois, N USA
East Scotia Basin 67 C7 undersea basin SE Scotia Sea
East Sea 130 A4 var. Sea of Japan, Rus. Yaponskoye More. Sea NW Pacific Ocean
East Siberian Sea 115 F1 Eng. East Siberian Sea. sea Arctic Ocean
East Siberian Sea see Vostochno-Sibirskoye More
East Timor 139 F5 var. Loro Sae; prev. Portuguese Timor, Timor Timur. country S Indonesia

EAST TIMOR
Southeast Asia

Official name Democratic Republic of Timor-Leste
Formation 2002 / 2002

EAST TIMOR
(continued)

Capital Dili
Population 1.2 million / 213 people per sq mile (82 people per sq km)
Total area 5756 sq. miles (14,874 sq. km)
Languages Tetum (Portuguese/Austronesian)*, Bahasa Indonesia, Portuguese*
Religions Roman Catholic 95%, Other (including Muslim and Protestant) 5%
Government Parliamentary system
Currency US dollar = 100 cents
Literacy rate 51%
Calorie consumption 2076 kilocalories

Eau Claire 40 A2 Wisconsin, N USA
Eau Claire, Lac à L' see St. Clair, Lake
Eauripik Rise 142 B2 undersea rise W Pacific Ocean
Ebensee 95 D6 Oberösterreich, N Austria
Eberswalde-Finow 94 D3 Brandenburg, E Germany
Ebetsu 130 D2 var. Ebetu. Hokkaidō, NE Japan
Ebetu see Ebetsu
Eblana see Dublin
Ebolowa 77 A5 Sud, S Cameroon
Ebon Atoll 144 D2 var. Epoon. atoll Ralik Chain, S Marshall Islands
Ebora see Évora
Eboracum see York
Ebro 93 E2 river NE Spain
Eburacum see York
Ebusus see Eivissa
Ebusus see Eivissa
Ebusus see Eivissa
Ecbatana see Hamadān
Ech Cheliff/Ech Chleff see Chlef
Echo Bay 37 E3 Northwest Territories, NW Canada
Echt 87 D5 Limburg, SE Netherlands
Ecija 92 D4 anc. Astigi. Andalucía, SW Spain
Eckengraf see Viesīte
Ecuador 60 B1 off. Republic of Ecuador. country NW South America

ECUADOR
South America

Official name Republic of Ecuador
Formation 1830 / 1942
Capital Quito
Population 14.7 million / 138 people per sq mile (53 people per sq km)
Total area 109,483 sq. miles (283,560 sq. km)
Languages Spanish*, Quechua, other Amerindian languages
Religions Roman Catholic 95%, Protestant, Jewish, and other 5%
Ethnic mix Mestizo 77%, White 11%, Amerindian 7%, Black 5%
Government Presidential system
Currency US dollar = 100 cents
Literacy rate 84%
Calorie consumption 2267 kilocalories

Ecuador, Republic of see Ecuador
Ed Da'ein 72 A4 Southern Darfur, W Sudan
Ed Damazin 72 C4 var. Ad Damazīn. Blue Nile, E Sudan
Ed Damer 72 C3 var. Ad Dāmir, Ad Damar. River Nile, NE Sudan
Ed Debba 72 B3 Northern, N Sudan
Ede 86 D4 Gelderland, C Netherlands
Ede 75 F5 Osun, SW Nigeria
Edéa 77 A5 Littoral, SW Cameroon
Edessa see Şanlıurfa
Edfu see Idfu
Edgeøya 83 G2 island S Svalbard
Edgware 89 A7 Harrow, SE England, United Kingdom
Edinburg 49 G5 Texas, SW USA
Edinburgh 88 C4 national capital S Scotland, United Kingdom
Edingen see Enghien
Edirne 116 A2 Eng. Adrianople; anc. Adrianopolis, Hadrianopolis. Edirne, NW Turkey
Edmonds 46 B2 Washington, NW USA
Edmonton 37 E5 province capital Alberta, SW Canada

Edmundston 39 E4 New Brunswick, SE Canada
Edna 49 G4 Texas, SW USA
Edolo 96 B1 Lombardia, N Italy
Edremit 116 A3 Balıkesir, NW Turkey
Edward, Lake 77 E5 var. Albert Edward Nyanza, Edward Nyanza, Lac Idi Amin, Lake Rutanzige. lake Uganda/Dem. Rep. Congo
Edward Nyanza see Edward, Lake
Edwards Plateau 49 F3 plain Texas, SW USA
Edzo 53 E4 prev. Rae-Edzo. Northwest Territories, NW Canada
Eeklo 87 B5 var. Eekloo. Oost-Vlaanderen, NW Belgium
Eekloo see Eeklo
Eems see Ems
Eersel 87 C5 Noord-Brabant, S Netherlands
Eesti Vabariik see Estonia
Efate 144 D4 var. Efate, Fr. Vaté; prev. Sandwich Island. island C Vanuatu
Efate see Efate
Effingham 40 B4 Illinois, N USA
Eforie-Sud 108 D5 Constanţa, E Romania
Egadi Is. 97 B7 island group S Italy
Ege Denizi see Aegean Sea
Eger 99 D6 Ger. Erlau. Heves, NE Hungary
Eger see Cheb, Czech Republic
Egeria Fracture Zone 141 C5 tectonic feature W Indian Ocean
Éghezèe 87 C6 Namur, C Belgium
Egina see Aígina
Egio see Aígio
Egmont see Taranaki, Mount
Egmont, Cape 150 C4 headland North Island, New Zealand
Egoli see Johannesburg
Egypt 72 B2 off. Arab Republic of Egypt, Ar. Jumhūrīyah Misr al 'Arabīyah, prev. United Arab Republic; anc. Aegyptus. country NE Africa

EGYPT
North Africa

Official name Arab Republic of Egypt
Formation 1936 / 1982
Capital Cairo
Population 82.5 million / 215 people per sq mile (83 people per sq km)
Total area 386,660 sq. miles (1,001,450 sq. km)
Languages Arabic*, French, English, Berber
Religions Muslim (mainly Sunni) 90%, Coptic Christian and other 10%
Ethnic mix Egyptian 99%, Nubian, Armenian, Greek, and Berber 1%
Government Transitional regime
Currency Egyptian pound = 100 piastres
Literacy rate 72%
Calorie consumption 3349 kilocalories

Eibar 93 E1 País Vasco, N Spain
Eibergen 86 E3 Gelderland, E Netherlands
Eidfjord 85 A5 Hordaland, S Norway
Fier-Berg see Suur Munamägi
Eifel 95 A5 plateau W Germany
Eiger 95 B7 mountain C Switzerland
Eigg 88 B3 island W Scotland, United Kingdom
Eight Degree Channel 132 B3 channel India/Maldives
Eighty Mile Beach 146 B4 beach Western Australia
Eijsden 87 D6 Limburg, SE Netherlands
Eilat see Elat
Eindhoven 87 D5 Noord-Brabant, S Netherlands
Eipel see Ipel'
Éire see Ireland
Éireann, Muir see Irish Sea
Eisenhüttenstadt 94 D4 Brandenburg, E Germany
Eisenmarkt see Hunedoara
Eisenstadt 95 E6 Burgenland, E Austria
Eisleben 94 C4 Sachsen-Anhalt, C Germany
Eivissa 93 G3 var. Iviza, Cast. Ibiza; anc. Ebusus. Ibiza, Spain, W Mediterranean Sea
Eivissa 93 G3 var. Iviza, Cast. Ibiza; anc. Ebusus. Ibiza, Spain, W Mediterranean Sea

Eivissa 93 G3 *var.* Iviza, *Cast.*
  Ibíza; *anc.* Ebusus. Ibiza, Spain,
  W Mediterranean Sea
Ejea de los Caballeros 93 E2 Aragón,
  NE Spain
Ejin Qi *see* Dalain Hob
Ekapa *see* Cape Town
Ekaterinodar *see* Krasnodar
Ekiatapskiy Khrebet *see* Ekvyvatapskiy
  Khrebet
Ekvyvatapskiy Khrebet 115 G1 *prev.*
  Ekiatapskiy Khrebet. *mountain range*
  NE Russian Federation
El 'Alamein *see* Al 'Alamayn
El Asnam *see* Chlef
Elat 119 B8 *var.* Eilat, Elath. Southern,
  S Israel
Elat, Gulf of *see* Aqaba, Gulf of
Elath *see* Elat, Israel
Elath *see* Al 'Aqabah, Jordan
El'Atrun 72 B3 Northern Darfur,
  NW Sudan
Elâzığ 117 E3 *var.* Elâzig, Elâziz. Elâzığ,
  E Turkey
Elba 96 B4 *island* Archipelago Toscano,
  C Italy
Elbasan 101 D6 *var.* Elbasani. Elbasan,
  C Albania
Elbasani *see* Elbasan
Elbe 80 D3 *Cz.* Labe. *river* Czech
  Republic/Germany
Elbert, Mount 44 C4 *mountain*
  Colorado, C USA
Elbing *see* Elbląg
Elbląg 98 C2 *var.* Elblag, *Ger.* Elbing.
  Warmińsko-Mazurskie, NE Poland
El Boulaïda/El Boulaïda *see* Blida
El'brus 111 A8 *var.* Gora El'brus.
  mountain SW Russian Federation
El'brus, Gora *see* El'brus
El Burgo de Osma 93 E2 Castilla y
  León, C Spain
Elburz Mountains 120 C2 *Eng.* Elburz
  Mountains. *mountain range* N Iran
Elburz Mountains *see* Alborz, Reshteh-ye
  Kūhhā-ye
El Cajon 47 C8 California, W USA
El Calafate 65 B7 *var.* Calafate. Santa
  Cruz, S Argentina
El Callao 59 E2 Bolívar, E Venezuela
El Campo 49 G4 Texas, SW USA
El Carmen de Bolívar 58 B2 Bolívar,
  NW Colombia
El Cayo *see* San Ignacio
El Centro 47 D8 California, W USA
Elche 93 F4 *Cat.* Elx; *anc.* Ilici, *Lat.* Illicis.
  Valenciana, E Spain
Elda 93 F4 Valenciana, E Spain
El Djazair *see* Alger
El Djelfa *see* Djelfa
Eldorado 64 E3 Misiones, NE Argentina
El Dorado 50 C3 Sinaloa, C Mexico
El Dorado 42 B2 Arkansas, C USA
El Dorado 45 F5 Kansas, C USA
El Dorado 59 F2 Bolívar, E Venezuela
El Dorado *see* California
Eldoret 73 C6 Rift Valley, W Kenya
Elektrostal' 111 B5 Moskovskaya
  Oblast', W Russian Federation
Elemi Triangle 73 B5 *disputed region*
  Kenya/Sudan
Elephant Butte Reservoir 48 C2
  reservoir New Mexico, SW USA
Élesd *see* Aleşd
Eleuthera Island 54 C1 *island*
  N Bahamas
El Fasher 72 A4 *var.* Al Fāshir. Northern
  Darfur, W Sudan
El Ferrol/El Ferrol del Caudillo *see*
  Ferrol
El Gedaref *see* Gedaref
El Geneina 72 A4 *var.* Ajjinena, Al-
  Genain, Al Junaynah. Western Darfur,
  W Sudan
Elgin 88 C3 NE Scotland, United
  Kingdom
Elgin 40 B3 Illinois, N USA
El Giza *see* Giza
El Goléa 70 D3 *var.* Al Golea. C Algeria
El Hank 74 D1 *cliff* N Mauritania
El Haseke *see* Al Ḥasakah
Elimberrum *see* Auch
Eliocroca *see* Lorca
Élisabethville *see* Lubumbashi
Elista 111 B7 Respublika Kalmykiya,
  SW Russian Federation
Elizabeth 149 B6 South Australia
Elizabeth City 43 G1 North Carolina,
  SE USA

Elizabethtown 40 C5 Kentucky, S USA
El-Jadida 70 C2 *prev.* Mazagan.
  W Morocco
Ełk 98 E2 *Ger.* Lyck. Warmińsko-
  mazurskie, NE Poland
Elk City 49 F1 Oklahoma, C USA
El Khalil *see* Hebron
El Khârga *see* Al Khārijah
Elkhart 40 C3 Indiana, N USA
El Khartûm *see* Khartoum
Elk River 45 F2 Minnesota, N USA
El Kuneitra *see* Al Qunayţirah
Ellás *see* Greece
Ellef Ringnes Island 37 E1 *island*
  Nunavut, N Canada
Ellen, Mount 44 B5 *mountain* Utah,
  W USA
Ellensburg 46 B2 Washington, NW USA
Ellesmere Island 37 F1 *island* Queen
  Elizabeth Islands, Nunavut, N Canada
Ellesmere, Lake 151 C6 *lake* South
  Island, New Zealand
Ellice Islands *see* Tuvalu
Elliston 149 A6 South Australia
Ellsworth Land 154 A3 *physical region*
  Antarctica
El Mahbas 70 B3 *var.* Mahbés.
  SW Western Sahara
El Mina 118 B4 *var.* Al Mīnā'.
  N Lebanon
El Minya *see* Al Minyā
Elmira 41 E3 New York, NE USA
El Mreyyé 74 D2 *desert* E Mauritania
Elmshorn 94 B3 Schleswig-Holstein,
  N Germany
El Muglad 72 B4 Southern Kordofan,
  C Sudan
El Obeid 72 B4 *var.* Al Obayyid, Al
  Ubayyid. Northern Kordofan, C Sudan
El Ouâdi *see* El Oued
El Oued 71 E2 *var.* Al Oued, El Ouâdi, El
  Wad. NE Algeria
Eloy 48 B2 Arizona, SW USA
El Paso 48 D3 Texas, SW USA
El Porvenir 53 G4 Kuna Yala, N Panama
El Progreso 52 C2 Yoro, NW Honduras
El Puerto de Santa María 92 C5
  Andalucía, S Spain
El Qâhira *see* Cairo
El Quneitra *see* Al Qunayţirah
El Quseir *see* Al Quşayr
El Quweira *see* Al Quwayrah
El Rama 53 E3 Región Autónoma
  Atlántico Sur, SE Nicaragua
El Real 53 H5 *var.* El Real de Santa María.
  Darién, SE Panama
El Real de Santa María *see* El Real
El Reno 49 F1 Oklahoma, C USA
El Salvador 52 B3 *off.* Republica de El
  Salvador. *country* Central America

EL SALVADOR
Central America

Official name Republic of El Salvador
Formation 1841 / 1841
Capital San Salvador
Population 6.2 million / 755 people
per sq mile (291 people per sq km)
Total area 8124 sq. miles (21,040 sq. km)
Languages Spanish
Religions Roman Catholic 80%,
Evangelical 18%, Other 2%
Ethnic mix Mestizo 90%,
White 9%, Amerindian 1%
Government Presidential system
Currency Salvadorean colón & US dollar =
100 centavos (colón); 100 cents (US dollar)
Literacy rate 84%
Calorie consumption 2574 kilocalories

El Salvador, Republica de *see* El Salvador
Elsass *see* Alsace
El Sáuz 50 C2 Chihuahua, N Mexico
El Serrat 91 A7 N Andorra Europe
Elst 86 D4 Gelderland, E Netherlands
El Sueco 50 C2 Chihuahua, N Mexico
El Suweida *see* As Suwaydā'
El Suweis *see* Suez
Eltanin Fracture Zone 153 E5 *tectonic
  feature* SE Pacific Ocean
El Tigre 59 E2 Anzoátegui, NE Venezuela
Elvas 92 C4 Portalegre, C Portugal
El Vendrell 93 G2 Cataluña, NE Spain
El Vigía 58 C2 Mérida, NW Venezuela
El Wad *see* El Oued
Elwell, Lake 44 B1 *reservoir* Montana,
  NW USA
Elx *see* Elche

Ely 47 D5 Nevada, W USA
El Yopal *see* Yopal
Emajõgi 106 D3 *Ger.* Embach. *river*
  SE Estonia
Emämrüd *see* Shāhrūd
Emämshahr *see* Shāhrūd
Emba 114 B4 *Kaz.* Embi. Aktyubinsk,
  W Kazakhstan
Embach *see* Emajõgi
Embi *see* Emba
Emden 94 A3 Niedersachsen,
  NW Germany
Emerald 148 D4 Queensland,
  E Australia
Emerald Isle *see* Montserrat
Emesa *see* Ḥimş
Emmaste 106 C2 Hiiumaa, W Estonia
Emmeloord 86 D2 Flevoland,
  N Netherlands
Emmen 86 E2 Drenthe, NE Netherlands
Emmendingen 95 A6 Baden-
  Württemberg, SW Germany
Emona *see* Ljubljana
Emonti *see* East London
Emory Peak 49 E4 *mountain* Texas,
  SW USA
Empalme 50 B2 Sonora, NW Mexico
Emperor Seamounts 113 G3 *seamount
  range* NW Pacific Ocean
Empire State of the South *see* Georgia
Emporia 45 F5 Kansas, C USA
Empty Quarter *see* Ar Rub' al Khālī
Ems 94 A3 *Dut.* Eems. *river*
  NW Germany
Enareträsk *see* Inarijärvi
Encamp 91 A8 Encamp, C Andorra
  Europe
Encarnación 64 D3 Itapúa, S Paraguay
Encinitas 47 C8 California, W USA
Encs 99 D6 Borsod-Abaúj-Zemplén,
  NE Hungary
Endeavour Strait 148 C1 *strait*
  Queensland, NE Australia
Enderbury Island 145 F3 *atoll* Phoenix
  Islands, C Kiribati
Enderby Land 154 C2 *physical region*
  Antarctica
Enderby Plain 154 D2 *abyssal plain*
  S Indian Ocean
Endersdorf *see* Jędrzejów
Enewetak Atoll 144 C1 *var.* Ānewetak,
  Eniwetok. *atoll* Ralik Chain,
  W Marshall Islands
Enfield 89 A7 United Kingdom
Engeten *see* Aiud
Enghien 87 B6 *Dut.* Edingen. Hainaut,
  SW Belgium
England 89 D5 *Lat.* Anglia. *cultural
  region* England, United Kingdom
Englewood 44 D4 Colorado, C USA
English Channel 89 D8 *var.* The
  Channel, *Fr.* la Manche. *channel*
  NW Europe
Engure 106 C3 W Latvia
Engures Ezers 106 B3 *lake* NW Latvia
Enguri 117 F1 *Rus.* Inguri. *river*
  NW Georgia
Enid 49 F1 Oklahoma, C USA
Enikale Strait *see* Kerch Strait
Eniwetok Atoll *see* Enewetak Atoll
En Nâqoûra 119 A5 *var.* An Nāqūrah.
  SW Lebanon
En Nazira *see* Natzrat
Ennedi 76 D2 *plateau* E Chad
Ennis 89 A6 *Ir.* Inis. Clare, W Ireland
Ennis 49 G3 Texas, SW USA
Enniskillen 89 B5 *var.* Inniskilling, *Ir.*
  Inis Ceithleann. SW Northern Ireland,
  United Kingdom
Enns 95 D6 *river* C Austria
Enschede 86 E3 Overijssel, E Netherlands
Ensenada 50 A1 Baja California Norte,
  NW Mexico
Entebbe 73 B6 S Uganda
Entroncamento 92 B3 Santarém,
  C Portugal
Enugu 75 G5 Enugu, S Nigeria
Epanomí 104 B4 Kentrikí Makedonía,
  N Greece
Epéna 77 B5 Likouala, NE Congo
Epi 144 D4 *var.* Épi. *island* C Vanuatu
Épi *see* Epi
Épinal 90 D4 Vosges, NE France
Epiphania *see* Ḥamāh
Epitoli *see* Tshwane
Epoon *see* Ebon Atoll
Epsom 89 A8 United Kingdom
Equality State *see* Wyoming
Equatorial Guinea 77 A5 *off.* Equatorial
  Guinea, Republic of. *country* C Africa

EQUATORIAL GUINEA
Central Africa

Official name Republic of
Equatorial Guinea
Formation 1968 / 1968
Capital Malabo
Population 700,000 / 65 people
per sq mile (25 people per sq km)
Total area 10,830 sq. miles (28,051 sq. km)
Languages Spanish*, Fang, Bubi, French*
Religions Roman Catholic 90%,
Other 10%
Ethnic mix Fang 85%, Other 11%, Bubi 4%
Government Presidential system
Currency CFA franc = 100 centimes
Literacy rate 93%
Calorie consumption Not available

Equatorial Guinea, Republic of *see*
  Equatorial Guinea
Erautini *see* Johannesburg
Erbil *see* Arbil
Erciş 117 F3 Van, E Turkey
Erdély *see* Transylvania
Erdélyi-Havasok *see* Carpaţii
  Meridionalii
Erdenet 127 E2 Orhon, N Mongolia
Erdi 76 C2 *plateau* NE Chad
Erdi Ma 76 D2 *desert* NE Chad
Erebus, Mount 154 B4 *volcano* Ross
  Island, Antarctica
Ereğli 116 C4 Konya, S Turkey
Erenhot 127 F2 *var.* Erlian. Nei Mongol
  Zizhiqu, NE China
Erfurt 94 C4 Thüringen, C Germany
Ergene Çayı *see* Ergene Irmaği
Ergene Irmaği 116 A2 *var.* Ergene Çayı.
  river NW Turkey
Ergun 127 F1 *var.* Labudalin; *prev.* Ergun
  Youqi. Nei Mongol Zizhiqu, N China
Ergun He *see* Argun
Ergun Youqi *see* Ergun
Erie 40 D3 Pennsylvania, NE USA
Érié, Lac *see* Erie, Lake
Erie, Lake 40 D3 *Fr.* Lac Érié. *lake*
  Canada/USA
Eritrea 72 C4 *off.* State of Eritrea, Êrtra.
  country E Africa

ERITREA
East Africa

Official name State of Eritrea
Formation 1993 / 2002
Capital Asmara
Population 5.4 million / 119 people
per sq mile (46 people per sq km)
Total area 46,842 sq. miles (121,320 sq. km)
Languages Tigrinya*, English*, Tigre,
Afar, Arabic*, Saho, Bilen, Kunama,
Nara, Hadareb
Religions Christian 50%, Muslim 48%,
Other 2%
Ethnic mix Tigray 50%, Tigre 31%, Other
9%, Afar 5%, Saho 5%
Government Transitional regime
Currency Nakfa = 100 cents
Literacy rate 67%
Calorie consumption 1640 kilocalories

Eritrea, State of *see* Eritrea
Erivan *see* Yerevan
Erlangen 95 C5 Bayern, S Germany
Erlau *see* Eger
Erlian *see* Erenhot
Ermelo 86 D3 Gelderland, C Netherlands
Ermióni 105 C6 Pelopónnisos, S Greece
Ermoúpoli 105 D6 *var.* Hermoupolis;
  prev. Ermoúpolis. Sýyros, Kykládes,
  Greece, Aegean Sea
Ermoúpolis *see* Ermoúpoli
Ernākulam 132 C3 Kerala, SW India
Erode 132 C2 Tamil Nādu, SE India
Erquelinnes 87 B7 Hainaut, S Belgium
Er-Rachidia 70 C2 *var.* Ksar al Soule.
  E Morocco
Er Rahad 72 B4 *var.* Ar Rahad. Northern
  Kordofan, C Sudan
Erromango 144 D4 *island* S Vanuatu
Ertis *see* Irtysh, C Asia
Êrtra *see* Eritrea
Erzerum *see* Erzurum
Erzgebirge *see* Erzurum
Erzincan 117 E3 *var.* Erzinjan. Erzincan,
  E Turkey
Erzinjan *see* Erzincan
Erzurum 117 E3 *prev.* Erzerum.
  Erzurum, NE Turkey

Esbjerg *85 A7* Syddtjylland, W Denmark
Esbo *see* Espoo
Escaldes *91 A8* Escaldes Engordany, C Andorra Europe
Escanaba *40 C2* Michigan, N USA
Escaut *see* Scheldt
Esch-sur-Alzette *87 D8* Luxembourg, S Luxembourg
Esclaves, Grand Lac des *see* Great Slave Lake
Escondido *47 C8* California, W USA
Escuinapa *50 D3* var. Escuinapa de Hidalgo. Sinaloa, C Mexico
Escuinapa de Hidalgo *see* Escuinapa
Escuintla *52 B2* Escuintla, S Guatemala
Escuintla *51 G5* Chiapas, SE Mexico
Esenguly *122 B3* Rus. Gasan-Kuli. Balkan Welaýaty, W Turkmenistan
Esfahān *120 C3* Eng. Isfahan; anc. Aspadana. Eşfahān, C Iran
Esh Sharā *see* Ash Sharāh
Esil *see* Ishim, Kazakhstan/Russian Federation
Eskimo Point *see* Arviat
Eskişehir *116 B3* var. Eskishehr. Eskişehir, W Turkey
Eskishehr *see* Eskişehir
Eslāmābād *see* Eslāmābād-e Gharb
Eslāmābād-e Gharb *120 C3* var. Eslāmābād; prev. Harunabad, Shāhābād. Kermānshāhān, W Iran
Esmeraldas *60 A1* Esmeraldas, N Ecuador
Esna *see* Isnā
España *see* Spain
Espanola *48 D1* New Mexico, SW USA
Esperance *147 B7* Western Australia
Esperanza *50 B2* Sonora, NW Mexico
Esperanza *154 A2* Argentinian research station Antarctica
Espinal *58 B3* Tolima, C Colombia
Espinhaço, Serra do *56 D4* mountain range SE Brazil
Espíritu Santo *63 F4* off. Estado do Espírito Santo. state E Brazil
Espíritu Santo *63 F4* off. Estado do Espírito Santo. region E Brazil
Espíritu Santo, Estado do *see* Espírito Santo
Espiritu Santo *144 C4* var. Santo. island W Vanuatu
Espoo *85 D6* Swe. Esbo. Etelä-Suomi, S Finland
Esquel *65 B6* Chubut, SW Argentina
Essaouira *70 B2* prev. Mogador. W Morocco
Esseg *see* Osijek
Es Semara *see* Smara
Essen *87 C5* Antwerpen, N Belgium
Essen *94 A4* var. Essen an der Ruhr. Nordrhein-Westfalen, W Germany
Essen an der Ruhr *see* Essen
Essequibo River *59 F3* river C Guyana
Es Suweida *see* As Suwaydā'
Estacado, Llano *49 E2* plain New Mexico/Texas, SW USA
Estados, Isla de los *65 C8* prev. Eng. Staten Island. island S Argentina
Estância *63 G3* Sergipe, E Brazil
Estelí *52 D3* Estelí, NW Nicaragua
Estella *93 E1* Bas. Lizarra. Navarra, N Spain
Estepona *92 D5* Andalucía, S Spain
Estevan *37 F5* Saskatchewan, S Canada
Estland *see* Estonia
Estonia *106 D2* off. Republic of Estonia, Est. Eesti Vabariik, Ger. Estland, Latv. Igaunija; prev. Estonian SSR, Rus. Estonskaya SSR. country NE Europe

Estonian SSR *see* Estonia
Estonia, Republic of *see* Estonia
Estonskaya SSR *see* Estonia
Estrela, Serra da *92 C3* mountain range C Portugal
Estremadura *see* Extremadura
Estremoz *92 C4* Évora, S Portugal
Eszék *see* Osijek
Esztergom *99 C6* Ger. Gran; anc. Strigonium. Komárom-Esztergom, N Hungary
Étalle *87 D8* Luxembourg, SE Belgium
Etāwah *134 D3* Uttar Pradesh, N India
Ethiopia *73 C5* off. Federal Democratic Republic of Ethiopia; prev. Abyssinia, People's Democratic Republic of Ethiopia. country E Africa

Ethiopia, Federal Democratic Republic of *see* Ethiopia
Ethiopian Highlands *73 C5* var. Ethiopian Plateau. plateau N Ethiopia
Ethiopian Plateau *see* Ethiopian Highlands
Ethiopia, People's Democratic Republic of *see* Ethiopia
Mount Etna *97 C7* Eng. Mount Etna. volcano Sicilia, Italy, C Mediterranean Sea
Etna, Mount *see* Etna, Monte
Etosha Pan *78 B3* salt lake N Namibia
Etoumbi *77 B5* Cuvette Ouest, NW Congo
Etsch *see* Adige
Et Tafila *see* Aţ Ţafīlah
Ettelbrück *87 D8* Diekirch, C Luxembourg
'Eua *145 E5* prev. Middleburg Island. island Tongatapu Group, SE Tonga
Euboea *105 C5* Lat. Euboea. island C Greece
Euboea *see* Évvoia
Eucla *147 D6* Western Australia
Euclid *40 D3* Ohio, N USA
Eufaula *49 G1* var. Eufaula Reservoir. reservoir Oklahoma, C USA
Eufaula Reservoir *see* Eufaula Lake
Eugene *46 B3* Oregon, NW USA
Eumolpias *see* Plovdiv
Eupen *87 D6* Liège, E Belgium
Euphrates *112 B4* Ar. Al-Furāt, Turk. Firat Nehri. river SW Asia
Eureka *47 A5* California, W USA
Eureka *44 A1* Montana, NW USA
Europa Point *93 H5* headland S Gibraltar
Europe *80* continent
Eutin *94 C2* Schleswig-Holstein, N Germany
Euxine Sea *see* Black Sea
Evansdale *45 G3* Iowa, C USA
Evanston *40 B3* Illinois, N USA
Evanston *44 B4* Wyoming, C USA
Evansville *40 B5* Indiana, N USA
Eveleth *45 G1* Minnesota, N USA
Everard, Lake *149 A6* salt lake South Australia
Everest, Mount *126 B5* Chin. Qomolangma Feng, Nep. Sagarmāthā. mountain China/Nepal
Everett *46 B2* Washington, NW USA
Everglades, The *43 F5* wetland Florida, SE USA
Evje *85 A6* Aust-Agder, S Norway
Evmolpia *see* Plovdiv

Évora *92 B4* anc. Ebora, Lat. Liberalitas Julia. Évora, C Portugal
Évreux *90 C3* anc. Civitas Eburovicum. Eure, N France
Évros *see* Maritsa
Évry *90 E2* Essonne, N France
Ewarton *54 B5* C Jamaica
Excelsior Springs *45 F4* Missouri, C USA
Exe *89 C7* river SW England, United Kingdom
Exeter *89 C7* anc. Isca Damnoniorum. SW England, United Kingdom
Exmoor *89 C7* moorland SW England, United Kingdom
Exmouth *146 A4* Western Australia
Exmouth *89 C7* SW England, United Kingdom
Exmouth Gulf *146 A4* gulf Western Australia
Exmouth Plateau *141 E5* undersea plateau E Indian Ocean
Extremadura *92 C3* var. Estremadura. autonomous community W Spain
Exuma Cays *54 C1* islets C Bahamas
Exuma Sound *54 C1* sound C Bahamas
Eyre Mountains *151 A7* mountain range South Island, New Zealand
Eyre North, Lake *149 A5* salt lake South Australia
Eyre Peninsula *149 A6* peninsula South Australia
Eyre South, Lake *149 A5* salt lake South Australia
Ezo *see* Hokkaidō

F

Faadhippolhu Atoll *132 B4* var. Fadiffolu, Lhaviyani Atoll. atoll N Maldives
Fabens *48 D3* Texas, SW USA
Fada *76 C2* Borkou-Ennedi-Tibesti, E Chad
Fada-Ngourma *75 E4* E Burkina Faso
Fadiffolu *see* Faadhippolhu Atoll
Faenza *96 C3* anc. Faventia. Emilia-Romagna, N Italy
Faeroe-Iceland Ridge *80 C1* undersea ridge NW Norwegian Sea
Faeroe Islands *83 E5* Dan. Færøerne, Faer. Føroyar. Danish external territory N Atlantic Ocean
Færøerne *see* Faeroe Islands
Faeroe-Shetland Trough *80 C2* trough NE Atlantic Ocean
Faetano *96 E2* E San Marino
Făgăraş *108 C4* Ger. Fogarasch, Hung. Fogaras. Braşov, C Romania
Fagibina, Lake *see* Faguibine, Lac
Fagne *87 C7* hill range S Belgium
Faguibine, Lac *75 E3* var. Lake Fagibina. lake NW Mali
Fahlun *see* Falun
Fahraj *120 E4* Kermān, SE Iran
Faial *92 A5* var. Ilha do Faial. island Azores, Portugal, NE Atlantic Ocean
Faial, Ilha do *see* Faial
Faifo *see* Hôi An
Fairbanks *36 D3* Alaska, USA
Fairfield *47 B6* California, W USA
Fair Isle *88 D2* island NE Scotland, United Kingdom
Fairlie *151 B6* Canterbury, South Island, New Zealand
Fairmont *45 F3* Minnesota, N USA
Faisalābād *134 C2* prev. Lyallpur. Punjab, NE Pakistan
Faizābād *135 E3* Uttar Pradesh, N India
Faizabad/Faizābād *see* Feyzābād
Fakaofo Atoll *145 F3* island SE Tokelau
Falam *136 A3* Chin State, W Myanmar (Burma)
Falconara Marittima *96 C3* Marche, C Italy
Falkenau an der Eger *see* Sokolov
Falkland Islands *65 D7* var. Falklands, Islas Malvinas. UK dependent territory SW Atlantic Ocean
Falkland Plateau *57 D7* var. Argentine Rise. undersea feature SW Atlantic Ocean
Falklands *see* Falkland Islands
Falknov nad Ohří *see* Sokolov
Fallbrook *47 C8* California, W USA
Falmouth *54 A4* W Jamaica
Falmouth *89 C7* SW England, United Kingdom

Falster *85 B8* island SE Denmark
Fălticeni *108 C3* Hung. Falticsén. Suceava, NE Romania
Falticsén *see* Fălticeni
Falun *85 C6* var. Fahlun. Kopparberg, C Sweden
Famagusta *see* Gazimağusa
Famagusta Bay *102 C5* var. Famagusta Bay, Gk. Kólpos Ammóchostos. bay E Cyprus
Famagusta Bay *see* Gazimağusa Körfezi
Famenne *87 C7* physical region SE Belgium
Fang *136 C3* Chiang Mai, NW Thailand
Fanning Island *see* Tabuaeran
Fanø *96 C3* island W Denmark
Farafangana *79 G4* Fianarantsoa, SE Madagascar
Farāh *122 D4* var. Farah, Fararud. Farāh, W Afghanistan
Farah Rud *122 D4* river W Afghanistan
Faranah *74 C4* Haute-Guinée, S Guinea
Fararud *see* Farāh
Farasan, Jaza'ir *121 A6* island group SW Saudi Arabia
Farewell, Cape *150 C4* headland South Island, New Zealand
Farewell, Cape *see* Nunap Isua
Fargo *45 F2* North Dakota, N USA
Farg'ona *123 F2* Rus. Fergana; prev. Novyy Margilan. Farg'ona Viloyati, E Uzbekistan
Faribault *45 F2* Minnesota, N USA
Farīdābād *134 D3* Haryāna, N India
Farkhor *123 E3* Rus. Parkhar. SW Tajikistan
Farmington *45 G5* Missouri, C USA
Farmington *48 C1* New Mexico, SW USA
Faro *92 B5* Faro, S Portugal
Farquhar Group *79 G2* island group S Seychelles
Fars, Khalīj-e *see* Persian Gulf
Farvel, Kap *see* Nunap Isua
Fastiv *109 E2* Rus. Fastov. Kyyivs'ka Oblast', NW Ukraine
Fastov *see* Fastiv
Fauske *84 C3* Nordland, C Norway
Faventia *see* Faenza
Faxa Bay *see* Faxaflói
Faxaflói *82 D5* Eng. Faxa Bay. bay W Iceland
Faya *76 C2* prev. Faya-Largeau, Largeau. Borkou-Ennedi-Tibesti, N Chad
Faya-Largeau *see* Faya
Fayetteville *42 A1* Arkansas, C USA
Fayetteville *43 F1* North Carolina, SE USA
Fdérick *see* Fdérik
Fdérik *74 C2* var. Fdérick, Fr. Fort Gouraud. Tiris Zemmour, NW Mauritania
Fear, Cape *43 F2* headland Bald Head Island, North Carolina, SE USA
Fécamp *90 B3* Seine-Maritime, N France
Fédala *see* Mohammedia
Federal Capital Territory *see* Australian Capital Territory
Fehérgyarmat *99 E6* Szabolcs-Szatmár-Bereg, E Hungary
Fehértemplom *see* Bela Crkva
Fehmarn *94 C2* island N Germany
Fehmarn Belt *94 C2* Dan. Femern Bælt, Ger. Fehmarnbelt. strait Denmark / Germany
Fehmarnbelt *see* Fehmarn Belt/Femer Bælt
Feijó *62 C2* Acre, W Brazil
Feilding *150 D4* Manawatu-Wanganui, North Island, New Zealand
Feira *see* Feira de Santana
Feira de Santana *63 G3* var. Feira. Bahia, E Brazil
Feizābād *123 F3* var. Faizabad, Faizābād, Feyzābād, Feyzabad; prev. Feyzābād. Badakhshān, NE Afghanistan
Feketehalom *see* Codlea
Felanitx *93 G3* Mallorca, Spain, W Mediterranean Sea
Felidhu Atoll *132 B4* atoll C Maldives
Felipe Carrillo Puerto *51 H4* Quintana Roo, SE Mexico
Felixstowe *89 E6* E England, United Kingdom
Fellin *see* Viljandi
Felsőbánya *see* Baia Sprie
Felsőmuzslya *see* Mužlja
Femunden *85 B5* lake S Norway
Fénérive *see* Fenoarivo Atsinanana

Fengcheng *128 D3 var.* Feng-cheng, Fenghwangcheng. Liaoning, NE China
Feng-cheng *see* Fengcheng
Fenghwangcheng *see* Fengcheng
Fengtien *see* Liaoning, China
Fengtien *see* Shenyang, China
Fenoarivo Atsinanana *79 G3 prev./Fr.* Fénérive. Toamasina, E Madagascar
Fens, The *89 E6 wetland* E England, United Kingdom
Feodosiya *109 F5 var.* Kefe, *It.* Kaffa; *anc.* Theodosia. Avtonomna Respublika Krym, S Ukraine
Ferdinand *see* Montana, Bulgaria
Ferdinandsberg *see* Oţelu Roşu
Féres *104 D3* Anatolikí Makedonía kai Thráki, NE Greece
Fergana *see* Farg'ona
Fergus Falls *45 F2* Minnesota, N USA
Ferizaj *101 D5 Serb.* Uroševac. C Kosovo
Ferkessédougou *74 D4* N Côte d'Ivoire
Fermo *96 C4 anc.* Firmum Picenum. Marche, C Italy
Fernandina, Isla *60 A5 var.* Narborough Island. *island* Galápagos Islands, Ecuador, E Pacific Ocean
Fernando de Noronha *63 H2 island* E Brazil
Fernando Po/Fernando Póo *see* Bioco, Isla de
Ferrara *96 C2 anc.* Forum Alieni. Emilia-Romagna, N Italy
Ferreñafe *60 B3* Lambayeque, W Peru
Ferro *see* Hierro
Ferrol *92 B1 var.* El Ferrol; *prev.* El Ferrol del Caudillo. Galicia, NW Spain
Fertő *see* Neusiedler See
Ferwerd *see* Ferwert
Ferwert *86 D1 Dutch.* Ferwerd. Fryslân, N Netherlands
Fès *70 C2 Eng.* Fez. N Morocco
Feteşti *108 D5* Ialomiţa, SE Romania
Fethiye *116 B4* Muğla, SW Turkey
Fetlar *88 D1 island* NE Scotland, United Kingdom
Feyzābād *see* Feizābād
Feyzābād *see* Feizābād
Fez *see* Fès
Fianarantsoa *79 F3* Fianarantsoa, C Madagascar
Fianga *76 B4* Mayo-Kébbi, SW Chad
Fier *101 C6 var.* Fieri. Fier, SW Albania
Fieri *see* Fier
Figeac *91 C5* Lot, S France
Figig *see* Figuig
Figueira da Foz *92 B3* Coimbra, W Portugal
Figueres *93 G2* Cataluña, E Spain
Figuig *70 D2 var.* Figig. E Morocco
Fiji *145 E5 off.* Sovereign Democratic Republic of Fiji, *Fij.* Viti. *country* SW Pacific Ocean

FIJI
Australasia & Oceania

Official name Republic of the Fiji Islands
Formation 1970 / 1970
Capital Suva
Population 900,000 / 128 people per sq mile (49 people per sq km)
Total area 7054 sq. miles (18,270 sq. km)
Languages Fijian, English*, Hindi, Urdu, Tamil, Telugu
Religions Hindu 38%, Methodist 37%, Roman Catholic 9%, Muslim 8%, Other 8%
Ethnic mix Melanesian 51%, Indian 44%, Other 5%
Government Transitional regime
Currency Fiji dollar = 100 cents
Literacy rate 94%
Calorie consumption 2996 kilocalories

Fiji, Sovereign Democratic Republic of *see* Fiji
Filadelfia *52 D4* Guanacaste, W Costa Rica
Filiaşi *108 B5* Dolj, SW Romania
Filipstad *85 B6* Värmland, C Sweden
Finale Ligure *96 A3* Liguria, NW Italy
Finchley *89 A7* United Kingdom
Findlay *40 C4* Ohio, N USA
Finike *116 B4* Antalya, SW Turkey
Finland *84 D4 off.* Republic of Finland, *Fin.* Suomen Tasavalta, Suomi. *country* N Europe

FINLAND
Northern Europe

Official name Republic of Finland
Formation 1917 / 1947
Capital Helsinki
Population 5.4 million / 46 people per sq mile (18 people per sq km)
Total area 130,127 sq. miles (337,030 sq. km)
Languages Finnish*, Swedish*, Sámi
Religions Evangelical Lutheran 83%, Other 15%, Orthodox Christian 1%, Roman Catholic 1%
Ethnic mix Finnish 93%, Other (including Sámi) 7%
Government Parliamentary system
Currency Euro = 100 cents
Literacy rate 99%
Calorie consumption 3240 kilocalories

Finland, Gulf of *85 D6 Est.* Soome Laht, *Fin.* Suomenlahti, *Ger.* Finnischer Meerbusen, *Rus.* Finskiy Zaliv, *Swe.* Finska Viken. *gulf* E Baltic Sea
Finland, Republic of *see* Finland
Finnischer Meerbusen *see* Finland, Gulf of
Finnmarksvidda *84 D2 physical region* N Norway
Finska Viken/Finskiy Zaliv *see* Finland, Gulf of
Finsterwalde *94 D4* Brandenburg, E Germany
Fiordland *151 A7 physical region* South Island, New Zealand
Fiorina *96 E1* NE San Marino
Firat Nehri *see* Euphrates
Firenze *96 C3 Eng.* Florence; *anc.* Florentia. Toscana, C Italy
Firmum Picenum *see* Fermo
First State *see* Delaware
Fischbacher Alpen *95 E7 mountain range* E Austria
Fischhausen *see* Primorsk
Fish *78 B4 var.* Vis. *river* S Namibia
Fishguard *89 C6 Wel.* Abergwaun. SW Wales, United Kingdom
Fisterra, Cabo *92 B1 headland* NW Spain
Fitzroy Crossing *146 C3* Western Australia
Fitzroy River *146 C3 river* Western Australia
Fiume *see* Rijeka
Flagstaff *48 B2* Arizona, SW USA
Flanders *see* Vlaanderen
Flandre *see* Vlaanderen
Flathead Lake *44 B1 lake* Montana, NW USA
Flat Island *128 C8 island* NE Spratly Islands
Flatts Village *42 B5 var.* The Flatts Village. C Bermuda
Flensburg *94 B2* Schleswig-Holstein, N Germany
Flessingue *see* Vlissingen
Flickertail State *see* North Dakota
Flinders Island *149 C8 island* Furneaux Group, Tasmania, SE Australia
Flinders Ranges *149 B6 mountain range* South Australia
Flinders River *148 C3 river* Queensland, NE Australia
Flin Flon *37 F5* Manitoba, C Canada
Flint *40 C3* Michigan, N USA
Flint Island *145 G4 island* Line Islands, E Kiribati
Floreana, Isla *see* Santa María, Isla
Florence *42 C1* Alabama, S USA
Florence *43 F2* South Carolina, SE USA
Florence *see* Firenze
Florencia *58 B4* Caquetá, S Colombia
Florentia *see* Firenze
Flores *52 B1* Petén, N Guatemala
Flores *139 E5 island* Nusa Tenggara, C Indonesia
Flores *92 A5 island* Azores, Portugal, NE Atlantic Ocean
Flores, Laut *see* Flores Sea
Flores Sea *138 D5 Ind.* Laut Flores. *sea* C Indonesia
Floriano *63 F2* Piauí, E Brazil
Florianópolis *63 F5 prev.* Destêrro. *state capital* Santa Catarina, S Brazil
Florida *64 D4* Florida, S Uruguay
Florida *43 E4 off.* State of Florida, *also known as* Peninsular State, Sunshine State. *state* SE USA

Florida Bay *43 E5 bay* Florida, SE USA
Florida Keys *43 E5 island group* Florida, SE USA
Florida, Straits of *54 B1 strait* Atlantic Ocean/Gulf of Mexico
Flórina *104 B4 var.* Phlórina. Dytikí Makedonía, N Greece
Florissant *45 G4* Missouri, C USA
Floúda, Akrotírio *105 D7 headland* Astypálaia, Kykládes, Greece, Aegean Sea
Flushing *see* Vlissingen
Flylân *see* Vlieland
Foča *100 C4 var.* Srbinje. SE Bosnia and Herzegovina
Focşani *108 C4* Vrancea, E Romania
Fogaras/Fogarasch *see* Făgăraş
Foggia *97 D5* Puglia, SE Italy
Fogo *74 A3 island* Ilhas de Sotavento, SW Cape Verde
Foix *91 B6* Ariège, S France
Folégandros *105 C7 island* Kykládes, Greece, Aegean Sea
Foleyet *38 C4* Ontario, S Canada
Foligno *96 C4* Umbria, C Italy
Folkestone *89 E7* SE England, United Kingdom
Fond du Lac *40 B2* Wisconsin, N USA
Fongafale *145 E3 var.* Funafuti. *country capital* (Tuvalu) Funafuti Atoll, SE Tuvalu
Fonseca, Golfo de *see* Fonseca, Gulf of
Fonseca, Gulf of *52 C3 Sp.* Golfo de Fonseca. *gulf* C Central America
Fontainebleau *90 C3* Seine-et-Marne, N France
Fontenay-le-Comte *90 B4* Vendée, NW France
Fontvieille *91 B8* SW Monaco Europe
Fonyód *99 C7* Somogy, W Hungary
Foochow *see* Fuzhou
Foochow *see* Fuzhou
Forchheim *95 C5* Bayern, SE Germany
Forel, Mont *82 D4 mountain* SE Greenland
Forfar *88 C3* E Scotland, United Kingdom
Forge du Sud *see* Dudelange
Forlì *96 C3 anc.* Forum Livii. Emilia-Romagna, N Italy
Formentera *93 G4 anc.* Ophiusa, *Lat.* Frumentum. *island* Islas Baleares, Spain, W Mediterranean Sea
Formosa *64 D2* Formosa, NE Argentina
Formosa/Formo'sa *see* Taiwan
Formosa, Serra *63 E3 mountain range* C Brazil
Formosa Strait *see* Taiwan Strait
Foroyar *see* Faeroe Islands
Forrest City *42 B1* Arkansas, C USA
Fort Albany *38 C3* Ontario, C Canada
Fortaleza *61 F2* Pando, N Bolivia
Fortaleza *63 G2 prev.* Ceará. *state capital* Ceará, NE Brazil
Fort-Archambault *see* Sarh
Fort-Bayard *see* Zhanjiang
Fort-Cappolani *see* Tidjikja
Fort Charlet *see* Djanet
Fort-Chimo *see* Kuujjuaq
Fort Collins *44 D4* Colorado, C USA
Fort-Crampel *see* Kaga Bandoro
Fort Davis *49 E3* Texas, SW USA
Fort-de-France *55 H4 prev.* Fort-Royal. *dependent territory capital* (Martinique) W Martinique
Fort Dodge *45 F3* Iowa, C USA
Fortescue River *146 A4 river* Western Australia
Fort-Foureau *see* Kousséri
Fort Frances *38 A3* Ontario, S Canada
Fort Good Hope *37 E3 var.* Rádeyilikóé. Northwest Territories, NW Canada
Fort Gouraud *see* Fdérik
Forth *88 C4 river* C Scotland, United Kingdom
Forth, Firth of *88 C4 estuary* E Scotland, United Kingdom
Fortín General Eugenio Garay *see* General Eugenio A. Garay
Fort Jameson *see* Chipata
Fort-Lamy *see* Ndjamena
Fort Lauderdale *43 F5* Florida, SE USA
Fort Liard *37 E4 var.* Liard. Northwest Territories, W Canada
Fort Madison *45 G4* Iowa, C USA
Fort McMurray *37 E4* Alberta, C Canada
Fort McPherson *36 D3 var.* McPherson. Northwest Territories, NW Canada
Fort Morgan *44 D4* Colorado, C USA

Fort Myers *43 E5* Florida, SE USA
Fort Nelson *37 E4* British Columbia, W Canada
Fort Peck Lake *44 C1 reservoir* Montana, NW USA
Fort Pierce *43 F4* Florida, SE USA
Fort Providence *37 E4 var.* Providence. Northwest Territories, W Canada
Fort-Repoux *see* Akjoujt
Fort Rosebery *see* Mansa
Fort Rousset *see* Owando
Fort-Royal *see* Fort-de-France
Fort St. John *37 E4* British Columbia, W Canada
Fort Scott *45 F5* Kansas, C USA
Fort Severn *38 C2* Ontario, C Canada
Fort-Shevchenko *114 A4* Mangistau, W Kazakhstan
Fort-Sibut *see* Sibut
Fort Simpson *37 E4 var.* Simpson. Northwest Territories, W Canada
Fort Smith *37 E4* Northwest Territories, W Canada
Fort Smith *42 B1* Arkansas, C USA
Fort Stockton *49 E3* Texas, SW USA
Fort-Trinquet *see* Bîr Mogreïn
Fort Vermilion *37 E4* Alberta, W Canada
Fort Victoria *see* Masvingo
Fort Walton Beach *42 C3* Florida, SE USA
Fort Wayne *40 C4* Indiana, N USA
Fort William *88 C3* N Scotland, United Kingdom
Fort Worth *49 G2* Texas, SW USA
Fort Yukon *36 D3* Alaska, USA
Forum Alieni *see* Ferrara
Forum Livii *see* Forlì
Fossa Claudia *see* Chioggia
Fougamou *77 A6* Ngounié, C Gabon
Fougères *90 B3* Ille-et-Vilaine, NW France
Fou-hsin *see* Fuxin
Foulwind, Cape *151 B5 headland* South Island, New Zealand
Foumban *76 A4* Ouest, NW Cameroon
Fou-shan *see* Fushun
Foveaux Strait *151 A8 strait* S New Zealand
Foxe Basin *37 G3 sea* Nunavut, N Canada
Fox Glacier *151 B6* West Coast, South Island, New Zealand
Fraga *93 F2* Aragón, NE Spain
Fram Basin *155 C3 var.* Amundsen Basin. *undersea basin* Arctic Ocean
France *90 B4 off.* French Republic, *It./Sp.* Francia; *prev.* Gaul, Gaule, *Lat.* Gallia. *country* W Europe

FRANCE
Western Europe

Official name French Republic
Formation 987 / 1919
Capital Paris
Population 63.1 million / 297 people per sq mile (115 people per sq km)
Total area 211,208 sq. miles (547,030 sq. km)
Languages French*, Provençal, German, Breton, Catalan, Basque
Religions Roman Catholic 88%, Muslim 8%, Protestant 2%, Buddhist 1%, Jewish 1%
Ethnic mix French 90%, North African (mainly Algerian) 6%, German (Alsace) 2%, Breton (Other) (including Corsicans) 1%
Government Mixed presidential– parliamentary system
Currency Euro = 100 cents
Literacy rate 99%
Calorie consumption 3531 kilocalories

Franceville *77 B6 var.* Massoukou, Masuku. Haut-Ogooué, E Gabon
Francfort *see* Frankfurt am Main
Franche-Comté *90 D4 cultural region* E France
Francia *see* France
Francis Case, Lake *45 E3 reservoir* South Dakota, N USA
Francisco Escárcega *51 G4* Campeche, SE Mexico
Francistown *78 D3* North East, NE Botswana
Franconian Jura *see* Fränkische Alb
Frankenalb *see* Fränkische Alb

Frankenstein/Frankenstein in Schlesien see Ząbkowice Śląskie
Frankfort 40 C5 state capital Kentucky, S USA
Frankfort on the Main see Frankfurt am Main
Frankfurt see Frankfurt am Main, Germany
Frankfurt see Słubice, Poland
Frankfurt am Main 95 B5 var. Frankfurt, Fr. Francfort; prev. Eng. Frankfort on the Main. Hessen, SW Germany
Frankfurt an der Oder 94 D3 Brandenburg, E Germany
Fränkische Alb 95 C6 var. Frankenalb, Eng. Franconian Jura. mountain range S Germany
Franklin 42 C1 Tennessee, S USA
Franklin D. Roosevelt Lake 46 C1 reservoir Washington, NW USA
Franz Josef Land 114 D1 Eng. Franz Josef Land. island group N Russian Federation
Franz Josef Land see Frantsa-Iosifa, Zemlya
Fraserburgh 88 D3 NE Scotland, United Kingdom
Fraser Island 148 E4 var. Great Sandy Island. island Queensland, E Australia
Frauenbach see Baia Mare
Frauenburg see Saldus, Latvia
Fredericksburg 41 E5 Virginia, NE USA
Fredericton 39 F4 province capital New Brunswick, SE Canada
Frederikshåb see Paamiut
Frederikshald see Halden
Fredrikstad 85 B6 Østfold, S Norway
Freeport 54 C1 Grand Bahama Island, N Bahamas
Freeport 49 H4 Texas, SW USA
Free State see Maryland
Freetown 74 C4 country capital (Sierra Leone) W Sierra Leone
Freiburg see Freiburg im Breisgau, Germany
Freiburg im Breisgau 95 A6 var. Freiburg, Fr. Fribourg-en-Brisgau. Baden-Württemberg, SW Germany
Freiburg in Schlesien see Świebodzice
Fremantle 147 A6 Western Australia
Fremont 45 F4 Nebraska, C USA
French Guiana 59 H3 var. Guiana, Guyane. French overseas department N South America
French Guinea see Guinea
French Polynesia 143 F4 French overseas territory S Pacific Ocean
French Republic see France
French Somaliland see Djibouti
French Southern and Antarctic Territories 141 B7 Fr. Terres Australes et Antarctiques Françaises. French overseas territory S Indian Ocean
French Sudan see Mali
French Territory of the Afars and Issas see Djibouti
French Togoland see Togo
Fresnillo 50 D3 var. Fresnillo de González Echeverría. Zacatecas, C Mexico
Fresnillo de González Echeverría see Fresnillo
Fresno 47 C6 California, W USA
Frías 64 C3 Catamarca, N Argentina
Fribourg-en-Brisgau see Freiburg im Breisgau
Friedek-Mistek see Frýdek-Místek
Friedrichshafen 95 B7 Baden-Württemberg, S Germany
Friendly Islands see Tonga
Frisches Haff see Vistula Lagoon
Frobisher Bay 82 B3 inlet Baffin Island, Nunavut, NE Canada
Frobisher Bay see Iqaluit
Frohavet 84 B4 sound C Norway
Frome, Lake 149 B6 salt lake South Australia
Frontera 51 G4 Tabasco, SE Mexico
Frontignan 91 C6 Hérault, S France
Frostviken see Kvarnbergsvattnet
Frøya 84 A4 island W Norway
Frumentum see Formentera
Frunze see Bishkek
Frýdek-Místek 99 C5 Ger. Friedek-Mistek. Moravskoslezský Kraj, E Czech Republic
Fu-chien see Fujian
Fu-chou see Fuzhou

Fu-chou see Fuzhou
Fuengirola 92 D5 Andalucía, S Spain
Fuerte Olimpo 64 D2 var. Olimpo. Alto Paraguay, NE Paraguay
Fuerte, Río 48 C5 river C Mexico
Fuerteventura 70 B3 island Islas Canarias, Spain, NE Atlantic Ocean
Fuhkien see Fujian
Fu-hsin see Fuxin
Fuji 131 D6 var. Huzi. Shizuoka, Honshū, S Japan
Fujian 128 D6 var. Fu-chien, Fuhkien, Fukien, Min, Fujian Sheng. province SE China
Fujian Sheng see Fujian
Mount Fuji 131 C6 var. Fujiyama, Eng. Mount Fuji. mountain Honshū, SE Japan
Fuji, Mount/Fujiyama see Mount Fuji
Fukang 126 C2 Xinjiang Uygur Zizhiqu, W China
Fukien see Fujian
Fukui 131 C6 var. Hukui. Fukui, Honshū, SW Japan
Fukuoka 131 A7 var. Hukuoka, hist. Najima. Fukuoka, Kyūshū, SW Japan
Fukushima 130 D4 var. Hukusima. Fukushima, Honshū, C Japan
Fulda 95 B5 Hessen, C Germany
Funafuti see Fongafale
Funafuti Atoll 145 E3 atoll C Tuvalu
Funchal 70 A2 Madeira, Portugal, NE Atlantic Ocean
Fundy, Bay of 39 F5 bay Canada/USA
Fünen see Fyn
Fünfkirchen see Pécs
Furnes see Veurne
Fürth 95 C5 Bayern, S Germany
Furukawa 130 D4 var. Hurukawa, Ōsaki. Miyagi, Honshū, C Japan
Fusan see Busan
Fushë Kosovë 101 D5 Serb. Kosovo Polje. C Kosovo
Fushun 128 D3 var. Fou-shan, Fu-shun. Liaoning, NE China
Fu-shun see Fushun
Fusin see Fuxin
Füssen 95 C7 Bayern, S Germany
Futog 100 D3 Vojvodina, NW Serbia
Futuna, Île 145 E4 island S Wallis and Futuna
Fuxin 128 D3 var. Fou-hsin, Fu-hsin, Fusin. Liaoning, NE China
Fuzhou 128 D6 var. Foochow, Fu-chou. province capital Fujian, SE China
Fuzhou 128 D6 var. Foochow, Fu-chou. province capital Fujian, SE China
Fyn 85 B8 Ger. Fünen. island C Denmark
FYR Macedonia/FYROM see Macedonia, FYR
Fyzabad see Feizābād

G

Gaafu Alifu Atoll see North Huvadhu Atoll
Gaalkacyo 73 E5 var. Galka'yo, It. Galcaio. Mudug, C Somalia
Gabela 78 B2 Cuanza Sul, W Angola
Gaberones see Gaborone
Gabès 71 E2 var. Qābis. E Tunisia
Gabès, Golfe de 71 F2 Ar. Khalīj Qābis. gulf E Tunisia
Gabon 77 B6 off. Gabonese Republic. country C Africa

GABON
Central Africa

Official name Gabonese Republic
Formation 1960 / 1960
Capital Libreville
Population 1.5 million / 15 people per sq mile (6 people per sq km)
Total area 103,346 sq. miles (267,667 sq. km)
Languages Fang, French*, Punu, Sira, Nzebi, Mpongwe
Religions Christian (mainly Roman Catholic) 55%, Traditional beliefs 40%, Other 4%, Muslim 1%
Government Presidential system
Currency CFA franc = 100 centimes
Literacy rate 88%
Calorie consumption 2745 kilocalories

Gabonese Republic see Gabon
Gaborone 78 C4 prev. Gaberones. country capital (Botswana) South East, SE Botswana
Gabrovo 104 D2 Gabrovo, N Bulgaria
Gadag 132 C1 Karnātaka, W India
Gades/Gadier/Gadir/Gadire see Cádiz
Gadsden 42 D2 Alabama, S USA
Gaeta 97 C5 Lazio, C Italy
Gaeta, Gulf of 97 C5 var. Gulf of Gaeta. gulf C Italy
Gaeta, Gulf of see Gaeta, Golfo di
Gäfle see Gävle
Gafsa 71 E2 var. Qafşah. W Tunisia
Gagnoa 74 D5 C Côte d'Ivoire
Gagra 117 E1 NW Georgia
Gaillac 91 C6 var. Gaillac-sur-Tarn. Tarn, S France
Gaillac-sur-Tarn see Gaillac
Gaillimh see Galway
Gaillimhe, Cuan na see Galway Bay
Gainesville 43 E3 Florida, SE USA
Gainesville 42 D2 Georgia, SE USA
Gainesville 49 G2 Texas, SW USA
Lake Gairdner 149 A6 salt lake South Australia
Gaizina Kalns see Gaiziņkalns
Gaiziņkalns 106 C3 var. Gaizina Kalns. mountain E Latvia
Galán, Cerro 64 B3 mountain NW Argentina
Galanta 99 C6 Hung. Galánta. Trnavský Kraj, W Slovakia
Galapagos Fracture Zone 153 E3 tectonic feature E Pacific Ocean
Galápagos Islands 153 F3 var. Islas de los Galápagos, Eng. Galapagos Islands, Tortoise Islands. island group Ecuador, E Pacific Ocean
Galápagos Islands see Colón, Archipiélago de
Galápagos, Islas de los see Colón, Archipiélago de
Galapagos Rise 153 F3 undersea rise E Pacific Ocean
Galashiels 88 C4 SE Scotland, United Kingdom
Galați 108 D4 Ger. Galatz. Galați, E Romania
Galatz see Galați
Galcaio see Gaalkacyo
Galesburg 40 B3 Illinois, N USA
Galicia 92 B1 anc. Gallaecia. autonomous community NW Spain
Galicia Bank 80 B4 undersea bank E Atlantic Ocean
Galilee, Sea of see Tiberias, Lake
Galka'yo see Gaalkacyo
Galkynyş 122 D3 prev. Rus. Deynau, Dyanev, Turkm. Dänew. Lebap Welaýaty, NE Turkmenistan
Gallaecia see Galicia
Galle 132 D4 prev. Point de Galle. Southern Province, SW Sri Lanka
Gallego Rise 153 F3 undersea rise E Pacific Ocean
Gallegos see Río Gallegos
Gallia see France
Gallipoli 97 E6 Puglia, SE Italy
Gällivare 84 C3 Lapp. Váhtjer. Norrbotten, N Sweden
Gallup 48 C1 New Mexico, SW USA
Galtat-Zemmour 70 B3 C Western Sahara
Galveston 49 H4 Texas, SW USA
Galway 89 A5 Ir. Gaillimh. W Ireland
Galway Bay 89 A6 Ir. Cuan na Gaillimhe. bay W Ireland
Gámas see Kaamanen
Gambell 36 C2 Saint Lawrence Island, Alaska, USA
Gambia 74 B3 off. Republic of The Gambia, The Gambia. country W Africa

GAMBIA
West Africa

Official name Republic of the Gambia
Formation 1965 / 1965
Capital Banjul
Population 1.8 million / 466 people per sq mile (180 people per sq km)
Total area 4363 sq. miles (11,300 sq. km)
Languages Mandinka, Fulani, Wolof, Jola, Soninke, English*
Religions Sunni Muslim 90%, Christian 8%, Traditional beliefs 2%
Ethnic mix Mandinka 42%, Fulani 18%,

GAMBIA
(continued)

Wolof 16%, Jola 10%, Serahuli 9%, Other 5%
Government Presidential system
Currency Dalasi = 100 butut
Literacy rate 46%
Calorie consumption 2643 kilocalories

Gambia 74 C3 Fr. Gambie. river W Africa
Gambia, Republic of The see Gambia
Gambia, The see Gambia
Gambie see Gambia
Gambier, Îles 143 G4 island group E French Polynesia
Gambo 77 B6 Plateaux, E Congo
Gamlakarleby see Kokkola
Gan 132 B5 Addu Atoll, C Maldives
Gan see Gansu, China
Gan see Jiangxi, China
Ganaane see Juba
Gäncä 117 G2 Rus. Gyandzha; prev. Kirovabad, Yelisavetpol. W Azerbaijan
Gand see Gent
Gandajika 77 D7 Kasai-Oriental, S Dem. Rep. Congo
Gander 39 G3 Newfoundland and Labrador, SE Canada
Gāndhīdhām 134 C4 Gujarāt, W India
Gandia 93 F3 prev. Gandía. Valenciana, E Spain
Gandía see Gandia
Ganges 135 F3 Ben. Padma. river Bangladesh/India
Ganges Cone see Ganges Fan
Ganges Fan 140 D4 var. Ganges Cone. undersea fan N Bay of Bengal
Ganges, Mouths of the 135 G4 delta Bangladesh/India
Gangra see Çankırı
Gangtok 135 F3 state capital Sikkim, N India
Gansos, Lago dos see Goose Lake
Gansu 128 B4 var. Gan, Gansu Sheng, Kansu. province N China
Gansu Sheng see Gansu
Gantsevichi see Hantsavichy
Ganzhou 128 D6 Jiangxi, S China
Gao 75 E3 Gao, E Mali
Gaocheng see Litang
Gaoual 74 C4 N Guinea
Gaoxiong 128 D6 var. Kaohsiung, Jap. Takao, Takow. S Taiwan
Gap 91 D5 anc. Vapincum. Hautes-Alpes, SE France
Gaplaňgyr Platosy 122 C2 Rus. Plato Kaplangky. ridge Turkmenistan/ Uzbekistan
Gar see Gar Xincun
Garabil Belentligi 122 D3 Rus. Vozvyshennost' Karabil'. mountain range S Turkmenistan
Garabogaz Aylagy 122 B2 Rus. Zaliv Kara-Bogaz-Gol. bay NW Turkmenistan
Garachiné 53 G5 Darién, SE Panama
Garagum 122 C3 var. Garagumy, Qara Qum, Eng. Black Sand Desert, Kara Kum; prev. Peski Karakumy. desert C Turkmenistan
Garagum Canal 122 D3 var. Kara Kum Canal, Rus. Karagumskiy Kanal, Karakumskiy Kanal. canal C Turkmenistan
Garagumy see Garagum
Gara Khitrino 104 D2 Shumen, NE Bulgaria
Gárasavvon see Kaaresuvanto
Garda, Lake 96 C2 var. Benaco, Eng. Lake Garda, Ger. Gardasee. lake NE Italy
Garda, Lake see Garda, Lago di
Gardasee see Garda, Lago di
Garden City 45 E5 Kansas, C USA
Garden State, The see New Jersey
Gardner Island see Nikumaroro
Garegegasnjárga see Karigasniemi
Gargždai 106 B3 Klaipėda, W Lithuania
Garissa 73 D6 Coast, E Kenya
Garland 49 G2 Texas, SW USA
Garoe see Garoowe
Garonne 91 B5 anc. Garumna. river S France
Garoowe 73 E5 var. Garoe. Nugaal, N Somalia
Garoua 76 B4 var. Garua. Nord, N Cameroon

Garry Lake *37 F3 lake* Nunavut, N Canada

Garsen *73 D6* Coast, S Kenya

Garua *see* Garoua

Garumna *see* Garonne

Garwolin *98 D4* Mazowieckie, E Poland

Gar Xincun *126 A4 prev.* Gar. Xizang Zizhiqu, W China

Gary *40 B3* Indiana, N USA

Garzón *58 B4* Huila, S Colombia

Gasan-Kuli *see* Esenguly

Gascogne *91 B6 Eng.* Gascony. *cultural region* S France

Gascony *see* Gascogne

Gascoyne River *147 A5 river* Western Australia

Gaspé *39 F3* Québec, SE Canada

Gaspé, Péninsule de *39 E4 var.* Péninsule de la Gaspésie. *peninsula* Québec, SE Canada

Gaspésie, Péninsule de la *see* Gaspé, Péninsule de

Gastonia *43 E1* North Carolina, SE USA

Gastoúni *105 B6* Dytikí Elláda, S Greece

Gatchina *110 B4* Leningradskaya Oblast', NW Russian Federation

Gatineau *38 D4* Québec, SE Canada

Gatooma *see* Kadoma

Gatún, Lake *53 F4 reservoir* C Panama

Gauhāti *see* Guwāhāti

Gauja *106 D3 Ger.* Aa. *river* Estonia/Latvia

Gaul/Gaule *see* France

Gauteng *see* Johannesburg, South Africa

Gāvbandī *120 D4* Hormozgān, S Iran

Gávdos *105 C8 island* SE Greece

Gavere *87 B6* Oost-Vlaanderen, NW Belgium

Gävle *85 C6 var.* Gäfle; *prev.* Gefle. Gävleborg, C Sweden

Gawler *149 B6* South Australia

Gaya *135 F3* Bihār, N India

Gaya *see* Kyjov

Gayndah *149 E5* Queensland, E Australia

Gaysin *see* Haysyn

Gaza *119 A6 Ar.* Ghazzah, *Heb.* 'Azza. NE Gaza Strip

Gaz-Achak *see* Gazojak

Gazandzhyk/Gazanjyk *see* Bereket

Gaza Strip *119 A7 Ar.* Qita Ghazzah. *disputed region* SW Asia

Gaziantep *116 D4 var.* Gazi Antep; *prev.* Aintab, Antep. Gaziantep, S Turkey

Gazi Antep *see* Gaziantep

Gazimağusa *102 D5 var.* Famagusta, *Gk.* Ammóchostos. E Cyprus

Gazli *122 D2* Buxoro Viloyati, C Uzbekistan

Gazojak *122 D2 Rus.* Gaz-Achak. Lebap Welaýaty, NE Turkmenistan

Gbanga *74 D5 var.* Gbarnga. N Liberia

Gbarnga *see* Gbanga

Gdańsk *98 C2 Fr.* Dantzig, *Ger.* Danzig. Pomorskie, N Poland

Gdan'skaya Bukhta/Gdańsk, Gulf of *see* Danzig, Gulf of

Gdańska, Zakota *see* Danzig, Gulf of

Gdingen *see* Gdynia

Gdynia *98 C2 Ger.* Gdingen. Pomorskie, N Poland

Gedaref *72 C4 var.* Al Qaḍārif, El Gedaref. Gedaref, E Sudan

Gediz *116 B3* Kütahya, W Turkey

Gediz Nehri *116 A3 river* W Turkey

Geel *87 C5 var.* Gheel. Antwerpen, N Belgium

Geelong *149 C7* Victoria, SE Australia

Ge'e'mu *see* Golmud

Gefle *see* Gävle

Geilo *85 A5* Buskerud, S Norway

Gejiu *128 B6 var.* Kochiu. Yunnan, S China

Gèkdepe *see* Gökdepe

Gela *97 C7 prev.* Terranova di Sicilia. Sicilia, Italy, C Mediterranean Sea

Geldermalsen *86 C4* Gelderland, C Netherlands

Geleen *87 D6* Limburg, SE Netherlands

Gelib *see* Jilib

Gellinsor *73 E5* Galguduud, C Somalia

Gembloux *87 C6* Namur, S Belgium

Gemena *77 C5* Equateur, NW Dem. Rep. Congo

Gem of the Mountains *see* Idaho

Gemona del Friuli *96 D2* Friuli-Venezia Giulia, NE Italy

Gem State *see* Idaho

Genalē Wenz *see* Juba

Genck *see* Genk

General Alvear *64 B4* Mendoza, W Argentina

General Carrera, Lago *see* Buenos Aires, Lago

General Eugenio A. Garay *64 C1 var.* Fortín General Eugenio Garay; *prev.* Yrendagüé. Nueva Asunción, NW Paraguay

General José F.Uriburu *see* Zárate

General Machado *see* Camacupa

General Santos *139 F3 off.* General Santos City. Mindanao, S Philippines

General Santos City *see* General Santos

Gênes *see* Genova

Geneva *see* Geneve

Geneva, Lake *95 A7 Fr.* Lac de Genève, Lac Léman, le Léman, *Ger.* Genfer See. *lake* France/Switzerland

Genève *95 A7 Eng.* Geneva, *Ger.* Genf, *It.* Ginevra. Genève, SW Switzerland

Genève, Lac de *see* Geneva, Lake

Genf *see* Genève

Genfer See *see* Geneva, Lake

Genichesk *see* Heniches'k

Genk *87 D6 var.* Genck. Limburg, NE Belgium

Gennep *86 D4* Limburg, SE Netherlands

Genoa *see* Genova

Genoa, Gulf of *96 A3 Eng.* Gulf of Genoa. *gulf* NW Italy

Genoa, Gulf of *see* Genova, Golfo di

Genova *102 D1 Eng.* Genoa; *anc.* Genua, *Fr.* Gênes. Liguria, NW Italy

Genovesa, Isla *60 B5 var.* Tower Island. *island* Galápagos Islands, Ecuador, E Pacific Ocean

Gent *87 B5 Eng.* Ghent, *Fr.* Gand. Oost-Vlaanderen, NW Belgium

Genua *see* Genova

Geok-Tepe *see* Gökdepe

George *78 C5* Western Cape, S South Africa

George *82 A4 river* Newfoundland and Labrador/Québec, E Canada

George, Lake *43 E3 lake* Florida, SE USA

Georgenburg *see* Jurbarkas

Georges Bank *35 D5 undersea bank* W Atlantic Ocean

George Sound *151 A7 sound* South Island, New Zealand

Georges River *148 D2 river* New South Wales, E Australia

Georgetown *59 F2 country capital* (Guyana) (Guyana) N Guyana

George Town *54 C2* Great Exuma Island, C Bahamas

George Town *54 B3 var.* Georgetown. *dependent territory capital* (Cayman Islands) Grand Cayman, SW Cayman Islands

George Town *138 B3 var.* Penang, Pinang, Peninsular Malaysia

Georgetown *43 F2* South Carolina, SE USA

Georgetown *see* George Town

George V Land *154 C4 physical region* Antarctica

Georgia *117 F2 off.* Republic of Georgia, *Geor.* Sak'art'velo, *Rus.* Gruzinskaya SSR, Gruziya. *country* SW Asia

GEORGIA
Southwest Asia

Official name Georgia
Formation 1991 / 1991
Capital Tbilisi
Population 4.3 million / 160 people per sq mile (62 people per sq km)
Total area 26,911 sq. miles (69,700 sq. km)
Languages Georgian*, Russian, Azeri, Armenian, Mingrelian, Ossetian, Abkhazian* *(in Abkhazia)*
Religions Georgian Orthodox 74%, Muslim 10%, Russian Orthodox 10%, Armenian Apostolic Church (Orthodox) 4%, Other 2%
Ethnic mix Georgian 84%, Armenian 6%, Azeri 6%, Russian 2%, Ossetian 1%, Other 1%
Government Presidential system
Currency Lari = 100 tetri
Literacy rate 99%
Calorie consumption 2743 kilocalories

Georgia *42 D2 off.* State of Georgia, *also known as* Empire State of the South, Peach State. *state* SE USA

Georgian Bay *40 D2 lake bay* Ontario, S Canada

Georgia, Republic of *see* Georgia

Georgia, Strait of *46 A1 strait* British Columbia, W Canada

Georgi Dimitrov *see* Kostenets

Georgiu-Dezh *see* Liski

Georg von Neumayer *154 A2 German research station* Antarctica

Gera *94 C4* Thüringen, E Germany

Geráki *105 B6* Pelopónnisos, S Greece

Geraldine *151 B6* Canterbury, South Island, New Zealand

Geraldton *147 A6* Western Australia

Geral, Serra *57 D5 mountain range* S Brazil

Gerede *116 C2* Bolu, N Turkey

Gereshk *122 D5* Helmand, SW Afghanistan

Gering *44 D3* Nebraska, C USA

German East Africa *see* Tanzania

Germanicopolis *see* Çankırı

Germanicum, Mare/German Ocean *see* North Sea

German Southwest Africa *see* Namibia

Germany *94 B4 off.* Federal Republic of Germany, Bundesrepublik Deutschland, *Ger.* Deutschland. *country* N Europe

GERMANY
Northern Europe

Official name Federal Republic of Germany
Formation 1871 / 1990
Capital Berlin
Population 82.1 million / 609 people per sq mile (235 people per sq km)
Total area 137,846 sq. miles (357,021 sq. km)
Languages German*, Turkish
Religions Protestant 34%, Roman Catholic 33%, Other 30%, Muslim 3%
Ethnic mix German 92%, Other European 3%, Other 3%, Turkish 2%
Government Parliamentary system
Currency Euro = 100 cents
Literacy rate 99%
Calorie consumption 3549 kilocalories

Germany, Federal Republic of *see* Germany

Geroliménas *105 B7* Pelopónnisos, S Greece

Gerona *see* Girona

Gerpinnes *87 C7* Hainaut, S Belgium

Gerunda *see* Girona

Gerze *116 D2* Sinop, N Turkey

Gesoriacum *see* Boulogne-sur-Mer

Gessoriacum *see* Boulogne-sur-Mer

Getafe *92 D3* Madrid, C Spain

Gevaş *117 F3* Van, SE Turkey

Gevgeli *see* Gevgelija

Gevgelija *101 E6 var.* Đevđelija, Djevdjelija, *Turk.* Gevgeli. SE Macedonia

Ghaba *see* Al Ghābah

Ghana *75 E5 off.* Republic of Ghana. *country* W Africa

GHANA
West Africa

Official name Republic of Ghana
Formation 1957 / 1957
Capital Accra
Population 25 million / 281 people per sq mile (109 people per sq km)
Total area 92,100 sq. miles (238,540 sq. km)
Languages Twi, Fanti, Ewe, Ga, Adangbe, Gurma, Dagomba (Dagbani), English*
Religions Christian 69%, Muslim 16%, Traditional beliefs 9%, Other 6%
Ethnic mix Akan 49%, Mole-Dagbani 17%, Ewe 13%, Other 9%, Ga and Ga-Adangbe 8%, Guan 4%
Government Presidential system
Currency Cedi = 100 pesewas
Literacy rate 67%
Calorie consumption 2934 kilocalories

Ghanzi *78 C3 var.* Khanzi. Ghanzi, W Botswana

Gharandal *119 B7* Al'Aqabah, SW Jordan

Gharbt, Jabal al *see* Liban, Jebel

Ghardaïa *70 D2* N Algeria

Gharvān *see* Gharyān

Gharyān *71 F2 var.* Gharvān. NW Libya

Ghawdex *see* Gozo

Ghazni *123 E4 var.* Ghazni. Ghaznī, E Afghanistan

Ghazzah *see* Gaza

Gheel *see* Geel

Ghent *see* Gent

Gheorgheni *108 C4 prev.* Gheorghieni, Sîn-Miclăuş, Ger. Niklasmarkt, *Hung.* Gyergyószentmiklós. Harghita, C Romania

Gheorghieni *see* Gheorgheni

Ghōriān *122 D4 prev.* Ghūrīān. Herāt, W Afghanistan

Ghūdara *123 F3 var.* Gudara, *Rus.* Kudara. SE Tajikistan

Ghurdaqah *see* Al Ghurdaqah

Ghūrīān *see* Ghōriān

Giamame *see* Jamaame

Giannitsá *104 B4 var.* Yiannitsá. Kentrikí Makedonía, N Greece

Gibraltar *93 G4 UK dependent territory* SW Europe

Gibraltar, Bay of *93 G5 bay* Gibraltar/SpainMediterranean Sea Atlantic Ocean

Gibraltar, Détroit de/Gibraltar, Estrecho de *see* Gibraltar, Strait of

Gibraltar, Strait of *92 C5 Fr.* Détroit de Gibraltar, *Sp.* Estrecho de Gibraltar. *strait* Atlantic Ocean/Mediterranean Sea

Gibson Desert *147 B5 desert* Western Australia

Giebnegáisi *see* Kebnekaise

Giedraičiai *107 C5* Utena, E Lithuania

Giessen *95 B5* Hessen, W Germany

Gifu *131 C6 var.* Gihu. Gifu, Honshū, SW Japan

Giganta, Sierra de la *50 B3 mountain range* NW Mexico

Gihu *see* Gifu

G'ijduvon *122 D2 Rus.* Gizhduvon. Buxoro Viloyati, C Uzbekistan

Gijón *92 D1 var.* Xixón. Asturias, NW Spain

Gila River *48 A2 river* Arizona, SW USA

Gilbert Islands *see* Tungaru

Gilbert River *148 C3 river* Queensland, NE Australia

Gilf Kebir Plateau *see* Haḍabat al Jilf al Kabīr

Gillette *44 D3* Wyoming, C USA

Gilolo *see* Halmahera, Pulau

Gilroy *47 B6* California, W USA

Gimie, Mount *55 F1 mountain* C Saint Lucia

Gimma *see* Jīma

Ginevra *see* Genève

Gingin *147 A6* Western Australia

Giohar *see* Jawhar

Gipeswic *see* Ipswich

Girardot *58 B3* Cundinamarca, C Colombia

Giresun *117 E2 var.* Kerasunt; *anc.* Cerasus, Pharnacia. Giresun, NE Turkey

Girgenti *see* Agrigento

Girin *see* Jilin

Girne *102 C5 Gk.* Kerýneia, Kyrenia. N Cyprus

Giron *see* Kiruna

Girona *93 G2 var.* Gerona; *anc.* Gerunda. Cataluña, NE Spain

Gisborne *150 E3* Gisborne, North Island, New Zealand

Gissar Range *123 E3 Rus.* Gissarskiy Khrebet. *mountain range* Tajikistan/Uzbekistan

Gissarskiy Khrebet *see* Gissar Range

Githio *see* Gýtheio

Giulianova *96 D4* Abruzzi, C Italy

Giumri *see* Gyumri

Giurgiu *108 C5* Giurgiu, S Romania

Giza *72 B1 var.* Al Jīzah, El Giza, Gizeh. N Egypt

Gizhduvon *see* G'ijduvon

Gizycko *98 D2 Ger.* Lötzen. Warmińsko-Mazurskie, NE Poland

Gjakovë *101 D5 Serb.* Ðakovica. W Kosovo

Gjeravicë *101 D5 Serb.* Ðeravica. *mountain* S Serbia

Gjilan *101 D5 Serb.* Gnjilane. E Kosovo

Gjinokastër *see* Gjirokastër

Gjirokastër *101 C7 var.* Gjirokastra; *prev.* Gjinokastër, *Gk.* Argyrokastron, *It.* Argirocastro. Gjirokastër, S Albania

Gjirokastra *see* Gjirokastër

Gjoa Haven *37 F3 var.* Uqsuqtuuq. King William Island, Nunavut, NW Canada

Gjøvik *85 B5* Oppland, S Norway
Glace Bay *39 G4* Cape Breton Island, Nova Scotia, SE Canada
Gladstone *148 E4* Queensland, E Australia
Gláma *85 B5 var.* Glommen. *river* S Norway
Glasgow *88 C4* S Scotland, United Kingdom
Glavn'a Morava *see* Velika Morava
Glazov *111 D5* Udmurtskaya Respublika, NW Russian Federation
Gleiwitz *see* Gliwice
Glendale *48 B2* Arizona, SW USA
Glendive *44 D2* Montana, NW USA
Glens Falls *41 F3* New York, NE USA
Glevum *see* Gloucester
Glina *100 B3 var.* Banijska Palanka. Sisak-Moslavina, NE Croatia
Glittertind *85 A5* mountain S Norway
Gliwice *99 C5 Ger.* Gleiwitz. Śląskie, S Poland
Globe *48 B2* Arizona, SW USA
Globino *see* Hlobyne
Głogau *see* Głogów
Głogów *98 B4 Ger.* Glogau, Glogow. Dolnośląskie, SW Poland
Glogow *see* Głogów
Glomma *see* Gláma
Glommen *see* Gláma
Gloucester *89 D6 hist.* Caer Glou, *Lat.* Glevum. C England, United Kingdom
Głowno *98 D4* Łódź, C Poland
Glubokoye *see* Hlybokaye
Glukhov *see* Hlukhiv
Gnesen *see* Gniezno
Gniezno *98 C3 Ger.* Gnesen. Weilkopolskie, C Poland
Gnjilane *see* Gjilan
Gobabis *78 B3* Omaheke, E Namibia
Gobi *126 D3 desert* China/Mongolia
Gobō *131 C6* Wakayama, Honshū, SW Japan
Godavari *124 B3 var.* Godavari. *river* C India
Godavari *see* Godávari
Godhavn *see* Qeqertarsuaq
Godhra *134 C4* Gujarāt, W India
Göding *see* Hodonín
Godoy Cruz *64 B4* Mendoza, W Argentina
Godthaab/Godthåb *see* Nuuk
Godwin Austen, Mount *see* K2
Goede Hoop, Kaap de *see* Good Hope, Cape of
Goeie Hoop, Kaap die *see* Good Hope, Cape of
Goeree *86 B4 island* SW Netherlands
Goes *87 B5* Zeeland, SW Netherlands
Goettingen *see* Göttingen
Gogebic Range *40 B1 hill range* Michigan/Wisconsin, N USA
Goiânia *63 E3 prev.* Goyania. *state capital* Goiás, C Brazil
Goiás *63 E3 off.* Estado de Goiás; *prev.* Goiaz, Goyaz. *region* C Brazil
Goiás *63 E3 off.* Estado de Goiás; *prev.* Goiaz, Goyaz. *state* C Brazil
Goiás, Estado de *see* Goiás
Goiaz *see* Goiás
Goidhoo Atoll *see* Horsburgh Atoll
Gojōme *130 D4* Akita, Honshū, NW Japan
Gökçeada *104 D4 var.* Imroz Adasī, *Gk.* Imbros. *island* NW Turkey
Gökdepe *122 C3 Rus.* Gēkdepe, Geok-Tepe. Ahal Welaýaty, C Turkmenistan
Göksun *116 D4* Kahramanmaraş, C Turkey
Gol *85 A5* Buskerud, S Norway
Golan Heights *119 B5 Ar.* Al Jawlān, *Heb.* HaGolan. *mountain range* SW Syria
Golaya Pristan *see* Hola Prystan'
Gołdap *98 E2 Ger.* Goldap. Warmińsko-Mazurskie, NE Poland
Gold Coast *149 E5 cultural region* Queensland, E Australia
Golden Bay *150 C4 bay* South Island, New Zealand
Golden State, The *see* California
Goldingen *see* Kuldīga
Goldsboro *43 F1* North Carolina, SE USA
Goleniów *98 B3 Ger.* Gollnow. Zachodnio-pomorskie, NW Poland
Gollnow *see* Goleniów
Golmo *see* Golmud

Golmud *126 D4 var.* Ge'e'mu, Golmo, *Chin.* Ko-erh-mu. Qinghǎi, C China
Golovanevsk *see* Holovanivs'k
Golub-Dobrzyń *98 C3* Kujawski-pomorskie, C Poland
Goma *77 E6* Nord-Kivu, NE Dem. Rep. Congo
Gombi *75 H4* Adamawa, E Nigeria
Gombroon *see* Bandar-e 'Abbās
Gomel' *see* Homyel'
Gomera *70 A3 island* Islas Canarias, Spain, NE Atlantic Ocean
Gómez Palacio *50 D3* Durango, C Mexico
Gonaïves *54 D3 var.* Les Gonaïves. N Haiti
Gonâve, Île de la *54 D3 island* C Haiti
Gondar *see* Gonder
Gonder *72 C4 var.* Gondar. Āmara, NW Ethiopia
Gondia *135 E4* Mahārāshtra, C India
Gonggar *126 C5 var.* Gyixong. Xizang Zizhiqu, W China
Gongola *75 G4 river* E Nigeria
Gongtang *see* Damxung
Gonni/Gónnos *see* Gónnoi
Gónnoi *104 B4 var.* Gonni, Gónnos; *prev.* Derelí. Thessalía, C Greece
Good Hope, Cape of *78 B5 Afr.* Kaap de Goede Hoop, Kaap die Goeie Hoop. *headland* SW South Africa
Goodland *44 D4* Kansas, C USA
Goondiwindi *149 D5* Queensland, E Australia
Goor *86 E3* Overijssel, E Netherlands
Goose Green *65 D7 var.* Prado del Ganso. East Falkland, Falkland Islands
Goose Lake *46 B4 var.* Lago dos Gansos. *lake* California/Oregon, W USA
Gopher State *see* Minnesota
Göppingen *95 B6* Baden-Württemberg, SW Germany
Góra Kalwaria *114 D4* Mazowieckie, C Poland
Gorakhpur *135 E3* Uttar Pradesh, N India
Gorany *see* Harany
Goražde *100 C4* Federacija Bosna I Hercegovina, SE Bosnia and Herzegovina
Gorbovichi *see* Harbavichy
Goré *76 C4* Logone-Oriental, S Chad
Gorē *73 C5* Oromīya, C Ethiopia
Gore *151 B7* Southland, South Island, New Zealand
Gorgān *120 D2 var.* Astarabad, Astrabad, Gurgan, *prev.* Asterābād; *anc.* Hyrcania. Golestán, N Iran
Gori *117 F2* C Georgia
Gorinchem *86 C4 var.* Gorkum. Zuid-Holland, C Netherlands
Goris *117 G3* SE Armenia
Gorki *see* Horki
Gor'kiy *see* Nizhniy Novgorod
Gorkum *see* Gorinchem
Görlitz *94 D4* Sachsen, E Germany
Görlitz *see* Zgorzelec
Gorlovka *see* Horlivka
Gorna Dzhumaya *see* Blagoevgrad
Gornja Mužlja *see* Mužlja
Gornji Milanovac *100 C4* Serbia, C Serbia
Gorodets *see* Haradzyets
Gorodishche *see* Horodyshche
Gorodnya *see* Horodnya
Gorodok *see* Haradok
Gorodok/Gorodok Yagellonski *see* Horodok
Gorontalo *139 E4* Sulawesi, C Indonesia
Gorontalo, Teluk *see* Tomini, Teluk
Gorssel *86 D3* Gelderland, E Netherlands
Goryn *see* Horyn'
Gorzów Wielkopolski *98 B3 Ger.* Landsberg, Landsberg an der Warthe. Lubuskie, W Poland
Gosford *149 D6* New South Wales, SE Australia
Goshogawara *130 D3 var.* Gosyogawara. Aomori, Honshū, C Japan
Gospić *100 A3* Lika-Senj, C Croatia
Gostivar *101 D6* W FYR Macedonia
Gosyogawara *see* Goshogawara
Göteborg *85 B7 Eng.* Gothenburg. Västra Götaland, S Sweden
Gotel Mountains *75 G5 mountain range* E Nigeria
Gotha *94 C4* Thüringen, C Germany
Gothenburg *see* Göteborg
Gotland *85 C7 island* SE Sweden

Goto-retto *131 A7 island group* SW Japan
Gotska Sandön *106 B1 island* SE Sweden
Gōtsu *131 B6 var.* Gôtu. Shimane, Honshū, SW Japan
Göttingen *94 B4 var.* Goettingen. Niedersachsen, C Germany
Gottschee *see* Kočevje
Gottwaldov *see* Zlín
Gôtu *see* Gōtsu
Gouda *86 C4* Zuid-Holland, C Netherlands
Gough Fracture Zone *67 C6 tectonic feature* S Atlantic Ocean
Gough Island *69 B8 island* Tristan da Cunha, S Atlantic Ocean
Gouin, Réservoir *38 D4 reservoir* Québec, SE Canada
Goulburn *149 D6* New South Wales, SE Australia
Goundam *75 E3* Tombouctou, NW Mali
Gouré *75 G3* Zinder, SE Niger
Goverla, Gora *see* Hoverla, Hora
Governador Valadares *63 F4* Minas Gerais, SE Brazil
Govi Altayn Nuruu *127 E3 mountain range* S Mongolia
Goya *64 D3* Corrientes, NE Argentina
Goyania *see* Goiânia
Goyaz *see* Goiás
Goz Beïda *76 C3* Ouaddaï, SE Chad
Gozo *97 C8 var.* Ghawdex. *island* N Malta
Graciosa *92 A5 var.* Ilha Graciosa. *island* Azores, Portugal, NE Atlantic Ocean
Graciosa, Ilha *see* Graciosa
Gradačac *100 C3* Federacija Bosna I Hercegovina, N Bosnia and Herzegovina
Gradaús, Serra dos *63 E3 mountain range* C Brazil
Gradiška *see* Bosanska Gradiška
Grafton *149 E5* New South Wales, SE Australia
Grafton *45 E1* North Dakota, N USA
Graham Land *154 A2 physical region* Antarctica
Grajewo *98 E3* Podlaskie, NE Poland
Grampian Mountains *88 C3 mountain range* C Scotland, United Kingdom
Gran *see* Esztergom, Hungary
Granada *52 D3* Granada, SW Nicaragua
Granada *92 D5* Andalucía, S Spain
Gran Canaria *70 A3 var.* Grand Canary. *island* Islas Canarias, Spain, NE Atlantic Ocean
Gran Chaco *64 D2 var.* Chaco. *lowland plain* South America
Grand Bahama Island *54 B1 island* N Bahamas
Grand Banks of Newfoundland *34 E4 undersea basin* NW Atlantic Ocean
Grand Bassa *see* Buchanan
Grand Canary *see* Gran Canaria
Grand Canyon *48 A1 canyon* Arizona, SW USA
Grand Canyon State *see* Arizona
Grand Cayman *54 B5 island* SW Cayman Islands
Grand Duchy of Luxembourg *see* Luxembourg
Grande, Bahía *65 B7 bay* S Argentina
Grande Comore *see* Ngazidja
Grande de Chiloé, Isla *see* Chiloé, Isla de
Grande Prairie *37 E4* Alberta, W Canada
Grand Erg Occidental *70 D3 desert* W Algeria
Grand Erg Oriental *71 E3 desert* Algeria/Tunisia
Rio Grande *51 E2 var.* Río Bravo, *Sp.* Río Bravo del Norte, Bravo del Norte. *river* Mexico/USA
Grande Terre *55 G3 island* E West Indies
Grand Falls *39 G3* Newfoundland, Newfoundland and Labrador, SE Canada
Grand Forks *45 E1* North Dakota, N USA
Grandichi *see* Hrandzichy
Grand Island *45 E4* Nebraska, C USA
Grand Junction *44 C4* Colorado, C USA
Grand Paradis *see* Gran Paradiso
Grand Rapids *40 C3* Michigan, N USA
Grand Rapids *45 F2* Minnesota, N USA
Grand-Saint-Bernard, Col du *see* Great Saint Bernard Pass
Grand-Santi *59 G3* W French Guiana
Granite State *see* New Hampshire
Gran Lago *see* Nicaragua, Lago de

Gran Malvina *see* West Falkland
Gran Paradiso *96 A2 Fr.* Grand Paradis. *mountain* NW Italy
Gran San Bernardo, Passo di *see* Great Saint Bernard Pass
Gran Santiago *see* Santiago
Grants *48 C2* New Mexico, SW USA
Grants Pass *46 B4* Oregon, NW USA
Granville *90 B3* Manche, N France
Gratianopolis *see* Grenoble
Gratz *see* Graz
Graudenz *see* Grudziądz
Graulhet *91 C6* Tarn, S France
Grave *86 D4* Noord-Brabant, SE Netherlands
Grayling *36 C2* Alaska, USA
Graz *95 E7 prev.* Gratz. Steiermark, SE Austria
Great Abaco *54 C1 var.* Abaco Island. *island* N Bahamas
Great Alföld *see* Great Hungarian Plain
Great Ararat *see* Büyükağrı Dağı
Great Australian Bight *147 D7 bight* S Australia
Great Barrier Island *150 D2 island* N New Zealand
Great Barrier Reef *148 D2 reef* Queensland, NE Australia
Great Basin *47 C5 basin* W USA
Great Bear Lake *37 E3 Fr.* Grand Lac de l'Ours. *lake* Northwest Territories, NW Canada
Great Belt *85 B8 var.* Store Bælt, *Eng.* Great Belt, Storebelt. *channel* Baltic Sea/Kattegat
Great Belt *see* Storebælt
Great Bend *45 E5* Kansas, C USA
Great Britain *see* Britain
Great Dividing Range *148 D4 mountain range* NE Australia
Greater Antilles *54 D3 island group* West Indies
Greater Caucasus *117 G2 mountain range* Azerbaijan/Georgia/Russian Federation Asia/Europe
Greater Sunda Islands *124 D5 var.* Sunda Islands. *island group* Indonesia
Great Exhibition Bay *150 C1 inlet* North Island, New Zealand
Great Exuma Island *54 C2 island* C Bahamas
Great Falls *44 B1* Montana, NW USA
Great Grimsby *see* Grimsby
Great Hungarian Plain *99 C7 var.* Great Alföld, Plain of Hungary, *Hung.* Alföld. *plain* SE Europe
Great Inagua *54 D2 var.* Inagua Islands. *island* S Bahamas
Great Indian Desert *see* Thar Desert
Great Khingan Range *127 G1 Eng.* Great Khingan Range. *mountain range* NE China
Great Khingan Range *see* Da Hinggan Ling
Great Lake *see* Tônlé Sap
Great Lakes *35 C5 lakes* Ontario, Canada/USA
Great Lakes State *see* Michigan
Great Meteor Seamount *see* Great Meteor Tablemount
Great Meteor Tablemount *66 B3 var.* Great Meteor Seamount. *seamount* E Atlantic Ocean
Great Nicobar *133 G3 island* Nicobar Islands, India, NE Indian Ocean
Great Plain of China *125 E2 plain* E China
Great Plains *45 E3 var.* High Plains. *plains* Canada/USA
Great Rift Valley *73 C5 var.* Rift Valley. *depression* Asia/Africa
Great Ruaha *73 C7 river* S Tanzania
Great Saint Bernard Pass *96 A1 Fr.* Col du Grand-Saint-Bernard, *It.* Passo del Gran San Bernardo. *pass* Italy/Switzerland
Great Salt Desert *see* Kavīr, Dasht-e
Great Salt Lake *44 A3 salt lake* Utah, W USA
Great Salt Lake Desert *44 A4 plain* Utah, W USA
Great Sand Sea *71 H3 desert* Egypt/Libya
Great Sandy Desert *146 C4 desert* Western Australia
Great Sandy Desert *see* Ar Rub' al Khālī
Great Sandy Island *see* Fraser Island
Great Slave Lake *37 E4 Fr.* Grand Lac des Esclaves. *lake* Northwest Territories, NW Canada

Great Socialist People's Libyan Arab Jamahiriya *see* Libya
Great Sound 42 A5 *sound* Bermuda, NW Atlantic Ocean
Great Victoria Desert 147 C5 *desert* South Australia/Western Australia
Great Wall of China 128 C4 *ancient monument* N China Asia
Great Yarmouth 89 E6 *var.* Yarmouth. E England, United Kingdom
Grebenka *see* Hrebinka
Gredos, Sierra de 92 D3 *mountain range* W Spain
Greece 105 A5 *off.* Hellenic Republic, *Gk.* Ellás; *anc.* Hellas. *country* SE Europe

GREECE
Southeast Europe

Official name Hellenic Republic
Formation 1829 / 1947
Capital Athens
Population 11.4 million / 226 people per sq mile (87 people per sq km)
Total area 50,942 sq. miles (131,940 sq. km)
Languages Greek*, Turkish, Macedonian, Albanian
Religions Orthodox Christian 98%, Muslim 1%, Other 1%
Ethnic mix Greek 98%, Other 2%
Government Parliamentary system
Currency Euro = 100 cents
Literacy rate 97%
Calorie consumption 3661 kilocalories

Greeley 44 D4 Colorado, C USA
Green Bay 40 B2 Wisconsin, N USA
Green Bay 40 B2 *lake bay* Michigan/Wisconsin, N USA
Greeneville 43 E1 Tennessee, S USA
Greenland 82 D3 *Dan.* Grønland, *Inuit* Kalaallit Nunaat. *Danish external territory* NE North America
Greenland Sea 83 F2 *sea* Arctic Ocean
Green Mountains 41 G2 *mountain range* Vermont, NE USA
Green Mountain State *see* Vermont
Greenock 88 C4 W Scotland, United Kingdom
Green River 44 B3 Wyoming, C USA
Green River 40 C5 *river* Kentucky, C USA
Green River 44 B4 *river* Utah, W USA
Greensboro 43 F1 North Carolina, SE USA
Greenville 42 B2 Mississippi, S USA
Greenville 43 F1 North Carolina, SE USA
Greenville 43 E1 South Carolina, SE USA
Greenville 49 G2 Texas, SW USA
Greenwich 89 B8 United Kingdom
Greenwood 42 B2 Mississippi, S USA
Greenwood 43 E2 South Carolina, SE USA
Gregory Range 148 C3 *mountain range* Queensland, E Australia
Greifenberg/Greifenberg in Pommern *see* Gryfice
Greifswald 94 D2 Mecklenburg-Vorpommern, NE Germany
Grenada 42 C2 Mississippi, S USA
Grenada 55 G5 *country* SE West Indies

GRENADA
West Indies

Official name Grenada
Formation 1974 / 1974
Capital St. George's
Population 109,011 / 832 people per sq mile (321 people per sq km)
Total area 131 sq. miles (340 sq. km)
Languages English*, English Creole
Religions Roman Catholic 68%, Anglican 17%, Other 15%
Ethnic mix Black African 82%, Mulatto (mixed race) 13%, East Indian 3%, Other 2%
Government Parliamentary system
Currency East Caribbean dollar = 100 cents
Literacy rate 96%
Calorie consumption 2456 kilocalories

Grenadines, The 55 H4 *island group* Grenada/St Vincent and the Grenadines
Grenoble 91 D5 *anc.* Cularo, Gratianopolis. Isère, E France
Gresham 46 B3 Oregon, NW USA

Grevená 104 B4 Dytikí Makedonía, N Greece
Grevenmacher 87 E8 Grevenmacher, E Luxembourg
Greymouth 151 B5 West Coast, South Island, New Zealand
Grey Range 149 C5 *mountain range* New South Wales/Queensland, E Australia
Greytown *see* San Juan del Norte
Griffin 42 D2 Georgia, SE USA
Grimari 76 C4 Ouaka, C Central African Republic
Grimsby 89 E5 *prev.* Great Grimsby. E England, United Kingdom
Grobin *see* Grobiņa
Grobiņa 106 B3 *Ger.* Grobin. W Latvia
Gródek Jagielloński *see* Horodok
Grodno *see* Hrodna
Grodzisk Wielkopolski 98 B3 Wielkopolskie, C Poland
Groesbeek 86 D4 Gelderland, SE Netherlands
Grójec 98 D4 Mazowieckie, C Poland
Groningen 86 E1 Groningen, NE Netherlands
Grønland *see* Greenland
Groote Eylandt 148 B2 *island* Northern Territory, N Australia
Grootfontein 78 B3 Otjozondjupa, N Namibia
Groot Karasberge 78 B4 *mountain range* S Namibia
Gros Islet 55 F1 N Saint Lucia
Grossa, Isola *see* Dugi Otok
Grossbetschkerek *see* Zrenjanin
Grosse Morava *see* Velika Morava
Grosser Sund *see* Suur Väin
Grosseto 96 B4 Toscana, C Italy
Grossglockner 95 C7 *mountain* W Austria
Grosskanizsa *see* Nagykanizsa
Gross-Karol *see* Carei
Grosskikinda *see* Kikinda
Grossmichel *see* Michalovce
Gross-Schlatten *see* Abrud
Grosswardein *see* Oradea
Groznyy 111 B8 Chechenskaya Respublika, SW Russian Federation
Grudovo *see* Sredets
Grudziądz 98 C3 *Ger.* Graudenz. Kujawsko-pomorskie, C Poland
Grums 85 B6 Värmland, C Sweden
Grünberg/Grünberg in Schlesien *see* Zielona Góra
Grüneberg *see* Zielona Góra
Gruzinskaya SSR/Gruziya *see* Georgia
Gryazi 111 B6 Lipetskaya Oblast', W Russian Federation
Gryfice 98 B2 *Ger.* Greifenberg, Greifenberg in Pommern. Zachodnio-pomorskie, NW Poland
Guabito 53 E4 Bocas del Toro, NW Panama
Guadalajara 50 D4 Jalisco, C Mexico
Guadalajara 93 E3 *Ar.* Wad Al-Hajarah; *anc.* Arriaca. Castilla-La Mancha, C Spain
Guadalcanal 144 C3 *island* C Solomon Islands
Guadalquivir 92 D4 *river* W Spain
Guadalupe 50 D3 Zacatecas, C Mexico
Guadalupe Peak 48 D3 *mountain* Texas, SW USA
Guadalupe River 49 G4 *river* SW USA
Guadarrama, Sierra de 93 E2 *mountain range* C Spain
Guadeloupe 55 H3 *French overseas department* E West Indies
Guadiana 92 C4 *river* Portugal/Spain
Guadix 93 E4 Andalucía, S Spain
Guaimaca 52 C2 Francisco Morazán, C Honduras
Guajira, Península de la 58 B1 *peninsula* N Colombia
Gualaco 52 D2 Olancho, C Honduras
Gualán 52 B2 Zacapa, C Guatemala
Gualdicciolo 96 D1 NW San Marino
Gualeguaychú 64 D4 Entre Ríos, E Argentina
Guam 144 B1 US *unincorporated territory* W Pacific Ocean
Guamúchil 50 C3 Sinaloa, C Mexico
Guanabacoa 54 B2 La Habana, W Cuba
Guanajuato 51 E4 Guanajuato, C Mexico
Guanare 58 C2 Portuguesa, N Venezuela
Guanare, Río 58 D2 *river* W Venezuela
Guangdong 128 C6 *var.* Guangdong Sheng, Kuang-tung, Kwangtung, Yue. *province* S China

Guangdong Sheng *see* Guangdong
Guangju *see* Gwangju
Guangxi *see* Guangxi Zhuangzu Zizhiqu
Guangxi Zhuangzu Zizhiqu 128 C6 *var.* Guangxi, Gui, Kwangsi, *Eng.* Kwangsi Chuang Autonomous Region. *autonomous region* S China
Guangyuan 128 B5 *var.* Kuang-yuan, Kwangyuan. Sichuan, C China
Guangzhou 128 C6 *var.* Kuang-chou, Kwangchow, *Eng.* Canton. *province capital* Guangdong, S China
Guantánamo 54 D3 Guantánamo, SE Cuba
Guantánamo, Bahia de 54 D3 *Eng.* Guantanamo Bay. *US military base* SE Cuba
Guantanamo Bay *see* Guantánamo, Bahia de
Guaporé, Rio 62 D3 *var.* Rio Iténez. *river* Bolivia/Brazil
Guarda 92 C3 Guarda, N Portugal
Guarumal 53 F5 Veraguas, S Panama
Guasave 50 C3 Sinaloa, C Mexico
Guatemala 52 A2 *off.* Republic of Guatemala. *country* Central America

GUATEMALA
Central America

Official name Republic of Guatemala
Formation 1838 / 1838
Capital Guatemala City
Population 14.8 million / 354 people per sq mile (136 people per sq km)
Total area 42,042 sq. miles (108,890 sq. km)
Languages Quiché, Mam, Cakchiquel, Kekchí, Spanish*
Religions Roman Catholic 65%, Protestant 33%, Other and nonreligious 2%
Ethnic mix Amerindian 60%, Mestizo 30%, Other 10%
Government Presidential system
Currency Quetzal = 100 centavos
Literacy rate 74%
Calorie consumption 2219 kilocalories

Guatemala Basin 35 B7 *undersea basin* E Pacific Ocean
Guatemala City *see* Ciudad de Guatemala
Guatemala, Republic of *see* Guatemala
Guaviare 56 B2 *off.* Comisaría Guaviare. *province* S Colombia
Guaviare, Comisaría *see* Guaviare
Guaviare, Río 58 D3 *river* E Colombia
Guayas, Macizo de las *see* Guiana Highlands
Guayaquil 60 A2 *var.* Santiago de Guayaquil. Guayas, SW Ecuador
Guayaquil, Gulf of 60 A2 *var.* Gulf of Guayaquil. *gulf* SW Ecuador
Guayaquil, Gulf of *see* Guayaquil, Golfo de
Guaymas 50 B2 Sonora, NW Mexico
Gubadag 122 C2 *Turkm.* Tel'man; *prev.* Tel'mansk. Daşoguz Welaýaty, N Turkmenistan
Guben 94 D4 *var.* Wilhelm-Pieck-Stadt. Brandenburg, E Germany
Gudara *see* Ghŭdara
Gudauta 117 E1 *prev.* Gudaut'a. NW Georgia
Gudaut'a *see* Gudauta
Guéret 90 C4 Creuse, C France
Guernsey 89 D8 *island* Channel Islands, NW Europe
Guerrero Negro 50 A2 Baja California Sur, NW Mexico
Gui *see* Guangxi Zhuangzu Zizhiqu
Guiana *see* French Guiana
Guiana Highlands 62 D1 *var.* Macizo de las Guayanas. *mountain range* N South America
Guiba *see* Juba
Guidder *see* Guider
Guider 76 B4 *var.* Guidder. Nord, N Cameroon
Guidimouni 75 G3 Zinder, S Niger
Guildford 89 D7 SE England, United Kingdom
Guilin 128 C6 *var.* Kuei-lin, Kweilin. Guangxi Zhuangzu Zizhiqu, S China
Guimarães 92 B2 *var.* Guimaráes. Braga, N Portugal
Guimaráes *see* Guimarães

Guinea 74 C4 *off.* Republic of Guinea, *var.* Guinée; *prev.* French Guinea, People's Revolutionary Republic of Guinea. *country* W Africa

GUINEA
West Africa

Official name Republic of Guinea
Formation 1958 / 1958
Capital Conakry
Population 10.2 million / 107 people per sq mile (41 people per sq km)
Total area 94,925 sq. miles (245,857 sq. km)
Languages Pulaar, Malinké, Soussou, French
Religions Muslim 85%, Christian 8%, Traditional beliefs 7%
Ethnic mix Peul 40%, Malinké 30%, Soussou 20%, Other 10%
Government Transitional regime
Currency Guinea franc = 100 centimes
Literacy rate 40%
Calorie consumption 2652 kilocalories

Guinea Basin 69 A5 *undersea basin* E Atlantic Ocean
Guinea-Bissau 74 B4 *off.* Republic of Guinea-Bissau, *Fr.* Guinée-Bissau, *Port.* Guiné-Bissau; *prev.* Portuguese Guinea. *country* W Africa

GUINEA-BISSAU
West Africa

Official name Republic of Guinea-Bissau
Formation 1974 / 1974
Capital Bissau
Population 1.5 million / 138 people per sq mile (53 people per sq km)
Total area 13,946 sq. miles (36,120 sq. km)
Languages Portuguese Creole, Balante, Fulani, Malinké, Portuguese*
Religions Traditional beliefs 50%, Muslim 40%, Christian 10%
Ethnic mix Balante 30%, Fulani 20%, Other 16%, Mandyako 14%, Mandinka 13%, Papel 7%
Government Transitional regime
Currency CFA franc = 100 centimes
Literacy rate 52%
Calorie consumption 2476 kilocalories

Guinea-Bissau, Republic of *see* Guinea-Bissau
Guinea, Gulf of 68 B4 *Fr.* Golfe de Guinée. *gulf* E Atlantic Ocean
Guinea, People's Revolutionary Republic of *see* Guinea
Guiné-Bissau *see* Guinea-Bissau
Guinée *see* Guinea
Guinée-Bissau *see* Guinea-Bissau
Guinée, Golfe de *see* Guinea, Gulf of
Güiria 59 E1 Sucre, NE Venezuela
Guiyang 128 B6 *var.* Kuei-Yang, Kuei-yang, Kueyang, Kweiyang; *prev.* Kweichu. *province capital* Guizhou, S China
Guizhou 128 B6 Guangdong, SE China
Gujarat 134 C4 *var.* Gujerat. *cultural region* W India
Gujerat *see* Gujarāt
Gujrānwāla 134 D2 Punjab, NE Pakistan
Gujrāt 134 D2 Punjab, E Pakistan
Gulbarga 132 C1 Karnātaka, C India
Gulbene 106 D3 *Ger.* Alt-Schwanenburg. NE Latvia
Gulf of Liaotung *see* Liaodong Wan
Gulfport 42 C3 Mississippi, S USA
Gulistan *see* Guliston
Guliston 123 E2 *Rus.* Gulistan. Sirdaryo Viloyati, E Uzbekistan
Gulja *see* Yining
Gulkana 36 D3 Alaska, USA
Gulu 73 B6 N Uganda
Gulyantsi 104 C1 Pleven, N Bulgaria
Guma *see* Pishan
Gumbinnen *see* Gusev
Gumpolds *see* Humpolec
Gümülcine/Gümüljina *see* Komotiní
Gümüşane *see* Gümüşhane
Gümüşhane 117 E3 *var.* Gümüşane, Gumushkhane. Gümüşhane, NE Turkey
Gumushkhane *see* Gümüşhane
Güney Doğu Toroslar 117 E4 *mountain range* SE Turkey

Gunnbjørn Fjeld 82 D4 var. Gunnbjörns Bjerge. *mountain* C Greenland
Gunnbjörns Bjerge *see* Gunnbjørn Fjeld
Gunnedah 149 D6 New South Wales, SE Australia
Gunnison 44 C5 Colorado, C USA
Gurbansoltan Eje 122 C2 *prev.* Ýylanly, *Rus.* Il'yaly. Daşoguz Welaýaty, N Turkmenistan
Gurbantünggüt Shamo 126 B2 *desert* W China
Gurgan *see* Gorgān
Guri, Embalse de 59 E2 *reservoir* E Venezuela
Gurkfeld *see* Krško
Gurktaler Alpen 95 D7 *mountain range* S Austria
Gürün 116 D3 Sivas, C Turkey
Gur'yev/Gur'yevskaya Oblast' *see* Atyrau
Gusau 75 G4 Zamfara, NW Nigeria
Gusev 106 B4 Ger. Gumbinnen. Kaliningradskaya Oblast', W Russian Federation
Gustavus 36 D4 Alaska, USA
Güstrow 94 C3 Mecklenburg-Vorpommern, NE Germany
Guta/Gúta *see* Kolárovo
Gütersloh 94 B4 Nordrhein-Westfalen, W Germany
Gutta *see* Kolárovo
Guttstadt *see* Dobre Miasto
Guwāhāti 135 G3 *prev.* Gauhāti. Assam, NE India
Guyana 59 F3 *off.* Co-operative Republic of Guyana; *prev.* British Guiana. *country* N South America

GUYANA
South America

Official name Cooperative Republic of Guyana
Formation 1966 / 1966
Capital Georgetown
Population 800,000 / 11 people per sq mile (4 people per sq km)
Total area 83,000 sq. miles (214,970 sq. km)
Languages English Creole, Hindi, Tamil, Amerindian languages, English*
Religions Christian 57%, Hindu 28%, Muslim 10%, Other 5%
Ethnic mix East Indian 43%, Black African 30%, Mixed race 17%, Amerindian 9%, Other 1%
Government Presidential system
Currency Guyanese dollar = 100 cents
Literacy rate 99%
Calorie consumption 2718 kilocalories

Guyana, Co-operative Republic of *see* Guyana
Guyane *see* French Guiana
Guymon 49 E1 Oklahoma, C USA
Güzelyurt 102 C5 Gk. Kólpos Mórfu, Morphou. W Cyprus
Gvardeysk 106 A4 Ger. Tapaiu. Kaliningradskaya Oblast', W Russian Federation
Gwādar 134 A3 var. Gwadur. Baluchistān, SW Pakistan
Gwadur *see* Gwādar
Gwalior 134 D3 Madhya Pradesh, C India
Gwanda 78 D3 Matabeleland South, SW Zimbabwe
Gwangju 129 E4 *off.* Kwangju-gwangyŏksi, var. Guangju, Kwangchu; *prev.* Kwangju, *Jap.* Kōshū. SW South Korea
Gwy *see* Wye
Gyandzha *see* Gäncä
Gyangzê 126 C5 Xizang Zizhiqu, W China
Gyaring Co 126 C5 *lake* W China
Gyêgu *see* Yushu
Gyergyószentmiklós *see* Gheorgheni
Gyixong *see* Gonggar
Gympie 149 E5 Queensland, E Australia
Gyomaendrőd 99 D7 Békés, SE Hungary
Gyöngyös 99 D6 Heves, NE Hungary
Győr 99 C6 Ger. Raab, Lat. Arrabona. Győr-Moson-Sopron, NW Hungary
Gytheio 105 B6 var. Githio; *prev.* Yíthion. Pelopónnisos, S Greece
Gyulafehérvár *see* Alba Iulia

Gyumri 117 F2 var. Giumri, Rus. Kumayri; *prev.* Aleksandropol', Leninakan. W Armenia
Gyzyrlabat *see* Serdar

H

Haabai *see* Ha'apai Group
Haacht 87 C6 Vlaams Brabant, C Belgium
Haaksbergen 86 E3 Overijssel, E Netherlands
Ha'apai Group 145 F4 var. Haabai. *island group* C Tonga
Haapsalu 106 D2 Ger. Hapsal. Läänemaa, W Estonia
Ha'Arava *see* 'Arabah, Wādī al
Haarlem 86 C3 prev. Harlem. Noord-Holland, W Netherlands
Haast 151 B6 West Coast, South Island, New Zealand
Hachijo-jima 131 D6 *island* Izu-shotō, SE Japan
Hachinohe 130 D3 Aomori, Honshū, C Japan
Hacıqabal 117 H3 prev. Qazimämmäd. SE Azerbaijan
Hadabat al Jilf al Kabīr 72 A2 var. Gilf Kebir Plateau. *plateau* SW Egypt
Hadama *see* Nazrēt
Hadejia 75 G4 Jigawa, N Nigeria
Hadejia 75 G3 *river* N Nigeria
Hadera 119 A6 var. Khadera; prev. Ḥadera. Ḥaifa, N Israel
Ḥadera *see* Hadera
Hadhdhunmathi Atoll 132 A5 *atoll* S Maldives
Ha Đông 136 D3 var. Hadong. Ha Tây, N Vietnam
Hadong *see* Ha Đông
Hadramaut 121 C6 Eng. Hadramaut. *mountain range* S Yemen
Hadramaut *see* Ḥaḍramawt
Hadrianopolis *see* Edirne
Haerbin/Haerhpin/Ha-erh-pin *see* Harbin
Hafnia *see* Denmark
Hafnia *see* København
Hafren *see* Severn
Hafun, Ras *see* Xaafuun, Raas
Hagåtña 144 B1 , var. Agaña. *dependent territory capital* (Guam) NW Guam
Hagerstown 41 F4 Maryland, NE USA
Ha Giang 136 D3 Ha Giang, N Vietnam
Hagios Evstrátios *see* Ágios Efstrátios
HaGolan *see* Golan Heights
Hagondange 90 D3 Moselle, NE France
Haguenau 90 E3 Bas-Rhin, NE France
Haibowan *see* Wuhai
Haicheng 128 D3 Liaoning, NE China
Haidarabad *see* Hyderābād
Haifa *see* Hefa
Haifa, Bay of *see* Mifrats Hefa
Haifong *see* Hai Phong
Haikou 128 C7 var. Hai-k'ou, Hoihow, Fr. Hoï-Hao. *province capital* Hainan, S China
Hai-k'ou *see* Haikou
Ḥā'il 120 B4 Ḥā'il, NW Saudi Arabia
Hailuoto 84 D4 Swe. Karlö. *island* W Finland
Hainan 128 B7 var. Hainan Sheng, Qiong. *province* S China
Hainan Dao 128 C7 *island* S China
Hainan Sheng *see* Hainan
Hainasch *see* Ainaži
Haines 36 D4 Alaska, USA
Hainichen 94 D4 Sachsen, E Germany
Hai Phong 136 D3 var. Haifong, Haiphong. N Vietnam
Haiphong *see* Hai Phong
Haiti 54 D3 *off.* Republic of Haiti. *country* C West Indies

HAITI
West Indies

Official name Republic of Haiti
Formation 1804 / 1844
Capital Port-au-Prince
Population 10.1 million / 949 people per sq mile (366 people per sq km)
Total area 10,714 sq. miles (27,750 sq. km)
Languages French Creole*, French*
Religions Roman Catholic 55%, Protestant 28%, Other (including Voodoo) 16%, Nonreligious 1%
Ethnic mix Black African 95%,

HAITI
(continued)

Mulatto (mixed race) and European 5%
Government Presidential system
Currency Gourde = 100 centimes
Literacy rate 62%
Calorie consumption 1979 kilocalories

Haiti, Republic of *see* Haiti
Haiya 72 C3 Red Sea, NE Sudan
Hajdúhadház 99 D6 Hajdú-Bíhar, E Hungary
Hajine *see* Abū Ḥardān
Hajnówka 98 E3 Ger. Hermhausen. Podlaskie, NE Poland
Hakodate 130 D3 Hokkaidō, NE Japan
Hal *see* Halle
Ḥalab 118 B2 Eng. Aleppo, Fr. Alep; anc. Beroea. Ḥalab, NW Syria
Hala'ib Triangle 72 C3 region SE Egypt
Ḥalāniyāt, Juzur al 121 D6 var. Jazā'ir Bin Ghalfān, Eng. Kuria Muria Islands. *island group* S Oman
Halberstadt 94 C4 Sachsen-Anhalt, C Germany
Halden 85 B6 prev. Fredrikshald. Østfold, S Norway
Halfmoon Bay 151 A8 var. Oban. Stewart Island, Southland, New Zealand
Haliacmon *see* Aliákmonas
Halifax 39 F4 *province capital* Nova Scotia, SE Canada
Halkida *see* Chalkída
Halle 87 B6 Fr. Hal. Vlaams Brabant, C Belgium
Halle 94 C4 var. Halle an der Saale. Sachsen-Anhalt, C Germany
Halle an der Saale *see* Halle
Halle-Neustadt 94 C4 Sachsen-Anhalt, C Germany
Halley 154 B2 UK research station Antarctica
Hall Islands 142 B2 *island group* C Micronesia
Halls Creek 146 C3 Western Australia
Halmahera, Laut 139 F4 Eng. Halmahera Sea. *sea* E Indonesia
Halmahera, Pulau 139 F3 prev. Djailolo, Gilolo, Jailolo. *island* E Indonesia
Halmahera Sea *see* Halmahera, Laut
Halmstad 85 B7 Halland, S Sweden
Ha Long 136 E3 prev. Hông Gai, var. Hon Gai, Hongay. Quang Ninh, N Vietnam
Hälsingborg *see* Helsingborg
Hamada 131 B6 Shimane, Honshū, SW Japan
Hamadān 120 C3 anc. Ecbatana. Hamadān, W Iran
Ḥamāh 118 B3 var. Hama; anc. Epiphania, Bibl. Hamath. Ḥamāh, W Syria
Hamamatsu 131 D6 var. Hamamatu. Shizuoka, Honshū, S Japan
Hamamatu *see* Hamamatsu
Hamar 85 B5 prev. Storhammer. Hedmark, S Norway
Hamath *see* Ḥamāh
Hamburg 94 B3 Hamburg, N Germany
Ḥamd, Wādī al 120 A4 *dry watercourse* W Saudi Arabia
Hämeenlinna 85 D5 Swe. Tavastehus. Etelä-Suomi, S Finland
HaMela h, Yam *see* Dead Sea
Hamersley Range 146 A4 *mountain range* Western Australia
Hamhŭng 129 E3 C North Korea
Hami 126 C3 var. Ha-mi, Uigh. Kumul, Qomul. Xinjiang Uygur Zizhiqu, NW China
Ha-mi *see* Hami
Hamilton 42 A5 *dependent territory capital* (Bermuda) C Bermuda
Hamilton 38 D5 Ontario, S Canada
Hamilton 150 D3 Waikato, North Island, New Zealand
Hamilton 88 C4 S Scotland, United Kingdom
Hamilton 42 C2 Alabama, S USA
Hamim, Wadi al 71 G2 *river* NE Libya
Hamis Musait *see* Khamīs Mushayt
Hamm 94 B4 var. Hamm in Westfalen. Nordrhein-Westfalen, W Germany
Ḥammāmāt, Khalīj al *see* Hammamet, Golfe de
Hammamet, Golfe de 102 D3 Ar. Khalīj al Ḥammāmāt. *gulf* NE Tunisia

Hammar, Hawr al 120 C3 *lake* SE Iraq
Hamm in Westfalen *see* Hamm
Hampden 151 B7 Otago, South Island, New Zealand
Hampstead 89 A7 Maryland, USA
Hamrun 102 B5 C Malta
Hāmūn, Daryācheh-ye *see* Şāberī, Hāmūn-e/Sīstān, Daryācheh-ye
Hamwih *see* Southampton
Hânceşti *see* Hînceşti
Hancewicze *see* Hantsavichy
Handan 128 C4 var. Han-tan. Hebei, E China
Haneda 130 A2 (Tōkyō) Tōkyō, Honshū, S Japan
Hanford 47 C6 California, W USA
Hangayn Nuruu 126 D2 *mountain range* C Mongolia
Hang-chou/Hangchow *see* Hangzhou
Hangö *see* Hanko
Hangzhou 128 D5 var. Hang-chou, Hangchow. *province capital* Zhejiang, SE China
Hania *see* Chaniá
Hanka, Lake *see* Khanka, Lake
Hanko 85 D6 Swe. Hangö. Etelä-Suomi, SW Finland
Han-kou/Han-k'ou/Hankow *see* Wuhan
Hanmer Springs 151 C5 Canterbury, South Island, New Zealand
Hannibal 45 G4 Missouri, C USA
Hannover 94 B3 Eng. Hanover. Niedersachsen, NW Germany
Hanöbukten 85 B7 bay S Sweden
Ha Nôi 136 D3 Eng. Hanoi, Fr. Hanoï. *country capital* (Vietnam) N Vietnam
Hanover *see* Hannover
Han Shui 127 E4 *river* C China
Han-tan *see* Handan
Hantsavichy 107 B6 Pol. Hancewicze, Rus. Gantsevichi. Brestskaya Voblasts', SW Belarus
Hanyang *see* Wuhan
Hanzhong 128 B5 Shaanxi, C China
Hāora 135 F4 prev. Howrah. West Bengal, NE India
Haparanda 84 D4 Norrbotten, N Sweden
Hapsal *see* Haapsalu
Haradok 107 E5 Rus. Gorodok. Vitsyebskaya Voblasts', N Belarus
Haradzyets 107 B6 Rus. Gorodets. Brestskaya Voblasts', SW Belarus
Haramachi 130 D4 Fukushima, Honshū, E Japan
Harany 107 D5 Rus. Gorany. Vitsyebskaya Voblasts', N Belarus
Harare 78 D3 prev. Salisbury. *country capital* (Zimbabwe) Mashonaland East, NE Zimbabwe
Harbavichy 107 E6 Rus. Gorbovichi. Mahilyowskaya Voblasts', E Belarus
Harbel 74 C5 W Liberia
Harbin 129 E2 var. Haerbin, Ha-erh-pin, Kharbin; prev. Haerhpin, Pingkiang, Pinkiang. *province capital* Heilongjiang, NE China
Hardangerfjorden 85 A6 *fjord* S Norway
Hardangervidda 85 A6 *plateau* S Norway
Hardenberg 86 E3 Overijssel, E Netherlands
Harelbeke 87 A6 var. Harlebeke. West-Vlaanderen, W Belgium
Harem *see* Ḥārim
Haren 86 E2 Groningen, NE Netherlands
Härer 73 D5 E Ethiopia
Hargeisa *see* Hargeysa
Hargeysa 73 D5 var. Hargeisa. Woqooyi Galbeed, NW Somalia
Hariana *see* Haryāna
Hari, Batang 138 B4 prev. Djambi. *river* Sumatera, W Indonesia
Ḥārim 118 B2 var. Harem. Idlib, W Syria
Harima-nada 131 B6 *sea* S Japan
Harirud 123 E4 var. Tedzhen, Turkm. Tejen. *river* Afghanistan/Iran
Harlan 45 F3 Iowa, C USA
Harlebeke *see* Harelbeke
Harlem *see* Haarlem
Harlingen 86 D2 Fris. Harns. Fryslân, N Netherlands
Harlingen 49 G5 Texas, SW USA
Harlow 89 E6 E England, United Kingdom
Harney Basin 46 B4 *basin* Oregon, NW USA
Härnösand 85 C5 var. Hernösand. Västernorrland, C Sweden

Harns see Harlingen
Harper 74 D5 var. Cape Palmas.
   NE Liberia
Harricana 38 D3 river Québec,
   SE Canada
Harris 88 B3 physical region
   NW Scotland, United Kingdom
Harrisburg 41 E4 state capital
   Pennsylvania, NE USA
Harrisonburg 41 E4 Virginia, NE USA
Harrison, Cape 39 F2 headland
   Newfoundland and Labrador, E Canada
Harris Ridge see Lomonosov Ridge
Harrogate 89 D5 N England, United
   Kingdom
Hârşova 108 D5 prev. Hîrsova.
   Constanţa, SE Romania
Harstad 84 C2 Troms, N Norway
Hartford 41 G3 state capital Connecticut,
   NE USA
Hartlepool 89 D5 N England, United
   Kingdom
Harunabad see Eslāmābād-e Gharb
Har Us Gol 126 C2 lake Hovd,
   W Mongolia
Har Us Nuur 126 C2 lake
   NW Mongolia
Harwich 89 E6 E England, United
   Kingdom
Haryāna 134 D2 var. Hariana. cultural
   region N India
Hashemite Kingdom of Jordan see
   Jordan
Hasselt 87 C6 Limburg, NE Belgium
Hassetché see Al Ḥasakah
Hasta Colonia/Hasta Pompeia see Asti
Hastings 150 A4 Hawke's Bay, North
   Island, New Zealand
Hastings 89 E7 SE England, United
   Kingdom
Hastings 45 E4 Nebraska, C USA
Haţeg 108 B4 Ger. Wallenthal, Hung.
   Hátszeg; prev. Hatzeg, Hötzing.
   Hunedoara, SW Romania
Hátszeg see Haţeg
Hattem 86 D3 Gelderland, E Netherlands
Hatteras, Cape 43 G1 headland North
   Carolina, SE USA
Hatteras Plain 35 D6 abyssal plain
   W Atlantic Ocean
Hattiesburg 42 C3 Mississippi, S USA
Hatton Bank see Hatton Ridge
Hatton Ridge 80 B2 var. Hatton Bank.
   undersea ridge N Atlantic Ocean
Hat Yai 137 C7 var. Ban Hat Yai.
   Songkhla, SW Thailand
Hatzeg see Haţeg
Hatzfeld see Jimbolia
Haugesund 85 A6 Rogaland, S Norway
Haukeligrend 85 A6 Telemark,
   S Norway
Haukivesi 85 E5 lake SE Finland
Hauraki Gulf 150 D2 gulf North Island,
   N New Zealand
Hauroko, Lake 151 A7 lake South
   Island, New Zealand
Hautes Fagnes 87 D6 Ger. Hohes Venn.
   mountain range E Belgium
Hauts Plateaux 70 D2 plateau Algeria/
   Morocco
Hauzenberg 95 D6 Bayern, SE Germany
Havana 35 D6 Illinois, N USA
Havana see La Habana
Havant 89 D7 S England, United
   Kingdom
Havelock 43 F1 North Carolina, SE USA
Havelock North 150 E4 Hawke's Bay,
   North Island, New Zealand
Haverfordwest 89 C6 SW Wales, United
   Kingdom
Havířov 99 C5 Moravskoslezský Kraj,
   E Czech Republic
Havre 44 C1 Montana, NW USA
Havre see le Havre
Havre-St-Pierre 39 F3 Québec,
   E Canada
Hawai'i 147 A8 off. State of Hawai'i,
   also known as Aloha State, Paradise
   of the Pacific, var. Hawaii. state USA,
   C Pacific Ocean
Hawai'i 147 B8 var. Hawaii. island
   Hawaiian Islands, USA, C Pacific Ocean
Hawai'ian Islands 152 E2 prev.
   Sandwich Islands. island group
   Hawaii, USA
Hawaiian Ridge 152 H4 undersea ridge
   N Pacific Ocean
Hawea, Lake 151 B6 lake South Island,
   New Zealand

Hawera 150 D4 Taranaki, North Island,
   New Zealand
Hawick 88 C4 SE Scotland, United
   Kingdom
Hawke Bay 150 E4 bay North Island,
   New Zealand
Hawkeye State see Iowa
Hawlēr see Arbīl
Hawthorne 47 C6 Nevada, W USA
Hay 149 C6 New South Wales,
   SE Australia
HaYarden see Jordan
Hayastani Hanrapetut'yun see Armenia
Hayes 38 B2 river Manitoba, C Canada
Hay River 37 E4 Northwest Territories,
   W Canada
Hays 45 E5 Kansas, C USA
Haysyn 108 D3 Rus. Gaysin. Vinnyts'ka
   Oblast', C Ukraine
Hazar 122 B2 prev. Rus. Cheleken.
   Balkan Welaýaty, W Turkmenistan
Heard and McDonald Islands 141 B7
   Australian external territory S Indian
   Ocean
Hearst 38 C4 Ontario, S Canada
Heart of Dixie see Alabama
Heathrow 89 A8 (London) SE England,
   United Kingdom
Hebei 128 C4 var. Hebei Sheng, Hopeh,
   Hopei, Ji; prev. Chihli. province
   E China
Hebei Sheng see Hebei
Hebron 119 A6 var. Al Khalīl, El Khalīl,
   Heb. Hevron; anc. Kiriath-Arba.
   S West Bank
Heemskerk 86 C3 Noord-Holland,
   W Netherlands
Heerde 86 D3 Gelderland, E Netherlands
Heerenveen 86 D2 Fris. It Hearrenfean.
   Fryslân, N Netherlands
Heerhugowaard 86 C2 Noord-Holland,
   NW Netherlands
Heerlen 87 D6 Limburg, SE Netherlands
Heerwegen see Polkowice
Hefa 119 A5 var. Haifa, hist. Caiffa,
   Caiphas; anc. Sycaminum. Haifa,
   N Israel
Hefa, Mifraz see Mifrats Hefa
Hefei 128 D5 var. Hofei, hist. Luchow.
   province capital Anhui, E China
Hegang 129 E2 Heilongjiang, NE China
Hei see Heilongjiang
Heide 94 B2 Schleswig-Holstein,
   N Germany
Heidelberg 95 B5 Baden-Württemberg,
   SW Germany
Heidenheim see Heidenheim an der
   Brenz
Heidenheim an der Brenz 95 B6 var.
   Heidenheim. Baden-Württemberg,
   S Germany
Hei-ho see Nagqu
Heilbronn 95 B5 Baden-Württemberg,
   SW Germany
Heilongjiang 128 D2 var. Hei,
   Heilongjiang Sheng, Hei-lung-chiang,
   Heilungkiang. province NE China
Heilong Jiang see Amur
Heilongjiang Sheng see Heilongjiang
Heiloo 86 C3 Noord-Holland,
   NW Netherlands
Heilsberg see Lidzbark Warmiński
Hei-lung-chiang/Heilungkiang see
   Heilongjiang
Heimdal 85 B5 Sør-Trøndelag, S Norway
Heinaste see Ainaži
Hekimhan 116 D3 Malatya, C Turkey
Helena 44 B2 state capital Montana,
   NW USA
Helensville 150 D2 Auckland, North
   Island, New Zealand
Helgoland Bay see Helgoländer Bucht
Helgoländer Bucht 94 A2 var.
   Helgoland Bay, Heligoland Bight. bay
   NW Germany
Heligoland Bight see Helgoländer Bucht
Heliopolis see Baalbek
Hellas see Greece
Hellenic Republic see Greece
Hellevoetsluis 86 B4 Zuid-Holland,
   SW Netherlands
Hellín 93 E4 Castilla-La Mancha,
   C Spain
Darya-ye Helmand 122 D5 var. Rūd-e
   Hīrmand. river Afghanistan/Iran
Helmantica see Salamanca
Helmond 87 D5 Noord-Brabant,
   S Netherlands

Helsingborg 85 B7 prev. Hälsingborg.
   Skåne, S Sweden
Helsingfors see Helsinki
Helsinki 85 D6 Swe. Helsingfors.
   country capital (Finland) Etelä-Suomi,
   S Finland
Heltau see Cisnădie
Helvetia see Switzerland
Henan 128 C5 var. Henan Sheng,
   Honan, Yu. province C China
Henderson 40 B5 Kentucky, S USA
Henderson 47 D7 Nevada, W USA
Henderson 49 F3 Texas, SW USA
Hendū Kosh see Hindu Kush
Hengchow see Hengyang
Hengduan Shan 128 A5 mountain range
   SW China
Hengelo 86 E3 Overijssel, E Netherlands
Hengnan see Hengyang
Hengyang 128 C6 var. Hengnan, Heng-
   yang; prev. Hengchow. Hunan, S China
Heng-yang see Hengyang
Heniches'k 109 F4 Rus. Genichesk.
   Khersons'ka Oblast', S Ukraine
Hennebont 90 A3 Morbihan, NW France
Henrique de Carvalho see Saurimo
Henzada see Hinthada
Herakleion see Irákleio
Herāt 122 D4 var. Herat; anc. Aria.
   Herāt, W Afghanistan
Heredia 53 E4 Heredia, C Costa Rica
Hereford 49 E2 Texas, SW USA
Herford 94 B4 Nordrhein-Westfalen,
   NW Germany
Héristal see Herstal
Herk-de-Stad 87 C6 Limburg,
   NE Belgium
Herlen Gol/Herlen He see Kerulen
Hermannstadt see Sibiu
Hermansverk 85 A5 Sogn Og Fjordane,
   S Norway
Hermhausen see Hajnówka
Hermiston 46 C2 Oregon, NW USA
Hermon, Mount 119 B5 Ar. Jabal ash
   Shaykh. mountain S Syria
Hermosillo 50 B2 Sonora, NW Mexico
Hernösand see Härnösand
Herrera del Duque 92 D3 Extremadura,
   W Spain
Herselt 87 C5 Antwerpen, C Belgium
Herstal 87 D6 Fr. Héristal. Liège,
   E Belgium
Herzogenbusch see 's-Hertogenbosch
Hesse see Hessen
Hessen 95 B5 Eng./Fr. Hesse. state
   C Germany
Hevron see Hebron
Heydebrech see Kędzierzyn-Koźle
Heydekrug see Šilutė
Heywood Islands 146 C3 island group
   Western Australia
Hibbing 45 F1 Minnesota, N USA
Hibernia see Ireland
Hidalgo del Parral 50 C2 var. Parral.
   Chihuahua, N Mexico
Hida-sanmyaku 131 C5 mountain range
   Honshū, S Japan
Hierosolyma see Jerusalem
Hierro 70 A3 var. Ferro. island Islas
   Canarias, Spain, NE Atlantic Ocean
High Atlas 70 C2 Eng. High Atlas.
   mountain range C Morocco
High Atlas see Haut Atlas
High Plains see Great Plains
High Point 43 E1 North Carolina,
   SE USA
Hiiumaa 106 C2 Ger. Dagden, Swe.
   Dagö. island W Estonia
Hikurangi 150 D2 Northland, North
   Island, New Zealand
Hildesheim 94 B4 Niedersachsen,
   N Germany
Hilla see Al Ḥillah
Hillaby, Mount 55 G1 mountain
   N Barbados
Hill Bank 52 C1 Orange Walk, N Belize
Hillegom 86 C3 Zuid-Holland,
   W Netherlands
Hilo 47 B8 Hawaii, USA, C Pacific Ocean
Hilton Head Island 43 E2 South
   Carolina, SE USA
Hilversum 86 C3 Noord-Holland,
   C Netherlands
Himalaya/Himalaya Shan see Himalayas
Himalayas 135 E2 var. Himalaya, Chin.
   Himalaya Shan. mountain range S Asia
Himeji 131 C6 var. Himezi. Hyōgo,
   Honshū, SW Japan

Himezi see Himeji
Ḥimş 118 B4 var. Homs; anc. Emesa.
   Ḥimş, C Syria
Hîncești 108 D4 var. Hâncești; prev.
   Kotovsk. C Moldova
Hinchinbrook Island 148 D3 island
   Queensland, NE Australia
Hinds 151 C6 Canterbury, South Island,
   New Zealand
Hindu Kush 123 F4 Per. Hendū Kosh.
   mountain range Afghanistan/Pakistan
Hinesville 43 E3 Georgia, SE USA
Hinnøya 84 C3 Lapp. Iinnasuolu. island
   C Norway
Hinson Bay 42 A5 bay W Bermuda
   W Atlantic Ocean
Hinthada 136 B4 var. Henzada.
   Ayeyarwady, SW Myanmar (Burma)
Hios see Chíos
Hîrfanlı Barajı 116 C3 reservoir
   C Turkey
Hîrmand, Rūd-e see Helmand, Darya-ye
Hirosaki 130 D3 Aomori, Honshū,
   C Japan
Hiroshima 131 B6 var. Hirosima.
   Hiroshima, Honshū, SW Japan
Hirosima see Hiroshima
**Hirschberg/Hirschberg im
   Riesengebirge/Hirschberg in
   Schlesien** see Jelenia Góra
Hirson 90 D3 Aisne, N France
Hîrşova see Hârşova
Hispalis see Sevilla
Hispana/Hispania see Spain
Hispaniola 56 B1 island Dominion
   Republic/Haiti
Hitachi 131 D5 var. Hitati. Ibaraki,
   Honshū, S Japan
Hitati see Hitachi
Hitra 84 A4 prev. Hitteren. island
   S Norway
Hitteren see Hitra
Hjälmaren 85 C6 Eng. Lake Hjalmar.
   lake C Sweden
Hjalmar, Lake see Hjälmaren
Hjørring 85 B7 Nordjylland, N Denmark
Hkakabo Razi 126 B3 mountain
   Myanmar (Burma)/China
Hlobyne 109 F2 Rus. Globino.
   Poltavs'ka Oblast', NE Ukraine
Hlukhiv 109 F1 Rus. Glukhov. Sums'ka
   Oblast', NE Ukraine
Hlybokaye 107 D5 Rus. Glubokoye.
   Vitsyebskaya Voblasts', N Belarus
Hoa Binh 136 D3 N Vietnam
Hoang Lien Son 136 D3 mountain range
   N Vietnam
Hobart 149 C8 prev. Hobarton, Hobart
   Town. state capital Tasmania,
   SE Australia
Hobarton/Hobart Town see Hobart
Hobbs 49 E3 New Mexico, SW USA
Hobro 85 A7 Nordjylland, N Denmark
Hô Chi Minh 137 E6 var. Ho Chi Minh
   City; prev. Saigon. S Vietnam
Ho Chi Minh City see Hô Chi Minh
Hodeida see Al Ḥudaydah
Hódmezővásárhely 99 D7 Csongrád,
   SE Hungary
Hodna, Chott El 102 C4 var. Chott
   el-Hodna, Ar. Shatt al-Hodna. salt
   lake N Algeria
Hodna, Chott el-/Hodna, Shatt al- see
   Hodna, Chott El
Hodonín 99 C5 Ger. Göding.
   Jihomoravský Kraj, SE Czech Republic
Hoei see Huy
Hoey see Huy
Hof 95 C5 Bayern, SE Germany
Hofei see Hefei
Hōfu 131 B7 Yamaguchi, Honshū,
   SW Japan
Hofuf see Al Hufūf
Hogoley Islands see Chuuk Islands
Hohensalza see Inowrocław
Hohenstadt see Zábřeh
Hohes Venn see Hautes Fagnes
Hohe Tauern 95 C7 mountain range
   W Austria
Hohhot 127 F3 var. Huhehot,
   Huhohaote, Mong. Kuku-khoto; prev.
   Kweisui, Kwesui. Nei Mongol Zizhiqu,
   N China
Hôi An 137 E5 prev. Faifo. Quang Nam-
   Đa Năng, C Vietnam
Hoï-Hao/Hoihow see Haikou
Hokianga Harbour 150 C2 inlet
   SE Tasman Sea
Hokitika 151 B5 West Coast, South
   Island, New Zealand

Hokkaido *130 C2 prev.* Ezo, Yeso, Yezo. *island* NE Japan

Hola Prystan' *109 E4 Rus.* Golaya Pristan. Khersons'ka Oblast', S Ukraine

Holbrook *48 B2* Arizona, SW USA

Holetown *55 G1 prev.* Jamestown. W Barbados

Holguín *54 C2* Holguín, SE Cuba

Holin Gol *127 G2 prev.* Hulingol. Nei Mongol Zizhiqu, N China

Hollabrunn *95 E6* Niederösterreich, NE Austria

Holland *see* Netherlands

Hollandia *see* Jayapura

Holly Springs *42 C1* Mississippi, S USA

Holman *37 E3* Victoria Island, Northwest Territories, N Canada

Holmsund *84 D4* Västerbotten, N Sweden

Holon *119 A6 var.* Kholon; *prev.* Ḥolon. Tel Aviv, C Israel

Ḥolon *see* Holon

Holovanivs'k *109 E3 Rus.* Golovanevsk. Kirovohrads'ka Oblast', C Ukraine

Holstebro *85 A7* Midtjylland, W Denmark

Holsteinborg/Holsteinsborg/ Holstenborg/Holstensborg *see* Sisimiut

Holyhead *89 C5 Wel.* Caer Gybi. NW Wales, United Kingdom

Hombori *75 E3* Mopti, S Mali

Homs *see* Al Khums, Libya

Homs *see* Ḥimṣ

Homyel' *107 D7 Rus.* Gomel'. Homyel'skaya Voblasts', SE Belarus

Honan *see* Henan, China

Honan *see* Luoyang, China

Hondo *49 F4* Texas, SW USA

Hondo *see* Honshū

Honduras *52 C2 off.* Republic of Honduras. *country* Central America

HONDURAS
Central America

Official name Republic of Honduras
Formation 1838 / 1838
Capital Tegucigalpa
Population 7.8 million / 181 people per sq mile (70 people per sq km)
Total area 43,278 sq. miles (112,090 sq. km)
Languages Spanish*, Garifuna (Carib), English Creole
Religions Roman Catholic 97%, Protestant 3%
Ethnic mix Mestizo 90%, Black 5%, Amerindian 4%, White 1%
Government Presidential system
Currency Lempira = 100 centavos
Literacy rate 84%
Calorie consumption 2694 kilocalories

Honduras, Golfo de *see* Honduras, Gulf of

Honduras, Gulf of *52 C2 Sp.* Golfo de Honduras. *gulf* W Caribbean Sea

Honduras, Republic of *see* Honduras

Honefoss *85 B6* Buskerud, S Norway

Honey Lake *47 B5 lake* California, W USA

Hon Gai *see* Ha Long

Hongay *see* Ha Long

Hông Gai *see* Ha Long

Hông Hà, Sông *see* Red River

Hong Kong *128 A1 Chin.* Xianggang. Hong Kong, S China

Hong Kong Island *128 B2 island* S China Asia

Honiara *144 C3 country capital* (Solomon Islands) Guadalcanal, C Solomon Islands

Honjō *130 D4 var.* Honzyô, Yurihonjô. Akita, Honshū, C Japan

Honolulu *47 A8 state capital* O'ahu, Hawaii, USA, C Pacific Ocean

Honshu *131 E5 var.* Hondo, Honsyū. *island* SW Japan

Honsyû *see* Honshū

Honte *see* Westerschelde

Honzyô *see* Honjō

Hoogeveen *86 E2* Drenthe, NE Netherlands

Hoogezand-Sappemeer *86 E2* Groningen, NE Netherlands

Hoorn *86 C3* Noord-Holland, NW Netherlands

Hoosier State *see* Indiana

Hopa *117 E2* Artvin, NE Turkey

Hope *36 C3* British Columbia, SW Canada

Hopedale *39 F2* Newfoundland and Labrador, NE Canada

Hopeh/Hopei *see* Hebei

Hopkinsville *40 B5* Kentucky, S USA

Horasan *117 F3* Erzurum, NE Turkey

Horizon Deep *152 D4 trench* W Pacific Ocean

Horki *107 E6 Rus.* Gorki. Mahilyowskaya Voblasts', E Belarus

Horlivka *109 G3 Rom.* Adâncata, *Rus.* Gorlovka. Donets'ka Oblast', E Ukraine

Hormoz, Tangeh-ye *see* Hormuz, Strait of

Hormuz, Strait of *120 D4 var.* Strait of Ormuz, *Per.* Tangeh-ye Hormoz. *strait* Iran/Oman

Cape Horn *65 C8 Eng.* Cape Horn. *headland* S Chile

Horn, Cape *see* Hornos, Cabo de

Hornsby *148 E1* New South Wales, SE Australia

Horodnya *109 E1 Rus.* Gorodnya. Chernihivs'ka Oblast', NE Ukraine

Horodok *108 B2 Pol.* Gródek Jagielloński, *Rus.* Gorodok, Gorodok Yagellonski. L'viv'ska Oblast', NW Ukraine

Horodyshche *109 E2 Rus.* Gorodishche. Cherkas'ka Oblast', C Ukraine

Horoshiri-dake *130 D2 var.* Horosiri Dake. *mountain* Hokkaidō, N Japan

Horosiri Dake *see* Horoshiri-dake

Horsburgh Atoll *132 A4 var.* Goidhoo Atoll. *atoll* N Maldives

Horseshoe Bay *42 A5 bay* W Bermuda

Horseshoe Seamounts *80 A4 seamount range* E Atlantic Ocean

Horsham *149 B7* Victoria, SE Australia

Horst *87 D5* Limburg, SE Netherlands

Horten *85 B6* Vestfold, S Norway

Horyn' *107 B7 Rus.* Goryn. *river* NW Ukraine

Hosingen *87 D7* Diekirch, NE Luxembourg

Hospitalet *see* L'Hospitalet de Llobregat

Hotan *126 B4 var.* Khotan, *Chin.* Ho-t'ien. Xinjiang Uygur Zizhiqu, NW China

Ho-t'ien *see* Hotan

Hoting *84 C4* Jämtland, C Sweden

Hot Springs *42 B1* Arkansas, C USA

Hötzing *see* Hateg

Houayxay *136 C3 var.* Ban Houayxay. Bokèo, N Laos

Houghton *40 B1* Michigan, N USA

Houilles *91 B5* Yvelines, Île-de-France, N France Europe

Houlton *41 H1* Maine, NE USA

Houma *42 B3* Louisiana, S USA

Houston *49 H4* Texas, SW USA

Hovd *126 C2 var.* Khovd, Kobdo; *prev.* Jirgalanta. Hovd, W Mongolia

Hove *89 E7* SE England, United Kingdom

Hoverla, Hora *108 C3 Rus.* Gora Goverla. *mountain* W Ukraine

Hovsgol, Lake *see* Hövsgöl Nuur

Hövsgöl Nuur *126 D1 var.* Lake Hovsgol. *lake* N Mongolia

Howa, Ouadi *see* Howar, Wâdi

Howar, Wadi *72 A3 var.* Ouadi Howa. *river* Chad/Sudan

Howrah *see* Hāora

Hoy *88 C2 island* N Scotland, United Kingdom

Hoyerswerda *94 D4 Lus.* Wojerecy. Sachsen, E Germany

Hpa-an *136 B4 var.* Pa-an. Kayin State, S Myanmar (Burma)

Hpyu *see* Phyu

Hradec Králové *99 B5 Ger.* Königgrätz. Královéhradecký Kraj, N Czech Republic

Hrandzichy *107 B5 Rus.* Grandichi. Hrodzyenskaya Voblasts', W Belarus

Hranice *99 C5 Ger.* Mährisch-Weisskirchen. Olomoucký Kraj, E Czech Republic

Hrebinka *109 E2 Rus.* Grebenka. Poltavs'ka Oblast', NE Ukraine

Hrodna *107 B5 Pol.* Grodno. Hrodzyenskaya Voblasts', W Belarus

Hrvatska *see* Croatia

Hsia-men *see* Xiamen

Hsiang-t'an *see* Xiangtan

Hsi Chiang *see* Xi Jiang

Hsing-K'ai Hu *see* Khanka, Lake

Hsi-ning/Hsining *see* Xining

Hsinking *see* Changchun

Hsin-yang *see* Xinyang

Hsu-chou *see* Xuzhou

Htawei *see* Dawei

Huacho *60 C4* Lima, W Peru

Hua Hin *see* Ban Hua Hin

Huaihua *128 C3* Hunan, S China

Huailai *128 C3 var.* Shacheng. Hebei, E China

Huainan *128 D5 var.* Huai-nan, Hwainan. Anhui, E China

Huai-nan *see* Huainan

Huajuapan *51 F5 var.* Huajuapan de León. Oaxaca, SE Mexico

Huajuapan de León *see* Huajuapan

Hualapai Peak *48 A2 mountain* Arizona, SW USA

Huallaga, Río *60 C3 river* N Peru

Huambo *78 B2* Port. Nova Lisboa. Huambo, C Angola

Huancavelica *60 D4* Huancavelica, SW Peru

Huancayo *60 D3* Junín, C Peru

Huang Hai *see* Yellow Sea

Huangshi *128 C5 var.* Huang-shih, Hwangshih. Hubei, C China

Huang-shih *see* Huangshi

Huanta *60 D4* Ayacucho, C Peru

Huánuco *60 C3* Huánuco, C Peru

Huanuni *61 F4* Oruro, W Bolivia

Huaral *60 C4* Lima, W Peru

Huarás *see* Huaraz

Huaraz *60 C3 var.* Huarás. Ancash, W Peru

Huarmey *60 C3* Ancash, W Peru

Huatabampo *50 C2* Sonora, NW Mexico

Hubli *132 B3* Karnātaka, SW India

Huddersfield *89 D5* N England, United Kingdom

Hudiksvall *85 C5* Gävleborg, C Sweden

Hudson Bay *37 G4 bay* NE Canada

Hudson Strait *37 H3 Fr.* Détroit d'Hudson. *strait* Northwest Territories/ Québec, NE Canada

Hudur *see* Xuddur

Huê *150 A4* Tha Thiên-Huê, C Vietnam

Huehuetenango *52 A2* Huehuetenango, W Guatemala

Huelva *92 C4 anc.* Onuba. Andalucía, SW Spain

Huesca *93 F2 anc.* Osca. Aragón, NE Spain

Huéscar *93 E4* Andalucía, S Spain

Hughenden *148 C3* Queensland, NE Australia

Hugo *49 G2* Oklahoma, C USA

Huíla Plateau *78 B2 plateau* S Angola

Huixtla *51 G5* Chiapas, SE Mexico

Hulingol *see* Holin Gol

Hull *38 D4* Québec, SE Canada

Hull *see* Kingston upon Hull

Hull Island *see* Orona

Hulst *87 B5* Zeeland, SW Netherlands

Hulun *see* Hulun Buir

Hulun Buir *127 F1 var.* Hailar; *prev.* Hulun. Nei Mongol Zizhiqu, N China

Hu-lun Ch'ih *see* Hulun Nur

Hulun Nur *127 F1 var.* Hu-lun Ch'ih; *prev.* Dalai Nor. *lake* NE China

Humaitá *62 D2* Amazonas, N Brazil

Humboldt River *47 C5 river* Nevada, W USA

Humphreys Peak *48 B1 mountain* Arizona, SW USA

Humpolec *99 B5 Ger.* Gumpolds, Humpoletz. Vysočina, C Czech Republic

Humpoletz *see* Humpolec

Hunan *128 C5 var.* Hunan Sheng. Xiang. *province* S China

Hunan Sheng *see* Hunan

Hunedoara *108 B4 Ger.* Eisenmarkt, *Hung.* Vajdahunyad. Hunedoara, SW Romania

Hünfeld *95 B5* Hessen, C Germany

Hungarian People's Republic *see* Hungary

Hungary *99 C6 off.* Republic of Hungary, *Ger.* Ungarn, *Hung.* Magyarország, *Rom.* Ungaria, *SCr.* Madarska, *Ukr.* Uhorshchyna; *prev.* Hungarian People's Republic. *country* C Europe

HUNGARY
Central Europe

Official name Republic of Hungary
Formation 1918 / 1947
Capital Budapest
Population 10 million / 280 people per sq mile (108 people per sq km)
Total area 35,919 sq. miles (93,030 sq. km)
Languages Hungarian (Magyar)*
Religions Roman Catholic 52%, Calvinist 16%, Other 15%, Nonreligious 14%, Lutheran 3%
Ethnic mix Magyar 90%, Roma 4%, German 3%, Serb 2%, Other 1%
Government Parliamentary system
Currency Forint = 100 fillér
Literacy rate 99%
Calorie consumption 3477 kilocalories

Hungary, Plain of *see* Great Hungarian Plain

Hungary, Republic of *see* Hungary

Hunjiang *see* Baishan

Hunter Island *149 B8 island* Tasmania, SE Australia

Huntington *40 D4* West Virginia, NE USA

Huntington Beach *47 B8* California, W USA

Huntly *150 D3* Waikato, North Island, New Zealand

Huntsville *42 D1* Alabama, S USA

Huntsville *49 G3* Texas, SW USA

Hurghada *see* Al Ghurdaqah

Huron *45 E3* South Dakota, N USA

Huron, Lake *40 D2 lake* Canada/USA

Hurukawa *see* Furukawa

Hurunui *151 C5 river* South Island, New Zealand

Húsavík *83 E4* Nordhurland Eystra, NE Iceland

Husté *see* Khust

Husum *94 B2* Schleswig-Holstein, N Germany

Huszt *see* Khust

Hutchinson *45 E5* Kansas, C USA

Hutchinson Island *43 F4 island* Florida, SE USA

Huy *87 C6 Dut.* Hoei, Hoey. Liège, E Belgium

Huzi *see* Fuji

Hvannadalshnúkur *83 E5 volcano* S Iceland

Hvar *100 B4 It.* Lesina; *anc.* Pharus. *island* S Croatia

Hwainan *see* Huainan

Hwange *78 D3 prev.* Wankie. Matabeleland North, W Zimbabwe

Hwang-Hae *see* Yellow Sea

Hwangshih *see* Huangshi

Hyargas Nuur *126 C2 lake* NW Mongolia

Hyderābād *134 D5 var.* Haidarabad. *state capital* Andhra Pradesh, C India

Hyderābād *134 B3 var.* Haidarabad. Sind, SE Pakistan

Hyères *91 D6* Var, SE France

Hyères, Îles d' *91 D6 island group* S France

Hypanis *see* Kuban'

Hyrcania *see* Gorgān

Hyvinge *see* Hyvinkää

Hyvinkää *85 D5 Swe.* Hyvinge. Etelä-Suomi, S Finland

I

Iader *see* Zadar

Ialomiţa *108 C5 river* SE Romania

Iaşi *108 D3 Ger.* Jassy. Iaşi, NE Romania

Ibadan *75 F5* Oyo, SW Nigeria

Ibagué *58 B3* Tolima, C Colombia

Ibar *see* Ibër

Ibarra *60 B1 var.* San Miguel de Ibarra. Imbabura, N Ecuador

Ibër *100 D4 Serb.* Ibar. *river* C Serbia

Iberia *see* Spain

Iberian Mountains *see* Ibérico, Sistema

Iberian Peninsula *80 B4 physical region* Portugal/Spain

Iberian Plain *80 B4 abyssal plain* E Atlantic Ocean

Iberia, Cordillera *see* Ibérico, Sistema

Ibérico, Sistema *93 E2 var.* Cordillera Ibérica, *Eng.* Iberian Mountains. *mountain range* NE Spain

Ibiza see Eivissa
Ibo see Sassandra
Ica 60 D4 Ica, SW Peru
Icaria see Ikaría
Içá, Rio 62 C2 var. Río Putumayo. river NW South America
Içá, Rio see Putumayo, Río
Içel see Mersin
Iceland 83 E4 off. Republic of Iceland, Dan. Island, Icel. Ísland. country N Atlantic Ocean

Iceland Basin 80 B1 undersea basin N Atlantic Ocean
Icelandic Plateau see Iceland Plateau
Iceland Plateau 155 B6 var. Icelandic Plateau. undersea plateau S Greenland Sea
Iceland, Republic of see Iceland
Iconium see Konya
Iculisma see Angoulême
Idabel 49 H2 Oklahoma, C USA
Idaho 46 D3 off. State of Idaho, also known as Gem of the Mountains, Gem State. state NW USA
Idaho Falls 46 E3 Idaho, NW USA
Idensalmi see Iisalmi
Idfû 72 B2 var. Edfu. SE Egypt
Idi Amin, Lac see Edward, Lake
Idini 74 B2 Trarza, W Mauritania
Idlib 118 B3 Idlib, NW Syria
Idre 85 B5 Dalarna, C Sweden
Iecava 106 C3 S Latvia
Ieper 87 A6 Fr. Ypres. West-Vlaanderen, W Belgium
Ierápetra 105 D8 Kríti, Greece, E Mediterranean Sea
Ierisós see Ierissós
Ierissós 104 C4 var. Ierisós. Kentrikí Makedonía, N Greece
Iferouâne 75 G2 Agadez, N Niger
Ifôghas, Adrar des 75 E2 var. Adrar des Iforas. mountain range NE Mali
Iforas, Adrar des see Ifôghas, Adrar des
Igarka 114 D3 Krasnoyarskiy Kray, N Russian Federation
Igaunija see Estonia
Iglau/Iglawa/Iglawa see Jihlava
Iglesias 97 A5 Sardegna, Italy, C Mediterranean Sea
Igloolik 37 G2 Nunavut, N Canada
Igoumenítsa 104 A4 Ípeiros, W Greece
Iguaçu, Rio 63 E4 Sp. Río Iguazú. river Argentina/Brazil
Iguaçu, Salto do 63 E4 Sp. Cataratas del Iguazú; prev. Victoria Falls. waterfall Argentina/Brazil
Iguala 51 E4 var. Iguala de la Independencia. Guerrero, S Mexico
Iguala de la Independencia see Iguala
Iguazú, Cataratas del see Iguaçu, Salto do
Iguazú, Río see Iguaçu, Rio
Iguid, Erg see Iguidi, 'Erg
Iguidi, 'Erg 70 C3 var. Erg Iguid. desert Algeria/Mauritania
Ihavandhippolhu Atoll 132 A3 var. Ihavandiffulu Atoll.
Ihavandiffulu Atoll see Ihavandhippolhu Atoll
Ihosy 79 F4 Fianarantsoa, S Madagascar
Iinnasuolu see Hinnøya
Iisalmi 84 E4 var. Idensalmi. Itä-Suomi, C Finland
IJmuiden 86 C3 Noord-Holland, W Netherlands
IJssel 86 D3 var. Yssel. river Netherlands
IJsselmeer 86 C2 prev. Zuider Zee. lake N Netherlands

IJsselmuiden 86 D3 Overijssel, E Netherlands
Ijzer 87 A6 river W Belgium
Ikaahuk see Sachs Harbour
Ikaluktutiak see Cambridge Bay
Ikaría 105 D6 var. Kariot, Nicaria, Nikaria; anc. Icaria. island Dodekánisa, Greece, Aegean Sea
Ikela 77 D6 Équateur, C Dem. Rep. Congo
Iki 131 A7 island SW Japan
Ilagan 139 E1 Luzon, N Philippines
Ilave 61 E4 Puno, S Peru
Iława 98 D3 Ger. Deutsch-Eylau. Warmińsko-Mazurskie, NE Poland
Ilebo 77 C6 prev. Port-Francqui. Kasai-Occidental, W Dem. Rep. Congo
Île-de-France 90 C3 cultural region N France
Ilerda see Lleida
Ilfracombe 89 C7 SW England, United Kingdom
Ílhavo 92 B2 Aveiro, N Portugal
Iliamna Lake 36 C3 lake Alaska, USA
Il'ichevsk see Illichivs'k, Ukraine
Ilici see Elche
Iligan 139 E2 off. Iligan City. Mindanao, S Philippines
Iligan City see Iligan
Illapel 64 B4 Coquimbo, C Chile
Illichivs'k 109 E4 Rus. Il'ichevsk. Odes'ka Oblast', SW Ukraine
Illicis see Elche
Illinois 40 A4 off. State of Illinois, also known as Prairie State, Sucker State. state C USA
Illinois River 40 B4 river Illinois, N USA
Illurco see Lorca
Illuro see Mataró
Ilo 61 E4 Moquegua, SW Peru
Iloilo 139 E2 off. Iloilo City. Panay Island, C Philippines
Iloilo City see Iloilo
Ilorin 75 F4 Kwara, W Nigeria
Ilovlya 111 B6 Volgogradskaya Oblast', SW Russian Federation
Iluh see Batman
Il'yaly see Gurbansoltan Eje
Imatra 85 E5 Etelä-Suomi, SE Finland
Imbros see Gökçeada
Imishli see İmişli
İmişli 117 H3 Rus. Imishli. C Azerbaijan
Imola 96 C3 Emilia-Romagna, N Italy
Imperatriz 63 F2 Maranhão, NE Brazil
Imperia 96 A3 Liguria, NW Italy
Impfondo 77 C5 Likouala, NE Congo
Imphāl 135 H3 state capital Manipur, NE India
Imroz Adası see Gökçeada
Inagua Islands see Little Inagua
Inagua Islands see Great Inagua
Inarijärvi 84 D2 Lapp. Aanaarjävri, Swe. Enareträsk. lake N Finland
Ináu see Ineu
Inawashiro-ko 131 D5 var. Inawasiro Ko. lake Honshū, C Japan
Inawasiro Ko see Inawashiro-ko
Íncesu 116 D3 Kayseri, Turkey Asia
Incheon 129 E4, Jap. Jinsen; prev. Chemulpo, Inch'ŏn. NW South Korea
Inch'ŏn see Incheon
Incudine, Monte 91 E7 mountain Corse, France, C Mediterranean Sea
Indefatigable Island see Santa Cruz, Isla
Independence 45 F4 Missouri, C USA
Independence Fjord 83 E1 fjord N Greenland
Independence Island see Malden Island
Independence Mountains 46 C4 mountain range Nevada, W USA

India see Indija
Indiana 40 B4 off. State of Indiana, also known as Hoosier State. state N USA
Indianapolis 40 C4 state capital Indiana, N USA
Indian Church 52 C1 Orange Walk, N Belize
Indian Desert see Thar Desert
Indianola 45 F4 Iowa, C USA
Indian Union see India
India, Republic of see India
India, Union of see India
Indigirka 115 F2 river NE Russian Federation
Indija 100 D3 Hung. India; prev. Indjija. Vojvodina, N Serbia
Indira Point 132 G3 headland Andaman and Nicobar Island, India, NE Indian Ocean
Indjija see Indija
Indomed Fracture Zone 141 B6 tectonic feature SW Indian Ocean
Indonesia 138 B4 off. Republic of Indonesia, Ind. Republik Indonesia; prev. Dutch East Indies, Netherlands East Indies, United States of Indonesia. country SE Asia

Indonesian Borneo see Kalimantan
Indonesia, Republic of see Indonesia
Indonesia, Republik see Indonesia
Indonesia, United States of see Indonesia
Indore 134 D4 Madhya Pradesh, C India
Indreville see Châteauroux
Indus 134 C2 Chin. Yindu He; prev. Yin-tu Ho. river S Asia
Indus Cone see Indus Fan
Indus Fan 112 C5 var. Indus Cone. undersea fan N Arabian Sea
Indus, Mouths of the 134 B4 delta S Pakistan
İnebolu 116 C2 Kastamonu, N Turkey
Ineu 108 A4 Hung. Borosjenő; prev. Ináu. Arad, W Romania
Infiernillo, Presa del 51 E4 reservoir S Mexico
Inglewood 46 D2 California, W USA
Ingolstadt 95 C6 Bayern, S Germany
Ingulets see Inhulets'
Inguri see Enguri
Inhambane 79 E4 Inhambane, SE Mozambique
Inhulets' 109 F3 Rus. Ingulets. Dnipropetrovs'ka Oblast', E Ukraine
I-ning see Yining
Inis see Ennis
Inis Ceithleann see Enniskillen
Inn 95 C6 river C Europe
Innaanganeq 82 C1 var. Kap York. headland NW Greenland

Inner Hebrides 88 B4 island group W Scotland, United Kingdom
Inner Islands 79 H1 var. Central Group. island group NE Seychelles
Innisfail 148 D3 Queensland, NE Australia
Inniskilling see Enniskillen
Innsbruch see Innsbruck
Innsbruck 95 C7 var. Innsbruch. Tirol, W Austria
Inoucdjouac see Inukjuak
Inowazlaw see Inowrocław
Inowrocław 98 C3 Ger. Hohensalza; prev. Inowrazlaw. Kujawski-pomorskie, C Poland
I-n-Sakane, 'Erg 75 E2 desert N Mali
I-n-Salah 70 D3 var. In Salah. C Algeria
Insterburg see Chernyakhovsk
Insula see Lille
Inta 110 E3 Respublika Komi, NW Russian Federation
Interamna see Teramo
Interamna Nahars see Terni
International Falls 45 F1 Minnesota, N USA
Inukjuak 38 D2 var. Inoucdjouac; prev. Port Harrison. Québec, NE Canada
Inuuvik see Inuvik
Inuvik 36 D3 var. Inuuvik. Northwest Territories, NW Canada
Invercargill 151 A7 Southland, South Island, New Zealand
Inverness 88 C3 N Scotland, United Kingdom
Investigator Ridge 141 D5 undersea ridge E Indian Ocean
Investigator Strait 149 B7 strait South Australia
Inyangani 78 D3 mountain NE Zimbabwe
Ioánnina 104 A4 var. Janina, Yannina. Ípeiros, W Greece
Iola 45 F5 Kansas, C USA
Ionia Basin see Ionian Basin
Ionian Basin 80 D5 var. Ionia Basin. undersea basin Ionian Sea, C Mediterranean Sea
Ionian Sea 103 E3 Gk. Iónio Pélagos, It. Mar Ionio. sea C Mediterranean Sea
Iónioi Nísoi 105 A5 Eng. Ionian Islands. region W Greece
Ionio, Mar/Iónio Pélagos see Ionian Sea
Íos 105 D6 var. Nio. island Kykládes, Greece, Aegean Sea
Íos 105 D6 var. Nio. island Kykládes, Greece, Aegean Sea
Íos 105 D6 var. Nio. island Kykládes, Greece, Aegean Sea
Ioulís 105 C6 prev. Kéa. Tziá, Kykládes, Greece, Aegean Sea
Iowa 45 F3 off. State of Iowa, also known as Hawkeye State. state C USA
Iowa City 45 G3 Iowa, C USA
Iowa Falls 45 G3 Iowa, C USA
Ipel' 99 C6 var. Ipoly, Ger. Eipel. river Hungary/Slovakia
Ipiales 58 A4 Nariño, SW Colombia
Ipoh 138 B3 Perak, Peninsular Malaysia
Ipoly see Ipel'
Ippy 76 C4 Ouaka, C Central African Republic
Ipswich 149 E5 Queensland, E Australia
Ipswich 89 E6 hist. Gipeswic. E England, United Kingdom
Iqaluit 37 H3 prev. Frobisher Bay. province capital Baffin Island, Nunavut, NE Canada
Iquique 64 B1 Tarapacá, N Chile
Iquitos 60 C1 Loreto, N Peru
Irákleio 105 D7 var. Herakleion, Eng. Candia; prev. Iráklion. Kríti, Greece, E Mediterranean Sea
Iráklion see Irákleio
Iran 120 C3 off. Islamic Republic of Iran; prev. Persia. country SW Asia

IRAN
(continued)

Arabic, Baluchi
Religions Shi'a Muslim 89%,
Sunni Muslim 9%, Other 2%
Ethnic mix Persian 51%, Azari 24%,
Other 10%, Lur and Bakhtiari 8%,
Kurdish 7%
Government Islamic theocracy
Currency Iranian rial = 100 dinars
Literacy rate 85%
Calorie consumption 3143 kilocalories

Iranian Plateau 120 D3 *var.* Plateau of
Iran. *plateau* N Iran
Iran, Islamic Republic of *see* Iran
Iran, Plateau of *see* Iranian Plateau
Irapuato 51 E4 Guanajuato, C Mexico
Iraq 120 B3 *off.* Republic of Iraq, *Ar.*
'Irāq. *country* SW Asia

IRAQ
Southwest Asia

Official name Republic of Iraq
Formation 1932 / 1990
Capital Baghdad
Population 32.7 million / 194 people
per sq mile (75 people per sq km)
Total area 168,753 sq. miles
(437,072 sq. km)
Languages Arabic*, Kurdish*, Turkic
languages, Armenian, Assyrian
Religions Shi'a Muslim 60%,
Sunni Muslim 35%, Other (including
Christian) 5%
Ethnic mix Arab 80%, Kurdish 15%,
Turkmen 3%, Other 2%
Government Parliamentary system
Currency New Iraqi dinar = 1000 fils
Literacy rate 78%
Calorie consumption 2197 kilocalories

'Irāq *see* Iraq
Iraq, Republic of *see* Iraq
Irbid 119 B5 Irbid, N Jordan
Irbil *see* Arbil
Ireland 89 A5 *off.* Republic of Ireland, *Ir.*
Éire. *country* NW Europe

IRELAND
Northwest Europe

Official name Ireland
Formation 1922 / 1922
Capital Dublin
Population 4.5 million / 169 people
per sq mile (65 people per sq km)
Total area 27,135 sq. miles (70,280 sq. km)
Languages English*, Irish Gaelic*
Religions Roman Catholic 87%,
Other and nonreligious 10%, Anglican 3%
Ethnic mix Irish 99%, Other 1%
Government Parliamentary system
Currency Euro = 100 cents
Literacy rate 99%
Calorie consumption 3617 kilocalories

Ireland 80 C3 *Lat.* Hibernia. *island*
Ireland/United Kingdom
Ireland, Republic of *see* Ireland
Irian *see* New Guinea
Irian Barat *see* Papua
Irian Jaya *see* Papua
Irian, Teluk *see* Cenderawasih, Teluk
Iringa 73 C7 Iringa, C Tanzania
Iriomote-jima 130 A4 *island* Sakishima-
shotō, SW Japan
Iriona 52 D2 Colón, NE Honduras
Irish Sea 89 C5 *Ir.* Muir Éireann. *sea*
C British Isles
Irkutsk 115 E4 Irkutskaya Oblast',
S Russian Federation
Irminger Basin *see* Reykjanes Basin
Iroise 90 A3 *sea* NW France
Iron Mountain 40 B2 Michigan, N USA
Ironwood 40 B1 Michigan, N USA
Irrawaddy 136 B2 *var.* Ayeyarwady.
river W Myanmar (Burma)
Irrawaddy, Mouths of the 137 A5 *delta*
SW Myanmar (Burma)
Irtish *see* Yertis
Irtysh *see* Yertis
Irun 93 E1 *Cast.* Irún. País Vasco,
N Spain
Irún *see* Irun
Iruña *see* Pamplona

Isabela, Isla 60 A5 *var.* Albemarle Island.
island Galápagos Islands, Ecuador,
E Pacific Ocean
Isaccea 108 D4 Tulcea, E Romania
Isachsen 37 F1 Ellef Ringnes Island,
Nunavut, N Canada
Ísafjördhur 83 E4 Vestfirdhir,
NW Iceland
Isbarta *see* İsparta
Isca Damnoniorum *see* Exeter
Ise 131 C6 Mie, Honshū, SW Japan
Iseghem *see* Izegem
Isère 91 D5 *river* E France
Isernia 97 D5 *var.* Æsernia. Molise,
C Italy
Ise-wan 131 C6 *bay* S Japan
Isfahan *see* Eşfahān
Isha Baydhabo *see* Baydhabo
Ishigaki-jima 130 A4 *island* Sakishima-
shotō, SW Japan
Ishikari-wan 130 C2 *bay* Hokkaidō,
NE Japan
Ishim 114 C4 Tyumenskaya Oblast',
C Russian Federation
Ishinomaki 130 D4 *var.* Isinomaki.
Miyagi, Honshū, C Japan
Ishkashim *see* Ishkoshim
Ishkoshim 123 F3 *Rus.* Ishkashim.
S Tajikistan
Isinomaki *see* Ishinomaki
Isiro 77 E5 Orientale, NE Dem. Rep.
Congo
Iskãr *see* Iskür
İskenderun 116 D4 *Eng.* Alexandretta.
Hatay, S Turkey
İskenderun Körfezi 118 A2 *Eng.* Gulf of
Alexandretta. *gulf* S Turkey
Iskur 104 C2 *var.* Iskãr. *river*
NW Bulgaria
Yazovir Iskur 104 B2 *prev.* Yazovir
Stalin. *reservoir* W Bulgaria
Isla Cristina 92 C4 Andalucía, S Spain
Isla de León *see* San Fernando
Islāmābād 134 C1 *country capital*
(Pakistan) Federal Capital Territory
Islāmābād, NE Pakistan
Island/Ísland *see* Iceland
Islay 88 B4 *island* SW Scotland, United
Kingdom
Isle 91 B5 *river* W France
Isle of Man 89 B5 *UK crown dependency*
NW Europe
Isles of Scilly 89 B8 *island group*
SW England, United Kingdom
Ismailia *see* Al Ismā'īlīya
Ismâ'ilîya *see* Al Ismā'īlīya
Ismid *see* İzmit
Isnã 72 B2 *var.* Esna. SE Egypt
Isoka 78 D1 Northern, NE Zambia
İsparta 116 B4 *var.* Isbarta. İsparta,
SW Turkey
İspir 117 E3 Erzurum, NE Turkey
Israel 119 A7 *off.* State of Israel, *var.*
Medinat Israel, *Heb.* Yisrael, Yisra'el.
country SW Asia

ISRAEL
Southwest Asia

Official name State of Israel
Formation 1948 / 1994
Capital Jerusalem (not internationally
recognized)
Population 7.6 million / 968 people
per sq mile (374 people per sq km)
Total area 8019 sq. miles (20,770 sq. km)
Languages Hebrew*, Arabic*,
Yiddish, German, Russian, Polish,
Romanian, Persian
Religions Jewish 76%, Muslim (mainly
Sunni) 16%, Other 4%, Druze 2%,
Christian 2%
Ethnic mix Jewish 76%, Arab 20%,
Other 4%
Government Parliamentary system
Currency Shekel = 100 agorot
Literacy rate 97%
Calorie consumption 3569 kilocalories

Israel, State of *see* Israel
Issa *see* Vis
Issiq Köl *see* Issyk-Kul', Ozero
Issoire 91 C5 Puy-de-Dôme, C France
Issyk-Kul' *see* Balykchy
Issyk-Kul', Ozero 123 G2 *var.* Issiq Köl,
Kir. Ysyk-Köl. *lake* E Kyrgyzstan
İstanbul 116 B2 *Bul.* Tsarigrad, *Eng.*
Istanbul, *prev.* Constantinople; *anc.*
Byzantium. İstanbul, NW Turkey

Istarska Županija *see* Istra
Istra 100 A2 *off.* Istarska Županija.
province NW Croatia
Istra 100 A3 *Eng.* Istria, *Ger.* Istrien.
cultural region NW Croatia
Istria/Istrien *see* Istra
Itabuna 63 G3 Bahia, E Brazil
Itagüí 58 B3 Antioquia, W Colombia
Itaipú, Represa de 63 E4 *reservoir* Brazil/
Paraguay
Itaituba 63 E2 Pará, NE Brazil
**Italia/Italiana, Republica/Italian
Republic, The** *see* Italy
Italian Somaliland *see* Somalia
Italy 96 C3 *off.* The Italian Republic, *It.*
Italia, Repubblica Italiana. *country*
S Europe

ITALY
Southern Europe

Official name Italian Republic
Formation 1861 / 1947
Capital Rome
Population 60.8 million / 536 people
per sq mile (207 people per sq km)
Total area 116,305 sq. miles
(301,230 sq. km)
Languages Italian*, German, French,
Rhaeto-Romanic, Sardinian
Religions Roman Catholic 85%,
Other and nonreligious 13%, Muslim 2%
Ethnic mix Italian 94%, Other 4%,
Sardinian 2%
Government Parliamentary system
Currency Euro = 100 cents
Literacy rate 99%
Calorie consumption 3627 kilocalories

Iténez, Río *see* Guaporé, Rio
Ithaca 41 E3 New York, NE USA
It Hearrenfean *see* Heerenveen
Itoigawa 131 C5 Niigata, Honshū,
C Japan
Itseqqortoormiit *see* Ittoqqortoormiit
Ittoqqortoormiit 83 E3 *var.*
Itseqqortoormiit, *Dan.* Scoresbysund,
Eng. Scoresby Sound. Tunu,
C Greenland
Iturup, Ostrov 130 E1 *island* Kuril'skiye
Ostrova, SE Russian Federation
Itzehoe 94 B2 Schleswig-Holstein,
N Germany
Ivalo 84 D2 *Lapp.* Avveel, Avvil. Lappi,
N Finland
Ivanava 107 B7 *Pol.* Janów, Janów
Poleski, *Rus.* Ivanovo. Brestskaya
Voblasts', SW Belarus
Ivangrad *see* Berane
Ivanhoe 149 C6 New South Wales,
SE Australia
Ivano-Frankivs'k 108 C2 *Ger.* Stanislau,
Pol. Stanisławów, *Rus.* Ivano-
Frankovsk; *prev.* Stanislav. Ivano-
Frankivs'ka Oblast', W Ukraine
Ivano-Frankovsk *see* Ivano-Frankivs'k
Ivanovo 111 B5 Ivanovskaya Oblast',
W Russian Federation
Ivanovo *see* Ivanava
Ivantsevichi/Ivatsevichi *see* Ivatsevichy
Ivatsevichy 107 B6 *Pol.* Iwacewicze, *Rus.*
Ivantsevichi, Ivatsevichi. Brestskaya
Voblasts', SW Belarus
Ivigtut *see* Ivittuut
Ivittuut 82 B4 *var.* Ivigtut. Kitaa,
S Greenland
Iviza *see* Eivissa\Ibiza
Ivory Coast *see* Côte d'Ivoire
Ivory Coast, Republic of the *see* Côte
d'Ivoire
Ivujivik 38 D1 Québec, NE Canada
Iwacewicze *see* Ivatsevichy
Iwaki 131 D5 Fukushima, Honshū,
N Japan
Iwakuni 131 B7 Yamaguchi, Honshū,
SW Japan
Iwanai 130 C2 Hokkaidō, NE Japan
Iwate 130 D3 Iwate, Honshū, N Japan
Ixtapa 51 E5 Guerrero, S Mexico
Ixtepec 51 F5 Oaxaca, SE Mexico
Iyo-nada 131 B7 *sea* S Japan
Izabal, Lago de 52 B2 *prev.* Golfo Dulce.
lake E Guatemala
Īzad Khvāst 120 D3 Fārs, C Iran
Izegem 87 A6 *prev.* Iseghem. West-
Vlaanderen, W Belgium
Izhevsk 111 D5 *prev.* Ustinov.
Udmurtskaya Respublika, NW Russian
Federation

Izmail *see* Izmayil
Izmayil 108 D4 *Rus.* Izmail. Odes'ka
Oblast', SW Ukraine
İzmir 116 A3 *prev.* Smyrna. İzmir,
W Turkey
İzmit 116 B2 *var.* Ismid; *anc.* Astacus.
Kocaeli, NW Turkey
İznik Gölü 116 B3 *lake* NW Turkey
Izu-hanto 131 D6 *peninsula* Honshū,
S Japan
Izu Shichito *see* Izu-shotō
Izu-shoto 131 D6 *var.* Izu Shichito.
island group S Japan
Izvor 104 B2 Pernik, W Bulgaria
Izyaslav 108 C2 Khmel'nyts'ka Oblast',
W Ukraine
Izyum 109 G2 Kharkivs'ka Oblast',
E Ukraine

J

Jabal ash Shifa 120 A4 *desert* NW Saudi
Arabia
Jabalpur 135 E4 *prev.* Jubbulpore.
Madhya Pradesh, C India
Jabbūl, Sabkhat al 118 B2 *sabkha*
NW Syria
Jablah 118 A3 *var.* Jeble, *Fr.* Djéblé. Al
Lādhiqīyah, W Syria
Jaca 93 F1 Aragón, NE Spain
Jacaltenango 52 A2 Huehuetenango,
W Guatemala
Jackson 42 B2 *state capital* Mississippi,
S USA
Jackson 45 H5 Missouri, C USA
Jackson 42 C1 Tennessee, S USA
Jackson Head 151 A6 *headland* South
Island, New Zealand
Jacksonville 43 E3 Florida, SE USA
Jacksonville 40 B4 Illinois, N USA
Jacksonville 43 F1 North Carolina,
SE USA
Jacksonville 49 G3 Texas, SW USA
Jacmel 54 D3 *var.* Jaquemel. S Haiti
Jacob *see* Nkayi
Jacobābād 134 B3 Sind, SE Pakistan
Jadotville *see* Likasi
Jadransko More/Jadransko Morje *see*
Adriatic Sea
Jaén 60 B2 Cajamarca, N Peru
Jaén 92 D4 Andalucía, SW Spain
Jaffna 132 D3 Northern Province,
N Sri Lanka
Jagannath *see* Puri
Jagdalpur 135 E5 Chhattisgarh, C India
Jagdaqi 127 G1 Nei Mongol Zizhiqu,
N China
Jagodina 100 D4 *prev.* Svetozarevo.
Serbia, C Serbia
Jahra *see* Al Jahrā'
Jailolo *see* Halmahera, Pulau
Jaipur 134 D3 *prev.* Jeypore. *state capital*
Rājasthān, N India
Jaisalmer 134 C3 Rājasthān, NW India
Jajce 100 B3 Federacija Bosna
I Hercegovina, W Bosnia and
Herzegovina
Jakarta 138 C5 *prev.* Djakarta, *Dut.*
Batavia. *country capital* (Indonesia)
Jawa, C Indonesia
Jakobstad 84 D4 *Fin.* Pietarsaari. Länsi-
Suomi, W Finland
Jakobstadt *see* Jēkabpils
Jalālābād 123 F4 *var.* Jalalabad,
Jelalabad. Nangarhār, E Afghanistan
Jalal-Abad *see* Dzhalal-Abad, Dzhalal-
Abadskaya Oblast', Kyrgyzstan
Jalandhar 134 D2 *prev.* Jullundur.
Punjab, N India
Jalapa 52 D3 Nueva Segovia,
NW Nicaragua
Jalpa 50 D4 Zacatecas, C Mexico
Jālū 71 G3 *var.* Jūla. NE Libya
Jaluit Atoll 144 D2 *var.* Jālwōj. *atoll*
Ralik Chain, S Marshall Islands
Jālwōj *see* Jaluit Atoll
Jamaame 73 D6 *It.* Giamame; *prev.*
Margherita. Jubbada Hoose, S Somalia
Jamaica 54 A4 *country* W West Indies

JAMAICA
West Indies

Official name Jamaica
Formation 1962 / 1962
Capital Kingston
Population 2.8 million / 670 people
per sq mile (259 people per sq km)

JAMAICA
(continued)

Total area 4243 sq. miles (10,990 sq. km)
Languages English Creole, English*
Religions Other and nonreligious 45%, Other Protestant 20%, Church of God 18%, Baptist 10%, Anglican 7%
Ethnic mix Black African 91%, Mulatto (mixed race) 7%, East Indian 1%, European and Chinese 1%
Government Parliamentary system
Currency Jamaican dollar = 100 cents
Literacy rate 86%
Calorie consumption 2807 kilocalories

Jamaica *56 A1 island* W West Indies
Jamaica Channel *54 D3 channel* Haiti/ Jamaica
Jamālpur *135 F3* Bihār, NE India
Jambi *138 B4 var.* Telanaipura; *prev.* Djambi. Sumatera, W Indonesia
Jamdena *see* Yamdena, Pulau
James Bay *38 C3 bay* Ontario/Québec, E Canada
James River *45 E2 river* North Dakota/ South Dakota, N USA
James River *41 E5 river* Virginia, NE USA
Jamestown *41 E3* New York, NE USA
Jamestown *45 E2* North Dakota, N USA
Jamestown *see* Holetown
Jammu *134 D2 prev.* Jummoo. *state capital* Jammu and Kashmir, NW India
Jammu and Kashmīr *134 D1 disputed region* India/Pakistan
Jāmnagar *134 C4 prev.* Navanagar. Gujarāt, W India
Jamshedpur *135 F4* Jhārkhand, NE India
Jamuna *see* Brahmaputra
Janaúba *63 F3* Minas Gerais, SE Brazil
Janesville *40 B3* Wisconsin, N USA
Janina *see* Ioánnina
Janischken *see* Joniškis
Jankovac *see* Jánoshalma
Jan Mayen *83 F4 Norwegian dependency* N Atlantic Ocean
Jánoshalma *99 C7 SCr.* Jankovac. Bács-Kiskun, S Hungary
Janów *see* Ivanava, Belarus
Janow/Janów *see* Jonava, Lithuania
Janów Poleski *see* Ivanava
Japan *130 C4 var.* Nippon, *Jap.* Nihon. *country* E Asia

JAPAN
East Asia

Official name Japan
Formation 1590 / 1972
Capital Tokyo
Population 126 million / 870 people per sq mile (336 people per sq km)
Total area 145,882 sq. miles (377,835 sq. km)
Languages Japanese*, Korean, Chinese
Religions Shinto and Buddhist 76%, Buddhist 16%, Other (including Christian) 8%
Ethnic mix Japanese 99%, Other (mainly Korean) 1%
Government Parliamentary system
Currency Yen = 100 sen
Literacy rate 99%
Calorie consumption 2723 kilocalories

Japan, Sea of *130 A4 var.* East Sea, *Rus.* Yapanskoye More. *sea* NW Pacific Ocean
Japan Trench *125 F1 trench* NW Pacific Ocean
Japen *see* Yapen, Pulau
Japiim *62 C2 var.* Máncio Lima. Acre, W Brazil
Japurá, Rio *62 C2 var.* Río Caquetá, Yapurá. *river* Brazil/Colombia
Japurá, Rio *see* Caquetá, Río
Jaqué *53 G5* Darién, SE Panama
Jaquemel *see* Jacmel
Jarablos *see* Jarābulus
Jarābulus *118 C2 var.* Jarablos, Jerablus, *Fr.* Djérablous. Ḥalab, N Syria
Jarbah, Jazīrat *see* Jerba, Île de
Jardines de la Reina, Archipiélago de los *54 B2 island group* C Cuba
Jarīd, Shaṭṭ al *see* Jerid, Chott el
Jarocin *98 C4* Wielkopolskie, C Poland
Jaroslau *see* Jarosław
Jarosław *99 E5 Ger.* Jaroslau, *Rus.* Yaroslav. Podkarpackie, SE Poland
Jarqo'rg'on *123 E3 Rus.* Dzharkurgan. Surkhondaryo Viloyati, S Uzbekistan
Jarvis Island *145 G2 US unincorporated territory* C Pacific Ocean
Jasło *99 D5* Podkarpackie, SE Poland
Jastrzębie-Zdrój *99 C5* Śląskie, S Poland
Jataí *63 E3* Goiás, C Brazil
Jativa *see* Xàtiva
Jauf *see* Al Jawf
Jaunpiebalga *106 D3* NE Latvia
Jaunpur *135 E3* Uttar Pradesh, N India
Java *152 A3* South Dakota, N USA
Javalambre *93 E3 mountain* E Spain
Java Sea *138 D4 Ind.* Laut Jawa. *sea* W Indonesia
Java Trench *124 D5 var.* Sunda Trench. *trench* E Indian Ocean
Jawa, Laut *see* Java Sea
Jawhar *73 D6 var.* Jowhar, *It.* Giohar. Shabeellaha Dhexe, S Somalia
Jaworów *see* Yavoriv
Jaya, Puncak *139 G4 prev.* Puntjak Carstensz, Puntjak Sukarno. *mountain* Papua, E Indonesia
Jayapura *139 H4 var.* Djajapura, *Dut.* Hollandia; *prev.* Kotabaru, Sukarnapura. Papua, E Indonesia
Jay Dairen *see* Dalian
Jayhawker State *see* Kansas
Jaz Murian, Hamun-e *120 E4 lake* SE Iran
Jebba *75 F4* Kwara, W Nigeria
Jebel, Bahr el *see* White Nile
Jeble *see* Jablah
Jedda *see* Jiddah
Jędrzejów *98 D4 Ger.* Endersdorf. Świętokrzyskie, C Poland
Jefferson City *45 G5 state capital* Missouri, C USA
Jega *75 F4* Kebbi, NW Nigeria
Jehol *see* Chengde
Jeju-do *129 E4 Jap.* Saishū; *prev.* Cheju-do, Quelpart. *island* S South Korea
Jeju Strait *129 E4 prev.* Cheju Strait. *strait* S South Korea
Jēkabpils *106 D4 Ger.* Jakobstadt. S Latvia
Jelalabad *see* Jalālābād
Jelenia Góra *98 B4 Ger.* Hirschberg, Hirschberg im Riesengebirge, Hirschberg in Riesengebirge, Hirschberg in Schlesien. Dolnośląskie, SW Poland
Jelgava *106 C3 Ger.* Mitau. C Latvia
Jemappes *87 B6* Hainaut, S Belgium
Jember *138 D5 prev.* Djember. Jawa, C Indonesia
Jena *94 C4* Thüringen, C Germany
Jenin *119 A6* N West Bank
Jerablus *see* Jarābulus
Jerada *70 D2* NE Morocco
Jérémie *54 D3* SW Haiti
Jerez *see* Jeréz de la Frontera, Spain
Jerez de la Frontera *92 C5 var.* Jerez; *prev.* Xeres. Andalucía, SW Spain
Jerez de los Caballeros *92 C4* Extremadura, W Spain
Jericho *119 B6 Ar.* Arīḥā, *Heb.* Yeriḥo. E West Bank
Jerid, Chott el *71 E2 var.* Shaṭṭ al Jarīd. *salt lake* SW Tunisia
Jersey *89 D8 uk crown dependency* Channel Islands, NW Europe
Jerusalem *103 H4 Ar.* Al Quds, Al Quds ash Sharīf, *Heb.* Yerushalayim; *anc.* Hierosolyma. *country capital* (Israel) Jerusalem, NE Israel
Jesenice *95 D7 Ger.* Assling. NW Slovenia
Jesselton *see* Kota Kinabalu
Jessore *135 G4* Khulna, W Bangladesh
Jesús María *64 C3* Córdoba, C Argentina
Jeypore *see* Jaipur, Rājasthān, India
Jhānsi *134 D3* Uttar Pradesh, N India
Jhārkhand *135 F4 cultural region* NE India
Jhelum *134 C2* Punjab, NE Pakistan
Ji *see* Hebei, China
Ji *see* Jilin, China
Jiangmen *128 C6* Guangdong, S China
Jiangsu *128 D4 var.* Chiang-su, Jiangsu Sheng, Kiangsu, Su. *province* E China
Jiangsu *see* Nanjing
Jiangsu Sheng *see* Jiangsu
Jiangxi *128 C6 var.* Chiang-hsi, Gan, Jiangxi Sheng, Kiangsi. *province* S China
Jiangxi Sheng *see* Jiangxi
Jiaxing *128 D5* Zhejiang, SE China
Jiayi *128 D6 var.* Chia-i, Chiai, Chiayi, Kiayi, *Jap.* Kagi. C Taiwan
Jibuti *see* Djibouti
Jiddah *121 A5 Eng.* Jedda. (Saudi Arabia) Makkah, W Saudi Arabia
Jih-k'a-tse *see* Xigazê
Jihlava *99 B5 Ger.* Iglau, *Pol.* Igława. Vysocina, S Czech Republic
Jilib *73 D6 It.* Gelib. Jubbada Dhexe, S Somalia
Jilin *128 E3 var.* Chi-lin, Girin, Kirin; *prev.* Yungki, Yunki. Jilin, NE China
Jilin *128 E3 var.* Chi-lin, Girin, Ji, Jilin Sheng, Kirin. *province* NE China
Jilin Sheng *see* Jilin
Jilong *128 D6 var.* Keelung, *Jap.* Kirun, Kirun', *prev.* Chilung, *prev. Sp.* Santissima Trinidad. N Taiwan
Jīma *73 C5 var.* Jimma, *It.* Gimma. Oromīya, C Ethiopia
Jimbolia *108 A4 Ger.* Hatzfeld, *Hung.* Zsombolya. Timiş, W Romania
Jiménez *50 D2* Chihuahua, N Mexico
Jimma *see* Jīma
Jimsar *126 C3* Xinjiang Uygur Zizhiqu, NW China
Jin *see* Shanxi
Jin *see* Tianjin Shi
Jinan *128 C4 var.* Chinan, Chi-nan, Tsinan. *province capital* Shandong, E China
Jingdezhen *128 C5* Jiangxi, S China
Jinghong *128 A6 var.* Yunjinghong. Yunnan, SW China
Jinhua *128 D5* Zhejiang, SE China
Jining *127 F3* Shandong, E China
Jinja *73 C6* S Uganda
Jinotega *52 D3* Jinotega, NW Nicaragua
Jinotepe *52 D3* Carazo, SW Nicaragua
Jinsen *see* Incheon
Jinzhong *128 C4 var.* Yuci. Shanxi, C China
Jinzhou *128 D3 var.* Chin-chou, Chinchow; *prev.* Chinhsien. Liaoning, NE China
Jirgalanta *see* Hovd
Jisr ash Shadadi *see* Ash Shadādah
Jiu *108 B5 Ger.* Schil, Schyl, *Hung.* Zsil, Zsily. *river* S Romania
Jiujiang *128 C5* Jiangxi, S China
Jixi *129 E2* Heilongjiang, NE China
Jīzān *121 B6 var.* Qīzān. Jīzān, SW Saudi Arabia
Jizzax *123 E2 Rus.* Dzhizak. Jizzax Viloyati, C Uzbekistan
João Belo *see* Xai-Xai
João Pessoa *63 G2 prev.* Paraíba. *state capital* Paraíba, E Brazil
Joazeiro *see* Juazeiro
Job'urg *see* Johannesburg
Jo-ch'iang *see* Ruoqiang
Jodhpur *134 C3* Rājasthān, NW India
Joensuu *85 E5* Itä-Suomi, SE Finland
Jōetsu *131 C5 var.* Zyôetu. Niigata, Honshū, C Japan
Jogjakarta *see* Yogyakarta
Johannesburg *78 D4 var.* Egoli, Erautini, Gauteng, *abbrev.* Job'urg. Gauteng, NE South Africa
Johannisburg *see* Pisz
John Day River *46 C3 river* Oregon, NW USA
John o'Groats *88 C2* N Scotland, United Kingdom
Johnston Atoll *143 E1 US unincorporated territory* C Pacific Ocean
Johor Baharu *see* Johor Bahru
Johor Bahru *138 B3 var.* Johor Baharu, Johore Bahru. Johor, Peninsular Malaysia
Johore Bahru *see* Johor Bahru
Johore Strait *138 A1 strait* Johor, Peninsular Malaysia, Malaysia/ Singapore Asia Andaman Sea/South China Sea
Joinvile *see* Joinville
Joinville *63 E4 var.* Joinvile. Santa Catarina, S Brazil
Jokkmokk *84 C3 Lapp.* Dálvvadis. Norrbotten, N Sweden
Jokyakarta *see* Yogyakarta
Joliet *40 B3* Illinois, N USA
Jonava *106 B4 Ger.* Janow, *Pol.* Janów. Kaunas, C Lithuania
Jonesboro *42 B1* Arkansas, C USA
Joniškis *106 C3 Ger.* Janischken. Šiaulai, N Lithuania
Jönköping *85 B7* Jönköping, S Sweden
Jonquière *39 E4* Québec, SE Canada
Joplin *45 F5* Missouri, C USA
Jordan *119 B6 off.* Hashemite Kingdom of Jordan, *Ar.* Al Mamlaka al Urdunīya al Hashemīyah, Al Urdunn; *prev.* Transjordan. *country* SW Asia

JORDAN
Southwest Asia

Official name Hashemite Kingdom of Jordan
Formation 1946 / 1967
Capital Amman
Population 6.3 million / 183 people per sq mile (71 people per sq km)
Total area 35,637 sq. miles (92,300 sq. km)
Languages Arabic*
Religions Muslim (mainly Sunni) 92%, Christian 6%, Other 2%
Ethnic mix Arab 98%, Circassian 1%, Armenian 1%
Government Monarchy
Currency Jordanian dinar = 1000 fils
Literacy rate 92%
Calorie consumption 2977 kilocalories

Jordan *119 B5 Ar.* Urdunn, *Heb.* HaYarden. *river* SW Asia
Jorhāt *135 H3* Assam, NE India
Jos *75 G4* Plateau, C Nigeria
Joseph Bonaparte Gulf *146 D2 gulf* N Australia
Jos Plateau *75 G4 plateau* C Nigeria
Jotunheimen *85 A5 mountain range* S Norway
Joûnié *118 A4 var.* Junīyah. W Lebanon
Joure *86 D2 Fris.* De Jouwer. Fryslân, N Netherlands
Joutseno *85 E5* Etelä-Suomi, SE Finland
Jowhar *see* Jawhar
J.Storm Thurmond Reservoir *see* Clark Hill Lake
Juan Aldama *50 D3* Zacatecas, C Mexico
Juan de Fuca, Strait of *46 A1 strait* Canada/USA
Juan Fernandez Islands *57 A6 Eng.* Juan Fernandez Islands. *island group* W Chile
Juan Fernandez Islands *see* Juan Fernández, Islas
Juazeiro *63 G2 prev.* Joazeiro. Bahia, E Brazil
Juazeiro do Norte *63 G2* Ceará, E Brazil
Juba *73 B5 var.* Jūbā. *country capital* (South Sudan) Central Equatoria, S South Sudan
Juba *73 D6 Amh.* Genalē Wenz, *It.* Guiba, *Som.* Ganaane, Webi Jubba. *river* Ethiopia/Somalia
Jubba, Webi *see* Juba
Jubbulpore *see* Jabalpur
Júcar *93 E3 var.* Jucar. *river* C Spain
Juchitán *51 F5 var.* Juchitán de Zaragosa. Oaxaca, SE Mexico
Juchitán de Zaragosa *see* Juchitán
Judayyidat Hāmir *120 B3* Al Anbār, S Iraq
Judenburg *95 D7* Steiermark, C Austria
Jugoslavija *see* Serbia
Juigalpa *52 D3* Chontales, S Nicaragua
Juiz de Fora *63 F4* Minas Gerais, SE Brazil
Jujuy *see* San Salvador de Jujuy
Jūlā *see* Jālū, Libya
Julia Beterrae *see* Béziers
Juliaca *61 E4* Puno, SE Peru
Juliana Top *59 G3 mountain* C Suriname
Julianehåb *see* Qaqortoq
Julio Briga *see* Bragança
Juliobriga *see* Logroño
Juliomagus *see* Angers
Jullundur *see* Jalandhar
Jumilla *93 E4* Murcia, SE Spain
Jummoo *see* Jammu
Jumna *see* Yamuna
Jumporn *see* Chumphon
Junction City *45 F4* Kansas, C USA
Juneau *36 D4 state capital* Alaska, USA
Junín *64 C4* Buenos Aires, E Argentina
Junīyah *see* Joûnié
Junkseylon *see* Phuket
Jur *73 B5 river* W South Sudan
Jura *90 D4 cultural region* E France
Jura *95 A7 var.* Jura Mountains. *mountain range* France/Switzerland

Jura 88 B4 island SW Scotland, United Kingdom
Jura Mountains see Jura
Jurbarkas 106 B4 Ger. Georgenburg, Jurburg. Tauragė, W Lithuania
Jurburg see Jurbarkas
Jūrmala 106 C3 C Latvia
Juruá, Rio 62 C2 var. Río Yuruá. river Brazil/Peru
Juruena, Rio 62 D3 river W Brazil
Jutiapa 52 B2 Jutiapa, S Guatemala
Juticalpa 52 D2 Olancho, C Honduras
Jutland see Jylland
Juvavum see Salzburg
Južna Morava 101 E5 Ger. Südliche Morava. river SE Serbia
Jwaneng 78 C4 Southern, S Botswana
Jylland 85 A7 Eng. Jutland. peninsula W Denmark
Jyrgalan see Dzhergalan
Jyväskylä 85 D5 Länsi-Suomi, C Finland

K

K2 126 A4 Chin. Qogir Feng, Eng. Mount Godwin Austen. mountain China/Pakistan
Kaafu Atoll see Male' Atoll
Kaaimanston 59 G3 Sipaliwini, N Suriname
Kaakhka see Kaka
Kaala see Caála
Kaamanen 84 D2 Lapp. Gámas. Lappi, N Finland
Kaapstad see Cape Town
Kaaresuvanto 84 C3 Lapp. Gárassavon. Lappi, N Finland
Kabale 73 B6 SW Uganda
Kabinda 77 D7 Kasai-Oriental, SE Dem. Rep. Congo
Kabinda see Cabinda
Kâbol see Kābul
Kabompo 78 C2 river W Zambia
Kābul 123 E4 prev. Kābol. country capital (Afghanistan) Kābul, E Afghanistan
Kābul 123 E4 var. Daryā-ye Kābul. river Afghanistan/Pakistan
Kābul, Daryā-ye see Kābul
Kabwe 78 D2 Central, C Zambia
Kachchh, Gulf of 134 B4 var. Gulf of Cutch, Gulf of Kutch. gulf W India
Kachchh, Rann of 134 B4 var. Rann of Kachh, Rann of Kutch. salt marsh India/Pakistan
Kachh, Rann of see Kachchh, Rann of
Kadan Kyun 137 B5 prev. King Island. island Mergui Archipelago, S Myanmar (Burma)
Kadavu 145 E4 prev. Kandavu. island S Fiji
Kadoma 78 D3 prev. Gatooma. Mashonaland West, C Zimbabwe
Kadugli 72 B4 Southern Kordofan, S Sudan
Kaduna 75 G4 Kaduna, C Nigeria
Kadzhi-Say see Bokonbayevo
Kaédi 74 C3 Gorgol, S Mauritania
Kaffa see Feodosiya
Kafue 78 D2 Lusaka, SE Zambia
Kafue 78 C2 river C Zambia
Kaga Bandoro 76 C4 prev. Fort-Crampel. Nana-Grébizi, C Central African Republic
Kagan see Kogon
Kâghet 74 D1 var. Karet. physical region N Mauritania
Kagi see Jiayi
Kagoshima 131 B8 var. Kagosima. Kagoshima, Kyūshū, SW Japan
Kagoshima-wan 131 A8 bay SW Japan
Kagosima see Kagoshima
Kagul see Cahul
Darya-ye Kahmard 123 E4 prev. Darya-i-surkhab. river NE Afghanistan
Kahramanmaraş 116 D4 var. Kahraman Maraş, Maraş, Marash. Kahramanmaraş, S Turkey
Kaiapoi 151 C6 Canterbury, South Island, New Zealand
Kaifeng 128 C4 Henan, C China
Kai, Kepulauan 139 F4 prev. Kei Islands. island group Maluku, SE Indonesia
Kaikohe 150 C2 Northland, North Island, New Zealand
Kaikoura 151 C5 Canterbury, South Island, New Zealand

Kaikoura Peninsula 151 C5 peninsula South Island, New Zealand
Kainji Lake see Kainji Reservoir
Kainji Reservoir 75 F4 var. Kainji Lake. reservoir W Nigeria
Kaipara Harbour 150 C2 harbour North Island, New Zealand
Kairouan 71 E2 var. Al Qayrawān. E Tunisia
Kaisaria see Kayseri
Kaiserslautern 95 A5 Rheinland-Pfalz, SW Germany
Kaišiadorys 107 B5 Kaunas, S Lithuania
Kaitaia 150 C2 Northland, North Island, New Zealand
Kajaani 84 E4 Swe. Kajana. Oulu, C Finland
Kajan see Kayan, Sungai
Kajana see Kajaani
Kajisay see Bokonbayevo
Kaka 122 C2 Rus. Kaakhka. Ahal Welaýaty, S Turkmenistan
Kake 36 D4 Kupreanof Island, Alaska, USA
Kakhovka 109 F4 Khersons'ka Oblast', S Ukraine
Kakhovs'ke Vodoskhovyshche 109 F4 Rus. Kakhovskoye Vodokhranilishche. reservoir SE Ukraine
Kakhovskoye Vodokhranilishche see Kakhovs'ke Vodoskhovyshche
Kākināda 132 D1 prev. Cocanada. Andhra Pradesh, E India
Kakshaal-Too, Khrebet see Kokshaal-Tau
Kaktovik 36 D2 Alaska, USA
Kalaallit Nunaat see Greenland
Kalahari Desert 78 B4 desert Southern Africa
Kalaikhum see Qal'aikhum
Kalámai see Kalámata
Kalamariá 104 B4 Kentrikí Makedonía, N Greece
Kalamás 104 A4 var. Thiamis; prev. Thýamis. river W Greece
Kalámata 105 B6 prev. Kalámai. Pelopónnisos, S Greece
Kalamazoo 40 C3 Michigan, N USA
Kalambaka see Kalampáka
Kálamos 105 C5 Attikí, C Greece
Kalampáka 104 B4 var. Kalambaka. Thessalía, C Greece
Kalanchak 109 F4 Khersons'ka Oblast', S Ukraine
Kalarash see Călăraşi
Kalasin 136 D4 var. Muang Kalasin. Kalasin, E Thailand
Kālat 134 B2 var. Kelat, Khelat. Baluchistān, SW Pakistan
Kalāt see Qalāt
Kalbarri 147 A5 Western Australia
Kalecik 116 C3 Ankara, N Turkey
Kalemie 77 E6 prev. Albertville. Katanga, SE Dem. Rep. Congo
Kale Sultanie see Çanakkale
Kalgan see Zhangjiakou
Kalgoorlie 147 B6 Western Australia
Kalima 77 D6 Maniema, E Dem. Rep. Congo
Kalimantan 138 D4 Eng. Indonesian Borneo. geopolitical region Borneo, C Indonesia
Kalinin see Tver'
Kaliningrad 106 A4 Kaliningradskaya Oblast', W Russian Federation
Kaliningrad see Kaliningradskaya Oblast'
Kaliningradskaya Oblast' 106 B4 var. Kaliningrad. province and enclave W Russian Federation
Kalinkavichy 107 C7 Rus. Kalinkovichi. Homyel'skaya Voblasts', SE Belarus
Kalinkovichi see Kalinkavichy
Kalisch/Kalish see Kalisz
Kalispell 44 B1 Montana, N USA
Kalisz 98 C4 Ger. Kalisch, Rus. Kalish; anc. Calisia. Wielkopolskie, C Poland
Kalix 84 D4 Norrbotten, N Sweden
Kalixälven 84 D3 river N Sweden
Kallaste 106 E3 Ger. Krasnogor. Tartumaa, SE Estonia
Kallavesi 85 E5 lake SE Finland
Kalloní 105 D5 Lésvos, E Greece
Kalmar 85 C7 var. Calmar. Kalmar, S Sweden
Kalmthout 87 C5 Antwerpen, N Belgium
Kalpáki 104 A4 Ípeiros, W Greece
Kalpeni Island 132 B3 island Lakshadweep, India, N Indian Ocean
Kaltdorf see Pruszków

Kaluga 111 B5 Kaluzhskaya Oblast', W Russian Federation
Kalush 108 C2 Pol. Kalusz. Ivano-Frankivs'ka Oblast', W Ukraine
Kałusz see Kalush
Kalutara 132 D4 Western Province, SW Sri Lanka
Kalvarija 107 B5 Pol. Kalwaria. Marijampolė, S Lithuania
Kalwaria see Kalvarija
Kalyān 134 C5 Mahārāshtra, W India
Kálymnos 105 D6 var. Kálimnos. island Dodekánisa, Greece, Aegean Sea
Kama 110 D4 river NW Russian Federation
Kamarang 59 F3 W Guyana
Kambryk see Cambrai
Kamchatka 115 G3 Eng. Kamchatka. peninsula E Russian Federation
Kamchatka see Kamchatka, Poluostrov
Kamenets-Podol'skiy see Kam"yanets'-Podil's'kyy
Kamenka Dneprovskaya see Kam"yanka-Dniprovs'ka
Kamenskoye see Romaniv
Kamensk-Shakhtinskiy 111 B6 Rostovskaya Oblast', SW Russian Federation
Kamina 77 D7 Katanga, S Dem. Rep. Congo
Kamishli see Al Qāmishlī
Kamloops 37 E5 British Columbia, SW Canada
Kammu Seamount 152 C2 guyot N Pacific Ocean
Kampala 73 B6 country capital (Uganda) S Uganda
Kâmpóng Cham 137 D6 prev. Kompong Cham. Kâmpóng Cham, C Cambodia
Kâmpóng Chhnăng 137 D6 prev. Kompong. Kâmpóng Chhnăng, C Cambodia
Kâmpóng Saôm see Sihanoukville
Kâmpóng Spoe see Kâmpóng Spœ
Kâmpóng Spœ 137 D6 prev. Kompong Speu. Kâmpóng Spœ, S Cambodia
Kâmpóng Thum 137 D5 var. Kompong Thom. Kâmpóng Thum, C Cambodia
Kâmpóng Trâbêk 137 D5 prev. Phumǐ Kâmpóng Trâbêk, Phum Kompong Trabek. Kâmpóng Thum, C Cambodia
Kâmpôt 137 D6 Kâmpôt, SW Cambodia
Kampuchea see Cambodia
Kampuchea, Democratic see Cambodia
Kampuchea, People's Democratic Republic of see Cambodia
Kam"yanets'-Podil's'kyy 108 C3 Rus. Kamenets-Podol'skiy. Khmel'nyts'ka Oblast', W Ukraine
Kam"yanka-Dniprovs'ka 109 F3 Rus. Kamenka Dneprovskaya. Zaporiz'ka Oblast', SE Ukraine
Kamyshin 111 B6 Volgogradskaya Oblast', SW Russian Federation
Kanaky see New Caledonia
Kananga 77 D6 prev. Luluabourg. Kasai-Occidental, S Dem. Rep. Congo
Kanara see Karnātaka
Kanash 111 C5 Chuvashskaya Respublika, W Russian Federation
Kanazawa 131 C5 Ishikawa, Honshū, SW Japan
Kanbe 136 B4 Yangon, SW Myanmar (Burma)
Kānchipuram 132 C2 prev. Conjeeveram. Tamil Nādu, SE India
Kandahār 123 E5 Per. Qandahār. Kandahār, S Afghanistan
Kandalaksa see Kandalaksha
Kandalaksha 110 B2 var. Kandalaksa, Fin. Kantalahti. Murmanskaya Oblast', NW Russian Federation
Kandangan 138 D4 Borneo, C Indonesia
Kandau see Kandava
Kandava 106 C3 Ger. Kandau. W Latvia
Kandavu see Kadavu
Kandi 75 F4 N Benin
Kandy 132 D3 Central Province, C Sri Lanka
Kane Fracture Zone 66 B4 fracture zone NW Atlantic Ocean
Kāne'ohe 47 A8 var. Kaneohe. O'ahu, Hawaii, USA, C Pacific Ocean
Kanestron, Akrotírio see Palioúri, Akrotírio
Kanëv see Kaniv
Kanevskoye Vodokhranilishche see Kaniv's'ke Vodoskhovyshche
Kangān see Bandar-e Kangān

Kangaroo Island 149 A7 island South Australia
Kangertittivaq 83 E4 Dan. Scoresby Sund. fjord E Greenland
Kangikajik 83 E4 var. Kap Brewster. headland E Greenland
Kaniv 109 E2 Rus. Kanëv. Cherkas'ka Oblast', C Ukraine
Kaniv's'ke Vodoskhovyshche 109 E2 Rus. Kanevskoye Vodokhranilishche. reservoir C Ukraine
Kanjiža 100 D2 Ger. Altkanischa, Hung. Magyarkanizsa, Ókanizsa; prev. Stara Kanjiža. Vojvodina, N Serbia
Kankaanpää 85 D5 Länsi-Suomi, SW Finland
Kankakee 40 B3 Illinois, N USA
Kankan 74 D4 E Guinea
Kannur 132 B2 prev. Cannanore, Jagatsinghapur. Kerala, SW India
Kano 75 G4 Kano, N Nigeria
Kānpur 135 E3 Eng. Cawnpore. Uttar Pradesh, N India
Kansas 45 F5 off. State of Kansas, also known as Jayhawker State, Sunflower State. state C USA
Kansas City 45 F4 Kansas, C USA
Kansas City 45 F4 Missouri, C USA
Kansas River 45 F5 river Kansas, C USA
Kansk 115 E4 Krasnoyarskiy Kray, S Russian Federation
Kansu see Gansu
Kantalahti see Kandalaksha
Kántanos 105 C7 Kríti, Greece, E Mediterranean Sea
Kantemirovka 111 B6 Voronezhskaya Oblast', W Russian Federation
Kantipur see Kathmandu
Kanton 145 F3 var. Abariringa, Canton Island; prev. Mary Island. atoll Phoenix Islands, C Kiribati
Kanye 78 C4 Southern, SE Botswana
Kaohsiung see Gaoxiong
Kaolack 74 B3 var. Kaolak. W Senegal
Kaolak see Kaolack
Kaolan see Lanzhou
Kaoma 78 C2 Western, W Zambia
Kapelle 87 B5 Zeeland, SW Netherlands
Kapellen 87 C5 Antwerpen, N Belgium
Kapka, Massif du 76 C2 mountain range E Chad
Kaplangky, Plato see Gaplaňgyr Platosy
Kapoeas see Kapuas, Sungai
Kapoeta 73 C5 Eastern Equatoria, SE South Sudan
Kaposvár 99 C7 Somogy, SW Hungary
Kappeln 94 B2 Schleswig-Holstein, N Germany
Kaproncza see Koprivnica
Kapstad see Cape Town
Kapsukas see Marijampolė
Kaptsevichy 107 C7 Rus. Koptsevichi. Homyel'skaya Voblasts', SE Belarus
Kapuas, Sungai 138 C4 prev. Kapoeas. river Borneo, C Indonesia
Kapuskasing 38 C4 Ontario, S Canada
Kapyl' 107 C6 Rus. Kopyl'. Minskaya Voblasts', C Belarus
Kara-Balta 123 F2 Chuyskaya Oblast', N Kyrgyzstan
Karabil', Vozvyshennost' see Garabil Belentligi
Kara-Bogaz-Gol, Zaliv see Garabogaz Aylagy
Karabük 116 C2 Karabük, NW Turkey
Karachi 134 B3 Sind, SE Pakistan
Karácsonkő see Piatra-Neamţ
Karadeniz Boğazı see İstanbul Boğazı
Karaferiye see Véroia
Karaganda 114 C4 Kaz. Qaraghandy; prev. Karaganda. Karagandy, C Kazakhstan
Karaginskiy, Ostrov 115 H2 island E Russian Federation
Karagumskiy Kanal see Garagum Kanaly
Karak see Al Karak
Karakax see Moyu
Karakılısse see Ağrı
Karakol 123 G2 var. Karakolka. Issyk-Kul'skaya Oblast', NE Kyrgyzstan
Karakol 123 G2 prev. Przheval'sk. Issyk-Kul'skaya Oblast', NE Kyrgyzstan
Karakolka see Karakol
Karakoram Range 134 D1 mountain range C Asia
Karaköse see Ağrı
Karakul' see Qarokŭl, Tajikistan

Kara Kum *see* Garagum
Kara Kum Canal/Karakumskiy Kanal
 see Garagum Kanaly
Karakumy, Peski *see* Garagum
Karamai *see* Karamay
Karaman *116 C4* Karaman, S Turkey
Karamay *126 B2 var.* Karamai,
 Kelamayi; *prev. Chin.* K'o-la-ma-i.
 Xinjiang Uygur Zizhiqu, NW China
Karamea Bight *151 B5* gulf South Island,
 New Zealand
Karapelit *104 E1 Rom.* Stejarul.
 Dobrich, NE Bulgaria
Kara-Say *123 G2* Issyk-Kul'skaya
 Oblast', NE Kyrgyzstan
Karasburg *78 B4* Karas, S Namibia
Kara Sea *114 D2 Eng.* Kara Sea. *sea*
 Arctic Ocean
Kara Sea *see* Karskoye More
Kara Strait *110 E2 Eng.* Kara Strait.
 strait N Russian Federation
Kara Strait *see* Karskiye Vorota, Proliv
Karatau *114 C5 Kaz.* Qarataū. Zhambyl,
 S Kazakhstan
Karavás *105 B7* Kýthira, S Greece
Karbalā' *120 B3 var.* Kerbala, Kerbela.
 Karbalā', S Iraq
Kardeljevo *see* Ploče
Kardhítsa *see* Karditsa
Karditsa *105 B5 var.* Kardhítsa.
 Thessalía, C Greece
Kärdla *106 C2 Ger.* Kertel. Hiiumaa,
 W Estonia
Karet *see* Kâghet
Kargı *116 C2* Çorum, N Turkey
Kargilik *see* Yecheng
Kariba *78 D2* Mashonaland West,
 N Zimbabwe
Kariba, Lake *78 D3* reservoir Zambia/
 Zimbabwe
Karibib *78 B3* Erongo, C Namibia
Karies *see* Karyés
Karigasniemi *84 D2* Lapp.
 Garegegasnjárga. Lappi, N Finland
Karimata, Selat *138 C4* strait
 W Indonesia
Karimnagar *134 D5* Andhra Pradesh,
 C India
Karin *72 D4* Woqooyi Galbeed,
 N Somalia
Kariot *see* Ikaría
Káristos *see* Kárystos
Karkinits'ka Zatoka *109 E4 Rus.*
 Karkinitskiy Zaliv. *gulf* S Ukraine
Karkinitskiy Zaliv *see* Karkinits'ka
 Zatoka
Karkük *see* Kirkūk
Karleby *see* Kokkola
Karl-Marx-Stadt *see* Chemnitz
Karló *see* Hailuoto
Karlovac *100 B3 Ger.* Karlstadt, *Hung.*
 Károlyváros. Karlovac, C Croatia
Karlovy Vary *99 A5 Ger.* Karlsbad;
 prev. Eng. Carlsbad. Karlovarský Kraj,
 W Czech Republic
Karlsbad *see* Karlovy Vary
Karlsburg *see* Alba Iulia
Karlskrona *85 C7* Blekinge, S Sweden
Karlsruhe *95 B6 var.* Carlsruhe. Baden-
 Württemberg, SW Germany
Karlstad *85 B6* Värmland, C Sweden
Karlstadt *see* Karlovac
Karnál *134 D2* Haryāna, N India
Karnātaka *132 C1 var.* Kanara; *prev.*
 Maisur, Mysore. *cultural region*
 W India
Karnobat *104 D2* Burgas, E Bulgaria
Karnul *see* Kurnool
Karol *see* Carei
Károly-Fehérvár *see* Alba Iulia
Károlyváros *see* Karlovac
Karpaten *see* Carpathian Mountains
Kárpathos *105 E7* Kárpathos, SE Greece
Kárpathos *105 E7 It.* Scarpanto;
 anc. Carpathos, Carpathus. *island*
 SE Greece
Karpaty *see* Carpathian Mountains
Karpenísi *105 B5 prev.* Karpenísion.
 Stereá Elláda, C Greece
Karpenísion *see* Karpenísi
Karpilovka *see* Aktsyabrski
Kars *117 F3 var.* Qars. Kars,
 NE Turkey
Karsau *see* Kārsava
Kārsava *106 D4 Ger.* Karsau; *prev. Rus.*
 Korsovka. E Latvia
Karshi *see* Qarshi, Uzbekistan
Karyés *104 C4 var.* Karies. Ágion Óros,
 N Greece

Kárystos *105 C6 var.* Káristos. Évvoia,
 C Greece
Kasai *77 C6 var.* Cassai, Kassai. *river*
 Angola/Dem. Rep. Congo
Kasaji *77 D7* Katanga, S Dem. Rep.
 Congo
Kasama *78 D1* Northern, N Zambia
Kasan *see* Koson
Kāsaragod *132 B2* Kerala, SW India
Kashan *see* Košice
Kāshān *120 C3* Eşfahān, C Iran
Kashgar *see* Kashi
Kashi *126 A3 Chin.* Kaxgar, K'o-shih,
 Uigh. Kashgar. Xinjiang Uygur Zizhiqu,
 NW China
Kasi *see* Vārānasi
Kasongo *77 D6* Maniema, E Dem.
 Rep. Congo
Kasongo-Lunda *77 C7* Bandundu,
 SW Dem. Rep. Congo
Kásos *105 D7* island S Greece
Kaspiy Mangy Oypaty *see* Caspian
 Depression
Kaspiysk *111 B8* Respublika Dagestan,
 SW Russian Federation
Kaspiyskoye More/Kaspiy Tengizi *see*
 Caspian Sea
Kassa *see* Košice
Kassai *see* Kasai
Kassala *72 C4* Kassala, E Sudan
Kassel *94 B4 prev.* Cassel. Hessen,
 C Germany
Kasserine *71 E2 var.* Al Qaşrayn.
 W Tunisia
Kastamonu *116 C2 var.* Castamoni,
 Kastamuni. Kastamonu, N Turkey
Kastamuni *see* Kastamonu
Kastaneá *see* Kastaniá
Kastaniá *104 B4 prev.* Kastaneá. Kentrikí
 Makedonía, N Greece
Kastélli *see* Kíssamos
Kastoría *104 B4* Dytikí Makedonía,
 N Greece
Kástro *105 C6* Sífnos, Kykládes, Greece,
 Aegean Sea
Kastsyukovichy *107 E7 Rus.*
 Kostyukovichi. Mahilyowskaya
 Voblasts', E Belarus
Kastsyukowka *107 D7 Rus.*
 Kostyukovka. Homyel'skaya Voblasts',
 SE Belarus
Kasulu *73 B7* Kigoma, W Tanzania
Kasumiga-ura *131 D5* lake Honshū,
 S Japan
Katahdin, Mount *41 G1* mountain
 Maine, NE USA
Katalla *36 C3* Alaska, USA
Katana *see* Qaţanā
Katanning *147 B7* Western Australia
Katawaz *see* Zarghūn Shahr
Katchall Island *133 F3* island Nicobar
 Islands, India, NE Indian Ocean
Kateríni *104 B4* Kentrikí Makedonía,
 N Greece
Katha *136 B2* Sagaing, N Myanmar
 (Burma)
Katherine *148 A2* Northern Territory,
 N Australia
Kathmandu *124 C3 prev.* Kantipur.
 country capital (Nepal) Central,
 C Nepal
Katikati *150 D3* Bay of Plenty, North
 Island, New Zealand
Katima Mulilo *78 C3* Caprivi,
 NE Namibia
Katiola *74 D4* C Côte d'Ivoire
Káto Achaḯa *105 B5 var.* Kato Ahaia,
 Káto Akhaḯa. Dytikí Elláda, S Greece
Kato Ahaia/Káto Akhaḯa *see* Káto Achaḯa
Katoúna *105 A5* Dytikí Elláda,
 C Greece
Katowice *99 C5 Ger.* Kattowitz. Śląskie,
 S Poland
Katsina *75 G3* Katsina, N Nigeria
Kattakurgan *see* Kattaqo'rg'on
Kattaqo'rg'on *123 E2 Rus.* Kattakurgan.
 Samarqand Viloyati, C Uzbekistan
Kattavía *105 E7* Ródos, Dodekánisa,
 Greece, Aegean Sea
Kattegat *85 B7 Dan.* Kattegatt. *strait*
 N Europe
Kattegatt *see* Kattegat
Kattowitz *see* Katowice
Kaua'i *47 A7 var.* Kauai. *island*
 Hawaiian Islands, Hawai'i, USA,
 C Pacific Ocean
Kauai *see* Kaua'i
Kauen *see* Kaunas
Kaufbeuren *95 C6* Bayern, S Germany

Kaunas *106 B4 Ger.* Kauen, *Pol.* Kowno;
 prev. Rus. Kovno. Kaunas, C Lithuania
Kavadar *see* Kavadarci
Kavadarci *101 E6 Turk.* Kavadar.
 C Macedonia
Kavaja *see* Kavajë
Kavajë *101 C6 It.* Cavaia, Kavaja.
 Tiranë, W Albania
Kavakli *see* Topolovgrad
Kavála *104 C3 prev.* Kaválla. Anatolikí
 Makedonía kai Thráki, NE Greece
Kavali *132 D2* Andhra Pradesh, E India
Kaválla *see* Kavála
Kavango *see* Cubango/Okavango
Kavaratti Island *132 A3* island
 Lakshadweep, Lakshadweep, SW India
 Asia N Indian Ocean
Kavarna *104 E2* Dobrich, NE Bulgaria
Kavengo *see* Cubango/Okavango
Kavir, Dasht-e *120 D3 var.* Great Salt
 Desert. *salt pan* N Iran
Kavkaz *see* Caucasus
Kawagoe *131 D5* Saitama, Honshū,
 S Japan
Kawasaki *130 A2* Kanagawa, Honshū,
 S Japan
Kawerau *150 E3* Bay of Plenty, North
 Island, New Zealand
Kaxgar *see* Kashi
Kaya *75 E3* C Burkina Faso
Kayan *136 B4* Yangon, SW Myanmar
 (Burma)
Kayan, Sungai *138 D3 prev.* Kajan. *river*
 Borneo, C Indonesia
Kayes *74 C3* Kayes, W Mali
Kayseri *116 D3 var.* Kaisaria; *anc.*
 Caesarea Mazaca, Mazaca. Kayseri,
 C Turkey
Kazach'ye *115 F2* Respublika Sakha
 (Yakutiya), NE Russian Federation
**Kazakhskaya SSR/Kazakh Soviet
 Socialist Republic** *see* Kazakhstan
Kazakhstan *114 B4 off.* Republic of
 Kazakhstan, *var.* Kazakstan, *Kaz.*
 Qazaqstan, Qazaqstan Respublikasy;
 prev. Kazakh Soviet Socialist Republic,
 Rus. Kazakhskaya SSR. *country* C Asia

KAZAKHSTAN
Central Asia

Official name Republic of Kazakhstan
Formation 1991 / 1991
Capital Astana
Population 16.2 million / 15 people
 per sq mile (6 people per sq km)
Total area 1,049,150 sq. miles
 (2,717,300 sq. km)
Languages Kazakh*, Russian, Ukrainian,
 German, Uzbek, Tatar, Uighur
Religions Muslim (mainly Sunni) 47%,
 Orthodox Christian 44%, Other 9%
Ethnic mix Kazakh 57%, Russian 27%,
 Other 8%, Uzbek 3%, Ukrainian 3%,
 German 2%
Government Presidential system
Currency Tenge = 100 tiyn
Literacy rate 99%
Calorie consumption 3284 kilocalories

Kazakhstan, Republic of *see* Kazakhstan
Kazakh Uplands *114 C4 Eng.* Kazakh
 Uplands, Kirghiz Steppe. *uplands*
 C Kazakhstan
Kazakh Uplands *see* Saryarka
Kazakstan *see* Kazakhstan
Kazan' *111 C5* Respublika Tatarstan,
 W Russian Federation
Kazandzhik *see* Bereket
Kazanlik *see* Kazanlŭk
Kazanlŭk *104 D2 prev.* Kazanlik. Stara
 Zagora, C Bulgaria
Kazatin *see* Kozyatyn
Kazbegi *see* Kazbek
Kazbek *117 F1 var.* Kazbegi, *Geor.*
 Mqinvartsveri. mountain N Georgia
Kāzerūn *120 D4* Fārs, S Iran
Kazvin *see* Qazvin
Kéa *see* Tziá
Kéa *see* Ioulís
Kea, Mauna *47 B8* mountain Hawai'i,
 USA
Kéamu *see* Aneityum
Kearney *45 E4* Nebraska, C USA
Keban Barajı *117 E3* reservoir C Turkey
Kebkabiya *72 A4* Northern Darfur,
 W Sudan
Kebnekaise *84 C3 Lapp.* Giebnegáisi.
 mountain N Sweden

Kecskemét *99 D7* Bács-Kiskun,
 C Hungary
Kediri *138 D5* Jawa, C Indonesia
Kędzierzyn-Kozle *99 C5 Ger.*
 Heydebrech. Opolskie, S Poland
Keelung *see* Jilong
Keetmanshoop *78 B4* Karas, S Namibia
Kefallinía *see* Kefallonía
Kefallonía *105 A5 var.* Kefallinía.
 island Iónia Nisiá, Greece,
 C Mediterranean Sea
Kefe *see* Feodosiya
Kegel *see* Keila
Kehl *95 A6* Baden-Württemberg,
 SW Germany
Kei Islands *see* Kai, Kepulauan
Keijō *see* Seoul
Keila *106 D2 Ger.* Kegel. Harjumaa,
 NW Estonia
Keïta *75 F3* Tahoua, C Niger
Keith *149 B7* South Australia
Këk-Art *123 G2 prev.* Alaykel', Alay-
 Kuu. Oshskaya Oblast', SW Kyrgyzstan
Kékes *99 C6* mountain N Hungary
Kelamayi *see* Karamay
Kelang *see* Klang
Kelat *see* Kālat
Kelifskiy Uzboy *see* Kelif Uzboýy
Kelif Uzboýy *122 D3 Rus.* Kelifskiy
 Uzboy. *salt marsh* E Turkmenistan
Kelkit Çayı *117 E3 river* N Turkey
Kelmė *106 B4* Šiauliai, C Lithuania
Kélo *76 B4* Tandjilé, SW Chad
Kelowna *37 E5* British Columbia,
 SW Canada
Kelso *46 B2* Washington, NW USA
Keltsy *see* Kielce
Keluang *138 B3 var.* Kluang. Johor,
 Peninsular Malaysia
Kem' *110 B3* Respublika Kareliya,
 NW Russian Federation
Kemah *117 E3* Erzincan, E Turkey
Kemaman *see* Cukai
Kemerovo *114 D4 prev.* Shcheglovsk.
 Kemerovskaya Oblast', C Russian
 Federation
Kemi *84 D4* Lappi, NW Finland
Kemijärvi *84 D3* river NW Finland
Kemijärvi *84 D3 Swe.* Kemiträsk. Lappi,
 N Finland
Kemijoki *84 D3* river NW Finland
Kemin *123 G2 prev.* Bystrovka.
 Chuyskaya Oblast', N Kyrgyzstan
Kemins Island *see* Nikumaroro
Kemiträsk *see* Kemijärvi
Kemmuna *102 A5 var.* Comino. *island*
 C Malta
Kempele *84 D4* Oulu, C Finland
Kempten *95 B7* Bayern, S Germany
Kendal *89 D5* NW England, United
 Kingdom
Kendari *139 E4* Sulawesi, C Indonesia
Kenedy *49 G4* Texas, SW USA
Kenema *74 C4* SE Sierra Leone
Këneurgench *see* Köneürgench
Kenge *77 C6* Bandundu, SW Dem.
 Rep. Congo
Kengtung *136 C3* Shan State, E Myanmar
 (Burma)
Kénitra *70 C2 prev.* Port-Lyautey.
 NW Morocco
Kennett *45 H5* Missouri, C USA
Kennewick *46 C2* Washington, NW USA
Kenora *38 A3* Ontario, S Canada
Kenosha *40 B3* Wisconsin, N USA
Kentau *114 B5* Yuzhnyy Kazakhstan,
 S Kazakhstan
Kentucky *40 C5 off.* Commonwealth
 of Kentucky, also known as Bluegrass
 State. *state* C USA
Kentucky Lake *40 B5* reservoir
 Kentucky/Tennessee, S USA
Kenya *73 C6 off.* Republic of Kenya.
 country E Africa

KENYA
East Africa

Official name Republic of Kenya
Formation 1963 / 1963
Capital Nairobi
Population 41.6 million / 190 people
 per sq mile (73 people per sq km)
Total area 224,961 sq. miles
 (582,650 sq. km)
Languages Kiswahili*, English*, Kikuyu,
 Luo, Kalenjin, Kamba
Religions Christian 80%, Muslim 10%,
 Traditional beliefs 9%, Other 1%
Ethnic mix Other 28%, Kikuyu 22%,

204

KENYA *(continued)*
Luhya 14%, Luo 14%, Kalenjin 11%,
Kamba 11%
Government Mixed Presidential–
Parliamentary system
Currency Kenya shilling = 100 cents
Literacy rate 87%
Calorie consumption 2090 kilocalories

Kenya, Mount *see* Kirinyaga
Kenya, Republic of *see* Kenya
Keokuk *45 G4* Iowa, C USA
Kéos *see* Tziá
Kępno *98 C4* Wielkopolskie,
C Poland
Keppel Island *see* Niuatoputapu
Kerak *see* Al Karak
Kerala *132 C2* *cultural region* S India
Kerasunt *see* Giresun
Keratéa *105 C6* *var.* Keratea. Attikí,
C Greece
Keratea *see* Keratéa
Kerbala/Kerbela *see* Karbalāʾ
Kerch *109 G5* *Rus.* Kerch′. Avtonomna
Respublika Krym, SE Ukraine
Kerch′ *see* Kerch
**Kerchens′ka Protska/Kerchenskiy
Proliv** *see* Kerch Strait
Kerch Strait *109 G4* *var.* Bosporus
Cimmerius, Enikale Strait, *Rus.*
Kerchenskiy Proliv, *Ukr.* Kerchens′ka
Protska. *strait* Black Sea/Sea of Azov
Keremitlik *see* Lyulyakovo
Kerguelen *141 C7* *island* C French
Southern and Antarctic Territories
Kerguelen Plateau *141 C7* *undersea
plateau* S Indian Ocean
Kerí *105 A6* Zákynthos, Iónia Nisiá,
Greece, C Mediterranean Sea
Kerikeri *150 D2* Northland, North
Island, New Zealand
Kerkenah, Îles de *102 D4* *var.* Kerkenna
Islands, *Ar.* Juzur Qarqannah. *island
group* E Tunisia
Kerkenna Islands *see* Kerkenah, Îles de
Kerki *see* Atamyrat
Kérkira *see* Kérkyra
Kerkrade *87 D6* Limburg,
SE Netherlands
Kerkuk *see* Kirkūk
Kérkyra *104 A4* *var.* Kérkira, *Eng.*
Corfu. Kérkyra, Iónia Nisiá, Greece,
C Mediterranean Sea
Kermadec Islands *152 C4* *island group*
New Zealand, SW Pacific Ocean
Kermadec Trench *143 E4* *trench*
SW Pacific Ocean
Kermān *120 D3* *var.* Kirman; *anc.*
Carmana. Kermān, C Iran
Kermānshāh *120 C4* *var.*
Qahremānshahr; *prev.* Bākhtarān.
Kermānshāhān, W Iran
Kerrville *49 F4* Texas, SW USA
Kertel *see* Kärdla
Kerulen *127 E2* *Chin.* Herlen He, *Mong.*
Herlen Gol. *river* China/Mongolia
Kerýneia *see* Girne
Kesennuma *130 D4* Miyagi, Honshū,
C Japan
Keszthely *99 C7* Zala, SW Hungary
Ketchikan *36 D4* Revillagigedo Island,
Alaska, USA
Kętrzyn *98 D2* *Ger.* Rastenburg.
Warmińsko-Mazurskie, NE Poland
Kettering *89 D6* C England, United
Kingdom
Kettering *40 C4* Ohio, N USA
Keupriya *see* Primorsko
Keuruu *85 D5* Länsi-Suomi, C Finland
Keweenaw Peninsula *40 B1* *peninsula*
Michigan, N USA
Key Largo *43 F5* Key Largo, Florida,
SE USA
Keystone State *see* Pennsylvania
Key West *43 E5* Florida Keys, Florida,
SE USA
Kezdivásárhely *see* Târgu Secuiesc
Khabarovsk *115 G4* Khabarovskiy Kray,
SE Russian Federation
Khachmas *see* Xaçmaz
Khadera *see* Hadera
Khairpur *134 B3* Sind, SE Pakistan
Khalij *see* Khvoy
Khalīj *var.* *gulf* NE Egypt
Khalkidhikí *see* Chalkidikí
Khalkís *see* Chalkída

Gulf of Khambhat *134 C4* *Eng.* Gulf of
Cambay. *gulf* W India
Khamīs Mushayṭ *121 B6* *var.* Hamīs
Musait. ʿAsīr, SW Saudi Arabia
Khānābād *123 E3* Kunduz,
NE Afghanistan
Khān al Baghdādī *see* Al Baghdādī
Khandwa *134 D4* Madhya Pradesh,
C India
Khanh Hung *see* Soc Trăng
Khaniá *see* Chaniá
Khanka, Lake *129 E2* *var.* Hsing-K′ai
Hu, Lake Hanka, *Chin.* Xingkai Hu,
Rus. Ozero Khanka. *lake* China/
Russian Federation
Khanka, Ozero *see* Khanka, Lake
Khankendi *see* Xankändi
Khanthabouli *see* Savannakhét
Khanty-Mansiysk *114 C3* *prev.*
Ostyako-Voguls′k. Khanty-Mansiyskiy
Avtonomnyy Okrug-Yugra, C Russian
Federation
Khān Yūnis *119 A7* *var.* Khān Yūnus.
S Gaza Strip
Khān Yūnus *see* Khān Yūnis
Khanzi *see* Ghanzi
Kharagpur *135 F4* West Bengal,
NE India
Kharbin *see* Harbin
Kharkiv *109 G2* *Rus.* Khar′kov.
Kharkivs′ka Oblast′, NE Ukraine
Khar′kov *see* Kharkiv
Kharmanli *104 D3* Khaskovo, S Bulgaria
Khartoum *72 B4* *var.* El Khartûm,
Khartum. *country capital* (Sudan)
Khartoum, C Sudan
Khartum *see* Khartoum
Khasavyurt *111 B8* Respublika Dagestan,
SW Russian Federation
Khash, Dasht-e *122 D5* *Eng.* Khash
Desert. *desert* SW Afghanistan
Khash Desert *see* Khash, Dasht-e
Khashim Al Qirba/Khashm al Qirbah
see Khashm el Girba
Khashm el Girba *72 C4* *var.* Khashim
Al Qirba, Khashm al Qirbah. Kassala,
E Sudan
Khaskovo *104 D3* Khaskovo, S Bulgaria
Khaybar, Kowtal-e *see* Khyber Pass
Khaydarkan *123 F2* *var.* Khaydarken.
Batkenskaya Oblast′, SW Kyrgyzstan
Khaydarken *see* Khaydarkan
Khazar, Baḥr-i/Khazar, Daryā-ye *see*
Caspian Sea
Khelat *see* Kālat
Kherson *109 E4* Khersons′ka Oblast′,
S Ukraine
Kheta *115 E2* *river* N Russian Federation
Khíos *see* Chíos
Khirbet el ʿAujā et Taḥtā *119 E7* E West
Bank Asia
Khiva/Khiwa *see* Xiva
Khmel′nits′kiy *see* Khmel ′nyts′kyy
Khmel ′nyts′kyy *108 C2* *Rus.*
Khmel′nitskiy; *prev.* Proskurov.
Khmel′nyts′ka Oblast′, W Ukraine
Khodasy *107 E6* *Rus.* Khodosy.
Mahilyowskaya Voblasts′, E Belarus
Khodoriv *108 C2* *Pol.* Chodorów,
Rus. Khodorov. L′vivs′ka Oblast′,
NW Ukraine
Khodorov *see* Khodoriv
Khodosy *see* Khodasy
Khodzhent *see* Khujand
Khoi *see* Khvoy
Khojend *see* Khujand
Khokand *see* Qoʾqon
Kholm *see* Chełm
Kholm *see* Holon
Khoms *see* Al Khums
Khong Sedone *see* Muang Khôngxédôn
Khon Kaen *136 D4* *var.* Muang Khon
Kaen. Khon Kaen, E Thailand
Khor *115 G4* Khabarovskiy Kray,
SE Russian Federation
Khorat *see* Nakhon Ratchasima
Khorog *see* Khorugh
Khorugh *123 F3* *Rus.* Khorog.
S Tajikistan
Khôst *123 F4* *prev.* Khowst. Khōst,
E Afghanistan
Khotan *see* Hotan
Khouribga *70 B2* C Morocco
Khovd *see* Hovd
Khoy *see* Khvoy
Khoyniki *107 D8* Homyel′skaya
Voblasts′, SE Belarus
Khudzhand *see* Khujand

Khujand *123 E2* *var.* Khodzhent,
Khojend, *Rus.* Khudzhand; *prev.*
Leninabad, *Taj.* Leninobod.
N Tajikistan
Khulm *123 E3* *var.* Tashqurghan; *prev.*
Kholm. Balkh, N Afghanistan
Khulna *135 G4* Khulna, SW Bangladesh
Khums *see* Al Khums
Khust *108 B3* *var.* Husté, *Cz.* Chust,
Hung. Huszt. Zakarpats′ka Oblast′,
W Ukraine
Khvoy *120 C2* *var.* Khoi, Khoy.
Āzarbāyjān-e Bakhtari, NW Iran
Khyber Pass *134 C1* *var.* Kowtal-e
Khaybar. *pass* Afghanistan/Pakistan
Kiangmai *see* Chiang Mai
Kiang-ning *see* Nanjing
Kiangsi *see* Jiangxi
Kiangsu *see* Jiangsu
Kiáto *105 B6* *prev.* Kiáton. Pelopónnisos,
S Greece
Kiáton *see* Kiáto
Kiayi *see* Jiayi
Kibangou *77 B6* Niari, SW Congo
Kibombo *77 D6* Maniema, E Dem.
Rep. Congo
Kibris/Kibris Cumhuriyeti *see* Cyprus
Kičevo *101 D6* SW FYR Macedonia
Kidderminster *89 D6* C England, United
Kingdom
Kiel *94 B2* Schleswig-Holstein,
N Germany
Kielce *98 D4* *Rus.* Keltsy. Świętokrzyskie,
C Poland
Kieler Bucht *94 B2* *bay* N Germany
Kiev *see* Kyyiv
Kiev Reservoir *109 E1* *Eng.* Kiev
Reservoir, *Rus.* Kiyevskoye
Vodokhranilishche. *reservoir*
N Ukraine
Kiev Reservoir *see* Kyyivs′ke
Vodoskhovyshche
Kiffa *74 C3* Assaba, S Mauritania
Kigali *77 B6* *country capital* (Rwanda)
C Rwanda
Kigoma *73 B7* Kigoma, W Tanzania
Kihnu *106 C2* *var.* Kihnu Saar, *Ger.*
Kühnö. *island* SW Estonia
Kihnu Saar *see* Kihnu
Kii-suido *131 C7* *strait* S Japan
Kikinda *100 D3* *Ger.* Grosskikinda,
Hung. Nagykikinda; *prev.* Velika
Kikinda. Vojvodina, N Serbia
Kikládhes *see* Kykládes
Kikwit *77 C6* Bandundu, W Dem.
Rep. Congo
Kilien Mountains *see* Qilian Shan
Kilimane *see* Quelimane
Kilimanjaro *69 E5* *region* E Tanzania
Kilimanjaro *73 C7* *var.* Uhuru Peak.
volcano NE Tanzania
Kilingi-Nõmme *106 D3* *Ger.* Kurkund.
Pärnumaa, SW Estonia
Kilis *116 D4* Kilis, S Turkey
Kiliya *108 D4* *Rom.* Chilia-Nouă.
Odes′ka Oblast′, SW Ukraine
Kilkenny *89 B6* *Ir.* Cill Chainnigh.
Kilkenny, S Ireland
Kilkís *104 B3* Kentrikí Makedonía,
N Greece
Killarney *89 A6* *Ir.* Cill Airne. Kerry,
SW Ireland
Killeen *49 G3* Texas, SW USA
Kilmain *see* Quelimane
Kilmarnock *88 C4* W Scotland, United
Kingdom
Kilwa *see* Kilwa Kivinje
Kilwa Kivinje *73 C7* *var.* Kilwa. Lindi,
SE Tanzania
Kimberley *78 C4* Northern Cape,
C South Africa
Kimberley Plateau *146 C3* *plateau*
Western Australia
Kimch′aek *129 E3* *prev.* Sŏngjin.
E North Korea
Kími *see* Kými
Kinabalu, Gunung *138 D3* *mountain*
East Malaysia
Kindersley *37 F5* Saskatchewan,
S Canada
Kindia *74 C4* Guinée-Maritime,
SW Guinea
Kindley Field *42 A4* *air base*
E Bermuda
Kindu *77 D6* *prev.* Kindu-Port-Empain.
Maniema, C Dem. Rep. Congo
Kindu-Port-Empain *see* Kindu
Kineshma *111 C5* Ivanovskaya Oblast′,
W Russian Federation

King Charles Islands *see* Kong Karls
Land
King Christian IX Land *see* Kong
Christian IX Land
King Frederik VI Coast *see* Kong
Frederik VI Kyst
King Frederik VIII Land *see* Kong
Frederik VIII Land
King Island *149 B8* *island* Tasmania,
SE Australia
King Island *see* Kadan Kyun
Kingissepp *see* Kuressaare
Kingman *48 A1* Arizona, SW USA
Kingman Reef *145 E2* *US territory*
C Pacific Ocean
Kingsford Smith *148 E2* (Sydney) New
South Wales, SE Australia
King′s Lynn *89 E6* *var.* Bishop′s Lynn,
Kings Lynn, Lynn, Lynn Regis.
E England, United Kingdom
Kings Lynn *see* King′s Lynn
King Sound *146 B3* *sound* Western
Australia
Kingsport *43 E1* Tennessee,
S USA
Kingston *54 B5* *country capital*
(Jamaica) E Jamaica
Kingston *38 D5* Ontario, SE Canada
Kingston *41 F3* New York, NE USA
Kingston upon Hull *89 D5* *var.* Hull.
E England, United Kingdom
Kingston upon Thames *89 A8*
SE England, United Kingdom
Kingstown *55 H4* *country capital*
(Saint Vincent and the Grenadines)
Saint Vincent, Saint Vincent and the
Grenadines
Kingstown *see* Dún Laoghaire
Kingsville *49 G5* Texas, SW USA
King William Island *37 F3* *island*
Nunavut, N Canada
Kinneret, Yam *see* Tiberias, Lake
Kinrooi *87 D5* Limburg, NE Belgium
Kinshasa *77 B6* *prev.* Léopoldville.
country capital (Dem. Rep. Congo)
Kinshasa, W Dem. Rep. Congo
Kintyre *88 B4* *peninsula* W Scotland,
United Kingdom
Kinyeti *73 B5* *mountain* S South Sudan
Kiparissia *see* Kyparissía
Kipili *73 B7* Rukwa, W Tanzania
Kipushi *77 D8* Katanga, SE Dem. Rep.
Congo
Kirdzhali *see* Kŭrdzhali
Kirghizia *see* Kyrgyzstan
Kirghiz Range *123 F2* *Rus.* Kirgizskiy
Khrebet; *prev.* Alexander Range.
mountain range Kazakhstan/
Kyrgyzstan
Kirghiz SSR *see* Kyrgyzstan
Kirghiz Steppe *see* Saryarka
Kirgizskaya SSR *see* Kyrgyzstan
Kirgizskiy Khrebet *see* Kirghiz Range
Kiriath-Arba *see* Hebron
Kiribati *145 F2* *off.* Republic of Kiribati.
country C Pacific Ocean

KIRIBATI
Australasia & Oceania

Official name Republic of Kiribati
Formation 1979 / 1979
Capital Bairiki (Tarawa Atoll)
Population 101,998 / 372 people
per sq mile (144 people per sq km)
Total area 277 sq. miles (717 sq. km)
Languages English*, Kiribati
Religions Roman Catholic 55%,
Kiribati Protestant Church 36%, Other 9%
Ethnic mix Micronesian 99%, Other 1%
Government Nonparty system
Currency Australian dollar = 100 cents
Literacy rate 99%
Calorie consumption 2866 kilocalories

Kiribati, Republic of *see* Kiribati
Kırıkhan *116 D4* Hatay, S Turkey
Kırıkkale *116 C3* *province* C Turkey
Kirin *see* Jilin
Kirinyaga *73 C6* *prev.* Mount Kenya.
volcano C Kenya
Kirishi *110 B4* *var.* Kirisi.
Leningradskaya Oblast′, NW Russian
Federation
Kirisi *see* Kirishi
Kiritimati *145 G2* *prev.* Christmas
Island. *atoll* Line Islands, E Kiribati
Kirkenes *84 E2* *Fin.* Kirkkoniemi.
Finnmark, N Norway

Kirk-Kilissa see Kırklareli
Kirkkoniemi see Kirkenes
Kirkland Lake 38 D4 Ontario, S Canada
Kırklareli 116 A2 prev. Kirk-Kilissa.
  Kırklareli, NW Turkey
Kirkpatrick, Mount 154 B3 mountain
  Antarctica
Kirksville 45 G4 Missouri, C USA
Kirkūk 120 B3 var. Karkūk, Kerkuk. At
  Ta'mím, N Iraq
Kirkwall 88 C2 NE Scotland, United
  Kingdom
Kirkwood 45 G4 Missouri, C USA
Kir Moab/Kir of Moab see Al Karak
Kirov 111 C5 prev. Vyatka. Kirovskaya
  Oblast', NW Russian Federation
Kirovabad see Gäncä
Kirovakan see Vanadzor
Kirovo-Chepetsk 111 D5 Kirovskaya
  Oblast', NW Russian Federation
Kirovohrad 109 E3 Rus. Kirovograd;
  prev. Kirovo, Yelizavetgrad,
  Zinov'yevsk. Kirovohrads'ka Oblast',
  C Ukraine
Kirovo/Kirovograd see Kirovohrad
Kírthar Range 134 B3 mountain range
  S Pakistan
Kiruna 84 C3 Lapp. Giron. Norrbotten,
  N Sweden
Kirun/Kirun' see Jilong
Kisalföld see Little Alföld
Kisangani 77 D5 prev. Stanleyville.
  Orientale, NE Dem. Rep. Congo
Kishinev see Chişinău
Kislovodsk 111 B7 Stavropol'skiy Kray,
  SW Russian Federation
Kismaayo 73 D6 var. Chisimayu,
  Kismayu, It. Chisimaio. Jubbada
  Hoose, S Somalia
Kismayu see Kismaayo
Kíssamos 105 C7 prev. Kastélli. Kríti,
  Greece, E Mediterranean Sea
Kissidougou 74 C4 Guinée-Forestière,
  S Guinea
Kissimmee, Lake 43 E4 lake Florida,
  SE USA
Kistna see Krishna
Kisumu 73 C6 prev. Port Florence.
  Nyanza, W Kenya
Kisvárda 99 E6 Ger. Kleinwardein.
  Szabolcs-Szatmár-Bereg, E Hungary
Kita 74 D3 Kayes, W Mali
Kitab see Kitob
Kitakyūshū 131 A7 var. Kitakyūsyū.
  Fukuoka, Kyūshū, SW Japan
Kitakyūsyū see Kitakyūshū
Kitami 130 D2 Hokkaidō, NE Japan
Kitchener 38 C5 Ontario, S Canada
Kithnos see Kýthnos
Kitimat 36 D4 British Columbia,
  SW Canada
Kitinen 84 D3 river N Finland
Kitob 123 E3 Rus. Kitab. Qashqadaryo
  Viloyati, S Uzbekistan
Kitwe 78 D2 var. Kitwe-Nkana.
  Copperbelt, C Zambia
Kitwe-Nkana see Kitwe
Kitzbüheler Alpen 95 C7 mountain
  range W Austria
Kivalina 36 C2 Alaska, USA
Kívalo 84 D3 ridge C Finland
Kivertsy 108 C1 Pol. Kiwerce, Rus.
  Kivertsy. Volyns'ka Oblast',
  NW Ukraine
Kiwerce see Kivertsi
Kivu, Lac see Kivu, Lake
Kivu, Lake 77 E6 Fr. Lac Kivu. lake
  Rwanda/Dem. Rep. Congo
Kiwerce see Kivertsi
Kiyev see Kyyiv
Kiyevskoye Vodokhranilishche see
  Kyyivs'ke Vodoskhovyshche
Kızıl Irmak 116 C3 river C Turkey
Kizil Kum see Kyzyl Kum
Kizyl-Arvat see Serdar
Kjølen see Kölen
Kladno 99 A5 Středočeský, NW Czech
  Republic
Klagenfurt 95 D7 Slvn. Celovec.
  Kärnten, S Austria
Klaipėda 106 B3 Ger. Memel. Klaipėda,
  NW Lithuania
Klamath Falls 46 B4 Oregon, NW USA
Klamath Mountains 46 A4 mountain
  range California/Oregon, W USA
Klang 138 B3 var. Kelang; prev. Port
  Swettenham. Selangor, Peninsular
  Malaysia
Klarälven 85 B6 river Norway/Sweden

Klatovy 99 A5 Ger. Klattau. Plzeňský
  Kraj, W Czech Republic
Klattau see Klatovy
Klausenburg see Cluj-Napoca
Klazienaveen 86 E2 Drenthe,
  NE Netherlands
Kleines Ungarisches Tiefland see
  Little Alföld
Klein Karas 78 B4 Karas, S Namibia
Kleinwardein see Kisvárda
Kleisoúra 105 A5 Ípeiros, W Greece
Klerksdorp 78 D4 North-West, N South
  Africa
Klimavichy 107 E7 Rus. Klimovichi.
  Mahilyowskaya Voblasts', E Belarus
Klimovichi see Klimavichy
Klintsy 111 A5 Bryanskaya Oblast',
  W Russian Federation
Klisura 104 C2 Plovdiv, C Bulgaria
Ključ 100 B3 Federacija Bosna I
  Hercegovina, NW Bosnia and
  Herzegovina
Kłobuck 98 C4 Śląskie, S Poland
Klosters 95 B7 Graubünden,
  SE Switzerland
Kluang see Keluang
Kluczbork 98 C4 Ger. Kreuzburg,
  Kreuzburg in Oberschlesien. Opolskie,
  S Poland
Klyuchevskaya Sopka, Vulkan 115 H3
  volcano E Russian Federation
Knin 100 B4 Šibenik-Knin, S Croatia
Knjaževac 100 E4 Serbia, E Serbia
Knokke-Heist 87 A5 West-Vlaanderen,
  NW Belgium
Knoxville 42 D1 Tennessee, S USA
Knud Rasmussen Land 82 D1 physical
  region N Greenland
Kn) Ng Ng 122 D2 Rus. Kagan. Buxoro
  Viloyati, C Uzbekistan
Kobdo see Hovd
Kōbe 131 C6 Hyōgo, Honshū,
  SW Japan
København 85 B7 Eng. Copenhagen;
  anc. Hafnia. country capital (Denmark)
  Sjælland, København, E Denmark
Kobenni 74 D3 Hodh el Gharbi,
  S Mauritania
Koblenz 95 A5 prev. Coblenz, Fr.
  Coblence; anc. Confluentes. Rheinland-
  Pfalz, W Germany
Kobrin see Kobryn
Kobryn 107 A6 Rus. Kobrin. Brestskaya
  Voblasts', SW Belarus
Kobuleti 117 F2 prev. K'obulet'i.
  W Georgia
K'obulet'i see Kobuleti
Kočani 101 E6 NE FYR Macedonia
Kočevje 95 D8 Ger. Gottschee. S Slovenia
Koch Bihār 135 G3 West Bengal,
  NE India
Kochchi Kochi
Kochi 132 C3 prev. Cochin, var. Kochchi.
  Kerala, SW India
Kōchi 131 B7 var. Kôti. Kôchi, Shikoku,
  SW Japan
Kochiu see Gejiu
Kodiak 36 C3 Kodiak Island, Alaska,
  USA
Kodiak Island 36 C3 island Alaska, USA
Koedoes see Kudus
Koeln see Köln
Koepang see Kupang
Ko-erh-mu see Golmud
Koetai see Mahakam, Sungai
Koetaradja see Banda Aceh
Kōfu 131 D5 var. Kôhu. Yamanashi,
  Honshū, S Japan
Kogarah 148 E2 New South Wales,
  E Australia
Kogon 122 D2 Rus. Kagan. Buxoro
  Viloyati, C Uzbekistan
Kōhalom see Rupea
Kohima 135 H3 state capital Nāgāland,
  E India
Koh I Noh see Büyükağrı Dağı
Kohtla-Järve 106 E2 Ida-Virumaa,
  NE Estonia
Kôhu see Kōfu
Kokand see Qo'qon
Kokchetav see Kokshetau
Kokkola 84 D4 Swe. Karleby; prev. Swe.
  Gamlakarleby. Länsi-Suomi, W Finland
Koko 75 F4 Kebbi, W Nigeria
Kokomo 40 C4 Indiana, N USA
Koko Nor see Qinghai Hu, China
Koko Nor see Qinghai, China
Kokrines 36 C2 Alaska, USA
Kokshaal-Tau 123 G2 Rus. Khrebet
  Kakshaal-Too. mountain range China/
  Kyrgyzstan

Kokshetau 114 C4 Kaz. Kökshetaü; prev.
  Kokchetav. Kokshetau, N Kazakhstan
Kökshetaü see Kokshetau
Koksijde 87 A5 West-Vlaanderen,
  W Belgium
Koksoak 38 D2 river Québec, E Canada
Kokstad 78 D5 KwaZulu/Natal, E South
  Africa
Kolaka 139 E4 Sulawesi, C Indonesia
K'o-la-ma-i see Karamay
Kola Peninsula 110 C2 Eng. Kola
  Peninsula. peninsula NW Russian
  Federation
Kola Peninsula see Kol'skiy Poluostrov
Kolari 84 D3 Lappi, NW Finland
Kolárovo 99 C6 Ger. Gutta; prev.
  Guta, Hung. Gúta. Nitriansky Kraj,
  SW Slovakia
Kolberg see Kołobrzeg
Kolda 74 C3 S Senegal
Kolding 85 A7 Syddanmark, C Denmark
Kölen 81 E1 Nor. Kjølen. mountain
  range Norway/Sweden
Kolguyev, Ostrov 110 C2 island
  NW Russian Federation
Kolhāpur 132 B1 Mahārāshtra, SW India
Kolhumadulu 132 A5 var. Thaa Atoll.
  atoll S Maldives
Kolín 99 B5 Ger. Kolin. Střední Čechy,
  C Czech Republic
Kolka 106 C2 NW Latvia
Kolkasrags 106 C2 prev. Eng. Cape
  Domesnes. headland NW Latvia
Kollam 132 C3 prev. Quilon. Kerala,
  SW India
Kolmar see Colmar
Köln 94 A4 var. Koeln, Eng./Fr. Cologne;
  prev. Cöln; anc. Colonia Agrippina,
  Oppidum Ubiorum. Nordrhein-
  Westfalen, W Germany
Koło 98 C3 Wielkopolskie, C Poland
Kołobrzeg 98 B2 Ger. Kolberg.
  Zachodnio-pomorskie, NW Poland
Kolokani 74 D3 Koulikoro, W Mali
Kolomea see Kolomyya
Kolomna 111 B5 Moskovskaya Oblast',
  W Russian Federation
Kolomyya 108 C3 Ger. Kolomea. Ivano-
  Frankivs'ka Oblast', W Ukraine
Kolosjoki see Nikel'
Kolozsvár see Cluj-Napoca
Kolpa 100 A2 Ger. Kulpa, SCr. Kupa.
  river Croatia/Slovenia
Kolpino 110 B4 Leningradskaya Oblast',
  NW Russian Federation
Kólpos Mórfu see Güzelyurt
Kolwezi 77 D7 Katanga, S Dem. Rep.
  Congo
Kolyma 115 G2 river NE Russian
  Federation
Komatsu 131 C5 var. Komatu. Ishikawa,
  Honshū, SW Japan
Komatu see Komatsu
Kommunizm, Qullai see Ismoili Somoní,
  Qullai
Komoé 75 E4 var. Komoé Fleuve.
  river E Côte d'Ivoire
Komoé Fleuve see Komoé
Komotau see Chomutov
Komotiní 104 D3 var. Gümüljina, Turk.
  Gümülcine. Anatolikí Makedonía kai
  Thráki, NE Greece
Kompong see Kâmpóng Chhnăng
Kompong Cham see Kâmpóng Cham
Kompong Som see Sihanoukville
Kompong Speu see Kâmpóng Spoe
Komrat see Comrat
Komsomolets, Ostrov 115 E1 island
  Severnaya Zemlya, N Russian
  Federation
Komsomol'sk-na-Amure 115 G4
  Khabarovskiy Kray, SE Russian
  Federation
Kondolovo 104 E3 Burgas, E Bulgaria
Kondopoga 110 B3 Respublika Kareliya,
  NW Russian Federation
Kondoz see Kunduz
Kondoz 122 C2 var. Köneürgench,
  Rus. Këneurgench; prev. Kunya-
  Urgench. Daşoguz Welaýaty,
  N Turkmenistan
Köneürgench 122 C2 var. Köneürgench,
  Rus. Këneurgench; prev. Kunya-
  Urgench. Daşoguz Welaýaty,
  N Turkmenistan

Kong Frederik VI Kyst 82 C4 Eng. King
  Frederik VI Coast. physical region
  SE Greenland
Kong Karls Land 83 G2 Eng. King
  Charles Islands. island group
  SE Svalbard
Kongo see Congo (river)
Kongolo 77 D6 Katanga, E Dem. Rep.
  Congo
Kongor 73 B5 Jonglei, S South Sudan
Kong Oscar Fjord 83 E3 fjord
  E Greenland
Kongsberg 85 B6 Buskerud, S Norway
Kŏng, Tônlé 137 E5 var. Xê Kong. river
  Cambodia/Laos
Kong, Xé see Kŏng, Tônlé
Königgrätz see Hradec Králové
Königshütte see Chorzów
Konin 98 C3 Ger. Kuhnau.
  Weilkopolskie, C Poland
Koninkrijk der Nederlanden see
  Netherlands
Konispol 101 C7 var. Konispoli. Vlorë,
  S Albania
Konispoli see Konispol
Kónitsa 104 A4 Ípeiros, W Greece
Konitz see Chojnice
Konjic 100 C4 Federacija Bosna I
  Hercegovina, S Bosnia and
  Herzegovina
Konosha 110 C4 Arkhangel'skaya
  Oblast', NW Russian Federation
Konotop 109 F1 Sums'ka Oblast',
  NE Ukraine
Konstantinovka see Kostyantynivka
Konstanz 95 B7 var. Constanz, Eng.
  Constance, hist. Kostnitz; anc.
  Constantia. Baden-Württemberg,
  S Germany
Konstanza see Constanţa
Konya 116 C4 var. Konieh, prev. Konia;
  anc. Iconium. Konya, C Turkey
Kopaonik 101 D5 mountain range
  S Serbia
Kopar see Koper
Koper 95 D8 It. Capodistria; prev. Kopar.
  SW Slovenia
Köpetdag Gershi 122 C3 mountain
  range Iran/Turkmenistan
Köpetdag Gershi/Kopetdag, Khrebet
  see Koppeh Dāgh
Koppeh Dāgh 120 D2 Rus. Khrebet
  Kopetdag, Turkm. Köpetdag Gershi.
  mountain range Iran/Turkmenistan
Kopreinitz see Koprivnica
Koprivnica 100 B2 Ger. Kopreinitz,
  Hung. Kaproncza. Koprivnica-
  Križevci, N Croatia
Köprülü see Veles
Koptsevichi see Kaptsevichy
Kopyl' see Kapyl'
Korat see Nakhon Ratchasima
Korat Plateau 136 D4 plateau
  E Thailand
Korba 135 E4 Chhattīsgarh, C India
Korça see Korçë
Korçë 101 D6 var. Korça, Gk. Korytsa,
  It. Corizza; prev. Koritsa. Korçë,
  SE Albania
Korčula 100 B4 It. Curzola; anc. Corcyra
  Nigra. island S Croatia
Korea Bay 127 G3 bay China/North
  Korea
**Korea, Democratic People's Republic
  of** see North Korea
Korea, Republic of see South Korea
Korea Strait 131 A7 Jap. Chōsen-kaikyō,
  Kor. Taehan-haehyŏp. channel Japan/
  South Korea
Korhogo 74 D4 N Côte d'Ivoire
Kórinthos 105 B6 anc. Corinthus Eng.
  Corinth. Pelopónnisos, S Greece
Koritsa see Korçë
Kōriyama 131 D5 Fukushima, Honshū,
  C Japan
Korla 126 C3 Chin. K'u-erh-lo. Xinjiang
  Uygur Zizhiqu, NW China
Körmend 99 B7 Vas, W Hungary
Koróni 105 B6 Pelopónnisos,
  S Greece
Koror 144 A2 (Palau) Oreor, N Palau
Körös see Križevci
Korosten' 108 D1 Zhytomyrs'ka Oblast',
  NW Ukraine
Koro Toro 76 C2 Borkou-Ennedi-
  Tibesti, N Chad
Korsovka see Kārsava
Kortrijk 87 A6 Fr. Courtrai. West-
  Vlaanderen, W Belgium

Koryak Range 115 H2 *var.* Koryakskiy
   Khrebet, *Eng.* Koryak Range. *mountain*
   range NE Russian Federation
Koryak Range *see* Koryakskoy
   e Nagor'ye
Koryakskiy Khrebet *see* Koryakskoye
   Nagor'ye
Koryazhma 110 C4 Arkhangel'skaya
   Oblast', NW Russian Federation
Korytsa *see* Korçë
Kos 105 E6 Kos, Dodekánisa, Greece,
   Aegean Sea
Kos 105 E6 *It.* Coo; *anc.* Cos. *island*
   Dodekánisa, Greece, Aegean Sea
Ko-saki 131 A7 *headland* Nagasaki,
   Tsushima, SW Japan
Kościan 98 B4 *Ger.* Kosten.
   Wielkopolskie, C Poland
Kościerzyna 98 C2 Pomorskie,
   NW Poland
Kosciusko, Mount *see* Kosciuszko,
   Mount
Kosciuszko, Mount 149 C7 *prev.* Mount
   Kosciusko. *mountain* New South
   Wales, SE Australia
K'o-shih *see* Kashi
Koshikijima-retto 131 A8 *var.*
   Kosikizima Rettô. *island group*
   SW Japan
Kôshū *see* Gwangju
Košice 99 D6 *Ger.* Kaschau, *Hung.* Kassa.
   Košický Kraj, E Slovakia
Kosikizima-rettô *see*
   Koshikijima-rettô
Köslin *see* Koszalin
Koson 123 E3 *Rus.* Kasan. Qashqadaryo
   Viloyati, S Uzbekistan
Kosovo 101 D5 *prev.* Autonomous
   Province of Kosovo and Metohija.
   country SE Europe

KOSOVO (not yet fully recognized)
Southeast Europe

Official name Republic of Kosovo
Formation 2008 / 2008
Capital Prishtinë
Population 1.73 million / 412 people
   per sq mile (159 people per sq km)
Total area 4212 sq miles (10,908 sq km)
Languages Albanian*, Serbian*, Bosniak,
   Gorani, Roma, Turkish
Religions Muslim 92%, Roman
   Catholic 4%, Orthodox Christian 4%
Ethnic mix Albanian 92%, Serb 4%,
   Bosniak and Gorani 2%, Turkish 1%,
   Roma 1%
Government Parliamentary system
Currency Euro = 100 cents
Literacy rate 92%
Calorie consumption Not available

Kosovo and Metohija, Autonomous
   Province of *see* Kosovo
Kosovo Polje *see* Fushë Kosovë
Kosovska Mitrovica *see* Mitrovicë
Kosrae 144 C2 *prev.* Kusaie. *island*
   Caroline Islands, E Micronesia
Kossou, Lac de 74 D5 *lake* C Côte
   d'Ivoire
Kostanay 114 C4 *var.* Kustanay, *Kaz.*
   Qostanay. Kostanay, N Kazakhstan
Kosten *see* Kościan
Kostenets 104 C2 *prev.* Georgi Dimitrov.
   Sofiya, W Bulgaria
Kostnitz *see* Konstanz
Kostroma 111 B4 Kostromskaya Oblast',
   NW Russian Federation
Kostyantynivka 109 G3 *Rus.*
   Konstantinovka. Donets'ka Oblast',
   SE Ukraine
Kostyukovichi *see* Kastsyukovichy
Kostyukovka *see* Kastsyukowka
Koszalin 98 B2 *Ger.* Köslin. Zachodnio-
   pomorskie, NW Poland
Kota 134 D3 *prev.* Kotah. Rājasthān,
   N India
Kota Baharu *see* Kota Bharu
Kota Bahru *see* Kota Bharu
Kotabaru *see* Jayapura
Kota Bharu 138 B3 *var.* Kota Baharu,
   Kota Bahru. Kelantan, Peninsular
   Malaysia
Kotaboemi *see* Kotabumi
Kotabumi 138 B4 *prev.* Kotaboemi.
   Sumatera, W Indonesia
Kotah *see* Kota
Kota Kinabalu 138 D3 *prev.* Jesselton.
   Sabah, East Malaysia

Kotel'nyy, Ostrov 115 E2 *island*
   Novosibirskiye Ostrova, N Russian
   Federation
Kotka 85 E5 Etelä-Suomi, S Finland
Kotlas 110 C4 Arkhangel'skaya Oblast',
   NW Russian Federation
Kotonu *see* Cotonou
Kotor 101 C5 *It.* Cattaro.
   SW Montenegro
Kotovs'k 108 D3 *Rus.* Kotovsk. Odes'ka
   Oblast', SW Ukraine
Kotovsk *see* Hînceşti
Kottbus *see* Cottbus
Kotto 76 D4 *river* Central African
   Republic/Dem. Rep. Congo
Kotuy 115 E2 *river* N Russian
   Federation
Koudougou 75 E4 C Burkina Faso
Koulamoutou 77 B6 Ogooué-Lolo,
   C Gabon
Koulikoro 74 D3 Koulikoro, SW Mali
Koumra 76 C4 Moyen-Chari, S Chad
Kourou 59 H3 N French Guiana
Kousséir *see* Al Quşayr
Kousséri 76 B3 *prev.* Fort-Foureau.
   Extrême-Nord, NE Cameroon
Koutiala 74 D4 Sikasso, S Mali
Kouvola 85 E5 Etelä-Suomi, S Finland
Kovel' 108 C1 *Pol.* Kowel. Volyns'ka
   Oblast', NW Ukraine
Kovno *see* Kaunas
Koweit *see* Kuwait
Kowel *see* Kovel'
Kowloon 128 A2 Hong Kong, S China
Kowno *see* Kaunas
Kozáni 104 B4 Dytikí Makedonía,
   N Greece
Kozara 100 B3 *mountain range*
   NW Bosnia and Herzegovina
Kozarska Dubica *see* Bosanska Dubica
Kozhikode 132 C2 *var.* Calicut. Kerala,
   SW India
Kozu-shima 131 D6 *island* E Japan
Kozyatyn 108 D2 *Rus.* Kazatin.
   Vinnyts'ka Oblast', C Ukraine
Kpalimé 75 E5 *var.* Palimé. SW Togo
Krâchéh 137 D6 *prev.* Kratie. Krâchéh,
   E Cambodia
Kragujevac 100 D4 Serbia, C Serbia
Krainburg *see* Kranj
Kra, Isthmus of 137 B6 *isthmus*
   Malaysia/Thailand
Krakau *see* Kraków
Kraków 99 D5 *Eng.* Cracow, *Ger.*
   Krakau; *anc.* Cracovia. Małopolskie,
   S Poland
Králánh 137 D5 Siĕmréab,
   NW Cambodia
Kralendijk 100 D4 *dependent territory*
   capital (Netherlands) Bonaire
Kraljevo 100 D4 *prev.* Rankovićevo.
   Serbia, C Serbia
Kramators'k 109 G3 *Rus.* Kramatorsk.
   Donets'ka Oblast', SE Ukraine
Kramatorsk *see* Kramators'k
Kramfors 85 C5 Västernorrland,
   C Sweden
Kranéa *see* Kraniá
Kraniá 104 B4 *var.* Kranéa. Dytikí
   Makedonía, N Greece
Kranj 95 D7 *Ger.* Krainburg.
   NW Slovenia
Kranz *see* Zelenogradsk
Kráslava 106 D4 SE Latvia
Krasnaye 107 C5 *Rus.* Krasnoye.
   Minskaya Voblasts', C Belarus
Krasnoarmeysk 111 C6 Saratovskaya
   Oblast', W Russian Federation
Krasnodar 111 A7 *prev.* Ekaterinodar,
   Yekaterinodar. Krasnodarskiy Kray,
   SW Russian Federation
Krasnodon 109 H3 Luhans'ka Oblast',
   E Ukraine
Krasnogor *see* Kallaste
Krasnogvardeyskoye *see*
   Krasnohvardiys'ke
Krasnohvardiys'ke 109 F4 *Rus.*
   Krasnogvardeyskoye. Avtonomna
   Respublika Krym, S Ukraine
Krasnokamensk 115 F4 Zabaykal'skiy
   Kray, S Russian Federation
Krasnokamsk 111 D5 Permskiy Kray,
   W Russian Federation
Krasnoperekops'k 109 F4 *Rus.*
   Krasnoperekopsk. Avtonomna
   Respublika Krym, S Ukraine
Krasnoperekopsk *see* Krasnoperekops'k
Krasnostav *see* Krasnystaw
Krasnovodsk *see* Türkmenbaşy

Krasnovodskiy Zaliv *see* Türkmenbaşy
   Aylagy
Krasnowodsk Aylagy *see* Türkmenbaşy
   Aylagy
Krasnoyarsk 114 D4 Krasnoyarskiy
   Kray, S Russian Federation
Krasnoye *see* Krasnaye
Krasnystaw 98 E4 *Rus.* Krasnostav.
   Lubelskie, SE Poland
Krasnyy Kut 111 C6 Saratovskaya
   Oblast', W Russian Federation
Krasnyy Luch 109 H3 *prev.*
   Krindachevka. Luhans'ka Oblast',
   E Ukraine
Kratie *see* Krâchéh
Krăvanh, Chuŏr Phnum 137 C6 *Eng.*
   Cardamom Mountains, *Fr.* Chaîne
   des Cardamomes. *mountain range*
   W Cambodia
Krefeld 94 A4 Nordrhein-Westfalen,
   W Germany
Kreisstadt *see* Krosno Odrzańskie
Kremenchug *see* Kremenchuk
Kremenchugskoye Vodokhranilishche/
   Kremenchuk Reservoir *see*
   Kremenchuts'ke Vodoskhovyshche
Kremenchuk 109 F2 *Rus.* Kremenchug.
   Poltavs'ka Oblast', NE Ukraine
Kremenchuk Reservoir 109 F2
   Eng. Kremenchuk Reservoir, *Rus.*
   Kremenchugskoye Vodokhranilishche.
   reservoir C Ukraine
Kremenets' 108 C2 *Pol.* Krzemieniec,
   Rus. Kremenets. Ternopil's'ka Oblast',
   W Ukraine
Kremennaya *see* Kreminna
Kreminna 109 G2 *Rus.* Kremennaya.
   Luhans'ka Oblast', E Ukraine
Kresena *see* Kresna
Kresna 104 C3 *var.* Kresena.
   Blagoevgrad, SW Bulgaria
Kretikon Delagos *see* Kritikó Pélagos
Kretinga 106 B3 *Ger.* Krottingen.
   Klaipėda, NW Lithuania
Kreutz *see* Cristuru Secuiesc
Kreuz *see* Križevci, Croatia
Kreuz *see* Risti, Estonia
Kreuzburg/Kreuzburg in
   Oberschlesien *see* Kluczbork
Krichëv *see* Krychaw
Krievija *see* Russian Federation
Krindachevka *see* Krasnyy Luch
Krishna 132 C1 *prev.* Kistna. *river*
   C India
Krishnagiri 132 C2 Tamil Nādu,
   SE India
Kristiania *see* Oslo
Kristiansand 85 A6 *var.* Christiansand.
   Vest-Agder, S Norway
Kristianstad 85 B7 Skåne, S Sweden
Kristiansund 84 A4 *var.* Christiansund.
   Møre og Romsdal, S Norway
Krivoy Rog *see* Kryvyy Rih
Križevci 100 D4 *Ger.* Kreuz, *Hung.*
   Körös. Varaždin, NE Croatia
Krk 100 A3 *It.* Veglia; *anc.* Curicta.
   island NW Croatia
Kroatien *see* Croatia
Krolevets' 109 F1 *Rus.* Krolevets.
   Sums'ka Oblast', NE Ukraine
Krolevets *see* Krolevets'
Królewska Huta *see* Chorzów
Kronach 95 C5 Bayern, E Germany
Kronstadt *see* Braşov
Kroonstad 78 D4 Free State, C South
   Africa
Kropotkin 111 A7 Krasnodarskiy Kray,
   SW Russian Federation
Krosno 99 D5 *Ger.* Krossen.
   Podkarpackie, SE Poland
Krosno Odrzańskie 98 B3 *Ger.* Crossen,
   Kreisstadt. Lubuskie, W Poland
Krossen *see* Krosno
Krottingen *see* Kretinga
Krško 95 E8 *Ger.* Gurkfeld; *prev.* Videm-
   Krško. E Slovenia
Krugloye *see* Kruhlaye
Kruhlaye 107 D6 *Rus.* Krugloye.
   Mahilyowskaya Voblasts', E Belarus
Kruja *see* Krujë
Krujë 101 C6 *var.* Kruja, *It.* Croia.
   Durrës, C Albania
Krummau *see* Český Krumlov
Krung Thep, Ao 137 C5 *var.* Bight of
   Bangkok. *bay* S Thailand
Krung Thep Mahanakhon *see* Ao
   Krung Thep
Krupki 107 D6 Minskaya Voblasts',
   C Belarus

Krušné Hory *see* Erzgebirge
Krychaw 107 E7 *Rus.* Krichëv.
   Mahilyowskaya Voblasts', E Belarus
Kryms'ki Hory 109 F5 *mountain range*
   S Ukraine
Kryms'kyy Pivostriv 109 F5 *peninsula*
   S Ukraine
Krynica 99 D5 *Ger.* Tannenhof.
   Małopolskie, S Poland
Kryve Ozero 109 E3 Odes'ka Oblast',
   SW Ukraine
Kryvyy Rih 109 F3 *Rus.* Krivoy Rog.
   Dnipropetrovs'ka Oblast', SE Ukraine
Krzemieniec *see* Kremenets'
Ksar al Kabir *see* Ksar-el-Kebir
Ksar al Soule *see* Er-Rachidia
Ksar-el-Kebir 70 C2 *var.* Alcázar,
   Ksar al Kabir, Ksar-el-Kébir, *Ar.*
   Al-Ksar al-Kebir, Al-Qsar al-Kbir, *Sp.*
   Alcazarquivir. NW Morocco
Ksar-el-Kébir *see* Ksar-el-Kebir
Kuala Dungun *see* Dungun
Kuala Lumpur 138 B3 *country capital*
   (Malaysia) Kuala Lumpur, Peninsular
   Malaysia
Kuala Terengganu 138 B3 *var.* Kuala
   Trengganu. Terengganu, Peninsular
   Malaysia
Kualatungkal 138 B4 Sumatera,
   W Indonesia
Kuang-chou *see* Guangzhou
Kuang-hsi *see* Guangxi Zhuangzu Zizhiqu
Kuang-tung *see* Guangdong
Kuang-yuan *see* Guangyuan
Kuantan 138 B3 Pahang, Peninsular
   Malaysia
Kuba *see* Quba
Kuban' 109 G5 *var.* Hypanis. *river*
   SW Russian Federation
Kubango *see* Cubango/Okavango
Kuching 138 C3 *prev.* Sarawak. Sarawak,
   East Malaysia
Küchnay Darwēshān 122 D5 *prev.*
   Kūchnay Darweyshān. Helmand,
   S Afghanistan
Kūchnay Darweyshān *see* Küchnay
   Darwēshān
Kuçova *see* Kuçovë
Kuçovë 101 C6 *var.* Kuçova; *prev.* Qyteti
   Stalin. Berat, C Albania
Kudara *see* Ghūdara
Kudus 138 C5 *prev.* Koedoes. Jawa,
   C Indonesia
Kuei-lin *see* Guilin
Kuei-Yang/Kuei-yang *see* Guiyang
K'u-erh-lo *see* Korla
Kueyang *see* Guiyang
Kugaaruk 37 G3 *prev.* Pelly Bay.
   Nunavut, N Canada
Kugluktuk 53 E3 *var.* Qurlurtuuq; *prev.*
   Coppermine. Nunavut, NW Canada
Kuhmo 84 E4 Oulu, E Finland
Kuhnau *see* Konin
Kühnö *see* Kihnu
Kuibyshev *see* Kuybyshevskoye
   Vodokhranilishche
Kuito 78 B2 *Port.* Silva Porto. Bié,
   C Angola
Kuji 130 D3 *var.* Kuzi. Iwate, Honshū,
   C Japan
Kukës 101 D5 *var.* Kukësi. Kukës,
   NE Albania
Kukësi *see* Kukës
Kukong *see* Shaoguan
Kukukhoto *see* Hohhot
Kula Kangri 135 G3 *var.* Kulhakangri.
   mountain Bhutan/China
Kuldiga 106 B3 *Ger.* Goldingen.
   W Latvia
Kuldja *see* Yining
Kulhakangri *see* Kula Kangri
Kullorsuaq 82 D2 *var.* Kuvdlorssuak.
   Kitaa, C Greenland
Kulm *see* Chełmno
Kulmsee *see* Chełmża
Kŭlob 123 F3 *Rus.* Kulyab.
   SW Tajikistan
Kulpa *see* Kolpa
Kulu 116 C3 Konya, W Turkey
Kulunda Steppe *see* Ravnina Kulyndy
Kulundinskaya Ravnina *see* Ravnina
   Kulyndy
Kulyab *see* Kŭlob
Kum *see* Qom
Kuma 111 B7 *river* SW Russian
   Federation
Kumamoto 131 A7 Kumamoto, Kyūshū,
   SW Japan
Kumanova *see* Kumanovo

Kumanovo 101 E5 Turk. Kumanova.
N Macedonia
Kumasi 75 E5 prev. Coomassie. C Ghana
Kumayri see Gyumri
Kumba 77 A5 Sud-Ouest, W Cameroon
Kumertau 111 D6 Respublika
Bashkortostan, W Russian Federation
Kumillā see Comilla
Kumo 75 G4 Gombe, E Nigeria
Kumon Range 136 B2 mountain range
N Myanmar (Burma)
Kumul see Hami
Kunashiri see Kunashir, Ostrov
Kunashir, Ostrov 130 E1 var. Kunashiri.
island Kuril'skiye Ostrova, SE Russian
Federation
Kunda 106 E2 Lääne-Virumaa,
NE Estonia
Kunduz 123 E3 prev. Kondoz. province
NE Afghanistan
Kunene 69 C6 var. Kunene. river
Angola/Namibia
Kunene see Cunene
Kungsbacka 85 B7 Halland, S Sweden
Kungur 111 D5 Permskiy Kray,
NW Russian Federation
Kunlun Mountains see Kunlun Shan
Kunlun Shan 126 B4 Eng. Kunlun
Mountains. mountain range NW China
Kunming 128 B6 var. K'un-ming; prev.
Yunnan. province capital Yunnan,
SW China
K'un-ming see Kunming
Kununurra 146 D3 Western Australia
Kunya-Urgench see Köneürgenç
Kuopio 85 E5 Itä-Suomi, C Finland
Kupa see Kolpa
Kupang 139 E5 prev. Koepang. Timor,
C Indonesia
Kup″yans'k 109 G2 Rus. Kupyansk.
Kharkivs'ka Oblast', E Ukraine
Kupyansk see Kup″yans'k
Kür see Kura
Kura 117 H3 Az. Kür, Geor. Mtkvari,
Turk. Kura Nehri. river SW Asia
Kura Nehri see Kura
Kurashiki 131 B6 var. Kurasiki.
Okayama, Honshū, SW Japan
Kurasiki see Kurashiki
Kurdistan 117 F4 cultural region SW Asia
Kürdzhali 104 D3 var. Kirdzhali.
Kūrdzhali, S Bulgaria
Kure 131 B7 Hiroshima, Honshū,
SW Japan
Küre Dağları 116 C2 mountain range
N Turkey
Kuressaare 106 C2 Ger. Arensburg; prev.
Kingissepp. Saaremaa, W Estonia
Kureyka 112 D2 river N Russian
Federation
Kurgan-Tyube see Qŭrghonteppa
Kuria Muria Islands see Ḩalāniyāt,
Juzur al
Kurile Islands 115 H4 Eng. Kurile
Islands. island group SE Russian
Federation
Kurile Islands see Kuril'skiye Ostrova
Kurile-Kamchatka Depression see
Kurile Trench
Kurile Trench 113 F3 var. Kurile-
Kamchatka Depression. trench
NW Pacific Ocean
Kuril'sk 130 E1 Jap. Shana. Kuril'skiye
Ostrova, Sakhalinskaya Oblast',
SE Russian Federation
Ku-ring-gai 148 E1 New South Wales,
E Australia
Kurisches Haff see Courland Lagoon
Kurkund see Kilingi-Nõmme
Kurnool 132 C1 var. Karnul. Andhra
Pradesh, S India
Kursk 111 A6 Kurskaya Oblast',
W Russian Federation
Kurskiy Zaliv see Courland Lagoon
Kuršumlija 101 D5 Serbia, S Serbia
Kurtbunar see Tervel
Kuruktag 126 C3 mountain range
NW China
Kurume 131 A7 Fukuoka, Kyūshū,
SW Japan
Kurupukari 59 F3 C Guyana
Kusaie see Kosrae
Kushiro 130 D2 var. Kusiro. Hokkaidō,
NE Japan
Kushka see Serhetabat
Kusiro see Kushiro
Kuskokwim Mountains 36 C3
mountain range Alaska, USA

Kustanay see Kostanay
Küstence/Küstendje see Constanța
Kütahya 116 B3 prev. Kutaia. Kütahya,
W Turkey
Kutai see Mahakam, Sungai
Kutaisi 117 F2 W Georgia
Kūt al 'Amārah see Al Kūt
Kut al Imara see Al Kūt
Kutaradja/Kutaraja see Banda Aceh
Kutch, Gulf of see Kachchh, Gulf of
Kutch, Rann of see Kachchh, Rann of
Kutina 100 B3 Sisak-Moslavina,
NE Croatia
Kutno 98 C3 Łódzkie, C Poland
Kuujjuaq 39 E2 prev. Fort-Chimo.
Québec, E Canada
Kuusamo 84 E3 Oulu, E Finland
Kuvango see Cubango
Kuvdlorssuak see Kullorsuaq
Kuwait 120 C4 off. State of Kuwait, var.
Dawlat al Kuwait, Koweit, Kuwait.
country SW Asia

KUWAIT
Southwest Asia

Official name State of Kuwait
Formation 1961 / 1961
Capital Kuwait City
Population 2.8 million / 407 people
per sq mile (157 people per sq km) / 96%
Total area 6880 sq. miles (17,820 sq. km)
Languages Arabic*, English
Religions Sunni Muslim 45%, Shi'a
Muslim 40%, Christian, Hindu,
and other 15%
Ethnic mix Kuwaiti 45%, Other Arab 35%,
South Asian 9%, Other 7%, Iranian 4%
Government Monarchy
Currency Kuwaiti dinar = 1000 fils
Literacy rate 94%
Calorie consumption 3681 kilocalories

Kuwait see Al Kuwayt
Kuwait City see Al Kuwayt
Kuwait, Dawlat al see Kuwait
Kuwait, State of see Kuwait
Kuwajleen see Kwajalein Atoll
Kuwayt 120 C3 Maysān, E Iraq
Kuweit see Kuwait
Kuybyshev see Samara
Kuybyshev Reservoir 111 C5 var.
Kuibyshev, Eng. Kuybyshev Reservoir.
reservoir W Russian Federation
Kuybyshev Reservoir see
Kuybyshevskoye Vodokhranilishche
Kuytun 126 B2 Xinjiang Uygur Zizhiqu,
NW China
Kuzi see Kuji
Kuznetsk 111 B6 Penzenskaya Oblast',
W Russian Federation
Kuźnica 98 E2 Białystok, NE Poland
Europe
Kvaløya 84 C2 island N Norway
Kvarnbergsvattnet 84 B4 var.
Frostviken. lake N Sweden
Kvarner 100 A3 var. Carnaro, It.
Quarnero. gulf W Croatia
Kvitøya 83 G1 island NE Svalbard
Kwajalein Atoll 144 C1 var. Kuwajleen.
atoll Ralik Chain, C Marshall Islands
Kwando see Cuando
Kwangchow see Guangzhou
Kwangchu see Gwangju
Kwangju see Gwangju
Kwangsi/Kwangsi-Chuang see Gwangju
Kwango 77 C7 Port. Cuango. river
Angola/Dem. Rep. Congo
Kwango see Cuango
Kwangsi/Kwangsi Chuang
Autonomous Region see Guangxi
Zhuangzu Zizhiqu
Kwangtung see Guangdong
Kwangyuan see Guangyuan
Kwanza see Cuanza
Kweichu see Guiyang
Kweilin see Guilin
Kweisui see Hohhot
Kweiyang see Guiyang
Kwekwe 78 D3 prev. Que Que. Midlands,
C Zimbabwe
Kwesui see Hohhot
Kwidzyń 98 C2 Ger. Marienwerder.
Pomorskie, N Poland
Kwigillingok 36 C3 Alaska,
USA
Kwilu 77 C6 river W Dem. Rep. Congo
Kwito see Cuito
Kyabé 76 C4 Moyen-Chari, S Chad

Kyaikkami 137 B5 prev. Amherst. Mon
State, S Myanmar (Burma)
Kyaiklat 136 B4 Ayeyarwady,
SW Myanmar (Burma)
Kyaikto 136 B4 Mon State, S Myanmar
(Burma)
Kyakhta 115 E5 Respublika Buryatiya,
S Russian Federation
Kyaukse 136 B3 Mandalay, C Myanmar
(Burma)
Kyjov 99 C5 Ger. Gaya. Jihomoravský
Kraj, SE Czech Republic
Kými 105 C5 prev. Kími. Évvoia,
C Greece
Kyōngsŏng see Seoul
Kyōto 131 C6 Kyōto, Honshū, SW Japan
Kyparissía 105 B6 var. Kiparissía.
Pelopónnisos, S Greece
Kypros see Cyprus
Kyrá Panagía 105 C5 island Vóreies
Sporádes, Greece, Aegean Sea
Kyrenia see Girne
Kyrgyz Republic see Kyrgyzstan
Kyrgyzstan 123 F2 off. Kyrgyz Republic,
var. Kirghizia; prev. Kirgizskaya SSR,
Kirghiz SSR, Republic of Kyrgyzstan.
country C Asia

KYRGYZSTAN
Central Asia

Official name Kyrgyz Republic
Formation 1991 / 1991
Capital Bishkek
Population 5.4 million / 70 people
per sq mile (27 people per sq km) / 34%
Total area 76,641 sq. miles (198,500 sq. km)
Languages Kyrgyz*, Russian*, Uzbek,
Tatar, Ukrainian
Religions Muslim (mainly Sunni) 70%,
Orthodox Christian 30%
Ethnic mix Kyrgyz 69%, Uzbek 14%,
Russian 9%, Other 6%, Dungan 1%,
Uighur 1%
Government Presidential system
Currency Som = 100 tyiyn
Literacy rate 99%
Calorie consumption 2791 kilocalories

Kyrgyzstan, Republic of see Kyrgyzstan
Kythira 105 C7 var. Kíthira, It. Cerigo,
Lat. Cythera. island S Greece
Kíthnos 105 C6 Kýnthnos, Kykládes,
Greece, Aegean Sea
Kythnos 105 C6 var. Kíthnos, Thermiá,
It. Termia; anc. Cythnos. island
Kyklådes, Greece, Aegean Sea
Kythréa see Değirmenlik
Kyushu 131 B7 var. Kyûsyû. island
SW Japan
Kyushu-Palau Ridge 125 F3 var.
Kyusyu-Palau Ridge. undersea ridge
W Pacific Ocean
Kyustendil 104 B2 anc. Pautalia.
Kyustendil, W Bulgaria
Kyûsyû see Kyūshū
Kyusyu-Palau Ridge see Kyushu-Palau
Ridge
Kyyiv 109 E2 Eng. Kiev, Rus. Kiyev.
country capital (Ukraine) Kyyivs'ka
Oblast', N Ukraine
Kyzyl 114 D4 Respublika Tyva, C Russian
Federation
Kyzyl Kum 122 D2 var. Kizil Kum,
Qizil Qum, Uzb. Qizilqum. desert
Kazakhstan/Uzbekistan
Kyzylorda 114 B5 var. Kzyl-Orda, Qizil
Orda, Qyzylorda; prev. Kzylorda,
Perovsk. Kyzylorda, S Kazakhstan
Kyzylrabot see Qizilrabot
Kyzyl-Suu 123 G2 prev. Pokrovka.
Issyk-Kul'skaya Oblast', NE Kyrgyzstan
Kzyl-Orda see Kyzylorda
Kzylorda see Kyzylorda

L

Laaland see Lolland
La Algaba 92 C4 Andalucía, S Spain
Laarne 87 B5 Oost-Vlaanderen,
NW Belgium
La Asunción 59 E1 Nueva Esparta,
NE Venezuela
Laatokka see Ladozhskoye, Ozero
Laâyoune 70 B3 var. Aaiun. country
capital (Western Sahara) NW
NW Western Sahara
La Banda Oriental see Uruguay

la Baule-Escoublac 90 A4 Loire-
Atlantique, NW France
Labé 74 C4 NW Guinea
Labe see Elbe
Laborca see Laborec
Laborec 99 E5 Hung. Laborca. river
E Slovakia
Labrador 39 F2 cultural region
Newfoundland and Labrador,
SW Canada
Labrador Basin 34 E3 var. Labrador Sea
Basin. undersea basin Labrador Sea
Labrador Sea 82 A4 sea NW Atlantic
Ocean
Labrador Sea Basin see Labrador Basin
Labudalin see Ergun
Labutta 137 A5 Ayeyarwady,
SW Myanmar (Burma)
Laç 101 C6 var. Laci. Lezhë, C Albania
La Calera 64 B4 Valparaíso, C Chile
La Carolina 92 D4 Andalucía, S Spain
Laccadive Islands 132 A3 Eng. Laccadive
Islands. island group India, N Indian
Ocean
**Laccadive Islands/Laccadive Minicoy
and Amindivi Islands, the** see
Lakshadweep
La Ceiba 52 D2 Atlántida, N Honduras
Lachanás 104 B3 Kentrikí Makedonía,
N Greece
La Chaux-de-Fonds 95 A7 Neuchâtel,
W Switzerland
Lachlan River 149 C6 river New South
Wales, SE Australia
Laci see Laç
la Ciotat 91 D6 anc. Citharista. Bouches-
du-Rhône, SE France
Lacobriga see Lagos
La Concepción 53 E5 var. Concepción.
Chiriquí, W Panama
La Concepción 58 C1 Zulia,
NW Venezuela
La Condamine 91 C8 W Monaco
Laconia 41 G2 New Hampshire, NE USA
La Crosse 40 A2 Wisconsin, N USA
La Cruz 52 D4 Guanacaste, NW Costa
Rica
La Ladoga 110 B3 Eng. Lake Ladoga,
Fin. Laatokka. lake NW Russian
Federation
Ladoga, Lake see Ladozhskoye, Ozero
Ladysmith 40 B2 Wisconsin, N USA
Lae 144 B3 Morobe, W Papua New
Guinea
La Esperanza 52 C2 Intibucá,
SW Honduras
Lafayette 40 C4 Indiana, N USA
Lafayette 42 B3 Louisiana, S USA
La Fé 54 A2 Pinar del Río, W Cuba
Lafia 75 G4 Nassarawa, C Nigeria
la Flèche 90 B4 Sarthe, NW France
Lagdo, Lac de 76 B4 lake N Cameroon
Laghouat 70 D2 N Algeria
Lagos 75 F5 Lagos, SW Nigeria
Lagos 92 B5 anc. Lacobriga. Faro,
S Portugal
Lagos de Moreno 51 E4 Jalisco,
SW Mexico
Lagouira 70 A4 SW Western Sahara
La Grande 46 C3 Oregon, NW USA
La Guaira 66 B4 Distrito Federal,
N Venezuela
Lagunas 64 B1 Tarapacá, N Chile
Lagunillas 61 G4 Santa Cruz, SE Bolivia
La Habana 54 B2 var. Havana. country
capital (Cuba) Ciudad de La Habana,
W Cuba
Lahat 138 B4 Sumatera, W Indonesia
La Haye see 's-Gravenhage
Laholm 85 B7 Halland, S Sweden
Lahore 134 D2 Punjab, NE Pakistan
Lahr 95 A6 Baden-Württemberg,
S Germany
Lahti 85 D5 Swe. Lahtis. Etelä-Suomi,
S Finland
Lahtis see Lahti
Lai 76 B4 prev. Behagle, De Behagle.
Tandjilé, S Chad
Laibach see Ljubljana
Lai Châu 136 D3 Lai Châu, N Vietnam
Laila see Laylā
La Junta 44 D5 Colorado, C USA
Lake Charles 42 A3 Louisiana, S USA
Lake City 43 E3 Florida, SE USA
Lake District 89 C5 physical region
NW England, United Kingdom
Lake Havasu City 48 A2 Arizona,
SW USA
Lake Jackson 49 H4 Texas, SW USA

Lakeland *43 E4* Florida, SE USA
Lakeside *47 C8* California, W USA
Lake State *see* Michigan
Lakewood *44 D4* Colorado, C USA
Lakhnau *see* Lucknow
Lakonikós Kólpos *105 B7 gulf* S Greece
Lakselv *84 D2 Lapp.* Leavdnja. Finnmark, N Norway
la Laon *see* Laon
Lalibela *72 C4* Āmara, Ethiopia
La Libertad *52 B1* Petén, N Guatemala
La Ligua *64 B4* Valparaíso, C Chile
Lalín *92 C1* Galicia, NW Spain
Lalitpur *135 F3* Central, C Nepal
La Louvière *87 B6* Hainaut, S Belgium
la Maddalena *96 A4* Sardegna, Italy, C Mediterranean Sea
la Manche *see* English Channel
Lamar *44 D5* Colorado, C USA
La Marmora, Punta *97 A5 mountain* Sardegna, Italy, C Mediterranean Sea
La Massana *91 A8* La Massana, W Andorra Europe
Lambaréné *77 A6* Moyen-Ogooué, W Gabon
Lamego *92 C2* Viseu, N Portugal
Lamesa *49 E3* Texas, SW USA
Lamezia Terme *97 D6* Calabria, SE Italy
Lamía *105 B5* Stereá Elláda, C Greece
Lamoni *45 F4* Iowa, C USA
Lampang *136 C4 var.* Muang Lampang. Lampang, NW Thailand
Lámpeia *105 B6* Dytikí Elláda, S Greece
Lanbi Kyun *137 B6 prev.* Sullivan Island. *island* Mergui Archipelago, S Myanmar (Burma)
Lancang Jiang *see* Mekong
Lancaster *89 D5* NW England, United Kingdom
Lancaster *47 C7* California, W USA
Lancaster *41 F4* Pennsylvania, NE USA
Lancaster Sound *37 F2 sound* Nunavut, N Canada
Lan-chou/Lan-chow/Lanchow *see* Lanzhou
Landao *see* Lantau Island
Landen *87 C6* Vlaams Brabant, C Belgium
Lander *44 C3* Wyoming, C USA
Landerneau *90 A3* Finistère, NW France
Landes *91 B5 cultural region* SW France
Land of Enchantment *see* New Mexico
The Land of Opportunity *see* Arkansas
Land of Steady Habits *see* Connecticut
Land of the Midnight Sun *see* Alaska
Landsberg *see* Gorzów Wielkopolski, Lubuskie, Poland
Landsberg an der Warthe *see* Gorzów Wielkopolski
Land's End *89 B8 headland* SW England, United Kingdom
Landshut *95 C6* Bayern, SE Germany
Langar *123 E2 Rus.* Lyangar. Navoiy Viloyati, C Uzbekistan
Langfang *128 D4* Hebei, E China
Langkawi, Pulau *137 B7 island* Peninsular Malaysia
Langres *90 D4* Haute-Marne, N France
Langsa *138 A3* Sumatera, W Indonesia
Lang Shan *127 E3 mountain range* N China
Lang Son *136 D3 var.* Langson. Lang Sơn, N Vietnam
Langson *see* Lang Sơn
Lang Suan *137 B6* Chumphon, SW Thailand
Languedoc *91 C6 cultural region* S France
Länkäran *117 H3 Rus.* Lenkoran'. S Azerbaijan
Lansing *40 C3 state capital* Michigan, N USA
Lanta, Ko *137 B7 island* S Thailand
Lantau Island *128 A2 Cant.* Tai Yue Shan, *Chin.* Landao. *island* Hong Kong, S China
Lan-ts'ang Chiang *see* Mekong
Lantung, Gulf of *see* Liaodong Wan
Lanzarote *70 B3 island* Islas Canarias, Spain, NE Atlantic Ocean
Lanzhou *128 B4 var.* Lan-chou, Lanchow, Lan-chow; *prev.* Kaolan. *province capital* Gansu, C China
Lao Cai *136 D3* Lao Cai, N Vietnam
Laodicea/Laodicea ad Mare *see* Al Lādhiqīyah
Laoet *see* Laut, Pulau
Laon *90 D3 var.* la Laon; *anc.* Laudunum. Aisne, N France

Lao People's Democratic Republic *see* Laos
La Orchila, Isla *58 D1 island* N Venezuela
La Oroya *60 C3* Junín, C Peru
Laos *136 D4 off.* Lao People's Democratic Republic. *country* SE Asia

LAOS
Southeast Asia

Official name Lao People's Democratic Republic
Formation 1953 / 1953
Capital Vientiane
Population 6.3 million / 71 people per sq mile (27 people per sq km)
Total area 91,428 sq. miles (236,800 sq. km)
Languages Lao*, Mon-Khmer, Yao, Vietnamese, Chinese, French
Religions Buddhist 65%, Other (including animist) 34%, Christian 1%
Ethnic mix Lao Loum 66%, Lao Theung 30%, Lao Soung 2%, Other 2%
Government One-party state
Currency New kip = 100 at
Literacy rate 73%
Calorie consumption 2377 kilocalories

La Palma *53 G5* Darién, SE Panama
La Palma *70 A3 island* Islas Canarias, Spain, NE Atlantic Ocean
La Paz *61 F4 var.* La Paz de Ayacucho. *country capital* (Bolivia-legislative and administrative capital) La Paz, W Bolivia
La Paz *50 B3* Baja California Sur, NW Mexico
La Paz, Bahía de *50 B3 bay* NW Mexico
La Paz de Ayacucho *see* La Paz
La Pérouse Strait *130 D1 Jap.* Sōya-kaikyō, *Rus.* Proliv Laperuza. *strait* Japan/Russian Federation
Laperuza, Proliv *see* La Pérouse Strait
Lápithos *see* Lapta
Lapland *84 D3 Fin.* Lappi, *Swe.* Lappland. *cultural region* N Europe
La Plata *64 D4* Buenos Aires, E Argentina
La Plata *see* Sucre
La Pola *92 D1 prev.* Pola de Lena. Asturias, N Spain
Lappeenranta *85 E5 Swe.* Villmanstrand. Etelä-Suomi, SE Finland
Lappi/Lappland *see* Lapland
Lappo *see* Lapua
Lapta *102 C5 Gk.* Lápithos. NW Cyprus
Laptev Sea *115 E2 Eng.* Laptev Sea. *sea* Arctic Ocean
Laptev Sea *see* Laptevykh, More
Lapua *85 D5 Swe.* Lappo. Länsi-Suomi, W Finland
Lapurdum *see* Bayonne
Łapy *98 E3* Podlaskie, NE Poland
La Quiaca *64 C2* Jujuy, N Argentina
L'Aquila *96 C4 var.* Aquila, Aquila degli Abruzzi. Abruzzo, C Italy
Laracha *92 B1* Galicia, NW Spain
Laramie *44 C4* Wyoming, C USA
Laramie Mountains *44 C3 mountain range* Wyoming, C USA
Laredo *93 E1* Cantabria, N Spain
Laredo *49 F5* Texas, SW USA
La Réunion *see* Réunion
Largeau *see* Faya
Largo *43 E4* Florida, SE USA
Largo, Cayo *54 B2 island* W Cuba
Lario *see* Como, Lago di
La Rioja *64 C3* La Rioja, NW Argentina
La Rioja *93 E2 autonomous community* N Spain
Lárisa *104 B4 var.* Larissa. Thessalía, C Greece
Larissa *see* Lárisa
Lärkäna *134 B3 var.* Larkhana. Sind, SE Pakistan
Larkhana *see* Lärkäna
Lárnaca *102 C5 var.* Larnaca, Larnax. SE Cyprus
Larnax *see* Lárnaca
la Rochelle *90 B4 anc.* Rupella. Charente-Maritime, W France
la Roche-sur-Yon *90 B4 prev.* Bourbon Vendée, Napoléon-Vendée. Vendée, NW France
La Roda *93 E3* Castilla-La Mancha, C Spain

La Romana *55 E3* E Dominican Republic
Larvotto *91 C8* N Monaco Europe
La-sa *see* Lhasa
Las Cabezas de San Juan *92 C5* Andalucía, S Spain
Las Cruces *48 D3* New Mexico, SW USA
La Serena *64 B3* Coquimbo, C Chile
La Seu d'Urgell *93 G1 var.* La Seu d'Urgell; *prev.* Seo de Urgel. Cataluña, NE Spain
La Seu d'Urgell *see* La Seu d'Urgell
la Seyne-sur-Mer *91 D6* Var, SE France
Lashio *136 B3* Shan State, E Myanmar (Burma)
Lashkar Gäh *122 D5 var.* Lash-Kar-Gar'. Helmand, S Afghanistan
Lash-Kar-Gar' *see* Lashkar Gäh
La Sila *97 D6 mountain range* SW Italy
La Sirena *52 D3* Región Autónoma Atlántico Sur, E Nicaragua
La Solana *93 E4* Castilla-La Mancha, C Spain
Las Lomitas *64 D2* Formosa, N Argentina
Las Palmas *70 A3 var.* Las Palmas de Gran Canaria. Gran Canaria, Islas Canarias, Spain, NE Atlantic Ocean
Las Palmas de Gran Canaria *see* Las Palmas
La Spezia *96 B3* Liguria, NW Italy
Lassa *see* Lhasa
Las Tablas *53 F5* Los Santos, S Panama
Last Frontier, The *see* Alaska
Las Tunas *54 C2 var.* Victoria de las Tunas. Las Tunas, E Cuba
Las Vegas *47 D7* Nevada, W USA
Latacunga *60 B1* Cotopaxi, C Ecuador
la Teste *91 B5* Gironde, SW France
Latina *97 C5 prev.* Littoria. Lazio, C Italy
La Tortuga, Isla *59 E1 var.* Isla Tortuga. *island* N Venezuela
La Tuque *39 E4* Québec, SE Canada
Latvia *106 C3 off.* Republic of Latvia, *Ger.* Lettland, *Latv.* Latvija, Latvijas Republika; *prev.* Latvian SSR, *Rus.* Latviyskaya SSR. *country* NE Europe

LATVIA
Northeast Europe

Official name Republic of Latvia
Formation 1991 / 1991
Capital Riga
Population 2.2 million / 88 people per sq mile (34 people per sq km)
Total area 24,938 sq. miles (64,589 sq. km)
Languages Latvian*, Russian
Religions Other 43%, Lutheran 24%, Roman Catholic 18%, Orthodox Christian 15%
Ethnic mix Latvian 59%, Russian 28%, Belarussian 4%, Other 4%, Ukrainian 3%, Polish 2%
Government Parliamentary system
Currency Lats = 100 santimi
Literacy rate 99%
Calorie consumption 2923 kilocalories

Latvian SSR/Latvija/Latvijas Republika/Latviyskaya SSR *see* Latvia
Latvia, Republic of *see* Latvia
Laudunum *see* Laon
Laudus *see* St-Lô
Lauenburg/Lauenburg in Pommern *see* Lębork
Lau Group *145 E4 island group* E Fiji
Lauis *see* Lugano
Launceston *149 C8* Tasmania, SE Australia
La Unión *52 C2* Olancho, C Honduras
La Unión *93 F4* Murcia, SE Spain
Laurel *42 C3* Mississippi, S USA
Laurel *44 C2* Montana, NW USA
Laurentian Highlands *see* Laurentian Mountains
Laurentian Mountains *39 E3 var.* Laurentian Highlands, *Fr.* Les Laurentides. *plateau* Newfoundland and Labrador/Québec, Canada
Laurentides, Les *see* Laurentian Mountains
Lauria *97 D6* Basilicata, S Italy
Laurinburg *43 F1* North Carolina, SE USA
Lauru *see* Choiseul
Lausanne *95 A7 It.* Losanna. Vaud, SW Switzerland

Laut, Pulau *138 D4 prev.* Laoet. *island* Borneo, C Indonesia
Laval *38 D4* Québec, SE Canada
Laval *90 B3* Mayenne, NW France
La Vall d'Uixó *93 F3 var.* Vall D'Uxó. Valenciana, E Spain
La Vega *55 E3 var.* Concepción de la Vega. C Dominican Republic
La Vila Joiosa *see* Villajoyosa
Lávrio *105 C6 prev.* Lávrion. Attikí, C Greece
Lávrion *see* Lávrio
Lawrence *41 G3* Massachusetts, NE USA
Lawrenceburg *42 C1* Tennessee, S USA
Lawton *49 F2* Oklahoma, C USA
La Yarada *61 E4* Tacna, SW Peru
Laylá *121 C5 var.* Laila. Ar Riyāḍ, C Saudi Arabia
Lazarev Sea *154 B1 sea* Antarctica
Lázaro Cárdenas *51 E5* Michoacán, SW Mexico
Leal *see* Lihula
Leamhcán *see* Lucan
Leamington *38 C5* Ontario, S Canada
Leavdnja *see* Lakselv
Lebak *139 E3* Mindanao, S Philippines
Lebanese Republic *see* Lebanon
Lebanon *45 G5* Missouri, C USA
Lebanon *41 G2* New Hampshire, NE USA
Lebanon *46 B3* Oregon, NW USA
Lebanon *118 A4 off.* Lebanese Republic, *Ar.* Al Lubnān, *Fr.* Liban. *country* SW Asia

LEBANON
Southwest Asia

Official name Republic of Lebanon
Formation 1941 / 1941
Capital Beirut
Population 4.3 million / 1089 people per sq mile (420 people per sq km)
Total area 4015 sq. miles (10,400 sq. km)
Languages Arabic*, French, Armenian, Assyrian
Religions Muslim 60%, Christian 39%, Other 1%
Ethnic mix Arab 95%, Armenian 4%, Other 1%
Government Parliamentary system
Currency Lebanese pound = 100 piastres
Literacy rate 90%
Calorie consumption 3153 kilocalories

Lebanon, Mount *see* Liban, Jebel
Lebap *122 D2* Lebapskiy Velayat, NE Turkmenistan
Lebedin *see* Lebedyn
Lebedyn *109 F2 Rus.* Lebedin. Sums'ka Oblast', NE Ukraine
Lębork *98 C2 var.* Lębórk, *Ger.* Lauenburg, Lauenburg in Pommern. Pomorskie, N Poland
Lebrija *92 C5* Andalucía, S Spain
Lebu *65 A5* Bío Bío, C Chile
le Cannet *91 D6* Alpes-Maritimes, SE France
Le Cap *see* Cap-Haïtien
Lecce *97 E6* Puglia, SE Italy
Lechainá *105 B6 var.* Lehena, Lekhainá. Dytikí Elláda, S Greece
Ledo Salinarius *see* Lons-le-Saunier
Leduc *37 E5* Alberta, SW Canada
Leech Lake *45 F2 lake* Minnesota, N USA
Leeds *89 D5* N England, United Kingdom
Leek *86 E2* Groningen, NE Netherlands
Leer *94 A3* Niedersachsen, NW Germany
Leeuwarden *86 D1 Fris.* Ljouwert. Fryslân, N Netherlands
Leeuwin, Cape *142 A5 headland* Western Australia
Leeward Islands *55 G3 island group* E West Indies
Leeward Islands *see* Sotavento, Ilhas de
Lefkáda *105 A5 prev.* Levkás. Lefkáda, Iónia Nisiá, Greece, C Mediterranean Sea
Lefkáda *105 A5 It.* Santa Maura, *prev.* Levkás; *anc.* Leucas. *island* Iónia Nisiá, Greece, C Mediterranean Sea
Lefká Óri *105 C7 mountain range* Kríti, Greece, E Mediterranean Sea
Lefkímmi *105 A5 var.* Levkímmi. Kérkyra, Iónia Nisiá, Greece, C Mediterranean Sea
Lefkosía/Lefkoşa *see* Nicosia
Legaceaster *see* Chester
Legaspi *see* Legazpi City

Leghorn see Livorno
Legnica 98 B4 Ger. Liegnitz.
Dolnośląskie, SW Poland
le Havre 90 B3 Eng. Havre; prev. le
Havre-de-Grâce. Seine-Maritime,
N France
le Havre-de-Grâce see le Havre
Lehena see Lecháiná
Leicester 89 D6 Lat. Batae Coritanorum.
C England, United Kingdom
Leiden 86 B3 prev. Leyden; anc.
Lugdunum Batavorum. Zuid-Holland,
W Netherlands
Leie 90 D2 Fr. Lys. river Belgium/France
Leinster 89 B6 Ir. Cúige Laighean.
cultural region E Ireland
Leipsic see Leipzig
Leipsoí 105 E6 island Dodekánisa,
Greece, Aegean Sea
Leipzig 94 C4 Pol. Lipsk, hist. Leipsic;
anc. Lipsia. Sachsen, E Germany
Leiria 92 B3 anc. Collipo. Leiria,
C Portugal
Leirvik 85 A6 Hordaland, S Norway
Lek 86 C4 river SW Netherlands
Lekhainá see Lecháiná
Lekhchevo 104 C2 Montana,
NW Bulgaria
Leksand 85 C5 Dalarna, C Sweden
Lel'chitsy see Lyel'chytsy
le Léman see Geneva, Lake
Lelystad 86 D3 Flevoland, C Netherlands
Léman, Lac see Geneva, Lake
le Mans 90 B3 Sarthe, NW France
Lemberg see L'viv
Lemesós 102 C5 var. Limassol.
SW Cyprus
Lemhi Range 46 D3 mountain range
Idaho, C USA North America
Lemnos see Límnos
Lemovices see Limoges
Lena 115 F3 river NE Russian Federation
Lena Tablemount 141 B7 seamount
S Indian Ocean
Len Dao 128 C8 island S Spratly Islands
Leninabad see Khujand
Leninakan see Gyumri
Lenine 109 G5 Rus. Lenino. Avtonomna
Respublika Krym, S Ukraine
Leningor see Leninogorsk
Leningrad see Sankt-Peterburg
Leningradskaya 154 B4 Russian research
station Antarctica
Lenino see Lenine, Ukraine
Leninobod see Khujand
Leninogorsk see Ridder
Leninpol' 123 F2 Talasskaya Oblast',
NW Kyrgyzstan
Lenin-Turkmenski see Türkmenabat
Lenkoran' see Länkäran
Lenti 99 B7 Zala, SW Hungary
Lentia see Linz
Leoben 95 E7 Steiermark, C Austria
León 51 E4 var. León de los Aldamas.
Guanajuato, C Mexico
León 52 C3 León, NW Nicaragua
León 92 D1 Castilla y León, NW Spain
León de los Aldamas see León
Leonídi see Leonídio
Leonídio 105 B6 var. Leonídi.
Pelopónnisos, S Greece
Léopold II, Lac see Mai-Ndombe, Lac
Léopoldville see Kinshasa
Lepe 92 C4 Andalucía, S Spain
Lepel' see Lyepyel'
le Portel 90 C2 Pas-de-Calais, N France
Le Puglie see Puglia
le Puy 91 C5 prev. le Puy-en-Velay, hist.
Anicium, Podium Anicensis. Haute-
Loire, C France
le Puy-en-Velay see le Puy
Léré 76 B4 Mayo-Kébbi, SW Chad
Lérida see Lleida
Lerma 92 D2 Castilla y León, N Spain
Leros 105 D6 island Dodekánisa, Greece,
Aegean Sea
Lerrnayin Gharabakh see
Nagorno-Karabakh
Lerwick 88 D1 NE Scotland, United
Kingdom
Lesbos 116 A3 anc. Lesbos. island
E Greece
Lesbos see Lésvos
Les Cayes see Cayes
Les Gonaïves see Gonaïves
Leshan 128 B5 Sichuan, C China
les Herbiers 90 B4 Vendée, NW France
Lesh/Leshi see Lezhë
Lesina see Hvar

Leskovac 101 E5 Serbia, SE Serbia
Lesnoy 114 C3 Sverdlovskaya Oblast',
C Russian Federation
Lesotho 78 D4 off. Kingdom of Lesotho;
prev. Basutoland. country S Africa

LESOTHO
Southern Africa

Official name Kingdom of Lesotho
Formation 1966 / 1966
Capital Maseru
Population 2.2 million / 188 people
per sq mile (72 people per sq km)
Total area 11,720 sq. miles (30,355 sq. km)
Languages English*, Sesotho*, isiZulu
Religions Christian 90%, Traditional
beliefs 10%
Ethnic mix Sotho 99%, European
and Asian 1%
Government Parliamentary system
Currency Loti & South African rand =
100 lisente
Literacy rate 90%
Calorie consumption 2371 kilocalories

Lesotho, Kingdom of see Lesotho
les Sables-d'Olonne 90 B4 Vendée,
NW France
Lesser Antarctica see West Antarctica
Lesser Antilles 55 G4 island group
E West Indies
Lesser Caucasus 117 F2 Rus. Malyy
Kavkaz. mountain range SW Asia
Lesser Khingan Range see Xiao Hinggan
Ling
Lesser Sunda Islands 139 E5 Eng.
Lesser Sunda Islands. island group
C Indonesia
Lesser Sunda Islands see Nusa Tenggara
Leszno 98 B4 Ger. Lissa. Wielkopolskie,
C Poland
Lethbridge 37 E5 Alberta, SW Canada
Lethem 59 F3 S Guyana
Leti, Kepulauan 139 F5 island group
E Indonesia
Letpadan 136 B4 Bago, SW Myanmar
(Burma)
Letsôk-aw Kyun 137 B6 var. Letsutan
Island; prev. Domel Island. island
Mergui Archipelago, S Myanmar
(Burma)
Letsutan Island see Letsôk-aw Kyun
Lettland see Latvia
Lëtzebuerg see Luxembourg
Leucas see Lefkáda
Leuven 87 C6 Fr. Louvain, Ger. Löwen.
Vlaams Brabant, C Belgium
Leuze see Leuze-en-Hainaut
Leuze-en-Hainaut 87 B6 var. Leuze.
Hainaut, SW Belgium
Léva see Levice
Levanger 84 B4 Nord-Trøndelag,
C Norway
Levelland 49 E2 Texas, SW USA
Leverkusen 94 A4 Nordrhein-Westfalen,
W Germany
Levice 99 C6 Ger. Lewentz, Hung. Léva,
Lewenz. Nitriansky Kraj, SW Slovakia
Levin 150 D4 Manawatu-Wanganui,
North Island, New Zealand
Levkás see Lefkáda
Levkímmi see Lefkímmi
Lewentz/Lewenz see Levice
Lewis, Isle of 88 B2 island NW Scotland,
United Kingdom
Lewis Range 44 B1 mountain range
Montana, NW USA
Lewiston 46 C2 Idaho, NW USA
Lewiston 41 G2 Maine, NE USA
Lewistown 44 C1 Montana,
NW USA
Lexington 40 C5 Kentucky, S USA
Lexington 45 E4 Nebraska, C USA
Leyden see Leiden
Leyte 139 E2 island C Philippines
Leżajsk 99 E5 Podkarpackie, SE Poland
Lezha see Lezhë
Lezhë 101 C6 var. Lezha; prev. Lesh,
Leshi. Lezhë, NW Albania
Lhasa 126 C5 var. La-sa, Lassa. Xizang
Zizhiqu, W China
Lhaviyani Atoll see Faadhippolhu Atoll
Lhazê 126 C5 var. Quxar. Xizang
Zizhiqu, China E Asia
L'Hospitalet de Llobregat 93 G2 var.
Hospitalet. Cataluña, NE Spain
Liancourt Rocks 131 A5 island group
Japan/South Korea

Lianyungang 128 D4 var. Xinpu.
Jiangsu, E China
Liao see Liaoning
Liaodong Wan 127 G3 Eng. Gulf of
Lantung, Gulf of Liaotung. gulf
NE China
Liao He 125 E1 river NE China
Liaoning 128 D3 var. Liao, Liaoning
Sheng, Shengking, hist. Fengtien,
Shenking. province NE China
Liaoning Sheng see Liaoning
Liaoyuan 129 E3 var. Dongliao, Shuang-
liao, Jap. Chengchiatun. Jilin, NE China
Liard see Fort Liard
Liban see Lebanon
Liban, Jebel 118 B4 Ar. Jabal al Gharbt,
Jabal Lubnān, Eng. Mount Lebanon.
mountain range C Lebanon
Libau see Liepāja
Libby 44 A1 Montana, NW USA
Liberal 45 E5 Kansas, C USA
Liberalitas Julia see Évora
Liberec 98 B4 Ger. Reichenberg.
Liberecký Kraj, N Czech Republic
Liberia 52 D4 Guanacaste, NW Costa
Rica
Liberia 74 C5 off. Republic of Liberia.
country W Africa

LIBERIA
West Africa

Official name Republic of Liberia
Formation 1847 / 1847
Capital Monrovia
Population 4.1 million / 110 people
per sq mile (43 people per sq km)
Total area 43,000 sq. miles (111,370 sq. km)
Languages Kpelle, Vai, Bassa, Kru, Grebo,
Kissi, Gola, Loma, English*
Religions Christian 40%, Traditional
beliefs 40%, Muslim 20%
Ethnic mix Indigenous tribes (12 groups)
49%, Kpelle 20%, Bassa 16%,
Gio 8%, Krou 7%
Government Presidential system
Currency Liberian dollar = 100 cents
Literacy rate 59%
Calorie consumption 2261 kilocalories

Liberia, Republic of see Liberia
Libian Desert see Libyan Desert
Libīyah, Aş Şahrā' al see Libyan Desert
Libourne 91 B5 Gironde, SW France
Libreville 77 A5 country capital (Gabon)
Estuaire, NW Gabon
Libya 71 F3 prev. Great Socialist People's
Libyan Arab Jamahiriya, Al Jamāhīrīyah
al 'Arabīyah al Lībīyah ash Sha'bīyah
al Ishtirākīy, Libyan Arab Republic.
country N Africa

LIBYA
North Africa

Official name Libya
Formation 1951 / 1951
Capital Tripoli
Population 6.4 million / 9 people
per sq mile (4 people per sq km)
Total area 679,358 sq. miles
(1,759,540 sq. km)
Languages Arabic*, Tuareg
Religions Muslim (mainly Sunni) 97%,
Other 3%
Ethnic mix Arab and Berber 97%,
Other 3%
Government Transitional regime
Currency Libyan dinar = 1000 dirhams
Literacy rate 89%
Calorie consumption 3157 kilocalories

Libyan Arab Republic see Libya
Libyan Desert 71 H4 var. Libian Desert,
Ar. Aş Şahrā' al Lībīyah. desert N Africa
Libyan Plateau 103 F4 var. Ad Diffah.
plateau Egypt/Libya
Lichtenfels 95 C5 Bayern, SE Germany
Lichtenvoorde 86 E4 Gelderland,
E Netherlands
Lichuan 128 C5 Hubei, C China
Lida 107 B5 Hrodzyenskaya Voblasts',
W Belarus
Lidhorikíon see Lidoríki
Lidköping 85 B6 Västra Götaland,
S Sweden
Lidokhorikion see Lidoríki
Lidoríki 105 B5 prev. Lidhorikíon,
Lidokhorikion. Stereá Elláda, C Greece

Lidzbark Warmiński 98 D2 Ger.
Heilsberg. Olsztyn, N Poland
Liechtenstein 94 D1 off. Principality of
Liechtenstein. country C Europe

LIECHTENSTEIN
Central Europe

Official name Principality of
Liechtenstein
Formation 1719 / 1719
Capital Vaduz
Population 36,713 / 592 people
per sq mile (229 people per sq km)
Total area 62 sq. miles (160 sq. km)
Languages German*, Alemannish
dialect, Italian
Religions Roman Catholic 79%,
Other 13%, Protestant 8%
Ethnic mix Liechtensteiner 66%,
Other 12%, Swiss 10%, Austrian 6%,
German 3%, Italian 3%
Government Parliamentary system
Currency Swiss franc = 100 rappen/
centimes
Literacy rate 99%
Calorie consumption Not available

Liechtenstein, Principality of see
Liechtenstein
Liège 87 D6 Dut. Luik, Ger. Lüttich.
Liège, E Belgium
Liegnitz see Legnica
Lienz 95 D7 Tirol, W Austria
Liepāja 106 B3 Ger. Libau. W Latvia
Lietuva see Lithuania
Lievenhof see Līvāni
Liezen 95 D7 Steiermark, C Austria
Liffey 89 B6 river Ireland
Lifou 144 D5 island Îles Loyauté, E New
Caledonia
Liger see Loire
Ligure, Appennino 96 A2 Eng. Ligurian
Mountains. mountain range NW Italy
Ligure, Mar see Ligurian Sea
Ligurian Mountains see Ligure,
Appennino
Ligurian Sea 96 A3 Fr. Mer
Ligurienne, It. Mar Ligure. sea
N Mediterranean Sea
Ligurienne, Mer see Ligurian Sea
Lihu'e 47 A1 var. Lihue. Kaua'i,
Hawaii, USA
Lihue see Lihu'e
Lihula 106 D2 Ger. Leal. Läänemaa,
W Estonia
Liivi Laht see Riga, Gulf of
Likasi 77 D7 prev. Jadotville. Shaba,
SE Dem. Rep. Congo
Liknes 85 A6 Vest-Agder, S Norway
Lille 90 C2 var. l'Isle, Dut. Rijssel, Flem.
Ryssel, prev. Lisle; anc. Insula. Nord,
N France
Lillehammer 85 B5 Oppland, S Norway
Lillestrøm 85 B6 Akershus, S Norway
Lilongwe 79 E2 country capital (Malawi)
Central , W Malawi
Lilybaeum see Marsala
Lima 60 C4 country capital (Peru)
Lima, W Peru
Limanowa 99 D5 Małopolskie, S Poland
Limassol see Lemesós
Limerick 89 A6 Ir. Luimneach. Limerick,
SW Ireland
Limín Vathéos see Sámos
Límnos 103 F3 anc. Lemnos. island
E Greece
Limoges 91 C5 anc. Augustoritum
Lemovicensium, Lemovices. Haute-
Vienne, C France
Limón 53 E4 var. Puerto Limón. Limón,
E Costa Rica
Limón 52 D2 Colón, NE Honduras
Limonum see Poitiers
Limousin 91 C5 cultural region C France
Limoux 91 C6 Aude, S France
Limpopo 78 D3 var. Crocodile. river
S Africa
Linares 64 B4 Maule, C Chile
Linares 51 E3 Nuevo León, NE Mexico
Linares 92 D4 Andalucía, S Spain
Lincoln 89 D5 anc. Lindum, Lindum
Colonia. E England, United Kingdom
Lincoln 41 H3 Maine, NE USA
Lincoln 45 F4 state capital Nebraska,
C USA
Lincoln Sea 34 D2 sea Arctic Ocean
Linden 59 F3 E Guyana
Líndhos see Líndos

Lindi *73 D8* Lindi, SE Tanzania
Líndos *105 E7 var.* Líndhos.
Dodekánisa, Greece, Aegean Sea
Lindum/Lindum Colonia *see*
Lincoln
Line Islands *145 G3 island group*
E Kiribati
Lingeh *see* Bandar-e Lengeh
Lingen *94 A3 var.* Lingen an der Ems.
Niedersachsen, NW Germany
Lingen an der Ems *see* Lingen
Lingga, Kepulauan *138 B4 island group*
W Indonesia
Lingling *129 C6 prev.* Yongzhou,
Zhishan. Hunan, S China
Linköping *85 C6* Östergötland,
S Sweden
Linz *95 D6 anc.* Lentia. Oberösterreich,
N Austria
Lion, Gulf of *91 C7 Eng.* Gulf of Lion,
Gulf of Lions; *anc.* Sinus Gallicus. *gulf*
S France
Lion, Gulf of/Lions, Gulf of *see* Lion,
Golfe du
Liozno *see* Lyozna
Lipari *97 D6 island* Isole Eolie,
S Italy
Lipari Islands/Lipari, Isole *see* Eolie,
Isole
Lipetsk *111 B5* Lipetskaya Oblast',
W Russian Federation
Lipno *98 C3* Kujawsko-pomorskie,
C Poland
Lipova *108 A4 Hung.* Lippa. Arad,
W Romania
Lipovets *see* Lypovets'
Lippa *see* Lipova
Lipsia/Lipsk *see* Leipzig
Lira *73 B6* N Uganda
Lisala *77 C5* Equateur, N Dem. Rep.
Congo
Lisboa *92 B4 Eng.* Lisbon; *anc.* Felicitas
Julia, Olisipo. *country capital*
(Portugal) Lisboa, W Portugal
Lisbon *see* Lisboa
Lisichansk *see* Lysychans'k
Lisieux *90 B3 anc.* Noviomagus.
Calvados, N France
Liski *111 B6 prev.* Georgiu-Dezh.
Voronezhskaya Oblast', W Russian
Federation
Lisle/l'Isle *see* Lille
Lismore *149 E5* New South Wales,
SE Australia
Lissa *see* Vis, Croatia
Lissa *see* Leszno, Poland
Lisse *86 C3* Zuid-Holland,
W Netherlands
Litang *128 A5 var.* Gaocheng. Sichuan,
C China
Litani, Nahr el *119 B5 var.* Nahr al
Litant. *river* C Lebanon
Litant, Nahr al *see* Litani, Nahr el
Litauen *see* Lithuania
Lithgow *149 D6* New South Wales,
SE Australia
Lithuania *106 B4 off.* Republic of
Lithuania, *Ger.* Litauen, *Lith.* Lietuva,
Pol. Litwa, *Rus.* Litva; *prev.* Lithuanian
SSR, *Rus.* Litovskaya SSR. *country*
NE Europe

Lithuanian SSR *see* Lithuania
Lithuania, Republic of *see* Lithuania
Litóchoro *104 B4 var.* Litohoro,
Litókhoron. Kentrikí Makedonía,
N Greece
Litohoro/Litókhoron *see* Litóchoro
Litovskaya SSR *see* Lithuania

Little Alföld *99 C6 Ger.* Kleines
Ungarisches Tiefland, *Hung.* Kisalföld,
Slvk. Podunajská Rovina. *plain*
Hungary/Slovakia
Little Andaman *133 F2 island* Andaman
Islands, India, NE Indian Ocean
Little Barrier Island *150 D2 island*
N New Zealand
Little Bay *93 H5 bay* Alboran Sea,
Mediterranean Sea
Little Cayman *54 B3 island* E Cayman
Islands
Little Falls *45 F2* Minnesota, N USA
Littlefield *49 E2* Texas, SW USA
Little Inagua *54 D2 var.* Inagua Islands.
island S Bahamas
Little Minch, The *88 B3 strait*
NW Scotland, United Kingdom
Little Missouri River *44 D2 river*
NW USA
Little Nicobar *133 G3 island* Nicobar
Islands, India, NE Indian Ocean
Little Rhody *see* Rhode Island
Little Rock *42 B1 state capital* Arkansas,
C USA
Little Saint Bernard Pass *91 D5 Fr.* Col
du Petit St-Bernard, *It.* Colle del Piccolo
San Bernardo. *pass* France/Italy
Little Sound *42 A5 bay* Bermuda,
NW Atlantic Ocean
Littleton *44 D4* Colorado, C USA
Littoria *see* Latina
Litva/Litwa *see* Lithuania
Liu-chou/Liuchow *see* Liuzhou
Liuzhou *128 C6 var.* Liu-chou, Liuchow.
Guangxi Zhuangzu Zizhiqu, S China
Livanátai *see* Livanátes
Livanátes *105 B5 prev.* Livanátai. Stereá
Elláda, C Greece
Līvāni *106 D4 Ger.* Lievenhof. SE Latvia
Liverpool *39 F5* Nova Scotia, SE Canada
Liverpool *89 C5* NW England, United
Kingdom
Livingston *44 B2* Montana,
NW USA
Livingston *49 H3* Texas, SW USA
Livingstone *49 H3 var.* Maramba.
Southern, S Zambia
Livingstone *78 C3 var.* Maramba.
Southern, S Zambia
Livingstone Mountains *151 A7*
mountain range South Island, New
Zealand
Livno *100 B4* Federicija Bosna
I Hercegovina, SW Bosnia and
Herzegovina
Livojoki *84 D4 river* C Finland
Livonia *40 C3* Michigan, N USA
Livorno *96 B3 Eng.* Leghorn. Toscana,
C Italy
Lixian Jiang *see* Black River
Lixoúri *105 A5 prev.* Lixoúrion.
Kefallinía, Iónia Nisiá, Greece,
C Mediterranean Sea
Lixoúrion *see* Lixoúri
Lizarra *see* Estella
Ljouwert *see* Leeuwarden
Ljubelj *see* Loibl Pass
Ljubljana *95 D7 Ger.* Laibach, *It.*
Lubiana; *anc.* Aemona, Emona.
country capital (Slovenia) C Slovenia
Ljungby *85 B7* Kronoberg, S Sweden
Ljusdal *85 C5* Gävleborg, C Sweden
Ljusnan *85 C5 river* C Sweden
Llanelli *89 C6 prev.* Llanelly. SW Wales,
United Kingdom
Llanelly *see* Llanelli
Llanes *92 D1* Asturias, N Spain
Llanos *58 D2 physical region* Colombia/
Venezuela
Lleida *93 F2 Cast.* Lérida; *anc.* Ilerda.
Cataluña, NE Spain
Llucmajor *93 G3* Mallorca, Spain,
W Mediterranean Sea
Loaita Island *128 C8 island* W Spratly
Islands
Loanda *see* Luanda
Lobatse *78 C4 var.* Lobatsi. Kgatleng,
SE Botswana
Lobatsi *see* Lobatse
Löbau *94 D4* Sachsen, E Germany
Lobito *78 B2* Benguela, W Angola
Lob Nor *see* Lop Nur
Lobositz *see* Lovosice
Loburi *see* Lop Buri
Locarno *95 B8 Ger.* Luggarus. Ticino,
S Switzerland
Lochem *86 E3* Gelderland, E Netherlands
Lockport *41 E3* New York, NE USA

Lodja *77 D6* Kasai-Oriental, C Dem.
Rep. Congo
Lodwar *73 C6* Rift Valley, NW Kenya
Łódź *98 D4 Rus.* Lodz. Łódź, C Poland
Loei *136 C4 var.* Loey, Muang Loei.
Loei, C Thailand
Loey *see* Loei
Lofoten *84 B3 var.* Lofoten Islands.
island group C Norway
Lofoten Islands *see* Lofoten
Logan *44 B3* Utah, W USA
Logan, Mount *36 D3 mountain* Yukon
Territory, W Canada
Logroño *93 E1 anc.* Vareia, *Lat.*
Juliobriga. La Rioja, N Spain
Loibl Pass *95 D7 Ger.* Loiblpass, *Slvn.*
Ljubelj. *pass* Austria/Slovenia
Loiblpass *see* Loibl Pass
Loikaw *136 B4* Kayah State, C Myanmar
(Burma)
Loire *90 B4 var.* Liger. *river* C France
Loja *60 B2* Loja, S Ecuador
Lokitaung *73 C5* Rift Valley, NW Kenya
Lokoja *75 G4* Kogi, C Nigeria
Loksa *106 E2 Ger.* Loxa. Harjumaa,
NW Estonia
Lolland *85 B8 prev.* Laaland. *island*
S Denmark
Lom *104 C1 prev.* Lom-Palanka.
Montana, NW Bulgaria
Lomami *77 D6 river* C Dem. Rep. Congo
Lomas *60 D4* Arequipa, SW Peru
Lomas de Zamora *64 D4* Buenos Aires,
E Argentina
Lombardia *96 B2 Eng.* Lombardy.
region N Italy
Lombardy *see* Lombardia
Lombok, Pulau *138 D5 island* Nusa
Tenggara, C Indonesia
Lomé *75 F5 country capital* (Togo)
S Togo
Lomela *77 D6* Kasai-Oriental, C Dem.
Rep. Congo
Lommel *87 C5* Limburg, N Belgium
Lomond, Loch *88 B4 lake* C Scotland,
United Kingdom
Lomonosov Ridge *155 B3 var.* Harris
Ridge, *Rus.* Khrebet Homonsova.
undersea ridge Arctic Ocean
Lomonsova, Khrebet *see* Lomonosov
Ridge
Lom-Palanka *see* Lom
Lompoc *47 B7* California, W USA
Lom Sak *136 C4 var.* Muang Lom Sak.
Phetchabun, C Thailand
Łomża *98 D3 Rus.* Lomzha. Podlaskie,
NE Poland
Lomzha *see* Łomża
London *89 A7 anc.* Augusta, *Lat.*
Londinium. *country capital*
(United Kingdom) SE England,
United Kingdom
London *38 C5* Ontario, S Canada
London *40 C5* Kentucky, S USA
Londonderry *88 B4 var.* Derry, *Ir.* Doire.
NW Northern Ireland, United Kingdom
Londonderry, Cape *146 C2 cape*
Western Australia
Londrina *63 E4* Paraná, S Brazil
Lone Star State *see* Texas
Long Bay *43 F2 bay* W Jamaica
Long Beach *47 C8* California, W USA
Longford *89 B5 Ir.* An Longfort.
Longford, C Ireland
Long Island *54 D2 island* C Bahamas
Long Island *41 G4 island* New York,
NE USA
Longlac *38 C3* Ontario, S Canada
Longmont *44 D4* Colorado, C USA
Longreach *148 C4* Queensland,
E Australia
Long Strait *115 G1 Eng.* Long Strait.
strait NE Russian Federation
Long Strait *see* Longa, Proliv
Longview *49 H3* Texas, SW USA
Longview *46 B2* Washington, NW USA
Long Xuyên *137 D6 var.* Longxuyen. An
Giang, S Vietnam
Longxuyen *see* Long Xuyên
Longyan *128 D6* Fujian, SE China
Longyearbyen *83 G2 dependent
territory capital* (Svalbard) Spitsbergen,
W Svalbard
Lons-le-Saunier *90 D4 anc.* Ledo
Salinarius. Jura, E France
Lop Buri *137 C5 var.* Loburi. Lop Buri,
C Thailand

Lop Nor *see* Lop Nur
Lop Nur *126 C3 var.* Lob Nor, Lop Nor,
Lo-pu Po. *seasonal lake* NW China
Loppersum *86 E1* Groningen,
NE Netherlands
Lo-pu Po *see* Lop Nur
Lorca *93 E4 Ar.* Lurka; *anc.* Eliocroca,
Lat. Illurco. Murcia, S Spain
Lord Howe Island *142 C4 island*
E Australia
Lord Howe Rise *142 C4 undersea rise*
SW Pacific Ocean
Loreto *50 B3* Baja California Sur,
NW Mexico
Lorient *90 A3 prev.* l'Orient. Morbihan,
NW France
l'Orient *see* Lorient
Lorn, Firth of *88 B4 inlet* W Scotland,
United Kingdom
Loro Sae *see* East Timor
Lörrach *95 A7* Baden-Württemberg,
S Germany
Lorraine *90 D3 cultural region*
NE France
Los Alamos *48 C1* New Mexico, SW USA
Los Amates *52 B2* Izabal, E Guatemala
Los Ángeles *65 B5* Bío Bío, C Chile
Los Angeles *47 C7* California, W USA
Losanna *see* Lausanne
Lošinj *100 A3 Ger.* Lussin, *It.* Lussino.
island W Croatia
Loslau *see* Wodzisław Śląski
Los Mochis *50 C3* Sinaloa, C Mexico
Losonc/Losontz *see* Lučenec
Los Roques, Islas *58 D1 island group*
N Venezuela
Lot *91 B5 cultural region* S France
Lot *91 B5 river* S France
Lotagipi Swamp *73 C5 wetland* Kenya/
Sudan
Lötzen *see* Giżycko
Loualaba *see* Lualaba
Louangnamtha *136 C3 var.* Luong Nam
Tha. Louang Namtha, N Laos
Louangphabang *124 D3 var.*
Louangphrabang, Luang Prabang.
Louangphabang, N Laos
Louangphrabang *see* Louangphabang
Loubomo *see* Dolisie
Loudéac *90 A3* Côtes d'Armor,
NW France
Loudi *128 C5* Hunan, S China
Louga *74 B3* NW Senegal
Louisiade Archipelago *144 B4 island
group* SE Papua New Guinea
Louisiana *42 A2 off.* State of Louisiana,
also known as Creole State, Pelican
State. *state* S USA
Louisville *40 C5* Kentucky, S USA
Louisville Ridge *143 E4 undersea ridge*
S Pacific Ocean
Loup River *45 E4 river* Nebraska, C USA
Lourdes *91 B6* Hautes-Pyrénées, S France
Lourenço Marques *see* Maputo
Louth *89 E5* E England, United Kingdom
Loutrá *104 C4* Kentrikí Makedonía,
N Greece
Louvain *see* Leuven
Louvain-la Neuve *87 C6* Walloon
Brabant, C Belgium
Louviers *90 C3* Eure, N France
Lovech *104 C2* Lovech, N Bulgaria
Loveland *44 D4* Colorado, C USA
Lovosice *98 A4 Ger.* Lobositz. Ústecký
Kraj, NW Czech Republic
Lóvua *78 C1* Moxico, E Angola
Lowell *41 G3* Massachusetts, NE USA
Löwen *see* Leuven
Lower California *48 A4 Eng.* Lower
California. *peninsula* NW Mexico
Lower California *see* Baja California
Lower Hutt *151 D5* Wellington, North
Island, New Zealand
Lower Lough Erne *89 A5 lake*
SW Northern Ireland, United Kingdom
Lower Red Lake *45 F1 lake* Minnesota,
N USA
Lower Rhine *see* Neder Rijn
Lower Tunguska *115 E3 Eng.* Lower
Tunguska. *river* N Russian Federation
Lower Tunguska *see* Nizhnyaya
Tunguska
Lowestoft *89 E6* E England, United
Kingdom
Loxa *see* Loksa
Lo-yang *see* Luoyang
Loyauté, Îles *144 D5 island group* S New
Caledonia
Loyev *see* Loyew

Loyew *107 D8 Rus.* Loyev. Homyel'skaya Voblasts', SE Belarus
Loznica *100 C3* Serbia, W Serbia
Lu *see* Shandong, China
Lualaba *77 D6 Fr.* Loualaba. *river* SE Dem. Rep. Congo
Luanda *78 A1 var.* Loanda, *Port.* São Paulo de Loanda. *country capital* (Angola) Luanda, NW Angola
Luang Prabang *see* Louangphabang
Luang, Thale *137 C7 lagoon* S Thailand
Luangua, Rio *see* Luangwa
Luangwa *73 B8 var.* Aruángua, Rio Luangua. *river* Mozambique/Zambia
Luanshya *78 D2* Copperbelt, C Zambia
Luarca *92 C1* Asturias, N Spain
Lubaczów *99 E5 var.* Lúbaczów. Podkarpackie, SE Poland
L'uban' *98 B4* Leningradskaya Oblast', Russian Federation
Lubānas Ezers *see* Lubāns
Lubango *78 B2 Port.* Sá da Bandeira. Huíla, SW Angola
Lubāns *106 D4 var.* Lubānas Ezers. *lake* E Latvia
Lubao *77 D6* Kasai-Oriental, C Dem. Rep. Congo
Lübben *94 D4* Brandenburg, E Germany
Lübbenau *94 D4* Brandenburg, E Germany
Lubbock *49 E2* Texas, SW USA
Lübeck *94 C2* Schleswig-Holstein, N Germany
Lubelska, Wyżyna *98 E4 plateau* SE Poland
Lüben *see* Lubin
Lubiana *see* Ljubljana
Lubin *98 B4 Ger.* Lüben. Dolnośląskie, SW Poland
Lublin *98 E4 Rus.* Lyublin. Lubelskie, E Poland
Lubliniec *98 C4* Śląskie, S Poland
Lubnān, Jabal *see* Liban, Jebel
Lubny *109 F2* Poltavs'ka Oblast', NE Ukraine
Lubsko *98 B4 Ger.* Sommerfeld. Lubuskie, W Poland
Lubumbashi *77 E8 prev.* Élisabethville. Shaba, SE Dem. Rep. Congo
Lubutu *77 D6* Maniema, E Dem. Rep. Congo
Luca *see* Lucca
Lucan *89 B5 Ir.* Leamhcán. Dublin, E Ireland
Lucanian Mountains *see* Lucano, Appennino
Lucano, Appennino *97 D5 Eng.* Lucanian Mountains. *mountain range* S Italy
Lucapa *78 C1 var.* Lukapa. Lunda Norte, NE Angola
Lucca *96 B3 anc.* Luca. Toscana, C Italy
Lucea *54 A4* W Jamaica
Lucena *139 E1 off.* Lucena City. Luzon, N Philippines
Lucena *92 D4* Andalucía, S Spain
Lucena City *see* Lucena
Lučenec *99 D6 Ger.* Losontz, *Hung.* Losonc. Banskobystrický Kraj, C Slovakia
Lucentum *see* Alicante
Lucerna/Lucerne *see* Luzern
Luchow *see* Hefei
Łuck *see* Luts'k
Lucknow *135 E3 var.* Lakhnau. *state capital* Uttar Pradesh, N India
Lüda *see* Dalian
Luda Kamchiya *104 D2 river* E Bulgaria
Ludasch *see* Luduş
Lüderitz *78 B4 prev.* Angra Pequena. Karas, SW Namibia
Ludhiāna *134 D2* Punjab, N India
Ludington *40 C2* Michigan, N USA
Ludsan *see* Ludza
Luduş *108 B4 Ger.* Ludasch, *Hung.* Marosludas. Mureş, C Romania
Ludvika *85 C6* Dalarna, C Sweden
Ludwigsburg *95 B6* Baden-Württemberg, SW Germany
Ludwigsfelde *94 D3* Brandenburg, NE Germany
Ludwigshafen *95 B5 var.* Ludwigshafen am Rhein. Rheinland-Pfalz, W Germany
Ludwigshafen am Rhein *see* Ludwigshafen
Ludwigslust *94 C3* Mecklenburg-Vorpommern, N Germany
Ludza *106 D4 Ger.* Ludsan. E Latvia

Luebo *77 C6* Kasai-Occidental, SW Dem. Rep. Congo
Luena *78 C2 var.* Lwena, *Port.* Luso. Moxico, E Angola
Lufira *77 E7 river* SE Dem. Rep. Congo
Lufkin *49 H3* Texas, SW USA
Luga *110 A4* Leningradskaya Oblast', NW Russian Federation
Lugano *95 B8 Ger.* Lauis. Ticino, S Switzerland
Lugansk *see* Luhans'k
Lugdunum *see* Lyon
Lugdunum Batavorum *see* Leiden
Lugenda, Rio *79 E2 river* N Mozambique
Luggarus *see* Locarno
Lugh Ganana *see* Luuq
Lugo *92 C1 anc.* Lugus Augusti. Galicia, NW Spain
Lugoj *108 A4 Ger.* Lugosch, *Hung.* Lugos. Timiş, W Romania
Lugos/Lugosch *see* Lugoj
Lugus Augusti *see* Lugo
Luguvallium/Luguvallum *see* Carlisle
Luhans'k *109 H3 Rus.* Lugansk; *prev.* Voroshilovgrad. Luhans'ka Oblast', E Ukraine
Luimneach *see* Limerick
Lukapa *see* Lucapa
Lukenie *77 C6 river* C Dem. Rep. Congo
Lukovit *104 C2* Lovech, N Bulgaria
Łuków *98 E4 Ger.* Bogendorf. Lubelskie, E Poland
Lukuga *77 D7 river* SE Dem. Rep. Congo
Luleå *84 D4* Norrbotten, N Sweden
Luleälven *84 C3 river* N Sweden
Lulonga *77 C5 river* NW Dem. Rep. Congo
Lulua *77 D7 river* S Dem. Rep. Congo
Luluabourg *see* Kananga
Lumber State *see* Maine
Lumbo *79 F2* Nampula, NE Mozambique
Lumsden *151 A7* Southland, South Island, New Zealand
Lund *85 B7* Skåne, S Sweden
Lüneburg *94 C3* Niedersachsen, N Germany
Lunga, Isola *see* Dugi Otok
Lungkiang *see* Qiqihar
Lungué-Bungo *78 C2 var.* Lungwebungu. *river* Angola/Zambia
Lungwebungu *see* Lungué-Bungo
Luninets *see* Luninyets
Łuniniec *see* Luninyets
Luninyets *107 B7 Pol.* Łuniniec, *Rus.* Luninets. Brestskaya Voblasts', SW Belarus
Lunteren *86 D4* Gelderland, C Netherlands
Luong Nam Tha *see* Louangnamtha
Luoyang *128 C4 var.* Honan, Lo-yang. Henan, C China
Lupatia *see* Altamura
Lúrio *79 F2* Nampula, NE Mozambique
Lúrio, Rio *79 E2 river* NE Mozambique
Lurka *see* Lorca
Lusaka *78 D2 country capital* (Zambia) Lusaka, SE Zambia
Lushnja *see* Lushnjë
Lushnjë *101 C6 var.* Lushnja. Fier, C Albania
Luso *see* Luena
Lussin/Lussino *see* Lošinj
Lüt, Baḥrat/Lut, Bahret *see* Dead Sea
Lut, Dasht-e *120 D3 var.* Kavīr-e Lūt. *desert* E Iran
Lutetia/Lutetia Parisiorum *see* Paris
Lūt, Kavīr-e *see* Lut, Dasht-e
Luton *89 D6* E England, United Kingdom
Łutselk'e *37 F4 prev.* Snowdrift. Northwest Territories, W Canada
Luts'k *108 C1 Pol.* Łuck, *Rus.* Lutsk. Volyns'ka Oblast', NW Ukraine
Lutsk *see* Luts'k
Lüttich *see* Liège
Lützow-Holm Bay *154 C2 var.* Lützow-Holm Bay. *bay* Antarctica
Lützow-Holm Bay *see* Lützow-Holm Bukta
Luuq *73 D6 It.* Lugh Ganana. Gedo, SW Somalia
Luvua *77 D7 river* SE Dem. Rep. Congo
Luwego *73 C8 river* S Tanzania
Luxembourg *87 D8 country capital* (Luxembourg) Luxembourg, S Luxembourg
Luxembourg *87 D8 off.* Grand Duchy of Luxembourg, *var.* Lëtzebuerg, Luxembourg. *country* NW Europe

Luxemburg *see* Luxembourg
Luxor *72 B2 Ar.* Al Uqsur. E Egypt
Luza *110 C4* Kirovskaya Oblast', NW Russian Federation
Luz, Costa de la *92 C5 coastal region* SW Spain
Luzern *95 B7 Fr.* Lucerne, *It.* Lucerna. Luzern, C Switzerland
Luzon *139 E1 island* N Philippines
Luzon Strait *125 E3 strait* Philippines/Taiwan
L'viv *108 B2 Ger.* Lemberg, *Pol.* Lwów, *Rus.* L'vov. L'vivs'ka Oblast', W Ukraine
L'vov *see* L'viv
Lwena *see* Luena
Lwów *see* L'viv
Lyakhavichy *107 B6 Rus.* Lyakhovichi. Brestskaya Voblasts', SW Belarus
Lyakhovichi *see* Lyakhavichy
Lyallpur *see* Faisalābād
Lyangar *see* Langar
Lyck *see* Ełk
Lycksele *84 C4* Västerbotten, N Sweden
Lycopolis *see* Asyūt
Lyel'chytsy *107 C7 Rus.* Lel'chitsy. Homyel'skaya Voblasts', SE Belarus
Lyepyel' *107 D5 Rus.* Lepel'. Vitsyebskaya Voblasts', N Belarus
Lyme Regis *89 C7 bay* S England, United Kingdom
Lynchburg *41 E5* Virginia, NE USA
Lynn *see* King's Lynn
Lynn Lake *37 F4* Manitoba, C Canada
Lynn Regis *see* King's Lynn
Lyon *91 D5 Eng.* Lyons; *anc.* Lugdunum. Rhône, E France
Lyons *see* Lyon
Lyozna *107 E6 Rus.* Liozno. Vitsyebskaya Voblasts', NE Belarus
Lypovets' *108 D2 Rus.* Lipovets. Vinnyts'ka Oblast', C Ukraine
Lys *see* Leie
Lysychans'k *109 H3 Rus.* Lisichansk. Luhans'ka Oblast', E Ukraine
Lyttelton *151 C6* South Island, New Zealand
Lyublin *see* Lublin
Lyubotin *see* Lyubotyn
Lyubotyn *109 G2 Rus.* Lyubotin. Kharkivs'ka Oblast', E Ukraine
Lyulyakovo *104 E2 prev.* Keremitlik. Burgas, E Bulgaria
Lyusina *107 B6 Rus.* Lyusino. Brestskaya Voblasts', SW Belarus
Lyusino *see* Lyusina

M

Maale *see* Male'
Ma'ān *119 B7* Ma'ān, SW Jordan
Maardu *106 D2 Ger.* Maart. Harjumaa, NW Estonia
Ma'aret-en-Nu'man *see* Ma'arrat an Nu'mān
Ma'arrat an Nu'mān *118 B3 var.* Ma'aret-en-Nu'man, Fr.* Maarret enn Naamâne. Idlib, NW Syria
Maarret enn Naamâne *see* Ma'arrat an Nu'mān
Maart *see* Maardu
Maas *see* Meuse
Maaseik *87 D5 prev.* Maeseyck. Limburg, NE Belgium

Maastricht *87 D6 var.* Maestricht; *anc.* Traiectum ad Mosam, Traiectum Tungorum. Limburg, SE Netherlands
Macao *129 C6 Chin.* Aomen, *Port.* Macau. Guangdong, SE China
Macapá *63 E1 state capital* Amapá, N Brazil
Macarsca *see* Makarska
Macassar *see* Makassar
Macău *see* Makó, Hungary
Macau *see* Macao
MacCluer Gulf *see* Berau, Teluk
Macdonnell Ranges *146 D4 mountain range* Northern Territory, C Australia
Macedonia *see* Macedonia, FYR
Macedonia, FYR *101 D6 off.* the Former Yugoslav Republic of Macedonia, *var.* Macedonia, *Mac.* Makedonija, *abbrev.* FYR Macedonia, FYROM. *country* SE Europe

Macedonia, the Former Yugoslav Republic of *see* Macedonia, FYR
Maceió *63 G3 state capital* Alagoas, E Brazil
Machachi *60 B1* Pichincha, C Ecuador
Machala *60 B2* El Oro, SW Ecuador
Machanga *79 E3* Sofala, E Mozambique
Machilipatnam *132 D1 var.* Bandar Masulipatnam. Andhra Pradesh, E India
Machiques *58 C2* Zulia, NW Venezuela
Macías Nguema Biyogo *see* Bioco, Isla de
Măcin *108 D5* Tulcea, SE Romania
Mackay *148 D4* Queensland, NE Australia
Mackay, Lake *146 C4 salt lake* Northern Territory/Western Australia
Mackenzie *37 E3 river* Northwest Territories, NW Canada
Mackenzie Bay *154 D3 bay* Antarctica
Mackenzie Mountains *36 D3 mountain range* Northwest Territories, NW Canada
Macleod, Lake *146 A4 lake* Western Australia
Macomb *40 A4* Illinois, N USA
Macomer *97 A5* Sardegna, Italy, C Mediterranean Sea
Mâcon *91 D5 anc.* Matisco, Matisco Ædourum. Saône-et-Loire, C France
Macon *42 D2* Georgia, SE USA
Macon *45 G4* Missouri, C USA
Macquarie Ridge *154 C5 undersea ridge* SW Pacific Ocean
Macuspana *51 G4* Tabasco, SE Mexico
Ma'dabā *119 B6 var.* Mādabā, Madeba; *anc.* Medeba. Ma'dabā, NW Jordan
Mādabā *see* Ma'dabā
Madagascar *79 F3 off.* Democratic Republic of Madagascar, *Malg.* Madagasikara; *prev.* Malagasy Republic. *country* W Indian Ocean

MADAGASCAR
(continued)

Christian (mainly Roman Catholic) 41%,
Muslim 7%
Ethnic mix Other Malay 46%,
Merina 26%, Betsimisaraka 15%,
Betsileo 12%, Other 1%
Government Transitional regime
Currency Ariary = 5 irairnbilanja
Literacy rate 64%
Calorie consumption 2117 kilocalories

Madagascar 79 F3 *island* W Indian
Ocean
Madagascar Basin 69 E7 *undersea basin*
W Indian Ocean
Madagascar, Democratic Republic of
see Madagascar
Madagascar Plateau 69 E7 *var.*
Madagascar Ridge, Madagascar
Rise, *Rus.* Madagaskarskiy Khrebet.
undersea plateau W Indian Ocean
Madagascar Rise/Madagascar Ridge *see*
Madagascar Plateau
Madagasikara *see* Madagascar
Madagaskarskiy Khrebet *see*
Madagascar Plateau
Madang 144 B3 Madang, N Papua
New Guinea
Madanīyīn *see* Médenine
Maḏarska *see* Hungary
Made 86 C4 Noord-Brabant,
S Netherlands
Madeba *see* Ma'dabā
Madeira 70 A2 *var.* Ilha de Madeira.
island Madeira, Portugal, NE Atlantic
Ocean
Madeira, Ilha de *see* Madeira
Madeira Plain 66 C3 *abyssal plain*
E Atlantic Ocean
Madeira, Rio 62 D2 *var.* Río Madera.
river Bolivia/Brazil
Madeleine, Îles de la 39 F4 *Eng.*
Magdalen Islands. *island group*
Québec, E Canada
Madera 47 B6 California, W USA
Madera, Río *see* Madeira, Rio
Madhya Pradesh 135 E4 *prev.* Central
Provinces and Berar. *cultural region*
C India
Madīnat ath Thawrah 118 C2 *var.* Ath
Thawrah. Ar Raqqah, N Syria
Madioen *see* Madiun
Madison 45 F3 South Dakota, N USA
Madison 40 B3 *state capital* Wisconsin,
N USA
Madiun 138 D5 *prev.* Madioen. Jawa,
C Indonesia
Madoera *see* Madura, Pulau
Madona 106 D4 *Ger.* Modohn. E Latvia
Madras *see* Tamil Nādu
Madras *see* Chennai
Madre de Dios, Río 61 E3 *river* Bolivia/
Peru
Madre del Sur, Sierra 51 E5 *mountain
range* S Mexico
Madre, Laguna 51 F3 *lagoon* NE Mexico
Madre, Laguna 49 G5 *lagoon* Texas,
SW USA
Madre Occidental, Sierra 50 C3 *var.*
Western Sierra Madre. *mountain range*
C Mexico
Madre Oriental, Sierra 51 E3 *var.*
Eastern Sierra Madre. *mountain range*
C Mexico
Madre, Sierra 52 B2 *var.* Sierra
de Soconusco. *mountain range*
Guatemala/Mexico
Madrid 92 D3 *country capital* (Spain)
Madrid, C Spain
Madura *see* Madurai
Madurai 132 C3 *prev.* Madura,
Mathurai. Tamil Nādu, S India
Madura, Pulau 138 D5 *prev.* Madoera.
island C Indonesia
Maebashi 131 D5 *var.* Maebasi,
Mayebashi. Gunma, Honshū, S Japan
Maebasi *see* Maebashi
Mae Khong *see* Mekong
Mae Nam Nan 136 C4 *var.* Nan
NW Thailand
Mae Nam Yom 136 C4 *river* W Thailand
Maeseyck *see* Maaseik
Maestricht *see* Maastricht
Maéwo 144 D4 *prev.* Aurora. *island*
C Vanuatu
Mafia 73 D7 *island* E Tanzania

Mafraq/Muḩāfaẓat al Mafraq *see* Al
Mafraq
Magadan 115 G3 Magadanskaya Oblast',
E Russian Federation
Magallanes *see* Punta Arenas
Magallanes, Estrecho de *see* Magellan,
Strait of
Magangué 58 B2 Bolívar, N Colombia
Magdalena 61 F3 El Beni, N Bolivia
Magdalena 50 B1 Sonora, NW Mexico
Isla Magdalena 50 B3 *island*
NW Mexico
Magdalena, Río 58 B2 *river* C Colombia
Magdalen Islands *see* Madeleine,
Îles de la
Magdeburg 94 C4 Sachsen-Anhalt,
C Germany
Magelang 138 C5 Jawa, C Indonesia
Magellan, Strait of 65 B8 *Sp.* Estrecho de
Magallanes. *strait* Argentina/Chile
Magerøy *see* Magerøya
Magerøya 84 D1 *var.* Magerøy, *Lapp.*
Máhkarávju. *island* N Norway
Maggiore, Lago *see* Maggiore, Lake
Maggiore, Lake 96 B1 *It.* Lago Maggiore.
lake Italy/Switzerland
Maglaj 100 C3 Federacija Bosna
I Hercegovina, N Bosnia and
Herzegovina
Maglie 97 E6 Puglia, SE Italy
Magna 44 B4 Utah, W USA
Magnesia *see* Manisa
Magnitogorsk 114 B4 Chelyabinskaya
Oblast', C Russian Federation
Magnolia State *see* Mississippi
Magta' Lahjar 74 C3 *var.* Magta Lahjar,
Magta' Lahjar, Magtá Lahjar. Brakna,
SW Mauritania
Magway 136 A3 *var.* Magwe. Magway,
W Myanmar (Burma)
Magyar-Becse *see* Bečej
Magyarkanizsa *see* Kanjiža
Magyarország *see* Hungary
Mahajanga 79 F2 *var.* Majunga.
Mahajanga, NW Madagascar
Mahakam, Sungai 138 D4 *var.* Koetai,
Kutai. *river* Borneo, C Indonesia
Mahalapye 78 D3 *var.* Mahalatswe.
Central, SE Botswana
Mahalatswe *see* Mahalapye
Mahān 120 D3 Kermān, E Iran
Mahanadi 135 F4 *river* E India
Mahārāshtra 134 D5 *cultural region*
W India
Mahbés *see* El Mahbas
Mahbūbnagar 134 D5 Andhra Pradesh,
C India
Mahdia 71 F2 *var.* Al Mahdīyah,
Mehdia. NE Tunisia
Mahé 79 H1 *island* Inner Islands,
NE Seychelles
Mahia Peninsula 150 E4 *peninsula*
North Island, New Zealand
Mahilyow 107 D6 *Rus.* Mogilëv.
Mahilyowskaya Voblasts', E Belarus
Máhkarávju *see* Magerøya
Mahmūd-e 'Erāqī *see* Mahmūd-e Rāqī
Mahmūd-e Rāqī 123 E4 *var.* Mahmūd-e
'Erāqī. Kāpīsā, NE Afghanistan
Mahón *see* Maó
Mähren *see* Moravia
Mährisch-Weisskirchen *see* Hranice
Maicao 58 C1 La Guajira, N Colombia
Mai Ceu/Mai Chio *see* Maych'ew
Maīdān Shahr 123 E4 *var.* Maydān
Shahr; *prev.* Meydān Shahr. Wardak,
E Afghanistan
Maidstone 89 E7 SE England, United
Kingdom
Maiduguri 75 H4 Borno, NE Nigeria
Mailand *see* Milano
Maïmāna *see* Maïmanah
Maïmanah 122 D3 *var.* Maimāna,
Maymana; *prev.* Meymaneh. Fāryāb,
NW Afghanistan
Main 95 B5 *river* C Germany
Mai-Ndombe, Lac 77 C6 *prev.* Lac
Léopold II. *lake* W Dem. Rep. Congo
Maine 41 G2 *off.* State of Maine, *also
known as* Lumber State, Pine Tree
State. *state* NE USA
Maine 90 B3 *cultural region* NW France
Maine, Gulf of 41 H2 *gulf* NE USA
Mainland 88 C2 *island* N Scotland,
United Kingdom
Mainland 88 D1 *island* NE Scotland,
United Kingdom
Mainz 95 B5 *Fr.* Mayence. Rheinland-
Pfalz, SW Germany

Maio 74 A3 *var.* Mayo. *island* Ilhas de
Sotavento, SE Cape Verde
Maisur *see* Mysore, India
Maisur *see* Karnātaka, India
Maizhokunggar 126 C5 Xizang Zizhiqu,
W China
Majorca 93 G3 *Eng.* Majorca; *anc.*
Baleares Major. *island* Islas Baleares,
Spain, W Mediterranean Sea
Majorca *see* Mallorca
Mājro *see* Majuro Atoll
Majunga *see* Mahajanga
Majuro Atoll 144 D2 *var.* Mājro. *atoll*
Ratak Chain, SE Marshall Islands
Makale *see* Mek'elē
Makarov Basin 155 B3 *undersea basin*
Arctic Ocean
Makarska 100 B4 *It.* Macarsca. Split-
Dalmacija, SE Croatia
Makasar *see* Makassar
Makasar, Selat *see* Makassar Straits
Makassar 139 E4 *var.* Macassar,
Makasar; *prev.* Ujungpandang.
Sulawesi, C Indonesia
Makassar Straits 138 D4 *Ind.* Makasar
Selat. *strait* C Indonesia
Makay 79 F3 *var.* Massif du Makay.
mountain range SW Madagascar
Makay, Massif du *see* Makay
Makedonija *see* Macedonia, FYR
Makeni 74 C4 C Sierra Leone
Makeyevka *see* Makiyivka
Makhachkala 114 A4 *prev.* Petrovsk-
Port. Respublika Dagestan, SW Russian
Federation
Makin 144 D2 *prev.* Pitt Island. *atoll*
Tungaru, W Kiribati
Makira *see* San Cristobal
Makiyivka 109 G3 *Rus.* Makeyevka;
prev. Dmitriyevsk. Donets'ka Oblast',
E Ukraine
Makkah 121 A5 *Eng.* Mecca. Makkah,
W Saudi Arabia
Makkovik 39 F2 Newfoundland and
Labrador, NE Canada
Makó 99 D7 *Rom.* Macău. Csongrád,
SE Hungary
Makoua 77 B5 Cuvette, C Congo
Makran Coast 120 E4 *coastal region*
SE Iran
Makrany 107 A6 *Rus.* Mokrany.
Brestskaya Voblasts', SW Belarus
Mākū 120 B2 Āzarbāyjān-e Gharbī,
NW Iran
Makurdi 75 G4 Benue, C Nigeria
Mala *see* Malaita, Solomon Islands
Malabār Coast 132 B3 *coast* SW India
Malabo 77 A5 *prev.* Santa Isabel.
country capital (Equatorial Guinea)
Isla de Bioco, NW Equatorial
Guinea
Malaca *see* Málaga
Malacca, Strait of 138 B3 *Ind.* Selat
Malaka. *strait* Indonesia/Malaysia
Malacka *see* Malacky
Malacky 99 C6 *Hung.* Malacka.
Bratislavský Kraj, W Slovakia
Maladyechna 107 C5 *Pol.* Molodeczno,
Rus. Molodechno. Minskaya Voblasts',
C Belarus
Málaga 92 D5 *anc.* Malaca. Andalucía,
S Spain
Malagarasi River 73 B7 *river*
W Tanzania Africa
Malagasy Republic *see* Madagascar
Malaita 144 C3 *var.* Mala. *island*
N Solomon Islands
Malakal 73 B5 Upper Nile, NE South
Sudan
Malakula *see* Malekula
Malang 138 D5 Jawa, C Indonesia
Malange *see* Malanje
Malanje 78 B1 *var.* Malange. Malanje,
NW Angola
Mälaren 85 C6 *lake* C Sweden
Malatya 117 E4 *anc.* Melitene. Malatya,
SE Turkey
Mala Vyska 109 E3 *Rus.* Malaya Viska.
Kirovohrads'ka Oblast', S Ukraine
Malawi 79 E1 *off.* Republic of Malaŵi;
prev. Nyasaland, Nyasaland
Protectorate. *country* S Africa

MALAWI
Southern Africa

Official name Republic of Malawi
Formation 1964 / 1964
Capital Lilongwe
Population 15.4 million / 424 people

MALAWI
(continued)

per sq mile (164 people per sq km)
Total area 45,745 sq. miles (118,480 sq. km)
Languages Chewa, Lomwe, Yao, Ngoni,
English*
Religions Protestant 55%,
Roman Catholic 20%, Muslim 20%,
Traditional beliefs 5%
Ethnic mix Bantu 99%, Other 1%
Government Presidential system
Currency Malawi kwacha = 100 tambala
Literacy rate 74%
Calorie consumption 2318 kilocalories

Malawi, Lake *see* Nyasa, Lake
Malawi, Republic of *see* Malawi
Malaya Viska *see* Mala Vyska
Malay Peninsula 124 D4 *peninsula*
Malaysia/Thailand
Malaysia 138 B3 *off.* Malaysia, *var.*
Federation of Malaysia; *prev.* the
separate territories of Federation of
Malaya, Sarawak and Sabah (North
Borneo) and Singapore. *country*
SE Asia

MALAYSIA
Southeast Asia

Official name Federation of Malaysia
Formation 1963 / 1965
Capital Kuala Lumpur;
Putrajaya (administrative)
Population 28.9 million / 228 people
per sq mile (88 people per sq km)
Total area 127,316 sq. miles (329,750 sq. km)
Languages Bahasa Malaysia*, Malay,
Chinese, Tamil, English
Religions Muslim (mainly Sunni) 61%,
Buddhist 19%, Christian 9%, Hindu 6%,
Other 5%
Ethnic mix Malay 53%, Chinese 26%,
Indigenous tribes 12%, Indian 8%,
Other 1%
Government Parliamentary system
Currency Ringgit = 100 sen
Literacy rate 92%
Calorie consumption 2902 kilocalories

Malaysia, Federation of *see* Malaysia
Malbork 98 C2 *Ger.* Marienburg,
Marienburg in Westpreussen.
Pomorskie, N Poland
Malchin 94 C3 Mecklenburg-
Vorpommern, N Germany
Malden 45 H5 Missouri, C USA
Malden Island 145 G3 *prev.*
Independence Island. *atoll* E Kiribati
Maldives 132 A4 *off.* Maldivian Divehi,
Republic of Maldives. *country* N Indian
Ocean

MALDIVES
Indian Ocean

Official name Republic of Maldives
Formation 1965 / 1965
Capital Male'
Population 394,491 / 3400 people
per sq mile (1315 people per sq km)
Total area 116 sq. miles (300 sq. km)
Languages Dhivehi (Maldivian)*, Sinhala,
Tamil, Arabic
Religions Sunni Muslim 100%
Ethnic mix Arab–Sinhalese–Malay 100%
Government Presidential system
Currency Rufiyaa = 100 laari
Literacy rate 97%
Calorie consumption 2720 kilocalories

Maldives, Republic of *see* Maldives
Maldivian Divehi *see* Maldives
Male' 132 B4 *Div.* Maale. *country capital*
(Maldives) Male' Atoll, C Maldives
Male' Atoll 132 A4 *var.* Kaafu Atoll. *atoll*
C Maldives
Malekula 144 D4 *var.* Malakula; *prev.*
Mallicolo. *island* W Vanuatu
Malesina 105 C5 Stereá Ellāda,
E Greece
Malheur Lake 46 C3 *lake* Oregon,
NW USA
Mali 75 E3 *off.* Republic of Mali, *Fr.*
République du Mali; *prev.* French
Sudan, Sudanese Republic. *country*
W Africa

MALI
West Africa

Official name Republic of Mali
Formation 1960 / 1960
Capital Bamako
Population 15.8 million / 34 people per sq mile (13 people per sq km)
Total area 478,764 sq. miles (1,240,000 sq. km)
Languages Bambara, Fulani, Senufo, Soninke, French*
Religions Muslim (mainly Sunni) 90%, Traditional beliefs 6%, Christian 4%
Ethnic mix Bambara 52%, Other 14%, Fulani 11%, Saracolé 7%, Soninka 7%, Tuareg 5%, Mianka 4%
Government Transitional regime
Currency CFA franc = 100 centimes
Literacy rate 23%
Calorie consumption 2624 kilocalories

Malik, Wadi al *see* Milk, Wadi el
Mali Kyun *137 B5 var.* Tavoy Island. *island* Mergui Archipelago, S Myanmar (Burma)
Malin *see* Malyn
Malindi *73 D7* Coast, SE Kenya
Malines *see* Mechelen
Mali, Republic of *see* Mali
Mali, République du *see* Mali
Malkiye *see* Al Mālikīyah
Malko Tŭrnovo *104 E3* Burgas, E Bulgaria
Mallaig *88 B3* N Scotland, United Kingdom
Mallawī *72 B2 var.* Mallawi. C Egypt
Mallawi *see* Mallawī
Mallicolo *see* Malekula
Malmberget *84 C3 Lapp.* Malmivaara. Norrbotten, N Sweden
Malmédy *87 D6* Liège, E Belgium
Malmivaara *see* Malmberget
Malmö *85 B7* Skåne, S Sweden
Maloelap *see* Maloelap Atoll
Maloelap Atoll *144 D1 var.* Maḷoeḷap. *atoll* E Marshall Islands
Małopolska, Wyżyna *98 D4 plateau* S Poland
Malozemel'skaya Tundra *110 D3 physical region* NW Russian Federation
Malta *106 D4* SE Latvia
Malta *44 C1* Montana, NW USA
Malta *97 C8 off.* Republic of Malta. *country* C Mediterranean Sea

MALTA
Southern Europe

Official name Republic of Malta
Formation 1964 / 1964
Capital Valletta
Population 400,000 / 3226 people per sq mile (1250 people per sq km)
Total area 122 sq. miles (316 sq. km)
Languages Maltese*, English*
Religions Roman Catholic 98%, Other and nonreligious 2%
Ethnic mix Maltese 96%, Other 4%
Government Parliamentary system
Currency Euro = 100 cents
Literacy rate 92%
Calorie consumption 3438 kilocalories

Malta *97 C8 island* Malta, C Mediterranean Sea
Malta, Canale di *see* Malta Channel
Malta Channel *97 C8 It.* Canale di Malta. *strait* Italy/Malta
Malta, Republic of *see* Malta
Maluku, Laut *see* Molucca Sea
Malung *85 B6* Dalarna, C Sweden
Malventum *see* Benevento
Malvina, Isla Gran *see* West Falkland
Malvinas, Islas *see* Falkland Islands
Malyn *108 D2 Rus.* Malin. Zhytomyrs'ka Oblast', N Ukraine
Malyy Kavkaz *see* Lesser Caucasus
Mamberamo, Sungai *139 H4 river* Papua, E Indonesia
Mambij *see* Manbij
Mamonovo *106 A4 Ger.* Heiligenbeil. Kaliningradskaya Oblast', W Russian Federation
Mamoré, Río *61 F3 river* Bolivia/Brazil
Mamou *74 C4* W Guinea
Mamoudzou *79 F2 dependent territory capital* (Mayotte) C Mayotte

Mamuno *78 C3* Ghanzi, W Botswana
Manacor *93 G3* Mallorca, Spain, W Mediterranean Sea
Manado *139 F3 prev.* Menado. Sulawesi, C Indonesia
Managua *52 D3 country capital* (Nicaragua) Managua, W Nicaragua
Managua, Lake *52 C3 var.* Xolotlán. *lake* W Nicaragua
Manakara *79 G4* Fianarantsoa, SE Madagascar
Manama *see* Al Manāmah
Mananjary *79 G3* Fianarantsoa, SE Madagascar
Manáos *see* Manaus
Manapouri, Lake *151 A7 lake* South Island, New Zealand
Manar *see* Mannar
Manas, Gora *123 E2 mountain* Kyrgyzstan/Uzbekistan
Manaus *62 D2 prev.* Manáos. *state capital* Amazonas, NW Brazil
Manavgat *116 B4* Antalya, SW Turkey
Manbij *118 C2 var.* Mambij, *Fr.* Membidj. Ḩalab, N Syria
Manchester *89 D5 Lat.* Mancunium. NW England, United Kingdom
Manchester *41 G3* New Hampshire, NE USA
Man-chou-li *see* Manzhouli
Manchurian Plain *125 E1 plain* NE China
Máncio Lima *see* Japiim
Mancunium *see* Manchester
Mand *see* Mand, Rūd-e
Mandalay *136 B3* Mandalay, C Myanmar (Burma)
Mandan *45 E2* North Dakota, N USA
Mandeville *54 B5* C Jamaica
Mándra *105 C6* Attikí, C Greece
Rud-e Mand *120 D4 var.* Mand. *river* S Iran
Mandurah *147 A6* Western Australia
Manduria *97 E5* Puglia, SE Italy
Mandya *132 C2* Karnātaka, C India
Manfredonia *97 D5* Puglia, SE Italy
Mangai *77 C6* Bandundu, W Dem. Rep. Congo
Mangaia *145 G5 island group* S Cook Islands
Mangalia *108 D5 anc.* Callatis. Constanța, SE Romania
Mangalmé *76 C4* Guéra, SE Chad
Mangalore *132 B2* Karnātaka, W India
Manguang *see* Bloemfontein
Mango *see* Sansanné-Mango, Togo
Mangoky *79 F3 river* W Madagascar
Manhattan *45 F4* Kansas, C USA
Manicouagan, Réservoir *38 D3 lake* Québec, E Canada
Manihiki *145 G4 atoll* N Cook Islands
Manihiki Plateau *143 E3 undersea plateau* C Pacific Ocean
Maniitsoq *82 C3 var.* Manîtsoq, *Dan.* Sukkertoppen. Kitaa, S Greenland
Manila *139 E1 off.* City of Manila. *country capital* (Philippines) Luzon, N Philippines
Manila, City of *see* Manila
Manisa *116 A3 var.* Manissa, *prev.* Saruhan; *anc.* Magnesia. Manisa, W Turkey
Manissa *see* Manisa
Manitoba *37 F5 province* S Canada
Manitoba, Lake *37 F5 lake* Manitoba, S Canada
Manitoulin Island *38 C4 island* Ontario, S Canada
Manîtsoq *see* Maniitsoq
Manizales *58 B3* Caldas, W Colombia
Manjimup *147 A7* Western Australia
Mankato *45 F3* Minnesota, N USA
Manlleu *93 G2* Cataluña, NE Spain
Manly *148 E1* Iowa, C USA
Manmād *134 C5* Mahārāshtra, W India
Mannar *132 C3 var.* Manar. Northern Province, NW Sri Lanka
Mannar, Gulf of *132 C3 gulf* India/Sri Lanka
Mannheim *95 B5* Baden-Württemberg, SW Germany
Manono *77 E7* Shaba, SE Dem. Rep. Congo
Manosque *91 D6* Alpes-de-Haute-Provence, SE France
Manra *145 F3 prev.* Sydney Island. *atoll* Phoenix Islands, C Kiribati

Mansa *78 D2 prev.* Fort Rosebery. Luapula, N Zambia
Mansel Island *37 G3 island* Nunavut, NE Canada
Mansfield *40 D4* Ohio, N USA
Manta *60 A2* Manabí, W Ecuador
Manteca *47 B6* California, W USA
Mantoue *see* Mantova
Mantova *96 B2 Eng.* Mantua, *Fr.* Mantoue. Lombardia, NW Italy
Mantua *see* Mantova
Manuae *145 G4 island* S Cook Islands
Manukau *see* Manurewa
Manurewa *150 D3 var.* Manukau. Auckland, North Island, New Zealand
Manzanares *93 E3* Castilla-La Mancha, C Spain
Manzanillo *54 C3* Granma, E Cuba
Manzanillo *50 D4* Colima, SW Mexico
Manzhouli *127 F1 var.* Man-chou-li. Nei Mongol Zizhiqu, N China
Mao *76 B3* Kanem, W Chad
Maó *93 H3 Cast.* Mahón, *Eng.* Port Mahon; *anc.* Portus Magonis. Menorca, Spain, W Mediterranean Sea
Maoke, Pegunungan *139 H4 Dut.* Sneeuw-gebergte, *Eng.* Snow Mountains. *mountain range* Papua, E Indonesia
Maoming *128 C6* Guangdong, S China
Mapmaker Seamounts *125 F1 seamount range* N Pacific Ocean
Maputo *78 D4 prev.* Lourenço Marques. *country capital* (Mozambique) Maputo, S Mozambique
Marabá *63 F2* Pará, NE Brazil
Maracaibo *58 C1* Zulia, NW Venezuela
Maracaibo, Gulf of *see* Venezuela, Golfo de
Maracaibo, Lake *58 C2 var.* Lake Maracaibo. *inlet* NW Venezuela
Maracaibo, Lake *see* Maracaibo, Lago de
Maracay *58 D2* Aragua, N Venezuela
Marada *see* Marādah
Marādah *71 G3 var.* Marada. N Libya
Maradi *75 G3* Maradi, S Niger
Maragha *see* Marāgheh
Marāgheh *120 C2 var.* Maragha. Āzarbāyjān-e Khāvarī, NW Iran
Marajó, Baía de *61 F1 bay* N Brazil
Marajó, Ilha de *61 E1 island* N Brazil
Marakesh *see* Marrakech
Maramba *see* Livingstone
Maramba *see* Livingstone
Maranhão *63 F2 off.* Estado do Maranhão. *state* E Brazil
Maranhão *63 F2 off.* Estado do Maranhão. *region* E Brazil
Maranhão, Estado do *see* Maranhão
Marañón, Río *60 B2 river* N Peru
Marathon *38 C4* Ontario, S Canada
Marathón *see* Marathónas
Marathónas *105 C5 prev.* Marathón. Attikí, C Greece
Märäzä *see* Qobustan
Marbella *92 D5* Andalucía, S Spain
Marble Bar *146 B4* Western Australia
Marburg *see* Marburg an der Lahn, Germany
Marburg *see* Maribor, Slovenia
Marburg an der Lahn *94 B4 hist.* Marburg. Hessen, W Germany
March *see* Morava
Marche *96 C3 Eng.* Marches. *region* C Italy
Marche *91 C5 cultural region* C France
Marche-en-Famenne *87 C7* Luxembourg, SE Belgium
Marchena, Isla *60 B5 var.* Bindloe Island. *island* Galápagos Islands, Ecuador, E Pacific Ocean
Marches *see* Marche
Mar Chiquita, Laguna *64 C3 lake* C Argentina
Marcounda *see* Markounda
Mardan *134 C1* Khyber Pakhtunkhwa, N Pakistan
Mar del Plata *65 D5* Buenos Aires, E Argentina
Mardin *117 E4* Mardin, SE Turkey
Maré *144 D5 island* Îles Loyauté, E New Caledonia
Marea Neagrǎ *see* Black Sea
Mareeba *148 D3* Queensland, NE Australia
Marek *see* Dupnitsa
Marganets *see* Marhanets'
Margarita, Isla de *59 E1 island* N Venezuela

Margate *89 E7 prev.* Mergate. SE England, United Kingdom
Margherita *see* Jamaame
Margherita, Lake *73 C5 Eng.* Lake Margherita, *It.* Abbaia. *lake* SW Ethiopia
Margherita, It. *see* Ābaya Hāyk'
Marghita *108 B3 Hung.* Margitta. Bihor, NW Romania
Margitta *see* Marghita
Marhanets' *109 F3 Rus.* Marganets. Dnipropetrovs'ka Oblast', E Ukraine
María Cleofas, Isla *50 C4 island* C Mexico
Maria Island *149 C8 island* Tasmania, SE Australia
María Madre, Isla *50 C4 island* C Mexico
María Magdalena, Isla *50 C4 island* C Mexico
Mariana Trench *125 G4 var.* Challenger Deep. *trench* W Pacific Ocean
Mariánské Lázně *99 A5 Ger.* Marienbad. Karlovarský Kraj, W Czech Republic
Marías, Islas *50 C4 island group* C Mexico
Maria-Theresiopel *see* Subotica
Maribor *95 E7 Ger.* Marburg. NE Slovenia
Marica *see* Maritsa
Maridi *73 B5* Western Equatoria, SW South Sudan
Marie Byrd Land *154 A3 physical region* Antarctica
Marie-Galante *55 G4 var.* Ceyre to the Caribs. *island* SE Guadeloupe
Marienbad *see* Mariánské Lázně
Mariental *78 B4* Hardap, SW Namibia
Marienburg *see* Alūksne, Latvia
Marienburg *see* Malbork, Poland
Marienburg in Westpreussen *see* Malbork
Marienhausen *see* Viļaka
Marijampolė *106 B4 prev.* Kapsukas. Marijampolė, S Lithuania
Marília *63 E4* São Paulo, S Brazil
Marín *92 B1* Galicia, NW Spain
Mar'ina Gorka *see* Mar"ina Horka
Mar"ina Horka *107 C6 Rus.* Mar'ina Gorka. Minskaya Voblasts', C Belarus
Maringá *63 E4* Paraná, S Brazil
Marion *45 G3* Iowa, C USA
Marion *40 D4* Ohio, N USA
Marion, Lake *43 E2 reservoir* South Carolina, SE USA
Mariscal Estigarribia *64 D2* Boquerón, NW Paraguay
Maritsa *104 D3 var.* Marica, *Gk.* Évros, *Turk.* Meriç; *anc.* Hebrus. *river* SW Europe
Maritzburg *see* Pietermaritzburg
Mariupol' *109 G4 prev.* Zhdanov. Donets'ka Oblast', SE Ukraine
Marka *73 D6 var.* Merca. Shabeellaha Hoose, S Somalia
Markham, Mount *154 B4 mountain* Antarctica
Markounda *76 C4 var.* Marcounda. Ouham, NW Central African Republic
Marktredwitz *95 C5* Bayern, E Germany
Marlborough *148 D4* Queensland, E Australia
Marmande *see* Marmande
Marmande *91 B5 anc.* Marmanda. Lot-et-Garonne, SW France
Sea of Marmara *116 A2 Eng.* Sea of Marmara. *sea* NW Turkey
Marmara, Sea of *see* Marmara Denizi
Marmaris *116 A4* Muğla, SW Turkey
Marne *90 C3 cultural region* N France
Marne *90 D3 river* N France
Maro *76 C4* Moyen-Chari, S Chad
Maroantsetra *79 G2* Toamasina, NE Madagascar
Maromokotro *79 G2 mountain* N Madagascar
Maroni *59 G3 Dut.* Marowijne. *river* French Guiana/Suriname
Maroshevíz *see* Toplița
Marosludas *see* Luduş
Marosvásárhely *see* Târgu Mureş
Marotiri *143 F4 var.* Îlots de Bass, Morotiri. *island group* Îles Australes, SW French Polynesia

Maroua 76 B3 Extrême-Nord, N Cameroon
Marowijne see Maroni
Marquesas Fracture Zone 153 E3 fracture zone E Pacific Ocean
Marquette 40 B1 Michigan, N USA
Marrakech 70 C2 var. Marakesh, Eng. Marrakesh; prev. Morocco. W Morocco
Marrakesh see Marrakech
Marrawah 149 C8 Tasmania, SE Australia
Marree 149 B5 South Australia
Marsá al Burayqah 71 G3 var. Al Burayqah. N Libya
Marsabit 73 C6 Eastern, N Kenya
Marsala 97 B7 anc. Lilybaeum. Sicilia, Italy, C Mediterranean Sea
Marsberg 94 B4 Nordrhein-Westfalen, W Germany
Marseille 91 D6 Eng. Marseilles; anc. Massilia. Bouches-du-Rhône, SE France
Marseilles see Marseille
Marshall 45 F2 Minnesota, N USA
Marshall 49 H2 Texas, S USA
Marshall Islands 144 C1 off. Republic of the Marshall Islands. country W Pacific Ocean

MARSHALL ISLANDS
Australasia & Oceania

Official name Republic of the Marshall Islands
Formation 1986 / 1986
Capital Majuro
Population 68,480 / 978 people per sq mile (378 people per sq km)
Total area 70 sq. miles (181 sq. km)
Languages Marshallese*, English*, Japanese, German
Religions Protestant 90%, Roman Catholic 8%, Other 2%
Ethnic mix Micronesian 90%, Other 10%
Government Presidential system
Currency US dollar = 100 cents
Literacy rate 91%
Calorie consumption Not available

Marshall Islands, Republic of the see Marshall Islands
Marshall Seamounts 125 H3 seamount range SW Pacific Ocean
Marsh Harbour 54 C1 Great Abaco, W Bahamas
Martaban see Mottama
Martha's Vineyard 41 G3 island Massachusetts, NE USA
Martigues 91 D6 Bouches-du-Rhône, SE France
Martin 99 C5 Ger. Sankt Martin, Hung. Turócszentmárton; prev. Turčiansky Svätý Martin. Zilinský Kraj, N Slovakia
Martinique 55 G4 French overseas department E West Indies
Martinique Channel see Martinique Passage
Martinique Passage 55 G4 var. Dominica Channel, Martinique Channel. channel Dominica/ Martinique
Marton 150 D4 Manawatu-Wanganui, North Island, New Zealand
Martos 92 D4 Andalucía, S Spain
Marungu 77 E2 mountain range SE Dem. Rep. Congo
Mary 122 D3 prev. Merv. Mary Welaýaty, S Turkmenistan
Maryborough 149 D4 Queensland, E Australia
Maryborough see Port Laoise
Mary Island see Kanton
Maryland 41 E5 off. State of Maryland, also known as America in Miniature, Cockade State, Free State, Old Line State. state NE USA
Maryland, State of see Maryland
Maryville 45 F4 Missouri, C USA
Maryville 42 D1 Tennessee, S USA
Masai Steppe 73 C7 grassland NW Tanzania
Masaka 73 B6 SW Uganda
Masallı 117 H3 Rus. Masally. S Azerbaijan
Masally see Masallı
Masasi 73 C8 Mtwara, SE Tanzania
Masawa/Massawa see Mits'iwa
Masaya 52 D3 Masaya, W Nicaragua

Mascarene Basin 141 B5 undersea basin W Indian Ocean
Mascarene Islands 79 H4 island group W Indian Ocean
Mascarene Plain 141 B5 abyssal plain W Indian Ocean
Mascarene Plateau 141 B5 undersea plateau W Indian Ocean
Maseru 78 D4 country capital (Lesotho) W Lesotho
Mas-ha 119 D7 W West Bank Asia
Mashhad 120 E2 var. Meshed. Khorāsān-Razavī, NE Iran
Masindi 73 B6 W Uganda
Masira see Maşīrah, Jazīrat
Masira, Gulf of 121 E5 var. Gulf of Masira. bay E Oman
Masira, Gulf of see Maşīrah, Khalīj
Maşīrah, Jazīrat 121 E5 var. Masira. island E Oman
Masis see Büyükağrı Dağı
Maskat see Masqaţ
Mason City 45 F3 Iowa, C USA
Masqaţ 121 E5 var. Maskat, Eng. Muscat. country capital (Oman) NE Oman
Massa 96 B3 Toscana, C Italy
Massachusetts 41 G3 off. Commonwealth of Massachusetts, also known as Bay State, Old Bay State, Old Colony State. state NE USA
Massenya 76 B3 Chari-Baguirmi, SW Chad
Massif Central 91 C5 plateau C France
Massilia see Marseille
Massoukou see Franceville
Mastanli see Momchilgrad
Masterton 151 D5 Wellington, North Island, New Zealand
Masty 107 B5 Rus. Mosty. Hrodzyenskaya Voblasts', W Belarus
Masuda 131 B6 Shimane, Honshū, SW Japan
Masuku see Franceville
Masvingo 78 D3 prev. Fort Victoria, Nyanda, Victoria. Masvingo, SE Zimbabwe
Maşyāf 118 B3 Fr. Misiaf. Ḥamāh, C Syria
Matadi 77 B6 Bas-Congo, W Dem. Rep. Congo
Matagalpa 52 D3 Matagalpa, C Nicaragua
Matale 132 D3 Central Province, C Sri Lanka
Matam 74 C3 NE Senegal
Matamata 150 D3 Waikato, North Island, New Zealand
Matamoros 50 D3 Coahuila, NE Mexico
Matamoros 51 E2 Tamaulipas, C Mexico
Matane 39 E4 Québec, SE Canada
Matanzas 54 B2 Matanzas, NW Cuba
Matara 132 D4 Southern Province, S Sri Lanka
Mataram 138 D5 Pulau Lombok, C Indonesia
Mataró 93 G2 anc. Illuro. Cataluña, E Spain
Mataura 151 B7 Southland, South Island, New Zealand
Mataura 151 B7 river South Island, New Zealand
Mata Uta see Matā'utu
Matā'utu 145 E4 var. Mata Uta. dependent territory capital (Wallis and Futuna) Île Uvea, Wallis and Futuna
Matera 97 E5 Basilicata, S Italy
Mathurai see Madurai
Matianus see Orūmīyeh, Daryācheh-ye
Matías Romero 51 F5 Oaxaca, SE Mexico
Matisco/Matisco Ædourum see Mâcon
Mato Grosso 63 E3 off. Estado de Mato Grosso; prev. Matto Grosso. state W Brazil
Mato Grosso 63 E3 off. Estado de Mato Grosso; prev. Matto Grosso. region W Brazil
Mato Grosso do Sul 63 E4 off. Estado de Mato Grosso do Sul. state S Brazil
Mato Grosso do Sul 63 E4 off. Estado de Mato Grosso do Sul. region S Brazil
Mato Grosso do Sul, Estado de see Mato Grosso do Sul
Mato Grosso, Estado de see Mato Grosso
Mato Grosso, Planalto de 56 C4 plateau C Brazil
Matosinhos 92 B2 prev. Matozinhos. Porto, NW Portugal

Matozinhos see Matosinhos
Matsue 131 B6 var. Matsuye, Matue. Shimane, Honshū, SW Japan
Matsumoto 131 C5 var. Matumoto. Nagano, Honshū, S Japan
Matsuyama 131 B7 var. Matuyama. Ehime, Shikoku, SW Japan
Matsuye see Matsue
Matterhorn 95 A8 It. Monte Cervino. mountain Italy/Switzerland
Matthews Ridge 59 F2 N Guyana
Matthew Town 54 D2 Great Inagua, S Bahamas
Matto Grosso see Mato Grosso
Matucana 60 C4 Lima, W Peru
Matue see Matsue
Matumoto see Matsumoto
Maturín 59 E2 Monagas, NE Venezuela
Matuyama see Matsuyama
Mau 135 E4 var. Maunāth Bhanjan. Uttar Pradesh, N India
Maui 47 B8 island Hawai'i, USA, C Pacific Ocean
Maun 78 C3 North-West, C Botswana
Maunāth Bhanjan see Mau
Mauren 94 E1 NE Liechtenstein Europe
Maurice see Mauritius
Mauritania 74 C2 off. Islamic Republic of Mauritania, Ar. Mūrītānīyah. country W Africa

MAURITANIA
West Africa

Official name Islamic Republic of Mauritania
Formation 1960 / 1960
Capital Nouakchott
Population 3.5 million / 9 people per sq mile (3 people per sq km)
Total area 397,953 sq. miles (1,030,700 sq. km)
Languages Hassaniyah Arabic*, Wolof, French
Religions Sunni Muslim 100%
Ethnic mix Maure 81%, Wolof 7%, Tukolor 5%, Other 4%, Soninka 3%
Government Presidential system
Currency Ouguiya = 5 khoums
Literacy rate 58%
Calorie consumption 2856 kilocalories

Mauritania, Islamic Republic of see Mauritania
Mauritius 79 H3 off. Republic of Mauritius, Fr. Maurice. country W Indian Ocean

MAURITIUS
Indian Ocean

Official name Republic of Mauritius
Formation 1968 / 1968
Capital Port Louis
Population 1.3 million / 1811 people per sq mile (699 people per sq km)
Total area 718 sq. miles (1860 sq. km)
Languages French Creole, Hindi, Urdu, Tamil, Chinese, English*, French
Religions Hindu 48%, Roman Catholic 24%, Muslim 17%, Protestant 9%, Other 2%
Ethnic mix Indo-Mauritian 68%, Creole 27%, Sino-Mauritian 3%, Franco-Mauritian 2%
Government Parliamentary system
Currency Mauritian rupee = 100 cents
Literacy rate 88%
Calorie consumption 2993 kilocalories

Mauritius 141 B5 island W Indian Ocean
Mauritius, Republic of see Mauritius
Mawlamyang see Mawlamyine
Mawlamyine 136 B4 var. Mawlamyaing, Moulmein. Mon State, S Myanmar (Burma)
Mawson 154 D2 Australian research station Antarctica
Mayadin see Al Mayādīn
Mayaguana 54 D2 island SE Bahamas
Mayaguana Passage 54 D2 passage SE Bahamas
Mayagüez 55 F3 W Puerto Rico
Mayamey 120 D2 Semnān, N Iran
Maya Mountains 52 B2 Sp. Montañas Mayas. mountain range Belize/ Guatemala
Mayas, Montañas see Maya Mountains

Maych'ew 72 C4 var. Mai Chio, It. Mai Ceu. Tigray, N Ethiopia
Maydān Shahr see Maīdān Shahr
Mayebashi see Maebashi
Mayence see Mainz
Mayfield 151 B6 Canterbury, South Island, New Zealand
Maykop 111 A7 Respublika Adygeya, SW Russian Federation
Maymana see Maīmanah
Maymyo see Pyin-Oo-Lwin
Mayo see Maio
Mayor Island 150 D3 island NE New Zealand
Mayor Pablo Lagerenza see Capitán Pablo Lagerenza
Mayotte 79 F2 French territorial collectivity E Africa
May Pen 54 B5 C Jamaica
Mayyit, Al Bahr al see Dead Sea
Mazabuka 78 D2 Southern, S Zambia
Mazaca see Kayseri
Mazagan see El-Jadida
Mazar-e Sharif 123 E3 var. Mazār-i Sharif. Balkh, N Afghanistan
Mazār-i Sharif see Mazar-e Sharif
Mazatlán 50 C3 Sinaloa, C Mexico
Mažeikiai 106 B3 Telšiai, NW Lithuania
Mazirbe 106 C2 NW Latvia
Mazra'a see Al Mazra'ah
Mazury 98 D3 physical region NE Poland
Mazyr 107 C7 Rus. Mozyr'. Homyel'skaya Voblasts', SE Belarus
Mbabane 78 D4 country capital (Swaziland) NW Swaziland
Mbacké see Mbaké
Mbaïki 77 C5 var. M'Baiki. Lobaye, SW Central African Republic
M'Baiki see Mbaïki
Mbaké 74 B3 var. Mbacké. W Senegal
Mbala 78 D1 prev. Abercorn. Northern, NE Zambia
Mbale 73 C6 E Uganda
Mbandaka 77 C5 prev. Coquilhatville. Equateur, NW Dem. Rep. Congo
M'Banza Congo 78 B1 var. Mbanza Congo; prev. São Salvador, São Salvador do Congo. Dem. Rep. Congo, NW Angola
Mbanza-Ngungu 77 B6 Bas-Congo, W Dem. Rep. Congo
Mbarara 73 B6 SW Uganda
Mbé 76 B4 Nord, N Cameroon
Mbeya 73 C7 Mbeya, SW Tanzania
Mbomou/M'Bomu/Mbomu see Bomu
Mbour 74 B3 W Senegal
Mbuji-Mayi 77 D7 prev. Bakwanga. Kasai-Oriental, S Dem. Rep. Congo
McAlester 49 G2 Oklahoma, C USA
McAllen 49 G5 Texas, SW USA
McCamey 49 E3 Texas, SW USA
McComb 42 B3 Mississippi, S USA
McCook 45 E4 Nebraska, C USA
McKean Island 145 E3 island Phoenix Islands, C Kiribati
Mount McKinley 36 C3 var. Denali. mountain Alaska, USA
McKinley Park 36 C3 Alaska, USA
M'Clintock Channel 37 F2 channel Nunavut, N Canada
McMinnville 46 B3 Oregon, NW USA
McMurdo 154 B4 US research station Antarctica
McPherson 45 E5 Kansas, C USA
McPherson see Fort McPherson
Mdantsane 78 D5 Eastern Cape, SE South Africa
Mead, Lake 47 D6 reservoir Arizona/ Nevada, W USA
Mecca see Makkah
Mechelen 87 C5 Eng. Mechlin, Fr. Malines. Antwerpen, C Belgium
Mechlin see Mechelen
Mecklenburger Bucht 94 C2 bay N Germany
Mecsek 99 C7 mountain range SW Hungary
Medan 138 B3 Sumatera, E Indonesia
Medeba see Ma'dabā
Medellín 58 B3 Antioquia, NW Colombia
Médenine 71 F2 var. Madanīyīn. SE Tunisia
Medeshamstede see Peterborough
Medford 46 B4 Oregon, NW USA
Medgidia 108 D5 Constanța, SE Romania
Medgyes see Mediaș

Mediaş 108 B4 Ger. Mediasch, Hung. Medgyes. Sibiu, C Romania
Mediasch see Mediaş
Medicine Hat 37 F5 Alberta, SW Canada
Medina see Al Madinah
Medinaceli 93 E2 Castilla y León, N Spain
Medina del Campo 92 D2 Castilla y León, N Spain
Medinat Israel see Israel
Mediolanum see Saintes, France
Mediolanum see Milano, Italy
Mediomatrica see Metz
Mediterranean Sea 102 D3 Fr. Mer Méditerranée. sea Africa/Asia/Europe
Méditerranée, Mer see Mediterranean Sea
Médoc 91 B5 cultural region SW France
Medvezh'yegorsk 110 B3 Respublika Kareliya, NW Russian Federation
Meekatharra 147 B5 Western Australia
Meemu Atoll see Mulakatholhu
Meerssen 87 D6 var. Mersen. Limburg, SE Netherlands
Meerut 134 D2 Uttar Pradesh, N India
Megáli Préspa, Límni see Prespa, Lake
Meghālaya 113 G3 cultural region NE India
Mehdia see Mahdia
Meheso see Mi'ēso
Me Hka see Nmai Hka
Mehriz 120 D3 Yazd, C Iran
Mehtar Lām 123 F4 var. Mehtarlām, Meterlam, Metharlam, Metharlam. Laghmān, E Afghanistan
Mehtarlām see Mehtar Lām
Meiktila 136 B3 Mandalay, C Myanmar (Burma)
Méjico see Mexico
Mejillones 64 B2 Antofagasta, N Chile
Mek'elē 72 C4 var. Makale. Tigray, N Ethiopia
Mékhé 74 B3 NW Senegal
Mekong 124 D3 var. Lan-ts'ang Chiang, Cam. Mékôngk, Chin. Lancang Jiang, Lao. Mènam Khong, Nam Khong, Th. Mae Nam Khong, Tib. Dza Chu, Vtn. Sông Tiên Giang. river SE Asia
Mékôngk see Mekong
Mekong, Mouths of the 137 E6 delta S Vietnam
Melaka 138 B3 var. Malacca. Melaka, Peninsular Malaysia
Melaka, Selat see Malacca, Strait of
Melanesia 144 D3 island group W Pacific Ocean
Melanesian Basin 142 C2 undersea basin W Pacific Ocean
Melbourne 149 C7 state capital Victoria, SE Australia
Melbourne 43 E4 Florida, SE USA
Meleda see Mljet
Melghir, Chott 71 E2 var. Chott Melrhir. salt lake E Algeria
Melilla 80 B5 anc. Rusaddir, Russadir. Melilla, Spain, N Africa
Melilla 70 D2 enclave Spain, N Africa
Melita 37 F5 Manitoba, S Canada
Melita see Mljet
Melitene see Malatya
Melitopol' 109 F4 Zaporiz'ka Oblast', SE Ukraine
Melle 87 B5 Oost-Vlaanderen, NW Belgium
Mellerud 85 B6 Västra Götaland, S Sweden
Mellieħa 102 B5 E Malta
Mellizo Sur, Cerro 65 A7 mountain S Chile
Melo 64 E4 Cerro Largo, NE Uruguay
Melodunum see Melun
Melrhir, Chott see Melghir, Chott
Melsungen 94 B4 Hessen, C Germany
Melun 90 C3 anc. Melodunum. Seine-et-Marne, N France
Melville Bay/Melville Bugt see Qimusseriarsuaq
Melville Island 146 D2 island Northern Territory, N Australia
Melville Island 37 E2 island Parry Islands, Northwest Territories, NW Canada
Melville, Lake 39 F2 lake Newfoundland and Labrador, E Canada
Melville Peninsula 37 G3 peninsula Nunavut, NE Canada
Melville Sound see Viscount Melville Sound
Membidj see Manbij

Memel see Neman, NE Europe
Memel see Klaipeda, Lithuania
Memmingen 95 B6 Bayern, S Germany
Memphis 42 C1 Tennessee, S USA
Menaam see Menaldum
Menado see Manado
Ménaka 75 F3 Goa, E Mali
Menaldum 86 D1 Fris. Menaam. Fryslân, N Netherlands
Mènam Khong see Mekong
Mendaña Fracture Zone 153 F4 fracture zone E Pacific Ocean
Mende 91 C5 anc. Mimatum. Lozère, S France
Mendeleyev Ridge 155 B2 undersea ridge Arctic Ocean
Mendocino Fracture Zone 152 D2 fracture zone NE Pacific Ocean
Mendoza 64 B4 Mendoza, W Argentina
Menemen 116 A3 İzmir, W Turkey
Menengiyn Tal 127 F2 plain E Mongolia
Menongue 78 B2 var. Vila Serpa Pinto, Port. Serpa Pinto. Cuando Cubango, C Angola
Mentawai, Kepulauan 138 A4 island group W Indonesia
Meppel 86 D2 Drenthe, NE Netherlands
Meran see Merano
Merano 96 C1 Ger. Meran. Trentino-Alto Adige, N Italy
Merca see Marka
Mercedes 64 D3 Corrientes, NE Argentina
Mercedes 64 D4 Soriano, SW Uruguay
Meredith, Lake 49 E1 reservoir Texas, SW USA
Merefa 109 G2 Kharkivs'ka Oblast', E Ukraine
Mergate see Margate
Mergui see Myeik
Mergui Archipelago see Myeik Archipelago
Mérida 51 H3 Yucatán, SW Mexico
Mérida 92 C4 anc. Augusta Emerita. Extremadura, W Spain
Mérida 58 C2 Mérida, W Venezuela
Meridian 42 C2 Mississippi, S USA
Mérignac 91 B5 Gironde, SW France
Merín, Laguna see Mirim Lagoon
Merkulovichi see Myerkulavichy
Merowe 72 B3 Northern, N Sudan
Merredin 147 B6 Western Australia
Mersen see Meerssen
Mersey 89 C5 river NW England, United Kingdom
Mersin 116 C4 var. İçel. İçel, S Turkey
Mêrsrags 106 C3 NW Latvia
Meru 73 C6 Eastern, C Kenya
Merv see Mary
Merzifon 116 D2 Amasya, N Turkey
Merzig 95 A5 Saarland, SW Germany
Mesa 48 B2 Arizona, SW USA
Meseritz see Międzyrzecz
Meshed see Mashhad
Mesopotamia 53 C5 var. Mesopotamia Argentina. physical region NE Argentina
Mesopotamia Argentina see Mesopotamia
Messalo, Rio 79 E2 var. Mualo. river NE Mozambique
Messana/Messene see Messina
Messina 97 D7 var. Messana, Messene; anc. Zancle. Sicilia, Italy, C Mediterranean Sea
Messina see Musina
Messina, Strait of 97 D7 Eng. Strait of Messina. strait SW Italy
Messina, Strait of see Messina, Stretto di
Messini 105 B6 Pelopónnisos, S Greece
Mesta see Néstos
Mestghanem see Mostaganem
Mest'ia 117 F1 prev. Mestia, var. Mestiya. N Georgia
Mestia see Mest'ia
Mestiya see Mest'ia
Mestre 96 C2 Veneto, NE Italy
Metairie 42 B3 Louisiana, S USA
Metán 64 C2 Salta, N Argentina
Metapán 52 B2 Santa Ana, NW El Salvador
Meta, Río 58 D3 river Colombia/Venezuela
Meterlam see Mehtar Lām
Methariam/Metharlam see Mehtar Lām
Metis see Metz
Metković 100 B4 Dubrovnik-Neretva, SE Croatia

Métsovo 104 B4 prev. Métsovon. Ípeiros, C Greece
Métsovon see Métsovo
Metz 90 D3 anc. Divodurum Mediomatricum, Mediomatrica, Metis. Moselle, NE France
Meulaboh 138 A3 Sumatera, W Indonesia
Meuse 87 C6 Dut. Maas. river W Europe
Mexcala, Río see Balsas, Río
Mexicali 50 A1 Baja California Norte, NW Mexico
Mexicanos, Estados Unidos see Mexico
México 51 E4 var. Ciudad de México, Eng. Mexico City. country capital (Mexico) México, C Mexico
Mexico 45 G4 Missouri, C USA
Mexico 50 C3 off. United Mexican States, var. Méjico, México, Sp. Estados Unidos Mexicanos. country N Central America

MEXICO
North America

Official name United Mexican States
Formation 1836 / 1848
Capital Mexico City
Population 115 million / 156 people per sq mile (60 people per sq km)
Total area 761,602 sq. miles (1,972,550 sq. km)
Languages Spanish*, Nahuatl, Mayan, Zapotec, Mixtec, Otomi, Totonac, Tzotzil, Tzeltal
Religions Roman Catholic 77%, Other 14%, Protestant 6%, Nonreligious 3%
Ethnic mix Mestizo 60%, Amerindian 30%, European 9%, Other 1%
Government Presidential system
Currency Mexican peso = 100 centavos
Literacy rate 93%
Calorie consumption 3146 kilocalories

México see Mexico
Mexico City see México
México, Golfo de see Mexico, Gulf of
Mexico, Gulf of 51 F2 Sp. Golfo de México. gulf W Atlantic Ocean
Meyadine see Al Mayādīn
Meydān Shahr see Maidān Shahr
Meymaneh see Maimanah
Mezen' 110 D3 river NW Russian Federation
Mezőtúr 99 D7 Jász-Nagykun-Szolnok, E Hungary
Mġarr 102 A5 Gozo, N Malta
Miadzioł Nowy see Myadzyel
Miahuatlán 51 F5 var. Miahuatlán de Porfirio Díaz. Oaxaca, SE Mexico
Miahuatlán de Porfirio Díaz see Miahuatlán
Miami 43 F5 Florida, SE USA
Miami 49 G1 Oklahoma, C USA
Miami Beach 43 F5 Florida, SE USA
Miāneh 120 C2 var. Miyāneh. Āzarbāyjān-e Sharqī, NW Iran
Mianyang 128 B5 Sichuan, C China
Miastko 98 C2 Ger. Rummelsburg in Pommern. Pomorskie, N Poland
Mi Chai see Nong Khai
Michalovce 99 E5 Ger. Grossmichel, Hung. Nagymihály. Košický Kraj, E Slovakia
Michigan 40 C1 off. State of Michigan, also known as Great Lakes State, Lake State, Wolverine State. state N USA
Michigan, Lake 40 C2 lake N USA
Michurin see Tsarevo
Michurinsk 111 B5 Tambovskaya Oblast', W Russian Federation
Micoud 55 F2 SE Saint Lucia
Micronesia 144 B1 off. Federated States of Micronesia. country W Pacific Ocean
Micronesia 144 C1 island group W Pacific Ocean

MICRONESIA
Australasia & Oceania

Official name Federated States of Micronesia
Formation 1986 / 1986
Capital Palikir (Pohnpei Island)
Population 106,487 / 393 people per sq mile (152 people per sq km)
Total area 271 sq. miles (702 sq. km)
Languages Trukese, Pohnpeian,

MICRONESIA
(continued)

Kosraean, Yapese, English*
Religions Roman Catholic 50%, Protestant 47%, Other 3%
Ethnic mix Chuukese 49%, Pohnpeian 24%, Other 14%, Kosraean 6%, Yapese 5%, Asian 2%
Government Nonparty system
Currency US dollar = 100 cents
Literacy rate 81%
Calorie consumption Not available

Micronesia, Federated States of see Micronesia
Mid-Atlantic Cordillera see Mid-Atlantic Ridge
Mid-Atlantic Ridge 66 C3 var. Mid-Atlantic Cordillera, Mid-Atlantic Rise, Mid-Atlantic Swell. undersea ridge Atlantic Ocean
Mid-Atlantic Rise/Mid-Atlantic Swell see Mid-Atlantic Ridge
Middelburg 87 B5 Zeeland, SW Netherlands
Middelharnis 86 B4 Zuid-Holland, SW Netherlands
Middelkerke 87 A5 West-Vlaanderen, W Belgium
Middle America Trench 35 B7 trench E Pacific Ocean
Middle Andaman 133 F2 island Andaman Islands, India, NE Indian Ocean
Middle Atlas 70 C2 Eng. Middle Atlas. mountain range N Morocco
Middle Atlas see Moyen Atlas
Middleburg Island see 'Eua
Middle Congo see Congo (Republic of)
Middlesboro 40 C5 Kentucky, S USA
Middlesbrough 89 D5 N England, United Kingdom
Middletown 41 F4 New Jersey, NE USA
Middletown 41 F3 New York, NE USA
Mid-Indian Basin 141 C5 undersea basin N Indian Ocean
Mid-Indian Ridge 141 C5 var. Central Indian Ridge. undersea ridge C Indian Ocean
Midland 38 D5 Ontario, S Canada
Midland 40 C3 Michigan, N USA
Midland 49 E3 Texas, SW USA
Mid-Pacific Mountains 152 C2 var. Mid-Pacific Seamounts. seamount range NW Pacific Ocean
Mid-Pacific Seamounts see Mid-Pacific Mountains
Midway Islands 152 D2 US territory C Pacific Ocean
Miechów 99 D5 Małopolskie, S Poland
Międzyrzec Podlaski 98 E3 Lubelskie, E Poland
Międzyrzecz 98 B3 Ger. Meseritz. Lubuskie, W Poland
Mielec 99 D5 Podkarpackie, SE Poland
Miercurea-Ciuc 108 C4 Ger. Szeklerburg, Hung. Csíkszereda. Harghita, C Romania
Mieres del Camín 92 D1 var. Mieres del Camino. Asturias, NW Spain
Mieres del Camino see Mieres del Camín
Mi'ēso 73 D5 var. Meheso, Miesso. Oromiya, C Ethiopia
Miesso see Mi'ēso
Mifrats Hefa 119 A5 Eng. Bay of Haifa; prev. MifraẕHefa. bay N Israel
Miguel Asua 50 D3 var. Miguel Auza. Zacatecas, C Mexico
Miguel Auza see Miguel Asua
Mijdrecht 86 C3 Utrecht, C Netherlands
Mikashevichi see Mikashevichy
Mikashevichy 107 C7 Pol. Mikaszewicze, Rus. Mikashevichi. Brestskaya Voblasts', SW Belarus
Mikaszewicze see Mikashevichy
Mikhaylovgrad see Montana
Mikhaylovka 111 B6 Volgogradskaya Oblast', SW Russian Federation
Míkonos see Mýkonos
Mikre 104 C2 Lovech, N Bulgaria
Mikun' 110 D4 Respublika Komi, NW Russian Federation
Mikuni-sanmyaku 131 D5 mountain range N Honshū, N Japan Asia
Mikura-jima 131 D6 island E Japan
Milagro 60 B2 Guayas, SW Ecuador
Milan see Milano

Milange 79 E2 Zambézia,
NE Mozambique
Milano 96 B2 *Eng.* Milan, *Ger.* Mailand;
anc. Mediolanum. Lombardia, N Italy
Milas 116 A4 Muğla, SW Turkey
Milashavichy 107 C7 *Rus.* Milashevichi.
Homyel'skaya Voblasts', SE Belarus
Milashevichi *see* Milashavichy
Mildura 149 C6 Victoria, SE Australia
Mile *see* Mili Atoll
Miles 149 D5 Queensland, E Australia
Miles City 44 C2 Montana, NW USA
Milford *see* Milford Haven
Milford Haven 89 C6 *prev.* Milford.
SW Wales, United Kingdom
Milford Sound 151 A6 Southland, South
Island, New Zealand
Milford Sound 151 A6 *inlet* South
Island, New Zealand
Milḩ, Baḩr al *see* Razāzah, Buḩayrat ar
Mili Atoll 144 D2 *var.* Mile. *atoll* Ratak
Chain, SE Marshall Islands
Mil'kovo 115 H3 Kamchatskiy Kray,
E Russian Federation
Milk River 37 E5 Alberta, SW Canada
Milk River 44 C1 *river* Montana,
NW USA
Milk, Wadi el 88 B4 *var.* Wadi al Malik.
river C Sudan
Milledgeville 43 E2 Georgia, SE USA
Mille Lacs Lake 45 F2 *lake* Minnesota,
N USA
Millennium Island 143 F3 *prev.*
Caroline Island, Thornton Island. *atoll*
Line Islands, E Kiribati
Millerovo 111 B6 Rostovskaya Oblast',
SW Russian Federation
Mílos 105 C6 *island* Kykládes, Greece,
Aegean Sea
Mílos 105 C6 *island* Kykládes, Greece,
Aegean Sea
Mílos 105 C7 *island* Kykládes, Greece,
Aegean Sea
Milton 151 B7 Otago, South Island,
New Zealand
Milton Keynes 89 D6 SE England,
United Kingdom
Milwaukee 40 B3 Wisconsin, N USA
Mimatum *see* Mende
Min *see* Fujian
Minā' Qābūs 140 B3 NE Oman
Minas Gerais 63 F3 *off.* Estado de Minas
Gerais. *state* E Brazil
Minas Gerais 63 F3 *off.* Estado de Minas
Gerais. *region* E Brazil
Minas Gerais, Estado de *see* Minas Gerais
Minatitlán 51 F4 Veracruz-Llave,
E Mexico
Minbu 136 A3 Magway, W Myanmar
(Burma)
Minch, The 88 B3 *var.* North Minch.
strait NW Scotland, United Kingdom
Mindanao 139 F2 *island* S Philippines
Mindanao Sea *see* Bohol Sea
Mindelheim 95 C6 Bayern, S Germany
Mindello *see* Mindelo
Mindelo 74 A2 *var.* Mindello; *prev.* Porto
Grande. São Vicente, N Cape Verde
Minden 94 B4 *anc.* Minthun. Nordrhein-
Westfalen, NW Germany
Mindoro 139 E2 *island* N Philippines
Mindoro Strait 139 E2 *strait*
W Philippines
Mineral Wells 49 F2 Texas, SW USA
Mingäçevir 117 G2 *Rus.* Mingechaur,
Mingechevir. C Azerbaijan
Mingãora *see* Saïdu
Mingechaur/Mingechevir *see*
Mingäçevir
Mingora *see* Saïdu
Minho 92 B2 *former province* N Portugal
Minho 92 B2 *Sp.* Miño. *river* Portugal/
Spain
Minho, Rio *see* Miño
Minicoy Island 132 B3 *island* SW India
Minius *see* Miño
Minna 75 G4 Niger, C Nigeria
Minneapolis 45 F2 Minnesota, N USA
Minnesota 45 F2 *off.* State of Minnesota,
also known as Gopher State. New
England of the West, North Star State.
state N USA
Miño 92 B2 *var.* Mino, Minius, *Port.* Rio
Minho. *river* Portugal/Spain
Miño *see* Minho, Rio
Minorca 93 H3 *Eng.* Minorca; *anc.*
Balearis Minor. *island* Islas Baleares,
Spain, W Mediterranean Sea
Minorca *see* Menorca

Minot 45 E1 North Dakota, N USA
Minsk 107 C6 *country capital* (Belarus)
Minskaya Voblasts', C Belarus
Minskaya Wzvyshsha 107 C6 *mountain
range* C Belarus
Mińsk Mazowiecki 98 D3 *var.* Nowo-
Minsk. Mazowieckie, C Poland
Minthun *see* Minden
Minto, Lac 38 D2 *lake* Québec, C Canada
Minya *see* Al Minyā
Miraflores 50 C3 Baja California Sur,
NW Mexico
Miranda de Ebro 93 E1 La Rioja,
N Spain
Mirgorod *see* Myrhorod
Miri 138 D3 Sarawak, East Malaysia
Mirim Lagoon 63 E5 *var.* Lake Mirim,
Sp. Laguna Merín. *lagoon* Brazil/
Uruguay
Mirim, Lake *see* Mirim Lagoon
Mírina *see* Mýrina
Mírjäveh 120 E4 Sīstān va Balūchestān,
SE Iran
Mirny 154 C3 *Russian research station*
Antarctica
Mirnyy 115 F3 Respublika Sakha
(Yakutiya), NE Russian Federation
Mīrpur Khās 134 B3 Sind, SE Pakistan
Mirtoan Sea 105 C6 *Eng.* Mirtoan Sea;
anc. Myrtoum Mare. *sea* S Greece
Mirtoan Sea *see* Mirtóo Pélagos
Misiaf *see* Maşyāf
Miskito Coast *see* La Mosquitia
Miskitos, Cayos 53 E2 *island group*
NE Nicaragua
Miskolc 99 D6 Borsod-Abaúj-Zemplén,
NE Hungary
Misool, Pulau 139 F4 *island* Maluku,
E Indonesia
Mişrātah 71 F2 *var.* Misurata. NW Libya
Mission 49 G5 Texas, SW USA
Mississippi 42 B2 *off.* State of
Mississippi, *also known as* Bayou State,
Magnolia State. *state* SE USA
Mississippi Delta 42 B4 *delta* Louisiana,
S USA
Mississippi River 35 C6 *river* C USA
Missoula 44 B1 Montana, NW USA
Missouri 45 F5 *off.* State of Missouri,
also known as Bullion State, Show Me
State. *state* C USA
Missouri River 45 E3 *river* C USA
Mistassini, Lac 38 D3 *lake* Québec,
SE Canada
Mistelbach an der Zaya 95 E6
Niederösterreich, NE Austria
Misti, Volcán 61 E4 *volcano* S Peru
Misurata *see* Mişrātah
Mitau *see* Jelgava
Mitchell 149 D5 Queensland, E Australia
Mitchell 45 E3 South Dakota, N USA
Mitchell, Mount 43 E1 *mountain* North
Carolina, SE USA
Mitchell River 148 C2 *river* Queensland,
NE Australia
Mi Tho *see* My Tho
Mitilíni *see* Mytilíni
Mitrovica/Mitrovicë *see* Kosovska
Mitrovica, Serbia
Mitrovica/Mitrowitz *see* Sremska
Mitrovica, Serbia
Mitrovicë 101 D5 *Serb.* Mitrovica,
Kosovska Mitrovica, Titova Mitrovica.
N Kosovo
Mits'iwa 72 C4 *var.* Masawa, Massawa.
E Eritrea
Mitspe Ramon 119 A7 *prev.* Mizpe
Ramon. Southern, S Israel
Mittelstadt *see* Baia Sprie
Mitú 58 C4 Vaupés, SE Colombia
Mitumba, Chaîne des/Mitumba Range
see Mitumba, Monts
Mitumba Range 77 E7 *var.* Chaîne des
Mitumba, Mitumba Range. *mountain
range* E Dem. Rep. Congo
Miueru Wantipa, Lake 77 E7 *lake*
N Zambia
Miyake-jima 131 D6 *island* Sakishima-
shotō, SW Japan
Miyako 130 D4 Iwate, Honshū, C Japan
Miyakonojō 131 B8 *var.* Miyakonojo.
Miyazaki, Kyūshū, SW Japan
Miyakonzyô *see* Miyakonojō
Miyāneh *see* Miāneh
Miyazaki 131 B8 Miyazaki, Kyūshū,
SW Japan
Mizil 108 C5 Prahova, SE Romania
Miziya 104 C1 Vratsa, NW Bulgaria

Mizpe Ramon *see* Mitspe Ramon
Mjøsa 85 B6 *var.* Mjøsen. *lake* S Norway
Mjøsen *see* Mjøsa
Mladenovac 100 D4 Serbia, C Serbia
Mława 98 D3 Mazowieckie, C Poland
Mljet 101 B5 *It.* Meleda; *anc.* Melita.
island S Croatia
Mmabatho 78 C4 North-West, N South
Africa
Moab 44 B5 Utah, W USA
Moa Island 148 C1 *island* Queensland,
NE Australia
Moanda 77 B6 *var.* Mouanda. Haut-
Ogooué, SE Gabon
Moba 77 E7 Katanga, E Dem. Rep. Congo
Mobay *see* Montego Bay
Mobaye 77 C5 Basse-Kotto, S Central
African Republic
Moberly 45 G4 Missouri, C USA
Mobile 42 C3 Alabama, S USA
Mobutu Sese Seko, Lac *see* Albert, Lake
Moçâmedes *see* Namibe
Mochudi 78 C4 Kgatleng,
SE Botswana
Mocímboa da Praia 79 F2 *var.* Vila de
Mocímboa da Praia. Cabo Delgado,
N Mozambique
Môco 78 B2 *var.* Morro de Môco.
mountain W Angola
Mocoa 58 A4 Putumayo, SW Colombia
Môco, Morro de *see* Môco
Mocuba 79 E3 Zambézia,
NE Mozambique
Modena 96 B3 *anc.* Mutina. Emilia-
Romagna, N Italy
Modesto 47 B6 California, W USA
Modica 97 C7 *anc.* Motyca. Sicilia, Italy,
C Mediterranean Sea
Modimolle 78 D4 *prev.* Nylstroom.
Limpopo, NE South Africa
Modohn *see* Madona
Modriča 100 C3 Republika Srpska,
N Bosnia and Herzegovina
Moe 149 C7 Victoria, SE Australia
Møen *see* Møn, Denmark
Moero, Lac *see* Mweru, Lake
Moeskroen *see* Mouscron
Mogadiscio/Mogadishu *see* Muqdisho
Mogador *see* Essaouira
Mogilëv *see* Mahilyow
Mogilev-Podol'skiy *see*
Mohyliv-Podil's'kyy
Mogilno 98 C3 Kujawsko-pomorskie,
C Poland
Moḩammadābād-e Rīgān 120 E4
Kermān, SE Iran
Mohammedia 70 C2 *prev.* Fédala.
NW Morocco
Mohave, Lake 47 D7 *reservoir* Arizona/
Nevada, W USA
Mohawk River 41 F3 *river* New York,
NE USA
Mohéli *see* Mwali
Mohns Ridge 83 F3 *undersea ridge*
Greenland Sea/Norwegian Sea
Moho 61 E4 Puno, SE Peru
Mohoro 73 C7 Pwani, E Tanzania
Mohyliv-Podil's'kyy 108 D3 *Rus.*
Mogilev-Podol'skiy. Vinnyts'ka
Oblast', C Ukraine
Moi 85 A6 Rogaland, S Norway
Moili *see* Mwali
Mo i Rana 84 C3 Nordland, C Norway
Moisaküla 106 D3 *Ger.* Moiseküll.
Viljandimaa, S Estonia
Moiseküll *see* Mõisaküla
Moissac 91 B6 Tarn-et-Garonne,
S France
Mojácar 93 E5 Andalucía, S Spain
Mojave Desert 47 D7 *plain* California,
W USA
Mokrany *see* Makrany
Moktama *see* Mottama
Mol 87 C5 *prev.* Moll. Antwerpen,
N Belgium
Moldavia *see* Moldova
Moldavian SSR/Moldavskaya SSR *see*
Moldova
Moldotau, Khrebet *see* Moldo-Too,
Khrebet
Moldo-Too, Khrebet 123 G2 *prev.*
Khrebet Moldotau. *mountain range*
C Kyrgyzstan
Moldova 108 D3 *off.* Republic of
Moldova, *var.* Moldavia; *prev.*
Moldavian SSR, *Rus.* Moldavskaya SSR.
country SE Europe

MOLDOVA
Southeast Europe

Official name Republic of Moldova
Formation 1991 / 1991
Capital Chisinau
Population 3.5 million / 269 people
per sq mile (104 people per sq km)
Total area 13,067 sq. miles (33,843 sq. km)
Languages Moldovan*, Ukrainian, Russian
Religions Orthodox Christian 93%, Other
6%, Baptist 1%
Ethnic mix Moldovan 84%, Ukrainian 7%,
Gagauz 5%, Russian 2%, Bulgarian 1%,
Other 1%
Government Parliamentary system
Currency Moldovan leu = 100 bani
Literacy rate 99%
Calorie consumption 2707 kilocalories

Moldova Nouă 108 A4 *Ger.*
Neumoldowa, *Hung.* Újmoldva.
Caraş-Severin, SW Romania
Moldova, Republic of *see* Moldova
Moldoveanul *see* Vârful Moldoveanu
Molfetta 97 E5 Puglia, SE Italy
Moll *see* Mol
Mollendo 61 E4 Arequipa, SW Peru
Mölndal 85 B7 Västra Götaland,
S Sweden
Molochans'k 109 G4 *Rus.* Molochansk.
Zaporiz'ka Oblast', SE Ukraine
Molodechno/Molodeczno *see*
Maladzyechna
Molodezhnaya 154 C2 *Russian research
station* Antarctica
Moloka'i 128 B4 *var.* Molokai. *island*
Hawaiian Islands, Hawai'i, USA
Molokai Fracture Zone 153 E2 *tectonic
feature* NE Pacific Ocean
Molopo 78 C4 *seasonal river* Botswana/
South Africa
Mólos 105 B5 Stereá Elláda,
C Greece
Molotov *see* Severodvinsk,
Arkhangel'skaya Oblast', Russian
Federation
Molotov *see* Perm', Permskaya Oblast',
Russian Federation
Moluccas 139 F4 *Dut.* Molukken, *Eng.*
Moluccas; *prev.* Spice Islands. *island
group* E Indonesia
Molucca Sea 139 F4 *Ind.* Laut Maluku.
sea E Indonesia
Molukken *see* Maluku
Mombasa 73 D7 Coast, SE Kenya
Mombetsu *see* Monbetsu
Momchilgrad 104 D3 *prev.* Mastanli.
Kŭrdzhali, S Bulgaria
Møn 85 B8 *prev.* Möen. *island*
SE Denmark
Mona, Canal de la *see* Mona Passage
Monaco 91 E6 var. Monaco-Ville; *anc.*
Monoecus. *country capital* (Monaco)
S Monaco
Monaco 91 E6 *off.* Principality of
Monaco. *country* W Europe

MONACO
Southern Europe

Official name Principality of Monaco
Formation 1861 / 1861
Capital Monaco-Ville
Population 30,510 / 40,680 people per
sq mile (15,646 people per sq km)
Total area 0.75 sq. miles (1.95 sq. km)
Languages French*, Italian,
Monégasque, English
Religions Roman Catholic 89%,
Protestant 6%, Other 5%
Ethnic mix French 47%, Other 21%,
Italian 16%, Monégasque 16%
Government Mixed monarchical–
parliamentary system
Currency Euro = 100 cents
Literacy rate 99%
Calorie consumption Not available

Monaco *see* München
Monaco, Port de 91 C8 *bay* S Monaco
W Mediterranean Sea
Monaco, Principality of *see* Monaco
Monaco-Ville *see* Monaco
Monahans 49 E3 Texas,
SW USA
Mona, Isla 55 E3 *island* W Puerto Rico

Mona Passage 55 E3 *Sp.* Canal de la Mona. *channel* Dominican Republic/ Puerto Rico
Monastir *see* Bitola
Monbetsu 130 D2 *var.* Mombetsu, Monbetu. Hokkaidō, NE Japan
Monbetu *see* Monbetsu
Moncalieri 96 A2 Piemonte, NW Italy
Monchegorsk 110 C2 Murmanskaya Oblast', NW Russian Federation
Monclova 50 D2 Coahuila, NE Mexico
Moncton 39 F4 New Brunswick, SE Canada
Mondovì 96 A2 Piemonte, NW Italy
Monfalcone 96 D2 Friuli-Venezia Giulia, NE Italy
Monforte de Lemos 92 C1 Galicia, NW Spain
Mongo 76 C3 Guéra, C Chad
Mongolia 126 C2 *Mong.* Mongol Uls. *country* E Asia

MONGOLIA
East Asia

Official name Mongolia
Formation 1924 / 1924
Capital Ulan Bator
Population 2.8 million / 5 people per sq mile (2 people per sq km)
Total area 604,247 sq. miles (1,565,000 sq. km)
Languages Khalkha Mongolian*, Kazakh, Chinese, Russian
Religions Tibetan Buddhist 50%, Nonreligious 40%, Shamanist and Christian 6%, Muslim 4%
Ethnic mix Khalkh 95%, Kazakh 4%, Other 1%
Government Mixed presidential– parliamentary system
Currency Tugrik (tögrög) = 100 möngö
Literacy rate 98%
Calorie consumption 2434 kilocalories

Mongolia, Plateau of 124 D1 *plateau* E Mongolia
Mongol Uls *see* Mongolia
Mongora *see* Saidu
Mongos, Chaine des *see* Bongo, Massif des
Mongu 78 C2 Western, W Zambia
Monkchester *see* Newcastle upon Tyne
Monkey Bay 79 E2 Southern, SE Malawi
Monkey River *see* Monkey River Town
Monkey River Town 52 C2 *var.* Monkey River. Toledo, SE Belize
Monoecus *see* Monaco
Mono Lake 47 C6 *lake* California, W USA
Monostor *see* Beli Manastir
Monóvar 93 F4 *Cat.* Monòver. Valenciana, E Spain
Monòver *see* Monóvar
Monroe 42 B2 Louisiana, S USA
Monrovia 74 C5 *country capital* (Liberia) W Liberia
Mons 87 B6 *Dut.* Bergen. Hainaut, S Belgium
Monselice 96 C2 Veneto, NE Italy
Montana 104 C2 *prev.* Ferdinand, Mikhaylovgrad. Montana, NW Bulgaria
Montana 44 B1 *off.* State of Montana, *also known as* Mountain State, Treasure State. *state* NW USA
Montargis 90 C4 Loiret, C France
Montauban 91 B6 Tarn-et-Garonne, S France
Montbéliard 90 D4 Doubs, E France
Mont Cenis, Col du 91 D5 *pass* E France
Mont-de-Marsan 91 B6 Landes, SW France
Monteagudo 61 G4 Chuquisaca, S Bolivia
Montecarlo 91 C8 Misiones, NE Argentina
Monte Caseros 64 D3 Corrientes, NE Argentina
Monte Cristi 54 D3 *var.* San Fernando de Monte Cristi. NW Dominican Republic
Monte Croce Carnico, Passo di *see* Plöcken Pass
Montegiardino 96 E2 SE San Marino
Montego Bay 54 A4 *var.* Mobay. W Jamaica
Montélimar 91 D5 *anc.* Acunum Acusio, Montilium Adhemari. Drôme, E France

Montemorelos 51 E3 Nuevo León, NE Mexico
Montenegro 101 C5 *Serb.* Crna Gora. *country* SW Europe

MONTENEGRO
Southeast Europe

Official name Montenegro
Formation 2006 / 2006
Capital Podgorica
Population 600,000 / 113 people per sq mile (43 people per sq km)
Total area 5332 sq. miles (13,812 sq. km)
Languages Montenegrin*, Serbian, Albanian, Bosniak, Croatian
Religions Orthodox Christian 74%, Muslim 18%, Roman Catholic 4%, Other 4%
Ethnic mix Montenegrin 43%, Serb 32%, Other 12%, Bosniak 8%, Albanian 5%
Government Parliamentary system
Currency Euro = 100 cents
Literacy rate 98%
Calorie consumption 2887

Monte Patria 64 B3 Coquimbo, N Chile
Monterey 47 B6 California, W USA
Monterey *see* Monterrey
Monterey Bay 47 A6 *bay* California, W USA
Montería 58 B2 Córdoba, NW Colombia
Montero 61 G4 Santa Cruz, C Bolivia
Monterrey 51 E3 *var.* Monterey. Nuevo León, NE Mexico
Montes Claros 63 F3 Minas Gerais, SE Brazil
Montevideo 64 D4 *country capital* (Uruguay) Montevideo, S Uruguay
Montevideo 45 F2 Minnesota, N USA
Montgenèvre, Col de 91 D5 *pass* France/Italy
Montgomery 42 D2 *state capital* Alabama, S USA
Montgomery *see* Sāhiwal
Monthey 95 A7 Valais, SW Switzerland
Montilium Adhemari *see* Montélimar
Montluçon 90 C4 Allier, C France
Montoro 92 D4 Andalucía, S Spain
Montpelier 41 G2 *state capital* Vermont, NE USA
Montpellier 91 C6 Hérault, S France
Montréal 39 E4 *Eng.* Montreal. Québec, SE Canada
Montrose 88 D3 E Scotland, United Kingdom
Montrose 44 C5 Colorado, C USA
Montserrat 55 G3 *var.* Emerald Isle. *UK dependent territory* E West Indies
Monywa 136 B3 Sagaing, C Myanmar (Burma)
Monza 96 B2 Lombardia, N Italy
Monze 78 D2 Southern, S Zambia
Monzón 93 F2 Aragón, NE Spain
Moonie 149 D5 Queensland, E Australia
Moon-Sund *see* Väinameri
Moora 147 A6 Western Australia
Moore 49 G1 Oklahoma, C USA
Moore, Lake 147 B6 *lake* Western Australia
Moorhead 45 F2 Minnesota, N USA
Moose 38 C3 *river* Ontario, S Canada
Moosehead Lake 41 G1 *lake* Maine, NE USA
Moosonee 38 C3 Ontario, SE Canada
Mopti 75 E3 Mopti, C Mali
Moquegua 61 E4 Moquegua, SE Peru
Mora 85 C5 Dalarna, C Sweden
Morales 52 C2 Izabal, E Guatemala
Morant Bay 54 B5 E Jamaica
Moratalla 93 E4 Murcia, SE Spain
Morava 99 C5 *var.* March. *river* C Europe
Morava *see* Moravia, Czech Republic
Morava *see* Velika Morava, Serbia
Moravia 99 B5 *Cz.* Morava, *Ger.* Mähren. *cultural region* E Czech Republic
Moray Firth 88 C3 *inlet* N Scotland, United Kingdom
Morea *see* Pelopónnisos
Moreau River 44 D2 *river* South Dakota, N USA
Moree 149 D5 New South Wales, SE Australia
Morelia 51 E4 Michoacán, S Mexico
Morena, Sierra 92 C4 *mountain range* S Spain
Moreni 108 C5 Dâmbovița, S Romania

Morgan City 42 B3 Louisiana, S USA
Morghāb, Daryā-ye *see* Murgap
Morioka 130 D4 Iwate, Honshū, C Japan
Morlaix 90 A3 Finistère, NW France
Mormon State *see* Utah
Mornington Abyssal Plain 67 A7 *abyssal plain* SE Pacific Ocean
Mornington Island 148 B2 *island* Wellesley Islands, Queensland, N Australia
Morocco 70 B3 *off.* Kingdom of Morocco, *Ar.* Al Mamlakah. *country* N Africa

MOROCCO
North Africa

Official name Kingdom of Morocco
Formation 1956 / 1969
Capital Rabat
Population 32.3 million / 187 people per sq mile (72 people per sq km)
Total area 172,316 sq. miles (446,300 sq. km)
Languages Arabic*, Tamazight (Berber), French, Spanish
Religions Muslim (mainly Sunni) 99%, Other (mostly Christian) 1%
Ethnic mix Arab 70%, Berber 29%, European 1%
Government Mixed monarchical– parliamentary system
Currency Moroccan dirham = 100 centimes
Literacy rate 56%
Calorie consumption 3264 kilocalories

Morocco *see* Marrakech
Morocco, Kingdom of *see* Morocco
Morogoro 73 C7 Morogoro, E Tanzania
Moro Gulf 139 E3 *gulf* S Philippines
Morón 54 C2 Ciego de Ávila, C Cuba
Mörön 126 D2 Hövsgöl, N Mongolia
Morondava 79 F3 Toliara, W Madagascar
Moroni 79 F2 *country capital* (Comoros) Grande Comore, NW Comoros
Morotai, Pulau 139 F3 *island* Maluku, E Indonesia
Morotiri *see* Marotiri
Morphou *see* Güzelyurt
Morrinsville 150 D3 Waikato, North Island, New Zealand
Morris 45 F2 Minnesota, N USA
Morris Jesup, Kap 83 E1 *headland* N Greenland
Morvan 90 D4 *physical region* C France
Moscow 46 C2 Idaho, NW USA
Moscow *see* Moskva
Mosel 95 A5 *Fr.* Moselle. *river* W Europe
Mosel *see* Moselle
Moselle 87 E8 *Ger.* Mosel. *river* W Europe
Moselle *see* Mosel
Mosgiel 151 B7 Otago, South Island, New Zealand
Moshi 73 C7 Kilimanjaro, NE Tanzania
Mosjøen 84 B4 Nordland, C Norway
Moskovskiy *see* Moskva
Moskva 111 B5 *Eng.* Moscow. *country capital* (Russian Federation) Gorod Moskva, W Russian Federation
Moskva 123 E3 *Rus.* Moskovskiy; *prev.* Chubek. SW Tajikistan
Moson and Magyaróvár *see* Mosonmagyaróvár
Mosonmagyaróvár 99 C6 *Ger.* Wieselburg-Ungarisch-Altenburg; *prev.* Moson and Magyaróvár, *Ger.* Wieselburg and Ungarisch-Altenburg. Győr-Moson-Sopron, NW Hungary
Mosquito Coast 53 E3 *var.* Miskito Coast, *Eng.* Mosquito Coast. *coastal region* E Nicaragua
Mosquito Coast *see* La Mosquitia
Mosquito Gulf 53 F4 *Eng.* Mosquito Gulf. *gulf* N Panama
Mosquito Gulf *see* Mosquitos, Golfo de los
Moss 85 B6 Østfold, S Norway
Mossâmedes *see* Namibe
Mosselbaai 78 C5 *var.* Mosselbai, *Eng.* Mossel Bay. Western Cape, SW South Africa
Mosselbai/Mossel Bay *see* Mosselbaai
Mossendjo 77 B6 Niari, SW Congo

Mossoró 63 G2 Rio Grande do Norte, NE Brazil
Most 98 A4 *Ger.* Brüx. Ústecký Kraj, NW Czech Republic
Mosta 102 B5 *var.* Musta. C Malta
Mostaganem 70 D2 *var.* Mestghanem. NW Algeria
Mostar 100 C4 Federacija Bosna I Hercegovina, S Bosnia and Herzegovina
Mosty *see* Masty
Mosul *see* Al Mawşil
Mota del Cuervo 93 E3 Castilla-La Mancha, C Spain
Motagua, Río 52 B2 *river* Guatemala/ Honduras
Mother of Presidents/Mother of States *see* Virginia
Motril 92 D5 Andalucía, S Spain
Motru 108 B4 Gorj, SW Romania
Mottama 136 B4 *var.* Martaban, Moktama. Mon State, S Myanmar (Burma)
Motueka 151 C5 Tasman, South Island, New Zealand
Motul 51 H3 *var.* Motul de Felipe Carrillo Puerto. Yucatán, SE Mexico
Motul de Felipe Carrillo Puerto *see* Motul
Motyca *see* Modica
Mouanda *see* Moanda
Mouhoun *see* Black Volta
Mouila 77 A6 Ngounié, C Gabon
Moukden *see* Shenyang
Mould Bay 37 E2 Prince Patrick Island, Northwest Territories, N Canada
Moulins 90 C4 Allier, C France
Moulmein *see* Mawlamyine
Moundou 76 B4 Logone-Occidental, SW Chad
Moŭng Roessei 137 D5 Bătdâmbâng, W Cambodia
Moun Hou *see* Black Volta
Mountain Home 42 B1 Arkansas, C USA
Mountain State *see* Montana
Mountain State *see* West Virginia
Mount Cook 151 B6 Canterbury, South Island, New Zealand
Mount Desert Island 41 H2 *island* Maine, NE USA
Mount Gambier 149 B7 South Australia
Mount Isa 148 B3 Queensland, C Australia
Mount Magnet 147 B5 Western Australia
Mount Pleasant 45 G4 Iowa, C USA
Mount Pleasant 40 C3 Michigan, N USA
Mount Vernon 40 B5 Illinois, N USA
Mount Vernon 46 B1 Washington, NW USA
Mourdi, Dépression du 76 C2 *desert lowland* Chad/Sudan
Mouscron 87 A6 *Dut.* Moeskroen. Hainaut, W Belgium
Mouse River *see* Souris River
Moussoro 76 B3 Kanem, W Chad
Moyen-Congo *see* Congo (Republic of)
Mo'ynoq 122 C1 *Rus.* Muynak. Qoraqalpog'iston Respublikasi, NW Uzbekistan
Moyobamba 60 B2 San Martín, NW Peru
Moyu 126 B3 *var.* Karakax. Xinjiang Uygur Zizhiqu, NW China
Moyynkum, Peski 123 F1 *Kaz.* Moyynqum. *desert* S Kazakhstan
Moyynqum *see* Moyynkum, Peski
Mozambique, Lakandranon' i *see* Mozambique Channel
Mozambique 79 E3 *off.* Republic of Mozambique; *prev.* People's Republic of Mozambique, Portuguese East Africa. *country* S Africa

MOZAMBIQUE
Southern Africa

Official name Republic of Mozambique
Formation 1975 / 1975
Capital Maputo
Population 23.9 million / 79 people per sq mile (30 people per sq km)
Total area 309,494 sq. miles (801,590 sq. km)
Languages Makua, Xitsonga, Sena, Lomwe, Portuguese*
Religions Traditional beliefs 56%, Christian 30%, Muslim 14%
Ethnic mix Makua Lomwe 47%, Tsonga 23%, Malawi 12%, Shona 11%,

MOZAMBIQUE
(continued)

Yao 4%, Other 3%
Government Presidential system
Currency New metical = 100 centavos
Literacy rate 55%
Calorie consumption 2112 kilocalories

Mozambique Basin *see* Natal Basin
Mozambique, Canal de *see* Mozambique Channel
Mozambique Channel 79 E3 *Fr.* Canal de Moçambique, *Mal.* Lakandranon' i Mozambika. *strait* W Indian Ocean
Mozambique, People's Republic of *see* Mozambique
Mozambique Plateau 69 D7 *var.* Mozambique Rise. *undersea plateau* SW Indian Ocean
Mozambique, Republic of *see* Mozambique
Mozambique Rise *see* Mozambique Plateau
Mozyr' *see* Mazyr
Mpama 77 B6 *river* C Congo
Mpika 78 D2 Northern, NE Zambia
Mqinvartsveri *see* Kazbek
Mragowo 98 D2 *Ger.* Sensburg. Warmińsko-Mazurskie, NE Poland
Mthatha 78 D5 *prev.* Umtata. Eastern Cape, SE South Africa
Mtkvari *see* Kura
Mtwara 73 D8 Mtwara, SE Tanzania
Mualo *see* Messalo, Rio
Muang Chiang Rai *see* Chiang Rai
Muang Kalasin *see* Kalasin
Muang Khammouan *see* Thakhèk
Muang Không 137 D5 Champasak, S Laos
Muang Khôngxédôn 137 D5 *var.* Khong Sedone. Salavan, S Laos
Muang Khon Kaen *see* Khon Kaen
Muang Lampang *see* Lampang
Muang Loei *see* Loei
Muang Lom Sak *see* Lom Sak
Muang Nakhon Sawan *see* Nakhon Sawan
Muang Namo 136 C3 Oudômxai, N Laos
Muang Nan *see* Nan
Muang Phalan 136 D4 *var.* Muang Phalane. Savannakhét, S Laos
Muang Phalane *see* Muang Phalan
Muang Phayao *see* Phayao
Muang Phitsanulok *see* Phitsanulok
Muang Phrae *see* Phrae
Muang Roi Et *see* Roi Et
Muang Sakon Nakhon *see* Sakon Nakhon
Muang Samut Prakan *see* Samut Prakan
Muang Sing 136 C3 Louang Namtha, N Laos
Muang Ubon *see* Ubon Ratchathani
Muang Xaignabouri *see* Xaignabouli
Muar 138 B3 *var.* Bandar Maharani. Johor, Peninsular Malaysia
Mucojo 79 F2 Cabo Delgado, N Mozambique
Mudanjiang 127 B3 *var.* Mu-tan-chiang. Heilongjiang, NE China
Mudon 137 B5 Mon State, S Myanmar (Burma)
Muenchen *see* München
Muenster *see* Münster
Mufulira 78 D2 Copperbelt, C Zambia
Mughla *see* Muğla
Muğla 116 A4 *var.* Mughla. Muğla, SW Turkey
Muḩ, Sabkhat al 118 C3 *lake* C Syria
Muhu Väin *see* Väinameri
Muisne 60 A1 Esmeraldas, NW Ecuador
Mukacheve 108 B3 *Hung.* Munkács, *Rus.* Mukachevo. Zakarpats'ka Oblast', W Ukraine
Mukachevo *see* Mukacheve
Mukalla *see* Al Mukallā
Mukden *see* Shenyang
Mula 93 E4 Murcia, SE Spain
Mulakatholhu 132 B4 *var.* Meemu Atoll, Mulaku Atoll. *atoll* C Maldives
Mulaku Atoll *see* Mulakatholhu
Muleshoe 49 E2 Texas, SW USA
Mulhacén 93 E5 *var.* Cerro de Mulhacén. *mountain* S Spain
Mulhacén, Cerro de *see* Mulhacén
Mülhausen *see* Mulhouse

Mülheim 95 A6 *var.* Mulheim an der Ruhr. Nordrhein-Westfalen, W Germany
Mulheim an der Ruhr *see* Mülheim
Mulhouse 90 E4 *Ger.* Mülhausen. Haut-Rhin, NE France
Müller-gerbergte *see* Muller, Pegunungan
Muller, Pegunungan 138 D4 *Dut.* Müller-gerbergte. *mountain range* Borneo, C Indonesia
Mull, Isle of 88 B4 *island* W Scotland, United Kingdom
Mulongo 77 D7 Katanga, SE Dem. Rep. Congo
Multān 134 C2 Punjab, E Pakistan
Mumbai 134 C5 *prev.* Bombay. *state capital* Mahārāshtra, W India
Munamägi *see* Suur Munamägi
Münchberg 95 C5 Bayern, E Germany
München 95 C6 *var.* Muenchen, *Eng.* Munich, *It.* Monaco. Bayern, SE Germany
Muncie 40 C4 Indiana, N USA
Mungbere 77 E5 Orientale, NE Dem. Rep. Congo
Mu Nggava *see* Rennell
Munich *see* München
Munkács *see* Mukacheve
Münster 94 A4 *var.* Muenster, Münster in Westfalen. Nordrhein-Westfalen, W Germany
Munster 89 A6 *Ir.* Cúige Mumhan. *cultural region* S Ireland
Münster in Westfalen *see* Münster
Muong Xiang Ngeun 136 C4 *var.* Xieng Ngeun. Louangphabang, N Laos
Muonio 84 D3 Lappi, N Finland
Muonioälv/Muoniojoki *see* Muonionjoki
Muoniojoki 84 D3 *var.* Muoniojoki, *Swe.* Muonioälv. *river* Finland/Sweden
Muqät 119 C5 Al Mafraq, E Jordan
Muqdisho 73 D6 *Eng.* Mogadishu, *It.* Mogadiscio. *country capital* (Somalia) Banaadir, S Somalia
Mur 95 E7 *SCr.* Mura. *river* C Europe
Mura *see* Mur
Muradiye 117 F3 Van, E Turkey
Murapara *see* Murupara
Murata 96 E2 S San Marino
Murchison River 147 A5 *river* Western Australia
Murcia 93 F4 Murcia, SE Spain
Murcia 93 E4 *autonomous community* SE Spain
Mureş 108 A4 *river* Hungary/Romania
Murfreesboro 42 D1 Tennessee, S USA
Murgab *see* Murghob
Murgap 122 D3 Mary Welaýaty, S Turkmenistan
Murgap 122 D3 *var.* Deryasy Murgap, Murghab, *Pash.* Daryā-ye Morghāb, *Rus.* Murgab. *river* Afghanistan/ Turkmenistan
Murghob 123 F3 *Rus.* Murgab. SE Tajikistan
Murgon 149 E5 Queensland, E Australia
Müritäniyah *see* Mauritania
Müritz 94 C3 *var.* Müritzee. *lake* NE Germany
Müritzee *see* Müritz
Murmansk 110 C2 Murmanskaya Oblast', NW Russian Federation
Murmashi 110 C2 Murmanskaya Oblast', NW Russian Federation
Murom 111 B5 Vladimirskaya Oblast', W Russian Federation
Muroran 130 D3 Hokkaidō, NE Japan
Muros 92 B1 Galicia, NW Spain
Murray Fracture Zone 153 E2 *fracture zone* NE Pacific Ocean
Murray Range *see* Murray Ridge
Murray Ridge 112 C5 *var.* Murray Range. *undersea ridge* N Arabian Sea
Murray River 149 B6 *river* SE Australia
Murrumbidgee River 149 C6 *river* New South Wales, SE Australia
Murska Sobota 95 E7 *Ger.* Olsnitz. NE Slovenia
Murupara 150 E3 *var.* Murapara. Bay of Plenty, North Island, New Zealand
Murwāra 135 E4 Madhya Pradesh, N India
Murwillumbah 149 E5 New South Wales, SE Australia
Murzuq, Edeyin *see* Murzuq, Idhān
Murzuq, Idhān 71 F4 *var.* Edeyin Murzuq. *desert* SW Libya

Mürzzuschlag 95 E7 Steiermark, E Austria
Muş 117 F3 *var.* Mush. Muş, E Turkey
Musa, Gebel 72 C2 *var.* Gebel Mûsa. *mountain* NE Egypt
Mûsa, Gebel *see* Musa, Jabal
Musala 104 B3 *mountain* W Bulgaria
Muscat *see* Masqaţ
Muscat and Oman *see* Oman
Muscatine 45 G3 Iowa, C USA
Musgrave Ranges 147 D5 *mountain range* South Australia
Musina 78 D3 *prev.* Messina. Limpopo, NE South Africa
Muskegon 40 C3 Michigan, N USA
Muskogean *see* Tallahassee
Muskogee 49 G1 Oklahoma, C USA
Musoma 73 C6 Mara, N Tanzania
Musta *see* Mosta
Mustafa-Pasha *see* Svilengrad
Musters, Lago 65 B6 *lake* S Argentina
Muswellbrook 149 D6 New South Wales, SE Australia
Mut 116 C4 İçel, S Turkey
Mu-tan-chiang *see* Mudanjiang
Mutare 78 D3 *var.* Mutari; *prev.* Umtali. Manicaland, E Zimbabwe
Mutari *see* Mutare
Mutina *see* Modena
Mutsu-wan 130 D3 *bay* N Japan
Muttonbird Islands 151 A8 *island group* SW New Zealand
Mu Us Shadi 127 E3 *var.* Ordos Desert; *prev.* Mu Us Shamo. *desert* N China
Mu Us Shamo *see* Mu Us Shadi
Muy Muy 52 D3 Matagalpa, C Nicaragua
Muynak *see* Mo'ynoq
Mužlja 100 D3 *Hung.* Felsőmuzslya; *prev.* Gornja Mužlja. Vojvodina, N Serbia
Mwali 79 F2 *var.* Moili, *Fr.* Mohéli. *island* S Comoros
Mwanza 73 B6 Mwanza, NW Tanzania
Mweka 77 C6 Kasai-Occidental, C Dem. Rep. Congo
Mwene-Ditu 77 D7 Kasai-Oriental, S Dem. Rep. Congo
Mweru, Lake 77 D7 *var.* Lac Moero. *lake* Dem. Rep. Congo/Zambia
Myadel' *see* Myadzyel
Myadzyel 107 C5 Pol. Miadzioł Nowy, *Rus.* Myadel'. Minskaya Voblasts', N Belarus
Myanaung 136 B4 Ayeyarwady, SW Myanmar (Burma)
Myanmar 136 A3 *off.* Union of Myanmar. *country* SE Asia. *See also* Burma

MYANMAR (BURMA)
Southeast Asia

Official name Union of Myanmar
Formation 1948 / 1948
Capital Nay Pyi Taw
Population 48.3 million / 190 people per sq mile (73 people per sq km)
Total area 261,969 sq. miles (678,500 sq. km)
Languages Burmese*, Shan, Karen, Rakhine, Chin, Yangbye, Kachin, Mon
Religions Buddhist 89%, Christian 4%, Muslim 4%, Other 2%, Animist 1%
Ethnic mix Burman (Bamah) 68%, Other 12%, Shan 9%, Karen 7%, Rakhine 4%
Government Presidential system
Currency Kyat = 100 pyas
Literacy rate 92%
Calorie consumption 2493 calories

Myaungmya 136 A4 Ayeyarwady, SW Myanmar (Burma)
Myaydo *see* Aunglan
Myeik 137 B6 *var.* Mergui. Tanintharyi, S Myanmar (Burma)
Myeik Archipelago 137 B6 *var.* Mergui Archipelago. *island group* S Myanmar (Burma)
Myerkulavichy 107 D7 *Rus.* Merkulovichi. Homyel'skaya Voblasts', SE Belarus
Myingyan 136 B3 Mandalay, C Myanmar (Burma)
Myitkyina 136 B2 Kachin State, N Myanmar (Burma)
Mykolayiv 109 E4 *Rus.* Nikolayev. Mykolayivs'ka Oblast', S Ukraine
Mykonos 105 D6 *var.* Míkonos. *island* Kykládes, Greece, Aegean Sea

Myrhorod 109 F2 *Rus.* Mirgorod. Poltavs'ka Oblast', NE Ukraine
Mýrina 104 D4 *var.* Mírina. Límnos, SE Greece
Myrtle Beach 43 F2 South Carolina, SE USA
Mýrtos 105 D8 Kríti, Greece, E Mediterranean Sea
Myrtoan Mare *see* Mirtóo Pélagos
Myślibórz 98 B3 Zachodnio-pomorskie, NW Poland
Mysore 132 C2 *var.* Maisur. Karnātaka, W India
Mysore *see* Karnātaka
My Tho 137 E6 *var.* Mi Tho. Tiên Giang, S Vietnam
Mytilene *see* Mytilíni
Mytilíni 105 D5 *var.* Mitilíni; *anc.* Mytilene. Lésvos, E Greece
Mzuzu 79 E2 Northern, N Malawi

N

Naberezhnyye Chelny 111 D5 *prev.* Brezhnev. Respublika Tatarstan, W Russian Federation
Nablus 119 A6 *var.* Nābulus, *Heb.* Shekhem; *anc.* Neapolis, *Bibl.* Shechem. N West Bank
Nābulus *see* Nablus
Nacala 79 F2 Nampula, NE Mozambique
Na-Ch'ii *see* Nagqu
Nada *see* Danzhou
Nadi 145 E4 *prev.* Nandi. Viti Levu, W Fiji
Nadur 102 A5 Gozo, N Malta
Nadvirna 108 C3 *Pol.* Nadwórna, *Rus.* Nadvornaya. Ivano-Frankivs'ka Oblast', W Ukraine
Nadvoitsy 110 B3 Respublika Kareliya, NW Russian Federation
Nadvornaya/Nadwórna *see* Nadvirna
Nadym 114 C3 Yamalo-Nenetskiy Avtonomnyy Okrug, N Russian Federation
Náfpaktos 105 B5 *var.* Návpaktos. Dytikí Elláda, C Greece
Náfplio 105 B6 *prev.* Návplion. Pelopónnisos, S Greece
Naga 139 E2 *off.* Naga City; *prev.* Nueva Caceres. Luzon, N Philippines
Naga City *see* Naga
Nagano 131 C5 Nagano, Honshū, S Japan
Nagaoka 131 D5 Niigata, Honshū, C Japan
Nagara Pathom *see* Nakhon Pathom
Nagara Sridharmaraj *see* Nakhon Si Thammarat
Nagara Svarga *see* Nakhon Sawan
Nagasaki 131 A7 Nagasaki, Kyūshū, SW Japan
Nagato 131 A7 Yamaguchi, Honshū, SW Japan
Nägercoil 132 C3 Tamil Nādu, SE India
Nagorno-Karabakh 117 G3 *var.* Nagorno- Karabakhskaya Avtonomnaya Oblast, *Arm.* Lerrnayin Gharabakh, *Az.* Dağlıq Quarabağ, *Rus.* Nagornyy Karabakh. *former autonomous region* SW Azerbaijan
Nagorno- Karabakhskaya Avtonomnaya Oblast *see* Nagorno-Karabakh
Nagornyy Karabakh *see* Nagorno-Karabakh
Nagoya 131 C6 Aichi, Honshū, SW Japan
Nāgpur 134 D4 Mahārāshtra, C India
Nagqu 126 C5 Chin. Na-Ch'ii; *prev.* Hei-ho. Xizang Zizhiqu, W China
Nagybánya *see* Baia Mare
Nagybecskerek *see* Zrenjanin
Nagydisznód *see* Cisnădie
Nagyenyed *see* Aiud
Nagykálló 99 E6 Szabolcs-Szatmár-Bereg, E Hungary
Nagykanizsa 99 C7 *Ger.* Grosskanizsa. Zala, SW Hungary
Nagykároly *see* Carei
Nagykikinda *see* Kikinda
Nagykőrös 99 D7 Pest, C Hungary
Nagymihály *see* Michalovce
Nagysurány *see* Šurany
Nagyszalonta *see* Salonta
Nagyszeben *see* Sibiu
Nagyszentmiklós *see* Sânnicolau Mare
Nagyszőllős *see* Vynohradiv
Nagyszombat *see* Trnava
Nagytapolcsány *see* Topoľčany

Nagyvárad see Oradea
Naha 130 A3 Okinawa, Okinawa, SW Japan
Nahariya 119 A5 prev. Nahariyya. Northern, N Israel
Nahariyya see Nahariya
Nahuel Huapí, Lago 63 B5 lake W Argentina
Nain 39 F2 Newfoundland and Labrador, NE Canada
Nāʾīn 120 D3 Eşfahān, C Iran
Nairobi 69 E5 country capital (Kenya) Nairobi Area, S Kenya
Nairobi 73 C6 Nairobi Area, S Kenya
Naissus see Niš
Najaf see An Najaf
Najima see Fukuoka
Najin 129 E3 NE North Korea
Najrān 121 B6 var. Abā as Suʿūd. Najrān, S Saudi Arabia
Nakambé see White Volta
Nakamura 131 B7 var. Shimanto. Kōchi, Shikoku, SW Japan
Nakatsugawa 131 C6 var. Nakatugawa. Gifu, Honshū, SW Japan
Nakatugawa see Nakatsugawa
Nakhichevan' see Naxçıvan
Nakhodka 115 G5 Primorskiy Kray, SE Russian Federation
Nakhon Pathom 137 C5 var. Nagara Pathom, Nakorn Pathom. Nakhon Pathom, W Thailand
Nakhon Ratchasima 137 C5 var. Khorat, Korat. Nakhon Ratchasima, E Thailand
Nakhon Sawan 137 C5 var. Muang Nakhon Sawan, Nagara Svarga. Nakhon Sawan, W Thailand
Nakhon Si Thammarat 137 C7 var. Nagara Sridharmaraj, Nakhon Sithamnaraj. Nakhon Si Thammarat, SW Thailand
Nakhon Sithamnaraj see Nakhon Si Thammarat
Nakorn Pathom see Nakhon Pathom
Nakuru 73 C6 Rift Valley, SW Kenya
Nalʾchik 111 B8 Kabardino-Balkarskaya Respublika, SW Russian Federation
Nālūt 71 F2 NW Libya
Namakan Lake 40 A1 lake Canada/USA
Namangan 123 F2 Namangan Viloyati, E Uzbekistan
Nambala 78 D2 Central, C Zambia
Nam Co 126 C5 lake W China
Nam Đinh 136 D3 Nam Ha, N Vietnam
Namib Desert 78 B3 desert W Namibia
Namibe 78 A2 Port. Moçâmedes, Mossâmedes. Namibe, SW Angola
Namibia 78 B3 off. Republic of Namibia, var. South West Africa, Afr. Suidwes-Afrika, Ger. Deutsch-Südwestafrika; prev. German Southwest Africa, South-West Africa. country S Africa

NAMIBIA
Southern Africa

Official name	Republic of Namibia
Formation	1990 / 1994
Capital	Windhoek
Population	2.3 million / 7 people per sq mile (3 people per sq km)
Total area	318,694 sq. miles (825,418 sq. km)
Languages	Ovambo, Kavango, English*, Bergdama, German, Afrikaans
Religions	Christian 90%, Traditional beliefs 10%
Ethnic mix	Ovambo 50%, Other tribes 22%, Kavango 9%, Damara 7%, Herero 7%, Other 5%
Government	Presidential system
Currency	Namibian dollar & South African rand = 100 cents
Literacy rate	88%
Calorie consumption	2151 kilocalories

Namibia, Republic of see Namibia
Nam Khong see Mekong
Namnetes see Nantes
Namo see Namu Atoll
Nam Ou 136 C3 river N Laos
Nampa 46 D3 Idaho, NW USA
Nampula 79 E2 Nampula, NE Mozambique
Namsos 84 B4 Nord-Trøndelag, C Norway
Nam Tha 136 C4 river N Laos

Namu Atoll 144 D2 var. Namo. atoll Ralik Chain, C Marshall Islands
Namur 87 C6 Dut. Namen. Namur, SE Belgium
Namyit Island 128 C8 island S Spratly Islands
Nan 136 C4 var. Muang Nan. Nan, NW Thailand
Nanaimo 36 D5 Vancouver Island, British Columbia, SW Canada
Nanchang 128 C5 var. Nan-ch'ang, Nanch'ang-hsien. province capital Jiangxi, S China
Nan-ch'ang see Nanchang
Nanch'ang-hsien see Nanchang
Nan-ching see Nanjing
Nancy 90 D3 Meurthe-et-Moselle, NE France
Nandaime 52 D3 Granada, SW Nicaragua
Nanded 134 D5 Mahārāshtra, C India
Nandi see Nadi
Nándorhegy see Oţelu Roşu
Nandyāl 132 C1 Andhra Pradesh, E India
Nan Hai see South China Sea
Naniwa see Ōsaka
Nanjing 128 D5 var. Nan-ching, Nanking; prev. Chianning, Chian-ning, Kiang-ning, Jiangsu. province capital Jiangsu, E China
Nanking see Nanjing
Nanning 128 B6 var. Nan-ning; prev. Yung-ning. Guangxi Zhuangzu Zizhiqu, S China
Nan-ning see Nanning
Nanortalik 82 C5 Kitaa, S Greenland
Nanpan Jiang 136 D2 river S China
Nanping 128 D6 var. Nan-p'ing; prev. Yenping. Fujian, SE China
Nan-p'ing see Nanping
Nansei Syotō Trench see Ryukyu Trench
Nansen Basin 155 C4 undersea basin Arctic Ocean
Nansen Cordillera 155 B3 var. Arctic Mid Oceanic Ridge, Nansen Ridge. seamount range Arctic Ocean
Nansen Ridge see Nansen Cordillera
Nansha Qundao see Spratly Islands
Nanterre 90 D1 Hauts-de-Seine, N France
Nantes 90 B4 Bret. Naoned; anc. Condivincum, Namnetes. Loire-Atlantique, NW France
Nantucket Island 41 G3 island Massachusetts, NE USA
Nanumaga 145 E3 var. Nanumanga. atoll NW Tuvalu
Nanumanga see Nanumaga
Nanumea Atoll 145 E3 atoll NW Tuvalu
Nanyang 128 C5 var. Nan-yang. Henan, C China
Nan-yang see Nanyang
Naoned see Nantes
Napa 47 B6 California, W USA
Napier 150 E4 Hawke's Bay, North Island, New Zealand
Naples 43 E5 Florida, SE USA
Naples see Napoli
Napo 56 A3 province NE Ecuador
Napoléon-Vendée see la Roche-sur-Yon
Napoli 97 C5 Eng. Naples, Ger. Neapel; anc. Neapolis. Campania, S Italy
Napo, Río 60 C1 river Ecuador/Peru
Naracoorte 149 B7 South Australia
Naradhivas see Narathiwat
Narathiwat 137 C7 var. Naradhivas. Narathiwat, SW Thailand
Narbada see Narmada
Narbo Martius see Narbonne
Narbonne 91 C6 anc. Narbo Martius. Aude, S France
Narborough Island see Fernandina, Isla
Nares Abyssal Plain see Nares Plain
Nares Plain 35 E6 var. Nares Abyssal Plain. abyssal plain NW Atlantic Ocean
Nares Strait see Nares Strait
Nares Strait 82 D1 Dan. Nares Stræde. strait Canada/Greenland
Narew 98 E3 river E Poland
Narmada 124 B3 var. Narbada. river C India
Narova see Narva
Narovlya 107 C8 Rus. Narovlya. Homyel'skaya Voblasts', SE Belarus
Närpes 85 D5 Fin. Närpiö. Länsi-Suomi, W Finland
Närpiö see Närpes

Narrabri 149 D6 New South Wales, SE Australia
Narrogin 147 B6 Western Australia
Narva 106 E2 Ida-Virumaa, NE Estonia
Narva 106 E2 prev. Narova. river Estonia/Russian Federation
Narva Bay 106 E2 Est. Narva Laht, Ger. Narwa-Bucht, Rus. Narvskiy Zaliv. bay Estonia/Russian Federation
Narva Laht see Narva Bay
Narva Reservoir 106 E2 Est. Narva Veehoidla, Rus. Narvskoye Vodokhranilishche. reservoir Estonia/Russian Federation
Narva Veehoidla see Narva Reservoir
Narvik 84 C3 Nordland, C Norway
Narvskiy Zaliv see Narva Bay
Narvskoye Vodokhranilishche see Narva Reservoir
Narwa-Bucht see Narva Bay
Nar'yan-Mar 110 D3 prev. Beloshchel'ye, Dzerzhinsky. Nenetskiy Avtonomnyy Okrug, NW Russian Federation
Naryn 123 G2 Narynskaya Oblast', C Kyrgyzstan
Nassau 54 C1 country capital (Bahamas) New Providence, N Bahamas
Nāsaud 108 B3 Ger. Nussdorf, Hung. Naszód. Bistriţa-Năsăud, N Romania
Nase see Naze
Nāshik 134 C5 prev. Nāsik. Mahārāshtra, W India
Nashua 41 G3 New Hampshire, NE USA
Nashville 42 C1 state capital Tennessee, S USA
Näsijärvi 85 D5 lake SW Finland
Nāsik see Nāshik
Nasir, Buhayrat/Nâşir,Buḥeiret see Nasser, Lake
Nāsiri see Ahvāz
Nasiriya see An Nāşirīyah
Nasser, Lake 72 B3 var. Buhayrat Nasir, Buḥayrat Nāşir, Buḥeiret Nâşir. lake Egypt/Sudan
Naszód see Nāsăud
Nata 78 C3 Central, NE Botswana
Natal 63 G2 state capital Rio Grande do Norte, E Brazil
Natal Basin 141 A6 var. Mozambique Basin. undersea basin W Indian Ocean
Natanya see Netanya
Natchez 42 B3 Mississippi, S USA
Natchitoches 42 A2 Louisiana, S USA
Nathanya see Netanya
Natitingou 75 F4 NW Benin
Natsrat see Natzrat
Natuna Islands see Natuna, Kepulauan
Natuna, Kepulauan 124 D4 var. Natuna Islands. island group W Indonesia
Naturaliste Plateau 141 E6 undersea plateau E Indian Ocean
Natzrat 119 A5 var. Natsrat, Ar. En Nazira, Eng. Nazareth; prev. Nazerat. Northern, N Israel
Naugard see Nowogard
Naujamiestis 106 C4 Panevėžys, C Lithuania
Nauru 144 D2 off. Republic of Nauru; prev. Pleasant Island. country W Pacific Ocean

NAURU
Australasia & Oceania

Official name	Republic of Nauru
Formation	1968 / 1968
Capital	Yaren District
Population	9378 / 1158 people per sq mile (447 people per sq km)
Total area	8.1 sq. miles (21 sq. km)
Languages	Nauruan*, Kiribati, Chinese, Tuvaluan, English
Religions	Nauruan Congregational Church 60%, Roman Catholic 35%, Other 5%
Ethnic mix	Nauruan 93%, Chinese 5%, European 1%, Other Pacific islanders 1%
Government	Nonparty system
Currency	Australian dollar = 100 cents
Literacy rate	95%
Calorie consumption	Not available

Nauru, Republic of see Nauru
Nauta 60 C2 Loreto, N Peru
Navahrudak 107 B6 Pol. Nowogródek, Rus. Novogrudok. Hrodzyenskaya Voblasts', W Belarus
Navanagar see Jāmnagar

Navapolatsk 107 D5 Rus. Novopolotsk. Vitsyebskaya Voblasts', N Belarus
Navarra 93 E2 Eng./Fr. Navarre. autonomous community N Spain
Navarre see Navarra
Navassa Island 54 C3 US unincorporated territory C West Indies
Navoi see Navoiy
Navoiy 123 E2 Rus. Navoi. Navoiy Viloyati, C Uzbekistan
Navojoa 50 C2 Sonora, NW Mexico
Navolat see Navolato
Navolato 50 C3 var. Navolat. Sinaloa, C Mexico
Návpaktos see Náfpaktos
Návplion see Náfplio
Nawabashah see Nawābshāh
Nawābshāh 134 B3 var. Nawabashah. Sind, S Pakistan
Naxçıvan 117 G3 Rus. Nakhichevan'. SW Azerbaijan
Náxos 105 D6 var. Naxos. Náxos, Kykládes, Greece, Aegean Sea
Náxos 105 D6 island Kykládes, Greece, Aegean Sea
Nayoro 130 D2 Hokkaidō, NE Japan
Nay Pyi Taw 136 B4 country capital (Myanmar (Burma)) Mandalay, C Myanmar (Burma)
Nazareth see Natzrat
Nazca 60 D4 Ica, S Peru
Nazca Ridge 57 A5 undersea ridge E Pacific Ocean
Naze 130 B3 var. Nase. Kagoshima, Amami-ōshima, SW Japan
Nazerat see Natzrat
Nazilli 116 A4 Aydın, SW Turkey
Nazrēt 73 C5 var. Adama, Hadama. Oromīya, C Ethiopia
N'Dalatando 78 B1 Port. Salazar, Vila Salazar. Cuanza Norte, NW Angola
Ndélé 76 C4 Bamingui-Bangoran, N Central African Republic
Ndende 77 B6 Ngounié, S Gabon
Ndindi 77 A6 Nyanga, S Gabon
Ndjamena 76 B3 var. N'Djamena; prev. Fort-Lamy. country capital (Chad) Chari-Baguirmi, W Chad
N'Djamena see Ndjamena
Ndjolé 77 A5 Moyen-Ogooué, W Gabon
Ndola 78 D2 Copperbelt, C Zambia
Ndzouani see Nzwani
Neagh, Lough 89 B5 lake E Northern Ireland, United Kingdom
Néa Moudánia 104 C4 var. Néa Moudhaniá. Kentrikí Makedonía, N Greece
Néa Moudhaniá see Néa Moudánia
Neapel see Napoli
Neápoli 104 B4 prev. Neápolis. Dytikí Makedonía, N Greece
Neápoli 105 D8 Kríti, Greece, E Mediterranean Sea
Neápoli 105 C7 Pelopónnisos, S Greece
Neápolis see Neápoli, Greece
Neapolis see Napoli, Italy
Neapolis see Nablus, West Bank
Near Islands 36 A2 island group Aleutian Islands, Alaska, USA
Néa Zíchni 104 C3 var. Néa Zíkhni; prev. Néa Zíkhna. Kentrikí Makedonía, NE Greece
Néa Zíkhna/Néa Zíkhni see Néa Zíchni
Nebaj 52 B2 Quiché, W Guatemala
Nebitdag see Balkanabat
Neblina, Pico da 62 C1 mountain NW Brazil
Nebraska 44 D4 off. State of Nebraska, also known as Blackwater State, Cornhusker State, Tree Planters State. state C USA
Nebraska City 45 F4 Nebraska, C USA
Neches River 49 H3 river Texas, SW USA
Neckar 95 B6 river SW Germany
Necochea 65 D5 Buenos Aires, E Argentina
Nederland 86 Netherlands
Neder Rijn 86 D4 Eng. Lower Rhine. river C Netherlands
Nederweert 87 D5 Limburg, SE Netherlands
Neede 86 E3 Gelderland, E Netherlands
Neerpelt 87 D5 Limburg, NE Belgium
Neftekamsk 111 D5 Respublika Bashkortostan, W Russian Federation
Neftezavodsk see Seýdi
Negara Brunei Darussalam see Brunei
Negēlē 73 D5 var. Negelli, It. Neghelli. Oromīya, C Ethiopia

Negelli see Negēlē
Negev 119 A7 Eng. Negev. desert S Israel
Negev see HaNegev
Neghelli see Negēlē
Negomane 79 E2 var. Negomano. Cabo Delgado, N Mozambique
Negomano see Negomane
Negombo 132 C3 Western Province, SW Sri Lanka
Negotin 100 E4 Serbia, E Serbia
Negra, Punto 60 A3 headland NW Peru
Negreşti see Negreşti-Oaş
Negreşti-Oaş 108 B3 Hung. Avasfelsőfalu; prev. Negreşti. Satu Mare, NE Romania
Negro, Río 65 C5 river E Argentina
Negro, Río 62 D1 river N South America
Negro, Río 64 D4 river Brazil/Uruguay
Negros 139 E2 island C Philippines
Nehbandān 120 E3 Khorāsān, E Iran
Neijiang 128 B5 Sichuan, C China
Neiva 58 B3 Huila, S Colombia
Nellore 132 D2 Andhra Pradesh, E India
Nelson 151 C5 Nelson, South Island, New Zealand
Nelson 37 G4 river Manitoba, C Canada
Néma 74 D3 Hodh ech Chargui, SE Mauritania
Neman 106 B4 Ger. Ragnit. Kaliningradskaya Oblast', W Russian Federation
Neman 106 A4 Bel. Nyoman, Ger. Memel, Lith. Nemunas, Pol. Niemen. river NE Europe
Nemausus see Nîmes
Neméa 105 B6 Pelopónnisos, S Greece
Nemetocenna see Arras
Nemours 90 C3 Seine-et-Marne, N France
Nemunas see Neman
Nemuro 130 E2 Hokkaidō, NE Japan
Neochóri 105 B5 Dytikí Elláda, C Greece
Nepal 135 E3 off. Nepal. country S Asia

NEPAL
South Asia

Official name Nepal
Formation 1769 / 1769
Capital Kathmandu
Population 30.5 million / 577 people per sq mile (223 people per sq km)
Total area 54,363 sq. miles (140,800 sq. km)
Languages Nepali*, Maithili, Bhojpuri
Religions Hindu 81%, Buddhist 11%, Muslim 4%, Other (including Christian) 4%
Ethnic mix Other 52%, Chhetri 16%, Hill Brahman 13%, Tharu 7%, Magar 7%, Tamang 5%
Government Transitional regime
Currency Nepalese rupee = 100 paisa
Literacy rate 59%
Calorie consumption 2443 kilocalories

Nepal see Nepal
Nereta 106 C4 S Latvia
Neretva 100 C4 river Bosnia and Herzegovina/Croatia
Neris 107 C5 Bel. Viliya, Pol. Wilia; prev. Pol. Wilja. river Belarus/Lithuania
Neris see Viliya
Nerva 92 C4 Andalucía, S Spain
Neryungri 115 F4 Respublika Sakha (Yakutiya), NE Russian Federation
Neskaupstadhur 83 E5 Austurland, E Iceland
Ness, Loch 88 C3 lake N Scotland, United Kingdom
Nesterov see Zhovkva
Néstos 104 C3 Bul. Mesta, Turk. Kara Su. river Bulgaria/Greece
Nesvizh see Nyasvizh
Netanya 119 A6 var. Natanya, Nathanya. Central, C Israel
Netherlands 86 C3 off. Kingdom of the Netherlands, var. Holland, Dut. Koninkrijk der Nederlanden, Nederland. country NW Europe

NETHERLANDS
Northwest Europe

Official name Kingdom of the Netherlands
Formation 1648 / 1839
Capital Amsterdam; The Hague (administrative)
Population 16.7 million / 1275 people

NETHERLANDS
(continued)

per sq mile (492 people per sq km)
Total area 16,033 sq. miles (41,526 sq. km)
Languages Dutch*, Frisian
Religions Roman Catholic 36%, Other 34%, Protestant 27%, Muslim 3%
Ethnic mix Dutch 82%, Other 12%, Surinamese 2%, Turkish 2%, Moroccan 2%
Government Parliamentary system
Currency Euro = 100 cents
Literacy rate 99%
Calorie consumption 3261 kilocalories

Netherlands East Indies see Indonesia
Netherlands Guiana see Suriname
Netherlands, Kingdom of the see Netherlands
Netherlands New Guinea see Papua
Nettilling Lake 37 G3 lake Baffin Island, Nunavut, N Canada
Netze see Noteć
Neu Amerika see Puławy
Neubrandenburg 94 D3 Mecklenburg-Vorpommern, NE Germany
Neuchâtel 95 A7 Ger. Neuenburg. Neuchâtel, W Switzerland
Neuchâtel, Lac de 95 A7 Ger. Neuenburger See. lake W Switzerland
Neuenburg see Neuchâtel
Neuenburger See see Neuchâtel, Lac de
Neufchâteau 87 D8 Luxembourg, SE Belgium
Neugradisk see Nova Gradiška
Neuhof see Zgierz
Neukuhren see Pionerskiy
Neumarkt see Târgu Secuiesc, Covasna, Romania
Neumarkt see Târgu Mureş
Neumoldowa see Moldova Nouă
Neumünster 94 B2 Schleswig-Holstein, N Germany
Neunkirchen 95 A5 Saarland, SW Germany
Neuquén 65 B5 Neuquén, SE Argentina
Neuruppin 94 C3 Brandenburg, NE Germany
Neusalz an der Oder see Nowa Sól
Neu Sandec see Nowy Sącz
Neusatz see Novi Sad
Neusiedler See 95 E6 Hung. Fertő. lake Austria/Hungary
Neusohl see Banská Bystrica
Neustadt see Baia Mare, Maramureş, Romania
Neustadt see Neustadt an der Weinstrasse
Neustadt an der Haardt see Neustadt an der Weinstrasse
Neustadt an der Weinstrasse 95 B5 prev. Neustadt an der Haardt, hist. Niewenstat; anc. Nova Civitas. Rheinland-Pfalz, SW Germany
Neustadtl see Novo mesto
Neustettin see Szczecinek
Neustrelitz 94 D3 Mecklenburg-Vorpommern, NE Germany
Neutra see Nitra
Neu-Ulm 95 B6 Bayern, S Germany
Neuwied 95 A5 Rheinland-Pfalz, W Germany
Neuzen see Terneuzen
Nevada 47 C5 off. State of Nevada, also known as Battle Born State, Sagebrush State, Silver State. state W USA
NevadaSierra 92 D5 mountain range S Spain
Nevada, Sierra 47 C6 mountain range W USA
Nevers 90 C4 anc. Noviodunum. Nièvre, C France
Neves 76 E2 São Tomé, S Sao Tome and Principe, Africa
Nevinnomyssk 111 B7 Stavropol'skiy Kray, SW Russian Federation
Nevşehir 116 C3 var. Nevsehir. Nevşehir, C Turkey
Newala 73 C8 Mtwara, SE Tanzania
New Albany 40 C5 Indiana, N USA
New Amsterdam 59 G3 E Guyana
Newark 41 F4 New Jersey, NE USA
New Bedford 41 G3 Massachusetts, NE USA
Newberg 46 B3 Oregon, NW USA
New Bern 43 F1 North Carolina, SE USA
New Braunfels 49 G4 Texas, SW USA
Newbridge 89 B6 Ir. An Droichead Nua. Kildare, C Ireland
New Britain 144 B3 island E Papua New Guinea

New Brunswick 39 E4 Fr. Nouveau-Brunswick. province SE Canada
New Caledonia 144 D4 var. Kanaky, Fr. Nouvelle-Calédonie. French overseas territory SW Pacific Ocean
New Caledonia 144 C5 island SW Pacific Ocean
New Caledonia Basin 142 C4 undersea basin W Pacific Ocean
Newcastle 149 D6 New South Wales, SE Australia
Newcastle see Newcastle upon Tyne
Newcastle upon Tyne 88 D4 var. Newcastle, hist. Monkchester, Lat. Pons Aelii. NE England, United Kingdom
New Delhi 134 D3 country capital (India) Delhi, N India
New England of the West see Minnesota
Newfoundland 39 G3 Fr. Terre-Neuve. island Newfoundland and Labrador, SE Canada
Newfoundland and Labrador 39 F2 Fr. Terre Neuve. province E Canada
Newfoundland Basin 66 B3 undersea feature NW Atlantic Ocean
New Georgia Islands 144 C3 island group NW Solomon Islands
New Glasgow 39 F4 Nova Scotia, SE Canada
New Goa see Panaji
New Guinea 144 A3 Dut. Nieuw Guinea, Ind. Irian. island Indonesia/Papua New Guinea
New Hampshire 41 F2 off. State of New Hampshire, also known as Granite State. state NE USA
New Haven 41 G3 Connecticut, NE USA
New Hebrides see Vanuatu
New Iberia 42 B3 Louisiana, S USA
New Ireland 144 C3 island NE Papua New Guinea
New Jersey 41 F4 off. State of New Jersey, also known as The Garden State. state NE USA
Newman 146 B4 Western Australia
Newmarket 89 E6 E England, United Kingdom
New Mexico 48 C2 off. State of New Mexico, also known as Land of Enchantment, Sunshine State. state SW USA
New Orleans 42 B3 Louisiana, S USA
New Plymouth 150 C4 Taranaki, North Island, New Zealand
Newport 89 D7 S England, United Kingdom
Newport 41 C7 SE Wales, United Kingdom
Newport 40 C4 Kentucky, S USA
Newport 41 G2 Vermont, NE USA
Newport News 41 F5 Virginia, NE USA
New Providence 54 C1 island N Bahamas
Newquay 89 C7 SW England, United Kingdom
Newry 89 B5 Ir. An tIúr. SE Northern Ireland, United Kingdom
New Sarum see Salisbury
New Siberian Islands 115 F1 Eng. New Siberian Islands. island group N Russian Federation
New Siberian Islands see Novosibirskiye Ostrova
New South Wales 149 C6 state SE Australia
Newton 45 G3 Iowa, C USA
Newton 45 F5 Kansas, C USA
Newtownabbey 89 B5 Ir. Baile na Mainistreach. E Northern Ireland, United Kingdom
New Ulm 45 F2 Minnesota, N USA
New York 41 F4 New York, NE USA
New York 41 F3 state NE USA
New Zealand 150 A4 country SW Pacific Ocean

NEW ZEALAND
Australasia & Oceania

Official name New Zealand
Formation 1947 / 1947
Capital Wellington
Population 4.4 million / 42 people per sq mile (16 people per sq km)
Total area 103,737 sq. miles (268,680 sq. km)
Languages English*, Maori*
Religions Anglican 24%, Other 22%, Presbyterian 18%, Nonreligious 16%,

NEW ZEALAND
(continued)

Roman Catholic 15%, Methodist 5%
Ethnic mix European 75%, Maori 15%, Other 7%, Samoan 3%
Government Parliamentary system
Currency New Zealand dollar = 100 cents
Literacy rate 99%
Calorie consumption 3172 kilocalories

Neyveli 132 C2 Tamil Nādu, SE India
Nezhin see Nizhyn
Ngangze Co 126 B5 lake W China
Ngaoundéré 76 B4 var. N'Gaoundéré. Adamaoua, N Cameroon
N'Gaoundéré see Ngaoundéré
Ngazidja 79 F2 Fr. Grande Comore, var. Njazidja. island NW Comoros
N'Giva 78 B3 var. Ondjiva, Port. Vila Pereira de Eça. Cunene, S Angola
Ngo 77 B6 Plateaux, SE Congo
Ngoko 77 B5 river Cameroon/Congo
Ngourti 75 H3 Diffa, E Niger
Nguigmi 75 H3 var. N'Guigmi. Diffa, SE Niger
N'Guigmi see Nguigmi
N'Gunza see Sumbe
Nguru 75 G3 Yobe, NE Nigeria
Nha Trang 137 E6 Khanh Hoa, S Vietnam
Niagara Falls 38 D5 Ontario, S Canada
Niagara Falls 41 E3 New York, NE USA
Niagara Falls 40 D3 waterfall Canada/USA
Niamey 75 F3 country capital (Niger) Niamey, SW Niger
Niangay, Lac 75 E3 lake E Mali
Nia-Nia 77 E5 Orientale, NE Dem. Rep. Congo
Nias, Pulau 138 A3 island W Indonesia
Nicaea see Nice
Nicaragua 52 D3 off. Republic of Nicaragua. country Central America

NICARAGUA
Central America

Official name Republic of Nicaragua
Formation 1838 / 1838
Capital Managua
Population 5.9 million / 129 people per sq mile (50 people per sq km)
Total area 49,998 sq. miles (129,494 sq. km)
Languages Spanish*, English Creole, Miskito
Religions Roman Catholic 80%, Protestant Evangelical 17%, Other 3%
Ethnic mix Mestizo 69%, White 17%, Black 9%, Amerindian 5%
Government Presidential system
Currency Córdoba oro = 100 centavos
Literacy rate 80%
Calorie consumption 2517 kilocalories

Lake Nicaragua 52 D4 var. Cocibolca, Gran Lago, Eng. Lake Nicaragua. lake S Nicaragua
Nicaragua, Lake see Nicaragua, Lago de
Nicaragua, Republic of see Nicaragua
Nicaria see Ikaría
Nice 91 D6 It. Nizza; anc. Nicaea. Alpes-Maritimes, SE France
Nicephorium see Ar Raqqah
Nicholas II Land see Severnaya Zemlya
Nicholls Town 54 C1 Andros Island, NW Bahamas
Nicobar Islands 124 B4 island group India, E Indian Ocean
Nicosia 102 C5 Gk. Lefkosía, Turk. Lefkoşa. country capital (Cyprus) C Cyprus
Nicoya 52 D4 Guanacaste, W Costa Rica
Nicoya, Golfo de 52 D5 gulf W Costa Rica
Nicoya, Península de 52 D4 peninsula NW Costa Rica
Nida 106 A3 Ger. Nidden. Klaipėda, SW Lithuania
Nidaros see Trondheim
Nidden see Nida
Nidzica 98 D3 Ger. Niedenburg. Warmińsko-Mazurskie, NE Poland
Niedenburg see Nidzica
Niedere Tauern 99 A6 mountain range C Austria
Niemen see Neman
Nieśwież see Nyasvizh

Nieuw Amsterdam 59 G3 Commewijne, NE Suriname
Nieuw-Bergen 86 D4 Limburg, SE Netherlands
Nieuwegein 86 C4 Utrecht, C Netherlands
Nieuw Guinea see New Guinea
Nieuw Nickerie 59 G3 Nickerie, NW Suriname
Niewenstat see Neustadt an der Weinstrasse
Niğde 116 C4 Niğde, C Turkey
Niger 75 F3 off. Republic of Niger. country W Africa

NIGER
West Africa

Official name Republic of Niger
Formation 1960 / 1960
Capital Niamey
Population 16.1 million / 33 people per sq mile (13 people per sq km)
Total area 489,188 sq. miles (1,267,000 sq. km)
Languages Hausa, Djerma, Fulani, Tuareg, Teda, French*
Religions Muslim 99%, Other (including Christian) 1%
Ethnic mix Hausa 53%, Djerma and Songhai 21%, Tuareg 11%, Fulani 7%, Kanuri 6%, Other 2%
Government Presidential system
Currency CFA franc = 100 centimes
Literacy rate 30%
Calorie consumption 2489 kilocalories

Niger 75 F4 river W Africa
Nigeria 75 F4 off. Federal Republic of Nigeria. country W Africa

NIGERIA
West Africa

Official name Federal Republic of Nigeria
Formation 1960 / 1961
Capital Abuja
Population 162 million / 462 people per sq mile (178 people per sq km)
Total area 356,667 sq. miles (923,768 sq. km)
Languages Hausa, English*, Yoruba, Ibo
Religions Muslim 50%, Christian 40%, Traditional beliefs 10%
Ethnic mix Other 29%, Hausa 21%, Yoruba 21%, Ibo 18%, Fulani 11%
Government Presidential system
Currency Naira = 100 kobo
Literacy rate 61%
Calorie consumption 2711 kilocalories

Nigeria, Federal Republic of see Nigeria
Niger, Mouths of the 75 F5 delta S Nigeria
Niger, Republic of see Niger
Nihon see Japan
Niigata 131 D5 Niigata, Honshū, C Japan
Niihama 131 B7 Ehime, Shikoku, SW Japan
Ni'ihau 47 A7 var. Niihau. island Hawai'i, USA, C Pacific Ocean
Nii-jima 131 D6 island E Japan
Nijkerk 86 D3 Gelderland, C Netherlands
Nijlen 87 C5 Antwerpen, N Belgium
Nijmegen 86 D4 Ger. Nimwegen; anc. Noviomagus. Gelderland, SE Netherlands
Nikaria see Ikaría
Nikel' 110 C2 Finn. Kolosjoki. Murmanskaya Oblast', NW Russian Federation
Nikiniki 139 E5 Timor, S Indonesia
Niklasmarkt see Gheorgheni
Nikolainkaupunki see Vaasa
Nikolayev see Mykolayiv
Nikol'sk see Ussuriysk
Nikol'sk-Ussuriyskiy see Ussuriysk
Nikopol' 109 F3 Dnipropetrovs'ka Oblast', SE Ukraine
Nikšić 101 C5 C Montenegro
Nikumaroro 145 E3 ; prev. Gardner Island. atoll Phoenix Islands, C Kiribati
Nikunau 145 E3 var. Nukunau; prev. Byron Island. atoll Tungaru, W Kiribati
Nile 72 B2 former province NW Uganda
Nile 68 D3 Ar. Nahr an Nil. river N Africa

Nile Delta 72 B1 delta N Egypt
Nîl, Nahr an see Nile
Nîmes 91 C6 anc. Nemausus, Nismes. Gard, S France
Nimwegen see Nijmegen
Nine Degree Channel 132 B3 channel India/Maldives
Ninetyeast Ridge 141 D5 undersea feature E Indian Ocean
Ninety Mile Beach 150 C1 beach North Island, New Zealand
Ningbo 128 D5 var. Ning-po, Yin-hsien; prev. Ninghsien. Zhejiang, SE China
Ning-hsia see Ningxia
Ninghsien see Ningbo
Ning-po see Ningbo
Ningsia/Ningsia Hui/Ningsia Hui Autonomous Region see Ningxia
Ningxia 128 B4 off. Ningxia Huizu Zizhiqu, var. Ning-hsia, Ningsia, Eng. Ningsia Hui, Ningsia Hui Autonomous Region. autonomous region N China
Ningxia Huizu Zizhiqu see Ningxia
Nio see Íos
Niobrara River 45 E3 river Nebraska/Wyoming, C USA
Nioro 74 D3 var. Nioro du Sahel. Kayes, W Mali
Nioro du Sahel see Nioro
Niort 90 B4 Deux-Sèvres, W France
Nipigon 38 B4 Ontario, S Canada
Nipigon, Lake 38 B3 lake Ontario, S Canada
Nippon see Japan
Niš 101 E5 Eng. Nish, Ger. Nisch; anc. Naissus. Serbia, SE Serbia
Niṣab 120 B4 Al Ḥudūd ash Shamālīyah, N Saudi Arabia
Nisch/Nish see Niš
Nisibin see Nusaybin
Nísiros see Nísyros
Nisko 98 E4 Podkrapackie, SE Poland
Nismes see Nîmes
Nistru see Dniester
Nísyros 105 E7 var. Nisiros. island Dodekánisa, Greece, Aegean Sea
Nitra 99 C6 Ger. Neutra, Hung. Nyitra. Nitriansky Kraj, SW Slovakia
Nitra 99 C6 Ger. Neutra, Hung. Nyitra. river W Slovakia
Niuatobutabu see Niuatoputapu
Niuatoputapu 145 E4 var. Niuatobutabu; prev. Keppel Island. island N Tonga
Niue 145 F4 self-governing territory in free association with New Zealand S Pacific Ocean
Niulakita 145 E3 var. Nurakita. atoll S Tuvalu
Niutao 145 E3 atoll NW Tuvalu
Nivernais 90 C4 cultural region C France
Nizāmābād 134 D5 Andhra Pradesh, C India
Nizhnegorskiy see Nyzhn'ohirs'kyy
Nizhnekamsk 111 C5 Respublika Tatarstan, W Russian Federation
Nizhnevartovsk 114 D3 Khanty-Mansiyskiy Avtonomnyy Okrug-Yugra, C Russian Federation
Nizhniy Novgorod 111 C5 prev. Gor'kiy. Nizhegorodskaya Oblast', W Russian Federation
Nizhniy Odes 110 D4 Respublika Komi, NW Russian Federation
Nizhyn 109 E1 Rus. Nezhin. Chernihivs'ka Oblast', NE Ukraine
Nizza see Nice
Njazidja see Ngazidja
Njombe 73 C8 Iringa, S Tanzania
Nkayi 77 B6 prev. Jacob. Bouenza, S Congo
Nkongsamba 76 A4 var. N'Kongsamba. Littoral, W Cameroon
N'Kongsamba see Nkongsamba
Nmai Hka 136 B2 var. Me Hka. river N Myanmar (Burma)
Nobeoka 131 B7 Miyazaki, Kyūshū, SW Japan
Noboribetsu 130 D3 var. Noboribetu. Hokkaidō, NE Japan
Noboribetu see Noboribetsu
Nogales 50 B1 Sonora, NW Mexico
Nogales 48 B3 Arizona, SW USA
Nogal Valley see Dooxo Nugaaleed
Noire, Rivi`ere see Black River
Nokia 85 D5 Länsi-Suomi, W Finland
Nokou 76 B3 Kanem, W Chad

Nola 77 B5 Sangha-Mbaéré, SW Central African Republic
Nolinsk 111 C5 Kirovskaya Oblast', NW Russian Federation
Nongkaya see Nong Khai
Nong Khai 136 C4 var. Mi Chai, Nongkaya. Nong Khai, E Thailand
Nonouti 144 D2 prev. Sydenham Island. atoll Tungaru, W Kiribati
Noord-Beveland 86 B4 var. North Beveland. island SW Netherlands
Noordwijk aan Zee 86 C3 Zuid-Holland, W Netherlands
Noordzee see North Sea
Nora 85 C6 Örebro, C Sweden
Norak 123 E3 Rus. Nurek. W Tajikistan
Nord 83 F1 Avannaarsua, N Greenland
Nordaustlandet 83 G1 island NE Svalbard
Norden 94 A3 Niedersachsen, NW Germany
Norderstedt 94 B3 Schleswig-Holstein, N Germany
Nordfriesische Inseln see North Frisian Islands
Nordhausen 94 C4 Thüringen, C Germany
Nordhorn 94 A3 Niedersachsen, NW Germany
Nord, Mer du see North Sea
Nord-Ouest, Territoires du see Northwest Territories
Nordsee/Nordsjøen/Nordsøen see North Sea
Norfolk 45 E3 Nebraska, C USA
Norfolk 41 F5 Virginia, NE USA
Norfolk Island 142 D4 Australian external territory SW Pacific Ocean
Norfolk Ridge 142 D4 undersea feature W Pacific Ocean
Norge see Norway
Norias 49 G5 Texas, SW USA
Noril'sk 114 D3 Krasnoyarskiy Kray, N Russian Federation
Norman 49 G1 Oklahoma, C USA
Normandes, Îles see Channel Islands
Normandie 90 B3 Eng. Normandy. cultural region N France
Normandy see Normandie
Normanton 148 C3 Queensland, NE Australia
Norrköping 85 C6 Östergötland, S Sweden
Norrtälje 85 C6 Stockholm, C Sweden
Norseman 147 B6 Western Australia
Norske Havet see Norwegian Sea
North Albanian Alps 101 C5 Alb. Bjeshkët e Namuna, SCr. Prokletije. mountain range SE Europe
Northallerton 89 D5 N England, United Kingdom
Northam 147 A6 Western Australia
North America 34 continent
Northampton 89 D6 C England, United Kingdom
North Andaman 133 D1 island Andaman Islands, India, NE Indian Ocean
North Australian Basin 141 E5 Fr. Bassin Nord de l' Australie. undersea feature E Indian Ocean
North Bay 38 D4 Ontario, S Canada
North Beveland see Noord-Beveland
North Borneo see Sabah
North Cape 150 C1 headland North Island, New Zealand
North Cape 84 D1 Eng. North Cape. headland N Norway
North Cape see Nordkapp
North Carolina 43 E1 off. State of North Carolina, also known as Old North State, Tar Heel State, Turpentine State. state SE USA
North Channel 40 D2 lake channel Canada/USA
North Charleston 43 F2 South Carolina, SE USA
North Dakota 44 D2 off. State of North Dakota, also known as Flickertail State, Peace Garden State, Sioux State. state N USA
North Devon Island see Devon Island
North East Frontier Agency/North East Frontier Agency of Assam see Arunāchal Pradesh
Northeast Providence Channel 54 C1 channel N Bahamas

Northeim 94 B4 Niedersachsen, C Germany
Northern Cook Islands 145 F4 island group N Cook Islands
Northern Dvina 110 C4 var. Northern Dvina. river NW Russian Federation
Northern Dvina see Severnaya Dvina
Northern Ireland 88 B4 var. The Six Counties. cultural region Northern Ireland, United Kingdom
Northern Mariana Islands 142 B1 US commonwealth territory W Pacific Ocean
Northern Rhodesia see Zambia
Northern Sporades 105 C5 var. Vóreioi Sporádes, Vórioi Sporádhes, Eng. Northern Sporades. island group E Greece
Northern Sporades see Vóreies Sporádes
Northern Territory 144 A5 territory N Australia
North European Plain 81 E3 plain N Europe
Northfield 45 F2 Minnesota, N USA
North Fiji Basin 142 D3 undersea feature N Coral Sea
North Frisian Islands 94 B2 var. Nordfriesische Inseln. island group N Germany
North Huvadhu Atoll 132 B5 var. Gaafu Alifu Atoll. atoll S Maldives
North Island 150 B2 island N New Zealand
North Korea 129 E3 off. Democratic People's Republic of Korea, Kor. Chosŏn-minjujuŭi-inmin-kanghwaguk. country E Asia

NORTH KOREA
East Asia

Official name Democratic People's Republic of Korea
Formation 1948 / 1953
Capital Pyongyang
Population 24.5 million / 527 people per sq mile (203 people per sq km)
Total area 46,540 sq. miles (120,540 sq. km)
Languages Korean*
Religions Atheist 100%
Ethnic mix Korean 100%
Government One-party state
Currency North Korean won = 100 chon
Literacy rate 99%
Calorie consumption 2078 kilocalories

North Little Rock 42 B1 Arkansas, C USA
North Minch see Minch, The
North Mole 93 G4 harbour wall NW Gibraltar Europe
North Platte 45 E4 Nebraska, C USA
North Platte River 44 D4 river C USA
North Pole 155 B3 pole Arctic Ocean
North Saskatchewan 37 F5 river Alberta/Saskatchewan, S Canada
North Sea 80 D3 Dan. Nordsøen, Dut. Noordzee, Fr. Mer du Nord, Ger. Nordsee, Nor. Nordsjøen; prev. German Ocean, Lat. Mare Germanicum. sea NW Europe
North Siberian Lowland 115 E2 var. North Siberian Plain, Eng. North Siberian Lowland. lowlands N Russian Federation
North Siberian Lowland/North Siberian Plain see Severo-Sibirskaya Nizmennost'
North Star State see Minnesota
North Taranaki Bight 150 C3 gulf North Island, New Zealand
North Uist 88 B3 island NW Scotland, United Kingdom
Northwest Atlantic Mid-Ocean Canyon 34 E4 undersea feature N Atlantic Ocean
North West Highlands 88 C3 mountain range N Scotland, United Kingdom
Northwest Pacific Basin 113 G4 undersea feature N Pacific Ocean
Northwest Territories 37 E3 Fr. Territoires du Nord-Ouest. territory NW Canada
Northwind Plain 155 B2 undersea feature Arctic Ocean
Norton Sound 36 C2 inlet Alaska, USA
Norway 85 A5 off. Kingdom of Norway, Nor. Norge. country N Europe

NORWAY
Northern Europe

Official name Kingdom of Norway
Formation 1905 / 1905
Capital Oslo
Population 4.9 million / 41 people
per sq mile (16 people per sq km)
Total area 125,181 sq. miles (324,220 sq. km)
Languages Norwegian* (Bokmål
"book language" and Nynorsk
"new Norsk"), Sámi
Religions Evangelical Lutheran 88%,
Other and nonreligious 8%, Muslim 2%,
Pentecostal 1%, Roman Catholic 1%
Ethnic mix Norwegian 93%, Other 6%,
Sámi 1%
Government Parliamentary system
Currency Norwegian krone = 100 øre
Literacy rate 99%
Calorie consumption 3453 kilocalories

Norway, Kingdom of *see* Norway
Norwegian Basin 83 F4 *undersea feature*
NW Norwegian Sea
Norwegian Sea 83 F4 *var.* Norske Havet.
sea NE Atlantic Ocean
Norwich 89 E6 E England, United
Kingdom
Nösen *see* Bistriţa
Noshiro 130 D4 *var.* Nosiro; *prev.*
Noshirominato. Akita, Honshū,
C Japan
Noshirominato/Nosiro *see* Noshiro
Nosivka 109 E1 *Rus.* Nosovka.
Chernihivs'ka Oblast', NE Ukraine
Nosovka *see* Nosivka
Noşratābād 120 E3 Sīstān va
Balūchestān, E Iran
Nossob 78 C4 *river* E Namibia
Noteć 98 C3 *Ger.* Netze. *river*
NW Poland
Nóties Sporádes *see* Dodekánisa
Nottingham 89 D6 C England, United
Kingdom
Nouâdhibou 74 B2 *prev.* Port-Étienne.
Dakhlet Nouâdhibou, W Mauritania
Nouakchott 74 B2 *country capital*
(Mauritania) Nouakchott District,
SW Mauritania
Nouméa 144 C5 *dependent territory
capital* (New Caledonia) Province Sud,
S New Caledonia
Nouveau-Brunswick *see* New Brunswick
Nouvelle-Calédonie *see* New Caledonia
Nouvelle Écosse *see* Nova Scotia
Nova Civitas *see* Neustadt an der
Weinstrasse
Nova Gorica 95 D8 W Slovenia
Nova Gradiška 100 C3 *Ger.* Neugradisk,
Hung. Újgradiska. Brod-Posavina,
NE Croatia
Nova Iguaçu 63 F4 Rio de Janeiro,
SE Brazil
Nova Lisboa *see* Huambo
Novara 96 B2 *anc.* Novaria. Piemonte,
NW Italy
Novaria *see* Novara
Nova Scotia 33 F4 *Fr.* Nouvelle Écosse.
province SE Canada
Nova Scotia 33 E5 *physical region*
SE Canada
Novaya Sibir', Ostrov 115 F1 *island*
Novosibirskiye Ostrova, NE Russian
Federation
Novaya Zemlya 110 D1 *island group*
N Russian Federation
Novaya Zemlya Trough *see* East Novaya
Zemlya Trough
Novgorod *see* Velikiy Novgorod
Novi Grad *see* Bosanski Novi
Novi Iskŭr 104 C2 Sofiya-Grad,
W Bulgaria
Noviodunum *see* Nevers, Nièvre,
France
Noviomagus *see* Lisieux, Calvados,
France
Noviomagus *see* Nijmegen, Netherlands
Novi Pazar 101 D5 *Turk.* Yenipazar.
Serbia, S Serbia
Novi Sad 100 D3 *Ger.* Neusatz, *Hung.*
Újvidék. Vojvodina, N Serbia
Novoazovs'k 109 G4 *Rus.* Novoazovsk.
Donets'ka Oblast', E Ukraine
Novocheboksarsk 111 C5 Chuvashskaya
Respublika, W Russian Federation
Novocherkassk 111 B7 Rostovskaya
Oblast', SW Russian Federation

Novodvinsk 110 C3 Arkhangel'skaya
Oblast', NW Russian Federation
Novograd-Volynskiy *see*
Novohrad-Volyns'kyy
Novogrudok *see* Navahrudak
Novohrad-Volyns'kyy 108 D2 *Rus.*
Novograd-Volynskiy. Zhytomyrs'ka
Oblast', N Ukraine
Novokazalinsk *see* Ayteke Bi
Novokuznetsk 114 D4 *prev.* Stalinsk.
Kemerovskaya Oblast', S Russian
Federation
Novolazarevskaya 154 C2 *Russian
research station* Antarctica
Novo mesto 95 E8 *Ger.* Rudolfswert;
prev. Ger. Neustadtl. SE Slovenia
Novomoskovsk 111 B5 Tul'skaya
Oblast', W Russian Federation
Novomoskovs'k 109 F3 *Rus.*
Novomoskovsk. Dnipropetrovs'ka
Oblast', E Ukraine
Novopolotsk *see* Navapolatsk
Novoradomsk *see* Radomsko
Novo Redondo *see* Sumbe
Novorossiysk 111 A7 Krasnodarskiy
Kray, SW Russian Federation
Novoshakhtinsk 111 B6 Rostovskaya
Oblast', SW Russian Federation
Novosibirsk 114 D4 Novosibirskaya
Oblast', C Russian Federation
Novotroitsk 111 D6 Orenburgskaya
Oblast', W Russian Federation
Novotroitskoye *see* Novotroyits'ke,
Ukraine
Novotroyits'ke 109 F4 *Rus.*
Novotroitskoye. Khersons'ka Oblast',
S Ukraine
Novo-Urgench *see* Urganch
Novovolyns'k 108 C1 *Rus.* Novovolynsk.
Volyns'ka Oblast', NW Ukraine
Novy Dvor 107 B6 *Rus.* Novyy Dvor.
Hrodzyenskaya Voblasts', W Belarus
Novyy Bug *see* Novyy Buh
Novyy Buh 109 E3 *Rus.* Novyy Bug.
Mykolayivs'ka Oblast', S Ukraine
Novyy Dvor *see* Novy Dvor
Novyy Margilan *see* Farg'ona
Novyy Uzen' *see* Zhanaozen
Nowa Sól 98 B4 *var.* Nowasól, *Ger.*
Neusalz an der Oder. Lubuskie,
W Poland
Nowasól *see* Nowa Sól
Nowogard 98 B2 *var.* Nowógard, *Ger.*
Naugard. Zachodnio-pomorskie,
NW Poland
Nowogródek *see* Navahrudak
Nowo-Minsk *see* Mińsk Mazowiecki
Nowy Dwór Mazowiecki 98 D3
Mazowieckie, C Poland
Nowy Sącz 99 D5 *Ger.* Neu Sandec.
Małopolskie, S Poland
Nowy Tomyśl 98 B3 *var.* Nowy Tomysl.
Wielkopolskie, C Poland
Nowy Tomysl *see* Nowy Tomyśl
Noyon 90 C3 Oise, N France
Nsanje 79 E3 Southern, S Malawi
Nsawam 75 E5 SE Ghana
Ntomba, Lac 77 C6 *var.* Lac Tumba.
lake NW Dem. Rep. Congo
Nubian Desert 72 B3 *desert*
NE Sudan
Nu Chiang *see* Salween
Nu'eima 119 E7 E West Bank Asia
Nueva Caceres *see* Naga
Nueva Gerona 54 B2 Isla de la Juventud,
S Cuba
Nueva Rosita 50 D2 Coahuila,
NE Mexico
Nuevitas 54 C2 Camagüey, E Cuba
Nuevo, Bajo 53 G1 *island* NW Colombia
South America
Nuevo Casas Grandes 50 C1 Chihuahua,
N Mexico
Nuevo, Golfo 65 C6 *gulf* S Argentina
Nuevo Laredo 51 E2 Tamaulipas,
NE Mexico
Nui Atoll 145 E3 *atoll* W Tuvalu
Nu Jiang *see* Salween
Nûk *see* Nuuk
Nukha *see* Şäki
Nuku'alofa 145 E5 *country capital*
(Tonga) Tongatapu, S Tonga
Nukufetau Atoll 145 E3 *atoll* C Tuvalu
Nukulaelae Atoll 145 E3 *var.* Nukulailai.
atoll E Tuvalu
Nukulailai *see* Nukulaelae Atoll
Nukunau *see* Nikunau
Nukunonu Atoll 145 E3 *island*
C Tokelau

Nukus 122 C2 Qoraqalpog'iston
Respublikasi, W Uzbekistan
Nullarbor Plain 147 C6 *plateau* South
Australia/Western Australia
Nunap Isua 82 C5 *var.* Uummannarsuaq,
Dan. Kap Farvel, *Eng.* Cape Farewell.
cape S Greenland
Nunavut 37 F3 *territory* N Canada
Nuneaton 89 D6 C England, United
Kingdom
Nunivak Island 36 B2 *island* Alaska,
USA
Nunspeet 86 D3 Gelderland,
E Netherlands
Nuoro 97 A5 Sardegna, Italy,
C Mediterranean Sea
Nuqui 58 A3 Chocó, W Colombia
Nurakita *see* Niulakita
Nurata *see* Nurota
Nurek *see* Norak
Nuremberg *see* Nürnberg
Nurmes 84 F4 Itä-Suomi, E Finland
Nürnberg 95 C5 *Eng.* Nuremberg.
Bayern, S Germany
Nurota 123 E2 *Rus.* Nurata. Navoiy
Viloyati, C Uzbekistan
Nusaybin 117 F4 *var.* Nisibin. Manisa,
SE Turkey
Nussdorf *see* Năsăud
Nutmeg State *see* Connecticut
Nuuk 82 C4 *var.* Nûk, *Dan.* Godthaab,
Godthåb. *dependent territory capital*
(Greenland) Kitaa, SW Greenland
Nyagan' 114 C3 Khanty-Mansiyskiy
Avtonomnyy Okrug-Yugra, N Russian
Federation
Nyainqentanglha Shan 126 C5
mountain range W China
Nyala 72 A4 Southern Darfur, W Sudan
Nyamapanda 78 D3 Mashonaland East,
NE Zimbabwe
Nyamtumbo 73 C8 Ruvuma, S Tanzania
Nyanda *see* Masvingo
Nyandoma 110 C4 Arkhangel'skaya
Oblast', NW Russian Federation
Nyantakara 73 B7 Kagera, NW Tanzania
Nyasa, Lake 79 E2 *var.* Lake Malawi;
prev. Lago Nyassa. *lake* E Africa
Nyasaland/Nyasaland Protectorate
see Malawi
Nyassa, Lago *see* Nyasa, Lake
Nyasvizh 107 C6 *Pol.* Nieśwież, *Rus.*
Nesvizh. Minskaya Voblasts', C Belarus
Nyaunglebin 136 B4 Bago, SW Myanmar
(Burma)
Nyeri 73 C6 Central, C Kenya
Nyíregyháza 99 D6 Szabolcs-Szatmár-
Bereg, NE Hungary
Nyitra *see* Nitra
Nykøbing 85 B8 Sjælland, SE Denmark
Nyköping 85 C6 Södermanland,
S Sweden
Nylstroom *see* Modimolle
Nyngan 149 D6 New South Wales,
SE Australia
Nyoman *see* Neman
Nyurba 115 F3 Respublika Sakha
(Yakutiya), NE Russian Federation
Nyzhn'ohirs'kyy 109 F4 *Rus.*
Nizhnegorskiy. Avtonomna Respublika
Krym, S Ukraine
NZ *see* New Zealand
Nzega 73 C7 Tabora, C Tanzania
Nzérékoré 74 D4 SE Guinea
Nzwani 79 F2 *Fr.* Anjouan, *var.*
Ndzouani. *island* SE Comoros

O

Oa'hu 47 A7 *var.* Oahu. *island* Hawai'ian
Islands, Hawai'i, USA
Oak Harbor 46 B1 Washington,
NW USA
Oakland 47 B6 California, W USA
Oamaru 151 B7 Otago, South Island,
New Zealand
Oaxaca 51 F5 *var.* Oaxaca de Juárez; *prev.*
Antequera. Oaxaca, SE Mexico
Oaxaca de Juárez *see* Oaxaca
Ob' 112 C2 *river* C Russian Federation
Obal' 107 D5 *Rus.* Obol'. Vitsyebskaya
Voblasts', N Belarus
Oban 88 C4 W Scotland, United
Kingdom
Oban *see* Halfmoon Bay
Obando *see* Puerto Inírida
Obdorsk *see* Salekhard
Óbecse *see* Bečej

Obeliai 106 C4 Panevėžys, NE Lithuania
Oberhollabrunn *see* Tulln
Ob', Gulf of 114 D3 *Eng.* Gulf of Ob. *gulf*
N Russian Federation
Ob', Gulf of *see* Obskaya Guba
Obidovichi *see* Abidavichy
Obihiro 130 D2 Hokkaidō, NE Japan
Obo 76 D4 Haut-Mbomou, E Central
African Republic
Obock 72 D4 E Djibouti
Obol' *see* Obal'
Oborniki 98 C3 Wielkolpolskie,
W Poland
Obrovo *see* Abrova
Ob' Tablemount 141 B7 *undersea
feature* S Indian Ocean
Ocala 43 E4 Florida, SE USA
Ocaña 58 B2 Norte de Santander,
N Colombia
Ocaña 92 D3 Castilla-La Mancha,
C Spain
O Carballiño 92 C1 *Cast.* Carballiño.
Galicia, NW Spain
Occidental, Cordillera 58 B2 *mountain
range* W South America
Occidental, Cordillera 61 E4 *mountain
range* Bolivia/Chile
Ocean Falls 36 D5 British Columbia,
SW Canada
Ocean Island *see* Banaba
Oceanside 47 C8 California, W USA
Ocean State *see* Rhode Island
Ochakiv 109 E4 *Rus.* Ochakov.
Mykolayivs'ka Oblast', S Ukraine
Ochakov *see* Ochakiv
Ochamchira *see* Ochamchire
Ochamchire 117 E2 *Rus.* Ochamchira;
prev. Och'amch'ire. W Georgia
Och'amch'ire *see* Ochamchire
Ocho Rios 54 B4 C Jamaica
Ochrida *see* Ohrid
Ochrida, Lake *see* Ohrid, Lake
Ocotal 52 D3 Nueva Segovia,
NW Nicaragua
Ocozocuautla 51 G5 Chiapas, SE Mexico
October Revolution Island 115 E2
Eng. October Revolution Island.
island Severnaya Zemlya, N Russian
Federation
October Revolution Island *see*
Oktyabr'skoy Revolyutsii, Ostrov
Ocú 53 F5 Herrera, S Panama
Ōdate 130 D3 Akita, Honshū, C Japan
Ödemiş 116 A4 İzmir, SW Turkey
Ödenburg *see* Sopron
Odenpäh *see* Otepää
Odense 85 B7 Syddtjylland, C Denmark
Oder 98 B3 *Cz./Pol.* Odra. *river*
C Europe
Oderhaff *see* Szczeciński, Zalew
Odesa 109 E4 *Rus.* Odessa. Odes'ka
Oblast', SW Ukraine
Odessa 49 E3 Texas, SW USA
Odessa *see* Odesa
Odessus *see* Varna
Odienné 74 D4 NW Côte d'Ivoire
Odisha *see* Orissa
Ödöngk 137 D6 Kâmpóng Spoe,
S Cambodia
Odoorn 86 E2 Drenthe, NE Netherlands
Odra *see* Oder
Oesel *see* Saaremaa
Of 117 E2 Trabzon, NE Turkey
Ofanto 97 D5 *river* S Italy
Offenbach 95 B5 *var.* Offenbach am
Main. Hessen, W Germany
Offenbach am Main *see* Offenbach
Offenburg 95 B6 Baden-Württemberg,
SW Germany
Ogaadeen *see* Ogaden
Ogaden 73 D5 *Som.* Ogaadeen. *plateau*
Ethiopia/Somalia
Ōgaki 131 C6 Gifu, Honshū, SW Japan
Ogallala 44 D4 Nebraska, C USA
Ogbomoso 75 F4 *var.* Ogmoboso. Oyo,
W Nigeria
Ogden 44 B4 Utah, W USA
Ogdensburg 41 F2 New York,
NE USA
Ogmoboso *see* Ogbomosho
Ogulin 100 A3 Karlovac, NW Croatia
Ohio 40 C4 *off.* State of Ohio, *also known
as* Buckeye State. *state* N USA
Ohio River 40 C4 *river* N USA
Ohlau *see* Oława
Ohri *see* Ohrid
Ohrid 101 D6 *Turk.* Ochrida, Ohri.
SW FYR Macedonia

Ohrid, Lake 101 D6 *var.* Lake Ochrida, *Alb.* Liqeni i Ohrit, *Mac.* Ohridsko Ezero. *lake* Albania/FYR Macedonia
Ohridsko Ezero/Ohrit, Liqeni i *see* Ohrid, Lake
Ohura 150 D3 Manawatu-Wanganui, North Island, New Zealand
Oirschot 87 C5 Noord-Brabant, S Netherlands
Oise 90 C3 *river* N France
Oistins 55 G2 S Barbados
Ōita 131 B7 Ōita, Kyūshū, SW Japan
Ojinaga 50 D2 Chihuahua, N Mexico
Ojos del Salado, Cerro 64 B3 *mountain* W Argentina
Okaihau 150 C2 Northland, North Island, New Zealand
Okanizsa *see* Kanjiža
Okāra 134 C2 Punjab, E Pakistan
Okavaggo *see* Cubango/Okavango
Okavango *see* Cubango
Okavango Delta 78 C3 *wetland* N Botswana
Okayama 131 B6 Okayama, Honshū, SW Japan
Okazaki 131 C6 Aichi, Honshū, C Japan
Okeechobee, Lake 43 E4 *lake* Florida, SE USA
Okefenokee Swamp 43 E3 *wetland* Georgia, SE USA
Okhotsk 115 G3 Khabarovskiy Kray, E Russian Federation
Okhotsk, Sea of 113 F3 *sea* NW Pacific Ocean
Okhtyrka 109 F2 *Rus.* Akhtyrka. Sums'ka Oblast', NE Ukraine
Oki-guntō *see* Oki-shotō
Okinawa 130 A3 *island* SW Japan
Okinawa-shoto 130 A3 *island group* Nansei-shotō, SW Japan Asia
Oki-shoto 131 B6 *var.* Oki-guntō. *island group* SW Japan
Oklahoma 49 F2 *off.* State of Oklahoma, *also known as* The Sooner State. *state* C USA
Oklahoma City 49 G1 *state capital* Oklahoma, C USA
Okmulgee 49 G1 Oklahoma, C USA
Oktyabr'skiy 111 D6 Volgogradskaya Oblast', W Russian Federation
Oktyabr'skiy *see* Aktsyabrski
Okulovka 110 B4 *var.* Okulovka. Novgorodskaya Oblast', W Russian Federation
Okulovka *see* Okulovka
Okushiri-to 130 C3 *var.* Okusiri Tô. *island* NE Japan
Okusiri Tô *see* Okushiri-tō
Oláh-Toplicza *see* Topliţa
Öland 85 C7 *island* S Sweden
Olavarría 65 D5 Buenos Aires, E Argentina
Oława 98 C4 *Ger.* Ohlau. Dolnośląskie, SW Poland
Olbia 97 A5 *prev.* Terranova Pausania. Sardegna, Italy, C Mediterranean Sea
Old Bay State/Old Colony State *see* Massachusetts
Old Dominion *see* Virginia
Oldebroek 86 D3 Gelderland, E Netherlands
Oldenburg 94 B3 Niedersachsen, NW Germany
Oldenburg 94 C2 *var.* Oldenburg in Holstein. Schleswig-Holstein, N Germany
Oldenburg in Holstein *see* Oldenburg
Oldenzaal 86 E3 Overijssel, E Netherlands
Old Harbour 54 B5 C Jamaica
Old Line State *see* Maryland
Old North State *see* North Carolina
Olëkma 115 F4 *river* C Russian Federation
Olëkminsk 115 F3 Respublika Sakha (Yakutiya), NE Russian Federation
Oleksandriva 109 E3 *Rus.* Aleksandrovka. Kirovohrads'ka Oblast', C Ukraine
Oleksandriya 109 F3 *Rus.* Aleksandriya. Kirovohrads'ka Oblast', C Ukraine
Olenegorsk 110 C2 Murmanskaya Oblast', NW Russian Federation
Olenëk 115 E3 Respublika Sakha (Yakutiya), NE Russian Federation
Olenëk 115 E3 *river* NE Russian Federation
Oléron, Île d' 91 A5 *island* W France

Olevs'k 108 D1 *Rus.* Olevsk. Zhytomyrs'ka Oblast', N Ukraine
Olevsk *see* Olevs'k
Ölgiy 126 C2 Bayan-Ölgiy, W Mongolia
Olhão 92 B5 Faro, S Portugal
Olifa 78 B3 Kunene, NW Namibia
Ólimbos *see* Ólympos
Olimpo *see* Fuerte Olimpo
Olisipo *see* Lisboa
Olita *see* Alytus
Oliva 93 F4 Valenciana, E Spain
Olivet 90 C4 Loiret, C France
Olmalig 123 E2 *Rus.* Almalyk. Toshkent Viloyati, E Uzbekistan
Olmütz *see* Olomouc
Olomouc 99 C5 *Ger.* Olmütz, *Pol.* Ołomuniec. Olomoucký Kraj, E Czech Republic
Olomuniec *see* Olomouc
Olonets 110 B3 Respublika Kareliya, NW Russian Federation
Olovyannaya 115 F4 Zabaykal'skiy Kray, S Russian Federation
Olpe 94 B4 Nordrhein-Westfalen, W Germany
Olshanka *see* Vil'shanka
Olsnitz *see* Murska Sobota
Olsztyn 98 D2 *Ger.* Allenstein. Warmińsko-Mazurskie, N Poland
Olt 108 D5 *var.* Oltul, *Ger.* Alt. *river* S Romania
Olteniţa 108 C5 *prev. Eng.* Oltenitsa; *anc.* Constantiola. Călăraşi, SE Romania
Oltenitsa *see* Olteniţa
Oltul *see* Olt
Olvera 92 D5 Andalucía, S Spain
Ol'viopol' *see* Pervomays'k
Olympia 46 B2 *state capital* Washington, NW USA
Olympic Mountains 46 A2 *mountain range* Washington, NW USA
Olympus, Mount 104 B4 *var.* Ólimbos, *Eng.* Mount Olympus. *mountain* N Greece
Omagh 89 B5 *Ir.* An Ómaigh. W Northern Ireland, United Kingdom
Omaha 45 F4 Nebraska, C USA
Oman 120 D6 *off.* Sultanate of Oman, *Ar.* Salţanat 'Umān; *prev.* Muscat and Oman. *country* SW Asia

OMAN
Southwest Asia

Official name Sultanate of Oman
Formation 1951 / 1951
Capital Muscat
Population 2.8 million / 34 people per sq mile (13 people per sq km)
Total area 82,031 sq. miles (212,460 sq. km)
Languages Arabic*, Baluchi, Farsi, Hindi, Punjabi
Religions Ibadi Muslim 75%, Other Muslim and Hindu 25%
Ethnic mix Arab 88%, Baluchi 4%, Persian 3%, Indian and Pakistani 3%, African 2%
Government Monarchy
Currency Omani rial = 1000 baisa
Literacy rate 87%
Calorie consumption Not available

Oman, Gulf of 120 E4 *Ar.* Khalīj 'Umān. *gulf* N Arabian Sea
Oman, Sultanate of *see* Oman
Omboué 77 A6 Ogooué-Maritime, W Gabon
Omdurman 72 B4 *var.* Umm Durmān. Khartoum, C Sudan
Ometepe, Isla de 52 D4 *island* S Nicaragua
Ommen 86 E3 Overijssel, E Netherlands
Omsk 114 C4 Omskaya Oblast', C Russian Federation
Ōmuta 131 A7 Fukuoka, Kyūshū, SW Japan
Onda 93 F3 Valenciana, E Spain
Ondjiva *see* N'Giva
Öndörhaan 127 E2 *var.* Undur Khan; *prev.* Tsetsen Khan. Hentiy, E Mongolia
Onega 110 C3 Arkhangel'skaya Oblast', NW Russian Federation
Onega 110 B4 *river* NW Russian Federation
Lake Onega 110 B4 *Eng.* Lake Onega. *lake* NW Russian Federation
Onega, Lake *see* Onezhskoye Ozero
Onex 95 A7 Genève, SW Switzerland
Ongole 132 D1 Andhra Pradesh, E India

Onitsha 75 G5 Anambra, S Nigeria
Onon Gol 127 E2 *river* N Mongolia
Onslow 146 A4 Western Australia
Onslow Bay 43 F1 *bay* North Carolina, E USA
Ontario 38 B3 *province* S Canada
Ontario, Lake 41 E3 *lake* Canada/USA
Onteniente *see* Ontinyent
Ontinyent 93 F4 *var.* Onteniente. Valenciana, E Spain
Ontong Java Rise 125 H4 *undersea feature* W Pacific Ocean
Onuba *see* Huelva
Oodeypore *see* Udaipur
Oos-Londen *see* East London
Oostakker 87 B5 Oost-Vlaanderen, NW Belgium
Oostburg 87 B5 Zeeland, SW Netherlands
Oostende 87 A5 *Eng.* Ostend, *Fr.* Ostende. West-Vlaanderen, NW Belgium
Oosterbeek 86 D4 Gelderland, SE Netherlands
Oosterhout 86 C4 Noord-Brabant, S Netherlands
Opatija 100 A2 *It.* Abbazia. Primorje-Gorski Kotar, NW Croatia
Opava 99 C5 *Ger.* Troppau. Moravskoslezský Kraj, E Czech Republic
Ópazova *see* Stara Pazova
Opelika 42 D2 Alabama, S USA
Opelousas 42 B3 Louisiana, S USA
Ophiusa *see* Formentera
Opmeer 86 C2 Noord-Holland, NW Netherlands
Opochka 110 A4 Pskovskaya Oblast', W Russian Federation
Opole 98 C4 *Ger.* Oppeln. Opolskie, S Poland
Oporto *see* Porto
Opotiki 150 E3 Bay of Plenty, North Island, New Zealand
Oppeln *see* Opole
Oppidum Ubiorum *see* Köln
Oqtosh 123 E2 *Rus.* Aktash. Samarqand Viloyati, C Uzbekistan
Oradea 108 B3 *prev.* Oradea Mare, *Ger.* Grosswardein, *Hung.* Nagyvárad. Bihor, NW Romania
Oradea Mare *see* Oradea
Orahovac *see* Rahovec
Oral *see* Ural'sk
Oran 70 D2 *var.* Ouahran, Wahran. NW Algeria
Orange 91 D6 New South Wales, SE Australia
Orange 91 D6 *anc.* Arausio. Vaucluse, SE France
Orangeburg 43 E2 South Carolina, SE USA
Orange Cone *see* Orange Fan
Orange Fan 69 C7 *var.* Orange Cone. *undersea feature* SW Indian Ocean
Orange Mouth/Orangemund *see* Oranjemund
Orange River 78 B4 *Afr.* Oranjerivier. *river* S Africa
Orange Walk 52 C1 Orange Walk, N Belize
Oranienburg 94 D3 Brandenburg, NE Germany
Oranjemund 78 B4 *var.* Orangemund; *prev.* Orange Mouth. Karas, SW Namibia
Oranjerivier *see* Orange River
Oranjestad 55 E5 *dependent territory capital* (Aruba) W Aruba
Orany *see* Varėna
Oraşul Stalin *see* Braşov
Oravicabánya *see* Oraviţa
Oraviţa 108 A4 *Ger.* Orawitza, *Hung.* Oravicabánya. Caraş-Severin, SW Romania
Orawitza *see* Oraviţa
Orbetello 96 B4 Toscana, C Italy
Orcadas 154 A1 *Argentinian research station* South Orkney Islands, Antarctica
Orchard Homes 44 B1 Montana, NW USA
Ordino 91 A8 Ordino, NW Andorra Europe
Ordos Desert *see* Mu Us Shadi
Ordu 116 D2 *anc.* Cotyora. Ordu, N Turkey
Ordzhonikidze 109 F3 Dnipropetrovs'ka Oblast', E Ukraine

Ordzhonikidze *see* Vladikavkaz, Russian Federation
Ordzhonikidze *see* Yenakiyeve, Ukraine
Orealla 59 G3 E Guyana
Örebro 85 C6 Örebro, C Sweden
Oregon 46 B3 *off.* State of Oregon, *also known as* Beaver State, Sunset State, Valentine State, Webfoot State. *state* NW USA
Oregon City 46 B3 Oregon, NW USA
Oregon, State of *see* Oregon
Orekhov *see* Orikhiv
Orël 111 B5 Orlovskaya Oblast', W Russian Federation
Orem 44 B4 Utah, W USA
Ore Mountains 95 C5 *Cz.* Krušné Hory, *Eng.* Ore Mountains. *mountain range* Czech Republic/Germany
Ore Mountains *see* Erzgebirge/Krušné Hory
Orenburg 111 D6 *prev.* Chkalov. Orenburgskaya Oblast', W Russian Federation
Orense *see* Ourense
Orestiáda 104 D3 *prev.* Orestiás. Anatolikí Makedonía kai Thráki, NE Greece
Orestiás *see* Orestiáda
Organ Peak 48 D3 *mountain* New Mexico, SW USA
Orgeyev *see* Orhei
Orhei 108 D3 *var.* Orheiu, *Rus.* Orgeyev. N Moldova
Orheiu *see* Orhei
Oriental, Cordillera 60 D3 *mountain range* Bolivia/Peru
Oriental, Cordillera 58 B3 *mountain range* C Colombia
Orihuela 93 F4 Valenciana, E Spain
Orikhiv 109 G3 *Rus.* Orekhov. Zaporiz'ka Oblast', SE Ukraine
Orinoco, Río 59 E2 *river* Colombia/Venezuela
Orissa 137 E4 *var.* Odisha. *cultural region* NE India
Orissaar *see* Orissaare
Orissaare 106 C2 *Ger.* Orissaar. Saaremaa, W Estonia
Oristano 97 A5 Sardegna, Italy, C Mediterranean Sea
Orito 58 A4 Putumayo, SW Colombia
Orizaba, Volcán Pico de 35 C7 *var.* Citlaltépetl. *mountain* S Mexico
Orkney *see* Orkney Islands
Orkney Islands 88 C2 *var.* Orkney, Orkneys. *island group* N Scotland, United Kingdom
Orkneys *see* Orkney Islands
Orlando 43 E4 Florida, SE USA
Orléanais 90 C4 *cultural region* C France
Orléans 90 C4 *anc.* Aurelianum. Loiret, C France
Orléansville *see* Chlef
Orly 90 E2 (Paris) Essonne, N France
Orlya 107 B6 Hrodzyenskaya Voblasts', W Belarus
Ormsö *see* Vormsi
Ormuz, Strait of *see* Hormuz, Strait of
Örnsköldsvik 85 C5 Västernorrland, C Sweden
Orolaunum *see* Arlon
Orol Dengizi *see* Aral Sea
Oromocto 39 F4 New Brunswick, SE Canada
Orona 145 F3 *prev.* Hull Island. *atoll* Phoenix Islands, C Kiribati
Oropeza *see* Cochabamba
Orosirá Rodhópis *see* Rhodope Mountains
Orpington 89 B8 United Kingdom
Orschowa *see* Orşova
Orsha 107 E6 Vitsyebskaya Voblasts', NE Belarus
Orsk 114 B4 Orenburgskaya Oblast', W Russian Federation
Orşova 108 A4 *Ger.* Orschowa, *Hung.* Orsova. Mehedinţi, SW Romania
Ortelsburg *see* Szczytno
Orthez 91 B6 Pyrénées-Atlantiques, SW France
Ortona 96 D4 Abruzzo, C Italy
Oruba *see* Aruba
Oruro 61 F4 Oruro, W Bolivia
Oryokko *see* Yalu
Oss 86 D4 Noord-Brabant, S Netherlands
Ōsaka 131 C6 *hist.* Naniwa. Ōsaka, Honshū, SW Japan
Ōsaki *see* Furukawa

Osa, Península de 53 E5 peninsula S Costa Rica
Osborn Plateau 141 D5 undersea feature E Indian Ocean
Osca see Huesca
Ösel see Saaremaa
Osh 123 F2 Oshskaya Oblast', SW Kyrgyzstan
Oshawa 38 D5 Ontario, SE Canada
Oshikango 78 B3 Ohangwena, N Namibia
O-shima 131 D6 island S Japan
Oshkosh 40 B2 Wisconsin, N USA
Oshmyany see Ashmyany
Osiek see Osijek
Osijek 100 C3 prev. Osiek, Osjek, Ger. Esseg, Hung. Eszék. Osijek-Baranja, E Croatia
Osipenko see Berdyans'k
Osipovichi see Asipovichy
Osjek see Osijek
Oskaloosa 45 G4 Iowa, C USA
Oskarshamn 85 C7 Kalmar, S Sweden
Öskemen see Ust'-Kamenogorsk
Oskil 109 G2 Rus. Oskil. river Russian Federation/Ukraine
Oskil see Oskil
Oslo 85 B6 prev. Christiania, Kristiania. country capital (Norway) Oslo, S Norway
Osmaniye 116 D4 Osmaniye, S Turkey
Osnabrück 94 A3 Niedersachsen, NW Germany
Osogov Mountains 104 B3 var. Osogovske Planine, Osogovski Planina, Mac. Osogovski Planini. mountain range Bulgaria/FYR Macedonia
Osogovske Planine/Osogovski Planina/ Osogovski Planini see Osogov Mountains
Oşorhei see Târgu Mureş
Osorno 65 B5 Los Lagos, C Chile
Ossa, Serra d' 92 C4 mountain range SE Portugal
Ossora 115 H2 Krasnoyarskiy Kray, E Russian Federation
Ostee see Baltic Sea
Ostend/Ostende see Oostende
Oster 109 E1 Chernihivs'ka Oblast', N Ukraine
Östermyra see Seinäjoki
Osterode/Osterode in Ostpreussen see Ostróda
Österreich see Austria
Östersund 85 C5 Jämtland, C Sweden
Ostia Aterni see Pescara
Ostiglia 96 C2 Lombardia, N Italy
Ostrava 99 C5 Moravskoslezský Kraj, E Czech Republic
Ostróda 98 D3 Ger. Osterode, Osterode in Ostpreussen. Warmińsko-Mazurskie, NE Poland
Ostrołęka 98 D3 Ger. Wiesenhof, Rus. Ostrolenka. Mazowieckie, C Poland
Ostrolenka see Ostrołęka
Ostrov 110 A4 Latv. Austrava. Pskovskaya Oblast', W Russian Federation
Ostrovets see Ostrowiec Świętokrzyski
Ostrovnoy 110 C2 Murmanskaya Oblast', NW Russian Federation
Ostrów see Ostrów Wielkopolski
Ostrowiec see Ostrowiec Świętokrzyski
Ostrowiec Świętokrzyski 98 D4 var. Ostrowiec, Rus. Ostrovets. Świętokrzyskie, C Poland
Ostrów Mazowiecka 98 D3 var. Ostrów Mazowiecki. Mazowieckie, NE Poland
Ostrów Mazowiecki see Ostrów Mazowiecka
Ostrowo see Ostrów Wielkopolski
Ostrów Wielkopolski 98 C4 var. Ostrów, Ger. Ostrowo. Wielkopolskie, C Poland
Ostyako-Vogulsk see Khanty-Mansiysk
Osum see Osumit, Lumi i
Osumi-shoto 131 A8 island group Kagoshima, Nansei-shotō, SW Japan Asia East China Sea Pacific Ocean
Osumit, Lumi i 101 D7 var. Osum. river SE Albania
Osuna 92 D4 Andalucía, S Spain
Oswego 41 F2 New York, NE USA
Otago Peninsula 151 B7 peninsula South Island, New Zealand
Otaki 150 D4 Wellington, North Island, New Zealand
Otaru 130 C2 Hokkaidō, NE Japan
Otavalo 60 B1 Imbabura, N Ecuador

Otavi 78 B3 Otjozondjupa, N Namibia
Oţelu Roşu 108 B4 Ger. Ferdinandsberg, Hung. Nándorhgy. Caras-Severin, SW Romania
Otepää 106 D3 Ger. Odenpäh. Valgamaa, SE Estonia
Oti 75 E4 river N Togo
Otira 151 C6 West Coast, South Island, New Zealand
Otjiwarongo 78 B3 Otjozondjupa, N Namibia
Otorohanga 150 D3 Waikato, North Island, New Zealand
Otranto, Canale d' see Otranto, Strait of
Otranto, Strait of 101 C6 It. Canale d'Otranto. strait Albania/Italy
Otrokovice 99 C5 Ger. Otrokowitz. Zlínský Kraj, E Czech Republic
Otrokowitz see Otrokovice
Ōtsu 131 C6 var. Ōtu. Shiga, Honshū, SW Japan
Ottawa 38 D5 country capital (Canada) Ontario, SE Canada
Ottawa 40 B3 Illinois, N USA
Ottawa 45 F5 Kansas, C USA
Ottawa 41 E2 Fr. Outaouais. river Ontario/Québec, SE Canada
Ottawa Islands 38 C1 island group Nunavut, C Canada
Ottignies 87 C6 Wallon Brabant, C Belgium
Ottumwa 45 G4 Iowa, C USA
Ōtu see Ōtsu
Ouachita Mountains 42 A1 mountain range Arkansas/Oklahoma, C USA
Ouachita River 42 B2 river Arkansas/ Louisiana, C USA
Ouagadougou 75 E4 var. Wagadugu. country capital (Burkina Faso) C Burkina Faso
Ouahigouya 75 E3 NW Burkina Faso
Ouahran see Oran
Oualâta 74 D3 var. Oualata. Hodh ech Chargui, SE Mauritania
Ouanary 59 H3 E French Guiana
Ouanda Djallé 76 D4 Vakaga, NE Central African Republic
Ouarâne 74 D2 desert C Mauritania
Ouargla 71 E2 var. Wargla. NE Algeria
Ouarzazate 70 C3 S Morocco
Oubangui 77 C5 Fr. Oubangui. river C Africa
Oubangui see Ubangi
Oubangui-Chari see Central African Republic
Oubangui-Chari, Territoire de l' see Central African Republic
Oudjda see Oujda
Ouessant, Île d' 90 A3 Eng. Ushant. island NW France
Ouésso 77 B5 Sangha, NW Congo
Oujda 70 D2 Ar. Oudjda, Ujda. NE Morocco
Oujeft 74 C2 Adrar, C Mauritania
Oulu 84 D4 Swe. Uleåborg. Oulu, C Finland
Oulujärvi 84 D4 Swe. Uleträsk. lake C Finland
Oulujoki 84 D4 Swe. Uleälv. river C Finland
Ounasjoki 84 D3 river N Finland
Ounianga Kébir 76 C2 Borkou-Ennedi-Tibesti, N Chad
Oup see Auob
Oupeye 87 D6 Liège, E Belgium
Our 87 D6 river NW Europe
Ourense 92 C1 Cast. Orense, Lat. Aurium. Galicia, NW Spain
Ourique 92 B4 Beja, S Portugal
Ours, Grand Lac de l' see Great Bear Lake
Ourthe 87 D7 river E Belgium
Ouse 89 D5 river N England, United Kingdom
Outaouais see Ottawa
Outer Hebrides 88 B3 var. Western Isles. island group NW Scotland, United Kingdom
Outer Islands 79 G1 island group SW Seychelles Africa W Indian Ocean
Ouvéa 144 D5 island Îles Loyauté, NE New Caledonia
Ouyen 149 C6 Victoria, SE Australia
Ovalle 64 B3 Coquimbo, N Chile
Ovar 92 B2 Aveiro, N Portugal
Overflakkee 86 B4 island SW Netherlands
Overijse 87 C6 Vlaams Brabant, C Belgium

Oviedo 92 C1 anc. Asturias. Asturias, NW Spain
Ovilava see Wels
Ovruch 108 D1 Zhytomyrs'ka Oblast', N Ukraine
Owando 77 B5 prev. Fort Rousset. Cuvette, C Congo
Owase 131 C6 Mie, Honshū, SW Japan
Owatonna 45 F3 Minnesota, N USA
Owen Fracture Zone 140 B4 tectonic feature W Arabian Sea
Owen, Mount 151 C5 mountain South Island, New Zealand
Owensboro 40 B5 Kentucky, S USA
Owen Stanley Range 144 B3 mountain range S Papua New Guinea
Owerri 75 G5 Imo, S Nigeria
Owo 75 F5 Ondo, SW Nigeria
Owyhee River 46 C4 river Idaho/Oregon, NW USA
Oxford 151 C6 Canterbury, South Island, New Zealand
Oxford 89 D6 Lat. Oxonia. S England, United Kingdom
Oxkutzcab 51 H4 Yucatán, SE Mexico
Oxnard 47 B7 California, W USA
Oxonia see Oxford
Oxus see Amu Darya
Oyama 131 D5 Tochigi, Honshū, S Japan
Oyem 77 B5 Woleu-Ntem, N Gabon
Oyo 77 B6 Cuvette, C Congo
Oyo 75 F4 Oyo, W Nigeria
Ozark 42 D3 Alabama, S USA
Ozark Plateau 45 G5 plain Arkansas/ Missouri, C USA
Ozarks, Lake of the 45 F5 reservoir Missouri, C USA
Ozbourn Seamount 152 D4 undersea feature W Pacific Ocean
Ózd 99 D6 Borsod-Abaúj-Zemplén, NE Hungary

P

Paamiut 82 B4 var. Påmiut, Dan. Frederikshåb. S Greenland
Pa-an see Hpa-an
Pabianice 98 C4 Łódzki, Poland
Pabna 135 G4 Rajshahi, W Bangladesh
Pacaraima, Sierra/Pacaraim, Serra see Pakaraima Mountains
Pachuca 51 E4 var. Pachuca de Soto. Hidalgo, C Mexico
Pachuca de Soto see Pachuca
Pacific-Antarctic Ridge 154 B5 undersea feature S Pacific Ocean
Pacific Ocean 152 D3 ocean
Padalung see Phatthalung
Padang 138 B4 Sumatera, W Indonesia
Paderborn 94 B4 Nordrhein-Westfalen, NW Germany
Padma see Brahmaputra
Padma see Ganges
Padova 96 C2 Eng. Padua; anc. Patavium. Veneto, NE Italy
Padre Island 49 G5 island Texas, SW USA
Padua see Padova
Paducah 40 B5 Kentucky, S USA
Paeroa 150 D3 Waikato, North Island, New Zealand
Páfos 102 C5 var. Paphos. W Cyprus
Pag 100 A3 It. Pago. island Zadar, C Croatia
Page 48 B1 Arizona, SW USA
Pago see Pag
Pago Pago 145 F4 dependent territory capital (American Samoa) Tutuila, W American Samoa
Pahiatua 150 D4 Manawatu-Wanganui, North Island, New Zealand
Pahsien see Chongqing
Paide 106 D2 Ger. Weissenstein. Järvamaa, N Estonia
Paihia 150 D2 Northland, North Island, New Zealand
Päijänne 85 D5 lake S Finland
Paine, Cerro 65 A7 mountain S Chile
Painted Desert 48 B1 desert Arizona, SW USA
Paisance see Piacenza
Paisley 88 C4 W Scotland, United Kingdom
País Vasco 93 E1 cultural region N Spain
Paita 60 B3 Piura, NW Peru
Pakanbaru see Pekanbaru

Pakaraima Mountains 59 E3 var. Serra Pacaraim, Sierra Pacaraima. mountain range N South America
Pakistan 134 A2 off. Islamic Republic of Pakistan, var. Islami Jamhuriya e Pakistan. country S Asia

PAKISTAN
South Asia

Official name Islamic Republic of Pakistan
Formation 1947 / 1971
Capital Islamabad
Population 177 million / 594 people per sq mile (229 people per sq km)
Total area 310,401 sq. miles (803,940 sq. km)
Languages Punjabi, Sindhi, Pashtu, Urdu*, Baluchi, Brahui
Religions Sunni Muslim 77%, Shi'a Muslim 20%, Hindu 2%, Christian 1%
Ethnic mix Punjabi 56%, Pathan (Pashtun) 15%, Sindhi 14%, Mohajir 7%, Baluchi 4%, Other 4%
Government Presidential system
Currency Pakistani rupee = 100 paisa
Literacy rate 56%
Calorie consumption 2423 kilocalories

Pakistan, Islamic Republic of see Pakistan
Pakistan, Islami Jamhuriya e see Pakistan
Paknam see Samut Prakan
Pakokku 136 A3 Magway, C Myanmar (Burma)
Pak Phanang 137 C7 var. Ban Pak Phanang. Nakhon Si Thammarat, SW Thailand
Pakruojis 106 C4 Šiauliai, N Lithuania
Paks 99 C7 Tolna, S Hungary
Paksé see Pakxé
Pakxé 137 D5 var. Paksé. Champasak, S Laos
Palafrugell 93 G2 Cataluña, NE Spain
Palagruža 101 B5 It. Pelagosa. island SW Croatia
Palaiá Epídavros 105 C6 Pelopónnisos, S Greece
Palaiseau 90 D2 Essonne, N France
Palamós 93 G2 Cataluña, NE Spain
Palamuse 106 E2 Ger. Sankt-Bartholomäi. Jõgevamaa, E Estonia
Palanka see Bačka Palanka
Pālanpur 134 C4 Gujarāt, W India
Palantia see Palencia
Palapye 78 D3 Central, SE Botswana
Palau 144 A2 var. Belau. country W Pacific Ocean

PALAU
Australasia & Oceania

Official name Republic of Palau
Formation 1994 / 1994
Capital Melekeok
Population 21,032 / 107 people per sq mile (41 people per sq km)
Total area 177 sq. miles (458 sq. km)
Languages Palauan*, English*, Japanese, Angaur, Tobi, Sonsorolese
Religions Christian 66%, Modekngei 34%
Ethnic mix Palauan 74%, Filipino 16%, Other 6%, Chinese and other Asian 4%
Government Nonparty system
Currency US dollar = 100 cents
Literacy rate 98%
Calorie consumption Not available

Palawan 139 E2 island W Philippines
Palawan Passage 138 D2 passage W Philippines
Paldiski 106 D2 prev. Baltiski, Eng. Baltic Port, Ger. Baltischport. Harjumaa, NW Estonia
Palembang 138 B4 Sumatera, W Indonesia
Palencia 92 D2 anc. Palantia, Pallantia. Castilla y León, NW Spain
Palerme see Palermo
Palermo 97 C7 Fr. Palerme; anc. Panhormus, Panormus. Sicilia, Italy, C Mediterranean Sea
Pāli 134 C3 Rājasthān, N India
Palikir 144 C2 country capital (Micronesia) Pohnpei, E Micronesia
Palimé see Kpalimé

225

Palioúri, Akrotírio 104 C4 var.
Akrotírio Kanestron. *headland*
N Greece
Palk Strait 132 C3 *strait* India/Sri Lanka
Pallantia *see* Palencia
Palliser, Cape 151 D5 *headland* North
Island, New Zealand
Palma 93 G3 var. Palma de Mallorca.
Mallorca, Spain, W Mediterranean Sea
Palma del Río 92 D4 Andalucía,
S Spain
Palma de Mallorca *see* Palma
Palmar Sur 53 E5 Puntarenas,
SE Costa Rica
Palma Soriano 54 C3 Santiago de Cuba,
E Cuba
Palm Beach 148 E1 New South Wales,
E Australia
Palmer 154 A2 US research station
Antarctica
Palmer Land 154 A3 *physical region*
Antarctica
Palmerston 145 F4 *island*
S Cook Islands
Palmerston *see* Darwin
Palmerston North 150 D4 Manawatu-
Wanganui, North Island, New Zealand
The Palmetto State *see* South Carolina
Palmi 97 D7 Calabria, SW Italy
Palmira 58 B3 Valle del Cauca,
W Colombia
Palm Springs 47 D7 California,
W USA
Palmyra *see* Tudmur
Palmyra Atoll 145 G2 *US privately
owned unincorporated territory*
C Pacific Ocean
Palo Alto 47 B6 California, W USA
Paloe *see* Denpasar, Bali, C Indonesia
Paloe *see* Palu
Palu 139 E4 *prev.* Paloe. Sulawesi,
C Indonesia
Pamiers 91 B6 Ariège, S France
Pamir 123 F3 var. Daryā-ye Pāmīr, Taj.
Dar"yoi Pomir. *river* Afghanistan/
Tajikistan
Pāmir, Daryā-ye *see* Pamir
Pamir/Pāmir, Daryā-ye *see* Pamirs
Pamirs 123 F3 Pash. Daryā-ye Pāmīr,
Rus. Pamir. *mountain range* C Asia
Pāmiut *see* Paamiut
Pamlico Sound 43 G1 *sound* North
Carolina, SE USA
Pampa 49 E1 Texas, SW USA
Pampa Aullagas, Lago *see* Poopó, Lago
Pampas 64 C4 *plain* C Argentina
Pampeluna *see* Pamplona
Pamplona 58 C2 Norte de Santander,
N Colombia
Pamplona 93 E1 Basq. Iruña, prev.
Pampeluna; anc. Pompaelo. Navarra,
N Spain
Panaji 132 B1 var. Pangim, Panjim, New
Goa. *state capital* Goa, W India
Panama 53 G4 var. Ciudad de Panama,
Eng. Panama City. *country capital*
(Panama) Panamá, C Panama
Panama 53 G5 off. Republic of Panama.
country Central America

PANAMA
Central America

Official name Republic of Panama
Formation 1903 / 1903
Capital Panama City
Population 3.6 million / 123 people
per sq mile (47 people per sq km)
Total area 30,193 sq. miles (78,200. sq. km)
Languages English Creole,
Spanish*, Amerindian languages,
Chibchan languages
Religions Roman Catholic 84%,
Protestant 15%, Other 1%
Ethnic mix Mestizo 70%, Black 14%,
White 10%, Amerindian 6%
Government Presidential system
Currency Balboa = 100 céntimos
Literacy rate 94%
Calorie consumption 2606 kilocalories

Panama Basin 35 C8 *undersea feature*
E Pacific Ocean
Panama Canal 53 F4 *canal* E Panama
Panama City 42 D3 Florida, SE USA
Panama City *see* Panama
Gulf of Panama 53 G5 var. Gulf of
Panama. *gulf* S Panama
Panama, Gulf of *see* Panamá, Golfo de

Isthmus of Panama 53 G4 Eng. Isthmus
of Panama; prev. Isthmus of Darien.
isthmus E Panama
Panama, Isthmus of *see* Panama,
Istmo de
Panama, Republic of *see* Panama
Panay Island 139 E2 *island* C Philippines
Pančevo 100 D3 Ger. Pantschowa, Hung.
Pancsova. Vojvodina, N Serbia
Pancsova *see* Pančevo
Paneas *see* Bāniyās
Panevėžys 106 C4 Panevėžys,
C Lithuania
Pangim *see* Panaji
Pangkalpinang 138 C4 Pulau Bangka,
W Indonesia
Pang-Nga *see* Phang-Nga
Panhormus *see* Palermo
Panjim *see* Panaji
Panopolis *see* Akhmîm
Pánormos 105 C7 Kríti, Greece,
E Mediterranean Sea
Panormus *see* Palermo
Pantanal 63 E3 var. Pantanalmato-
Grossense. *swamp* SW Brazil
Pantanalmato-Grossense *see* Pantanal
Pantelleria, Isola di 97 B7 *island*
SW Italy
Pantschowa *see* Pančevo
Pánuco 51 E3 Veracruz-Llave,
E Mexico
Pao-chi/Paoki *see* Baoji
Paola 102 B5 E Malta
Pao-shan *see* Baoshan
Pao-t'ou/Paotow *see* Baotou
Papagayo, Golfo de 52 C4 *gulf*
NW Costa Rica
Papakura 150 D3 Auckland, North
Island, New Zealand
Papantla 51 F4 var. Papantla de Olarte.
Veracruz-Llave, E Mexico
Papantla de Olarte *see* Papantla
Papeete 145 H4 *dependent territory
capital* (French Polynesia) Tahiti,
W French Polynesia
Paphos *see* Páfos
Papile 106 B3 Šiauliai, NW Lithuania
Papillion 45 F4 Nebraska, C USA
Papua 139 H4 var. Irian Barat, West
Irian, West New Guinea, West Papua;
prev. Dutch New Guinea, Irian Jaya,
Netherlands New Guinea. *province*
E Indonesia
Papua and New Guinea, Territory of *see*
Papua New Guinea
Papua, Gulf of 144 B3 *gulf* S Papua
New Guinea
Papua New Guinea 144 B3 off.
Independent State of Papua New
Guinea; prev. Territory of Papua and
New Guinea. *country* NW Melanesia

PAPUA NEW GUINEA
Australasia & Oceania

Official name Independent State
of Papua New Guinea
Formation 1975 / 1975
Capital Port Moresby
Population 7 million / 40 people
per sq mile (15 people per sq km)
Total area 178,703 sq. miles
(462,840 sq. km)
Languages Pidgin English, Papuan,
English*, Motu, 800 (est.) native languages
Religions Protestant 60%, Roman
Catholic 37%, Other 3%
Ethnic mix Melanesian and mixed
race 100%
Government Parliamentary system
Currency Kina = 100 toea
Literacy rate 60%
Calorie consumption 2193 kilocalories

**Papua New Guinea, Independent State
of** *see* Papua New Guinea
Papuk 100 C3 *mountain range*
NE Croatia
Pará 63 E3 off. Estado do Pará. *state*
NE Brazil
Pará 63 E2 off. Estado do Pará. *region*
NE Brazil
Pará *see* Belém
Paracel Islands 125 E3 *disputed territory*
SE Asia
Paraćin 100 D4 Serbia, C Serbia
Pará, Estado do *see* Pará
Paragua, Río 59 E3 *river* SE Venezuela

Paraguay 64 C2 *country* C South
America

PARAGUAY
South America

Official name Republic of Paraguay
Formation 1811 / 1938
Capital Asunción
Population 6.6 million / 43 people
per sq mile (17 people per sq km)
Total area 157,046 sq. miles
(406,750 sq. km)
Languages Guaraní, Spanish*, German
Religions Roman Catholic 90%,
Protestant (including Mennonite) 10%
Ethnic mix Mestizo 91%, Other 7%,
Amerindian 2%
Government Presidential system
Currency Guaraní = 100 céntimos
Literacy rate 95%
Calorie consumption 2518 kilocalories

Paraguay 64 D2 var. Río Paraguay. *river*
C South America
Paraguay, Río *see* Paraguay
Paraíba/Parahyba *see* Paraíba
Paraíba 63 G2 off. Estado da Paraíba;
prev. Parahiba, Parahyba. *state* E Brazil
Paraíba 63 G2 off. Estado da Paraíba;
prev. Parahiba, Parahyba. *region*
E Brazil
Paraíba *see* João Pessoa
Paraíba, Estado da *see* Paraíba
Parakou 75 F4 C Benin
Paramaribo 59 G3 *country capital*
(Suriname) Paramaribo, N Suriname
Paramushir, Ostrov 115 H3 *island*
SE Russian Federation
Paraná 63 E4 Entre Ríos, E Argentina
Paraná 63 E5 off. Estado do Paraná.
state S Brazil
Paraná 63 E5 off. Estado do Paraná.
region S Brazil
Paraná 57 C5 var. Alto Paraná. *river*
C South America
Paraná, Estado do *see* Paraná
Paranésti 104 C3 var. Paranestio.
Anatolikí Makedonía kai Thráki,
NE Greece
Paranestio *see* Paranésti
Paraparaumu 151 D5 Wellington, North
Island, New Zealand
Parchim 94 C3 Mecklenburg-
Vorpommern, N Germany
Parczew 98 E4 Lubelskie, E Poland
Pardubice 99 B5 Ger. Pardubitz.
Pardubický Kraj, C Czech Republic
Pardubitz *see* Pardubice
Parechcha 107 B5 Pol. Porzecze, Rus.
Porech'ye. Hrodzyenskaya Voblasts',
W Belarus
Parecis, Chapada dos 62 D3 var. Serra
dos Parecis. *mountain range* W Brazil
Parecis, Serra dos *see* Parecis, Chapada
dos
Parenzo *see* Poreč
Parepare 139 E4 Sulawesi, C Indonesia
Párga 105 A5 Ípeiros, W Greece
Paria, Golfo de *see* Paria, Gulf of
Paria, Gulf of 59 E1 var. Golfo de Paria.
gulf Trinidad and Tobago/Venezuela
Parika 59 F2 NE Guyana
Paris 90 D1 anc. Lutetia, Lutetia
Parisiorum, Parisii. *country capital*
(France) Paris, N France
Paris 49 G2 Texas, SW USA
Parisii *see* Paris
Parkersburg 40 D4 West Virginia,
NE USA
Parkes 149 D6 New South Wales,
SE Australia
Parkhar *see* Farkhor
Parma 96 B2 Emilia-Romagna, N Italy
Parnahyba *see* Parnaíba
Parnaíba 63 F2 var. Parnahyba. Piauí,
E Brazil
Pärnau *see* Pärnu
Pärnu 106 D2 Ger. Pernau, Latv.
Pērnava; prev. Rus. Pernov. Pärnumaa,
SW Estonia
Pärnu 106 D2 var. Parnu Jõgi, Ger.
Pernau. *river* SW Estonia
Pärnu-Jaagupi 106 D2 Ger. Sankt-
Jakobi. Pärnumaa, SW Estonia
Parnu Jõgi *see* Pärnu
Pärnu Laht 106 D2 Ger. Pernauer Bucht.
bay SW Estonia
Paropamisus Range *see* Sefid Kūh,
Selseleh-ye

Páros 105 C6 *island* Kykládes, Greece,
Aegean Sea
Parral 64 B4 Maule, C Chile
Parral *see* Hidalgo del Parral
Parramatta 148 D1 New South Wales,
SE Australia
Parras 50 D3 var. Parras de la Fuente.
Coahuila, NE Mexico
Parras de la Fuente *see* Parras
Parsons 45 F5 Kansas, C USA
Pasadena 47 C7 California, W USA
Pasadena 49 H4 Texas, SW USA
Pașcani 108 C3 Hung. Páskán. Iași,
NE Romania
Pasco 46 C2 Washington, NW USA
Pasewalk 94 D3 Mecklenburg-
Vorpommern, NE Germany
Pashkeni *see* Bolyarovo
Pasinler 117 F3 Erzurum, NE Turkey
Páskán *see* Pașcani
Pasłęk 98 D2 Ger. Preußisch Holland.
Warmińsko-Mazurskie, NE Poland
Pasni 134 A3 Baluchistān, SW Pakistan
Paso de Indios 65 B6 Chubut,
S Argentina
Passarowitz *see* Požarevac
Passau 95 D6 Bayern, SE Germany
Passo Fundo 63 E5 Rio Grande do
Sul, S Brazil
Pastavy 107 C5 Pol. Postawy, Rus.
Postavy. Vitsyebskaya Voblasts',
NW Belarus
Pastaza, Río 60 B2 *river* Ecuador/Peru
Pasto 58 A4 Nariño, SW Colombia
Pasvalys 106 C4 Panevėžys, N Lithuania
Patagonia 57 B7 *physical region*
Argentina/Chile
Patalung *see* Phatthalung
Patani *see* Pattani
Patavium *see* Padova
Patea 150 D4 Taranaki, North Island,
New Zealand
Paterson 41 F3 New Jersey, NE USA
Pathein 136 A4 var. Bassein.
Ayeyarwady, SW Myanmar (Burma)
Pátmos 105 D6 *island* Dodekánisa,
Greece, Aegean Sea
Patna 135 F3 Azimabad. *state capital*
Bihār, N India
Patnos 117 F3 Ağrı, E Turkey
Patos, Lagoa dos 63 E5 *lagoon*
S Brazil
Pátra 105 B5 Eng. Patras; prev. Pátrai.
Dytikí Elláda, S Greece
Pátrai/Patras *see* Pátra
Pattani 137 C7 var. Patani. Pattani,
SW Thailand
Pattaya 137 C5 Chon Buri, S Thailand
Patuca, Río 52 D2 *river* E Honduras
Pau 91 B6 Pyrénées-Atlantiques,
SW France
Paulatuk 37 E3 Northwest Territories,
NW Canada
Paungde 136 B4 Bago, C Myanmar
(Burma)
Pautalia *see* Kyustendil
Pavia 96 B2 anc. Ticinum. Lombardia,
N Italy
Pāvilosta 106 B3 W Latvia
Pavlikeni 104 D2 Veliko Tŭrnovo,
N Bulgaria
Pavlodar 114 C4 Pavlodar,
NE Kazakhstan
Pavlograd *see* Pavlohrad
Pavlohrad 109 G3 Rus. Pavlograd.
Dnipropetrovs'ka Oblast', E Ukraine
Pawai, Pulau 138 A2 *island*
SW Singapore Asia
Pawn, Nam 136 B3 *river* C Myanmar
(Burma)
Pax Augusta *see* Badajoz
Pax Julia *see* Beja
Paxoí 105 A5 *island* Iónia Nisiá, Greece,
C Mediterranean Sea
Payo Obispo *see* Chetumal
Paysandú 64 D4 Paysandú, W Uruguay
Pazar 117 E2 Rize, NE Turkey
Pazardzhik 104 C3 prev. Tatar
Pazardzhik. Pazardzhik, SW Bulgaria
Peace Garden State *see* North Dakota
Peach State *see* Georgia
Pearl Islands 53 G5 Eng. Pearl Islands.
island group SE Panama
Pearl Islands *see* Perlas, Archipiélago
de las
Pearl Lagoon 53 E3 Eng. Pearl Lagoon.
lagoon E Nicaragua
Pearl Lagoon *see* Perlas, Laguna de

Pearl River *42 B3 river* Louisiana/
Mississippi, S USA
Pearsall *49 F4* Texas, SW USA
Peawanuk *38 C2 river* Ontario, S Canada
Peć *see* Pejë
Pechora *110 D3* Respublika Komi,
NW Russian Federation
Pechora *110 D3 river* NW Russian
Federation
Pechora Sea *110 D2 Eng.* Pechora Sea.
sea NW Russian Federation
Pechora Sea *see* Pechorskoye More
Pecos *49 F3* Texas, SW USA
Pecos River *49 E3 river* New Mexico/
Texas, SW USA
Pécs *99 C7 Ger.* Fünfkirchen, *Lat.*
Sopianae. Baranya, SW Hungary
Pedra Lume *74 A3* Sal, NE Cape Verde
Pedro Cays *54 C3 island group* Greater
Antilles, S Jamaica North America
N Caribbean Sea W Atlantic Ocean
Pedro Juan Caballero *64 D2* Amambay,
E Paraguay
Peer *87 D5* Limburg, NE Belgium
Pegasus Bay *151 C6 bay* South Island,
New Zealand
Pegu *see* Bago
Pehuajó *64 C4* Buenos Aires, E Argentina
Pei-ching *see* Beijing/Beijing Shi
Peine *94 B3* Niedersachsen, C Germany
Pei-p'ing *see* Beijing/Beijing Shi
Peipsi Järv/Peipus-See *see* Peipus, Lake
Peipus, Lake *106 E3 Est.* Peipsi Järv, *Ger.*
Peipus-See, *Rus.* Chudskoye Ozero.
lake Estonia/Russian Federation
Peiraiás *105 C6 prev.* Piraiévs, *Eng.*
Piraeus. Attikí, C Greece
Pejë *101 D5 Serb.* Peć. W Kosovo
Pēk *see* Phônsaven
Pekalongan *138 C4* Jawa, C Indonesia
Pekanbaru *138 B3 var.* Pakanbaru.
Sumatera, W Indonesia
Pekin *40 B4* Illinois, N USA
Peking *see* Beijing/Beijing Shi
Pelagie *97 B8 island group* SW Italy
Pelagosa *see* Palagruža
Pelican State *see* Louisiana
Pelly Bay *see* Kugaaruk
Pélmonostor *see* Beli Manastir
Peloponnese *105 B6 var.* Morea, *Eng.*
Peloponnese; *anc.* Peloponnesus.
peninsula S Greece
Peloponnese/Peloponnesus *see*
Pelopónnisos
Pematangsiantar *138 B3* Sumatera,
W Indonesia
Pemba *79 F2 prev.* Port Amelia,
Porto Amélia. Cabo Delgado,
NE Mozambique
Pemba *73 D7 island* E Tanzania
Pembroke *38 D4* Ontario, SE Canada
Penang *see* Pinang, Pulau, Peninsular
Malaysia
Penang *see* George Town
Penas, Golfo de *65 A7 gulf* S Chile
Penderma *see* Bandırma
Pendleton *46 C3* Oregon, NW USA
Pend Oreille, Lake *46 D2 lake* Idaho,
NW USA
Peneius *see* Pineiós
Peng-pu *see* Bengbu
Penibético, Sistema *see* Béticos, Sistemas
Peniche *92 B3* Leiria, W Portugal
Peninsular State *see* Florida
Pennine, Alpes/Pennine, Alpi *see*
Pennine Alps
Pennine Alps *95 A8 Fr.* Alpes Pennines,
It. Alpi Pennine, *Lat.* Alpes Penninae.
mountain range Italy/Switzerland
Pennine Chain *see* Pennines
Pennines *89 D5 var.* Pennine Chain.
mountain range N England, United
Kingdom
Pennines, Alpes *see* Pennine Alps
Pennsylvania *41 E4 off.* Commonwealth
of Pennsylvania, *also known as*
Keystone State. *state* NE USA
Penobscot River *41 G2 river* Maine,
NE USA
Penong *149 A6* South Australia
Penonomé *53 F5* Coclé, C Panama
Penrhyn *145 G3 atoll* N Cook Islands
Penrhyn Basin *143 F3 undersea feature*
C Pacific Ocean
Penrith *148 D1* New South Wales,
SE Australia
Penrith *89 D5* NW England, United
Kingdom

Pensacola *42 C3* Florida, SE USA
Pentecost *144 D4 Fr.* Pentecôte. *island*
C Vanuatu
Pentecôte *see* Pentecost
Penza *111 C6* Penzenskaya Oblast',
W Russian Federation
Penzance *89 C7* SW England, United
Kingdom
Peoria *40 B4* Illinois, N USA
Perchtoldsdorf *95 E6* Niederösterreich,
NE Austria
Percival Lakes *146 C4 lakes* Western
Australia
Perdido, Monte *93 F1 mountain*
NE Spain
Perece Vela Basin *see* West Mariana
Basin
Pereira *58 B3* Risaralda, W Colombia
Peremyshl *see* Przemyśl
Pergamino *64 C4* Buenos Aires,
E Argentina
Périgueux *91 C5 anc.* Vesuna.
Dordogne, SW France
Perito Moreno *65 B6* Santa Cruz,
S Argentina
Perleberg *94 C3* Brandenburg,
N Germany
Perlepe *see* Prilep
Perm' *114 C3 prev.* Molotov. Permskiy
Kray, NW Russian Federation
Pernambuco *63 G2 off.* Estado de
Pernambuco. *region* E Brazil
Pernambuco *63 G2 off.* Estado de
Pernambuco. *state* E Brazil
Pernambuco *see* Recife
Pernambuco Abyssal Plain *see*
Pernambuco Plain
Pernambuco, Estado de *see*
Pernambuco
Pernambuco Plain *67 C5 var.*
Pernambuco Abyssal Plain. *undersea
feature* E Atlantic Ocean
Pernau *see* Pärnu
Pernauer Bucht *see* Pärnu Laht
Pērnava *see* Pärnu
Pernik *104 B2 prev.* Dimitrovo. Pernik,
W Bulgaria
Pernov *see* Pärnu
Perote *51 F4* Veracruz-Llave, E Mexico
Pérouse *see* Perugia
Perovsk *see* Kyzylorda
Perpignan *91 C6* Pyrénées-Orientales,
S France
Perryton *49 F1* Texas, SW USA
Perryville *45 H5* Missouri, C USA
Persia *see* Iran
Persian Gulf *120 C4 var.* Gulf, The,
Ar. Khalīj al 'Arabī, *Per.* Khalīj-e Fars.
gulf SW Asia
Perth *147 A6 state capital* Western
Australia
Perth *88 C4* C Scotland,
United Kingdom
Perth Basin *141 E6 undersea feature*
SE Indian Ocean
Peru *60 C3 off.* Republic of Peru. *country*
S South America

PERU
South America

Official name Republic of Peru
Formation 1824 / 1941
Capital Lima
Population 29.4 million / 59 people
per sq mile (23 people per sq km)
Total area 496,223 sq. miles
(1,285,200 sq. km)
Languages Spanish*, Quechua*, Aymara
Religions Roman Catholic 81%, Other 19%
Ethnic mix Amerindian 45%,
Mestizo 37%, White 15%, Other 3%
Government Presidential system
Currency New sol = 100 céntimos
Literacy rate 90%
Calorie consumption 2563 kilocalories

Peru *see* Beru
Peru Basin *67 A5 undersea feature*
E Pacific Ocean
Peru-Chile Trench *56 A4 undersea
feature* E Pacific Ocean
Perugia *96 C4 Fr.* Pérouse; *anc.* Perusia.
Umbria, C Italy
Perugia, Lake of *see* Trasimeno, Lago
Peru, Republic of *see* Peru
Perusia *see* Perugia
Péruwelz *87 B6* Hainaut, SW Belgium

Pervomays'k *109 E3 prev.* Ol'viopol'.
Mykolayivs'ka Oblast', S Ukraine
Pervyy Kuril'skiy Proliv *115 H3 strait*
E Russian Federation
Pesaro *96 C3 anc.* Pisaurum. Marche,
C Italy
Pescara *96 D4 anc.* Aternum, Ostia
Aterni. Abruzzo, C Italy
Peshāwar *134 C1* Khyber Pakhtunkhwa,
N Pakistan
Peshkopi *101 C6 var.* Peshkopia,
Peshkopija. Dibër, NE Albania
Peshkopia/Peshkopija *see* Peshkopi
Pessac *91 B5* Gironde, SW France
Petach-Tikva *see* Petah Tikva
Petah Tikva *119 A6 var.* Petach-Tikva,
Petah Tiqva, Petakh Tikva; *prev.* Petaẖ
Tiqwa. Tel Aviv, C Israel
Petah Tiqwa *see* Petah Tikva
Petakh Tikva/Petah Tiqva *see* Petah
Tikva
Pétange *87 D8* Luxembourg,
SW Luxembourg
Petchaburi *see* Phetchaburi
Peterborough *149 B6* South Australia
Peterborough *38 D5* Ontario, SE Canada
Peterborough *89 E6 prev.*
Medeshamstede. E England, United
Kingdom
Peterhead *88 D3* NE Scotland, United
Kingdom
Peter I Øy *154 A3 Norwegian
dependency* Antarctica
Petermann Bjerg *83 E3 mountain*
C Greenland
Petersburg *41 E5* Virginia, NE USA
Peters Mine *59 F3 var.* Peter's Mine.
N Guyana
Petit St-Bernard, Col du *see* Little Saint
Bernard Pass
Peto *51 H4* Yucatán, SE Mexico
Petoskey *40 C2* Michigan, N USA
Petra *see* Wādī Mūsā
Petrich *104 C3* Blagoevgrad,
SW Bulgaria
Petrikau *see* Piotrków Trybunalski
Petrikov *see* Pyetrykaw
Petrinja *100 B3* Sisak-Moslavina,
C Croatia
Petroaleksandrovsk *see* To'rtko'l
Petrodvorets *110 B4 Fin.* Pietarhovi.
Leningradskaya Oblast', NW Russian
Federation
Petrograd *see* Sankt-Peterburg
Petrokov *see* Piotrków Trybunalski
Petropavl *114 C4 Kaz.* Petropavl.
Severnyy Kazakhstan, N Kazakhstan
Petropavlovsk-Kamchatskiy *115
H3* Kamchatskiy Kray, E Russian
Federation
Petropavlovsk *see* Petropavl
Petroşani *108 B4 var.* Petroşeni,
Ger. Petroschen, *Hung.* Petrozsény.
Hunedoara, W Romania
Petroschen/Petroşeni *see* Petroşani
Petroskoi *see* Petrozavodsk
Petrovgrad *see* Zrenjanin
Petrovsk-Port *see* Makhachkala
Petrozavodsk *114 B2 Fin.* Petroskoi.
Respublika Kareliya, NW Russian
Federation
Petrozsény *see* Petroşani
Pettau *see* Ptuj
Pevek *115 G1* Chukotskiy Avtonomnyy
Okrug, NE Russian Federation
Pezinok *99 C6 Ger.* Bösing, *Hung.* Bazin.
Bratislavský Kraj, W Slovakia
Pforzheim *95 B6* Baden-Württemberg,
SW Germany
Pfungstadt *95 B5* Hessen, W Germany
Phangan, Ko *137 C6 island* SW Thailand
Phang-Nga *137 B7 var.* Pang-Nga,
Phangnga. Phangnga, SW Thailand
Phangnga *see* Phang-Nga
Phan Rang/Phanrang *see* Phan Rang-
Thap Cham
Phan Rang-Thap Cham *137 E6 var.*
Phanrang, Phan Rang, Phan Rang
Thap Cham. Ninh Thuận, S Vietnam
Phan Thiết *137 E6* Bình Thuận,
S Vietnam
Pharnacia *see* Giresun
Pharus *see* Hvar
Phatthalung *137 C7 var.* Padalung,
Patalung. Phatthalung, SW Thailand
Phayao *136 C4 var.* Muang Phayao.
Phayao, NW Thailand
Phenix City *42 D2* Alabama, S USA
Phet Buri *see* Phetchaburi

Phetchaburi *137 C5 var.* Bejraburi,
Petchaburi, Phet Buri. Phetchaburi,
SW Thailand
Philadelphia *41 F4* Pennsylvania,
NE USA
Philadelphia *see* 'Amman
Philippine Basin *125 F3 undersea
feature* W Pacific Ocean
Philippine Islands *139 E1 island group*
W Pacific Ocean
Philippines *139 E1 off.* Republic of the
Philippines. *country* SE Asia

PHILIPPINES
Southeast Asia

Official name Republic of the Philippines
Formation 1946 / 1946
Capital Manila
Population 84.9 million / 824 people
per sq mile (318 people per sq km)
Total area 115,830 sq. miles
(300,000 sq. km)
Languages Filipino, English, Tagalog,
Cebuano, Ilocano, Hiligaynon, many
other local languages
Religions Roman Catholic 81%,
Protestant 9%, Muslim 5%,
Other (including Buddhist) 5%
Ethnic mix Other 34%, Tagalog 28%,
Cebuano 13%, Ilocano 9%, Hiligaynon 8%,
Bisaya 8%
Government Presidential system
Currency Philippine peso = 100 centavos
Literacy rate 95%
Calorie consumption 2580 kilocalories

Philippine Sea *125 F3 sea* W Pacific
Ocean
Philippines, Republic of the *see*
Philippines
Philippine Trench *142 A1 undersea
feature* W Philippine Sea
Philippopolis *see* Plovdiv
Phitsanulok *136 C4 var.* Bisnulok,
Muang Phitsanulok, Pitsanulok.
Phitsanulok, C Thailand
Phlórina *see* Flórina
Phnom Penh *see* Phnum Penh
Phnum Penh *137 D6 var.* Phnom
Penh. *country capital* (Cambodia)
Phnum Penh,
S Cambodia
Phoenix *48 B2 state capital* Arizona,
SW USA
Phoenix Islands *145 E3 island group*
C Kiribati
Phôngsali *136 C3 var.* Phong Saly.
Phôngsali, N Laos
Phong Saly *see* Phôngsali
Phônsaven *136 D4 var.* Pēk, Xieng
Khouang; *prev.* Xiangkhoang.
Xiangkhoang, N Laos
Phou Louang *see* Annamite Mountains
Phrae *136 C4 var.* Muang Phrae, Prae.
Phrae, NW Thailand
Phra Nakhon Si Ayutthaya *see*
Ayutthaya
Phra Thong, Ko *137 B6 island*
SW Thailand
Phuket *137 B7 var.* Bhuket, Puket, *Mal.*
Ujung Salang; *prev.* Junkseylon, Salang.
Phuket, SW Thailand
Phuket, Ko *137 B7 island* SW Thailand
Phumĭ Kâmpóng Trâbêk *see* Kâmpóng
Trâbêk
Phumĭ Sâmraông *see* Sâmraông
Phum Kompong Trabek *see* Kâmpóng
Trâbêk
Phum Samrong *see* Sâmraông
Phu Vinh *see* Tra Vinh
Phyu *136 B4 var.* Hpyu, Pyu. Bago,
C Myanmar (Burma)
Piacenza *96 B2 Fr.* Paisance; *anc.*
Placentia. Emilia-Romagna, N Italy
Piatra-Neamţ *108 C4 Hung.*
Karácsonkő. Neamţ, NE Romania
Piauhy *see* Piauí
Piauí *63 F2 off.* Estado do Piauí; *prev.*
Piauhy. *state* E Brazil
Piauí *63 F2 off.* Estado do Piauí; *prev.*
Piauhy. *region* E Brazil
Piauí, Estado do *see* Piauí
Picardie *90 C3 Eng.* Picardy. *cultural
region* N France
Picardy *see* Picardie
Piccolo San Bernardo, Colle di *see* Little
Saint Bernard Pass
Pichilemu *64 B4* Libertador, C Chile

Pico *92 A5 var.* Ilha do Pico. *island*
Azores, Portugal, NE Atlantic Ocean
Pico, Ilha do *see* Pico
Picos *63 F2* Piauí, E Brazil
Picton *151 C5* Marlborough, South
Island, New Zealand
Piedmont *see* Piemonte
Piedras Negras *51 E2 var.* Ciudad
Porfírio Díaz. Coahuila, NE Mexico
Pielavesi *84 D4 lake* C Finland
Pielinen *84 E4 var.* Pielisjärvi. *lake*
E Finland
Pielisjärvi *see* Pielinen
Piemonte *96 A2 Eng.* Piedmont. *region*
NW Italy
Pierre *45 E3 state capital* South Dakota,
N USA
Pieštany *99 C6 Ger.* Pistyan, *Hung.*
Pöstyén. Tranavský Kraj, W Slovakia
Pietarhovi *see* Petrodvorets
Pietari *see* Sankt-Peterburg
Pietarsaari *see* Jakobstad
Pietermaritzburg *78 C5 var.*
Maritzburg. KwaZulu/Natal, E South
Africa
Pietersburg *see* Polokwane
Bay of Pigs *54 B2 Eng.* Bay of Pigs. *bay*
SE Cuba
Pigs, Bay of *see* Cochinos, Bahía de
Pihkva Järv *see* Pskov, Lake
Pijijiapán *51 G5* Chiapas, SE Mexico
Pikes Peak *44 C5 mountain* Colorado,
C USA
Pikeville *40 D5* Kentucky, S USA
Pikinni *see* Bikini Atoll
Piła *98 B3 Ger.* Schneidemühl.
Wielkopolskie, C Poland
Pilar *64 D3 var.* Villa del Pilar.
Ñeembucú, S Paraguay
Pilcomayo, Rio *57 C5 river* C South
America
Pílos *see* Pýlos
Pilsen *see* Plzeň
Pilzno *see* Plzeň
Pinang *see* Pinang, Pulau, Peninsular
Malaysia
Pinang *see* George Town
Pinang, Pulau *138 B3 var.* Penang,
Pinang; *prev.* Prince of Wales Island.
island Peninsular Malaysia
Pinar del Río *54 A2* Pinar del Río,
W Cuba
Píndhos/Píndhos Óros *see* Píndos
Pindus Mountains *104 A4 var.* Píndhos
Óros, *Eng.* Pindus Mountains; *prev.*
Píndhos. *mountain range* C Greece
Pindus Mountains *see* Píndos
Pine Bluff *42 B2* Arkansas, C USA
Pine Creek *146 D2* Northern Territory,
N Australia
Pinega *110 C3 river* NW Russian
Federation
Pineiós *104 B4 var.* Piniós; *anc.* Peneius.
river C Greece
Pineland *49 H3* Texas, SW USA
Pínes, Akrotírio *104 C4 var.* Akrotírio
Pínnes. *headland* N Greece
Pines, The Isle of the *see* Juventud,
Isla de la
Pine Tree State *see* Maine
Pingdingshan *128 C4* Henan, C China
Pingkiang *see* Harbin
Ping, Mae Nam *136 B4 river* W Thailand
Piniós *see* Pineiós
Pinkiang *see* Harbin
Pínnes, Akrotírio *see* Pínes, Akrotírio
Pinos, Isla de *see* Juventud, Isla de la
Pinotepa Nacional *51 F5 var.* Santiago
Pinotepa Nacional. Oaxaca, SE Mexico
Pinsk *107 B7 Pol.* Pińsk. Brestskaya
Voblasts', SW Belarus
Pinta, Isla *57 A5 var.* Abingdon. *island*
Galápagos Islands, Ecuador, E Pacific
Ocean
Piombino *96 B3* Toscana, C Italy
Pioneer Mountains *46 D3 mountain
range* Montana, N USA North America
Pionerskiy *106 A4 Ger.* Neukuhren.
Kaliningradskaya Oblast', W Russian
Federation
Piotrków Trybunalski *98 D4 Ger.*
Petrikau, *Rus.* Petrokov. Łódzkie,
C Poland
Piraeus/Piraiévs *see* Peiraiás
Pírgos *see* Pýrgos
Pirineos *see* Pyrenees
Piripiri *63 F2* Piauí, E Brazil
Pirna *94 D4* Sachsen, E Germany
Pirot *101 E5* Serbia, SE Serbia

Piryatin *see* Pyryatyn
Pisa *96 B3 var.* Pisae. Toscana, C Italy
Pisae *see* Pisa
Pisaurum *see* Pesaro
Pisco *60 D4* Ica, SW Peru
Písek *99 A5* Budějovický Kraj, S Czech
Republic
Pishan *126 A3 var.* Guma. Xinjiang
Uygur Zizhiqu, NW China
Pishpek *see* Bishkek
Pistoia *96 B3 anc.* Pistoria, Pistoriæ.
Toscana, C Italy
Pistoria/Pistoriæ *see* Pistoia
Pistyan *see* Piešt'any
Pisz *98 D3 Ger.* Johannisburg.
Warmińsko-Mazurskie, NE Poland
Pita *74 C4* NW Guinea
Pitalito *58 B4* Huila, S Colombia
Pitcairn Island *143 G4 island* S Pitcairn
Islands
Pitcairn Islands *143 G4 UK dependent
territory* C Pacific Ocean
Piteå *84 D4* Norrbotten, N Sweden
Piteşti *108 B5* Argeş, S Romania
Pitsanulok *see* Phitsanulok
Pitt Island *see* Makin
Pittsburg *45 F5* Kansas, C USA
Pittsburgh *41 E4* Pennsylvania, NE USA
Pittsfield *41 F3* Massachusetts, NE USA
Piura *60 B2* Piura, NW Peru
Pivdennyy Buh *109 E3 Rus.* Yuzhnyy
Bug. *river* S Ukraine
Placentia *see* Piacenza
Placetas *54 B2* Villa Clara, C Cuba
Plainview *49 E2* Texas, SW USA
Planeta Rica *58 B2* Córdoba,
NW Colombia
Planken *94 E1* C Liechtenstein Europe
Plano *49 G2* Texas, SW USA
Plasencia *92 C3* Extremadura, W Spain
Plate, River *64 D4 var.* River Plate.
estuary Argentina/Uruguay
Plate, River *see* Plata, Rio de la
Platinum *36 C3* Alaska, USA
Plattensee *see* Balaton
Platte River *45 E4 river* Nebraska, C USA
Plattsburgh *41 F2* New York, NE USA
Plauen *95 C5 var.* Plauen im Vogtland.
Sachsen, E Germany
Plauen im Vogtland *see* Plauen
Pļaviņas *106 D4 Ger.* Stockmannshof.
S Latvia
Plây Cu *see* Plei Ku
Pleasant Island *see* Nauru
Plei Ku *137 E5 prev.* Plây Cu. Gia Lai,
C Vietnam
Plenty, Bay of *150 E3 bay* North Island,
New Zealand
Plérin *90 A3* Côtes d'Armor, NW France
Plesetsk *110 C3* Arkhangel'skaya Oblast',
NW Russian Federation
Pleshchenitsy *see* Plyeshchanitsy
Pleskau *see* Pskov
Pleskauer See *see* Pskov, Lake
Pleskava *see* Pskov
Pleszew *98 C4* Wielkopolskie, C Poland
Pleven *104 C2 prev.* Plevna. Pleven,
N Bulgaria
Plevlja/Plevlje *see* Pljevlja
Plevna *see* Pleven
Pljevlja *100 C4 prev.* Plevlja, Plevlje.
N Montenegro
Plocce *see* Ploče
Ploče *100 B4 It.* Plocce; *prev.* Kardeljevo.
Dubrovnik-Neretva, SE Croatia
Płock *98 D3 Ger.* Plozk. Mazowieckie,
C Poland
Plöcken Pass *95 C7 Ger.* Plöckenpass,
It. Passo di Monte Croce Carnico. *pass*
SW Austria
Plöckenpass *see* Plöcken Pass
Ploeşti *see* Ploieşti
Ploieşti *108 C5 prev.* Ploeşti. Prahova,
SE Romania
Plomári *105 D5 prev.* Plomárion.
Lésvos, E Greece
Plomárion *see* Plomári
Płońsk *98 D3* Mazowieckie, C Poland
Plovdiv *104 C3 prev.* Eumolpias;
anc. Evmolpia, Philippopolis, *Lat.*
Trimontium. Plovdiv, C Bulgaria
Plozk *see* Płock
Plungė *106 B3* Telšiai, W Lithuania
Plyeshchanitsy *107 D5 Rus.*
Pleshchenitsy. Minskaya Voblasts',
N Belarus
Plymouth *89 C7* SW England, United
Kingdom
Plymouth *see* Brades

Plzeň *99 A5 Ger.* Pilsen, *Pol.* Pilzno.
Plzeňský Kraj, W Czech Republic
Po *80 D4 river* N Italy
Pobedy, Pik *126 B3 Chin.* Tomür Feng.
mountain China/Kyrgyzstan
Po, Bocche del *see* Po, Foci del
Pocahontas *42 B1* Arkansas, C USA
Pocatello *46 E4* Idaho, NW USA
Pochinok *111 A5* Smolenskaya Oblast',
W Russian Federation
Pocking *95 D6* Bayern, SE Germany
Poděbrady *99 B5 Ger.* Podiebrad.
Středočeský Kraj, C Czech Republic
Podgorica *101 C5 prev.* Titograd.
country capital (Montenegro)
S Montenegro
Podiebrad *see* Poděbrady
Podil's'ka Vysochina *108 D3 plateau*
W Ukraine
Podium Anicensis *see* le Puy
Podol'sk *111 B5* Moskovskaya Oblast',
W Russian Federation
Podravska Slatina *see* Slatina
Podujevě *101 D5 Serb.* Podujevo.
N Kosovo
Podujevo *see* Podujevě
Podunajská Rovina *see* Little Alföld
Poetovio *see* Ptuj
Pogradec *101 D6 var.* Pogradeci. Korçë,
SE Albania
Pogradeci *see* Pogradec
Pohjanlahti *see* Bothnia, Gulf of
Pohnpei *144 C2 prev.* Ponape Ascension
Island. *island* E Micronesia
Poictiers *see* Poitiers
Poinsett, Cape *154 D4 headland*
Antarctica
Point de Galle *see* Galle
Pointe-à-Pitre *55 G3* Grande Terre,
C Guadeloupe
Pointe-Noire *77 B6* Kouilou, S Congo
Point Lay *36 C2* Alaska, USA
Poitiers *90 B4 anc.* Poictiers; *anc.*
Limonum. Vienne, W France
Poitou *90 B4 cultural region* W France
Pokhará *135 E3* Western, C Nepal
Pokrovka *see* Kyzyl-Suu
Pokrov's'ke *109 G3 Rus.* Pokrovskoye.
Dnipropetrovs'ka Oblast', E Ukraine
Pokrovskoye *see* Pokrov's'ke
Pola *see* Pula
Pola de Lena *see* La Pola
Poland *98 B4 off.* Republic of Poland,
var. Polish Republic, *Pol.* Polska,
Rzeczpospolita Polska; *prev. Pol.* Polish
Rzeczpospolita Ludowa, The Polish
People's Republic. *country* C Europe

POLAND
Northern Europe

Official name Republic of Poland
Formation 1918 / 1945
Capital Warsaw
Population 38.3 million / 326 people
per sq mile (126 people per sq km)
Total area 120,728 sq. miles
(312,685 sq. km)
Languages Polish*
Religions Roman Catholic 93%, Other and
nonreligious 5%, Orthodox Christian 2%
Ethnic mix Polish 98%, Other 2%
Government Parliamentary system
Currency Zloty = 100 groszy
Literacy rate 99%
Calorie consumption 3392 kilocalories

Poland, Republic of *see* Poland
Polatlı *116 C3* Ankara, C Turkey
Polatsk *107 D5 Rus.* Polotsk.
Vitsyebskaya Voblasts', N Belarus
Pol-e Khomrī *see* Pol-e Khumrī
Poli *see* Pólis
Polikastro/Polikastron *see* Polýkastro
Polikrayshte *104 D2* Veliko Türnovo,
N Bulgaria
Pólis *102 C5 var.* Poli. W Cyprus
Polish People's Republic, The *see*
Poland
Polish Republic *see* Poland
Polkowice *98 B4 Ger.* Heerwegen.
Dolnośląskie, SW Poland
Pollença *93 G3* Mallorca, Spain,
W Mediterranean Sea
Pologi *see* Polohy
Polohy *109 G3 Rus.* Pologi. Zaporiz'ka
Oblast', SE Ukraine
Polokwane *78 D4 prev.* Pietersburg.
Limpopo, NE South Africa

Polonne *108 D2 Rus.* Polonnoye.
Khmel'nyts'ka Oblast', NW Ukraine
Polonnoye *see* Polonne
Polotsk *see* Polatsk
**Polska/Polska, Rzeczpospolita/Polska
Rzeczpospolita Ludowa** *see* Poland
Polsko Kosovo *104 C2* Ruse, N Bulgaria
Poltava *109 F2* Poltavs'ka Oblast',
NE Ukraine
Poltoratsk *see* Aşgabat
Põlva *106 E3 Ger.* Pölwe. Põlvamaa,
SE Estonia
Põlwe *see* Põlva
Polyarnyy *110 C2* Murmanskaya Oblast',
NW Russian Federation
Polýkastro *104 B3 var.* Polikastro; *prev.*
Polikastron. Kentrikí Makedonía,
N Greece
Polynesia *143 F4 island group* C Pacific
Ocean
Pomeranian Bay *94 D2 Ger.*
Pommersche Bucht, *Pol.* Zatoka
Pomorska. *bay* Germany/Poland
Pomir, Dar"yoi *see* Pamir/Pāmir,
Darya-ye
Pommersche Bucht *see* Pomeranian Bay
Pomorska, Zatoka *see* Pomeranian Bay
Pomorskiy Proliv *110 D2 strait*
NW Russian Federation
Po, Mouth of the *96 C2 var.* Bocche del
Po. *river* NE Italy
Pompaelo *see* Pamplona
Pompano Beach *43 F5* Florida, SE USA
Ponape Ascension Island *see* Pohnpei
Ponca City *49 G1* Oklahoma, C USA
Ponce *55 F3* C Puerto Rico
Pondicherry *132 C2 var.* Puducherri,
Fr. Pondichéry. Pondicherry, SE India
Ponferrada *92 C1* Castilla y León,
NW Spain
Poniatowa *98 E4* Lubelskie, E Poland
Pons Aelii *see* Newcastle upon Tyne
Pons Vetus *see* Pontevedra
Ponta Delgada *92 B5* São Miguel,
Azores, Portugal, NE Atlantic Ocean
Ponta Grossa *63 E4* Paraná, S Brazil
Pontarlier *90 D4* Doubs, E France
Ponteareas *92 B2* Galicia, NW Spain
Ponte da Barca *92 B2* Viana do Castelo,
N Portugal
Pontevedra *92 B1 anc.* Pons Vetus.
Galicia, NW Spain
Pontiac *40 D3* Michigan, N USA
Pontianak *138 C4* Borneo, C Indonesia
Pontisarae *see* Pontoise
Pontivy *90 A3* Morbihan, NW France
Pontoise *90 C3 anc.* Briva Isarae, Cergy-
Pontoise, Pontisarae. Val-d'Oise,
N France
Ponziane Island *97 C5 island* C Italy
Poole *89 D7* S England, United Kingdom
Poona *see* Pune
Poopó, Lago *61 F4 var.* Lago Pampa
Aullagas. *lake* W Bolivia
Popayán *58 B4* Cauca, SW Colombia
Poperinge *87 A6* West-Vlaanderen,
W Belgium
Poplar Bluff *45 G5* Missouri, C USA
Popocatépetl *51 E4 volcano* S Mexico
Popper *see* Poprad
Poprad *99 D5 Ger.* Deutschendorf,
Hung. Poprád. Prešovský Kraj,
E Slovakia
Poprád *99 D5 Ger.* Popper, *Hung.*
Poprád. *river* Poland/Slovakia
Porbandar *134 B4* Gujarāt, W India
Porcupine Plain *80 B3 undersea feature*
E Atlantic Ocean
Pordenone *96 C2 anc.* Portenau. Friuli-
Venezia Giulia, NE Italy
Poreč *100 A2 It.* Parenzo. Istra,
NW Croatia
Porech'ye *see* Parechcha
Pori *85 D5 Swe.* Björneborg. Länsi-
Suomi, SW Finland
Porirua *151 D5* Wellington, North
Island, New Zealand
Porkhov *110 A4* Pskovskaya Oblast',
W Russian Federation
Porlamar *59 E1* Nueva Esparta,
NE Venezuela
Póros *105 C6* Póros, S Greece
Póros *105 A5* Kefallinía, Iónia Nisiá,
Greece, C Mediterranean Sea
Porsangenfjorden *84 D2 Lapp.*
Porsáŋgguvuotna. *fjord* N Norway
Porsáŋgguvuotna *see* Porsangenfjorden
Porsgrunn *85 B6* Telemark, S Norway
Portachuelo *61 G4* Santa Cruz, C Bolivia

Portadown 89 B5 *Ir.* Port An Dúnáin. S Northern Ireland, United Kingdom
Portalegre 92 C3 *anc.* Ammaia, Amoea. Portalegre, E Portugal
Port Alexander 36 D4 Baranof Island, Alaska, USA
Port Alfred 78 D5 Eastern Cape, S South Africa
Port Amelia *see* Pemba
Port An Dúnáin *see* Portadown
Port Angeles 46 B1 Washington, NW USA
Port Antonio 54 B5 NE Jamaica
Port Arthur 49 H4 Texas, SW USA
Port Augusta 149 B6 South Australia
Port-au-Prince 54 D3 *country capital* (Haiti) C Haiti
Port Blair 133 F2 Andaman and Nicobar Islands, SE India
Port Charlotte 43 E4 Florida, SE USA
Port Darwin *see* Darwin
Port d'Envalira 91 B8 E Andorra Europe
Port Douglas 148 D3 Queensland, NE Australia
Port Elizabeth 78 C5 Eastern Cape, S South Africa
Portenau *see* Pordenone
Porterville 47 C7 California, W USA
Port-Étienne *see* Nouâdhibou
Port Florence *see* Kisumu
Port-Francqui *see* Ilebo
Port-Gentil 77 A6 Ogooué-Maritime, W Gabon
Port Harcourt 75 G5 Rivers, S Nigeria
Port Hardy 36 D5 Vancouver Island, British Columbia, SW Canada
Port Harrison *see* Inukjuak
Port Hedland 146 B4 Western Australia
Port Huron 40 D3 Michigan, N USA
Portimão 92 B4 *var.* Vila Nova de Portimão. Faro, S Portugal
Port Jackson 148 E1 *harbour* New South Wales, E Australia
Portland 149 B7 Victoria, SE Australia
Portland 41 G2 Maine, NE USA
Portland 46 B3 Oregon, NW USA
Portland 49 G4 Texas, SW USA
Portland Bight 54 B5 *bay* S Jamaica
Portlaoighise *see* Port Laoise
Port Laoise 89 B6 *var.* Portlaoise, *Ir.* Portlaoighise; *prev.* Maryborough. C Ireland
Portlaoise *see* Port Laoise
Port Lavaca 49 G4 Texas, SW USA
Port Lincoln 149 A6 South Australia
Port Louis 79 H3 *country capital* (Mauritius) NW Mauritius
Port-Lyautey *see* Kénitra
Port Macquarie 149 E6 New South Wales, SE Australia
Port Mahon *see* Maó
Portmore 54 B5 C Jamaica
Port Moresby 144 B3 *country capital* (Papua New Guinea) Central/National Capital District, SW Papua New Guinea
Port Natal *see* Durban
Porto 92 B2 *Eng.* Oporto; *anc.* Portus Cale. Porto, NW Portugal
Porto Alegre 63 E5 *var.* Pôrto Alegre. *state capital* Rio Grande do Sul, S Brazil
Porto Alegre 76 E2 São Tomé, S Sao Tome and Principe, Africa
Porto Alegre 76 E2 São Tomé, S Sao Tome and Principe, Africa
Porto Alexandre *see* Tombua
Porto Amélia *see* Pemba
Porto Bello *see* Portobelo
Portobelo 53 G4 *var.* Porto Bello, Puerto Bello. Colón, N Panama
Port O'Connor 49 G4 Texas, SW USA
Porto Edda *see* Sarandë
Portoferraio 96 B4 Toscana, C Italy
Port-of-Spain 55 H5 *country capital* (Trinidad and Tobago) Trinidad, Trinidad and Tobago
Porto Grande *see* Mindelo
Portogruaro 96 C2 Veneto, NE Italy
Porto-Novo 75 F5 *country capital* (Benin) S Benin
Porto Rico *see* Puerto Rico
Porto Santo 70 A2 *var.* Ilha do Porto Santo. *island* Madeira, Portugal, NE Atlantic Ocean
Porto Santo, Ilha do *see* Porto Santo
Porto Torres 97 A5 Sardegna, Italy, C Mediterranean Sea

Porto Velho 62 D2 *var.* Velho. *state capital* Rondônia, W Brazil
Portoviejo 60 A2 *var.* Puertoviejo. Manabí, W Ecuador
Port Pirie 149 B6 South Australia
Port Rex *see* East London
Port Said *see* Bûr Sa'îd
Portsmouth 89 D7 S England, United Kingdom
Portsmouth 41 G3 New Hampshire, NE USA
Portsmouth 40 D4 Ohio, N USA
Portsmouth 41 F5 Virginia, NE USA
Port Stanley *see* Stanley
Port Sudan 72 C3 Red Sea, NE Sudan
Port Swettenham *see* Klang/Pelabuhan Klang
Port Talbot 89 C7 S Wales, United Kingdom
Portugal 92 B3 *off.* Portuguese Republic. *country* SW Europe

PORTUGAL
Southwest Europe

Official name	The Portuguese Republic
Formation	1139 / 1640
Capital	Lisbon
Population	10.7 million / 301 people per sq mile (116 people per sq km)
Total area	35,672 sq. miles (92,391 sq. km)
Languages	Portuguese*
Religions	Roman Catholic 92%, Protestant 4%, Nonreligious 3%, Other 1%
Ethnic mix	Portuguese 98%, African and other 2%
Government	Parliamentary system
Currency	Euro = 100 cents
Literacy rate	95%
Calorie consumption	3617 kilocalories

Portuguese East Africa *see* Mozambique
Portuguese Guinea *see* Guinea-Bissau
Portuguese Republic *see* Portugal
Portuguese Timor *see* East Timor
Portuguese West Africa *see* Angola
Portus Cale *see* Porto
Portus Magnus *see* Almería
Portus Magonis *see* Maó
Port-Vila 144 D4 *var.* Vila. *country capital* (Vanuatu) Éfaté, C Vanuatu
Porvenir 61 E3 Pando, NW Bolivia
Porvenir 65 B8 Magallanes, S Chile
Porvoo 85 E6 *Swe.* Borgå. Etelä-Suomi, S Finland
Porzecze *see* Parechcha
Posadas 64 D3 Misiones, NE Argentina
Poschega *see* Požega
Posen *see* Poznań
Posnania *see* Poznań
Postavy/Postawy *see* Pastavy
Posterholt 87 D5 Limburg, SE Netherlands
Postojna 95 D8 *Ger.* Adelsberg, *It.* Postumia. SW Slovenia
Postumia *see* Postojna
Pöstyén *see* Piešt'any
Potamós 105 C7 Antikýthira, S Greece
Potentia *see* Potenza
Potenza 97 D5 *anc.* Potentia. Basilicata, S Italy
Poti 117 F2 *prev.* P'ot'i. W Georgia
P'ot'i *see* Poti
Potiskum 75 G4 Yobe, NE Nigeria
Potomac River 41 E5 *river* NE USA
Potosí 61 F4 Potosí, S Bolivia
Potsdam 94 D3 Brandenburg, NE Germany
Potwar Plateau 134 C2 *plateau* NE Pakistan
Poŭthĭsăt 137 D6 *prev.* Pursat. Poŭthĭsăt, W Cambodia
Po, Valle del *see* Po Valley
Po Valley 96 C2 *It.* Valle del Po. *valley* N Italy
Považská Bystrica 99 C5 *Ger.* Waagbistritz, *Hung.* Vágbeszterce. Trenčiansky Kraj, W Slovakia
Poverty Bay 150 E4 *inlet* North Island, New Zealand
Póvoa de Varzim 92 B2 Porto, NW Portugal
Powder River 44 D2 *river* Montana/ Wyoming, NW USA
Powell 44 C2 Wyoming, C USA
Powell, Lake 44 B5 *lake* Utah, W USA
Požarevac 100 D4 *Ger.* Passarowitz. Serbia, NE Serbia
Poza Rica 51 F4 *var.* Poza Rica de Hidalgo. Veracruz-Llave, E Mexico

Poza Rica de Hidalgo *see* Poza Rica
Požega 100 D4 *prev.* Slavonska Požega, *Ger.* Poschega, *Hung.* Pozsega. Požega-Slavonija, NE Croatia
Požega 100 D4 Serbia
Poznań 98 C3 *Ger.* Posen, Posnania. Wielkolpolskie, C Poland
Pozoblanco 92 D4 Andalucía, S Spain
Pozsega *see* Požega
Pozsony *see* Bratislava
Pozzallo 97 C8 Sicilia, Italy, C Mediterranean Sea
Prachatice 99 A5 *Ger.* Prachatitz. Jihočeský Kraj, S Czech Republic
Prachatitz *see* Prachatice
Prado del Ganso *see* Goose Green
Prae *see* Phrae
Prag/Praga/Prague *see* Praha
Praha 99 A5 *Eng.* Prague, *Ger.* Prag, *Pol.* Praga. *country capital* (Czech Republic) Středočeský Kraj, NW Czech Republic
Praia 74 A3 *country capital* (Cape Verde) Santiago, S Cape Verde
Prairie State *see* Illinois
Prathet Thai *see* Thailand
Prato 96 B3 Toscana, C Italy
Pratt 45 E5 Kansas, C USA
Prattville 42 D2 Alabama, S USA
Pravda 104 D1 *prev.* Dogrular. Silistra, NE Bulgaria
Pravia 92 C1 Asturias, N Spain
Preny *see* Prienai
Prenzlau 94 D3 Brandenburg, NE Germany
Prerau *see* Přerov
Přerov 99 C5 *Ger.* Prerau. Olomoucký Kraj, E Czech Republic
Preschau *see* Prešov
Prescott 48 B2 Arizona, SW USA
Preševo 101 D5 Serbia, SE Serbia
Presidente Epitácio 63 E4 São Paulo, S Brazil
Presidente Stroessner *see* Ciudad del Este
Prešov 99 D5 *var.* Preschau, *Ger.* Eperies, *Hung.* Eperjes. Prešovský Kraj, E Slovakia
Prespa, Lake 101 D6 *Alb.* Liqen i Prespës, *Gk.* Límni Megáli Préspa, Límni Prespa, *Mac.* Prespansko Ezero, *Serb.* Prespansko Jezero. *lake* SE Europe
Prespa, Limni/Prespansko Ezero/ Prespansko Jezero/Prespës, Liqen i *see* Prespa, Lake
Presque Isle 41 H1 Maine, NE USA
Pressburg *see* Bratislava
Preston 89 D5 NW England, United Kingdom
Prestwick 88 C4 W Scotland, United Kingdom
Pretoria 78 D4 *see also.* Tshwane. *country capital* (South Africa) (admin. capital) NE South Africa
Preussisch Eylau *see* Bagrationovsk
Preußisch Holland *see* Pasłęk
Preussisch-Stargard *see* Starogard Gdański
Prévéza 105 A5 Ípeiros, W Greece
Pribilof Islands 36 A3 *island group* Alaska, USA
Priboj 100 C4 Serbia, W Serbia
Price 44 B4 Utah, W USA
Prichard 42 C3 Alabama, S USA
Priekulė 106 B3 *Ger.* Prökuls. Klaipėda, W Lithuania
Prienai 107 B5 *Pol.* Preny. Kaunas, S Lithuania
Prieska 78 C4 Northern Cape, C South Africa
Prijedor 100 B3 Republika Srpska, NW Bosnia and Herzegovina
Prijepolje 100 D4 Serbia, W Serbia
Prikaspiyskaya Nizmennost' *see* Caspian Depression
Prilep 101 D6 *Turk.* Perlepe. S FYR Macedonia
Priluki *see* Pryluky
Primorsk 106 A4 *Ger.* Fischhausen. Kaliningradskaya Oblast', W Russian Federation
Primorsko 104 E2 *prev.* Keupriya. Burgas, E Bulgaria
Primorsk/Primorskoye *see* Prymors'k
Prince Albert 37 F5 Saskatchewan, S Canada
Prince Edward Island 39 F4 *Fr.* Île-du Prince-Édouard. *province* SE Canada

Prince Edward Islands 69 E8 *island group* S South Africa
Prince George 37 E5 British Columbia, SW Canada
Prince of Wales Island 148 B1 *island* Queensland, E Australia
Prince of Wales Island 37 F2 *island* Queen Elizabeth Islands, Nunavut, NW Canada
Prince of Wales Island *see* Pinang, Pulau
Prince Patrick Island 37 E2 *island* Parry Islands, Northwest Territories, NW Canada
Prince Rupert 36 D4 British Columbia, SW Canada
Prince's Island *see* Príncipe
Princess Charlotte Bay 148 C2 *bay* Queensland, NE Australia
Princess Elizabeth Land 154 C3 *physical region* Antarctica
Príncipe 77 A5 *var.* Príncipe Island, *Eng.* Prince's Island. *island* N Sao Tome and Principe
Príncipe Island *see* Príncipe
Prinzapolka 53 E3 Región Autónoma Atlántico Norte, NE Nicaragua
Pripet 107 C7 *Bel.* Prypyats', *Ukr.* Pryp"yat'. *river* Belarus/Ukraine
Pripet Marshes 107 B7 *wetland* Belarus/ Ukraine
Prishtinë 101 D5 *Serb.* Priština. C Kosovo
Priština *see* Prishtinë
Privas 91 D5 Ardèche, E France
Prizren 101 D5 S Kosovo
Probolinggo 138 D5 Jawa, C Indonesia
Probstberg *see* Wyszków
Progreso 51 H3 Yucatán, SE Mexico
Prokhladnyy 111 B8 Kabardino-Balkarskaya Respublika, SW Russian Federation
Prokletije *see* North Albanian Alps
Prökuls *see* Priekulė
Prokuplje 101 D5 Serbia, SE Serbia
Prome *see* Pyay
Promyshlennyy 110 E3 Respublika Komi, NW Russian Federation
Prościejów *see* Prostějov
Proskurov *see* Khmel 'nyts'kyy
Prossnitz *see* Prostějov
Prostějov 99 C5 *Ger.* Prossnitz, *Pol.* Prościejów. Olomoucký Kraj, E Czech Republic
Provence 91 D6 *cultural region* SE France
Providence 41 G3 *state capital* Rhode Island, NE USA
Providence *see* Fort Providence
Providencia, Isla de 53 F3 *island* NW Colombia, Caribbean Sea
Provideniya 155 B1 Chukotskiy Avtonomnyy Okrug, NE Russian Federation
Provo 44 B4 Utah, W USA
Prudhoe Bay 36 D2 Alaska, USA
Prusa *see* Bursa
Pruszków 98 D3 *Ger.* Kaltdorf. Mazowieckie, C Poland
Prut 108 D4 *Ger.* Pruth. *river* E Europe
Pruth *see* Prut
Pružana *see* Pruzhany
Pruzhany 107 B6 *Pol.* Pružana. Brestskaya Voblasts', SW Belarus
Prychornomor'ska Nyzovyna *see* Black Sea Lowland
Prydniprovs'ka Nyzovyna/ Prydniaprowskaja Nizina *see* Dnieper Lowland
Prydz Bay 154 D3 *bay* Antarctica
Pryluky 109 E2 *Rus.* Priluki. Chernihivs'ka Oblast', NE Ukraine
Prymors'k 109 G4 *Rus.* Primorsk; *prev.* Primorskoye. Zaporiz'ka Oblast', SE Ukraine
Pryp"yat'/Prypyats' *see* Pripet
Przemyśl 99 E5 *Rus.* Peremyshl. Podkarpackie, C Poland
Przheval'sk *see* Karakol
Psará 105 D5 *island* E Greece
Psel 109 F2 *Rus.* Psël. *river* Russian Federation/Ukraine
Psël *see* Psel
Pskov 114 B2 *Ger.* Pleskau, *Latv.* Pleskava. Pskovskaya Oblast', W Russian Federation
Pskov, Lake 106 E3 *Est.* Pihkva Järv, *Ger.* Pleskauer See, *Rus.* Pskovskoye Ozero. *lake* Estonia/Russian Federation
Pskovskoye Ozero *see* Pskov, Lake
Ptich' *see* Ptsich

229

Ptsich *107 C7 Rus.* Ptich'. Homyel'skaya Voblasts', SE Belarus
Ptsich *107 C7 Rus.* Ptich'. *river* SE Belarus
Ptuj *95 E7 Ger.* Pettau; *anc.* Poetovio. NE Slovenia
Pucallpa *60 C3* Ucayali, C Peru
Puck *98 C2* Pomorskie, N Poland
Pudasjärvi *84 D4* Oulu, C Finland
Puebla *51 F4 var.* Puebla de Zaragoza. Puebla, S Mexico
Puebla de Zaragoza *see* Puebla
Pueblo *44 D5* Colorado, C USA
Puerto Acosta *61 E4* La Paz, W Bolivia
Puerto Aisén *65 B6* Aisén, S Chile
Puerto Ángel *51 F5* Oaxaca, SE Mexico
Puerto Argentino *see* Stanley
Puerto Ayacucho *58 D3* Amazonas, SW Venezuela
Puerto Baquerizo Moreno *60 B5 var.* Baquerizo Moreno. Galápagos Islands, Ecuador, E Pacific Ocean
Puerto Barrios *52 C2* Izabal, E Guatemala
Puerto Bello *see* Portobelo
Puerto Berrío *58 B2* Antioquia, C Colombia
Puerto Cabello *58 D1* Carabobo, N Venezuela
Puerto Cabezas *53 E2 var.* Bilwi. Región Autónoma Atlántico Norte, NE Nicaragua
Puerto Carreño *58 D3* Vichada, E Colombia
Puerto Cortés *52 C2* Cortés, NW Honduras
Puerto Cumarebo *58 C1* Falcón, N Venezuela
Puerto Deseado *65 C7* Santa Cruz, SE Argentina
Puerto Escondido *51 F5* Oaxaca, SE Mexico
Puerto Gallegos *see* Río Gallegos
Puerto Inírida *58 D3 var.* Obando. Guainía, E Colombia
Puerto La Cruz *59 E1* Anzoátegui, NE Venezuela
Puerto Lempira *53 E2* Gracias a Dios, E Honduras
Puerto Limón *see* Limón
Puertollano *92 D4* Castilla-La Mancha, C Spain
Puerto López *58 C1* La Guajira, N Colombia
Puerto Maldonado *61 E3* Madre de Dios, E Peru
Puerto México *see* Coatzacoalcos
Puerto Montt *65 B5* Los Lagos, C Chile
Puerto Natales *65 B7* Magallanes, S Chile
Puerto Obaldía *53 H5* Kuna Yala, NE Panama
Puerto Plata *55 E3 var.* San Felipe de Puerto Plata. N Dominican Republic
Puerto Presidente Stroessner *see* Ciudad del Este
Puerto Princesa *139 E2 off.* Puerto Princesa City. Palawan, W Philippines
Puerto Princesa City *see* Puerto Princesa
Puerto Príncipe *see* Camagüey
Puerto Rico *55 F3 off.* Commonwealth of Puerto Rico; *prev.* Porto Rico. *US commonwealth territory* C West Indies
Puerto Rico *56 B1 island* C West Indies
Puerto Rico, Commonwealth of *see* Puerto Rico
Puerto Rico Trench *56 B1 trench* NE Caribbean Sea
Puerto San José *see* San José
Puerto San Julián *65 B7 var.* San Julián. Santa Cruz, SE Argentina
Puerto Suárez *61 H4* Santa Cruz, E Bolivia
Puerto Vallarta *50 D4* Jalisco, SW Mexico
Puerto Varas *65 B5* Los Lagos, C Chile
Puerto Viejo *53 E4* Heredia, NE Costa Rica
Puertoviejo *see* Portoviejo
Puget Sound *46 B1 sound* Washington, NW USA
Puglia *97 E5 var.* Le Puglie, *Eng.* Apulia. *region* SE Italy
Pukaki, Lake *151 B6 lake* South Island, New Zealand
Pukekohe *150 D3* Auckland, North Island, New Zealand

Puket *see* Phuket
Pukhavichy *107 C6 Rus.* Pukhovichi. Minskaya Voblasts', C Belarus
Pukhovichi *see* Pukhavichy
Pula *100 A3 It.* Pola; *prev.* Pulj. Istra, NW Croatia
Pulaski *40 D5* Virginia, NE USA
Puławy *98 D4* Lubelskie, E Poland
Pul-e Khumrī *123 E4 prev.* Pol-e Khomrī. Baghlān, NE Afghanistan
Pulj *see* Pula
Pullman *46 C2* Washington, NW USA
Pułtusk *98 D3* Mazowieckie, C Poland
Puná, Isla *60 A2 island* SW Ecuador
Pune *134 C5 prev.* Poona. Poona, W India
Punjab *134 C2 prev.* West Punjab, Western Punjab. *province* E Pakistan
Puno *61 F4* Puno, SE Peru
Punta Alta *65 C5* Buenos Aires, E Argentina
Punta Arenas *65 B8 prev.* Magallanes. Magallanes, S Chile
Punta Gorda *52 C2* Toledo, SE Belize
Punta Gorda *53 E4* Región Autónoma Atlántico Sur, SE Nicaragua
Puntarenas *52 D4* Puntarenas, W Costa Rica
Punto Fijo *58 C1* Falcón, N Venezuela
Pupuya, Nevado *61 E4 mountain* W Bolivia
Puri *135 F5 var.* Jagannath. Orissa, E India
Puriramya *see* Buriram
Purmerend *86 C3* Noord-Holland, C Netherlands
Pursat *see* Poŭthĭsăt, Poŭthĭsăt, W Cambodia
Purus, Rio *62 C2 var.* Río Purús. *river* Brazil/Peru
Pusan *see* Busan
Pusan-gwangyŏksi *see* Busan
Pushkino *see* Bilăsuvar
Püspökladány *99 D6* Hajdú-Bihar, E Hungary
Putorana, Gory/Putorana Mountains *see* Putorana, Plato
Putorana Mountains *115 E3 var.* Gory Putorana, *Eng.* Putorana Mountains. *mountain range* N Russian Federation
Putrajaya *138 B3 country capital* (Malaysia) (administrative) Kuala Lumpur, Peninsular Malaysia
Puttalam *132 C3* North Western Province, W Sri Lanka
Puttgarden *94 C2* Schleswig-Holstein, N Germany
Putumayo, Río *58 B5 var.* Içá, Rio. *river* NW South America
Putumayo, Río *see* Içá, Rio
Puurmani *106 D2 Ger.* Talkhof. Jõgevamaa, E Estonia
Pyatigorsk *111 B7* Stavropol'skiy Kray, SW Russian Federation
P'yatykhatky *109 F3 Rus.* Pyatikhatki. Dnipropetrovs'ka Oblast', E Ukraine
Pyay *136 B4 var.* Prome, Pye. Bago, C Myanmar (Burma)
Pye *see* Pyay
Pyetrykaw *107 C7 Rus.* Petrikov. Homyel'skaya Voblasts', SE Belarus
Pyin-Oo-Lwin *136 B3 var.* Maymyo. Mandalay, C Myanmar (Burma)
Pýlos *105 B6 var.* Pilos. Pelopónnisos, S Greece
P'yŏngyang *129 E3 var.* P'yŏngyang-si, *Eng.* Pyongyang. *country capital* (North Korea) SW North Korea
P'yŏngyang-si *see* P'yŏngyang
Pyramid Lake *47 C5 lake* Nevada, W USA
Pyrenaei Montes *see* Pyrenees
Pyrenees *102 B2 Fr.* Pyrénées, *Sp.* Pirineos; *anc.* Pyrenaei Montes. *mountain range* SW Europe
Pýrgos *105 B6 var.* Pírgos. Dytikí Elláda, S Greece
Pyritz *see* Pyrzyce
Pyryatyn *109 E2 Rus.* Piryatin. Poltavs'ka Oblast', NE Ukraine
Pyrzyce *98 B3 Ger.* Pyritz. Zachodnio-pomorskie, NW Poland
Pyu *see* Phyu
Pyuntaza *136 B4* Bago, SW Myanmar (Burma)

Q

Qāʻ al Jafr *119 C7 lake* S Jordan
Qaanaaq *82 D1 var.* Qânâq, *Dan.* Thule. Avannaarsua, N Greenland
Qab ā tiya *119 E6* N West Bank Asia
Qābis *see* Gabès
Qābis, Khalij *see* Gabès, Golfe de
Qacentina *see* Constantine
Qafṣah *see* Gafsa
Qagan Us *see* Dulan
Qahremānshahr *see* Kermānshāh
Qaidam Pendi *126 C4 basin* C China
Qal'aikhum *123 F3 Rus.* Kalaikhum. S Tajikistan
Qalāt *123 E5 Per.* Kalāt. Zābul, S Afghanistan
Qalʻat Bīshah *121 B5* ʻAsīr, SW Saudi Arabia
Qalqīlya *see* Qalqīlya
Qalqīlya *119 D6 var.* Qalqiliya. Central, W West Bank Asia
Qamanittuaq *see* Baker Lake
Qamdo *126 D5* Xizang Zizhiqu, W China
Qamishly *see* Al Qāmishlī
Qânâq *see* Qaanaaq
Qaqortoq *82 C4 Dan.* Julianehåb. Kitaa, S Greenland
Qaraghandy/Qaraghandy Oblysy *see* Karagandy
Qara Qum *see* Garagum
Qarataū *see* Karatau, Zhambyl, Kazakhstan
Qarkilik *see* Ruoqiang
Qarokŭl *123 F3 Rus.* Karakul'. E Tajikistan
Qarqannah, Juzur *see* Kerkenah, Îles de
Qars *see* Kars
Qarshi *123 E3 Rus.* Karshi; *prev.* Bek-Budi. Qashqadaryo Viloyati, S Uzbekistan
Qasigiannguit *see* Qasigiannguit
Qasigiannguit *82 C3 var.* Qasigianguit, *Dan.* Christianshåb. Kitaa, C Greenland
Qaşr al Farāfirah *72 B2 var.* Qasr Farâfra. W Egypt
Qasr Farāfra *see* Qaşr al Farāfirah
Qaṭanā *119 B5 var.* Katana. Rif Dimashq, S Syria
Qatar *120 C4 off.* State of Qatar, *Ar.* Dawlat Qaṭar. *country* SW Asia

QATAR
Southwest Asia

Official name	State of Qatar
Formation	1971 / 1971
Capital	Doha
Population	1.9 million / 447 people per sq mile (173 people per sq km)
Total area	4416 sq. miles (11,437 sq. km)
Languages	Arabic*
Religions	Muslim (mainly Sunni) 95%, Other 5%
Ethnic mix	Qatari 20%, Indian 20%, Other 20%, Nepalese 13%, Filipino 10%, Other 10%, Pakistani 7%
Government	Monarchy
Currency	Qatar riyal = 100 dirhams
Literacy rate	95%
Calorie consumption	Not available

Qatar, State of *see* Qatar
Qattara Depression *72 A1 var.* Munkhafaḍ al Qaṭṭārah *var.* Monkhafad el Qaṭṭâra, *Eng.* Qattara Depression. *desert* NW Egypt
Qattara Depression/Qaṭṭārah, Munkhafaḍ al *see* Qaṭṭārah, Munkhafaḍ al
Qaṭṭārah, Monkhafad el *see* Qaṭṭārah, Munkhafaḍ al
Qausuitup *see* Resolute
Qazaqstan/Qazaqstan Respublikasy *see* Kazakhstan
Qazimämmäd *see* Hacıqabal
Qazris *see* Cáceres
Qazvīn *120 C2 var.* Kazvin. Qazvīn, N Iran
Qena *see* Qinā
Qeqertarsuaq *see* Qeqertarsuaq
Qeqertarsuaq *82 C3 var.* Qeqertarssuaq, *Dan.* Godhavn. Kitaa, S Greenland
Qeqertarsuaq *82 C3 island* W Greenland

Qeqertarsuup Tunua *82 C3 Dan.* Disko Bugt. *inlet* W Greenland
Qerveh *see* Qorveh
Qeshm *120 D4 var.* Jazīreh-ye Qeshm, Qeshm Island. *island* S Iran
Qeshm Island/Qeshm, Jazīreh-ye *see* Qeshm
Qilian Shan *126 D3 var.* Kilien Mountains. *mountain range* N China
Qimusseriarsuaq *82 C2 Dan.* Melville Bugt, *Eng.* Melville Bay. *bay* NW Greenland
Qinā *72 B2 var.* Qena; *anc.* Caene, Caenepolis. E Egypt
Qing *see* Qinghai
Qingdao *128 D4 var.* Ching-Tao, Ch'ing-tao, Tsingtao, Tsintao, *Ger.* Tsingtau. Shandong, E China
Qinghai *126 C4 var.* Chinghai, Koko Nor, Qing, Qinghai Sheng, Tsinghai. *province* C China
Qinghai Hu *126 D4 var.* Ch'ing Hai, Tsing Hai, *Mong.* Koko Nor. *lake* C China
Qinghai Sheng *see* Qinghai
Qinhuangdao *128 D3* Hebei, E China
Qinzhou *128 B6* Guangxi Zhuangzu Zizhiqu, S China
Qiong *see* Hainan
Qiqihar *128 D2 var.* Ch'i-ch'i-ha-erh, Tsitsihar; *prev.* Lungkiang. Heilongjiang, NE China
Qira *126 B4* Xinjiang Uygur Zizhiqu, NW China
Qita Ghazzah *see* Gaza Strip
Qitai *126 C3* Xinjiang Uygur Zizhiqu, NW China
Qīzān *see* Jīzān
Qizil Orda *see* Kyzylorda
Qizil Qum/Qizilqum *see* Kyzyl Kum
Qizilrabot *123 G3 Rus.* Kyzylrabot. SE Tajikistan
Qobustan *117 H2 prev.* Märäzä. E Azerbaijan
Qogir Feng *see* K2
Qom *120 C3 var.* Kum, Qum. Qom, N Iran
Qomolangma Feng *see* Everest, Mount
Qomul *see* Hami
Qoʻqon *123 F2 var.* Khokand, *Rus.* Kokand. Farg'ona Viloyati, E Uzbekistan
Qorveh *120 C3 var.* Qerveh, Qurveh. Kordestān, W Iran
Qostanay/Qostanay Oblysy *see* Kostanay
Qoubaïyât *118 B4 var.* Al Qubayyāt. N Lebanon
Qoussantina *see* Constantine
Quang Ngai *137 E5 var.* Quangngai, Quang Nghia. Quang Ngai, C Vietnam
Quangngai *see* Quang Ngai
Quang Nghia *see* Quang Ngai
Quan Long *see* Ca Mau
Quanzhou *128 D6 var.* Ch'uan-chou, Tsinkiang; *prev.* Chin-chiang. Fujian, SE China
Quanzhou *128 C6* Guangxi Zhuangzu Zizhiqu, S China
Qu'Appelle *37 F5 river* Saskatchewan, S Canada
Quarles, Pegunungan *139 E4 mountain range* Sulawesi, C Indonesia
Quarnero *see* Kvarner
Quartu Sant' Elena *97 A6* Sardegna, Italy, C Mediterranean Sea
Quba *117 H2 Rus.* Kuba. N Azerbaijan
Qubba *see* Ba'qūbah
Québec *39 E4 var.* Quebec. *province capital* Québec, SE Canada
Québec *38 D3 var.* Quebec. *province* SE Canada
Queen Charlotte Islands *36 C5 Fr.* Îles de la Reine-Charlotte. *island group* British Columbia, SW Canada
Queen Charlotte Sound *36 C5 sea area* British Columbia, W Canada
Queen Elizabeth Islands *37 E1 Fr.* Îles de la Reine-Elisabeth. *island group* Nunavut, N Canada
Queensland *148 B4 state* N Australia
Queenstown *151 B7* Otago, South Island, New Zealand
Queenstown *78 D5* Eastern Cape, S South Africa
Quelimane *79 E3 var.* Kilimane, Kilmain, Quilimane. Zambézia, NE Mozambique

Quelpart *see* Jeju-do
Quepos *53 E4* Puntarenas, S Costa Rica
Que Que *see* Kwekwe
Quera *see* Chur
Querétaro *51 E4* Querétaro de Arteaga, C Mexico
Quesada *53 E4* var. Ciudad Quesada, San Carlos. Alajuela, N Costa Rica
Quetta *134 B2* Baluchistān, SW Pakistan
Quetzalcoalco *see* Coatzacoalcos
Quezaltenango *52 A2* var. Quetzaltenango. Quezaltenango, W Guatemala
Quibdó *58 A3* Chocó, W Colombia
Quilimane *see* Quelimane
Quillabamba *60 D3* Cusco, C Peru
Quilon *see* Kollam
Quimper *90 A3* anc. Quimper Corentin. Finistère, NW France
Quimper Corentin *see* Quimper
Quimperlé *90 A3* Finistère, NW France
Quincy *40 A4* Illinois, N USA
Qui Nhon/Quinhon *see* Quy Nhơn
Quissico *79 E4* Inhambane, S Mozambique
Quito *60 B1* country capital (Ecuador) Pichincha, N Ecuador
Qulyndy Zhazyghy *see* Ravnina Kulyndy
Qum *see* Qom
Qurein *see* Al Kuwayt
Qŭrghonteppa *123 E3* Rus. Kurgan-Tyube. SW Tajikistan
Qurlurtuuq *see* Kugluktuk
Qurveh *see* Qorveh
Quşayr *see* Al Quşayr
Quxar *see* Lhazê
Quy Nhơn *137 E5* var. Quinhon, Qui Nhon. Bình Định, C Vietnam
Qyteti Stalin *see* Kuçovë
Qyzylorda *see* Kyzylorda

R

Raab *100 B1* Hung. Rába. river Austria/Hungary
Raab *see* Rába
Raab *see* Győr
Raahe *84 D4* Swe. Brahestad. Oulu, W Finland
Raalte *86 D3* Overijssel, E Netherlands
Raamsdonksveer *86 C4* Noord-Brabant, S Netherlands
Raasiku *106 D2* Ger. Rasik. Harjumaa, NW Estonia
Rába *99 B7* Ger. Raab. river Austria/Hungary
Rába *see* Raab
Rabat *70 C2* var. al Dar al Baida. country capital (Morocco) NW Morocco
Rabat *102 B5* W Malta
Rabat *see* Victoria
Rabbah Ammon/Rabbath Ammon *see* 'Amman
Rabinal *52 B2* Baja Verapaz, C Guatemala
Rabka *99 D5* Małopolskie, S Poland
Râbniţa *see* Rîbniţa
Rabyanah Ramlat *71 G4* var. Rebiana Sand Sea, Şaḥrā' Rabyānah. desert SE Libya
Rabyānah, Şaḥrā' *see* Rabyanah, Ramlat
Răcari *see* Durankulak
Race, Cape *39 H3* headland Newfoundland, Newfoundland and Labrador, E Canada
Rach Gia *137 D6* Kiên Giang, S Vietnam
Rach Gia, Vinh *137 D6* bay S Vietnam
Racine *40 B3* Wisconsin, N USA
Rácz-Becse *see* Bečej
Rădăuţi *108 C3* Ger. Radautz, Hung. Rádóc. Suceava, N Romania
Radautz *see* Rădăuţi
Rádeyilikóé *see* Fort Good Hope
Rádóc *see* Rădăuţi
Radom *98 D4* Mazowieckie, C Poland
Radomsko *98 D4* Rus. Novoradomsk. Łódzkie, C Poland
Radomyshl' *108 D2* Zhytomyrs'ka Oblast', N Ukraine
Radoviš *101 E6* prev. Radovište. E Macedonia
Radovište *see* Radoviš
Radviliškis *106 B4* Šiauliai, N Lithuania
Radzyń Podlaski *98 E4* Lubelskie, E Poland
Rae-Edzo *see* Edzo

Raetihi *150 D4* Manawatu-Wanganui, North Island, New Zealand
Rafa *see* Rafah
Rafaela *64 C3* Santa Fe, E Argentina
Rafah *119 A7* var. Rafa, Rafaḥ, Heb. Rafiaḥ, Raphiah. SW Gaza Strip
Rafḥah *120 B4* Al Ḥudūd ash Shamālīyah, N Saudi Arabia
Rafiaḥ *see* Rafah
Raga *73 A5* Western Bahr el Ghazal, W South Sudan
Ragged Island Range *54 C2* island group S Bahamas
Ragnit *see* Neman
Ragusa *97 C7* Sicilia, Italy, C Mediterranean Sea
Ragusa *see* Dubrovnik
Rahachow *107 D7* Rus. Rogachëv. Homyel'skaya Voblasts', SE Belarus
Rahaeng *see* Tak
Rahaṭ, Ḥarrat *121 B5* lava flow W Saudi Arabia
Rahīmyār Khān *134 C3* Punjab, SE Pakistan
Rahovec *101 D5* Serb. Orahovac. W Kosovo
Raiatea *145 G4* island Îles Sous le Vent, W French Polynesia
Rāichūr *132 C1* Karnātaka, C India
Raidestos *see* Tekirdağ
Rainier, Mount *34 A4* volcano Washington, NW USA
Rainy Lake *38 A4* lake Canada/USA
Raipur *135 E4* Chhattīsgarh, C India
Rājahmundry *135 E5* Andhra Pradesh, E India
Rajang *see* Rajang, Batang
Rajang, Batang *138 D3* var. Rajang. river East Malaysia
Rājapālaiyam *132 C3* Tamil Nādu, SE India
Rājasthān *134 C3* cultural region NW India
Rājkot *134 C4* Gujarāt, W India
Rāj Nāndgaon *135 E4* Chhattīsgarh, C India
Rajshahi *135 G3* prev. Rampur Boalia. Rajshahi, W Bangladesh
Rakahanga *145 F3* atoll N Cook Islands
Rakaia *151 B6* river South Island, New Zealand
Rakka *see* Ar Raqqah
Rakke *106 E2* Lääne-Virumaa, NE Estonia
Rakvere *106 E2* Ger. Wesenberg. Lääne-Virumaa, N Estonia
Raleigh *43 F1* state capital North Carolina, SE USA
Ralik Chain *144 D1* island group Ralik Chain, W Marshall Islands
Ramadi *see* Ar Ramādī
Râmnicul-Sărat *see* Râmnicu Sărat
Râmnicu Sărat *108 C4* prev. Râmnicul-Sărat, Rîmnicu-Sărat. Buzău, E Romania
Râmnicu Vâlcea *108 B4* prev. Rîmnicu Vîlcea. Vâlcea, C Romania
Rampur Boalia *see* Rajshahi
Ramree Island *136 A4* island W Myanmar (Burma)
Ramtha *see* Ar Ramthā
Rancagua *64 B4* Libertador, C Chile
Rānchi *135 F4* Jhārkhand, N India
Randers *85 B7* Midtjylland, C Denmark
Ráneš *see* Ringvassøya
Rangiora *151 C6* Canterbury, South Island, New Zealand
Rangitikei *150 D4* river North Island, New Zealand
Rangoon *see* Yangon
Rangpur *135 G3* Rajshahi, N Bangladesh
Rankin Inlet *37 G3* Nunavut, C Canada
Rankovićevo *see* Kraljevo
Ranong *137 B6* Ranong, SW Thailand
Rapa Nui *see* Pascua, Isla de
Raphiah *see* Rafah
Rapid City *44 D3* South Dakota, N USA
Räpina *106 E3* Ger. Rappin. Põlvamaa, SE Estonia
Rapla *106 D2* Ger. Rappel. Raplamaa, NW Estonia
Rappel *see* Rapla
Rappin *see* Räpina
Rarotonga *145 G5* island S Cook Islands, C Pacific Ocean
Ra's al 'Ain *see* Ra's al 'Ayn
Ra's al 'Ayn *118 D1* var. Ras al Ain. Al Ḥasakah, N Syria
Ra's an Naqb *119 B7* Ma'ān, S Jordan

Raseiniai *106 B4* Kaunas, C Lithuania
Rasht *120 C2* var. Resht. Gīlān, NW Iran
Rasik *see* Raasiku
Râşnov *108 C4* prev. Rîşno, Rozsnyó, Hung. Barcarozsnyó. Braşov, C Romania
Rastenburg *see* Kętrzyn
Ratak Chain *144 D1* island group Ratak Chain, E Marshall Islands
Ratān *85 C5* Jämtland, C Sweden
Rat Buri *see* Ratchaburi
Ratchaburi *137 C5* var. Rat Buri. Ratchaburi, W Thailand
Ratisbon/Ratisbona/Ratisbonne *see* Regensburg
Rat Islands *36 A2* island group Aleutian Islands, Alaska, USA
Ratlām *134 D4* prev. Rutlam. Madhya Pradesh, C India
Ratnapura *132 D4* Sabaragamuwa Province, S Sri Lanka
Raton *48 D1* New Mexico, SW USA
Rättvik *85 C5* Dalarna, C Sweden
Raudhatain *see* Ar Rawḍatayn
Raufarhöfn *83 E4* Nordhurland Eystra, NE Iceland
Raukawa *see* Cook Strait
Raukumara Range *150 E3* mountain range North Island, New Zealand
Rāulakela *see* Rourkela
Rauma *85 D5* Swe. Raumo. Länsi-Suomi, SW Finland
Raumo *see* Rauma
Rāurkela *135 F4* var. Rāulakela, Rourkela. Orissa, E India
Ravenna *96 C3* Emilia-Romagna, N Italy
Ravi *134 C2* river India/Pakistan
Ravnina Kulyndy *114 C4* prev. Kulunda Steppe, Kaz. Qulyndy Zhazyghy, Rus. Kulundinskaya Ravnina. grassland Kazakhstan/Russian Federation
Rāwalpindi *134 C1* Punjab, NE Pakistan
Rawa Mazowiecka *98 D4* Łódzkie, C Poland
Rawicz *98 C4* Ger. Rawitsch. Wielkopolskie, C Poland
Rawitsch *see* Rawicz
Rawlins *44 C3* Wyoming, C USA
Rawson *65 C6* Chubut, SE Argentina
Rayak *118 B4* var. Rayaq, Riyāq. E Lebanon
Rayaq *see* Rayak
Rayong *137 C5* Rayong, S Thailand
Razazah, Buhayrat ar *120 B3* var. Baḥr al Milḥ. lake C Iraq
Razdolnoye *see* Rozdol'ne
Razelm, Lacul *see* Razim, Lacul
Razgrad *104 D2* Razgrad, N Bulgaria
Razim, Lacul *108 D5* prev. Lacul Razelm. lagoon NW Black Sea
Reading *89 D7* S England, United Kingdom
Reading *41 F4* Pennsylvania, NE USA
Realicó *64 C4* La Pampa, C Argentina
Reăng Kesei *137 D5* Bătdâmbâng, W Cambodia
Greater Antarctica *see* East Antarctica
Rebecca, Lake *147 C6* lake Western Australia
Rebiana Sand Sea *see* Rabyānah, Ramlat
Rebun-to *130 C2* island NE Japan
Rechitsa *see* Rechytsa
Rechytsa *107 D7* Rus. Rechitsa. Brestskaya Voblasts', SW Belarus
Recife *63 G2* prev. Pernambuco. state capital Pernambuco, E Brazil
Recklinghausen *94 A4* Nordrhein-Westfalen, W Germany
Recogne *87 C7* Luxembourg, SE Belgium
Reconquista *64 D3* Santa Fe, C Argentina
Red Deer *37 E5* Alberta, SW Canada
Redding *47 B5* California, W USA
Redon *90 B4* Ille-et-Vilaine, NW France
Red River *24 C2* var. Yuan, Chin. Yuan Jiang, Vtn. Sông Hồng Hà. river China/Vietnam
Red River *35 C6* river S USA
Red River *42 D3* river Louisiana, S USA
Red Sea *72 C3* var. Sinus Arabicus. sea Africa/Asia
Red Wing *45 G2* Minnesota, N USA
Reefton *151 C5* West Coast, South Island, New Zealand
Refahiye *117 E3* Erzincan, C Turkey

Regensburg *95 C6* Eng. Ratisbon, Fr. Ratisbonne, hist. Ratisbona; anc. Castra Regina, Reginum. Bayern, SE Germany
Regenstauf *95 C6* Bayern, SE Germany
Rêgistân *122 D5* var. Registan prev. Rigestân. S Afghanistan
Reggane *70 D3* C Algeria
Reggio *see* Reggio nell'Emilia
Reggio Calabria *see* Reggio di Calabria
Reggio di Calabria *97 D7* var. Reggio Calabria, Gk. Rhegion; anc. Regium, Rhegium. Calabria, SW Italy
Reggio Emilia *see* Reggio nell'Emilia
Reggio nell'Emilia *96 B2* var. Reggio Emilia, abbrev. Reggio; anc. Regium Lepidum. Emilia-Romagna, N Italy
Reghin *108 C4* Ger. Sächsisch-Reen, Hung. Szászrégen; prev. Reghinul Săsesc, Ger. Sächsisch-Regen. Mureş, C Romania
Reghinul Săsesc *see* Reghin
Regina *37 F5* province capital Saskatchewan, S Canada
Reginum *see* Regensburg
Registan *see* Rêgistân
Regium *see* Reggio di Calabria
Regium Lepidum *see* Reggio nell'Emilia
Rehoboth *78 B3* Hardap, C Namibia
Rehovot *119 A6* prev. Reḥovot. Central, C Israel
Reḥovot *see* Rehovot
Reichenau *see* Bogatynia, Poland
Reichenberg *see* Liberec
Reid *147 D6* Western Australia
Reikjavik *see* Reykjavík
Ré, Île de *90 A4* island W France
Reims *90 D3* Eng. Rheims; anc. Durocortorum, Remi. Marne, N France
Reindeer Lake *37 F4* lake Manitoba/Saskatchewan, C Canada
Reine-Charlotte, Îles de la *see* Queen Charlotte Islands
Reine-Élisabeth, Îles de la *see* Queen Elizabeth Islands
Reinga, Cape *150 C1* headland North Island, New Zealand
Reinosa *92 D1* Cantabria, N Spain
Reka *see* Rijeka
Rekhovot *see* Rehovot
Reliance *37 F4* Northwest Territories, C Canada
Remi *see* Reims
Rendina *see* Rentína
Rendsburg *94 B2* Schleswig-Holstein, N Germany
Rengat *138 B4* Sumatera, W Indonesia
Reni *108 D4* Odes'ka Oblast', SW Ukraine
Rennell *144 C4* var. Mu Nggava. island S Solomon Islands
Rennes *90 B3* Bret. Roazon; anc. Condate. Ille-et-Vilaine, NW France
Reno *47 C5* Nevada, W USA
Renqiu *128 C2* Hebei, E China
Rentína *105 B5* var. Rendina. Thessalía, C Greece
Reps *see* Rupea
Repulse Bay *37 G3* Northwest Terretories, N Canada
Reschitza *see* Reşiţa
Resht *see* Rasht
Resicabánya *see* Reşiţa
Resistencia *64 D3* Chaco, NE Argentina
Reşiţa *108 A4* Ger. Reschitza, Hung. Resicabánya. Caraş-Severin, W Romania
Resolute *37 F2* Inuit Qausuittuq. Cornwallis Island, Nunavut, N Canada
Resolution Island *39 E1* island Nunavut, NE Canada
Resolution Island *151 A7* island SW New Zealand
Réunion *79 H4* off. La Réunion. French overseas department W Indian Ocean
Réunion *141 B5* island W Indian Ocean
Reus *93 F2* Cataluña, E Spain
Reutlingen *95 B6* Baden-Württemberg, S Germany
Reuver *87 D5* Limburg, SE Netherlands
Reval/Revel *see* Tallinn
Revillagigedo Island *50 B5* island Alexander Archipelago, Alaska, USA
Rexburg *46 E3* Idaho, NW USA
Reyes *61 F3* El Beni, NW Bolivia
Rey, Isla del *53 G5* island Archipiélago de las Perlas, SE Panama
Reykjanes Basin *82 C5* var. Irminger Basin. undersea basin N Atlantic Ocean

Reykjanes Ridge *80 A1 undersea ridge* N Atlantic Ocean
Reykjavík *83 E5 var.* Reikjavík. *country capital* (Iceland) Höfudhborgarsvaedhi, W Iceland
Reynosa *51 E2* Tamaulipas, C Mexico
Rezā'īyeh, Daryācheh-ye *see* Orūmīyeh, Daryācheh-ye
Rezé *90 A4* Loire-Atlantique, NW France
Rēzekne *106 D4 Ger.* Rositten; *prev. Rus.* Rezhitsa. SE Latvia
Rezhitsa *see* Rēzekne
Rezovo *104 E3 Turk.* Rezve. Burgas, E Bulgaria
Rezve *see* Rezovo
Rhaedestus *see* Tekirdağ
Rhegion/Rhegium *see* Reggio di Calabria
Rheims *see* Reims
Rhein *see* Rhine
Rhine *94 A3 var.* Rheine in Westfalen. Nordrhein-Westfalen, NW Germany
Rheine in Westfalen *see* Rheine
Rheinisches Schiefergebirge *95 A5 var.* Rhine State Uplands, *Eng.* Rhenish Slate Mountains. *mountain range* W Germany
Rhenish Slate Mountains *see* Rheinisches Schiefergebirge
Rhin *see* Rhine
Rhine *80 D4 Dut.* Rijn, *Fr.* Rhin, *Ger.* Rhein. *river* W Europe
Rhinelander *40 B2* Wisconsin, N USA
Rhine State Uplands *see* Rheinisches Schiefergebirge
Rho *96 B2* Lombardia, N Italy
Rhode Island *41 G3 off.* State of Rhode Island and Providence Plantations, *also known as* Little Rhody, Ocean State. *state* NE USA
Rhodes *105 E7 var.* Ródhos, *Eng.* Rhodes, *It.* Rodi; *anc.* Rhodos. *island* Dodekánisa, Greece, Aegean Sea
Rhodes *see* Ródos
Rhodesia *see* Zimbabwe
Rhodope Mountains *104 C3 var.* Rodhópi Óri, *Bul.* Rhodope Planina, Rodopi, *Gk.* Orosirá Rodhópis, *Turk.* Dospad Dagh. *mountain range* Bulgaria/Greece
Rhodope Planina *see* Rhodope Mountains
Rhône *80 C4 river* France/Switzerland
Rhum *88 B3 var.* Rum. *island* W Scotland, United Kingdom
Ribble *89 D5 river* NW England, United Kingdom
Ribeira *see* Sanata Uxía de Ribeira
Ribeirão Preto *63 F4* São Paulo, S Brazil
Riberalta *61 F2* El Beni, N Bolivia
Ribniţa *108 D3 var.* Rábniţa, *Rus.* Rybnitsa. NE Moldova
Rice Lake *40 A2* Wisconsin, N USA
Richard Toll *74 B3* N Senegal
Richfield *44 B4* Utah, W USA
Richland *46 C2* Washington, NW USA
Richmond *151 C5* Tasman, South Island, New Zealand
Richmond *40 C5* Kentucky, S USA
Richmond *41 E5 state capital* Virginia, NE USA
Richmond Range *151 C5 mountain range* South Island, New Zealand
Ricobayo, Embalse de *92 C2 reservoir* NW Spain
Ricomagus *see* Riom
Ridder *114 D4 prev.* Leninogorsk, *Kaz.* Leningor. Vostochnyy Kazakhstan, E Kazakhstan
Ridgecrest *47 C7* California, W USA
Ried *see* Ried im Innkreis
Ried im Innkreis *95 D6 var.* Ried. Oberösterreich, NW Austria
Riemst *87 D6* Limburg, NE Belgium
Riesa *94 D4* Sachsen, E Germany
Rift Valley *see* Great Rift Valley
Riga *106 C3 Eng.* Riga. *country capital* (Latvia) C Latvia
Rigaer Bucht *see* Riga, Gulf of
Riga, Gulf of *106 C3 Est.* Liivi Laht, *Ger.* Rigaer Bucht, *Latv.* Rīgas Jūras Līcis, *Rus.* Rizhskiy Zaliv; *prev. Est.* Riia Laht. *gulf* Estonia/Latvia
Rīgas Jūras Līcis *see* Riga, Gulf of
Rigestān *see* Rēgestān
Riia Laht *see* Riga, Gulf of
Riihimäki *85 D5* Etelä-Suomi, S Finland

Rijeka *100 A2 Ger.* Sankt Veit am Flaum, *It.* Fiume, *Slvn.* Reka; *anc.* Tarsatica. Primorje-Gorski Kotar, NW Croatia
Rijn *see* Rhine
Rijssel *see* Lille
Rijssen *86 E3* Overijssel, E Netherlands
Rimah, Wadi ar *120 B4 var.* Wādī ar Rummah. *dry watercourse* C Saudi Arabia
Rimini *96 C3 anc.* Ariminum. Emilia-Romagna, N Italy
Râmnicu-Sărat *see* Râmnicu Sărat
Râmnicu Vâlcea *see* Râmnicu Vâlcea
Rimouski *39 E4* Québec, SE Canada
Ringebu *85 B5* Oppland, S Norway
Ringen *see* Rõngu
Ringkøbing Fjord *85 A7 fjord* W Denmark
Ringvassøya *84 C2 Lapp.* Ráneš. *island* N Norway
Rio *see* Rio de Janeiro
Riobamba *60 B1* Chimborazo, C Ecuador
Rio Branco *56 B3 state capital* Acre, W Brazil
Rio Branco, Território de *see* Roraima
Río Bravo *51 E2* Tamaulipas, C Mexico
Río Cuarto *64 C4* Córdoba, C Argentina
Rio de Janeiro *63 F4 var.* Rio. *state capital* Rio de Janeiro, SE Brazil
Rio de Janeiro *63 E5 var.* Rio. *state* SE Brazil
Río Gallegos *65 B7 var.* Gallegos, Puerto Gallegos. Santa Cruz, S Argentina
Río Grande *50 D3* Zacatecas, C Mexico
Rio Grande do Norte *63 G2 off.* Estado do Rio Grande do Norte. *state* E Brazil
Rio Grande do Norte *63 G2 off.* Estado do Rio Grande do Norte. *region* E Brazil
Rio Grande do Norte, Estado do *see* Rio Grande do Norte
Rio Grande do Sul *63 E5 off.* Estado do Rio Grande do Sul. *state* S Brazil
Rio Grande do Sul *63 E5 off.* Estado do Rio Grande do Sul. *region* S Brazil
Rio Grande do Sul, Estado do *see* Rio Grande do Sul
Rio Grande Plateau *see* Rio Grande Rise
Rio Grande Rise *57 E6 var.* Rio Grande Plateau. *undersea plateau* SW Atlantic Ocean
Ríohacha *58 B1* La Guajira, N Colombia
Río Lagartos *51 H3* Yucatán, SE Mexico
Riom *91 C5 anc.* Ricomagus. Puy-de-Dôme, C France
Río Verde *51 E4 var.* Rioverde. San Luis Potosí, C Mexico
Rioverde *see* Río Verde
Ripoll *93 G2* Cataluña, NE Spain
Rishiri-to *132 D2 var.* Risiri Tô. *island* NE Japan
Risiri Tô *see* Rishiri-tō
Rişno *see* Rişnov
Risti *106 D2 Ger.* Kreuz. Läänemaa, W Estonia
Rivas *52 D4* Rivas, SW Nicaragua
Rivera *64 D3* Rivera, NE Uruguay
River Falls *40 A2* Wisconsin, N USA
Riverside *47 C7* California, W USA
Riverton *151 A7* Southland, South Island, New Zealand
Riverton *44 C3* Wyoming, C USA
Rivière-du-Loup *39 E4* Québec, SE Canada
Rivne *108 D2 Pol.* Równe, *Rus.* Rovno. Rivnens'ka Oblast', NW Ukraine
Rivoli *96 A2* Piemonte, NW Italy
Riyadh/Riyāḍ, Minţaqat ar *see* Ar Riyāḍ
Riyāq *see* Rayak
Rize *117 E2* Rize, NE Turkey
Rizhao *128 D4* Shandong, E China
Rizhskiy Zaliv *see* Riga, Gulf of
Rkíz *74 C3* Trarza, W Mauritania
Road Town *55 F3 dependent territory capital* (British Virgin Islands) Tortola, C British Virgin Islands
Roanne *91 C5 anc.* Rodunma. Loire, E France
Roanoke *41 E5* Virginia, NE USA
Roanoke River *43 F1 river* North Carolina/Virginia, SE USA
Roatán *52 C2 var.* Coxen Hole, Coxin Hole. Islas de la Bahía, N Honduras
Roat Kampuchea *see* Cambodia
Roazon *see* Rennes
Robbie Ridge *143 E3 undersea ridge* W Pacific Ocean
Robert Williams *see* Caála

Robinson Range *147 B5 mountain range* Western Australia
Robson, Mount *37 E5 mountain* British Columbia, SW Canada
Robstown *49 G4* Texas, SW USA
Roca Partida, Isla *50 B5 island* W Mexico
Rocas, Atol das *63 G2 island* E Brazil
Rochefort *87 C7* Namur, SE Belgium
Rochefort *90 B4 var.* Rochefort sur Mer. Charente-Maritime, W France
Rochefort sur Mer *see* Rochefort
Rochester *45 G3* Minnesota, N USA
Rochester *41 G2* New Hampshire, NE USA
Rocheuses, Montagnes/Rockies *see* Rocky Mountains
Rockall Bank *80 B2 undersea bank* N Atlantic Ocean
Rockall Trough *80 B2 trough* N Atlantic Ocean
Rockdale *148 E2* Texas, SW USA
Rockford *40 B3* Illinois, N USA
Rockhampton *148 D4* Queensland, E Australia
Rock Hill *43 E1* South Carolina, SE USA
Rockingham *147 A6* Western Australia
Rock Island *40 B3* Illinois, N USA
Rock Sound *54 C1* Eleuthera Island, C Bahamas
Rock Springs *44 C3* Wyoming, C USA
Rockstone *59 F3* C Guyana
Rocky Mount *43 F1* North Carolina, SE USA
Rocky Mountains *34 B4 var.* Rockies, *Fr.* Montagnes Rocheuses. *mountain range* Canada/USA
Roden *86 E2* Drenthe, NE Netherlands
Rodez *91 C5 anc.* Segodunum. Aveyron, S France
Rodhópi Óri *see* Rhodope Mountains
Ródhos/Rodi *see* Rhodes
Rodopi *see* Rhodope Mountains
Rodosto *see* Tekirdağ
Rodunma *see* Roanne
Roermond *87 D5* Limburg, SE Netherlands
Roeselare *87 A6 Fr.* Roulers; *prev.* Rousselaere. West-Vlaanderen, W Belgium
Rogachëv *see* Rahachow
Rogatica *100 C4* Republika Srpska, SE Bosnia and Herzegovina
Rogers *42 A1* Arkansas, C USA
Roger Simpson Island *see* Abemama
Roi Ed *see* Roi Et
Roi Et *137 D5 var.* Muang Roi Et, Roi Ed. Roi Et, E Thailand
Roja *106 C2* NW Latvia
Rokiškis *106 C4* Panevėžys, NE Lithuania
Rokycany *99 A5 Ger.* Rokytzan. Plzeňský Kraj, W Czech Republic
Rokytzan *see* Rokycany
Rôlas, Ilha das *76 E2 island* S Sao Tome and Principe, Africa, E Atlantic Ocean
Rolla *45 G5* Missouri, C USA
Röm *see* Rømø
Roma *96 C4 Eng.* Rome. *country capital* (Italy) Lazio, C Italy
Roma *149 D5* Queensland, E Australia
Roman *104 C2* Vratsa, NW Bulgaria
Roman *108 C4 Hung.* Románvásár. Neamţ, NE Romania
Romania *108 B4 Bul.* Rumūniya, *Ger.* Rumänien, *Hung.* Románia, *Rom.* România, *SCr.* Rumunjska, *Ukr.* Rumuniya, *prev.* Republica Socialistă România, Roumania, Rumania, Socialist Republic of Romania, *Rom.* Rominia. *country* SE Europe

ROMANIA
Southeast Europe

Official name Romania
Formation 1878 / 1947
Capital Bucharest
Population 21.4 million / 241 people per sq mile (93 people per sq km)
Total area 91,699 sq. miles (237,500 sq. km)
Languages Romanian*, Hungarian (Magyar), Romani, German
Religions Romanian Orthodox 87%, Protestant 5%, Roman Catholic 5%, Greek Orthodox 1%, Greek Catholic (Uniate) 1%, Other 1%
Ethnic mix Romanian 89%, Magyar 7%,

ROMANIA
(continued)

Roma 2%, Other 2%
Government Presidential system
Currency New Romanian leu = 100 bani
Literacy rate 98%
Calorie consumption 3487 kilocalories

România, Republica Socialistă *see* Romania
Romania, Socialist Republic of *see* Romania
Romaniv *109 F3 Rus.* Dneprodzerzhinsk, *prev.* Dniprodzerzhyns'k, *prev.* Kamenskoye. Dnipropetrovs'ka Oblast', E Ukraine
Románvásár *see* Roman
Rome *42 D2* Georgia, SE USA
Rome *see* Roma
Rominia *see* Romania
Romny *109 F2* Sums'ka Oblast', NE Ukraine
Rømø *85 A7 Ger.* Röm. *island* SW Denmark
Roncador, Serra do *56 D4 mountain range* C Brazil
Ronda *92 D5* Andalucía, S Spain
Rondônia *62 D3 off.* Estado de Rondônia; *prev.* Território de Rondônia. *state* W Brazil
Rondônia *62 D3 off.* Estado de Rondônia; *prev.* Território de Rondônia. *region* W Brazil
Rondônia, Estado de *see* Rondônia
Rondônia, Território de *see* Rondônia
Rondonópolis *63 E3* Mato Grosso, W Brazil
Rongelap Atoll *144 D1 var.* Rönlap. *atoll* Ralik Chain, NW Marshall Islands
Rõngu *106 D3 Ger.* Ringen. Tartumaa, SE Estonia
Rönlap *see* Rongelap Atoll
Rønne *85 B8* Bornholm, E Denmark
Ronne Ice Shelf *154 A3 ice shelf* Antarctica
Roosendaal *87 C5* Noord-Brabant, S Netherlands
Roosevelt Island *154 B4 island* Antarctica
Roraima *62 D1 off.* Estado de Roraima; *prev.* Território de Rio Branco, Território de Roraima. *state* N Brazil
Roraima *62 D1 off.* Estado de Roraima; *prev.* Território de Rio Branco, Território de Roraima. *region* N Brazil
Roraima, Estado de *see* Roraima
Roraima, Mount *59 E3 mountain* N South America
Roraima, Território de *see* Roraima
Røros *85 B5* Sør-Trøndelag, S Norway
Ross *151 B6* West Coast, South Island, New Zealand
Rosa, Lake *54 D2 lake* Great Inagua, S Bahamas
Rosario *64 D4* Santa Fe, C Argentina
Rosario *64 D2* San Pedro, C Paraguay
Rosario *see* Rosarito
Rosarito *50 A1 var.* Rosario. Baja California Norte, NW Mexico
Roscianum *see* Rossano
Roscommon *40 C2* Michigan, N USA
Roseau *55 G4 prev.* Charlotte Town. *country capital* (Dominica) SW Dominica
Roseburg *46 B4* Oregon, NW USA
Rosenau *see* Brașov
Rosenberg *49 G4* Texas, SW USA
Rosenberg *see* Ružomberok, Slovakia
Rosengarten *94 B3* Niedersachsen, N Germany
Rosenheim *95 C6* Bayern, S Germany
Rosia *93 H5* W Gibraltar Europe
Rosia Bay *93 H5 bay* SW Gibraltar Europe W Mediterranean Sea Atlantic Ocean
Roşiori de Vede *108 B5* Teleorman, S Romania
Rositten *see* Rēzekne
Roslavl' *111 A5* Smolenskaya Oblast', W Russian Federation
Rosmalen *86 C4* Noord-Brabant, S Netherlands
Rossano *97 E6 anc.* Roscianum. Calabria, SW Italy
Ross Ice Shelf *154 B4 ice shelf* Antarctica
Rossiyskaya Federatsiya *see* Russian Federation

Rosso *74 B3* Trarza, SW Mauritania
Rossosh' *111 B6* Voronezhskaya Oblast',
 W Russian Federation
Ross Sea *154 B4 sea* Antarctica
Rostak *see* Ar Rustāq
Rostock *95 C2* Mecklenburg-
 Vorpommern, NE Germany
Rostov *see* Rostov-na-Donu
Rostov-na-Donu *111 B7 var.* Rostov,
 Eng. Rostov-on-Don. Rostovskaya
 Oblast', SW Russian Federation
Rostov-on-Don *see* Rostov-na-Donu
Roswell *48 D2* New Mexico,
 SW USA
Rota *144 B1 island* S Northern Mariana
 Islands
Rotcher Island *see* Tamana
Rothera *154 A2 UK research station*
 Antarctica
Rotomagus *see* Rouen
Rotorua *150 D3* Bay of Plenty, North
 Island, New Zealand
Rotorua, Lake *150 D3 lake* North Island,
 New Zealand
Rotterdam *86 C4* Zuid-Holland,
 SW Netherlands
Rottweil *95 B6* Baden-Württemberg,
 S Germany
Rotuma *145 E4 island* NW Fiji Oceania
 S Pacific Ocean
Roubaix *90 C2* Nord, N France
Rouen *90 C3 anc.* Rotomagus. Seine-
 Maritime, N France
Roulers *see* Roeselare
Roumania *see* Romania
Round Rock *49 G3* Texas, SW USA
Rourkela *see* Räurkela
Rousselaere *see* Roeselare
Roussillon *91 C6 cultural region*
 S France
Rouyn-Noranda *38 D4* Québec,
 SE Canada
Rovaniemi *84 D3* Lappi, N Finland
Rovigno *see* Rovinj
Rovigo *96 C2* Veneto, NE Italy
Rovinj *100 A3 It.* Rovigno. Istra,
 NW Croatia
Rovno *see* Rivne
Rovuma, Rio *79 F2 var.* Ruvuma. *river*
 Mozambique/Tanzania
Rovuma, Rio *see* Ruvuma
Równe *see* Rivne
Roxas City *139 E2* Panay Island,
 C Philippines
Royale, Isle *40 B1 island* Michigan,
 N USA
Royan *91 B5* Charente-Maritime,
 W France
Rozdol'ne *109 F4 Rus.* Razdolnoye.
 Avtonomna Respublika Krym,
 S Ukraine
Rožňava *99 D6 Ger.* Rosenau, *Hung.*
 Rozsnyó. Košický Kraj,
 E Slovakia
Rózsahegy *see* Ružomberok
Rozsnyó *see* Rášno, Romania
Rozsnyó *see* Rožňava, Slovakia
Ruanda *see* Rwanda
Ruapehu, Mount *150 D4 volcano* North
 Island, New Zealand
Ruapuke Island *151 B8 island*
 SW New Zealand
Ruatoria *150 E3* Gisborne, North Island,
 New Zealand
Ruawai *150 D2* Northland, North Island,
 New Zealand
Rubezhnoye *see* Rubizhne
Rubizhne *109 H3 Rus.* Rubezhnoye.
 Luhans'ka Oblast', E Ukraine
Ruby Mountains *47 D5 mountain range*
 Nevada, W USA
Rucava *106 B3* SW Latvia
Rudensk *see* Rudzyensk
Rüdiškės *107 B5* Vilnius, S Lithuania
Rudnik *104 E2* Varna, E Bulgaria
Rudny *see* Rudnyy
Rudnyy *114 C4 var.* Rudny. Kostanay,
 N Kazakhstan
Rudolf, Lake *see* Turkana, Lake
Rudolfswert *see* Novo mesto
Rudzyensk *107 C6 Rus.* Rudensk.
 Minskaya Voblasts', C Belarus
Rufiji *73 C7 river* E Tanzania
Rufino *64 C4* Santa Fe, C Argentina
Rugāji *106 D4* E Latvia
Rügen *94 D2 headland* NE Germany
Ruggell *94 E1* N Liechtenstein
 Europe
Ruhja *see* Rūjiena

Ruhnu *106 C2 var.* Ruhnu Saar, *Swe.*
 Runö. *island* SW Estonia
Ruhnu Saar *see* Ruhnu
Rujen *see* Rūjiena
Rūjiena *106 D3 Est.* Ruhja, *Ger.* Rujen.
 N Latvia
Rukwa, Lake *73 B7 lake* SE Tanzania
Rum *see* Rhum
Ruma *100 D3* Vojvodina, N Serbia
Rumadiya *see* Ar Ramādī
Rumania/Rumänien *see* Romania
Rumbek *73 B5* El Buhayrat, C South
 Sudan
Rum Cay *54 D2 island* C Bahamas
Rumia *98 C2* Pomorskie, N Poland
Rummah, Wādī ar *see* Rimah, Wādī ar
Rummelsburg in Pommern *see*
 Miastko
Rumuniya/Rumūniya/Rumunjska
 see Romania
Runanga *151 B5* West Coast, South
 Island, New Zealand
Rundu *78 C3 var.* Runtu. Okavango,
 NE Namibia
Runö *see* Ruhnu
Runtu *see* Rundu
Ruoqiang *126 C3 var.* Jo-ch'iang, *Uigh.*
 Charkhlik, Charkhliq, Qarkilik.
 Xinjiang Uygur Zizhiqu, NW China
Rupea *108 C4 Ger.* Reps, *Hung.*
 Kőhalom; *prev.* Cohalm. Brașov,
 C Romania
Rupel *87 B5 river* N Belgium
Rupella *see* la Rochelle
Rupert, Rivière de *38 C3 river* Québec,
 C Canada
Rusaddir *see* Melilla
Ruschuk/Rusçuk *see* Ruse
Ruse *104 D1 var.* Ruschuk, Rustchuk,
 Turk. Rusçuk. Ruse, N Bulgaria
Russadir *see* Melilla
Russellville *42 A1* Arkansas, C USA
Russia *see* Russian Federation
Russian America *see* Alaska
Russian Federation *112 D2 off.* Russian
 Federation, *var.* Russia, *Latv.* Krievija,
 Rus. Rossiyskaya Federatsiya. *country*
 Asia/Europe

RUSSIAN FEDERATION
Europe / Asia

Official name Russian Federation
Formation 1480 / 1991
Capital Moscow
Population 143 million / 22 people
per sq mile (8 people per sq km)
Total area 6,592,735 sq. miles
(17,075,200 sq. km)
Languages Russian*, Tatar, Ukrainian,
Chavash, various other national languages
Religions Orthodox Christian 75%,
Muslim 14%, Other 11%
Ethnic mix Russian 80%, Other 12%,
Tatar 4%, Ukrainian 2%, Bashkir 1%,
Chavash 1%
Government Mixed Presidential–
Parliamentary system
Currency Russian rouble = 100 kopeks
Literacy rate 99%
Calorie consumption 3172 kilocalories

Russian Federation *see* Russian
 Federation
Rustaq *see* Ar Rustāq
Rustavi *117 G2 prev.* Rust'avi.
 SE Georgia
Rust'avi *see* Rustavi
Rustchuk *see* Ruse
Ruston *42 B2* Louisiana, S USA
Rutanzige, Lake *see* Edward, Lake
Rutba *see* Ar Ruṭbah
Rutlam *see* Ratlām
Rutland *41 F2* Vermont, NE USA
Rutog *126 A4 var.* Rutög, Rutok. Xizang
 Zizhiqu, W China
Rutok *see* Rutog
Ruvuma *69 E5 var.* Rio Rovuma. *river*
 Mozambique/Tanzania
Ruvuma, Rio *see* Rovuma, Rio
Ruwenzori *77 E5 mountain range* Dem.
 Rep. Congo/Uganda
Ruzhany *107 B6* Brestskaya Voblasts',
 SW Belarus
Ružomberok *99 C5 Ger.* Rosenberg,
 Hung. Rózsahegy. Žilinský Kraj,
 N Slovakia
Rwanda *73 B6 off.* Rwandese Republic;
 prev. Ruanda. *country* C Africa

RWANDA
Central Africa

Official name Republic of Rwanda
Formation 1962 / 1962
Capital Kigali
Population 10.9 million / 1132 people
per sq mile (437 people per sq km)
Total area 10,169 sq. miles (26,338 sq. km)
Languages Kinyarwanda*, French*,
Kiswahili, English*
Religions Christian 94%, Muslim 5%,
Traditional beliefs 1%
Ethnic mix Hutu 85%, Tutsi 14%,
Other (including Twa) 1%
Government Presidential system
Currency Rwanda franc = 100 centimes
Literacy rate 71%
Calorie consumption 2188 kilocalories

Rwandese Republic *see* Rwanda
Ryazan' *111 B5* Ryazanskaya Oblast',
 W Russian Federation
Rybach'ye *see* Balykchy
Rybinsk *110 B4 prev.* Andropov.
 Yaroslavskaya Oblast', W Russian
 Federation
Rybnik *99 C5* Śląskie, S Poland
Rybnitsa *see* Rîbniţa
Ryde *148 E1* United Kingdom
Ryki *98 D4* Lubelskie, E Poland
Rykovo *see* Yenakiyeve
Rypin *98 C3* Kujawsko-pomorskie,
 C Poland
Ryssel *see* Lille
Rysy *99 C5 mountain* S Poland
Ryukyu Islands *130 A2 Eng.* Ryukyu
 Islands. *island group* SW Japan
Ryukyu Islands *125 E3 Eng.* Ryukyu
 Islands. *island group* SW Japan
Ryukyu Islands *see* Nansei-shotō
Ryukyu Islands *see* Nansei-shotō
Ryukyu Trench *125 F3 var.* Nansei Syotō
 Trench. *trench* S East China Sea
Rzeszów *99 E5* Podkarpackie,
 SE Poland
Rzhev *110 B4* Tverskaya Oblast',
 W Russian Federation

S

Saale *94 C4 river* C Germany
Saalfeld *95 C5 var.* Saalfeld an der Saale.
 Thüringen, C Germany
Saalfeld an der Saale *see* Saalfeld
Saarbrücken *95 A6 Fr.* Sarrebruck.
 Saarland, SW Germany
Sääre *106 C2 var.* Sjar. Saaremaa,
 W Estonia
Saare *see* Saaremaa
Saaremaa *106 C2 Ger.* Oesel, Ösel; *prev.*
 Saare. *island* W Estonia
Saariselkä *84 D2 Lapp.* Suoločielgi.
 Lappi, N Finland
Sab' Ābār *118 C4 var.* Sab'a Biyar, Sa'b
 Bi'ār. Ḥimş, C Syria
Sab'a Biyar *see* Sab' Ābār
Šabac *100 D3* Serbia, W Serbia
Sabadell *93 G2* Cataluña, E Spain
Sabah *138 D3 prev.* British North
 Borneo, North Borneo. *state* East
 Malaysia
Sabanalarga *58 B1* Atlántico,
 N Colombia
Sabaneta *58 C1* Falcón, N Venezuela
Sabaria *see* Szombathely
Sab'atayn, Ramlat as *121 C6 desert*
 C Yemen
Sabaya *61 F4* Oruro, S Bolivia
Sa'b Bi'ār *see* Sab' Ābār
Saberi, Hamun-e *122 C5 var.*
 Daryācheh-ye Hāmun, Daryācheh-ye
 Sīstān. *lake* Afghanistan/Iran
Sabhā *71 F3* C Libya
Sabi *see* Save
Sabinas *51 E2* Coahuila, NE Mexico
Sabinas Hidalgo *51 E2* Nuevo León,
 NE Mexico
Sabine River *49 H3 river* Louisiana/
 Texas, SW USA
Sabkha *see* As Sabkhah
Sable, Cape *43 E5 headland* Florida,
 SE USA
Sable Island *39 G4 island* Nova Scotia,
 SE Canada
Şabyā *121 B6* Jīzān, SW Saudi Arabia

Sabzawar *see* Sabzevār
Sabzevār *120 D2 var.* Sabzawar.
 Khorāsān-Razavi, NE Iran
Sachsen *94 D4 Eng.* Saxony, *Fr.* Saxe.
 state E Germany
Sachs Harbour *37 E2 var.* Ikaahuk.
 Banks Island, Northwest Territories,
 N Canada
Sächsisch-Reen/Sächsisch-Regen
 see Reghin
Sacramento *47 B5 state capital*
 California, W USA
Sacramento Mountains *48 D2*
 mountain range New Mexico,
 SW USA
Sacramento River *47 B5 river* California,
 W USA
Sacramento Valley *47 B5 valley*
 California, W USA
Sá da Bandeira *see* Lubango
Şa'dah *121 B6* NW Yemen
Sado *see* Sadoga-shima
Sadoga-shima *131 C5 var.* Sado. *island*
 C Japan
Saena Julia *see* Siena
Safad *see* Tsefat
Ṣafāqis *see* Sfax
Ṣafāshahr *120 D3 var.* Deh Bīd. Fārs,
 C Iran
Safed *see* Tsefat
Säffle *85 B6* Värmland, C Sweden
Safford *48 C3* Arizona, SW USA
Safi *70 B2* W Morocco
Selseleh-ye Safīd Kūh *122 D4 Eng.*
 Paropamisus Range. *mountain range*
 W Afghanistan
Sagaing *136 B3* Sagaing, C Myanmar
 (Burma)
Sagami-nada *131 D6 inlet* SW Japan
Sagan *see* Żagań
Sāgar *134 D4 prev.* Saugor. Madhya
 Pradesh, C India
Sagarmāthā *see* Everest, Mount
Sagebrush State *see* Nevada
Saghez *see* Saqqez
Saginaw *40 C3* Michigan, N USA
Saginaw Bay *40 D2 lake bay* Michigan,
 N USA
Sagua la Grande *54 B2* Villa Clara,
 C Cuba
Sagunto *93 F3 Cat.* Sagunt, *Ar.*
 Murviedro; *anc.* Saguntum.
 Valenciana, E Spain
Sagunt/Saguntum *see* Sagunto
Sahara *68 B3 desert* Libya/Algeria
Sahara el Gharbiya *see* Şaḥrā' al
 Gharbīyah
Saharan Atlas *70 D2 var.* Saharan Atlas.
 mountain range Algeria/Morocco
Saharan Atlas *see* Atlas Saharien
Sahel *74 D3 physical region* C Africa
Sāḥiliyah, Jibāl as *118 B3 mountain*
 range NW Syria
Sāhīwāl *134 C2 prev.* Montgomery.
 Punjab, E Pakistan
Saīda *119 A5 var.* Şaydā, Sayida; *anc.*
 Sidon. W Lebanon
Sa'īdābād *see* Sīrjān
Saidpur *135 G3 var.* Syedpur. Rajshahi,
 NW Bangladesh
Saīdu *134 C1 var.* Mingora, Mongora;
 prev. Mingāora. Khyber Pakhtunkhwa,
 N Pakistan
Saigon *see* Hồ Chí Minh
Saimaa *85 E5 lake* SE Finland
St Albans *89 E6 anc.* Verulamium.
 E England, United Kingdom
Saint Albans *40 B5* West Virginia,
 NE USA
St Andrews *88 C4* E Scotland, United
 Kingdom
Saint Anna Trough *see* Svyataya Anna
 Trough
St. Ann's Bay *54 B4* C Jamaica
St. Anthony *39 G3* Newfoundland and
 Labrador, SE Canada
Saint Augustine *43 E3* Florida,
 SE USA
St Austell *89 C7* SW England, United
 Kingdom
St.Botolph's Town *see* Boston
St-Brieuc *90 A3* Côtes d'Armor,
 NW France
St. Catharines *38 D5* Ontario, S Canada
St-Chamond *91 C5* Loire, E France
Saint Christopher and Nevis,
 Federation of *see* Saint Kitts and Nevis

233

Saint Christopher-Nevis *see* Saint Kitts and Nevis
Saint Clair, Lake *40 D3 var.* Lac à L'Eau Claire. *lake* Canada/USA
St-Claude *91 D5 anc.* Condate. Jura, E France
Saint Cloud *45 F2* Minnesota, N USA
Saint Croix *55 F3 island* S Virgin Islands (US)
Saint Croix River *40 A2 river* Minnesota/Wisconsin, N USA
St David's Island *42 B5 island* E Bermuda
St-Denis *79 G4 dependent territory capital* (Réunion) NW Réunion
St-Dié *90 E4* Vosges, NE France
St-Egrève *91 D5* Isère, E France
Sainte Marie, Cap *see* Vohimena, Tanjona
Saintes *91 B5 anc.* Mediolanum. Charente-Maritime, W France
St-Étienne *91 D5* Loire, E France
St-Flour *91 C5* Cantal, C France
St-Gall/Saint Gall/St. Gallen *see* Sankt Gallen
St-Gaudens *91 B6* Haute-Garonne, S France
Saint George *149 D5* Queensland, E Australia
St George *42 B4* N Bermuda
Saint George *44 A5* Utah, W USA
St. George's *55 G5 country capital* (Grenada) SW Grenada
St-Georges *39 E4* Québec, SE Canada
St-Georges *59 H3* E French Guiana
Saint George's Channel *89 B6 channel* Ireland/Wales, United Kingdom
St George's Island *42 B4 island* E Bermuda
Saint Helena *69 B6 UK dependent territory* C Atlantic Ocean
St Helier *89 D8 dependent territory capital* (Jersey) S Jersey, Channel Islands
St.Iago de la Vega *see* Spanish Town
Saint Ignace *40 C2* Michigan, N USA
St-Jean, Lac *39 E4 lake* Québec, SE Canada
Saint Joe River *46 D2 river* Idaho, NW USA North America
St. John *39 F4* New Brunswick, SE Canada
Saint-John *see* Saint John
Saint John River *41 H1 Fr.* Saint-John. *river* Canada/USA
St John's *55 G3 country capital* (Antigua and Barbuda) Antigua, Antigua and Barbuda
St. John's *39 H3 province capital* Newfoundland and Labrador, E Canada
Saint Joseph *45 F4* Missouri, C USA
St Julian's *see* San Giljan
St Kilda *88 A3 island* NW Scotland, United Kingdom
Saint Kitts and Nevis *55 F3 off.* Federation of Saint Christopher and Nevis, *var.* Saint Christopher-Nevis. *country* E West Indies

SAINT KITTS & NEVIS
West Indies

Official name Federation of Saint Christopher and Nevis
Formation 1983 / 1983
Capital Basseterre
Population 50,726 / 365 people per sq mile (141 people per sq km)
Total area 101 sq. miles (261 sq. km)
Languages English*, English Creole
Religions Anglican 33%, Methodist 29%, Other 22%, Moravian 9%, Roman Catholic 7%
Ethnic mix Black 95%, Mixed race 3%, White 1%, Other and Amerindian 1%
Government Parliamentary system
Currency Eastern Caribbean dollar = 100 cents
Literacy rate 98%
Calorie consumption 2546 kilocalories

St-Laurent *see* St-Laurent-du-Maroni
St-Laurent-du-Maroni *59 H3 var.* St-Laurent. NW French Guiana
St-Laurent, Fleuve *see* St. Lawrence
St. Lawrence *39 E4 Fr.* Fleuve St-Laurent. *river* Canada/USA

St. Lawrence, Gulf of *39 F3 gulf* NW Atlantic Ocean
Saint Lawrence Island *36 B2 island* Alaska, USA
St-Lô *90 B3 anc.* Briovera, Laudus. Manche, N France
St-Louis *90 E4* Haut-Rhin, NE France
Saint Louis *74 B3* NW Senegal
Saint Louis *45 G4* Missouri, C USA
Saint Lucia *55 E1 country* SE West Indies

SAINT LUCIA
West Indies

Official name Saint Lucia
Formation 1979 / 1979
Capital Castries
Population 162,178 / 687 people per sq mile (266 people per sq km)
Total area 239 sq. miles (620 sq. km)
Languages English*, French Creole
Religions Roman Catholic 90%, Other 10%
Ethnic mix Black 83%, Mulatto (mixed race) 13%, Asian 3%, Other 1%
Government Parliamentary system
Currency Eastern Caribbean dollar = 100 cents
Literacy rate 95%
Calorie consumption 2710 kilocalories

Saint Lucia Channel *55 H4 channel* Martinique/Saint Lucia
St-Malo *90 B3* Ille-et-Vilaine, NW France
St-Malo, Golfe de *90 A3 gulf* NW France
Saint Martin *see* Sint Maarten
St.Matthew's Island *see* Zadetkyi Kyun
St.Matthias Group *144 B3 island group* NE Papua New Guinea
St. Moritz *95 B7 Ger.* Sankt Moritz, *Rmsch.* San Murezzan. Graubünden, SE Switzerland
St-Nazaire *90 A4* Loire-Atlantique, NW France
Saint Nicholas *see* São Nicolau
Saint-Nicolas *see* Sint-Niklaas
St-Omer *90 C2* Pas-de-Calais, N France
Saint Paul *45 F2 state capital* Minnesota, N USA
St-Paul, Île *141 C6 var.* St.Paul Island. *island* Île St-Paul, NE French Southern and Antarctic Territories Antarctica Indian Ocea
St.Paul Island *see* St-Paul, Île
St Peter Port *89 D8 dependent territory capital* (Guernsey) C Guernsey, Channel Islands
Saint Petersburg *43 E4* Florida, SE USA
Saint Petersburg *see* Sankt-Peterburg
St-Pierre and Miquelon *39 G4 Fr.* Îles St-Pierre et Miquelon. *French territorial collectivity* NE North America
St-Quentin *90 C3* Aisne, N France
Saint Thomas *see* São Tomé, Sao Tome and Principe
Saint Thomas *see* Charlotte Amalie, Virgin Islands (US)
Saint Ubes *see* Setúbal
Saint Vincent *55 G4 island* N Saint Vincent and the Grenadines
Saint Vincent *see* São Vicente
Saint Vincent and the Grenadines *55 H4 country* SE West Indies

SAINT VINCENT & THE GRENADINES
West Indies

Official name Saint Vincent and the Grenadines
Formation 1979 / 1979
Capital Kingstown
Population 103,537 / 790 people per sq mile (305 people per sq km)
Total area 150 sq. miles (389 sq. km)
Languages English*, English Creole
Religions Anglican 47%, Methodist 28%, Roman Catholic 13%, Other 12%
Ethnic mix Black 66%, Mulatto (mixed race) 19%, Other 12%, Carib 2%, Asian 1%
Government Parliamentary system
Currency Eastern Caribbean dollar = 100 cents
Literacy rate 88%
Calorie consumption 2914 kilocalories

Saint Vincent, Cape *see* São Vicente, Cabo de
Saint Vincent Passage *55 H4 passage* Saint Lucia/Saint Vincent and the Grenadines
Saint Yves *see* Setúbal
Saipan *142 B1 island/country capital* (Northern Mariana Islands) S Northern Mariana Islands
Saishū *see* Jeju-do
Sajama, Nevado *61 F4 mountain* W Bolivia
Sajószentpéter *99 D6* Borsod-Abaúj-Zemplén, NE Hungary
Sakākah *120 B4* Al Jawf, NW Saudi Arabia
Sakakawea, Lake *44 D1 reservoir* North Dakota, N USA
Sak'art'velo *see* Georgia
Sakata *130 D4* Yamagata, Honshū, C Japan
Sakhalin *115 G4 var.* Sakhalin. *island* SE Russian Federation
Sakhalin *see* Sakhalin, Ostrov
Sakhon Nakhon *see* Sakon Nakhon
Şäki *117 G2 Rus.* Sheki; *prev.* Nukha. NW Azerbaijan
Saki *see* Saky
Sakishima-shoto *130 A3 var.* Sakisima Syotō. *island group* SW Japan
Sakisima Syotō *see* Sakishima-shotō
Sakiz *see* Saqqez
Sakiz-Adasi *see* Chíos
Sakon Nakhon *136 D4 var.* Muang Sakon Nakhon, Sakhon Nakhon. Sakon Nakhon, E Thailand
Saky *109 F5 Rus.* Saki. Avtonomna Respublika Krym, S Ukraine
Sal *74 A3 island* Ilhas de Barlavento, NE Cape Verde
Sala *85 C6* Västmanland, C Sweden
Salacgrīva *106 C3 Est.* Salatsi. N Latvia
Sala Consilina *97 D5* Campania, S Italy
Salado, Río *62 D5 river* E Argentina
Salado, Río *64 C3 river* C Argentina
Salamá *52 B2* Baja Verapaz, C Guatemala
Salamanca *41 D6* Coquimbo, C Chile
Salamanca *92 D2 anc.* Helmantica, Salmantica. Castilla y León, NW Spain
Salamīyah *118 B3 var.* As Salamīyah. Ḩamāh, W Syria
Salang *see* Phuket
Salantai *106 B3* Klaipėda, NW Lithuania
Salatsi *see* Salacgrīva
Salavan *137 D5 var.* Saravan, Saravane. Salavan, S Laos
Salavat *111 D6* Respublika Bashkortostan, W Russian Federation
Sala y Gomez *153 F4 island* Chile, E Pacific Ocean
Sala y Gomez Fracture Zone *see* Sala y Gomez Ridge
Sala y Gomez Ridge *153 G4 var.* Sala y Gomez Fracture Zone. *fracture zone* SE Pacific Ocean
Salazar *see* N'Dalatando
Šalčininkai *107 C5* Vilnius, SE Lithuania
Salduba *see* Zaragoza
Saldus *106 B3 Ger.* Frauenburg. W Latvia
Sale *149 C7* Victoria, SE Australia
Salé *70 C2* NW Morocco
Salekhard *114 D3 prev.* Obdorsk. Yamalo-Nenetskiy Avtonomnyy Okrug, N Russian Federation
Salem *132 C2* Tamil Nādu, SE India
Salem *46 B3 state capital* Oregon, NW USA
Salerno *97 D5 anc.* Salernum. Campania, S Italy
Salerno, Gulf of *97 C5 Eng.* Gulf of Salerno. *gulf* S Italy
Salerno, Gulf of *see* Salerno, Golfo di
Salernum *see* Salerno
Salihorsk *107 C7 Rus.* Soligorsk. Minskaya Voblasts', S Belarus
Salima *79 E2* Central, C Malawi
Salina *45 E5* Kansas, C USA
Salina Cruz *51 F5* Oaxaca, SE Mexico
Salinas *60 A2* Guayas, W Ecuador
Salinas *47 B6* California, W USA
Salisbury *89 D7 var.* New Sarum. S England, United Kingdom
Salisbury *see* Harare
Sällan *see* Sørøya
Salliq *see* Coral Harbour

Sallyana *see* Şalyän
Salmantica *see* Salamanca
Salmon River *46 D3 river* Idaho, NW USA
Salmon River Mountains *46 D3 mountain range* Idaho, NW USA
Salo *85 D6* Länsi-Suomi, SW Finland
Salon-de-Provence *91 D6* Bouches-du-Rhône, SE France
Salonica/Salonika *see* Thessaloníki
Salonta *108 A3 Hung.* Nagyszalonta. Bihor, W Romania
Sal'sk *111 B7* Rostovskaya Oblast', SW Russian Federation
Salt *see* As Salţ
Salta *64 C2* Salta, NW Argentina
Saltash *89 C7* SW England, United Kingdom
Saltillo *51 E3* Coahuila, NE Mexico
Salt Lake City *44 B4 state capital* Utah, W USA
Salto *64 D4* Salto, N Uruguay
Salton Sea *47 D8 lake* California, W USA
Salvador *63 G3 prev.* São Salvador. *state capital* Bahia, E Brazil
Salween *124 C2 Bur.* Thanlwin, *Chin.* Nu Chiang, Nu Jiang. *river* SE Asia
Şalyän *135 E3 var.* Sallyana. Mid Western, W Nepal
Salzburg *95 D6 anc.* Juvavum. Salzburg, N Austria
Salzgitter *94 C4 prev.* Watenstedt-Salzgitter. Niedersachsen, C Germany
Salzwedel *94 C3* Sachsen-Anhalt, N Germany
Šamac *see* Bosanski Šamac
Samakhixai *see* Attapu
Samalayuca *50 C1* Chihuahua, N Mexico
Samar *139 F2 island* C Philippines
Samara *114 B3 prev.* Kuybyshev. Samarskaya Oblast', W Russian Federation
Samarang *see* Semarang
Samarinda *138 D4* Borneo, C Indonesia
Samarkand *see* Samarqand
Samarkandski/Samarkandskoye *see* Temirtau
Samarobriva *see* Amiens
Samarqand *123 E2 Rus.* Samarkand. Samarqand Viloyati, C Uzbekistan
Samawa *see* As Samāwah
Sambalpur *135 F4* Orissa, E India
Sambava *79 G2* Antsiranana, NE Madagascar
Sambir *108 B2 Rus.* Sambor. L'vivs'ka Oblast', NW Ukraine
Sambor *see* Sambir
Sambre *90 D2 river* Belgium/France
Samfya *78 D2* Luapula, N Zambia
Saminatal *94 E2 valley* Austria/Liechtenstein Europe
Samnān *see* Semnān
Sam Neua *see* Xam Nua
Samoa *145 E4 off.* Independent State of Samoa, *var.* Sāmoa; *prev.* Western Samoa. *country* W Polynesia

SAMOA
Australasia & Oceania

Official name Independent State of Samoa
Formation 1962 / 1962
Capital Apia
Population 200,000 / 183 people per sq mile (71 people per sq km)
Total area 1104 sq. miles (2860 sq. km)
Languages Samoan*, English*
Religions Christian 99%, Other 1%
Ethnic mix Polynesian 91%, Euronesian 7%, Other 2%
Government Parliamentary system
Currency Tala = 100 sene
Literacy rate 99%
Calorie consumption 2997 kilocalories

Sāmoa *see* Samoa
Samoa Basin *143 E3 undersea basin* W Pacific Ocean
Samoa, Independent State of *see* Samoa
Samobor *100 E2* C Croatia
Sámos *105 E6 prev.* Limín Vathéos. Sámos, Dodekánisa, Greece, Aegean Sea
Sámos *105 E6 island* Dodekánisa, Greece, Aegean Sea
Samothrace *see* Samothráki

Samothráki *104 D4* Samothráki,
NE Greece
Samothraki *104 C4 anc.* Samothrace.
island NE Greece
Sampit *138 C4* Borneo, C Indonesia
Sâmraông *137 D5 prev.* Phumĭ
Sâmraông, Phum Samrong. Siěmréab,
NW Cambodia
Samsun *116 D2 anc.* Amisus. Samsun,
N Turkey
Samt'redia *117 F2 prev.* Samtredia.
W Georgia
Samtredia *see* Samt'redia
Samui, Ko *137 C6 island* SW Thailand
Samut Prakan *137 C5 var.* Muang Samut
Prakan, Paknam. Samut Prakan,
C Thailand
San *74 D3* Ségou, C Mali
San *99 E5 river* SE Poland
Şan'ā' *121 B6 Eng.* Sana. *country capital*
(Yemen) W Yemen
Sana *100 B3 river* NW Bosnia and
Herzegovina
Sanae *154 B2 South African research
station* Antarctica
Sanaga *77 B5 river* C Cameroon
San Ambrosio, Isla *57 A5 Eng.* San
Ambrosio Island. *island* W Chile
San Ambrosio Island *see* San Ambrosio,
Isla
Sanandaj *120 C3 prev.* Sinneh.
Kordestān, W Iran
San Andrés, Isla de *53 F3 island*
NW Colombia, Caribbean Sea
San Andrés Tuxtla *51 F4 var.* Tuxtla.
Veracruz-Llave, E Mexico
San Angelo *49 F3* Texas, SW USA
San Antonio *52 B2* Toledo, C Belize
San Antonio *64 B4* Valparaíso, C Chile
San Antonio *49 F4* Texas, SW USA
San Antonio Oeste *65 C5* Río Negro,
E Argentina
San Antonio River *49 G4 river* Texas,
SW USA
Sanata Uxía de Ribeira *92 B1 var.*
Ribeira. Galicia, NW Spain
Sanáw *121 C6 var.* Sanaw. NE Yemen
San Benedicto, Isla *50 B4 island*
W Mexico
San Benito *52 B1* Petén, N Guatemala
San Benito *49 G5* Texas, SW USA
San Bernardino *47 C7* California,
W USA
San Blas *50 C3* Sinaloa, C Mexico
San Blas, Cape *42 D3 headland* Florida,
SE USA
San Blas, Cordillera de *53 G4 mountain
range* NE Panama
San Carlos *52 D4* Río San Juan,
S Nicaragua
San Carlos *48 B2* Arizona, SW USA
San Carlos *see* Quesada, Costa Rica
San Carlos de Ancud *see* Ancud
San Carlos de Bariloche *65 B5* Río
Negro, SW Argentina
San Carlos del Zulia *58 C2* Zulia,
W Venezuela
San Clemente Island *47 B8 island*
Channel Islands, California, W USA
San Cristóbal *58 C2* Táchira,
W Venezuela
San Cristóbal *144 C4 var.* Makira. *island*
SE Solomon Islands
San Cristóbal *see* San Cristóbal de
Las Casas
San Cristóbal De Las Casas *51 G5 var.*
San Cristóbal. Chiapas, SE Mexico
San Cristóbal, Isla *60 B5 var.* Chatham
Island. *island* Galápagos Islands,
Ecuador, E Pacific Ocean
Sancti Spíritus *54 B2* Sancti Spíritus,
C Cuba
Sandakan *138 D3* Sabah, East Malaysia
Sandalwood Island *see* Sumba, Pulau
Sandanski *104 C3 prev.* Sveti Vrach.
Blagoevgrad, SW Bulgaria
Sanday *88 D2 island* NE Scotland, United
Kingdom
Sanders *48 C2* Arizona, SW USA
Sand Hills *44 D3 mountain range*
Nebraska, C USA
San Diego *47 C8* California, W USA
Sandnes *85 A6* Rogaland, S Norway
Sandomierz *98 D4 Rus.* Sandomir.
Świętokrzyskie, C Poland
Sandomir *see* Sandomierz
Sandoway *see* Thandwe

Sandpoint *46 C1* Idaho, NW USA
Sand Springs *49 G1* Oklahoma, C USA
Sandusky *40 D3* Ohio, N USA
Sandvika *85 A6* Akershus, S Norway
Sandviken *85 C6* Gävleborg, C Sweden
Sandwich Island *see* Efate
Sandwich Islands *see* Hawai'ian Islands
Sandy Bay *93 H5* Saskatchewan,
C Canada
Sandy City *44 B4* Utah, W USA
Sandy Lake *38 B3 lake* Ontario,
C Canada
San Esteban *52 D2* Olancho, C Honduras
San Eugenio/San Eugenio del Cuareim
see Artigas
San Felipe *58 D1* Yaracuy,
NW Venezuela
San Felipe de Puerto Plata *see* Puerto
Plata
San Félix, Isla *57 A5 Eng.* San Felix
Island. *island* W Chile
San Felix Island *see* San Félix, Isla
San Fernando *92 C5 prev.* Isla de León.
Andalucía, S Spain
San Fernando *55 H5* Trinidad, Trinidad
and Tobago
San Fernando *46 D1* California,
W USA
San Fernando *58 D2 var.* San Fernando
de Apure. Apure, C Venezuela
San Fernando de Apure *see* San
Fernando
San Fernando del Valle de Catamarca
64 C3 var. Catamarca. Catamarca,
NW Argentina
San Fernando de Monte Cristi *see*
Monte Cristi
San Francisco *47 B6* California, W USA
San Francisco del Oro *50 C2*
Chihuahua, N Mexico
San Francisco de Macorís *55 E3*
C Dominican Republic
San Fructuoso *see* Tacuarembó
San Gabriel *60 B1* Carchi, N Ecuador
San Gabriel Mountains *46 E1 mountain
range* California, USA
Sangihe, Kepulauan *see* Sangir,
Kepulauan
San Giljan *102 B5 var.* St Julian's.
N Malta
Sangir, Kepulauan *139 F3 var.*
Kepulauan Sangihe. *island group*
N Indonesia
Sāngli *132 B1* Mahārāshtra, W India
Sangmélima *77 B5* Sud, S Cameroon
Sangre de Cristo Mountains *48 D1
mountain range* Colorado/New Mexico,
C USA
San Ignacio *52 B1 prev.* Cayo, El Cayo.
Cayo, W Belize
San Ignacio *61 F3* El Beni, N Bolivia
San Ignacio *50 B2* Baja California Sur,
NW Mexico
San Joaquin Valley *47 B7 valley*
California, W USA
San Jorge, Gulf of *65 C6 var.* Gulf of San
Jorge. *gulf* S Argentina
San Jorge, Gulf of *see* San Jorge, Golfo
San José *53 E4 country capital*
(Costa Rica) San José,
C Costa Rica
San José *61 G3 var.* San José de
Chiquitos. Santa Cruz, E Bolivia
San José *52 B3 var.* Puerto San José.
Escuintla, S Guatemala
San José *47 B6* California, W USA
San José *see* San José del Guaviare,
Colombia
San José de Chiquitos *see* San José
San José de Cúcuta *see* Cúcuta
San José del Guaviare *58 C4 var.* San
José. Guaviare, S Colombia
San Juan *64 B4* San Juan, W Argentina
San Juan *55 F3 dependent territory
capital* (Puerto Rico) NE Puerto Rico
San Juan Bautista *64 D3* Misiones,
S Paraguay
San Juan Bautista *see* Villahermosa
San Juan Bautista Tuxtepec *see* Tuxtepec
San Juan de Alicante *see* Sant Joan
d'Alacant
San Juan del Norte *53 E4 var.* Greytown.
Río San Juan, SE Nicaragua
San Juan de los Morros *58 D2 var.* San
Juan. Guárico, N Venezuela
San Juanito, Isla *50 C4 island* C Mexico

San Juan Mountains *48 D1 mountain
range* Colorado, C USA
San Juan, Río *53 E4 river* Costa Rica/
Nicaragua
San Juan River *48 C1 river* Colorado/
Utah, W USA
San Julián *see* Puerto San Julián
Sankt-Bartholomäi *see* Palamuse
Sankt Gallen *95 B7 var.* St. Gallen, *Eng.*
Saint Gall, *Fr.* St-Gall. Sankt Gallen,
NE Switzerland
Sankt-Georgen *see* Sfântu Gheorghe
Sankt-Jakobi *see* Pärnu-Jaagupi,
Pärnumaa, Estonia
Sankt Martin *see* Martin
Sankt Moritz *see* St. Moritz
Sankt-Peterburg *110 B4 prev.*
Leningrad, Petrograd, *Eng.*
Saint Petersburg, *Fin.* Pietari.
Leningradskaya Oblast', NW Russian
Federation
Sankt Pölten *95 E6* Niederösterreich,
N Austria
Sankt Veit an der Flaum *see* Rijeka
Sankuru *77 D6 river* C Dem. Rep. Congo
Şanlıurfa *117 E4 prev.* Sanli Urfa, Urfa;
anc. Edessa. Şanlıurfa, S Turkey
Sanli Urfa *see* Şanlıurfa
San Lorenzo *61 G5* Tarija, S Bolivia
San Lorenzo *60 A1* Esmeraldas,
N Ecuador
San Lorenzo, Isla *60 C4 island* W Peru
Sanlúcar de Barrameda *92 C5*
Andalucía, S Spain
San Luis *64 C4* San Luis, C Argentina
San Luis *52 B2* Petén, NE Guatemala
San Luis Obispo *47 B7* California,
W USA
San Luis Potosí *51 E3* San Luis Potosí,
C Mexico
San Luis Río Colorado *50 A1 var.*
San Luis Río Colorado. Sonora,
NW Mexico
San Luis Río Colorado *see* San Luis Río
Colorado
San Marcos *52 A2* San Marcos,
W Guatemala
San Marcos *49 G4* Texas, SW USA
San Marcos de Arica *see* Arica
San Marino *96 E1 country capital* (San
Marino) C San Marino
San Marino *96 D1 off.* Republic of San
Marino. *country* S Europe

SAN MARINO
Southern Europe

Official name Republic of San Marino
Formation 301 / 1631
Capital San Marino
Population 32,140 / 1339 people
per sq mile (527 people per sq km)
Total area 23.6 sq. miles (61 sq. km)
Languages Italian*
Religions Roman Catholic 93%,
Other and nonreligious 7%
Ethnic mix Sammarinese 88%,
Italian 10%, Other 2%
Government Parliamentary system
Currency Euro = 100 cents
Literacy rate 99%
Calorie consumption Not available

San Marino, Republic of *see* San Marino
San Martín *154 A2 Argentinian research
station* Antarctica
San Mateo *59 E2* Anzoátegui,
NE Venezuela
San Matías *61 H3* Santa Cruz, E Bolivia
San Matías, Gulf of *65 C5 var.* Gulf of
San Matias. *gulf* E Argentina
San Matías, Gulf of *see* San Matías, Golfo
Sanmenxia *128 C4 var.* Shan Xian.
Henan, C China
San Miguel *52 C3* San Miguel,
SE El Salvador
San Miguel *50 D2* Coahuila,
N Mexico
San Miguel de Ibarra *see* Ibarra
San Miguel de Tucumán *64 C3 var.*
Tucumán. Tucumán, N Argentina
San Miguelito *53 G4* Panamá, C Panama
San Miguel, Río *61 G3 river* E Bolivia
San Murezzan *see* St. Moritz
Sannär *see* Sennar
Sânnicolaul-Mare *see* Sânnicolau Mare

Sânnicolau Mare *108 A4 var.*
Sânnicolaul-Mare, *Hung.*
Nagyszentmiklós; *prev.* Sânniclăuş
Mare, Sinnicolau Mare. Timiş,
W Romania
Sanok *99 E5* Podkarpackie, SE Poland
San Pablo *61 F5* Potosí, S Bolivia
San Pedro *52 C1* Corozal, NE Belize
San-Pédro *74 D5* S Côte d'Ivoire
San Pedro *50 D3 var.* San Pedro de las
Colonias. Coahuila, NE Mexico
San Pedro de la Cueva *50 C2* Sonora,
NW Mexico
San Pedro de las Colonias *see* San Pedro
San Pedro de Lloc *60 B3* La Libertad,
NW Peru
San Pedro Mártir, Sierra *50 A1
mountain range* NW Mexico
San Pedro Sula *52 C2* Cortés,
NW Honduras
San Rafael *64 B4* Mendoza, W Argentina
San Rafael Mountains *47 C7 mountain
range* California, W USA
San Ramón de la Nueva Orán *64 C2*
Salta, N Argentina
San Remo *96 A3* Liguria, NW Italy
San Salvador *52 B3 country capital*
(El Salvador) San Salvador,
SW El Salvador
San Salvador *54 D2 prev.* Watlings
Island. *island* E Bahamas
San Salvador de Jujuy *64 C2 var.* Jujuy.
Jujuy, N Argentina
San Salvador, Isla *54 A4 island* Ecuador
Sansanné-Mango *75 E4 var.* Mango.
N Togo
Sansepolcro *96 C3* Toscana, C Italy
San Severo *97 D5* Puglia, SE Italy
Santa Ana *61 F3* El Beni, N Bolivia
Santa Ana *52 B3* Santa Ana,
NW El Salvador
Santa Ana *46 D2* California, W USA
Santa Ana de Coro *see* Coro
Santa Ana Mountains *46 E2 mountain
range* California, W USA
Santa Barbara *50 C2* Chihuahua,
N Mexico
Santa Barbara *47 C7* California, W USA
Santa Catalina de Armada *92 B1*
Galicia, NW Spain
Santa Catalina Island *47 B8 island*
Channel Islands, California, W USA
Santa Catarina *63 E5 off.* Estado de
Santa Catarina. *region* S Brazil
Santa Catarina *63 E5 off.* Estado de
Santa Catarina. *state* S Brazil
Santa Catarina, Estado de *see* Santa
Catarina
Santa Clara *54 B2* Villa Clara, C Cuba
Santa Clarita *46 D1* California, USA
Santa Cruz *76 E2* São Tomé, S Sao Tome
and Principe, Africa
Santa Cruz *47 B6* California, W USA
Santa Cruz *61 G4 department* E Bolivia
Santa Cruz Barillas *see* Barillas
Santa Cruz del Quiché *52 B2* Quiché,
W Guatemala
Santa Cruz de Tenerife *70 A3* Tenerife,
Islas Canarias, Spain, NE Atlantic Ocean
Santa Cruz, Isla *60 B5 var.* Indefatigable
Island, Isla Chávez. *island* Galápagos
Islands, Ecuador, E Pacific Ocean
Santa Cruz Islands *144 F3 island group*
E Solomon Islands
Santa Cruz, Río *65 B7 river* S Argentina
Santa Elena *52 B1* Cayo, W Belize
Santa Fe *48 D1 state capital* New Mexico,
SW USA
Santa Fe *64 C4* Santa Fe, C Argentina
Santa Fe de Bogotá *see* Bogotá
Santa Genoveva *50 B3* mountain
NW Mexico
Santa Isabel *144 C3 var.* Bughotu. *island*
N Solomon Islands
Santa Isabel *see* Malabo
Santa Lucia Range *47 B7 mountain
range* California, W USA
Santa Margarita, Isla *50 B3 island*
NW Mexico
Santa Maria *63 E5* Rio Grande do Sul,
S Brazil
Santa Maria *47 B7* California, USA
Santa Maria *92 A5 island* Azores,
Portugal, NE Atlantic Ocean
Santa Maria del Buen Aire *see* Buenos
Aires

235

Santa María, Isla 60 A5 var. Isla Floreana, Charles Island. island Galápagos Islands, Ecuador, E Pacific Ocean
Santa Marta 58 B1 Magdalena, N Colombia
Santa Maura see Lefkáda
Santa Monica 46 D1 California, W USA
Santana 76 E2 São Tomé, C Sao Tome and Principe, Africa
Santander 92 D1 Cantabria, N Spain
Santarém 63 E2 Pará, N Brazil
Santarém 92 B3 anc. Scalabis. Santarém, W Portugal
Santa Rosa 64 C4 La Pampa, C Argentina
Santa Rosa see Santa Rosa de Copán
Santa Rosa de Copán 52 C2 var. Santa Rosa. Copán, W Honduras
Santa Rosa Island 47 B8 island California, W USA
Sant Carles de la Rápida see Sant Carles de la Ràpita
Sant Carles de la Ràpita 93 F3 var. Sant Carles de la Rápida. Cataluña, NE Spain
Santiago 64 B4 var. Gran Santiago. country capital (Chile) Santiago, C Chile
Santiago 55 E3 var. Santiago de los Caballeros. N Dominican Republic
Santiago 53 F5 Veraguas, S Panama
Santiago 74 A3 var. São Tiago. island Ilhas de Sotavento, S Cape Verde
Santiago see Santiago de Cuba, Cuba
Santiago see Santiago de Compostela
Santiago de Compostela 92 B1 var. Santiago, Eng. Compostella; anc. Campus Stellae. Galicia, NW Spain
Santiago de Cuba 54 C3 var. Santiago. Santiago de Cuba, E Cuba
Santiago de Guayaquil see Guayaquil
Santiago del Estero 64 C3 Santiago del Estero, C Argentina
Santiago de los Caballeros see Santiago, Dominican Republic
Santiago de los Caballeros see Ciudad de Guatemala, Guatemala
Santiago Pinotepa Nacional see Pinotepa Nacional
Santiago, Río 60 B2 river N Peru
Santi Quaranta see Sarandë
Santissima Trinidad see Jilong
Sant Joan d'Alacant 93 F4 Cast. San Juan de Alicante. Valenciana, E Spain
Sant Julià de Lòria 91 A8 Sant Julià de Lòria, SW Andorra Europe
Santo see Espíritu Santo
Santo Antão 74 A2 island Ilhas de Barlavento, N Cape Verde
Santo António 76 E1 Príncipe, N Sao Tome and Principe, Africa
Santo Domingo 55 D3 prev. Ciudad Trujillo. country capital (Dominican Republic) SE Dominican Republic
Santo Domingo de los Colorados 60 B1 Pichincha, NW Ecuador
Santo Domingo Tehuantepec see Tehuantepec
Santos 63 F4 São Paulo, S Brazil
Santos Plateau 57 D5 undersea plateau SW Atlantic Ocean
Santo Tomé 64 D3 Corrientes, NE Argentina
Santo Tomé de Guayana see Ciudad Guayana
San Valentín, Cerro 65 A6 mountain S Chile
San Vicente 52 C3 San Vicente, C El Salvador
São Francisco, Rio 63 F3 river E Brazil
São Hill 73 C7 Iringa, S Tanzania
São João da Madeira 92 B2 Aveiro, N Portugal
São Jorge 92 A5 island Azores, Portugal, NE Atlantic Ocean
São Luís 63 F2 state capital Maranhão, NE Brazil
São Mandol see São Manuel, Rio
São Manuel, Rio 63 E3 var. São Mandol, Teles Pirés. river C Brazil
São Marcos, Baía de 63 F1 bay N Brazil

São Miguel 92 A5 island Azores, Portugal, NE Atlantic Ocean
Saona, Isla 55 E3 island SE Dominican Republic
Saône 91 D5 river E France
São Nicolau 74 A3 Eng. Saint Nicholas. island Ilhas de Barlavento, N Cape Verde
São Paulo 63 E4 state capital São Paulo, S Brazil
São Paulo 63 E4 off. Estado de São Paulo. region S Brazil
São Paulo 63 E4 off. Estado de São Paulo. state S Brazil
São Paulo de Loanda see Luanda
São Paulo, Estado de see São Paulo
São Pedro do Rio Grande do Sul see Rio Grande
São Roque, Cabo de 63 G2 headland E Brazil
São Salvador see Salvador, Brazil
São Salvador/São Salvador do Congo see M'Banza Congo, Angola
São Tiago see Santiago
São Tomé 77 A5 country capital (Sao Tome and Principe) São Tomé, S Sao Tome and Principe
São Tomé 76 E2 Eng. Saint Thomas. island S Sao Tome and Principe
Sao Tome and Principe 76 D1 off. Democratic Republic of Sao Tome and Principe. country E Atlantic Ocean

SÃO TOMÉ & PRÍNCIPE
West Africa

Official name The Democratic Republic of Sao Tome and Principe
Formation 1975 / 1975
Capital São Tomé
Population 200,000 / 539 people per sq mile (208 people per sq km)
Total area 386 sq. miles (1001 sq. km)
Languages Portuguese Creole, Portuguese*
Religions Roman Catholic 84%, Other 16%
Ethnic mix Black 90%, Portuguese and Creole 10%
Government Presidential system
Currency Dobra = 100 céntimos
Literacy rate 89%
Calorie consumption 2734 kilocalories

Sao Tome and Principe, Democratic Republic of see Sao Tome and Principe
São Tomé, Pico de 76 D2 mountain São Tomé, C Sao Tome and Principe, Africa
São Vicente 74 A3 Eng. Saint Vincent. island Ilhas de Barlavento, N Cape Verde
São Vicente, Cabo de 92 B5 Eng. Cape Saint Vincent, Port. Cabode São Vicente. cape S Portugal
São Vicente, Cabo de see São Vicente, Cabo de
Sápai see Sápes
Sapele 75 F5 Delta, S Nigeria
Sápes 104 D4 var. Sápai. Anatolikí Makedonía kai Thráki, NE Greece
Sapir 119 B7 prev. Sappir. Southern, S Israel
Sa Pobla 93 G3 Mallorca, Spain, W Mediterranean Sea
Sappir see Sapir
Sapporo 130 D2 Hokkaidō, NE Japan
Sapri 97 D6 Campania, S Italy
Sapulpa 49 G1 Oklahoma, C USA
Saqqez 120 C2 var. Saghez, Sakiz, Saqqiz. Kordestän, NW Iran
Saqqiz see Saqqez
Sara Buri 137 C5 var. Saraburi. Saraburi, C Thailand
Saraburi see Sara Buri
Saragossa see Zaragoza
Saragt see Sarahs
Saraguro 60 B2 Loja, S Ecuador
Sarahs 122 D3 var. Saragt, Rus. Serakhs. Ahal Welaýaty, S Turkmenistan
Sarajevo 100 C4 country capital (Bosnia and Herzegovina) Federacija Bosna I Hercegovina, SE Bosnia and Herzegovina
Sarakhs 120 E2 Khorāsān-Razavī, NE Iran

Saraktash 111 D6 Orenburgskaya Oblast', W Russian Federation
Saran' 114 C4 Kaz. Saran. Karagandy, C Kazakhstan
Saranda see Sarandë
Sarandë 101 C7 var. Saranda, It. Porto Edda; prev. Santi Quaranta. Vlorë, S Albania
Saransk 111 C5 Respublika Mordoviya, W Russian Federation
Sarasota 43 E4 Florida, SE USA
Saratov 114 B3 Saratovskaya Oblast', W Russian Federation
Saravan/Saravane see Salavan
Sarawak 138 D3 state East Malaysia
Sarawak see Kuching
Sarcelles 90 D1 Val-d'Oise, Île-de-France, N France Europe
Sardinia 97 A5 Eng. Sardinia. island Italy, C Mediterranean Sea
Sardinia see Sardegna
Sarera, Teluk see Cenderawasih, Teluk
Sargasso Sea 66 B4 sea W Atlantic Ocean
Sargodha 134 C2 Punjab, NE Pakistan
Sarh 76 C4 prev. Fort-Archambault. Moyen-Chari, S Chad
Sārī 120 D2 var. Sari, Sāri, Sāri. Māzandarān, N Iran
Saría 105 E7 island SE Greece
Sarıkamış 117 F3 Kars, NE Turkey
Sarıkol Range 123 G3 Rus. Sarykol'skiy Khrebet. mountain range China/Tajikistan
Sark 89 D8 Fr. Sercq. island Channel Islands
Şarkışla 116 D3 Sivas, C Turkey
Sarmiento 65 B6 Chubut, S Argentina
Sarnia 38 C5 Ontario, S Canada
Sarny 108 C1 Rivnens'ka Oblast', NW Ukraine
Sarochyna 107 D5 Rus. Sorochino. Vitsyebskaya Voblasts', N Belarus
Sarov 111 C5 prev. Sarova. Respublika Mordoviya, W Russian Federation
Sarova see Sarov
Sarpsborg 85 B6 Østfold, S Norway
Sarrebruck see Saarbrücken
Sartène 91 E7 Corse, France, C Mediterranean Sea
Sarthe 90 B4 river N France
Sárti 104 C4 Kentrikí Makedonía, N Greece
Saruhan see Manisa
Sarykol'skiy Khrebet see Sarikol Range
Sary-Tash 123 F2 Oshskaya Oblast', SW Kyrgyzstan
Saryyesik-Atyrau, Peski 123 G1 desert E Kazakhstan
Sasebo 131 A7 Nagasaki, Kyūshū, SW Japan
Saskatchewan 37 F5 province SW Canada
Saskatchewan 37 F5 river Manitoba/Saskatchewan, C Canada
Saskatoon 37 F5 Saskatchewan, S Canada
Sasovo 111 B5 Ryazanskaya Oblast', W Russian Federation
Sassandra 74 D5 S Côte d'Ivoire
Sassandra 74 D5 var. Ibo, Sassandra Fleuve. river S Côte d'Ivoire
Sassandra Fleuve see Sassandra
Sassari 97 A5 Sardegna, Italy, C Mediterranean Sea
Sassenheim 86 C3 Zuid-Holland, W Netherlands
Sassnitz 94 D2 Mecklenburg-Vorpommern, NE Germany
Sathmar see Satu Mare
Sátoraljaújhely 99 D6 Ger. Borsod-Abaúj-Zemplén, NE Hungary
Satpura Range 134 D4 mountain range C India
Satsuma-Sendai 131 A8 Kagoshima, Kyūshū, SW Japan
Satsunan-shoto 130 A3 island group Nansei-shotō, SW Japan Asia
Sattanen 84 D3 Lappi, NE Finland
Satu Mare 108 B3 Ger. Sathmar, Hung. Szatmárrnémeti. Satu Mare, NW Romania
Sau see Sava
Saudi Arabia 121 B5 off. Kingdom of Saudi Arabia, Al 'Arabīyah as Su'ūdīyah, Ar. Al Mamlakah al 'Arabīyah as Su'ūdīyah. country SW Asia

SAUDI ARABIA
Southwest Asia

Official name Kingdom of Saudi Arabia
Formation 1932 / 1932
Capital Riyadh
Population 28.1 million / 34 people per sq mile (13 people per sq km)
Total area 756,981 sq. miles (1,960,582 sq. km)
Languages Arabic*
Religions Sunni Muslim 85%, Shi'a Muslim 15%
Ethnic mix Arab 72%, Foreign residents (mostly south and southeast Asian) 20%, Afro-Asian 8%
Government Monarchy
Currency Saudi riyal = 100 halalat
Literacy rate 86%
Calorie consumption 3076 kilocalories

Saudi Arabia, Kingdom of see Saudi Arabia
Sauer see Sûre
Saugor see Sāgar
Saulkrasti 106 C3 C Latvia
Sault Sainte Marie 38 C4 Michigan, N USA
Sault Sainte Marie 40 C1 Michigan, N USA
Sault Ste. Marie 38 C4 Ontario, S Canada
Saumur 90 B4 Maine-et-Loire, NW France
Saurimo 78 C1 Port. Henrique de Carvalho, Vila Henrique de Carvalho. Lunda Sul, NE Angola
Sava 107 E6 Mahilyowskaya Voblasts', E Belarus
Savá 52 D2 Colón, N Honduras
Sava'i 145 E4 island NW Samoa
Savannah 43 E2 Georgia, SE USA
Savannah River 43 E2 river Georgia/South Carolina, SE USA
Savannakhét 136 D4 var. Khanthabouli. Savannakhét, S Laos
Savanna-La-Mar 54 A5 W Jamaica
Savaria see Szombathely
Save 100 B3 Eng. Save, Ger. Sau, Hung. Száva. river SE Europe
Save see Sava
Save, Rio 79 E3 var. Sabi. river Mozambique/Zimbabwe
Saverne 90 E3 var. Zabern; anc. Tres Tabernae. Bas-Rhin, NE France
Savigliano 96 A2 Piemonte, NW Italy
Savigsivik see Savissivik
Savinski see Savinskiy
Savinskiy 110 C3 var. Savinski. Arkhangel'skaya Oblast', NW Russian Federation
Savissivik 83 D1 var. Savigsivik. Avannaarsua, N Greenland
Savoie 91 D5 cultural region E France
Savona 96 A2 Liguria, NW Italy
Savu Sea 139 E5 Ind. Laut Sawu. sea S Indonesia
Sawakin see Suakin
Sawdiri see Sodiri
Sawhāj 72 B2 var. Sawhāj, var. Sohág, Suliag. C Egypt
Sawhāj see Sawhāj
Şawqirah 121 D6 var. Suqrah. S Oman
Sawu, Laut see Savu Sea
Saxe see Sachsen
Saxony see Sachsen
Sayaboury see Xaignabouli
Sayanskiy Khrebet 112 D3 mountain range S Russian Federation
Saýat 122 D3 Rus. Sayat. Lebap Welaýaty, E Turkmenistan
Sayaxché 52 B2 Petén, N Guatemala
Şaydā/Sayida see Saïda
Sayhūt 121 D6 E Yemen
Saynshand 127 E2 Dornogovĭ, SE Mongolia
Sayre 41 E3 Pennsylvania, NE USA
Say'ūn 121 C6 var. Saywūn. C Yemen
Saywūn see Say'ūn
Scalabis see Santarém
Scandinavia 66 D2 geophysical region NW Europe
Scarborough 89 D5 N England, United Kingdom
Scarpanto see Kárpathos
Scebeli see Shebeli
Schaan 94 E1 W Liechtenstein Europe

Schaerbeek *87 C6* Brussels, C Belgium
Schaffhausen *95 B7* Fr. Schaffhouse.
Schaffhausen, N Switzerland
Schaffhouse *see* Schaffhausen
Schagen *86 C2* Noord-Holland,
NW Netherlands
Schaulen *see* Šiauliai
Schebschi Mountains *see* Shebshi
Mountains
Scheessel *94 B3* Niedersachsen,
NW Germany
Schefferville *39 E2* Québec, E Canada
Schelde *see* Scheldt
Scheldt *87 B5* *Dut.* Schelde, *Fr.* Escaut.
river W Europe
Schell Creek Range *47 D5* *mountain
range* Nevada, W USA
Schenectady *41 F3* New York, NE USA
Schertz *49 G4* Texas, SW USA
Schiermonnikoog *86 D1* *Fris.*
Skiermûntseach. *island*
Waddeneilanden, N Netherlands
Schijndel *86 D4* Noord-Brabant,
S Netherlands
Schil *see* Jiu
Schiltigheim *90 E3* Bas-Rhin, NE France
Schivelbein *see* Świdwin
Schleswig *94 B2* Schleswig-Holstein,
N Germany
Schleswig-Holstein *94 B2* *state*
N Germany
Schlettstadt *see* Sélestat
Schlochau *see* Człuchów
Schneekoppe *see* Sněžka
Schneidemühl *see* Piła
Schoden *see* Skuodas
Schönebeck *94 C4* Sachsen-Anhalt,
C Germany
Schönlanke *see* Trzcianka
Schooten *see* Schoten
Schoten *87 C5* *var.* Schooten.
Antwerpen, N Belgium
Schouwen *86 B4* *island* SW Netherlands
Schwabenalb *see* Schwäbische Alb
Schwäbische Alb *95 B6* *var.*
Schwabenalb, *Eng.* Swabian Jura.
mountain range S Germany
Schwandorf *95 C5* Bayern, SE Germany
Schwaz *95 C7* Tirol, W Austria
Schweidnitz *see* Świdnica
Schweinfurt *95 B5* Bayern, SE Germany
Schweiz *see* Switzerland
Schwerin *94 C3* Mecklenburg-
Vorpommern, N Germany
Schwertberg *see* Świecie
Schwiebus *see* Świebodzin
Schwyz *95 B7* *var.* Schwiz. Schwyz,
C Switzerland
Schyl *see* Jiu
Scio *see* Chíos
Scoresby Sound/Scoresbysund *see*
Ittoqqortoormiit
Scoresby Sund *see* Kangertittivaq
Scotia Sea *57 C8* *sea* SW Atlantic Ocean
Scotland *88 C3* *cultural region* Scotland,
U K
Scott Base *154 B4* NZ research station
Antarctica
Scott Island *154 B5* *island* Antarctica
Scottsbluff *44 D3* Nebraska, C USA
Scottsboro *42 D1* Alabama, S USA
Scottsdale *48 B2* Arizona, SW USA
Scranton *41 F3* Pennsylvania, NE USA
Scrobesbyrig' *see* Shrewsbury
Scupi *see* Skopje
Scutari *see* Shkodër
Scutari, Lake *101 C5* *Alb.* Liqeni i
Shkodrës, *SCr.* Skadarsko Jezero. *lake*
Albania/Montenegro
Scyros *see* Skýros
Searcy *42 B1* Arkansas, C USA
Seattle *46 B2* Washington, NW USA
Sébaco *52 D3* Matagalpa, W Nicaragua
Sebaste/Sebastia *see* Sivas
Sebastián Vizcaíno, Bahía *50 A2* *bay*
NW Mexico
Sebastopol *see* Sevastopol'
Sebenico *see* Šibenik
Sechura, Bahía de *60 A3* *bay* NW Peru
Secunderābād *134 D5* *var.*
Sikandarabad. Andhra Pradesh, C India
Sedan *90 D3* Ardennes, N France
Seddon *151 D5* Marlborough, South
Island, New Zealand
Seddonville *151 C5* West Coast, South
Island, New Zealand
Sédhiou *74 B3* SW Senegal

Sedlez *see* Siedlce
Sedona *48 B2* Arizona, SW USA
Sedunum *see* Sion
Seeland *see* Sjælland
Seenu Atoll *see* Addu Atoll
Seesen *94 B4* Niedersachsen, C Germany
Segestica *see* Sisak
Segezha *110 B3* Respublika Kareliya,
NW Russian Federation
Seghedin *see* Szeged
Segna *see* Senj
Segodunum *see* Rodez
Ségou *74 D3* *var.* Segu. Ségou, C Mali
Segovia *92 D2* Castilla y León, C Spain
Segoviao Wangkí *see* Coco, Río
Segu *see* Ségou
Séguédine *75 H2* Agadez, NE Niger
Seguin *49 G4* Texas, SW USA
Segura *93 E4* *river* S Spain
Seinäjoki *85 D5* *Swe.* Östermyra. Länsi-
Suomi, W Finland
Seine *90 D1* *river* N France
Seine, Baie de la *90 B3* *bay* N France
Sekondi *see* Sekondi-Takoradi
Sekondi-Takoradi *75 E5* *var.* Sekondi.
S Ghana
Selânik *see* Thessaloníki
Selenga *127 E1* *Mong.* Selenge Mörön.
river Mongolia/Russian Federation
Selenge Mörön *see* Selenga
Sélestat *90 E4* *Ger.* Schlettstadt. Bas-
Rhin, NE France
Seleucia *see* Silifke
Selfoss *83 E5* Suðurland, SW Iceland
Sélibabi *74 C3* *var.* Sélibaby. Guidimaka,
S Mauritania
Sélibaby *see* Sélibabi
Selma *47 C6* California, W USA
Selway River *46 D2* *river* Idaho,
NW USA North America
Selwyn Range *148 B3* *mountain range*
Queensland, C Australia
Selzaete *see* Zelzate
Semarang *138 C5* *var.* Samarang. Jawa,
C Indonesia
Sembé *77 B5* Sangha, NW Congo
Semendria *see* Smederevo
Semey *114 D4* *prev.* Semipalatinsk.
Vostochnyy Kazakhstan, E Kazakhstan
Semezhevo *see* Syemyezhava
Seminole *49 E3* Texas, SW USA
Seminole, Lake *42 D3* *reservoir* Florida/
Georgia, SE USA
Semipalatinsk *see* Semey
Semnān *120 D3* *var.* Samnān. Semnān,
N Iran
Semois *87 C8* *river* SE Belgium
Sendai *130 D4* Miyagi, Honshū,
C Japan
Sendai-wan *130 D4* *bay* E Japan
Senec *99 C6* *Ger.* Wartberg, *Hung.* Szenc;
prev. Szempcz. Bratislavský Kraj,
W Slovakia
Senegal *74 B3* *off.* Republic of Senegal,
Fr. Sénégal. *country* W Africa

SENEGAL
West Africa

Official name Republic of Senegal
Formation 1960 / 1960
Capital Dakar
Population 12.8 million / 172 people
per sq mile (66 people per sq km)
Total area 75,749 sq. miles (196,190 sq. km)
Languages Wolof, Pulaar, Serer, Diola,
Mandinka, Malinké, Soninké, French*
Religions Sunni Muslim 95%, Christian
(mainly Roman Catholic) 4%, Traditional
beliefs 1%
Ethnic mix Wolof 43%, Serer 15%,
Peul 14%, Other 14%, Toucouleur 9%,
Diola 5%
Government Presidential system
Currency CFA franc = 100 centimes
Literacy rate 50%
Calorie consumption 2479 kilocalories

Senegal *74 B3* *Fr.* Sénégal. *river* W Africa
Senegal, Republic of *see* Senegal
Senftenberg *94 D4* Brandenburg,
E Germany
Senia *see* Senj
Senica *99 C6* *Ger.* Senitz, *Hung.* Szenice.
Trnavský Kraj, W Slovakia
Seniça *see* Sjenica
Senitz *see* Senica

Senj *100 A3* *Ger.* Zengg, *It.* Segna; *anc.*
Senia. Lika-Senj, NW Croatia
Senja *84 C2* *prev.* Senjen. *island*
N Norway
Senjen *see* Senja
Sejong City *128 E4* *country capital*
(South Korea) (administrative)
C South Korea
Senkaku-shoto *130 A3* *island group*
SW Japan
Senlis *90 C3* Oise, N France
Sennar *72 C4* *var.* Sannār. Sinnar,
C Sudan
Senones *see* Sens
Sens *90 C3* *anc.* Agendicum, Senones.
Yonne, C France
Sensburg *see* Mrągowo
Sên, Stœng *137 D5* *river* C Cambodia
Senta *100 D3* *Hung.* Zenta. Vojvodina,
N Serbia
Seo de Urgel *see* La Seu d'Urgell
Seoul *129 E4* *Jap.* Keijō; *prev.*
Kyŏngsŏng, Sŏul. *country capital*
(South Korea) NW South Korea
Sepik *144 B3* *river* Indonesia/
Papua New Guinea
Şepşi-Sângeorz/Sepsiszentgyörgy *see*
Sfântu Gheorghe
Sept-Îles *39 E3* Québec,
SE Canada
Seraing *87 D6* Liège, E Belgium
Serakhs *see* Sarahs
Seram, Laut *139 F4* *Eng.* Ceram Sea. *sea*
E Indonesia
Pulau Seram *139 F4* *var.* Serang,
Eng. Ceram. *island* Maluku,
E Indonesia
Serang *138 C5* Jawa, C Indonesia
Serang *see* Seram, Pulau
Serasan, Selat *138 C3* *strait* Indonesia/
Malaysia
Serbia *100 D4* *off.* Federal Republic
of Serbia; *prev.* Yugoslavia, *SCr.*
Jugoslavija. *country* SE Europe

SERBIA
Southeast Europe

Official name Republic of Serbia
Formation 2006 / 2008
Capital Belgrade
Population 9.9 million / 331 people
per sq mile (128 people per sq km)
Total area 29,905 sq miles (77,453 sq km)
Languages Serbian*, Hungarian (Magyar)
Religions Orthodox Christian 85%,
Roman Catholic 6%, Other 6%,
Muslim 3%
Ethnic mix Serb 83%, Other 10%,
Magyar 4%, Bosniak 2%, Roma 1%
Government Parliamentary system
Currency Dinar = 100 para
Literacy rate 98%
Calorie consumption 2823 kilocalories

Serbia, Federal Republic of *see* Serbia
Sercq *see* Sark
Serdar *122 C2* *prev. Rus.* Gyzyrlabat,
Kizyl-Arvat. Balkan Welaýaty,
W Turkmenistan
Serdica *see* Sofiya
Serdobol' *see* Sortavala
Serenje *78 D2* Central, E Zambia
Seres *see* Sérres
Seret/Sereth *see* Siret
Serhetabat *122 D4* *prev. Rus.*
Gushgy, Kushka. Mary Welaýaty,
S Turkmenistan
Sérifos *105 C6* *anc.* Seriphos. *island*
Kykládes, Greece, Aegean Sea
Seriphos *see* Sérifos
Serov *114 C3* Sverdlovskaya Oblast',
C Russian Federation
Serowe *78 D3* Central, SE Botswana
Serpa Pinto *see* Menongue
Serpent's Mouth, The *59 F2* *Sp.* Boca
de la Serpiente. *strait* Trinidad and
Tobago/Venezuela
Serpiente, Boca de la *see* Serpent's
Mouth, The
Serpukhov *111 B5* Moskovskaya Oblast',
W Russian Federation
Sérrai *see* Sérres
Serrana, Cayo de *53 F2* *island group*
NW Colombia South America
Serranilla, Cayo de *53 F2* *island
group* NW Colombia South America
Caribbean Sea
Serravalle *96 E1* N San Marino

Sérres *104 C3* *var.* Seres; *prev.* Sérrai.
Kentrikí Makedonía, NE Greece
Sesdlets *see* Siedlce
Sesto San Giovanni *96 B2* Lombardia,
N Italy
Sesvete *100 B2* Zagreb, N Croatia
Setabis *see* Xàtiva
Sète *91 C6* *prev.* Cette. Hérault, S France
Setesdal *85 A6* *valley* S Norway
Sétif *71 E2* *var.* Stif. N Algeria
Setté Cama *77 A6* Ogooué-Maritime,
SW Gabon
Setúbal *92 B4* *Eng.* Saint Ubes, Saint
Yves. Setúbal, W Portugal
Setúbal, Baía de *92 B4* *bay* W Portugal
Seul, Lac *38 B3* *lake* Ontario, S Canada
Sevan *117 G2* C Armenia
Sevan, Lake *117 G3* *Eng.* Lake Sevan,
Rus. Ozero Sevan. *lake* E Armenia
Sevan, Lake/Sevan, Ozero *see* Sevana
Lich
Sevastopol' *109 F5* *Eng.* Sebastopol.
Avtonomna Respublika Krym,
S Ukraine
Severn *38 B2* *river* Ontario, S Canada
Severn *89 D6* Wel. Hafren. *river*
England/Wales, United Kingdom
Severnaya Zemlya *115 E2* *var.* Nicholas
II Land. *island group* N Russian
Federation
Severnyy *110 E3* Respublika Komi,
NW Russian Federation
Severodonetsk *see* Syeverodonets'k
Severodvinsk *110 C3* *prev.* Molotov,
Sudostroy. Arkhangel'skaya Oblast',
NW Russian Federation
Severomorsk *110 C2* Murmanskaya
Oblast', NW Russian Federation
Seversk *114 D4* Tomskaya Oblast',
C Russian Federation
Sevier Lake *44 A4* *lake* Utah,
W USA
Sevilla *92 C4* *Eng.* Seville; *anc.* Hispalis.
Andalucía, SW Spain
Seville *see* Sevilla
Sevlievo *104 D2* Gabrovo,
N Bulgaria
Sevluš/Sevlyush *see* Vynohradiv
Seward's Folly *see* Alaska
Seychelles *79 G1* *off.* Republic of
Seychelles. *country* W Indian Ocean

SEYCHELLES
Indian Ocean

Official name Republic of Seychelles
Formation 1976 / 1976
Capital Victoria
Population 90,024 / 866 people
per sq mile (333 people per sq km)
Total area 176 sq. miles (455 sq. km)
Languages French Creole*,
English*, French*
Religions Roman Catholic 82%,
Anglican 6%, Other (including Muslim)
6%, Other Christian 3%, Hindu 2%,
Seventh-day Adventist 1%
Ethnic mix Creole 89%, Indian 5%,
Other 4%, Chinese 2%
Government Presidential system
Currency Seychelles rupee = 100 cents
Literacy rate 92%
Calorie consumption 2426 kilocalories

Seychelles, Republic of *see* Seychelles
Seydhisfjördhur *83 E5* Austurland,
E Iceland
Seýdi *122 D2* *Rus.* Seydi; *prev.*
Neftezavodsk. Lebap Welaýaty,
E Turkmenistan
Seyhan *see* Adana
Sfákia *see* Chóra Sfakíon
Sfântu Gheorghe *108 C4* *Ger.* Sankt-
Georgen, *Hung.* Sepsiszentgyörgy;
prev. Şepşi-Sângeorz, Sfintu Gheorghe.
Covasna, C Romania
Sfax *71 F2* *Ar.* Ṣafāqis. E Tunisia
Sfintu Gheorghe *see* Sfântu Gheorghe
's-Gravenhage *86 B4* *var.* Den Haag,
Eng. The Hague, *Fr.* La Haye.
country capital (Netherlands)
(seat of government)
Zuid-Holland,
W Netherlands
's-Gravenzande *86 B4* Zuid-Holland,
W Netherlands
Shaan/Shaanxi Sheng *see* Shaanxi

Shaanxi *128 B5 var.* Shaan, Shaanxi Sheng, Shan-hsi, Shenshi, Shensi. *province* C China
Shabani *see* Zvishavane
Shabeelle, Webi *see* Shebeli
Shache *126 A3 var.* Yarkant. Xinjiang Uygur Zizhiqu, NW China
Shacheng *see* Huailai
Shackleton Ice Shelf *154 D3 ice shelf* Antarctica
Shaddādī *see* Ash Shadādah
Shāhābād *see* Eslāmābād-e Gharb
Sha Hi *see* Orūmīyeh, Daryācheh-ye
Shahjahanabad *see* Delhi
Shahr-e Kord *120 C3 var.* Shahr Kord. Chahār Maḥall va Bakhtiārī, C Iran
Shahr Kord *see* Shahr-e Kord
Shāhrūd *120 D2 prev.* Emāmrūd, Emāmshahr. Semnān, N Iran
Shalkar *114 B4 var.* Chelkar. Aktyubinsk, W Kazakhstan
Shām, Bādiyat ash *see* Syrian Desert
Shana *see* Kuril'sk
Shandi *see* Shendi
Shandong *128 D4 var.* Lu, Shandong Sheng, Shantung. *province* E China
Shanghai *128 D5 var.* Shang-hai. Shanghai Shi, E China
Shangrao *128 D5* Jiangxi, S China
Shan-hsi *see* Shaanxi, China
Shan-hsi *see* Shanxi, China
Shannon *89 A6 Ir.* An tSionainn. *river* W Ireland
Shan Plateau *136 B3 plateau* E Myanmar (Burma)
Shansi *see* Shanxi
Shantar Islands *see* Shantarskiye Ostrova
Shantarskiye Ostrova *115 G3 Eng.* Shantar Islands. *island group* E Russian Federation
Shantou *128 D6 var.* Shan-t'ou, Swatow. Guangdong, S China
Shan-t'ou *see* Shantou
Shantung *see* Shandong
Shanxi *128 C4 var.* Jin, Shan-hsi, Shansi, Shanxi Sheng. *province* C China
Shan Xian *see* Sanmenxia
Shanxi Sheng *see* Shanxi
Shaoguan *128 C6 var.* Shao-kuan, *Cant.* Kukong; *prev.* Ch'u-chiang. Guangdong, S China
Shao-kuan *see* Shaoguan
Shaqrāʼ *120 B4* Ar Riyāḍ, C Saudi Arabia
Shaqrā *see* Shuqrah
Shar *114 D5 var.* Charsk. Vostochnyy Kazakhstan, E Kazakhstan
Shari *130 D2* Hokkaidō, NE Japan
Shari *see* Chari
Sharjah *see* Ash Shāriqah
Shark Bay *147 A5 bay* Western Australia
Sharqi, Al Jabal ash/Sharqi, Jebel esh *see* Anti-Lebanon
Shashe *78 D3 var.* Shashi. *river* Botswana/Zimbabwe
Shashi *see* Shashe
Shatskiy Rise *125 G1 undersea rise* N Pacific Ocean
Shawnee *49 G1* Oklahoma, C USA
Shaykh, Jabal ash *see* Hermon, Mount
Shchadryn *107 D7 Rus.* Shchedrin. Homyel'skaya Voblasts', SE Belarus
Shchedrin *see* Shchadryn
Shcheglovsk *see* Kemerovo
Shchëkino *111 B5* Tul'skaya Oblast', W Russian Federation
Shchors *109 E1* Chernihivs'ka Oblast', N Ukraine
Shchuchin *see* Shchuchyn
Shchuchinsk *114 C4 prev.* Shchuchye. Akmola, N Kazakhstan
Shchuchye *see* Shchuchinsk
Shchuchyn *107 B5 Pol.* Szczuczyn Nowogródzki, *Rus.* Shchuchin. Hrodzyenskaya Voblasts', W Belarus
Shebekino *111 A6* Belgorodskaya Oblast', W Russian Federation
Shebelë Wenz, Wabë *see* Shebeli
Shebeli *73 D5 Amh.* Wabë Shebelë Wenz, *It.* Scebeli, *Som.* Webi Shabeelle. *river* Ethiopia/Somalia
Sheberghān *see* Shibirghān
Sheboygan *40 B2* Wisconsin, N USA

Shebshi Mountains *76 A4 var.* Schebschi Mountains. *mountain range* E Nigeria
Shechem *see* Nablus
Shedadi *see* Ash Shadādah
Sheffield *89 D5* N England, United Kingdom
Shekhem *see* Nablus
Sheki *see* Şäki
Shelby *44 B1* Montana, NW USA
Sheldon *45 F3* Iowa, C USA
Shelekhov Gulf *115 G2 Eng.* Shelekhov Gulf. *gulf* E Russian Federation
Shelekhov Gulf *see* Shelikhova, Zaliv
Shendi *72 C4 var.* Shandī. River Nile, NE Sudan
Shengking *see* Liaoning
Shenking *see* Liaoning
Shenshi/Shensi *see* Shaanxi
Shenyang *128 D3 Chin.* Shen-yang, *Eng.* Moukden, Mukden; *prev.* Fengtien. *province capital* Liaoning, NE China
Shen-yang *see* Shenyang
Shepetivka *108 D2 Rus.* Shepetovka. Khmel'nyts'ka Oblast', NW Ukraine
Shepetovka *see* Shepetivka
Shepparton *149 C7* Victoria, SE Australia
Sherbrooke *39 E4* Québec, SE Canada
Shereik *72 C3* River Nile, N Sudan
Sheridan *44 C2* Wyoming, C USA
Sherman *49 G2* Texas, SW USA
's-Hertogenbosch *86 C4 Fr.* Bois-le-Duc, *Ger.* Herzogenbusch. Noord-Brabant, S Netherlands
Shetland Islands *88 D1 island group* NE Scotland, United Kingdom
Shevchenko *see* Aktau
Shibarghān *see* Shibirghān
Shiberghan/Shiberghān *see* Shibirghān
Shibetsu *130 D2 var.* Sibetu. Hokkaidō, NE Japan
Shibh Jazirat Sīnāʼ *see* Sinai
Shibirghān *123 E3 var.* Shibarghān, Shiberghan, Shiberghān; *prev.* Sheberghān. Jowzjān, N Afghanistan
Shibushi-wan *131 B8 bay* SW Japan
Shigatse *see* Xigazê
Shih-chia-chuang/Shihmen *see* Shijiazhuang
Shihezi *126 C2* Xinjiang Uygur Zizhiqu, NW China
Shiichi *see* Shyichy
Shijiazhuang *128 C4 var.* Shih-chia-chuang; *prev.* Shihmen. *province capital* Hebei, E China
Shikārpur *134 B3* Sind, S Pakistan
Shikoku *131 C7 var.* Sikoku. *island* SW Japan
Shikoku Basin *125 F2 var.* Sikoku Basin. *undersea basin* N Philippine Sea
Shikotan, Ostrov *130 E2 Jap.* Shikotan-tō. *island* NE Russian Federation
Shikotan-tō *see* Shikotan, Ostrov
Shilabo *73 D5* Sumalē, E Ethiopia
Shiliguri *135 F3 prev.* Siliguri. West Bengal, NE India
Shilka *115 F4 river* S Russian Federation
Shillong *135 G3 state capital* Meghālaya, NE India
Shimanto *see* Nakamura
Shimbir Berris *see* Shimbiris
Shimbiris *72 E4 var.* Shimbir Berris. *mountain* N Somalia
Shimoga *132 C2* Karnātaka, W India
Shimonoseki *131 A7 var.* Simonoseki, *hist.* Akamagaseki, Bakan. Yamaguchi, Honshū, SW Japan
Shinano-gawa *131 C5 var.* Sinano Gawa. *river* Honshū, C Japan
Shindand *122 D4 prev.* Shīndani. Herāt, W Afghanistan
Shīndand *see* Shindand
Shingū *131 C6 var.* Singû. Wakayama, Honshū, SW Japan
Shinjō *130 D4 var.* Sinzyô. Yamagata, Honshū, C Japan
Shinyanga *73 C7* Shinyanga, NW Tanzania
Shiprock *48 C1* New Mexico, SW USA
Shīrāz *120 D4 var.* Shīrāz. Fārs, S Iran
Shishchitsy *see* Shyshchytsy
Shivpuri *134 D3* Madhya Pradesh, C India
Shizugawa *130 D4* Miyagi, Honshū, NE Japan

Shizuoka *131 D6 var.* Sizuoka. Shizuoka, Honshū, S Japan
Shklov *see* Shklow
Shklow *107 D6 Rus.* Shklov. Mahilyowskaya Voblasts', E Belarus
Shkodër *101 C5 var.* Shkodra, *It.* Scutari, *SCr.* Skadar. Shkodër, NW Albania
Shkodra *see* Shkodër
Shkodrës, Liqeni i *see* Scutari, Lake
Shkumbi/Shkumbin *see* Shkumbinit, Lumi i
Shkumbinit, Lumi i *101 C6 var.* Shkumbi, Shkumbin. *river* C Albania
Sholāpur *see* Solāpur
Shostka *109 F1* Sums'ka Oblast', NE Ukraine
Show Low *48 B2* Arizona, SW USA
Show Me State *see* Missouri
Shpola *109 E3* Cherkas'ka Oblast', N Ukraine
Shqipëria/Shqipërisë, Republika e *see* Albania
Shreveport *42 A2* Louisiana, S USA
Shrewsbury *89 D6 hist.* Scrobesbyrig'. W England, United Kingdom
Shu *114 C5 Kaz.* Shū. Zhambyl, SE Kazakhstan
Shuang-liao *see* Liaoyuan
Shū, Kazakhstan *see* Shu
Shumagin Islands *36 B3 island group* Alaska, USA
Shumen *104 D2* Shumen, NE Bulgaria
Shumilina *107 E5 Rus.* Shumilino. Vitsyebskaya Voblasts', NE Belarus
Shumilino *see* Shumilina
Shunsen *see* Chuncheon
Shuqrah *121 B7 var.* Shaqrā. SW Yemen
Shwebo *136 B3* Sagaing, C Myanmar (Burma)
Shyichy *107 C7 Rus.* Shiichi. Homyel'skaya Voblasts', SE Belarus
Shymkent *114 B5 prev.* Chimkent. Yuzhnyy Kazakhstan, S Kazakhstan
Shyshchytsy *107 C6 Rus.* Shishchitsy. Minskaya Voblasts', C Belarus
Siam *see* Thailand
Siam, Gulf of *see* Thailand, Gulf of
Sian *see* Xi'an
Siang *see* Brahmaputra
Siangtan *see* Xiangtan
Šiauliai *106 B4 Ger.* Schaulen. Šiauliai, N Lithuania
Siazan' *see* Siyäzän
Sibay *111 D6* Respublika Bashkortostan, W Russian Federation
Šibenik *100 B4 It.* Sebenico. Šibenik-Knin, S Croatia
Siberia *115 E3 var.* Siberia. *physical region* NE Russian Federation
Siberia *see* Sibir'
Siberoet *see* Siberut, Pulau
Siberut, Pulau *138 A4 prev.* Siberoet. *island* Kepulauan Mentawai, W Indonesia
Sibi *134 B2* Baluchistān, SW Pakistan
Sibiti *77 B6* Lékoumou, S Congo
Sibiu *108 B4 Ger.* Hermannstadt, *Hung.* Nagyszeben. Sibiu, C Romania
Sibolga *138 B3* Sumatera, W Indonesia
Sibu *138 D3* Sarawak, East Malaysia
Sibut *76 C4 prev.* Fort-Sibut. Kémo, S Central African Republic
Sibuyan Sea *139 E2 sea* W Pacific Ocean
Sichon *137 C6 var.* Ban Sichon, Si Chon. Nakhon Si Thammarat, SW Thailand
Si Chon *see* Sichon
Sichuan *128 B5 var.* Chuan, Sichuan Sheng, Ssu-ch'uan, Szechuan, Szechwan. *province* C China
Sichuan Pendi *128 B5 basin* C China
Sichuan Sheng *see* Sichuan
Sicilian Channel *see* Sicily, Strait of
Sicily *97 C7 Eng.* Sicily; *anc.* Trinacria. *island* Italy, C Mediterranean Sea
Sicily, Strait of *97 B7 var.* Sicilian Channel. *strait* C Mediterranean Sea
Sicuani *61 E4* Cusco, S Peru
Sidári *104 A4* Kérkyra, Iónia Nisiá, Greece, C Mediterranean Sea
Sidas *138 C4* Borneo, C Indonesia
Siderno *97 D7* Calabria, SW Italy
Sidhirókastron *see* Sidirókastro
Sidi Barrāni *72 A1* NW Egypt
Sidi Bel Abbès *70 D2 var.* Sidi bel Abbès, Sidi-Bel-Abbès. NW Algeria

Sidirókastro *104 C3 prev.* Sidhirókastron. Kentrikí Makedonía, NE Greece
Sidley, Mount *154 B4 mountain* Antarctica
Sidney *44 D1* Montana, NW USA
Sidney *44 D4* Nebraska, C USA
Sidney *40 C4* Ohio, N USA
Sidon *see* Saïda
Sidra *see* Surt
Sidra/Sidra, Gulf of *see* Surt, Khalīj, N Libya
Siebenbürgen *see* Transylvania
Siedlce *98 E3 Ger.* Sedlez, *Rus.* Sesdlets. Mazowieckie, C Poland
Siegen *94 B4* Nordrhein-Westfalen, W Germany
Siemiatycze *98 E3* Podlaskie, NE Poland
Siena *96 B3 Fr.* Sienne; *anc.* Saena Julia. Toscana, C Italy
Sienne *see* Siena
Sieradz *98 C4* Sieradz, C Poland
Sierpc *98 D3* Mazowieckie, C Poland
Sierra Leone *74 C4 off.* Republic of Sierra Leone. *country* W Africa

SIERRA LEONE
West Africa

Official name Republic of Sierra Leone
Formation 1961 / 1961
Capital Freetown
Population 6 million / 217 people per sq mile (84 people per sq km)
Total area 27,698 sq. miles (71,740 sq. km)
Languages Mende, Temne, Krio, English*
Religions Muslim 60%, Christian 30%, Traditional beliefs 10%
Ethnic mix Mende 35%, Temne 32%, Other 21%, Limba 8%, Kuranko 4%
Government Presidential system
Currency Leone = 100 cents
Literacy rate 41%
Calorie consumption 2162 kilocalories

Sierra Leone Basin *66 C4 undersea basin* E Atlantic Ocean
Sierra Leone, Republic of *see* Sierra Leone
Sierra Leone Ridge *see* Sierra Leone Rise
Sierra Leone Rise *66 C4 var.* Sierra Leone Ridge, Sierra Leone Schwelle. *undersea rise* E Atlantic Ocean
Sierra Leone Schwelle *see* Sierra Leone Rise
Sierra Vista *48 B3* Arizona, SW USA
Sífnos *105 C6 anc.* Siphnos. *island* Kykládes, Greece, Aegean Sea
Sigli *138 A3* Sumatera, W Indonesia
Siglufjördhur *83 E4* Nordhurland Vestra, N Iceland
Signal Peak *48 A2 mountain* Arizona, SW USA
Signan *see* Xi'an
Signy *154 A2* UK research station South Orkney Islands, Antarctica
Siguatepeque *52 C2* Comayagua, W Honduras
Siguiri *74 D4* NE Guinea
Sihanoukville *137 D6 var.* Kâmpóng Saôm; *prev.* Kompong Som. Kâmpóng Saôm, SW Cambodia
Siilinjärvi *84 E4* Itä-Suomi, C Finland
Siirt *117 F4 var.* Sert; *anc.* Tigranocerta. Siirt, SE Turkey
Sikandarabad *see* Secunderābād
Sikasso *74 D4* Sikasso, S Mali
Sikeston *45 H5* Missouri, C USA
Sikhote-Alin', Khrebet *115 G4 mountain range* SE Russian Federation
Siking *see* Xi'an
Siklós *99 C7* Baranya, SW Hungary
Sikoku *see* Shikoku
Sikoku Basin *see* Shikoku Basin
Šilalė *106 B4* Tauragė, W Lithuania
Silchar *135 G3* Assam, NE India
Silesia *98 B4 physical region* SW Poland
Silifke *116 C4 anc.* Seleucia. Içel, S Turkey
Siliguri *see* Shiliguri
Siling Co *126 C5 lake* W China
Silinhot *see* Xilinhot
Silistra *104 E1 var.* Silistria; *anc.* Durostorum. Silistra, NE Bulgaria
Silistria *see* Silistra
Sillamäe *106 E2 Ger.* Sillamäggi. Ida-Virumaa, NE Estonia

Sillamäggi see Sillamäe
Sillein see Žilina
Šilutė *106 B4 Ger.* Heydekrug.
    W Lithuania
Silvan *117 E4* Diyarbakır, SE Turkey
Silva Porto see Kuito
Silver State see Colorado
Silver State see Nevada
Simanichy *107 C7 Rus.* Simonichi.
    Homyel'skaya Voblasts', SE Belarus
Simav *116 B3* Kütahya, W Turkey
Simav Çayı *116 A3 river* NW Turkey
Simbirsk see Ul'yanovsk
Simeto *97 C7 river* Sicilia, Italy,
    C Mediterranean Sea
Simeulue, Pulau *138 A3 island*
    NW Indonesia
Simferopol' *109 F5* Avtonomna
    Respublika Krym, S Ukraine
Simitla *104 C3* Blagoevgrad, SW Bulgaria
Şimlăul Silvaniei/Şimleul Silvaniei see
    Şimleu Silvaniei
Şimleu Silvaniei *108 B3 Hung.*
    Szilágysomlyó; *prev.* Şimlăul Silvaniei,
    Şimleul Silvaniei. Sălaj, NW Romania
Simonichi see Simanichy
Simonoseki see Shimonoseki
Simpelveld *87 D6* Limburg,
    SE Netherlands
Simplon Pass *95 B8 pass* S Switzerland
Simpson see Fort Simpson
Simpson Desert *148 B4 desert* Northern
    Territory/South Australia
Sinai *72 C2 var.* Sinai Peninsula, *Ar.*
    Shibh Jazīrat Sīnāʾ, Sīnā. *physical
    region* NE Egypt
Sinaia *108 C4* Prahova, SE Romania
Sinano Gawa see Shinano-gawa
Sīnā/Sinai Peninsula see Sinai
Sincelejo *58 B2* Sucre, NW Colombia
Sind see Sindh
Sindelfingen *95 B6* Baden-Württemberg,
    SW Germany
Sindh *134 B3 prev.* Sind. *province*
    SE Pakistan
Sindi *106 D2 Ger.* Zintenhof. Pärnumaa,
    SW Estonia
Sines *92 B4* Setúbal, S Portugal
Singan see Xi'an
Singapore *138 B3 country capital*
    (Singapore) (Singapore) S Singapore
Singapore *138 A1 off.* Republic of
    Singapore. *country* SE Asia

SINGAPORE
Southeast Asia

Official name Republic of Singapore
Formation 1965 / 1965
Capital Singapore
Population 5.2 million / 22,034 people
    per sq mile (8525 people per sq km)
Total area 250 sq. miles (648 sq. km)
Languages Mandarin*, Malay*,
    Tamil*, English*
Religions Buddhist 55%, Taoist 22%,
    Muslim 16%, Hindu, Christian, and Sikh 7%
Ethnic mix Chinese 74%, Malay 14%,
    Indian 9%, Other 3%
Government Parliamentary system
Currency Singapore dollar = 100 cents
Literacy rate 95%
Calorie consumption Not available

Singapore, Republic of see Singapore
Singen *95 B6* Baden-Württemberg,
    S Germany
Singida *73 C7* Singida, C Tanzania
Singkang *139 E4* Sulawesi, C Indonesia
Singkawang *138 C3* Borneo, C Indonesia
Singora see Songkhla
Singū see Shingū
Sining see Xining
Siniscola *97 A5* Sardegna, Italy,
    C Mediterranean Sea
Sinj *100 B4* Split-Dalmacija, SE Croatia
**Sinjajevina/Sinjai Uighur
    Autonomous Region** see Xinjiang
    Uygur Zizhiqu
Sinkiang see Sinnamary
Sinnamary *59 H3 var.* Sinnamarie.
    N French Guiana
Sinneh see Sanandaj
Sînnicolau Mare see Sânnicolau Mare
Sinoe, Lacul see Sinoe, Lacul
Sinoie, Lacul *108 D5 prev.* Lacul Sinoe.
    lagoon SE Romania

Sinop *116 D2 anc.* Sinope. Sinop,
    N Turkey
Sinope see Sinop
Sinsheim *95 B6* Baden-Württemberg,
    SW Germany
Sint Maarten *55 G3 Eng.* Saint
    Martin. *Dutch autonomous region*
    NE Caribbean Sea
Sint-Michielsgestel *86 C4* Noord-
    Brabant, S Netherlands
Sin-Miclăuş see Gheorgheni
Sint-Niklaas *87 B5 Fr.* Saint-Nicolas.
    Oost-Vlaanderen, N Belgium
Sint-Pieters-Leeuw *87 B6* Vlaams
    Brabant, C Belgium
Sintra *92 B3 prev.* Cintra. Lisboa,
    W Portugal
Sinujiif *73 E5* Nugaal, NE Somalia
Sinus Aelaniticus see Aqaba, Gulf of
Sinus Gallicus see Lion, Golfe du
Sinyang see Xinyang
Sinzyô see Shinjō
Sion *95 A7 Ger.* Sitten; *anc.* Sedunum.
    Valais, SW Switzerland
Sioux City *45 F3* Iowa, C USA
Sioux Falls *45 F3* South Dakota,
    N USA
Sioux State see North Dakota
Siphnos see Sífnos
Siping *128 D3 var.* Ssu-p'ing, Szeping;
    prev. Ssu-p'ing-chieh. Jilin, NE China
Siple, Mount *154 A4 mountain* Siple
    Island, Antarctica
Siquirres *53 E4* Limón, E Costa Rica
Siracusa *97 D7 Eng.* Syracuse. Sicilia,
    Italy, C Mediterranean Sea
Sir Edward Pellew Group *148 B2 island
    group* Northern Territory,
    NE Australia
Siret *108 C4 var.* Siretul, *Ger.* Sereth, *Rus.*
    Seret. *river* Romania/Ukraine
Siretul see Siret
Siria see Syria
Sirikit Reservoir *136 C4 lake*
    N Thailand
Sirjān *120 D4 prev.* Sa'īdābād. Kermān,
    S Iran
Sirna see Sýrna
Şırnak *117 F4* Şırnak, SE Turkey
Síros see Sýros
Sirte see Surt
Sirte, Gulf of *71 F2 Eng.* Gulf of Sidra,
    Gulf of Sirti, Sidra. *gulf* N Libya
Sirti, Gulf of see Surt, Khalīj
Sisak *100 B3 var.* Siscia, *Ger.* Sissek,
    Hung. Sziszek; *anc.* Segestica. Sisak-
    Moslavina, C Croatia
Siscia see Sisak
Sisimiut *82 C3 var.* Holsteinborg,
    Holsteinsborg, Holstenborg,
    Holstensborg. Kitaa, S Greenland
Sissek see Sisak
Sīstān, Daryācheh-ye see Şāberī,
    Hāmūn-e
Sitaş Cristuru see Cristuru Secuiesc
Siteía *105 D8 var.* Sitía. Kríti, Greece,
    E Mediterranean Sea
Sitges *93 G2* Cataluña, NE Spain
Sitía see Siteía
Sittang see Sittoung
Sittard *87 D5* Limburg, SE Netherlands
Sitten see Sion
Sittoung *136 B4 var.* Sittang. *river*
    S Myanmar (Burma)
Sittwe *136 A3 var.* Akyab. Rakhine State,
    W Myanmar (Burma)
Siuna *52 D3* Región Autónoma Atlántico
    Norte, NE Nicaragua
Siut see Asyūṭ
Sivas *116 D3 anc.* Sebastia, Sebaste.
    Sivas, C Turkey
Siverek *117 E4* Şanlıurfa, S Turkey
Siwa see Sīwah
Siwah *72 A2 var.* Siwa. NW Egypt
Six Counties, The see Northern Ireland
Six-Fours-les-Plages *91 D6* Var,
    SE France
Siyäzän *117 H2 Rus.* Siazan'.
    NE Azerbaijan
Sjar see Sääre
Sjenica *101 D5 Turk.* Seniça. Serbia,
    SW Serbia
Skadar see Shkodër
Skadarsko Jezero see Scutari, Lake
Skagerak see Skagerrak
Skagerrak *85 A6 var.* Skagerak. *channel*
    N Europe

Skagit River *46 B1 river* Washington,
    NW USA
Skalka *84 C3 Lapp.* Skalkká. *lake*
    N Sweden
Skalkká see Skalka
Skarżysko-Kamienna *98 D4*
    Świętokrzyskie, C Poland
Skaudvilė *106 B4* Tauragė, SW Lithuania
Skegness *89 E6* E England, United
    Kingdom
Skellefteå *84 D4* Västerbotten, N Sweden
Skellefteälven *84 C4 river* N Sweden
Ski *85 B6* Akershus, S Norway
Skíathos *105 C5* Skíathos, Vóreies
    Sporádes, Greece, Aegean Sea
Skidal' *107 B5 Rus.* Skidel'.
    Hrodzyenskaya Voblasts', W Belarus
Skidel' see Skidal'
Skiermonnikoog see Schiermonnikoog
Skierniewice *98 D3* Łódzkie,
    C Poland
Skiften *106 C1 strait* Finland Atlantic
    Ocean Baltic Sea Gulf of Bothnia/Gulf
    of Finland
Skíros see Skýros
Skópelos *105 C5* Skópelos, Vóreies
    Sporádes, Greece, Aegean Sea
Skopje *101 D6 var.* Üsküb, *Turk.* Üsküp,
    prev. Skoplje; *anc.* Scupi. *country
    capital* (Macedonia) N FYR Macedonia
Skoplje see Skopje
Skovorodino *115 F4* Amurskaya Oblast',
    SE Russian Federation
Skudeneshjorden *85 A6* S Norway
Skuodas *106 B3 Ger.* Schoden, *Pol.*
    Szkudy. Klaipėda, NW Lithuania
Skye, Isle of *88 B3 island* NW Scotland,
    United Kingdom
Skylge see Terschelling
Skýros *105 C5 var.* Skíros. Skńyros,
    Vóreies Sporádes, Greece, Aegean Sea
Skýros *105 C5 var.* Skíros; *anc.* Scyros.
    island Vóreies Sporádes, Greece,
    Aegean Sea
Slagelse *85 B7* Sjælland, E Denmark
Slatina *100 C3* Hung. Szlatina; *prev.*
    Podravska Slatina. Virovitica-
    Podravina, NE Croatia
Slatina *108 B5* Olt, S Romania
Slavgorod see Slawharad
Slavonski Brod *100 C3 Ger.* Brod, *Hung.*
    Bród; *prev.* Brod, Brod na Savi. Brod-
    Posavina, NE Croatia
Slavuta *108 C2* Khmel'nyts'ka Oblast',
    NW Ukraine
Slavyansk see Slov"yans'k
Slawharad *107 E7 Rus.* Slavgorod.
    Mahilyowskaya Voblasts', E Belarus
Sławno *98 C2* Zachodnio-pomorskie,
    NW Poland
Slēmānī see As Sulaymānīyah
Sliema *102 B5* N Malta
Sligo *89 A5 Ir.* Sligeach. Sligo,
    NW Ireland
Sliven *104 D2 var.* Slivno. Sliven,
    C Bulgaria
Slivnitsa *104 B2* Sofiya, W Bulgaria
Slivno see Sliven
Slobozia *108 C5* Ialomiţa, SE Romania
Slonim *107 B6 Pol.* Słonim.
    Hrodzyenskaya Voblasts', W Belarus
Słonim see Slonim
Slovakia *99 C6 off.* Slovenská Republika,
    Ger. Slowakei, *Hung.* Szlovákia, *Slvk.*
    Slovensko. *country* C Europe

SLOVAKIA
Central Europe

Official name Slovak Republic
Formation 1993 / 1993
Capital Bratislava
Population 5.5 million / 290 people
    per sq mile (112 people per sq km)
Total area 18,859 sq. miles (48,845 sq. km)
Languages Slovak*, Hungarian
    (Magyar), Czech
Religions Roman Catholic 69%,
    Nonreligious 13%, Other 10%,
    Greek Catholic (Uniate) 4%,
    Orthodox Christian 1%
Ethnic mix Slovak 86%, Magyar 10%,
    Roma 2%, Czech 1%, Other 1%
Government Parliamentary system
Currency Euro = 100 cents
Literacy rate 99%
Calorie consumption 2881 kilocalories

Slovak Ore Mountains see Slovenské
    rudohorie
Slovenia *95 D8 off.* Republic of Slovenia,
    Ger. Slowenien, *Slvn.* Slovenija. *country*
    SE Europe

SLOVENIA
Central Europe

Official name Republic of Slovenia
Formation 1991 / 1991
Capital Ljubljana
Population 2 million / 256 people
    per sq mile (99 people per sq km)
Total area 7820 sq. miles (20,253 sq. km)
Languages Slovenian*
Religions Roman Catholic 58%,
    Other 28%, Atheist 10%, Orthodox
    Christian 2%, Muslim 2%
Ethnic mix Slovene 83%, Other 12%,
    Serb 2%, Croat 2%, Bosniak 1%
Government Parliamentary system
Currency Euro = 100 cents
Literacy rate 99%
Calorie consumption 3275 kilocalories

Slovenia, Republic of see Slovenia
Slovenija see Slovenia
Slovenská Republika see Slovakia
Slovenské rudohorie *99 D6 Eng.* Slovak
    Ore Mountains, *Ger.* Slowakisches
    Erzgebirge, Ungarisches Erzgebirge.
    mountain range C Slovakia
Slovensko see Slovakia
Slov"yans'k *109 G3 Rus.* Slavyansk.
    Donets'ka Oblast', E Ukraine
Slowakei see Slovakia
Slowakisches Erzgebirge see Slovenské
    rudohorie
Slowenien see Slovenia
Słubice *98 B3 Ger.* Frankfurt. Lubuskie,
    W Poland
Sluch *108 D1 river* NW Ukraine
Słupsk *98 C2 Ger.* Stolp. Pomorskie,
    N Poland
Slutsk *107 C6* Minskaya Voblasts',
    S Belarus
Smallwood Reservoir *39 F2 lake*
    Newfoundland and Labrador, S Canada
Smara *70 B3 var.* Es Semara. N Western
    Sahara
Smarhon' *107 C5 Pol.* Smorgonie, *Rus.*
    Smorgon'. Hrodzyenskaya Voblasts',
    W Belarus
Smederevo *100 D4 Ger.* Semendria.
    Serbia, N Serbia
Smederevska Palanka *100 D4* Serbia,
    C Serbia
Smela see Smila
Smila *109 E2 Rus.* Smela. Cherkas'ka
    Oblast', C Ukraine
Smilten see Smiltene
Smiltene *106 D3 Ger.* Smilten. N Latvia
Smøla *84 A4 island* W Norway
Smolensk *111 A5* Smolenskaya Oblast',
    W Russian Federation
Smorgon'/Smorgonie see Smarhon'
Smyrna see Izmir
Snake *34 B4 river* Yukon Territory,
    NW Canada
Snake River *46 C3 river* NW USA
Snake River Plain *46 D4 plain* Idaho,
    NW USA
Sneek *86 D2 Fris.* Snits. Fryslân,
    N Netherlands
Sneeuw-gebergte see Maoke,
    Pegunungan
Sněžka *98 B4 Ger.* Schneekoppe, *Pol.*
    Śnieżka. *mountain* N Czech Republic/
    Poland
Śniardwy, Jezioro *98 D2 Ger.*
    Spirdingsee. *lake* NE Poland
Snieckus see Visaginas
Śnieżka see Sněžka
Snina *99 E5 Hung.* Szinna. Prešovský
    Kraj, E Slovakia
Snits see Sneek
Snowdonia *89 C6 mountain range*
    NW Wales, United Kingdom
Snowdrift see Łutselk'e
Snow Mountains see Maoke, Pegunungan
Snyder *49 F3* Texas, SW USA
Sobradinho, Barragem de see
    Sobradinho, Represa de
Sobradinho, Represa de *63 F2 var.*
    Barragem de Sobradinho. *reservoir*
    E Brazil

Sochi *111 A7* Krasnodarskiy Kray, SW Russian Federation
Société, Îles de la/Society Islands *see* Société, Archipel de la
Society Islands *145 G4 var.* Archipel de Tahiti, Îles de la Société, *Eng.* Society Islands. *island group* W French Polynesia
Soconusco, Sierra de *see* Madre, Sierra
Socorro *48 D2* New Mexico, SW USA
Socorro, Isla *50 B5* island W Mexico
Socotra *121 C7 var.* Sokotra, *Eng.* Socotra. *island* SE Yemen
Socotra *see* Suquṭrā
Soc Trăng *137 D6 var.* Khanh Hung. Soc Trăng, S Vietnam
Socuéllamos *93 E3* Castilla-La Mancha, C Spain
Sodankylä *84 D3* Lappi, N Finland
Sodari *see* Sodiri
Söderhamn *85 C5* Gävleborg, C Sweden
Södertälje *85 C6* Stockholm, C Sweden
Sodiri *72 B4 var.* Sawdiri, Sodari. Northern Kordofan, C Sudan
Soekaboemi *see* Sukabumi
Soemba *see* Sumba, Pulau
Soengaipenoeh *see* Sungaipenuh
Soerabaja *see* Surabaya
Soerakarta *see* Surakarta
Sofia *see* Sofiya
Sofiya *104 C2 var.* Sophia, *Eng.* Sofia, *Lat.* Serdica. *country capital* (Bulgaria) Sofiya-Grad, W Bulgaria
Sogamoso *58 B3* Boyacá, C Colombia
Sognefjorden *85 A5 fjord* NE North Sea
Sohâg *see* Sawhāj
Sohar *see* Şuḩār
Sohm Plain *66 B3 abyssal plain* NW Atlantic Ocean
Sohrau *see* Żory
Sokal' *108 C2 Rus.* Sokal. L'vivs'ka Oblast', NW Ukraine
Söke *116 A4* Aydın, SW Turkey
Sokhumi *117 E1 Rus.* Sukhumi. NW Georgia
Sokodé *75 F4* C Togo
Sokol *110 C4* Vologodskaya Oblast', NW Russian Federation
Sokółka *98 E3* Podlaskie, NE Poland
Sokolov *99 A5 Ger.* Falkenau an der Eger; *prev.* Falknov nad Ohří. Karlovarský Kraj, W Czech Republic
Sokone *74 B3* W Senegal
Sokoto *75 F3* Sokoto, NW Nigeria
Sokoto *75 F4 river* NW Nigeria
Sokotra *see* Suquṭrā
Solāpur *124 B3 var.* Sholāpur. Mahārāshtra, W India
Solca *108 C3 Ger.* Solka. Suceava, N Romania
Sol, Costa del *92 D5 coastal region* S Spain
Soldeu *91 B7* NE Andorra Europe
Solec Kujawski *98 C3* Kujawsko-pomorskie, C Poland
Soledad *58 B1* Atlántico, N Colombia
Isla Soledad *see* East Falkland
Soligorsk *see* Salihorsk
Solikamsk *114 C3* Permskiy Kray, NW Russian Federation
Sol'-Iletsk *111 D6* Orenburgskaya Oblast', W Russian Federation
Solingen *94 A4* Nordrhein-Westfalen, W Germany
Solka *see* Solca
Sollentuna *85 C6* Stockholm, C Sweden
Solo *see* Surakarta
Solok *138 B4* Sumatera, W Indonesia
Solomon Islands *144 C3 prev.* British Solomon Islands Protectorate. *country* W Solomon Islands N Melanesia W Pacific Ocean

SOLOMON ISLANDS
Australasia & Oceania

Official name Solomon Islands
Formation 1978 / 1978
Capital Honiara
Population 600,000 / 56 people per sq mile (21 people per sq km)
Total area 10,985 sq. miles (28,450 sq km)
Languages English*, Pidgin English, Melanesian Pidgin, c.120 others
Religions Church of Melanesia (Anglican) 34%, Roman Catholic 19%, South Seas

SOLOMON ISLANDS
(continued)

Evangelical Church 17%, Methodist 11%, Seventh-day Adventist 10%, Other 9%
Ethnic mix Melanesian 93%, Polynesian 4%, Micronesian 2%, Other 1%
Government Parliamentary system
Currency Solomon Islands dollar = 100 cents
Literacy rate 77%
Calorie consumption 2439 kilocalories

Solomon Islands *144 C3 island group* Papua New Guinea/Solomon Islands
Solomon Sea *144 B3 sea* W Pacific Ocean
Soltau *94 B3* Niedersachsen, NW Germany
Sol'tsy *110 A4* Novgorodskaya Oblast', W Russian Federation
Solun *see* Thessaloníki
Solwezi *78 D2* North Western, NW Zambia
Sōma *130 D4* Fukushima, Honshū, C Japan
Somalia *73 D5 off.* Somali Democratic Republic, *Som.* Jamuuriyada Demuqraadiga Soomaaliyeed, Soomaaliya; *prev.* Italian Somaliland, Somaliland Protectorate. *country* E Africa

SOMALIA
East Africa

Official name The Somali Democratic Republic
Formation 1960 / 1960
Capital Mogadishu
Population 9.6 million / 40 people per sq mile (15 people per sq km)
Total area 246,199 sq. miles (637,657 sq. km)
Languages Somali*, Arabic*, English, Italian
Religions Sunni Muslim 99%, Christian 1%
Ethnic mix Somali 85%, Other 15%
Government Transitional regime
Currency Somali shilin = 100 senti
Literacy rate 24%
Calorie consumption 1762 kilocalories

Somali Basin *69 E5 undersea basin* W Indian Ocean
Somali Democratic Republic *see* Somalia
Somaliland *73 D5 disputed territory* N Somalia
Somaliland Protectorate *see* Somalia
Sombor *100 C3 Hung.* Zombor. Vojvodina, NW Serbia
Someren *87 D5* Noord-Brabant, SE Netherlands
Somerset *42 A5 var.* Somerset Village. W Bermuda
Somerset *40 C5* Kentucky, S USA
Somerset Island *37 F2 island* Queen Elizabeth Islands, Nunavut, NW Canada
Somerset Village *see* Somerset
Somers Islands *see* Bermuda
Somerton *48 A2* Arizona, SW USA
Someş *108 B3 river* Hungary/Romania Europe
Somme *90 C2 river* N France
Sommerfeld *see* Lubsko
Somotillo *52 C3* Chinandega, NW Nicaragua
Somoto *52 D3* Madriz, NW Nicaragua
Songea *73 C8* Ruvuma, S Tanzania
Sŏngjin *see* Kimch'aek
Songkhla *137 C7 var.* Songkla, *Mal.* Singora. Songkhla, SW Thailand
Songkla *see* Songkhla
Sonoran Desert *48 A3 var.* Desierto de Altar. *desert* Mexico/USA
Sonsonate *52 B3* Sonsonate, W El Salvador
Soochow *see* Suzhou
Soomaaliya/Soomaaliyeed, Jamuuriyada Demuqraadiga *see* Somalia
Soome Laht *see* Finland, Gulf of
Sop Hao *136 D3* Houaphan, N Laos

Sophia *see* Sofiya
Sopianae *see* Pécs
Sopot *98 C2 Ger.* Zoppot. Pomorskie, N Poland
Sopron *99 B6 Ger.* Ödenburg. Győr-Moson-Sopron, NW Hungary
Sorau/Sorau in der Niederlausitz *see* Żary
Sorgues *91 D6* Vaucluse, SE France
Sorgun *116 D3* Yozgat, C Turkey
Soria *93 E2* Castilla y León, N Spain
Soroca *108 D3 Rus.* Soroki. N Moldova
Sorochino *see* Sarochyna
Soroki *see* Soroca
Sorong *139 F4* Papua, E Indonesia
Sørøy *see* Sørøya
Sørøya *84 C2 var.* Sørøy, *Lapp.* Sállan. *island* N Norway
Sortavala *110 B3 prev.* Serdobol'. Respublika Kareliya, NW Russian Federation
Sotavento, Ilhas de *74 A3 var.* Leeward Islands. *island group* S Cape Verde
Sotkamo *84 E4* Oulu, C Finland
Souanké *77 B5* Sangha, NW Congo
Soueida *see* As Suwaydā'
Soufli *104 D3 prev.* Souflíon. Anatolikí Makedonía kai Thráki, NE Greece
Souflíon *see* Soufli
Soufrière *55 F2* W Saint Lucia
Soukhné *see* As Sukhnah
Sŏul *see* Seoul
Soûr *119 A5 var.* Şūr; *anc.* Tyre. SW Lebanon
Souris River *45 E1 var.* Mouse River. *river* Canada/USA
Soúrpi *105 B5* Thessalía, C Greece
Sousse *71 F2 var.* Sūsah. NE Tunisia
South Africa *78 C4 off.* Republic of South Africa, *Afr.* Suid-Afrika. *country* S Africa

SOUTH AFRICA
Southern Africa

Official name Republic of South Africa
Formation 1934 / 1994
Capital Pretoria (Tshwane); Cape Town; Bloemfontein
Population 50.5 million / 107 people per sq mile (41 people per sq km)
Total area 471,008 sq. miles (1,219,912 sq. km)
Languages English, isiZulu, isiXhosa, Afrikaans, Sepedi, Setswana, Sesotho, Xitsonga, siSwati, Tshivenda, isiNdebele
Religions Christian 68%, Traditional beliefs and animist 29%, Muslim 2%, Hindu 1%
Ethnic mix Black 89%, White 9%, Asian 2%
Government Presidential system
Currency Rand = 100 cents
Literacy rate 89%
Calorie consumption 3017 kilocalories

South Africa, Republic of *see* South Africa
South America *56* continent
Southampton *89 D7 hist.* Hamwih, *Lat.* Clausentum. S England, United Kingdom
Southampton Island *37 G3 island* Nunavut, NE Canada
South Andaman *133 F2 island* Andaman Islands, India, NE Indian Ocean
South Australia *149 A5 state* S Australia
South Australian Basin *142 B5 undersea basin* SW Indian Ocean
South Bend *40 C3* Indiana, N USA
South Beveland *see* Zuid-Beveland
South Bruny Island *149 C8 island* Tasmania, SE Australia
South Carolina *43 E2 off.* State of South Carolina, *also known as* The Palmetto State. *state* SE USA
South Carpathians *see* Carpaţii Meridionalii
South China Basin *125 E4 undersea basin* SE South China Sea
South China Sea *125 E4 Chin.* Nan Hai, *Ind.* Laut Cina Selatan, *Vtn.* Biển Đông. *sea* SE Asia
South Dakota *44 D2 off.* State of South Dakota, *also known as* The Coyote State, Sunshine State. *state* N USA

Southeast Indian Ridge *141 D7 undersea ridge* Indian Ocean/Pacific Ocean
Southeast Pacific Basin *153 E5 var.* Belling Hausen Mulde. *undersea basin* SE Pacific Ocean
South East Point *149 C7 headland* Victoria, S Australia
Southend-on-Sea *89 E6* E England, United Kingdom
Southern Alps *151 B6 mountain range* South Island, New Zealand
Southern Cook Islands *145 F4 island group* S Cook Islands
Southern Cross *147 B6* Western Australia
Southern Indian Lake *37 F4 lake* Manitoba, C Canada
Southern Ocean *67 B7 ocean* Atlantic Ocean/Indian Ocean/Pacific Ocean
Southern Uplands *88 C4 mountain range* S Scotland, United Kingdom
South Fiji Basin *142 D4 undersea basin* S Pacific Ocean
South Geomagnetic Pole *154 B3 pole* Antarctica
South Georgia *57 D8 island* South Georgia and the South Sandwich Islands, SW Atlantic Ocean
South Goulburn Island *146 E2 island* Northern Territory, N Australia
South Huvadhu Atoll *132 A5 atoll* S Maldives
South Indian Basin *141 D7 undersea basin* Indian Ocean/Pacific Ocean
South Island *151 C6 island* S New Zealand
South Korea *129 E4 off.* Republic of Korea, *Kor.* Taehan Min'guk. *country* E Asia

SOUTH KOREA
East Asia

Official name Republic of Korea
Formation 1948 / 1953
Capital Seoul; Sejong City
Population 48.4 million / 1270 people per sq mile (490 people per sq km)
Total area 38,023 sq. miles (98,480 sq. km)
Languages Korean*
Religions Mahayana Buddhist 47%, Protestant 38%, Roman Catholic 11%, Confucianist 3%, Other 1%
Ethnic mix Korean 100%
Government Presidential system
Currency South Korean won = 100 chon
Literacy rate 99%
Calorie consumption 3200 kilocalories

South Lake Tahoe *47 C5* California, W USA
South Orkney Islands *154 A2 island group* Antarctica
South Ossetia *117 F2 former autonomous region* SW Georgia
South Pacific Basin *see* Southwest Pacific Basin
South Platte River *44 D4 river* Colorado/Nebraska, C USA
South Pole *154 B3 pole* Antarctica
South Sandwich Islands *57 D8 island group* SW Atlantic Ocean
South Sandwich Trench *57 E8 trench* SW Atlantic Ocean
South Shetland Islands *154 A2 island group* Antarctica
South Shields *88 D4* NE England, United Kingdom
South Sioux City *45 F3* Nebraska, C USA
South Sudan *73 B5 off.* Republic of South Sudan. *country* E Africa

SOUTH SUDAN
East Africa

Official name Republic of South Sudan
Formation 2011 / 2011
Capital Juba
Population 8.3 million / 33 people per sq mile (13 people per sq km)
Total area 244,777 sq. miles (644,329 sq. km)
Languages Arabic, Dinka, Nuer, Zande, Bari, Shilluk, Lotuko
Religions Over half of the population

SOUTH SUDAN
(continued)

follow Christian or traditional beliefs
Ethnic mix Dinka 40%, Nuer 15%,
Bari 10%, Shilluk/Anwak 10%,
Azande 10%, Arab 10%, Other 5%
Government Transitional regime
Currency South Sudan pound = 100
piastres
Literacy rate 37%
Calorie consumption Not available

South Taranaki Bight *150 C4 bight*
SE Tasman Sea
South Tasmania Plateau *see* Tasman
Plateau
South Uist *88 B3 island* NW Scotland,
United Kingdom
South-West Africa/South West Africa
see Namibia
South West Cape *151 A8 headland*
Stewart Island, New Zealand
Southwest Indian Ocean Ridge *see*
Southwest Indian Ridge
Southwest Indian Ridge *141 B6 var.*
Southwest Indian Ocean Ridge.
undersea ridge SW Indian Ocean
Southwest Pacific Basin *143 E4 var.*
South Pacific Basin. *undersea basin*
SE Pacific Ocean
Sovereign Base Area *102 C5 uk military
installation* S Cyprus
Soweto *78 D4* Gauteng,
NE South Africa
Sōya-kaikyō *see* La Pérouse Strait
Spain *92 D3 off.* Kingdom of Spain, *Sp.*
España; *anc.* Hispania, Iberia, *Lat.*
Hispania. *country* SW Europe

SPAIN
Southwest Europe

Official name Kingdom of Spain
Formation 1492 / 1713
Capital Madrid
Population 46.5 million / 241 people per
sq mile (93 people per sq km)
Total area 194,896 sq. miles
(2504,782 sq. km)
Languages Spanish*, Catalan*,
Galician*, Basque*
Religions Roman Catholic 96%, Other 4%
Ethnic mix Castilian Spanish 72%,
Catalan 17%, Galician 6%, Basque 2%,
Other 2%, Roma 1%
Government Parliamentary system
Currency Euro = 100 cents
Literacy rate 98%
Calorie consumption 3239 kilocalories

Spain, Kingdom of *see* Spain
Spalato *see* Split
Spanish Town *54 B5 hist.* St.Iago de la
Vega. C Jamaica
Sparks *47 C5* Nevada, W USA
Sparta *see* Spárti
Spartanburg *43 E1* South Carolina,
SE USA
Spárti *105 B6 Eng.* Sparta. Pelopónnisos,
S Greece
Spearfish *44 D2* South Dakota,
N USA
Speightstown *55 G1* NW Barbados
Spencer *45 F3* Iowa, C USA
Spencer Gulf *149 A6 gulf* South Australia
Spey *88 C3 river* NE Scotland, United
Kingdom
Spice Islands *see* Maluku
Spiess Seamount *67 C7 seamount*
S Atlantic Ocean
Spijkenisse *86 B4* Zuid-Holland,
SW Netherlands
Spíli *105 C8* Kríti, Greece,
E Mediterranean Sea
Spīn Būldak *123 E5 prev.* Spīn Būldak.
Kandahār, S Afghanistan
Spīn Būldak *see* Spīn Būldak
Spirdingsee *see* Śniardwy, Jezioro
Spitsbergen *83 F2 island* NW Svalbard
Split *100 B4 It.* Spalato. Split-Dalmacija,
S Croatia
Špogi *106 D4* SE Latvia
Spokane *46 C2* Washington, NW USA
Spratly Islands *138 B2 Chin.* Nansha
Qundao. *disputed territory* SE Asia
Spree *94 D4 river* E Germany

Springfield *40 B4 state capital* Illinois,
N USA
Springfield *41 G3* Massachusetts,
NE USA
Springfield *45 G5* Missouri, C USA
Springfield *40 C4* Ohio, N USA
Springfield *46 B3* Oregon, NW USA
Spring Garden *59 F2* NE Guyana
Spring Hill *43 E4* Florida, SE USA
Springs Junction *151 C5* West Coast,
South Island, New Zealand
Springsure *148 D4* Queensland,
E Australia
Sprottau *see* Szprotawa
Spruce Knob *41 E4 mountain* West
Virginia, NE USA
Srbinje *see* Foča
Srbobran *100 D3 var.* Bácsszenttamás,
Hung. Szenttamás. Vojvodina,
N Serbia
Srebrenica *100 C4* Republika Srpska,
E Bosnia and Herzegovina
Sredets *104 D2 prev.* Syulemeshlii. Stara
Zagora, C Bulgaria
Sredets *104 E2 prev.* Grudovo. Burgas,
E Bulgaria
Sremska Mitrovica *100 C3 prev.*
Mitrovica, *Ger.* Mitrowitz. Vojvodina,
NW Serbia
Srepok, Sông *see* Srêpôk, Tônle
Srêpôk, Tônle *137 E5 var.* Sông Srepok.
river Cambodia/Vietnam
Sri Aman *138 C3* Sarawak,
East Malaysia
Sri Jayewardenapura Kotte *132 D3
country capital* (Sri Lanka) (legislative)
Western Province, W Sri Lanka
Srikākulam *135 F5* Andhra Pradesh,
E India
Sri Lanka *132 D3 off.* Democratic
Socialist Republic of Sri Lanka; *prev.*
Ceylon. *country* S Asia

SRI LANKA
South Asia

Official name Democratic Socialist
Republic of Sri Lanka
Formation 1948 / 1948
Capital Colombo; Sri Jayewardenapura
Kotte
Population 21 million / 840 people
per sq mile (324 people per sq km)
Total area 25,332 sq. miles (65,610 sq. km)
Languages Sinhala*, Tamil*,
Sinhala-Tamil, English
Religions Buddhist 69%, Hindu 15%,
Muslim 8%, Christian 8%
Ethnic mix Sinhalese 74%, Tamil 18%,
Moor 7%, Other 1%
Government Mixed presidential–
parliamentary system
Currency Sri Lanka rupee = 100 cents
Literacy rate 91%
Calorie consumption 2426 kilocalories

**Sri Lanka, Democratic Socialist
Republic of** *see* Sri Lanka
Srinagarind Reservoir *137 C5 lake*
W Thailand
Srpska, Republika *100 B3 republic*
Bosnia and Herzegovina
Ssu-ch'uan *see* Sichuan
Ssu-p'ing/Ssu-p'ing-chieh *see* Siping
Stabroek *87 B5* Antwerpen,
N Belgium
Stade *94 B3* Niedersachsen,
NW Germany
Stadskanaal *86 E2* Groningen,
NE Netherlands
Stafford *89 D6* C England, United
Kingdom
Staicele *106 D3* N Latvia
Ştaierdorf-Anina *see* Anina
Stájerlakanina *see* Anina
Stakhanov *109 H3* Luhans'ka Oblast',
E Ukraine
Stalin *see* Varna
Stalinabad *see* Dushanbe
Stalingrad *see* Volgograd
Stalino *see* Donets'k
Stalinobod *see* Dushanbe
Stalinsk *see* Novokuznetsk
Stalinski Zaliv *see* Varnenski Zaliv
Stalin, Yazovir *see* Iskŭr, Yazovir
Stalowa Wola *98 E4* Podkarpackie,
SE Poland

Stamford *41 F3* Connecticut,
NE USA
Stampalia *see* Astypálaia
Stanislau *see* Ivano-Frankivs'k
Stanislav *see* Ivano-Frankivs'k
Stanisławów *see* Ivano-Frankivs'k
Stanke Dimitrov *see* Dupnitsa
Stanley *65 D7 var.* Port Stanley, Puerto
Argentino. *dependent territory capital*
(Falkland Islands) East Falkland,
Falkland Islands
Stanleyville *see* Kisangani
Stann Creek *see* Dangriga
Stanovoy Khrebet *113 E3 mountain
range* SE Russian Federation
Stanthorpe *149 D5* Queensland,
E Australia
Staphorst *86 D2* Overijssel,
E Netherlands
Starachowice *98 D4* Świętokrzyskie,
C Poland
Stara Kanjiža *see* Kanjiža
Stara Pazova *100 D3 Ger.* Altpasua,
Hung. Ópazova. Vojvodina, N Serbia
Stara Planina *see* Balkan Mountains
Stara Zagora *100 D2 Lat.* Augusta
Trajana. Stara Zagora, C Bulgaria
Starbuck Island *145 G3 prev.* Volunteer
Island. *island* E Kiribati
Stargard in Pommern *see* Stargard
Szczeciński
Stargard Szczeciński *98 B3 Ger.*
Stargard in Pommern. Zachodnio-
pomorskie, NW Poland
Stari Bečej *see* Bečej
Starobel'sk *see* Starobil's'k
Starobil's'k *109 H2 Rus.* Starobel'sk.
Luhans'ka Oblast', E Ukraine
Starobin *107 C7 var.* Starobyn.
Minskaya Voblasts', S Belarus
Starobyn *see* Starobin
Starogard Gdański *98 C2 Ger.*
Preussisch-Stargard. Pomorskie,
N Poland
Starokonstantinov *see* Starokostyantyniv
Starokostyantyniv *108 D2 Rus.*
Starokonstantinov. Khmel'nyts'ka
Oblast', NW Ukraine
Starominskaya *111 A7* Krasnodarskiy
Kray, SW Russian Federation
Staryya Darohi *107 C6 Rus.* Staryye
Dorogi. Minskaya Voblasts', S Belarus
Staryye Dorogi *see* Staryya Darohi
Staryy Oskol *111 B6* Belgorodskaya
Oblast', W Russian Federation
State College *41 E4* Pennsylvania,
NE USA
Staten Island *see* Estados, Isla de los
Statesboro *43 E2* Georgia, SE USA
States, The *see* United States of America
Staunton *41 E5* Virginia, NE USA
Stavanger *85 A6* Rogaland, S Norway
Stavers Island *see* Vostok Island
Stavropol' *111 B7 prev.* Voroshilovsk.
Stavropol'skiy Kray, SW Russian
Federation
Stavropol' *see* Tol'yatti
Steamboat Springs *44 C4* Colorado,
C USA
Steenwijk *86 D2* Overijssel,
N Netherlands
Steier *see* Steyr
Steierdorf/Steierdorf-Anina *see* Anina
Steinamanger *see* Szombathely
Steinkjer *84 B4* Nord-Trøndelag,
C Norway
Stejarul *see* Karapelit
Stendal *94 C3* Sachsen-Anhalt,
C Germany
Stepanakert *see* Xankändi
Stephenville *49 F3* Texas, SW USA
Sterling *44 D4* Colorado, C USA
Sterling *40 B3* Illinois, N USA
Sterlitamak *114 B3* Respublika
Bashkortostan, W Russian Federation
Stettin *see* Szczecin
Stettiner Haff *see* Szczeciński, Zalew
Stevenage *89 E6* E England, United
Kingdom
Stevens Point *40 B2* Wisconsin, N USA
Stewart Island *151 A8 island* S New
Zealand
Steyerlak-Anina *see* Anina
Steyr *95 D6 var.* Steier. Oberösterreich,
N Austria
St. Helena Bay *78 B5 bay* SW South
Africa

Stif *see* Sétif
Stillwater *49 G1* Oklahoma, C USA
Štip *101 E6* E FYR Macedonia
Stirling *88 C4* C Scotland, United
Kingdom
Stjørdalshalsen *84 B4* Nord-Trøndelag,
C Norway
St-Maur-des-Fossés *90 E2* Val-de-
Marne, Île-de-France, N France Europe
Stockach *95 B6* Baden-Württemberg,
S Germany
Stockholm *85 C6 country capital*
(Sweden) Stockholm, C Sweden
Stockmannshof *see* Pļaviņas
Stockton *47 B6* California, W USA
Stockton Plateau *49 E4 plain* Texas,
SW USA
Stœng Trêng *137 D5 prev.* Stung Treng.
Stœng Trêng, NE Cambodia
Stoke *see* Stoke-on-Trent
Stoke-on-Trent *89 D6 var.* Stoke.
C England, United Kingdom
Stolbce *see* Stowbtsy
Stolbtsy *see* Stowbtsy
Stolp *see* Słupsk
Stolpmünde *see* Ustka
Stómio *104 B4* Thessalía, C Greece
Store Bælt *see* Storebælt
Storebælt *see* Storebælt
Støren *85 B5* Sør-Trøndelag,
S Norway
Storfjorden *83 G2 fjord* S Norway
Storhammer *see* Hamar
Stornoway *88 B2* NW Scotland, United
Kingdom
Storsjön *85 B5 lake* C Sweden
Storuman *84 C4* Västerbotten,
N Sweden
Storuman *84 C4 lake* N Sweden
Stowbtsy *107 C6 Pol.* Stolbce, *Rus.*
Stolbtsy. Minskaya Voblasts',
C Belarus
Strabane *89 B5 Ir.* An Srath Bán.
W Northern Ireland, United Kingdom
Strakonice *99 A5 Ger.* Strakonitz.
Jihočeský Kraj, S Czech Republic
Strakonitz *see* Strakonice
Stralsund *94 D2* Mecklenburg-
Vorpommern, NE Germany
Stranraer *89 C5* S Scotland, United
Kingdom
Strasbourg *90 E3 Ger.* Strassburg; *anc.*
Argentoratum. Bas-Rhin, NE France
Strãşeni *108 D3 var.* Strasheny.
C Moldova
Strasheny *see* Strãşeni
Strasbourg *see* Strasbourg, France
Strassburg *see* Aiud, Romania
Stratford *150 D4* Taranaki, North Island,
New Zealand
Strathfield *148 E2* New South Wales,
E Australia
Straubing *95 C6* Bayern,
SE Germany
Strehaia *108 B5* Mehedinţi,
SW Romania
Strelka *114 D4* Krasnoyarskiy Kray,
C Russian Federation
Strigonium *see* Esztergom
Strofília *see* Strofyliá
Strofyliá *105 C5 var.* Strofilia. Évvoia,
C Greece
Stromboli *97 D6 island* Isole Eolie,
S Italy
Stromeferry *88 C3* N Scotland, United
Kingdom
Strömstad *85 B6* Västra Götaland,
S Sweden
Strömsund *84 C4* Jämtland, C Sweden
Struga *101 D6* SW FYR Macedonia
Strumica *101 E6* E FYR Macedonia
Struma *see* Strymónas
Strumyani *104 C3* Blagoevgrad,
SW Bulgaria
Strymónas *104 C3 Bul.* Struma. *river*
Bulgaria/Greece
Stryy *108 B2* L'vivs'ka Oblast',
NW Ukraine
Studholme *151 B6* Canterbury, South
Island, New Zealand
Stuhlweissenberg *see* Székesfehérvár
Stung Treng *see* Stœng Trêng
Sturgis *44 D3* South Dakota, N USA
Stuttgart *95 B6* Baden-Württemberg,
SW Germany
Stykkishólmur *83 E4* Vesturland,
W Iceland

Styr *108 C1 Rus.* Styr'. *river* Belarus/ Ukraine
Su *see* Jiangsu
Suakin *72 C3 var.* Sawakin. Red Sea, NE Sudan
Subačius *106 C4* Panevėžys, NE Lithuania
Subaykhān *118 E3* Dayr az Zawr, E Syria
Subotica *100 D2 Ger.* Maria-Theresiopel, *Hung.* Szabadka. Vojvodina, N Serbia
Suceava *108 C3 Ger.* Suczawa, *Hung.* Szucsava. Suceava, NE Romania
Su-chou *see* Suzhou
Suchow *see* Xuzhou, Jiangsu, China
Suchow *see* Suzhou, Jiangsu, China
Sucker State *see* Illinois
Sucre *61 F4 hist.* Chuquisaca, La Plata. *country capital* (Bolivia) (legal capital) Chuquisaca, S Bolivia
Suczawa *see* Suceava
Sudan *72 A4 off.* Republic of Sudan, *Ar.* Jumhuriyat as-Sudan; *prev.* Anglo-Egyptian Sudan. *country* N Africa

SUDAN
East Africa

Official name Republic of the Sudan
Formation 1956 / 2011
Capital Khartoum
Population 34 million / 47 people per sq mile (18 people per sq km)
Total area 728,722 sq. miles (1,861,481 sq. km)
Languages Arabic, Nubian, Beja, Fur
Religions Nearly the whole population is Muslim (mainly Sunni)
Ethnic mix Arab 60%, Other 18%, Nubian 10%, Beja 8%, Fur 3%, Zaghawa 1%
Government Presidential system
Currency New Sudanese pound = 100 piastres
Literacy rate 61%
Calorie consumption 2326 kilocalories

Sudanese Republic *see* Mali
Sudan, Jumhuriyat as- *see* Sudan
Sudan, Republic of *see* Sudan
Sudbury *38 C4* Ontario, S Canada
Sudd *73 B5 swamp region* C South Sudan
Sudeten *98 B4 var.* Sudetes, Sudetic Mountains, *Cz./Pol.* Sudety. *mountain range* Czech Republic/Poland
Sudetes/Sudetic Mountains/Sudety *see* Sudeten
Südkarpaten *see* Carpaţii Meridionalii
Südliche Morava *see* Južna Morava
Sudong, Pulau *138 A2 island* SW Singapore Asia
Sudostroy *see* Severodvinsk
Sue *73 B5 river* W South Sudan
Sueca *93 F3* Valenciana, E Spain
Sue Wood Bay *42 B5 bay* W Bermuda North America W Atlantic Ocean
Suez *72 B1 Ar.* As Suways, El Suweis. NE Egypt
Suez Canal *72 B1 Ar.* Qanāt as Suways. *canal* NE Egypt
Suez, Gulf of *see* Khalīj as Suways
Suğla Gölü *116 C4 lake* SW Turkey
Şuḩār *121 D5 var.* Sohar. N Oman
Sühbaatar *127 E1* Selenge, N Mongolia
Suhl *95 C5* Thüringen, C Germany
Suicheng *see* Suixi
Suid-Afrika *see* South Africa
Suidwes-Afrika *see* Namibia
Suixi *128 C6 var.* Suicheng. Guangdong, S China
Sujāwal *134 B3* Sind, SE Pakistan
Sukabumi *138 C5 prev.* Soekaboemi. Jawa, C Indonesia
Sukagawa *131 D5* Fukushima, Honshū, C Japan
Sukarnapura *see* Jayapura
Sukarno, Puntjak *see* Jaya, Puncak
Sukhne *see* As Sukhnah
Sukhona *110 C4 var. or* Tot'ma. *river* NW Russian Federation
Sukhumi *see* Sokhumi
Sukkertoppen *see* Maniitsoq
Sukkur *134 B3* Sind, SE Pakistan
Sukumo *131 B7* Kōchi, Shikoku, SW Japan

Sulaimaniya *see* As Sulaymānīyah
Sulaiman Range *134 C2 mountain range* C Pakistan
Sula, Kepulauan *139 E4 island group* C Indonesia
Sulawesi, Laut *see* Celebes Sea
Sulechów *98 B3 Ger.* Züllichau. Lubuskie, W Poland
Suliag *see* Sawhāj
Sullana *60 B2* Piura, NW Peru
Sullivan Island *see* Lanbi Kyun
Sulphur Springs *49 G2* Texas, SW USA
Sultānābād *see* Arāk
Sulu Archipelago *139 E3 island group* SW Philippines
Sülüktü *see* Sulyukta
Sulu, Laut *see* Sulu Sea
Sulu Sea *139 E2 var.* Laut Sulu. *sea* SW Philippines
Sulyukta *123 E2 Kir.* Sülüktü. Batkenskaya Oblast', SW Kyrgyzstan
Sumatra *137 B8 Eng.* Sumatra. *island* W Indonesia
Sumatra *see* Sumatera
Šumava *see* Bohemian Forest
Sumba, Pulau *139 E5 Eng.* Sandalwood Island; *prev.* Soemba. *island* Nusa Tenggara, C Indonesia
Sumba, Selat *139 E5 strait* Nusa Tenggara, S Indonesia
Sumbawanga *73 B7* Rukwa, W Tanzania
Sumbe *78 B2 var.* N'Gunza, *Port.* Novo Redondo. Cuanza Sul, W Angola
Sumeih *73 B5* Southern Darfur, S Sudan
Sumgait *see* Sumqayıt, Azerbaijan
Summer Lake *46 B4 lake* Oregon, NW USA
Summit *93 H5* Alaska, USA
Sumqayıt *117 H2 Rus.* Sumgait. E Azerbaijan
Sumy *109 F2* Sums'ka Oblast', NE Ukraine
Sunbury *149 C7* Victoria, SE Australia
Sunda Islands *see* Greater Sunda Islands
Sunda, Selat *138 B5 strait* Jawa/ Sumatera, SW Indonesia
Sunda Trench *see* Java Trench
Sunderland *88 D4 var.* Wearmouth. NE England, United Kingdom
Sundsvall *85 C5* Västernorrland, C Sweden
Sunflower State *see* Kansas
Sungaipenuh *138 B4 prev.* Soengaipenoeh. Sumatera, W Indonesia
Sunnyvale *47 A6* California, W USA
Sunset State *see* Oregon
Sunshine State *see* Florida
Sunshine State *see* New Mexico
Sunshine State *see* South Dakota
Suntar *115 F3* Respublika Sakha (Yakutiya), NE Russian Federation
Sunyani *75 E5* W Ghana
Suoločielgi *see* Saariselkä
Suomenlahti *see* Finland, Gulf of
Suomen Tasavalta/Suomi *see* Finland
Suomussalmi *84 E4* Oulu, E Finland
Suŏng *137 D6* Kâmpóng Cham, C Cambodia
Suoyarvi *110 B3* Respublika Kareliya, NW Russian Federation
Supe *60 C3* Lima, W Peru
Supérieur, Lac *see* Superior, Lake
Superior *40 A1* Wisconsin, N USA
Superior, Lake *40 B1 Fr.* Lac Supérieur. *lake* Canada/USA
Suqrah *see* Şawqirah
Şūr *121 E5* NE Oman
Şūr *see* Soûr
Surabaja *see* Surabaya
Surabaya *138 D5 prev.* Surabaja, Soerabaja. Jawa, C Indonesia
Surakarta *138 C5 Eng.* Solo; *prev.* Soerakarta. Jawa, S Indonesia
Šurany *99 C6 Hung.* Nagysurány. Nitriansky Kraj, SW Slovakia
Sürat *134 C4* Gujarāt, W India
Suratdhani *see* Surat Thani
Surat Thani *137 C6 var.* Suratdhani. Surat Thani, SW Thailand
Surazh *107 E5* Vitsyebskaya Voblasts', NE Belarus
Surdulica *101 E5* Serbia, SE Serbia

Sûre *87 D7 var.* Sauer. *river* W Europe
Surendranagar *134 C4* Gujarāt, W India
Surfers Paradise *149 E5* Queensland, E Australia
Surgut *114 D3* Khanty-Mansiyskiy Avtonomnyy Okrug-Yugra, C Russian Federation
Surin *137 D5* Surin, E Thailand
Surinam *see* Suriname
Suriname *59 G3 off.* Republic of Suriname, *var.* Surinam; *prev.* Dutch Guiana, Netherlands Guiana. *country* N South America

SURINAME
South America

Official name Republic of Suriname
Formation 1975 / 1975
Capital Paramaribo
Population 500,000 / 8 people per sq mile (3 people per sq km)
Total area 63,039 sq. miles (163,270 sq. km)
Languages Sranan (Creole), Dutch*, Javanese, Sarnami Hindi, Saramaccan, Chinese, Carib
Religions Hindu 27%, Protestant 25%, Roman Catholic 23%, Muslim 20%, Traditional beliefs 5%
Ethnic mix East Indian 27%, Creole 18%, Black 15%, Javanese 15%, Mixed race 13%, Other 6%, Amerindian 4%, Chinese 2%
Government Parliamentary system
Currency Suriname dollar = 100 cents
Literacy rate 95%
Calorie consumption 2548 kilocalories

Suriname, Republic of *see* Suriname
Sūriya/Sūriyah, Al-Jumhūrīyah al-'Arabīyah as- *see* Syria
Surkhab, Darya-i- *see* Kahmard, Daryā-ye
Surkhob *123 F3 river* C Tajikistan
Surt *71 G2 var.* Sidra, Sirte. N Libya
Surtsey *83 E5 island* S Iceland
Suruga-wan *131 D6 bay* SE Japan
Susa *96 A2* Piemonte, NE Italy
Sūsah *see* Sousse
Susanville *47 B5* California, W USA
Susitna *36 C3* Alaska, USA
Susteren *87 D5* Limburg, SE Netherlands
Susuman *115 G3* Magadanskaya Oblast', E Russian Federation
Sutlej *134 C2 river* India/Pakistan
Suur Munamägi *106 D3 var.* Munamägi, *Ger.* Eier-Berg. *mountain* SE Estonia
Suur Väin *106 C2 var.* Grosser Sund. *strait* W Estonia
Suva *145 E4 country capital* (Fiji) Viti Levu, W Fiji
Suvalkai/Suvalki *see* Suwałki
Suwałki *98 E2 Lith.* Suvalkai, *Rus.* Suvalki. Podlaskie, NE Poland
Suways, Qanāt as *see* Suez Canal
Suweida *see* As Suwaydā'
Suzhou *128 D5 var.* Soochow, Su-chou, Suchow; *prev.* Wuhsien. Jiangsu, E China
Svalbard *83 E1 Norwegian dependency* Arctic Ocean
Svartisen *84 C3 glacier* C Norway
Svay Riĕng *137 D6* Svay Riĕng, S Cambodia
Sveg *85 B5* Jämtland, C Sweden
Svenstavik *85 C5* Jämtland, C Sweden
Sverdlovsk *see* Yekaterinburg
Sverige *see* Sweden
Sveti Vrach *see* Sandanski
Svetlograd *111 B7* Stavropol'skiy Kray, SW Russian Federation
Svetlovodsk *see* Svitlovods'k
Svetozarevo *see* Jagodina
Svilengrad *104 D3 prev.* Mustafa-Pasha. Khaskovo, S Bulgaria
Svitlovods'k *109 F3 Rus.* Svetlovodsk. Kirovohrads'ka Oblast', C Ukraine
Svizzera *see* Switzerland
Svobodnyy *115 G4* Amurskaya Oblast', SE Russian Federation
Svyataya Anna Trough *155 C4 var.* Saint Anna Trough. *trough* N Kara Sea
Svyetlahorsk *107 D7 Rus.* Svetlogorsk. Homyel'skaya Voblasts', SE Belarus
Swabian Jura *see* Schwäbische Alb
Swakopmund *78 B3* Erongo, W Namibia

Swan Islands *53 E1 island group* NE Honduras North America
Swansea *89 C7 Wel.* Abertawe. S Wales, United Kingdom
Swarzędz *98 C3* Poznań, W Poland
Swatow *see* Shantou
Swaziland *78 D4 off.* Kingdom of Swaziland. *country* S Africa

SWAZILAND
Southern Africa

Official name Kingdom of Swaziland
Formation 1968 / 1968
Capital Mbabane
Population 1.2 million / 181 people per sq mile (70 people per sq km)
Total area 6704 sq. miles (17,363 sq. km)
Languages English*, siSwati*, isiZulu, Xitsonga
Religions Traditional beliefs 40%, Other 30%, Roman Catholic 20%, Muslim 10%
Ethnic mix Swazi 97%, Other 3%
Government Monarchy
Currency Lilangeni = 100 cents
Literacy rate 87%
Calorie consumption 2249 kilocalories

Swaziland, Kingdom of *see* Swaziland
Sweden *84 B4 off.* Kingdom of Sweden, *Swe.* Sverige. *country* N Europe

SWEDEN
Northern Europe

Official name Kingdom of Sweden
Formation 1523 / 1921
Capital Stockholm
Population 9.4 million / 59 people per sq mile (23 people per sq km)
Total area 173,731 sq. miles (449,964 sq. km)
Languages Swedish*, Finnish, Sámi
Religions Evangelical Lutheran 75%, Other 13%, Muslim 5%, Other Protestant 5%, Roman Catholic 2%
Ethnic mix Swedish 86%, Foreign-born or first-generation immigrant 12%, Finnish and Sámi 2%
Government Parliamentary system
Currency Swedish krona = 100 öre
Literacy rate 99%
Calorie consumption 3125 kilocalories

Sweden, Kingdom of *see* Sweden
Sweetwater *49 F3* Texas, SW USA
Świdnica *98 B4 Ger.* Schweidnitz. Wałbrzych, SW Poland
Świdwin *98 B2 Ger.* Schivelbein. Zachodnio-pomorskie, NW Poland
Świebodzice *98 B4 Ger.* Freiburg in Schlesien, Swiebodzice. Wałbrzych, SW Poland
Świebodzin *98 B3 Ger.* Schwiebus. Lubuskie, W Poland
Świecie *98 C3 Ger.* Schwertberg. Kujawsko-pomorskie, C Poland
Swindon *89 D7* S England, United Kingdom
Swinemünde *see* Świnoujście
Świnoujście *98 B2 Ger.* Swinemünde. Zachodnio-pomorskie, NW Poland
Swiss Confederation *see* Switzerland
Switzerland *95 A7 off.* Swiss Confederation, *Fr.* La Suisse, *Ger.* Schweiz, *It.* Svizzera; *anc.* Helvetia. *country* C Europe

SWITZERLAND
Central Europe

Official name Swiss Confederation
Formation 1291 / 1857
Capital Bern
Population 7.7 million / 501 people per sq mile (194 people per sq km)
Total area 15,942 sq. miles (41,290 sq. km)
Languages German*, Swiss-German, French*, Italian*, Romansh
Religions Roman Catholic 42%, Protestant 35%, Other and nonreligious 19%, Muslim 4%
Ethnic mix German 64%, French 20%, Other 9.5%, Italian 6%, Romansch 0.5%

SWITZERLAND
(continued)

Government Parliamentary system
Currency Swiss franc = 100
rappen/centimes
Literacy rate 99%
Calorie consumption 3454 kilocalories

Sycaminum see Hefa
Sydenham Island see Nonouti
Sydney 148 D1 state capital New South Wales, SE Australia
Sydney 39 G4 Cape Breton Island, Nova Scotia, SE Canada
Sydney Island see Manra
Syedpur see Saidpur
Syemyezhava 107 C6 Rus. Semezhevo. Minskaya Voblasts', C Belarus
Syene see Aswän
Syeverodonets'k 109 H3 Rus. Severodonetsk. Luhans'ka Oblast', E Ukraine
Syktyvkar 110 D4 prev. Ust'-Sysol'sk. Respublika Komi, NW Russian Federation
Sylhet 135 G3 Sylhet, NE Bangladesh
Synel'nykove 109 G3 Dnipropetrovs'ka Oblast', E Ukraine
Syowa 154 C2 Japanese research station Antarctica
Syracuse 41 E3 New York, NE USA
Syracuse see Siracusa
Syrdar'ya 114 B4 Sirdaryo Viloyati, E Uzbekistan
Syria 118 B3 off. Syrian Arab Republic, var. Siria, Syrie, Ar. Al-Jumhūrīyah al-'Arabīyah as-Sūrīyah, Sūrīya. country SW Asia

SYRIA
Southwest Asia

Official name Syrian Arab Republic
Formation 1941 / 1967
Capital Damascus
Population 20.8 million / 293 people per sq mile (113 people per sq km)
Total area 71,498 sq. miles (184,180 sq. km)
Languages Arabic*, French, Kurdish, Armenian, Circassian, Turkic languages, Assyrian, Aramaic
Religions Sunni Muslim 74%, Alawi 12%, Christian 10%, Druze 3%, Other 1%
Ethnic mix Arab 90%, Kurdish 9%, Armenian, Turkmen, and Circassian 1%
Government One-party state
Currency Syrian pound = 100 piastres
Literacy rate 84%
Calorie consumption 3212 kilocalories

Syrian Arab Republic see Syria
Syrian Desert 119 D5 Ar. Al Hamad, Bādiyat ash Shām. desert SW Asia
Syrie see Syria
Sýrna 105 E7 var. Sirna. island Kykládes, Greece, Aegean Sea
Sýros 105 C6 var. Síros. island Kykládes, Greece, Aegean Sea
Syulemeshlii see Sredets
Syvash, Zaliv see Syvash, Zatoka
Syvash, Zatoka 109 F4 Rus. Zaliv Syvash. inlet S Ukraine
Syzran' 111 C6 Samarskaya Oblast', W Russian Federation
Szabadka see Subotica
Szamotuły 98 B3 Poznań, W Poland
Szászrégen see Reghin
Szatmárrnémeti see Satu Mare
Száva see Sava
Szczecin 98 B3 Eng./Ger. Stettin. Zachodnio-pomorskie, NW Poland
Szczecinek 98 B2 Ger. Neustettin. Zachodnio-pomorskie, NW Poland
Szczeciński, Zalew 98 A2 var. Stettiner Haff, Ger. Oderhaff. bay Germany/ Poland
Szczuczyn Nowogródzki see Shchuchyn
Szczytno 98 D3 Ger. Ortelsburg. Warmińsko-Mazurskie, NE Poland
Szechuan/Szechwan see Sichuan
Szeged 99 D7 Ger. Szegedin, Rom. Seghedin. Csongrád, SE Hungary
Szegedin see Szeged
Székelykeresztúr see Cristuru Secuiesc

Székesfehérvár 99 C6 Ger. Stuhlweissenberg; anc. Alba Regia. Fejér, W Hungary
Szeklerburg see Miercurea-Ciuc
Szekler Neumarkt see Târgu Secuiesc
Szekszárd 99 C7 Tolna, S Hungary
Szempcz/Szenc see Senec
Szenice see Senica
Szenttamás see Srbobran
Szeping see Siping
Szilágysomlyó see Şimleu Silvaniei
Szinna see Snina
Sziszek see Sisak
Szitás-Keresztúr see Cristuru Secuiesc
Szkudy see Skuodas
Szlatina see Slatina
Szlovákia see Slovakia
Szolnok 99 D6 Jász-Nagykun-Szolnok, C Hungary
Szombathely 99 B6 Ger. Steinamanger; anc. Sabaria, Savaria. Vas, W Hungary
Szprotawa 98 B4 Ger. Sprottau. Lubuskie, W Poland
Sztálinváros see Dunaújváros
Szucsava see Suceava

T

Tabariya, Bahrat see Tiberias, Lake
Table Rock Lake 49 G1 reservoir Arkansas/Missouri, C USA
Tábor 99 B5 Jihočeský Kraj, S Czech Republic
Tabora 73 B7 Tabora, W Tanzania
Tabrīz 120 C2 var. Tebriz; anc. Tauris. Āžarbāyjān-e Sharqī, NW Iran
Tabuaeran 145 G2 prev. Fanning Island. atoll Line Islands, E Kiribati
Tabūk 120 A4 Tabūk, NW Saudi Arabia
Täby 85 C6 Stockholm, C Sweden
Tachau see Tachov
Tachov 99 A5 Ger. Tachau. Plveňský Kraj, W Czech Republic
Tacloban 139 F2 off. Tacloban City. Leyte, C Philippines
Tacloban City see Tacloban
Tacna 61 E4 Tacna, SE Peru
Tacoma 46 B2 Washington, NW USA
Tacuarembó 64 D4 prev. San Fructuoso. Tacuarembó, C Uruguay
Tademait, Plateau du 70 D3 plateau C Algeria
Tadmor/Tadmur see Tudmur
Tädpatri 132 C2 Andhra Pradesh, E India
Tadzhikistan see Tajikistan
Taegu see Daegu
Taehan-haehyŏp see Korea Strait
Taehan Min'guk see South Korea
Taejön see Daejeon
Tafassâsset, Ténéré du 75 G2 desert N Niger
Tafila / Ţafilah, Muḩāfaẓat aţ see Aţ Ţafilah
Taganrog 111 A7 Rostovskaya Oblast', SW Russian Federation
Taganrog, Gulf of 109 G4 Rus. Taganrogskiy Zaliv, Ukr. Tahanroz'ka Zatoka. gulf Russian Federation/ Ukraine
Taganrogskiy Zaliv see Taganrog, Gulf of
Taguatinga 63 F3 Tocantins, C Brazil
Tagus 92 C3 Port. Rio Tejo, Sp. Río Tajo. river Portugal/Spain
Tagus Plain 80 A4 abyssal plain E Atlantic Ocean
Tahanroz'ka Zatoka see Taganrog, Gulf of
Tahat 71 E4 mountain SE Algeria
Tahiti 145 H4 island Îles du Vent, W French Polynesia
Tahiti, Archipel de see Société, Archipel de la
Tahlequah 49 G1 Oklahoma, C USA
Tahoe, Lake 47 B5 lake California/ Nevada, W USA
Tahoua 75 F3 Tahoua, W Niger
Taichū see Taizhong
T'aichung see Taizhong
Taiden see Daejeon

Taieri 151 B7 river South Island, New Zealand
Taihape 150 D4 Manawatu-Wanganui, North Island, New Zealand
Taihoku see T'aipei
Taikyū see Daegu
Tailem Bend 149 B7 South Australia
Tainan 128 D6 prev. Dainan, T'ainan. S Taiwan
T'aipei 128 D6 Jap. Taihoku; prev. Daihoku. country capital (Taiwan) N Taiwan
Taiping 138 B3 Perak, Peninsular Malaysia
Taiwan 128 D6 off. Republic of China, var. Formosa, Formo'sa. country E Asia

TAIWAN
East Asia

Official name Republic of China (ROC)
Formation 1949 / 1949
Capital Taipei
Population 23.2 million / 1860 people per sq mile (718 people per sq km)
Total area 13,892 sq. miles (35,980 sq. km)
Languages Amoy Chinese, Mandarin Chinese*, Hakka Chinese
Religions Buddhist, Confucianist, and Taoist 93%, Christian 5%, Other 2%
Ethnic mix Han (pre-20th-century migration) 84%, Han (20th-century migration) 14%, Aboriginal 2%
Government Presidential system
Currency Taiwan dollar = 100 cents
Literacy rate 98%
Calorie consumption 2673 kilocalories

Taiwan see Taizhong
T'aiwan Haihsia/Taiwan Haixia see Taiwan Strait
Taiwan Strait 128 D6 var. Formosa Strait, Chin. T'aiwan Haihsia, Taiwan Haixia. strait China/Taiwan
Taiyuan 128 C4 var. T'ai-yuan, T'ai-yüan; prev. Yangku. province capital Shanxi, C China
T'ai-yuan/T'ai-yüan see Taiyuan
Taizhong 128 D6 Jap. Taichū; prev. T'aichung, Taiwan. C Taiwan
Ta'izz 121 B7 SW Yemen
Tajikistan 123 E3 off. Republic of Tajikistan, Rus. Tadzhikistan, Taj. Jumhurii Tojikiston; prev. Tajik S.S.R. country C Asia

TAJIKISTAN
Central Asia

Official name Republic of Tajikistan
Formation 1991 / 1991
Capital Dushanbe
Population 7 million / 127 people per sq mile (49 people per sq km)
Total area 55,251 sq. miles (143,100 sq. km)
Languages Tajik*, Uzbek, Russian
Religions Sunni Muslim 95%, Shi'a Muslim 3%, Other 2%
Ethnic mix Tajik 80%, Uzbek 15%, Other 3%, Russian 1%, Kyrgyz 1%
Government Presidential system
Currency Somoni = 100 diram
Literacy rate 99%
Calorie consumption 2106 kilocalories

Tajikistan, Republic of see Tajikistan
Tajik S.S.R see Tajikistan
Tajo, Río see Tagus
Tak 136 C4 var. Rahaeng. Tak, W Thailand
Takao see Gaoxing
Takaoka 131 C5 Toyama, Honshū, SW Japan
Takapuna 150 D2 Auckland, North Island, New Zealand
Takhiatash see Taxiatosh
Takhtakupyr see Taxtako'pir
Takikawa 130 D2 Hokkaidō, NE Japan
Takla Makan Desert 126 B3 Eng. Takla Makan Desert. desert NW China
Takla Makan Desert see Taklimakan Shamo
Takow see Gaoxing
Takutea 145 G4 island S Cook Islands

Talabriga see Aveiro, Portugal
Talabriga see Talavera de la Reina, Spain
Talachyn 107 D6 Rus. Tolochin. Vitsyebskaya Voblasts', NE Belarus
Talamanca, Cordillera de 53 E5 mountain range S Costa Rica
Talara 60 B2 Piura, NW Peru
Talas 123 F2 Talasskaya Oblast', NW Kyrgyzstan
Talaud, Kepulauan 139 F3 island group E Indonesia
Talavera de la Reina 92 D3 anc. Caesarobriga, Talibriga. Castilla-La Mancha, C Spain
Talca 64 B4 Maule, C Chile
Talcahuano 65 B5 Bío Bío, C Chile
Taldykorgan 114 C5 Kaz. Taldyqorghan; prev. Taldy-Kurgan. Taldykorgan, SE Kazakhstan
Taldy-Kurgan/Taldyqorghan see Taldykorgan
Ta-lien see Dalian
Taliq-an see Täloqän
Tal'ka 107 C6 Minskaya Voblasts', C Belarus
Talkhof see Puurmani
Tallahassee 42 D3 prev. Muskogean. state capital Florida, SE USA
Tall al Abyaḍ see At Tall al Abyaḍ
Tallin see Tallinn
Tallinn 106 D2 Ger. Reval, Rus. Tallin; prev. Revel. country capital (Estonia) Harjumaa, NW Estonia
Tall Kalakh 118 B4 var. Tell Kalakh. Ḩimṣ, C Syria
Tallulah 42 B2 Louisiana, S USA
Talnakh 114 D3 Krasnoyarskiy Kray, N Russian Federation
Tal'ne 109 E3 Rus. Tal'noye. Cherkas'ka Oblast', C Ukraine
Tal'noye see Tal'ne
Taloga 49 F1 Oklahoma, C USA
Täloqän 123 E3 var. Taliq-an. Takhār, NE Afghanistan
Talsen see Talsi
Talsi 106 C3 Ger. Talsen. NW Latvia
Taltal 64 B2 Antofagasta, N Chile
Talvik 84 D2 Finnmark, N Norway
Tamabo, Banjaran 138 D3 mountain range East Malaysia
Tamale 75 E4 C Ghana
Tamana 145 E3 prev. Rotcher Island. atoll Tungaru, W Kiribati
Tamanrasset 71 E4 var. Tamenghest. S Algeria
Tamar 89 C7 river SW England, United Kingdom
Tamar see Tudmur
Tamatave see Toamasina
Tamazunchale 51 E4 San Luis Potosí, C Mexico
Tambacounda 74 C3 SE Senegal
Tambov 111 B6 Tambovskaya Oblast', W Russian Federation
Tambura 73 B5 Western Equatoria, SW South Sudan
Tamchaket see Tâmchekkeţ
Tâmchekkeţ 74 C3 var. Tamchaket. Hodh el Gharbi, S Mauritania
Tamenghest see Tamanrasset
Tamil Nādu 132 C3 prev. Madras. cultural region SE India
Tam Ky 137 E5 Quang Nam-fa Năng, C Vietnam
Tammerfors see Tampere
Tampa 43 E4 Florida, SE USA
Tampa Bay 43 E4 bay Florida, SE USA
Tampere 85 D5 Swe. Tammerfors. Länsi-Suomi, W Finland
Tampico 51 E3 Tamaulipas, C Mexico
Tamworth 149 D6 New South Wales, SE Australia
Tanabe 131 C7 Wakayama, Honshū, SW Japan
Tana Bru 84 D2 Finnmark, N Norway
Tanais see Don
Lake Tana 72 C4 var. Lake Tana. lake NW Ethiopia
Tana, Lake see T'ana Häyk'

Tanami Desert 146 D3 *desert* Northern Territory, N Australia
Tananarive *see* Antananarivo
Ţăndărei 108 D5 Ialomiţa, SE Romania
Tandil 65 D5 Buenos Aires, E Argentina
Tandjoengkarang *see* Bandar Lampung
Tanega-shima 131 B8 *island* Nanseishotō, SW Japan
Tanen Taunggyi *see* Tane Range
Tane Range 136 B4 *Bur.* Tanen Taunggyi. *mountain range* W Thailand
Tanezrouft 70 D4 *desert* Algeria/Mali
Ţanf, Jabal aţ 118 D4 *mountain* SE Syria
Tanga 73 C7 Tanga, E Tanzania
Tanganyika and Zanzibar *see* Tanzania
Tanganyika, Lake 73 B7 *lake* E Africa
Tanger 70 C2 *var.* Tangiers, Tangier, *Fr./Ger.* Tangerk, *Sp.* Tánger; *anc.* Tingis. NW Morocco
Tangerk *see* Tanger
Tanggula Shan 126 C4 *mountain* W China
Tangier *see* Tanger
Tangiers *see* Tanger
Tangra Yumco 126 B5 *var.* Tangro Tso. *lake* W China
Tangro Tso *see* Tangra Yumco
Tangshan 128 D3 *var.* T'ang-shan. Hebei, E China
T'ang-shan *see* Tangshan
Tanimbar, Kepulauan 139 F5 *island group* Maluku, E Indonesia
Tanintharyi 137 B6 *var.* Tenasserim. Tanintharyi, S Myanmar (Burma)
Tanjungkarang/Tanjungkarang-Telukbetung *see* Bandar Lampung
Tanna 144 D4 *island* S Vanuatu
Tannenhof *see* Krynica
Tan-Tan 70 B3 SW Morocco
Tan-tung *see* Dandong
Tanzania 73 C7 *off.* United Republic of Tanzania, *Swa.* Jamhuri ya Muungano wa Tanzania; *prev.* German East Africa, Tanganyika and Zanzibar. *country* E Africa

TANZANIA
East Africa

Official name United Republic of Tanzania
Formation 1964 / 1964
Capital Dodoma
Population 46.2 million / 135 people per sq mile (52 people per sq km)
Total area 364,898 sq. miles (945,087 sq. km)
Languages Kiswahili*, Sukuma, Chagga, Nyamwezi, Hehe, Makonde, Yao, Sandawe, English*
Religions Christian 63%, Muslim 35%, Other 2%
Ethnic mix Native African (over 120 tribes) 99%, European, Asian, and Arab 1%
Government Presidential system
Currency Tanzanian shilling = 100 cents
Literacy rate 73%
Calorie consumption 2137 kilocalories

Tanzania, Jamhuri ya Muungano wa *see* Tanzania
Tanzania, United Republic of *see* Tanzania
Taoudenit *see* Taoudenni
Taoudenni 75 E2 *var.* Taoudenit. Tombouctou, N Mali
Tapa 106 E2 *Ger.* Taps. Lääne-Virumaa, NE Estonia
Tapachula 51 G5 Chiapas, SE Mexico
Tapaiu *see* Gvardeysk
Tapajós, Rio 63 E2 *var.* Tapajóz. *river* NW Brazil
Tapajóz *see* Tapajós, Rio
Taps *see* Tapa
Ţarābulus 71 F2 *var.* Ţarābulus al Gharb, *Eng.* Tripoli. *country capital* (Libya) NW Libya
Ţarābulus al Gharb *see* Ţarābulus
Ţarābulus/Ţarābulus ash Shām *see* Tripoli
Taraclia 108 D4 *Rus.* Tarakilya. S Moldova

Tarakilya *see* Taraclia
Mount Taranaki 150 C4 *var.* Egmont. *volcano* North Island, New Zealand
Tarancón 93 E3 Castilla-La Mancha, C Spain
Taranto 97 E5 *var.* Tarentum. Puglia, SE Italy
Taranto, Gulf of 97 E6 *Eng.* Gulf of Taranto. *gulf* S Italy
Taranto, Gulf of *see* Taranto, Golfo di
Tarapoto 60 C2 San Martín, N Peru
Tarare 91 D5 Rhône, E France
Tarascon 91 D6 Bouches-du-Rhône, SE France
Tarawa 144 D2 *atoll* Tungaru, W Kiribati
Taraz 114 C5 *prev.* Aulie Ata, Auliye-Ata, Dzhambul, Zhambyl. Zhambyl, S Kazakhstan
Tarazona 93 E2 Aragón, NE Spain
Tarbes 91 B6 *anc.* Bigorra. Hautes-Pyrénées, S France
Tarcoola 149 A6 South Australia
Taree 149 D6 New South Wales, SE Australia
Tarentum *see* Taranto
Târgoviște 108 C5 *prev.* Tîrgoviște. Dâmbovița, S Romania
Targu Jiu 108 B4 *prev.* Tîrgu Jiu. Gorj, W Romania
Târgul-Neamţ *see* Târgu-Neamţ
Târgul-Săcuiesc *see* Târgu Secuiesc
Târgu Mures 108 B4 *prev.* Oşorhei, Tîrgu Mures, *Ger.* Neumarkt, *Hung.* Marosvásárhely. Mureş, C Romania
Târgu-Neamţ 108 C3 *var.* Târgul-Neamţ; *prev.* Tîrgu-Neamţ. Neamţ, NE Romania
Târgu Ocna 108 C4 *Hung.* Aknavásár; *prev.* Tîrgu Ocna. Bacău, E Romania
Târgu Secuiesc 108 C4 *Ger.* Neumarkt, Szekler Neumarkt, *Hung.* Kezdivásárhely; *prev.* Chezdi-Oşorheiu, Târgul-Săcuiesc, Tîrgu Secuiesc. Covasna, E Romania
Tar Heel State *see* North Carolina
Tarija 61 G5 Tarija, S Bolivia
Tarim 121 C6 C Yemen
Tarim Basin 124 C2 *Eng.* Tarim Basin. *basin* NW China
Tarim Basin *see* Tarim Pendi
Tarim He 126 B3 *river* NW China
Tarma 60 C3 Junín, C Peru
Tarn 91 C6 *cultural region* S France
Tarn 91 C6 *river* S France
Tarnobrzeg 98 D4 Podkarpackie, SE Poland
Tarnopol *see* Ternopil'
Tarnów 99 D5 Małopolskie, S Poland
Tarraco *see* Tarragona
Tarragona 93 G2 *anc.* Tarraco. Cataluña, E Spain
Tarrasa *see* Terrassa
Tàrrega 93 F2 *var.* Tarrega. Cataluña, NE Spain
Tarsatica *see* Rijeka
Tarsus 116 C4 İçel, S Turkey
Tartous/Tartouss *see* Ţarţūs
Tartu 106 D3 *Ger.* Dorpat; *prev. Rus.* Yurev, Yury'ev. Tartumaa, SE Estonia
Ţarţūs 118 A3 *off.* Muḥāfaẓat Ţarţūs, *var.* Tartous, Tartus. *governorate* W Syria
Ţarţūs, Muḥāfaẓat *see* Ţarţūs
Ta Ru Tao, Ko 137 B7 *island* S Thailand Asia
Tarvisio 96 D2 Friuli-Venezia Giulia, NE Italy
Tarvisium *see* Treviso
Tashauz *see* Daşoguz
Tashi Chho Dzong *see* Thimphu
Tashkent *see* Toshkent
Tash-Kömür *see* Tash-Kumyr
Tash-Kumyr 123 F2 *Kir.* Tash-Kömür. Dzhalal-Abadskaya Oblast', W Kyrgyzstan
Tashqurghan *see* Khulm
Tasikmalaja *see* Tasikmalaya
Tasikmalaya 138 C5 *prev.* Tasikmalaja. Jawa, C Indonesia
Tasman Basin 142 C5 *var.* East Australian Basin. *undersea basin* S Tasman Sea

Tasman Bay 151 C5 *inlet* South Island, New Zealand
Tasmania 149 B8 *prev.* Van Diemen's Land. *state* SE Australia
Tasmania 152 B4 *island* SE Australia
Tasman Plateau 142 C5 *var.* South Tasmania Plateau. *undersea plateau* SW Tasman Sea
Tasman Sea 142 C5 *sea* SW Pacific Ocean
Tassili-n-Ajjer 71 E4 *plateau* E Algeria
Tatabánya 99 C6 Komárom-Esztergom, NW Hungary
Tatar Pazardzhik *see* Pazardzhik
Tathlith 121 B5 'Asīr, S Saudi Arabia
Tatra Mountains 99 D5 *Ger.* Tatra, *Hung.* Tátra, *Pol./Slvk.* Tatry. *mountain range* Poland/Slovakia
Tatra/Tátra *see* Tatra Mountains
Tatry *see* Tatra Mountains
Ta-t'ung/Tatung *see* Datong
Tatvan 117 F3 Bitlis, SE Turkey
Ta'ū 145 F4 *var.* Tau. *island* Manua Islands, E American Samoa
Taukum, Peski 123 G1 *desert* SE Kazakhstan
Taumarunui 150 D4 Manawatu-Wanganui, North Island, New Zealand
Taungdwingyi 136 B3 Magway, C Myanmar (Burma)
Taunggyi 136 B3 Shan State, C Myanmar (Burma)
Taungoo 136 B4 Bago, C Myanmar (Burma)
Taunton 89 C7 SW England, United Kingdom
Taupo 150 D3 Waikato, North Island, New Zealand
Taupo, Lake 150 D3 *lake* North Island, New Zealand
Tauragė 106 B4 *Ger.* Tauroggen. Tauragė, SW Lithuania
Tauranga 150 D3 Bay of Plenty, North Island, New Zealand
Tauris *see* Tabriz
Tauroggen *see* Tauragė
Taurus Mountains 116 C4 *Eng.* Taurus Mountains. *mountain range* S Turkey
Taurus Mountains *see* Toros Dağları
Tavas 116 B4 Denizli, SW Turkey
Tavastehus *see* Hämeenlinna
Tavira 92 C5 Faro, S Portugal
Tavoy *see* Dawei
Tavoy Island *see* Mali Kyun
Ta Waewae Bay 151 A7 *bay* South Island, New Zealand
Tawakoni, Lake 49 G2 *reservoir* Texas, SW USA
Tawau 138 D3 Sabah, East Malaysia
Ţawkar *see* Tokar
Tawzar *see* Tozeur
Taxco 51 E4 *var.* Taxco de Alarcón. Guerrero, S Mexico
Taxco de Alarcón *see* Taxco
Taxiatosh 122 C2 *Rus.* Takhiatash. Qoraqalpog'iston Respublikasi, W Uzbekistan
Taxtako'pir 122 D1 *Rus.* Takhtakupyr. Qoraqalpog'iston Respublikasi, NW Uzbekistan
Tay 88 C3 *river* C Scotland, United Kingdom
Taylor 49 G3 Texas, SW USA
Taymā' 120 A4 Tabūk, NW Saudi Arabia
Taymyr, Ozero 115 E2 *lake* N Russian Federation
Taymyr, Poluostrov 115 E2 *peninsula* N Russian Federation
Taz 114 D3 *river* N Russian Federation
Tbilisi 117 G2 *Eng.* Tiflis. *country capital* (Georgia) SE Georgia
Tchad *see* Chad
Tchad, Lac *see* Chad, Lake
Tchien *see* Zwedru
Tchongking *see* Chongqing
Tczew 98 C2 *Ger.* Dirschau. Pomorskie, N Poland
Te Anau 151 A7 Southland, South Island, New Zealand
Te Anau, Lake 151 A7 *lake* South Island, New Zealand
Teapa 51 G4 Tabasco, SE Mexico
Teate *see* Chieti

Tebingtinggi 138 B3 Sumatera, N Indonesia
Tebriz *see* Tabriz
Techirghiol 108 D5 Constanţa, SE Romania
Tecomán 50 D4 Colima, SW Mexico
Tecpan 51 E5 *var.* Tecpan de Galeana. Guerrero, S Mexico
Tecpan de Galeana *see* Tecpan
Tecuci 108 C4 Galaţi, E Romania
Tedzhen *see* Harīrūd/Tejen
Tedzhen *see* Tejen
Tees 89 D5 *river* N England, United Kingdom
Tefé 62 D2 Amazonas, N Brazil
Tegal 138 C4 Jawa, C Indonesia
Tegelen 87 D5 Limburg, SE Netherlands
Tegucigalpa *see* Toncontín
Teheran *see* Tehrān
Tehrān 120 C3 *var.* Teheran. *country capital* (Iran) Tehrän, N Iran
Tehuacán 51 F4 Puebla, S Mexico
Tehuantepec 51 F5 *var.* Santo Domingo Tehuantepec. Oaxaca, SE Mexico
Gulf of Tehuantepec 51 F5 *var.* Gulf of Tehuantepec. *gulf* S Mexico
Tehuantepec, Gulf of *see* Tehuantepec, Golfo de
Isthmus of Tehuantepec 51 F5 *var.* Isthmus of Tehuantepec. *isthmus* SE Mexico
Tehuantepec, Isthmus of *see* Tehuantepec, Istmo de
Tejen 122 C3 *Rus.* Tedzhen. Ahal Welaýaty, S Turkmenistan
Tejen *see* Harīrūd
Tejo, Rio *see* Tagus
Te Kao 150 C1 Northland, North Island, New Zealand
Tekax 51 H4 *var.* Tekax de Álvaro Obregón. Yucatán, SE Mexico
Tekax de Álvaro Obregón *see* Tekax
Tekeli 114 C5 Almaty, SE Kazakhstan
Tekirdağ 116 A2 *It.* Rodosto; *anc.* Bisanthe, Raidestos, Rhaedestus. Tekirdağ, NW Turkey
Te Kuiti 150 D3 Waikato, North Island, New Zealand
Tela 52 C2 Atlántida, NW Honduras
Telanaipura *see* Jambi
Tel Aviv-Jaffa *see* Tel Aviv-Yafo
Tel Aviv-Yafo 119 A6 *var.* Tel Aviv-Jaffa. Tel Aviv, C Israel
Teles Pirés *see* São Manuel, Rio
Telish 104 C2 *prev.* Azizie. Pleven, N Bulgaria
Tell Abiad/Tell Abyad *see* At Tall al Abyaḍ
Tell Kalakh *see* Tall Kalakh
Tell Shedadi *see* Ash Shadādah
Tel'man/Tel'mansk *see* Gubadag
Teloekbetoeng *see* Bandar Lampung
Telo Martius *see* Toulon
Telschen *see* Telšiai
Telšiai 106 B3 *Ger.* Telschen. Telšiai, NW Lithuania
Telukbetung *see* Bandar Lampung
Temerin 100 D3 Vojvodina, N Serbia
Temeschburg/Temeschwar *see* Timişoara
Temesvár/Temeswar *see* Timişoara
Temirtau 114 C4 *prev.* Samarkandski, Samarkandskoye. Karagandy, C Kazakhstan
Tempio Pausania 97 A5 Sardegna, Italy, C Mediterranean Sea
Temple 49 G3 Texas, SW USA
Temuco 65 B5 Araucanía, C Chile
Tenuka 151 B6 Canterbury, South Island, New Zealand
Ténénkou 74 D3 Mopti, C Mali
Ténéré 75 G3 *physical region* C Niger
Tenerife 70 A3 *island* Islas Canarias, Spain, NE Atlantic Ocean
Tengger Shamo 127 E3 *desert* N China
Tengréla 74 D4 *var.* Tingréla. N Côte d'Ivoire
Tenkodogo 75 E4 S Burkina Faso
Tennant Creek 148 A3 Northern Territory, C Australia

Tennessee 42 C1 off. State of Tennessee, also known as The Volunteer State. state SE USA
Tennessee River 42 C1 river S USA
Tenos see Tínos
Tepelena see Tepelenë
Tepelenë 101 C7 var. Tepelena, It. Tepeleni. Gjirokastër, S Albania
Tepeleni see Tepelenë
Tepic 50 D4 Nayarit, C Mexico
Teplice 98 A4 Ger. Teplitz; prev. Teplice-Šanov, Teplitz-Schönau. Ústecký Kraj, NW Czech Republic
Teplice-Šanov/Teplitz/Teplitz-Schönau see Teplice
Tequila 50 D4 Jalisco, SW Mexico
Teraina 145 G2 prev. Washington Island. atoll Line Islands, E Kiribati
Teramo 96 C4 anc. Interamna. Abruzzi, C Italy
Tercan 117 E3 Erzincan, NE Turkey
Terceira 92 A5 var. Ilha Terceira. island Azores, Portugal, NE Atlantic Ocean
Terceira, Ilha see Terceira
Terekhovka see Tsyerakhowka
Teresina 63 F2 var. Therezina. state capital Piauí, NE Brazil
Termez see Termiz
Termia see Kýthnos
Términos, Laguna de 51 G4 lagoon SE Mexico
Termiz 123 E3 Rus. Termez. Surkhondaryo Viloyati, S Uzbekistan
Termoli 96 D4 Molise, C Italy
Terneuzen 87 B5 var. Neuzen. Zeeland, SW Netherlands
Terni 96 C4 anc. Interamna Nahars. Umbria, C Italy
Ternopol' 108 C2 Pol. Tarnopol, Rus. Ternopol'. Ternopil's'ka Oblast', W Ukraine
Ternopol' see Ternopil'
Terracina 97 C5 Lazio, C Italy
Terranova di Sicilia see Gela
Terranova Pausania see Olbia
Terrassa 93 G2 Cast. Tarrasa. Cataluña, E Spain
Terre Adélie 154 C4 physical region Antarctica
Terre Haute 40 B4 Indiana, N USA
Terre Neuve see Newfoundland and Labrador
Terschelling 86 C1 Fris. Skylge. island Waddeneilanden, N Netherlands
Teruel 93 F3 anc. Turba. Aragón, E Spain
Tervel 104 E1 prev. Kurtbunar, Rom. Curtbunar. Dobrich, NE Bulgaria
Tervueren see Tervuren
Tervuren 87 C6 var. Tervueren. Vlaams Brabant, C Belgium
Teseney 72 C4 var. Tessenei. W Eritrea
Tessalit 75 E2 Kidal, NE Mali
Tessaoua 75 G3 Maradi, S Niger
Tessenderlo 87 C5 Limburg, NE Belgium
Tessenei see Teseney
Testigos, Islas los 59 E1 island group N Venezuela
Tete 79 E2 Tete, NW Mozambique
Teterow 94 C3 Mecklenburg-Vorpommern, NE Germany
Tétouan 70 C2 var. Tetouan, Tetuán. N Morocco
Tetovo 101 D5 Razgrad, N Bulgaria
Tetschen see Děčín
Tetuán see Tétouan
Teverya see Tverya
Te Waewae Bay 151 A7 bay South Island, New Zealand
Texarkana 42 A2 Arkansas, C USA
Texarkana 49 H2 Texas, SW USA
Texas 49 F3 off. State of Texas, also known as Lone Star State. state S USA
Texas City 49 H4 Texas, SW USA
Texel 86 C2 island Waddeneilanden, NW Netherlands
Texoma, Lake 49 G2 reservoir Oklahoma/Texas, C USA
Teziutlán 51 F4 Puebla, S Mexico
Thaa Atoll see Kolhumadulu
Thai, Ao see Thailand, Gulf of
Thai Binh 136 D3 Thai Binh, N Vietnam

Thailand 137 C5 off. Kingdom of Thailand, Th. Prathet Thai; prev. Siam. country SE Asia

THAILAND
Southeast Asia

Official name Kingdom of Thailand
Formation 1238 / 1907
Capital Bangkok
Population 69.5 million / 352 people per sq mile (136 people per sq km)
Total area 198,455 sq. miles (514,000 sq. km)
Languages Thai*, Chinese, Malay, Khmer, Mon, Karen, Miao
Religions Buddhist 95%, Muslim 4%, Other (including Christian) 1%
Ethnic mix Thai 83%, Chinese 12%, Malay 3%, Khmer and Other 2%
Government Parliamentary system
Currency Baht = 100 satang
Literacy rate 94%
Calorie consumption 2862 kilocalories

Thailand, Gulf of 137 C6 var. Gulf of Siam, Th. Ao Thai, Vtn. Vinh Thai Lan. gulf SE Asia
Thailand, Kingdom of see Thailand
Thai Lan, Vinh see Thailand, Gulf of
Thai Nguyên 136 D3 Bắc Thai, N Vietnam
Thakhèk 136 D4 var. Muang Khammouan. Khammouan, C Laos
Thamarid see Thamarīt
Thamarīt 121 D6 var. Thamarīd, Thumrayt. SW Oman
Thames 150 D3 Waikato, North Island, New Zealand
Thames 89 B8 river S England, United Kingdom
Thandwe 136 A4 var. Sandoway. Rakhine State, W Myanmar (Burma)
Thanh Hoa 136 D3 Thanh Hoa, N Vietnam
Thanintari Taungdan see Bilauktaung Range
Thanlwin see Salween
Thar Desert 134 C3 var. Great Indian Desert, Indian Desert. desert India/ Pakistan
Tharthar, Buhayrat ath 120 B3 lake C Iraq
Thásos 104 C4 Thásos, E Greece
Thásos 104 C4 island E Greece
Thaton 136 B4 Mon State, S Myanmar (Burma)
Thayetmyo 136 A4 Magway, C Myanmar (Burma)
The Crane 55 H2 var. Crane. S Barbados
The Dalles 46 B3 Oregon, NW USA
The Flatts Village see Flatts Village
The Hague see 's-Gravenhage
Theodosia see Feodosiya
The Pas 37 F5 Manitoba, C Canada
Therezina see Teresina
Thérma 105 D6 Ikaría, Dodekánisa, Greece, Aegean Sea
Thermaic Gulf 104 B4 Eng. Thermaic Gulf; anc. Thermaicus Sinus. gulf N Greece
Thermaic Gulf/Thermaicus Sinus see Thermaïkós Kólpos
Thermia see Kýthnos
Thérmo 105 B5 Dytikí Elláda, C Greece
The Rock 93 H4 New South Wales, SE Australia
The Sooner State see Oklahoma
Thessaloníki 104 C3 Eng. Salonica, Salonika, SCr. Solun, Turk. Selânik. Kentrikí Makedonía, N Greece
The Valley 55 G3 dependent territory capital (Anguilla) E Anguilla
The Village 49 G1 Oklahoma, C USA
The Volunteer State see Tennessee
Thiamis see Kalamás
Thian Shan see Tien Shan
Thibet see Xizang Zizhiqu
Thief River Falls 45 F1 Minnesota, N USA
Thienen see Tienen
Thiers 91 C5 Puy-de-Dôme, C France

Thiès 74 B3 W Senegal
Thikombia see Cikobia
Thimbu see Thimphu
Thimphu 135 G3 var. Thimbu; prev. Tashi Chho Dzong. country capital (Bhutan) W Bhutan
Thionville 90 D3 Ger. Diedenhofen. Moselle, NE France
Thíra 105 D7 Santoríni, Kykládes, Greece, Aegean Sea
Thíra 105 D7 Santoríni, Kykládes, Greece, Aegean Sea
Thíra 105 D7 Santoríni, Kykládes, Greece, Aegean Sea
Thiruvananthapuram 132 C3 prev. Trivandrum, var. Tiruvantapuram. state capital Kerala, SW India
Thitu Island 128 C8 island NW Spratly Islands
Tholen 86 B4 island SW Netherlands
Thomasville 42 D3 Georgia, SE USA
Thompson 37 F4 Manitoba, C Canada
Thonon-les-Bains 91 D5 Haute-Savoie, E France
Thorenburg see Turda
Thorlákshöfn 83 E5 Sudhurland, SW Iceland
Thorn see Toruń
Thornton Island see Millennium Island
Thorshavn see Tórshavn
Thospitis see Van Gölü
Thouars 90 B4 Deux-Sèvres, W France
Thoune see Thun
Thracian Sea 104 D4 Gk. Thrakikó Pélagos; anc. Thracium Mare. sea Greece/Turkey
Thracium Mare/Thrakikó Pélagos see Thracian Sea
Three Kings Islands 150 C1 island group N New Zealand
Thrissur 132 C3 prev. Trichūr. Kerala, SW India
Thuin 87 B7 Hainaut, S Belgium
Thule see Qaanaaq
Thumrayt see Thamarīt
Thun 95 A7 Fr. Thoune. Bern, W Switzerland
Thunder Bay 38 B4 Ontario, S Canada
Thuner See 95 A7 lake C Switzerland
Thung Song 137 C7 var. Cha Mai. Nakhon Si Thammarat, SW Thailand
Thurso 88 C2 N Scotland, United Kingdom
Thýamis see Kalamás
Tianjin 128 D4 var. Tientsin. Tianjin Shi, E China
Tianjin Shi 128 D4 var. Jin, Tianjin, T'ien-ching, Tientsin. municipality E China
Tian Shan see Tien Shan
Tianshui 128 B4 Gansu, C China
Tiba see Chiba
Tiber 96 C4 Eng. Tiber. river C Italy
Tiber see Tevere, Italy
Tiber see Tivoli, Italy
Tiberias see Tverya
Tiberias, Lake 119 B5 var. Chinnereth, Sea of Bahr Tabariya, Sea of Galilee, Ar. Bahrat Tabariya, Heb. Yam Kinneret. lake N Israel
Tibesti 76 C2 var. Tibesti Massif, Ar. Tibistī. mountain range N Africa
Tibesti Massif see Tibesti
Tibet see Xizang Zizhiqu
Tibetan Autonomous Region see Xizang Zizhiqu
Tibet, Plateau of 126 B4 var. Xizang Gaoyuan, Eng. Plateau of Tibet. plateau W China
Tibet, Plateau of see Qingzang Gaoyuan
Tibistī see Tibesti
Tibni see At Tibnī
Tiburón 50 B2 var. Isla del Tiburón. island NW Mexico
Tiburón, Isla del see Tiburón, Isla
Tichau see Tychy
Tichît 74 D2 var. Tichitt. Tagant, C Mauritania
Tichitt see Tichît
Ticinum see Pavia
Ticul 51 H3 Yucatán, SE Mexico

Tidjikdja see Tidjikja
Tidjikja 74 C2 var. Tidjikdja; prev. Fort-Cappolani. Tagant, C Mauritania
T'ien-ching see Tianjin Shi
Tienen 87 C6 var. Thienen, Fr. Tirlemont. Vlaams Brabant, C Belgium
Tiên Giang, Sông see Mekong
Tien Shan 126 B3 Chin. Thian Shan, Tian Shan, T'ien Shan, Rus. Tyan'-Shan'. mountain range C Asia
Tientsin see Tianjin
Tierp 85 C6 Uppsala, C Sweden
Tierra del Fuego 65 B8 island Argentina/ Chile
Tiflis see Tbilisi
Tifton 42 D3 Georgia, SE USA
Tifu 139 F4 Pulau Buru, E Indonesia
Tighina 108 D4 Rus. Bendery; prev. Bender. E Moldova
Tigranocerta see Siirt
Tigris 120 B2 Ar. Dijlah, Turk. Dicle. river Iraq/Turkey
Tiguentourine 71 E3 E Algeria
Ti-hua/Tihwa see Ürümqi
Tijuana 50 A1 Baja California Norte, NW Mexico
Tikhoretsk 111 A7 Krasnodarskiy Kray, SW Russian Federation
Tikhvin 110 B4 Leningradskaya Oblast', NW Russian Federation
Tiki Basin 143 G3 undersea basin S Pacific Ocean
Tikirarjuaq see Whale Cove
Tiksi 115 F2 Respublika Sakha (Yakutiya), NE Russian Federation
Tilburg 86 C4 Noord-Brabant, S Netherlands
Tilimsen see Tlemcen
Tilio Martius see Toulon
Tillabéri 75 E3 var. Tillabéry. Tillabéri, W Niger
Tillabéry see Tillabéri
Tílos 105 E7 island Dodekánisa, Greece, Aegean Sea
Timan Ridge 110 D3 Eng. Timan Ridge. ridge NW Russian Federation
Timan Ridge see Timanskiy Kryazh
Timaru 151 B6 Canterbury, South Island, New Zealand
Timbaki/Timbákion see Tympáki
Timbedgha 74 D3 var. Timbédra. Hodh ech Chargui, SE Mauritania
Timbédra see Timbedgha
Timbuktu see Tombouctou
Timiş 108 A4 county SW Romania
Timişoara 108 A4 Ger. Temeschwar, Temeswar, Hung. Temesvár; prev. Temeschburg. Timiş, W Romania
Timmins 38 C4 Ontario, S Canada
Timor 125 F5 island Nusa Tenggara, C Indonesia
Timor Sea 125 F5 sea E Indian Ocean
Timor Timur see East Timor
Timor Trench see Timor Trough
Timor Trough 125 F5 var. Timor Trench. trough NE Timor Sea
Timrå 85 C5 Västernorrland, C Sweden
Tindouf 70 C3 W Algeria
Tineo 92 C1 Asturias, N Spain
Tingis see Tanger
Tingo María 60 C3 Huánuco, C Peru
Tingréla see Tengréla
Tinhosa Grande 76 E2 island N Sao Tome and Príncipe, Africa, E Atlantic Ocean
Tinhosa Pequena 76 E1 island N Sao Tome and Príncipe, Africa, E Atlantic Ocean
Tinian 144 B1 island S Northern Mariana Islands
Tínos 105 D6 Tínos, Kykládes, Greece, Aegean Sea
Tínos 105 D6 anc. Tenos. island Kykládes, Greece, Aegean Sea
Tip 101 E6 Papua, E Indonesia
Tipitapa 52 D3 Managua, W Nicaragua
Tip Top Mountain 38 C4 mountain Ontario, S Canada
Tirana see Tiranë
Tiranë 101 C6 var. Tirana. country capital (Albania) Tiranë, C Albania

Tiraspol *108 D4 Rus.* Tiraspol'.
E Moldova
Tiraspol' *see* Tiraspol
Tiree *88 B3 island* W Scotland,
United Kingdom
Tîrgovişte *see* Târgovişte
Tîrgu Jiu *see* Targu Jiu
Tîrgu Mures *see* Târgu Mureş
Tîrgu-Neamţ *see* Târgu-Neamţ
Tîrgu Ocna *see* Târgu Ocna
Tîrgu Secuiesc *see* Târgu Secuiesc
Tîrlemont *see* Tienen
Tîrnavos *see* Týrnavos
Tîrnovo *see* Veliko Tŭrnovo
Tirol *95 C7 off.* Land Tirol, *var.* Tyrol, *It.*
Tirolo. *state* W Austria
Tirol, Land *see* Tirol
Tirolo *see* Tirol
Tirreno, Mare *see* Tyrrhenian Sea
Tiruchchirāppalli *132 C3 prev.*
Trichinopoly. Tamil Nādu,
SE India
Tiruppattūr *132 C2* Tamil Nādu,
SE India
Tiruvantapuram *see*
Thiruvanathapuram
Tisa *103 F1 Ger.* Theiss, *Rom./Slvn./*
SCr. Tisa, *Rus.* Tissa, *Ukr.* Tysa. *river*
SE Europe
Tisa *see* Tisza
Tiszakécske *99 D7* Bács-Kiskun,
C Hungary
Titano, Monte *96 E1 mountain*
C San Marino
Titicaca, Lake *61 E4 lake* Bolivia/
Peru
Titograd *see* Podgorica
Titose *see* Chitose
Titova Mitrovica *see* Mitrovicë
Titovo Užice *see* Užice
Titu *108 C5* Dâmboviţa, S Romania
Titule *77 D5* Orientale, N Dem. Rep.
Congo
Tiverton *89 C7* SW England, United
Kingdom
Tivoli *96 C4 anc.* Tiber. Lazio,
C Italy
Tizimín *51 H3* Yucatán, SE Mexico
Tizi Ouzou *71 E1 var.* Tizi-Ouzou.
N Algeria
Tizi-Ouzou *see* Tizi Ouzou
Tiznit *70 B3* SW Morocco
Tjilatjap *see* Cilacap
Tjirebon *see* Cirebon
Tlaquepaque *50 D4* Jalisco,
C Mexico
Tlaxcala *51 F4 var.* Tlaxcala, Tlaxcala de
Xicohténcatl. Tlaxcala, C Mexico
Tlaxcala de Xicohténcatl *see* Tlaxcala
Tlemcen *70 D2 var.* Tilimsen, Tlemsen.
NW Algeria
Tlemsen *see* Tlemcen
Toamasina *79 G3 prev./Fr.* Tamatave.
Toamasina, E Madagascar
Toba, Danau *138 B3 lake* Sumatera,
W Indonesia
Tobago *55 H5 island* NE Trinidad and
Tobago
Toba Kakar Range *134 B2 mountain*
range NW Pakistan
Tobol *see* Tobyl
Tobol'sk *114 C3* Tyumenskaya Oblast',
C Russian Federation
Tobruch/Tobruk *see* Ţubruq
Tobyl *114 C4 prev.* Tobol. *river*
Kazakhstan/Russian Federation
Tocantins *63 E3 off.* Estado do
Tocantins. *state* C Brazil
Tocantins *63 E3 off.* Estado do
Tocantins. *region* C Brazil
Tocantins, Estado do *see* Tocantins
Tocantins, Río *63 F2 river* N Brazil
Tocoa *52 D2* Colón, N Honduras
Tocopilla *64 B2* Antofagasta, N Chile
Todi *96 C4* Umbria, C Italy
Todos os Santos, Baía de *63 G3 bay*
E Brazil
Toetoes Bay *151 B8 bay* South Island,
New Zealand
Tofua *145 E4 island* Ha'apai Group,
C Tonga
Togo *75 E4 off.* Togolese Republic; *prev.*
French Togoland. *country* W Africa

TOGO
West Africa

Official name The Togolese Republic
Formation 1960 / 1960
Capital Lomé
Population 6.2 million / 295 people
per sq mile (114 people per sq km)
Total area 21,924 sq. miles (56,785 sq. km)
Languages Ewe, Kabye, Gurma, French*
Religions Christian 47%, Traditional
beliefs 33%, Muslim 14%, Other 6%
Ethnic mix Ewe 46%, Other African 41%,
Kabye 12%, European 1%
Government Presidential system
Currency CFA franc = 100 centimes
Literacy rate 57%
Calorie consumption 2363 kilocalories

Togolese Republic *see* Togo
Tojikiston, Jumhurii *see* Tajikistan
Tokanui *151 B7* Southland, South Island,
New Zealand
Tokar *72 C3 var.* Ţawkar. Red Sea,
NE Sudan
Tokat *116 D3* Tokat, N Turkey
Tokelau *145 E3 NZ overseas territory*
W Polynesia
Tőketerebes *see* Trebišov
Tokio *see* Tōkyō
Tokmak *109 G4 var.* Velykyy Tokmak.
Zaporiz'ka Oblast', SE Ukraine
Tokmak *see* Tomok
Tokoroa *150 D3* Waikato, North Island,
New Zealand
Tokounou *74 C4* C Guinea
Tokushima *131 C6 var.* Tokusima.
Tokushima, Shikoku, SW Japan
Tōkyō *130 A1 var.* Tokio. *country*
capital (Japan) Tōkyō, Honshū,
S Japan
Tōkyō-wan *130 A2 bay* S Japan
Tolbukhin *see* Dobrich
Toledo *92 D3 anc.* Toletum. Castilla-La
Mancha, C Spain
Toledo *40 D3* Ohio, N USA
Toledo Bend Reservoir *49 G3 reservoir*
Louisiana/Texas, SW USA
Toletum *see* Toledo
Toliara *79 F4 var.* Toliary; *prev.* Tuléar.
Toliara, SW Madagascar
Toliary *see* Toliara
Tolmein *see* Tolmin
Tolmin *95 D7 Ger.* Tolmein, *It.* Tolmino.
W Slovenia
Tolmino *see* Tolmin
Tolna *99 C7 Ger.* Tolnau. Tolna,
S Hungary
Tolnau *see* Tolna
Tolochin *see* Talachyn
Tolosa *93 E1* País Vasco, N Spain
Tolosa *see* Toulouse
Toluca *51 E4 var.* Toluca de Lerdo.
México, S Mexico
Toluca de Lerdo *see* Toluca
Tol'yatti *111 C6 prev.* Stavropol'.
Samarskaya Oblast', W Russian
Federation
Tomah *40 B2* Wisconsin,
N USA
Tomakomai *130 D2* Hokkaidō,
NE Japan
Tomar *92 B3* Santarém, W Portugal
Tomaschow *see* Tomaszów Mazowiecki
Tomaschow *see* Tomaszów Lubelski
Tomaszów *see* Tomaszów Mazowiecki
Tomaszów Lubelski *98 E4 Ger.*
Tomaschow. Lubelskie,
E Poland
Tomaszów Mazowiecka *see* Tomaszów
Mazowiecki
Tomaszów Mazowiecki *98 D4 var.*
Tomaszów Mazowiecka; *prev.*
Tomaszów, *Ger.* Tomaschow. Łódzkie,
C Poland
Tombigbee River *42 C3 river* Alabama/
Mississippi, S USA
Tombouctou *75 E3 Eng.* Timbuktu.
Tombouctou, N Mali
Tombua *78 A2 Port.* Porto Alexandre.
Namibe, SW Angola
Tomelloso *93 E3* Castilla-La Mancha,
C Spain
Tomini, Gulf of *see* Tomini, Teluk

Tomini, Teluk *139 E4 var.* Gulf of
Tomini; *prev.* Teluk Gorontalo. *bay*
Sulawesi, C Indonesia
Tomok *123 G2 prev.* Tokmak.
Chuyskaya Oblast', N Kyrgyzstan
Tomsk *114 D4* Tomskaya Oblast',
C Russian Federation
Tomür Feng *see* Pobedy, Pik
Toncontín *52 C3 prev.* Tegucigalpa.
country capital (Honduras) Francisco
Morazán, SW Honduras
Tonezh *see* Tonyezh
Tonga *145 E4 off.* Kingdom of Tonga,
var. Friendly Islands. *country*
SW Pacific Ocean

TONGA
Australasia & Oceania

Official name Kingdom of Tonga
Formation 1970 / 1970
Capital Nuku'alofa
Population 106,146 / 382 people
per sq mile (147 people per sq km)
Total area 289 sq. miles (748 sq. km)
Languages English*, Tongan*
Religions Free Wesleyan 41%, Other 17%,
Roman Catholic 16%, Church of Jesus
Christ of Latter-day Saints 14%,
Free Church of Tonga 12%
Ethnic mix Tongan 98%, Other 2%
Government Monarchy
Currency Pa'anga (Tongan dollar)
= 100 seniti
Literacy rate 99%
Calorie consumption Not available

Tonga, Kingdom of *see* Tonga
Tongatapu *145 E5 island* Tongatapu
Group, S Tonga
Tongatapu Group *145 E5 island group*
S Tonga
Tonga Trench *143 E3 trench* S Pacific
Ocean
Tongchuan *128 C4* Shaanxi,
C China
Tongeren *87 D6 Fr.* Tongres. Limburg,
NE Belgium
Tongking, Gulf of *128 B7 Chin.* Beibu
Wan, *Vtn.* Vinh Băc Bô. *gulf* China/
Vietnam
Tongliao *127 G2* Nei Mongol Zizhiqu,
N China
Tongres *see* Tongeren
Tongshan *see* Xuzhou, Jiangsu, China
Tongtian He *126 C4 var.* Zhi Qu. *river*
C China
Tonj *73 B5* Warap, W South Sudan
Tônlé Sap *137 D5 Eng.* Great Lake. *lake*
W Cambodia
Tonopah *47 C6* Nevada, W USA
Tonyezh *107 C7 Rus.* Tonezh.
Homyel'skaya Voblasts', SE Belarus
Tooele *44 B4* Utah, W USA
Toowoomba *149 E5* Queensland,
E Australia
Topeka *45 F4 state capital* Kansas,
C USA
Toplicza *see* Topliţa
Topliţa *108 C3 Ger.* Töplitz, *Hung.*
Maroshévíz; *prev.* Topliţa Română,
Hung. Oláh-Toplicza, Toplicza.
Harghita, C Romania
Topliţa Română/Töplitz *see* Topliţa
Topol'čany *99 C6 Hung.* Nagytapolcsány.
Nitriansky Kraj, W Slovakia
Topolovgrad *104 D3 prev.* Kavakli.
Khaskovo, S Bulgaria
Topolya *see* Bačka Topola
Top Springs Roadhouse *146 E3*
Northern Territory, N Australia
Torda *see* Turda
Torez *109 H3* Donets'ka Oblast',
SE Ukraine
Torgau *94 D4* Sachsen, E Germany
Torhout *87 A5* West-Vlaanderen,
W Belgium
Torino *96 A2 Eng.* Turin. Piemonte,
NW Italy
Tornacum *see* Tournai
Torneä *see* Tornio
Torneträsk *84 C3 lake* N Sweden
Tornio *84 D4 Swe.* Torneä. Lappi,
NW Finland
Tornionjoki *84 D3 river* Finland/Sweden

Tornionjoki *84 D3 river* Finland/
Sweden
Toro *92 D2* Castilla y León, N Spain
Toronto *38 D5 province capital* Ontario,
S Canada
Torquay *89 C7* SW England, United
Kingdom
Torrance *46 D2* California, W USA
Torre, Alto da *92 B3 mountain*
C Portugal
Torre del Greco *97 D5* Campania,
S Italy
Torrejón de Ardoz *93 E3* Madrid,
C Spain
Torrelavega *92 D1* Cantabria,
N Spain
Torrens, Lake *149 A6 salt lake* South
Australia
Torrent *93 F3 Cas.* Torrente, *var.*
Torrent de l'Horta. Valenciana,
E Spain
Torrent de l'Horta/Torrente *see*
Torrent
Torreón *50 D3* Coahuila, NE Mexico
Torres Strait *148 C1 strait* Australia/
Papua New Guinea
Torres Vedras *92 B3* Lisboa,
C Portugal
Torrington *44 D3* Wyoming,
C USA
Tórshavn *83 F5 Dan.* Thorshavn.
Dependent territory capital Faeroe
Islands
To'rtkok'l *122 D2 var.* Türtkül, *Rus.*
Turtkul'; *prev.* Petroaleksandrovsk.
Qoraqalpog'iston Respublikasi,
W Uzbekistan
Tortoise Islands *see* Colón,
Archipiélago de
Tortosa *93 F2 anc.* Dertosa. Cataluña,
E Spain
Tortue, Montagne *59 H3 mountain*
range C French Guiana
Tortuga, Isla *see* La Tortuga, Isla
Toruń *98 C3 Ger.* Thorn. Toruń,
Kujawsko-pomorskie, C Poland
Tõrva *106 D3 Ger.* Törwa. Valgamaa,
S Estonia
Tõrwa *see* Tõrva
Torzhok *110 B4* Tverskaya Oblast',
W Russian Federation
Tosa-wan *131 B7 bay* SW Japan
Toscana *96 B3 Eng.* Tuscany. *region*
C Italy
Toscano, Archipelago *96 B4 Eng.*
Tuscan Archipelago. *island group*
C Italy
Toshkent *123 E2 Eng./Rus.* Tashkent.
country capital (Uzbekistan) Toshkent
Viloyati, E Uzbekistan
Totana *93 E4* Murcia, SE Spain
Tot'ma *see* Sukhona
Totness *59 G3* Coronie, N Suriname
Tottori *131 B6* Tottori, Honshū,
SW Japan
Touâjîl *74 C2* Tiris Zemmour,
N Mauritania
Tougouri *71 E2* NE Algeria
Toukoto *74 C3* Kayes, W Mali
Toul *90 D3* Meurthe-et-Moselle,
NE France
Toulon *91 D6 anc.* Telo Martius, Tilio
Martius. Var, SE France
Toulouse *91 B6 anc.* Tolosa. Haute-
Garonne, S France
Toungoo *see* Taungoo
Touraine *90 B4 cultural region*
C France
Tourane *see* Đa Năng
Tourcoing *90 C2* Nord, N France
Tournai *87 A6 var.* Tournay, *Dut.*
Doornik; *anc.* Tornacum. Hainaut,
SW Belgium
Tournay *see* Tournai
Tours *90 B4 anc.* Caesarodunum,
Turoni. Indre-et-Loire, C France
Tovarkovskiy *111 B5* Tul'skaya Oblast',
W Russian Federation
Tower Island *see* Genovesa, Isla
Townsville *148 D3* Queensland,
NE Australia
Towoeti Meer *see* Towuti, Danau
Towraghoudī *122 D4* Herāt,
NW Afghanistan

Towson *41 F4* Maryland, NE USA
Towuti, Danau *139 E4* Dut. Towoeti
Meer. *lake* Sulawesi, C Indonesia
Toyama *131 C5* Toyama, Honshū,
SW Japan
Toyama-wan *131 B5* bay W Japan
Toyohara *see* Yuzhno-Sakhalinsk
Toyota *131 C6* Aichi, Honshū,
SW Japan
Tozeur *71 E2 var.* Tawzar. W Tunisia
Tråblous *see* Tripoli
Trabzon *117 E2* Eng. Trebizond; *anc.*
Trapezus. Trabzon, NE Turkey
Traiectum ad Mosam/Traiectum
Tungorum *see* Maastricht
Traiskirchen *95 E6* Niederösterreich,
NE Austria
Trajani Portus *see* Civitavecchia
Trajectum ad Rhenum *see* Utrecht
Trakai *107 C5* Ger. Traken, *Pol.* Troki.
Vilnius, SE Lithuania
Traken *see* Trakai
Tralee *89 A6 Ir.* Trá Lí. SW Ireland
Trá Lí *see* Tralee
Tralles Aydin *see* Aydın
Trang *137 C7* Trang, S Thailand
Transantarctic Mountains *154 B3*
mountain range Antarctica
Transilvania *see* Transylvania
Transilvaniei, Alpi *see* Carpaţii
Meridionalii
Transjordan *see* Jordan
Transsylvanische Alpen/
Transylvanian Alps *see* Carpaţii
Meridionalii
Transylvania *108 B4* Eng. Ardeal,
Transilvania, *Ger.* Siebenbürgen, *Hung.*
Erdély. *cultural region* NW Romania
Transylvanian Alps *108 B4 var.* Alpi
Transilvaniei, Carpaţii Sudici, *Eng.*
South Carpathians, Transylvanian Alps,
Ger. Südkarpaten, Transsylvanische
Alpen, *Hung.* Déli-Kárpátok, Erdélyi-
Havasok. *mountain range* C Romania
Trapani *97 B7 anc.* Drepanum. Sicilia,
Italy, C Mediterranean Sea
Trápeăng Vêng *see* Kâmpóng Thum
Trapezus *see* Trabzon
Traralgon *149 C7* Victoria, SE Australia
Trasimenischersee *see* Trasimeno, Lago
Trasimeno, Lago *96 C4* Eng. Lake
of Perugia, *Ger.* Trasimenischersee.
lake C Italy
Traù *see* Trogir
Traverse City *40 C2* Michigan,
N USA
Tra Vinh *137 D6 var.* Phu Vinh. Tra
Vinh, S Vietnam
Travis, Lake *49 F3 reservoir* Texas,
SW USA
Travnik *100 C4* Federacija Bosna
I Hercegovina, C Bosnia and
Herzegovina
Trbovlje *95 E7* Ger. Trifail. C Slovenia
Treasure State *see* Montana
Třebíč *99 B5* Ger. Trebitsch. Vysočina,
C Czech Republic
Trebinje *101 C5* Republika Srpska,
S Bosnia and Herzegovina
Trebišov *99 D6* Hung. Tőketerebes.
Košický Kraj, E Slovakia
Trebitsch *see* Třebíč
Trebnitz *see* Trzebnica
Tree Planters State *see* Nebraska
Trélazé *90 B4* Maine-et-Loire,
NW France
Trelew *65 C6* Chubut, SE Argentina
Tremelo *87 C5* Vlaams Brabant,
C Belgium
Trenčín *99 C5* Ger. Trentschin,
Hung. Trencsén. Trenčiansky Kraj,
W Slovakia
Trencsén *see* Trenčín
Trengganu, Kuala *see*
Kuala Terengganu
Trenque Lauquen *64 C4* Buenos Aires,
E Argentina
Trent *see* Trento
Trento *96 C2* Eng. Trent, *Ger.* Trient;
anc. Tridentum. Trentino-Alto Adige,
N Italy
Trenton *41 F4 state capital* New Jersey,
NE USA
Trentschin *see* Trenčín

Tres Arroyos *65 D5* Buenos Aires,
E Argentina
Treskavica *100 C4 mountain range*
SE Bosnia and Herzegovina
Tres Tabernae *see* Saverne
Treves/Trèves *see* Trier
Treviso *96 C2 anc.* Tarvisium. Veneto,
NE Italy
Trichinopoly *see* Tiruchchirāppalli
Trichūr *see* Thrissur
Tridentum/Trient *see* Trento
Trier *95 A5* Eng. Treves, *Fr.* Trèves; *anc.*
Augusta Treverorum. Rheinland-Pfalz,
SW Germany
Triesen *94 E2* SW Liechtenstein Europe
Triesenberg *94 E2* SW Liechtenstein
Trieste *96 D2* Slvn. Trst. Friuli-Venezia
Giulia, NE Italy
Trifail *see* Trbovlje
Tríkala *104 B4 prev.* Trikkala. Thessalía,
C Greece
Trikkala *see* Tríkala
Trimontium *see* Plovdiv
Trinacria *see* Sicilia
Trincomalee *132 D3 var.* Trinkomali.
Eastern Province, NE Sri Lanka
Trindade, Ilha da *67 C5 island* Brazil,
W Atlantic Ocean
Trinidad *61 F3* El Beni, N Bolivia
Trinidad *64 D4* Flores, S Uruguay
Trinidad *44 D5* Colorado, C USA
Trinidad *55 H5 island* C Trinidad and
Tobago
Trinidad and Tobago *55 H5 off.*
Republic of Trinidad and Tobago.
country SE West Indies

TRINIDAD & TOBAGO
West Indies

Official name Republic of Trinidad
and Tobago
Formation 1962 / 1962
Capital Port-of-Spain
Population 1.3 million / 656 people
per sq mile (253 people per sq km)
Total area 1980 sq. miles (5128 sq. km)
Languages English Creole, English*, Hindi,
French, Spanish
Religions Roman Catholic 26%,
Hindu 23%, Other and nonreligious 23%,
Anglican 8%, Baptist 7%, Pentecostal 7%,
Muslim 6%
Ethnic mix East Indian 40%, Black 38%,
Mixed race 20%, Other 2%
Government Parliamentary system
Currency Trinidad and Tobago dollar
= 100 cents
Literacy rate 99%
Calorie consumption 2751 kilocalories

Trinidad and Tobago, Republic of *see*
Trinidad and Tobago
Trinité, Montagnes de la *59 H3*
mountain range C French Guiana
Trinity River *49 G3 river* Texas, SW USA
Trinkomali *see* Trincomalee
Trípoli *105 B6 prev.* Trípolis.
Pelopónnisos, S Greece
Tripoli *118 B4 var.* Tarābulus, Ṭarābulus
ash Shām, Tråblous; *anc.* Tripolis.
N Lebanon
Tripoli *see* Ṭarābulus
Trípolis *see* Trípoli, Greece
Tripolis *see* Tripoli, Lebanon
Tristan da Cunha *69 B7 dependency of*
Saint Helena SE Atlantic Ocean
Triton Island *128 B7 island* S Paracel
Islands
Trivandrum *see* Thiruvananthapuram
Trnava *99 C6* Ger. Tyrnau, *Hung.*
Nagyszombat. Trnavský Kraj,
W Slovakia
Trnovo *see* Veliko Tŭrnovo
Trogir *100 B4* It. Traù. Split-Dalmacija,
S Croatia
Troglav *100 B4 mountain range* Bosnia and
Herzegovina/Croatia
Trois-Rivières *39 E4* Québec, SE Canada
Troki *see* Trakai
Trollhättan *85 B6* Västra Götaland,
S Sweden
Tromsø *84 C2 Fin.* Tromssa. Troms,
N Norway
Tromssa *see* Tromsø

Trondheim *84 B4* Ger. Drontheim; *prev.*
Nidaros, Trondhjem. Sør-Trøndelag,
S Norway
Trondheimsfjorden *84 B4 fjord*
S Norway
Trondhjem *see* Trondheim
Troódos *102 C5 var.* Troodos
Mountains. *mountain range*
C Cyprus
Troodos Mountains *see* Troódos
Troppau *see* Opava
Troy *42 D3* Alabama, S USA
Troy *41 F3* New York, NE USA
Troyan *104 C2* Lovech, N Bulgaria
Troyes *90 D3 anc.* Augustobona
Tricassium. Aube, N France
Trst *see* Trieste
Trstenik *100 E4* Serbia, C Serbia
Trucial States *see* United Arab Emirates
Trujillo *52 D2* Colón, NE Honduras
Trujillo *60 B3* La Libertad, NW Peru
Trujillo *92 C3* Extremadura, W Spain
Truk Islands *see* Chuuk Islands
Trün *104 B2* Pernik, W Bulgaria
Truro *39 F4* Nova Scotia, SE Canada
Truro *89 C7* SW England, United
Kingdom
Trzcianka *98 B3* Ger. Schönlanke. Pila,
Wielkopolskie, C Poland
Trzebnica *98 C4* Ger. Trebnitz.
Dolnośląskie, SW Poland
Tsalka *117 F2* S Georgia Asia
Tsamkong *see* Zhanjiang
Tsangpo *see* Brahmaputra
Tsarevo *104 E2 prev.* Michurin. Burgas,
E Bulgaria
Tsarigrad *see* İstanbul
Tsaritsyn *see* Volgograd
Tschakathurn *see* Čakovec
Tschaslau *see* Čáslav
Tschenstochau *see* Częstochowa
Tsefat *119 B5 var.* Safed, *Ar.* Safad; *prev.*
Zefat. Northern, N Israel
Tselinograd *see* Astana
Tsetsen Khan *see* Öndörhaan
Tsetserleg *126 D2* Arhangay,
C Mongolia
Tshela *77 B6* Bas-Congo, W Dem.
Rep. Congo
Tshikapa *77 C7* Kasai-Occidental,
SW Dem. Rep. Congo
Tshuapa *77 D6 river* C Dem. Rep.
Congo
Tshwane *78 D4 var.* Epitoli; *see also.*
Pretoria. *country capital* (South Africa)
(administrative capital)
Gauteng, NE South Africa
Tsinan *see* Jinan
Tsing Hai *see* Qinghai Hu, China
Tsinghai *see* Qinghai, China
Tsingtao/Tsingtau *see* Qingdao
Tsinkiang *see* Quanzhou
Tsintao *see* Qingdao
Tsitsihar *see* Qiqihar
Tsu *131 C6 var.* Tu. Mie, Honshū,
SW Japan
Tsugaru-kaikyo *130 C3 strait*
N Japan
Tsumeb *78 B3* Oshikoto, N Namibia
Tsuruga *131 C6 var.* Turuga. Fukui,
Honshū, SW Japan
Tsuruoka *130 D4 var.* Turuoka.
Yamagata, Honshū, C Japan
Tsushima *131 A7 var.* Tsushima-tō,
Tusima. *island group* SW Japan
Tsushima-tō *see* Tsushima
Tsyerakhowka *107 D8* Rus. Terekhovka.
Homyel'skaya Voblasts', SE Belarus
Tsyurupinsk *see* Tsyurupyns'k
Tsyurupyns'k *109 E4* Rus. Tsyurupinsk.
Khersons'ka Oblast', S Ukraine
Tu *see* Tsu
Tuamotu, Archipel des *see* Tuamotu, Îles
Tuamotu Fracture Zone *143 H3*
fracture zone E Pacific Ocean
Tuamotu Islands *145 H4 var.* Archipel
des Tuamotu, Dangerous Archipelago,
Tuamotu Islands. *island group*
N French Polynesia
Tuamotu Islands *see* Tuamotu, Îles
Tuapi *53 E2* Región Autónoma Atlántico
Norte, NE Nicaragua
Tuapse *111 A7* Krasnodarskiy Kray,
SW Russian Federation

Tuba City *48 B1* Arizona,
SW USA
Tubbergen *86 E3* Overijssel,
E Netherlands
Tubeke *see* Tubize
Tubize *87 B6* Dut. Tubeke. Walloon
Brabant, C Belgium
Tubmanburg *74 C5* NW Liberia
Ṭubruq *71 H2* Eng. Tobruk, *It.* Tobruch.
NE Libya
Tubuai, Îles/Tubuai Islands *see*
Australes, Îles
Tucker's Town *42 B5* E Bermuda
Tuckum *see* Tukums
Tucson *48 B3* Arizona, SW USA
Tucumán *see* San Miguel de Tucumán
Tucumcari *49 E2* New Mexico, S
W USA
Tucupita *59 E2* Delta Amacuro,
NE Venezuela
Tucuruí, Represa de *63 F2 reservoir*
NE Brazil
Tudela *93 E2* Basq. Tutera; *anc.* Tutela.
Navarra, N Spain
Tudmur *118 C3 var.* Tadmur, Tamar,
Gk. Palmyra, *Bibl.* Tadmor. Ḥimṣ,
C Syria
Tuguegarao *139 E1* Luzon,
N Philippines
Tuktoyaktuk *37 E3* Northwest
Territories, NW Canada
Tukums *106 C3* Ger. Tuckum.
W Latvia
Tula *111 B5* Tul'skaya Oblast', W Russian
Federation
Tulancingo *51 E4* Hidalgo, C Mexico
Tulare Lake Bed *47 C7 salt flat*
California, W USA
Tulcán *60 B1* Carchi, N Ecuador
Tulcea *108 D5* Tulcea, E Romania
Tul'chin *see* Tul'chyn
Tul'chyn *108 D3* Rus. Tul'chin.
Vinnyts'ka Oblast', C Ukraine
Tuléar *see* Toliara
Tulia *49 E2* Texas, SW USA
Tülkarm *119 D7* West Bank, Israel
Tulle *91 C5 anc.* Tutela. Corrèze,
C France
Tulln *95 E6 var.* Oberhollabrunn.
Niederösterreich, NE Austria
Tully *148 D3* Queensland,
NE Australia
Tulsa *49 G1* Oklahoma, C USA
Tuluá *58 B3* Valle del Cauca,
W Colombia
Tulun *115 E4* Irkutskaya Oblast',
S Russian Federation
Tumaco *58 A4* Nariño, SW Colombia
Tumba, Lac *see* Ntomba, Lac
Tumbes *60 A2* Tumbes, NW Peru
Tumkūr *132 C2* Karnātaka,
W India
Tumuc-Humac Mountains *63 E1 var.*
Serra Tumucumaque. *mountain range*
N South America
Tumucumaque, Serra *see* Tumuc-
Humac Mountains
Tunca Nehri *see* Tundzha
Tunduru *73 C8* Ruvuma,
S Tanzania
Tundzha *104 D3 Turk.* Tunca Nehri.
river Bulgaria/Turkey
Tungabhadra Reservoir *132 C2 lake*
S India
Tungaru *145 E2 prev.* Gilbert Islands.
island group W Kiribati
T'ung-shan *see* Xuzhou
Tungsten *36 D4* Northwest Territories,
W Canada
Tung-t'ing Hu *see* Dongting Hu
Tunis *71 E1 var.* Tūnis. *country capital*
(Tunisia) NE Tunisia
Tunis, Golfe de *102 D3 Ar.* Khalīj Tūnis.
gulf NE Tunisia
Tunisia *71 F2 off.* Tunisian Republic,
Ar. Al Jumhūrīyah at Tūnisīyah, *Fr.*
République Tunisienne. *country*
N Africa

TUNISIA
North Africa

Official name The Tunisian Republic
Formation 1956 / 1956
Capital Tunis

TUNISIA
(continued)

Population 10.6 million / 177 people
per sq mile (68 people per sq km)
Total area 63,169 sq. miles (163,610 sq. km)
Languages Arabic*, French
Religions Muslim (mainly Sunni) 98%,
Christian 1%, Jewish 1%
Ethnic mix Arab and Berber 98%,
Jewish 1%, European 1%
Government Transitional regime
Currency Tunisian dinar = 1000 millimes
Literacy rate 78%
Calorie consumption 3314 kilocalories

Tunisian Republic see Tunisia
Tunisienne, République see Tunisia
Tūnisīyah, Al Jumhūrīyah at see
Tunisia
Tūnis, Khalij see Tunis, Golfe de
Tunja 58 B3 Boyacá, C Colombia
Tuong Buong see Tương Đương
Tương Đương 136 D4 var. Tuong
Buong. Nghệ An, N Vietnam
Tüp see Tyup
Tupelo 42 C2 Mississippi, S USA
Tupiza 61 G5 Potosí, S Bolivia
Turabah 121 B5 Makkah, W Saudi
Arabia
Turangi 150 D4 Waikato, North Island,
New Zealand
Turan Lowland 122 C2 var. Turan Plain,
Kaz. Turan Oypaty, Rus. Turanskaya
Nizmennost', Turk. Turan Pesligi, Uzb.
Turan Pasttekisligi. plain C Asia
**Turan Oypaty/Turan Pesligi/Turan
Plain/Turanskaya Nizmennost'** see
Turan Lowland
Turan Pasttekisligi see Turan Lowland
Turayf 120 A3 Al Ḩudūd ash
Shamālīyah, NW Saudi Arabia
Turba see Teruel
Turbat 134 A3 Baluchistān,
SW Pakistan
Turčiansky Svätý Martin see Martin
Turda 108 B4 Ger. Thorenburg, Hung.
Torda. Cluj, NW Romania
Turek 98 C3 Wielkopolskie, C Poland
Turfan see Turpan
Turin see Torino
Turkana, Lake 73 C6 var. Lake Rudolf.
lake N Kenya
Turkestan see Turkistan
Turkey 116 B3 off. Republic of Turkey,
Turk. Türkiye Cumhuriyeti. country
SW Asia

TURKEY
Asia / Europe

Official name Republic of Turkey
Formation 1923 / 1939
Capital Ankara
Population 73.6 million / 248 people
per sq mile (96 people per sq km)
Total area 301,382 sq. miles
(780,580 sq. km)
Languages Turkish*, Kurdish,
Arabic, Circassian, Armenian, Greek,
Georgian, Ladino
Religions Muslim (mainly Sunni) 99%,
Other 1%
Ethnic mix Turkish 70%, Kurdish 20%,
Other 8%, Arab 2%
Government Parliamentary system
Currency new Turkish lira = 100 kurus
Literacy rate 91%
Calorie consumption 3666 kilocalories

Turkey, Republic of see Turkey
**Turkish Republic of Northern
Cyprus** 102 D5 disputed territory
Cyprus
Turkistan 114 B5 prev. Turkestan.
Yuzhnyy Kazakhstan, S Kazakhstan
Türkiye Cumhuriyeti see Turkey
Türkmenabat 122 D3 prev. Rus.
Chardzhev, Chardzhou, Chardzhui,
Lenin-Turkmenski, Turkm. Chärjew.
Lebap Welaýaty, E Turkmenistan
Türkmen Aylagy 122 B2 Rus.
Turkmenskiy Zaliv. lake gulf
W Turkmenistan
Turkmenbashi see Türkmenbaşy

Türkmenbaşy 122 B2 Rus.
Turkmenbashi; prev. Krasnovodsk.
Balkan Welaýaty, W Turkmenistan
Türkmenbasy Aylagy 122 A2 prev.
Rus. Krasnovodskiy Zaliv, Turkm.
Krasnowodsk Aylagy. lake Gulf
W Turkmenistan
Turkmenistan 122 B2; prev.
Turkmenskaya Soviet Socialist
Republic. country C Asia

TURKMENISTAN
Central Asia

Official name Turkmenistan
Formation 1991 / 1991
Capital Ashgabat
Population 5.1 million / 27 people
per sq mile (10 people per sq km)
Total area 188,455 sq. miles
(488,100 sq. km)
Languages Turkmen*, Uzbek, Russian,
Kazakh, Tatar
Religions Sunni Muslim 89%,
Orthodox Christian 9%, Other 2%
Ethnic mix Turkmen 85%, Other 6%,
Uzbek 5%, Russian 4%
Government One-party state
Currency Manat = 100 tenge
Literacy rate 99%
Calorie consumption 2878 kilocalories

**Turkmenskaya Soviet Socialist
Republic** see Turkmenistan
Turkmenskiy Zaliv see Türkmen
Aylagy
Turks and Caicos Islands 55 E2 UK
dependent territory N West Indies
Turku 85 D6 Swe. Åbo. Länsi-Suomi,
SW Finland
Turlock 47 B6 California, W USA
Turnagain, Cape 150 D4 headland
North Island, New Zealand
Turnau see Turnov
Turnhout 87 C5 Antwerpen,
N Belgium
Turnov 98 B4 Ger. Turnau. Liberecký
Kraj, N Czech Republic
Türnovo see Veliko Türnovo
Turnu Măgurele 108 B5 var. Turnu-
Măgurele. Teleorman, S Romania
Turnu Severin see Drobeta-Turnu
Severin
Turócszentmárton see Martin
Turoni see Tours
Turpan 126 C3 var. Turfan. Xinjiang
Uygur Zizhiqu, NW China
Turpan Depression see Turpan Pendi
Turpan Pendi 126 C3 Eng. Turpan
Depression. depression NW China
Turpentine State see North Carolina
Türtkül/Turtkul' see To'rtko'l
Turuga see Tsuruga
Turuoka see Tsuruoka
Tuscaloosa 42 C2 Alabama, S USA
Tuscan Archipelago see Toscano,
Archipelago
Tuscany see Toscana
Tusima see Tsushima
Tutela see Tulle, France
Tutela see Tudela, Spain
Tutera see Tudela
Tuticorin 132 C3 Tamil Nādu,
SE India
Tutrakan 104 D1 Silistra,
NE Bulgaria
Tutuila 145 F4 island W American
Samoa
Tuvalu 145 E3 prev. Ellice Islands.
country SW Pacific Ocean

TUVALU
Australasia & Oceania

Official name Tuvalu
Formation 1978 / 1978
Capital Fongafale, on Funafuti Atoll
Population 10,619 / 1062 people
per sq mile (408 people per sq km)
Total area 10 sq. miles (26 sq. km)
Languages Tuvaluan, Kiribati, English*
Religions Church of Tuvalu 97%,
Baha'i 1%, Seventh-day Adventist 1%,
Other 1%
Ethnic mix Polynesian 96%,
Micronesian 4%

TUVALU
(continued)

Government Nonparty system
Currency Australian dollar and Tuvaluan
dollar = 100 cents
Literacy rate 98%
Calorie consumption Not available

Tuwayq, Jabal 121 C5 mountain range
C Saudi Arabia
Tuxpan 50 D4 Jalisco, C Mexico
Tuxpan 50 D4 Nayarit, C Mexico
Tuxpán 51 F4 var. Tuxpán de Rodríguez
Cano. Veracruz-Llave, E Mexico
Tuxpán de Rodríguez Cano see
Tuxpán
Tuxtepec 51 F4 var. San Juan Bautista
Tuxtepec. Oaxaca, S Mexico
Tuxtla 51 G5 var. Tuxtla Gutiérrez.
Chiapas, SE Mexico
Tuxtla see San Andrés Tuxtla
Tuxtla Gutiérrez see Tuxtla
Tuy Hoa 137 E5 Phu Yên,
S Vietnam
Tuz, Lake 116 C3 lake C Turkey
Tver' 110 B4 prev. Kalinin. Tverskaya
Oblast', W Russian Federation
Tverya 119 B5 var. Tiberias; prev.
Teverya. Northern, N Israel
Twin Falls 46 D4 Idaho, NW USA
Tyan'-Shan' see Tien Shan
Tychy 99 D5 Ger. Tichau. Śląskie,
S Poland
Tyler 49 G3 Texas, SW USA
Tylos see Bahrain
Tympáki 105 C8 var. Timbaki;
prev. Timbákion. Kríti, Greece,
E Mediterranean Sea
Tynda 115 F4 Amurskaya Oblast',
SE Russian Federation
Tyne 88 D4 river N England, United
Kingdom
Tyôsi see Chōshi
Tyras see Dniester
Tyre see Soûr
Tyrnau see Trnava
Týrnavos 104 B4 var. Tírnavos.
Thessalía, C Greece
Tyrol see Tirol
Tyros see Bahrain
Tyrrhenian Sea 97 B6 It. Mare Tirreno.
sea N Mediterranean Sea
Tyumen' 114 C3 Tyumenskaya Oblast',
C Russian Federation
Tyup 123 G2 Kir. Tüp. Issyk-Kul'skaya
Oblast', NE Kyrgyzstan
Tywyn 89 C6 W Wales, United
Kingdom
Tzekung see Zigong
Tziá 105 C6 prev. Kéa, Kéos; anc. Ceos.
island Kykládes, Greece, Aegean Sea

U

UAE see United Arab Emirates
Uanle Uen see Wanlaweyn
Uaupés, Rio see Vaupés, Río
Ubangi-Shari see Central African
Republic
Ube 131 B7 Yamaguchi, Honshū,
SW Japan
Úbeda 93 E4 Andalucía, S Spain
Uberaba 63 F4 Minas Gerais,
SE Brazil
Uberlândia 63 F4 Minas Gerais, S
E Brazil
Ubol Rajadhani/Ubol Ratchathani see
Ubon Ratchathani
Ubon Ratchathani 137 D5 var.
Muang Ubon, Ubol Rajadhani, Ubol
Ratchathani, Udon Ratchathani.
Ubon Ratchathani, E Thailand
Ubrique 92 D5 Andalucía, S Spain
Ubsu-Nur, Ozero see Uvs Nuur
Ucayali, Río 60 D3 river C Peru
Uchiura-wan 130 D3 bay NW Pacific
Ocean
Uchkuduk see Uchquduq
Uchquduq 122 D2 Rus. Uchkuduk.
Navoiy Viloyati, N Uzbekistan
Uchtagan Gumy/Uchtagan, Peski see
Uçtagan Gumy

Uçtagan Gumy 122 C2 var. Uchtagan
Gumy, Rus. Peski Uchtagan. desert
NW Turkmenistan
Udaipur 134 C3 prev. Oodeypore.
Rājasthān, N India
Uddevalla 85 B6 Västra Götaland,
S Sweden
Udine 96 D2 anc. Utina. Friuli-Venezia
Giulia, NE Italy
Udintsev Fracture Zone 154 A5 tectonic
feature S Pacific Ocean
Udipi see Udupi
Udon Ratchathani see
Ubon Ratchathani
Udon Thani 136 C4 var. Ban Mak
Khaeng, Udorndhani. Udon Thani,
N Thailand
Udorndhani see Udon Thani
Udupi 132 B2 var. Udipi. Karnātaka,
SW India
Uele 77 D5 var. Welle. river NE Dem.
Rep. Congo
Uelzen 94 C3 Niedersachsen,
N Germany
Ufa 111 D6 Respublika Bashkortostan,
W Russian Federation
Ugâle 106 C2 NW Latvia
Uganda 73 B6 off. Republic of Uganda.
country E Africa

UGANDA
East Africa

Official name Republic of Uganda
Formation 1962 / 1962
Capital Kampala
Population 34.5 million / 448 people
per sq mile (173 people per sq km)
Total area 91,135 sq. miles (236,040 sq. km)
Languages Luganda, Nkole, Chiga, Lango,
Acholi, Teso, Logbara, English*
Religions Christian 85%, Muslim (mainly
Sunni) 12%, Other 3%
Ethnic mix Other 50%, Baganda 17%,
Banyakole 10%, Basoga 9%, Iteso 7%,
Bakiga 7%
Government Presidential system
Currency New Uganda shilling
= 100 cents
Literacy rate 74%
Calorie consumption 2260 kilocalories

Uganda, Republic of see Uganda
Uhorshchyna see Hungary
Uhuru Peak see Kilimanjaro
Uíge 78 B1 Port. Carmona, Vila
Marechal Carmona. Uíge,
NW Angola
Uinta Mountains 44 B4 mountain range
Utah, W USA
Uitenhage 78 C5 Eastern Cape, S South
Africa
Uithoorn 86 C3 Noord-Holland,
C Netherlands
Ujda see Oujda
Ujelang Atoll 144 C1 var. Wujlän. atoll
Ralik Chain, W Marshall Islands
Újgradiska see Nova Gradiška
Újmoldova see Moldova Nouă
Ujungpandang see Makassar
Ujung Salang see Phuket
Újvidék see Novi Sad
UK see United Kingdom
Ukhta 111 C5 Respublika Komi,
NW Russian Federation
Ukiah 47 B5 California, W USA
Ukmergė 106 C4 Pol. Wiłkomierz.
Vilnius, C Lithuania
Ukraina see Ukraine
Ukraine 108 C2 off. Ukraine, Rus.
Ukraina, Ukr. Ukrayina; prev.
Ukrainian Soviet Socialist Republic,
Ukrainskay S.S.R. country SE Europe

UKRAINE
Eastern Europe

Official name Ukraine
Formation 1991 / 1991
Capital Kiev
Population 45.2 million / 194 people
per sq mile (75 people per sq km)
Total area 233,089 sq. miles
(603,700 sq. km)
Languages Ukrainian*, Russian, Tatar
Religions Christian (mainly

UKRAINE
(continued)

Orthodox) 95%, Other 5%
Ethnic mix Ukrainian 78%, Russian 17%,
  Other 5%
Government Presidential system
Currency Hryvna = 100 kopiykas
Literacy rate 99%
Calorie consumption 3198 kilocalories

Ukraine *see* Ukraine
Ukrainian Soviet Socialist Republic
  see Ukraine
Ukrainskaya S.S.R/Ukrayina *see*
  Ukraine
Ulaanbaatar *127 E2 Eng.* Ulan Bator;
  prev. Urga. *country capital* (Mongolia)
  Töv, C Mongolia
Ulaangom *126 C2* Uvs,
  NW Mongolia
Ulan Bator *see* Ulaanbaatar
Ulanhad *see* Chifeng
Ulan-Ude *115 E4 prev.* Verkhneudinsk.
  Respublika Buryatiya, S Russian
  Federation
Uleälv *see* Oulujoki
Uleträsk *see* Oulujärvi
Ulft *86 E4* Gelderland, E Netherlands
Ullapool *88 C3* N Scotland, United
  Kingdom
Ulm *95 B6* Baden-Württemberg,
  S Germany
Ulsan *129 E4 Jap.* Urusan. SE South
  Korea
Ulster *89 B5 province* Northern Ireland,
  United Kingdom/Ireland
Ulungur Hu *126 B2 lake* NW China
Uluṟu *147 D5 var.* Ayers Rock. *monolith*
  Northern Territory, C Australia
Ul'yanovka *109 E3* Kirovohrads'ka
  Oblast', C Ukraine
Ul'yanovsk *111 C5 prev.* Simbirsk.
  Ul'yanovskaya Oblast', W Russian
  Federation
Umán *51 H3* Yucatán, SE Mexico
Uman' *109 E3 Rus.* Uman. Cherkas'ka
  Oblast', C Ukraine
Uman *see* Uman'
Umanak/Umanaq *see* Uummannaq
'Umān, Khalīj *see* Oman, Gulf of
'Umān, Salṭanat *see* Oman
Umbrian-Machigian Mountains *see*
  Umbro-Marchigiano, Appennino
Umbro-Marchigiano, Appennino
  96 C3 Eng. Umbrian-Machigian
  Mountains. *mountain range* C Italy
Umeå *84 C4* Västerbotten, N Sweden
Umeälven *84 C4 river* N Sweden
Umiat *36 D2* Alaska, USA
Umm Buru *72 A4* Western Darfur,
  W Sudan
Umm Durmān *see* Omdurman
Umm Ruwaba *72 C4 var.* Umm
  Ruwābah, Um Ruwāba. Northern
  Kordofan, C Sudan
Umm Ruwābah *see* Umm Ruwaba
Umnak Island *36 A3 island* Aleutian
  Islands, Alaska, USA
Um Ruwāba *see* Umm Ruwaba
Umtali *see* Mutare
Umtata *see* Mthatha
Una *100 B3 river* Bosnia and
  Herzegovina/Croatia
Unac *100 B3 river* W Bosnia and
  Herzegovina
Unalaska Island *36 A3 island* Aleutian
  Islands, Alaska, USA
'Unayzah *120 B4 var.* Anaiza. Al Qaṣīm,
  C Saudi Arabia
Unci *see* Almería
Uncía *61 F4* Potosí, C Bolivia
Uncompahgre Peak *44 B5 mountain*
  Colorado, C USA
Undur Khan *see* Öndörhaan
Ungaria *see* Hungary
Ungarisches Erzgebirge *see* Slovenské
  rudohorie
Ungarn *see* Hungary
Ungava Bay *39 E1 bay* Québec,
  E Canada
Ungava Peninsula *38 D1 peninsula*
  Québec, SE Canada
Ungeny *see* Ungheni

Ungheni *108 D3 Rus.* Ungeny.
  W Moldova
Unguja *see* Zanzibar
Üngüz Angyrsyndaky Garagum *122 C2*
  Rus. Zaunguzskiye Garagumy. *desert*
  N Turkmenistan
Ungvár *see* Uzhhorod
Unimak Island *36 B3 island* Aleutian
  Islands, Alaska, USA
Union *43 E1* South Carolina, SE USA
Union City *42 C1* Tennessee, S USA
Union of Myanmar *see* Burma
United Arab Emirates *121 C5 Ar.* Al
  Imārāt al 'Arabīyah al Muttaḥidah,
  abbrev. UAE; *prev.* Trucial States.
  country SW Asia

UNITED ARAB EMIRATES
Southwest Asia

Official name United Arab Emirates
Formation 1971 / 1972
Capital Abu Dhabi
Population 7.9 million / 245 people
  per sq mile (94 people per sq km)
Total area 32,000 sq. miles (82,880 sq. km)
Languages Arabic*, Farsi, Indian and
  Pakistani languages, English
Religions Muslim (mainly Sunni) 96%,
  Christian, Hindu, and other 4%
Ethnic mix Asian 60%, Emirian 25%,
  Other Arab 12%, European 3%
Government Monarchy
Currency UAE dirham = 100 fils
Literacy rate 90%
Calorie consumption 3245 kilocalories

United Arab Republic *see* Egypt
United Kingdom *89 B5 off.* United
  Kingdom of Great Britain and
  Northern Ireland, *abbrev.* UK. *country*
  NW Europe

UNITED KINGDOM
Northwest Europe

Official name United Kingdom of Great
  Britain and Northern Ireland
Formation 1707 / 1922
Capital London
Population 62.4 million / 669 people
  per sq mile (258 people per sq km)
Total area 94,525 sq. miles
  (244,820 sq. km)
Languages English*, Welsh* *(in Wales)*,
  Scottish Gaelic, Irish Gaelic
Religions Anglican 45%, Other and
  nonreligious 36%, Roman Catholic 9%,
  Presbyterian 4%, Muslim 3%,
  Methodist 2%, Hindu 1%
Ethnic mix English 80%, Scottish 9%,
  West Indian, Asian, and other 5%,
  Northern Irish 3%, Welsh 3%
Government Parliamentary system
Currency Pound sterling = 100 pence
Literacy rate 99%
Calorie consumption 3432 kilocalories

United Kingdom of Great Britain and
  Northern Ireland *see*
  United Kingdom
United Mexican States *see* Mexico
United Provinces *see* Uttar Pradesh
United States of America *35 B5 off.*
  United States of America, *var.* America,
  The States, *abbrev.* U.S., USA. *country*
  North America

UNITED STATES
North America

Official name United States of America
Formation 1776 / 1959
Capital Washington D.C.
Population 313 million / 88 people
  per sq mile (34 people per sq km)
Total area 3,717,792 sq. miles
  (9,626,091 sq. km)
Languages English, Spanish, Chinese,
  French, German, Tagalog, Vietnamese,
  Italian, Korean, Russian, Polish
Religions Protestant 52%, Roman
  Catholic 25%, Other and nonreligious
  20%, Jewish 2%, Muslim 1%
Ethnic mix White 62%, Hispanic 13%,
  Black American/African 13%, Other 7%,
  Asian 4%, Native American 1%

UNITED STATES
(continued)

Government Presidential system
Currency US dollar = 100 cents
Literacy rate 99%
Calorie consumption 3688 kilocalories

United States of America *see* United
  States of America
Unst *88 D1 island* NE Scotland, United
  Kingdom
Ünye *116 D2* Ordu, W Turkey
Upala *52 D4* Alajuela, NW Costa Rica
Upata *59 E2* Bolívar, E Venezuela
Upemba, Lac *77 D7 lake* SE Dem.
  Rep. Congo
Upernavik *82 C2 var.* Upernivik. Kitaa,
  C Greenland
Upernivik *see* Upernavik
Upington *78 C4* Northern Cape,
  W South Africa
Upolu *145 F4 island* SE Samoa
Upper Klamath Lake *46 A4 lake*
  Oregon, NW USA
Upper Lough Erne *89 A5 lake*
  SW Northern Ireland, United
  Kingdom
Upper Red Lake *45 F1 lake* Minnesota,
  N USA
Upper Volta *see* Burkina Faso
Uppsala *85 C6* Uppsala, C Sweden
Uqsuqtuuq *see* Gjoa Haven
Ural *114 B4 Kaz.* Zayyq. *river*
  Kazakhstan/Russian Federation
Ural Mountains *114 C3 var.* Ural'skiy
  Khrebet, *Eng.* Ural Mountains.
  mountain range Kazakhstan/Russian
  Federation
Ural Mountains *see* Ural'skiye Gory
Ural'sk *114 B3 Kaz.* Oral. Zapadnyy
  Kazakhstan, NW Kazakhstan
Ural'skiy Khrebet *see* Ural'skiye Gory
Uraricoera *62 D1* Roraima, N Brazil
Ura-Tyube *see* Ŭroteppa
Urbandale *45 F3* Iowa, C USA
Urdunn *see* Jordan
Uren' *111 C5* Nizhegorodskaya Oblast',
  W Russian Federation
Urga *see* Ulaanbaatar
Urganch *122 D2 Rus.* Urgench; *prev.*
  Novo-Urgench. Xorazm Viloyati,
  W Uzbekistan
Urgench *see* Urganch
Urgut *123 E3* Samarqand Viloyati,
  C Uzbekistan
Urmia, Lake *121 C2 var.* Matianus, Sha
  Hi, Urumi Yeh, *Eng.* Lake Urmia; *prev.*
  Daryācheh-ye Reẕā'iyeh. *lake*
  NW Iran
Urmia, Lake *see* Orūmīyeh,
  Daryācheh-ye
Uroševac *see* Ferizaj
Ŭroteppa *123 E2 Rus.* Ura-Tyube.
  NW Tajikistan
Uruapan *51 E4 var.* Uruapan del
  Progreso. Michoacán,
  SW Mexico
Uruapan del Progreso *see* Uruapan
Uruguai, Rio *see* Uruguay
Uruguay *64 D4 off.* Oriental Republic
  of Uruguay; *prev.* La Banda Oriental.
  country E South America

URUGUAY
South America

Official name Eastern Republic
  of Uruguay
Formation 1828 / 1828
Capital Montevideo
Population 3.4 million / 50 people
  per sq mile (19 people per sq km)
Total area 68,039 sq. miles (176,220 sq. km)
Languages Spanish*
Religions Roman Catholic 66%, Other
  and nonreligious 30%,
  Jewish 2%, Protestant 2%
Ethnic mix White 90%, Mestizo 6%,
  Black 4%
Government Presidential system
Currency Uruguayan peso
  = 100 centésimos
Literacy rate 98%
Calorie consumption 2808 kilocalories

Uruguay *64 D3 var.* Rio Uruguai, Río
  Uruguay. *river* E South America
Uruguay, Oriental Republic of *see*
  Uruguay
Uruguay, Río *see* Uruguay
Urumchi *see* Ürümqi
Urumi Yeh *see* Orūmīyeh, Daryācheh-ye
Ürümqi *126 C3 var.* Tihwa, Urumchi,
  Urumqi, Urumtsi, Wu-lu-k'o-mu-shih,
  Wu-lu-mu-ch'i; *prev.* Ti-hua. Xinjiang
  Uygur Zizhiqu, NW China
Urumtsi *see* Ürümqi
Urundi *see* Burundi
Urup, Ostrov *115 H4 island* Kuril'skiye
  Ostrova, SE Russian Federation
Urusan *see* Ulsan
Urziceni *108 C5* Ialomiţa,
  SE Romania
Usa *110 E3 river* NW Russian
  Federation
Uşak *116 B3 prev.* Ushak. Uşak,
  W Turkey
Ushak *see* Uşak
Ushant *see* Ouessant, Île d'
Ushuaia *65 B8* Tierra del Fuego,
  S Argentina
Usinsk *110 E3* Respublika Komi,
  NW Russian Federation
Üsküb/Üsküp *see* Skopje
Usmas Ezers *106 B3 lake* NW Latvia
Usol'ye-Sibirskoye *115 E4* Irkutskaya
  Oblast', C Russian Federation
Ussel *91 C5* Corrèze, C France
Ussuriysk *115 G5 prev.* Nikol'sk,
  Nikol'sk-Ussuriyskiy, Voroshilov.
  Primorskiy Kray, SE Russian
  Federation
Ustica *97 B6 island* S Italy
Ust'-Ilimsk *115 E4* Irkutskaya Oblast',
  C Russian Federation
Ústí nad Labem *98 A4 Ger.* Aussig.
  Ústecký Kraj, NW Czech Republic
Ustinov *see* Izhevsk
Ustka *98 C2 Ger.* Stolpmünde.
  Pomorskie, N Poland
Ust'-Kamchatsk *115 H2* Kamchatskiy
  Kray, E Russian Federation
Ust'-Kamenogorsk *114 D5 Kaz.*
  Öskemen. Vostochnyy Kazakhstan,
  E Kazakhstan
Ust'-Kut *115 E4* Irkutskaya Oblast',
  C Russian Federation
Ust'-Olenëk *115 E3* Respublika Sakha
  (Yakutiya), NE Russian Federation
Ustrzyki Dolne *99 E5* Podkarpackie,
  SE Poland
Ust'-Sysol'sk *see* Syktyvkar
Ust Urt *see* Ustyurt Plateau
Ustyurt Plateau *122 B1 var.* Ust
  Urt, *Uzb.* Ustyurt Platosi. *plateau*
  Kazakhstan/Uzbekistan
Ustyurt Platosi *see* Ustyurt Plateau
Usulután *52 C3* Usulután,
  SE El Salvador
Usumacinta, Río *52 B1 river*
  Guatemala/Mexico
Usumbura *see* Bujumbura
U.S./USA *see* United States of America
Utah *44 B4 off.* State of Utah, *also known*
  as Beehive State, Mormon State. *state*
  W USA
Utah Lake *44 B4 lake* Utah,
  W USA
Utena *106 C4* Utena, E Lithuania
Utica *41 F3* New York, NE USA
Utina *see* Udine
Utrecht *86 C4 Lat.* Trajectum ad
  Rhenum. Utrecht, C Netherlands
Utsunomiya *131 D5 var.* Utunomiya.
  Tochigi, Honshū, S Japan
Uttarakhand *135 E2 cultural region*
  N India
Uttar Pradesh *135 E3 prev.* United
  Provinces, United Provinces of Agra
  and Oudh. *cultural region* N India
Utunomiya *see* Utsunomiya
Uulu *106 D2* Pärnumaa, SW Estonia
Uummannaq *82 C3 var.* Umanak,
  Umanaq. Kitaa, C Greenland
Uummannarsuaq *see* Nunap Isua
Uvalde *49 F4* Texas,
  SW USA
Uvaravichy *107 D7 Rus.* Uvarovichi.
  Homyel'skaya Voblasts', SE Belarus

Uvarovichi *see* Uvaravichy
Uvea, Île 145 *E4 island* N Wallis and Futuna
Uvs Nuur 126 *C1 var.* Ozero Ubsu-Nur. *lake* Mongolia/Russian Federation
'Uwaynāt, Jabal al 88 *A3 var.* Jebel Uweinat. *mountain* Libya/Sudan
Uweinat, Jebel *see* 'Uwaynāt, Jabal al
Uyo 75 *G5* Akwa Ibom, S Nigeria
Uyuni 61 *F5* Potosí, W Bolivia
Uzbekistan 122 *D2 off.* Republic of Uzbekistan. *country* C Asia

UZBEKISTAN
Central Asia

Official name Republic of Uzbekistan
Formation 1991 / 1991
Capital Tashkent
Population 27.8 million / 161 people per sq mile (62 people per sq km)
Total area 172,741 sq. miles (447,400 sq. km)
Languages Uzbek*, Russian, Tajik, Kazakh
Religions Sunni Muslim 88%, Orthodox Christian 9%, Other 3%
Ethnic mix Uzbek 80%, Russian 6%, Other 6%, Tajik 5%, Kazakh 3%
Government Presidential system
Currency Sum = 100 tiyin
Literacy rate 99%
Calorie consumption 2618 kilocalories

Uzbekistan, Republic of *see* Uzbekistan
Uzhgorod *see* Uzhhorod
Uzhhorod 108 *B2 Rus.* Uzhgorod; *prev.* Ungvár. Zakarpats'ka Oblast', W Ukraine
Užice 100 *D4 prev.* Titovo Užice. Serbia, W Serbia

V

Vaal 78 *D4 river* C South Africa
Vaals 87 *D6* Limburg, SE Netherlands
Vaasa 85 *D5 Swe.* Vasa; *prev.* Nikolainkaupunki. Länsi-Suomi, W Finland
Vaassen 86 *D3* Gelderland, E Netherlands
Vác 99 *C6 Ger.* Waitzen. Pest, N Hungary
Vadodara 134 *C4 prev.* Baroda. Gujarāt, W India
Vaduz 94 *E2 country capital* (Liechtenstein) W Liechtenstein
Vág *see* Váh
Vágbeszterce *see* Považská Bystrica
Váh 99 *C5 Ger.* Waag, *Hung.* Vág. *river* W Slovakia
Váhtjer *see* Gällivare
Väinameri 106 *C2 prev.* Muhu Väin, *Ger.* Moon-Sund. *sea* E Baltic Sea
Vajdahunyad *see* Hunedoara
Valachia *see* Wallachia
Valday 110 *B4* Novgorodskaya Oblast', W Russian Federation
Valdecañas, Embalse de 92 *D3 reservoir* W Spain
Valdepeñas 93 *E4* Castilla-La Mancha, C Spain
Valdés, Península 65 *C6 peninsula* SE Argentina
Valdez 36 *C3* Alaska, USA
Valdia *see* Weldiya
Valdivia 65 *B5* Los Ríos, C Chile
Val-d'Or 38 *D4* Québec, SE Canada
Valdosta 43 *E3* Georgia, SE USA
Valence 91 *D5 anc.* Valentia, Valentia Julia, Ventia. Drôme, E France
Valencia 93 *F3* Valenciana, E Spain
Valencia 46 *D1* California, USA
Valencia 58 *D1* Carabobo, N Venezuela
Valencia, Gulf of 93 *F3 var.* Gulf of Valencia. *gulf* E Spain
Valencia, Gulf of *see* Valencia, Golfo de
Valenciana 93 *F3 var.* Valencia, *Cat.* València; *anc.* Valentia. *autonomous community* NE Spain
Valencia/València *see* Valenciana
Valenciennes 90 *D2* Nord, N France

Valentia *see* Valence, France
Valentia *see* Valenciana
Valentia Julia *see* Valence
Valentine State *see* Oregon
Valera 58 *C2* Trujillo, NW Venezuela
Valetta *see* Valletta
Valga 106 *D3 Ger.* Walk, *Latv.* Valka. Valgamaa, S Estonia
Valira 91 *A8 river* Andorra/Spain
Valjevo 100 *C4* Serbia, W Serbia
Valjok *see* Válljohka
Valka 106 *D3 Ger.* Walk. N Latvia
Valka *see* Valga
Valkenswaard 87 *D5* Noord-Brabant, S Netherlands
Valladolid 51 *H3* Yucatán, SE Mexico
Valladolid 92 *D2* Castilla y León, NW Spain
Vall D'Uxó *see* La Vall d'Uixó
Valle de La Pascua 58 *D2* Guárico, N Venezuela
Valledupar 58 *B1* Cesar, N Colombia
Vallejo 47 *B6* California, W USA
Vallenar 64 *B3* Atacama, N Chile
Valletta 97 *C8 prev.* Valetta. *country capital* (Malta) E Malta
Valley City 45 *E2* North Dakota, N USA
Válljohka 84 *D2 var.* Valjok. Finnmark, N Norway
Valls 93 *G2* Cataluña, NE Spain
Valmiera 106 *D3 Est.* Volmari, *Ger.* Wolmar. N Latvia
Valona *see* Vlorë
Valozhyn 107 *C5 Pol.* Wołożyn, *Rus.* Volozhin. Minskaya Voblasts', C Belarus
Valparaíso 64 *B4* Valparaíso, C Chile
Valparaiso 40 *C3* Indiana, N USA
Valverde del Camino 92 *C4* Andalucía, S Spain
Van 117 *F3* Van, E Turkey
Vanadzor 117 *F2 prev.* Kirovakan. N Armenia
Vancouver 36 *D5* British Columbia, SW Canada
Vancouver 46 *B3* Washington, NW USA
Vancouver Island 36 *D5 island* British Columbia, SW Canada
Vanda *see* Vantaa
Van Diemen Gulf 146 *D2 gulf* Northern Territory, N Australia
Van Diemen's Land *see* Tasmania
Vaner, Lake *see* Vänern
Vänern 85 *B6 Eng.* Lake Vaner; *prev.* Lake Vener. *lake* S Sweden
Vangaindrano 79 *G4* Fianarantsoa, SE Madagascar
Van Horn 48 *D3* Texas, SW USA
Lake Van 117 *F3 Eng.* Lake Van; *anc.* Thospitis. *salt lake* E Turkey
Van, Lake *see* Van Gölü
Vannes 90 *A3 anc.* Dariorigum. Morbihan, NW France
Vantaa 85 *D6 Swe.* Vanda. Etelä-Suomi, S Finland
Vanua Levu 145 *E4 island* N Fiji
Vanuatu 144 *C4 off.* Republic of Vanuatu; *prev.* New Hebrides. *country* SW Pacific Ocean

VANUATU
Australasia & Oceania

Official name Republic of Vanuatu
Formation 1980 / 1980
Capital Port Vila
Population 200,000 / 42 people per sq mile (16 people per sq km)
Total area 4710 sq. miles (12,200 sq. km)
Languages Bislama* (Melanesian pidgin), English*, French*, other indigenous languages
Religions Presbyterian 37%, Other 19%, Anglican 15%, Roman Catholic 15%, Traditional beliefs 8%, Seventh-day Adventist 6%
Ethnic mix ni-Vanuatu 94%, European 4%, Other 2%
Government Parliamentary system
Currency Vatu = 100 centimes
Literacy rate 82%
Calorie consumption 2841 kilocalories

Vanuatu, Republic of *see* Vanuatu
Van Wert 40 *C4* Ohio, N USA
Vapincum *see* Gap
Varaklāni 106 *D4* C Latvia
Vārānasi 135 *E3 prev.* Banaras, Benares, *hist.* Kasi. Uttar Pradesh, N India
Varangerfjorden 84 *E2* Lapp. Várjjatvuotna. *fjord* N Norway
Varangerhalvøya 84 *D2* Lapp. Várnjárga. *peninsula* N Norway
Varannó *see* Vranov nad Topl'ou
Varasd *see* Varaždin
Varaždin 100 *B2 Ger.* Warasdin, *Hung.* Varasd. Varaždin, N Croatia
Varberg 85 *B7* Halland, S Sweden
Vardar 101 *E6 Gk.* Axiós. *river* FYR Macedonia/Greece
Varde 85 *A7* Syddtjylland, W Denmark
Vareia *see* Logroño
Varéna 107 *B5 Pol.* Orany. Alytus, S Lithuania
Varese 96 *B2* Lombardia, N Italy
Vârful Moldoveanu 108 *B4 var.* Moldoveanul; *prev.* Vírful Moldoveanu. *mountain* C Romania
Várjjatvuotna *see* Varangerfjorden
Varkaus 85 *E5* Itä-Suomi, C Finland
Varna 104 *E2 prev.* Stalin; *anc.* Odessus. Varna, E Bulgaria
Varnenski Zaliv 104 *E2 prev.* Stalinski Zaliv. *bay* E Bulgaria
Várnjárga *see* Varangerhalvøya
Varshava *see* Warszawa
Vasa *see* Vaasa
Vasilíki 105 *A5* Lefkáda, Iónia Nisiá, Greece, C Mediterranean Sea
Vasilishki 107 *B5 Pol.* Wasiliszki. Hrodzyenskaya Voblasts', W Belarus
Vasil'kov *see* Vasyl'kiv
Vaslui 108 *D4* Vaslui, C Romania
Västerås 85 *C6* Västmanland, C Sweden
Vasyl'kiv 109 *E2 var.* Vasil'kov. Kyyivs'ka Oblast', N Ukraine
Vaté *see* Efate
Vatican City 97 *A7 off.* Vatican City. *country* S Europe

VATICAN CITY
Southern Europe

Official name State of the Vatican City
Formation 1929 / 1929
Capital Vatican City
Population 836 / 4918 people per sq mile (1900 people per sq km)
Total area 0.17 sq. miles (0.44 sq. km)
Languages Italian*, Latin*
Religions Roman Catholic 100%
Ethnic mix The current pope is German, though most popes for the last 500 years have been Italian. Cardinals are from many nationalities, but Italians form the largest group. Most of the resident lay persons are Italian
Government Papal state
Currency Euro = 100 cents
Literacy rate 99%
Calorie consumption Not available

Vatican City *see* Vatican City
Vatnajökull 83 *E5 glacier* SE Iceland
Vatter, Lake *see* Vättern
Vättern 85 *B6 Eng.* Lake Vatter; *prev.* Lake Vetter. *lake* S Sweden
Vaughn 48 *D2* New Mexico, SW USA
Vaupés, Río 58 *C4 var.* Rio Uaupés. *river* Brazil/Colombia
Vava'u Group 145 *E4 island group* N Tonga
Vavuniya 132 *D3* Northern Province, N Sri Lanka
Vawkavysk 107 *B6 Pol.* Wołkowysk, *Rus.* Volkovysk. Hrodzyenskaya Voblasts', W Belarus
Växjö 85 *C7 var.* Vexiö. Kronoberg, S Sweden
Vaygach, Ostrov 110 *E2 island* NW Russian Federation
Veendam 86 *E2* Groningen, NE Netherlands

Veenendaal 86 *D4* Utrecht, C Netherlands
Vega 84 *B4 island* C Norway
Veglia *see* Krk
Veisiejai 107 *B5* Alytus, S Lithuania
Vejer de la Frontera 92 *C5* Andalucía, S Spain
Veldhoven 87 *D5* Noord-Brabant, S Netherlands
Velebit 100 *A3 mountain range* C Croatia
Velenje 95 *E7 Ger.* Wöllan. N Slovenia
Veles 101 *E6 Turk.* Köprülü. C FYR Macedonia
Velho *see* Porto Velho
Velika Kikinda *see* Kikinda
Velika Morava 100 *D4 var.* Glavn'a Morava, Morava, *Ger.* Grosse Morava. *river* C Serbia
Velikaya 113 *G2 river* NE Russian Federation
Veliki Bečkerek *see* Zrenjanin
Velikiye Luki 110 *A4* Pskovskaya Oblast', W Russian Federation
Velikiy Novgorod 110 *B4 prev.* Novgorod. Novgorodskaya Oblast', W Russian Federation
Veliko Tŭrnovo 104 *D2 prev.* Tirnovo, Trnovo, Tŭrnovo. Veliko Tŭrnovo, N Bulgaria
Velingrad 104 *C3* Pazardzhik, C Bulgaria
Vel'ký Krtíš 99 *D6* Banskobystrický Kraj, C Slovakia
Vellore 132 *C2* Tamil Nādu, SE India
Velobriga *see* Viana do Castelo
Velsen *see* Velsen-Noord
Velsen-Noord 86 *C3 var.* Velsen. Noord-Holland, W Netherlands
Vel'sk 110 *C4 var.* Velsk. Arkhangel'skaya Oblast', NW Russian Federation
Velykyy Tokmak *see* Tokmak
Vendôme 90 *C4* Loir-et-Cher, C France
Venedig *see* Venezia
Vener, Lake *see* Vänern
Venetia *see* Venezia
Venezia 96 *C2 Eng.* Venice, *Fr.* Venise, *Ger.* Venedig; *anc.* Venetia. Veneto, NE Italy
Venezia, Golfo di *see* Venice, Gulf of
Venezuela 58 *D2 off.* Republic of Venezuela; *prev.* Estados Unidos de Venezuela, United States of Venezuela. *country* N South America

VENEZUELA
South America

Official name Bolivarian Republic of Venezuela
Formation 1830 / 1830
Capital Caracas
Population 29.4 million / 86 people per sq mile (33 people per sq km)
Total area 352,143 sq. miles (912,050 sq. km)
Languages Spanish*, Amerindian languages
Religions Roman Catholic 96%, Protestant 2%, Other 2%
Ethnic mix Mestizo 69%, White 20%, Black 9%, Amerindian 2%
Government Presidential system
Currency Bolívar fuerte = 100 céntimos
Literacy rate 93%
Calorie consumption 3014 kilocalories

Venezuela, Estados Unidos de *see* Venezuela
Venezuela, Gulf of 58 *C1 Eng.* Gulf of Maracaibo, Gulf of Venezuela. *gulf* NW Venezuela
Venezuela, Gulf of *see* Venezuela, Golfo de
Venezuelan Basin 56 *B1 undersea basin* E Caribbean Sea
Venezuela, Republic of *see* Venezuela
Venezuela, United States of *see* Venezuela
Venice 42 *C4* Louisiana, S USA
Venice *see* Venezia

Venice, Gulf of 96 C2 *It.* Golfo di Venezia, *Slvn.* Beneški Zaliv. *gulf* N Adriatic Sea
Venise *see* Venezia
Venlo 87 D5 *prev.* Venloo. Limburg, SE Netherlands
Venloo *see* Venlo
Venta 106 B3 *Ger.* Windau. *river* Latvia/Lithuania
Venta Belgarum *see* Winchester
Ventia *see* Valence
Ventimiglia 96 A3 Liguria, NW Italy
Ventspils 106 B2 *Ger.* Windau. NW Latvia
Vera 64 D3 Santa Fe, C Argentina
Veracruz 51 F4 *var.* Veracruz Llave. Veracruz-Llave, E Mexico
Veracruz Llave *see* Veracruz
Vercellae *see* Vercelli
Vercelli 96 A2 *anc.* Vercellae. Piemonte, NW Italy
Verdal *see* Verdalsøra
Verdalsøra 84 B4 *var.* Verdal. Nord-Trøndelag, C Norway
Verde, Cabo *see* Cape Verde
Verde, Costa 92 D1 *coastal region* N Spain
Verden 94 B3 Niedersachsen, NW Germany
Veria *see* Véroia
Verkhnedvinsk *see* Vyerkhnyadzvinsk
Verkhneudinsk *see* Ulan-Ude
Verkhoyanskiy Khrebet 115 F3 *mountain range* NE Russian Federation
Vermillion 45 F3 South Dakota, N USA
Vermont 41 F2 *off.* State of Vermont, *also known as* Green Mountain State. *state* NE USA
Vernal 44 B4 Utah, W USA
Vernon 49 F2 Texas, SW USA
Veröcze *see* Virovitica
Véroia 104 B4 *var.* Veria, Vérroia, *Turk.* Karaferiye. Kentrikí Makedonía, N Greece
Verona 96 C2 Veneto, NE Italy
Vérroia *see* Véroia
Versailles 90 D1 Yvelines, N France
Versecz *see* Vršac
Verulamium *see* St Albans
Verviers 87 D6 Liège, E Belgium
Vesdre 87 D6 *river* E Belgium
Veselinovo 104 D2 Shumen, NE Bulgaria
Vesontio *see* Besançon
Vesoul 90 D4 *anc.* Vesulium, Vesulum. Haute-Saône, E France
Vesterålen 84 B2 *island group* N Norway
Vestfjorden 84 C3 *fjord* C Norway
Vestmannaeyjar 83 E5 Suðurland, S Iceland
Vesulium/Vesulum *see* Vesoul
Vesuna *see* Périgueux
Vesuvius 97 D5 *Eng.* Vesuvius. *volcano* S Italy
Vesuvius *see* Vesuvio
Veszprém 99 C7 *Ger.* Veszprim. Veszprém, W Hungary
Veszprim *see* Veszprém
Vetrino 104 E2 Varna, E Bulgaria
Vetrino *see* Vyetryna
Vetter, Lake *see* Vättern
Veurne 87 A5 *var.* Furnes. West-Vlaanderen, W Belgium
Vexiö *see* Växjö
Viacha 61 F4 La Paz, W Bolivia
Viana de Castelo *see* Viana do Castelo
Viana do Castelo 92 B2 *var.* Viana de Castelo; *anc.* Velobriga. Viana do Castelo, NW Portugal
Vianen 86 C4 Utrecht, C Netherlands
Viangchan 136 C4 *Eng./Fr.* Vientiane. *country capital* (Laos) C Laos
Viangphoukha 136 C3 *var.* Vieng Pou Kha. Louang Namtha, N Laos
Viareggio 96 B3 Toscana, C Italy
Viborg 85 A7 Midtjylland, NW Denmark
Vic 93 G2 *var.* Vich; *anc.* Ausa, Vicus Ausonensis. Cataluña, NE Spain
Vicentia *see* Vicenza
Vicenza 96 C2 *anc.* Vicentia. Veneto, NE Italy

Vich *see* Vic
Vichy 91 C5 Allier, C France
Vicksburg 42 B2 Mississippi, S USA
Victoria 79 H1 *country capital* (Seychelles) Mahé, SW Seychelles
Victoria 36 D5 *province capital* Vancouver Island, British Columbia, SW Canada
Victoria 102 A5 *var.* Rabat. Gozo, NW Malta
Victoria 49 G4 Texas, SW USA
Victoria 149 C7 *state* SE Australia
Victoria *see* Masvingo, Zimbabwe
Victoria Bank *see* Vitória Seamount
Victoria de Durango *see* Durango
Victoria de las Tunas *see* Las Tunas
Victoria Falls 78 C3 Matabeleland North, W Zimbabwe
Victoria Falls 78 C2 *waterfall* Zambia/Zimbabwe
Victoria Falls *see* Iguaçu, Salto do
Victoria Island 37 F3 *island* Northwest Territories/Nunavut, NW Canada
Victoria, Lake 73 B6 *var.* Victoria Nyanza. *lake* E Africa
Victoria Land 154 C4 *physical region* Antarctica
Victoria Nyanza *see* Victoria, Lake
Victoria River 146 D3 *river* Northern Territory, N Australia
Victorville 47 C7 California, W USA
Vicus Ausonensis *see* Vic
Vicus Elbii *see* Viterbo
Vidalia 43 E2 Georgia, SE USA
Videm-Krško *see* Krško
Vídeň *see* Wien
Vidin 104 B1 *anc.* Bononia. Vidin, NW Bulgaria
Vidzy 107 C5 Vitsyebskaya Voblasts', NW Belarus
Viedma 65 C5 Río Negro, E Argentina
Vieja, Sierra 48 D3 *mountain range* Texas, SW USA
Vieng Pou Kha *see* Viangphoukha
Vienna *see* Wien, Austria
Vienna *see* Vienne, France
Vienne 91 D5 *anc.* Vienna. Isère, E France
Vienne 90 B4 *river* W France
Vientiane *see* Viangchan
Vientos, Paso de los *see* Windward Passage
Vierzon 90 C4 Cher, C France
Viesīte 106 C4 *Ger.* Eckengraf. S Latvia
Vietnam 136 D4 *off.* Socialist Republic of Vietnam, *Vtn.* Công Hoa Xa Hôi Chu Nghia Viêt Nam. *country* SE Asia

VIETNAM
Southeast Asia

Official name Socialist Republic of Vietnam
Formation 1976 / 1976
Capital Hanoi
Population 88.8 million / 707 people per sq mile (273 people per sq km)
Total area 127,243 sq. miles (329,560 sq. km)
Languages Vietnamese*, Chinese, Thai, Khmer, Muong, Nung, Miao, Yao, Jarai
Religions Buddhist 74%, Other 24%, Roman Catholic 7%, Cao Dai 3%, Protestant 2%
Ethnic mix Vietnamese 86%, Other 8%, Muong 2%, Tay 2%, Thai 2%
Government One-party state
Currency Dông = 10 hao = 100 xu
Literacy rate 93%
Calorie consumption 2690 kilocalories

Vietnam, Socialist Republic of *see* Vietnam
Vietri *see* Viêt Tri
Viêt Tri 136 D3 *var.* Vietri. Vinh Phu, N Vietnam
Vieux Fort 55 F2 S Saint Lucia
Vigo 92 B2 Galicia, NW Spain
Viipuri *see* Vyborg
Vijayawāda 132 D1 *prev.* Bezwada. Andhra Pradesh, SE India
Vila *see* Port-Vila
Vila Artur de Paiva *see* Cubango
Vila da Ponte *see* Cubango

Vila de João Belo *see* Xai-Xai
Vila de Mocímboa da Praia *see* Mocímboa da Praia
Vila do Conde 92 B2 Porto, NW Portugal
Vila do Zumbu 78 D2 *prev.* Vila do Zumbu, Zumbo. Tete, NW Mozambique
Vila do Zumbu *see* Vila do Zumbo
Vilafranca del Penedès 93 G2 *var.* Villafranca del Panadés. Cataluña, NE Spain
Vila General Machado *see* Camacupa
Vila Henrique de Carvalho *see* Saurimo
Viļaka 106 D4 *Ger.* Marienhausen. NE Latvia
Vilalba 92 C1 Galicia, NW Spain
Vila Marechal Carmona *see* Uíge
Vila Nova de Gaia 92 B2 Porto, NW Portugal
Vila Nova de Portimão *see* Portimão
Vila Pereira de Eça *see* N'Giva
Vila Real 92 C2 *var.* Vila Rial. Vila Real, N Portugal
Vila Rial *see* Vila Real
Vila Robert Williams *see* Caála
Vila Salazar *see* N'Dalatando
Vila Serpa Pinto *see* Menongue
Vileyka *see* Vilyeyka
Vilhelmina 84 C4 Västerbotten, N Sweden
Vilhena 62 D3 Rondônia, W Brazil
Vília 105 C5 Attikí, C Greece
Viliya 107 C5 *Lith.* Neris. *river* W Belarus
Viliya *see* Neris
Viljandi 106 D2 *Ger.* Fellin. Viljandimaa, S Estonia
Vilkaviškis 106 B4 *Pol.* Wyłkowyszki. Marijampolė, SW Lithuania
Villa Acuña 50 D2 *var.* Ciudad Acuña. Coahuila, NE Mexico
Villa Bella 61 F2 El Beni, N Bolivia
Villacarrillo 93 E4 Andalucía, S Spain
Villa Cecilia *see* Ciudad Madero
Villach 95 D7 *Slvn.* Beljak. Kärnten, S Austria
Villacidro 97 A5 Sardegna, Italy, C Mediterranean Sea
Villa Concepción *see* Concepción
Villa del Pilar *see* Pilar
Villafranca de los Barros 92 C4 Extremadura, W Spain
Villafranca del Panadés *see* Vilafranca del Penedès
Villahermosa 51 G4 *prev.* San Juan Bautista. Tabasco, SE Mexico
Villajoyosa 93 F4 *Cat.* La Vila Joïosa. Valenciana, E Spain
Villa María 64 C3 Córdoba, C Argentina
Villa Martín 61 F5 Potosí, SW Bolivia
Villa Mercedes 64 C4 *var.* Mercedes. San Luis, C Argentina
Villanueva 50 D3 Zacatecas, C Mexico
Villanueva de la Serena 92 C3 Extremadura, W Spain
Villanueva de los Infantes 93 E4 Castilla-La Mancha, C Spain
Villarrica 64 D2 Guairá, SE Paraguay
Villavicencio 58 B3 Meta, C Colombia
Villaviciosa 92 D1 Asturias, N Spain
Villazón 61 G5 Potosí, S Bolivia
Villena 93 F4 Valenciana, E Spain
Villeurbanne 91 D5 Rhône, E France
Villingen-Schwenningen 95 B6 Baden-Württemberg, S Germany
Villmanstrand *see* Lappeenranta
Vilna *see* Vilnius
Vilnius 107 C5 *Pol.* Wilno, *Ger.* Wilna; *prev. Rus.* Vilna. *country capital* (Lithuania) Vilnius, SE Lithuania
Vil'shanka 109 E3 *Rus.* Olshanka. Kirovohrads'ka Oblast', C Ukraine
Vilvoorde 87 C6 *Fr.* Vilvorde. Vlaams Brabant, C Belgium
Vilvorde *see* Vilvoorde
Vilyeyka 107 C5 *Pol.* Wilejka, *Rus.* Vileyka. Minskaya Voblasts', NW Belarus

Vilyuy 115 F3 *river* NE Russian Federation
Viña del Mar 64 B4 Valparaíso, C Chile
Vinarós 93 F3 Valenciana, E Spain
Vincennes 40 B4 Indiana, N USA
Vindhya Mountains *see* Vindhya Range
Vindhya Range 134 D4 *var.* Vindhya Mountains. *mountain range* N India
Vindobona *see* Wien
Vineland 41 F4 New Jersey, NE USA
Vinh 136 D4 Nghê An, N Vietnam
Vinh Loi *see* Bac Liêu
Vinishte 104 C2 Montana, NW Bulgaria
Vinita 49 G1 Oklahoma, C USA
Vinkovci 100 C3 *Ger.* Winkowitz, *Hung.* Vinkovce. Vukovar-Srijem, E Croatia
Vinkovce *see* Vinkovci
Vinnitsa *see* Vinnytsya
Vinnytsya 108 D2 *Rus.* Vinnitsa. Vinnyts'ka Oblast', C Ukraine
Vinogradov *see* Vynohradiv
Vinson Massif 154 A3 *mountain* Antarctica
Viranşehir 117 E4 Şanlıurfa, SE Turkey
Virful Moldoveanu *see* Vârful Moldoveanu
Virginia 45 G1 Minnesota, N USA
Virginia 41 E5 *off.* Commonwealth of Virginia, *also known as* Mother of Presidents, Mother of States, Old Dominion. *state* NE USA
Virginia Beach 41 F5 Virginia, NE USA
Virgin Islands *see* British Virgin Islands
Virgin Islands (US) 55 F3 *var.* Virgin Islands of the United States; *prev.* Danish West Indies. *US unincorporated territory* E West Indies
Virgin Islands of the United States *see* Virgin Islands (US)
Virôchey 137 E5 Rôtânôkiri, NE Cambodia
Virovitica 100 C2 *Ger.* Virovititz, *Hung.* Veröcze; *prev. Ger.* Werowitz. Virovitica-Podravina, NE Croatia
Virovititz *see* Virovitica
Virton 87 D8 Luxembourg, SE Belgium
Virtsu 106 D2 *Ger.* Werder. Läänemaa, W Estonia
Vis 100 B4 *It.* Lissa; *anc.* Issa. *island* S Croatia
Vis *see* Fish
Visaginas 106 C4 *prev.* Sniečkus. Utena, E Lithuania
Visākhapatnam 135 E5 *var.* Vishakhapatnam. Andhra Pradesh, SE India
Visalia 47 C6 California, W USA
Visby 85 C7 *Ger.* Wisby. Gotland, SE Sweden
Viscount Melville Sound 37 F2 *prev.* Melville Sound. *sound* Northwest Territories, N Canada
Visé 87 D6 Liège, E Belgium
Viseu 92 C3 *prev.* Vizeu. Viseu, N Portugal
Vishakhapatnam *see* Visākhapatnam
Vislinskiy Zaliv *see* Vistula Lagoon
Visoko 100 C4 Federacija Bosna I Hercegovina, C Bosnia and Herzegovina
Visttasjohka 84 D3 *river* N Sweden
Vistula 98 C2 *Eng.* Vistula, *Ger.* Weichsel. *river* C Poland
Vistula *see* Wisła
Vistula Lagoon 98 C2 *Ger.* Frisches Haff, *Pol.* Zalew Wiślany, *Rus.* Vislinskiy Zaliv. *lagoon* Poland/Russian Federation
Vitebsk *see* Vitsyebsk
Viterbo 96 C4 *anc.* Vicus Elbii. Lazio, C Italy
Viti *see* Fiji
Viti Levu 145 E4 *island* W Fiji
Vitim 115 F4 *river* C Russian Federation
Vitória 63 F4 *state capital* Espírito Santo, SE Brazil
Vitoria *see* Vitoria-Gasteiz
Vitoria Bank *see* Vitória Seamount
Vitória da Conquista 63 F3 Bahia, E Brazil

Vitoria-Gasteiz 93 E1 var. Vitoria, Eng.
  Vittoria. País Vasco, N Spain
Vitória Seamount 67 B5 var. Victoria
  Bank, Vitoria Bank. seamount
  C Atlantic Ocean
Vitré 90 B3 Ille-et-Vilaine, NW France
Vitsyebsk 107 E5 Rus. Vitebsk.
  Vitsyebskaya Voblasts', NE Belarus
Vittoria 97 C7 Sicilia, Italy,
  C Mediterranean Sea
Vittoria see Vitoria-Gasteiz
Vízcaya, Golfo de see Biscay, Bay of
Vizianagaram 135 E5 var. Vizianagram.
  Andhra Pradesh, E India
Vizianagram see Vizianagaram
Vjosës, Lumi i 101 C7 var. Vijosa,
  Vijosë, Gk. Aóos. river Albania/
  Greece
Vlaanderen 87 A6 Eng. Flanders, Fr.
  Flandre. cultural region Belgium/
  France
Vlaardingen 86 B4 Zuid-Holland,
  SW Netherlands
Vladikavkaz 111 B8 prev. Dzaudzhikau,
  Ordzhonikidze. Respublika Severnaya
  Osetiya, SW Russian Federation
Vladimir 111 B5 Vladimirskaya Oblast',
  W Russian Federation
Vladimirovka see Yuzhno-Sakhalinsk
Vladimir-Volynskiy see
  Volodymyr-Volyns'kyy
Vladivostok 115 G5 Primorskiy Kray,
  SE Russian Federation
Vlagtwedde 86 E2 Groningen,
  NE Netherlands
Vlasotince 101 E5 Serbia, SE Serbia
Vlieland 86 C1 Fris. Flylân. island
  Waddeneilanden, N Netherlands
Vlijmen 86 C4 Noord-Brabant,
  S Netherlands
Vlissingen 87 B5 Eng. Flushing, Fr.
  Flessingue. Zeeland, SW Netherlands
Vlodava see Włodawa
Vloně/Vlora see Vlorë
Vlorë 101 C7 prev. Vlonë, It. Valona,
  Vlora. Vlorë, SW Albania
Vlotslavsk see Włocławek
Vöcklabruck 95 D6 Oberösterreich,
  NW Austria
Vogelkop see Doberai, Jazirah
Vohimena, Tanjona 79 F4 Fr. Cap
  Sainte Marie. headland
  S Madagascar
Voiron 91 D5 Isère, E France
Vojvodina 100 D3 Ger. Wojwodina.
  Vojvodina, N Serbia
Volga 111 B7 river NW Russian
  Federation
Volga Uplands 81 G3 var. Volga
  Uplands. mountain range
  W Russian Federation
Volga Uplands see Privolzhskaya
  Vozvyshennost'
Volgodonsk 111 B7 Rostovskaya Oblast',
  SW Russian Federation
Volgograd 111 B7 prev. Stalingrad,
  Tsaritsyn. Volgogradskaya Oblast',
  SW Russian Federation
Volkhov 110 B4 Leningradskaya Oblast',
  NW Russian Federation
Volkovysk see Vawkavysk
Volmari see Valmiera
Volnovakha 109 G3 Donets'ka Oblast',
  SE Ukraine
Volodymyr-Volyns'kyy 108 C1 Pol.
  Włodzimierz, Rus. Vladimir-Volynskiy.
  Volyns'ka Oblast', NW Ukraine
Vologda 110 B4 Vologodskaya Oblast',
  W Russian Federation
Vólos 105 B5 Thessalía, C Greece
Volozhin see Valozhyn
Vol'sk 111 C6 Saratovskaya Oblast',
  W Russian Federation
Volta 75 E5 river SE Ghana
Volta Blanche see White Volta
Volta, Lake 75 E5 reservoir SE Ghana
Volta Noire see Black Volta
Volturno 97 D5 river S Italy
Volunteer Island see Starbuck Island
Volzhskiy 111 B6 Volgogradskaya
  Oblast', SW Russian Federation
Võnnu 106 E3 Ger. Wendau. Tartumaa,
  SE Estonia
Voorst 86 D3 Gelderland, E Netherlands

Voranava 107 C5 Pol. Werenów, Rus.
  Voronovo. Hrodzyenskaya Voblasts',
  W Belarus
Vorderrhein 95 B7 river SE Switzerland
Vóreioi Sporádes see Vóreies Sporádes
Vórioi Sporádhes see Vóreies Sporádes
Vorkuta 114 C2 Respublika Komi,
  NW Russian Federation
Vormsi 106 C2 var. Vormsi Saar,
  Ger. Worms, Swed. Ormsö. island
  W Estonia
Vormsi Saar see Vormsi
Voronezh 111 B6 Voronezhskaya
  Oblast', W Russian Federation
Voronovo see Voranava
Voroshilov see Ussuriysk
Voroshilovgrad see Luhans'k, Ukraine
Voroshilovsk see Stavropol', Russian
  Federation
Võru 106 D3 Ger. Werro. Võrumaa,
  SE Estonia
Vosges 90 E4 mountain range
  NE France
Vostochnyy Sayan 115 E4 Eng. Eastern
  Sayans, Mong. Dzüün Soyoni Nuruu.
  mountain range Mongolia/Russian
  Federation
Vostock Island see Vostok Island
Vostok 154 C3 Russian research station
  Antarctica
Vostok Island 145 G3 var. Vostock
  Island; prev. Stavers Island. island Line
  Islands, SE Kiribati
Voznesens'k 109 E3 Rus. Voznesensk.
  Mykolayivs'ka Oblast', S Ukraine
Vranje 101 E5 Serbia, SE Serbia
Vranov see Vranov nad Topľou
Vranov nad Topľou 99 D5 var. Vranov,
  Hung. Varannó. Prešovský Kraj,
  E Slovakia
Vratsa 104 C2 Vratsa, NW Bulgaria
Vrbas 100 D3 Vojvodina, NW Serbia
Vrbas 100 C3 river N Bosnia and
  Herzegovina
Vršac 100 E3 Ger. Werschetz, Hung.
  Versecz. Vojvodina, NE Serbia
Vsetín 99 C5 Ger. Wsetin. Zlínský Kraj,
  E Czech Republic
Vučitrn see Vushtrri
Vukovar 100 C3 Hung. Vukovár.
  Vukovar-Srijem, E Croatia
Vulcano, Isola 97 C7 island Isole
  Eolie, S Italy
Vung Tau 137 E6 prev. Fr. Cape Saint
  Jacques, Cap Saint-Jacques. Ba Ria-
  Vung Tau, S Vietnam
Vusan see Busan
Vushtrri 101 D5 Serb. Vučitrn.
  N Kosovo
Vyatka 111 C5 river NW Russian
  Federation
Vyatka see Kirov
Vyborg 110 B3 Fin. Viipuri.
  Leningradskaya Oblast', NW Russian
  Federation
Vyerkhnyadzvinsk 107 D5 Rus.
  Verkhnedvinsk. Vitsyebskaya
  Voblasts', N Belarus
Vyetryna 107 D5 Rus. Vetrino.
  Vitsyebskaya Voblasts', N Belarus
Vynohradiv 108 B3 Cz. Sevluš, Hung.
  Nagyszöllős, Rus. Vinogradov; prev.
  Sevlyush. Zakarpats'ka Oblast',
  W Ukraine

W

Wa 75 E4 NW Ghana
Waag see Váh
Waagbistritz see Považská Bystrica
Waal 86 C4 river S Netherlands
Wabash 40 C4 Indiana, N USA
Wabash River 40 B5 river N USA
Waco 49 G3 Texas, SW USA
Wad Al-Hajarah see Guadalajara
Waddān 71 F3 NW Libya
Waddenzee 86 C1 var. Wadden Zee.
  sea SE North Sea
Wadden Zee see Waddenzee
Waddington, Mount 36 D5 mountain
  British Columbia, SW Canada
Wadi as Sir 119 B6 var. Wadi es Sir.
  'Ammân, NW Jordan

Wadi es Sir see Wādī as Sīr
Wadi Halfa 72 B3 var. Wādī Ḥalfā'.
  Northern, N Sudan
Wādī Mūsā 119 B7 var. Petra. Ma'ān,
  S Jordan
Wad Madani see Wad Medani
Wad Medani 72 C4 var. Wad Madanī.
  Gezira, C Sudan
Waflia 139 F4 Pulau Buru, E Indonesia
Wagadugu see Ouagadougou
Wagga Wagga 149 C7 New South Wales,
  SE Australia
Wagin 147 B7 Western Australia
Wāh 134 C1 Punjab, NE Pakistan
Wahai 139 F4 Pulau Seram,
  E Indonesia
Wahaybah, Ramlat Al see Wahībah,
  Ramlat Āl
Wahiawā 47 A8 var. Wahiawa. O'ahu,
  Hawaii, USA, C Pacific Ocean
Wahibah, Ramlat Ahl see Wahībah,
  Ramlat Āl
Wahībah, Ramlat Āl var. Ramlat Ahl
  Wahibah, Ramlat Al Wahaybah, Eng.
  Wahībah Sands. desert N Oman
Wahībah Sands see Wahībah, Ramlat Āl
Wahpeton 45 F2 North Dakota,
  N USA
Wahran see Oran
Waiau 151 A7 river South Island, New
  Zealand
Waigeo, Pulau 139 G4 island Maluku,
  E Indonesia
Waikaremoana, Lake 150 E4 lake
  North Island, New Zealand
Wailuku 47 B8 Maui, Hawaii, USA,
  C Pacific Ocean
Waimate 151 B6 Canterbury, South
  Island, New Zealand
Waiouru 150 D4 Manawatu-Wanganui,
  North Island, New Zealand
Waipara 151 C6 Canterbury, South
  Island, New Zealand
Waipawa 150 E4 Hawke's Bay, North
  Island, New Zealand
Waipukurau 150 D4 Hawke's Bay,
  North Island, New Zealand
Wairau 151 C5 river South Island, New
  Zealand
Wairoa 150 E4 Hawke's Bay, North
  Island, New Zealand
Wairoa 150 D2 river North Island, New
  Zealand
Waitaki 151 B6 river South Island, New
  Zealand
Waitara 150 D4 Taranaki, North Island,
  New Zealand
Waitzen see Vác
Waiuku 150 D3 Auckland, North Island,
  New Zealand
Wakasa-wan 131 C6 bay C Japan
Wakatipu, Lake 151 A7 lake South
  Island, New Zealand
Wakayama 131 C6 Wakayama, Honshū,
  SW Japan
Wake Island 152 C2 US unincorporated
  territory NW Pacific Ocean
Wake Island 142 D1 atoll NW Pacific
  Ocean
Wakkanai 130 C1 Hokkaidō, NE Japan
Walachei/Walachia see Wallachia
Wałbrzych 98 B4 Ger. Waldenburg,
  Waldenburg in Schlesien. Dolnośląskie,
  SW Poland
Walcourt 87 C7 Namur, S Belgium
Wałcz 98 B3 Ger. Deutsch Krone.
  Zachodnio-pomorskie, NW Poland
Waldenburg/Waldenburg in Schlesien
  see Wałbrzych
Waldia see Weldiya
Wales 36 C2 Alaska, USA
Wales 89 C6 Wel. Cymru. cultural region
  Wales, United Kingdom
Walgett 149 D5 New South Wales,
  SE Australia
Walk see Valga, Estonia
Walk see Valka, Latvia
Walker Lake 47 C5 lake Nevada,
  W USA
Wallachia 108 B5 var. Walachia, Ger.
  Walachei, Rom. Valachia. cultural
  region S Romania
Walla Walla 46 C2 Washington,
  NW USA

Wallenthal see Haṭeg
Wallis and Futuna 145 E4 Fr. Territoire
  de Wallis et Futuna. French overseas
  territory C Pacific Ocean
Wallis et Futuna, Territoire de see
  Wallis and Futuna
Walnut Ridge 42 B1 Arkansas,
  C USA
Waltenberg see Zalău
Walthamstow 89 B7 Waltham Forest,
  SE England, United Kingdom
Walvisbaai see Walvis Bay
Walvis Bay 78 A4 Afr. Walvisbaai.
  Erongo, NW Namibia
Walvis Ridge 69 B7 var. Walvish Ridge.
  undersea ridge E Atlantic Ocean
Wan see Anhui
Wanaka 151 B6 Otago, South Island,
  New Zealand
Wanaka, Lake 151 A6 lake South Island,
  New Zealand
Wanchuan see Zhangjiakou
Wandel Sea 83 E1 sea Arctic Ocean
Wandsworth 89 A8 Wandsworth,
  SE England, United Kingdom
Wanganui 150 D4 Manawatu-
  Wanganui, North Island,
  New Zealand
Wangaratta 149 C7 Victoria,
  SE Australia
Wankie see Hwange
Wanki, Río see Coco, Río
Wanlaweyn 73 D6 var. Wanle Weyn,
  It. Uanle Uen. Shabeellaha Hoose,
  SW Somalia
Wanle Weyn see Wanlaweyn
Wanxian see Wanzhou
Wanzhou 128 B5 var. Wanxian.
  Chongqing Shi, C China
Warangal 135 E5 Andhra Pradesh,
  C India
Warasdin see Varaždin
Warburg 94 B4 Nordrhein-Westfalen,
  W Germany
Ware 37 E4 British Columbia,
  W Canada
Waremme 87 C6 Liège, E Belgium
Waren 94 C3 Mecklenburg-
  Vorpommern, NE Germany
Wargla see Ouargla
Warkworth 150 D2 Auckland, North
  Island, New Zealand
Warnemünde 94 C2 Mecklenburg-
  Vorpommern, NE Germany
Warner 49 G1 Oklahoma, C USA
Warnes 61 G4 Santa Cruz, C Bolivia
Warrego River 149 C5 seasonal river
  New South Wales/Queensland,
  E Australia
Warren 40 D3 Michigan, N USA
Warren 40 D3 Ohio, N USA
Warren 41 E3 Pennsylvania,
  NE USA
Warri 75 F5 Delta, S Nigeria
Warrnambool 149 B7 Victoria,
  SE Australia
Warsaw/Warschau see Warszawa
Warszawa 98 D3 Eng. Warsaw,
  Ger. Warschau, Rus. Varshava.
  country capital (Poland) Mazowieckie,
  C Poland
Warta 98 B3 Ger. Warthe. river
  W Poland
Wartberg see Senec
Warthe see Warta
Warwick 149 E5 Queensland,
  E Australia
Washington 44 A2 NE England, United
  Kingdom
Washington DC 41 E4 country capital
  (USA) District of Columbia, NE USA
Washington Island see Teraina
Washington, Mount 41 G2 mountain
  New Hampshire, NE USA
Wash, The 89 E6 inlet E England, United
  Kingdom
Wasiliszki see Vasilishki
Waspam 53 E2 var. Waspán. Región
  Autónoma Atlántico Norte,
  NE Nicaragua
Waspán see Waspam
Watampone 139 E4 var. Bone. Sulawesi,
  C Indonesia

Watenstedt-Salzgitter *see* Salzgitter
Waterbury *41 F3* Connecticut, NE USA
Waterford *89 B6* *Ir.* Port Láirge. Waterford, S Ireland
Waterloo *45 G3* Iowa, C USA
Watertown *41 F2* New York, NE USA
Watertown *45 F2* South Dakota, N USA
Waterville *41 G2* Maine, NE USA
Watford *89 A7* E England, United Kingdom
Watlings Island *see* San Salvador
Watsa *77 E5* Orientale, NE Dem. Rep. Congo
Watts Bar Lake *42 D1* *reservoir* Tennessee, S USA
Wau *73 B5* *var.* Wāw. Western Bahr el Ghazal, W South Sudan
Waukegan *40 B3* Illinois, N USA
Waukesha *40 B3* Wisconsin, N USA
Wausau *40 B2* Wisconsin, N USA
Waverly *45 G3* Iowa, C USA
Wavre *87 C6* Walloon Brabant, C Belgium
Wāw *see* Wau
Wawa *38 C4* Ontario, S Canada
Waycross *43 E3* Georgia, SE USA
Wearmouth *see* Sunderland
Webfoot State *see* Oregon
Webster City *45 F3* Iowa, C USA
Weddell Plain *154 A2* *abyssal plain* SW Atlantic Ocean
Weddell Sea *154 A2* *sea* SW Atlantic Ocean
Weener *94 A3* Niedersachsen, NW Germany
Weert *87 D5* Limburg, SE Netherlands
Weesp *86 C3* Noord-Holland, C Netherlands
Węgorzewo *98 D2* *Ger.* Angerburg. Warmińsko-Mazurskie, NE Poland
Weichsel *see* Wisła
Weimar *94 C4* Thüringen, C Germany
Weissenburg *see* Alba Iulia, Romania
Weissenburg in Bayern *95 C6* Bayern, SE Germany
Weissenstein *see* Paide
Weisskirchen *see* Bela Crkva
Weiswampach *87 D7* Diekirch, N Luxembourg
Wejherowo *98 C2* Pomorskie, NW Poland
Welchman Hall *55 G1* C Barbados
Weldiya *72 C4* *var.* Waldia, *It.* Valdia. Āmara, N Ethiopia
Welkom *78 D4* Free State, C South Africa
Welle *see* Uele
Wellesley Islands *148 B2* *island group* Queensland, N Australia
Wellington *151 D5* *country capital* (New Zealand) Wellington, North Island, New Zealand
Wellington *45 F5* Kansas, C USA
Wellington *see* Wellington, Isla
Wellington, Isla *65 A7* *var.* Wellington. *island* S Chile
Wells *46 D4* Nevada, W USA
Wellsford *150 D2* Auckland, North Island, New Zealand
Wells, Lake *147 C5* *lake* Western Australia
Wels *95 D6* *anc.* Ovilava. Oberösterreich, N Austria
Wembley *89 A8* Alberta, W Canada
Wemmel *87 B6* Vlaams Brabant, C Belgium
Wenatchee *46 B2* Washington, NW USA
Wenchi *75 E4* W Ghana
Wen-chou/Wenchow *see* Wenzhou
Wendau *see* Võnnu
Wenden *see* Cēsis
Wenzhou *128 D5* *var.* Wen-chou, Wenchow. Zhejiang, SE China
Werda *78 C4* Kgalagadi, S Botswana
Werder *see* Virtsu
Werenów *see* Voranava
Werkendam *86 C4* Noord-Brabant, S Netherlands
Werowitz *see* Virovitica
Werro *see* Võru

Werschetz *see* Vršac
Wesenberg *see* Rakvere
Weser *94 B3* *river* NW Germany
Wessel Islands *148 B1* *island group* Northern Territory, N Australia
West Antarctica *154 A3* *prev.* Lesser Antarctica. *physical region* Antarctica
West Australian Basin *see* Wharton Basin
West Bank *119 A6* *disputed region* SW Asia
West Bend *40 B3* Wisconsin, N USA
West Bengal *135 F4* *cultural region* NE India
West Cape *151 A7* *headland* South Island, New Zealand
West Des Moines *45 F3* Iowa, C USA
Westerland *94 B2* Schleswig-Holstein, N Germany
Western Australia *146 B4* *state* W Australia
Western Bug *see* Bug
Western Carpathians *99 E7* *mountain range* W Romania Europe
Western Desert *72 B2* *var.* Sahara el Gharbīya, *Eng.* Western Desert. *desert* C Egypt
Western Desert *see* Ṣaḥrā' al Gharbīyah
Western Dvina *85 E7* *Bel.* Dzvina, *Ger.* Düna, *Latv.* Daugava, *Rus.* Zapadnaya Dvina. *river* W Europe
Western Ghats *134 C5* *mountain range* SW India
Western Isles *see* Outer Hebrides
Western Punjab *see* Punjab
Western Sahara *70 B3* *disputed territory* N Africa
Western Samoa *see* Samoa
Western Sayans *114 D4* *Eng.* Western Sayans. *mountain range* S Russian Federation
Western Sayans *see* Zapadnyy Sayan
Western Scheldt *87 B5* *Eng.* Western Scheldt; *prev.* Honte. *inlet* S North Sea
Western Scheldt *see* Westerschelde
Western Sierra Madre *see* Madre Occidental, Sierra
West Falkland *65 C7* *var.* Gran Malvina, Isla Gran Malvina. *island* W Falkland Islands
West Fargo *45 F2* North Dakota, N USA
West Frisian Islands *86 C1* *Eng.* West Frisian Islands. *island group* N Netherlands
West Frisian Islands *see* Waddeneilanden
West Irian *see* Papua
Westliche Morava *see* Zapadna Morava
West Mariana Basin *142 B1* *var.* Perece Vela Basin. *undersea feature* W Pacific Ocean
West Memphis *42 B1* Arkansas, C USA
West New Guinea *see* Papua
Weston-super-Mare *89 D7* SW England, United Kingdom
West Palm Beach *43 F4* Florida, SE USA
West Papua *see* Papua
Westport *151 C5* West Coast, South Island, New Zealand
West Punjab *see* Punjab
West River *see* Xi Jiang
West Siberian Plain *114 C3* *Eng.* West Siberian Plain. *plain* C Russian Federation
West Siberian Plain *see* Zapadno-Sibirskaya Ravnina
West Virginia *40 D4* *off.* State of West Virginia, *also known as* Mountain State. *state* NE USA
Wetar, Pulau *139 F5* *island* Kepulauan Damar, E Indonesia
Wetzlar *95 B5* Hessen, W Germany
Wevok *36 C2* *var.* Wewuk. Alaska, USA
Wewuk *see* Wevok
Wexford *89 B6* *Ir.* Loch Garman. SE Ireland
Weyburn *37 F5* Saskatchewan, S Canada
Weymouth *89 D7* S England, United Kingdom

Wezep *86 D3* Gelderland, E Netherlands
Whakatane *150 E3* Bay of Plenty, North Island, New Zealand
Whale Cove *37 G3* *var.* Tikirarjuaq. Nunavut, C Canada
Whangarei *150 D2* Northland, North Island, New Zealand
Wharton Basin *141 D5* *var.* West Australian Basin. *undersea feature* E Indian Ocean
Whataroa *151 B6* West Coast, South Island, New Zealand
Wheatland *44 D3* Wyoming, C USA
Wheeler Peak *48 D1* *mountain* New Mexico, SW USA
Wheeling *40 D4* West Virginia, NE USA
Whitby *89 D5* N England, United Kingdom
Whitefish *44 B1* Montana, NW USA
Whitehaven *89 C5* NW England, United Kingdom
Whitehorse *36 D4* *territory capital* Yukon Territory, W Canada
White Nile *72 B4* *Ar.* Al Baḥr al Abyaḍ, An Nīl al Abyaḍ, *Bahr el Jebel.* *river* NE South Sudan
White Nile *72 B4* *var.* Bahr el Jebel. *river* S Sudan
White River *44 D3* *river* South Dakota, N USA
White Sea *110 C3* *Eng.* White Sea. *sea* NW Russian Federation
White Sea *see* Beloye More
White Volta *75 E4* *var.* Nakambé, *Fr.* Volta Blanche. *river* Burkina Faso/Ghana
Whitianga *150 D2* Waikato, North Island, New Zealand
Whitney, Mount *47 C6* *mountain* California, W USA
Whitsunday Group *148 D3* *island group* Queensland, E Australia
Whyalla *149 B6* South Australia
Wichita *45 F5* Kansas, C USA
Wichita Falls *49 F2* Texas, SW USA
Wichita River *49 F2* *river* Texas, SW USA
Wickenburg *48 B2* Arizona, SW USA
Wicklow *89 B6* *Ir.* Cill Mhantáin. *county* E Ireland
Wicklow Mountains *89 B6* *Ir.* Sléibhte Chill Mhantáin. *mountain range* E Ireland
Wieliczka *99 D5* Małopolskie, S Poland
Wieluń *98 C4* Sieradz, C Poland
Wien *95 E6* *Eng.* Vienna, Hung. Bécs, *Slvk.* Videň, *Slvn.* Dunaj; *anc.* Vindobona. *country capital* (Austria) Wien, NE Austria
Wiener Neustadt *95 E6* Niederösterreich, E Austria
Wierden *86 E3* Overijssel, E Netherlands
Wiesbaden *95 B5* Hessen, W Germany
Wieselburg and Ungarisch-Altenburg/ Wieselburg-Ungarisch-Altenburg *see* Mosonmagyaróvár
Wiesenhof *see* Ostrołęka
Wight, Isle of *89 D7* *island* United Kingdom
Wigorna Ceaster *see* Worcester
Wijchen *86 D4* Gelderland, SE Netherlands
Wijk bij Duurstede *86 D4* Utrecht, C Netherlands
Wilcannia *149 C6* New South Wales, SE Australia
Wilejka *see* Vilyeyka
Wilhelm, Mount *144 B3* *mountain* C Papua New Guinea
Wilhelm-Pieck-Stadt *see* Guben
Wilhelmshaven *94 B3* Niedersachsen, NW Germany
Wilia/Wilja *see* Neris
Wilkes Barre *41 F3* Pennsylvania, NE USA
Wilkes Land *154 C4* *physical region* Antarctica
Wiłkomierz *see* Ukmergė
Willard *48 D2* New Mexico, SW USA

Willcox *48 C3* Arizona, SW USA
Willebroek *87 B5* Antwerpen, C Belgium
Willemstad *55 E5* *dependent territory capital* (Netherlands) Curaçao
Williston *44 D1* North Dakota, N USA
Wilmington *41 F4* Delaware, NE USA
Wilmington *43 F2* North Carolina, SE USA
Wilmington *40 C4* Ohio, N USA
Wilna/Wilno *see* Vilnius
Wilrijk *87 C5* Antwerpen, N Belgium
Winchester *89 D7* *hist.* Wintanceaster, *Lat.* Venta Belgarum. S England, United Kingdom
Winchester *41 E4* Virginia, NE USA
Windau *see* Ventspils, Latvia
Windau *see* Venta, Latvia/Lithuania
Windhoek *78 B3* *Ger.* Windhuk. *country capital* (Namibia) Khomas, C Namibia
Windhuk *see* Windhoek
Windorah *148 C4* Queensland, C Australia
Windsor *38 C5* Ontario, S Canada
Windsor *89 D7* S England, United Kingdom
Windsor *41 G3* Connecticut, NE USA
Windward Islands *55 H4* *island group* E West Indies
Windward Islands *see* Barlavento, Ilhas de, Cape Verde
Windward Passage *54 D3* *Sp.* Paso de los Vientos. *channel* Cuba/Haiti
Winisk *38 C2* *prev.* Winisk. Ontario, C Canada
Winisk *see* Winisk
Winkowitz *see* Vinkovci
Winnebago, Lake *40 B2* *lake* Wisconsin, N USA
Winnemucca *47 C5* Nevada, W USA
Winnipeg *37 G5* *province capital* Manitoba, S Canada
Winnipeg, Lake *37 G5* *lake* Manitoba, C Canada
Winnipegosis, Lake *38 A3* *lake* Manitoba, C Canada
Winona *45 G3* Minnesota, N USA
Winschoten *86 E2* Groningen, NE Netherlands
Winsen *94 B3* Niedersachsen, N Germany
Winston Salem *43 E1* North Carolina, SE USA
Winsum *86 D1* Groningen, NE Netherlands
Wintanceaster *see* Winchester
Winterswijk *86 E4* Gelderland, E Netherlands
Winterthur *95 B7* Zürich, NE Switzerland
Winton *148 C4* Queensland, E Australia
Winton *151 A7* Southland, South Island, New Zealand
Wisby *see* Visby
Wisconsin *40 A2* *off.* State of Wisconsin, *also known as* Badger State. *state* N USA
Wisconsin Rapids *40 B2* Wisconsin, N USA
Wisconsin River *40 B3* *river* Wisconsin, N USA
Wiślany, Zalew *see* Vistula Lagoon
Wismar *94 C2* Mecklenburg-Vorpommern, N Germany
Wittenberge *94 C3* Brandenburg, N Germany
Wittlich *95 A5* Rheinland-Pfalz, SW Germany
Wittstock *94 C3* Brandenburg, NE Germany
W. J. van Blommesteinmeer *59 G3* *reservoir* E Suriname
Władysławowo *98 C2* Pomorskie, N Poland
Włocławek *98 C3* *Ger./Rus.* Vlotslavsk. Kujawsko-pomorskie, C Poland
Włodawa *98 E4* *Rus.* Vlodava. Lubelskie, SE Poland
Włodzimierz *see* Volodymyr-Volyns'kyy

Wlotzkasbaken 78 B3 Erongo, W Namibia
Wodonga 149 C7 Victoria, SE Australia
Wodzisław Śląski 99 C5 *Ger.* Loslau. Śląskie, S Poland
Wojerecy *see* Hoyerswerda
Wójja *see* Wotje Atoll
Wojwodina *see* Vojvodina
Woking 89 D7 SE England, United Kingdom
Wolf, Isla 60 A4 *island* Galápagos, Galápagos Islands, W Ecuador South America
Wolfsberg 95 D7 Kärnten, SE Austria
Wolfsburg 94 C3 Niedersachsen, N Germany
Wolgast 94 D2 Mecklenburg-Vorpommern, NE Germany
Wołkowysk *see* Vawkavysk
Wöllan *see* Velenje
Wollaston Lake 37 F4 Saskatchewan, C Canada
Wollongong 149 D6 New South Wales, SE Australia
Wolmar *see* Valmiera
Wołożyn *see* Valozhyn
Wolvega 86 D2 *Fris.* Wolvegea. Fryslân, N Netherlands
Wolvegea *see* Wolvega
Wolverhampton 89 D6 C England, United Kingdom
Wolverine State *see* Michigan
Wŏnsan 129 E3 SE North Korea
Woodburn 46 B3 Oregon, NW USA
Woodland 47 B5 California, W USA
Woodruff 40 B2 Wisconsin, N USA
Woods, Lake of the 38 A3 *Fr.* Lac des Bois. *lake* Canada/USA
Woodville 150 D4 Manawatu-Wanganui, North Island, New Zealand
Woodward 49 F1 Oklahoma, C USA
Worcester 78 C5 Western Cape, SW South Africa
Worcester 89 D6 *hist.* Wigorna Ceaster. W England, United Kingdom
Worcester 41 G3 Massachusetts, NE USA
Workington 89 C5 NW England, United Kingdom
Worland 44 C3 Wyoming, C USA
Wormatia *see* Worms
Worms 95 B5 *anc.* Augusta Vangionum, Borbetomagus, Wormatia. Rheinland-Pfalz, SW Germany
Worms *see* Vormsi
Worthington 45 F3 Minnesota, N USA
Wotje Atoll 144 D1 *var.* Wōjjā. *atoll* Ratak Chain, E Marshall Islands
Woudrichem 86 C4 Noord-Brabant, S Netherlands
Wrangel Island 115 F1 *Eng.* Wrangel Island. *island* NE Russian Federation
Wrangel Island *see* Vrangelya, Ostrov
Wrangel Plain 155 B2 *undersea feature* Arctic Ocean
Wrocław 98 C4 *Eng./Ger.* Breslau. Dolnośląskie, SW Poland
Września 98 C3 Wielkopolskie, C Poland
Wsetín *see* Vsetín
Wuchang *see* Wuhan
Wuday'ah 121 C6 *spring/well* S Saudi Arabia
Wuhai 127 E3 *var.* Haibowan. Nei Mongol Zizhiqu, N China
Wuhan 128 C5 *var.* Han-kou, Han-k'ou, Hanyang, Wuchang, Wu-han; *prev.* Hankow. *province capital* Hubei, C China
Wu-han *see* Wuhan
Wuhsien *see* Suzhou
Wuhsi/Wu-hsi *see* Wuxi
Wuhu 128 D5 *var.* Wu-na-mu. Anhui, E China
Wujlān *see* Ujelang Atoll
Wukari 75 G4 Taraba, E Nigeria
Wuliang Shan 128 A6 *mountain range* SW China

Wu-lu-k'o-mu-shi/Wu-lu-mu-ch'i *see* Ürümqi
Wu-na-mu *see* Wuhu
Wuppertal 94 A4 *prev.* Barmen-Elberfeld. Nordrhein-Westfalen, W Germany
Würzburg 95 B5 Bayern, SW Germany
Wusih *see* Wuxi
Wuxi 128 D6 *var.* Wuhsi, Wu-hsi, Wusih. Jiangsu, E China
Wuyi Shan 125 E3 *mountain range* SE China
Wye 89 C6 *Wel.* Gwy. *river* England/Wales, United Kingdom
Wyłkowyszki *see* Vilkaviškis
Wyndham 146 D3 Western Australia
Wyoming 40 C3 Michigan, N USA
Wyoming 44 B3 *off.* State of Wyoming, *also known as* Equality State. *state* C USA
Wyszków 98 D3 *Ger.* Probstberg. Mazowieckie, NE Poland

X

Xaafuun, Raas 72 E4 *var.* Ras Hafun. *cape* NE Somalia
Xaçmaz 117 H2 *Rus.* Khachmas. N Azerbaijan
Xaignabouli 136 C4 *prev.* Muang Xaignabouri, *Fr.* Sayaboury. Xaignabouli, N Laos
Xai-Xai 79 E4 *prev.* João Belo, Vila de João Belo. Gaza, S Mozambique
Xalapa 51 F4 Veracruz-Llave, Mexico
Xam Nua 136 D3 *var.* Sam Neua. Houaphan, N Laos
Xankändi 117 G3 *Rus.* Khankendi; *prev.* Stepanakert. SW Azerbaijan
Xánthi 104 C3 Anatolikí Makedonía kai Thráki, NE Greece
Xàtiva 93 F3 *Cas.* Xátiva; *anc.* Setabis, *var.* Jativa. Valenciana, E Spain
Xauen *see* Chefchaouen
Xäzär Dänizi *see* Caspian Sea
Xeres *see* Jerez de la Frontera
Xiaguan *see* Dali
Xiamen 128 D6 *var.* Hsia-men; *prev.* Amoy. Fujian, SE China
Xi'an 128 C4 *var.* Changan, Sian, Signan, Siking, Singan, Xian. *province capital* Shaanxi, C China
Xiang *see* Hunan
Xianggang *see* Hong Kong
Xiangkhoang *see* Phônsavan
Xiangtan 128 C5 *var.* Hsiang-t'an, Siangtan. Hunan, S China
Xiao Hinggan Ling 128 D2 *Eng.* Lesser Khingan Range. *mountain range* NE China
Xichang 128 B5 Sichuan, C China
Xieng Khouang *see* Phônsaven
Xieng Ngeun *see* Muang Xiang Ngeun
Xigazê 126 C5 *var.* Jih-k'a-tse, Shigatse, Xigaze. Xizang Zizhiqu, W China
Xi Jiang 124 D3 *var.* Hsi Chiang, *Eng.* West River. *river* S China
Xilinhot 127 F2 *var.* Silinhot. Nei Mongol Zizhiqu, N China
Xilokastro *see* Xylókastro
Xin *see* Xinjiang Uygur Zizhiqu
Xingkai Hu *see* Khanka, Lake
Xingu, Rio 63 E2 *river* C Brazil
Xingxingxia 126 D3 Xinjiang Uygur Zizhiqu, NW China
Xining 127 E4 *var.* Hsining, Hsi-ning, Sining. *province capital* Qinghai, C China
Xinjiang *see* Xinjiang Uygur Zizhiqu
Xinjiang Uygur Zizhiqu 126 B3 *var.* Sinkiang, Sinkiang Uighur Autonomous Region, Xin, Xinjiang. *autonomous region* NW China
Xinpu *see* Lianyungang
Xinxiang 128 C4 Henan, C China
Xinyang 128 C5 *var.* Hsin-yang, Sinyang. Henan, C China
Xinzo de Limia 92 C2 Galicia, NW Spain
Xiqing Shan 124 D2 *mountain range* C China
Xiva 122 D2 *Rus.* Khiva, Khiwa. Xorazm Viloyati, W Uzbekistan

Xixón *see* Gijón
Xizang *see* Xizang Zizhiqu
Xizang Gaoyuan *see* Qingzang Gaoyuan
Xizang Zizhiqu 126 B4 *var.* Thibet, Tibetan Autonomous Region, Xizang, *Eng.* Tibet. *autonomous region* W China
Xolotlán *see* Managua, Lago de
Xucheng *see* Xuwen
Xuddur 73 D5 *var.* Hudur, *It.* Oddur. Bakool, SW Somalia
Xuwen 128 C7 *var.* Xucheng. Guangdong, S China
Xuzhou 128 D4 *var.* Hsu-chou, Suchow, Tongshan; *prev.* T'ung-shan. Jiangsu, E China
Xylókastro 105 B5 *var.* Xilokastro. Pelopónnisos, S Greece

Y

Ya'an 128 B5 *var.* Yaan. Sichuan, C China
Yabēlo 73 C5 Oromīya, C Ethiopia
Yablis 53 E2 Región Autónoma Atlántico Norte, NE Nicaragua
Yablonovyy Khrebet 115 F4 *mountain range* S Russian Federation
Yabrai Shan 127 E3 *mountain range* NE China
Yafran 71 F2 NW Libya
Yaghan Basin 67 B7 *undersea feature* SE Pacific Ocean
Yagotin *see* Yahotyn
Yahotyn 109 E2 *Rus.* Yagotin. Kyyivs'ka Oblast', N Ukraine
Yahualica 50 D4 Jalisco, SW Mexico
Yakima 46 B2 Washington, NW USA
Yakima River 46 B2 *river* Washington, NW USA
Yakoruda 104 C3 Blagoevgrad, SW Bulgaria
Yaku-shima 131 B8 *island* Nansei-shotō, SW Japan
Yakutat 36 D4 Alaska, USA
Yakutsk 115 F3 Respublika Sakha (Yakutiya), NE Russian Federation
Yala 137 C7 Yala, SW Thailand
Yalizava 107 D6 *Rus.* Yelizovo. Mahilyowskaya Voblasts', E Belarus
Yalong Jiang 128 A5 *river* C China
Yalova 116 B3 Yalova, NW Turkey
Yalpug, Ozero *see* Yalpuh, Ozero
Yalpuh, Ozero 108 D4 *Rus.* Ozero Yalpug. *lake* SW Ukraine
Yalta 109 F5 Avtonomna Respublika Krym, S Ukraine
Yalu 125 E2 *Chin.* Yalu Jiang, *Jap.* Oryokko, *Kor.* Amnok-kang. *river* China/North Korea
Yalu Jiang *see* Yalu
Yamaguchi 131 B7 *var.* Yamaguti. Yamaguchi, Honshū, SW Japan
Yamal, Poluostrov 114 D2 *peninsula* N Russian Federation
Yamaniyah, Al Jumhūrīyah al *see* Yemen
Yambio 73 B5 *var.* Yambiyo. Western Equatoria, S South Sudan
Yambiyo *see* Yambio
Yambol 104 D2 *Turk.* Yanboli. Yambol, E Bulgaria
Yamdena, Pulau 139 G5 *prev.* Jamdena. *island* Kepulauan Tanimbar, E Indonesia
Yamoussoukro 74 D5 *country capital* (Côte d'Ivoire) C Côte d'Ivoire
Yamuna 134 D3 *prev.* Jumna. *river* N India
Yana 115 F2 *river* NE Russian Federation
Yanboli *see* Yambol
Yanbu' al Baḥr 121 A5 Al Madīnah, W Saudi Arabia
Yangambi 77 D5 Orientale, N Dem. Rep. Congo
Yangchow *see* Yangzhou
Yangiyo'l 123 E2 *Rus.* Yangiyul'. Toshkent Viloyati, E Uzbekistan
Yangiyul' *see* Yangiyo'l
Yangku *see* Taiyuan
Yangon 136 B4 *Eng.* Rangoon. Yangon, S Myanmar (Burma)

Yangtze 128 B5 *var.* Yangtze Kiang, *Eng.* Yangtze. *river* C China
Yangtze *see* Chang Jiang/Jinsha Jiang
Yangtze *see* Chang Jiang
Yangtze Kiang *see* Chang Jiang
Yangzhou 128 D5 *var.* Yangchow. Jiangsu, E China
Yankton 45 E3 South Dakota, N USA
Yannina *see* Ioánnina
Yanskiy Zaliv 113 F2 *bay* N Russian Federation
Yantai 128 D4 *var.* Yan-t'ai; *prev.* Chefoo, Chih-fu. Shandong, E China
Yaoundé 77 B5 *var.* Yaunde. *country capital* (Cameroon) Centre, S Cameroon
Yap 144 A1 *island* Caroline Islands, W Micronesia
Yapanskoye More East Sea/Japan, Sea of
Yapen, Pulau 139 G4 *prev.* Japen. *island* E Indonesia
Yap Trench 142 B2 *var.* Yap Trough. *undersea feature* SE Philippine Sea
Yapurá *see* Caquetá, Río, Brazil/Colombia
Yapurá *see* Japurá, Rio, Brazil/Colombia
Yaqui, Río 50 C2 *river* NW Mexico
Yaransk 111 C5 Kirovskaya Oblast', NW Russian Federation
Yarega 110 D4 Respublika Komi, NW Russian Federation
Yarkant *see* Shache
Yarlung Zangbo Jiang *see* Brahmaputra
Yarmouth 39 F5 Nova Scotia, SE Canada
Yarmouth *see* Great Yarmouth
Yaroslav *see* Jarosław
Yaroslavl' 110 B4 Yaroslavskaya Oblast', W Russian Federation
Yarumal 58 B2 Antioquia, NW Colombia
Yasyel'da 107 B7 *river* Brestskaya Voblasts', SW Belarus Europe
Yatsushiro 131 A7 *var.* Yatusiro. Kumamoto, Kyūshū, SW Japan
Yatusiro *see* Yatsushiro
Yaunde *see* Yaoundé
Yavari *see* Javari, Rio
Rio Yavari 62 C2 *var.* Yavarí. *river* Brazil/Peru
Yaviza 53 H5 Darién, SE Panama
Yavoriv 108 B2 Pol. Jaworów, *Rus.* Yavorov. L'vivs'ka Oblast', NW Ukraine
Yavorov *see* Yavoriv
Yazd 120 D3 *var.* Yezd. Yazd, C Iran
Yazoo City 42 B2 Mississippi, S USA
Yding Skovhøj 85 A7 *hill* C Denmark
Ýdra 105 C6 *var.* Ídhra. *island* Ýdra, S Greece
Ye 136 B5 Mon State, S Myanmar (Burma)
Yecheng 126 A3 *var.* Kargilik. Xinjiang Uygur Zizhiqu, NW China
Yefremov 111 B5 Tul'skaya Oblast', W Russian Federation
Yekaterinburg 114 C3 *prev.* Sverdlovsk. Sverdlovskaya Oblast', C Russian Federation
Yekaterinodar *see* Krasnodar
Yekaterinoslav *see* Dnipropetrovs'k
Yelets 111 B5 Lipetskaya Oblast', W Russian Federation
Yelisavetpol *see* Gäncä
Yelizavetgrad *see* Kirovohrad
Yelizovo *see* Yalizava
Yell 88 D1 *island* NE Scotland, United Kingdom
Yellowhammer State *see* Alabama
Yellowknife 37 E4 *territory capital* Northwest Territories, W Canada
Yellow River 128 C4 *var.* Yellow River. *river* C China
Yellow River *see* Huang He
Yellow Sea 128 D4 *Chin.* Huang Hai, *Kor.* Hwang-Hae. *sea* E Asia

Yellowstone River *44 C2 river* Montana/ Wyoming, NW USA
Yel'sk *107 C7* Homyel'skaya Voblasts', SE Belarus
Yelwa *75 F4* Kebbi, W Nigeria
Yemen *121 C7 off.* Republic of Yemen, *Ar.* Al Jumhuriyah al Yamaniyah, Al Yaman. *country* SW Asia

YEMEN
Southwest Asia

Official name Republic of Yemen
Formation 1990 / 1990
Capital Sana
Population 24.8 million / 114 people per sq mile (44 people per sq km)
Total area 203,849 sq. miles (527,970 sq. km)
Languages Arabic*
Religions Sunni Muslim 55%, Shi'a Muslim 42%, Christian, Hindu, and Jewish 3%
Ethnic mix Arab 99%, Afro-Arab, Indian, Somali, and European 1%
Government Transitional regime
Currency Yemeni rial = 100 fils
Literacy rate 62%
Calorie consumption 2109 kilocalories

Yemen, Republic of *see* Yemen
Yemva *110 D4 prev.* Zheleznodorozhnyy. Respublika Komi, NW Russian Federation
Yenakiyeve *109 G3 Rus.* Yenakiyevo; *prev.* Ordzhonikidze, Rykovo. Donets'ka Oblast', E Ukraine
Yenakiyevo *see* Yenakiyeve
Yenangyaung *136 A3* Magway, W Myanmar (Burma)
Yendi *75 E4* NE Ghana
Yengisar *126 A3* Xinjiang Uygur Zizhiqu, NW China
Yenierenköy *102 D4 var.* Yialousa, *Gk.* Agialoúsa. NE Cyprus
Yenipazar *see* Novi Pazar
Yenisey *114 D3 river* Mongolia/Russian Federation
Yenping *see* Nanping
Yeovil *89 D7* SW England, United Kingdom
Yeppoon *148 D4* Queensland, E Australia
Yerevan *117 F3 Eng.* Erivan. *country capital* (Armenia) C Armenia
Yeriho *see* Jericho
Yertis *114 C4 var.* Irtish, *Kaz.* Ertis; *prev.* Irtysh. *river* C Asia
Yerushalayim *see* Jerusalem
Yesil' *114 C4 Kaz.* Esil. *river* Kazakhstan/Russian Federation
Yeso *see* Hokkaidō
Yeu, Île d' *90 A4 island* NW France
Yevlakh *see* Yevlax
Yevlax *117 G2 Rus.* Yevlakh. C Azerbaijan
Yevpatoriya *109 F5* Avtonomna Respublika Krym, S Ukraine
Yeya *109 H4 river* SW Russian Federation
Yezerishche *see* Yezyaryshcha
Yezo *see* Hokkaidō
Yezyaryshcha *107 E5 Rus.* Yezerishche. Vitsyebskaya Voblasts', NE Belarus
Yialousa *see* Yenierenköy
Yiannitsá *see* Giannitsá
Yichang *128 C5* Hubei, C China
Yıldızeli *116 D3* Sivas, N Turkey
Yinchuan *128 B4 var.* Yinch'uan, Yin-ch'uan, Yinchwan. *province capital* Ningxia, N China
Yinchwan *see* Yinchuan
Yindu He *see* Indus
Yin-hsien *see* Ningbo
Yining *126 B2 var.* I-ning, *Uigh.* Gulja, Kuldja. Xinjiang Uygur Zizhiqu, NW China
Yin-tu Ho *see* Indus
Yisrael/Yisra'el *see* Israel
Yíthion *see* Gýtheio
Yogyakarta *138 C5 prev.* Djokjakarta, Jogjakarta, Jokyakarta. Jawa, C Indonesia

Yokohama *131 D5* Aomori, Honshū, C Japan
Yokohama *130 A2* Kanagawa, Honshū, S Japan
Yokote *130 D4* Akita, Honshū, C Japan
Yola *75 H4* Adamawa, E Nigeria
Yonago *131 B6* Tottori, Honshū, SW Japan
Yong'an *128 D6 var.* Yongan. Fujian, SE China
Yongzhou *see* Lingling
Yonkers *41 F3* New York, NE USA
Yonne *90 C4 river* C France
Yopal *58 C3 var.* El Yopal. Casanare, C Colombia
York *89 D5 anc.* Eboracum, Eburacum. N England, United Kingdom
York *45 E4* Nebraska, C USA
York, Cape *144 C1 headland* Queensland, NE Australia
York, Kap *see* Innaanganeq
Yorkton *37 F5* Saskatchewan, S Canada
Yoro *52 C2* Yoro, C Honduras
Yoshkar-Ola *111 C5* Respublika Mariy El, W Russian Federation
Yösönbulag *see* Altay
Youngstown *40 D4* Ohio, N USA
Youth, Isle of *54 A2 var.* Isla de Pinos, *Eng.* Isle of Youth; *prev.* The Isle of the Pines. *island* W Cuba
Youth, Isle of *see* Juventud, Isla de la
Ypres *see* Ieper
Yreka *46 B4* California, W USA
Yrendagüé *see* General Eugenio A. Garay
Yssel *see* IJssel
Ysyk-Köl *see* Issyk-Kul', Ozero
Ysyk-Köl *see* Balykchy
Yu *see* Henan
Yuan *see* Red River
Yuan Jiang *see* Red River
Yuba City *47 B5* California, W USA
Yucatán, Canal de *see* Yucatan Channel
Yucatan Channel *51 H3 Sp.* Canal de Yucatán. *channel* Cuba/Mexico
Yucatan Peninsula *35 C7 Eng.* Yucatan Peninsula. *peninsula* Guatemala/ Mexico
Yucatan Peninsula *see* Yucatán, Península de
Yuci *see* Jinzhong
Yue *see* Guangdong
Yue Shan, Tai *see* Lantau Island
Yueyang *128 C5* Hunan, S China
Yugoslavia *see* Serbia
Yukhavichy *107 D5 Rus.* Yukhovichi. Vitsyebskaya Voblasts', N Belarus
Yukhovichi *see* Yukhavichy
Yukon River *36 C2 river* Canada/USA
Yukon, Territoire du *see* Yukon Territory
Yukon Territory *36 D3 var.* Yukon, *Fr.* Territoire du Yukon. *territory* NW Canada
Yulin *128 C6* Guangxi Zhuangzu Zizhiqu, S China
Yuma *48 A2* Arizona, SW USA
Yumendong *128 A3 prev.* Laojunmiao. Gansu, N China
Yun *see* Yunnan
Yungki *see* Jilin
Yung-ning *see* Nanning
Yunjinghong *see* Jinghong
Yunki *see* Jilin
Yunnan *128 A6 var.* Yun, Yunnan Sheng, Yünnan, Yun-nan. *province* SW China
Yunnan *see* Kunming
Yunnan Sheng *see* Yunnan
Yünnan/Yun-nan *see* Yunnan
Yurev *see* Tartu
Yurihonjō *see* Honjō
Yuruá, Río *see* Juruá, Rio
Yury'ev *see* Tartu
Yushu *126 D4 var.* Gyêgu. Qinghai, C China
Yuty *64 D3* Caazapá, S Paraguay

Yuzhno-Sakhalinsk *115 H4 Jap.* Toyohara; *prev.* Vladimirovka. Ostrov Sakhalin, Sakhalinskaya Oblast', SE Russian Federation
Yuzhnyy Bug *see* Pivdennyy Buh
Yuzhou *see* Chongqing
Yylanly *see* Gurbansoltan Eje

Z

Zaandam *see* Zaanstad
Zaanstad *86 C3 prev.* Zaandam. Noord-Holland, C Netherlands
Zabaykal'sk *115 F5* Zabaykal'skiy Kray, S Russian Federation
Zabern *see* Saverne
Zabid *121 B7* W Yemen
Żabinka *see* Zhabinka
Ząbkowice *see* Ząbkowice Śląskie
Ząbkowice Śląskie *98 B4 var.* Ząbkowice, *Ger.* Frankenstein, Frankenstein in Schlesien. Dolnośląskie, SW Poland
Zábřeh *99 C5 Ger.* Hohenstadt. Olomoucký Kraj, E Czech Republic
Zacapa *52 B2* Zacapa, E Guatemala
Zacatecas *50 D3* Zacatecas, C Mexico
Zacatepec *51 E4* Morelos, S Mexico
Zacháro *105 B6 var.* Zaharo, Zakháro. Dytikí Elláda, S Greece
Zadar *100 A3 It.* Zara; *anc.* Iader. Zadar, SW Croatia
Zadetkyi Kyun *137 B6 var.* St.Matthew's Island. *island* Mergui Archipelago, S Myanmar (Burma)
Zafra *92 C4* Extremadura, W Spain
Żagań *98 B4 var.* Zagań, Żegań, *Ger.* Sagan. Lubuskie, W Poland
Zagazig *see* Az Zaqāziq
Zágráb *see* Zagreb
Zagreb *100 B2 Ger.* Agram, *Hung.* Zágráb. *country capital* (Croatia) Zagreb, N Croatia
Zagros Mountains *120 C3 Eng.* Zagros Mountains. *mountain range* W Iran
Zagros Mountains *see* Zāgros, Kūhhā-ye
Zaharo *see* Zacháro
Zāhedān *120 E4 var.* Zahidan; *prev.* Duzdab. Sīstān va Balūchestān, SE Iran
Zahidan *see* Zāhedān
Zaḥlah *see* Zahlé
Zahlé *118 B4 var.* Zaḥlah. C Lebanon
Záhony *99 E6* Szabolcs-Szatmár-Bereg, NE Hungary
Zaire *see* Congo (river)
Zaire *see* Congo (Democratic Republic of)
Zaječar *100 E4* Serbia, E Serbia
Zakataly *see* Zaqatala
Zakháro *see* Zacháro
Zakhidnyy Buh/Zakhodni Buh *see* Bug
Zākhō *120 B2 var.* Zākhū. Dahūk, N Iraq
Zākhū *see* Zākhō
Zakopane *99 D5* Małopolskie, S Poland
Zákynthos *105 A6 var.* Zákinthos, *It.* Zante. *island* Iónia Nísoi, Greece, C Mediterranean Sea
Zalaegerszeg *99 B7* Zala, W Hungary
Zalău *108 B3 Ger.* Waltenberg, *Hung.* Zilah; *prev. Ger.* Zillenmarkt. Sălaj, NW Romania
Ẕalim *121 B5* Makkah, W Saudi Arabia
Zambezi *78 D2 var.* Zambesi, Port. Zambeze. *river* S Africa
Zambia *78 C2 off.* Republic of Zambia; *prev.* Northern Rhodesia. *country* S Africa

ZAMBIA
Southern Africa

Official name Republic of Zambia
Formation 1964 / 1964
Capital Lusaka
Population 13.5 million / 47 people per sq mile (18 people per sq km)
Total area 290,584 sq. miles (752,614 sq. km)
Languages Bemba, Tonga, Nyanja, Lozi, Lala-Bisa, Nsenga, English*
Religions Christian 63%, Traditional

ZAMBIA
(continued)

beliefs 36%, Muslim and Hindu 1%
Ethnic mix Bemba 34%, Other African 26%, Tonga 16%, Nyanja 14%, Lozi 9%, European 1%
Government Presidential system
Currency Zambian kwacha = 100 ngwee
Literacy rate 71%
Calorie consumption 1879 kilocalories

Zambia, Republic of *see* Zambia
Zamboanga *139 E3 off.* Zamboanga City. Mindanao, S Philippines
Zamboanga City *see* Zamboanga
Zambrów *98 E3* Łomża, E Poland
Zamora *92 D2* Castilla y León, NW Spain
Zamora de Hidalgo *50 D4* Michoacán, SW Mexico
Zamość *98 E4 Rus.* Zamoste. Lubelskie, E Poland
Zamoste *see* Zamość
Zancle *see* Messina
Zanda *126 A4* Xizang Zizhiqu, W China
Zanesville *40 D4* Ohio, N USA
Zanjān *120 C2 var.* Zenjan, Zinjan. Zanjān, NW Iran
Zante *see* Zákynthos
Zanthus *147 C6* Western Australia, S Australia Oceania
Zanzibar *73 D7* Zanzibar, E Tanzania
Zanzibar *73 C7 Swa.* Unguja. *island* E Tanzania
Zaozhuang *128 D4* Shandong, E China
Zapadna Morava *100 D4 Ger.* Westliche Morava. *river* C Serbia
Zapadnaya Dvina *110 A4* Tverskaya Oblast', W Russian Federation
Zapadnaya Dvina *see* Western Dvina
Zapadnyy Bug *see* Bug
Zapala *65 B5* Neuquén, W Argentina
Zapiola Ridge *67 B6 undersea feature* SW Atlantic Ocean
Zapolyarnyy *110 C2* Murmanskaya Oblast', NW Russian Federation
Zaporizhzhya *109 F3 Rus.* Zaporozh'ye; *prev.* Aleksandrovsk. Zaporiz'ka Oblast', SE Ukraine
Zaporozh'ye *see* Zaporizhzhya
Zapotiltic *50 D4* Jalisco, SW Mexico
Zaqatala *117 G2 Rus.* Zakataly. NW Azerbaijan
Zara *116 D3* Sivas, C Turkey
Zara *see* Zadar
Zarafshan *see* Zarafshon
Zarafshon *122 D2 Rus.* Zarafshan. Navoiy Viloyati, N Uzbekistan
Zarafshon *see* Zeravshan
Zaragoza *93 F2 Eng.* Saragossa; *anc.* Caesaraugusta, Salduba. Aragón, NE Spain
Zarand *120 D3* Kermān, C Iran
Zaranj *122 D5* Nīmrōz, SW Afghanistan
Zarasai *106 C4* Utena, E Lithuania
Zárate *64 D4 prev.* General José F.Uriburu. Buenos Aires, E Argentina
Zarautz *93 E1 var.* Zarauz. País Vasco, N Spain
Zarauz *see* Zarautz
Zaraza *59 E2* Guárico, N Venezuela
Zarghūn Shahr *123 E4 var.* Katawaz. Paktīkā, SE Afghanistan
Zaria *75 G4* Kaduna, C Nigeria
Zarós *105 D8* Kríti, Greece, E Mediterranean Sea
Zarqa *see* Az Zarqā'
Zary *98 B4 Ger.* Sorau, Sorau in der Niederlausitz. Lubuskie, W Poland
Zaunguzskiye Garagumy *see* Üngüz Angyrsyndaky Garagum
Zavertse *see* Zawiercie
Zavet *104 D1* Razgrad, NE Bulgaria
Zavidovići *100 C3* Federacija Bosna I Hercegovina, N Bosnia and Herzegovina
Zawia *see* Az Zāwiyah
Zawiercie *98 D4 Rus.* Zavertse. Śląskie, S Poland
Zawilah *71 F3 var.* Zuwaylah, *It.* Zueila. C Libya
Zaysan Köl *see* Zaysan, Ozero

Zaysan, Ozero 114 D5 *Kaz.* Zaysan Köl. *lake* E Kazakhstan
Zayyq *see* Zhayyk
Zbarazh 108 C2 Ternopil's'ka Oblast', W Ukraine
Zduńska Wola 98 C4 Sieradz, C Poland
Zealand 85 B8 *Eng.* Zealand, *Ger.* Seeland. *island* E Denmark
Zealand *see* Sjælland
Zeebrugge 87 A5 West-Vlaanderen, NW Belgium
Zeewolde 86 D3 Flevoland, C Netherlands
Zefat *see* Tsefat
Żegań *see* Zagań
Zeiden *see* Codlea
Zeist 86 C4 Utrecht, C Netherlands
Zele 87 B5 Oost-Vlaanderen, NW Belgium
Zelenoborskiy 110 B2 Murmanskaya Oblast', NW Russian Federation
Zelenograd 111 B5 Moskovskaya Oblast', W Russian Federation
Zelenogradsk 106 A4 *Ger.* Cranz, Kranz. Kaliningradskaya Oblast', W Russian Federation
Zelle *see* Celle
Zel'va 107 B6 *Pol.* Zelwa. Hrodzyenskaya Voblasts', W Belarus
Zelwa *see* Zel'va
Zelzate 87 B5 *var.* Selzaete. Oost-Vlaanderen, NW Belgium
Žemaičių Aukštumas 106 B4 *physical region* W Lithuania
Zemst 87 C5 Vlaams Brabant, C Belgium
Zemun 100 D3 Serbia, N Serbia
Zengg *see* Senj
Zenica 100 C4 Federacija Bosna I Hercegovina, C Bosnia and Herzegovina
Zenta *see* Senta
Zeravshan 123 E3 *Taj./Uzb.* Zarafshon. *river* Tajikistan/Uzbekistan
Zevenaar 86 D4 Gelderland, SE Netherlands
Zevenbergen 86 C4 Noord-Brabant, S Netherlands
Zeya 113 E3 *river* SE Russian Federation
Zgerzh *see* Zgierz
Zgierz 98 C4 *Ger.* Neuhof, *Rus.* Zgerzh. Łódź, C Poland
Zgorzelec 98 B4 *Ger.* Görlitz. Dolnośląskie, SW Poland
Zhabinka 107 A6 *Pol.* Żabinka. Brestskaya Voblasts', SW Belarus
Zhambyl *see* Taraz
Zhanaozen 114 A4 *Kaz.* Zhangaözen; *prev.* Novyy Uzen'. Mangistau, W Kazakhstan
Zhangaözen *see* Zhanaozen
Zhangaqazaly *see* Ayteke Bi
Zhang-chia-k'ou *see* Zhangjiakou
Zhangdian *see* Zibo
Zhangjiakou 128 C3 *var.* Changkiakow, Zhang-chia-k'ou, *Eng.* Kalgan; *prev.* Wanchuan. Hebei, E China
Zhangzhou 128 D6 Fujian, SE China
Zhanjiang 128 C7 *var.* Chanchiang, Chan-chiang, Cant. Tsamkong, *Fr.* Fort-Bayard. Guangdong, S China
Zhaoqing 128 C6 Guangdong, S China

Zhayyk 112 B3 *var.* Zayyq, Ural. *river* Kazakhstan/Russian Federation
Zhdanov *see* Mariupol'
Zhe *see* Zhejiang
Zhejiang 128 D5 *var.* Che-chiang, Chekiang, Zhe, Zhejiang Sheng. *province* SE China
Zhejiang Sheng *see* Zhejiang
Zheleznodorozhnyy 106 A4 Irkutskaya Oblast', C Russian Federation
Zheleznodorozhnyy *see* Yemva
Zheleznogorsk 111 A5 Kurskaya Oblast', W Russian Federation
Zhëltyye Vody *see* Zhovti Vody
Zhengzhou 128 C4 *var.* Ch'eng-chou, Chengchow; *prev.* Chenghsien. *province capital* Henan, C China
Zhezkazgan 114 C4 *Kaz.* Zhezqazghan; *prev.* Dzhezkazgan. Karagandy, C Kazakhstan
Zhezqazghan *see* Zhezkazgan
Zhidachov *see* Zhydachiv
Zhishan *see* Lingling
Zhitkovichi *see* Zhytkavichy
Zhitomir *see* Zhytomyr
Zhlobin 107 D7 Homyel'skaya Voblasts', SE Belarus
Zhmerinka *see* Zhmerynka
Zhmerynka 108 D2 *Rus.* Zhmerinka. Vinnyts'ka Oblast', C Ukraine
Zhodino *see* Zhodzina
Zhodzina 107 D6 *Rus.* Zhodino. Minskaya Voblasts', C Belarus
Zholkev/Zholkva *see* Zhovkva
Zhonghua Renmin Gongheguo *see* China
Zhosaly 114 B4 *prev.* Dzhusaly. Kzylorda, SW Kazakhstan
Zhovkva 108 B2 *Pol.* Żółkiew, *Rus.* Zholkev, Zholkva; *prev.* Nesterov. L'vivs'ka Oblast', NW Ukraine
Zhovti Vody 109 F3 *Rus.* Zhëltyye Vody. Dnipropetrovs'ka Oblast', E Ukraine
Zhovtneve 109 E4 *Rus.* Zhovtnevoye. Mykolayivs'ka Oblast', S Ukraine
Zhovtnevoye *see* Zhovtneve
Zhi Qu *see* Tongtian He
Zhydachiv 108 B2 *Pol.* Żydaczów, *Rus.* Zhidachov. L'vivs'ka Oblast', NW Ukraine
Zhytkavichy 107 C7 *Rus.* Zhitkovichi. Homyel'skaya Voblasts', SE Belarus
Zhytomyr 108 D2 *Rus.* Zhitomir. Zhytomyrs'ka Oblast', NW Ukraine
Zibo 128 D4 *var.* Zhangdian. Shandong, E China
Zichenau *see* Ciechanów
Zielona Góra 98 B4 *Ger.* Grünberg, Grünberg in Schlesien, Grüneberg. Lubuskie, W Poland
Zierikzee 86 B4 Zeeland, SW Netherlands
Zigong 128 B5 *var.* Tzekung. Sichuan, C China
Ziguinchor 74 B3 SW Senegal
Zilah *see* Zalău
Žilina 99 C5 *Ger.* Sillein, *Hung.* Zsolna. Zílinský Kraj, N Slovakia
Zillenmarkt *see* Zalău
Zimbabwe 78 D3 *off.* Republic of Zimbabwe; *prev.* Rhodesia. *country* S Africa

ZIMBABWE
Southern Africa

Official name Republic of Zimbabwe
Formation 1980 / 1980
Capital Harare
Population 12.8 million / 86 people per sq mile (33 people per sq km)
Total area 150,803 sq. miles (390,580 sq. km)
Languages Shona, isiNdebele, English*
Religions Syncretic (Christian/traditional beliefs) 50%, Christian 25%, Traditional beliefs 24%, Other (including Muslim) 1%
Ethnic mix Shona 71%, Ndebele 16%, Other African 11%, White 1%, Asian 1%
Government Presidential system
Currency Zimbabwe dollar suspended in 2009; US dollar, South African rand, euro, UK pound, and Botswanan pula are legal tender
Literacy rate 91%
Calorie consumption 2219 kilocalories

Zimbabwe, Republic of *see* Zimbabwe
Zimnicea 108 C5 Teleorman, S Romania
Zimovniki 111 B7 Rostovskaya Oblast', SW Russian Federation
Zinder 75 G3 Zinder, S Niger
Zinov'yevsk *see* Kirovohrad
Zintenhof *see* Sindi
Zipaquira 58 B3 Cundinamarca, C Colombia
Zittau 94 D4 Sachsen, E Germany
Zlatni Pyasûtsi 104 E2 Dobrich, NE Bulgaria
Zlín 99 C5 *prev.* Gottwaldov. Zlínský Kraj, E Czech Republic
Złoczów *see* Zolochiv
Złotów 98 C3 Wielkopolskie, C Poland
Znamenka *see* Znam"yanka
Znam"yanka 109 F3 *Rus.* Znamenka. Kirovohrads'ka Oblast', C Ukraine
Żnin 98 C3 Kujawsko-pomorskie, C Poland
Zoetermeer 86 C4 Zuid-Holland, W Netherlands
Zólkiew *see* Zhovkva
Zolochev *see* Zolochiv
Zolochiv 109 G2 *Rus.* Zolochev. Kharkivs'ka Oblast', E Ukraine
Zolochiv 108 C2 *Pol.* Złoczów, *var.* Zolochev. L'vivs'ka Oblast', W Ukraine
Zolote 109 H3 *Rus.* Zolotoye. Luhans'ka Oblast', E Ukraine
Zolotonosha 109 E2 Cherkas'ka Oblast', C Ukraine
Zolotoye *see* Zolote
Zólyom *see* Zvolen
Zomba 79 E2 Southern, S Malawi
Zombor *see* Sombor
Zongo 77 C5 Équateur, N Dem. Rep. Congo
Zonguldak 116 C2 Zonguldak, NW Turkey
Zonhoven 87 D6 Limburg, NE Belgium
Zoppot *see* Sopot
Żory 99 C5 *var.* Zory, *Ger.* Sohrau. Śląskie, S Poland

Zouar 76 C2 Borkou-Ennedi-Tibesti, N Chad
Zouérat 74 C2 *var.* Zouérate, Zouîrât. Tiris Zemmour, N Mauritania
Zouérate *see* Zouérat
Zouîrât *see* Zouérat
Zrenjanin 100 D3 *prev.* Petrovgrad, Veliki Bečkerek, *Ger.* Grossbetschkerek, *Hung.* Nagybecskerek. Vojvodina, N Serbia
Zsil/Zsily *see* Jiu
Zsolna *see* Žilina
Zsombolya *see* Jimbolia
Zsupanya *see* Županja
Zubov Seamount 67 D5 *undersea feature* E Atlantic Ocean
Zueila *see* Zawīlah
Zug 95 B7 *Fr.* Zoug. Zug, C Switzerland
Zugspitze 95 C7 *mountain* S Germany
Zuid-Beveland 87 B5 *var.* South Beveland. *island* SW Netherlands
Zuider Zee *see* IJsselmeer
Zuidhorn 86 E1 Groningen, NE Netherlands
Zuidlaren 86 E2 Drenthe, NE Netherlands
Zula 72 C4 E Eritrea
Zumbo *see* Vila do Zumbo
Zundert 87 C5 Noord-Brabant, S Netherlands
Zunyi 128 B5 Guizhou, S China
Županja 100 C3 *Hung.* Zsupanya. Vukovar-Srijem, E Croatia
Zürich 95 B7 *Eng./Fr.* Zurich, *It.* Zurigo. Zürich, N Switzerland
Zurich, Lake 95 B7 *Eng.* Lake Zurich. *lake* NE Switzerland
Zürich, Lake *see* Zürichsee
Zurigo *see* Zürich
Zutphen 86 D5 Gelderland, E Netherlands
Zuwārah 71 F2 NW Libya
Zuwaylah *see* Zawīlah
Zuyevka 111 D5 Kirovskaya Oblast', NW Russian Federation
Zvenigorodka *see* Zvenyhorodka
Zvenyhorodka 109 E2 *Rus.* Zvenigorodka. Cherkas'ka Oblast', C Ukraine
Zvishavane 78 D3 *prev.* Shabani. Matabeleland South, S Zimbabwe
Zvolen 99 C6 *Ger.* Altsohl, *Hung.* Zólyom. Banskobystrický Kraj, C Slovakia
Zvornik 100 C4 E Bosnia and Herzegovina
Zwedru 74 D5 *var.* Tchien. E Liberia
Zwettl 95 E6 Wien, NE Austria
Zwevegem 87 A6 West-Vlaanderen, W Belgium
Zwickau 95 C5 Sachsen, E Germany
Zwolle 86 D3 Overijssel, E Netherlands
Żydaczów *see* Zhydachiv
Zyôetu *see* Jōetsu
Żyrardów 98 D3 Mazowieckie, C Poland
Zyryanovsk 114 D5 Vostochnyy Kazakhstan, E Kazakhstan

Key to map pages

North & West Asia 112-113

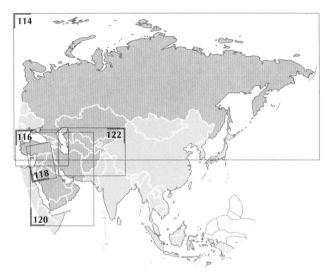

South & East Asia 124-125

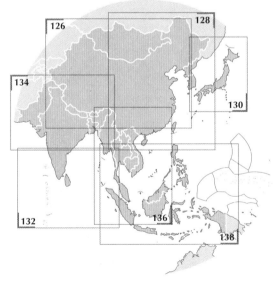